WHY?

Why read, or rather *study*, this book?

Because if you are interested in Magic, the Tarot or Occultism, you will sooner or later realize that it is very much the foundation upon which the Twentieth Century public rebirth of this subject has been raised.

While first published in four volumes in 1937–1940, most of the prominent writers and practitioners of Magic and the Occult Sciences since 1888 were trained in the system described in this book: Aleister Crowley, Dion Fortune, A. E. Waite, S. L. MacGregor Mathers—to name only a few of those directly involved.

This book is not *about* Magic, it is Magic. It is a valid training program that can be experienced by any reader who will employ his imagination to follow the drama of Initiation, and who will practice the simple and basic rituals described herein.

You may prefer to call what is described herein something other than "Magic". It is the essential technology for Spiritual Growth, Psychic Development, Success Training, Soul Therapy or any of dozens of other names we might consider. It is "the Yoga of the West".

Why should you study, and practice, Magic?

Because it is your birthright to become a Magician! The meaning of your life is found in growth, development, and self-transformation. To become a Magician is to become more than Human, for it is in the fulfillment of your human potential that your destiny is realized.

To become a Magician is to assume your proper place in the Universe. What that place is, only you can discover—but you will commune with the Spirit of Nature, you will know distant Stars, you will realize the Oneness of All Things.

ABOUT THE AUTHORS

Francis I. Regardie, born in London, England, November 17, 1907; died in Sedona, Arizona, March 10, 1985. Came to the United States in August 1921, educated in Washington D. C. and studied art in schools in Washington and Philadelphia. Returned to Europe in 1928 at the invitation of Aleister Crowley to work as his secretary and study with him. Returned to London as secretary to Thomas Burke 1932–34, and during that time wrote *A Garden of Pomegranates* and *The Tree of Life.*

In 1934 he was invited to join the Order of the Golden Dawn, Stella Matutina Temple, during which time he wrote *The Middle Pillar* and *The Art of True Healing,* and did the basic work for *The Philosopher's Stone.*

Returning to the United States in 1937 he entered Chiropractic College in New York, graduating in 1941, and published *The Golden Dawn.* Served in the U. S. Army 1942–1945, and then moved to Los Angeles where he opened a chiropractic practice and taught psychiatry. Upon retirement in 1981, he moved to Sedona.

During his lifetime, he studied psychoanalysis with Dr. E. Clegg and Dr. J. L. Bendit, and later studied psychotherapy under Dr. Nandor Fodor. His training encompassed Freudian, Jungian and Reichian methods.

As to who authored the various foundation rituals upon which the edifice of the Hermetic Order of the Golden Dawn was erected, debate will perhaps continue forever. One history is given in this book, and other histories have likewise been written and will continue to be written. Their authenticity does not rest upon their history, but history has proved their value. For 100 years this has been the Mother Lode of Western Esotericism.

Information about the contributors will be found in the Foreword and Appreciation. Letters addressed to the contributors in care of the Publisher will be forwarded to them. We cannot guarantee that every letter can be answered, but please include a self-addressed, stamped envelope for reply, or $1.00 to cover costs. To gain more information about the subject matter of this book, request a copy of *Llewellyn's New Times.*

Golden Dawn Associates
LLEWELLYN PUBLICATIONS
P. O. Box 64383, Dept. 663, St. Paul, MN 55164-0383, U.S.A.

ABOUT LLEWELLYN'S GOLDEN DAWN SERIES

Just as, 100 years ago, the original Order of the Golden Dawn *initiated* a powerful re-birth of interest in The Western Esoteric Tradition that has lasted through this day, so do we expect this new series of books to add new impetus to The Great Work itself among an ever broadening base of sincere students.

> *I further promise and swear that with the Divine Permission, I will, from this day forward, apply myself to the Great Work—which is: to purify and exalt my Spiritual Nature so that with the Divine Aid I may at length attain to be more than human, and thus gradually raise and unite myself to my Higher and Divine Genius, and that in this event I will not abuse the great power entrusted to me.*

With this oath, the *Adeptus Minor* of the Inner Order committed his/her self to undertake, consciously and deliberately, that which was ordained as the birthright of all Humanity: TO BECOME MORE THAN HUMAN!

It is this that is the ultimate message of Esotericism: that evolution continues, and that the purpose of each life is to grow into the Image set for us by our Creator: to attain and reveal our own Divinity.

These books and tapes will themselves make more easily accessible the Spiritual Technology that is inherent in the Golden Dawn System. It is a system that allows for individual as well as group endeavor; a system that works within or without an organized lodge; a system that is based on universal principles that will be shown to be global in their impact today.

And practical. The works in this series will be practical in their applications and requirements for application. You need neither to travel to the Mountain Top nor obtain any tool other than your own Consciousness. No garment need you other than that of your own Imagination. No authority need you other than that of your own True Will.

Set forth, then, into The New Dawn—a New Start on the greatest adventure there is: to become One with the Divine Genius.

Other Books by Israel Regardie

A Garden of Pomegranates
The Tree of Life
My Rosicrucian Adventure
The Art of True Healing
The Middle Pillar
The Philosopher's Stone
The Romance of Metaphysics
The Art and Meaning of Magic
Be Yourself, the Art of Relaxation
New Wings for Daedalus
Twelve Steps to Spiritual Enlightenment
The Eye in the Triangle
Roll Away the Stone
The Legend of Aleister Crowley
(with P.R. Stephensen)

Llewellyn's Golden Dawn Series

THE GOLDEN DAWN

A Complete Course in Practical Ceremonial Magic
Four Volumes in One

The Original Account of the Teachings,
Rites and Ceremonies of the
Hermetic Order of the Golden Dawn
(Stella Matutina)
as revealed by

ISRAEL REGARDIE

with further revision, expansion, and additional notes by
Israel Regardie, Cris Monnastre, and others,
under the editorship of
Carl Llewellyn Weschcke

Complete index compiled by David Godwin

Sixth Edition

1989
LLEWELLYN PUBLICATIONS
St. Paul, Minnesota, 55164-0383, U.S.A.

International Standard Book Number: 0-87542-663-8
Library of Congress Catalog Number: 86-15247

First Edition, (4 volumes) 1937-1940
Second Edition, Revised & Enlarged (2 Volumes) 1969
Third Edition, Revised & Enlarged (2 volumes) 1970
Fourth Edition, Revised & Enlarged (1 volume) 1971
Sixth Printing, 1984
Fifth Edition, Revised, Enlarged and Reset 1986
Second Printing, 1987
Third Printing, 1987
Fourth Printing, 1988
Fifth Printing, 1988
Sixth Edition, Revised and Expanded, 1989

Library of Congress Cataloging-in-Publication Data
Regardie, Israel.
The Golden Dawn.

1. Hermetic Order of the Golden Dawn. I. Title.
BF1623.R7R33 1986 135'.43 86-15247
ISBN 0-87542-663-8 (pbk)

Cover Art: Timothy Miske

Produced by Llewellyn Publications
Typography and Art property of Chester-Kent, Inc.

Published by
LLEWELLYN PUBLICATIONS
A Division of Chester-Kent, Inc.
P.O. Box 64383
St. Paul, MN 55164-0383, U.S.A.

Printed in the United States of America

DEDICATED

To all True Seekers of the Light

May what they find herein sustain them in their search for the Quintessence; the Stone of the Philosophers, true Wisdom and perfect Happiness, the *Summum Bonum.*

THE GOLDEN DAWN

"Howbeit we know after a time there will now be a general reformation, both of divine and human things, according to our desire and the expectation of others; for it is fitting that before the rising of the Sun there should appear and break forth *Aurora,* or some clearness, or divine light in the sky. And so, in the meantime, some few, which shall give their names, may join together, thereby to increase the number and respect of our Fraternity, and make a happy and wished for beginning of our Philosophical Canons, prescribed to us by our Brother R.C., and be partakers with us of our treasures (which can never fail or be wasted) in all humility and love, to be eased of this world's labours, and not walk so blindly in the knowledge of the wonderful works of God."

FAMA FRATERNITATIS, (1614)

FOREWORD AND APPRECIATION

Just about 100 years ago (in 1887) we had the beginnings of The Hermetic Order of the Golden Dawn. It was then that (according to history and "myth") Dr. William Westcott discovered a cipher manuscript that led to the founding of an English branch of *Die Goldene Dammerung* in 1888.

It was this Golden Dawn that attracted some of the most talented personalities of the time — including W. B. Yeats, Algernon Blackwood, Arthur Machen, Florence Farr, Annie Horniman, A. E. Waite, S. L. MacGregor Mathers, Dion Fortune and Aleister Crowley. And it was this Golden Dawn that itself provided a NEW DAWN for "occultism" in the early 20th century.

In the early 1900s, the original Order began to fragment. First Crowley published many of the G.D. rituals in *The Equinox* and left to form his own order, the A.A., in 1905. The original Isis-Urania Temple expelled Mathers, and then — as The Stella Matutina — under the direction of Waite, put more emphasis on mysticism than had the original G.D. Later Dion Fortune broke off from this Temple to form her own Inner Light group.

It was as a member of the Stella Matutina that Israel Regardie first published a nearly complete set of the rituals and teachings in 1937-40 as the first edition of this present work. Later he sold the copyrights for this and most of his other books at that time to the Aries Press, and I purchased them in 1968 and brought out the second edition, with new material from Regardie, in 1969.

As Sam Webster points out in the *Epilogue* to this fifth edition, this book has been the foundation for much of the "occult revival" of the last half of the twentieth century. It has provided resource materials for Wicca, the New Paganism, various magical groups, and for tens of thousands of serious students.

And as Cris Monnastre points out in her *Introduction,* it is now beginning to provide a structure into which modern psychology can flow to bring about a solution to the present world crisis which demands a dramatic expansion of consciousness and of the 'tools' of awareness.

It is the actual *"structured" experience* of magic — whether it be attained through group or solitary work — that is vital to the accelerated evolution of human consciousness beyond present limitations, and to the expansion of human awareness from communal to global dimensions. And it is this that is essential to avoidance of nuclear war and to the restoration of Nature to the environment and of humanity to Nature.

The Golden Dawn is a curriculum of study, a workbook to the Great Work, and Cris Monnastre has provided guidelines to the practical approach to the Work. I cannot emphasize enough the importance of personal work, for it is that — whether undertaken alone or with a group — that is important. Only personal work can accomplish true initiation.

And The Golden Dawn is a valid curriculum for personal work even for those associated with other than Golden Dawn groups or systems of magical study. One of the great messages of the New Age is that of eclecticism — *if it works, use it!* There are many other valuable and valid resources for our evolution, and in this time of "quickening", all are pertinent. But it is a personal and regular program of meditation that brings order to what otherwise might prove chaotic. Such a program, combined with the simple magical exercises of "The Middle Pillar" and "Banishing Ritual of the Pentagram", and the keeping of a journal will initiate your own journey to the Light!

I want to give special appreciation to the writers who have added important materials to this new edition, but I also want to give personal appreciation to Israel Regardie for having recognized in 1937 that the "time for secrecy" was over. The twentieth century is a time in which the knowledge of the past has to be brought forward and integrated into a new "common sense" upon which a new humanity can be built.

Once, years ago, when I first talked about buying the Golden Dawn copyrights from the Aries Press, another occult writer made a statement to the effect that no one could "own" this knowledge — *for it all came originally from God!* I think that concept describes exactly what we are dealing with: *true Spiritual Technology,* Treat it as such!

Throughout this edition we have retained the original pagination so that references to the original four volume edition could still be identified. I have made corrections to the original where they were needed, but unless important to the readers' perception I have not made changes to the style. In addition, I am very much indebted to Cris Monnastre, MaDhyan Anupassana, George Wilson, Hal Sundt and Sam Webster for their help and their contributions. In most cases these are identified by initials, along with my own, in footnotes.

And it is with a great deal of pleasure that I announce that Cris Monnastre has been instrumental in bringing together these, and other G.D. practitioners, who will be producing a future series of "Golden Dawn Manuals" to develop individual techniques and exercises for study and use.

Carl Llewellyn Weschcke
St. Paul, July 10, 1986

About the Contributors

Cris Monnastre, born April 2, 1946, is currently finishing a doctoral program in psychology with a specialty in clinical psychology. She is a therapist in the Los Angeles area and combines traditional therapy with Golden Dawn techniques. She is a poet, musician, and composer, and lives with her two sons, Aaron and Adam. She is interested in inquiries regarding Golden Dawn work and therapy. Please address letters to her care of Llewellyn Publications.

Hal Sundt, born August 14, 1950, B.A. in History presently working on Master's thesis regarding the Gnostic influence on Jacob Boehme and the Rosicricians. Has been studying/working with Golden Dawn groups for 12 years.

Sam Webster, 25, B.A. in English. A student of symbolism and consciousness. He is a practitioner of Thelemic Magick and affiliated with several branches of the O.T.O. and other Thelemic groups. During 1983-84 he traveled to study with magickal practitioners scattered around the country. Presently he is involved in generating grimoires for Egyptian and Thelemic Magicks. As a poet and storyteller, he attends festivals and gatherings to share his art.

George Wilson, 39, B.A. Philosophy, B.S. Nursing. Professionally was an RN with a psychiatric specialty. Recently retired to devote full time to occult studies. A student of mysticism for 20 years, "Kabbalah led to G.D. Obtained The Golden Dawn in 1970 and this was the focus of occult interests from that time on." Currently engaged in projects focusing on Color Scales, the Outer Order rituals, and the generation of Magic Squares.

Ma Dhyan Anupassana, aka Suzan Wilson, born August 26, 1954, Sannyasin of Bhagwan Shree Rajneesh, has studied Eastern Religion at San Diego State University and practiced various occult systems since 1972. Also a student and teacher of Iyengar Yoga. She is married to George Wilson. They have three sons and plan to emigrate to New Zealand as soon as possible where they will continue personal magickal work, writing, and teaching yoga.

Carl L. Weschcke, born September 10, 1930, B.S. in Business Administration, work toward doctorate in Philosophy, D. Ph. Mag. (Honorary), Certificate in Clinical Hypnosis. Lifelong student of the occult, starting with Theosophy, several years of work with Crowley materials and as a correspondence student with the Society of the Inner Light, study of Jungian psychology and yoga. High Priest in Wicca, and Administrator General Aurum Solis. President of Llewellyn Publications since 1960.

David Godwin, born in 1939 in Dallas, Texas, is a long-time student of esoteric lore. Learned and knowledgeable about cabalistic practices, he has successfully mastered them and written a classic treatise on the subject entitled *Godwin's Cabalistic Encyclopedia.* Out of print for several years, popular demand dictated that it be reprinted. It is now available again with new additions and information, from Llewellyn Publications.

Godwin has worked as a manual laborer, a newspaper reporter, an editor for a petrochemical magazine, a technical editor for two NASA contractors during the Apollo missions, a typesetter, a free-lance writer and a practicing astrologer. He has never been to a writers' workshop, owns no cats, and is entirely ignorant of the martial arts. Godwin believes in maintaining the open-minded, balanced attitude advocated by the middle path of cabalism.

HOW TO USE THIS BOOK

Normally speaking, "a book is a book . . . is a book" and no advice has to given about how it is used.

This book is different, for several reasons, and you will find advice on how to use it in the introductions by Cris Monnastre and Israel Regardie. Because it is a big book, and because it is both a text for study and a guide to practice as well as an encyclopedic reference work, you will use it many different ways.

In the Table of Contents, we have listed the major rituals in italics for easier location, and we have provided an extensive listing of the illustrations and tables to be make reference use easier and faster. Hopefully, in a subsequent edition, we will be able to provide a comprehensive index.

Page Numbers. There are two sets of them: those referring to this edition will be found at the top outer margin, or at the bottom center. Those that refer to the original four-volume edition may be found bracketed at the left margin to indicate approximately the location of the page break in the text. At the top of the page will be found reference to the original Volume and Book numbers. It is hoped in this way that references to the original edition found in other works may be easily located.

Corrections and Additions. Any book of this size can be expected to have some errors. We have corrected all those in the original edition that we could locate, and have subjected this edition to several proof-readings. Yet, we know that some will continue to be found. It is our hope that readers will consider this book so important that they will send us notes of such further corrections that we may make in future editions. We have also made some additions in the form of short introductions to some of the sections and as footnotes to the text where we felt clarification was needed.

Future Work. The Golden Dawn is a complete system of Ceremonial Magic. Within the system may be found the basic technologies of spiritual development and their practical application. Future books and tapes in this series will simplify and expand these techniques, including the initiatory rituals, for greater ease of study and use.

Lodges and Study Groups. The Golden Dawn system is not dependent on affiliation with any group proclaiming itself as "Golden Dawn" or "Rosicrucian". Nor, even though the initiatory rituals describe a lodge system, is group practice necessary for their enactment. All magic must ultimately take place in the psyche of the student. There are existing Golden Dawn Lodges, and Lodges and Study Groups of other organizations teaching ceremonial magic. Often the most practical way to make contact with a group is by placing an advertisement in a local New Age or Occult tabloid or magazine.

TABLE OF CONTENTS

Foreword and Appreciation, by Carl Llewellyn Weschcke ix
Introduction to Fifth Edition, by Cris Monnastre, 1986 xvii
Indexing the Golden Dawn, by David Godwin xxvii
Introduction to Second Edition, by Israel Regardie, 1968 1
Introduction to First Edition, by Israel Regardie, 1937 14

Volume I, Book One: Basic Knowledge and Practice
- First Knowledge Lecture 50
  - *Lesser Ritual of the Pentagram* 53
- Second Knowledge Lecture 60
- Third Knowledge Lecture 67
- Fourth Knowledge Lecture 69
- Fifth Knowledge Lecture 77
- Miscellany Omitted from Lectures 82
  - The Portal Work 87
    - *The Middle Pillar Exercise* 90
  - Concerning the Tree of Life 95
  - The Adeptus Minor Task 106

Volume II, Book Two: Rituals of the Outer Order
- Introduction to the Neophyte Ceremony, by Anupassana, 1986 114
  - *Neophyte Ritual* 116
- Introduction to the Elemental Grade Ceremonies, by Anupassana, 1986 136
  - *Zealator Ritual* 141
  - *Theoricus Ritual* 154
  - *Practicus Ritual* 166
  - *Philosophus Ritual* 181

Book Three: Rituals of the Inner Order
  - *Portal Ritual* 198
  - *Adeptus Minor Ritual* 221
  - *Equinox Ceremonies* 248
  - *Consecration and Corpus Christi Ceremony (with Opening by Watchtower)* 258
- Symbolism of the Seven Sides 266
- On the Use of the Vault 272

Volume III, Book Four: Primary Techniques of Magical Practice, and the Magical Weapons
  - *Ritual of the Pentagram* 280
  - *Supreme Invoking Ritual of the Pentagram* 285
  - *Ritual of the Hexagram* 287
  - *Lesser Ritual of the Hexagram* 296
- The Lotus Wand, and *Consecration Ritual* 302
  - *Ritual of the Rose Cross* 306
- The Rose Cross Lamen, and *Consecration Ritual* 310
- The Magic Sword, and *Consecration Ritual* 317
- The Four Elemental Weapons, and *Consecration Rituals* 320

Book Five: Details of the Principles and Symbolism of Ritual Magic
- Z.1 The Enterer of the Threshold 330
- Z.3 Symbolism of the Admission 363
- Z.2 Magical Formulae 376

Book Six: Ceremonial Magic in Practice
  - *Evocation Ritual* 402
  - *Talisman Consecration Ritual* 413
  - *Ritual for Invisibility* 423
  - *Ritual for Self-Transformation* 429
  - *Ritual for Spiritual Development* 435
  - *The Bornless Ritual for the Invocation of the Higher Genius* 442
  - *Requiem Ceremony* 447
- Preparation for Divination 451

Volume IV, Book Seven: Clairvoyance, Talismans, Sigils, Tattwas
Clairvoyance and Rising on the Planes 455
Skrying, Tattwa Visions, and Astral Travel 467
Talismans, Talismanic Figures, Sigils and Flashing Tablets 479
Polygons and Polygrams 505
Tattwas of the Eastern School 514
Book Eight: Divination
Geomancy 524
Book T — The Tarot, Description 540
Tarot Divination 566
The Tarot Trumps 588
The Tree of Life Projected in a Solid Sphere 594
Book Nine: Enochian Magic
Introduction to the Enochian System 624
The Book of the Concourse of Forces 630
The Forty-Eight Angelical Calls 671
Enochian Chess 683

Epilogue, by Sam Webster, 1986 697

ILLUSTRATIONS, LISTS, AND TABLES

The Curriculum of the Order 43
Elements, Signs, Triplicities 50
The Old Planets 51
The Sephiroth, in English and Hebrew 51
The Hebrew Alphabet, its Powers and Meanings 52
Invoking and Banishing Pentagrams 53-54
Alchemical Symbols 60
The Serpent on the Tree of Life 62
The Four Worlds of the Qabalah 63
The Ten Houses of the Material World 63
Divine Names Attributed to the Sephiroth 64
Planetary Names: Angel, Intelligence, Spirit 65
Fylfot Cross and the Caduceus 68
The Figures of Geomancy and Zodiacal Attributions 69
Planetary Numbers and Figures 70
Figures on the Admission Badges 70-71
Attributions of the Tarot Trumps: Path, Letter, Symbol 71
Tetragrammaton on the Tree 78
Figures on the Philosophus Admission Badge 79
Attributions of the Four Elements, Hebrew and English 80
Alchemical Attributions to the Tree of Life 82
The Qlippoth on the Tree: Names and Meanings 82
The Seven Palaces attributed to the Ten Sephiroth 82
Alchemical Terms and Symbols 84
Divine and Angelic Names by Zodiacal Correspondence 86
The Middle Pillar and Ten Sephiroth on the Human Body 89
The Four Colour Scales 99
The Four Elements and Spirit on the Body 100
Planetary Attributions to the Seven Apertures of the Head 103
Paintings on the Lid of the Pastos 112
Temple Diagram for Neophyte Ritual 116

Color Plates: Following Page 116

Banner of the East and West
The Garden of Eden Before the Fall (text reference 73)
The Garden of Eden After the Fall (text reference 76)
The Minutum Mundum

Temple Diagram for Neophyte Ritual—Second Part 122
Gestures and Signs 134-135
Temple Diagram for Zelator Ritual 141
Second Part 148
Temple Diagram for Theoricus Ritual 154
Second Part 161
Temple Diagram for Practicus Ritual 166
Path of Resh 173
In Sphere of Hod 176
Temple Diagram for Philosophus Ritual 181
Path of Tzaddi 186
Path of Peh 189
In Sphere of Netzach 192
Temple Diagram for Portal Ritual 198
Rite of the Pentagram and Five Paths 208
Temple Diagram for Adeptus Minor Ritual, First Part 222
Second Part 233
Third Part 238
Symbols in the Vault 243
Figures on Side of Pastos and Wall of the Vault 244
Signs and Symbols on the Pastos 245
Attributions of the Points of the Pentagram 281
Spirit Invoking and Banishing Pentagrams 281
Elemental Invoking and Banishing Pentagrams 282
Supreme Invoking Pentagrams 285-286
Invoking and Banishing Pentagrams 288-292
First and Second Forms of Hexagram: Fire and Earth 294
Third and Fourth Forms of Hexagram: Air and Water 295
Invoking and Banishing Hexagrams 296-298
The Lotus Wand 300
Petals of the Lotus 301
Invocations to the Forces of the Zodiac 305
Rose Cross Symbol 306
Rose Cross as Traced in Ritual 307
The Rose Cross Lamen 313
The Sword and the Four Elemental Weapons 321
Divine and Angelic Names upon the Weapons 324
Four Forms of the Cross 335
Magical Formula for Enterer Ceremony 379-380
Magical Formula for Evocation 380-384
Magaical Formula for Consecration of Talismans 384-387
Magical Formula for Invisibility 387-389
Magical Formula for Transformation 389-391
Magical Formula for Spiritual Development 391-393
Magical Formula for Divination 393-395
Magical Formula for Alchemical Operations 395-399
Altar Diagrams for Alchemical Operations 398
Tattwa Symbols 457
Complimentary Colors for Flashing Tablets 479
Sigils 483-485
Telesmatic Attributions of the Hebrew Letters 491
Cross of the Letters of the Divine Name 492
Geomantic Sigils 494
Attributions of the Enochian Letters 495
Geomantic Talisman 496
Qabalah of the Nine Chambers 497
Kameas (Magical Squares) and Sigils of the Planets 498-502
Names and Sigils of the Olympic Planetary Spirits 503

Polygons and Polygrams 505-513
The Swara in the Body 515
Descriptions of the Tattwas 518
Plan of Geomantic Divination 525
Geomantic Attributions 526-527
Signification of the 12 Houses of Heaven 530
Example of a Geomantic Map 531
Meanings of Geomantic Figures in the Houses 532-537
Tarot Attributions for the Significator 567
Method of Counting in Tarot Divination 568
First Tarot Cut (Tetragrammaton) 568
First Horse-shoe Layout 570
Second Tarot Cut (Twelve Houses) 571
Second Horse-shoe Layout 574
Third Horse-shoe Layout 575
Fourth Tarot Cut (Decanates) 577
Fourth Decanate Layout 577
Fifth Tarot Layout (Tree of Life) 580
Fifth Horse-shoe Layout 580
Rules for Tarot Divination 581-587
The Tree of Life Projection on the Planets' Sphere 595
Golden Dawn Symbol in the Decanates 602
S.A.'s Key Plan of Sephiroth 604
S.A.'s Key Plan of the Paths 605
S.A.'s Key Plan of the Tarot 606
The Course of the Aces 609
Table of Elements and Tarot Aces 610
Table Showing Elemental Qualities 612
Hourglass Symbol Connecting the Planes 614
The Convoluted Transmission of Forces 616
Direct, or Creeping Serpent, Formula 618
Looped, or Flying Serpent, Formula 619
Leaping Serpent Formula 620
Revolving, or Flowing Serpent, Formula 620
The Four Enochian Tablets 631-634
The Name of the King (Central Whorl) 636
The Six Seniors 636
Lesser Angle of Fire of Water Tablet 638
Method of Attributing Tetragrammaton 639-641
Decanate Attributions of Great Cross of the Air Tablet 645
Earth Angle of Water Tablet 645
The Tablet of Union 645
Tetragrammaton Attributions to Lesser Angles 646-647
Triangles of Enochian Squares 647
Triangles of Squares in Great Central Cross 648
Examples of Pyramids 649
Table of Attributions for Working out Squares 651
The Enochian Alphabet and English Equivalents 652
Direction of Forces in the Triangles 653
Sigils of the Angelic Tablets 657
Coptic Deities 663
The Egyptian Pyramid Gods Illustrated 664-665
Rules for the Practice of Enochian Magic 668-670
Index to Enochian Keys 672
Tablet of Union 674
Enochian Chess Board 689
Index 701

Introduction
To The Fifth Edition

"Inheritor of a Dying World, we call thee to the Living Beauty. Wanderer in the Wild Darkness, we call thee to the Gentle Light. Long hast thou dwelt in Darkness — Quit the Night and seek the Day."

With these poetic and deeply symbolic words, the three principal officers in the Neophyte Grade ceremony ritually bring the candidate into the Order of the Golden Dawn as well as *to the Light.* This is not unlike Edinger's explanation in *Ego and Archetype* of the circular development of the ego-Self axis of which the anima may be the bridge. The "Night" is the unconscious, and the "Day" increased consciousness. Edinger refers to an alternating process of ego-Self separation and ego-Self union as a spiral-like psychological development throughout all of life. Whereas this is natural to the human condition, *the system of the Golden Dawn acts as a precise catalytic agent which accelerates this growth toward Soul* much as a "hot house" or "grow light" influences the quality and development of plant growth. One may ask why the necessity for "acceleration." Considering the world's current political arena and that we are no longer, in a deeper reality, separate nations but a worldwide community, as much "consciousness" as possible is gravely necessary unto the very survival of our planet. Additionally, what with pervasive technological implementation, we also must establish and maintain connection with the instinctual, transpersonal, and powerfully "rooted" experience of the deeper layers of the unconscious. And for this, the Golden Dawn provides its wonderous reservoir of symbol, sacrament, and ceremonial.

It is important to establish that Israel Regardie did not look upon the Golden Dawn system as an abstruse or interesting "occult" oddity of the turn of this last century. In his initial introduction for the first publication of this book in the late nineteen thirties he writes, "It is for this reason that I hold that the Golden Dawn magic, the technique of initiation, is of supreme and inestimable importance to mankind at large. In it the work of academic psychology may find a logical conclusion and fruition, so that it may develop further its own particular contribution to modern life and culture. For this psycho-magical technique of ceremonial initiation indicates the solution of the 'anima' problem. 'Arise! Shine! For thy light is come!' " And Regardie unreservedly maintained this position until his death in 1985.

Thinking through and fully understanding the usage of such terms as "occult" or "magic" apart from their historically negative or even lurid connotations is fundamental. The association of these words with "black" magic or Satanism has uniformly been the result of hysteria, narcissistic theatrics, capitalization by the media, or psychosis. To truly explore the "dark arts" (or in other words, apprehend the archetype of the *shadow)* through systematic ritual work demands not only extraordinary knowledge, discipline, and training, but a great deal of plain hard work toward which would-be dabblers never seem inclined. For any of us to integrate our "darker" side is a lifelong and necessary process, *but a process which yields toward a more fullness of Self.* As Edinger comments, "All these aspects of the rejected shadow are equated with the 'King,' which means psychologically that acceptance of the shadow and compassion for the inferior man are equivalent to acceptance of the Self." The masses have projected (and not integrated) their shadow from the witch burnings of Salem to congressional hearings on censorship of lyrics in rock music. The "occult" means nothing more than the study of what is "hidden" beyond the perception of the five senses. Electricity could be construed as an "occult" force, and indeed to primitive man (as it manifested as an electrical storm) who partook of the mysterious since this was beyond the bounds of the ordinary. But electricity is no longer a "magical" force, for modern man has understood and harnessed it. So too, there are other forces beyond electricity and even nuclear power awaiting their further discovery and definition by man. And as Crowley articulated, "magic" means creating change through consciousness at will. The alchemist preceded the chemist, the astrologer the astronomer. *And the Magician is a threshold to an inner frontier which encompasses the limitless possibilities of the manifested and unknown universe as being contained, dormant, but inevitably actualized "within" the psyche.*

There is no better explanation of the structure, function, and basic concepts of the Golden Dawn system than in Regardie's introduction to the original edition of this book contained herein. This extensive and clarifying narrative demands rereading again and again. The Golden Dawn is a "system" of discovering, dialoguing, and even negotiating with the collective unconscious and is not a religion, philosophy or even a cult. As the candidate is about to take the obligation of the Neophyte, the Hierophant assures him or her that, "There is nothing contrary to your civil, moral, or religious duties in this Obligation." Furthermore, the Hierophant reminds the candidate to respect all religions, for each contains a spark of the divine.

The key theme in both the Neophyte Grade and the ritual of Adeptus Minor is that of being brought *to the Light.* This Light is also referred to as L.V.X. In the introduction to Volumes III and IV of *The Golden Dawn,* Regardie's excellent analysis of the keyword (I.N.R.I.) and subsequent gematric correspondences and conclusions will bear fruit from continued study and meditation regarding this Light. But a true "secret" of the entire system is that this Light is not a metaphysical or philosophically speculative construct meaning grace, spirituality, or healing (although the Light does bring all of these) but is *an ACTUAL FORCE which although independent of egoic man can be generated by man through the use of his consciousness to bring about CHANGE AT WILL!*

Although the so-called "new" physics has begun to come closer with any variety of theoretical models for this "force," the brilliant work of Fred Alan Wolf in such books as *Star Wave* has come closest to explaining L.V.X. and the paradigmatic raison d'etre for not only what the Golden Dawn is based upon, but why it "works"!

Wolf's work echoes Regardie's intuitive leap of fifty years ago when Regardie felt (as in the above quotation) that psychology would find its "logical conclusion and fruition" within the Golden Dawn system! Although Wolf makes no reference to the Golden Dawn or L.V.X. per se, he has dealt a death knell to a classical physics model of psychological theory while a quantum mechanics model has been astoundingly and secretly kerneled within the profound symbology and initiatory technique of the Golden Dawn system for countless years! To quote Wolf, "It is my dream that quantum physics will bridge the gap between science and mysticism. As such it must lead thinkers and researchers to a new view of human behavior. B.F. Skinner was not so wrong in attempting to deal with behavior scientifically, but he was the Newton of behaviorists. We now search for the Einstein and the Bohr of human behavior to develop the quantum model of human beings."

L.V.X. is generated in a number of ways and these are through ceremonial magic, the Middle Pillar technique, the Vibratory Formula of the Middle Pillar, and the Opening by Watchtower. Although Regardie published a progressive ritual use of the Opening by Watchtower in *Ceremonial Magic,* I would advise the beginning student to leave this particular ceremony strictly alone until he or she felt well within the initiatory containment and safety of the Second Order either through personal work or within an initiatory group. (Later in this introduction I will offer suggestions for the individual to plan a safe and successful approach to this Work overall.) This Light knows no moral or conscionable dictate. (Fire can burn your hand as surely as cook your favorite recipe!) But this is the "holy and formless fire" which either manifests in our external environment through the screen of our disciplined and CONSCIOUS image making (Crowley gave great emphasis to developing the concentrated image making aspect of consciousness) as well as through the automatic UNCONSCIOUS complexes of our personalities. And hence Regardie insisted upon some form of psychotherapeutic work once the unconscious had been activated by the ritual work since it was unlikely that the Neophyte had yet even knowledge of the possibility of control of image building with consciousness and what effect this could have on the personal life, let alone the discipline to implement it. The Neophyte was equally unlikely to be aware of the "sleeping dogs" (to use a phrase of Blavatsky's) or unconscious complexes of the personality and how those unknown parts of ourselves influence our lives.

This brings us to a discussion of "initiation". Initiation means "beginning" and if performed effectively, brings the candidate to an entirely new threshold and phase of experience. Initiation in itself does not bring "happiness" or "wishes come true." It is a starting point for difficult personal work ahead, and once the symbols are activated within the sphere of the candidate, it can mean many months, even years of difficult inward personal labor from one Grade to the next. The INNER completion of a ritual Grade does in fact bring a new awareness, more personal freedom from automatic parts of oneself, increased control over conscious image building, and a greater power, but with most of us this is usually hard won and painful. As to who is capable of initiating, the question of "succession" or "lineage" or the "transfer of power" has been debated for years regarding its pros and cons. Ultimately, the only person who can truly initiate another is one who has not only done the work pertaining to the particular Grade, but for the complete Order into which he or she initiates someone else. Unless the totality of the symbols are within the sphere of sensation of the initiator, little will be activated within the candidate and the ritual will be shallow theatrics. As Jung wrote in a foreword to a book of Michael Fordham's "The treatment of the transference reveals in a pitiless light what the healing agent really is: it is the degree to which the analyst himself can cope with his own psychic problems." Just as the analyst can no more guide an analysand through territory he or she has never struggled with or confronted within him or herself, so too the initiator's effectiveness rests upon how well he or she has built the "Temple not made with hands" within his or her own psyche.

In the late 1960's, the seeds of my destiny were actively fertilized toward what I much later understood as my personal "dance" with the unconscious, the process of magical initiation, the Golden Dawn system, and the Western Mystery Tradition. In the earlier part of 1969, I had had a brief, albeit intoxicating, exposure to Jungian analysis in San Francisco. In the latter part of 1969, by way of a powerful and unusual synchronicity, I had been told about a Los Angeles organization called Builders of the Adytum which had been founded by Paul Foster Case (who I was to much later find out had been a participant in a Golden Dawn Temple of the earlier 1900's). It took a full year for these connections to ripen before I embarked upon Case's excellent correspondence lessons in a committed way. His work introduced me to an exciting and enriching world of the symbolism of Tarot, Qabalah, and basic ritual. These lessons provided me with a solid foundation which has played a significant part in my magical career ever since.

In that first year, I had a profound sense of a sudden major change of consciousness which manifested as frequent mystical-like experiences and a daily and pervasive "feeling" of numinosity regarding my experience of life around and within me. As I look back on my early journal entries during this year, on the surface they appear naive, almost child-like as to the extent of a new found trust in the transpersonal and a "sweetness" and joy with life. This was not unlike what Regardie had referred to in *The Eye And The Triangle* as the "awakening" which comes unbidden and cannot be determined by good works, conscious wishes, or the best of intentions. My former way of experiencing life was over and behind me. I had truly become a fresh inquisitive Child of the Universe. I enjoyed this upwelling type of experience almost daily for at least a year as an infant enjoys suckling the warm nourishing breast. But the Child was to grow into greater consciousness and Light, and although the Child leads with delight, sparkle, and vivaciousness; responsibility, hard work, and even the pain of struggle and loss are inevitable once psychic contact with the gods presents the challenge toward further consciousness and inner growth beyond the safety of womb, new birth and breast.

In the fall of 1971, I had "accidentally" noticed a copy of Llewellyn's then current edition of Regardie's *The Golden Dawn* in a bookstore. I perused these books with a combination of awe, confusion, and reverence. The material was abstruse, and I remember while looking through its pages that I had a fleeting moment of fear (an Alice falling down the rabbit hole!!) as well as a sense of recognition, and realization that this information would thoroughly upset my current constructs of viewing life. My "rational" side felt ready for a fall! I left the books remaining on the store shelf!

Over the next several weeks, Regardie's writing became intensely more visible to me through any variety of additional "accidents." In early October, without my requesting, a stranger spontaneously gave me Regardie's telephone number and encouraged me to contact him. I spoke with Regardie for the first time on October 9, 1971. I wrote in my journal simply that day "I seek Initiation." I wrote further, "How sweet the Rose." I had virtually no idea at the time how powerful these simple words, their meaning, and the images they engendered were to become for me over the next 15 years! On the evening of October 20, 1971 I had had my most powerful and perhaps last mystical experience of this earlier period. While meditating on the Tarot Trump, "The Hermit," I was aware of a separate "consciousness" other than my own which I sensed clearly communicating the following via an inner awareness: "Come! Join Me at the Summit, and we shall watch the Dawn come upon us before others even know the Hour of Awakening is at hand. Run! Hurry! So that you too might sing with Me and rejoice in the Morning Light!" Two days later I sat opposite Regardie in his office in Studio City, California. I was 25 years of age, and I knew absolutely nothing about the Hermetic Order of the Golden Dawn!

I knew that Regardie had been practicing as a Reichian therapist at that time and my initial meeting with him was for purposes of introducing myself, inquiring about Reichian technique, and exploring with him why he felt psychotherapy was of such importance along with a magical regimen. I was too shy to venture any serious questions about the nature of magic, and the few I hinted toward he avoided completely. Midway through my time with him, he had me read aloud from *Light On The Path* by Mabel Collins. Although a lengthy passage, it is well worth quoting here since it gives the student the first inkling of the personal Genius or more poetically, the Holy Guardian Angel.

Stand aside in the coming battle, and though thou fightest be not thou the warrior. Look for the warrior and let him fight in thee. Take his orders for battle and obey them. Obey him not as though he were a general, but as though he were thyself and his spoken words were the utterance of thy secret desires; for he is thyself, yet infinitely wiser and stronger than thyself. Look for him, else in the fever and hurry of the fight thou mayest pass him; and he will not know thee unless thou knowest him. If thy cry reach his listening ear then will he fight in thee and fill the dull void within. And if this is so, then canst thou go through the fight cool and unwearied, standing aside and letting him battle for thee. Then it will be impossible for thee to strike one blow amiss. But if thou look not for him, if thou pass him by, then there is no safeguard for thee. Thy brain will reel, thy heart grow uncertain, and in the dust of the battlefield thy sight and senses will fail, and thou wilt not know thy friends from thy emenies.

He is thyself, yet thou art finite and liable to error. He is eternal and is sure. He is eternal truth. When once he has entered thee and become thy warrior, he will never utterly desert thee, and at the day of the great peace he will become one with thee.

I entered into Reichian therapy with Regardie for a period of approximately two years. Apart from Reich's method of therapy, he also incorporated some basic pranayama yoga techniques and chiropractic adjustments. But he also occasionally worked at activating one chakra located below my breastbone and above my solar plexus which on the Tree of Life would correspond to Tiphareth. Within a brief time, I felt the "streamings" referred to by Reich in his writings and others who have experienced this kind of therapeutic work. But the experience of this particular chakra being activated was beyond description! On one occasion I experienced an actual glowing, pulsating sphere within the center of my body which felt like an electrified tennis ball!

Years later, however, I am convinced that this kind of occurrence was not just the result of Regardie's success as a good Reichian therapist, but also due to many years of his own dedicated work with the Middle Pillar technique which he frequently referred to as the "sine qua non" of all magical work. In other words, Regardie was able, by a kind of process of induction, to begin to open me up to the entrance of powerful healing creative energy from profoundly deep reservoirs of the unconscious (and in the absence of verbal therapy!). Wilhelm Reich had called this energy "orgone" and, in his opinion, it is what numberless generations before revered and worshipped as "God." A Jungian may call this Soul, Self, or "meaning" depending upon individual interpretation. Or a Freudian may relate to this phenomenon as a release of libido. But the Magician calls this experience and influx of energy L.V.X. and with proper training and dedication, is able to release it him or herself WITHOUT THE AID OF AN OUTSIDE PERSON OR AGENCY!

Regardie had a phenomenal ability in generating this kind of energy quickly and efficiently. However, once in 1982 he confided to me that if any person worked the Middle Pillar technique twice daily for a significant period of time, that the same result would eventually occur. If this daily work were combined with sustained relaxation and prolonged rhythmic deep breathing, one could, in effect, *become one's OWN "Hierophant"* and trust that one's personal Genius would guide one within the pure intention of sincere effort.

Several months into my therapeutic work with Regardie, he one day suddenly placed a copy of Crowley's *The Holy Books* in my hands. I had read very little of Crowley at that time. He asked me to open the book at random and suggested that by doing so, I mught have a more conscious sense of my "Dharma" or destiny. I opened to the Path of Tav, the Path of Saturn, the Astral plane, and the Path of the unconscious. My "dance" with the inner life, the nonrational and unconscious life has blessedly unfolded ever since!

My therapy with Regardie ended in 1974 and for the next two years we were occasionally in contact with each other. I then moved out of the Los Angeles area, and we maintained a correspondence for several years. Throughout this time, he still continued to be reticent regarding any discussion of magical matters. In 1979, while I was experiencing anxiety and an acute depression, he suggested I begin working the Banishing Ritual of the Pentagram daily for a full year and in complete silence during that time. The tide had turned, and this was my true entry into practical magic!

In 1981, Regardie gave me a gift of approximately 200 pieces of his lifelong magical paraphernalia and equipment which is currently in a bank vault and will eventually be sent as a gift to the Warburg Institute in London, England for preservation and future generations to appreciate and experience. At this same time, Regardie had also made a gift of his practical alchemical equipment to another friend. He had secretly maintained an alchemical laboratory in a garage adjacent his house for nearly 10 years! Although Regardie's earlier conceptions pertaining to the "Stone of the Wise" reflected that the alchemical process was one of spiritual transformation, in the latter years before he died he changed his thinking and did believe in an actual "philosopher's stone." He had told me about such a Stone where one took off slight shaving with a sharp knife and mixed them with a small amount of white wine to be ingested daily. He also had several physicists and mathematicians around the country quietly working toward a scientific solution of the "Stone of the Wise." This was not an aging man's fantasy attempting to defy death's inevitability. Metaphorically, this was a Leonardo DaVinci who was making "intuitive drawings" of his conception of the "flying machine"!

Between 1981 and 1983, I studied magic under Regardie in his home and personal Temple in Sedona, Arizona. Hundreds of hours of personal instruction, stimulating conversation, practical ritual, magical drill, and warm companionship replaced his reticence of discussing magical topics 10 years before! This time with him had been a period of true asylum for me, and experiencing the pristine though primitive atmosphere of his home in Sedona with its "red rock" landscapes and quiet lifestyle contributed to the romantic conception of the "magical retirement."

In the summer of 1983, Regardie and I traveled to Fiji, Australia and New Zealand for magical as well as personal reasons. His magical career had turned full circle with his re-connection with the Felkin's legacy in New Zealand, and powerful feelings and memories were stirred within him with a disquieting poignancy. He had once remarked that the "giants" of magic had all died, and while in New Zealand reflected upon who would continue on with the work he had so carefully helped to preserve over the past fifty years. In New Zealand, I purchased a novel by Mary Renault which I read on the tedious plane ride. Its title proved to be predictive. When Regardie and I returned to the United States, I was never to see him again. He died two years later. The novel I read was entitled *The King Must Die.*

Regardie's work and legacy is that he established a bridge from the Victorian magicians to the modern day inquiring student. But the crucial question is how does that student approach and benefit from this vast and complex wealth of symbology and ritual without the aid of a guide or the support of a working group. And more importantly, how does the Golden Dawn system successfully make a "difference" in the individual's usual way of experiencing life. I am convinced that by working assiduously, or as Crowley would say "Work... Work blindly, foolishly, misguidedly, it doesn't matter in the end. Work in itself has absolute virtue" is an essential attitude to be taken toward this work. And hard work it is!

I know of two women who intuitively decided to perform the Neophyte ceremony, imagining the roles of the officers while acting as Neophyte. Although they had no duly installed Hierophant presiding, and may not have understood the magical formulae underlying their action at the time, the results were remarkable in terms of their individual magical growth and eventually being linked with an active Temple.

Upon approaching this book, I would make the following suggestions. For the first several weeks, read Regardie's introduction to the original edition contained herein. I would suggest several careful readings since this gives the student an overview of the history, structure, and function of not only the Hermetic Order of the Golden Dawn but of the Great Work itself. Allow this material to settle deeply into consciousness by reflecting, meditating, or associating any variety of images or ideas to it. Then I would suggest reading the First Knowledge lecture and then immediately begin the task of memorizing the Hebrew alphabet and its correspondences, both found within the First Knowledge Lecture. Within this system, the Hebrew alphabet has no connotation of religion or sect. Its letters are considered "generic" and "holy" symbols — powerful doorways into the inner world — and are not associated with dogma or esoteric religious organization. A convenient way of memorizing these letters is to place them on "flash" cards, not unlike what we have all become acquainted with in elementary school or in foreign language courses as a means of acquiring vocabulary.

The next step is to acquire a notebook of some kind and begin a magical journal which must be kept daily, even if it is only to quickly jot down that no work was accomplished on a given day or that one was ill. I have heard so many excuses throughout the years that journal keeping is cumbersome, purposeless, or simply not convenient, but the journal is essential. Not only is it a means of keeping track of one's progress, but it becomes the means for an active dialogue with the inner world and one's unconscious. The way in which a journal is kept can be as varied as is appropriate to any one personality, but apart from the date and time and a record of one's magical work; dreams, fantasies, body sensations, events of the day, synchronicities, astrological aspects and transits, and spontaneous imagery can all be incorporated at the choice of the student.

At this point, I would suggest the student make a full year's commitment to performing the Banishing Ritual of the Pentagram twice a day. And this should be done with a vow to silence, meaning that one does not discuss one's personal work with friends, even if they be of likemindedness. The purpose of this is to begin building with "thought," that is, by paying "attention" to a particular system of symbols they are then "built" within the "sphere of sensation" or aura much as a sculptor creates with clay. The Astral Light as termed by French occultist Eliphas Levi (Louis Alphonse Constant) is malleable by FOCUSED and CONCENTRATED thought! The symbols thus created within the aura act as doorways for healing, inspiration, protection, and guidance and prevent emotional and psychological contagion. How many of us have felt depleted by being around a depressed person or otherwise influenced by a negative environment.

Using the description of this ritual in the First Knowledge lecture as a guide, with right hand at full extension straight ahead, the Banishing Pentagram begins just opposite the left hip tracing a large inverted "V" down to the right hip crossing up to and outwards from the left shoulder, over to the right shoulder, and then most importantly reconnecting at the starting point. The dagger is never lowered and also traces a circle connecting each pentagram. The tracing is imagined as blue flame flecked with gold, not unlike a gas flame. The four archangels are imagined as towering figures which bring a refreshing Air from the East, cleansing Water from the West, purifying Fire from the South, and Earth as a stabilizer in perseverance from the North. The ritual is performed without expecting results, change, or power, but quietly persevered in for a full year while carefully noting how it affects the personality and outer life. Ideally, the ritual should be performed in the same location apart from the gaze of others, and if possible, in a place set apart from day to day interference.

At this point, I would then suggest the student read the Neophyte Ritual slowly, carefully, and contemplatively over the period of at least a month while still maintaining daily devotion to the Banishing Ritual of the Pentagram and persevering in the memorization work discussed above. It is within this ritual that are the formulae for future practical magical operations as well as it being the engine whereby the candidate is brought to the Light. The importance of this ritual cannot be emphasized enough, not only in its content, but in the movements and identities of the officers as well as a kind of "glamour" that is created by a number of the speeches. Although the style of writing is at times oblique, this is not only a ritual to be understood in terms of its content, but to be additionally "experienced" devoid of rational explanation of content! And the writing style facilitates this greatly. Toward the end of this month, the student may wish to add the Neophyte meditation which also is contained within the First Knowledge lecture. Although Regardie was never particularly attracted to or impressed by these simple meditations at the end of each Knowledge Lecture, I have found them of immense value.

This then is a suggested schema for approaching each of the elemental rituals and Knowledge Lectures in the Outer Order that follow the Neophyte Ritual. The elemental rituals have been criticized from a variety of courts as to their superficiality or continued maintenance of Victorian occult "claptrap." Nothing could be further from the truth! Anyone who would make such allegations has not experienced these rituals in full Temple again and again and seen their worth, stimulating possibility, and enduring freshness. If the student would persevere slowly and with discipline in the above for at least six months, a very firm foundation would be laid indeed! At that point, a study of the Inner Order rituals and the material of Books Four, Five, and Six will not only be easier to comprehend, but a fertile inner "soil" within the psyche will have been well prepared for the planting of powerful inner life generating seeds. At this point the student should begin to pay persistent attention to the "Z" documents, appreciating that a lifetime will never exhaust their amazing wealth of possibilities and inspiration. Finally, echoing Regardie's earlier warning, and a fair warning it is, the Enochian system of magic should be left strictly alone until one has left no other stone unturned in this book to the point where every correspondence is memorized, every technique understood, and every ritual experienced.

The above suggestions presuppose that the student will be working alone, and working alone can be very effective. Taking steps toward one's Holy Guardian Angel or personal Genius through attention to this inner awareness, inspiration, and guidance. The "Right" persons or situation will automatically be available for the individual as he or she is ready for them, as in the often quoted occult aphorism, paraphrased: when the student is ready, the teacher will appear. So there should be a relaxed attitude toward persisting in the work and knowing that one is guided in spite of oneself! However, the student may eventually be brought into contact with a group and the following are important issues to reflect upon. ALL groups have a hierarchy or "pecking" order even if this may be heatedly denied by the group. Regardie felt that the Golden Dawn system was particularly effective in activating the darker or unknown parts of each member. While this may be true, it has been my observation that ANY group (be it even most benign and well-intentioned in its purpose) still grapples with projections of all kinds and ultimately with the issue of POWER! A talented and creative professor of mine once commented to me several years ago that the next great frontier for psychological research (beyond the current fascination with sex roles) was power! Participation in group effort automatically calls for multiple parental and sibling projections and each person's genetic material comes into play. The student's only safeguard in these situations is "consciousness," which is not easily come by! Regardie felt the only way for these conflicts to be worked through was for the individual to be in psychotherapy in tandem with magical work. His adamant insistence upon this is something to be seriously examined.

While driving back to his home from Flagstaff, Arizona one day through a tentative drizzling rain, Regardie had confided to me that it had taken him about seven years to recover from his breach with Crowley. At some point, Dion Fortune had offered him rest and asylum in her country home in the neighborhood of Glastonbury in England. There the younger Regardie went to heal and plan his life further. Fortune was fascinated by this "new" brand of self-exploration called Freudian "analysis" and even went so far as to engage in being (what was then called) a "lay" analyst. This term meant that the analyst was not bound by the training, educational, or licensure restrictions which were adopted in the United States sometime after World War II, but instead studied privately under a mentor who more often than not was one's own analyst. I would speculate that Fortune was a significant influence on Regardie at that time in terms of aiding him toward a different kind of explanation of the chaos and abandonment he had been experiencing up to that point as well as helping him to forage an expanded understanding of the future direction of his life within the containment of his interests in magic and mysticism.

Regardie experienced Jungian analysis in London and Reichian therapy later in New York City. While he maintained a profound respect for Jung's theoretical concepts, he felt that Reichian technique was infinitely more effective than free association, dream interpretation, or a verbal analysis of the transference. While both approaches to therapy have their merits and limitations, I am more convinced that the "match" between therapist and client is a more salient issue than orientation. I would suggest that the student who engages in therapy in tandem with magical work read the first edition of Robert Langs' *Psychotherapy, A Basic Text,* as a guide, paying particular attention to what Langs refers to as the "framework." The "framework" (or Jungian "temenos") is universal and essential, and depending on how well a therapist maintains it, determines the outcome and effectiveness of therapy.

In Regardie's first edition of *The Middle Pillar* in 1938 he wrote, "These ideas are mentioned not because a systematic union of Magic and Psychology will be here presented, but in the hope that this effort will spur some psychologist acquainted with magical and mystical techniques to attempt such a task. Whoever does succeed in welding the two indissolubly together, to him mankind will ever be grateful." And so this book has great value for therapists as well to explore its content for fresh ideas and catalytic suggestions toward innovative research. Jung's *The Psychology of Transference* is immeasureably illuminated by Golden Dawn concepts of Rosicruciannism and alchemy. When Jung speaks of the "rose" in this work, by interpreting that rose as the Rose Cross of the Inner Order, one's associations and insights are deeply enriched knowing that this is not an abstruse alchemical reference, but a powerful engine for any variety of practical purpose. Additionally, Edinger's development of such themes in *Ego and Archetype* as the "blood of Christ" or the four elements is markedly enhanced when understood with the respective Golden Dawn concepts pertaining to the Hebrew letter "Shin" or the significance of the four elements on the altar in the Neophyte Hall.

The Current of The Hermetic Order the Golden Dawn is alive with a brilliant blaze re-ignited by Regardie's patient tending to it over the past 50 years when many a storm threatened to extinguish it when it became a small spark. And the student will *find* that Current by personal inner work and not through external organizations, initiations for a fee, or publicized Grade attainments. As Paul Foster Case wrote in *The True and Invisible Rosicrucian Order,* "There is a true Rosicrucian Order. If you are duly and truly prepared, you will undoubtedly make contact . . . in due season . . . I do not condemn pretenders. They condemn themselves."

Llewellyn Publications and Carl L. Weschcke are to be congratulated on this special presentation of the first paperback edition of this significant work. That the original pagination has been maintained for purposes of reference and future research is only one example that points to the long standing commitment of Llewellyn to high standards and impeccable quality. Many people have played an invaluable and special role in my life since 1980, and I would like to acknowledge some of them now. The contributing editors to this edition: Anupassana, George Wilson, and Hal Sundt have taken immense time and responsibility for making this an unparallelled edition of critical and extended material. Adam Forrest has been my faithful Golden Dawn companion and guide, and Chic Cicero has achieved attainments in actualizing Golden Dawn symbolism seldom possible. I also wish to thank Stephan Hoeller, for the first Light, Don Kraig for stimulating conversation and ideas, and my dear friends in New Mexico for bringing me closer to the Feminine. Finally, I wish to heartfully thank Richard Auger Ph.D. for his patient participation in my own perilous "Night Sea Journey."

When Regardie finished his introduction to the original edition, he concluded with the words that his work was done. My work, your work, all of us as true fratres and sorores who seek the Ruby Rose, the Cross of Gold, and the True Stone of the Wise . . . our Work too, just begun!

Cris Monnastre
Corpus Christi
Los Angeles, 1986

INDEXING THE GOLDEN DAWN
by David Godwin

I must admit that, when Carl Weschcke asked me to do an index for *The Golden Dawn*—a job for which I eagerly volunteered—I underestimated the effort involved and the amount of time required to complete such a project. I thought I had a fair grasp of the methods and teachings of the Order, but preparing an index taught me that I didn't know quite as much as I supposed! I knew, of course, that the Golden Dawn had an elaborate system of correspondences—but even I did not begin to guess *how* elaborate! It was partly to dispel similar confusion on the part of others that this index was prepared. I learned a great deal in the process and therefore have no cause to regret any of it.

It is now possible, however—as one small example—to trace the use of each magical implement, each oft-repeated invocation, each name of each spiritual entity, and even each use of each element, planet, Sephira, and Zodiacal sign in either a grade ceremony or one of the example rituals such as evocation or charging a talisman. The index contains many cross-references. I hope the reader will be patient with these and study them, because they are the key to the whole system. It would have necessitated an index twice this size if they had not been used, and the Order's system of correspondences definitely required them. For example, there are over 120 subheadings under the listing for the element of Air—intimidating at first glance, but *it lets you find what you want!* If you want to know the appropriate Enochian call for the Air angle of the Water tablet without having to skim through the book to find it, here it is. A quick glance down the column of subheadings will also give you all the correspondences and meanings of the element, many of which may surprise you as they did me. You may find yourself saying, as I did, "How about that!" or "I never thought of that before!" Of course, the same thing is true for each of the elements as well as the planets, Sephiroth, Tarot cards, ceremonies—whatever your interest may be at the moment.

Let it be said at the outset that several key terms used throughout the book have *not* been indexed: consciousness, Genius, God, Great Work, Higher Self, Higher Soul, Light, Magic of Light, Qabalah, etc. These terms occur so frequently that any mere list of page numbers would be so lengthy as to be meaningless. Citations for these words belong more properly in a concordance than in an index designed to help the student find and research various concepts. In a sense, they may be said to epitomize the subject of the entire work. If this statement is true of any one word more than any other, that word would be "Light." Of course! That's what it's all about.

In this index, variant spellings are cross-referenced, or, if very similar, given in parentheses. The Golden Dawn documents make use of many spelling variations, particularly in the case of Coptic names. When these documents were written, there was no standardized system of transliteration from languages such as Hebrew, Aramaic, and Coptic that do not (or did not) use the Roman alphabet. Hence the name spelled in Hebrew as *aleph lamed* was rendered both "Al" and "El." The Hebrew letter *shin,* normally representing an "sh" sound, was commonly translitered as "sch"—a practice which supports the order's claims of a German connection. This is to say nothing of the differences between the usual Golden Dawn spellings and those of more modern authors, not indicated in this index, such as the Golden Dawn's "Qlippoth" vs. Gershom Scholem's "kelippot." Enochian words and names were usually spelled phonetically, and opinions differed then as now as to the proper pronunciation, so that John Dee's "Ol sonf vorsg" becomes "Ol sonuf vaorsagi" or some variant thereof, and the name "Ikzhikal" becomes "Ic Zod Heh Chal." This index follows Golden Dawn usage, with the pure Enochian form cross-referenced where it is otherwise almost unrecognizable.

There is some inconsistency concerning whether Enochian names are to be written in all capital letters or with an initial capital only. I have usually followed the latter procedure as being more readable (for example, "Exarp" instead of "EXARP").

Something also needs to be said about the court cards of the Tarot. There has been--and still is—a certain amount of confusion arising from the differences between Golden Dawn terminology and the traditional designations. In the Golden Dawn system, the Kings become Princes, and the Knights become Kings! A. E. Waite, who used the traditional terminology in his book on the Tarot and in his very popular Tarot deck, to avoid giving away the secrets of the order, nevertheless tipped his hand when he said that the Kings are to be used as significators for young men and the Knights for men over forty. Such a procedure makes no particular sense unless you know the Golden Dawn system.

The following table may help to clarify matters.

Traditional	*Golden Dawn*	*Letter of Tetragrammaton*
King	Prince	Vav
Queen	Queen	Heh
Knight	King	Yod
Page or Knave	Princess	Heh final

Unfortunately, the Golden Dawn documents themselves contribute to this confusion by appearing to be, on the surface at least, somewhat inconsistent. In this index, I have tried to clarify matters by citing "Kings," for example, as "Kings (Princes)."

The section entitled "The Tree of Life as Projected in a Solid Sphere" (pages 594-621) has been, in all previous editions published by Llewellyn and others, overflowing with mistakes and typos. I assume that these errors must have been in the original document that Regardie first published in the '30s.

Most of the errors were in the names of the constellations, which are in Latin. Mathers, the author of the original document, knew Latin well enough, so I assume the mistakes were copying errors made as the document was passed along, and that the copy which finally reached Regardie was rather corrupt.

The names of the constellations have changed in the last hundred years, paticularly in the Southern hemisphere; I have attempted to research such changes in Richard Hinckley Allen's *Star Names.* Nevertheless, making all such allowances, there were still many mistakes and several instances of what amounted to gibberish. The document as it stood would certainly have proved a puzzle to anyone actually attempting to use it as intended. Much time would have been wasted researching non-existent constellation names in an attempt to correlate the cards of the Tarot with the sphere of the heavens. For example, the constellation Pyxis Nautica ("the mariner's compass") appeared as "Pisces Nautica" ("the mariner's fishes"). What fish were doing on board the ship Argo, the larger constellation of which Pyxis Nautica is a part, I can't tell you. I don't recollect that Jason was on a fishing trip. There were also several constellations listed as "Pisces" which should have been "Piscis" (singular, just one fish), such as "Piscis Australis." It was plain that "Pisces Volcan" should have been "Piscis Volans," the flying fish, now known simply as "Volans."

Something like the discrepancy involved between "Camelopardus" vs. "Camelopardalis" was no problem; the constellation has been known by both these names at various times. But there is no such star group as Rhombus (p. 600, #40). It should have been part of the preceding name—"Reticulum Rhomboidalis." On the next page, the name "Naochi" was listed. There is not now and never has been a star or constellation called "Naochi." The best I could make out of this was that "Naochi" was originally part of the previous name, Columba, in the form "Columba Noae," Noah's dove, an older name for the constellation.

To avoid confusion by anyone referring to an earlier edition, I have attempted to cross-reference all the old, corrupted names of the constellations. For example, there are entries such as *Pyxis Nautica ("Pisces Nautica")* and *Pisces Nautica—see Pyxis Nautica.*

Unfortunately, it was largely unavoidable to incorporate the 19th-century sexism of the Golden Dawn documents into this index. The order was ahead of its time in recognizing the importance of the feminine aspect of deity, admitting women to membership, and recommending that certain officers of the order be women. Nevertheless, "man" is still used as a generic term for "human being" (as in Mathers' document, "The Microcosm-Man"), and, as just one other example, nearly all references to Egyptian deities, whether female or male, are to "Egyptian gods." I have adhered to Golden Dawn terminology to avoid confusion.

Using the Index:

Numbers in parentheses refer to the original volume number and pagination. Roman numerals refer to the Foreword and Appreciation by Carl Llewellyn Weschcke and to the Introduction to the Fifth Edition by Cris Monnastre, the latter of which is a personal account of her encounter with Israel Regardie and experience with the Golden Dawn system. Pages 1-48 consist of introductory material by Israel Regardie and contain much valuable information and commentary.

All readers may not be familiar with the notation *"passim,"* which occurs frequently throughout this index. It means "here and there," and it indicates that the indexed item occurs on every page included in the notation *(passim)*, but that those pages do not constitute a continuous discussion of that item alone. For example, 201-5 *passim* means that the indexed word occurs on pages 201, 202, 203, 204, and 205, but in the course of a discussion of a more inclusive topic. The most frequent example would be an officer in a ritual. The general topic is the ritual itself (for example, "Adeptus Minor ritual, 221-47"), but the officer's appearances and speeches occur on almost every page (for example, "Adept, Second, in Adeptus Minor ritual, 221-42 *passim*, 246, 247").

The letter "n" following a page reference indicates that the item appears in a footnote on that page but not anywhere else on the page.

A note on using these cross-references: if items are separated by commas (as in "*see also* Enochian, angels"), the first word listed refers to the main heading and any subsequent words refer to subheadings in that listing rather than to a separate citation. Separate listings, on the other hand, are separated by semicolons (for example, "*see also* keyword analysis; Opening by Watchtower"). Naturally, the two methods are sometimes combined, as in "*see also* Knights (Kings); Tarot, court cards." This means to consult the listing for "Knights (Kings)" (under "K") and the subheading "court cards" under "Tarot" (listed under "T"), but it does not mean to look for "court cards" under "C."

I apologize to the more scholarly for taking the space to explain all this, but I do not wish to puzzle anyone who is not familiar with these usages.

—David Godwin

INTRODUCTION TO THE SECOND EDITION

Volume I

It would be trite to say that life is a strange, wonderful and mysterious process. But it is! In his *Triumphal Chariot of Antimony,* the alchemist Basil Valentine describes his antimony as a deadly poison on the one hand, yet, when purified alchemically, as a potent medicament on the other. Apparently this *Golden Dawn* material has to be described in rather the same way—reminding me of an old adage concerning money. It passes through the lives of an infinite number of people to change their lives catalytically, but in the process always remaining untouched itself.

At the same time, it recalls to mind several letters that were received years ago following the publication of the first of the four volumes in the original edition. Anyone would have thought, judging from the tone of some of these letters, that I had become exalted to the throne of God Almighty himself. Even a few came from active Order members scattered in various parts of the world, corroborating many of the critical allegations made earlier in *My Rosicrucian Adventure.* Though the latter book was published independently of *The Golden Dawn,* it was originally written to serve as an introduction to the whole body of Order teaching.

On the other hand, there was a long letter from the late Captain J. Langford Garstin, under his Order sacramental name, chiding me severely for publishing the secret teachings of the Order, and asking me in the future never again to refer to the Order by name. And, strangely enough, one of the last letters received from Aleister Crowley before we became estranged (as described in *The Eye in the Triangle)* stated two things. First, in connection with my statement that one of the officiating officers had hurried through an initiatory ritual as though reading a batch of grocery bills—he remarked that I should have rudely told him to go to Jericho, or words to that effect. And secondly, relative to the material itself, he roundly scolded me, stating I had absolutely no right whatsoever to have published this material and to have broken my sacred obligation to secrecy. Many decades earlier, he had published these same Order teachings in the *Equinox*—only under direct command from the Secret Chiefs of the Order, at least that was his claim.

If Aleister Crowley disapproved of my action, I have to be egostistical enough to assume that my editorial job was far better than his own with his amanuensis of that time, Captain J. F. C. Fuller. My version certainly was more orderly, more adherent to the *letter* of the Order system, and unmarred by too many extraneous comments and some hideous garbling.

So there we are. Some approved of the publication of these books; a very few disapproved. That's all there is to it.

Whatever I have done in the past, has been done. I have, basically, no regrets. Perhaps the only fleeting or hesitant regret that I do have is a doubt as to whether publication has actually done much good, whether students at large were able to utilize the system in the manner I had hoped for. This is a serious doubt; oral instruction is invaluable, and should be given only under the guidance of a teacher, or within the framework of an Order.

The past two or three decades have revealed something else as a definite disadvantage. The average student approaching *The Golden Dawn* has simply been overwhelmed by the sheer weight and wealth of original teaching material. As he glances through the large four-volume set, understanding but little of it, he becomes altogether confused, thrust headlong into despair, and does not pause long enough to study the system in small sections until he does discover its intent and purpose.

In the Order—or *any* occult organization for that matter—no student was ever bombarded with too much study material at the beginning. He is spoonfed small doses, as it were, monthly. Some critics regard this procedure as a "come on," as bait merely to keep the student paying his monthly dues for long periods of time. In some instances, this may well be true. On the contrary, it is sometimes given in this form, I am sure, so that the student can study a little of it at a time, transmuting it into personal property by assimilating it piecemeal into his own psychic structure. Then more teaching was assigned, and so on. Periodically an examination, oral and written, was given, not to grade the student in conventional terms, nor to put him on the spot, but to ascertain whether or not he had grasped and understood the preceding lessons.

This procedure is not possible in a book like *The Golden Dawn.* Of course it could have been re-written in lesson form with the above intent in mind, cautioning the student not to proceed until he had thoroughly grasped each segment of the work. But it was not done that way.

Under these circumstances, therefore, it remains only for the intelligent student to work out his own study technique or regimen. If he is not astute enough to perceive the practicality or necessity of the above, then quite evidently he is not intelligent enough to deal with the material itself, and it should not be in his possession at all.

This is the counsel I would give to the serious student of the Great Work. Study the contents of the first two volumes, now combined to form a single book, as if you were a member of an Order, and were receiving a monthly monogram or lesson from headquarters. Glance through *all* the material once or twice just to get the drift of it, and then allocate to yourself *a few pages only* at a time.

If these pages are not clear at first, which is more than likely, then I would strongly suggest supplementing them with additional reading. First of all, I would recommend an old book of mine, *The Garden of Pomegranates.* This is a simple outline of the Qabalah comprising the backbone of the Order philosophy. It has been out of print for several years. Thanks to Llewellyn Publications it is on its way back into circulation once more in a new edition. It should prove a useful guide through the initial knowledge lectures of the Order as given in volume one of *The Golden Dawn.*

In particular, two Order papers in this volume are supremely important documents. They are *The Path of the Chameleon* (p. 95) which deals comprehensively with the Tree of Life, and another one entitled *The Microcosm* (p. 100). It is my suggestion that they should be studied over and over again, if necessary using *The Garden of Pomegranates* as a companion and as an aid to simplification. Sometimes the language of S. Liddell MacGregor Mathers, who apparently was the author of these papers, was not as simple as it might have been. Be that as it may, nothing should deter the serious student from extracting the last drop of intellectual nutriment from these papers.

There is also the new edition of *The Tree of Life* (Samuel Weiser, New York, 1968), which provides an elementary introduction to magical procedures, the heart and core of the practical work of the Order. With these two simple books, and only a few pages of *The Golden Dawn* handled at any single time, most of the complex problems should be eliminated.

Such a course is analogous to the procedure used in driving across the country, say from Los Angeles to New York City, approximately three thousand miles. This is a considerable distance. But by setting intermediate goals and marking them on your road maps the journey is made much easier. Then each day one aims not for New York but for the next town or city, perhaps three or four hundred miles from your present stop. In this way, the limited objective is easily reached without the driver being overwhelmed by the enormity of the distance to his final goal, New York City.

Much the same progress should be followed here where the study material is concerned. Make sure you allow enough time for this initial material to be absorbed before you press onward. More haste means less speed. Take your time. There is no hurry. In many such cliches, there is a profound wisdom.

In the opening passages of the very first initiatory ritual of the Order is found the remarkable phrase "By names and images are all powers awakened and reawakened."

This simple phrase sets the stage, as it were, for all subsequent Order teaching. In effect it reveals the essential fact involved in all practical magical work. Most of the later instructions merely elaborate the necessity for the correct vibration of the highest Divine Names, and the building up in the imagination of pictures of one kind or another. In all of the major rituals, and in all such instructions as those on talismans and telesmatic images, the basic factors are those mentioned in the very simple phrase given above. Never let it be forgotten, when apparently submerged in a mass of complicated attributions and technical details, that the essence of magic is simple. So simple in fact, that a vast amount of self-discipline and training is required to make it effective.

The counsel given in the Portal document (p. 175 of volume One), preparing the student for the Adept grade is of the greatest importance here. It should be read, reread, and then studied some more.

One of the items referred to for the first time in this Portal document is "building the Tree of Life in the aura." I have found this rudimentary scheme so useful and so important in my own growth and development that it came to have tremendous significance in my own daily practice. There is rarely a time when I permit myself to fall asleep at night without "lighting the lamp above my head", as I personally describe for myself the formulation of Kether. *This powerful magical technique is vital and I cannot recommend it too highly.* I have elaborated this rudimentary outline considerably in a simple little manual I wrote over thirty years ago entitled *The Art of True Healing.* It should also prove useful to the student just getting the feel of these magico-mystical methods.

This particular Portal document is one of the most practical of all in *The Golden Dawn* curriculum. The reader should study it almost beyond all else, applying its recommendations in his efforts to integrate *The Golden Dawn* teachings into his life and mind. Its counsel is invaluable. If only the students who had written to me to complain of the overwhelming quantity and quality of teaching, had first heeded its instructions and counsel, their opinion might have been different. It is a sensible and rational approach to a vast subject with almost infinite ramifications.

Once this counsel has been well heeded, and closely adhered to, then the student could start dealing with the simplest elements of ritual and ceremonial procedures. An attempt to handle the complex initiatory rituals of the Grades without proper preparation and guidance, can only end in failure. Much the same is true of the complicated ceremonies described in the third volume. Leave them severely alone until you have studied them sufficiently to know what you are doing. This may take considerable time.

Start off first with what is known as the Lesser Banishing Ritual of the Pentagram (p. 106, Volume I). This is a simple procedure. Follow the written instructions to the letter—literally, and then the ritual itself will present no difficulties. Problems only arise when the student propels himself in to these activities without proper study and preparation. Stay with this simple ritual until you become expert. Then begin to practice what should be done with the imagination as you make the appropriate gestures with your outstretched arm (without a magical weapon—that comes later), and the appropriate movements around your own axis or around the room where you work. Do not leave the topic until absolute perfection has been obtained, else you may be obliged to return and master it before you can proceed to more advanced matters.

Then experiment with the simple Rose-Cross Ritual (p. 46 of Volume III). Though this ritual is described in a later volume than the two now under discussion, it could well be taken out of context and mastered at the same time as the Pentagram Ritual. This ritual of the Rose-Cross teaches the formulation of the symbol in the four corners of the room, as well as above and below the axis where you stand. It results in surrounding yourself with the traditional symbol. It will provide basic discipline in at least three important matters:

1. Tracing geometrical figures with the hand.
2. Imagining them clearly in your mind.
3. Vibrating the appropriate names.

A simple instruction on the latter process is to be found in the Portal paper already mentioned, as well as in several other very important documents scattered through the remaining volumes. Study could be supplemented by consulting another old book of mine *The Middle Pillar* (Llewellyn Publications, St. Paul, 1970), which summarizes most of the Order teachings on this topic.

The meditations given in Volume I are relatively simple, though some of the descriptive material attached to them are not likely to be applicable to the beginner. In addition to these, or else as an alternative, I would like to recommend a series of meditations or psychophysical exercises which could do much to prepare the student in a more dynamic way for this phase of things. They are to be found in a little book recently written by me called *Twelve Steps to Spiritual Enlightenment* (Sangreal Foundation, Texas, 1969). It should prove useful in this connection.

It might also be worthwhile for the student really to start studying the initiatory rituals, beginning naturally with the 0=0 or Neophyte degree. Again, I would counsel patience. Do not hurry. Read the ritual many times in order to clearly understand its importance, its theme of bringing the candidate to the Light, and what is involved in the various movements of the officers. Only when thoroughly conversant with these ideas, should the student attempt to place himself in his imagination within the ritualistic movements themselves. This should be done in segments, a little at a time, until he feels at ease practicing the ritualistic movements in his imagination. The same type of procedure should be followed with each of the following elemental initiations.

Naturally, this involves a great deal of effort and time, and should be extended over many weeks or months. Hurrying through it in order to get to the next grade will only defeat your own purpose, and you will derive next to nothing from what you do. Again and again, it has to be stated—*Make haste slowly!* Don't hurry.

Some of the speeches made by various officers during the ceremonies are magnificent and are well worth memorizing. The adoration that is a constant through all the rituals and which is of Gnostic origin is certainly one of these:

> Holy art thou, Lord of the Universe.
> Holy art thou, whom Nature hath not formed.
> Holy art thou, the Vast and the Mighty One.
> Lord of the Light and the Darkness.

Another lovely passage which deserves a place in all of one's private devotions and spiritual exercises is this one:

> Glory be to Thee, Father of the Undying. For thy Glory flows out rejoicing, to the ends of the earth.

Perhaps one of the most important of these passages to be memorized, and which is unequivocally at the core of all the Qabalistic teaching in the Order is the excerpt from the Neophyte ritual:

> Unbalanced Power is the ebbing away of life.

Unbalanced Mercy is weakness and the fading out of the Will.
Unbalanced Severity is cruelty and the barrenness of Mind.

A whole textbook could be elaborated on this one simple piece of teaching. Since the Order system is replete with such choice gems, it is clear that volumes would be required to elaborate the beauty and full meaning of its teaching.

Still another dynamic passage which could be incorporated into one's daily practice of the Middle Pillar technique:

I come in the power of the Light.
I come in the Light of Wisdom.
I come in the Mercy of the Light.
The Light hath healing in its Wings!

All of these are beautiful and their eloquence lingers with deep feeling in my memory. In one's private spritiual work, a place could be found for many of them. As one progresses in the Path of Light, they take on more significance and radiance, tending to evoke higher states of consciousness.

I should like to add a little more to the general counsel of this all-important Portal document. If the student has not recently brushed up on his anatomy and physiology, the essentials of which are absolutely necessary parts of the intellectual armamentarium of a well-educated person, I should like to recommend an excellent manual which has impressed me and which should answer the average need rather well. It is Logan Clendenning's *The Human Body*. It once appeared in a paperback edition which was rapidly sold out. I am hoping it will soon be reprinted in a similar edition.

The following books are recommended in lieu of those mentioned in the text. From my viewpoint, they are more up-to-date and therefore more useful.

For a general outline of psychological functioning, I would suggest *Psychology* by Norman Munn (Houghton Mifflin, Boston). On the dynamic side, *An Elementary Textbook of Psychoanalysis* by Charles Brenner (Anchor Books, New York, 1957) is superb, to be followed by *Man and His Symbols* edited by Carl G. Jung (Doubleday, New York, 1964).

The Function of the Orgasm by Wilhelm Reich (Orgone Institute Press, New York, 1942) is a *must*. A cheaper paperback edition has appeared since that date. I consider it a necessity, because, without intending to do so, Reich has succeeded in building a bridge between the modern psychologies and occultism. Were he alive, he would have a fit to learn of this interpretation—but fit or no fit, it is still a fact. What he had to say, and the therapeutic method he developed and called vegetotherapy, have been found of inestimable value in my life, and the two hundred hours of therapy I had years ago comprise an experience that today, in retrospect, I would not be without.

With these materials in mind, the serious student might well be persuaded, as I was once, to enter psychotherapy. It is of small consequence what analytical school he selects. All are useful. All provide help for the student in his search for the Light, and serve as excellent preparation for the serious discipline of Magic and self-knowledge.

Where the divinatory techniques are concerned, the counsel given in the Portal paper under consideration is still valid. Newer and better books on astrology have been published since that Portal paper was first written. Dane Rudhyar's *Astrology of Personality* is an excellent textbook for the inquisitive student. The author regards astrology as the "algebra of life" which gives meaningful relationships to the events of life.

A more comprehensive but less philosophical text is the *A to Z Horoscope Maker and Delineator* by Llewellyn George (Llewellyn Publications, St. Paul). These two should be studied together.

With regard to alchemy, while some of the basic definitions of the so-called

Knowledge lectures are accurate enough so far as generalizations go, they may be of small value when examining classical spagyric texts. The later work of the Order is also surprisingly vague on alchemy, and contributes little to clarify understanding. Some extraneous help is obviously required on this topic. I strongly recommend *The Alchemist's Handbook* by Frater Albertus (Paracelsus Research Society, Salt Lake City, 1964). While lacking in literary style, it is nevertheless one of the most complete introductions to alchemy I have ever found, providing as it does, an ABC of practical instruction. I know of no other that even attempts this task.

The Order instructions on Geomancy are in the fourth volume of the original edition (Volume II of this new one). I mention it here, albeit prematurely, because the Portal paper brings up the topic. There is no equivalent instruction elsewhere. I grew to like this as a divinatory method, using and experimenting with it extensively for several years. It can be operated swiftly and easily to get a direct "yes" or "no" answer, though a great many more details can be elicited with but little application and study.

In spite of A. E. Waite's stuffiness and turgidity, his short method of Tarot divination using a ten card layout, as described towards the end of his book *A Pictorial Key to the Tarot* (University Books, New York), is a useful, simple and direct method. It can and should, of course, be supplemented by some of the brief Order definitions as laid down in the second volume of this edition. Practice will demonstrate its value. The unsuspecting student will rapidly discover his intuition and psychic faculties will undergo a marked stimulation and development by the use of these methods.

Insofar as the Portal document suggests the student reflect on "words and the power of words," I am reminded of something I have long wanted to say, but somehow neglected. I would like strongly to recommend *The Miracle of Language* by Charlton Laird (Premier Books, New York, 1953), a superb piece of writing, with deep insight and humor, relative to the origins of our own language. And secondly, the topic of general semantics is an absolute necessity for the serious student on the Path. *Language in Action* by S. I. Hayakawa (Harcourt Brace, New York, 1939) is a lucid, insightful introduction to a difficult subject, which should be followed by *People in Quandaries* by Wendell Johnson (Harper, New York, 1946).

Few mystics or occult teachers have taken general semantics to their bosoms. Most of them, I fancy, know nothing about the subject. A few hold it in disdain, perhaps out of fear. With considerable pleasure, I urge every student to read *The Problem of Good and Evil* or *The Christos* by Vitvan (School of the Natural Order, Baker, Nevada). Both of these books attempt to correlate the ancient wisdom both of the East and the West with the techniques of Count Korzybski who developed general semantics. Reading this literature should considerably broaden the mental and spiritual horizons of the sincere and serious student. It will also help him keep a level head where the occult jungle is concerned, so that he will not fall prey to the vast mass of fantasy and hysteria which have sadly infiltrated this field.

If it appears that in dealing with this opening volume of *The Golden Dawn* I have done little else than recommend a wide selection of books, I had a purpose in so doing. Those books suggested are excellent additions to the basic requisites of a sound occult library. Secondly, they may succeed in training the would-be mystic and student of magic to be skeptical, well-informed, and intuitive all at the same time. Thirdly, they will go far towards disciplining his mind, enabling him to manage more intelligently this mass of material subsumed under the words *The Golden Dawn*.

Such a preparation is not easily come by, and for that reason should not be lightly treated.

November 25, 1968
ISRAEL REGARDIE

NOTE TO THIRD EDITION

As a final word I should like to add that the Introduction written for the original edition is still important, in my estimation. It should certainly be studied by the new student. When stimulated by enquiries from correspondents in various countries all over the world, I have often returned to it myself, reading it with renewed interest as though written by other than myself long ago. Composed under trying circumstances, it succeeded in conveying nonetheless the essential facts surrounding the history and noble teaching of the Order.

I do not think the Order will have good reason for disowning it, should this book survive and be read a century or two from today. It emphasizes the fundamental theme of Order teaching—"Long hast thou dwelt in darkness. Quit the Night and seek the Day."

I pray this will never be forsaken.

November 14, 1969

INTRODUCTION TO THE SECOND EDITION

Volume II

This second volume (comprising Volumes III and IV of the first edition) should present little problem to the student who has scrupulously followed the counsel detailed in the Introduction to the first volume (Volumes I and II of the first edition). Exactly the same procedure should be followed where this particular volume is concerned as with the first.

These volumes are nothing less than an ENCYCLOPEDIA OF PRACTICAL OCCULTISM, and the wise student will regard them as absolutely that, and perhaps a good deal more. Most phases of the ancient knowledge are explored and described in full in one document or another. They need to be read and studied and practised over a long period of time for their usefulness fully to be realized. An encyclopedia should be handled with loving care; how much more so then, an encyclopedia which elaborates so many hitherto obscure aspects of the secret knowledge?

"Before all things are the Chaos, the Darkness and the Gates of the Land of the Night." Thus runs one excerpt from a ritual in this particular volume. It is particularly apt. All the ritual workings and descriptions of the magical rubrics to be employed will at first appear utterly chaotic and without meaning. Only with consistent effort and a well-laid out plan of study and practice will this chaos gradually lift to be replaced by enlightenment, order, and meaning.

"After the formless and the Void and the Darkness, then cometh the knowledge of the Light"

Let the student therefore give himself ample time to study casually at first this next volume—remembering that it contains the last two volumes of the old edition, replete with the most illuminating material conceivable, which requires to be understood thoroughly. Even after the lapse of forty years, when I first became aware of this teaching through Aleister Crowley's several volumes of *The Equinox,* I still thrill inwardly with spiritual excitement as I glance through the volumes to be commented on. I can wish no less for the sincere student who is willing to devote time and effort to comprehending the nature of this magical system.

The first two documents that should be thoroughly studied are the descriptions of the usages of the Pentagram and Hexagram. The language is unnecessarily archaic, and one of the aids to comprehension that I would suggest is this: *After reading it many, many times so as to be quite sure that the contents are understood, try to rewrite the instructions in simple every-day English.* This is not as difficult as it sounds. The benefit to be derived from this is an increase in understanding far greater than anything you would initially expect.

In the earlier volume, there was a lesser form of Pentagram ritual given for daily usage, together with the simple Rose-Cross ritual. If the student has followed this recommendation, by the time he gets to studying this present volume, he should be quite expert in tracing these lineal figures. All that is required now is a slight expansion of his already existent knowledge, to incorporate the new but basic data to be found in these two documents. The rewriting that the student will do is to enable him to omit all extraneous and unnecessary verbiage, leaving the essence of the instruction uncomplicated and simple. It will be this simple material which needs to be assimilated to the previously learned data.

Continuing with the study of the rituals, let the student study the beautiful simplicity of the construction of such rituals as are intended for the consecration of the various weapons or instruments that are to be used. There is no need to rush headlong into making the instruments. Delay this process for a while until the meaning of the ceremonies is assimilated into the psyche. Again, I would suggest that the student select a simple consecration ceremony, such as that for the Lotus Wand, and analyze it with as much attention and care as he would have done the Neophyte Ritual in the preceding volume. Apart from all else, it lays down the simplest possible forms or principles upon which ceremonies should be constructed.

Though the manufacture of the elemental weapons is a simple enough procedure, although a time-consuming one, these should be postponed until all the consecration ceremonies have been studied closely enough to have yielded their ultimate secrets. There are far more complicated rituals depicted in Volume III (old edition) but these particular shorter consecration ceremonies take the prize for simplicity, sincerity and efficacy. I was particularly impressed by the skill and ingenuity involved in the writing, for example, of the consecration ceremony for the four elemental weapons. Its virtuosity renders it altogether unique.

These matters make one ponder anew the origins of The Golden Dawn and its teachings. What McGregor Mather has written and published is of course good; of this there is little question. But not one of his three published works—*The Kabbalah Unveiled, The Greater Key of King Solomon,* and *The Sacred Magic of Abramelin*—bears the intrinsic stamp of genius or uniqueness. Nothing that Dr. William Wynn Westcott wrote is exempt from the same criticism. His book on the Kaballah is simple, clear and informative—but it bears no resemblance to the peculiar quality or character of the Golden Dawn documents which I suggest contain the hallmarks of genius. Whoever was the originator of the Golden Dawn system left the mark both of genius and uniqueness on every phase of the work. He is still unknown—he, or a line of continental Rosicrucian Adepts, or? . . . we do not know!

Volume III (of the first edition) contains the Z—2 document, which the student will recognize as being a finely structured analysis of the Neophyte Ritual, breaking it down into several movements and sections. This then serves as the basis for the construction of several elaborate types of ceremonial. These will be altogether without meaning until and unless the student has thoroughly studied the Neophyte Ritual. Nor will it convey much if he has neglected to master the basic principles of the Qabalah, particularly the dynamics involved in Tetragrammaton, the four-lettered Name—and how, by the descent of the Divine Fire, it becomes converted into the Pentagrammaton, With a display of great erudition, even the letter Shin representing the divine fire becomes classified according to the Three Mother letters, *(Aleph, Mem, Shin*—Air, Water, and Fire), each serving as the basis of a distinct type of ritual.

This document is one of the intrinsic signs of the genius of the G. D. I have been impressed by its magnificence as well as practicality for nearly forty years, when I first discovered it in *Equinox 3.* Time has not diminished the lustre, nor familiarity its mark of uniqueness.

Z—1 is an important paper descriptive of the Neophyte Ritual, given to the newly inducted Adeptus Minor for whom it discloses a depth of symbolism and a wealth of practical formulae he could never have previously thought possible. The beginner who glances through this grade initiation may perceive very little in it, until he studies this particular document. It explains the meaning and purpose of the manifold symbols employed, the regalia worn by the officers, and the various movements made by the officiants. A companion document Z—3 explains the symbolism of the admission of the Candidate. I still find this an extremely interesting document that reveals level upon level of insight, no matter how many years elapse between readings. An occasional perusal of its material will prevent the student from taking a prosaic attitude towards this and other initiatory rituals. Both of these papers are among the most important of all Order documents, since so many general magical formulae are there described. They pertain to a great many magical matters, other than initiation.

As an aside, for the serious student who is interested in making comparisons and drawing deductions, I recommend a slim volume entltled *The Ceremony of Initiation* by W. L. Wilmshurst, an eminent British Freemason. This little volume, though privately printed in 1953, is available to the general public, being obtainable through J. M. Watkins, London. It purports to be an analysis and commentary on Masonic initiations. Its similarity to the Z—2 document is startling, though the latter is of course written on a much deeper level than its Masonic equivalent, and is esoterically slanted. But without knowing anything about Masonry, the student could read this volume side by side with Z—2, and develop a very clear idea of the nature of Masonic initiation.

Other papers in this final volume are still no less valuable than the day they were first published. Those on clairvoyance, astral projection, and skrying are still the most complete instructions on these subject yet written. I doubt if much can be added to them, or whether they can be improved upon. Even a great deal of Aleister Crowley's later magical writing, which is always excellent, does not elaborate very much more on some of this basic Golden Dawn magical teaching.

The material in the 4th Volume (first edition) or the last half of this present Volume II (second edition) is of maximum importance. *Here are to be found the ground rules as it were governing magic in all of its many branches.*

Would you know what a talisman is? And how it is constructed? The necessary information is to be found here. Sigils—what they are, and how made, are also elucidated in this volume. Full instruction in all such matters is given in several documents republished in this volume. There is no other text which is as explicit. Francis Barrett's *The Magus* and Henry Cornelius Agrippa's far older work on magical philosophy give the sigils derived from the magic squares, but neither is particularly explicit in description, etc. This deficiency is repaired in these G. D. manuscripts.

Is it divination that interests you? The Order method of Tarot reading is second to none.

In the first place, the description of the cards themselves is unique. From these descriptions the enterprising student could draw or paint a pack for himself. Whether he produces a finely polished, artistic pack or a set of crude amateurish drawings as I have, makes no difference. The effort alone will have made strong multi-sensory impressions on his psyche. These will be drawn upon, consciously or unconsciously, when divining.

Furthermore, some of the character descriptions given of the Court cards give one pause. These are evidently not the work of a mere gypsy fortune teller. They betray sound psychological insights of an unusually penetrating nature, and many a professional writer has drawn on them in one way or another. I know at least a couple of books which have used them at great length, though without acknowledgement, but in this instance that does not mean very much.

Some abstruse teaching relative to the Tarot and other germane matters is scattered through several of these Order documents. One matter which I have never seen taken up by astrological writers is that concerning starting the Zodiac with the Star Regulus in Leo. The teaching emphasizes that were this done, the constellations and the signs would coincide.

"Within the Zodiac," wrote Louis MacNiece in his book *Astrology*, "there are twelve constellations . . . These bear the same names as the twelve signs used by the astrologers, but astrologically they have nothing to do with the case. If you are told that the Sun was in that particular sign when you were born between March 31 and April 30—this does not mean that you were born under the actual group of *stars* known as Aries. Once upon a time the Sun *was* (or appeared to be) among that group at that time of year, but he is not there now, thanks to what is known as the 'precession of the equinoxes' (a very slow shift in the sky pattern, as observed from the earth, that takes 25,800 years to come full circle). The signs that most modern astrologers deal with are 12 exactly equal sections of the total circle of the Zodiac. Each section measures 30° and it makes no difference what fixed stars are contained in it.

"This disconcerting fact provides ready ammunition for opponents of astrology . . ."

As all students of the subject know, due to the precession of the Equinoxes, the signs and the constellations are now separated by as much as a whole sign. This has led to two distinct schools in astrology, the *Tropical* and the *Sidereal*. The adoption of the Order recommendation, could lead to some closing of the distance between these two approaches.

One of the things that slightly puzzles me occasionally is the frequency with which the almost wholly untutored beginner invariably selects the Enochian system to start with. He is intrigued by its mystery and its complexity. It is the most complicated of the Order sub-systems, and really is used as the basis for synthesizing all the previously given knowledge of the Order. Qabalah, Tarot, Geomancy, skrying, ritual magic, etc. are all drawn together and worked up into a single majestic system. Therefore to appreciate it, one must have acquired a good working knowledge of all the partial systems. As such, it is the province of the seasoned veteran in occult matters, of the mature well-informed student, certainly not the tyro.

In Crowley's A.A. (which he founded on what he thought and hoped were the ashes of the G.D.), this kind of selection would not altogether have been frowned on. In fact, one of the cardinal rules which was never to have been abrogated, was that the Probationer should personally select from all that he has read, anything that personally appeals to him. And for one year he was required to do whatever practices his own ingenium selected.

But the A.A. is not the Golden Dawn, even though it has its roots deeply buried in the fertile soil that was prepared by Mathers and Westcott. Nor is the G.D. completely dead. I am glad to hear periodically that there is a Temple here and there which still continues to use the time-honored methods. Under these circumstances, someone has to try and drum some rationality into the beginning student whose enthusiasm and fanaticism may well run away with him. For this reason, I suggest the Enochian system—rich, suggestive and powerful that it is—be left alone until a great deal of prior knowledge and magical experience be obtained.

The Adeptus Minor obligation contains the following clause, which is the quintessence of the entire Golden Dawn magical work:

> I further promise and swear that with the Divine Permission I will, from this day forward, apply myself to the Great Work—which is, to purify and exalt my Spiritual Nature so that with the Divine Aid I may at length attain to be more than human, and thus gradually raise and unite myself to my Higher and Divine Genius, and that in this event I will not abuse the great power entrusted to me.

Many years after Crowley had become exposed to this obligation, and had labored hard on the road to magical accomplishment, he took this obligation and translated it as seeking and acquiring the Knowledge and Conversation of the Holy Guardian Angel. In the use of this archaic language, he merely followed McGregor Mathers who had translated into English *The Sacred Magic of Abramelin the Mage,* where this phrase was first used.

As the Tiphareth clause of the obligation, it is the most important one of all the ten clauses. And in one way or another, its fulfillment is pointed to in nearly every important phase of the Order work. Regardless of which phase you may think of—skrying in the spirit-vision, ceremonial magic, formation of telesmatic images, etc.—this one goal is in the background, giving meaning and substance to all else. No matter, then, what aspect of the work the student devotes himself to, he should never lose sight of this one clause, and the goal to which it refers.

One particular passage in Z—2 found immediately after its opening confirms this notion in a specially powerful way. Describing the temple in reference to the Sephiroth, it says:

> The Temple as arranged in the Neophyte Grade of the Order of the Golden Dawn in the Outer, is placed looking towards the YH or YHVH in Malkuth in Assiah. That is, as Y and H answer unto the Sephiroth Chokmah and Binah in the Tree, (and unto Abba and Aima, through whose knowledge alone that of Kether may be obtained) even so, the Sacred Rites of the Temple may gradually, as it were, *in spite of himself,* lead the Neophyte unto the knowledge of his Higher Self.

(Italics mine.)

There are several other passages confirmatory of this important set of ideas. One of them relates to the Hierophants' wand which "represents him as touching thereby the Divine Light of Kether and attracting through the Middle Pillar to Malkuth." Another concerns the so-called Banner of the East which "affirms the mode of action employed by the Divine Light in its operation by the Forces of Nature. Upon it is the symbol of the Macrocosm so colored as to affirm the action of the Fire of the Spirit through the Waters of Creation under the harmony of the Golden Cross of the Reconciler . . . *The whole represents the ascent of the Initiate into Perfect Knowledge of the Light."*

(Italics mine.)

In the Adeptus Minor Ritual is to be found the analysis of the so-called keyword *I.N.R.I.* It is found in several places thereafter; its very frequency should make the student suspect its importance. Few, however, take time out to apply basic Qabalistic and magical principles to elucidate its meaning. So in order to convey some idea of elementary meanings, I have decided to show the student what can be done with these four English letters *I.N.R.I.* They are, of course, the initials of a Latin phrase once placed by the Romans at the head of the Cross representing the phrase "Jesus of Nazareth, King of the Jews." Several other theological meanings to these letters have been given at different periods in history by various groups of people and scholars.

For example, the medieval alchemists suggested that *I.N.R.I.* meant "Igne Natura Renovatur Integra." "The whole of Nature is renewed by Fire."

Another example of about the same period elaborated the four letters to "Igne Nitrum Raris Invenitum," translated as "shining (or glittering) is rarely found in fire."

The Jesuits in their day interpreted it as "Justum Necare Regis Impius"—"It is just to kill an impious king."

J.S.M. Ward in his book *Freemasonry and the Ancient Gods* gives yet another example:

I. Yam=Water
N. Nour=Fire
R. Ruach=Air
I. Yebeshas=Earth

Thus the four letters may be used as Hebrew initials of the four ancient elements.

In the nineteenth century when the Hermetic Order of the Golden Dawn came to be formed, these letters were picked up and integrated into the complex structure of the Order symbolism. To understand the interpretation used by the Order, we need only the most superficial knowledge of the basic attributions given in the Sepher Yetzirah, the Tarot pack of cards, a smattering of Gnosticism and astrology. The first gesture is to convert the four letters into their Hebrew equivalents and then to direct Yetziratic attributions, as follows:

I.	=	Yod	=	Virgo
N	=	Nun	=	Scorpio
R.	=	Resh	=	Sun
I.	=	Yod	=	Virgo

The final "I", being repetitious, is dropped, only to be picked up again in a later place in order to extend the significance of the meanings derived from the analysis.

This breakdown, though not getting us very far, is nonetheless highly suggestive. Elementary astrology will extend the meaning a little. Virgo represents the virginal sign of nature itself. Scorpio is the sign of death and transformation; sex is involved here as well. Sol, the Sun, is the source of light and life to all on earth; it is the centre of our solar system. All the so-called resurrection gods are known to be solar connected. The Sun was thought to die every winter when vegetation perished and the earth became cold and barren. Every Spring, when the Sun returned, green life was restored to the Earth.

In various of the grade rituals as well as the elementary knowledge lectures of the Order, we find the following which we can add to the data already obtained:

Virgo=Isis—who was Nature, the Mother of all things.
Scorpio=Apophis—death, the destroyer.
Sol=Osiris—slain and risen, the Egyptian resurrection and vegetative God.

Here we now begin to get a definite sequence of ideas that proves somewhat meaningful. The simplicity of a natural state of affairs in, shall we say, the Garden of Eden representing the springtime of mankind, is shattered by the intrusion of the knowledge of Good and Evil, sexual perception. This is due to the intervention of the destroyer Apophis, the Red Dragon, or Lucifer, the Lightbearer, who changed all things—by illuminating all things. Thus the Fall—as well as the Fall of the year. This is succeeded by the advent of Osiris the resurrection God who is quoted as stating: "This is my body, which I destroy in order that it may be renewed." He is the symbolic prototype of the perfected solar Man, who suffered through earthly experience, was glorified by trial, was betrayed and killed, and then rose again to renew all things.

The final analysis of the keyword sums up the formula with the initials *I*sis, *A*pophis, *O*siris=*IAO,* the supreme God of the Gnostics. (IAO is pronounced ee—ah—oh!)

Since the Sun is the giver of life and light, the formula must refer to Light as the redeemer. The Order was predicated on the age-old process of bringing Light to the natural man. In other words, it taught a psycho-spiritual technique leading to illumination, to enlightenment. In this connection, one should always remember those beautiful versicles about the Light in the opening chapter of the Gospel according to St. John.

In the very first or Neophyte Ritual of the Golden Dawn, the candidate is startled to hear the strangely-worded invocation "Khabs Am Pekht. Konx om Pax. Light in Extension." In other words, may you too receive the benediction of the Light, and undergo the mystical experience, the goal of all our work.

"The enlightenment by a ray of the divine light which transforms the psychic nature of many may be an article of faith," says Hans Jonas in his excellent book *The Gnostic Religion*, "but it may also be an experience . . . Annihilation and deification of the person are fused in the spiritual ecstasis which purports to experience the immediate presence of the acosmic essence.

"In the gnostic context, this transfiguring face-to-face experience is *Gnosis* in the most exalted sense of the term, since it is knowledge of the unknowable . . . The mystical *gnosis theou*—direct beholding of the divine reality—is itself an earnest of the consummation to come. It is transcendence become immanent; and although prepared for by human acts of self-modification which induce the proper disposition, the event itself is one of divine activity and grace. It is this as much a 'being known' by God as a 'knowing' him, and in this ultimate mutuality the 'gnosis' is beyond the terms of 'knowledge' properly speaking . . ."

Since this is the basic theme recurrent through all the Golden Dawn rituals and teaching, we would expect to find it repeated and expanded in the analysis of the Keyword of the Adeptus Minor grade. And of course it is there, clearly defined.

The word 'Light' is translated into *LVX*, the Latin word for Light. A series of physical mimes or gestures are employed by the officiants to represent the descent of this Light, as well as to summarize the symbolism of the previous findings.

So one Adept or officiant raises his right arm directly in the air above him, while extending his left arm straight outwards (as though to make a left turn when driving a car). This forms by shape the letter 'L'.

A second Adept raises his arms as though in supplication above his head—the letter 'V'.

The third Adept extends his arms outwards forming a Cross.

All together finally cross their arms on their chests, forming the letter 'X'.

(A single person may of course perform the identical gestures.)

The letters form 'LVX' which is now interpreted as the 'Light of the Cross'. It is so interpreted because the letters 'INRI' were initially found on the Cross, as well as because *LVX* means Light. Finally the letters 'LVX' themselves are portions of one type or another of the Cross.

A process of repetition is followed in order to synthesize all these variegated ideas and gestures, and to add one more mime to replace the second 'I' that was eliminated for being repetitious.

As the 'L' sign is being made, the Adept says: "The Sign of the Mourning of Isis." This expresses the sorrow of Isis on learning that Osiris had been slain by Set or Apophis.

As the 'V' sign is made, the Adept says: "The Sign of Apophis and Typhon." These are other names for Set, the brother and murderer of Osiris, whose body was so mutilated that only the phallus could be found by Isis who had searched all over creation for him.

As the Adept spreads his arms outward from the shoulders forming actively the

Cross, he says: "The Sign of Osiris Slain."

Then crossing one arm over the other on the chest, he adds: "And risen. Isis, Apophis, Osiris, IAO."

Thus what started out to be a simple abbreviation of a traditional Latin sentence on the Cross above the head of Jesus, has now evolved by a Qabalistic process of exegesis into a complex series of evocative ideas and symbolic gestures which extend tremendously the root idea. And by knowing these ideas, the gestures may be used practically to aspire to the illumination it suggests. This is the essential value of the sacramental actions.

The Rosicrucian equivalent of this formula is found in the Fama Fraternatitas, one of the original three classical Rosicrucian documents. Ex Deo Nascimur. In Jesu Morimur. Per spiritus sanctus reviviscimus. "From God are we born. In Christ we die. We are revived by the Holy Spirit."

Nor is this all. If we take 'LVX' as symbols of Roman numerals, we have 65. This number, therefore, attains the symbolic equivalent of Light, gnosis and illumination.

The Adeptus Minor obligation imposed on the candidate during the ritual initiation, obligates him, as already demonstrated, to aspire and work and practise so that by enlightenment he may one day "become more than human." This is the Qabalistic philosophy summarized in the statement that the Adept seeks to unite himself to his higher soul or his higher Self, symbolized again in the Hebrew word *Adonai.* All the above notions therefore are synthesized in this word *Adonai,* literally translated "My Lord." Its Hebrew letters are:

Aleph *Daleth* *Nun* *Yod*
1 + 4 + 50 + 10 = 65.

This number is also that of *LVX* Light. Qabalistically the process enables us to perceive a necessary connection between *Adonai* and the Light, their identity. From here we can move in a variety of exegetical directions.

But enough has been said, I hope, to show the student not to accept superficially any phase of the Rituals and the teachings, but to subject them to the most exacting scrutiny.

November 25, 1968
ISRAEL REGARDIE

<13> **INTRODUCTION TO THE FIRST EDITION**

It was in the year 1890 that Dr. Franz Hartmann, in an endeavour to provide a simple outline of the vicissitudes of what came to be known as the Rosicrucian Order, wrote a book entitled *In the Pronaos of the Temple.* The central figure of this history was a monk, Fr. R. C.—described in the earliest Rosicrucian manifesto the *Fama Fraternitatis* as the "pious, spiritual and highly-illuminated Father . . . It is said that he was a German nobleman who had been educated in a convent, and that long before the time of the Reformation he had made a pilgrimage to the Holy Land in company with another brother of this convent, and that while at Damascus they had been initiated by some learned Arabs into the mysteries of the secret science. After remaining three years at Damascus, they went to Fez, in Africa, and there they obtained still more knowledge of magic, and of the relations existing between the macrocosm and microcosm. After having also travelled in Spain, he returned to Germany, where he founded a kind of convent called *Sanctus Spiritus,* and remained there writing his secret science and continuing his studies. He then accepted as his assistants, at first, three, and after-
<14> wards, four more monks from the same convent in which he had been educated, and thus founded the first society of the Rosicrucians. They then laid down the results of their science in books, which are said to be still in existence, and in the hands of some Rosicrucians. It is then said that 120 years after his death, the

entrance to his tomb was discovered. A stair-case led into a subterranean vault, at the door of which was written, *Post annos CXX patebo.* There was a light burning in the vault, which, however, became extinct as soon as it was approached. The vault had seven sides and seven angles, each side being five feet wide and eight feet high. The upper part represented the firmament, the floor, the earth, and they were laid out in triangles, while each side was divided into ten squares. In the middle was an altar, bearing a brass plate, upon which were engraved the letters, *A.C.R.C.*, and the words *Hoc Universi Compendium vivus mihi Sepulchrum feci.* In the midst were four figures surrounded by the words, *Nequaquam Vacuum. Legis Jugum. Libertas Evangelii. Dei Gloria Intacta.* Below the altar was found the body of *Rosenkreutz,* intact, and without any signs of putrefaction. In his hand was a book of parchment, with golden letters marked on the cover with a T, and at the end was written, *Ex Deo nascimur. In Jesus morimur. Per Spiritum Sanctum reviviscimus."*

It was upon this schema and from this original body, to state it briefly, that the Hermetic Order of the Golden Dawn claimed direct descent. Its history lecture, however, volunteered very few verifiable details as to the historical facts which, from the scholarly point of view, we should be acquainted with—the details for
<15> example of the line of descent from, say, 1614 to 1865. Current within the present day Order was the belief that at various dates within the period named, the Order as an organised body of students ceased to exist. Instead, there was an oral continuation of teaching from isolated initiates here, there and everywhere, until more recent times when religious and political conditions did not militate against the advisability of formulating a group. With the institution of a definite body, the original system of grades was re-established, and the systems of Alchemy, the Qabalah and Magic once more were taught to zealous, aspiring Neophytes. As a cloak to their activities, they likewise continued in the early agreement of the Order which was:

"*First,* that none of them should profess any other thing than to cure the sick, and that gratis.

Second, None of the posterity should be constrained to wear one certain kind of habit, but therein to follow the custom of the country.

Third, that every year, upon the day C. they should meet together at the house *Sanctus Spiritus,* or write the cause of his absence.

Fourth, Every Brother should look about for a worthy person who, after his decease, might succeed him.

Fifth, The word R. C. should be their seal, mark, and character.

Sixth, The Fraternity should remain secret one hundred years.

With this preliminary account, we may turn to the claims of the Order within the more historical times of the late 19th century, though unfortunately, these claims are no more verifiable and certainly no clearer than those which characterised its beginning.

<16> "The Order of the Golden Dawn," narrates the history lecture of that Order, "is an Hermetic Society whose members are taught the principles of Occult Science and the Magic of Hermes. During the early part of the second half of last century, several eminent Adepti and Chiefs of the Order in France and England died, and their death caused a temporary dormant condition of Temple work.

"Prominent among the Adepti of our Order and of public renown were Eliphas Levi the greatest of modern French magi; Ragon, the author of several books of occult lore; Kenneth M. Mackenzie, author of the famous and learned Masonic Encyclopaedia; and Frederick Hockley possessed of the power of vision in the crystal, and whose manuscripts are highly esteemed. These and other contemporary Adepti of this Order received their knowledge and power from predecessors of equal and even of greater eminence. They received indeed and have handed down to us their doctrine and system of Theosophy and Hermetic Science and the higher Alchemy from a long series of practised investigators whose origin is traced to the Fratres Roseae Crucis of Germany, which association was founded by one Christian Rosenkreutz about the year 1398 A. D.

"The Rosicrucian revival of Mysticism was but a new development of the vastly older wisdom of the Qabalistic Rabbis and of that very ancient secret knowledge, the Magic of the Egyptians, in which the Hebrew Pentateuch tells you that Moses the founder of the Jewish system was 'learned', that is, in which he had been initiated."

In a slender but highly informative booklet entitled *Data of the History of*
<17> *the Rosicrucians* published in 1916 by the late Dr. William Wynn Westcott, we
find the following brief statement: "In 1887 by permission of S.D.A. a continental Rosicrucian Adept, the Isis-Urania Temple of Hermetic Students of the G.D. was formed to give instruction in the mediaeval Occult sciences. Frates M.E.V. with S.A. and S.R.M.D. became the chiefs, and the latter wrote the rituals in modern English from old Rosicrucian mss. (the property of S.A.) supplemented by his own literary researches."

In these two statements is narrated the beginning of the Hermetic Order of the Golden Dawn — an organisation which has exerted a greater influence on the development of Occultism since its revival in the last quarter of the 19th century than most people can realise. There can be little or no doubt that the Golden Dawn is, or rather was until very recently, the sole depository of magical knowledge, the only Occult Order of any real worth that the West in our time has known. A great many other occult organisations owe what little magical knowledge is theirs to leakages issuing from that Order and from its renegade members.

The membership of the Golden Dawn was recruited from every circle, and it was represented by dignified professions as well as by all the arts and sciences, to make but little mention of the trades and business occupations. It included physicians, psychologists, clergymen, artists and philosophers. And normal men and women, humble and unknown, from every walk of life have drawn inspiration from its font of wisdom, and undoubtedly many would be happy to recognise and admit the enormous debt they owe it.

<18> As an organisation, it preferred after the fashion of its mysterious parent
always to shroud itself in an impenetrable cloak of mystery. Its teaching and methods of instruction were stringently guarded by serious penalties attached to the most awe-inspiring obligations in order to ensure that secrecy. So well have these obligations, with but one or two exceptions, been kept that the general public knows next to nothing about the Order, its teaching, or the extent and nature of its membership. Though this book will touch upon the teaching of the Golden Dawn, concerning its membership as a whole the writer will have nothing to say, except perhaps to repeat what may already be more or less well-known. For instance, it is common knowledge that W. B. Yeats, Arthur Machen and, if rumour may be trusted, the late Arnold Bennett were at one time among its members, together with a good many other writers and artists.

With regard to the names given in Dr. Westcott's statement it is necessary that we bestow to them some little attention in order to unravel, so far as may be possible, the almost inextricable confusion which has characterised every previous effort to detail the history of the Order. M.E.V. was the motto chosen by Dr. William Robert Woodman, an eminent Freemason of the last century. Sapere Aude and Non Omnis Moriar were the two mottos used by Dr. Westcott, an antiquarian, scholar, and coroner by profession. S. R. M. D. or S'Rhiogail Ma Dhream was the motto of S. L. MacGregor Mathers, the translator of *The Greater Key of King Solomon,* the *Book of the Sacred Magic of Abramelin the Mage,* and *The Kabbalah Unveiled,* which latter consisted of certain
<19> portions of the Zohar prefixed by an introduction of high erudition. He also

employed the Latin motto Deo Duce Comite Ferro. S. D. A. was the abbreviation of the motto Sapiens Dominabitur Astris chosen by a Fraulein Anna Sprengel of Nuremburg, Germany. Such were the actors on this occult stage, this the *dramatis personae* in the background of the commencement of the Order. More than any other figures who may later have prominently figured in its government and work, these are the four outstanding figures publicly involved in the English foundation of what came to be known as The Hermetic Order of the Golden Dawn.

How the actual instigation of the Order came to pass is not really known. Or rather, because of so many conflicting stories and legends the truth is impossible to discover. At any rate, so far as England is concerned, without a doubt we must seek for its origin in the Societas Rosicruciana in Anglia. This was an organisation formulated in 1865 by eminent Freemasons, some of them claiming authentic Rosicrucian initiation from continental authorities. Amongst those who claimed such initiation was one Kenneth H. Mackenzie, a Masonic scholar and encyclopaedist, who had received his at the hands of a Count Apponyi in Austria. The objects of this Society which confined its membership to Freemasons in good standing, was "to afford mutual aid and encouragement in working out the great problems of Life, and in discovering the secrets of nature; to facilitate the study of the systems of philosophy founded upon the Kaballah and the doctrines of Hermes Trismegistus." Dr. Westcott also remarks that
today its Fratres "are concerned in the study and administration of medi-
<20> cines, and in their manufacture upon old lines; they also teach and practise the
curative effects of coloured light, and cultivate mental processes which are believed to induce spiritual enlightenment and extended powers of the human senses, especially in the directions of clairvoyance and clairaudience."

The first Chief of this Society, its Supreme Magus so-called, was one Robert Wentworth Little who is said to have rescued some old rituals from a certain Masonic storeroom, and it was from certain of those papers that the Society's rituals were elaborated. He died in 1878, and in his stead was appointed Dr. William R. Woodman. Both Dr. Westcott and MacGregor Mathers were prominent and active members of this body. In fact, the former became Supreme Magus upon Woodman's death, the office of Junior Magus being conferred upon Mathers. One legend has it that one day Westcott discovered in his library a series of cipher manuscripts, and in order to decipher them he enlisted the aid of MacGregor Mathers. It is said that this library was that of the Societas Rosicruciana in Anglia, and it is likewise asserted that those cipher manuscripts were among the rituals and documents originally rescued by Robert Little from Freemason's Hall. Yet other accounts have it that Westcott or a clerical friend found the manuscripts on a bookstall in Farringdon Street. Further apocryphal legends claim that they were found in the library of books and manuscripts inherited from the mystic and clairvoyant, Frederick Hockley, who died in 1885. Whatever the real origin of these mysterious cipher manuscripts, when eventually deciphered with
the aid of MacGregor Mathers, they were alleged to have contained the
<21> address of a Fraulein Anna Sprengel who purported to be a Rosicrucian
Adept, in Nuremburg. Here was a discovery which, naturally, not for one moment was neglected. Its direct result was a lengthy correspondence with Fraulein Sprengel, culminating in the transmission of authority to Woodman, Westcott and Mathers, to formulate in England a semi-public occult organisation which was to employ an elaborate magical ceremonial, Qabalistic teaching, and a comprehensive scheme of spiritual training. Its foundation was designed to include both men and women on a basis of perfect equality in contradistinction to the policy of the Societas Rosicruciana in Anglia which was comprised wholly of Freemasons. Thus, in 1887, the Hermetic Order of the Golden Dawn was established. Its first English Temple, Isis-Urania, was opened in the following year.

There is a somewhat different version as to its origin, having behind it the authority of Frater F. R., the late Dr. Felkin, who was the Chief of the Stella Matutina as well as a member of the Societas Rosicruciana. According to his account, and the following words are substantially his own, prior to 1880 members of the Rosicrucian Order on the Continent selected with great care their own candidates whom they thought suitable for personal instruction. For these pupils they were each individually responsible, the pupils thus selected being trained by them in the theoretical traditional knowledge now used in the Outer Order. After some three or more years of intensive private study these pupils were presented to the Chiefs of the Order, and if approved and passed by examination, they then received their initiation into the Order of the Roseae Rubeae et Aureae Crucis.

<22> The political state of Europe in the nineteenth century was such that the strictest secrecy as to the activities of these people was very necessary. England, however, where many Masonic bodies and semi-private organisations were flourishing without interference, was recognised as having far greater freedom and liberty than the countries in which the continental Adepts were domiciled. Some, but by no means all, suggested therefore that in England open Temple work might be inaugurated. And Dr. Felkin here adds, though without the least word of explanation as to what machinery was set in motion towards the attainment of that end, "and so it was . . . It came about then that Temples arose in London, Bradford, Weston-super-Mare, and Edinburgh. The ceremonies we have were elaborated from cipher manuscripts, and all went well for a time."

Since the history of the Hermetic Order of the Golden Dawn subsequent to this period has already been narrated elsewhere there is little need to repeat it. Those who may be interested in a detailed meticulous history of the Rosicrucian claim as it has existed in Europe during the past three hundred years are advised to consult Arthur Edward Waite's *The Brotherhood of the Rosy Cross.* While in my small work *My Rosicrucian Adventure* the events that occurred to the Golden Dawn, culminating in this present publication of its teaching and rituals, are delineated at some length. The motives which have confirmed me in this decision to act contrary to the obligation of secrecy are there presented and discussed. And with these directions, let us pass from historical bones to what is the dynamic life and soul of the Order, its teaching and ceremonial technique of initiation.

§

<23> Before one can grasp the nature of ceremonial initiation, which was the assumed function of the Golden Dawn, a few fundamental notions of the philosophy underlying its practice must be grasped. The basic theory of the Order system was such as to identify certain of the grades with various spritual principles existing in the universe. Hence a philosophy which describes, classifies, and purports to understand the nature of the universe must be studied before the significance of the grades can be appreciated. One of the most important backgrounds of the system is the scheme of the Qabalah, a Jewish system described at length in my *Tree of Life* and the knowledge lectures herein. Since it is primarily a mystical method, the Qabalah has innumerable points of identity with the more ancient systems elaborated by other peoples in other parts of the world. Its most important root concept is that the ultimate root from which this universe, with all things therein, has evolved is *Ain Soph Aour,* Infinite or Limitless Light. So far as our minds are capable of conceiving such metaphysical abstractions, this is to be understood as an infinite ocean of brilliance wherein all things are held as within a matrix, from which all things were evolved, and it is that divine goal to which all life and all beings eventually must return.

Issuing from or within this Boundless Light, there manifests what is called the Tree of Life. Qabalists have produced a conventional glyph indicating thereupon ten numerations or *Sephiroth* which are the branches of that Tree growing or evolving

<24> within space, ten different modes of the manifestation of its radiation — ten varying degrees of but one ubiquitous substance-principle.

The first of these numerations is called *Kether,* the Crown, and is the first manifestation from the Unknown, a concentration of its Infinite Light. As the radiant apex of this heavenly tree, it is the deepest sense of selfhood and the ultimate root of substance. It constitutes the divine centre of human consciousness, all the other principles which comprise what we call man being rather like so many layers of an onion around a central core. From this metaphysical and universal centre duality issues, two distinct principles of activity, the one named *Chokmah,* Wisdom, and the other *Binah,* Understanding. Here we have the roots of polarity, male and female, positive and negative, fire and water, mind and matter, and these two ideas are the noumena of all the various opposites in life of which we have cognisance.

These three emanations are unique in a special way, and they especially symbolise that "Light which shineth in darkness," the Light of the spiritual Self. As Light shines into darkness, illuminating it without suffering a diminution of its own existence, so the workings of the Supernals, as these three Sephiroth are called, overflow from their exuberant being without thereby diminishing in any degree the reality or infinite vitality of their source. They are considered hence to have but little relation with the inferior Sephiroth which issue from them, except as stem and root. Yet though hardly in any philosophic relation to our phenomenal universe, we find when engaged in magical working that it is customary — even necessary — to open ourselves by invocation to its influence so that this divine power of the Supernal
<25> Light, descending through the human mind, may sanctify and accomplish the
object of the ceremony itself. The Supernals are often portrayed diagrammatically and symbolically as a woman clothed with the Sun, stars above her head and the moon at her feet — the typical *anima* figure of modern psychology.

She represents thus that First Matter of the Alchemists, the description of which given by Thomas Vaughan in his *Coelum Terrae* is interesting to quote as indicating further the nature and qualities of the Supernals: "A most pure sweet virgin, for nothing as yet hath been generated out of her... She yields to nothing but love, for her end is generation, and that was never yet performed by violence. He that knows how to wanton and toy with her, the same shall receive all her treasures. First, she sheds at her nipples a thick heavy water, but white as any snow; the philosophers call it Virgin's Milk. Secondly, she gives him blood from her very heart; it is a quick, heavenly fire; some improperly call it their sulphur. Thirdly and lastly, she presents him with a secret crystal, of more worth and lustre than the white rock and all her rosials. This is she, and these are her favours."

From this first triad, a second triad of emanations is reflected or projected downwards into a more coarse degree of substance. They likewise reflect the negative and positive qualities of two of the Supernals with the addition of a third factor, a resultant which acts as a reconciling principle. In passing, I should add that planetary attributions are given to these Sephiroth as expressing the type of their operation. *Kether* is Spirit, *Chokmah* refers to the Zodiac, and *Binah* is attributed to Saturn.

<26> The fourth Sephirah is *Chesed,* meaning Grace or Mercy; also *Gedulah* is its other name, meaning Greatness, and to it is referred the astrological quality called Jupiter. Its concept is one of construction, expansion and solidification.

Geburah is the fifth enumeration, Power of Might, and it is a symbol of creative power and force. Its planetary attribution is Mars, its quality being that destructive force which demolishes all forms and ideas when their term of usefulness and healthy life is done. It symbolises not so much a fixed state of things, as an act, a further passage and transition of potentiality into actuality.

Six is the harmonising and reconciling Sephirah, *Tiphareth.* The word itself means beauty and harmony. It is attributed to the Sun, the lord and centre of our solar system. Just as *Kether* referred to the most secret depths of the Unconscious, the core of man's life, so *Tiphareth* is its reflection, the ego, the ordinary human consciousness. This Sephirah completes the second triad, which is a triad of consciousness, as the first triad of the Supernal Light may be considered the triad of that which is supremely divine, the Superconscious.

Netzach, Victory, to which the planet Venus is referred, is the first Sephirah of the third and reflected triad, and marks an entirely different order of things. Here we enter the elemental sphere, where Nature's forces have their sway. It is also the region in the human sphere of what we may term the Unconscious. The magical tradition classifies this Unconsciousness into several strata, and to each of them is attributed some one of the four elements, Fire, Water, Air and Earth. *Netsach* is attributed
<27> to the element of Fire, and so far as concerns the classification of man's principles, it represents his emotional life.

Its opposite pole on the Tree of Life, is *Hod,* which means Splendour, which receives the attribution of the planet Mercury. Its element is Water, and its action represents fluidic mind, the thinking, logical capacity in man, as well as what may be called his magical or nervous force — what the Hindu systems denominate as Prana.

The third of that triad is *Yesod,* the Foundation, the ninth Sephirah, the operation of the Sphere of the Moon. This is the airy sphere of the fourth dimension, termed in occultism the Astral plane. Here we find the subtle electro-magnetic substance into which all the higher forces are focussed, the ether, and it constitutes the basis or final model upon which the physical world is built. Its elemental attribution is that of Air, ever flowing, shifting, and in a constant flux — yet because of that flux, in perpetual stability. Just as the tremendous speed of the particles insures the stability of the atom, so the fleeting forms and motion of *Yesod* in all its implications constitute the permanence and surety of the physical world.

Pendant to these three triads is *Malkuth,* the Kingdom, referred to the element of Earth, the synthesis or vehicle of the other elements and planets. *Malkuth* is the physical world, and in man represents his physical body and brain, the Temple of the Holy Ghost — the actual tomb of the allegorical Christian Rosenkreutz.

These Sephiroth are not to be construed as ten different portions of objective space, each separated by millions and millions of miles —though of course
<28> they must have their correspondences in different parts of space. They are, rather, serial concepts, each condition or state or serial concept enclosing the other. Each Sephirah, be it spiritual, ethereal, or physical, has its own laws, conditions, and "times," if one may borrow terminology from Dunne's *Experiment with Time.* The distinction between them is one of quality and density of substance. The difference may well be one of dimension, besides representing different type-levels of consciousness, the "lower" worlds or Sephiroth being interpenetrated or held by the "higher." Thus *Kether,* the Crown, is in *Malkuth,* as one axiom puts it, by virtue of the fact that its substance is of an infinitely rare, attenuated, and ethereal nature, while *Malkuth,* the physical universe is enclosed within the all-pervading spirit which is *Kether* in precisely the same way that Dunne conceives Time No. 1, to be enclosed or contained, or moving as a field of experience, within Serial Time No. 2.

So far as concerns the Supernals, for these are the ideas which must principally interest us, the Qabalah teaches us that they comprise an abstract impersonal principle. That is, it is explained as an exalted condition of consciousness rather than of substance; an essence or spirit which is everywhere and at all times expressed in terms of Light. In one sense, and from a comparative point of view, it may help our understanding if we imagine it to have certain similarities to what our leading Analytical Psychologists call the Collective Unconscious.

Though wholly impersonal in itself, and without characteristics that are readily
understandable to the ordinary mind, the Supernals are, to all intents and
<29> purposes, what is commonly thought of as God. In the Tibetan Buddhist sys-
tem, an analogous concept is *Sunyata,* the Void. And the realisation of the Void through Yoga processes and the technical meditations of the Sangha is, to quote Dr. Evan-Wentz's book *The Tibetan Book of the Dead,* to attain "the unconditioned Dharmakaya, or the Divine Body of Truth, the primordial state of uncreatedness, of the Supramundane *Bodhic,* All-consciousness —Buddhahood." In man, this Light is represented by the very deepest levels of his Unconscious — a mighty activity within his soul, which one magical system calls the higher and Divine Genius. Though the Golden Dawn rituals persistently use phraseology which implies the belief in a personal God, that usage to my mind is a poetic or dramatic convention. A number of its very fine invocations are addressed to a deity conceived of in a highly individualistic and personal manner, yet if the student bears in mind the several Qabalistic definitions, these rituals take on added and profound meaning from a purely psychological point of view. That is, they are seen to be technical methods of exalting the individual consciousness until it comes to a complete realisation of its own divine root, and that universal pure essence of mind which ultimately it is.

It may be convenient for the reader if I tabulate the names of the Sephiroth with the Grades employed in the Golden Dawn, together with a few important attributions:

<30> 1. Kether. The Crown. Spirit.	Ipsissmus	⑩ = [1]
2. Chokmah. Wisdom.	Magus	⑨ = [2]
3. Binah. Understanding.	Magister Templi	⑧ = [3]
4. Chesed. Mercy.	Adeptus Exemptus	⑦ = [4]
5. Geburah. Might.	Adeptus Major	⑥ = [5]
6. Tiphareth. Harmony.	Adeptus Minor	⑤ = [6]
7. Netzach. Victory. Fire.	Philosophus	④ = [7]
8. Hod. Splendour. Water.	Practicus	③ = [8]
9. Yesod. Foundation. Air.	Theoricus	② = [9]
10. Malkuth. Kingdom. Earth.	Zelator	① = [10]

In the consideration of the grades, I shall not discuss any others than those existing between Zelator and Adeptus Minor. My reason for doing so is that it is impossible for the ordinary individual to understand those above the grade of Adeptus Minor, and individuals who lay claim openly to such exalted grades, by that very act place a gigantic question mark against the validity of their attainment. He that is exalted is humble. And to have tasted that which is conveyed by the Adeptus Minor grade is so lofty an experience that few in their right minds, unless they were extremely saintlike in character, would consider themselves as having passed officially to a higher spiritual state.

Before proceeding to an analysis of the grades, and the ceremonies which were
supposed to confer them, it has been thought advisable to consider the nature
<31> of initiation itself, which was the avowed function and purpose of the Order.

What exactly is Initiation? Those of us who have read some of the neo-occult and pseudo-Theosophical literature will also have heard the word initiation just too often to feel wholly at ease. Lesser Initiations and Greater Initiations have been written of at some length. But the entire subject was surrounded with that vague air of mystery, that halo of sanctity and ambiguity whose only excuse can be ignorance on the part of the writers thereof. The degree of phantasy and attenuated sentimentality which has obtained expression from these sources, plus the real lack of knowledge as to the objects of these degrees and mysteries, act as a constant source of irritation. Particularly, when we remember that they were issued to satisfy people spiritually hungry, and yearning with an indescribable hunger for but a few crumbs of the divine wisdom.

Learned dissertations have been published describing in great detail the folk customs of Australian aborigines and Polynesian and other primitive peoples. All the strange habits and unfamiliar rites of these tribes are paraded before our gaze — from their hour of birth, through the vicissitudes of their emotional life, to the moment of death and interrment. We are asked to accept that these are initiations. The sole import attached to the word "initiation" in this connection is that of the formal acceptance of a boy at puberty, for example, into the communal life of his people.

Moreover, Jane E. Harrison, Sir J. G. Frazer and a host of other excellent scholars have provided us with a wealth of anthropological data so far as the Greeks
<32> and Romans of another day are concerned. Some knowledge of their religious
rites and observances is displayed. The daily habits of the people are carefully noted and recorded in many a tome.

They also describe, though more haltingly and with rather less confidence, the circumstances surrounding the Ancient Mystery Cults. The symbolism of these mystery religions was, we see, in certain aspects uniform. All were dramas of redemption, plans of salvation, ways of purgation. Degrees of initiation, baptism by water, a mystical meal for the privileged, dramatic plays depicting the life and death of some god or other — these are the familiar incidents of the cults described by our scholars.

But the obvious question arises, what spiritual value have such things for us? Do they help our own interior development so that we may solve our personal problems and handle more satisfactorily the rather difficult process of living today? And is this sort of thing what the Adepts of old implied by initiation? And if this is all there is to it, why should so many moderns have been so curiously perturbed and excited by it all. Some other meaning must be latent herein; some other purpose to the rite must have been understood by their original observers whereby they were spiritually assisted and aided not only to deal adequately with life but to further the conquest and manifestation of their own latent spiritual nature.

For despite every record, and every learned attempt to penetrate into the significance of these rites, as to the exact procedure of the Theurgic technique we still obtain no lasting satisfaction, or understanding. There was undoubtedly a secret
<33> about these celebrations, both ethnic and early Christian, which no exoteric
record has divulged or common sense, so-called, succeeded wholly to explain away. And the reason no doubt it this. Though the early writers felt no hesitancy in expounding certain principles of the philosophy of their Mysteries, none felt it incumbent upon himself to record in black and white the practical details of the magical technique. Hence it is, in the absence of a description of the practical elements of these rites, that our scholars, anthropologists and philosophers do not feel inclined to attach much significance to the ancient Mysteries other than an ordinary religious or philosophic one. That is, it is their belief that ordinary notions of an advanced theological or philosophical nature were promulgated therein. For I may add in passing the complete esoteric technique of initiation has never previously passed into open publication. It has been reserved in all secrecy for initiates of the sacred schools of Magic. While various documents explaining the principia of this wisdom were circulated amongst the members of these schools, the oaths of secrecy attaching to their receipt was such that in recent times, as I have said, few lay exponents of the ancient religions and philosophies have never so much as suspected the existence of these

principia.

The root of the word itself means "to begin," "to commence anew." Initiation is thus the beginning of a new phase or attitude to life, the entry, moreover, into an entirely new type of existence. Its characteristic is the opening of the mind to an awareness of other levels of consciousness, both within and without. Initiation means above all spiritual growth — a definite mark in the span of human life.

<34> Now one of the best methods for bringing about this stimulus of the inner life, so that one does really begin or enter upon an entirely new existence characterised by an awareness of higher principles within, is the Ceremonial technique. By this we mean that a Ceremony is arranged in which certain ideas, teaching and admonitions are communicated to the candidate in dramatic form in a formally prepared Temple or Lodge room. Nor is this all — otherwise, no claim could be made on behalf of Magic that it really and not merely figuratively initiates. For the utterance of an injunction does not necessarily imply that it can sink sufficiently deeply into consciousness so as to arouse into renewed activity the dormant spiritual qualities. And we have already witnessed the invalidity and spiritual bankruptcy of innumerable organisations, religious, secular, and fraternal so-called, which have their own rituals and yet, taking them by and large, have produced very few initiates or spiritually-minded men and women, saints or adepts of any outstanding merit.

The efficacy of an initiation ceremony depends almost exclusively on the initiator. What is it that bestows the power of successful initiation? This power comes from either having had it awakened interiorly at the hands of some other competent initiator, or that a very great deal of magical and meditation work has successfully been performed. It is hardly necessary at this juncture to labour at a description of these exercises and technical processes of development which were undertaken by candidates and would-be initiators. These have been delineated at length elsewhere, both in my *Tree of Life,* and in an incomparably fine form in the Golden Dawn
<35> documents presented herein. But it is necessary to emphasize the fact that an
anterior personal training and prolonged magical effort are the sole means by which one is enabled so to awaken the dormant spiritual life of another that he may well and truly be called "initiated."

Now we know from an examination of the above mentioned documents and of ancient literature that the object of the Theurgic art, as the magical concept of initiation was then termed, was so to purify the personality that that which was there imprisoned could spring into open manifestation. As one of the alchemical expositors has expressed it: "Within the material extreme of this life, *when it is purified,* the Seed of the Spirit is at last found." The entire object of all magical and alchemical processes is the purification of the natural man, and by working upon his nature to extract the pure gold of spiritual attainment. This is initiation.

§

These Golden Dawn rituals and ceremonies of initiation are worthy of a great deal of study and attention. It is my sincere and fervent hope that meditation and a close examination will be made of the text. Now, if we examine these texts carefully, we shall find that we can epitomise in a single word the entire teaching and ideal of those rituals. If one idea more than any other is persistently stressed from the beginning that idea is in the word *Light.* From the candidate's first reception in the Hall of the Neophytes when the Hierophant adjures him with these words: "Child of Earth, long hast thou dwelt in darkness. Quit the night and seek the day," to the
<36> transfiguration in the Vault ceremony, the whole system has as its objective
the bringing down of the Light. For it is by that Light that the golden banner of the inner life may be exalted; it is in light where lies healing and the power of growth. Some vague intimation of the power and splendour of that glory is first given to the

aspirant in the Neophyte Grade when, rising from his knees at the close of the invocation, the Light is formulated above his head in the symbol of the White Triangle by the union of the implements of the three chief officers. By means of the Adeptus Minor ritual, which identifies him with the Chief Officer, he is slain as though by the destructive force of his lower self. After being symbolically buried, triumphantly he rises from the tomb of Osiris in a glorious resurrection through the descent of the white Light of the Spirit. The intervening grades occupy themselves with the analysis of that Light as it vibrates between the light and the darkness, and with the establishment within the candidate's personal sphere of the rays of the many-coloured rainbow of promise.

"Before all things," commences a phrase in one ritual, "are the chaos, the darkness, and the Gates of the Land of Night." It is in this dark chaotic night so blindly called life, a night in which we struggle, labour and war incessantly for no reasonable end, that we ordinary human beings stumble and proceed about our various tasks. These gates of the far-flung empire of the night indeed refer eloquently to the material bondage which we ourselves have created — a bondage whereby we are tied to our circumstances, to our selves, to trial of every kind, bound to the very things we so despise and hate. It is not until we have clearly realised that we are
<37> enmeshed in darkness, an interior darkness, that we can commence to seek
for that alchemical solvent which shall disperse the night, and call a halt to the continual projection outwards of the blackness which blinds our souls. As in the Buddhist scheme, where the first noble truth is sorrow, so not until we have been brought by experience to understand life as sorrow, can we hope for the cessation of its dread ravage. Only then does the prospect open of breaking the unconscious projection, the ending of which discloses the world and the whole of life in a totally different light. "One thing only, brother, do I proclaim," said the Buddha, "now as before. Suffering and deliverance from suffering."

These restricting circumstances and bonds are only the gates of the wilderness. The use of the word "gate" implies a means both of egress and ingress. By these gates we have entered, and by them also may we go out if so we choose, to enter the brilliance of the dawning Sun, and perchance greet the rising of the spiritual splendour. For "after the formless, the void, and the darkness, then cometh the knowledge of the Light." As intimated above, one first must have realised that one's soul is lost in darkness before a remedy can be sought to that irresponsible *participation mystique*, the unconscious projection outwards of interior confusion, and aspire to that divine land which is, metaphorically, the place of one's birth. In that land is no darkness, no formlessness, no chaos. It is the place of the Light itself — that Light "which no wind can extinguish, which burns without wick or fuel."

Being "brought to the Light" then is a very apposite description of the
<38> function of Initiation. It is the Great Work. There is no ambiguity in the con-
ception of the Rituals, for it appears throughout the entire work from Neophyte to Adeptus Minor and perhaps beyond. For the Path is a journeying upwards on the ladder of existence to the crown of the Tree of Life, a journey where every effort made and every step taken brings one a little nearer to the true glory of the Clear Light. As we know, the experience of the rising of the Light in both vision and waking state is common to mystics of every age and of every people. It must be an experience of the greatest significance in the treading of the Path because its appearance seems always and everywhere an unconditional psychic thing. It is an experience which defies definition, as well in its elementary flashes as in its most advanced transports. No code of thought, philosophy or religion, no logical process can bind it or limit it or express it. But always it represents, spiritually, a marked attainment, a liberation from the turmoil of life and from psychic complications and, as Dr. C. G. Jung has expressed the matter, it "thereby frees the inner personality from emotional and imaginary

entanglements, creating thus a unity of being which is universally felt as a release." It is the attainment of spiritual puberty, marking a significant stage in growth.

Symptomatic of this stage of interior growth is the utter transformation that comes over what previously appeared to be "the chaos, the darkness, and the Gates of the Land of Night." While man is assumed into godhead, and the divine spirit is brought down into manhood, a new heaven and a new earth make their appearance,
and familiar objects take on a divine radiance as though illumined by an inter-
<39> nal spiritual light. And this is what, in part at any rate, was meant by the old
alchemists, for the finding of the Philosopher's Stone converts all base metals into the purest gold. In his book *Centuries of Meditation,* Thomas Traherne gives an interesting description of the rapture of the inner personality, its reaction to the world, when it is freed by the mystical experience from all entanglements. He says: "The corn was orient and immortal wheat, which never should be reaped, nor was ever sown. I thought it had stood from everlasting to everlasting. The dust and the stones of the street were as precious as gold; the gates were at first the end of the world. The green trees when I saw them first through one of the gates, transported and ravished me, their sweetness and unusual beauty made my heart to leap, and almost mad with ecstasy, they were such strange and wonderful things. The men! O what venerable and reverent creatures did the aged seem! Immortal Cherubim! And the young men glittering and sparkling angels, and maids, strange seraphic pieces of life and beauty. Boys and girls tumbling in the street, and playing, were moving jewels . . . I knew not that they were born or should die. But all things abided eternally as they were in their proper places. Eternity was manifest in the Light of the Day, and something infinite behind everything appeared . . ."

And to illustrate the magical attitude towards life and the world when initiation has produced its true result, there is another exalted panegyric by Traherne which I cannot desist from quoting. For let me add that Magic does not countenance a retreat
from life, an escape from the turmoils of practical life. It seeks only to trans-
<40> mute what formerly was dross into gold. Initiation has as its object the com-
mencement of a new life, to transform the base and low into the pure and unutterably splendid. "All appeared new and strange at first, inexpressibly rare and delightful and beautiful. I was a little stranger which at my entrance into the world was saluted and surrounded with innumerable joys. My knowledge was Divine; I knew by intuition those things which since my Apostacy I collected again by the highest reason. My very ignorance was advantageous. I seemed as one brought into the state of innocence. All things were spotless and pure and glorious; yea, and infinitely mine and joyful and precious. I knew not that there were any sins, or complaints or laws. I dreamed not of poverties, contentions, or vices. All tears and quarrels were hidden from my eyes. Everything was at rest, free and immortal. I knew nothing of sickness or death or exaction. In the absence of these I was entertained like an angel with the works of God in their splendour and glory; I saw all in the peace of Eden . . . All Time was Eternity, and a perpetual Sabbath . . ."

Such is the stone of the Philosophers, the Quintessence, the Summum Bonum, true wisdom and perfect happiness.

Psellus, the Neoplatonist, has written that the function of Initiatory Magic was "to initiate or perfect the human soul by the powers of materials here on earth; for the supreme faculty of the soul cannot by its own guidance aspire to the sublimest intuition and to the comprehension of Divinity." It is a commonplace aphorism in Occultism that "Nature unaided fails." That is to say that the natural life, if left to itself, and
isolated from the impact of a higher type of life or consciousness, can only
<41> produce a commonplace thing of the natural life. It reminds us of the senti-
ment of the alchemists who expressed contempt of their first matter as it existed in its natural or impure state, in the condition where it normally is found. But

this first matter, cleansed and purified by the psycho-chemical art of alchemy, that is to say by Initiation —is that which is transformed into the most precious thing in the whole world. But until cleansed and purified it is of little or no value. Nature, however, aided where she had left off by wise and devout men, may surpass herself. And this is why Psellus claims that the soul of itself and by itself is not able to attain to divinity unless and until it is guided by Initiates and thus enfolded into another life. It is to effect this integration, to bring about this initiation, this exaltation of the consciousness above its natural state to the light divine, that the magical system of the Golden Dawn, or of any other legitimate initiating system, owes its existence. The function of every phase of its work, the avowed intention of its principal rituals, and the explicit statement of its teaching, is to assist the candidate by his own aspirations to find that unity of being which is the inner Self, the pure essence of mind, the Buddha-nature. Not only does the system imply this by its ritualistic movements and axiomata, but there are clear and unmistakable passages where these ideas are given unequivocal expression. Thus, we find it written that the entire object of initiation and mystical teaching is "by the intervention of the symbol, ceremonial and sacrament, so to lead the soul that it may be withdrawn from the attraction of matter and delivered from the absorption therein, whereby it walks in somnambulism, knowing
<42> not whence it cometh nor whither it goeth." And moreover, in the same
Ritual, celebrated at the autumnal and vernal Equinoxes, the Chief Adept officiating recites an invocation beseeching guidance for the newly-installed Hierophant. It is asked "that he may well and worthily direct those who have been called from the tribulation of the darkness into the Light of this little kingdom of Thy love. And vouchsafe also, that going forward in love for Thee, through him and with him, they may pass from the Desire of Thy house into the Light of Thy presence." This is succeeded by sentences read by the Second and Third Adepti: "The desire of Thy house hath eaten me up," and "I desire to be dissolved and to be with Thee."

And finally, that not the least vestige of misunderstanding or misconception may remain as to the objects of this divine Theurgy, let me reproduce one last quotation from this same ritual. Referring to the Supernals and the Temple that in old time was built on high, the speech adds: "The holy place was made waste and the Sons of the house of Wisdom were taken away into the captivity of the senses. We have worshipped since then in a house made with hands, receiving a sacramental ministration by a derived Light in place of the cohabiting Glory. And yet, amidst Signs and symbols the tokens of the Higher presence have never been wanting in our hearts. By the waters of Babylon we have sat down and wept, but we have ever remembered Zion; and that memorial is a witness testifying that we shall yet return with exultation into the house of our Father."

Thus and unmistakably is the true object of the Great Work set before us, and we shall do well ever to keep eye and aspiration firmly fixed thereto. For while the
<43> road to the spiritual Zion demands great exertion, and because it is a way that
at times proceeds by devious routes, there is great temptation to linger by the roadside, to stroll down pleasant side-lanes, or to play absent-mindedly with toys or staves cut but to assist our forward march. But if we forget not to what noble city the winding path leads us, little danger can overtake any who pursue it steadfast to the end. It is only when the abiding city is forgotten that the road becomes hard, and the way beset by unseen danger and difficulty.

Prior to attempting to describe a few of the salient points of the Rituals —briefly, for since they appear within these volumes, they must be individually studied and experienced so that an individual point of view may be acquired — it may be advisable to devote a few explanatory words to the Art of Ceremonial Initiation itself.

A useful and significant preface may be taken from Dr. Jung's commentary to Wilhelm's translation of *The Secret of The Golden Flower,* where there is much that explains the ritualistic functions of Magic. "Magical practices are," he declares, "the projections of psychic events which, in cases like these, exert a counter influence on the soul, and act like a kind of enchantment of one's own personality. That is to say, by means of these concrete performances, the attention or better said the interest, is brought back to an inner sacred domain which is the source and goal of the soul. This inner domain contains the unity of life and consciousness which, though once possessed, has been lost and must now be found again."

From one point of view the officers employed in these Rituals represent
<44> just such psychic projections. They represent, even as figures in dreams do,
different aspects of man himself — personifications of abstract psychological principles inhering within the human spirit. Through the admittedly artificial or conventional means of a dramatic projection of these personified principles in a well-ordered ceremony a reaction is induced in consciousness. This reaction is calculated to arouse from their dormant condition those hitherto latent faculties represented objectively in the Temple of Initiation by the officers. Without the least conscious effort on the part of the aspirant, an involuntary current of sympathy is produced by this external delineation of spiritual parts which may be sufficient to accomplish the purpose of the initiation ceremony. The aesthetic appeal to the imagination — quite apart from what could be called the intrinsic magical virtue with which the G. D. documents Z. 1. and Z. 3. deal at some length — stirs to renewed activity the life of the inner domain. And the entire action of this type of dramatic ritual is that the soul may discover itself exalted to the heights, and during that mystical elevation receive the rushing forth of the Light.

Applying these ideas then, to the Neophyte or ⓪=0⃞ — so called because it is not attributed to any of the enumerations or Sephiroth on the Tree of Life since it is a preliminary or probationary grade — we find that the Kerux is an officer who personifies the reasoning faculties. He represents that intelligent active part of the mind which functions ever in obedience to the Will — the Qabalistic *Ruach,* in a word. The
higher part of that mind, the aspiring, sensitive, and the intuitive conscious-
<45> ness is represented by the Hegemon, who seeks the rising of the Light. And
the Hierophant, in this initial ceremony of Neophyte, acts on behalf of the higher spiritual soul of man himself, that divine self of which too rarely, if ever at all, we become aware. "The essence of mind is intrinsically pure," is a definition of the Bodhisattva Sila Sutra, and it is this essential state of enlightenment, this interior Self, Osiris glorified through trial and perfected by suffering, which is represented by the Hierophant on the dais. He is seated in the place of the rising Sun, on the throne of the East, and with but two or three exceptions never moves from that station in the Temple. As the Qabalah teaches, the everlasting abode of the Higher Self is in the Eden of Paradise, the supernal sanctuary which is ever guarded from chaos by the flaming sword of the Kerubim whirling every way on the borders of the abyss. From that aloof spiritual stronghold it gazes down upon its vehicle, the lower man, evolved for the purpose of providing it with experience — involved in neither its struggles or tribulations, yet, from another point of view, suffering acutely thereby. And seldom does that Genius leave its palace of the stars except when, voluntarily, the lower self opens itself to the higher by an act of sincerest aspiration of self-sacrifice, which alone makes possible the descent of the Light within our hearts and minds. Thus when the Hierophant leaves the Throne of the East, he represents that Higher Self in action, and as Osiris marks the active descent of the Supernal splendour. For he says, as he leaves the dais with wand uplifted: "I come in the Power of the Light. I come in the Light of
Wisdom. I come in the Mercy of the Light. The Light hath healing in its wings."
<46> And having brought the Light to the aspirant, he returns to his throne, as
though that divine Genius of whom he is the symbol awaited the deliberate willing return of the aspirant himself to the everlasting abode of the Light.

Even in the communication of the usual claptrap of secret societies, the signs and grips, all these are explained solely in terms of the quest for the Light. Also the various groupings of officers and their movements in the Temple are not without profound meaning. These should be sought out, since they constantly reiterate the implicit purpose of the rite. Thus, at the altar, the three principal officers form about the candidate a Triad, representing in symbolic formation again the Supernal clear Light of the Void, and this also is represented by the number of the circumambulations about the confines of the Temple. The white cord bound thrice about the waist has reference to the same set of ideas. Even upon the altar of the Temple are symbols indicating the rise of Light. A red calvary cross of six squares as symbolic of harmony and equilibrium is placed above a white triangle — the emblem of the Golden Dawn. They form the symbol of the Supernal Sephiroth which are the dynamic life and root of all things, while in man they constitute that triad of spiritual faculties which is the intrinsically pure essence of mind. Hence the triangle is a fitting emblem of the Light. And the place of the Cross above the Triangle suggests not the domination of the sacred spirit, but its equilibriation and harmony in the heart of man. Despite the fact that the whole of this intricate symbolism can hardly be realised by the candidate at the time of his initiation, its intrinsic value is such that unconsciously as an organised body of sug-
<47> gestion it is perceived and noted and strikes the focal centre.

We are taught by tradition that the entire object of the sacred rites was the purification of the soul so that its power could gradually dissolve the impediments of, and percolate through, the heavy body and opaque brain. "Know" says Synesius, "that the Quintessence and hidden thing of our stone is nothing else than our viscous celestial and glorious soul *drawn out of its minera by our magistery.*" Hence the entire trend of the preliminary Neophyte grade of the Golden Dawn is towards the purification of the personality. It fulfills the testimony of the Hermetic Art so that the Light within could be fermented and perfected by the ceremonial method of initiation. Purification and consecration — this is the insistent and uncompromising theme caught by the candidate's ear. "Unpurified and unconsecrated thou canst not enter our sacred Hall!" Fire and water assist in these several consecrations until, eventually, the candidate is placed in the position of balanced power, between the two Pillars, where the first link is effected with his higher and divine Genius.

§

The Neophyte Ritual really stands by itself. It is an introductory ceremony shadowing forth all the major formulae and techniques. With the Adeptus Minor ritual it is concerned almost entirely with the Light itself. The five grades that are placed between them have as their object the awakening of the elemental bases of what must develop into the instrument of the higher. Awakened and purified,
<48> they may be consecrated to the Great Work, in order that they may become
worthy vehicles for the indwelling of the Light. First, however, it is necessary that they be awakened. For, psychological truism that it is, until their presence is realised their transmutation cannot be accomplished. In symbolic form and pageantry, the ceremony of each grade calls forth the spirits of a particular element. And as a steel placed in close proximity to a magnet receives some degree of its magnetism, and comparable to the electrical phenomenon of induction, so the presence of power induces power. Contact with the appropriate type of elemental force produces an identical type of reaction within the sphere of the Neophyte, and it is thus that growth and advancement proceeds. The speeches of the officers deal almost exclusively with the knowledge pertaining to that element and grade, and excerpts from fragmentary remains of the ancient Mysteries and from certain of the books of the Qabalah do much towards producing an impressive atmosphere.

The element offered for the work of transmutation in the Grade of Zelator is the

earthy part of the Candidate. The ritual symbolically admits him to the first rung of that mighty ladder whose heights are obscured in the Light above. This first rung is the lowest sphere of the conventional Tree of Life, *Malkuth,* the *Sanctum Regnum.* To it are ascribed the first grade of Zelator, and the element of Earth. Herein, after the Earth elementals are invoked, the Candidate is ceremonially brought to three stations, the first two being those of evil and the presence divine. At each of these stations the Guardians reject him at the point of the sword, urging him in his unprepared
<49> state to return. His third attempt to go forward places him in a balanced position, the path of equilibrium, the Middle Way, where he is received. And a way is cleared for him by the Hierophant, who again represents the celestial soul of things. During his journey along that path, the stability of earth is established within him, that eventually it may prove an enduring temple of the Holy Spirit.

Some have criticised these elemental grades a little harshly and severely; others have rejected them entirely. In a letter sent to me from a former Praemonstrator of one G. D. Temple, these rituals too were condemned in that they were said to be simply a parade, redundant and verbose, of the occult knowledge that one of the Chiefs possessed at that time. In one sense, of course, what those critics claim is perfectly true. The principal formulae and teaching are concealed in the preliminary Neophyte Grade and that of Adeptus Minor. It is the development of the ideas in these ceremonies which constitutes the Great Work — the disclosure of the essence of mind, the invocation of the higher Genius. These, however, are the high ends and the final goals of the mystic term. Notwithstanding his limitations these are ultimates to which every man must work. Meanwhile, in order to render that attainment possible in its fullest sense, several important matters require attention. The personality must be harmonised. Every element therein demands equilibriation in order that illumination ensuing from the magical work may not produce fanaticism and pathology instead of Adeptship and integrity. Balance is required for the accomplishment of the Great Work. "Equilibrium is the basis of the soul." Therefore, the four grades of
<50> Earth, Air, Water and Fire plant the seeds of the microcosmic pentagram, and above them is placed, in the Portal ceremony, the Crown of the Spirit, the quintessence, added so that the elemental vehemence may be tempered, to the end that all may work together in balanced disposition. These grades are therefore an important and integral part of the work, despite shortsighted hostile criticism. To compare them, however, with those which precede and follow, is symptomatic of an intellectual confusion of function. It is rather as if one said that milk is more virtuous than Friday — which, naturally, is absurd. Yet similar comparisons in magical matters are constantly being made without exciting ridicule. It is obvious that different categories may not be so compared. The purpose of the Neophyte ritual is quite distinct from that of Zelator, and it is mistaken policy to compare them. What rightly could be asked is whether the Zelator and the other elemental grades accomplish what they purport to do. That is another matter. The concensus of experienced opinion is on the whole that they do, and I am content for the time being to accept that authority.

The candidate by these grades is duly prepared, so it is argued, to enter the immeasurable region, to begin to analyse and comprehend the nature of the Light which has been vouchsafed him. The first three elemental grades could be taken just as quickly as the candidate, at the discretion of the Chiefs, desired. There were no requirements other than to indicate by examination that the appropriate meditations had been performed and certain items of Qabalistic knowledge necessary to the magical routine committed to memory.

<51> Before proceeding further in the analysis of the grades, there is one rather fine prose passage in the Zelator grade which must be given here — a passage of beauty, high eloquence, and lofty significance. "And Tetragrammaton

placed Kerubim at the East of the Garden of Eden and a Flaming Sword which turned every way to keep the path of the Tree of Life, for He has created Nature that man being cast out of Eden may not fall into the Void. He has bound man with the stars as with a chain. He allures him with scattered fragments of the Divine Body in bird and beast and flower. And He laments over him in the Wind and in the Sea and in the Birds. And when the times are ended, He will call the Kerubim from the East of the Garden, and all shall be consumed and become infinite and holy."

It would be a happy task, were it advisable, to devote several pages of this introduction to praising the excellence of what are called the four elemental prayers. Each one of the elemental Initiation ceremonies closes with a long prayer of invocation which issues, as it were, from the heart of the elements themselves. These must be silently read, continuously meditated upon and frequently heard fully to be appreciated, when the reader will find his own personal reactions crystallising. Recited by the Hierophant at the end of the ceremony, these prayers voice the inherent aspiration of the elements towards the goal they are striving in their own way to reach, for here they are conceived as blind dumb forces both within and without the personal sphere of man. They are given assistance by the human beings who, having invoked them and used their power, strive to repay in some way the debt owed to these other struggling lives.

<52> The grade after the Earth ceremony is that of Theoricus. It is referred to the Ninth Sephirah on the Tree of Life, *Yesod,* the Foundation, and to it are attributed the sphere of the operation of Luna and the element Air. Here the candidate is conducted to the stations of the four Kerubim, the Angelic choir of Yesod. The Kerubim are defined in that ritual as the presidents of the elemental forces, the vivified powers of the letters of Tetragrammaton operating in the Elements. Over each of these rules some one of the four letters of the mirific word and the Kerubim. It is always through the power and authority and symbol of the Kerub that the elemental spirits and their rulers are invoked. In this ritual, as in all the others, important practical formulae of ceremonial magic are concealed.

At this juncture, of the ceremony, with the Airy elements vibrating about him and through him, the Zelator is urged to be "prompt and active as the Sylphs, but avoid frivolity and caprice. Be energetic and strong as the Salamanders but avoid irritability and ferocity. Be flexible and attentive to images, like the Undines, but avoid idleness and changeability. Be laborious and patient like the Gnomes, but avoid grossness and avarice. So shalt thou gradually develop the powers of thy soul and fit thyself to command the spirits of the elements."

In each of the grades, several drawings and diagrams are exhibited, each one conveying useful knowledge and information required in the upward quest. The Tarot Keys are also dealt with, as indicating pictorially the stages of that journey, and depicting the story of the soul. It may not be possible because of the exigencies of space to reproduce in these volumes a pack of Tarot cards based upon esoteric
<53> descriptions — though I should very much liked to have done so. But by using
the Waite and the available French and Italian packs, and by comparing them with the accounts given in the rituals, the imagination of the reader will render this omission unimportant.

The third grade is that of Practicus referred to the Sephirah *Hod,* the Splendour, the lowest of the Sephiroth on the left hand side of the Tree, the Pillar of Severity. Its attributions refer to the sphere of the operation of Mercury, but more especially to the element of Water which in this ceremony is invoked to power and presence. As I have previously remarked, and it bears constant reiteration, the Tree of Life and the Qabalistic scheme as a whole should be carefully studied so that the aptness of the attributions both to the Sephiroth and the Paths may be fully appreciated. Two Paths lead to the Sphere of Splendour, the Path of Fire from Malkuth, and the Path of the reflection of the sphere of the Sun from Yesod. Water is germinative and maternal, whilst Fire is paternal and fructifying. It is from their interior stimulation and union, the alchemical trituration, that the higher life is born, even as has been said, "Except ye be baptised with water and the Spirit ye cannot enter the Kingdom of heaven."

Therefore in this grade, the Candidate is led to the sphere of stagnant water which by the presence of solar and fiery elements is vitalised and rendered a perfect creative base. Most of the speeches in this ritual are depicted as issuing from the Samothracian Kabiri, the deluge Gods, though the main body of the ritual consists of
the sonorous and resonant versicles of the *Chaldaean Oracles*, the translation, I
<54> believe, of Dr. Westcott, with a few modifications authorised by Mathers.
Briefly, the entire symbolism of the Practicus grade is summarised by the position on the altar of the principal Golden Dawn emblems so arranged that "the cross above the Triangle represents the power of the Spirit rising above the triangle of the Waters." That also indicates the immediate task of the Candidate. At this juncture, too, the diagrams displayed begin to take on especial significance, and though their theme apparently is biblical in nature, accompanied by explanations in a curious phraseology consonant therewith, they are nevertheless highly suggestive, as containing the elements of a profound psychology. After this grade follows an automatic wait of three months, referred to the regimen of the elements, a period as it were of silent incubation, during which time the rituals were given to the candidate that he may make copies for his own private use and study.

The fourth grade of Philosophus carries the candidate one step further. The Sephirah involved is *Netsach*, Victory, to which is referred the operation of the planet Venus and the element of Fire, while the paths that connect to the lower rungs of the ladder are principally of a watery nature. Thus the elements encountered are of an identical nature with those of the preceding grade, but their order and power is quite reversed. Previously the water was predominant. Now the Fire rages and whirls in lurid storm, with water only as the complementary element whereon it may manifest, and in order that due equilibrium may be maintained, as it is written: — "The *Ruach Elohim* moved upon the face of the Waters." These two are the primary terrestrial
elements which, intelligently controlled and creatively employed may lead
<55> eventually to the restoration of the Golden Age. By their transmutation a new
paradise may be re-created from the darkness and chaos into which formerly it had fallen. For the Light may not legitimately be called forth upon man, nor dwell within him, until chaos has been turned into equilibrium of complete realisation and enlightenment. Not until order has been restored to the lower elements of his earthy kingdom, neither peace nor inner security may be his rightful lot.

The symbols depicted while traversing the Path of Peh, which joins the spheres of Fire and Water, indicate the results as it were of the first stages of the Path, for the Tarot card shown demonstrates the destruction of a Tower by lightning. The three holes blasted in the walls symbolise the Supernal Triad, the establishment of the divine through and following the destruction of the outer self. Though Fire and Water, warmth and moisture, are essentially creative, their stimulation within the being of the Neophyte draws his attention, perhaps for the first time, to the chaotic condition of his natural existence, and the complete psychic muddle into which his ignorance and spiritual impotence have stranded him. Evocative of the highest within his soul, these elements equally call forth that which is base and low. The result of the first step is analytical, an unbalancing, the levelling down of all that man formerly held true and holy — the chaos, the darkness, and the Gates of the Land of Night. An unhappy state, but a very necessary one if progress is to be made and if the preliminary chaos is to be transcended. From these ruins may be erected the new temple of Light, for it is always from the rubbish heap that are selected the materials for the

<56> manifestation of god-head. These symbols have a dual reference. Not only do they refer to the epochs of creative evolution whose memory has long since faded even from the visible memory of nature, but also to the recapitulations of these periods within personal progress on the Path. "The Aspirant on the threshold of Initiation," observes Crowley very aptly, "finds himself assailed by the 'complexes' which have corrupted him, their externalisation excruciating him, and his agonised reluctance to their elimination plunging him into such ordeals that he seems (both to himself and to others) to have turned from a noble and upright man into an unutterable scoundrel." These are the experiences and events which occur to every aspirant when initiation forces the realisation upon him that "all is sorrow." In fact, it is my belief that the criterion or hall mark of successful initiation is the occurrence of these or similar experiences. The whole universe, under the stimulation of the magical elements and inward analysis, seems to tumble like a pack of cards crazily about one's feet. This is the *solve* half of the alchemical *solve et coagula* formula.

Analysis must precede synthesis. Corruption is the primitive base from which the pure gold of the spirit is drawn. Moreover the alchemical treatises are eloquent in their description of the poisonous nature of this condition which, though extremely unpleasant, is a highly necessary one, and success in its production is at least one symptom of good working. It is held that the highest results may not be obtained until this particular type of change has occurred. So far as the nature of the environment and the creative power of the personal self permits, the task implied by the
<57> *coagula* formula is to assemble them and remould them nearer to the heart's
desire. And here again, the alchemists are adamant in their insistence upon the aphorism that "Nature unaided fails." For the alchemist, so the tradition asserts, commences his work where Nature has left off. And were this *solve* phenomenon to occur spontaneously in the course of nature, the result and the outcome — the coagulation of previously dissolved elements — would not be very dissimilar to that which previously existed. But with the technique of initiation, the chaos is lifted up and fermented so to speak, that from it, with the aid of the invoked white Light of the divine Spirit, a higher species of being, illumined and enlightened, may develop.

In two Altar diagrams — one called the Garden of Eden, shown in the Practicus grade, and the other called The Fall shown in the Philosophus grade, all these ideas are expanded and synthesized. They should be carefully studied and receive long meditation, for in them are many clues to the spiritual and psychological problems which beset the traveller on the Path, and they resume the entire philosophy of Magic. Many hints, moreover, which may be found useful as assisting meditation are contained in *The 'Curse' from a Philosophical Point of View* in the second volume of Blavatsky's *Secret Doctrine* in connection with the Prometheus myth and the awakening of Manas, mind.

Since both of these diagrams may be found reproduced in the body of the text very little by way of prolonged explanation need here be said. The first depicts a personified representation of the three fundamental principles in Man. Each of these is apparently separate, functioning independently on its own plane without co-
<58> operation with, because apparently unaware of, either the higher or the
lower. Principally, it represents man in the now departed morning of the race, in the primal rounds of evolutionary effort when self-consciousness had not yet been won by self-induced and self-devised efforts, and when peace and harmony prevailed both within and without by right of heritage rather than through personal labour. The diagram appears in the Water grade of Practicus, since Water is a fitting representation of this placid peace. At the summit of the diagram stands the Apocalyptic woman clothed with the Sun of glory, crowned with the twelve stars, and the moon lying at her feet. Her symbolism pertains to the supernal essence of mind, representing thus the type and symbol of the glittering Augoeides, the *Neschamah*.

Speaking of an analogous psychological conception in his commentary to *The Secret of the Golden Flower*, Dr. C. G. Jung remarks that this figure represents "a line or principle of life that strives after superhuman, shining heights." At the base of the tree stands Eve, the *Nephesch* or unconscious who, in opposition to this divine Genius, stands for the dark, "earthborn, feminine principle with its emotionality and instinctiveness reaching far back into the depths of time, and into the roots of physiological continuity." Between the two stands Adam, supported by the fundamental strength of Eve, the *Ruach* or Ego not yet awakened to a realisation of its innate power and possibility. From the larger point of view he represents the race as a whole and "is the personified symbol of the collective Logos, the 'Host', and of the Lords of Wisdom or the Heavenly Man, who incarnated in humanity." Otherwise he represents
<59> the individual Candidate on the Path, prior to the awakening of the "sleeping dogs" within his being, to use Blavatsky's apt expression.

Beneath these three figures sleeps a coiled dragon, silent, unawakened. None it would seem is aware of that latent power, titanic and promethean, coiled beneath — the active magical power centered in man, his libido, neutral, of vast potentialities but neither good nor evil in itself.

Very similar in some respects is the diagram revealed in the Philosophus Grade. As the divine peace of the Garden of Eden was manifested during the Water grade, so in this Grade of Philosophus, the power of Fire is shown to have called forth catastrophe. Formerly coiled beneath the tree, the hydra-headed dragon in this Diagram has usurped its proper place. Its several horned heads wind their way up into the very structure of the Tree of Life, even unto *Daath* at the foot of the Supernals. Lured downwards by the tree of knowledge — and remembering in what sense the Bible speaks of the verb "to know," we gather that the root of the trouble was an imperfect apprehension of creative power — towards the "darkly splendid world wherein continually lieth a faithless depth," Eve, the lower self, ceases to give support to Adam. She has yielded to the awful fascination of the awakening psyche. Far easier is it to fall than to climb to the distant heights. Yet only from one viewpoint is the Fall catastrophic. The awareness of the rise of the Dragon endows man also with consciousness of power — and power is life and progress. The Dragon stands as the symbol of the great enemy to be overcome, and, as the task of equilibration proceeds, the great prize awaiting success.

<60> The Fall as a state of consciousness is analagous to that condition described by various mystics as the dark Night of the Soul. It is accompanied by a sense of intolerable dryness, a dreaded awareness of the fact that all the powers of the soul seem dead, and the mind's vision closed in dumb protest, as it were, against the harsh discipline of the Work itself. A thousand and one seductions will tend to lure the candidate from the contemplation of the magical goal, and there will be presented to him a thousand and one means of breaking in spirit his vow to "persevere in the divine science" without breaking it in letter. And it will appear that the mind itself will run riot and become unstable, warning the candidate that it were better for him to enjoy a lull in his magical operations. This state is allegorically referred to by the alchemists in their descriptions of the poisonous Dragon which follows upon the corruption of their First Matter. Vaughan calls it: "a horrible devouring Dragon — creeping and weltering in the bottom of her cave, without wings. Touch her not by any means, not so much as with thy hands, for there is not upon earth such a violent, transcendent poison." But as the mystics teach, if this condition be patiently endured, it passes, a higher spiritual consciousness gradually dawning in the heart and mind. So also in the alchemical writings, we find that Vaughan observes: "As thou hast begun so proceed, and this Dragon will turn to a Swan, but more white than the hovering virgin snow when it is not yet sullied with the earth."

The Qabalistic Sephirah of *Daath* is the conjunction of Chokmah and Binah on

the Tree of Life, the child of Wisdom and Understanding —knowledge. It
<61> refers to the symbolic sphere formed within or above the *Ruach* by means of
experience obtained, and this assimilated becomes transmuted into intuition and faculty of mind. But fundamentally it is the ascent of the Dragon or, if you wish, an upwelling of the Unconscious archetypes — a highly dangerous and unbalancing ascent, until they are assimilated to consciousness — which first renders *Daath* a possibility. It is the Fall which is responsible for the acquisition of self-knowledge. "Thus it stands proven" claims Blavatsky, "that Satan, or the red *Fiery* Dragon, the 'Lord of Phosphorus' and *Lucifer,* or 'Light-bearer,' is in us; it is our Mind — our temptor and Redeemer, our intelligent liberator and saviour from pure animalism."

In the evolutionary scheme, the Fall occurs through a higher type of intelligence coming into close contact with nascent humanity, thus stimulating the psyche of the race — or so the magical tradition has it. The recapitulation of this process within the individual sphere of consciousness proceeds through the technique of initiation whereby the Red Dragon is stirred into activity through contact with the fructifying powers of the elements, invoked through the skill and power of a trained initiator. The use of the divine prerogative, brought about by the magic of every-day experience, the awakening of *Daath,* brings disaster at first because the awakened psyche is imperfectly understood and so abused for personal ends. But that very disaster and that abuse confers the consciousness of self, and is instrumental, at least in part of breaking up the primitive *participation mystique.* Consequently, the realisation of
sorrow as it impinges on the ego, or at least the sense of personal mental and
<62> emotional discomfort, and an understanding of its causes, invariably con-
stitute the first impetus to perform the Great Work, even as it comprises the motive first to seek the services and aid of the analytical psychologist. This impetus and this self-consciousness are the prime implications of *Daath.* Its signification is a higher type of consciousness, the beginning of a spiritual rebirth. It acts as a self-evolved link between the higher Genius, on the one hand, at peace in its Supernal abode, and, on the other hand, the human soul bound by its Fall to the world of illusion and sense and matter. Not until that self-consciousness and acquired knowledge are turned to noble and altruistic ends, so long will sorrow and suffering be the inevitable result. Continually will the Red Dragon, the inverted power of the eros, ravish the little kingdom of self until such time as we open ourselves to the deepest levels of our unconsciousness, reconciling and uniting them with our conscious outlook, thus conquering the foe by driving it back to its proper realm. In such a way may we use, but neither ignore nor repress, the experience of life and its fruit to transcend our own personal limitations and attain to a *participation mystique* on a higher and self-conscious level.

Let me quote a few especially appropriate lines from Jung in connection with this Fall, when the fundamental basis of the *Ruach* has been attracted to the kingdom of shells and when *Malkuth* has been disassociated from the other Sephiroth: "Consciousness thus torn from its roots and no longer able to appeal to the authority of the primordial images, possesses a Promethean freedom, it is true, but it also partakes of
the nature of a godless *hybris.* It soars above the earth, even above mankind,
<63> but the danger of capsizing is there, not for every individual to be sure, but
collectively for the weak members of such a society, who again Promethean-like, are bound by the unconscious to the Caucasus."

For the Adept to be cut off from his roots, from contact with the vitalising and necessary basis of his Unconsciousness, will never do. He must unite and integrate the various levels of his entire Tree. His task must be to train and develop the titanic forces of his own underworld, so that they become as a powerful but docile beast whereon he may ride.

§

The Adeptus minor grade continues the theme of these two diagrams. Escorted into the Vault, the Aspirant is shown the lid of the Tomb of Osiris, the Pastos, wherein is buried our Father, Christian Rosenkreutz, and on that lid is a painting which brings fulfillment as it were to the narrative of the preceding diagrams. It is divided into two sections. The lower half of the painting depicts a figure of Adam, similar to his presentation in the Practicus grade diagram, though here the heads of the Dragon are falling back from the Tree, showing the Justified One, the illuminated adept, by his immolation and self-sacrifice rescuing the fallen kingdom of his natural self from the clutches of an outraged eros. But above this, as though to show the true nature behind the deceptive appearance of things is illustrated a noble figure of majesty and divinity described in the Ritual in these words. "And being turned I saw seven golden
<64> Light-bearers, and in the midst of the Light-bearers, one like unto the Ben
Adam, clothed with a garment down to the feet, and girt with a golden girdle. His head and his hair were white as snow, and his eyes as flaming fire; his feet like unto fine brass as if they burned in a furnace. And his voice as the sound of many waters. And he had in his right hand seven stars and out of his mouth went the Sword of Flame, and his countenance was as the Sun in his strength."

It is to effect this redemption of the personality, to regenerate the power of the dragon, and attempt to bring the individual to some realisation of his potential godhead, that is the object of the Adeptus Minor Ceremony.

It is for this reason that I hold that the Golden Dawn magic, the technique of initiation, is of supreme and inestimable importance to mankind at large. In it the work of academic psychology may find a logical conclusion and fruition, so that it may develop further its own particular contribution to modern life and culture. For this psycho-magical technique of ceremonial initiation indicates the psychological solution of the *anima* problem. "Arise! Shine! For thy light is come!"

Between the grade of Philosophus and the Portal, an interval of seven months was prescribed, the regimen of the planets. During that period, devised to assist the gradual fructification of the seeds planted within, a review was advised of all the preceding studies. Such a review certainly was imperative. As one of the Chiefs of the Order expressed it:—"Remember that there is hardly a circumstance in the rituals even of the First Order which has not its special meaning and application, and
<65> which does not conceal a potent magical formula. These ceremonies have
brought thee into contact with certain forces which thou hast now to learn to awaken in thyself, and to this end, read, study and re-read that which thou hast already received. Be not sure even after the lapse of much time that thou hast fully discovered all that is to be learned from these. And to be of use unto thee, this must be the work of thine own inner self, thine own and not the work of another for thee so that thou mayest gradually attain to the knowledge of the Divine Ones."

The Grade of the Portal, which conferred upon the Candidate the title of Lord of the Paths of the Portal of the Vault of the Adepti, is not referred to a Sephirah as such. It may, however, be considered as an outer court to Tiphareth, exactly as the Adeptus Minor ceremony may be considered Tiphareth within. Its technical attribution is the element of Akasa, Spirit or Ether which is magically invoked by the usual procedure of invoking pentagrams and the vibration of divine names following upon the conjuration of the powers of the four subsidiary elements. To this grade, there is attached no elemental prayer as in the former grades, but there is one remarkable invocation employed which bears quoting here. In full Temple, the English version is not used, but it is vibrated in the original Enochian or Angelic tongue — a language which is at once sonorous, vibrant and dramatically impressive. The following is the full version of which an abridged one was normally used in the Temple: "I reign over you, (here

the Order version names the three Archangels of the element) saith the God of Justice in power exalted above the firmament of wrath. In whose hands the Sun is as a
<66> sword and the Moon as a through-thrusting fire. Who measureth your garments in the midst of my vestures and trussed you together as the palms of my hands. Whose seat I garnished with the fire of gathering. Who beautified your garments with admiration. To whom I made a law to govern the holy ones, and delivered you a rod with the ark of knowledge. Moreover, ye lifted up your voices and sware obedience and faith to him that liveth and triumpheth. Whose beginning is not nor end cannot be. Who shineth as a flame in the midst of your palaces and reigneth amongst you as the balance of righteousness and truth. Move therefore and show yourselves. Open the mysteries of your creation. Be friendly unto me, for I am the servant of the same your God, a true worshipper of the Highest."

This grade, referred to the veil *Paroketh,* which separates the First and Second Orders, is intermediate between the purely elemental grades and the spiritual grade of Adeptus Minor. A crown to the four lower elements, this Rite formulates above Earth, Air, Water and Fire, the uppermost point of the Pentagram, revealing the administration of the Light over and through the kingdom of the natural world. It concerns itself with the recapitulation of the former grades, co-ordinating and equilibriating the elemental self which, symbolically sacrificed upon the mystical altar, is offered to the service of the higher Genius. In that grade, too, aspiration to the divine is strongly stressed as the faculty by which the veil of the inner sanctuary may be rent. It is the way to realisation. The five Paths leading from the grades of the First to the Second Orders are symbolically traversed, and their symbols impressed within the sphere of sensation.

<67> A gestation period of at least nine months had to elapse prior to initiation to the grade of Adeptus Minor, and since there can be no misunderstanding the purpose and nature of this beautiful ceremony it requires the minimum of comment from my pen. It explains itself completely in one of the speeches: "Buried with that Light in a mystical death, rising again in a mystical resurrection, cleansed and purified through him our Master, O Brother of the Cross of the Rose. Like him, O Adepts of all ages, have ye toiled. Like him have ye suffered tribulation. Poverty, torture and death have ye passed through; they have been but the purification of the gold. In the alembic of thine heart through the athanor of affliction, seek thou the true stone of the wise."

The form of this ritual is beautiful in its simplicity and warrants a brief description. First of all, the candidate is led in, arrayed with insignia and badges and calling himself by his various titles and mottos. But he is warned that not in any vainglorious spirit are the mysteries to be approached, but in simplicity alone. This is the signal for him to be divested of all his ornaments and insignia, and by the Temple entrance, just prior to being bound upon a large upstanding cross of wood, he stands alone, clad in a simple unornamented black gown. The reader is earnestly recommended to study this Ritual again and again, until almost it becomes a part of his very life, incorporated into the fabric of his being, for herein are highly important and significant formulae of mystical aspiration and of practical magic. In it is exemplified the technical "Dying God" formula about which in *The Golden Bough* Frazer has written so eloquently.

Examples of this are to be found in every mythology and every mystical
<68> religion that our world has ever known. But I doubt that it has ever attained to a more clarified and definite espression than in this ceremony of the Adeptus Minor grade. For we are clearly taught by precept and by example that we are, in essence, gods of great power and spirituality who died to the land of our birth in the Garden of Hesperides, and mystically dying descended into hell. And moreover the ritual demonstrates that like Osiris, Christ, and Mithra, and many another type of god-man, we too may rise from the tomb and become aware of our true divine

natures. The principal clause of the lengthy Obligation assumed while bound to the cross, indicating the trend of its teaching, and the import of its objective, is: "I further solemnly promise and swear that, with the Divine permission, I will from this day forward apply myself unto the Great Work, which is so to purify and exalt my spritual nature that with Divine aid I may at length attain to be more than human and thus gradually raise and unite myself to my higher and divine Genius, and that in this event, I will not abuse the great power entrusted to me."

The preface to the assumption of the obligation is under these circumstances a tremendously impressive occurrence, and few could fail to be even faintly moved by it. It consists of an invocation of an Angelic power: "In the divine name IAO, I invoke Thee thou great avenging Angel HUA, that thou mayest invisibly place thy hand upon the head of this Aspirant in attestation of his obligation . . ."

It is not difficult to realise that this is a critical and important phase of the ceremony. During this obligation, because of the symbolism attached to it and because of the active aspiration which is induced at this juncture, illumination
<69> may quite easily occur. In one of the documents describing certain effects ensuing from this initiation, one of the Chiefs has written, that the object of the ceremony conceived as a whole "is especially intended to effect the change of the consciousness into the *Neschamah,* and there are three places where this can take place. The first is when the aspirant is on the cross, because he is so exactly fulfilling the symbol of the abnegation of the lower self and the Union with the higher."

The Obligation assumed, the candidate is now removed from the cross, and the Officers then narrate to him the principal facts in the history of the founder of the Order — Christian Rosenkreutz. On a previous page was given a summary of these historical facts. When the History lecture mentions the discovery of the Vault wherein the Tomb and body of the illustrious Father were discovered, one of the initiating adepts draws aside a curtain, admitting the candidate to a chamber erected in the midst of the Temple similar to that described in the lecture. A few words roughly describing it may not be considered amiss. As a climax to the very simple Temple furniture of the Outer grades, it comes as a psychological spasm and as a highly significant symbol. The vault itself is a small seven-sided chamber, each side representing one of the seven planets, with their host of magical correspondences. The mediaeval Rosicrucian manifesto the *Fama Fraternitatis,* translated in Arthur Edward Waite's *Real History of the Rosicrucians,* describes it at great length, though I shall here quote but briefly: "We opened the door, and there appeared to our sight a vault of seven sides and seven corners, every side five foot broad and the height of eight foot. Although the
<70> sun never shined in this vault, nevertheless it was enlightened with another Sun, which had learned this from the sun, and was situated in the upper part of the centre of the ceiling. In the midst, instead of a tomb-stone, was a round altar . . . Now, as we had not yet seen the dead body of our careful and wise Father, we therefore removed the altar aside; then we lifted up a strong plate of brass, and found a fair and worthy body, whole and unconsumed. . . ."

Around this fundamental symbolism, the Golden Dawn adepts, displaying a genius of extraordinary insight and synthesis, had built a most awe-inspiring superstructure. The usual Order symbolism of the Light was represented by a white triangle centred by the Rose — this placed upon the ceiling. The floor design was so painted as to represent the Red Dragon and the forces of the primitive archetypes upon which the candidate trod as emblematic of his conquest. Placed in the centre of the Vault was the Pastos of Rosenkreutz — though the Pastos is also referred to as the Tomb of Osiris the Justified One. Both of these beings may be considered as the type and symbol of the higher and divine Genius. Immediately above this coffin rested the circular altar mentioned in the Fama. It bore paintings of the Kerubic emblems, and upon these were placed the four elemental weapons and a cross, the symbol of

resurrection. At one point in the ceremony, the acting Hierophant, or Chief Adept as he is now called, is interred in the Pastos as though to represent the aspirant's higher Self which is hidden and confined within the personality, itself wandering blindly, lost in the dark wilderness. The whole concatenation of symbols is an elaborate and dramatic portrayal of the central theme of the Great Work. In a word, it depicts
<71> the spiritual rebirth or redemption of the candidate, his resurrection from the dark tomb of mortality through the power of the holy Spirit.

In the symbol of the Vault, the psychologist no doubt will see a highly interesting and complex array of Mother symbols, traces of which, used in very much the same way, may be found in the literary fragments we inherit from the mystery cults of antiquity. It would be possible, and quite legitimate so to interpret the Vault. For even the Order interpretation refers the Vault in its entirety to the Isis of Nature, the great and powerful mother of mankind and all that is. And an analysis of the separate parts of the Vault — the Venus door, the Pastos, the two Pillars — would subscribe to that view. For regeneration and the second birth have always as creative psychological states been associated with the Mother. And it may be recalled that the *Neschamah* or that principle in man which constantly strives for the superhuman shining heights, is always portrayed as a feminine principle, passive, intuitive and alluring. Whilst the universal counterpart of this human principle, represented on the Tree of Life by the Supernals, is always described by the mediaeval alchemists as a virginal figure, from whose life and substance all things have issued, and through whose agency man is brought to the second birth.

The reader is earnestly recommended to study this Ritual again and again until almost it becomes a part of his very life, incorporated into the very fabric of his being. Very little aesthetic appreciation will be required to realise that in this and the other rituals are passages of divine beauty and high eloquence. And the least
<72> learned will find ideas of especial appeal to him, as the scholar and the profound mystic will perceive great depth and erudition in what may appear on the surface as simple statement. Properly performed, with initiated technique and insight, these rituals are stately ceremonies of great inspiration and enlightenment.

The apparent complexity of the above delineated scheme may be thought by some individuals to be entirely too complicated for modern man and not sufficiently simple in nature. While one can deeply sympathise with the ideas of the extreme simplicity cult in Mysticism, nevertheless it is evident that the complex and arduous nature of the routine is no fault of Magic. Man himself is responsible for this awkward situation. To be purified was considered by the alchemists and the Theurgists of a bygone day as not nearly enough. That purification and consecration was required to be repeated and repeated, again and again. Because of countless centuries of evolution and material development — sometimes in quite false directions — man has spiritually repressed himself, and thus gradually forgotten his true divine nature. Meanwhile, as a sort of compensation for this loss, he has developed a complexity of physical and psychic constitution for dealing adequately with the physical world. Hence, methods of spiritual development refusing to admit the reality of that many-principled organisation may not be recognised as valid, for the sole reason that man is not a simple being. Fundamentally and at root he may be simple; but in actuality he is not. Having strayed from his roots, and lost his spiritual birthright in a jungle of delusion, it is not always easy to re-discover those roots or to find the way out from the Gates of the Land of Night.

<73> In contradistinction to the above mentioned type of amorphous mystical doctrine, Magic *does* recognise the many-faceted nature of man. If that intricate structure so painfully constructed be considered an evil, as some seem to think, it is a necessary evil. It is one to be faced and used. Therefore Magic connives by its technique to use, develop, and improve each of these several principles to its highest

degree of perfection. "Thou must prepare thyself" councils Vaughan "till thou art conformable to Him Whom thou wouldst entertain, and that in every respect. Fit thy roof to thy God in what thou canst, and in what thou canst not He will help thee. When thou hast thus set thy house in order, do not think thy Guest will come without invitation. Thou must tire Him out with pious importunities.

> Perpetual knockings at His door,
> Tears sullying his transparent rooms,
> Sighs upon sighs; weep more and more—
> He comes.

This is the way thou must walk in, which if thou dost thou shall perceive a sudden illustration, and there shall then abide in thee fire with light, wind with fire, power with wind, knowledge with power, and with knowledge an integrity of sober mind!"

Not enough is it to be illuminated. The problem is not quite as simple as that. It is in vain that the wine of the Gods is poured into broken bottles. Each part of the soul, each elemental aspect of the entire man must be strengthened and transmuted and brought into equilibrium and harmony with the others. Integration must be
<74> the rule of the initiate, not pathology. In such a vehicle made consecrate and truly holy by this equilibriation, the higher Genius may find a worthy and fit dwelling. This and this alone, may ever constitute the true nature of initiation.

§

With each of the grades just described, a certain amount of personal work was provided, principally of a theoretical kind. The basic ideas of the Qabalah were imparted by means of so-called knowledge lectures, together with certain important symbols and significant names in Hebrew were required to be memorised. The lamens —insignia worn over the heart — of the various Officers were referred in divers ways to the Tree of Life, thus explaining after a fashion the function of that particular office in the Temple of Initiation. Each path traversed, and every grade entered, had a so-called Admission Badge. This usually consisted of one of the many forms of the Cross, and of symbols of the type of the Swastika, truncated Pyramid, and so forth. To these astrological and elemental attributions were referred. Most of these symbols possess great value, and since they repeatedly recur under different guises through the stages of personal magical work undertaken after the Adeptus Minor grade, they should receive the benefit of prolonged brooding and meditation.

Three of the most important items of personal study to be accomplished while in the First or Outer Order, apart from the memorisation of the rudiments of the Qabalah were: (a) The practice of the Pentagram Ritual with the Qabalistic
<75> Cross, (b) Tattwa Vision, and (c) Divination by Geomancy and the simple Tarot method described by Waite in his *Key to the Tarot.*

The Pentagram Ritual was taught to the Neophyte immediately after his initiation in order that he might "form some idea of how to attract and come into communication with spiritual and invisible things." Just as the Neophyte Ceremony of admission contains the essential symbolism of the Great Work, shadowing forth symbolically the commencement of certain formulae of the Magic of Light, so potential within the Pentagram Ritual and the Qabalistic Cross are the epitomes of the whole of that work. In all magical procedure it is fundamental, for it is a gesture of upraising the human consciousness to its own root of perfection and enlightenment by which the sphere of sensation and every act performed under its surveillance are sanctified. Thus it should precede every phase of magical work, elementary as well as advanced. The written rubric has previously appeared in my *Tree of Life,* and I may now add a word or two concerning the further directions which are orally imparted to the Candidate after his admission.

The prime factor towards success in that exercise is to imagine that the astral form is capable of expansion, that it grows tall and high, until at length it has the semblance of a vast angelic figure, whose head towers amongst the distant stars of heaven. When this imaginative expansion of consciousness produces the sense that the height is enormous, with the Earth as a tiny globe revolving beneath the feet, then above the head should be perceived or formulated a descending ray of brilliant Light.

As the candidate marks the head and then the breast, so should this brilliance
<76> descend, even down to his feet, a descending shaft of a gigantic cross of Light.

The act of marking the shoulders right and left whilst vibrating the Sephirotic names, traces the horizontal shaft of the cross, equilibriating the Light within the sphere of sensation. Since it has been argued above that the Great Work consists in the search for the Light, this ritual truly and completely performed leads to the accomplishment of that Work and the personal discovery of the Light. The Pentagrams trace a cleansing and protecting circle of force invoked by the four Names of four letters each about the limits of the personal sphere, and the archangels are called, by vibration, to act as great stabilising influences.

The study of the different types of divination may seem difficult to understand in an Order which purported to teach methods of spiritual development. Many will no doubt be rather perplexed by this. Divination usually is said to refer exclusively to the low occult arts, to fortune-telling, and the prognostication of the future. Actually, however, so far as the Order is concerned, the principal object for these practical methods is that they stimulate, as few exercises can, the faculties of clairvoyance, imagination, and intuition. Though certain readings or interpretations to the geomantic and Tarot symbols may be found in the appropriate text books, these rule of thumb methods do not conduce to the production of an accurate delineation of the spiritual causes behind material events. These interpretations are usual to the beginner in the art, for he requires a foundation of the principal definitions employed upon which his own meditations can build. These textual delineations in actual
<77> practice serve only as a base for the working of the inner faculties, provides
for them a thrust-block as it were from which they may "kick-off." In short, the effort to divine by these methods calls into operation the intuitive and imaginative faculties to a very large extent. Everyone without exception has this faculty of divining in some degree, varying only in his ability to make it manifest. In most people it is wholly dormant.

Again, while divination as an artificial process may be wholly unnecessary and a hindrance to the refined perceptions of a fully developed Adept, who requires no such convention to ascertain whence a thing comes and whither it is going, yet these aids and stimuli have their proper place for the Neophyte. For those in training they are not only legitimate but useful and necessary. It may be interesting for the reader to attempt to acquire intuitive knowledge on any matter without the divinatory aids first, and it will be seen how extremely difficult it is to get started, to pick upon any one fact or incident which shall act as a prompt or a starter of the interior mechanism. Having failed in this way, let him see how much further he really may go by the judicious and sensible use of one of the Order methods. There is no doubt that the opening of the mind to an intuitive perception is considerably aided by these methods. And this is particularly true with regard to the rather lengthy Tarot method which was given to the initiate while engaged in the fulfilment of his Adeptus Minor curriculum. Like all magical techniques, divination is open to abuse. The fact, however, that abuse is possible does not, as again and again must be reiterated, fully condemn the abused technique. The application of common sense to the magical art is as necessary as it is to all else.

<78> There was a movement on foot in one of the Temples a little while ago to

eliminate the study and practice of Geomancy from the scheme of training of the Outer Order. The prevailing tendency is so to simplify the road to Adeptship as to reduce the practical requisites to an absolute minimum by eliminating every phase of the work which does not come "naturally," and whose study might involve hard work. Most of the newly admitted candidates to this Temple within the past five years or more are utterly without any practical acquaintance with this technique.

Originally, Astrology was taught as part of the regular routine. All instruction on this subject seems now to have been thoroughly extirpated from the Order papers. Perhaps in this particular instance the omission is just as well. For recent years have seen a great deal of meticulous attention paid to this study by sincere and honest researchers, and there have been published many first-rate books explaining its intricacies. All that the Order demands of the Adeptus Minor is that he should be able to draw up a map showing the position of Planets and Signs, preparatory to certain operations requiring the invocation of Zodiacal forces.

Tattwa vision requires but little mention in this place, for full instructions in this technical method of acquiring clairvoyance may be seen in a later volume. They are compiled from a number of documents and verbal instructions obtaining within the Order. Since these oral "tid-bits" and papers were very scattered, it has been found necessary to reorganise the whole matter. In that restatement, however, I have exercised no originality nor uttered personal viewpoints on any phase of the
<79> technique, confining my labour solely to re-writing the material in my possession. It may be interesting for the psychological critic to reflect upon the fact that it was this technique to which most members of the Order devoted the greatest attention — the only technique in which, more than any other single branch of the work, there is greater opportunity for deception and self-deception. While in many ways the Order technique may appear different from the vision method described in my *Tree of Life,* both are essentially the same. For they teach the necessity of an imaginative formation of an intellectual or astral form, the Body of Light, for the purpose of exploring the different regions of the Tree of Life or the several strata of one's own psychic make-up. The simpler aspects of this investigation are taught just after the grade of Philosophus, though naturally the full possibilities of this method and the complete details on the technical side do not reveal themselves until the teaching of the Second Order has been received.

In addition to these technical methods there were meditations on the symbols and ideas of the whole system, and it was quite frequently suggested that the student go through the ceremonies, after having taken the grades, and build them up in his imagination so that he re-lives them as vividly as when he was in the Temple. The practical exercise that accompanied the Portal grade was one in which the aspirant built up, again in the imagination, a symbolic form of the Qabalistic Tree of Life, paying at first particular attention to the formulation of the Middle Pillar in the sphere of sensation or aura. This latter was conceived to be an ovoid shape of subtle
<80> matter, and the imaginative formulation of the various Sephiroth therein whilst vibrating the appropriate Divine Names went far towards opening, in a safe and balanced way, the psycho-spiritual centres of which the Sephiroth were but symbols. This technique, with the so-called Vibratory Formula of the Middle Pillar which is a development therefrom, I consider to be one of the most important practical systems employed in the Order. Though the documents describe it in a very rudimentary and sketchy fashion, nevertheless it is capable of expansion in several quite astonishing directions. I have discussed and expanded this technique at considerable length in my book *The Art of True Healing.*

So far, I have confined myself to a bird's eye view of the routine as established in the First or Outer Order of the Golden Dawn. The graduated training of the entire Outer was intended as a preparation for the practical work to be performed in the

Inner or Second Order of the Roseae Rubeae et Aureae Crucis. The assignation of personal magical work seems deliberately to have been postponed until after the Vault reception. It was held that the Ceremony formulated a link between the Aspirant and his Augoeides, that connection serving therefore as a guide and a powerful protection which is clearly required in the works of Ceremonial Magic. Since at the commencement of each serious operation the Initiate must needs exalt himself towards his higher and divine Genius that through him may flow the divine power which alone is capable of producing a pure magical work, the initial forging of that link is a matter of supreme importance.

Let me now detail the curriculum of work prescribed in the Second
<81> Order. The training of the Adeptus Minor consisted of eight separate items, and I quote the following from a syllabus "A—General Orders," now in circulation.

"*Part One. A. Preliminary.* Receive and copy: Notes on the Obligation. The Ritual of the ⑤ = [6] Grade. The manuscript, Sigils from the Rose. The Minutum Mundum. Having made your copies of these and returned the originals you should study them in order to prepare to sit for the written examination. You must also arrange with the Adept in whose charge you are, about your examination in the Temple on the practical work."

"*Part Two.* Receive the Rituals of the Pentagram and Hexagram. Copy and learn them. You can now sit for the written examination in these subjects and complete 'A' by arranging to be tested in your practical knowledge in the Temple.

"*Part One. B. Implements.* Receive the Rituals of the Lotus Wand, Rose Cross, Sword, and the Elemental Weapons. Copy and return them. There is a written examination on the above subjects — that is on the construction, symbolism, and use of these objects, and the general nature of a consecration ceremony and the forming of invocations. This can be taken before the practical work of making is begun or at any stage during it.

"*Part Two.* This consists in the making of the Implements which must be passed as suitable before the consecration is arranged for, in the presence of a Chief or other qualified Adept. The making and consecration are done in the order given above unless it is preferred to do all the practical work first, and make arrangements for consecration as convenient.

<82> "*Part One. G. Neophyte Formulae.* Receive and copy Z. 1. on the symbols and formulae of the Neophyte Ritual. Z. 3, the symbolism of the Neophyte in this Ceremony. Copy the God-form designs of the Neophyte Ritual. The written examination on the Z. manuscripts may now be taken.

"*Part Two.* To describe to the Chief or other suitable Adept in the Temple the arrangement of the Astral Temple and the relative position of the Forms in it. To build up any God-form required, using the correct Coptic Name."

The above three sections, A. B. G., completed the course prescribed for the Zelator Adeptus Minor, the first sub-grade. The passing of these examinations, conferred the qualification for holding the office of Hierophant, that is the initiator, in the Outer Order of the G. D.

"*Part One. C. Psychic.* This consists in a written examination in the Tattwa system. Its method of use, and an account of any one vision you have had from any card.

"*Part Two.* This consists in making a set of Tattwa cards, if you have not already done so, and sending them to be passed by the Chief or other Adept appointed. To take the examiner on a Tattwic journey, instructing him as if he were a student and vibrating the proper names for a selected symbol.

"*Part One. D. Divination.* Receive and study the Tarot system, making notes of the principal attributions of the Inner method.

<83> *"Part Two. Practical.* On a selected question, either your own, or the examiner's, to work out a Divination first by Geomancy, then by Horary Astrology, then by the complete inner Tarot system, and send in a correlated account of the result.

"Part One. F. Angelic Tablets. Receive and make copies of the Enochian Tablets, the Ritual of the Concourse of the Forces, and the Ritual of the making of the Pyramid, Sphinx, and God-form for any square. A written examination on these subjects may now be taken.

"Part Two. Make and colour a pyramid for a selected square, and to make the God-form and Sphinx suitable to it, and to have this passed by an Adept. To prepare a Ritual for practical use with this square, and in the presence of a Chief or other Adept appointed to build it up astrally and describe the vision produced. To study and play Enochian chess, and to make one of the Chess boards and a set of Chessmen.

"Part One. E. Talismans. Receive a manuscript on the making and consecrating of Talismans. Gather Names, Sigils, etc., for a Talisman for a special purpose. Make a design for both designs of it and send it in for a Chief to pass. Make up a special ritual for consecrating to the purpose you have in mind and arrange a time with the Chief for the Ceremony of Consecration.

"H. Consecration and Evocation. Subject: A ceremony on the formulae of Ritual Z. 2. Must be prepared before Examiner and must meet with his approval as to method, execution and effect."

<84> In the early Temples there was also issued a catalogue of manuscripts, enumerating in alphabetical order the documents circulated amongst the Zelatores Adepti Minores.

A. General Orders. The Curriculum of Work prescribed.
B. The Lesser and Supreme Rituals of the Pentagram.
C. The Rituals of the Hexagram.
D. Description of Lotus Wand, and Ritual of Consecration.
E. Description of Rose Cross and the Ritual of Consecration.
F. Sigils from the Rose.
G. Sword and Four Implements, with Consecration Ritual.
H. Clavicula Tabularum Enochi.
J. Notes on the Obligation of the Adeptus Minor.
K. Consecration Ceremony of the Vault.
L. History Lecture.
M. Hermes Vision, and Lineal Figures of the Sephiroth.
N. O. P. Q. R. Complete Treatise on the Tarot, with Star Maps.
S. The Attributions of the Enochian Tablets.
T. The Book of The Angelical Keys or Calls.
U. Lecture on Man, the Microcosm.
W. Hodos Chamelionis, the Minutum Mundum.
X. The Egyptian God-forms as applied to the Enochian Squares.
Y. Enochian Chess.
Z. Symbolism of the Temple, Candidate, and Ritual of the Neophyte grade.

<85> All the documents from A to Z listed above will be found reproduced in these volumes, though I have not retained that particular order. The sole omissions are the documents lettered H. J. L. and part of M.

"J" consists simply of an elaborated commentary upon the Adeptus Minor Obligation, written in a florid ponderous style reminiscent of Eliphas Levi-cum-Arthur Edward Waite.

"H" Clavicula Tabularum Enochi, is a more or less lengthy manuscript, turgid and archaic, for the most part repeating, though not as clearly, the contents of "S, The Book of the Concourse of the Forces." Incidentally, this document is practically a verbatim duplicate of part of a lengthy manuscript to be found in the Manuscript Library of the British Museum, Sloane 307. A good deal of the advice given is typically mediaeval, and definitely unsound from a spiritual viewpoint, and is certainly not in accord with the general lofty tenor of the remaining Order teaching. It explains how to find precious metals and hidden treasure, and how to drive away the elemental guardians thereof. It is an inferior piece of work — as also is the document "L", and so I have decided to omit both.

"M" has two sections, the Hermes Vision which I do propose to give, and the Lineal Figures of the Sephiroth. Because of the extreme complexity of the latter, and because it will be impossible to reproduce the several geometrical drawings in colour which accompany that manuscript, the writer has deemed it sufficient to restate it in a general manner as a note to the instruction on Telesmatic Images.

<86> The whole of the above decribed material I have arranged and classified in an entirely different way. The contents of these volumes will be found divided up into so many chapters or separate books, each complete by itself. And the material in each book will be seen to be consistent and appertain to parts of the magical technique which are placed with it. The Table of Contents describes my method of arrangement.

Clearly from these disclosures there may be drastic results. But the good, I trust, will immeasurably and ultimately outweigh whatever evil may come. That some careless people will hurt themselves and burn their fingers experimenting with matters not wholly understood seems almost inevitable. Theirs, however, will be the fault. For the formulae of Magic require intensive study prior to experimental work. And since all the important formulae are given in their entirety, and nothing withheld that is of the least value, there should be no excuse for anybody harming himself. No serious hurt should come to anyone. On the contrary, the gain to those serious students of Magic and Mysticism who have initiative and yet refuse to involve themselves with corrupt occult orders, and it is to these that I fain would speak, should be immeasurable.

You are being given a complete system of attainment. This you must study and develop at your own leisure, appyling it in your own particular way. The system is complete and effectual, as well as noble. The grade rituals as I shall reproduce them have been tampered with, in some cases unintelligently. Their efficacy, however, is not impaired, for the principal portion of those grade rituals, which teaches
<87> the art of invocation, is intact. So that the unwise editing that they have received in the past several years has not actually damaged them; all that has been removed are a few items, more or less important, of Qabalistic knowledge. If the reader feels that these might be value to him, and for the sake of tolerable completeness would like to have them, by studying such Qabalistic texts as the *Zohar* and the *Sepher Yetzirah* both of which are now in English translation, or some such work as Waite's *Holy Kaballah,* he will be in possession of the fundamental facts. It is in other parts of the Order work that injudicious tampering has been at work. Most of this is now restored and I believe that this book is an accurate representation of the whole of the Order work from Neophyte to Theoricus Adeptus Minor.

Some portions of the manuscripts have required editing, principally from the literary point of view. Whole paragraphs have had to be deleted, others shortened, sentences made more clear, the redundant use of many words eliminated, and a general coordination of the manuscripts undertaken. Certain other sections — those dealing at length with Talismans, Sigils, Clairvoyance, Geomancy and the Enochian Tablets — have been completely rewritten to render them more coherent. But nothing that is essential or vital to the magical tenor or understanding of any document will be omitted, changed or altered. This I avow and publicly swear. Where personally I have seen fit to make comment on any matter in order to clarify the issue or to indicate its antecedents, or connections in other parts of the work, that comment or remark is so marked by me with initials.

<88> Let me therefore urge upon the sincere reader whose wish it is to study this magical system, to pay great attention to the scheme of the grade rituals, to obtain a bird's eye view of the whole, to study every point, its movement and teaching. This should be repeated again and again, until the mind moves easily from one point of the ritual to another. The synthetic outline of those rituals presented in this Introduction should be found helpful as assisting in this task. Let him also study the diagrams of the Temple lay-out, and build up in his imagination a clear and vivid picture of that Temple together with the appropriate officers and their movements. Then it will be an easy matter to devise a simple form of self-initiation. It will be simple to adapt the text to solo performance. But a careful scrutiny and examination of the entire system should long precede any effort to do practical work, if serious harm and danger is to be avoided. The language needs first of all to be mastered, and the symbolic ideas of the whole system assimilated and incorporated into the very fibre of one's being. Intellectual acquaintance with every aspect of the subject is just as necessary as personal integrity and selfless devotion to an ideal. Sincerity is indeed the most trustworthy shield and buckler that any student may possess, but if he neglects the intellectual mastery of the subject, he will soon discover where his heel of Achilles is located. But these two combined are the only safeguards, the fundamental requisites to an insight into the significance of Magic. Not only are they the only sure foundation, but they conduce to the continual recollection of the goal at the end, which understanding arises through penetrating to the root of the matter, without which the student may stray but too readily from the narrow way stretching
<89> before him. No matter how brilliant his intellectual capacity, no matter how ardent his sincerity or potent his dormant magical power, always must he remember that they matter absolutely in no way unless applied to the Great Work — the knowledge and conversation of the Higher and Divine Genius. "Power without wisdom," said a poet, "is the name of Death." And as Frater D. D. C. F. so rightly said of one phase of magical work, but which has its application to the whole scheme, "Know thou that this is not to be done lightly for thine amusement or experiment, seeing that the forces of Nature were not created to be thy plaything or toy. Unless thou doest thy practical magical works with solemnity, ceremony and reverence, thou shalt be like an infant playing with fire, and thou shalt bring destruction upon thyself." In deviation from these injunctions lie the only actual dangers in the divine science.

One of the essentials of preliminary work, is the committing to memory of the important correspondences and attributions. And I cannot insist too strongly that this is fundamental. The student must make himself familiar first of all with the Hebrew Alphabet, and learn how to write the names of the Sephiroth and Deity Names in that tongue — he will realise their value when he approaches the practical work of invocation. Much time should be spent studying and meditating upon the glyph of the Tree of Life and memorising all the important attributions — divine Names, names of Archangels, Angels and Spheres and elements. All the symbols referred to the lamens of the officers should be carefully meditated upon, as also the various
<90> admission badges, and other symbols given in the knowledge lectures. Above all, a great deal of time and attention should be paid to the Middle Pillar technique and the Vibratory Formulae of divine names.

The student can easily adapt any fair-sized room to the exigencies of a Temple. The writer has worked in one hardly larger than a long cupboard, about ten feet long by six or seven wide. All furniture from the centre should be cleared away, leaving a central space in which one may freely move and work. A small table covered with a black cloth will suffice for the Altar, and the two Pillars may be dispensed with but formulated in the imagination as present. He may find it very useful to paint flashing Angelic Tablets according to the instructions found elsewhere, as well as the Banners of the East and West, placing these in the appropriate cardinal quarters of his improvised Temple. If he is able to obtain small plaster-casts of the heads of the Kerubim — the lion, the eagle, bull and man — and place these in the proper stations, they will be found together with the Tablets to impart a considerable amount of magical vitality and atmosphere to the Temple. What actually they do bestow is rather subtle, and perhaps indefinable. They are not absolute essentials, however, and may be dispensed with. But since Magic works by the intervention of symbol and emblem, the surrounding of the student's sphere with the correct forms of magical symbolism, assists in the impressing of those symbols within the aura or sphere of sensation, the true magical Temple. This may be left to the ingenium and the convenience of the student himself to discover after having made a close examination of the documents involved.

<91> Another matter upon which brief comment must be made concerns the Instruments. It would have given me great pleasure to have had illustrations of these reproduced in colour, for only thus can one appreciate their significance and the part they play in ceremonial. But this unfortunately has not been possible. Thus they are given only in black and white, which obviously cannot impart anything but the merest fraction of their actual beauty and suggestiveness. And I impress upon the serious student, even implore him, to betake upon himself the trouble of making these instruments himself. They are very simple to fashion. And the results obtained, to say little of the knowledge acquired or the intuitive processes that somehow are stimulated by that effort, are well worth even a great deal of bother. To adopt temporarily part of the terminology now current among analytical psychologists, and identify the latent spiritual self of man with what is known as the Unconscious, then be it remembered that this vast subterranean stream of vitality and memory and inspiration can only be reached by means of a symbol. For the latter, states Jung, "is the primitive expression of the Unconscious, while on the other hand it is an idea corresponding to the highest intuition produced by consciousness." Thus these weapons and magical instruments are symbolic representations of psychic events, of forces inhering within the potentiality of the inner man. By means of their personal manufacture, magical consecration and continual employment they may be made to affect and stimulate the dormant side of man's nature. It is an interesting fact that in his practice, Jung encouraged his patients to paint symbolic designs which some-
<92> times were comparable to the Eastern mandalas. It seems that the effort to paint these designs had the effect of straightening out stresses and knots in the unconscious, thus accomplishing the therapeutic object of the analysis. And not only were they thus means of self-expression but these designs produced a counter-effect of fascinating, healing and stimulating to renewed activity the hitherto unmanifested psyche.

With the exception that the ordinary magical student is not neurotic or psychopathic, the techniques are rather similar. For the magical tradition has always insisted upon the routine to be followed by the aspirant to that art. He was required to fashion the implements himself, and the more laborious he found that task, with the greater difficulties thrown before him, by so much more were those efforts of spiritual value. For not only are these instruments symbols or expressions of inner realities, but what is infinitely more of practical worth, their actual projection in this way from within outwards, the physical fashioning and painting of these instruments, also works an effect. They bring to life the man that was asleep. They react upon their maker. They become powerful magical agents, true talismans of power.

Thus, the Lotus Wand is declared in the Ritual to have the colours of the twelve

signs of the Zodiac painted on its stem, and it is surmounted by the Lotus flower of Isis. It symbolises the development of creation. The Wand has ever been a symbol of the magical Will, the power of the spirit in action. And its description in the instruction on the Lotus Wand is such that it is seen to embrace the whole of nature — the Sephiroth, the spiritual aspects of the elements, and the action of the Sun
<93> upon all life by a differentiating process. Even as the whole of nature is the
embodiment of a dynamic will, the visible form and vehicle of a spiritual consciousness. The Lotus flower grows from the darkness and gloom of the secret depths, through the waters, ever striving to open its blossoms on the surface of the waters to the rays of light of the Sun. So is the true magical or spiritual will secreted within the hidden depths of the soul of man. Unseen, sometimes unknown and unsuspected, it lies latent though the whole of the life. By these rites of Magic, its symbols and exercises, we are enabled to assist its growth and development, by piercing through the outer husks of the restricting shell, until it bursts into full bloom — the flower of the human spirit, the Lotus of the higher Soul. "Look for the flower to bloom in the silence . . . It shall grow, it will shoot up, it will make branches and leaves and form buds while the storm continues, while the battle lasts . . . It is the flower of the soul that has opened." Note, moreover, the description of and the comment made by Jung to a symbolic design brought to him by one of his patients, evidently a design like to the Lotus Wand, for he says: "The plant is frequently a structure in brilliant fiery colours and is shown growing out of a bed of darkness and carrying the blossom of light at the top, a symbol similar to the Christmas tree." This is highly suggestive, and students both of Yoga and Magic will find in this curious indications of the universality of cogent symbols. Magical processes and symbols are, in short, receiving confirmation at the hands of experimental psychology. It remains for the reader to benefit thereby.

<94> The Rose-Cross is a Lamen or badge synthesising a vast concourse of
ideas, representing in a single emblem the Great Work itself — the harmonious reconciliation in one symbol of diverse and apparently contradictory concepts, the reconciliation of divinity and manhood. It is a highly important symbol to be worn over the heart during every important operation. It is a glyph, in one sense, of the higher Genius to whose knowledge and conversation the student is eternally aspiring. In the Rituals it is described as the Key of Sigils and Rituals.

The Sword is a weapon symbolising the critical dispersive faculty of the mind. It is used where force and strength are required, more particularly for banishing than for invoking — as though conscious intellection were allied to the power of Will. When employed in certain magical ceremonies with the point upwards, its nature is transformed into an instrument similar to the Wand. The Elemental weapons of the Wand, Cup, Dagger, and Pentacle are symbolical representations of the forces employed for the manifestation of the inner self, the elements required for the incarnation of the divine. They are attributed to the four letters of Tetragrammaton. All of these are worth making, and by creating them and continually employing them intelligently in the ways shown by the various rituals, the student will find a new power developing within him, a new centre of life building itself up from within.

One last word of caution. Let me warn the student against attempting difficult and complex ceremonies before he has mastered the more simple ones. The syllabus provided on a former page for the use of the Minor Adept grades the work
<95> rather well. The consecration ceremonies for the magical implements are, of
their kind, excellent examples of ceremonial work. Classical in nature, they are simple in structure and operation, and provide a harmonious and easily flowing ritual. A good deal of experience should be obtained with the constant use of these and similar types which the student should himself construct along these lines. A

variety of things may occur to his mind for which a variety of operations may be performed. This of course, applies only to that phase of his studies when the preliminary correspondences and attributions have been thoroughly memorised and what is more, understood, and when the meditations have been performed. This likewise is another matter upon which too much emphasis cannot be laid.

Above all, the Pentagram and Hexagram rituals should be committed to memory so that no effort is required to recall at a moment's notice the points or angles of these figures from which the invocation of a certain force commences. Short ceremonies should be devised having as their object the frequent use of these lineal figures so that they become a part of the very manner in which the mind works during ceremonial. After some time has elapsed, and after considerable experience with the more simple consecration formulae, the student feeling more confident of himself and his ritualistic capacity, let him turn to the complex ceremonies whose formulae are summarised in the manuscripts Z. 2. These require much preparation, intensive study, and a great deal of rehearsal and experience. Moreover, he must not be disappointed if, at first, the results fall short of his anticipations. Persistence is an admirable and
<96> necessary virtue, particularly in Magic. And let him endeavour to penetrate
into the reasons for the apparent worthlessness or puerility of the aims of these formulae, such as transformation, evocation, invisibility, by reflection on the spiritual forces which must flow through him in order to effect such ends. And let him beware of the booby trap which was set up in the Order — of doing but one of these ceremonies, or superficially employing any phase of the system as though to pass an examination, and considering in consequence that he is the master of the technique.

My work is now done.

"Let us work, therefore, my brethren and effect righteousness, because the Night cometh when no man shall labour . . . May the Light which is behind the veil shine through you from your throne in the East on the Fratres and Sorores of the Order and lead them to the perfect day, when the glory of this world passes and a great light shines over the splendid sea."

BOOK ONE

<99> **BOOK ONE**

First Knowledge Lecture

1. The Four Elements of the Ancients are duplicated conditions of:

Heat and Dryness	Fire	△
Heat and Moisture	Air	🜁
Cold and Dryness	Earth	🜃
Cold and Moisture	Water	▽

2. The Signs of the Zodiac are twelve:

1. Aries, *the Ram*	♈
2. Taurus, *The Bull*	♉
3. Gemini, *The Twins*	♊
4. Cancer, *The Crab*	♋
5. Leo, *The Lion*	♌
6. Virgo, *The Virgin*	♍
7. Libra, *The Scales*	♎
8. Scorpio, *The Scorpion*	♏
9. Sagittarius, *The Archer*	♐
10. Capricorn, *The Goat*	♑
11. Aquarius, *The Water-Bearer*	♒
12. Pisces, *The Fishes*	♓

These Twelve Signs are distributed among the Four Triplicities,
<100> or sets of three Signs, each being attributed to one of the Four Elements, and they represent the operation of the elements in the Zodiac.

Thus to Fire belong Aries, Leo, Sagittarius:	♈ : ♌ : ♐
Thus to Earth belong Taurus, Virgo, Capricornus:	♉ : ♍ : ♑
Thus to Air belong Gemini, Libra, Aquarius:	♊ : ♎ : ♒
Thus to Water belong Cancer, Scorpio, Pisces.	♋ : ♏ : ♓

3. To the Ancients,
six Planets were known, besides THE SUN, which they classed with the Planets. They also assigned certain planetary values to the North and

South NODES of the MOON — that is, the points where her orbit touches that of the Ecliptic.

These they named

Caput Draconis ☊ *Head of the Dragon* and
Cauda Draconis ☋ *Tail of the Dragon*

Since the discovery of two more distant Planets Neptune and Uranus or Herschel, these two terms have been partially replaced by them.

The effect of *Caput Draconis* is similar to that of ♆.

The effect of *Cauda Draconis* is similar to that of ♅.

<101> The Old Planets *are:*

Saturn	♄	*Sol*	☉
Jupiter	♃	*Venus*	♀
Mars	♂	*Mercury*	☿

Luna ——— ☽ The Moon

4. The Hebrew Alphabet

is given on page 103. Each letter represents a number and has also a meaning.

Five letters

have a different shape when written at the end of a word and also a different number.

Mem ם (final) Of these finals, Mem is distinguished by being the only *oblong* letter.

ך : ן : ף : ץ The other four—Kaph, Nun, Pe, Tzaddi, have tails which should come below the line as shown.

Hebrew and Chaldee letters are written from right to left.

The Hebrew Qabalists

referred the highest and most abstract ideas to the *Emanations of Deity* or *Sephiroth.* They made them *ten* in number. Each one is a *Sephira,* and when arranged in a certain manner they form *The Tree of Life.*

Hebrew letters are holy symbols. They should be carefully drawn and square.

<102> The Sephiroth *are:*

1. Kether	K-Th-R	—*The Crown*	כתר
2. Chokmah	Ch-K-M-H	—*Wisdom*	חכמה
3. Binah	B-I-N-H	—*Understanding*	בינה
4. Chesed	Ch-S-D	—*Mercy*	חסד
5. Geburah	G-B-U-R-H	—*Severity*	גבורה
6. Tipareth	Th-Ph-A-R-Th	—*Beauty*	תפארת
7. Netzach	N-Ts-Ch	—*Victory*	נצח
8. Hod	H-O-D	—*Glory*	הוד
9. Yesod	Y-S-O-D	—*The Foundation*	יסוד
10. Malkuth	M-L-K-U-Th	—*The Kingdom*	מלכות

The *Dagesh* or pointing which represents the vowel sounds in modern Hebrew script is not given. It was a later invention to standardise pronunciation and is described in Hebrew grammars.*

<103>

THE HEBREW ALPHABET

Letter	Power	Value	Final	Name	Meaning
א	A	1		Aleph	Ox
ב	B,V	2		Beth	House
ג	G,Gh	3		Gimel	Camel
ד	D,Dh	4		Daleth	Door
ה	H	5		He	Window
ו	O,U,V	6		Vau	Pin or Hook
ז	Z	7		Zayin	Sword or Armour
ח	Ch	8		Cheth	Fence, Enclosure
ט	T	9		Teth	Snake
י	I,Y	10		Yod	Hand
כ	K,Kh	20,500	ך	Kaph	Fist
ל	L	30		Lamed	Ox Goad
מ	M	40,600	ם	Mem	Water
נ	N	50,700	ן	Nun	Fish
ס	S	60		Samekh	Prop
ע	Aa,Ngh	70		Ayin	Eye
פ	P,Ph	80,800	ף	Pe	Mouth
צ	Tz	90,900	ץ	Tzaddi	Fish-hook
ק	Q	100		Qoph	Ear. Back of head
ר	R	200		Resh	Head
ש	S,Sh	300		Shin	Tooth
ת	T,Th	400		Tau	Cross

<105>

MEDITATION No. 1

Let the Neophyte

consider a point as defined in mathematics—having position, but no magnitude—and let him note the ideas to which this gives rise. Concentrating his faculties on this, as a focus, let him endeavour to realise the *immanance* of the *Divine* throughout *Nature,* in all her aspects.

*Readers of the above who have perused my *Tree of Life* and *Garden of Pomegranates* will
<104> note the difference in Hebrew pronunciation, and in order to avoid any further confusion an explanatory note must here be added. As is true of every language, in Hebrew there are several quite distinct dialects. There are, however, two principal ones which should be mentioned. The Ashkenazic, a dialect mostly in employment in Germany, Poland, and Russia; and the Sephardic used in Spain, Portugal, and the Mediterranean generally. Now since the Qabalah attained its prominence in Spain, most Qabalists have employed the Sephardic dialect. Personally I have found that the Ashkenazic dialect answers more nearly than the other to the requirements of transliteration into English, and many problems that have assailed modern students would have been non-existent had they known of the pronunciation which I employed in my former works. Actually, however, the student must discover which of these two suits his own personal predilection and answers to the necessity imposed by the results of study and experience. The Order teaching employs the Sephardic pronunciation, and I have not ventured to interfere with that in any way at all. I simply mention the matter here to render impossible the likelihood of confusion arising. I.R.

Begin by finding a position, balanced, but sufficiently comfortable. Breathe rhythmically until the body is still and the mind quiet. Keep this state for a few minutes at first—and for longer as you get more used to preventing the mind from wandering. Think now of the subject for meditation in a general way—then choose out one thought or image and follow that to its conclusion.

The simplest rhythm for the beginner is the Fourfold Breath.

1. Empty the lungs and remain thus while counting 4.
2. Inhale, counting 4 so that you feel filled with breath to the throat.
3. Hold this breath while counting 4.
4. Exhale, counting 4 till the lungs are empty.

This should be practised, counting slowly or quickly till you obtain a rhythm that suits you—one that is comforting and stilling.

Having attained this, count the breath thus for two or three minutes, till you feel quiet, and then proceed with the meditation.

<106> THE QABALISTIC CROSS AND LESSER RITUAL OF THE PENTAGRAM

Take a steel dagger in the right hand. Face East.

Invoking

Begin here

Touch thy forehead
and say ATEH *(thou art)*

Touch thy breast
and say MALKUTH *(the Kingdom)*

Touch thy right shoulder
and say VE-GEBURAH *(and the Power)*

Touch thy left shoulder
and say VE-GEDULAH *(and the Glory)*

Clasp thy hands before thee
and say LE-OLAM *(for ever)*

Dagger between fingers, point up
and say AMEN.

Make in the Air toward the East the invoking PENTAGRAM as shown and, bringing the point of the dagger to the centre of the Pentagram, vibrate the DEITY NAME —YOD HE VAU HE—imagining that your voice carries forward to the East of the Universe.

Holding the dagger out before you, go to the South, make the Pentagram and vibrate similarly the deity name—ADONAI.

Go to the West, make the Pentagram and vibrate EHEIEH.

Go to the North, make the Pentagram and vibrate AGLA.

<107> Return to the East and complete your circle by bringing the dagger point to the centre of the first Pentagram.

Stand with arms outstretched in the form of a cross and say:—

BEFORE ME	RAPHAEL
BEHIND ME	GABRIEL
AT MY RIGHT HAND	MICHAEL
AT MY LEFT HAND	AURIEL

BEFORE ME FLAMES THE PENTAGRAM—
BEHIND ME SHINES THE SIX-RAYED STAR

Again make the Qabalistic Cross as directed above, saying ATEH, etc.

For Banishing use the same Ritual, but reversing the direction of the lines of the Pentagram.

<108> THE USES OF THE PENTAGRAM RITUAL

1. As a form of prayer the invoking ritual should be used in the morning the banishing in the evening.

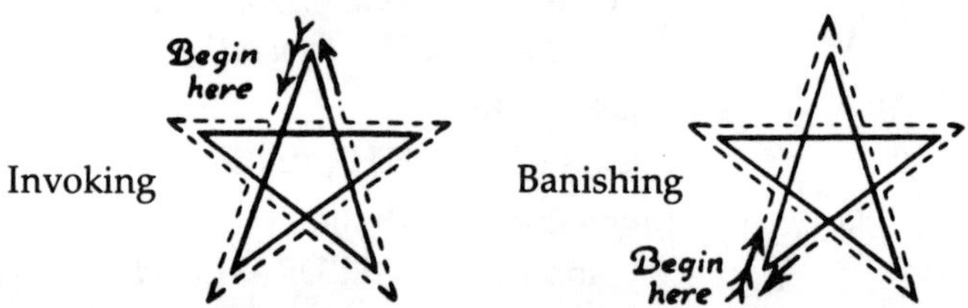

The NAMES should be pronounced inwardly in the breath vibrating it as much as possible and feeling that the whole body throbs with the sound and sends out a wave of vibration directed to the ends of the quarter.

2. As a protection against impure magnetism, the Banishing Ritual can be used to get rid of obsessing or disturbing thoughts. Give a mental image to your obsession and imagine it formulated before you. Project it out of your aura with the Saluting Sign of a Neophyte, and when it is away about three feet, prevent its return with the Sign of Silence.

   Now imagine the form in the East before you and do the Banishing Ritual of the Pentagram to disintegrate it, seeing it, in your mind's eye, dissolving on the further side of your ring of flame.

3. It can be used as an exercise in concentration. Seated in meditation or lying down, formulate yourself standing up in robes and holding a dagger.

   Put your consciousness in this form and go to the East. Make
<109> yourself 'feel' there by touching the wall, opening your eyes, stamping on the floor, etc.

Begin the Ritual and go round the room mentally vibrating the words and trying to feel them as coming from the form.

Finish in the East and try to see your results in the Astral Light, then walk back and stand behind the head of your body and let yourself be reabsorbed.

(In the introduction, page 106, I have given instructions for the performance of the Qabalistic Cross. When tracing the Pentagrams, the imagination should be exerted to visualize them as flaming stars all about one. The impression should be of a fire ring studded in four places with stars of flame.

Likewise, when vibrating the angelic names, the student should endeavour to imagine four vast towering figures about him. But see further in my book "The Middle Pillar." I.R.)

<110>

THE PILLARS

In the explanation of the Symbols of the Grade of Neophyte, your attention has been directed to the general mystical meaning of the Two pillars called in the Ritual the "Pillars of Hermes" of "Seth" and of "Solomon." In the 9th chapter of the Ritual of the Dead they are referred to as the "Pillars of Shu," the "Pillars of the Gods of the Dawning Light," and also as "the North and Southern Columns of the Gate of the Hall of Truth." In the 125th Chapter, they are represented by the sacred gateway, the door to which the aspirant is brought when he has completed the negative confession. The archaic pictures on the one Pillar are painted in black upon a white ground, and those on the other in white upon a black ground, in order to express the interchange and reconciliation of opposing forces and the eternal balance of light and darkness which gives force to visible nature.

The black cubical bases represent darkness and matter wherein the Spirit, the *Ruach Elohim,* began to formulate the Ineffable NAME, that Name which the ancient Rabbis have said "rushes through the universe," that Name before which the Darkness rolls back at the birth of time.

The flaming red triangular capitals which crown the summit of the Pillars represent the Triune manifestation of the Spirit of Life, the Three Mothers of the Sepher Yetsirah, the Three Alchemical Principles of Nature, the Sulphur, the Mercury and the Salt.

Each Pillar is surmounted by its own light-bearer veiled from the material world.

At the base of both Pillars rise the Lotus flowers, symbols of regeneration and metempsychosis. The archaic illustrations are taken from
<111> vignettes of the 17th and 125th chapter of the Ritual of the Dead, the
Egyptian Book of the *Per-em-Hru* or the *Book of Coming Forth into the Day,* the oldest book in the world as yet discovered. The Recension of the Priests of ON is to be found in the walls of the Pyramids of the Kings of the 5th and 6th Dynasties at Sakarah, the recension of the 11th and 12th Dynasties on the sarcophagi of that period, and the Theban recension of the

18th Dynasty and onward is found on papyri, both plain and illuminated. No satisfactory translation of these books is available, none having been yet attempted by a scholar having the qualifications of mystic as well as Egyptologist.

The Ritual of the Dead, generally speaking, is a collection of hymns and prayers in the form of a series of ceremonial Rituals to enable the man to unite himself with Osiris the Redeemer. After this union he is no longer called the man, but Osiris, with whom he is now symbolically identified. "That they also may be One of us," said the Christ of the New Testament. "I am Osiris" said the purified and justified man, his soul luminous and washed from sin in the immortal and uncreated light, united to Osiris, and thereby justified, and the son of God; purified by suffering, strengthened by opposition, regenerate through self-sacrifice. Such is the subject of the great Egyptian Ritual.

The 17th Chapter of the Theban recension consists of a very ancient text with several commentaries, also extremely old, and some prayers, none of which come into the scheme of the original text. It has, together with the 12th chapter, been very carefully translated for the purpose of this lecture by the
V. H. Frater M. W. T., and the V. H. Soror S. S. D. D. has made many
<112> valuable suggestions with regard to the interpretation. The Title
and Preface of the 17th Chapter reads:

"Concerning the exaltation of the Glorified Ones, of Coming and Going forth in the Divine Domain, of the Genies of the Beautiful land of Amentet. Of coming forth in the light of Day in any form desired, of Hearing the Forces of Nature by being enshrined as a living Bai."

And the rubric is:

"The united with Osiris shall recite it when he has entered the Harbour. May glorious things be done thereby upon earth. May all the words of the Adept be fulfilled."

Owing to the complex use of symbols, the ritual translation of the Chapter can only be understood by perpetual reference to the ancient Egyptian commentaries, and therefore the following paraphrase has been put together to convey to modern minds as nearly as possible the ideas conceived by the old Egyptians in this glorious triumphal song of the Soul of Man made one with Osiris, the Redeemer.

"I am TUM made One with all things.

"I have become NU. I am RA in his rising ruling by right of his Power. I am the Great God self-begotten, even NU, who pronounced His Names, and thus the Circle of the Gods was created.

"I am Yesterday and know Tomorrow. I can never more be overcome. I know the secret of Osiris, whose being is perpetually revered of RA. I have finished the work which was planned at the Beginning, I am the Spirit made manifest, and armed with two vast eagle's plumes. Isis and Nephthys are their names, made One with Osiris.

"I claim my inheritance. My sins have been uprooted and my
<113> passions overcome. I am Pure White. I dwell in Time. I live through
Eternity, when Initiates make offering to the Everlasting Gods. I

have passed along the Pathway. I know the Northern and the Southern Pillars, the two Columns at the Gateway of the Hall of Truth.

"Stretch unto me your hands, O ye Dwellers in the centre. For I am transformed to a God in your midst. Made One with Osiris, I have filled the eye socket in the day of the morning when Good and Evil fought together.

"I have lifted up the cloud-veil in the Sky of the Storm. Till I saw RA born again from out the Great Waters. His strength is my strength, and my strength is His strength. Homage to you, Lords of Truth, chiefs who Osiris rules. Granting release from Sin, Followers of Ma where rest is Glorious. Whose Throne Anubis built in the day when Osiris said:

"Lo! A man wins his way to Amentet. I come before you, to drive away my faults. As ye did to the Seven Glorious Ones who follow their Lord Osiris. I am that Spirit of Earth and Sun.

"Between the Two Pillars of Flame. I am RA when he fought beneath the Ashad Tree, destroying the enemies of the Ancient of Days. I am the Dweller in the Egg. I am he who turns in the Disc. I shine forth from the Horizon, as the gold from the mine. I float through the Pillars of SHU in the ether. Without a peer among the Gods. The Breath of my mouth is as a flame. I light upon the Earth with my glory. Eye cannot gaze on my daring beams, as they reach through the Heavens and lick up the Nile with tongues of flame. I am strong upon Earth with the strength of RA. I have come into Harbour as
Osiris made perfect. Let priestly offerings be made to me as one in
<114> the train of the ancient of Days. I brood as the Divine Spirit. I move in
the firmness of my Strength. I undulate as the Waves that vibrate
through Eternity. Osiris has been claimed with acclamation, and ordained to rule among the Gods. Enthroned in the Domain of Horus where the Spirit and the Body are united in the presence of the Ancient of Days. Blotted out are the sins of his body in passion. He has passed the Eternal Gate, and has received the New Year Feast with Incense, at the marriage of Earth with Heaven.

"TUM has built his Bridal Chamber. RURURET has founded his shrine. The Procession's completed. HORUS has purified, SET has consecrated, SHU made one with OSIRIS, has entered his heritage.

"As TUM he has entered the Kingdom to complete union with the Invisible. Thy Bride, O Osiris, is Isis, who mourned Thee when she found Thee slain. In Isis, thou art born again. From Nephthys is thy nourishment. They cleansed thee in thy Heavenly Birth. Youth waits upon thee, ardour is ready at thy hand. And their arms shall uphold thee for millions of years. Initiates surround Thee and Thine enemies are cast down. The Powers of Darkness are destroyed. The Companions of Thy Joys are with Thee. Thy Victories in the Battle await their reward in the Pillar. The Forces of Nature obey Thee. Thy Power is exceeding great. The Gods curse him that curseth Thee. Thine Aspirations are fulfilled. Thou art the Mistress of Splendour. They are destroyed who barred Thy way."

The 125th Chapter is concerned with the entry of an Initiate into the Hall of the Two Columns of Justice, and commenced with a most beautiful and

symbolic description of Death, as a journey from the barren
<115> wilderness of Earth, to the Glorious Land which lies beyond. The
literal translation of the opening lines is as follows:

"I have come from afar to look upon thy beauties. My hands salute Thy Name of Justice. I have come from afar, where the Acacia Tree grew not. Where the tree thick with leaves is not born. Where there come not beams from herb or grass. I have entered the Place of Mystery. I have communed with Set. Sleep came upon me, I was wrapped therein, bowing down before the hidden things. I was ushered into the House of Osiris. I saw the marvels that were there. The Princes of the Gates in their Glory."

The illustrations in this chapter represent the Hall of Truth as seen through the open leaves of its door. The Hall is presided over by a God who holds his right hand over the cage of a hawk, and his left over the food of eternity. On each side of the God is a cornice crowned by a row of alternate feathers and Uraei symbolising justice and fiery power. The door leaf which completes the right hand of a stall is called "Possessor of Truth controlling the Feet," while that on the left is "Possessor of strength, binding the male and female animals." The 42 Judges of the Dead are represented as seated in a long row, and each of them has to be named, and the Sin over which he presided has been denied.

This chapter describes the introduction of the initiate into the Hall of Truth by ANUBIS, who, having questioned the aspirant, receives from him an account of his initiation, and is satisfied by his right to enter. He states that
he has been taken into the ante-chamber of the Temple and there
<116> stripped and blind-folded, he had to grope for the entrance of the
Hall, and having found it, he was reclothed and anointed in the presence of the Initiated. He is then asked for the Pass-words and demands that his Soul should be weighed in the Great Balance of the Hall of Truth, whereupon ANUBIS again interrogates him concerning the symbolism of the door of the Hall, and his answers being found correct, ANUBIS says: "Pass on, thou knowest it."

Among other things the Initiate states that he has been purified four times, the same number of times that the Neophyte is purified and consecrated in the ceremony of the Neophyte. He then makes the long Negative Confession, stating to each Judge in turn that he is innocent of that form of Sin over which he judges. Then he invokes the Judges to do him justice, and afterwards describes how he had washed in the washing place of the South, and rested in the North, in the place called "Son of the Deliverers" and he becomes the Dweller under the Olive Tree of Peace, and how he was given a tall flame of fire and a sceptre of cloud which he preserved in the salting tank in which mummies were swathed. And he found there another sceptre called "Giver of Breath" and with that he extinguished the flame and shattered the sceptre of cloud, and made a lake of it. The initiate is then brought to the actual Pillars, and has to name them and their parts under the symbol of the Scales of a Balance. He also has to name the Guardian of the Gateway, who prevents his passage, and when all these are propitiated, the plea of the Hall itself cries out against his steps, saying "Because I am silent, because I am pure," and it must know that his aspirations are pure enough and high

enough for him to be allowed to tread upon it. He is then allowed to
<117> announce to Thoth that he is clean from all evil, and has overcome
the influence of the planets, and THOTH says to him: "Who is He whose Pylons are of Flame, whose walls of Living Uraei, and the flames of whose House are streams of Water?" And the Initiate replies "Osiris!"

And it is immediately proclaimed: "Thy meat shall be from the Infinite, and thy drink from the Infinite. Thou art able to go forth to the sepulchral feasts on earth, for thou hast overcome."

Thus, these two chapters, which are represented by their illustrations upon the Pillars, represent the advance and purification of the Soul and its union with Osiris, the Redeemer, in the Golden Dawn of the Infinite Light, in which the Soul is transfigured, knows all, and can do all, for it is made One with the Eternal God.

KHABS AM PEKHT
KONX OM PAX
LIGHT IN EXTENSION!

<119> SECOND KNOWLEDGE LECTURE

The Names and Alchemical Symbols of the Three Principles of Nature *are:—*

SULPHUR 🜍 MERCURY ☿ SALT 🜔

The Metals Attributed to the Planets in Alchemy *are:—*

LEAD	♄	GOLD	☉
TIN	♃	COPPER or BRASS	♀
IRON	♂	QUICKSILVER	☿
		SILVER ☽	

The following terms are used in books about Alchemy. They have the meanings given below.

Sol Philosophorum

The Pure Living Alchemical Spirit of *Gold*—the Refined Essence of Heat and Fire.

Luna Philosophorum

The Pure Living Alchemical Spirit of *Silver*—the Refined Essence of Heat and Moisture.

<120> The Green Lion

The Stem and Root of the Radical Essence of Metals.

The Black Dragon

Death—Putrefaction—Decay.

The King

Red—The Qabalistic *Miscroprosopus.*
Tiphareth—analogous to *Gold* and the *Sun.*

The Queen

White—The Qabalistic *Bride of Microprosopus,*
Malkah—analogous to *Silver* and the *Moon.*

The Four Orders of the Elementals Are:

1. The Spirits of the Earth — *Gnomes*
2. The Spirits of the Air — *Sylphs*
3. The Spirits of the Water — *Undines*
4. The Spirits of the Fire — *Salamanders*

These are the Essential Spiritual Beings called upon to praise *God* in the *'Benedicite Omnia Opera.'*

The Kerubim are the Living Powers of Tetragrammaton on the Material Plane and the *Presidents of the Four Elements.*

They operate through the *Fixed* or *Kerubic Signs* of the *Zodiac* and are thus symbolised and attributed:—

Kerub *of* Air—*Man*—Aquarius	♒
Kerub *of* Fire—*Lion*—Leo	♌
Kerub *of* Earth—*Bull*—Taurus	♉
Kerub *of* Water—*Eagle*—Scorpio	♏ or

Tetragrammaton means Four-Lettered Name and refers to the
<121> Unpronounceable Name of *God* symbolised by Jehovah.

The Laver of Water of Purification refers to the Waters of *Binah,* the Female Power reflected in the Waters of Creation.

The Altar of Burnt Offering for the sacrifice of animals symbolises the *Qlippoth* or Evil Demons of the plane contiguous to and below the Material Universe. It points out that our passions should be sacrificed.

The Qlippoth are the Evil Demons of Matter and the Shells of the Dead.

The Altar of Incense in the Tabernacle was overlaid with gold. Ours is Black to symbolise our work which is to separate the philosophic Gold from the Black Dragon of Matter.

This altar diagram (page 123) shows the Ten Sephiroth with all the
<122> connecting Paths numbered and lettered, and the Serpent winding
over each Path. Around each Sephirah are written the Names of the Deity, Archangel and Angelic Host attributed to it. The Twenty Two Paths are bound together by the Serpent of Wisdom. It unites the Paths but does not touch any of the Sephiroth, which are linked by the Flaming Sword.

The Flaming Sword is formed by the natural order of the Tree of Life. It resembles a flash of Lightning.

Together the Sephiroth and the Twenty Two Paths form the 32 Paths of the Sepher Yetzirah or Book of Formation.

The Two pillars either side of the Altar represent:

Active: The White Pillar on the South Side.
Male.
Adam.
Pillar of Light and Fire.
Right Kerub.
Metatron.

<123>

THE SERPENT ON THE TREE OF LIFE

Passive: The Black Pillar on the North Side.
Female.
Eve.
Pillar of Cloud.
Left Kerub.
Sandalphon.

<124> THE SECOND MEDITATION

LET THE ZELATOR meditate on a straight line. Let him take a ruler or a pencil and by moving it a distance equal to its length, outline a square.

Having done this, let him, after quieting his mind with the rhythmic breathing taught in the first meditation, mentally formulate a cube, and endeavor to discover the significance of this figure and its correspondences.

Let him meditate upon minerals and crystals, choosing especially a crystal of SALT,and entering into it, actually feel himself of crystalline formation.

Looking out on the Universe from this standpoint, let him identify himself with the EARTH SPIRITS in love and sympathy, recalling as far as he can their prayer as said in the closing of the Zelator Grade.

Let him meditate upon the EARTH TRIPLICITY, visualising the symbols of a BULL—a VIRGIN—a GOAT which stand for KERUBIC EARTH—MUTABLE EARTH—CARDINAL EARTH.

For the above terms consult a simple astrology manual. Make notes of the ideas and pictures which arise in your mind.

The Four Worlds of the Qabalah are:

<125> ATZILUTH, Archtypal—Pure Deity. אצילות
BRIAH, Creative—Archangelic. בריאה
YETZIRAH, Formative—Angelic. יצירה
ASSIAH, Action—Matter, Man, Shells, Demons. עשיה

The Ten Houses, or Heavens, of Assiah, the Material World are:

1. Primum Mobile, Rashith ha Gilgalim. ראשית הגלגלים
2. Sphere of the Zodiac, Mazloth. מזלות
3. Sphere of Saturn, Shabbathai. שבתאי
4. Sphere of Jupiter, Tzedek. צדק
5. Sphere of Mars, Madim. מדים
6. Sphere of the Sol, Shemesh. שמש
7. Sphere of Venus, Nogah. נוגה
8. Sphere of Mercury, Kokab. כוכב
9. Sphere of Luna, Levanah. לבנה
10. Sphere of the Elements, Olam Yesodoth*. עולם יסודות

(*This is sometimes rendered Cholem Yesodoth, and translated "The Breaker of Foundations." I am pretty certain that this is a mistake no doubt due to a printer's error in reproducing "Ch" in place of "Gh," the latter being intended for "Ayin.")

<126>

THE DIVINE NAMES ATTRIBUTED TO THE SEPHIROTH

No. of Sephirah	Divine Name (Atziluth)	Archangelic Name (Briah)	Choir of Angels (Yetsirah)
1. Kether	Eheieh אהיה	Metatron מטטרון	Chayoth ha-Qadesh חיות הקדש
2. Chokmah	Yah יה	Raziel רזיאל	Auphanim אופנים
3. Binah	Yhvh Elohim יהוה אלהים	Tzaphqiel צפקיאל	Aralim אראלים
4. Chesed	El אל	Tzadqiel צדקיאל	Chashmalim חשמלים
5. Geburah	Elohim Gibor אלהים גבור	Kamael כמאל	Seraphim שרפים
6. Tiphareth	Yhvh Eloah Vedaath יהוה אלוה ודעת	Raphael רפאל	Melekim מלכים
7. Netzach	Yhvh Tzabaoth יהוה צבאות	Haniel האניאל	Elohim אלהים
8. Hod	Elohim Tzabaoth אלהים צבאות	Michael מיכאל	Beni Elohim בני אלהים
9. Yesod	Shaddai El Chai שדי אלחי	Gabriel גבריאל	Kerubim כרובים
10. Malkuth	Adonai ha-Aretz אדני הארץ	Sandalphon סנדלפון	Ashim אשים

NOTE: *The student should himself draw several Trees of Life, and upon them place the above names in proper order. Only by doing this will he learn of their significance.* I. R.

<127>

PLANETARY NAMES

	Name of Planet in Hebrew	Angel	Intelligence	Spirit
♄	Shabbathai	Cassiel	Agiel אגיאל	Zazel זאזל
♃	Tzedek	Sachiel	Iophiel יהפיאל	Hismael הסמאל
♂	Madim	Zamael	Graphiel גראפיאל	Bartzabel ברצבאל
☉	Shemesh	Michael	Nakhiel נכיאל	Sorath סורת
♀	Nogah	Hanael	Hagiel הגיאל	Kedemel קדמאל
☿	Kokab	Raphael	Tiriel טיריאל	Taphthartharath תפתרתרת
☽	Levanah	Gabriel	Malkah be Tarshisim ve-ad Ruachoth Schechalim מלכא בתרשיסים ועד רוחות שחלים	Schad Barschemoth ha-Shartathan שד ברשמעת השרתתו

The traditional Tarot consists of a pack of 78 cards made up of
<128> Four Suits of 14 cards each, together with 22 Trumps, or Major Arcana, which tell the story of the Soul.

Each suit consists of ten numbered cards, as in the modern playing cards, but there are four instead of three honours: King or Knight, Queen, Prince or Emperor, Princess or Knave.

The Four Suits Are:

1. *Wands* or Sceptres comparable to Diamonds.
2. *Cups* or Chalices comparable to Hearts.
3. *Swords* comparable to Spades.
4. *Pentacles* or Coins comparable to Clubs.

<129> THIRD KNOWLEDGE LECTURE

THE SOUL is divided by the Qabalists into three Principal Parts:—

1. NESCHAMAH The Highest Part, answering to the Three Supernals.
2. RUACH The Middle Part, answering to the six Sephiroth from CHESED to YESOD, inclusive.
3. NEPHESCH The lowest, answering to MALKUTH.

NESCHAMAH answers to the higher aspirations of the Soul.

RUACH answers to the mind and reasoning powers.

NEPHESCH answers to the animal instincts.

CHIAH answers to CHOKMAH, YECHIDAH TO KETHER, while NESCHAMAH itself is referred to BINAH.

The Sepher Yetzirah divides the Hebrew Letters into three Classes of Three, Seven, and Twelve.

Three Mothers	א : מ : ש
Seven Double Letters	בגדכפרת
Twelve Single Letters	הוזחטילנסעצק

The Holy Place embraces the symbolism of the 22 Letters.

<130> The Table of Shew-Bread, the Single Letters.

The Altar of Incense the Three Mothers.

Astral Spirits are those belonging to the Astral Plane. Such are false and illusionary forms, shells of the dead, and Ghosts and Phantoms.

Elemental Spirits are those belonging to the nature of the Elements; some are good and some are evil.

An Angel is a pure and high Spirit of unmixed good in office and operation.

In the Tarot, the ten small cards of each suit refer to the Sephiroth. The four suits refer to the Letters of Tetragrammaton thus:—

Sceptres or Wands to	Yod
Cups	Heh
Swords	Vau
Pentacles	Heh (final)

The Four Suits also refer to the Four Worlds of the Qabalists thus:—

Sceptres to	Atziluth
Cups	Briah
Swords	Yetzirah
Pentacles	Assiah

The Honours of the Tarot Pack are, as it were, the Vice-gerants of the Great Name, in the Qabalistic World to which each suit is referred. They also symbolise Father, Mother, Son, Daughter, Birth, Life, Death, Resurrection.

<131>

THE FYLFOT CROSS

The 17 Squares out of a square of lesser squares, refer to the *Sun* in the twelve Signs of the Zodiac and the Four Elements:

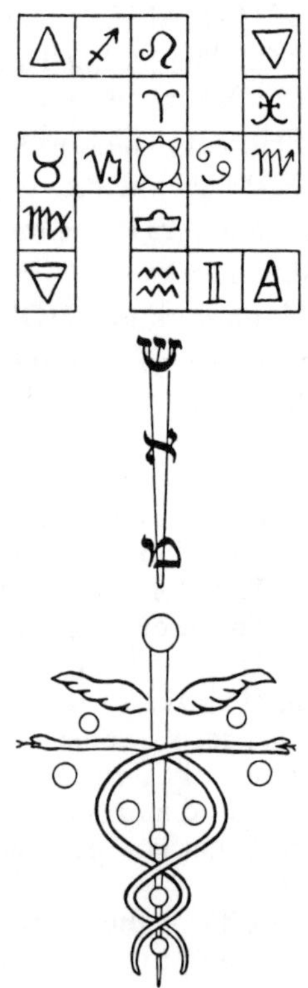

This form of the Caduceus of Hermes is that of the Three Mother Letters placed on one another thus:

The Caduceus has another meaning on the *Tree of Life.* The upper part wings touch *Chokmah* and *Binah:* These are the Three Supernals.

The Seven lower Sephiroth are embraced by the twin Serpents whose heads rest upon *Chesed* and *Geburah.*

<132> The meaning of *Luna* on the *Tree of Life* is thus:

In its increase it embraces the side of Mercy; in its decrease the side of Severity, and at the full, it reflects the *Sun of Tiphareth.*

<133>

MEDITATION

Let the Theoricus practise the Moon Breath, while saying mentally the word AUM: (Moon breath is through the left nostril only.)

Let him meditate upon the waxing and waning crescents, while visualising a silver crescent upon an indigo background.

Let him now call before his mind the Signs of the Airy Triplicity ♊ ♎ ♒ and enclosed in these, let him meditate upon the numbers nine and five and therewith the forms of the Pentagram and Pentangle.

Let him now rise in imagination above the mineral world into the world of trees and flowers and identify himself in love and sympathy with the Powers of the Elements behind these.

Let him realise the mental world where mind rules over matter, and let him meditate upon the ideas of appearance and reality.

<135> FOURTH KNOWLEDGE LECTURE

The Figures of Geomancy
and Their Zodiacal Attributions

• • • • •	Puer	♈	• • • • •	Puella	♎
• • • • • •	Amissio	♉	• • • • • • •	Rubeus	♏
• • • • • • •	Albus	♊	• • • • • •	Acquisitio	♐
• • • • • • • •	Populus	♋	• • • • • •	Carcer	♑
• • • •	Via	♋	• • • • • • •	Tristitia	♒
• • • • • •	Fortuna Major	♌	• • • • • • •	Laetitia	♓
• • • • • •	Fortuna Minor	♌	• • • • •	Caput Draconis	☊
• • • • • •	Conjunctio	♍	• • • • •	Cauda Draconis	☋

<136> The numbers and lineal figures appropriate to the planets are:

Saturn	3	Triangle
Jupiter	4	Square
Mars	5	Pentagram
Sun	6	Hexagram
Venus	7	Heptagram
Mercury	8	Octagram
Moon	9	Enneagram

THE MAGICAL SQUARES OF THE PLANETS are formed of the squares of the number of the planet, arranged so as to yield the same number each way. The number of the sum of each column of figures and the number of the total of all the numbers of the square, are also numbers especially attached to the Planet. Thus the number of the Planet SATURN is 3, square 9, sum of all columns vertical, horizontal and diagonal 15; total sum of all numbers, 45.

These numbers are then formed into Divine and Spirit Names, as is demonstrated in that section of this book dealing with sigils.

<137> THE SOLID GREEK CUBICAL CROSS, the Admission Badge for the Path of Tau, is composed of 22 squares, answering to the 22 letters of the Hebrew Alphabet.

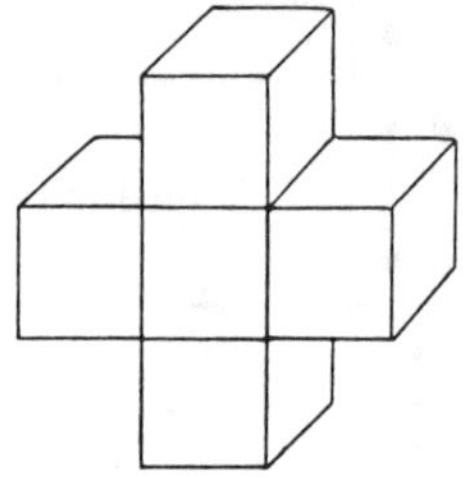

THE SOLID TRIANGLE OR TETRAHEDRON, or Pyramid of Fire, the Admission Badge for the Path of Shin, represents the Simple Fire of Nature and the Latent or Hidden Fire.

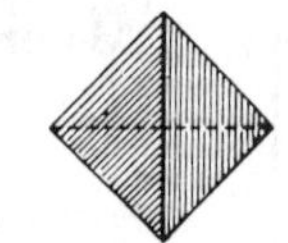

The three upper triangles refer to Fire — Solar, Volcanic and Astral, while the lowest or basal triangle represents the latent heat.

THE GREEK CROSS of 13 Squares, the Admission Badge for the Path of Resh, is referred to the Sun in the Twelve Signs of the Zodiac, and also in the midst of the Four Elements.

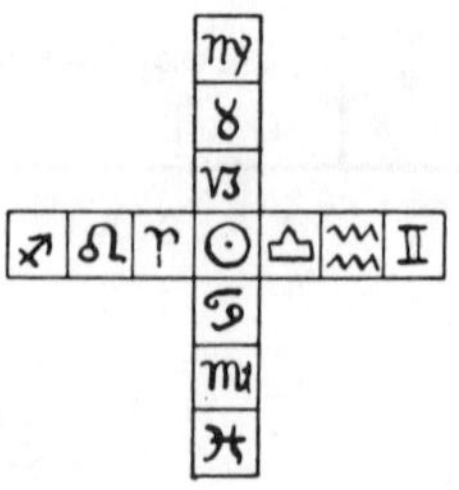

<138> THE CUP OF STOLISTES, the Admission Badge to the Grade of ③ = [8], is thus referred to the Tree of Life. It embraces nine of the Sephiroth, exclusive of *Kether.*

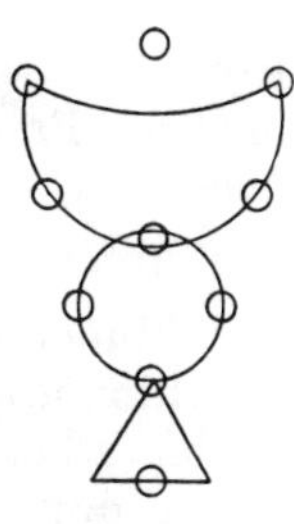

Yesod and *Malkuth* are referred to the triangle below, the former to the apex, the latter to the base. Like the Caduceus, it further represents the Three Elements: Water, Fire and Air. The Crescent refers to the Waters Above the Firmament, the sphere to the Firmament, and the basal triangle to the consuming Fire, which is opposed to the Fire symbolised by the upper part of the Caduceus.

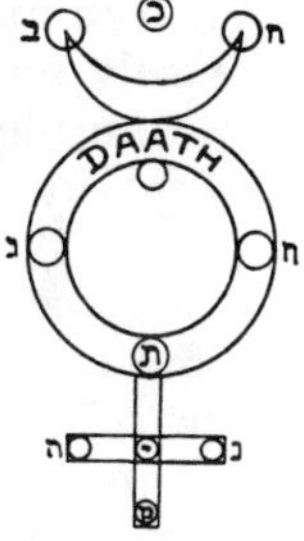

THE SYMBOL of MERCURY on the Tree of Life Enbraces all but *Kether.* The horns spring from *Daath* (Knowledge) which is not, properly speaking, a Sephira, but rather a conjunction of *Chokmah* and *Binah.*

<139>

ATTRIBUTION OF THE TAROT TRUMPS

Path	*No.*	*Tarot Trump*	*Letter*	*Symbol*
11	0	The Foolish Man	א	△
12	1	The Juggler	ב	☿
13	2	The High Priestess	ג	☽
14	3	The Empress	ד	♀
15	4	The Emperor	ה	♈
16	5	The Hierophant	ו	♉
17	6	The Lovers	ז	♊
18	7	The Chariot	ח	♋
19	8	Strength (Justice)	ט	♌
20	9	The Hermit (Prudence)	י	♍
21	10	The Wheel of Fortune	כ	♃
22	11	Justice (Strength)	ל	♎
23	12	The Hanged Man	מ	▽
24	13	Death	נ	♏
25	14	Temperance	ס	♐
26	15	The Devil	ע	♑
27	16	Tower Struck by Lightning	פ	♂
28	17	The Star	צ	♒
29	18	The Moon	ק	♓
30	19	The Sun	ר	☉
31	20	Last Judgment	ש	△
32	21	The Universe.	ת	♄

<140>

MEDITATION

Let the Practicus meditate upon the Symbols of the Rhomboid and the Vesica.

Let him seek out their meanings and correspondences.

Let him contemplate the Symbol Mercury and the Number 8.

Let him now learn to control his emotions, on no account giving way to anger, hatred and jealousy, but to turn the force he hitherto expended in these directions towards the attainment of perfection, that the malarial marsh of his nature may become a clear and limpid lake, reflecting the Divine Nature truly and without distortion.

Let him identify himself with the Powers of Water, considering the Water Triplicity in all its aspects, with its attributions and correspondences.

<141>

NOTES ON THE TAROT

by Frater S.R.M.D.

In the Tree of Life in the Tarot, each path forms the connecting link between two of the Sephiroth. The King and the Queen are the correlations of the *Abba* and the *Aima* in that suit; the Knight or Prince answers to Microprosopus, and the Knave or Princess which was anciently a female figure, is referred to the Bride, *Kallah* or *Malkah.*

Combining, then, the material attributions of the Sephiroth and the Path, it results that:

0. Fool=The Crown of Wisdom, the Primum Mobile, acting through the Air on the Zodiac.
1. The Juggler=The Crown of Understanding, the beginning of material production, the Primum Mobile acting through the Philosophic Mercury on Saturn.
2. High Priestess=The Crown of Beauty, the beginning of Sovereignty and Beauty, the Primum Mobile, acting through the Moon on the Sun.
3. Empress=The Wisdom of Understanding, the Union of the powers of Origination and Production; the Sphere of the Zodiac acting through Venus upon Saturn.
4. Emperor=The Wisdom of Sovereignty and Beauty, and the originator of them; the Sphere of the Zodiac acting through Aries upon the Sun, and initiating Spring.

<142> 5. Hierophant=The Wisdom and fountain of Mercy, the Sphere of the Zodiac acting through Taurus upon Jupiter.

6. The Lovers=The Understanding of Beauty and Production of Beauty and Sovereignty. Saturn acting through Gemini upon Sol.
7. Chariot=Understanding acting upon Severity. Saturn acting through Cancer upon Mars.
8. Strength=Fortitude. Mercy tempering Severity. The Glory of Strength. Jupiter acting through Leo upon Mars.
9. Hermit=The Mercy of Beauty, the Magnificence of Sovereignty, Jupiter acting through Virgo upon Sol.
10. Wheel of Fortune=The Mercy and Magnificence of Victory. Jupiter acting through Jupiter direct upon Venus.
11. Justice=The Severity of Beauty and Sovereignty. Mars acting through Libra upon Sol.

12. The Hanged Man=The Severity of Splendour. Execution of Judgment. Mars acting through Water upon Mercury.
13. Death=The Sovereignty and result of Victory. Sol acting through Scorpio upon Venus, or Osiris under the destroying power of Typhon afflicting Isis.

<143> 14. Temperance=The Beauty of a firm Basis. The Sovereignty of Fundamental Power. Sol acting through Sagittarius upon Luna.

15. The Devil=The Sovereignty and Beauty of Material (and therefore false) splendour. Sol acting through Capricorn upon Mercury.
16. The Tower=The Victory over Splendour. Venus acting through Mars upon Mercury. Avenging force.
17. Star=The Victory of Fundamental Strength. Venus acting through Aquarius upon Luna. Hope.
18. Moon=The Victory of the Material. Venus acting through Pisces upon the Cosmic Elements, deceptive effect of the apparent power of Material Forces.
19. Sun=The Splendour of the Material World. Mercury acting through the Sun upon the Moon.
20. Judgment=The Splendour of the Material World. Mercury acting through Fire upon the Cosmic Elements.
21. Universe=The Foundation of the Cosmic Elements and of the Material World. Luna acting through Saturn upon the Elements.

<144> THE GARDEN OF EDEN BEFORE THE FALL

This diagram is described in the Practicus Ritual. It shows in a glyph the teaching proper to the Practicus on entering the Sephirah HOD which he has reached by the Paths of SHIN and RESH from MALKUTH and YESOD respectively.

At the summit are the THREE SUPERNAL SEPHIROTH summed up into ONE—AIMA ELOHIM, the Mother Supernal—The Woman of the Apocalypse (Chap. 12) clothed with the SUN, the MOON under her feet, and on her head the Crown of Twelve Stars.

It is written 'So the Name JEHOVAH is joined to the Name ELOHIM, for JEHOVAH planted a Garden Eastward in Eden.'

From the Three Supernals follow the other Sephiroth of THE TREE OF LIFE. Below the TREE, proceeding from MALKUTH is THE TREE OF KNOWLEDGE of GOOD AND of EVIL which is between the Tree of Life and the World or Assiah or Shells, represented by the Coiled Up DRAGON with Seven Heads and Ten Horns—being the Seven Infernal Palaces and the Ten Averse Sephiroth. (These are described in the text of the Rituals but are not read to the Candidate at his Grade. When studying this diagram, these descriptions should be looked up, but they are not required for the exam.)

The River NAHER flows forth from the Supernal Eden and in DAATH it is divided into Four Heads:—

PISON: Fire—flowing to GEBURAH where there is Gold.
<145> GIHON: Water—the Waters of Mercy, flowing into CHESED.
HIDDIKEL: Air—flowing into TIPHARETH.
PHRATH (Euphrates): Earth — flowing into MALKUTH.

It is written "In DAATH the Depths are broken up and the Clouds drop down dew."

The word *Naher* has the meaning 'perennial stream'—'never failing waters' as opposed to other words meaning Torrent or Brook.

The River going out of Eden is the River of the Apocalypse, the Waters of Life, clear as crystal proceeding from the Throne, on either side of the Tree of Life, bearing all manner of Fruit.

Thus the Rivers form a Cross and on it The GREAT ADAM, the SON who is to rule the Nations, was extended from TIPHARETH and his arms stretch out to GEBURAH AND GEDULAH, and in MALKUTH is EVE, supporting with her hands the TWO PILLARS.

<146> ON THE GENERAL GUIDANCE AND PURIFICATION OF THE SOUL

Learn first, O Practicus of our Ancient Order, that true Equilibrium is the basis of the Soul. If thou thyself hast not a sure foundation, whereon wilt thou stand to direct the forces of Nature?

Know then that as Man is born into this world amidst the darkness of Nature and the strife of contending forces, so must his first endeavour be to seek the Light through their reconciliation. Thus, thou who hast trial and trouble of this life, rejoice because of them, for in them is strength, and by their means is a pathway opened unto that Light Divine.

How should it be otherwise, O man, whose life is but a day in Eternity, a drop in the Ocean of Time? How, if thy trials were not many, couldst thou purge thy soul from the dross of Earth?

Is it but now that the higher life is beset with dangers and difficulties; hath it not been ever thus with the Sages and Hierophants of the Past? They have been persecuted and reviled, they have been tormented of men, yet through this has their glory increased. Rejoice, therefore, O Initiate, for the greater thy trial, the brighter thy triumph. When men shall revile thee and speak against thee falsely, hath not the Master said "Blessed art thou." Yet, O Practicus, let thy victories bring thee not vanity, for with increase of knowledge should come increase of wisdom. He who knows little, thinketh he knows much; but he who knoweth much hath learned his own ignorance. Seest thou a Man wise in his own conceit? There is more hope of a fool than of him.

Be not hasty to condemn other's sin. How knowest thou that in
<147> their place thou couldst have resisted the temptation? And even were it so, why shouldst thou despise one who is weaker than thyself? Be thou well sure of this, that in slander and self-righteousness is sin. Pardon therefore the sinner, but encourage not the sin. The Master condemned not the adulterous woman, but neither did he encourage her to commit the sin.

Thou therefore who desirest magical gifts, be sure that thy soul is firm and steadfast, for it is by flattering thy weakness that the Evil One will gain power over thee. Humble thyself before thy God, yet fear neither man nor spirit. Fear is failure and the forerunner of failure; and courage is the beginning of virtue. Therefore fear not the Spirits, but be firm and courteous with them, for thou hast no right either to despise or to revile them, and this too may lead thee into sin. Command and banish the Evil ones. Curse them by the Great Names of God, if need be; but neither mock nor revile them, for so assuredly thou wilt be led into error.

A man is what he maketh himself within the limits fixed by his inherited destiny; he is a part of mankind. His actions affect not himself only, but also those with whom he is brought into contact, either for good or for evil.

Neither worship nor neglect the physical body, which is thy temporary connection with the outer and material world. Therefore let thy mental equilibrium be above disturbances by material events. Restrain the animal passions and nourish the higher aspirations; the emotions are purified by suffering.

Do good unto others for God's sake, not for reward, not for gratitude
from them, not for sympathy. If thou art generous, thou wilt not long
<148> for thine ears to be tickled by expressions of gratitude. Remember
that unbalanced force is evil, that unbalanced severity is but cruelty and oppression, but that also unbalanced Mercy is but weakness which would allow and abet evil.

True prayer is as much action as Word; it is Will. The Gods will not do for man what his Higher Powers can do for himself, if he cultivate Will and Wisdom. Remember that this Earth is but an atom in the Universe, and thou thyself but an atom thereon. And that even couldst thou become the God of this Earth whereon thou crawlest and grovellest, thou wouldst even then be but an atom and one among many. Nevertheless, have the greatest self-respect, and to that end sin not against thyself. The sin which is unpardonable is knowingly and wilfully to reject spiritual truth, but every sin and act leaveth its effect.

To obtain magical Power, learn to control thought. Admit only true ideas which are in harmony with the end desired, and not every stray and contradictory idea that presents itself. Fixed thought is a means to an end; therefore pay attention to the power of silent thought and meditation. The material act is but the outward expression of the thought, and therefore it hath been said that "the thought of foolishness is sin." Thought therefore is the commencement of action, and if a chance thought can produce much effect, what cannot fixed thought do? Therefore, as has been already said, establish thyself firmly in the Equilibrium of Forces, in the centre of the cross of the elements, that Cross from whose centre the creative word issued in the birth of the dawning universe.

As it was said unto thee in the Grade of Theoricus: "Be thou
<149> therefore prompt and active as the Sylphs, but avoid frivolity and
caprice. Be energetic and strong like the Salamanders, but avoid irritability and ferocity. Be flexible and attentive to images like the Undines, but avoid idleness and changeability. Be laborious and patient like the Gnomes, but avoid grossness and avarice." So shalt thou gradually develop the powers of thy Soul and fit thyself to command the spirits of the elements.

For wert thou to summon the Gnomes to pander to thy avarice, thou wouldst no longer command them, but they would command thee. Wouldst thou abuse the pure creatures of God's creation to fill thy coffers and to satisfy thy lust for Gold? Wouldst thou defile the Spirits of driving Fire to serve thy wrath and hatred? Wouldst thou violate the purity of the Souls of the Water to pander to thy lust and debauchery? Wouldst thou force the Spirits of the evening breeze to minister to thy folly and caprice?

Know that with such desires thou canst but attract the evil and not the good, and in that can the evil will have power over thee.

In true religion there is no sect. Therefore take heed that thou blaspheme not the name by which another knoweth his God for if thou doest this thing in Jupiter, thou wilt blaspheme YHVH; and in Osiris YEHESHUAH.

"Ask of God and ye shall have,
Seek and ye shall find.
Knock, and it shall be opened unto you."

<150> THE GARDEN OF EDEN AFTER THE FALL

This diagram is described in the Philosophus Ritual. It shows in a glyph the teaching proper to a Philosophus on entering the Sephirah NETZACH which he has reached by the Three Paths of QOPH, TZADDI, AND PEH from the SEPHIROTH—MALKUTH, YESOD and HOD respectively.

The Great Goddess EVE, being tempted by the fruits of the TREE OF KNOWLEDGE whose branches tend upwards to the seven lower Sephiroth, but also downward to the Kingdom of Shells, reached down to them and the two pillars were left unsupported.

Then the Sephirotic Tree was shattered. She fell and with her fell the Great ADAM. And the Great Red Dragon arose with his seven heads and ten horns, and EDEN was desolated—and the folds of the Dragon enclosed MALKUTH and linked it to the Kingdom of the Shells.

And the heads of the Dragon rose into the seven lower Sephiroth, even up to DAATH at the feet of Aima Elohim.

Thus were the four Rivers of EDEN desecrated and the Dragon Mouth gave forth the Infernal Waters in DAATH—and this is LEVIATHAN, The Piercing and Crooked Serpent.

But TETRAGRAMMATON ELOHIM placed the Four Letters YHVH of the NAME and the Flaming Sword of the Ten Sephiroth between the devastated Garden and the Supernal Eden, that this should not be involved in the Fall of ADAM.

And it became necessary that a Second Adam should arise to
<151> restore the System, and thus, as ADAM had been spread on the
Cross of the Four Rivers, so the Second ADAM should be crucified on the Infernal Rivers of the four armed Cross of DEATH—yet to do this He must descend into the lowest, even MALKUTH the Earth, and be born of her. (Psalm 74. 'Thou breakest the Heads of Leviathan in pieces.')

And on the Dragon Heads were the names of the eight Kings of EDOM and on his horns the names of the Eleven Dukes of EDOM, for DAATH having developed in the Dragon a new Head, the Seven Headed Dragon with Ten Horns became Eight Headed and Eleven Horned. (Genesis, 36:31 to 43. Chronicles 1: 43 to 54.)

NOTE: The Edomites were the descendants of Esau who sold his birthright. Their Kings came to symbolise unlawful and chaotic forces.

<153> FIFTH KNOWLEDGE LECTURE

AZOTH is a word formed from the initial and final letters of the Greek, Latin and Hebrew Alphabets thus:—A and Z, Aleph and Tau, Alpha and Omega. It is used with various meanings by different writers but generally signifies *Essence.*

The following names occur in Qabalistic writings:—

AIN—the Negative	אין	(Nothing—Not)
AIN SOPH	אין סוף	(Limitless)
AIN SOPH AUR	אין סוף אור	(The Limitless Light)

These are the Veils of the Negative Existence depending from Kether. ARIK ANPIN אריך אנפין—MACROPROSOPUS or The Vast Countenance is a title of Kether, and another of its titles is the Ancient of Days, AATIK YOMIN עתיך יומין

Kether or the Vast Countenance emanates first as ABBA, the Supernal Father, and AIMA the Supernal Mother.

ABBA אבבא The Supernal Father is referred to YOD of Tetragrammaton, and

AIMA אימא The Supernal Mother is referred to HEH.

ELOHIM אלהים is a name given to these two Persons united.

As Elohim they become the parents of THE SON ZAUIR
<155> ANPIN זאויר אנפין, also called MICROPROSOPUS or the LESSER COUNTENANCE.

ABBA is referred to YOD and the Sephira CHOKMAH. AIMA is referred to HEH and the Sephirah BINAH. ZAUIR ANPIN is referred to the six Sephiroth—Chesed, Geburah, Tiphareth, Netzach, Hod, and Yesod, and of these especially to TIPHARETH.

MALKAH מלכה The Queen, and KALAH כלה The Bride are titles of MALKUTH considered as the Spouse of Zauir Anpin, the Microprosopus.

The Letters of the Name YHVH contain these meanings, thus:—

YOD is referred to ABBA.	HEH to AIMA.
VAU to ZAUIR ANPIN.	HEH (final) to MALKAH.

These Letters are also referred to the Four Worlds and the Four Suits of the Tarot thus:—

YOD	ATZILUTH	WANDS
HEH	BRIAH	CUPS
VAU	YETZIRAH	SWORDS
HEH (f)	ASSIAH	PENTACLES

In each of the Four Worlds are the Ten Sephiroth of that World, and each Sephirah has its own ten Sephiroth, making 400 Sephiroth in all — the number of the letter TAU, The Cross, The Universe, the Completion of all Things.

<154>

TETRAGRAMMATON ON THE TREE

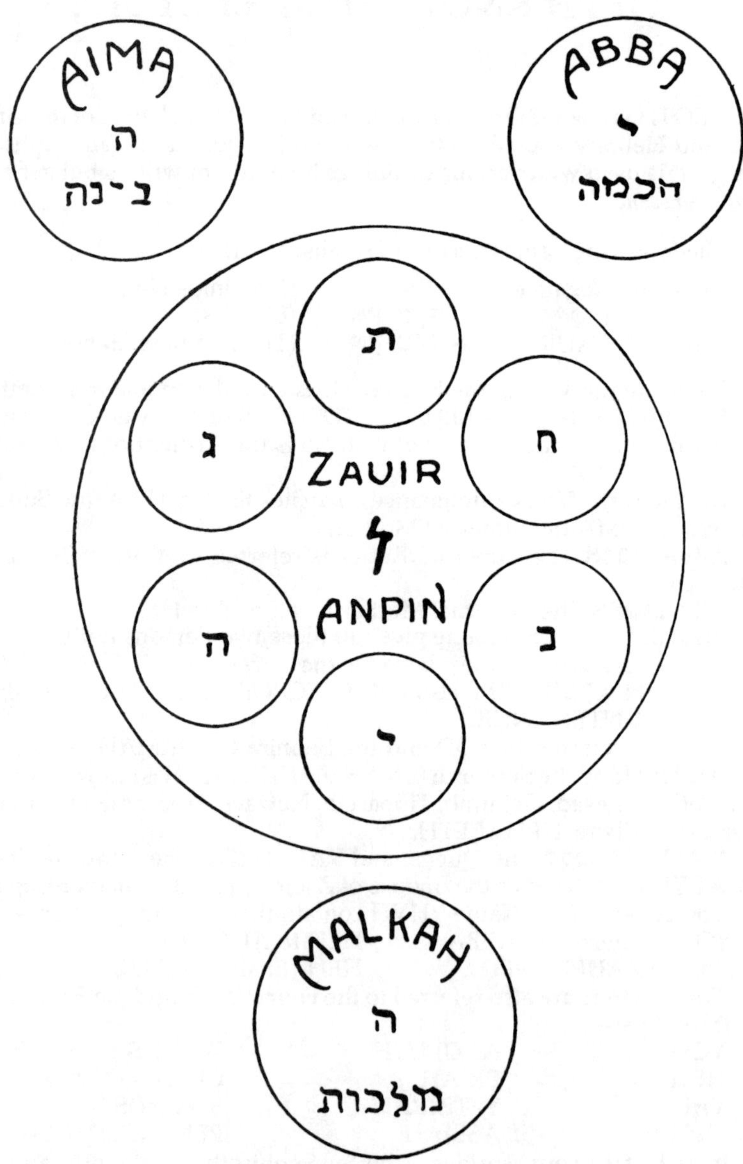

The Tarot is thus referred to The Tree of Life:

The Four Aces are placed on the Throne of Kether — the
<156> remaining small cards of the suit desired on the respective
Sephiroth, 2 on Chokmah, 3 on Binah, etc. The 22 *Trumps* are then

arranged on the Paths between them, according to the Letters to which they correspond.

The King and Queen of the suit are placed beside *Chokmah* and *Binah* respectively; the *Knight* and *Knave* by *Tiphareth* and *Malkuth.*

The Tarot Trumps thus receive the equilibrium of the Sephiroth they connect.

The Admission Badges used in the grade of *Philosophus* are as follows:

The Calvary Cross of Twelve Squares, admitting to the Path of *Qoph,* the 29th Path, refers to the Zodiac and to the Eternal River of Eden divided into Four Heads:

Nahar — The River ________________ נהר
1. Hiddikel ________________ חדקל
2. Pison ________________ פישון
3. Gihon ________________ גיהון
4. Phrath ________________ פרת

The Pyramid of the Four Elements admits to the Path of *Tzaddi,* the 28th Path.

On the sides are the Hebrew Names of the Elements. On the apex is the word *Eth* — Essence, and on the base the word *Olam* meaning World.

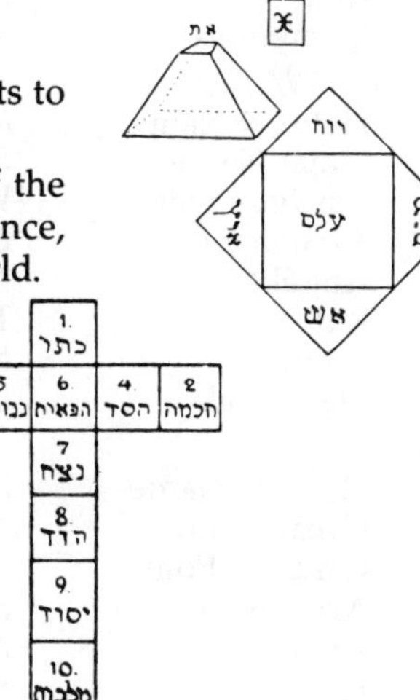

<157> The Calvary Cross of Ten Squares admits to the Path of Peh, Mars — the 27th Path. The Ten Squares are referred to the Ten Sephiroth in balanced disposition. It is also the opened out form of the double Cube of the Altar of Incense.

The Cross of the Hegemon's Badge admits to the Grade of Philosophus. This cross embraces Tiphareth, Netzach, Hod and Yesod, and rests upon Malkuth. The Calvary Cross of Six Squares also refers to the six Sephiroth of Microprosopus and is the opened out form of the cube.

<158> The Symbol of Venus on the Tree of Life embraces the whole Ten Sephiroth. It is a fitting emblem of the Isis of Nature. As it contains all the Sephiroth its circle should be made larger than that of Mercury.

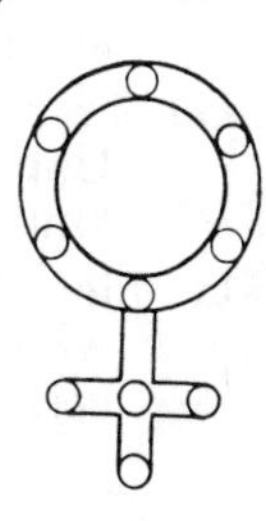

NAMES especially connected with the Four Elements:—

EARTH:		
Hebrew Name	*Aretz* or *Ophir*	ארץ : עפיר
Great Name	*Adonai ha-Aretz*	ארני הארץ
Cardinal Point	North. *Tzaphon*	צפון
Archangel	*Auriel*	אוריאל
Angel	*Phorlakh*	פורלאך
Ruler	*Kerub*	כרוב
King	*Ghob*	
Elementals	*Gnomes*	
AIR:		
Hebrew Name	*Ruach*	רוח
Great Name	*Shaddai El Chai*	שרי אל חי
Cardinal Point	East. *Mizrach*	מזרח
Archangel	*Raphael*	רפאל
Angel	*Chassan*	חשן
Ruler	*Ariel*	אריאל
King	*Paralda*	
Elementals	*Sylphs*	
<159> WATER:		
Hebrew Name	*Maim*	מים
Great Name	*Elohim Tzabaoth*	אלהים צבאות
Cardinal Point	West. *Maarab*	מע רב
Archangel	*Gabriel*	גבריאל
Angel	*Taliahad*	טליהד
Ruler	*Tharsis*	תרשים
King	*Nichsa*	
Elementals	*Undines*	
FIRE:		
Hebrew Name	*Asch*	אש
Great Name	*Yhvh Tzabaoth*	יהוה צבאות
Cardinal Point	South. *Darom*	דרום
Archangel	*Michael*	מיכאל
Angel	*Aral*	אראל
King	*Seraph*	שרף
Ruler	*Djin*	
Elementals	*Salamanders*	

<160>

MEDITATION

LET THE PHILOSOPHUS meditate upon the symbol of the Fire Triangle in all its aspects.

Let him contemplate the symbol of the Planet VENUS until he realises the Universal Love which would express itself in perfect service to all mankind and which embraces Nature both visible and invisible.

Let him identify himself with the powers of FIRE, consecrating himself wholly until the Burnt Sacrifice is consummated and the Christ is conceived by the Spirit.

Let him meditate upon the Triplicity of Fire—its attributes and correspondences.

<161> THE DIAGRAMS

As confusion is found to exist with regard to the Right and Left Pillars of the Sephiroth on the Tree of Life in relation to the right and left sides of a man, and as to the phases of the Moon—you must note:

That in every diagram and picture, the right hand side of the observer is next to the Pillar of Mercy—Chokmah, Chesed, and Netzach; while the Pillar of Severity is on the observer's left hand. Yet when you apply the Tree of Life to yourself, your right side, arm, and leg represent the side of Strength and Severity, Binah, Geburah and Hod, and your left side refers to the Pillar of Mercy. So that when you look at a diagram, you are looking, as it were, at a man facing you, that your right side faces his left. His Merciful side forms the right hand Pillar in front of you, so that it is as if you looked at yourself in a mirror.

Just as the man looks at you, so does the Moon look at you and so you say that the Moon in her increase is on the side of Mercy, the right hand pillar of the Sephiroth; and in her decrease, the crescent is on the left hand Pillar of Severity.

A Diagram, then, is a picture of a Man or the Moon facing you. The Temple Pillars are similar:

Black Pillar	Severity	Left	North
White Pillar	Mercy	Right	South
Black Pillar	Boaz	Stolistes	
White Pillar	Jachin	Dadouchos	

That is, the white Mercy or Jachin Pillar is on your right hand as
<162> you approach the Altar from the West and from the Hiereus. (See
Chronicles II. iii, 17.) "And call the Name on the right hand (of him who enters) Jachin, and the Name of that on the left, Boaz."

Now Boaz = Strength, Severity, Binah, Black Pillar, and Jachin = White Pillar of Mercy.

So in making the Qabalistic Cross on your breast it is correct to touch the Forehead and say *Ateh*—Thou art; the Heart—*Malkuth;* Right Shoulder, *ve-Geburah;* left shoulder *ve-Gedulah,* and with the fingers clasped on the breast say, *Le, olahm, amen!*

(Note: The following items and attributions are those which were formerly eliminated from the so-called knowledge lectures and rituals. They have been assembled here and added as an appendix since this was assumed to be more satisfactory than inserting them once again into the knowledge lectures. I. R.)

<163> TWO FURTHER ALCHEMICAL ATTRIBUTIONS TO THE TREE OF LIFE

1. Kether	Mercury	The Metallic Root
2. Chokmah	Salt	Lead
3. Binah	Sulphur	Tin
4. Chesed	Silver	Silver
5. Geburah	Gold	Gold
6. Tiphareth	Iron	Iron
7. Netzach	Copper	Hermaphroditical Brass
8. Hod	Tin	Brass
9. Yesod	Lead	Mercury
10. Malkuth	Mercury Philosophorum	Medicina Metallorum

THE QLIPPOTH ON THE TREE OF LIFE

1. Kether	Thaumiel—The two contending Forces
2. Chokmah	Ghogiel—The Hinders
3. Binah	Satariel—The Concealers
4. Chesed	Agshekeloh—The Breakers in Pieces
5. Geburah	Golohab—The Burners
6. Tiphareth	Tagiriron—The Disputers
7. Netzach	Gharab Tzerek—The Ravens of Death
8. Hod	Samael—The Liar or Poison of God
9. Yesod	Gamaliel—The Obscene Ones
10. Malkuth	Lilith—Queen of the Night and of Demons

<164>

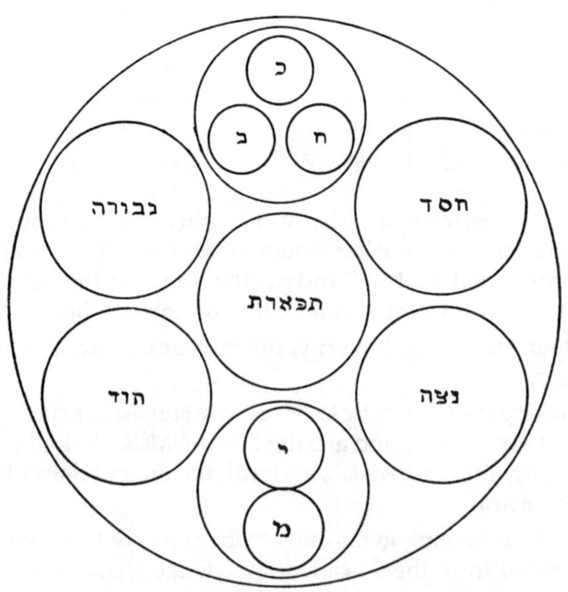

The Seven Palaces attributed to the Ten Sephiroth

<165> THE ASTROLOGICAL SYMBOLS OF THE PLANETS

These are derived from the three primary forms of the Cross, the Crescent and the Circle, either singly or in combination.

The Circle denotes Sun and Gold; the Crescent the Moon and Silver, respectively analogous to the Red and White Alchemical natures.

The Cross is the symbol of corrosion. The corrosion of metals is usually of the complementary colour to that to which they naturally approximate. Thus Copper, which is reddish, becomes green in its corrosion of verdigris, etc.

Mercury is the only planet which unites these three primary forms in one symbol. Saturn is composed of the cross and the crescent showing that Lead is corrosive internally and Luna externally. Jupiter is the reverse. Mars is Solar externally but corrosive externally.

Venus is opposite. Copper is externally of the nature of Gold, but internally corrosive. Hence the name of the Sphere of Venus is *Nogah*—denoting External Splendour but internal corruption.

The Serpent Nehushtan, which Moses made when the Children of Israel were bitten by Serpents of Fire in the Wilderness, is the Serpent of the Paths of the Tree. And he set it on a pole—that is, twined it round the middle Pillar of the Sephiroth. And the word used in the passage in Numbers 21 for Fiery Serpents is the same as the Name of the Angels of Geburah, the same spelling, the same pointing, Seraphim. Round the Middle Pillar of the Sephiroth, because that is the Reconciler between the Fires of Geburah or Severity, and the Waters of Chesed or Mercy—and hence it is said in the New
<166> Testament that it is a type of Christ, the Reconciler. And the serpent
is of Brass, the Metal of Venus, whose Sphere is called Nogah, or External Splendour, as shewn further by the Alchemical Symbol of Venus, wherein the Circle of the Sun is exalted above the Cross of Corrosion. And therefore it is said in the Zohar that "Alone of the Shells is the Serpent Nogah found in Holiness" and he is called the Balance of Justice. Why, then, is he called the External or False Splendour? Because he indeed uniteth the Paths, but comprehendeth not the Sephiroth. Nevertheless, he is also the Celestial Serpent of Wisdom. But the Serpent of the Temptation is the Serpent of the Tree of Knowledge of Good and of Evil, and not that of the Tree of Life.

Here is a method of writing Hebrew words by the Yetsiratic attribution of the Alphabet, whence results some curious hieroglyphic symbolism. Thus Tetragrammaton will be written by Virgo, Aries, Taurus, Aries. *Eheieh,* by Air, Aries, Virgo, Aries. From *Yeheshua,* the Qabalistic mode of spelling Jesus, which is simply the Tetragrammaton with the letter Shin placed therein, we obtain a very peculiar combination—Virgo, Aries, Fire, Taurus, Aries. Virgo born of a Virgin, Aries the Sacrificial Lamb, Fire the Fire of the Holy Spirit, Taurus the Ox of the Earth in whose Manger He was laid, and lastly Aries the flocks of sheep whose Herdsmen came to worship Him. *Elohim* yields Air, Libra, Aries, Virgo, Water—the Firmament, the Balanced Forces, the Fire of the Spirit (For Aries is a fiery Sign), operating in the Zodiac, the Fire God dess, and the Waters of Creation.

<167> *The terms* Raven or Crow, Lion and Eagle have various Alchemical significations. Generally

Raven—Initiation through blackness
Lion—Heat and sulphurous action
Eagle—Sublimation

One great difference between Chemical and Alchemical processes is that Alchemy only employs a gradual heat continually but carefully increased, and does not commence with violent heat.

The Cucurbite is a glass boiler attached to the lower part of the Alembic. It consists of a tube, a head, and a receiver added thereto for purposes of distillation.

The Athanor or Philosophical Furnace is to produce a graduated heat.

The Balneum Mariae is the modern water bath—a vessel of hot water in which was placed the vessel to be heated.

The Balneum Arenae or sand bath is a vessel of sand in which is placed the vessel to receive a dry heat.

The Philosophic Egg is an oval glass vessel in which is placed the water or liquid to be acted upon, and which may be hermetically sealed.

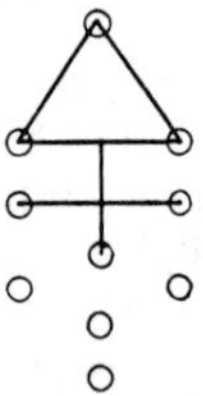

<168> *This represents the Alchemical Symbol of Sulphur* on the Tree of Life. It does not touch the four lower Sephiroth. The Cross terminates in Tiphareth, whereby, as it were, the Supernal Triangle is to be grasped, and Tiphareth is the purified Man.

The Hexagram of Tiphareth is formed from the Pillars on each side. In Chesed is the Water triangle, in Geburah the Fire triangle. And Tiphareth unites and reconciles them so as to form a reconciliation between them in the form of the hexagram.

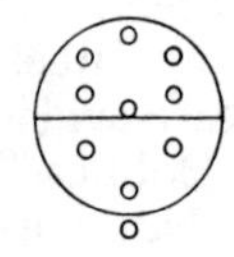

The Symbol of Salt on the Tree of Life embraces all the Sephiroth but Malkuth, and is as it were, the Reconciler between the Sulphur and Mercury. The horizontal dividing line implies the precept of Hermes "as above so below."

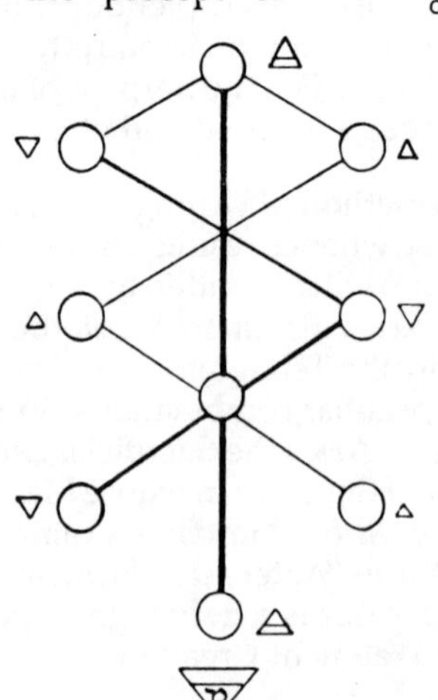

<169> *The drawing represents the Trinity* operating through the Sephiroth and reflected downwards in the four triangles of the Elements. Air is reflected from Kether through Tiphareth to Yesod. Water is reflected from Binah through Chesed to Hod; Fire is reflected from Chokmah through Geburah to Netzach; while Earth is Malkuth, the receptacle of the other Three.

(Note: The following Angelic Names have been assembled and
<170> tabulated systematically from a Philosophus manuscript entitled "The Lecture on the Shemhamphoresch." This document deals principally with the traditional modes of forming Angelic Names. It describes how various verses are taken from the book of Exodus, and by methods of permutation, are formed into seventy-two names of three letters each. To each of these names is added the suffix *Yeh* or *El,* thus yielding angelic names and formulae. These seventy-two Angels are allotted to each quinary, or division of 5°, in the celestial heavens, so that with the other names a very complete hierarchy is given. Thus every Sign of the Zodiac has an Archangel, Angel, Angel of its corresponding house, and a vast sub-hierarchy.

Too much space would have been consumed to detail the methods by which these names are given. So I have contented myself to list, simply, all the Archangelic and Angelic Names of the twelve Zodiacal Signs, and state that they are very important names, and their arrangement should be carefully studied. The documents on Tarot attribute two of these Angels to each of the 36 small cards, and the anglicised transliteration of their names will there be found. But I have thought it advisable here to give the Hebrew letters and spelling so that the student may have them at his hand when dealing with the matters of Sigils and Telesmatic Images, which are, as elsewhere explained, formed from the Hebrew spellings. I. R.)

Divine and Angelic Names

Sign	Name in Hebrew	Divine Name	Arch-angel	Angel	Angel ruling the House corresponding	Decan	Angel ruling Decan	Angel ruling Quinance
<171>						♂	זור	והואל דניאל
♈	טלה	יהוה	מלכידאל	שרחיאל	איאל	☉	בהחמי	החשיה עממיה
						♀	כנדר	ננאאל ניתאל
						☿	כרדמרי	מבהיה פויאל
♉	שור	יהחו	אסמודאל	ארזיאל	טואל	☽	מנחראי	נממיה יילאל
						♄	יסגנזן	הרחאל מצראל
						♃	סגרש	ומבאל יההאל
♊	תאומים	יוהה	אמבריאל	סראיאל	גיאל	♂	שגרני	ענואל מחיאל
						☉	ביתור	דמביה מנקאל
<172>						♀	מתראוש	איעאל חבויה
♋	סרטן	הוהי	מוריאל	פכיאל	כעאל	☿	רהדע	ראהאל יבמיה
						☽	אלינכיר	הייאל מומיה
						♄	לוסנהר	והויה יליאל
♌	אריה	הויה	ורכיאל	שרטיאל	עואל	♃	זחעי	סיטאל עלמיה
						♂	סחיבה	מהשיה ללהאל
						☉	אננאורה	אכאיה כהתאל
♍	בתולה	ההוי	המליאל	שלתיאל	ויאל	♀	ראיהוה	הזיאל אלדיה
						☿	מספר	לאויה ההעיה
<173>						☽	טרסני	יזלאל מבהאל
♎	מאזנים	והיה	זוריאל	חדקיאל	יהאל	♄	סהרנץ	הריאל הקמיה
						♃	שהדר	לאויה כליאל
						♂	כמוץ	לוויה פהליה
♏	עקרב	וההי	ברכיאל	סאיציאל	סוסול	☉	נינדוהר	נלכאל יייאל
						♀	נתרודיאל	מלהאל ההויה
						☿	משרית	נתהיה האאיה
♐	קשת	ויהה	ארוכיאל	סמקיאל	סויעסאל	☽	והרין	ירתאל שאהיה
						♄	אבוהא	רייאל אומאל
<174>						♃	מסנין	לכבאל ושריה
♑	גדי	היהו	הנאל	סריטיאל	כשניעיה	♂	יסיסיה	יחויה להחיה
						☉	יסגדיברודיאל	כוקיה מנדאל
						☿	ססמם	אניאל חעמיה
♒	דלי	היוה	כאמבריאל	צכמקיאל	אנסואל	♀	אבדרון	רהעאל ייזאל
						☽	גרודיאל	הההאל מוכאל
						♄	בחלמי	ווליה ילהיה
♓	דגים	ההיו	אמניציאל	וכביאל	פשיאל	♃	אורון	סאליה עריאל
						♂	סטריף	עשליה מיהאל

<175>

ON THE WORK TO BE UNDERTAKEN BETWEEN PORTAL AND ⑤—[6]

The work comes under six headings as follows:

1. A Thesis on the Rituals.
2. A meditation on the crosses which have been used as admission badges in the Grades. This is a preparation for the meditation which precedes the ⑤—[6] Grade and should be applied for when you have been a Portal Member for seven months.
3. A complete diagram of The Tree of Life.
4. The practice of control of the Aura.
5. The placing of The Tree of Life in the Aura.
6. Tattwas—Astrology—Divination.

1. The Thesis. Read the rituals. Build them up in imagination. Compare the Opening and Closing in the various Grades. Note the general underlying scheme for each Elemental Grade—and note where the differences occur. Follow the careers of the various Officers. Note at what Grade an Officer disappears.

Make a precis of each Ritual so that the general scheme becomes apparent. This is of the greatest assistance when you are called on to take Office because you will not then need to follow everything in the Ritual but need only turn to the page where your Office is mentioned and when you have no more to say, you can turn to the Closing and put the Ritual aside till required for that. Ability to do this and to move correctly in the
<176> Temple adds greatly to the harmony and repose of the whole Ceremony.

Note the positions of the various officers—what mathematical shapes they make among themselves from time to time as they take up their places in the Temple. It may be a triangle, a cross, a pentagram, etc.

Read the speeches carefully, and read them sometimes aloud so that you get familiar with the sound of your own voice in saying the words. Note that some speeches are designed to create atmosphere by their archaic form and should be read rhythmically and sonorously, while others are informative and should be read in such a way as to make their points clear.

Examples of archaic passages are challenges of Gods: "Thou canst not pass the Gate of the Western Heaven unless thou canst tell me my Name." And the speeches of the Kabiri in the Grades of Practicus and Philosophus. Information is given in speeches about Tarot Keys and diagrams.

Note the technique for traversing the various Paths—the words, and the badges with which the Path is entered, the length of the circumambulation and the special symbolism described therein.

Let all these things soak into your mind, make notes as ideas occur to you—and presently your personal reaction to the Grades will crystallise out and you will be able to write your thesis.

2. Make a list and drawings of the crosses which have been given you as Admission Badges throughout the Grades, from the Swastika of the
<177> Zelator to the Five-squared cross which you put on as you stood at
the Altar at the second point of the Portal Grade. Read what is said of them in the Rituals and knowledge lectures, and make notes about them.

3. The Tree of Life. This should be done fairly large in order that the writing and symbols should be clear. It is essential to show the Deity Names, Names of Archangels and Angels in Hebrew in the Sephiroth, and to number the Paths and give their attributions. Apart from this, the Tree should be your personal synthesis of the Order symbolism as it applies to the Tree of Life. Colours may be used.

4. Control of the Aura. If you are not already familiar with the parts of your own body such as nervous system, respiratory system, digestive system, get some simple text-book such as is used in ambulance work, or attend a course of first-aid lectures so that, before starting to work on your subtle body, you may know something about your physical body.

Your physical body is interpenetrated by a subtle body or aura which also surrounds the physical body like an egg of light. You should now begin to practise controlling this aura or Sphere of Sensation. This means that you must first try to get your emotional reactions under conscious control. Instead of automatically liking this, disliking that, you must try to understand the mechanism which underlies these feelings. To assist you in this, the study of psychology is recommended. There are many books on the subject, of which the following are easy to understand and clearly stated.

Psychology by Wm. McDougall (Home University Library).
<178> *Psychoanalysis for Normal People* by Geraldine Coster.
Psycho-Synthesis by the Dean of Chester Cathedral.
Machinery of the Mind by Violet Firth.

Having built up some idea of the mechanism of your mental processes, you should now try to make yourself negative or positive at will towards people or ideas. If you are likely to meet someone who always makes you argumentative and irritable, decide that your aura is closed to their power of irritating you and that your mind will not be disturbed by what they say. It is good sometimes to listen to views with which you disagree to teach you not only to make no verbal response, but to keep your feelings in abeyance also. In this way you come to learn how much of your disagreement is due to prejudice or personal factors, and how much to your regard for abstract truth.

Again, sometimes practise opening your aura to people or ideas in an endeavour to see things from another's point of view.

The practice of deep breathing is also of help in establishing poise and in controlling nervousness. It is good to expand the chest to its fullest extent and then to expand the diaphragm below the ribs as well and then to let the breath out slowly and steadily on a vowel sound such as ah or 'O'.

If you are nervy, you will find that your breathing is shallow and that your muscles are tense. You tend to clench your hands and tighten
<179> up the abdominal muscles. To cure this, take a deep breath to full
capacity, hold it while tensing and relaxing alternately the abdominal muscles. Do this (i.e. the tensing and relaxing of the muscles) three

<180> THE MIDDLE PILLAR AND THE HUMAN BODY

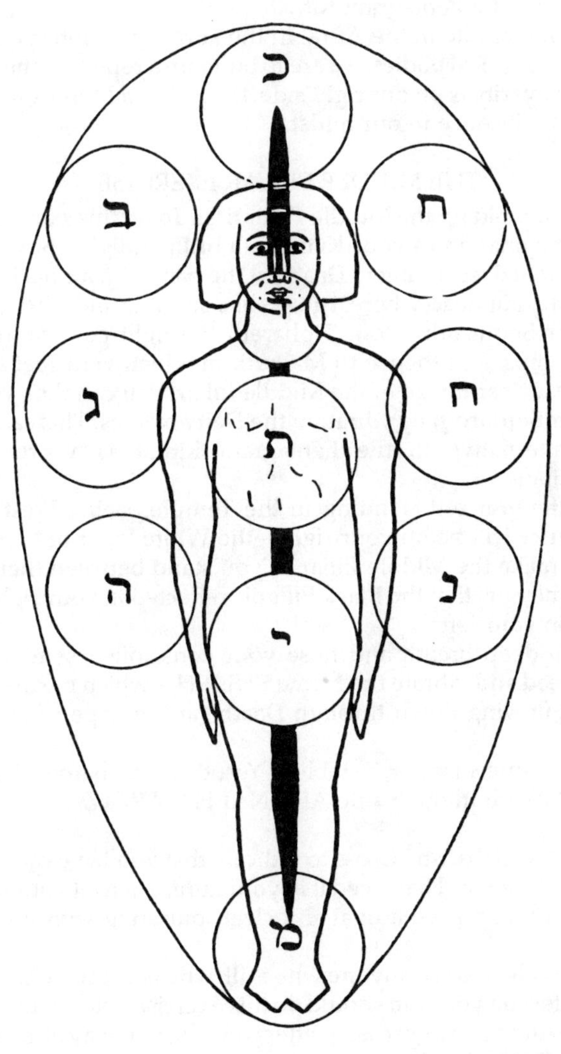

times and then relax completely into a chair. Allow all your muscles to go limp and let your breath out to the last gasp. Do the whole process three times, if necessary. It is designed to stimulate the solar plexus which is the heart of the nervous system which governs emotion.

Another good exercise is to say the Deity Names aloud. Take a deep breath and say them softly, smoothly and slowly, imagining the while that your voice travels out to the confines of the Universe. This can be done in conjunction with the Pentagram Ritual.

5. The Tree of Life in the Aura. In the aura which interpenetrates and surrounds our physical bodies, we are to build up a replica of the Tree of Life. The Pillar of Severity is on our right side, the Pillar of Mercy on our left, and the Pillar of Benificence in our midst.

THE MIDDLE PILLAR EXERCISE

It is best to build up the Middle Pillar first. To do this stand up and raise yourself in imagination to your Kether—a brilliant light above your head. Imagine this light descending to Daath, at the nape of your neck, and thence to Tiphareth in your heart where it glows like sunlight and whence it radiates into the other Sephiroth. From Tiphareth the light goes to Yesod in the region of the hips, and thence to Malkuth in which your feet are planted. Having made a clear image of the Middle Pillar, you can then establish the other Sephiroth by vibrating the Deity Names. This can be done as
<181> an alternative to the Pentagram Ritual as a preparation for meditation.

1. Imagine yourself standing in the Temple, facing West. The Black Pillar of Severity will be on your right—the White Pillar of Mercy on your left. You will make the Middle Pillar as you stand between them.

2. Imagine now that the Black Pillar is reflected in your right side—the White Pillar in your left.

3. Take a deep breath and raise your consciousness to your Kether above your head and vibrate the Name EHEIEH—which means I am. Imagine the Light flowing down through Daath (at the nape of your neck) to Tiphareth.

4. In the same manner, establish Yesod in the name SHADDAI EL CHAI, and Malkuth in the Name ADONAI HA-ARETZ.

5. Make the Qabalistic Cross to indicate that you have called down the Light of your Kether and balanced it in your aura. Then let your imagination dwell on the aura and see it oval and clear, pulsating with the glow from Tiphareth.

If you are called to see anyone who is ill, who is depressed, or who has a depressing effect on you, you should do this exercise beforehand. In the case of the person who has a depressing effect on you, you may also imagine that your aura is hardened at the edge so that they are unable to penetrate it, and so deplete you of vitality (which is generally what such sensations mean).

In all these practices it is well to remember that 'Strength is in Silence.' If you talk about them, save to your Chief, or if you try to analyse their
<182> effects, you will not benefit by them. Try them with simple faith and

in silence for a year before rationalising them.

It is better at first to keep your aura to yourself, rather than to try to flow out towards others. Unless you are particularly vital and well-balanced, you will only waste energy. So-called modes of healing and of 'doing good to others' should be eschewed for a time. Such methods have a technique of their own and required trained and balanced minds and bodies to carry them out. Get yourself right first before you attempt to interfere with others in any way but the ordinary ways of kindly decent society.

When you have practised the exercise of the Middle Pillar for some time and can visualise it easily, you can establish the other Sephiroth.

6. Tattwas—Astrology—Divination. The Tattwas are designed to assist you in your researches into the Soul of Nature. They are at first done with a senior member, and later can be done alone or with a companion of your own Grade. They should never be allowed to become uncontrolled day-dreams. The method taught should be strictly adhered to—a definite time, preferably in the morning being set aside—and they should not be attempted when you are feeling tired or when your mind is too occupied with other things to let you 'get away.' They should not be done too frequently—once in three weeks or a month is enough, once a week if time and circumstances permit. Notes of the pictures and symbols seen should be kept together in a book.

Astrology. This should be done as time permits. The subject is
<183> vast and highly technical, and can be studied fully through the
various schools and correspondence classes if you are interested in it. From the Order Lectures you should be able to set up a true birth horoscope for any place and any time. You can practise setting up horoscopes for the cases given in Alan Leo's little book *1001 Notable Nativities* and see whether you can tell for what the horoscope was remarkable. You should attempt the reading of a horoscope for someone you know and then get the data for someone about whom you know nothing, and see whether you can give a reading which satisfies their friends.

The Order requires only that you should be able to set up an accurate horoscope and that you should know how to work out the aspects and how to make a simple assessment of the good and bad factors in a horary figure. If Astrology interests you further, it is a very fascinating field of research.

Divination. You may try to develop your intuition by the use of horary and natal astrology, geomancy, and the reading of the Tarot Cards by the method given in the small book by Mr. A. E. Waite.

You are advised to attempt only questions in which you are not emotionally involved because methods of divination can be a fruitful source of self-deception to those who are psychic but not self-knowing. If you are given to having intuitions you must learn to say not only 'I was right about that' but also 'I was quite wrong about that,' and if you advertise only successes (as is usual) at the bar of your own conscience, learn to assess them honestly.

The interval of time between Portal and ⑤—[6] should be given
<184> to the study of the whole make-up of yourself. All these methods are
designed to assist you to get as far as you can along the road to self-

knowledge.

You are to realise the different layers of your being—some of which you have been led through symbolically in the Outer Grades—"Which in one sense quitteth not Malkuth"—the Kingdom of yourself.

This line of thought, coupled with the study of the Rituals, may lead you to realise what it was you gathered together in the first point of the Portal Ritual, and what it is you are trying to perfect to lay on the Altar of the Spirit.

(Note: The reader or student who is interested particularly in this subject of the Sphere of Sensation, or aura as it is called, would be well-advised to study very carefully the Order Tarot teaching. There is much in that set of documents which concerns the application of the idealogy of the Qabalistic Tree of Life to a sphere. In that case the Pillar arrangement becomes slightly altered or extended so as to produce 4 Pillars about an invisible axis, the Middle Pillar. There is also much profound wisdom in the very skeletal attributions of the five divisions of the Tarot Pack to the surface or parts of the solid sphere. The Aces to the North pole, and the 36 decanate Cards to the South pole up to the Ecliptic, while in between range the Princess cards which are the Thrones of the Aces, the other Court cards, and the Trumps. The studied application of this intricate scheme to the extended arrangement of the Tree of Life, and thence to the human personality and sphere
<185> in all its branches will yield a wealth of significant material.

I have also elaborated this scheme in two books. In *The Art of True Healing* I have dealt with the Aura and the Middle Pillar solely from the therapeutic point of view. My other book, *The Middle Pillar,* considers the technique from a considerably wider view. Moreover it attempts to associate the results of training with the terminology of Analytical Psychology. I. R.)

We are told in the Portal that the nine months' wait which must intervene before the Portal is again opened for the Aspirant has a correspondence to the nine months of gestation before birth. As the unborn child, stage by stage, grows through the ancestral history of the race so the Candidate in the Portal by a single circumambulation for each, recalls his past Grades and, at the end of the first point regards their symbols upon the Altar as parts of his body, and contemplates them as coming together in one place—the unity of his person.

In the second point, he sacrifices his name—symbol of his idea of himself in order that the idea of a new self and a new consciousness may be attained.

This has a correspondence in the birth of a child. It emerges from the membranes and placenta which hitherto have been its body and source of life and finds itself not 'dead' after the dread change, but translated to a larger consciousness.

Thus the Portal foreshadows the kind of change and development necessary for understanding the symbolism of the ⑤ = [6].

We do not know what consciousness the unborn child has—how far it

<186> has choice in its development—through what agency it unfolds the potencies of its tiny seed and draws to itself the necessary materials for growth. The miracle happens—and gives us courage to believe that a similar miracle is even now enacting whereby a body will be ready for us when this, which seems so real to us, shall share the same fate as the placenta and membranes which 'die' at our birth.

But tradition, as embodied in our Order and shown somewhat less directly in the revealed religions, teaches that this development can be assisted by conscious effort—indeed, that there comes a time when this effort must be made through the body and mind we are now endowed with. And realising that we are indeed in a Path of Darkness groping for Light, we must feel our way to an understanding of the meaning of life—the reason for death.

To those who feel the call to make this effort, comes the Order with a series of pictures, symbolic of the growth of the soul to new life. The meditations given with each Grade are designed to lead the mind towards ideas which will assist in self-knowledge—universal impersonal ideas which each must find in his own way—'the secrets which cannot be told save to those who know them already.'

The Aspirant is led to look backwards. First he must acknowledge his debt to evolution through which has been perfected the instrument wherein his mind works and gathers material. Then, through meditation, he is led to see himself as not only self-conscious—as one who receives impressions—one who criticises and watches—one whose will is interfered
<187> with—one who is misunderstood—one to whom others are 'persons' or masks (from Latin *Persona,* a mask)—but, standing outside himself, he now becomes one who endeavours to sense how his mask appears to others—sees himself as part of the consciousness of others, as one who impresses, one who is criticised and watched, one who interferes with the will of others, one who misunderstands.

He may recall periods in his life when his convictions were sure, his judgments harsh and unjust, his actions shameful, and view himself in that picture dispassionately as an entity operative in the give and take of life, something growing and as outside the category of blame as is the bitterness of unripe fruit.

As the knowledge of his place and relative importance in the Universe matures, he will attain strength to be honest with himself—ashamed of nothing he finds in his mind—one watching the antics of his personality with tolerant amusement—yet always learning.

He will reflect on words, and the power of words. He will catch himself weaving them—twisting their meaning—deceiving himself and others with them. He will catch himself under obsession to them—he will see how they fix and make possible the recall of events and emotions, and with this knowledge he will become aware of how his words affect other people.

As he begins to realise the tremendous miracle of words, the magic both good and evil of human communion by words, he will begin to grasp why the Order reiterates the importance of silence. The true Magician must understand his tools and, in periods of silence, he must contemplate words as one of them.

As he thus traverses the long road to dispassionate self-
<188> knowledge, and no longer has to waste energy in doing battle for and indulging wounded feelings in defence of a totally false idea of himself, he is led to meditate on the varied symbols of the cross, and from this to contemplate the Crucified One, revealed to the West as Jesus of Nazareth.

This life and the sayings of Jesus given in the Meditation should be studied and pictured in the mind.

The mind must be taught to die to useless churnings over past things and vain apprehensions about future things. This is difficult, for human phantasies die hard, but once the effort is made, however transient the result, it becomes easier with time to replace wasteful thoughts with those that cluster round a powerful symbol of eternal truth.

As the time for the ⑤=[6] Ceremony approaches, the Aspirant should withdraw as far as may be from externals that these symbols may work in his mind.

He will find them waiting on the threshold of his mind ready to tell their story as he walks about or is occupied in mechanical tasks. Once a place has been made for them no 'time' is required to develop them. They grow in the waste places.

Definite times, too should be set aside for Meditation wherein ideas may be formulated as far as possible.

Before going to sleep, the Aspirant should do the Pentagram
<189> Ritual and impress on his mind that he must recall on waking any teaching that has been given him in dream or vision. This may be assisted, if on waking, he calls before his mind the Sun rising, thinly veiled in clouds.

This should be done at least the week preceding the Grade.

The Ceremony will be a true initiation for the Aspirant only in so far as he has prepared himself to receive it.

Like a word, it is a symbol, the communication of whose essence depends on the understanding and experience of the recipient.

<190>

MEDITATION

LET THE ASPIRANT meditate upon the Cross in its various forms and aspects as shown in the Admission Badges throughout the Grades.

Let him consider the necessity and prevalence of sacrifice throughout nature and religion.

Let him realise the saying of the Master 'Whosoever shall save his life shall lose it, and whosoever shall lose his life shall save it.'

'Except a corn of wheat fall into the ground and die, it abideth alone, but if it die, it bringeth forth much fruit.'

Let him endeavour to realise his own place and relative importance in the Universe, striving to stand outside himself and allowing only such claims as he would allow to another.

Let him carefully abstain from talking of himself, his feelings or experiences that he may gain continence of speech, and learn to control the wasteful activities of his mind.

Let him contemplate the Sun as thinly veiled in clouds.

<191> CONCERNING THE TREE OF LIFE

This is the Book of the Path of the Chameleon—the knowledge of the colours of the forces which lie beyond the physical universe. Study thou well that saying of Hermes 'that which is below is like that which is above,' for if that which is below is conformed according to the Law of the Concealed One—Great is his Name—be thou well assured that the closer thou adherest unto the Law of the Universe in thy working, by so much the more is thy Magical working just and true.

Recall what was said unto thee in the Ritual of the Paths of the Portal of the Vault of the Adepti. 'Therefore, by the straight and narrow path of Samekh, let the Philosophus advance like the arrow from the Bow of Qesheth.' Now Qesheth the Bow is the Rainbow of Promise stretched above the earth, whose name is formed from the letters of the Paths leading from Malkuth. If then it be by the Path of Samekh that the Philosophus should advance to the knowledge of the Adept, turning aside neither unto the right hand nor unto the left, whereon are the evil and threatening symbols of Death and the Devil, he must have a perfect and absolute knowledge of the Bow, ere he can follow the Path of the Arrow. But the Bow is of brilliant and perfect colour, whose analysis and synthesis yield others of the same scale, and hence is this book entitled "The Book of the Path of the Chameleon"—that Path, namely which ascendeth alone through the force of Qesheth, the Bow.

And if thy knowledge and application of the outer knowledge, which thou hast already learned, be faulty and incorrect how wilt thou be
<192> able to keep thyself from turning aside unto thy hurt? Therefore,
learn not knowledge by rote only as an unreasoning child, but meditate, search out and compare, and to the end, see that thou think but little of thyself—for only he that humbleth himself shall be exalted. Magical knowledge is not given unto thee to tickle thy vanity and conceit, but that by its means, thou mayest purify and equilibriate thy spiritual nature and honour the Vast and Concealed One.

This is the explanation of the first diagram of the Paths—the Sephiroth being in the feminine scale and the Paths in the masculine or King's scale. It is the Key of the Forces which lie in Qesheth the Bow. Treasure it in thy heart and mark it well, seeing that therein is the key of nature. Meditate on it and reveal it not unto the profane, for many and great are its mysteries.

NOTE: There are four scales of colour which correspond to the Four Worlds. They are:

The King Scale	*Atziluth*	*Wands*	*Yod*	*Fire*
The Queen Scale	*Briah*	*Cups*	*Heh*	*Water*
The Prince Scale	*Yetzirah*	*Swords*	*Vau*	*Air*
The Princess Scale	*Assiah*	*Pentacles*	*Heh*	*Earth*

The Colors differ according to the World or aspect of the *Great Name* they represent:

Thus Samekh in:	
The King Scale is	Deep Blue
The Queen Scale is	Yellow
The Prince Scale is	Green
The Princess Scale is	Grey Blue

<193> Tiphareth in:	
The King Scale is	Rose
The Queen Scale is	Gold
The Prince Scale is	Pink
The Princess Scale is	Tawny Yellow

The Tree of Life for the use of an Adeptus Minor is compounded of the first two scales. The Sephiroth are in the feminine, passive, or Queen Scale. The paths are in the masculine, active, or King Scale. It thus represents the forces of Atziluth in the Paths uniting the Sephiroth as reflected in the Briatic World, one of the possible arrangements of the powers inherent in Yod He of the Great Name.

First are the Feminine colours of the Sephiroth, the Queen's Scale. In Kether is the Divine White Brilliance, the scintillation and corruscation of the Divine Glory—that Light which lighteth the universe—that Light which surpasseth the glory of the Sun and beside which the light of mortals is but darkness, and concerning which it is not fitting that we should speak more fully. And the Sphere of its Operation is called *Rashith Ha-Gilgalim*—the beginning of whirling (or whirls, or whorls), the Primum Mobile or First Mover, which bestoweth the gift of life in all things and filleth the whole Universe. And *Eheieh* is the Name of the Divine Essence in Kether; and its Archangel is the Prince of Countenances—Metatron or Metraton, He who bringeth others before the face of God. And the Name of its Order of Angels is called *Chaioth ha-Qadesh,* the Holy Living Creatures, which are also called the Order of Seraphim.

In Chokmah is a cloud-like grey which containeth various
<194> colours and is mixed with them, like a transparent pearl-hued mist,
yet radiating withal, as if behind it there was a brilliant glory. And the Sphere of its influence is in *Masloth,* the Starry Heaven, wherein it disposeth the forms of things. And *Yah* is the Divine Ideal Wisdom, and its Archangel is *Ratziel,* the Prince or Princes of the knowledge of hidden and concealed things, and the name of its Order of Angels is *Auphanim,* the Wheels or the Whirling Forces which are also called the Order of Kerubim.

In Binah is a thick darkness which yet veileth the Divine Glory in which all colours are hidden, wherein is mystery and depth and silence, and yet, it is the habitation of the Supernal Light. There is the Supernal Triad completed. And the Sphere of its Operation is *Shabbathai,* or rest, and it giveth forms and similitudes unto chaotic matter and it ruleth the sphere of action of the planet

Saturn. And *Jehovah Elohim* is the perfection of Creation and the Life of the World to Come. And its Archangel is *Tzaphqiel,* the Prince of the Spiritual Strife against Evil, and the Name of the Order of Angels is *Aralim,* the Strong and Mighty Ones who are also called the Order of Thrones. The Angel *Jophiel* is also referred unto Binah.

In Chokmah is the Radix of blue and thence is there a blue colour pure and primitive, and glistening with a spiritual Light which is reflected unto *Chesed.* And the Sphere of its Operation is called *Tzedek* or Justice and it fashioneth the images of material things, bestowing peace and mercy; and it ruleth the sphere of the action of the planet Jupiter. And *Al* is the title
<195> of a God strong and mighty, ruling in Glory, Magnificence and
Grace. And the Archangel of Chesed is *Tzadkiel,* the prince of Mercy and Beneficence, and the Name of the Order of Angels is *Chashmalim* Brilliant Ones, who are also called the Order of Dominions or Dominations. The Sephira Chesed is also called Gedulah or Magnificence and Glory.

In Binah is the Radix of Red, and therein is there a red colour, pure and scintillating and flashing with flame which is reflected unto *Geburah.* The Sphere of its Operation is called *Madim* or violent rushing Force and it bringeth fortitude, and war and strength and slaughter, as it were, the flaming Sword of an avenging God. And it ruleth the Sphere of Action of the Planet Mars. And *Elohim Gibor* is the Elohim, Mighty and Terrible, judging and avenging evil, ruling in wrath and terror and storm, and at whose steps are lightning and flame. And its Archangel is *Kamael* the Prince of Strength and Courage, and the Name of the Order of Angels is *Seraphim* the Flaming Ones who are also called the Order of Powers. The Sephira *Chesed* is also called *Gedulah* or Magnificense and Glory, and the Sephira *Geburah* is also called *Pachad* Terror and Fear.

In Kether is the Radix of a Golden Glory and thence is there a pure, primitive and sparkling, gleaming golden yellow which is reflected unto *Tiphareth.* Thus is the *first reflected Triad* completed. And the Sphere of its operation is that of *Shemesh,* the Solar Light, and bestoweth Life, Light and Brilliancy in metallic matter, and it ruleth the sphere of action of the Sun. And *Yhvh Eloha va-Daath* is a God of Knowledge and Wisdom, ruling over the Light of the Universe; and its Archangel is *Raphael,* the Prince of
<196> Brightness, Beauty and Life. And the Name of the Order of Angels is
Melechim or *Malakim,* that is Kings or Angelic Kings, who are also called the Order of Virtues, Angels and Rulers. The Angels Peniel and Pelial are also referred unto this Sephira. It especially rules the Mineral world.

The beams of Chesed and of Tiphareth meet in *Netzach* and thence in *Netzach* arises a green, pure, brilliant, liquid, and gleaming like an emerald. And the Sphere of its operations is that of *Nogah* of External Splendour, producing zeal, love, harmony, and it ruleth the Sphere of Action of the Planet Venus and the nature of the vegetable World. And *Jehovah Tzabaoth* is a God of Hosts and of Armies, of Triumph and of Victory, ruling the Universe in Justice and Eternity. And its Archangel *Hanial* is the Prince of Love and Harmony, and the Name of the Order of Angels is *Elohim* or Gods who are also called the Order of Principalities. The Angel *Cerviel* is also referred unto this Sephira.

The beams of *Geburah* and *Tiphareth* meet in *Hod* and thence arises in *Hod* a brilliant pure and flashing orange tawny. And the Sphere of its Operation is that of *Kokab,* the stellar light, bestowing elegance, swiftness, and scientific knowledge and art, and constancy of speech, and it ruleth the sphere of the action of the planet Mercury. And *Elohim Tzabaoth* is also a God of Hosts and of Armies, of Mercy and of Agreement, of Praise and Honour, ruling the Universe in Wisdom and Harmony. And its Archangel is *Michael,* the Prince of Splendour and of Wisdom, and the Name of Order of Angels is *Beni Elohim,* or Sons of the Gods, who are also called the Order of Archangels.

The beams of Chesed and Geburah meet in *Yesod* and thence
<197> ariseth in *Yesod* a brilliant deep violet-purple or puce, and thus is the
third Triad completed. And the sphere of its operation is that of *Levanah,* the Lunar beam, bestowing change, increase and decrease upon created things and it ruleth the Sphere of Action of the Moon and the nature of mankind. And *Shaddai* is a God who sheddeth benefits, Omnipotent and Satisfying, and *Al Chai* is the God of Life, the Living One. Its Archangel is *Gabriel* the Prince of Change and Alteration. And the name of the Order of Angels is *Kerubim* or Kerubic ones who are also called the Order of Angels.

And from the rays of this Triad there appear three colours in *Malkuth* together with a fourth which is their synthesis. Thus from the orange tawny of Hod and the green nature of Netzach, there goeth forth a certain greenish 'citrine' colour, yet pure and translucent withal. From the orange tawny of Hod mingled with the puce of Yesod there goeth forth a certain red russet brown, 'russet' yet gleaming with a hidden fire. And from the green of Netzach and the puce of Yesod there goeth forth a certain other darkening green 'olive' yet rich and glowing withal. And the synthesis of all these is a blackness which bordereth upon the Qlippoth.

Thus are the colours of the Sephiroth completed in their feminine or Rainbow scale.

Moreover, though the Tree of Life operates through all the Ten Sephiroth, yet it is referred in a special manner to Tiphareth. Also, though the branches of the Tree of Knowledge of Good and Evil stretch into the seven lower Sephiroth and downwards into the Kingdom of Shells, yet it
<198> is referred especially unto Malkuth. Similarly with Netzach and
Hod, the right and left columns of the Sephiroth are referred respectively thereto.

In Malkuth, *Adonai ha-Aretz* is God, the Lord and King, ruling over the Kingdom and Empire which is the Visible Universe.

And *Cholem Yesodoth* the Breaker of Foundations, (or *Olam Yesodoth*—the World of the Elements) is the Name of the Sphere of Operation of Malkuth which is called the Sphere of the Elements from which all things are formed, and its Archangels are three:—*Metatron,* the Prince of Countenance reflected from Kether, and *Sandalphon,* the Prince of Prayer (feminine), and *Nephesch ha Messiah,* the Soul of the Reconciler for Earth. And the Order of Angels is *Ashim* or Flames of Fire, as it is written 'Who maketh his Angels Spirits and his Ministers as a flaming Fire,' and these are also called the Order of Blessed Souls, or of the Souls of the Just made Perfect.

(Note the Three Archangels attributed to Malkuth with reference to Christian symbolism in regard to Our Father, Our Lady, and Our Lord.)

The following table consists of a classification of the scales of colour in each of the Four Worlds. The numbers 1-10 refer to the Sephiroth, and those from 11-32 inclusive to the Paths.

<199-200-201-202>

THE FOUR COLOUR SCALES

	YOD—FIRE	HEH—WATER	VAU—AIR	HEH (final) EARTH
	King Scale (Atsiluth)	Queen Scale (Briah)	Emperor or Prince (Yetsirah)	Empress or Knave (Assiah)
	Wands	Cups	Swords	Pentacles
1	Brilliance	White Brilliance	White Brilliance	White flecked gold
2	Soft Blue	Grey	Bluish Mother of pearl	White flecked red, blue, yellow
3	Crimson	Black	Dark Brown	Grey flecked pink
4	Deep Violet	Blue	Deep Purple	Deep azure flecked yellow
5	Orange	Scarlet-red	Bright Scarlet	Red flecked black
6	Clear pink rose	Yellow (gold)	Rich Salmon	Gold amber
7	Amber	Emerald	Bright Yellow Green	Olive flecked gold
8	Violet-purple	Orange	Red Russet	Yellow-brown flecked white
9	Indigo	Violet	Very Dark purple	Citrine flecked azure
10	Yellow	Citrine, olive, russet, black	4 colours fl. gold	Black rayed yellow
11	Bright-pale yellow	Sky-blue	Blue-emerald green	Emerald flecked gold
12	Yellow	Purple	Grey	Indigo-rayed violet
13	Blue	Silver	Cold Pale Blue	Silver rayed sky-blue
14	Emerald Green	Sky Blue	Early Spring Green	Bright rose of cerise rayed pale yellow
15	Scarlet	Red	Brilliant Flame	Glowing Red
16	Red Orange	Deep Indigo	Deep warm olive	Rich Brown
17	Orange	Pale Mauve	New yellow	Reddish grey inclined to mauve
18	Amber	Maroon	Rich bright Russet	Dark greenish-brown
19	Greenish-Yellow	Deep Purple	Grey	Reddish-amber
20	Yellowish-Green	Slate Grey	Green Grey	Plum Colour
21	Violet	Blue	Rich Purple	Bright blue rayed Yellow
22	Emerald-Green	Blue	Deep blue green	Pale Green
23	Deep blue	Sea-Green	Deep olive green	White flecked purple like mother of pearl
24	Green-blue	Dull brown	Very dark Brown	Livid Indigo brown-black-beetle
25	Blue	Yellow	Green	Dark vivid-blue
26	Indigo	Black	Blue black	Cold-dark-grey near black
27	Scarlet	Red	Venetian Red	Bright red rayed azure or emerald
28	Violet	Sky blue	Bluish Mauve	White tinged purple
29	Ultra Violet Crimson	Buff flecked silver-white	Light translucent Pinkish brown	Stone Colour
30	Orange	Gold yellow	Rich amber	Amber rayed red
31	Glowing scarlet-Orange	Vermillion	Scarlet flecked gold	Vermillion flecked crimson and Emerald
32	Indigo	Black	Blue black	Black rayed blue
31	Citrine, olive, russet black	Amber	Dark Brown	Black and yellow
32	White, merging Grey	Deep purple (nearly black)	7 prismatic colours. violet outside	White, red, yellow, blue black (outside)
Daath	Lavender	Grey White	Pure Violet	Grey flecked gold

<203>

THE MICROCOSM—MAN

Thou shalt know that the whole Sphere of Sensation which surroundeth the whole physical body of a man is called "The Magical Mirror of the Universe." For therein are represented all the occult forces of the Universe projected as on a sphere, convex to the outer, but concave to man. This sphere surroundeth the physical body of a man as the Celestial Heavens do the body of a Star or a Planet, having their forces mirrored in its atmosphere. Therefore its allotment or organization is the copy of that Greater World or Macrocosm. In this "Magical Mirror of the Universe," therefore, are the Ten Sephiroth projected in the form of the Tree of Life as in a solid sphere. (See also the Astronomic view of the Tarot in Part Eight.)

A man's physical body is within the Ten Sephiroth projected in a sphere. The divisions and parts of the body are formed from the Sephiroth of the Tree of Life, thus.

Kether is *above* the Crown of the Head, and represents a crown which indeed is powerful, but requires one worthy to wear it. In the crown of the head is placed the faculty of Neschamah, which is the power of Aspiration unto that which is beyond. This power of Neschamah is especially attributed unto the Supernal Triad in Assiah, of which there are three manifestations which are included in the general concept, Neschamah.

From Chokmah and Binah are formed the sides of the brain and head. Therein exist the intellectual faculties of Wisdom and Understanding, shining into illuminating their inferior, the Ruach. They are the man-
<204> sions of the practical administration of the intellect, whose physical shewing forth is by reflection in Ruach. In the Magical Mirror of the Universe, or the Sphere of Sensation, Man is placed between four pillars of the Tree of Life as projected in a sphere. These keep their place and *move not.* But the Man himself places in his Sphere of Sensation that point of the Zodiac which ascended at the moment of his birth and conception (for the same degree of the Zodiac ascendeth at both, otherwise the birth could not take place). That is to say that at those times the same degree of the Zodiac is ascending in the East of the Heavens of the Star whereon he is incarnated. Thus doth he remain during that incarnation facing that particular point in his sphere of sensation. That is to say, this sphere *doth not revolve* about the physical body.

From Chesed and Geburah are formed the arms. Therein exist the faculties of operative action, wherefore at their extremities are the symbols of the Four Elements and the Spirit, thus:—

Thumb..........Spirit
3rd Finger..........Fire
Index Finger..........Water
Little Finger..........Air
Second Finger..........Earth

The arms are the manifestors of the executive power of the Ruach, and therein are the faculties of touch strongly expressed.

From Tiphareth is formed the trunk of the body, free from the
<205> members,and therein as in a receptacle of influences are situated
the vital organs.

The blood is Spirit mingled with and governing the watery principle. The lungs are the receptacles of Air which tempereth the blood as the wind doth the waves of the sea—the mephitic impurities of the blood in its traversal of the body requiring the dispersing force of the Air, even as the sea, under a calm, doth putrify and become mephitic.

The heart is the great centre of the action of Fire, lending its terrible energy as an impulse unto the others. Thence cometh from the fiery nature the red colour of the blood.

The part above the heart is the chief abode of the *Ruach,* as there receiving and concentrating the other expressions of its Sephiroth. This part is the central citadel of the body and is the particular abode of the lower and more physical will. The higher will is in the Kether of the body. For the higher will to manifest, it must be reflected into the lower will by Neschamah. This lower will is immediately potent in the lower membranes and thus, in the region about the heart, is the lower will seated like the King of the body upon its throne.

The concentration of the other faculties of the *Ruach* in and under the presidency of the Will, at the same time reflecting the administrative governance of Chokmah and Binah, is what is called the human consciousness. That is, a reflection of the two creative Sephiroth under the presidency
of the Four Elements, or the reflection of *Aima* and *Abba* as the
<206> parents of the human Jehovah. But the human Neschamah *exists*
only when the higher Will is reflected by the agency of aspiration from Kether into the lower body, and when the flaming letter Shin is placed like a crown on the head of Microprosopus. Thus only doth the human will become the receptacle of the higher Will and the action of Neschamah is the link therewith. The lower will is the human Jehovah—an angry and jealous God, the Shaker of the Elements, the manifestor in the life of the body. But illuminated by the higher Will, he becometh Yeheshuah, no longer angry and jealous, but the self-sacrificer and the Atoning and Reconciling One.

This as regards the action of the more physical man.

Unto this *Ruach* also are presented the reflections of the Macrocosmic Universe in the Sphere of Sensation. They surround the *Ruach* which, in the natural man, feeleth them but vaguely and comprehendeth them not. The faculties of the Earth are shown forth in the organs which digest and putrify, casting forth the impurities, even as the Earth is placed above the Qlippoth.

Thou wilt say, then, that the Ruach cannot be the reasoning mind, seeing that it reflecteth its reason from Chokmah and Binah — but it is the executive faculty which reasoneth, which worketh with and combineth the faculties reflected into it. The reasoning mind, therefore, is that which useth and combineth the Principia of Chokmah and Binah so that the parts of Chokmah and Binah which touch the Ruach are the initiators of the reasoning power. The reason itself is a process and but a simulacrum of the action of the higher Wisdom and Understanding. For the Air is not the Light—only the

<207> translator of the Light. Yet without the Air, the operations of the
Light could not so well be carried out. The word *Ruach,* Spirit, also meaneth Air. It is like a thing that goeth out thou knowest not whither, and cometh in thou knowest not whence.

'The wind bloweth where it listeth, and thou hearest the sound thereof, but canst not tell whence it cometh nor whither it goeth. So is every one that is born of the Spirit.'

This Air, the *Ruach,* permeateth the whole physical body but its concentrated influence is about the heart. Yet, were it not for the boundary force of Chokmah and Binah above, of the sphere of sensation surrounding it, and of Malkuth below, the *Ruach* could not concentrate under the presidency of the Name, and the life of the body would cease.

Thus far concerning the Ruach as a *whole,* that is, the action of the Will in Tiphareth.

From Netzach and Hod are formed the thighs and legs, and they terminate in the symbols of five, as do the arms; but they are not so moveable, owing to the effect of Malkuth. In them are placed the faculties of support and firmness and balance; and they show the more physical qualities of the *Ruach.* In them is the sustaining force of the *Ruach.* They are the affirmation of the Pillars of the Sephiroth, as answering to the Passive, the arms more answering to the two pillars which are Active. They are the columns of the Human Temple.

From Yesod are formed the generative and excretory organs,
<208> and therein is the seat of the lower desires, as bearing more on the
double nature of, on the one hand, the rejection of the Qlippoth, and on the other hand the simulacrum of the vital forces in Tiphareth. It is the special seat of the automatic consciousness. That is, not the Will, but the *simulacrum* of the Will in Tiphareth. Yesod is the lowest of the Sephiroth of the Ruach, and representeth "Fundamental Action." It therefore governeth generation. In Yesod is therefore the automatic consciousness or simulacrum of the Will. This automatic consciousness is to the Nephesch what the *Daath* action is to the *Ruach.* Thus, therefore, there being a simulacrum or reflection of the heart and vital organs in the parts governed by Yesod, if the consciousness of the Tiphareth be given unto this wholly, it shall pave the way for disease and death. For this will be a withdrawing of the vital forces of the Name, which are in the citadel of Tiphareth, to locate them in Yesod, which is a more easily attacked position. For the automatic consciousness is the translator of the Ruach unto the Nephesch.

From Malkuth is formed the whole physical body under the command and presidency of the Nephesch. The Nephesch is the subtle body of refined astral Light upon which, as on an invisible pattern, the physical body is extended. The physical body is permeated throughout by the rays of the Ruach, of which it is the material completion. The Nephesch shineth through the Material body and formeth the Magical Mirror or Sphere of Sensation. This Magical Mirror or Sphere of Sensation is an imitation or copy of the Sphere
of the Universe. The space between the physical body and the
<209> boundary of the sphere of Sensation is occupied by the ether of the
astral world; that is to say, the container or recipient of the Astral

Rays of the Macrocosm.

The Nephesch is divided into its seven Palaces, combining the Sephirotic influences in their most material forms. That is, the world of passions dominated by the Ruach, or by the world which is beyond. That is, its Sephiroth are passionate, expressing a passionate dominion. Thus, its three Supernal Sephiroth, Kether, Chokmah and Binah, are united in a sense of feeling and comprehending impressions. Its Chesed is expressed by laxity of action. Its Geburah by violence of action. Its Tiphareth is expressed by more or less sensual contemplation of beauty, and love of vital sensation. Its Hod and Netzach, by physical well-being and health. Its Yesod, by physical desires and gratifications. Its Malkuth, by absolute increase and domination of matter in the material body.

The Nephesch is the real, the actual body, of which the material body is only the result through the action of Ruach, which by the aid of the Nephesch, formeth the material body by the rays of Ruach, which do not ordinarily proceed beyond the limits of the physical body. That is to say, in the ordinary man the rays of Ruach rarely penetrate into the sphere of Sensation.

Shining through infinite worlds, and darting its rays through the confines of space, in this Sphere of Sensation is a faculty placed even as a light is placed within a lantern. This is a certain sense placed in an aperture of the upper part of the Ruach wherein act the rays from Chokmah and Binah which govern the reason—*Daath.* This faculty can be thrown
<210> downwards into the Ruach, and thence can radiate into the
Nephesch. It consists of seven manifestations answering to the Hexagram, and is like the Soul of Microprosopus or the Elohim of the human Tetragrammaton. Therefore in the head, which is its natural and chief seat, are formed the seven apertures of the head. This is the Spiritual Consciousness as distinct from the human consciousness. It is manifested in 7 as just said or in 8 if *Daath* be included. The Father is the Sun (Chokmah). The Mother is the Moon (Binah). The Wind beareth it in his bosom, (Ruach). Its Nurse is the Earth (Nephesch). The power is manifested when it can be vibrated through the Earth.

The following is the true attribution of the seven apertures of the head:

Right Ear	*Saturn*	Left Ear	*Jupiter*
Right Eye	*Sol*	Left Eye	*Luna*
Mouth	*Mercury* (who is the messenger of the Gods)		
Right Nostril	*Mars*	Left Nostril	*Venus*

These latter represent here the sonoriferous sense. The right and left eye, the luminous sense, as the Sun and Moon are the luminaries of the Macrocosm. The right and left nostrils through which the breath passes, giving strength to the physical body, are under Mars and Venus. The mouth is under Mercury, the messenger and the Speaker.

This spiritual consciousness is a focus of the action of *Neschamah.* The lower will-power should control the descent of this spiritual consciousness

into the *Ruach,* and thence into the *Nephesch,* for the consciousness
<211> must descend into the *Nephesch* before the images of the Sphere of Sensation can be perceived. For it is only the rays of this consciousness permeating the *Ruach* that can take cognisance thereof. This faculty of the spiritual consciousness is the seat of Thought. *Thought* is a *Light* proceeding from the radiation of this spiritual consciousness, traversing the *Ruach* as Light traverseth Air, and encountering thereafter the symbols reflected in the sphere of Sensation, or magical mirror of the Universe. These symbols are by its radiation (i.e. that of the Thought) reflected again into the Spiritual Consciousness where they are subjected unto the action of the *Reasoning Mind* and of the *Lower Will.* That is, in the ordinary natural man when awake, the thought acteth through the *Ruach,* subject when there to the action of the Lower Will, and submitted to the reasoning power derived as aforesaid from Chokmah and Binah. But in the ordinary man when sleeping, and in the madman, the idiot, and the drunkard, the process is not quite the same. In the sleeping man, the concentration of the *Ruach* in his heart during the waking time hath produced a weakening of the action of the *Ruach* in its subsidiary Sephiroth in the Physical Body. To preserve the salutary conjunction of the *Ruach* with the *Nephesch* in the physical body (whose limits are fixed by the Sephiroth of the Ruach) it is necessary to weaken the concentration in Tiphareth to repair the strain which is produced by the concentration of the *Ruach* therein during the waking state. This reflux of the *Ruach* into its subsidiary Sephiroth produceth naturally a weakening of the Lower Will; and the *Ruach,* therefore, doth not reflect so clearly the Reasoning
<212> Faculty. Wherefore, the thought of the spiritual consciousness reflecteth the image in a confused series, which are only partially realised by the lower will. (This is as regards the ordinary natural man in sleep.)

In the madman, as considered apart from obsession (thought-obsession is frequently the accompaniment of mania, and still more frequently its cause) the thought and lower will are very strongly exercised to the detriment of the reasoning faculty. That is, that there is an alliance between the two former which overpowereth the action of Chokmah and Binah in the latter.

Monomania is shown in the consideration of only one certain symbol which is too attractive to the Will. A chain of thought is therefore simply a graduated vibration arising from the contact of a ray of thought with a symbol. If controlled by the reasoning power and licensed by the Will, such vibrations will be balanced and of equal length. But if uncontrolled by the lower Will and the Reason, they will be unbalanced and inharmonious. (That is, of uneven length.)

In the case of the drunkard, the equilibrium of the Sphere of Sensation and consequently of the Nephesch, is disturbed. In consequence the thought rays are shaken at each vibration, so that the sphere of sensation of the Nephesch is caused to rock and waver at the extremities of the Physical Body where the Ruach action is bounded. The thought therefore is dazzled by the symbols of the Sphere of Sensation, in the same way as the eyes can be dazzled in front of a mirror if the latter be shaken or waved. The sensation

<213> therefore then conveyed by the thoughts is that of the Sphere of Sensation oscillating and almost revolving about the physical body, bringing giddiness, sickness, vertigo and the loss of idea of place and position. Nearly the same may be said of Seasickness, and the action of certain drugs.

Restoration of the equilibrium of the Sphere of Sensation after this naturally produceth a slackening of the concentration of the Ruach in Tiphareth, whence sleep is an absolute necessity to the drunkard. This is so imperative that he cannot fight against the need. If he does so, or if this condition be constantly repeated, the thought rays are launched through the Sphere of Sensation so irregularly and so violently that they pass its boundary without either the lower Will or the Reasoning Power or even the Thought itself consenting thereto; and the latter is therefore without the protection of the will. Thence arise the conditions of delirium tremens, and an opening is made in the Sphere of Sensation which is unguarded, and through which hostile influences may enter. But this latter cometh under the head of obsession.

All thought action in the spiritual consciousness originateth in radiation, and radiation is as inseparable from the spiritual consciousness as it is from Light.

This Spiritual Consciousness is the focus of the action of *Neschamah.* The spiritual consciousness is, in its turn, the Throne or Vehicle of the Life of the Spirit which is *Chiah;* and these combined form the Chariot of that Higher Will which is in *Kether.* Also it is the peculiar faculty of *Neschamah* to aspire unto that which is beyond. The Higher Will manifests itself through *Yechidah.*

The *Chiah* is the real Life Principle, as distinct from the more
<214> illusionary life of the Physical Body. The Shining Flame of the
Divine Fire, the *Kether* of the Body, is the Real Self of the Incarnation. Yet but few of the sons of men know it or feel its presence. Still less do they believe in or comprehend those Higher Potencies—Angelic, Archangelic or Divine, of which the manifestation directly touching *Yechidah* is the Higher Genius.

This *Yechidah* in the ordinary man can but rarely act through the spiritual consciousness, seeing that for it to do so the King of the Physical Body, that is the Lower Will, must rise from his Throne to acknowledge his superior. That is the reason why, in some cases, in sleep only doth the Higher Will manifest itself by dream unto the ordinary man. In other cases it may be manifested; at times through the sincere practice of religious rites, or in cases where the opportunity for self-sacrifice occurreth. In all these cases the Lower Will hath for a moment recognised a higher form of itself, and the YHVH of the man hath reflected from the Eternal Lord of the Higher Life. This *Yechidah* is the only part of the man which can truly say—EHEIEH, I am. This is then but the Kether of the Assiah of the Microcosm, that is, it is the highest part of man as Man. It is that which toucheth, or is the manifestation of a higher and greater range of Being. This Yechidah is at the same time the Higher Human Self and the Lower Genius, the God of the Man, the Atziluth of his Assiah, even as Chiah and Neschamah form his Briah, and Ruach his Yetzirah. This is the Higher Will and the Divine Consciousness, as Daath is the Spiritual Consciousness, Tiphareth the Human Consciousness, and Yesod the Automatic Consciousness.

It is the Divine Consciousness because it is the only part of man
<215> which can touch the All-potent forces. Behind Yechidah are Angelic
and Archangelic Forces of which Yechidah is the manifestor. It is therefore the Lower Genius or Viceroy of the Higher Genius which is beyond, an Angel Mighty and Terrible. This Great Angel is the Higher Genius, beyond which are the Archangelic and Divine.

Recall the Tiphareth clause of an Adeptus Minor: "I further solemnly promise and swear that with the divine permission I will from this day forward apply myself unto the Great Work which is so to purify and exalt my spiritual nature, that with the Divine Aid I may at length attain to be more than Human, and thus gradually raise and unite myself to my Higher and Divine Genius, and that in this event, I will not abuse the great power entrusted unto me."

Note that this clause answereth unto Tiphareth, seeing that it is the Lower Will that must apply itself unto this work, because it is the King of the Physical Man. All the Shining Ones (whom we call Angels) are microcosms of the Macrocosm Yetzirah, even as Man is the microcosm of the Macrocosm of Assiah. All Archangelic forms are microcosms of the Macrocosm of Briah, and the Gods of the Sephiroth are consequently the Microcosms of the Macrocosm of Atziluth. Therefore apply this perfecting of the Spiritual Nature as the preparation of the Pathway for the Shining Light, the Light Divine.

The evil persona of a man is in the Sphere of the Qlippoth, and the devils
are the Microcosms of the Macrocosm of the Qlippoth. This evil per-
<216> sona hath its parts and divisions, and of it the part which toucheth
the Malkuth of the Nephesch is its Kether. Tremble therefore at the evil forces which be in thy own evil persona. And as above the Kether of a Man are his Angelic and other forms, so below the Malkuth of the Evil Persona are awful forms, dangerous even to express or think of.

<217>

TASK UNDERTAKEN BY THE ADEPTUS MINOR

This, then, is the task to be undertaken by the Adeptus Minor. To expel from the Sephiroth of the Nephesch the usurpation by the evil Sephiroth; to balance the action of the Sephiroth of the Ruach in those of the Nephesch. To prevent the Lower Will and Human Consciousness from falling into and usurping the place of the Automatic Consciousness. To render the King of the Body, the Lower Will, obedient to and anxious to execute the commands of the Higher Will, that he be neither a usurper of the faculties of the Higher, nor a sensual despot—but an Initiated Ruler, and an anointed King, the viceroy and representative of the Higher Will, because inspired thereby, in his Kingdom which is man. Then shall it happen that the Higher Will, i.e., the Lower Genius, shall descend into the Royal Habitation, so that the Higher Will and the Lower Will shall be as one, and the Higher Genius shall descend into the Kether of the Man, bringing with him the tremendous illumination of his Angelic Nature. And the Man shall become what is said of Enoch. "And

Chanokh made himself to walk with God, and he was not, for God took him." (Genesis, V. v. 24.)

Then also this shalt thou know, that the Nephesch of the Man shall become as the Genius of the Evil Persona, so that the evil persona itself shall be as the power of the Divine in the Qlippoth, as it is said: "Whither shall I go from thy Spirit, or whither from thy Presence shall I flee? If I ascend up to Heaven, thou art there. If I make my bed in Hell, behold thou art there." (Ps. cxxxix.)

Therefore even the Evil Persona is not so evil when it fulfileth
<218> its work. For it is the beginning of a dim reflection of the Light unto
the Qlippoth, and this is what is hidden in the saying that "Typhon is the brother of Osiris." Hear thou, then, a mystery of the knowledge of evil. The ⑤ = 6 Ritual of the Adeptus Minor saith that even the "Evil helpeth forward the Good." When the evil Sephiroth are expelled from the Nephesch into the Evil Persona, they are, in a sense, equilibriated therein. The evil persona can be rendered as a great and strong, yet trained, animal whereupon the man rideth, and it then becometh a strength unto his physical base of action. This Mystery shalt thou keep from the knowledge of the First Order, and still more from that of the Outer World, that is as a formula, seeing that it is a dangerous secret.

Now then shalt thou begin to understand the saying "He descended into Hell," and also to comprehend in part this strength, and thus begin to understand the necessity of evil unto the material creation. Wherefore, also, revile not overmuch the evil forces, for they have also a place and a duty, and in this consisteth their right to be. But check their usurpation, and cast them down unto their plane. Unto *this* end, curse them by the mighty names if need be, but thou shalt not revile them for their condition, for thus also shalt thou be led into error.

There is also a great mystery that the Adeptus Minor must know, viz.:

How the spiritual consciousness can act around and beyond the sphere of Sensation. "Thought" is a mighty force when projected with all the strength of the lower Will under the guidance of the reasoning faculty and
illuminated by the Higher Will. Therefore, it is that, in thy occult
<219> working, thou art advised to invoke the Divine and Angelic Names,
so that thy Lower Will may willingly receive the influx of the Higher Will, which is also the Lower Genius behind which are the all-potent forces. This, therefore, is the magical manner of operation of the Initiate when "skrying" in the spirit vision. Through his own arcane wisdom, he knows the disposition and correspondences of the Forces of the Macrocosmos. Selecting not many, but one symbol, and that balanced and with its correlatives, then sendeth he a thought-ray from his Spiritual Consciousness, illuminated by his Higher Will, directly unto the part of his Sphere of Sensation which is consonant with the symbol employed. There, as in a mirror, doth he perceive its properties as reflected from the Macrocosmos, shining forth into the Infinite Abyss of the Heavens. Thence can he follow the ray of reflection therefrom, and while concentrating his united consciousness at that point of his sphere of sensation, can receive the direct reflection of the ray from the

Macrocosmos. Thus receiving the direct ray as then reflected into his Thought, he can unite himself with the ray of his Thought so as to make one continuous ray from the corresponding point of the Macrocosmos unto the centre of his consciousness. If, instead of concentrating at that actual point of the sphere of Sensation he shall retain the thought-ray only touching the sphere of sensation at that point, he shall, it is true, perceive the reflection of the Macrocosmic Ray *answering* to that symbol in the sphere of his Consciousness. But he shall receive this reflection tinctured much by his own nature, and therefore to an extent untrue, because his united con-
<220> sciousnesses have not been able to focus along the thought-ray at
the circumference of the Sphere of sensation. And this is the reason why there are so many and multifarious errors in untrained spirit visions. For the untrained seer, even supposing him free from the delusions of obsession, doth not know or understand how to unite his consciousnesses and the harmonies between his own sphere of sensation, and the universe, the macrocosmos. Therefore is it so necessary that the Adeptus Minor should correctly understand the principia and axiomata of our secret knowledge, which are contained in our Rituals and Lectures.

OF TRAVELING IN THE SPIRIT VISION

The symbol, place, direction, or Plane being known whereon it is desired to act, a thought-ray as before is sent unto the corresponding part of the Sphere of Sensation of the Nephesch. The Thought-Ray is sent like an arrow from the bow, right through the circumference of the Sphere of Sensation direct unto the place desired. Arrived there, a sphere of astral Light is formed by the agency of the Lower Will, illuminated by the Higher Will, and acting through the spiritual consciousness by reflection along the Thought-Ray. This sphere of Astral Light is partly drawn from the surrounding atmosphere. This sphere being formed, a simulacrum of the person of the Skryer is reflected into it along the thought-ray, and this united consciousness is then projected therein. This Sphere is then a duplicate, by reflection, of the Sphere of Sensation. As it is said: "Believe thyself to be in a place and thou art there." In this Astral Projection, however, a certain part of the consciousness must remain in the body to protect the Thought-Ray beyond the
<221> Sphere of Sensation (as well as the Sphere itself at that point of
departure of the Thought-Ray) from attack by any hostile force, so that the consciousness in this projection is not quite so strong as the consciousness when concentrated in the natural body in ordinary life. The return taketh place with a reversal of this process, and save to persons whose Nephesch and physical body are exceptionally strong and healthy, the whole operation of skrying and traveling in the Spirit Vision is of course fatiguing.

Also there is another mode of astral projection which can be used by the more practised and advanced Adept. This consisteth in forming first a sphere from his own Sphere of Sensation, casting his reflection therein, and then projecting this whole sphere to the desired place, as in the previous method.

But this is not easy to be done by any but the practised operator.

Thus far, regarding Skrying and Travelling in the Spirit Vision.

(These instructions are considerably amplified with practical examples in a later volume dealing with Astral vision and clairvoyance. I. R.)

<222> CONCERNING THE MICROCOSMS OF MACROCOSM

As thou well knowest there be many and numberless other inhabitants of the Macrocosmos besides Man, Angels, and Devils. The animals are microcosms in a sense, yet not so complete as man. In them are many and great mysteries. They also have their magical mirror or sphere of sensation. But its polarisation is usually *horizontal* rather than *perpendicular,* and this is owing to the Sephiroth not being shown therein. This Sphere, then, is not bounded by the Sephirothic columns, but they are especially governed by the Stellar System without the Sephiroth. They are therefore ruled by the Paths, rather than by the Sephiroth, and are consequently classed each under an Element or a Planet, and a Sign. Thus each followeth a formula which may be translated into letters, and these again form a vibratory name. As it is written: "And Adam gave names unto all the cattle and to the fowl of the air, and to every beast of the field." (Gen. II, v. 20.) Yet they are ruled by the name YHVH, though classed rather by one or more of its letters:

Thus, Fish, etc., are under the influence of Water
Birds are under the influence of Air
Quadrupeds are under the influence of Fire
Creeping things and insects are under the influence of Earth

There are some which partake of two elements, but in them one element is usually chief, and besides the Elements, each is under a Planet and a Sign.

The vegetable kingdom is again under a somewhat different
<223> Law. These are under a Planet and a Sign, a planet first differentiated by a Sign.

The Mineral Kingdom is under the Signs only. Vegetables have a Sphere of Sensation, but corresponding only to the Planets and Zodiacal Signs. The Minerals have also a Sphere which correspondeth unto the Signs only. But the metals are under the Planets only, and therein is the difference between them and the Minerals, wherefore also are they stronger. Shining Stones are especially under the Light; and they are, as it were, centres for the action thereof in the darkness of matter, as it is said: "My light is concealed in all that shineth." (This passage is believed to be from the Zend-Avesta.) They are therefore under the rule of the three active elements with an earthy base.

Shining through all things as a whole, are the rays of the Macrocosmos. Besides these classes of life there be multitudinous existences representing Forces of the Macrocosm, each with its own microcosm. Such are Elemental Spirits, Planetary Spirits, Olympic Spirits, Fays, Arch-Fays, Genii, and many other potencies which cannot be classed under these forms.

Thus the Macrocosmic Universe is one vast infinite sphere containing so many and diverse infinite microcosmic forms, of which the perfect knowledge is only known unto the advanced Adept.

Also it shall here suffice to say that thou shalt make a distinction between the Four-handed race (the quadrumana, Apes and monkeys)
<224> which be midway between Man and Beast and other animals. For
they be neither the one or the other, but are the fallen and debased result of a most ancient magical effect to formulate a material and immediate link between the human and animal microcosms. This is elsewhere treated of, and it shall here be sufficient to say that they are *not* an *ascent*, from the beast unto the Man, but a mistaken magical fall from a man unto a beast. Anciently they were a terrible power upon this planet, as then having more of the man than of the animal, whereas now they have more of the animal than of Man. The ancient traditions of their primal conditions are preserved unto this day in the legends of ogres and, in certain records, cannibalism and its rites.

Regarding the beasts, they are, for the most part, easily obsessed, and they have not the spiritual responsibility of the man. Their nature is not evil, but, following a natural law—seeing that man is head of the Assiatic creation—so the animal is higher than the vegetables or mineral. Also bear thou well in mind that the race of the transformers are given unto cruelty. Such are above all the race of creeping things. As Man hath his Ruach which is upright in the Tree of Life, so hath the beast his Ruach which is horizontal; as it is said: "The Ruach of a man which goeth upwards (i.e. directeth itself upwards), and the Ruach of the beast which goeth downwards (or crosswise) in the Earth." The Neschamah in the Beast is not. The beast consisteth of a Ruach and a Nephesch with a rudimentary Daath or Spiritual Consciousness. This Daath ever seeketh that which is beyond it and thence are beasts not responsible, but are submitted unto obsession, and herein is a great mystery. Man, therefore, is placed at the head of the beasts. Woe, woe,
<225> unto him if he teacheth their elementary Daath cruelty and injustice
instead of mercy and justice. For the Man is a God unto the Beast, and the aspiration of the Beast is toward the Man, and great is the office of the Beast, for he prepareth the foundation for the man. Man is responsible for creation, and since he was originally placed in creation to be its Lord, as *he is,* so will the creation follow him. And thus it is possible for the *Genius of a Nation* to change the climate of a country, and the nature of the beasts therein. Men fell from primal estate, and then they who were formless became imaged in form, deformed. And this is a mystery of the Demonic Plane which entereth not into this section.

The Elemental Spirits and other of their kind are an organisation not quite so complete as man. In spiritual consciousness more keen, and yet in some ways his spiritual superior though organically his inferior. They are the formers of the primal Man, that is the Elementary Man, and they have other and greater offices, for in them are many worlds and ranks and spheres. They are as the younger man (i.e. child) and towards them also is Man responsible, and he hath wrought them much injustice.

<226> OF OBSESSION, TRANCE, DEATH

Obsession always entereth through a cutting off of the Higher from the Lower Will, and it is ordinarily first induced by a Thought-Ray of the Spiritual consciousness (whence one danger of evil thoughts) ill-governed, penetrating the Sphere of Sensation and admitting another potency, either human embodied, or human disembodied, elemental or demonic. The first action of such a force is to flatter the lower will, until he shall have established firmly an entrance into the Sphere of Sensation, and thus shall cause a strain on the Nephesch which shall render the Ruach less concentrated. As soon as the Ruach is sufficiently dispersed to repair the strain on the physical body, the lower will is weakened, and is soon seized upon and bound by the invader. Whence arise the sensations of chill and drowsiness which are the usual forerunners of obsession. Now to yield the force necessary to overpower the lower will from any chance of communication with the higher the obsessing idea proceeds by seizing upon the Daath, and this consequently is the great point of attack, especially the part in the physical body which is at the back of the head about the junction with the Spine. Now unless the lower Will shall voluntarily endeavour to restore the connection, it is impossible for the Higher Will to intervene, seeing that the Lower Will is King of the Physical Body. Remember that no obsessing force can overpower the lower will, if that shall bravely and in spite of all opposition aspire unto the Higher Will.

Trance may arise from the action of obsession, or from the ac-
<227> tion of the Higher Will, therefore its aspects are varied.

Death superveneth in the natural man, when the mental action of the Ruach and the Nephesch is definitely and thoroughly interrupted in the physical body. In the Adept death can only supervene when the Higher Will consenteth thereto, and herein is implied the whole Mystery of the Elixir of Life.

End of Volume One

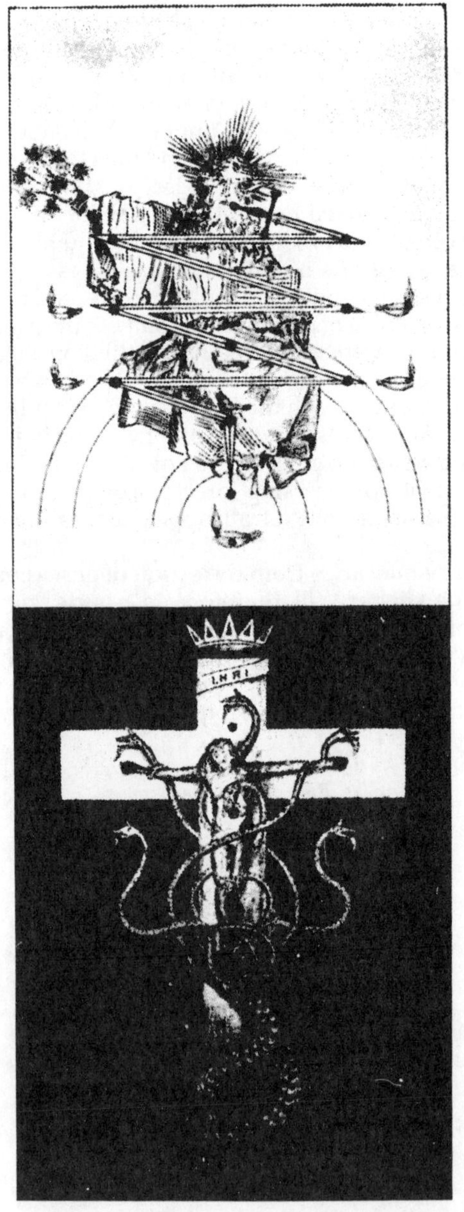

The Lid of the Pastos

BOOK TWO

RITUALS OF THE FIRST ORDER
THE STELLA MATUTINA
OR
GOLDEN DAWN

INTRODUCTION TO THE NEOPHYTE CEREMONY

GOD FORMS AND STATIONS IN THE ⓪ = 0⃞

The Opening of the Hall of the Neophytes and the Ceremony of Initiation into the ⓪ = 0⃞ Grade describe the essential formula of the Outer Order work and set in motion the energies necessary for the aspirant's spiritual growth. The setting is Ancient Egyptian, particularly referred to the 125th Chapter of the *Egyptian Book of the Dead,* and the ⓪ = 0⃞ Hall is also called "The Hall of Maat", the "Hall of Two Truths", and the "Hall of Dual Manifestation". The Hall of Maat is the scene for the weighing of the Soul where the crucial judgement of the deceased is made. Just as the deceased Ani's soul hangs in the balance, the soul and aspiration of the candidate for ⓪ = 0⃞ Grade of Neophyte hang between light and dark, evolution or devolution.

The numerous gods of the Egyptian judgement are represented in the ⓪ = 0⃞ by the stations of the officers, their functions and movements in the temple. These stations and the god-forms attributed are fully described in the "Z" documents, (later chapters in this book.)[1] All are well worth the time to read carefully — ". . . therefore learn not as an unreasoning child, but meditate, search out and compare . . ."[2]

Besides the seven officers and their corresponding god-forms, there are Invisible Stations, with associated deities, which do not move in the temple and are very significant as representing the balance of opposing forces in the Hall of Two Truths. The Invisible Station corresponding to the Yesod, the 9th Sephirah on the Tree of Life, immediately East of the Altar which is in the upper region of Malkuth in the ⓪ = 0⃞ temple, is the abode of a Set-like god-form associated with the Evil Triad and at the same time with a dark reptilian god associated with Typhon (see description of three animals in one, in "Z. 3". He is the Accusor, the Evil Genius, who would bind the candidate's soul in darkness with forces of the Qlippoth. In the Neophyte Initiation the Accusor rises from the base of the Altar at the time of the soul's greatest danger. During this vulnerable time, four Invisible Stations attributed to the Sons of Horus[3] protect the vital organs, symbolic of the essential life forces, until after the Oath has been taken and judgement has been passed.

Before the Hierophant administers the Oath he leaves the Throne of the East. The god-form of Osiris, represented by the Hierophant on the Throne, remains there maintaining the balance of forces in the temple. As the Hierophant passes between the Pillars on the way to the Altar, he assumes a second form of his Office which is having consented to take the obligation, is unprepared for this most delicate phase of initiation. Thrice bound and hoodwinked, the seeker is braver than he knows, uninitiated and in ignorance, totally dependent on the surrounding balance of forces. The Hierophant's Office now represents the candidate's Higher and Divine Genius, which in his blindness he cannot realize himself. Standing upon the Station of Typhon/Set during the weighing of the soul, the Hierophant, as the

[1]Vol. 3 Book 5, pages 81 and 152.
[2]Quoted from Vol. 1 Book 1 *Concerning the Tree of Life.*
[3]Vol. 3 Book 5, p. 124 *The Canopic Gods*

Higher Self, steps upon and keeps down the Evil Triad until the danger is passed. However "well prepared" or knowledgeable before initiation, the critical choice of the aspirant's soul is the same for everyone, and is especially equal in the equilibrating system of the Golden Dawn.

Also present for the judgement, disappearing after the Oath, are the Invisible Stations of the 42 Assessors. These god-forms are more like accusors than assessors, as the deceased in the *Book of the Dead* is required to deny to each one of them a particular crime or fault in the "Negative Confession". In the ⓪ = [0] temple these gods are represented through visualization by the officers, reinforced by other members present. Contemplation of these and the other god-forms and stations will enhance experience of the ceremony and facilitate the establishing of the Neophyte energies in all participants.

THE TREE OF LIFE IN THE TEMPLES OF THE OUTER ORDER

The representation of the Tree of Life in the Outer Order temples reflects the harmony and balance of that simple and infinite diagram. The philosophy of the Qabalah is expressed in the temple's changing patterns throughout the grade rituals and in the rhythm of activity within the rituals individually. Regardless of nationality, religion, language, etc. of the god-forms and forces represented, they are consistently balanced and in alignment with the different levels of manifestation in the temple and on the Tree, in their attributes, functions and with the magical purpose of the ceremonies. Systematically working through the grades can provide unexpected insights, new perspectives and a broader understanding of the synthesis of magical, religious, scientific aspects of the Great Work as it relates to the growth and processing of the aspiring student.

The four Sephiroth of the ⓪ = [0] are the only ones shown in the Outer Order temples. The stations and officers as appropriate, follow the Tree thru the Elemental Grades from ⓪ = [0] to ④ = [7]. Malkuth is the Sephirah of the Neophyte and Zelator grades, Theoricus is in Yesod, Practicus in Hod, Philosophus in Netzach. In a sense all Outer Order ceremonies take place in Malkuth as they never leave the world of Assiah represented macrocosmically by Malkuth.

The floor plan of the temple as an ideal, geometrically perfect reality may not be visible in the less than perfect surroundings of the participants' living room, bedroom, union hall, or whatever place has been chosen for a ceremony. There are significant connections to be discovered in the arrangement of the temple. Experimentation and application of number systems, including the Hebrew alphabet and numbers, and geometrical concepts like the symbols introduced as Meditations in the Knowledge Lectures of each grade can lead students to leaps in understanding of the relationships between the Qabalah and the Golden Dawn system. Practice in drawing the Tree in different ways, connecting paths with Sephiroth in the endless variety of patterns, will aid in determining a satisfactory geometric model and a method of drawing the Tree which students of the Qabalah and the Golden Dawn will use countless times. The potential for discovery is exponential with conscious, receptive experience of the rituals — literally walking the Paths — and dedicated, directed study, assimilating and synthesizing knowledge and experience over time.

Anupassana, May 4, 1986

<11> NEOPHYTE 0 = 0 GRADE OF THE ORDER OF THE STELLA MATUTINA

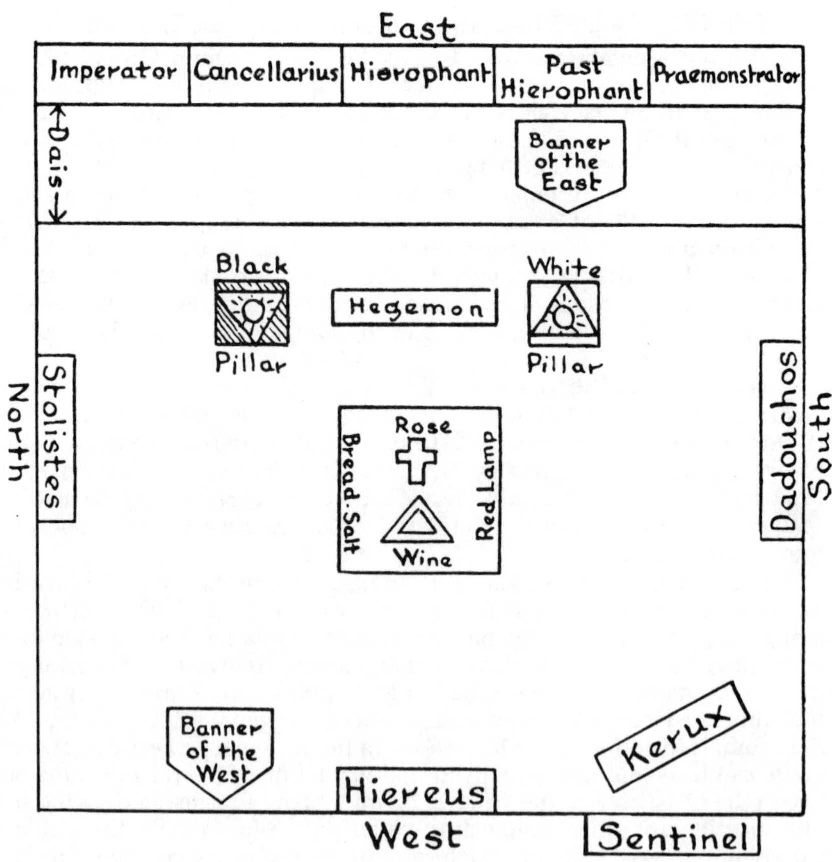

<12> *OFFICERS:*

On the Dais:

Imperator — Cancellarius — Past Hierophant — Praemonstrator.
Hierophant (Red Cloak,[1] Lamen, Sceptre).

In the Hall:

Hiereus (Black Cloak, Lamen, Sword).
Hegemon (White Cloak, Lamen, Sceptre).
Kerux (Lamen, Lamp and Wand).
Stolistes (Lamen, Cup of Lustral Water).
Dadouchos (Lamen, Thurible).
Sentinel (Lamen, Sword).

REQUIRED:

For the Altar:

Red Cross andWhite Triangle. Red Rose. Red Lamp. Cup of Wine.
Paten of Bread and Salt.

For the Candidate:

Black Robe and Red Shoes.[2] Hoodwink, Rope. Neophyte Sash.

For the Temple:

Chemical Change.[3]

OPENING OF THE ⓪ = 0 GRADE

When the Members are assembled and robed, Hierophant gives one knock and each is seated in his proper place, and the Officers rise.

Members present, but not taking on office, do not rise except for Adorations to the East or when asked for the Signs. They stand after the Hierophant says: "Let us adore the Lord of the Universe and Space" and face East, remaining so to the end of the Adoration. These non-participating members do not circumambulate with the Officers, but when they have occasion to move in the Temple, they do so in the direction of the SUN and make the Sign of the Enterer[4] *on passing the Throne of the East whether the Hierophant is there or not. The Sign of the Enterer is made in the direction of movement except when entering or leaving the Hall, when it is made towards the East or when asked to give the Signs, and then it is made*
<13> *towards the Altar.* 1 — *This sign represents one knock made by rapping the base of Sceptre or shaft of wand or the pommel of sword on a table or side-altar.*

---

[1]Cloaks—See page 111, Vol. III—are worn over the basic robe. Members of the Outer Order wear black robes while members of the Inner Order wear White Robes. G.W.

[2]Or red slippers, or red socks. G.W.

[3]See page 38. Dissolve a small amount of Sodium Salicylate in one glass of water, and a small amount of ferric Ammonium Sulfate in a second glass of water. Both glasses will continue to exhibit the clear transparency of water; however, when either is poured into the other, the liquid will change into a blood red color. A little experimentation beforehand will assure that the best shade of red and avoid such disconcerting experience as having the fluid change back to a clear fluid (e.g. when there is too little of one of the two ingredients). G.W.

[4]In the original, the first sign reference was to the Neophyte Sign and the second was to the Grade Sign. Only the Sign of the Enterer is made when passing the Throne of the East. To project into the vortex about the temple energy received from the Throne at the point of the rending of the Veil. To make the Sign of Silence, after making the Sign of the Enterer, would block the flow of this energy and actually be counterproductive to what you wish to accomplish in the circumambulation. G.W.

Hiero *(one knock)*
Kerux on hearing the Hierophant's knock, goes to the North East, to Hierophant's right, faces West, raising his Lamp and Wand and says:

Kerux HEKAS! HEKAS! ESTE BEBELOI!
Kerux returns to his place.
Hierophant rises with one knock.

Hiero *(knocks)* Fratres and Sorores of the .... Temple of the Order of the Stella Matutina, assist me to open the Hall of the Neophytes. Frater Kerux, see that the Hall is properly guarded.
Kerux goes to the door and gives one knock. Sentinel replies with one knock.

Kerux Very Honoured Hierophant, the Hall is properly guarded.
He salutes the Hierophant's Throne. Remains by door.

Hiero Honoured Hierus, guard the hither side of the portal and assure yourself that all present have witnessed the Stella Matutina.
Hiereus goes to the door, stands before it with Sword erect, Kerux being on his right with Lamp and Wand, and says:

Hiereus Fratres and Sorores of the Order of the Stella Matutina, give the Signs of a Neophyte.
This done, Hiereus gives Signs towards Hierophant, and says:
Very Honoured Hierophant, all present have been so honoured.

<14> *Hiereus and Kerux return to their places.*
Hierophant gives the Sign of the Enterer towards the West, but NOT the Sign of Silence.

Hiero Let the number of Officers in this degree and the nature of their Offices be proclaimed once again, that the Powers whose images they are may be re-awakened in the spheres of those present and in the Sphere of this Order — for by Names and Images are all Powers awakened and re-awakened.
He makes the Sign of Silence.
Honoured Hiereus, how many Chief Officers are there in this Grade?

Hiereus There are three Chief Officers; the Hierophant, the Hiereus, and the Hegemon.

Hiero Is there any peculiarity in these Names?

Hiereus They all commence with the letter 'H'.

Hiero Of what is this Letter a symbol?

Hiereus Of life; because the Letter 'H' is our mode of representing the ancient Greek aspirate or breathing, and Breath is the evidence of Life.

Hiero How many lesser Officers are there?

Hiereus There are three besides the Sentinel; the Kerux, the Stolistes, and the Dadouchos.
The Sentinel is without the Portal of the Hall and has a Sword in his hand to keep out intruders. It is his duty to prepare the Candidate.

Hiero Frater Dadouchos, your station and duties?

Dad My station is in the South to symbolise Heat and Dryness, and my duty is to see that the Lamps and Fires of the Temple are ready at the

GARDEN OF EDEN AFTER THE FALL

Refer to page 76.

GARDEN OF EDEN BEFORE THE FALL

Refer to page 73.

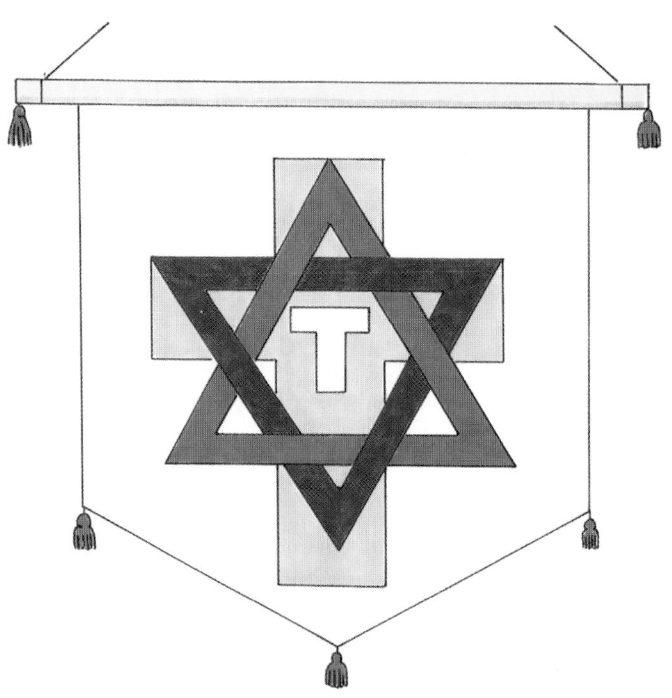

THE BANNER OF THE EAST

THE BANNER OF THE WEST

Refer to page 117.

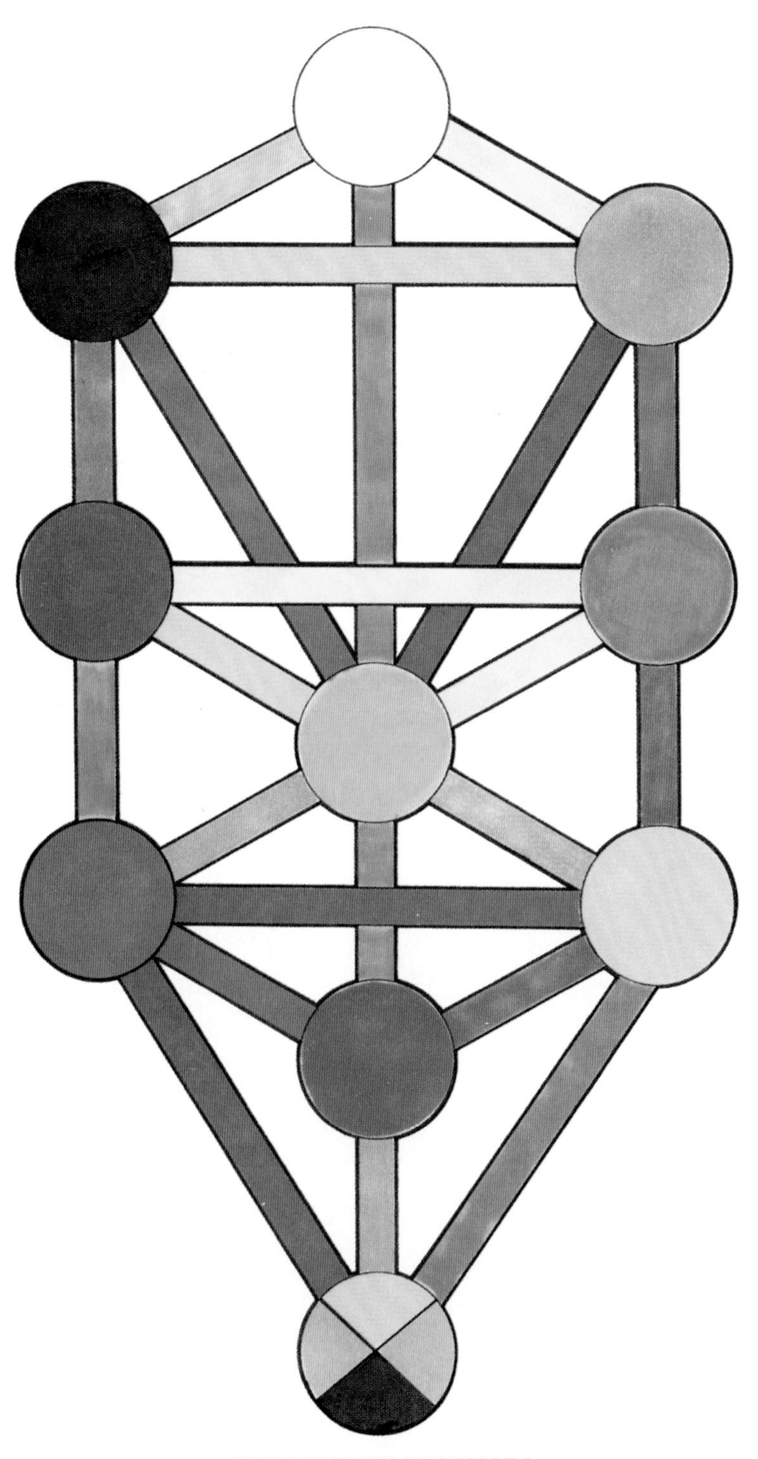

THE MINUTUM MUNDUM

Refer to page 95-98.

opening, to watch over the Censer and the Incense and to consecrate
<15> the Hall and the Fratres and Sorores and the Candidate with Fire.

Hiero Frater Stolistes, your station and duties?

Stol My station is in the North to symbolise Cold and Moisture, and my duties are to see that Robes and Collars and Insignia of the Officers are ready at the Opening, to watch over the Cup of Lustral Water and to purify the Hall and the Fratres and Sorores and the Candidate with Water.

Hiero Frater Kerux, your station and duties?

Kerux My place is within the portal. My duties are to see that the furniture of the Hall is properly arranged at the Opening, to guard the inner side of the portal, to admit the Fratres and Sorores, and to watch over the reception of the Candidate; to lead all Mystic Circumambulations carrying the Lamp of my Office, and to make all reports and announcements. My Lamp is the symbol of the Hidden Knowledge, and my Wand is the symbol of its directing power.

Hiero Honoured Hegemon, your station and duties?

Heg My station is between the Two Pillars of Hermes and Solomon and my face is towards the cubical Altar of the Universe. My duty is to watch over the Gate-way of the Hidden Knowledge for I am the reconciler between Light and Darkness. I watch over the preparation of the Candidate and assist in his reception and I lead him in the Path that conducts from Darkness to Light. The White Colour of my
<16> Robe is the colour of Purity, my ensign of office is a Mitre-headed sceptre to symbolise religion which guides and regulates life, and my Office symbolises those higher aspirations of the soul which should guide its action.

Hiero Honoured Hiereus, your station and duties?

Hiereus *(holds Sword and Banner)* My station is on the Throne of the West and is a symbol of increase of Darkness and decrease of Light and I am the Master of Darkness. I keep the Gateway of the West and watch over the reception of the Candidate and over the lesser officers in the doing of their work. My black Robe is an image of the Darkness that was upon the Face of the Waters. I carry the Sword of Judgment and the Banner of the Evening Twilight, which is the Banner of the West, and I am called Fortitude by the Unhappy.

Hierophant stands holding Sceptre and Banner of the East.

Hiero My station is on the Throne of the East in the place where the Sun rises, and I am the Master of the Hall, governing it according to the laws of the Order, as HE whose Image I am, is the Master of all who work for the Hidden Knowledge. My robe is red because of Uncreated Fire and Created Fire, and I hold the Banner of the Morning Light which is the Banner of the East. I am called Power and Mercy and Light and Abundance, and I am the Expounder of the Mysteries.

He sits down.

<17> Frater Stolistes and Frater Dadouchos, I command you to purify and consecrate the Hall with Water and with Fire.

Stolistes goes to the East, faces Hierophant, and making a cross in the Air with his Cup, sprinkles a few drops of Water three times towards the East. He passes to the South, West and North, repeating the purification in each quarter and returns to the East to complete the circle. He then holds the Cup on high and says.

Stol I purify with Water.

Dadouchos follows Stolistes when he goes to the East, and when Stolistes has gone to the South, Dadouchos faces East, raises his Censer and swings it thrice towards the East. He then goes to the South, West and North repeating the censing at each quarter and returns to the East where he completes the circle and raising the Censer says:

Dad I consecrate with Fire.

Stolistes and Dadouchos return to their places.

Hiero Let the Mystic Circumambulation take place in the Pathway of LIGHT.

Hierophant stands holding the Sceptre in his right hand, the Banner of the East in his left. Kerux goes to the North-East with Lamp and Wand. Then follow Hegemon, Hierus with Banner and Sword, Stolistes with Cup. Dadouchos with Censer and last, Sentinel with Sword. They all line up in this order behind the Kerux who leads the procession past Hierophant, making the Signs of Horus and Harpocrates as he passes. Each Officer in turn

<18> *does the same.*

Hierus falls out as soon as he reaches his Throne. Hegemon returns to his place after passing Hierophant twice. The other Officers pass Hierophant three times and then take their places as they come to them.

The Mystical Circumambulation symbolical of the Rise of LIGHT is accomplished. Let us adore the Lord of the Universe and Space.

Members rise. All face East and make the Saluting or the Enterer (Horus) Sign following the lead of Hierophant. The Sign of Silence is made at the end of the Prayer.

Holy art Thou, Lord of the Universe! *(Salute)*
Holy art Thou, Whom Nature hath not Formed! *(Salute)*
Holy art Thou, the Vast and the Mighty One! *(Salute)*
Lord of the Light and of the Darkness! *(Sign of Silence)*

Hierophant, Hierus and Hegemon raise Wands and Sword in salute, and sink them.

All face as usual but remain standing.

Frater Kerux, in the Name of the Lord of the Universe, I command you to declare that I have opened the Hall of the Neophytes.

Kerux goes North-East, faces West, and raising his Wand says:

Kerux In the Name of the Lord of the Universe, Who works in Silence and Whom naught but Silence can express, I declare that the Sun has arisen and the Shadows flee away.

<19> *Kerux returns to his place.*

Hierophant knocks. 1 Hiereus knocks. 1 Hegemon knocks. 1

Hiero (knocks and says:) KHABS.

Hiereus *(knocks)* AM.

Heg *(knocks)* PEKHT.

Hiereus *(knocks)* KONX.
Heg *(knocks)* OM.
Hiero *(knocks)* PAX.
Heg *(knocks)* LIGHT.
Hiero *(knocks)* IN.
Hiereus *(knocks)* EXTENSION.

The Knocks are given before the Words are said. When the battery is completed, all make the Signs towards the Altar and then sit down. Kerux removes the Rose, Cup, Paten of Bread and Salt and the Lamp from the Altar, leaving the Cross and Triangle only. He sees that a hassock is in readiness at the West for the Candidate to kneel on.

Hiero Fratres and Sorores of the .... Temple of the Order of the Stella Matutina, I have received a Dispensation from the Greatly Honoured Chiefs of the Second Order, to admit .... to the ⓪ = [0] Degree of Neophyte. Honoured Hegemon, bid the Candidate prepare for the Ceremony of his admission, and superintend his preparation.

Hegemon rises and removes his chair from between the Pillars and goes out followed by Sentinel, who carries the Hood-wink and Rope. Hegemon sees
<20> *that the Candidate is properly robed and hood-winked and that the Rope goes three times round his waist.*

He then leads Candidate to Door, and gives one knock.

Heg *(one knock on the door)*
Kerux *(one knock from within)* The Candidate seeks for entrance.
Hiero I give permission to admit .... who now loses his name and will henceforth be known among us as .... Let the Stolistes and the Dadouchos assist in the reception.

Stolistes and Dadouchos stand behind Kerux who is facing the entrance, ready to open the door. As soon as Candidate is well in the Hall, these three Officers stand before him in triangular formation, and Sentinel is behind him. The Officers then say their words in turn.

Heg Inheritor of a Dying World, arise and enter the Darkness.
Stol The Mother of Darkness hath blinded him with her Hair.
Dad The Father of Darkness hath hidden him under His Wings.
Hiero His limbs are still weary from the wars which were in Heaven.
Kerux Unpurified and Unconsecrated, thou canst not enter our Sacred Hall.

Stolistes comes forward and dipping his thumb in the lustral water, makes with it a Cross on the Candidate's brow and sprinkles him three times, saying:

Stol I purify thee with Water.
<21> *Dadouchos comes forward and makes a Cross over Candidate with his censer, and waving it three times, says:*

Dad I consecrate thee with Fire.
Hiero Conduct the Candidate to the foot of the Altar.
Inheritor of a Dying World, why seekest thou to enter our Sacred Hall? Why seekest thou admission to our Order?

Hegemon speaks for Candidate.

Heg My Soul wanders in Darkness and seeks the Light of the Hidden Knowledge, and I believe that in this Order Knowledge of that Light may be obtained.

Hiero We hold your signed pledge to keep secret everything that relates to this Order. I now ask you, are you willing to take a solemn Obligation in the presence of this Assembly, to keep the secrets and Mysteries of our Order inviolate?

Heg *(prompts Candidate to say)* I am.

Hiero There is nothing contrary to your civil, moral or religious duties in this Obligation. Although the Magical virtues can indeed awaken into momentary life in the wicked and foolish hearts, they cannot reign in any heart that has not the natural virtues to be their throne.

He Who is the Fountain of the Spirit of Man and of Things, came not to break, but to fulfill the Law. Are you ready to take this Oath.

Cand. *(prompted by Hegemon)* I am ready.

Hiero Then you will kneel on both your knees.

Hierophant comes to the East of the Altar with his Sceptre. Hegemon assists
<22> *Candidate to kneel, and stands right of Candidate. Hiereus stands to left.*
Kerux, Stolistes and Dadouchos complete the Hexagram of Officers as shown below.

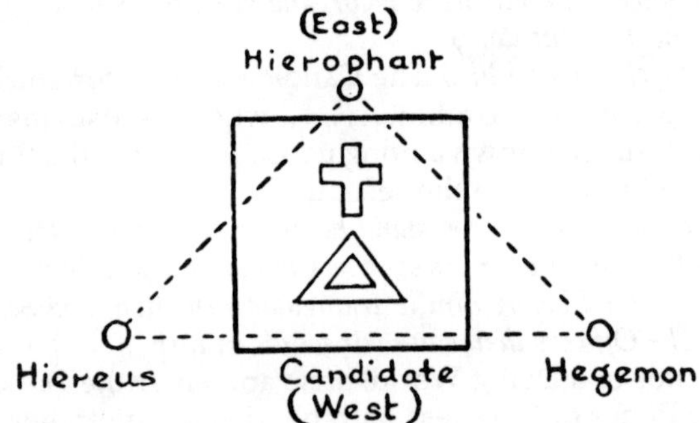

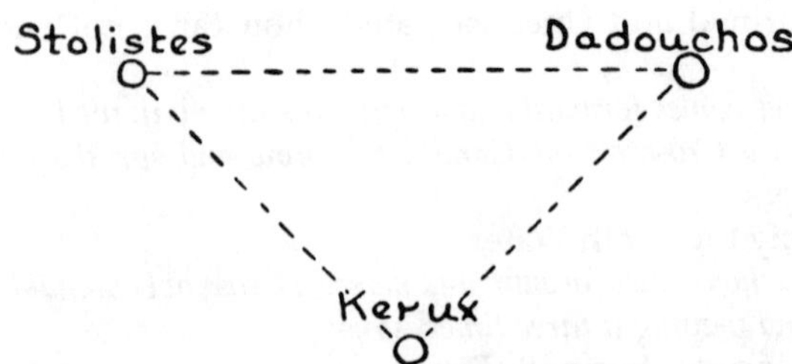

Hiero Give me your right hand which I place upon this Holy Symbol. Place your left hand in mine, bow your head, repeat your full name by which you are known on earth, and say after me:

I........ in the Presence of the LORD of the Universe, Who works in

Silence and Whom naught but Silence can express, and in this Hall of the Neophytes of the STELLA MATUTINA, regularly assembled under Warrant from the Greatly Honoured Chiefs of the Second Order, do, of my own freewill, hereby and hereon, most solemnly
<23> promise to keep secret this Order, its Name, the Names of its Members and the proceedings that take place at its meetings, from every person in the world who has not been initiated into it; nor will I discuss them with any Member who has not the Pass-word for the time being, or who has resigned, demitted or been expelled.
I undertake to maintain a kindly and benevolent relation with all the Fratres and Sorores of this Order.
I solemnly promise to keep secret any information I may have gathered concerning this Order before taking this Oath.
I solemnly promise that any Ritual or lecture placed in my care or any cover containing them, shall bear the official label of this Order.
I will neither copy nor allow to be copied, any manuscript, until I have obtained permission of the Second Order, lest our Secret Knowledge be revealed through my neglect.
I solemnly promise not to suffer myself to be placed in such a state of passivity, that any uninitiated person or power may cause me to lose control of my words or actions.
I solemnly promise to persevere with courage and determination in the labours of the Divine Science, even as I shall persevere with courage and determination through this Ceremony which is their Image — and I will not debase my mystical knowledge in the labour of Evil Magic at any time tried or under any temptation.
<24> I swear upon this Holy Symbol to observe all these things without evasion, equivocation, or mental reservation, under the penalty of being expelled from this Order for my perjury and my offence.
Furthermore, if I break this, my Magical Obligation, I submit myself, by my own consent, to a Stream of Power, set in motion by the Divine Guardians of this Order, Who live in the Light of their Perfect Justice, and before Whom my Soul now stands.

They journey as upon the Winds—
They strike where no man strikes—
They slay where no man slays—

and, as I bow my neck under the Sword of the Hiereus, so do I commit myself unto their Hands for vengeance or reward.

So help me my Mighty and Secret Soul, and the Father of my Soul Who works in Silence and Whom naught but Silence can express.

Hiereus, at the words "Bow my neck" places the flat of his Sword on the nape of Candidate's neck.

Rise, Neophyte, of the ⓪ = 0 Grade of the Order of the Stella Matutina.

Hierophant returns to his Throne.

Hiereus removes hassock and returns to his Throne.

Hegemon assists Candidate to rise.
The other Officers resume their seats.

Honoured Hegemon, you will now place the Neophyte in the Northern part of the Hall — the place of Forgetfulness, Dumbness
<25> and Necessity, and of the greatest symbolical Darkness.

Hegemon takes Candidate to the North and faces him East. Kerux goes with Lamp and Wand to the North East. Stolistes and Dadouchos stand ready to follow in the Procession.

Hiero The Voice of my Undying and Secret Soul said unto me—"Let me enter the Path of Darkness and, peradventure, there shall I find the Light. I am the only Being in an Abyss of Darkness; from an Abyss of Darkness came I forth ere my birth, from the Silence of a Primal Sleep.

And the Voice of Ages answered to my Soul—'I am He who formulates in Darkness—the Light that shineth in Darkness, yet the Darkness comprehendeth it not.' "

Let the Mystical Circumambulation take place in the Path of Knowledge that leadeth unto Light, with the Lamp of Hidden Knowledge to guide us.

Kerux leads forward, followed by Hegemon with Candidate—Stolistes and Dadouchos coming last. As they pass Hierophant gives one knock, just as Candidate passes. They pass on by South and West and passing Hiereus he also gives one knock as Candidate passes. They pass on by the North and on passing East again Hierophant gives one knock as Candidate passes. Kerux stops in the South after the second passing of Hierophant and barring the way with his Wand, says:

Kerux Unpurified and Unconsecrated, thou canst not enter the path of the West!

<26> *Stolistes comes forward and dipping his thumb in Water, makes a Cross on Candidate's brow, sprinkles three times and says:*

Stol I purify thee with Water.

Dadouchos comes forward, censes in the form of a cross, and waves incense three times, and says:

Dad I consecrate thee with Fire.

Stolistes and Dadouchos then step back to their places in the procession.

Heg Child of Earth, twice purified and twice consecrated, thou mayest approach the Gate-way of the West.

Kerux leads the Procession to Throne of Hiereus. Hegemon raises the hoodwink for a moment. Hiereus stands threatening with his sword.

Hiereus Thou canst not pass by me, saith the Guardian of the West, unless thou canst tell me my name.

Heg Darkness is thy Name, thou Great One of the Paths of the Shades.

Hiereus Thou hast known me now, so pass thou on. Fear is failure so be thou without fear. For he who trembles at the Flame and at the Flood and at the Shadows of the Air, hath no part in God.

Kerux leads on. They pass Hierophant who gives one knock. Hiereus gives one knock as they pass. After this passing, Kerux halts in the North, and raises his Wand.

Kerux Unpurified and unconsecrated, thou canst not enter the Path of the East!

Stol I purify thee with Water. *Cross and sprinkling as before)*

<27> *Dad* I consecrate thee with Fire. *(Cross and censing as before)*

Heg Child of Earth, thrice purified and thrice Consecrated, thou mayest approach the Gate-way of the East!

Kerux leads the procession forward to Hierophant who stands threatening with his Sceptre. The Hood-wink is again raised for a moment.

Hiero Thou canst not pass by me, saith the Guardian of the East, unless thou canst tell me my Name.

Heg Light dawning in Darkness is thy Name, the Light of a Golden Day!

Hiero Unbalanced Power is the ebbing away of Life.
Unbalanced Mercy is weakness and the fading out of the Will.
Unbalanced Severity is cruelty and the barrenness of Mind.
Thou hast known me now, so pass thou on to the Cubical Altar of the Universe.

The Hood-wink is replaced.

Kerux leads the Procession to the Altar. Candidate is placed exactly West of the Altar — Hegemon on his right — Hiereus on his left; Kerux, Stolistes and Dadouchos at the rear form a supporting triangle. Hierophant, holding Sceptre in his right hand and the Banner of the East in his left, advances between the pillars and comes to the East of the Altar, saying:

I come in the Power of the Light.
I come in the Light of Wisdom.
I come in the Mercy of the Light.
The Light hath Healing in its Wings.

<28> *The Officers now form a Hexagram round the Altar. Hiereus holds his Sword in his right hand, the Banner of the West in his left. All the Officers except Hierophant kneel down. Candidate is assisted to kneel. Hierophant stands, raising his hands, holding Sceptre and Banner for the Invocation as follows.*

Lord of the Universe — the Vast and the Mighty One!
Ruler of the Light and of the Darkness!
We adore Thee and We invoke Thee!
Look with favour on this Neophyte who now kneeleth before Thee.
And grant Thine aid unto the higher aspirations of his Soul,
So that he may prove a true and faithful Frater Neophyte among us.
To the glory of Thine Ineffable Name. Amen!

All rise, Candidate is assisted to rise and is brought close to the Altar. Hierophant, Hiereus, and Hegemon raise their Wands and Sword to touch each other over the head of Candidate. Kerux, at the word "Darkness" removes the hood-wink.

Heg Inheritor of a Dying World, we call thee to the Living Beauty.

Hiereus Wanderer in the Wild Darkness, we call thee to the Gentle Light. *(Hood-wink removed)*

Hiero Long hast thou dwelt in Darkness —
Quit the Night and seek the Day.

Heg
Hiereus } *(together)* We receive thee into the Order of the Stella Matutina.
Hiero

<29> *Hiero* KHABS.

Hiereus *AM.*

Heg PEKHT.

Hiereus KONX.

Heg OM.

Hiero PAX.

Heg LIGHT.

Hiero IN.

Hiereus EXTENSION.

The Officers take down their Sceptres and Sword. Kerux moves to North East of the Altar and raises his Lamp. Hierophant points to the Lamp to direct Candidate's attention.

Hiero In all thy wandering in Darkness, the Lamp of the Kerux went before thee, though it was not seen by thine eyes. It is the Symbol of the Light of the Hidden Knowledge.

The Officers return to their places, Hierophant to his Throne. Hegemon and Candidate remain West of the Altar.

Let the Neophyte be led to the East of the Altar.

Hegemon places him to the East, near but not between the Pillars, and then takes his place outside the White Pillar.

Honoured Hiereus, give the Neophyte the Secret Signs, Token and Words, together with the present pass-word of the ⓪ = 0 Grade of the Stella Matutina.

Place him between the Mystical Pillars and superintend his fourth and final Consecration.

Hiereus passes by the North to the Black Pillar. He comes round to the East.
<30> *Hegemon advances to meet him and take from him his Sword and Banner. Hiereus steps between the Pillars, and facing Candidate, says:*

Hiereus Frater ...., I shall now proceed to instruct you in the secret Step, Signs, Grip and Words of this Grade.

Firstly, advance your left foot a short space, as if entering a portal. This is the Step.

The Signs are two. The First or Saluting Sign is given thus: Lean forward and stretch both arms out thus: *(make Neophyte do this)*. It alludes to your condition in a state of Darkness, groping for Light.

The second Sign is the Sign of Silence, and is given by placing the left fore-finger on your lip thus *(makes Neophyte do it)*. It is the position shown in many ancient statues of Harpocrates, and it alludes to the strict silence you have sworn to maintain concerning everything connected with this Order. The first sign is always answered by the second.

The Grip or Token is given thus: Advance your left foot touching mine, toe and heel, extend your right hand to grasp mine, fail, try again, and then succeed in touching the fingers only. It alludes to the seeking guidance in Darkness.

The Grand Word is Har-Par-Krat, and it is whispered in this position mouth to ear, in syllables. *(They exchange the Word)* It is the Egyptian Name for the God of Silence, and should always remind you of the strict silence you have sworn to maintain.

<31> The Pass-Word is .... It is periodically changed each Equinox, so that a Member who has resigned, demitted or been expelled, may be in ignorance of the existing Pass-Word.

I now place you between the two Pillars of Hermes and of Solomon in the symbolical Gateway of Occult Wisdom.

Hiereus leads Neophyte forward and then takes back the Sword and Banner as Hegemon hands them to him. He stands North East of the Black Pillar and says:

Let the final Consecration take place.

Stolistes and Dadouchos come forward and purify and consecrate the Hall as in the Opening, but on returning to the East, Stolistes turns round to Neophyte, makes a cross of Water on his brow, sprinkles three times, and says:

Stol I purify thee with Water.

Dadouchos likewise turns round from the East and says after making a cross and censing three times:

Dad I consecrate thee with Fire. *(They return to their places)*

Hiero Honoured Hegemon, I command you to remove the Rope, last remaining symbol of the Path of Darkness, and to invest our Frater with the Badge of this degree.

Hegemon comes forward and hands his Sceptre and Ritual to Hiereus. He removes the Rope and puts on the Sash over the left shoulder.

<32> *Heg* By command of the Very Honoured Hierophant, I invest you with the Badge of this degree. It symbolises Light dawning in Darkness.

Takes Sceptre, etc. and returns to White Pillar.

Hiero Let the Mystical Circumambulation take place in the Path-way of Light.

Kerux goes to the North East. Hegemon takes Candidate behind Black Pillar, and stands behind Kerux. Hiereus comes next, followed by Stolistes and Dadouchos. Kerux leads off, all salute on passing Hierophant who stands holding Sceptre and Banner as in the Opening. Hiereus drops out on reaching his Throne. Hegemon returns to between the Pillars after passing Hierophant twice. He directs Neophyte to follow Kerux, who with the other Officers passes Hierophant thrice. After the third passing, Hierophant says:

Take your place North West of the Stolistes.

Kerux indicates this and goes on followed by Stolistes who falls out in the North and returns to his place.

Hegemon replaces his chair between the Pillars and sits down. Kerux replaces the Rose, Lamp, Cup and Paten in their proper places on the Altar.

All are seated.

The Three Fold Cord bound about your waist, was an image of the three-fold bondage of Mortality, which amongst the Initiated is called earthly or material inclination, that has bound into a narrow
<33> place the once far-wandering Soul; and the Hood-wink was an image of the Darkness, of Ignorance, or Mortality that has blinded men to the Happiness and Beauty their eyes once looked upon.

The Double Cubical Altar in the centre of the Hall, is an emblem of visible Nature or the Material Universe, concealing within herself the mysteries of all dimensions, while revealing her surface to the exterior senses. It is a double cube because, as the Emerald Tablet has said "The things that are below are a reflection of the things that are above." The world of men and women created to unhappiness is a reflection of the World of Divine Beings created to Happiness. It is described in the SEPHER YETSIRAH, or The Book of Formation, as "An Abyss of Height" and as an "Abyss of Depth", "An Abyss of the East" and "An Abyss of the West", "An Abyss of the North" and "An Abyss of the South." The Altar is black because, unlike Divine Beings who unfold in the Element of Light, the Fires of Created Beings arise from Darkness and Obscurity.

On the Altar is a White Triangle to be the Image of that Immortal Light, that Triune Light, which moved in Darkness and formed the World of Darkness and out of Darkness. There are two contending Forces and One always uniting them. And these Three have their Image in the three-fold Flame of our Being and in the three-fold wave of the sensual world.

<34> *Hierophant stands in the form of Cross, saying:*

Glory be to Thee, Father of the Undying. For Thy Glory flows out rejoicing, to the ends of the Earth!

He reseats himself.

The Red Cross above the White Triangle, is an Image of Him Who was unfolded in the Light. At its East, South, West and North Angles are a Rose, Fire, Cup of Wine and Bread and Salt. These allude to the Four Elements, Air, Fire, Water, Earth.

The Mystical Words — Khabs Am Pekht — are ancient Egyptian, and are the origin of the Greek "Konx Om Pax" which was uttered at the Eleusinian Mysteries. A literal translation would be "Light Rushing Out in One Ray" and they signify the same form of Light as that symbolised by the Staff of the Kerux.

East of the Double Cubical Altar, of created things, are the Pillars of Hermes and of Solomon. On these are painted certain Hieroglyphics from the 17th and the 125th Chapters of the *Book of the Dead.* They are the symbols of the two powers of Day and Night, Love and Hate, Work and Rest, the subtle force of the Lodestone and the Eternal out-pouring and in-pouring of the Heart of God.

The Lamps that burn, though with a veiled light, upon their summits show that the Pathway to Hidden Knowledge, unlike the Pathway of
<35> Nature — which is a continual undulation, the winding hither and

thither of the Serpent — is the straight and narrow way between them.

It was because of this that I passed between them, when you came to the Light, and it was because of this that you were placed between them to receive the Final Consecration.

Two contending Forces and one which unites them eternally. Two basal angles of the triangle and one which forms the apex. Such is the origin of Creation — it is the Triad of Life.

My Throne at the Gate of the East is the Place of the Guardian of the Dawning Sun.

The Throne of the Hiereus at the Gate of the West is the Place of the Guardian against the Multitudes that sleep through the Light and awaken at the Twilight.

The Throne of the Hegemon seated between the Columns is the Place of Balanced Power, between the Ultimate Light and the Ultimate Darkness. These meanings are shown in detail and by the colour of our robes.

The Wand of the Kerux is the Beam of Light from the Hidden Wisdom, and his Lamp is an emblem of the Ever-burning Lamp of the Guardian of the Mysteries.

The Seat of the Stolistes at the Gate of the North is the Place of the Guardian of the Cauldron and the Well of Water — of Cold and Moisture. The Seat of the Dadouchos at the Gate of the South is the Place of the Guardian of the Lake of Fire and the Burning Bush.

<36> Frater Kerux, I command you to declare that the Neophyte has been initiated into the Mysteries of the ⓪ = [0] Grade.

Kerux advances to the North East, faces West, raises his Wand, and says:

Kerux In the Name of the Lord of the Universe, Who works in Silence and Whom naught but Silence can express, and by command of the Very Honoured Hierophant, hear ye all, that I proclaim that .... who will henceforth be known to you by the Motto ...., has been duly admitted to the ⓪ = [0] Grade as a Neophyte of the Order of the Stella Matutina.

Kerux returns to his Place.

Hiero Honoured Hiereus, I delegate to you the duty of pronouncing a short address to our Frater on his admission.

Hiereus Frater ...., it is my duty to deliver this exhortation to you. Remember your Obligation in this Order to secrecy — for Strength is in Silence, and the Seed of Wisdom is sown in Silence and grows in Darkness and Mystery.

Remember that you hold all Religions in reverence, for there is none but contains a Ray from the Ineffable Light that you are seeking. Remember the penalty that awaits the breaker of his Oath. Remember the Mystery that you have received, and that the Secret of Wisdom can be discerned only from the place of Balanced Powers.

Study well the Great Arcanum of the proper equilibrium of Severity
<37> and Mercy, for either unbalanced is not good. Unbalanced Severity
is cruelty and oppression; unbalanced Mercy is but weakness and

would permit Evil to exist unchecked, thus making itself, as it were, the accomplice of that Evil.

Remember that things Divine are not attained by mortals who understand the Body alone, for only those who are lightly armed can attain the summit.

Remember that God alone is our Light and the Bestower of Perfect Wisdom, and that no mortal power can do more than bring you to the Pathway of that Wisdom, which he could, if it so pleased him, put into the heart of a child. For as the whole is greater than the part, so are we but Sparks from the unsupportable Light which is in Him.

The ends of the Earth are swept by the Borders of His Garment of Flame — from Him all things proceed, and unto Him all things return.

Therefore, we invoke Him. Therefore even the Banner of the East falls in adoration before Him.

Hiero Before you can ask to pass to a higher Grade, you will have to commit certain rudiments of Occult Knowledge to memory. A manuscript lecture in these subjects will be supplied you by the Chief in whose charge they are. When you can pass an examination in this elementary Qabalistic knowledge, you will inform the Member in whose charge you are, and arrangements will be made for you to sit for examination. If you are found perfect you will then apply for
<38> admission to the next Degree. Remember, that without a Dispensation from the Second Order, no person can be admitted or advanced to a Grade of the First Order.

Kerux conducts Neophyte to his table and gives him one of the small dishes of solution to hold.

Kerux Nature is harmonious in all her workings, and that which is above is as that which is below. Thus also, the Truths which by material Science we investigate, are but special examples of the all-pervading Laws of the Universe. So, within this pure and limpid fluid, lie hidden and unperceived of mortal eyes, the elements bearing the semblance of blood, even as within the mind and brain of the Initiate lie concealed the Divine Secrets of the Hidden Knolwedge. Yet if the Oath be forgotten, and the solemn pledge broken, then that which is secret shall be revealed, even as this pure fluid reveals the semblance of blood.

Kerux adds fluid from the other dish.

Let this remind thee ever, O Neophyte, how easily by a careless or unthinking word, thou mayst betray that which thou hast sworn to keep secret and mayst reveal the Hidden Knowledge imparted to thee, and planted in thy brain and in thy mind. And let the hue of blood remind thee that if thou shalt fail in this thy oath of secrecy, thy blood may be poured out and thy body broken; for heavy is the penalty exacted by the Guardians of the Hidden Knowledge from those who wilfully betray their trust.

<39> *Hierophant comes to the table. The Register is signed.*

Hiero Resume your seat, and remember that your admission to this Order does not give you the right to initiate any other person without a Dispensation from the Greatly Honoured Chiefs of the Second Order.

Kerux directs Neophyte to his seat.

Hierophant returns to the dais.

CLOSING OF THE NEOPHYTE GRADE

Hiero *(gives knock* ו*)*

Kerux goes to the North East, faces West, and raising Lamp and Wand, says:

Kerux HEKAS! HEKAS! ESTE BEBELOI!

He returns to his place.

Hiero Fratres and Sorores of the . . . . . . Temple of the Order of the Stella Matutina, assist me to close the Hall of the Neophytes.

All rise. Neophyte is directed to rise by Stolistes.

Hiereus *(knocks)* ו

Heg *(knocks)* ו

Kerux *(knocks)* ו

Sentinel *(knocks)* ו

Hiero Frater Kerux, see that the Hall is properly guarded.

Kerux The Hall is properly guarded, Very Honoured Hierophant.

Hiero Honoured Hiereus, assure yourself that all present have beheld the Stella Matutina.

<40> *Hiereus* Fratres and Sorores, give the signs. *(done)* Very Honoured Hierophant, all present have been so honoured.

Hiero Let the Hall be purified by Water and by Fire.

Stol I purify with Water. *(Purifying as in the Opening)*

Dad I consecrate with Fire. *(Consecrating as in the Opening)*

Hiero Let the Mystical Reverse Circumambulation take place in the Pathway of Light.

Kerux goes by the South to the South East.

Hegemon goes to the North and leads the new Neophyte by West and South, directing him to follow Hegemon in the Procession.

Hiereus follows Neophyte and Stolistes follows Hiereus, accompanied or followed by Dadouchos, and Sentinel ends the Procession. As they pass the Hierophant, who is standing and holding the Banner of the East in his left hand, the Sceptre in his right, they make the Neophyte Signs. Hiereus drops out when his Throne is reached. Hegemon passes Hierophant twice and then takes his place between the Pillars, directing Neophyte to follow Kerux who, after the third passing of Hierophant, directs Neophyte to his seat, the other Officers dropping out as their places are reached.

The Mystical Circumambulation is accomplished. It is the symbol of Fading Light. Let us adore the Lord of the Universe.

All turn East. Stolistes directs Neophyte to rise and face East. Hierophant
<41> *faces East, making the salute at each adoration — the others, Officers and Members repeating it also.*

Holy art Thou, Lord of the Universe! *(salute)*

Holy art Thou, Whom nature hath not formed! *(salute)*
Holy art Thou, the Vast and the Mighty One! *(salute)*
Lord of the Light and of the Darkness! *(Sign of Silence)*
Nothing now remains but to partake together in silence, of the Mystic Repast, composed of the symbols of the Four Elements, and to remember our pledge of secrecy.

All are seated.

Hierophant puts down his Sceptre and returns the Banner of the East to its place. He goes to the West of the Altar and facing East gives the Saluting Sign but not the Sign of Silence, and taking up the Rose says:

I invite you to inhale with me the perfume of this Rose, as a symbol of Air. *(smells Rose)*

To feel with me the warmth of this sacred Fire. *(spreads his hands over it)*

To eat with me this Bread and Salt as types of Earth. *(dips bread in Salt and eats)*

And finally to drink with me this Wine, the consecrated emblem of Elemental Water. *(makes a Cross with the Cup and drinks)*

Hierophant puts down the Cup between the Cross and Triangle. He comes East of the Altar and faces West.

<42> *The Praemonstrator then comes to the West of the Altar and makes the Saluting Sign. Hierophant replies with the Sign of Silence and then hands the Elements, beginning with the Rose which Praemonstrator smells and returns; then feels the warmth of the Lamp, eats the Bread and Salt and receives from the Hierophant the Cup with which he makes a Cross, and having drunk, returns it. Hierophant then passes by West and South to his Throne. Praemonstrator then comes to the East of the Altar. Imperator comes to the West, exchanges Signs and partakes. He returns to his place — after serving Cancellarius who in turn serves Past Hierophant. After the Chiefs, the Officers partake in this order: Hiereus, Hegemon, Stolistes, Dadouchos. Whan all the Officers except Kerux have partaken, the Inner Members in order of seniority of admission, partake but do not wait for instruction in this. If there is a pause, one comes forward. Next come the Members of the Outer in the same manner — the Neophytes coming last piloted by Hegemon or any Officer appointed. The Order of procedure for Outer members is: Philosophi, Practici, Theorici, Zelatores, Neophytes. When the last Neophyte stands East of the Altar, Kerux comes to the West, exchanges the Signs and partakes. (Hegemon directs Neophyte to return to his place as soon as Kerux takes the Cup.) Kerux, on receiving the Cup, drains it, inverts it, and says:*

Kerux It is finished!

<43> *Kerux replaces the Cup and returns to his place.*

All rise.

Hiero *(knocks)* ו TETELESTAI!

Hiereus *(knocks)* ו

Heg *(knocks)* ו

Hiero *(knocks)* Khabs. *Hiereus (knocks)* Am. *Heg (knocks)* Pekht.

Hiereus *(knocks)* Konx. *Heg (knocks)* Om. *Hierophant (knocks)* Pax.

Heg *(knocks)* Light *Hiero (knocks)* In *Hiereus (knocks)* Extension.
All make the Signs towards the Altar.

Hiero May what we have partaken maintain us in our search for the QUINTESSENCE, the Stone of the Philosophers. True Wisdom, Perfect Happiness, the SUMMUM BONUM.
Officers remain in the Temple while the new Neophyte is led out by Kerux.

(Note: Full instructions as to the magical work performed by the officers during the ceremony are given in documents Z.[1] and Z.[3]. These latter will be found in Volume III of this work. I. R.)

The Neophyte Signs

Signs of Elemental Grades

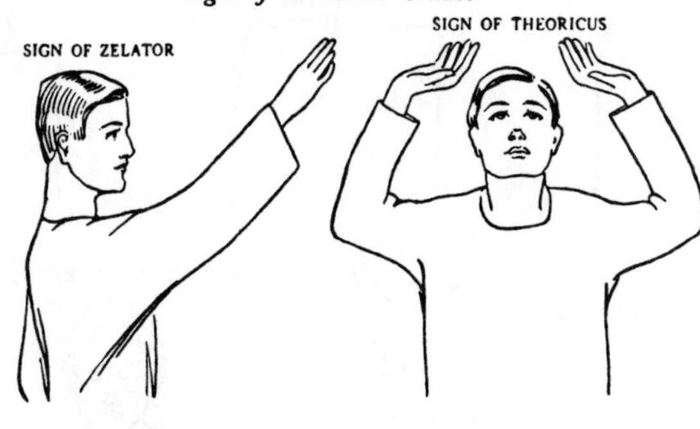

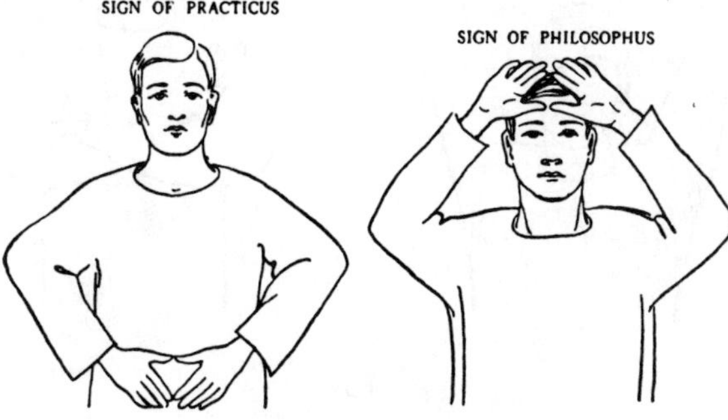

The Portal Signs

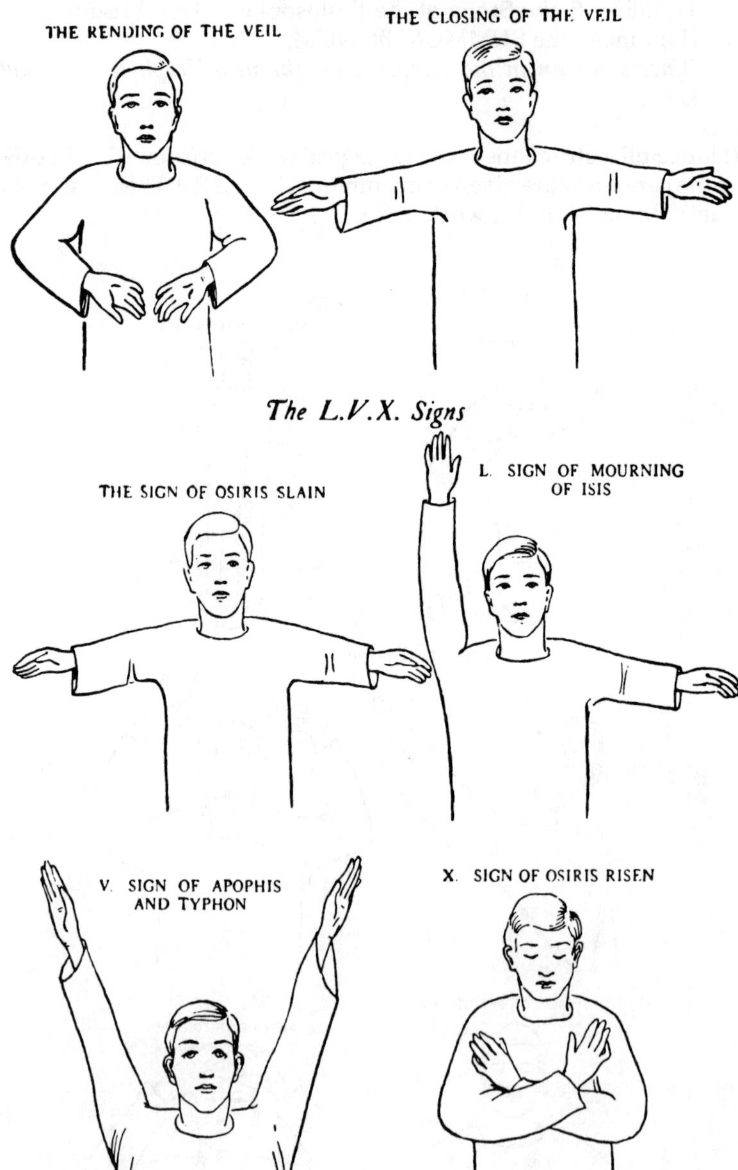

INTRODUCTION TO THE ELEMENTAL GRADE CEREMONIES

The initiation ceremonies of the Zelator, Theoricus, Practicus and Philosophus grades are each referred to one of the four elements of Tetragrammaton—YHVH—beginning with the last, Earth, Air, Water and Fire respectively. As a whole these grades represent the fundamental work of the Outer Order which is to equilibrate the elemental forces in the working temple and in the psyches of individuals, whether participating as officers or as aspiring candidates for advancement.

These ceremonies will be referred to here generally as the Grade Ceremonies for the purpose of providing an overall description of the ritual patterns repeated and expounded in progression thru the Outer Order. To provide ceremonies which can be read and performed from the text, lengthy explanations concerning the many details of performance are not practical. At the same time, familiarity with the essential formula and basic understanding prior to attempting the ceremonies will effect a smooth flow of ritual work enhancing effectiveness. This also makes it easier for participants to become aware of specific relationships and symbolism described by precise ritual activity within the basic framework of the Grade Ceremonies.

Study of the pattern common to all four would also aid in memorization of the ceremonies. Performance of any magickal working from memory is a realizable ideal worth some time and effort as the subtleties of the energies at work are more easily perceived when the mind is free from chores like finding the right page, reading instructions or wondering why you're standing and everyone else is sitting. The further participants can get from ordinary day to day consciousness the more receptive they can become to the extraordinary influences which are only available to the intuitiveless intellectual faculties.

Much can be understood only by experience as an initiate, then as different officers, and in the steeping of students in the study and practice of the Grade Ceremonies, individually and/or collectively, over a period of time. Don't be discouraged by errors during ceremony — They are sure to occur. To let imperfection stop the aspiring student would end the spiritual journey at the very first step which recognizes and accepts human ignorance and error.

As the dedicated student continues to patiently aspire to be more than human, to transcend physical limitations, while forgiving himself for mistakes and setbacks along the way, the ceremonies will become increasingly precise and effective. Regular repetition awakens and establishes the energies gradually through sincere sustained effort. When a mistake is made during ritual work, simply return to the point immediately preceding the error with as little disruption as possible and carefully repeat from there after making certain of the correct procedure. Hopefully, no matter how elevated by study and initiation the student's understanding may become, he will discover that the Grade Ceremonies are not to be learned, performed, perfected and left behind; the potential for insight is endless, with levels upon levels of meaning and symbol never exhausted, always new.

Initiation into the Elemental Grades is a starting point from which students may begin to comprehend the wholeness of the Outer Order. By the synthesis of the four elements, in relation to the Hall of the Neophytes and as a preparation for Inner Order Initiation and work, continuous integration will dynamically balance the forces in the entire being.

The Openings and Closings of each grade follow a similar format which is relatively easy to follow and brief to carry out. There are a few points of etiquette appropriate to anyone involved whether in a group or alone, as an officer or observer, which add significance to the ceremony and emphasize the special existence of the spiritual temple wherever it is located.

The intention behind special names, clothing, movement — i.e. everything concerning ritual work — is to produce a state of mind quite different from the ordinary non-ritual state. These special signals, in association with all that is done in performing the ceremonies, cultivate a "habit" which will trigger participants to assume this state of mind spontaneously in preparation for magickal work. Students can, with a little imagination, find numerous ways of consciously producing mental receptivity to the intended work. One could begin by quieting the mind with rhythmic breathing and meditation on an appropriate image; for example, a great preparation for a Grade Ceremony would be to contemplate the appropriate symbolism as in the Meditation given in each Grade's Knowledge Lecture.* Groups or individuals may decide upon a special rite of entry into the temple signaling commencement of ceremonial behavior when all is ready to begin.

A quiet, though not somber, mood should be encouraged, limiting extraneous speech, movement and noise. Make doubly sure all is arranged and supplies available as needed before starting to avoid last minute shuffling. Lock doors, draw curtains, take the phone off the hook and in general insure as much as possible that there will be no rude or embarrassing interruptions. Discretion in magickal activities, as is advised in the ⓪ = 0 Initiation so emphatically, is as important to the unseen workings and effectiveness of ceremony as the secrecy of the visible, physical location of the temple is to the protection from unwanted observation, eavesdropping, or even deliberate interference.

In any temple of the Outer Order, the Sign of the Enterer or Projecting Sign is given toward the East upon entering and the Sign of Silence given when leaving. These Signs, special to the ⓪ = 0 Grades of Neophyte are used in the Elemental Ceremonies in a specific way, as the interpenetration of the ⓪ = 0 which encompasses the whole, is followed through the Outer Order. These Signs are not given for grade identification in the Elemental Ceremonies but as signals to indicate the beginning and ending of individual events, usually by an officer. Non-officiating members move very little or not at all in the temple but when necessary movement is always clockwise and the Projecting Sign is given in that direction when passing the East. Upon returning to seat or station the Sign of Silence is given signifying completion of that activity. Officers give the Sign of the Enterer toward the Hierophant before beginning any movement, before addressing the Hierophant and in

*Vol. I Book I, page 99.

response to the Hierophant's commands or directives. This is done by rising in place (without holding instruments) facing the East and giving the Sign. Then the officer may take up instrument, speak or move as needed. Upon completion of speech or action the Sign of Silence is given before the next activity begins. Opening the Activity with Projection of energy from the Officer's Station toward the East, carrying out the duty, then Closing with the Sign of Silence to end the energy flow which the Projecting Sign begins creates a precision in the ritual work, and helps define individual duties of officers and parts of ceremony.

THE BASIC STRUCTURE OF THE GRADE CEREMONIES

Opening

1. The Hierophant knocks once to signal the onset of the Ceremony when the temple is ready: members robed, seated and quiet; lamps, candles, incense lit; officers at stations wearing appropriate lamens, nemysses, mantles; with copies of the ritual if needed. The Hiero. tells the officers to assist in Opening the Grade and directs either the Kerux (in ① = [2] and ② = [9]) or the Hegemon (in ③ = [8] and ④ = [7]) to check the temple door. This is done without opening the temple door because the office of Sentinel, open to the members of the Neophyte Grade, is dropped from all grades after ⓪ = [0]

2. The Hierophant tells Hiereus to see that all present are members of that Grade. Hiereus rises, giving Sign of Enterer. Then holding his Sword upright, Hiereus asks the members to give the Sign of the grade, which all members (except the Hiereus and Hierophant) give toward the Altar. Hiereus puts down Sword and gives the Grade Sign after the other members before assuring the Hiero. that all present are members of the Grade, and then gives the Sign of Silence to signal completion of his duty. The Hiero. then gives the Grade Sign towards the Altar, alone.

3. The Stolistes and Dadouchos, stations and offices open to Zelators (members of the ① = [10] grade), purify and consecrate the temple Opening of the ① = [10] grade. These officers and their functions are dropped from the remaining higher grade rituals, as the Sentinel is from the ① = [10]. The office of Kerux is omitted likewise from the ③ = [8] grade of Practicus, as the station apropos to ② = [9]. The Ceremonies of ③ = [8] and ④ = [7] are performed with the Chief Officers only.

4. The Hiereus and/or Hegemon name the Element and any Planet, Path(s) and Spheres associated with Path(s) at Hierophant's request. Officers are seated at this time and the short responses by Heg. and/or Hier. are given from their stations without rising, giving ⓪ = [0] Signs.

5. The Hierophant knocks once and stands to announce the Adoration to the East. All members stand, face East, and give the Sign of the Grade, remaining in that position for the duration of the Hierophant's prayer. After "Amen!" all release Grade Sign and remain standing quietly, facing East.

6. The Hierophant now goes to the quarter of the temple appropriate to the Grade, and faces the Enochian Tablet in that direction. The officers follow, and stand in balanced arrangement behind him, forming a Hexagram, facing as the Hierophant. The Tablet should be positioned and centered in that

direction, if possible, with the center of the tablet at eye level. A symbol of the Element of the grade is before the Tablet on a small table or side altar. The Hierophant hands Sceptre to officer on his right, takes up the symbol, gestures with it three times towards the Tablet: left, right, then center, and proclaims the invokation of the element by the Divine God Name given to the Sephirah of the Grade. Replacing the symbol before the Tablet, the Hierophant takes his Sceptre again in order to trace the invoking figure.

The invokation is performed by tracing certain figures in the air in front of and concentric to the Enochian Tablet. With the Sceptre the Hierophant first traces the Circle which will contain the Invoking Pentagrams and confine the invoked force of the Element to the quarter. This Invoking Circle is traced in a clockwise direction beginning at the left, or North, as if the top of the Circle represented the East. The Circle is visualized in brilliant white light and is traced from the North edge past the top, completing one full rotation at the top, or East. This principle of invoking energy is represented in the Opening of the ⓪= [0] by the Mystical Circumambulation which also begins in the North led by the Kerux, and describes one complete round on the return to the East. Both Circles symbolize the Rising of Light which precedes invokation, and provides the container where the invoked forces are concentrated and focused in the formula of the Magic of Light. The Circle is traced silently, then the Hiero. lowers the Sceptre to the position where the Invoking Pentagram of Spirit will begin. Whether the Spirit invoked is active or passive depends upon the nature of the Element to be invoked. (A description of both the Active and Passive Spirit Pentagrams and how to trace them is given in a later chapter — see page 9, Volume III.) The Spirit Pentagram, active or passive, is visualized in white light, within the Circle already traced, and is "charged" by thrusting the Sceptre toward the center, visualizing the figure glowing strongly in the astral light, the brilliance of the Pentagram flaring brightly at the force of the Hiero.'s projection.

The Hierophant then begins the Invoking Pentagram of the Element, following the Circle around with Sceptre from the angle where the Spirit Pentagram ended to the angle where the Pentagram of the Element begins (see page 13, Volume III for specific instructions on invoking the Elements by Pentagram). The Pentagram of the Element is visualized in the color of that element as described in the lecture on the Supreme Ritual of the Pentagram and "charged" in the same manner as the Pentagram of Spirit. Both Invoking Pentagrams are traced in silence.

Vibrating forcefully, using a full breath, the Hierophant invokes by the Divine Names and Images of the Grade, with Sceptre raised toward the direction of invokation.

Again handing his Sceptre to the officer on his right, the hiero. takes up the symbol in front of the Tablet and with it traces the Kerubic Sign of the element in the center of the Pentagram already traced, "charging" the Sign as before. Then, vibrating fully, he invokes in the names of the Archangel, in the three Great Secret Names of God, and in that of the King of the Tablet. The Hiero. replaces the symbol, takes his Sceptre, and all officers return to their stations. The non-officiating members who have been standing, facing the direction of invokation throughout, are also seated as before.

7. In the name of the Divine Name or Grand Word of the Grade, the Hierophant declares the temple open in the particular grade.
8. Hierophant, Hiereus, and Hegemon, in that order, give the Knocks of the Grade in succession, each completing the alarm before the next begins. Thus the opening of the Grade Ceremony is completed.

Initiation into the Elemental Grades
1. Hierophant announces dispensation to advance the candidate for the grade. Hegemon rises and salutes Hierophant with the Sign of the Enterer or Projecting Sign, answering the command to prepare the candidate. If the Hegemon passes the East on the way to the door, moving always clockwise around the temple, the Projecting Sign of the Enterer is given as in ⓪ = [0] circumambulation. The Sign of Silence is given toward the East before leaving the temple to prepare the candidate, who is always hoodwinked at first part of the ceremony of advancement. The Hegemon gives the candidate an admission badge to hold in the right hand and gives the knocks of the grade, called 'the alarm', when ready to enter.
2. The candidate is tested in the Token, Step, Grand Word, Mystic Number, and Mystic Password of his present grade.
3. The candidate pledges secrecy concerning the mysteries of this grade, going to the Quarter appropriate to the grade and making the pledge there toward the Tablet. The hoodwink is then removed.
4. The candidate is placed between the Pillars, facing a Portal in the grade to which he seeks admission, represented by the Hebrew letter pictured in the correct direction in relation to the temple. This is a Path on the Tree of Life, in relation to the Sephirah the temple is in.
5. Circumambulations are made in the Rituals of the Paths, the candidate visits the stations, hears speeches of the officers, see diagrams of the Tree and the Garden of Eden in relationship to the Path.
6. In the East, the Hierophant explains symbolism of the admission badge to that particular Path or Sephirah, and the admission badge is set aside. The symbolism of the Path is explained.
7. Hierophant takes candidate to the West of the Altar and describes, and explains, the symbolism on the Altar, including a Tarot Key on the Path. Also explains other Temple symbolism.
8. Hierophant confers the title Lord or Lady of the (number) Path. Candidate is led out between Path working and reception into the Grade.

Reception into the Sephirah of the Grade
1. The candidate is instructed in knocks, or alarm, of grade and gives them in order to be admitted. He also holds the Admission Badge.
2. Candidate is shown past and future Paths to and from the grade. Hiereus explains symbolism of the Admission Badge in this reception into the grade (which is represented in all four grades by the officers' lamens: in the ① = [10] by the Hiereus Lamen or Fylfot Cross; in ② = [9] by the Kerux Lamen or Caduceus; in ③ = [8] by the Stolistes Lamen; in ④ = [7] by the Hegemon's Lamen).
3. The candidate stands West of the Altar with Hierophant, who speaks on the symbolism of the Garden of Eden particularly referred to in the grade;

also the Planets, Paths, Sephirah and other Qabalistic correspondences; the Sign, Number, Grand Word, Password and Mystic Title. The Sash of the grade is described and bestowed.

4. Facing the direction of the Tablet in the grade, Hierophant gives the candidate the symbolism of the Element, the three Names of God, and the name of the King from the Enochian Tablet.

5. Next the symbolism of Cross, Triangle, etc. on the Altar are explained by the Hierophant.

6. The Hegemon gives his speech on the symbolism of the Sephirah, the Planet, and indicates the Kamea, Sigils and Signs appropriate, as displayed in the temple.

7. The Hierophant confers Mystic Title of Grade upon the candidate and gives the symbol of the Element, which is its name in Hebrew, and proclaims him or her Lord or Lady of (number) Paths.

Closing

1. The Hierophant knocks to announce Closing. All rise.
2. Temple security is seen to, the door checked as in the Opening.
3. Hierophant knocks once and all face East for the Adoration. All Salute the East with the Grade Sign after "Amen".
4. Hierophant goes to the Quarter and Tablet appropriate to the Grade, and officers arrange themselves behind him as in Opening.
5. Hierophant knocks once and then announces the Elemental Prayer, which all recite together.
6. After the Prayer, Hierophant makes Banishing Pentagrams, first of Spirit, active or passive, then of the Element — tracing and charging each with Sceptre before the Tablet.
7. Hierophant then gives License to Depart, after which all return to places.
8. Hierophant declares the temple closed.
9. Chief officers give knocks as in Opening, with base of Sceptre or Sword on floor.

—Anupassana
May, 1986

<44>

CEREMONY OF THE ZELATOR ① = ⑩ GRADE

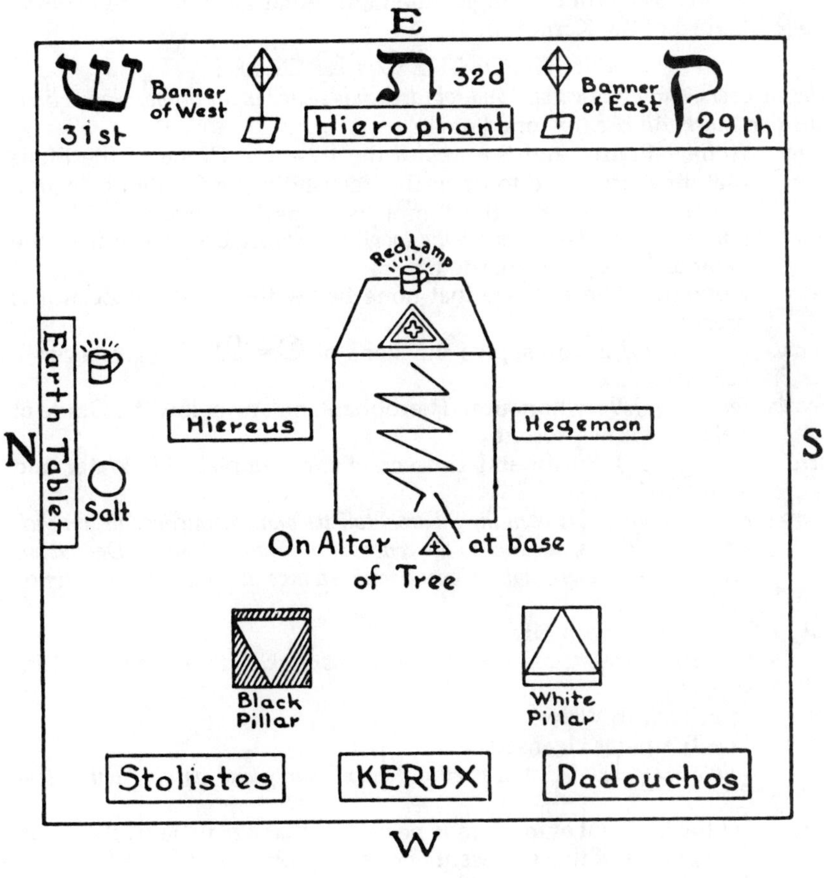

<45> OFFICERS —

Hierophant, Hiereus, Hegemon, Kerux, Stolistes, Dadouches.[1]

TEMPLE —

Arranged as in Diagram.

REQUIRED —

For the Candidate:

Hoodwink, Zelator Sash.

For the Temple:

Fylfot Cross, Three Portal Symbols, Shewbread Diagram, Candle-stick Diagram, Earth Tablet, Altar Diagrams.

For the Altar:

Red Cross, White Triangle, Red Light, Altar Diagram (the Flaming Sword of the Kerubim).

OPENING OF THE ① = [10] GRADE

(The members, having assembled and robed, each is seated in his proper place. Hiero. gives one knock. All rise. ⌉ = one knock.

Hiero *(sitting)* Fratres and Sorores of the ① = [10] Grade of the Stella Matutina, assist me to open the Temple in the Grade of Zelator. Frater Kerux, see that the Temple is properly guarded.

Kerux *(knocks once without opening the door),* Very Honoured Hirophant, the Temple is properly guarded.

Hiero Honoured Hiereus, see that none below the Grade of Zelator is present.

Hiereus Fratres and Sorores, give the signs of ① = [10]. *(All give signs of Zelator.)*

Hiereus *(gives sign)* Very honoured Hierophant, no one below the Grade of Zelator is now present.

Hiero *(giving sign)* Purify and consecrate the Temple with Water and with Fire.

<46> *Kerux advances between the Pillars. Stolistes and Dadouchos, one on each side of the Pillars, advance to the centre of the Hall. All salute. Dadouchos makes cross in air with Censer, and swings it forward three times, saying:*

Dad I consecrate with Fire.

Stolistes makes Cross with Cup, and sprinkles thrice towards East, saying:

Stol I purify with Water.

Kerux The Temple is cleansed.

Salute ① = [10]. *All three retire, Kerux leading and passing with* ⓪ = [0].

Hiero Let the Element of this Grade be named that it may be awakened in the spheres of those present and in the sphere of the Order.

Heg The Element of Earth.

Hiero *(gives one knock)* Let us adore the Lord and King of Earth.

All face East.

[1]In the earlier editions, an error was perpetuated with regard to the participation of the officers, and the role of certain of them in this ritual. See the Introduction to this section by Anupassana.

Hiero Adonai ha-Aretz.* Adonai Melekh.* Unto Thee be the Kingdom and the Power *(cross on self)* and the Glory.

Malkuth, Geburah, Gedulah.

He makes Cross and Circle with Sceptre before him as he says Malkuth, etc.

The Rose of Sharon and the Lily of the Valley, Amen.

All give Zelator Signs. Hiero goes to North, and sprinkles Salt before the Tablet, saying:

Hiero Let the Earth Adore Adonai!

Hierophant leaves his place and goes to North. He stands facing the centre of
<47> *the Tablet of the North and at a convenient distance therefrom, say six feet. Hiereus takes his place at the right of Hiero. Hegemon on left of Hiero; Stolistes behind Hiereus, Dadouchos behind Hegemon. All Officers face North. Hierophant makes sign in front of, and concentric with Tablet of the North, an invoking Pentagram of Earth, saying:*

Hiero And the Elohim said, "Let us make Adam in our Image, after our likeness and let him have dominion over the fish of the sea and over the fowl of the air and over the cattle and over all the earth, and over every creeping thing that creepeth over the Earth." And the Elohim created Eth ha-Adam in their own Image, in the Image of the Elohim created they them. In the name of Adonai Melekh and of the Bride and Queen of the Kingdom, Spirits of Earth adore Adonai!

Hierophant hands his Sceptre to Hiereus and, taking his Sword, makes the Ox ♉ in centre of Pentagram, saying:

Hiero In the Name of Auriel, the Great Archangel of Earth, and by the sign of the Head of the Ox — Spirits of Earth, adore Adonai!

Hierophant returns Sword to Hiereus and takes Mitre-headed Sceptre from Hegemon, and makes Cross in the air, saying:

In the Names and Letters of the Great Northern Quadrangle, Spirits of Earth, adore Adonai!

Hiero returns Sceptre to Hegemon, and takes Cup from Stolistes, making cross, and sprinkling thrice to North, saying:

<48> In the Three Great Secret Names of God, borne upon the Banners of the North — EMOR DIAL HECTEGA — Spirits of Earth, adore Adonai!

Hiero returns Cup to Stol and takes Censer from Dad, and making three forward swings, says: In the name of IC ZOD HEH CHAL, Great King of the North, Spirits of Earth adore Adonai!

Hiero returns Censer to Dad, and takes back Sceptre from Hiereus, returns to Throne. All Officers return to places. All members face as usual.

Hiero In the name of ADONAI HA-ARETZ, I declare this Temple duly opened in the ① = ⑩ Grade of Zelator.

Hiero IIII III III
Hiereus IIII III III
Heg IIII III III

*All god names and words of power used in ceremonies are "vibrated" (or intoned) forcefully, using a complete breath to pronounce the word during an entire exhalation. P.M.

ADVANCEMENT — FIRST PART

Hierophant sits East of Altar, Hiereus North, and Hegemon South.

Hiero Fratres and Sorores, our Frater (Soror) having made such progress in the Paths of Occult Science as has enabled him (her) to pass an examination in the required knowledge, is now eligible for advancement to this Grade, and I have duly received a dispensation from the Greatly Honoured Chiefs of the Second Order to admit him (her) in due form. Honoured Hegemon, superintend the preparation of the Neophyte and give the customary alarm.

<49> *Hegemon salutes with ① = [10] sign, and leaves the room by South and West. Hegemon prepares Neophyte who wears sash of ⓪ = [0] Grade and is blindfolded. He carries the Fylfot Cross in right hand. Hegemon instructs Neophyte in knocks of the Grade. Kerux opens the door to be just ajar.*

Heg Let me enter the Portal of Wisdom.

Kerux I will.

Opens door and admits them. Kerux having turned down lights previously.

Hiero Except Adonai build the house, their labour is but lost that build it. Except Adonai keep the City, the Watchman waketh in vain. Frater (Soror) Neophyte, by what aid dost thou seek admission to the ① = [10] Grade of Zelator of the Stella Matutina?

Heg *(for Neophyte)* By the guidance of Adonai; by the possession of the necessary knowledge; by the dispensation of the Greatly Honoured Chiefs of the Second Order; by the signs and tokens of the ① = [10] Grade. By this symbol of the Hermetic Cross.

Kerux takes Cross from Neophyte.

Hiero Give the step and signs of a Neophyte.

Neophyte gives them.

Hiero Frater Kerux, receive from the Neophyte the Token, Grand Word, and Password of the ① = [10] Grade.

Kerux places himself in front of Neo. and says:

Kerux Give me the grip of the Neophyte. *(done)*
Give me the Word. *(done)*

<50> Give me the Pass-word *(done)*

Having received it, he turns to Hiero, gives Grade Salute, and says:

Kerux Very Honoured Hierophant, I have received them.

Hiero *(to Hegemon)* Lead the Neophyte to the West and set him between the Mystic Pillars, with his face towards the East.

Hegemon places Neophyte between the Pillars, and remains behind him.

Frater (Soror) .... will you pledge yourself to maintain the same secrecy regarding the Mysteries of this Grade as you are pledged to maintain regarding those of the ⓪ = [0] Grade — never to reveal them to the world, and not even to confer them upon a Neophyte without a dispensation from the Greatly Honoured Chiefs of the Second Order?

Neo I will.

Hiero Then you will kneel on both your knees, lay your right hand on the ground, and say: — "I swear by the Earth whereon I kneel." *(done)*

Let the symbol of blindness be removed.

Hegemon unbinds Neo's eyes. Kerux turns up lights. Hegemon goes back to his proper place. Neophyte remains kneeling between the Pillars with his hand on the ground. Kerux takes the Salt from before the Tablet of the North, and passing round the Altar with Sol stands in front of Neophyte facing him and holds the Salt in front of him.

Take Salt with your left hand and cast it to the North; say "Let
<51> the Powers of Earth witness my pledge."

Done. Kerux replaces Salt, and returns to his place.

Let the Neophyte rise and let him be purified with Water and consecrated with Fire, in confirmation of his pledge, and in the Name of the Lord of the Universe who works in silence and whom naught but silence can express.

Dad. comes forward round South Pillar, stands before Neo. and makes three forward swings of censer, saying:

Dad In the name of the Lord of the Universe who works in silence and whom naught but silence can express, I consecrate thee with Fire.

Dadouchos returns by way he came. Stolistes comes round North Pillar, stands before Neophyte, makes cross on forehead, sprinkles thrice, saying:

Stol In the Name of the Lord of the Universe Who works in Silence and Whom naught but Silence can express, I purify thee with Water.

Returns to place as he came.

Hiero The ① = [10] Grade of Neophyte is a preparation for other Grades, a threshold before our discipline, and it shows by its imagery, the Light of the Hidden Knowledge dawning in the Darkness of Creation; and you are now to begin to analyse and comprehend the Nature of that Light. To this end, you stand between the Pillars, in the Gateway where the secrets of the ⓪ = [0] Grade were communicated to you.

<52> Prepare to enter the Immeasurable region.

And Tetragrammaton Elohim planted a Garden Eastward in Eden, and out of the ground made Tetragrammaton Elohim to grow every tree that is pleasant to the sight and good for food; the Tree of Life also, in the midst of the Garden, and the Tree of Knowledge of Good and of Evil. This is the Tree that has two Paths, and it is the Tenth Sephirah Malkuth, and it has about it seven Columns, and the Four Splendours whirl around it as in the Vision of the Mercabah of Ezekiel; and from Gedulah it derives an influx of Mercy, and from Geburah an influx of Severity, and the Tree of the Knowledge of Good and of Evil shall it be until it is united with the Supernals in Daath.

But the Good which is under it is called the Archangel Metatron, and the Evil is called the Archangel Samael, and between them lies the straight and narrow way where the Archangel Sandalphon keeps watch. The Souls and the Angels are above its branches, and the Qlippoth or Demons dwell under its roots.

Let the Neophyte enter the Pathway of Evil.

Kerux takes his place in front of Neophyte, leads him in a N. E. direction towards the Hiereus, halts, and steps out of the direct line between Hiereus and Neophyte.

Hiereus Whence comest thou?

Kerux I come from between the two Pillars and I seek the light of the Hidden Knowledge in the Name of Adonai.

<53> *Hiereus* And the Great Angel Samael answered, and said: I am the Prince of Darkness and of Night. The foolish and rebellious gaze upon the face of the created World, and find therein nothing but terror and obscurity. It is to them the Terror of Darkness and they are as drunken men stumbling in the Darkness.

Return, for thou canst not pass by.

Kerux leads Neo. back as he came, to between the Pillars.

Hiero Let the Neophyte enter the Pathway of Good.

Kerux leads Neophyte S. E., and halts opposite Hegemon, stepping aside from before Neo.

Heg Whence comest thou?

Kerux I come from between the Pillars, and I seek the Light of the Hidden Knowledge in the Name of Adonai.

Heg The Great Angel Metatron answered, and said: I am the Angel of the Presence Divine. The Wise gaze upon the created world and behold there the dazzling image of the Creator. Not yet can thine eyes bear that dazzling Image. Return, for thou canst not pass by.

Kerux turns and leads Neophyte back between the Pillars.

Hiero Let the Neophyte enter the straight and narrow Pathway which turns neither to the right hand nor to the left hand.

Kerux leads Neophyte directly up centre of Hall until he is near the Altar, halts, steps aside from before Neophyte, leaving him to face Altar unobstructed.

<54> *Hiereus, Hegemon (together)* Whence comest thou?

(They cross Sceptre and Sword before Altar.)

Kerux I come from between the Pillars and I seek the Light of the Hidden Knowledge in the Name of Adonai.

Hierophant advances to East of Altar with Sceptre, which he thrusts between Sword of Hiereus and Sceptre of Hegemon, and raising it to an angle of 45° says:

Hiero But the Great Angel Sandalphon said: I am the reconciler for Earth, and the Celestial Soul therein. Form is invisible alike in Darkness and in blinding Light. I am the left hand Kerub of the Ark and the Feminine Power, as Metatron is the right hand Kerub and the Masculine Power, And I prepare the way to the Celestial Light.

Hegemon and Hiereus step back to South and North of Altar respectively. Hiero takes Neo by right hand with his left, and pointing to the Altar and Diagram says:

And Tetragrammaton placed Kerubim at the East of the Garden of Eden and a Flaming Sword which turned every way to keep the Path of the Tree of Life, for He has created Nature that Man being cast out of Eden may not fall into the Void. He has bound Man with the Stars as with a chain. He allures him with Scattered Fragments of the Divine body in bird and beast and flower, and He laments over him in the Wind and in the Sea and in the birds. When the times are
<55> ended, He will call the Kerubim from the East of the Garden, and all shall be consumed and become Infinite and Holy.

Receive now the secrets of this Grade.* The step is thus given — 6 by 6 — showing you have passed the threshold. The Sign is given by raising the right hand to an angle of 45°. It is the position in which the Hierophant interposed for you between the Hiereus and the Hegemon. The Token is given by grasping fingers, the thumb touching thumb to form a triangle. It refers to the Ten Sephiroth. The Word is ADONAI HA—ARETZ, and means Adonai the Lord of the Earth, to which Element this Grade is allotted. The Mystic Number is 55, and from it is formed the Pass-word *Nun He.* It means Ornament, and when given is lettered separately. The Badge of this Grade, is the sash of the Neophyte with the narrow white border, a red cross within the Triangle, and the number ① within a circle and [10] within a square, one on each side of the triangle.

He invests Neophyte with the sash, and points out the Three Portals, saying:

The Three Portals facing you in the East, are the Gates of the Paths leading to the three further Grades, which with the Zelator and the Neophyte forms the first and lowest Order of our Fraternity. Furthermore, they represent the Paths which connect the Tenth Sephirah Malkuth with the other Sephiroth. The letters Tau, Qoph and Shin make the word Quesheth — a Bow, the reflection of the
<56> Rainbow of Promise stretched over our Earth, and which is about the Throne of God.

Hegemon points out the Flaming Sword, saying:

Heg This drawing of the Flaming Sword of the Kerubim, is a representation of the Guardians of the Gates of Eden, just as the Hiereus and Hegemon symbolise the Two Paths of the Tree of the Knowledge of Good and of Evil.

Hiereus In this Grade, the red Cross is placed within the White Triangle upon the Altar, and it is thus the symbol of the Banner of the West. The Triangle refers to the Three Paths and the Cross to the Hidden Knowledge. The Cross and the Triangle together represent Life and Light.

Hiero points out the Tablet of the North, saying:

Hiero This Grade is especially referred to the Element of Earth, and therefore, one of its principal emblems is the Great Watch Tower or

*This entire section—from this point to ending sentence at the top of page 57—is better placed in the second part of the Zelator's reception into the grade, which is when the secrets are given. See note to page 65. P.M.

Terrestrial Tablet of the North. It is the Third or Great Northern Quadrangle or Earth Tablet, and it is one of the four Great Tablets of the Elements said to have been given to Enoch by the Great Angel Ave. It is divided within itself into four lesser angles. The Mystic letters upon it form various Divine and Angelic Names, in what our tradition calls the Angelic secret language. From it are drawn the Three Holy Secret Names of God EMOR DIAL HECTEGA which are borne upon the Banners of the North, and there are also number-
<57> less names of Angels, Archangels, and Spirits ruling the Element of Earth.

Kerux comes forward and hands Fylfot Cross to Hiero:

Hiero The Hermetic Cross, which is also called Fylfot, Hammer of Thor, and Swastika, is formed of 17 Squares out of a square of 25 lesser squares. These 17 represent the Sun, the Four Elements, and the Twelve Signs of the Zodiac. In this Grade, the lights on the Pillars are unshaded, showing that you have quitted the Darkness of the outer world. You will leave the Temple for a short time.

Kerux takes Neophyte out.

<58>

SECOND PART

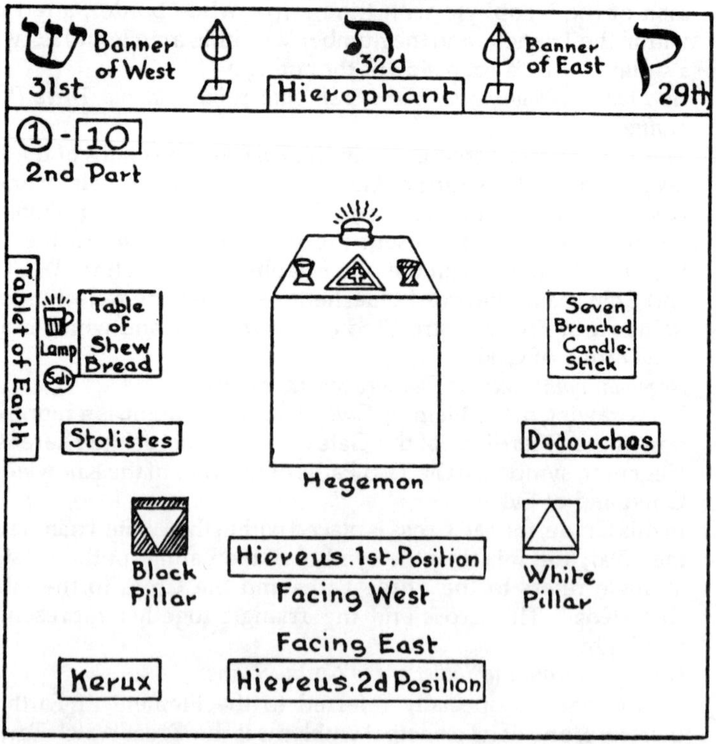

Temple arranged as in Diagram.

Hiero Frater Kerux, when the Neophyte gives the proper alarm, you will admit him. Fraters Stolistes and Dadouchos, assist the Kerux in the reception.

Kerux goes out and instructs Neophyte in the knocks. Stol. and Dad. take up positions so as to face Neophyte as he enters Hall. Kerux opens door and
<59> *admits Neo., but does not stand in front of him.*

Hiero Frater......, as in the Grade of Neophyte, you came out of the World to the Gateway of Hidden Knowledge, so in this Grade you pass through the Gate-way and come into the Holy Place. You are now in the Court of the Tabernacle, where stood the Altar of Burnt Offering, whereon was offered the Sacrifices of animals, which symbolised the Qlippoth or Evil Demons who inhabit the plane contiguous to and below the Material Universe.

Dadouchos makes Cross in air with Censer, and censes Neophyte in silence with three forward swings.

Hiero Between the Altar and the entrance into the Holy Place, stood the Laver of Brass wherein the priests washed before entering the Tabernacle. It was the symbol of the Waters of Creation.

Stol. makes cross with water on Neophyte's forehead and sprinkles thrice in silence.

Having made offering at the Altar of Burnt Sacrifice, and having been cleansed at the Laver of Brass, the Priest then entered the Holy Place.

Kerux takes Neophyte behind Pillars to North. Stolistes and Dadouchos return to their places. Hiereus takes his stand between the Pillars (Kerux having removed the chair) facing Neophyte. He guards the path with his Sword and says:

<60> *Hiereus* Thou canst not pass the Gateway which is between the Pillars, unless thou canst give the Signs and Words of a Neophyte.

Neophyte gives them, and instructed by Kerux, advances to a position between the Pillars. Hiereus returns to his place. Hegemon comes forward, stands East of Pillars, facing Neophyte, and bars the way into the Temple with Sceptre, saying:

Heg Thou canst not enter the Holy Place, unless thou canst give the Sign and Grip of a Zelator.

Neophyte gives them. Kerux resumes his seat after handing Neophyte over to charge of Hegemon. Heg. leads Neophyte to North, and says:

Heg To the Northern side of the Holy Place, stood the Table of Shewbread. The drawing before you represents its occult meaning. On it twelve loaves were laid as emblems of the Bread of life, and it is an image of the Mystery of the Rose of Creation. The 12 circles are the 12 Signs of the Zodiac, while the Lamp in the centre is symbolic of the Sun, which is the source of heat and life. The Four Triangles whose twelve angles each touch one of the 12 circles are those of Fire, Earth, Air, and Water, and allude to the four Triplicities of the Zodiacal Signs. The Triangle inscribed within each of the 12 circles, alludes to the 3 Decanates, or phases of ten degrees of each sign. On one side of each Triangle is the Permutation of the Divine Name Yod Heh Vau Heh, which is referred to that particular sign, while in the
<61> opposite side of it is the name of one of the 12 Tribes which is also attributed to it.

Now the 22 sounds and letters of the Hebrew Alphabet are the foundations of all things. Three Mothers, Seven Double and Twelve Simples. The Twelve Simple letters are allotted to the 12 directions in space, and those diverge to Infinity, and are in the arms of the Eternal. These Twelve Letters He designed and combined, and formed with them the Twelve Celestial Constellations of the Zodiac. They are over the Universe as a King upon his throne, and they are in the revolution of the year as a King traversing his dominions, and they are in the heart of man as a King in warfare.

And the Twelve Loaves are the images of those ideas, and are the outer petals of the Rose; while within are the Four Archangels ruling over the Four Quarters, and the Kerubic emblems of the Lion, Man, Bull and Eagle.

Around the great central Lamp which is an image of the Sun, is the Great Mother of Heaven, symbolised by the letter Heh, the first of the Simple letters, and by its number 5, the Pentagram, Malkah the Bride, ruling in her Kingdom Malkuth, crowned with a crown of Twelve Stars.

These Twelve Circles further represent the 12 Foundations of the Holy City of the Apocalypse, while in Christian Symbolism the Sun and the Twelve Signs are referred to Christ and His Twelve Apostles.

<62> *Hegemon leads Neophyte to Hiereus and then returns to his place and is seated. Hiereus leads Neophyte to the South, and says:*

Hiereus On the Southern side of the Holy Place stood the Seven-Branched Candlestick, wherein was burned pure olive oil. It is an image of the Mystery of the Elohim, the Seven Creative Ideas. The symbolic drawing before you represents its occult meaning. The Seven Circles which surround the Heptagram, represent the Seven Planets and the Seven Qabalistic Palaces of Assiah, the Material World — which answer to the Seven Apocalytic Churches which are in Asia or Assiah — as these again allude to the Seven Lamps before the Throne on another Plane.

Within each circle is a triangle to represent the Three Fold Creative Idea operating in all things. On the right hand side of each is the Hebrew Name of the Angel who governs the Planet; on the left side is the Hebrew Name of the sphere of the Planet itself; while the Hebrew letter beneath the base is one of the duplicated letters of the Hebrew Alphabet which refer to the Seven Planets.

The Seven Double Letters of the Hebrew Alphabet have each two sounds associated with them, one hard, and one soft. They are called "double", because each letter represents a contrary or permutation, thus: Life and Death; Peace and War; Wisdom and Folly; Riches and Poverty; Grade and Indignity; Fertility and Solitude; Power and Servitude.

<63> These Seven letters point out 7 localities; Zenith, Nadir, East, West, North, South, and the Place of Holiness in the midst sustaining all things. The Archetypal Creator designed, produced, combined and

formed with them the Planets of the Universe, the Days of the Week, and in Man, the Gate of the Soul. He has loved and blessed the number 7 more than all things under His Throne. The powers of these 7 letters are also shown forth in the 7 Palaces of Assiah, and the Seven Stars of that Vision are the 7 Archangels who rule them.

He leads Neophyte to W. of Altar, and returns to his place, and is seated. Hierophant comes to E. of Altar, takes censer from Altar, and holding it with chain short, makes cross and three forward swings, replaces it, and says:

Hiero Before the Veil of the Holy of Holies, stood the Altar of Incense, of which this Altar is an image. It was of the form of a double cube, thus representing material form as a reflection and duplication of that which is Spiritual. The sides of the Altar, together with the top and bottom, consist of ten squares, thus symbolising the Ten Sephiroth of which the basal one is Malkuth, the realisation of the rest upon the material plane, behind which the others are concealed. For were this double cube raised in the air immediately above your head, you would but see the single square forming the lowest side, the others from their position being concealed from you. Just so, behind the material Universe, lies the concealed form of the Majesty of God.

<64> The Altar of Incense was overlaid with Gold to represent the highest degree of purity, but the Altar before you is black to represent the terrestrial Earth. Learn then, to separate the pure from the impure, and refine the Gold of the Spirit from the Black Dragon, the corruptible body. Upon the Cubical Altar, were Fire, Water, and Incense, the Three Mother Letters of the Hebrew Alphabet; Aleph, Mem, and Shin. Mem is silent, Shin is sibilant, and Aleph is the tongue of a balance between these contraries in equilibrium, reconciling and mediating between them. In this is a great Mystery, very admirable and recondite. The Fire produced the Heavens, the Water, the Earth, and the Air is the reconciler between them. In the year, they bring forth the hot, the cold, and the temperate seasons, and in man, they are imaged in the head, the chest, and the trunk.

I now confer upon you the Mystic Title of Periclinus de Faustis, which signifies that on this Earth you are in a wilderness, far from the Garden of the Happy.

And I give you the symbol of ARETZ which is the Hebrew name for Earth, to which the ① = ⑩ Grade of Zelator is referred. The word Zelator is derived from the ancient Egyptian Zaruator, signifying "Searcher of Athor", Goddess of Nature; but others assign to it the meaning of the zealous student whose first duty was to blow the Athanor of Fire which heated the Crucible of the Alchemist.

<65> *Hierophant resumes seat on Dais: Kerux leads new Zelator to seat in North West.*

Hiero Frater Kerux, you have my command to declare that our Frater has been duly admitted to the ① = ⑩ Grade of Zelator.

Kerux comes to N. W. of Hierophant, faces West, raises Wand and says:

Kerux In the Name of ADONAI MELEKH, and by command of the Very Honoured Hierophant, hear ye all that I proclaim that Frater. . . . . .

has been duly admitted to the ① = [10] Grade of Zelator, and that he has obtained the Mystic Title of Periclinus (Pericline) de Faustis and the symbol of Aretz.

*He returns to his place by E, saluting, and by S. and W.**

Hiero In the Zelator Grade, the symbolism of the Tenth Sephirah Malkuth is especially shown, as well as the Tenth Path of the Sepher Yetsirah. Among other Mystic Titles, Malkuth is called SHAAR, the Gate, which by metathesis becomes ASHUR, meaning the number Ten. Also in Chaldee it is called THRAA, The Gate, which has the same number as the Great Name ADONAI, written in full: Aleph, Daleth, Nun, Yod, which both equal 671 in total numeration. It is also called the "Gate of Death", "The Gate of Tears", and the "Gate of Justice", the "Gate of Prayer", and "The Gate of the Daughter of the Mighty Ones". It is also called "The Gate of the Garden of Eden" and the Inferior Mother, and in Christian symbolism, it is connected with
<66> the Three Holy Women at the foot of the Cross. The Tenth Path of the Sepher Yetsirah which answereth to Malkuth is called "The Resplendent Intelligence", because if exalts above every head and sitteth upon the Throne of Binah. It illuminateth the Splendour of all the Lights, (the Zohar ME-OUROTH) and causeth the current of the Divine Influx to descend from the Prince of Countenances, the Great Archangel Metatron.

Frater . . . . . . before you can be eligible for advancement to the next Grade of ② = [9], you will be required to pass an examination in certain subjects. A manuscript on these will be supplied to you. When you are well satisfied that you are well informed on these, notify the Officer in charge.

CLOSING

Hiero Fratres and Sorores, assist me to close this Temple in the ① = [10] Grade of Zelator.

All rise.

Frater Kerux, see that the Temple is properly guarded.

Kerux *(on inner side of the door, knocks. Sentinel knocks.)* Very Honoured Hierophant, the Temple is properly guarded.

Hiero Let us adore the Lord and King of Earth.

All face East.

ADONAI HA-ARETZ, ADONAI MELEKH, Blessed be Thy Name unto the countless ages. Amen.

<67> *Gives Sign. All give sign and face as usual. Hiero. leaves his Throne and passes to the North, standing before the Tablet of the North, Hiereus stands on right of Hiero; Hegemon left; Kerux behind Hiero; Stolistes behind Hiereus, Dadouchos behind Hegemon.*

Hiero Let us rehearse the prayer of the Earth Spirits.

O Invisible King, Who, taking the Earth for Foundation, didst hollow its depths to fill them with Thy Almighty Power. Thou Whose Name shaketh the Arches of the World, Thou who causest the Seven

*It is at this point that the Secrets related on page 55 would be better place. P.M.

Metals to flow in the veins of the rocks, King of the Seven Lights, Rewarder of the subterranean Workers, lead us into the desirable Air and into the Realm of Splendour. We watch and we labour unceasingly, we seek and we hope, by the twelve stones of the Holy City, by the buried Talismans, by the Axis of the Loadstone which passes through the centre of the Earth — O Lord, O Lord, O Lord! Have pity upon those who suffer. Expand our hearts, unbind and upraise our minds, enlarge our natures.

O Stability and Motion! O Darkness veiled in Brilliance! O Day clothed in Night! O Master who never dost withhold the wages of Thy Workmen! O Silver Whiteness — O Golden Splendour! O Crown of Living and Harmonious Diamond! Thou who wearest the Heavens on Thy Finger like a ring of Sapphire! Thou Who hidest beneath the Earth in the Kingdom of Gems, the marvellous Seed of
<68> the Stars! Live, reign, and be Thou the Eternal Dispenser of the Treasures whereof Thou hast made us the Wardens.

Depart ye in peace unto your abodes. May the blessing of Adonai be upon you. *(Makes Banishing Pentagram of Earth.)* Be there peace between us and you, and be ye ready to come when ye are called.

All return to their places and face as usual.

Hiero In the Name of ADONAI MELEKH, I declare this Temple closed in the Grade of Zelator.

Hiero וווו ו וו ווו

Hiereus וווו ו וו וווו

Heg וווו ו וו ווו

Candidate is let out by Hegemon.

<69>

CEREMONY
OF THE
② = [9] GRADE OF THEORICUS

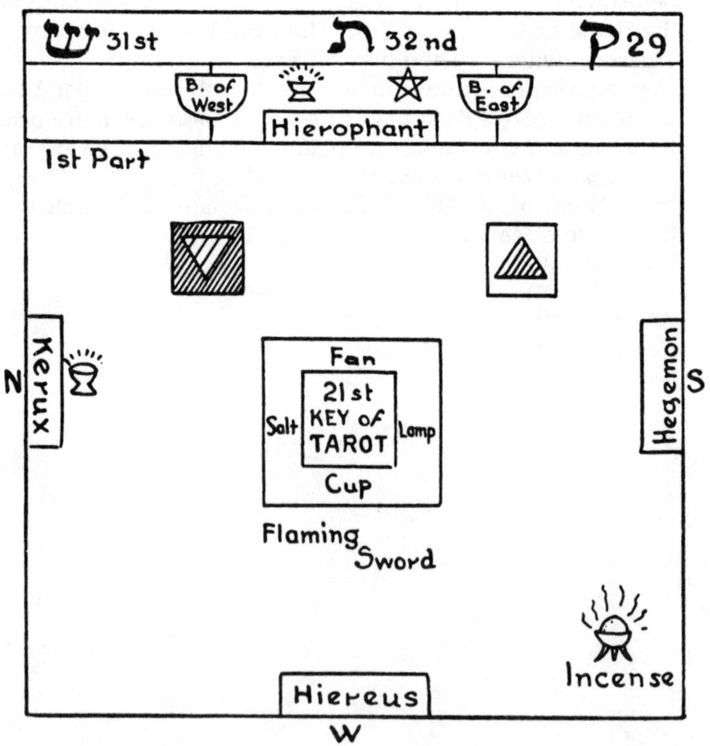

<70> *Requirements:*

In the East — Pentacle, Banner of East and West.

On the Altar — Fan, Lamp, Cup, Salt, surrounding the Altar Diagram of the Universe.

For the Zelator — Hoodwink, Cubical Cross (1st point); Caduceus (2nd point).

OPENING

Temple arranged as in diagram for the 32nd Path. Members assembled and clothed. Lamp on Altar lighted. Members present, but not taking office, rise at the words "Let us adore the Lord and King of Air" and face East, remaining so to the end of the invokation. They do the same at the closing, but otherwise do not move from their places. (∩ = one knock)

Hiero *(knocks)* Fratres and Sorores of the Order of the STELLA MATUTINA in the Outer, assist me to open the Temple in the Theoricus Grade. Frater KERUX, see that the Temple is properly guarded.

Kerux goes to door, sees that it is closed, knocks, and says:

Kerux *(knocks)* Very Honoured Hierophant, the Temple is properly guarded. *(returns to his place.)*

Hiero Honoured Hiereus, see that none below the Grade of Theoricus is present.

Hiereus Fratres and Sorores, give the Signs of the ② = [9] Grade. *(done)* Very Honoured Hierophant, all present have attained the Grade of Theoricus. *(Salutes with ② = [9] Sign.)*

<71> *Hiero* Honoured Hegemon, to what particular Element is this Grade attributed?

Heg To the Element of Air.

Hiero Honoured Hiereus, to what Planet does this Grade especially refer?

Hiereus To the Moon.

Hiero Honoured Hegemon, what path is attached to this Grade?

Heg The 32nd Path of TAU.

Hiero Honoured Hiereus, to what does it allude?

Hiereus To the Universe as composed of the Four Elements — to the KERUBIM, the QLIPPOTH and the Astral Plane, and the reflection of the sphere of SATURN.

Hiero *(knocks) (All rise and face East.)* Let us adore the Lord and King of Air!

Hierophant makes circle with Sceptre towards E.

Hiero SHADDAI EL CHAI, Almighty and Ever-lasting — Ever-Living be Thy Name, Ever Magnified in the Life of All. Amen.

All Salute. Hiero remains facing E. Hiereus advances to W. of Altar. Hegemon and Kerux advance and stand at the outer sides of the Pillars. All face E. Hiero makes invoking Pentagrams within a circle before the Air Tablet.

Hiero And the ELOHIM said—"Let us make ADAM in Our Image, after our likeness, and let them have dominion over the Fowl of the Air."

In the Name YOD HE VAU HE and in the Name of SHADDAI EL CHAI Spirits of Air adore your Creator.

<72> *Takes up Pentacle and at the words "Head of the Man" makes the sign Aquarius before Tablet.*

Hiero In the Name of RAPHAEL, the Great Archangel of Air, and in the Sign of the Head of the Man ≈, Spirits of Air adore your Creator!
Makes Cross with Pentacle.

Hiero In the Name and Letters of the Great Eastern Quadrangle, revealed unto ENOCH by the Great Angel AVE, Spirits of Air adore your Creator!

Hiero *(holding Pentacle on High)* In the Three Great Secret Names of God, borne on the Banners of the East, ORO IBAH AOZPI, Spirits of Air adore your Creator! In the Name of BATAIVAH, Great King of the East, Spirits of Air, adore your Creator!
Replaces Pentacle. All return to places.

Hiero In the Name of SHADDAI EL CHAI, I declare this Temple opened in the ② = [9] Grade of Theoricus.

Hiero 111 111 111
Hiereus 111 111 111
Heg 111 111 111

Ceremony of Advancement in the Path of TAU

Hiero *(knocks)* Fratres and Sorores, our Frater (Soror)......having made such progress in the Paths of Occult Knowledge as has enabled him to pass an examination in the requisite knowledge, is now eligible for advancement to the Grade of Theoricus, and I have duly received a dispensation from the Greatly Honoured Chiefs of the
<73> Second Order, to advance him in due form.
Honoured Hegemon, superintend the preparation of the Zelator and give the customary alarm.
Hegemon rises and saluting, quits the Temple. He prepares the Zelator by seeing he is robed and wearing his sash, presents him with Greek Cubical Cross, Hood-winks him and comes to the door, giving the knock.
Kerux meanwhile, places FAN by Hierophant; LAMP by Hegemon; CUP by Hiereus; and SALT by his own place. Kerux, on hearing the alarm, opens the door and allows Hegemon to enter with Zelator, and then closes it.

Heg QUIT THE MATERIAL AND SEEK THE SPIRITUAL.

Hiero Conduct the Zelator to the East.
Zelator is led between the Pillars to Hierophant's Throne, Kerux standing on his right, Hegemon on his left. Kerux takes Cubical Cross from him.

Hiero Give me the Step and Sign of a Zelator. *(done)*
Give me the Grip or Token. *(done)*
Give me the Grand Word. (ADONAI HA-ARETZ) Mystic Title (Periclinus de Faustis) and the Mystic Number (55) of a Zelator. What is the Pass-Word formed from the Mystic Number? (Nun Heh)
(This is done, Hegemon prompting if necessary)

Hiero Frater Periclinus de Faustis, do you solemnly pledge yourself to

maintain the same strict secrecy regarding the Mysteries of the
<74> 32nd Path of the ②=[9] Grade of Theoricus, which you have already sworn to maintain regarding those of the preceding Grades?

Zelator I do. *(Kerux gives back Cross to Zelator.)*

Hiero Then you will stretch out your hand, holding the Cubical Cross towards Heaven and say: "I swear by the Firmament of Heaven."

This is done — Zelator repeating the words.

Hiero Let the hood-wink be removed.

Done. Hegemon returns to his place in the South. Kerux is now in charge of Zelator.

Hiero Stretch forth your right hand, holding the Cubicle Cross towards the East, in the position of the Zelator Sign, saying: "Let the Powers of Air witness my pledge." *(done)*

Hiero *(knocks)* Facing you are the Portals of the 31st, 32nd, and 29th Paths leading from the Grade of Zelator to the three other Grades which are beyond. The only Path now open to you, however, is the 32nd, which leads to the ②= [9] of Theoricus, and which you must traverse before arriving at that Grade.

Take in your right hand, the Cubical Cross and in your left the Banner of Light *(gives it to him)* and follow your Guide, Anubis the Guardian, who leads you from the material to the spiritual.

Kerux Anubis the Guardian said to the Aspirant, "Let us enter the Presence of the Lord of Truth. Arise and follow me."

Kerux turns to the right, and leads Zelator round the Hall once slowly, while
<75> *Hiereus reads. Hierophant rises with Banner of West in Left Hand —Fan in right.*

Hiereus The Sphinx of Egypt spake and said: "I am the synthesis of the Elemental Forces. I am also the symbol of Man. I am Life and I am Death. I am the Child of the Night of Time."

As Kerux and Zelator approach the East, Hierophant bars the Way with Banner of the West and FAN.

Hiero The Priest with the Mask of OSIRIS spake and said: "Thou canst not pass the Gate of the Eastern Heaven unless thou canst tell me my Name."

Kerux Thou art NU, Goddess of the Firmament of Air. Thou art HORMAKU, Lord of the Eastern Sun.

Hiero In what Signs and Symbols do ye come?

Kerux In the Letter Aleph. In the Banner of Light, and the symbol of the Equated Forces.

Hierophant stands back and signs Aquarius ≈ before Zelator with FAN.

Hiero In the Sign of the MAN, Child of AIR, thou art Purified. Pass Thou on.

Gives Banner of the West to Kerux who leads Zelator on, and hands the Banner to Hegemon in passing, while Hiereus again reads:

Hiereus I am OSIRIS, the Soul in twin aspect, united to the Higher by purification, perfected by suffering, glorified through trial. I have come where the Great GODS are, through the Power of the Mighty Name.

Kerux and Zelator have now reached Hegemon who bars their way, Lamp in
<76> *right hand — Banner of West in left hand.*

Heg The Priest with the mask of the LION, spake and said: "Thou canst not pass by the Gate of the Southern Heaven unless thou canst tell me my Name."

Kerux MAU the Lion, Very Powerful, Lord of FIRE, is Thy Name. Thou art RA, the Sun in his Strength.

Heg In what Signs and Symbols do ye come?

Kerux In the Letter SHIN; in the Banner of the East, and the Symbol of the Cubical Cross.

Heg *(standing back and signing Leo ♌ before Zelator with Lamp)* In the Sign of the LION, Child of Fire, thou art purified. Pass thou on.

He replaces Lamp and takes the place of Kerux, who returns to his seat in the North. Hegemon leads Zelator past Hiereus, to whom he hands Banner of the West. Meanwhile, Hiereus reads for the third time, Hegemon being careful to lead Zelator slowly round the Temple, returning to Hiereus when the speech is finished.

Hiereus *(as they go round the third time)* I have passed through the Gates of the Firmament. Give me your hands, for I am made as ye, Ye Lords of Truth! For Ye are the formers of the Soul.

Hiereus puts down Sword and stands with CUP in right hand, Banner of West in left, barring the way of Hegemon and Zelator.

Hiereus The Priest with the Mask of the EAGLE spake and said: "Thou canst not pass the Gate of the Western Heaven, unless thou canst tell me my Name."

<77> *Heg* HEKA, Mistress of HESUR, Ruler of Water, is Thy Name. Thou art TOUM, the Setting Sun.

Hiereus In what Signs and Symbols do ye come?

Heg In the Letter MEM;* in the Banner of Light; and the Symbol of the Twenty-two Letters.

Hiereus *(standing back and making Sign of EAGLE over Zelator with CUP)* In the Sign of the EAGLE, Child of Water, thou art purified. Pass thou on.

He gives Banner of West to Hegemon who continues to circumambulate with Zelator, giving Banner of West to Kerux as he passes him. Hiereus reads as they go round the fourth time, while Kerux rises with SALT in his right hand, the Banner of the West in left.

Hiereus *(as they go round)* O Lord of the Universe — Thou art above all things and Thy Name is in all things; and before Thee, the Shadows of Night roll back and the Darkness hasteth away.

Kerux *(barring the way with SALT and Banner of West)* The Priest with the Mask of the OX, spake and said: "Thou canst not pass the Gate of the Northern Heaven, unless thou canst tell me my Name."

Heg SATEM, in the abode of SHU, the Bull of Earth, is Thy Name. Thou art KEPHRA, the Sun at Night.

*The "Mother Letters" are given as relating to the Primary Elements appropriate to each quarter, i.e. Aleph, East; Shin, South; Mem, West; and all three together in the North to symbolize the physical universe which manifests by their union, the combined elements. P.M.

Kerux In what Signs and Symbols do ye come?

Heg In the Letters Aleph, Mem, and Shin, and in the symbols of Banner and Cross.

Kerux *(standing back, and signs TAURUS ♉ over Zelator with Salt)* In the Sign of
<78> the Head of the OX, Child of the Elements, thou art purified. Pass thou on.

Hegemon leads the Zelator to Hierophant between the Pillars, Kerux accompanies them with Banner of West, which he hands to Hierophant to replace on stand. Hegemon now hands up Banner of East which Zelator has been holding. This is also replaced. Hegemon hands Cubical Cross to Hierophant. Kerux collects the Fan, Lamp, Cup and Salt and replaces them in their right places on the Altar, round the Diagram.

Hiero (holding Cubical Cross) The Cubical Cross is a fitting emblem of the equilibrated and balanced forces of the Elements. It is composed of 22 squares externally, thus referring to the 22 letters that are placed thereon. Twenty-two are the letters of the Eternal Voice, in the Vault of Heaven; in the depth of Earth; in the Abyss of Water; in the All-Presence of Fire. Heaven cannot speak their fullness — Earth cannot utter it. Yet hath the Creator bound them in all things. He hath mingled them in Water. He hath whirled them aloft in Fire. He hath sealed them in the Air of Heaven. He hath distributed them through the Planets. He hath assigned unto them the Twelve Constellations of the Universe. *(Places Cross aside)*

The 32nd Path of the Sepher Yetzirah, which answereth unto MALKUTH and the Letter TAU, is called the Administrative Intelligence, and it is so-called because it directeth and associateth in
<79> all their operations, the Seven Planets, even all of them in their own due courses. To it, therefore, is attributed the due knowledge of the Seven Abodes of ASSIAH, the Material World, which are symbolised in the Apocalypse by the Seven Churches.

It refers to the Universe as composed of the Four Elements, to the KERUBIM, to the QLIPPOTH, and to the Astral Plane. It is the Reflection of the Sphere of Saturn. It represents the connecting and binding link between the Material and Formative Worlds, Assiah and Yetsirah, and necessarily passes through the Astral Plane, the Abode of the Elementals and the Shells of the Dead. It is the Rending of the Veil of the Tabernacle, whereon the Kerubim and the Palm Trees are depicted. It is the Passing of the Gate of Eden.

Hierophant rises and leads Zelator to the West of Altar. He draws attention to the Key of the Universe.

These ideas are symbolically resumed in the representation of the Twenty First Key of the TAROT, in front of you. Within the oval formed of the 72 circles, is a female form, nude save for a scarf that floats round her. She is crowned with the Lunar Crescent of ISIS, and holds in her hands, two wands. Her legs form a cross. She is the Bride of Apocalypse, the Kabbalistic Queen of the Canticles, the Egyptian ISIS or Great Feminine Kerubic Angel SANDALPHON on the left hand of the Mercy Seat of the Ark

<80> The Wands are the directing forces of the positive and negative currents. The Seven Pointed Heptagram or Star alludes to the Seven Palaces of Assiah; the crossed legs to the symbol of the Four Letters of the Name.

The surmounting crescent receives alike the influences of Geburah and Gedulah. She is the synthesis of the 32nd Path, uniting Malkuth to Yesod.

The oval of the 72 smaller circles refers to the SCHEMHAMPORESCH, or Seventy-two fold Name of the Deity. The twelve larger circles form the Zodiac. At the angles are the Four KERUBIM which are the vivified powers of the letters of the Name YOD HE VAU HE operating in the Elements, through which you have just symbolically passed in the preceding Ceremony.

The Fan, Lamp, Cup and Salt represent the four Elements themselves whose inhabitants are the Sylphs, Salamanders, Undines and Gnomes.

Be thou, therefore, prompt and active as the Sylphs, but avoid frivolity and caprice.

Be energetic and strong as the Salamanders, but avoid irritability and ferocity. Be flexible and attentive to images, like the Undines, but avoid idleness and changeability; be laborious and patient like the Gnomes, but avoid grossness and avarice.

<81> So shalt thou gradually develop the powers of thy soul, and fit thyself to command the Spirits of the Elements.

The Altar, as in the preceding degree, represents the Material Universe. On its right is symbolically the Garden of Eden, represented by the station of Hegemon, while on its left is symbolically GEHENNA, the Abode of Shells, represented by the station of Kerux.

(Hierophant returns to his throne. Kerux steps forward and stands at Zelator's left hand.)

I have much pleasure in conferring on you the Title of Lord of the 32nd Path.

You will now quit the Temple for a short time, and on your return the Ceremony of your Reception into the ② = 9 Grade of Theoricus will be proceeded with.

Kerux leads Zelator out.

<82> SECOND PART

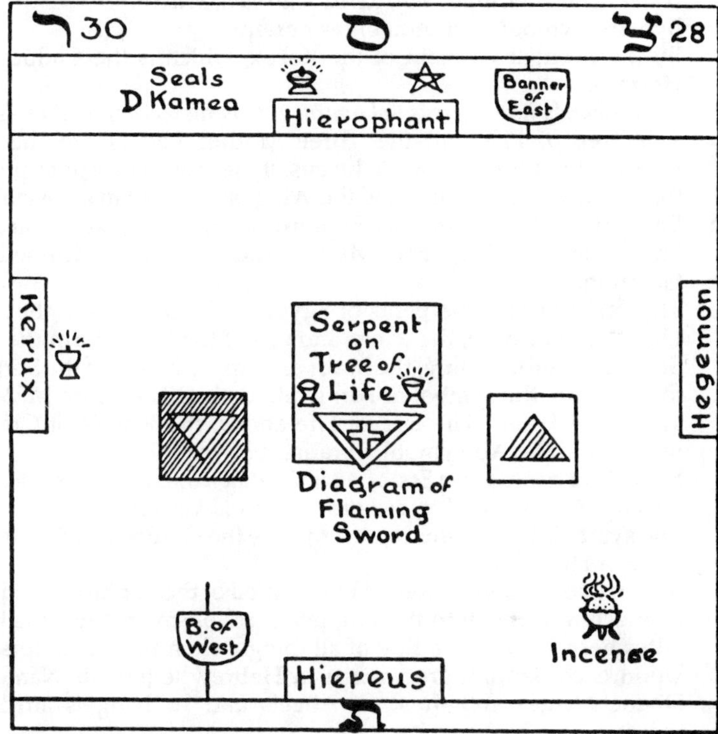

Temple arranged as in diagram.
Kerux takes up CADUCEUS Badge.

Hiero Frater Kerux, you have my commands to instruct the Zelator in the proper alarm, and to present him with the necessary Admission Badge.
Honoured Hegemon, guard the Portal and admit them on giving the proper alarm.

<83> *Kerux takes Caduceus Admission Badge and brings Zelator to the door to give the knocks. Hegemon opens the door and leads Zelator in a little way and faces him to Hierophant.*

Hiero Frater Periclinus de Faustis, as in the Zelator Grade there were given the symbolical representations of the Tree of the Knowledge of Good and Evil, of the Gate of Eden and of the Holy Place, so in this Grade of Theoricus, the Sanctum Sanctorum with the Ark and the Kerubim is shown, as well as the Garden of Eden with which it coincides; while in the 32nd Path leading hereunto, through which you have just symbolically passed, the Kerubic Guardians are represented, and the Palm Trees or Trees of Progression in the Garden of Eden. Honoured Hegemon, conduct the Zelator to the West, and place him thus before the Portal of the 32nd Path of TAU by which he has symbolically entered.

(Done. Zelator faced to West, Kerux returns to place.)

Hiereus By what symbol dost thou enter herein?

Heg By the peculiar emblem of the Kerux, which is the Caduceus of Hermes.

Zelator hands it to Hiereus, who turns it towards Zelator, and reads:

Hiereus The Tree of Life and the Three Mother Letters are the Keys wherewith to unlock the Caduceus of Hermes. The upper point of the Wand rests on Kether, and the Wings stretch out to Chokmah and
<84> Binah, the Three Supernal Sephiroth. The lower seven are embraced by the Serpents, whose heads fall upon Chesed and Geburah.

They are the Twin Serpents of Egypt — the currents of the Astral Light. Furthermore, the wings and top of the Wand form the letter Shin, the symbol of Fire; the heads and upper halves of the Serpents form Aleph, the symbol of Air; while their tails enclose MEM, the symbol of Water. The Fire of Life above, the Waters of Creation below, and the Air symbol vibrating between them.

Hierophant comes to the East of Altar. Hegemon directs Zelator to face him from the West of the Altar, and then returns to his place.

Hiero The symbols before you represent alike the Garden of Eden and the Holy of Holies.

Before you stands the Tree of Life formed of the Sephiroth and their connecting Paths. Into its complete symbolism, it is impossible to enter here, for it is the Key of all things when rightly understood. Upon each Sephira are written in Hebrew letters, its Name, the Divine Names and those of Angels and Archangels attributed thereto.

The connecting Paths are twenty-two in number and are distinguished by the Twenty-Two Letters of the Hebrew Alphabet, making with the Ten Sephiroth themselves the Thirty-two Paths of Wisdom of the Sepher Yetsirah.

The course of the Hebrew Letters, as placed on the paths, forms as you see, the Symbol of the Serpent of Wisdom, while the natural
<85> succession of the Sephiroth forms the Flaming Sword, and the course of the Lightning Flash, as shown in the drawing below.

The Cross within the Triangle, Apex downwards, placed upon the Altar at the base of the Tree of Life, refers to the Four Rivers of Paradise, while the angles of the triangles refer to the Three Sephiroth, Netzach, Hod, and Yesod. The Two Pillars, right and left of the Tree are the symbols of Active and Passive, Male and Female, Adam and Eve. They also allude to the Pillars of Fire and Cloud which guided the Israelites in the wilderness, and the hot and moist natures are further marked by the Red Lamp and the Cup of Water.

The Pillars further represent the Two Kerubim of the Ark — the right, Metatron, Male — and the left, Sandalphon, Female.

Above them ever burn the Lamps of their Spiritual Essence, of which they are partakers in the Eternal Uncreated One.

Hierophant stands in the Sign of Theoricus.

Glory be unto Thee, Lord of the Land of Life, for Thy Splendour filleth the Universe.

After a short pause, Hierophant comes to the West of the Altar, and says:

The ② = [9] Grade of Theoricus is referred to YESOD, as the Zelator Grade is to Malkuth. The Path between them is assigned to the Letter TAU, whose portal you now see in the West, and through which you have just symbolically passed.

<86> To this Grade, as to those preceding it, certain Signs and Tokens are attributed. They consist of a Sign, Token, Grand Word, Mystic Number and Pass-word formed therefrom.

The Sign is thus given. Stand with feet together and raise both arms upwards and back, palms up, as if supporting a weight, thus ♆ . It represents you in the Path of YESOD, supporting the Pillars of Mercy and Severity. It is the Sign made by the Greek God ATLAS, who supported the Universe on his shoulders and whom Hercules was directed to emulate. It is the ISIS of Nature, supporting the Heavens.

The Grip is that of the First Order which you received in the preceding Grade.

The Grand Word is a name of Seven Letters, SHADDAI EL CHAI, which means the Almighty and Living One.

The MYSTIC NUMBER is 45, and from it is formed the Pass-Word which is MEM HE, the Secret Name of the World of Formation. It should be lettered separately when given.

Unto this Grade and unto the Sephirah YESOD, the ninth Path of the Sepher Yetsirah is referred. It is called the Pure and Clear Intelligence, and it is so called because it purifieth and maketh clear the Sephiroth, proveth and emendeth the forming of their representation, and disposeth their duties or harmonies, wherein they combine, without mutilation or division. The Distinguishing Badge of this Grade, which you are now entitled to wear is the Sash of the
<87> Zelator, with the addition of a white cross above the triangle and the numbers ② and [9] in a circle and square respectively, left and right of its summit — and beneath the triangle, the number 32 between two narrow parallel white lines. The meaning of the Tablet of Earth was explained to you in the preceding Grade.

Hierophant returns to East and sits down. Hegemon guides Zelator to him.

The Three Portals facing you are the Gates of Paths leading from this Grade. That on the right connects with the Grade of Philosophus, that on your left with the Grade of Practicus, while the central one leads to the Portal.

This Grade especially refers to the Element of AIR, and therefore the Great Watch-Tower or Terrestrial Tablet of the East forms one of its principal emblems. It is one of the Four Great Tablets delivered unto

Enoch by the Great Angel Ave.

From it are drawn the Three Holy Secret Names of God, ORO IBAH AOZPI, which are borne upon the Banners of the East, and number less Divine and Angelic Names which appertain unto the Element of Air.

To the MOON, also, is this Grade related. Its Kamea or Mystical Square is shown in the East, with Seals and Names appropriate thereto.

It is also shown inscribed upon the Tree of Life, whereon its crescent in increase represents the side of Mercy — in decrease the side of Severity, while at the full it reflects the Sun of Tipareth.

<88> *Hegemon conducts Zelator to a seat West of the Altar.*

I now congratulate you on having attained the Grade of Theroicus and in recognition thereof, I confer upon you the Mystic Title of PORAIOS DE REJECTIS which means "Brought From Among The Rejected", and I give you the Symbol of RUACH, which is the Hebrew name for Air.

(Knocks) Frater Kerux, you have my command to declare that the Zelator has been duly advanced to the Grade of THEORICUS.

Kerux In the name of SHADDAI EL CHAI, and by command of the Very Honoured Hierophant, hear ye all that I proclaim that our Frater..... having made sufficient progress in the study of Occult Science, has been duly advanced to the Grade of ② = [9] of Theoricus, Lord of the 32nd Path, and that he has received the Mystic Title of PORAIOS DE REJECTIS, and the symbol of Ruach.

Hiero Frater. . . . . .before you are eligible for advancement to the next Grade, you must be perfect in certain subjects, a manuscript of which will be supplied to you.

CLOSING

Hiero *(knocks)* Assist me to close the Temple in the Grade of Theoricus.

All rise.

Frater Kerux, see that the Temple is properly guarded. *(done)*

<89> *Kerux (knocks)* Very Honoured Hierophant, the Temple is properly guarded.

Hiero *(knocks)* Let us adore the Lord and King of AIR.

All face East. New Theoricus is directed to stand facing East.

ADORATION

Hiero SHADDAI EL CHAI, Almighty and Everliving, blessed be Thy Name unto the countless ages. Amen.

All salute. Officers form in the East as in Opening. Members stand facing East. Hiereus remains standing just behind new Theoricus.

Hiero *(knocks)* Let us rehearse the Prayer of the Sylphs or Air Spirits.

SPIRIT OF LIFE! Spirit of Wisdom! Whose breath giveth forth and withdraweth the form of all things:

THOU, before Whom the life of beings is but a shadow which changeth, and a vapour which passeth:

THOU, Who mountest upon the clouds, and Who walkest upon the Wings of the Wind.

THOU, Who breathest forth Thy Breath, and endless space is peopled:

THOU, Who drawest in Thy Breath, and all that cometh from Thee, returneth unto Thee!

CEASELESS MOTION, in Eternal Stability, be Thou eternally blessed!

<90> We praise Thee and we bless Thee in the Changeless Empire of Created Light, of Shades, of Reflections, and of Images —

And we aspire without cessation unto Thy Immutable and Imperishable Brilliance.

Let the Ray of Thy Intelligence and the warmth of Thy Love penetrate even unto us!

Then that which is Volatile shall be Fixed; the Shadow shall be a Body; the Spirit of Air shall be a Soul; the Dream shall be a Thought.

And no more shall we be swept away by the Tempest, but we shall hold the Bridles of the Winged Steeds of Dawn.

And we shall direct the course of the Evening Breeze to fly before Thee!

O SPIRIT of Spirits! O Eternal Soul of Souls!

O IMPERISHABLE Breath of Life! O Creative Sigh! O Mouth which breathest forth and withdrawest the life of all beings, in the flux and reflux of Thine Eternal Word, which is the Divine Ocean of Movement and of Truth!

Hierophant makes with Sceptre the Banishing Circle and Pentagrams in the Air before the Tablet.

Depart ye in peace unto your habitations. May the blessing of YOD HE VAU HE rest with ye. Be there peace between us and you, and be ye ready to come when ye are called.

All return to their places.

<91> In the Name of SHADDAI EL CHAI, I declare this Temple closed in the ② = [9] Grade of Theoricus.

Hiero ııı ııı ııı

Hiereus ııı ııı ııı

Heg ııı ııı ııı

Kerux leads out new Theoricus.

<92>

CEREMONY
OF THE
③ = 8 GRADE OF PRACTICUS

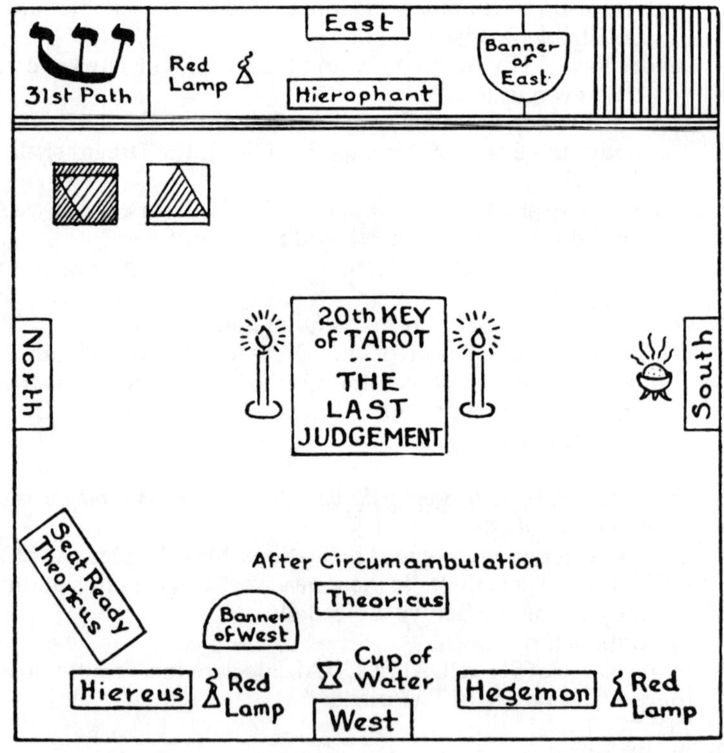

<93> OPENING

Temple arranged for the 31 PATH.

Hiero *(knocks)* Fratres and Sorores of the . . . . . .Temple of the STELLA MATUTINA in the Outer, assist me to open the Temple in the Three equals Eight Grade of PRACTICUS. Honoured Hegemon, see that the Temple is properly guarded.

This is done.

Heg Very Honoured Hierophant, the Temple is properly guarded.

Hiero Honoured Hiereus, see that none below the Grade of Practicus is present.

Hiereus Fratres and Sorores, give the Sign of the Practicus. *(done)* Very Honoured Hierophant, all present have attained the Three equals Eight Grade. *(Salutes)*

Hiero Honoured Hegemon, to what particular Element is this Grade attributed?

Heg To the Element of Water.

Hiero Honoured Hiereus, to what Planet does this Grade especially refer?

Hiereus To the Planet Mercury.

Hiero Honoured Hegemon, what Paths are attached to this Grade?

Heg The 31st and 30th Paths of SHIN and RESH.

Hiero Honoured Hiereus, to what does the 31st Path refer?

Hiereus To the Reflection of the Sphere of FIRE.

Hiero Honoured Hegemon, to what does the 30th Path allude?

<94> *Heg* To the Reflection of the Sphere of the SUN.

All rise and face East.

Hiero Let us adore the Lord and King of Water.

ELOHIM TZABAOTH — Elohim of Hosts! Glory be unto the RUACH ELOHIM who moved upon the Face of the Waters of Creation, Amen!

All salute. Hierophant quits his Throne and goes to the West. He stands before the Tablet of Water before which a Cup of Water is placed. He makes in the air over the Tablet the Invoking Circle and Pentagrams of Water.

And Elohim said, "Let us make Adam in our Image, after our likeness and let them have dominion over the Fish of the Sea. In the Name of A L Strong and Powerful, and in the name of ELOHIM TZABAOTH, Spirits of Water adore your Creator!

Takes Cup from before the Tablet and makes therewith the Sign of the EAGLE in the air before it.

In the Name of GABRIEL, the Great Archangel of Water, and in the Sign of the EAGLE, Spirits of Water Adore your Creator!

Makes a Cross with the Cup.

In the Name and letters of the Great Western Quadrangle revealed unto Enoch by the Great Angel Ave, Spirits of Water adore your Creator!

Holds Cup on high.

In the Three Great Secret Names of God, borne upon the banners of

the West — EMPEH ARSEL GAIOL — Spirits of Water adore your
<95> Creator! in the Name RA-AGIOSEL, Great King of the West, Spirits of Water adore your Creator!

Hierophant replaces the Cup and returns to his place. All return to their places.

In the name of ELOHIM TZABAOTH, I declare the Temple opened in the Three equals Eight Grade of Practicus.

Hiero ו ווו ו ווו

Hiereus ו ווו ו ווו

Heg ו ווו ו ווו

THE THIRTY FIRST PATH

Hiero Fratres and Sorores, our Frater (or Soror)...... having made such progress in the Path of Occult Science as has enabled him to pass an examination in the requisite knowledge, is now eligible for advancement to the Grade of Practicus, and I have duly received a dispensation from the Greatly Honoured Chiefs of the Second Order, to advance him in due form.

Honoured Hegemon, superintend the preparation of the Theoricus and give the customary alarm.

Hegemon rises. He proceeds to leave the Temple, pausing before Hierophant's Throne to salute with the Grade Sign. The Theoricus should be robed and wearing the Sash of his Grade. Hegemon gives him the Badge — The Solid Triangular Pyramid — hoodwinks him, and leads him to the door. Hegemon gives the alarm — ו ווו ו ווו. *Hiereus opens the door, admits them, and returns to his seat.*

<96> *Heg* His Throne was like a Fiery Flame and the Wheels as Burning Fire.

Hegemon conducts the Theoricus to the WEST and takes the Pyramid. Theoricus is faced towards Hiereus who rises.

Hiereus Give me the Sign of the Grade of Theoricus. Give me the Grip. Give the Grand Word. *(This is given, Hegemon prompting if necessary. Shaddai El Chai.)* The Mystic Number (45), and Pass word *(Mem-He)*. Give me also the Mystic Title and Symbol you received in that Grade.

Theo Poraios de Rejectis. Ruach. *(Prompted if necessary.)*

Hiero Poraios de Rejectis, do you solemnly pledge yourself to maintain the same strict secrecy regarding the Mysteries of the 31st and 30th Paths of this Grade of Practicus which you have already sworn to maintain respecting those of the preceding Grades?

Theo I do. *(Theoricus is faced West before Tablet by Hegemon.)*

Hiero Then you will stretch forth your hand in the position of the Saluting Sign of a Neophyte and say: "I swear by the Abyss of the Waters."

(Done — Theoricus repeating the words.)

Let the Hood-wink be removed.

Done. Hegemon places in his hand the cup of Water before the Tablet.

Sprinkle with your hand a few drops of Water towards the Tablet of
<97> Water in the West and say: "Let the Powers of Water witness my

pledge."

Done. Theoricus repeats the words. Hegemon replaces Cup.

Conduct the Theoricus to the East and place him between the Mystical Pillars. *(done)*

Before you are the Portals of the 31st, 32nd, and 29th paths. Of these, as you already know, the central one leads to the Grade of Theoricus from that of Zelator. The one on your left hand now open to you, is the 31st, which leads from the One equals Ten of Zelator to the Three equals Eight of Practicus.

Take in your right hand the Pyramid of Flame, and follow your Guide, AXIOKERSA, the KABIR, who leads you through the Path of FIRE.

Hegemon leads the Theoricus between the Pillars, past Hierophant, making the Saluting Sign of a Neophyte in passing, circumambulates the Hall and halts at Hierophant's Throne. Hierophant rises as they approach, red lamp in hand.

AXIEROS, the FIRST KABIR, spake unto Kasmillos the Candidate, and said: "I am the apex of the Pyramid of Flame. I am the Solar Fire pouring forth its beams upon the lower World — Life-giving, Light-producing. By what symbol dost thou seek to pass by?"

Heg By the symbol of the Pyramid of Flame.

Hiero Hear Thou the voice of AXIEROS, the First KABIR: "The Mind of the Father whirled forth in reechoing roar — comprehending by in-
<98> vincible Will, ideas omniform, which flying forth from that One Fountain issued. For, from the Father alike were the Will and the End, by which yet they are connected with the Father, according to alternating Life through varying vehicles.

But as they were divided asunder, being by Intellectual Fire distributed into other Intellectuals. For the King of all previously placed before the polymorphous World, by which the Universe shines forth decked with ideas all various, of which the Foundation is One and Alone. From this: the others rush forth distributed and separated through the various bodies of the Universe and are borne in swarms through its vast Abysses, ever whirling forth in Illimitable Radiation.

They are Intellectual Conceptions from the Paternal Fountain, partaking abundantly of the Brilliance of Fire in the culmination of Unresting Time.

But the Primary, Self-Perfect Fountain of the Father pours forth these Primogenial Ideas. These being many, ascend flashingly into the Shining World and in them are contained the Three Supernals — because it is the Operator — because it is the Giver of the Life-bearing Fire — because it filleth the Life-producing Bosom of Hecate — and it instilleth into the Synoches, the enlivening strength of Fire, endued with Mighty Power.

<99> The Creator of all, Self-operating, formed the World, and there was a certain mass of Fire, and all these self-operating He produced, so that the Cosmic Body might be completely conformed — that the

Cosmos might be manifest and not appear membranous.

And He fixed a vast multitude of in-wandering stars, not by a strain laborious and hurtful, but to uphold them with stability, void of movement — forcing Fire forward into Fire."

Hereunto is the speech of AXIEROS.

Hegemon leads Theoricus to the seat of Hiereus who rises holding his red Lamp. They halt before him.

Hiereus AXIOKERSOS, the Second KABIR, spake to Kasmillos the Candidate and said: "I am the left basal angle of the Triangle of Flame. I am the Fire Volcanic and Terrestrial, flashingly flaming through Abysses of Earth — Fire-rending — Fire penetrating — tearing asunder the curtain of Matter — Fire constrained — Fire tormented — raging and whirling in lurid storm. By what sign dost thou seek to pass by?

Heg By the Symbol of the Pyramid of Flame.

Hegemon returns to his place — signing Theoricus to remain.

Hiereus Hear thou the voice of AXIOKERSOS, the Second KABIR: "For not in Matter did the Fire which is in the Beyond First enclose His Power in acts, but in Mind; for the Former of the Fiery World is the Mind of Mind, Who first sprang from Mind, clothing the one Fire with the
<100> other Fire, binding them together so that He might mingle the fountainous craters while preserving unsullied the brilliance of His own Fire — and thence a Fiery Whirlwind drawing down the brilliance of the Flashing Flame — penetrating the Abysses of the Universe; thencefrom downwards all extend their wondrous rays, abundantly animating Light, Fire, Aether and the Universe.

From Him leap forth all relentless thunders, and the whirlwind-wrapped, storm-enrolled Bosom of the All-splendid Strength of Hecate, Father-begotten, and He who encircleth the Brilliance of Fire and the Strong Spirit of the Poles, all fiery beyond."

Hereunto is the speech of AXIOKERSOS.

Hiereus leads Theoricus round to Hegemon who rises with Lamp.

Heg AXIOKERSA, the Third KABIR, spake to Kasmillos the Candidate, and said: "I am the Right Basal Angle of the Triangle of Flame. I am the Fire astral and fluid, winding and corruscating through the Firmament. I am the Life of beings — the vital heat of existence. By what Sign dost thou seek to pass by?"

Hiereus prompts Theoricus and returns to his place after placing a seat West of the Altar for Theoricus.

Theo By the Symbol of the Pyramid of Flame.

Heg Hear Thou the voice of AXIOKERSA, the Third KABIR: "The Father hath withdrawn Himself but hath not shut up His Own Fire in His
<101> Intellectual Power. All things are sprung from that One Fire, for all things did the Father of all things perfect, and delivered them over to the Second Mind Whom all races of men call First. The Mind of the Father riding on the subtle girders which glitter with the tracings of inflexible and relentless Fire.

The Soul, being a brilliant Fire, by the Power of the Father remaineth immortal and is Mistress of Life, and filleth up the many recesses of the Bosom of the World, the channels being intermixed, wherein she performeth the works of Incorruptible Fire." Hereunto is the speech of AXIOKERSA.

Hegemon places Theoricus in the seat in the West facing Hierophant.

Hiero Stoop not down unto the darkly splendid World wherein continually lieth a faithless Depth, and Hades wrapped in clouds delighting in unintelligible images, precipitous, winding, a black ever-rolling Abyss, ever espousing a Body, unluminous, formless and void.

Nature persuadeth us that there are pure daemons and that even the evil germs of Matter may alike become useful and good. But these are Mysteries which are evolved in the profound abyss of the Mind.

Such a Fire existeth extending through the rushings of Air or even a Fire formless whence cometh the Image of a Voice, or even a flashing Light, abounding, whirling forth, crying aloud. Also there is the
<102> vision of the Fire-flashing Courser of Light, or of a Child borne aloft on the shoulders of the Celestial Steed, fiery or clothed in gold, or naked and shooting with a bow, shafts of light, and standing on the shoulders of a horse.

But if thy meditation prolongeth itself, thou shalt unite all these symbols in the form of a LION.

Then when no longer are visible to thee the Vault of the Heavens, and the Mass of the Earth; when to Thee, the Stars have lost their light and the Lamp of the Moon is veiled; when the Earth abideth not and around thee is the Lightning Flame — then call not before thyself the Visible Image of the Soul of Nature, for thou must not behold it ere thy body is purged by the Sacred Rites — since, ever dragging down the Soul and leading it from the Sacred Things, from the confines of Matter, arise the terrible Dog-faced Demons, never showing true image unto mortal gaze.

So therefore first the priest who governeth the works of Fire must sprinkle with the lustral water of the Loud, Resounding Sea.

Labour thou around the Strophalos of Hecate. When thou shalt see a terrestrial Demon approaching, cry aloud and sacrifice the Stone MNIZOURIN.

Change not the barbarous Names of Evocation, for they are Names Divine, having in the Sacred Rites a power ineffable. And when,
<103> after all the phantoms have vanished, thou shalt see that Holy and Formless Fire — that Fire which darts and flashes through the Hidden Depths of the Universe, Hear Thou the Voice of Fire.

Hereunto is the speech of Kabir.

Hegemon conducts the Theoricus to the foot of Hierophant's Throne, and taking the Triangular Pyramid, hands it to Hierophant.

The Solid Triangular Pyramid is an appropriate hieroglyph of Fire. It is formed of four triangles, three visible and one concealed, which yet is the synthesis of the rest. The three visible triangles represent Fire, Solar, Volcanic, and Astral, while the fourth represents the latent Heat — AUD, active — AUB, passive — AUR, equilibrated — while ASCH is the name of Fire.

(Puts Pyramid aside.)

The Thirty First Path of the Sepher Yetsirah which answereth unto the Letter SHIN is called The Perpetual Intelligence, and it is so-called because it regulateth the proper motion of the Sun and the Moon in their proper order, each in an orbit convenient for it.

It is therefore a reflection of the Sphere of Fire, and the Path connecting the Material Universe as depicted in Malkuth with the Pillar of Severity and the side of Geburah, through the Sephirah HOD.

Hierophant rises. Hegemon steps back and when he has descended from the Dais, indicates to Theoricus to follow him. He leads Theoricus to the West of
<104> *the Altar, Hegemon follows and stands on the South Side — Hierophant being on the North.*

Before you upon the Altar, is the Twentieth Key of the TAROT, which symbolically represents these ideas. To the uninitiated eye it apparently represents The Last Judgment with an angel blowing a trumpet and the Dead rising from their tombs — but its meaning is far more occult and recondite than this, for it is a glyph of the powers of Fire.

The Angel encircled by the rainbow, whence leap corruscations of Fire, and crowned with the Sun, represents MICHAEL, the Great Archangel, the Ruler of Solar Fire.

The Serpents which leap in the rainbow are symbols of the Fiery Seraphim. The Trumpet represents the influence of the Spirit descending from BINAH, while the Banner with the Cross refers to the Four Rivers of Paradise and the Letters of the Holy Name.

He is also AXIEROS, the first of the Samothracian Kabiri, as well as Zeus and Osiris.

The left hand figure below, rising from the Earth is SAMAEL, the Ruler of Volcanic Fire. He is also AXIOKERSOS, the Second Kabir, Pluto and Typhon.

The right hand figure below is ANAEL, the Ruler of Astral Light. She is also AXIOKERSA, the Third Kabir, Ceres and Persephone, Isis and Nephthys. She is, therefore, represented in duplicate form, and rising from the waters. Around both these figures dart flashes of Lightning.

<105> These three principle figures form the Fire Triangle, and further represent Fire operating in the other Three Elements of Earth, Air, and Water.

The central lower figure with his back turned, and his arms in the Sign of the Two equals Nine, is AREL, the Ruler of latent heat. He is rising from the Earth as if to receive the properties of the other three. He is also KASMILLOS, the Candidate in the Samothracian Mysteries, and the Horus of Egypt. He rises from the rock-hewn cubical Tomb and he also alludes to the Candidate who traverses the Path of Fire. The three lower figures represent the Hebrew letter SHIN, to which Fire is especially referred. The seven Hebrew Yods allude to the Sephiroth operating in each of the Planets and to the Schemhamphoresch.

Hierophant returns to his Throne. Hegemon comes round to the North of the Altar, and stands before Theoricus, who remains in the West.

I have much pleasure in conferring on you the Title of Lord of the Thirty First Path.

You will now quit the Temple for a short time, and on your return the ceremony of your passage of the Thirtieth Path will take place.

Theoricus is led out by Hegemon who makes the Neophyte sign on passing Hierophant's Throne. Theoricus should also do this.

<106> THE THIRTIETH PATH OF RESH

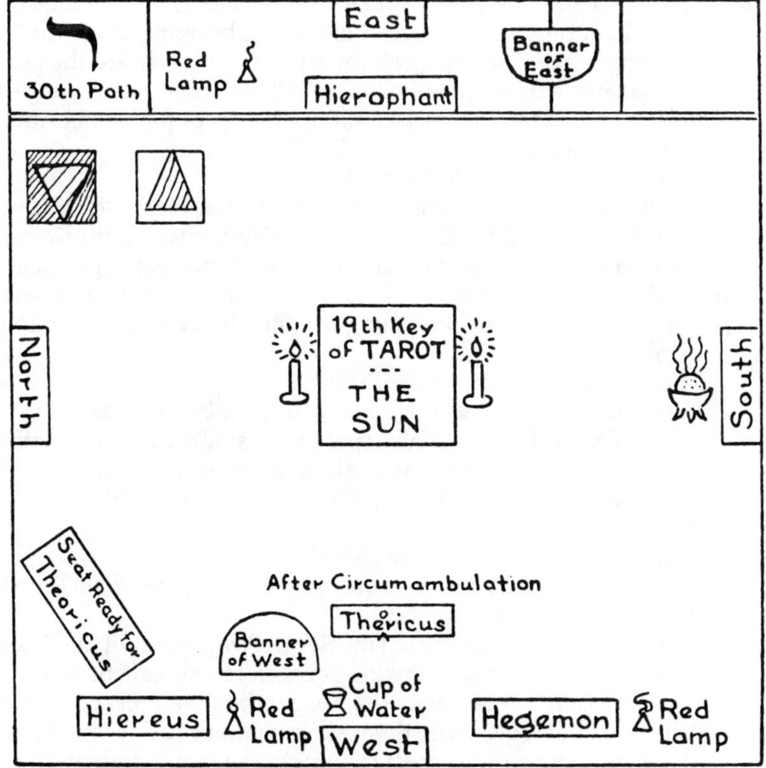

Temple arranged as in Diagram. Portal RESH shown.

Hiero Honoured Hegemon, you have my commands to present the Theoricus with the necessary admission Badge and to admit him.

Hegemon rises and goes to the East where he salutes in the Three equals Eight. He then admits Theoricus after having given him The Greek Cross of

<107> *Thirteen Squares. As he brings him in, Hegemon says:*

Heg Behold He hath placed His Tabernacle in the Sun.

He leads Theoricus to the North East, and places him facing the Pillars.

Hiero *(knocks)* Frater Poraios de Rejectis, before you in the East lie the Portals of the 30th, 25th, and 28th Paths leading from the Two equals Nine Grade of Theoricus to those Grades which are beyond. Of these, the only one now open to you, is the Thirtieth which leads to the Three equals Eight Grade of Practicus. Take in your right hand the Solar Greek Cross, and follow your Guide through the Pathway of the Sun.

Heg Before the Intellectual Whirlings of Intellectual Fire, all things are subservient through the Will of the Father of All.

Hegemon leads Theoricus between Pillars and halts before Hierophant, who rises, red Lamp in hand.

Hiero AXIEROS, the First Kabir, spake unto Kasmillos the Candidate and said: "I am the Sun in greatest elevation, bringing upon Earth the ripening heat —fructifying all things — urging forward the growth of vegetable nature, Life-giving, Light-producing — crowning summer with golden harvest, and filling the lap of plenteous Autumn with the Purple vintage of the Vine."

Thus far the voice of AXIEROS!

Hegemon leads Theoricus to the Seat of Hiereus who rises with red Lamp.

<108> *Hiereus* AXIOKERSOS, the Second Kabir, spake unto Kasmillos the Candidate, and said: "I am the Sun in greatest depression beneath the Equator when cold is greatest and heat is least —withdrawing his light in darkening winter, the Dweller in mist and storm."

Thus far the voice of AXIOKERSOS.

Hegemon leads Theoricus to his own seat and taking red Lamp says:

Heg AXIOKERSA, the Third Kabir spake to Kasmillos the Candidate and said: "I am the Sun in Equinox, initiating Summer or heralding Winter — mild and genial in operation, giving forth or withdrawing the vital heat of life."

Thus far the voice of AXIOKERSA!

Hiereus places a seat West of the Altar. Hegemon indicates this to Theoricus. All are seated, facing Hierophant.

Hiero The Father of All congregated the Seven Firmaments of the Cosmos, circumscribing the Heaven with convex form. He constituted, a Septenary of Wandering Existences, suspending their disorder in well-disposed zones. He made them six in number and for the seventh, he cast into the midst thereof the Fire of the Sun — into that Centre from which all lines are equal — that the Swift Sun may come around that Centre eagerly urging itself towards that Centre of Resounding Light. As rays of light, His locks flow forth, stretching to the confines of Space, and of the Solar Circles, and of the Lunar flashings and of the Aerial Recesses, the Melody of the Aether and of
<109> the Sun and of the Passages of the Moon and of the Air.

The wholeness of the Sun is in the supermundane orders, for

therein a Solar World and endless Light subsist. The Sun more true measureth all things by time, for He is the Time of Time, and his disc is in the Starless above the inerratic Sphere, and he is the centre of the Triple World. The Sun is Fire and the Dispenser of Fire. He is also the channel for the Higher Fire.

O Aether, Sun and Spirit of the Moon, ye are the Leaders of Air. And the Great Goddess bringeth forth the vast Sun and the brilliant Moon and the wide Air, and the lunar Course and the Solar Pole. She collecteth it, receiving the melody of the Aether and of the Sun and of the Moon, and of whatsoever is contained in air.

Unwearied doth Nature rule over the Worlds and Works, so that the Period of all things may be accomplished. And above the shoulders of the Great Goddess, is Nature in her vastness exalted.

Thus far the voice of the Kabiri.

Hegemon conducts Theoricus to Hierophant, to whom he hands the Solar Greek Cross.

The Solar Greek Cross is formed of thirteen squares which fitly refer to the Sun's motion through the Zodiac, these Signs being further arranged in the arms of the Cross according to the Four Elements with the Sun in the centre and representing that luminary as the centre of the whole. The Thirtieth Path of the Sepher Yetzirah which
<110> answereth to the Letter Resh is called the Collecting Intelligence, and it is so called because from it the Astrologers deduce the judgment of the Stars, and of the Celestial Signs, and the perfections of their science according to the rules of their resolutions. It is therefore the Reflection of the Sphere of the Sun and the Path connecting YESOD with HOD — Foundation with Splendour.

Hierophant rises. Hegemon and Theoricus step back and follow him to the Altar where he places Theoricus in the West, Hierophant North, Hegemon South.

Before you upon the Altar is the Nineteenth Key of TAROT which symbolically resumes these ideas. The Sun has twelve principal rays which represent the Twelve Signs of the Zodiac. They are alternately waved and salient as symbolising the alternation of the masculine and feminine natures. These again are subdivided into the 36 Decanates or sets of ten degrees in the Zodiac, and these again into 72, typifying the 72 quinances or sets of five, and the 72-fold Name Schemhamphoresch. Thus the Sun embraces the whole creation in its rays.

The seven Hebrew Yods on each side, falling through the air, refer to the Solar influence descending. The Wall is the Circle of the Zodiac, and the stones are its various degrees and divisions.

The two children standing respectively on Water and Earth repre-
<111> sent the generating influence of both, brought into action by the rays of the Sun. They are the two inferior and passive Elements, as the Sun and Air above them are the superior and active Elements of Fire and Air. Furthermore, these two children resemble the Sign Gemini which unites the Earthy Sign of Taurus with the Watery Sign Cancer,

and this Sign was, by the Greeks and Romans, referred to Apollo and the Sun.

Hierophant returns to his Throne. Hegemon comes to the North by Theoricus who remains in the West.

I have much pleasure in conferring upon you the title of Lord of the Thirtieth Path. You will now quit the Temple for a short time, and on your return the Ceremony of your reception into the Grade of Three equals Eight will take place.

<112> TEMPLE IN HOD
ARRANGED AS IN DIAGRAM

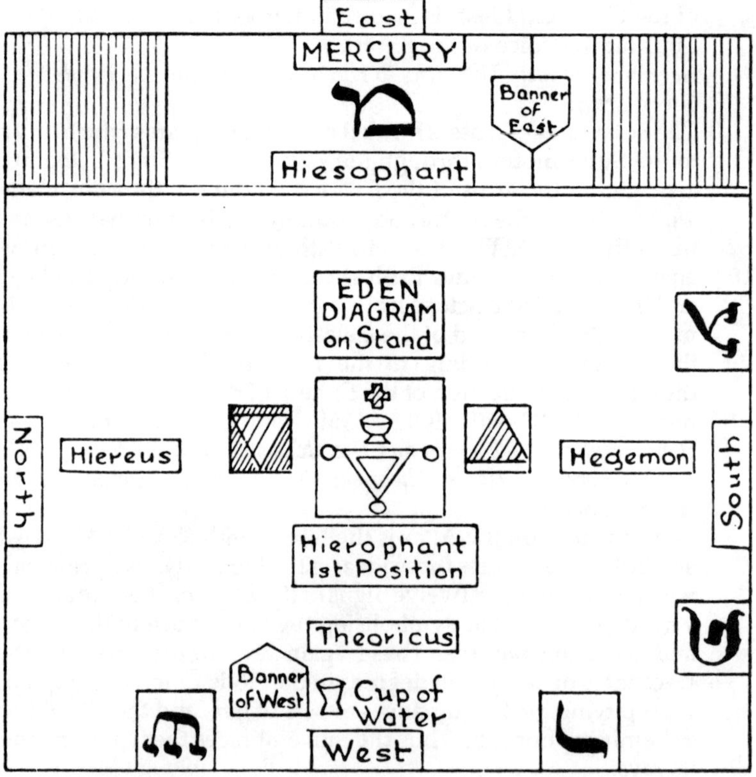

Hiero Honoured Hegemon, instruct the Theoricus in the proper alarm, present him with the necessary Admission Badge, and admit him.

Hegemon takes the Badge, the Cup of Stolistes, and brings Theoricus, telling him to knock 1 111 1 111

Place the Theoricus before the Portal of the 31st Path by which he
<113> has symbolically entered this Grade from the One equals Ten of Zelator. *(done)*

Place the Theoricus now before the portal of the 30th Path by which he has symbolically entered this Grade from the Two equals Nine of Theoricus. *(done)*

Hiereus By what Symbol dost thou enter herein?

Heg By the Peculiar Emblem of the Stolistes, the Cup of Water.

Hiereus The Cup of the Stolistes partakes in part of the Symbolism of the Laver of Moses and the Sea of Solomon. On the Tree of Life, it embraces nine of the Sephiroth, exclusive of Kether. Yesod and Malkuth form the triangle below, the former the apex, the latter the base. Like Caduceus, it further represents the Three Elements of Water, Air, and Fire. The Crescent is the Water which is above the Firmament, the Circle is the Firmament, and the Triangle the consuming Fire below, which is opposed to the Celestial Fire symbolised by the upper part of the Caduceus.

Hiereus puts admission badge aside. Hegemon directs Theoricus to Hierophant whose chair should now be moved back towards the West, and placed in readiness for the Candidate at the Closing. Hiereus and Hegemon stand either side of the Altar, facing it.

Before you is represented the symbolism of the Garden of Eden. At the summit is the Supernal Eden, containing the Three Supernal Sephiroth, summed up and contained in Aima Elohim, the Mother
<114> Supernal, the Woman of the twelfth chapter of the Apocalypse, crowned with the Sun and the Moon under her feet, and upon her head the Crown of Twelve Stars, Kether. And whereas the Name, YOD HE VAU HE, is joined to the name Elohim, when it is said Tetragrammaton Elohim planted a Garden Eastward in Eden, so this represents the power of the Father joined thereto in the Glory from the Face of the Ancient of Days. And in the Garden was the Tree of the Knowledge of Good and of Evil, which latter is from Malkuth, which is the lowest Sephirah between the rest of the Sephiroth and the Kingdom of Shells, which latter is represented by the Great Red Dragon coiled beneath, having Seven Heads (the Seven Infernal Palaces) and Ten Horns — (The Ten Averse Sephiroth of Evil, contained in the Seven Palaces).

And a River Naher went forth out of Eden, namely from the Supernal Triad, to water the Garden (the rest of the Sephiroth), and from thence it was divided into Four Heads in Daath, whence it is said "In Daath the Depths are broken up and the clouds drop down dew." The first Head is PISON, which flows into Geburah (whence there is Gold.) It is the River of Fire. The Second Head is GIHON, the River of Waters, flowing into Chesed. The Third is HIDDEKEL, the River of Air, flowing into Tiphareth, and the Fourth which receiveth the virtues of the other three, is PHRATH, Euphrates, which floweth down
<115> upon the Earth. This River going forth out of Eden is the River of the Apocalypse, the Waters of Life, clear as crystal proceeding out of the Throne of God and the Lamb, on either side of which was the Tree of Life, bearing Twelve manner of Fruits. And thus do the Rivers of Eden form a Cross, and on that Cross the Great ADAM, the Son who

was to rule the Nations with a Rod of Iron, is extended from Tiphareth and his arms stretch out to Gedulah and Geburah, and in Malkuth is Eve, Mother of all, the Completion of all, and above the Universe she supporteth with her hands the Eternal Pillars of the Sephiroth. As it was said to you in the Thirtieth Path, "And above the shoulders of that Great Goddess is Nature in her vastness exalted."

The Three equals Eight Grade of Practicus is referred to the Sephirah Hod and the Thirtieth and Thirty First Paths — those of Resh and Shin are bound thereto.

The Sign of this Grade is given thus. With the hands together, raise the arms till the elbows are level with the shoulders. With the thumbs and fore-fingers make a triangle on your breast thus *(showing it)* — a triangle apex downwards. This represents the Element of Water, to which this Grade is attributed.

The Grip or Token is the general Grip of the First Order. The Grand Word is a Name of ten letters, ELOHIM TZABAOTH, which means Lord of Hosts. The Mystic Number is 36, and from it is formed the Pass-word of this Grade which is ELOAH, one of the Divine Names.
<116> It should be lettered separately when given thus — Aleph, Lamed He. Unto this Grade and unto the Sephirah Hod, the Eighth Path of the Sepher Yetsirah is referred. It is called the absolute or perfect Path, because it is the means of the Primordial, which hath no root to which it may be established, except in the penetralia of that Gedulah (Magnificence) which emanate from the subsisting properties thereof.

The distinguishing badge of this Grade which you are now entitled to wear, is the sash of the Theoricus with the addition of a purple cross above the white cross and the numbers three and eight within a circle and a square respectively, left and right of its summit — and below the number 32, the numbers 30 and 31 in purple between two narrow purple lines.

This grade is especially referred to the Element of Water and therefore the Great Watch Tower of Tablet of the West forms one of its principal emblems.

Hierophant and Theoricus turn towards it.

It is known as the Second or Great Western Quadrangle or Tablet of Water, and it is one of the Four Great Tablets delivered unto Enoch by the Great Angel Ave. From it are drawn the Three Holy Secret Names of God — EMPEH ARSEL GAIOL — which are borne upon the Banners of the West, and numberless Divine and Angelic Names which appertain unto the element of Water. The meanings of the
<117> Tablets of Earth and Air were explained to you in the preceding Grades.

Turning to the Altar, Hierophant indicates the Cross and Triangle.

The Cross above the Triangle represents the power of the Spirit of Life rising above the triangle of the Waters and reflecting the Triune therein, as further marked by the Lamps at the angles. While the Cup of Water placed at the junction of the Cross and Triangle represents the maternal Letter MEM.

Hierophant returns to his Throne in the East. Hegemon indicates the seat West of the Altar to Theoricus who sits down. Hegemon comes round the Altar and removes the diagram stand, placing it in the South West, and returns to his place. All are seated.

The Portals in the East and South East are those of the Paths which conduct to higher Grades, while that in the South leads to the Four equals Seven of Philosophus, the highest Grade in the First Order.

This grade of Practicus is especially related to the Planet MERCURY, whose Kamea, or Mystical Square, together with Seals and Names formed from it, is shown in the East. The Symbol of Mercury when inscribed on the Tree of Life is also shown. It embraces all but Kether. The horns spring from DAATH, which is not properly a Sephirah, but rather the conjunction of Chokmah and Binah.

<118> I now congratulate you on having passed through the Ceremony of Three equals Eight of Practicus, and in recognition thereof, I confer upon you the Mystic Title of MONOCRIS DE ASTRIS, which means "Unicorn from the Stars"; and I give you the Symbol of MAIM which is the Hebrew Name for Water. *(knocks)* In the Name of ELOHIM TZABAOTH, I now proclaim that you have been duly advanced to the Grade of Three equals Eight of Practicus, and that you are Lord of the Thirtieth and Thirty First Paths.

CLOSING

Hiero *(knocks)* Assist me to close this Temple in the Three equals Eight Grade of Practicus.

All rise. The New Practicus is signed to rise.

Honoured Hegemon, see that the Temple is properly guarded. *(done)*

Heg Very Honoured Hierophant, the Temple is properly guarded.

Hiero Let us adore the Lord and King of water! *(knock)*

All face East.

Hiero Let ELOHIM TZABAOTH be praised unto the Countless Ages of Time, Amen!

Hegemon removes the seat of Practicus to the North, and leads Practicus to the East of Altar, where he stands facing West. Hierophant goes to the west before the Tablet of Water. All face West — Members arranging themselves in balanced disposition, facing West.

<119> *Hiero (knocks)* Let us rehearse the Prayer of the Undines or Water spirits!

Terrible King of the Sea, Thou who holdest the Keys of the Cataracts of Heaven, and who enclosest the subterranean Waters in the cavernous hollows of Earth. King of the Deluge and of the Rains of Spring. Thou who openest the sources of the rivers and of the fountains; Thou who commandest moisture which is, as it were, the Blood of the Earth, to become the sap of the plants. We adore Thee and we invoke Thee. Speak Thou unto us, Thy Mobile and changeful creatures, in the Great Tempests, and we shall tremble before Thee. Speak to us also in the murmur of the limpid Waters, and we shall desire Thy love.

O Vastness! wherein all the rivers of Being seek to lose themselves — which renew themselves ever in Thee! O Thou Ocean of Infinite Perfection ! O Height which reflectest Thyself in the Depth! O Depth which exhalest into the Height! Lead us into the true life, through intelligence, through love! Lead us unto immortality through sacrifice, that we may be found worthy to offer one day unto Thee, the Water, the Blood and the Tears, for the Remission of Sins! Amen.

Hierophant makes with his Sceptre, the Banishing Circle and Pentagrams in the Air before the Tablet.

Depart ye in peace unto your Habitations. May the blessing of
<120> Elohim Tzabaoth be upon you. Be there peace between us and you,
and be ye ready to come when ye are called! *(knock)*

All return to their places — Practicus being directed to West of Altar, facing West.

Hiero ו ווו ו ווו
Hiereus ו ווו ו ווו
Heg ו ווו ו ווו

Hegemon leads out the new Practicus. They give the Neophyte Sign as they pass Hierophant.

<121> # CEREMONY
OF THE
④ = [7] GRADE OF PHILOSOPHUS

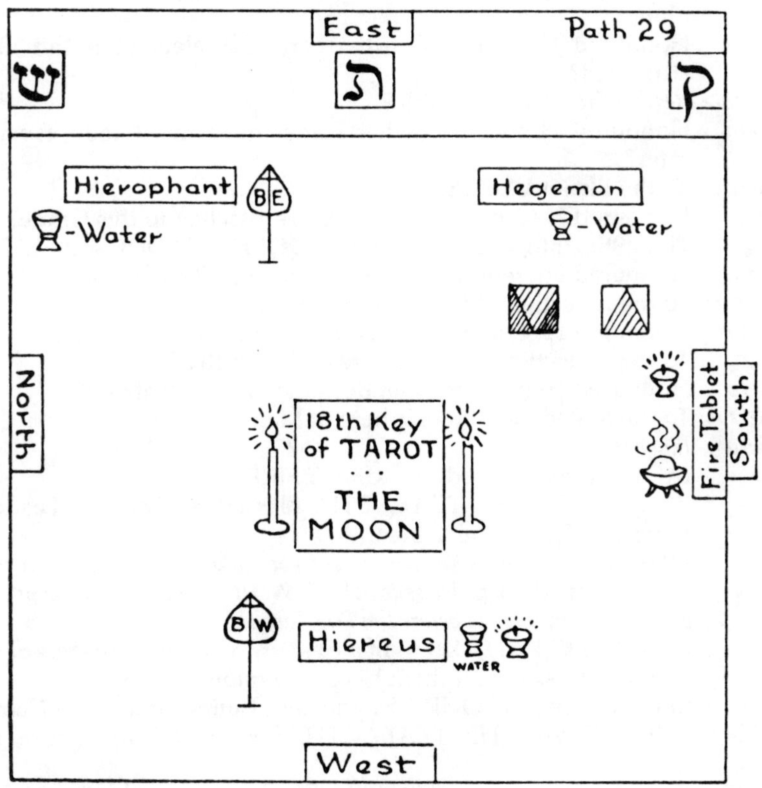

<122> THE OPENING

Arrangement of the Temple for the Opening and for the Path of Qoph. There are three Officers — Hierophant, Hiereus and Hegemon. The Throne of the Hierophant, beside which is a Cup of Water and the Banner of the East, is placed before the Dais N. E. The seat of the Hegemon is before the Dais in the S. E., that of Hiereus in the West. Each Officer has a Cup of Water. The Pillars are placed about three feet in front of Hegemon's seat, and behind her is displayed the Letter Qoph. The Altar in the Centre of the Hall is supplied with a candle on either side. On it is the Tarot Key of the Path — THE MOON. The Elemental lights are lit. Incense is burning in the South. This Sign ו *represents one knock. The Grade Knock is* ווו ווו ו.

Members are assembled and clothed. Hierophant knocks. All rise.

Hiero *(knock)* Honoured Fratres and Sorores, assist me to open the Temple in the ④ = ⑦ Grade of Philosophus. Honoured Hegemon, see that the Temple is properly guarded. *(done)*

Heg Very Honoured Hierophant, the Temple is properly guarded.

Hiero Honoured Hiereus, see that none below the Grade of Philosophus is present.

Hiereus Honoured Fratres, give the signs of the ④ = ⑦. *(done)* Very honoured Hierophant, all present have attained the Grade of Philosophus.

Hiero Honoured Hegemon, to what particular element is this Grade attributed?

<123> *Heg* To the Element of FIRE.

Hiero Honoured Hiereus, to what Planet does this Grade especially refer?

Hiereus To the Planet VENUS.

Hiero Honoured Hegemon, what Paths are attached to this Grade?

Heg The 29th, 28th, and 27th Paths of QOPH, TZADDI, and PEH.

Hiero Honoured Hiereus, to what does the 29th Path allude?

Hiereus To the reflection of the Sphere of PISCES.

Hiero Honoured Hegemon, to what does the 28th Path allude?

Heg To the Reflection of the Sphere of AQUARIUS.

Hiero Honoured Hiereus, to what does the 27th Path allude?

Hiereus To the Reflection of the Sphere of Mars

Hiero *(knock)*

Let us adore the Lord and King of FIRE.

YOD HE VAU HE TZABAOTH. Blessed be Thou — Leader of Armies is Thy Name, Amen!

All salute. Hiero quits his Throne and goes to the South. Hegemon stands behind him in the S. E., Hiereus in the S. W. Hierophant makes the invoking Pentagrams in a circle before the Fire Tablet.

And ELOHIM said, "Let us make Adam in our own Image, after our own likeness, and let them have Dominion."

In the Name of ELOHIM, Mighty and Ruling, and in the Name of
<124> YOD HE VAU HE TZABAOTH, Spirits of FIRE, adore your Creator!

Hierophant takes incense from before Fire Tablet, and makes the sign Leo in the air before it.

In the Name of MICHAEL, the Great Archangel of Fire, and in the Sign of the ♌ Lion, Spirits of Fire, adore your Creator!

Makes Cross with Incense.

In the Name and letters of the Great Southern Quadrangle revealed unto ENOCH by the Great Angel AVE, Spirits of Fire, adore your Creator!

Holds Incense on high.

In the Three Great Secret Names of God borne upon the Banners of the South — OIP TEAA PEDOCE — Spirits of FIRE adore your Creator!

In the Name of EDELPERNA, Great King of the South, Spirits of

Fire, adore your Creator!
Replaces Incense and returns to place.
All return to places.
In the name of YOD HE VAU HE TZABAOTH, I declare this Temple opened in the ④ = [7] Grade of PHILOSOPHUS.

Hiero ווו ווו ו
Hiereus ווו ווו ו
Heg ווו ווו ו

THE 29TH PATH OF QOPH

Hiero Fratres and Sorores, our Frater. . . . . .having made such progress in the Paths of Occult Science as has enabled him to pass the examina-
<125> tion in the requisite knowledge, and further, having been a Member of the ③ = [8] Grade of Practicus for a period of three months, is now eligible for advancement to the Grade of Philosophus and I have duly received a dispensation from the Greatly Honoured Chiefs of the Second Order, to advance him in due form. Honoured Hegemon, superintend the preparation of the Practicus and give the customary alarm.
Hegemon rises, salutes Hierophant, quits the Temple, and sees that the Practicus is robed and wearing the sash of the ③ = [8] Grade. She hoodwinks him and places in his hand the admission badge. She leads him to the Temple door and gives the alarm saying, as they enter:

Heg And the Ruach Elohim moved upon the Face of the Waters.
Hiereus admits them and returns to his place. Hegemon leads Practicus to the South by the Tablet of Fire, faces him East and takes away Cross.

Hiero Give the Hegemon the Signs and Words of this Grade.

Heg Give me the Sign of the ③ = [8] Grade. The Grip or Token—the Grand Word *(Elohim Tzabaoth)* The Mystic Number (36) and the Pass-Word *(Aleph Lamed He)* of the Grade of Practicus.

Hiero Give me also the Mystic Title and Symbol you received in that Grade *(Monocris de Astris. Maim.)*
This done, Hegemon faces Practicus to the Fire Tablet.
<126> Frater Monocris de Astris, do you solemnly pledge yourself to maintain the same strict secrecy regarding the Mysteries of the 29th, 28th, and 27th Paths and of the ④ = [7] Grade of Philosophus which you have already sworn to maintain respecting those of the preceding Grades?

Practicus (prompted if necessary) I do.

Hiero Then you will stretch your arms above your head to their full limit and say: "I swear by the Torrent of FIRE."
Practicus repeats words.
Let the hood-wink be removed.
Done. Hegemon gives Practicus the incense from before the Tablet.
Wave the incense before the Tablet of Fire and say: "Let the Powers of Fire witness my pledge."
Done. Practicus repeats words. Hegemon replaces incense.
Conduct the Practicus to the East and place him between the Mystic

Pillars. *(done)* Before you are the Portals of the 31st, 32nd, and 29th PATHS as in the Grade of Zelator. The two former you have already traversed, and the Portal of the 29th PATH leading to the Grade of Philosophus is now open to you. Take in your right hand the Calvary Cross of Twelve Squares and follow your guide through the Path of the Waters.

Hegemon circumambulates Temple once with Practicus, having given him the Calvary Cross to carry. As they approach the East for the second time,
<127> *Hierophant rises holding up Cup of Water. Hegemon and Practicus halt.*

The priest with the Mask of OSIRIS spake and said: I am Water, stagnant and silent and still, reflecting all, concealing all. I am the Past — I am the Inundation. He who riseth from the Great Water is my Name. Hail unto ye, Dwellers of the Land of Night! For the rending of Darkness is near.

Heg. leads Practicus round to Hiereus who rises cup in hand as they approach. Hegemon and Practicus halt before him.

Hiereus The Priest with the Mask of HORUS spake and said: I am Water, turbid and troubled. I am the Banisher of Peace in the vast abode of the Waters. None is so strong that can withstand the Great Waters — the Vastness of their Terror — the Magnitude of their Fear — the Roar of their Thundering Voice. I am the Future, mist-clad and shrouded in gloom. I am the Recession of the Torrent. The storm veiled in Terror is my Name. Hail unto the Mighty Powers of Nature and the Chiefs of the Whirling Storm!

Hegemon takes Practicus round to his own seat, takes up Cup and says:

Heg The Priestess with the Mask of ISIS spake and said: The traveller through the Gates of Anubis is my Name. I am Water, pure and limpid ever flowing on toward the sea. I am the Ever-passing Present that stands in the place of the Past. I am the Fertilised land. Hail unto
<128> thee Dwellers of the Wings of the Morning!

Heg. replaces Cup and leads Practicus to a seat West of the Altar, and returns to place.

Hiero *(rising)* I arise in the place of the Gathering of the Waters, through the rolled back Cloud of Night. From the Father of Waters went forth the Spirit, rending asunder the veils of Darkness. And there was but a Vastness of Silence and of Depth in the place of the Gathering Waters. Terrible was the Silence of that Uncreated World — Immeasurable the depth of that Abyss. And the Countenances of Darkness half-formed arose — they abode not — they hasted away — and in the Darkness of Vacancy, the Spirit moved and the Lightbearers existed for a space.

I have said Darkness of Darkness — are not the Countenances of Darkness fallen with Kings? Do the Sons of the Night of Time last for ever? And have they not yet passed away? Before all things are the Waters and the Darkness and the Gates of the Land of Night. And the CHAOS cried aloud for the Unity of Form — and the Face of the ETERNAL arose. Before the Glory of that Countenance the Night rolled back and the Darkness hasted away. In the Waters beneath

was that Face reflected, in the Formless Abyss of the Void. From those Eyes darted rays of terrible splendour which crossed with the currents reflected. That Brow and those Eyes formed the triangle of the Measureless Heavens —and their reflections formed the
<129> triangle of the Measureless Waters. And thus was formulated the Eternal Hexad — the number of the Dawning Creation.

Hegemon conducts the Practicus to the foot of Hiero's throne — handing to Hiero the Calvary Cross of twelve squares.

The Calvary Cross of Twelve Squares fitly represents the ZODIAC which embraces the Waters of Nu as the ancient Egyptians called the Heavens, the Waters which be above the Firmament. It also alludes to the Eternal River of Eden, divided into four Heads which find their correlations in the four triplicities of the Zodiac.

Places Cross aside.

The 29th PATH of the Sepher Yetsirah which answereth unto the letter QOPH is called the Corporeal Intelligence — and it is so called because it forms the very body which is so formed beneath the whole Order of the Worlds and the increment of them. It is therefore the reflection of the Watery Sign of Pisces and the Path connecting the material universe as depicted in Malkuth with the Pillar of Mercy and the side of Chesed, through the Sephirah NETZACH, and through it do the Waters of Chesed flow down.

Hiero, Hegemon and Practicus come to the West of the Altar.

Before you upon the Altar is the 18th Key of TAROT which symbolically resumes these Ideas. It represents the MOON with four Hebrew YODS like drops of dew falling, two dogs, two Towers, a
<130> winding Path leading to the Horizon, and, in the fore-ground, Water with a Crayfish crawling through it to the land.

The Moon is in its increase on the side of Mercy, Gedulah, and from it proceed sixteen principal and sixteen secondary rays, which make 32, the number of the Paths of Yetsirah. She is the Moon at the feet of the Woman of Revelations, ruling equally over the cold and moist natures and the passive elements of Earth and Water. It is to be noted that the symbol of the Sign is formed of two lunar crescents bound together. It thus shows the lunar nature of the Sign. The Dogs are the Jackals of the Egyptian ANUBIS, guarding the Gates of the East and of the West, shown by the two Towers between which lies the Path of all the heavenly bodies ever rising in the East and setting in the west. The Cray-fish is the Sign Cancer and was anciently the Scarabeus or Khephera, the emblem of the Sun below the Horizon as he ever is when the Moon is increasing above. Also, when the Sun is in the Sign Pisces the Moon will be well in her increase in Cancer as shown by the Cray-fish emblem.

Hiero returns to place. Hegemon remains with Practicus West of Altar.

I have now much pleasure in conferring upon you the title of LORD of the 29th PATH. You will now quit the Temple for a short time, and on your return the Ceremony of your passage of the 28th PATH will take place.

Hegemon conducts Practicus out.

<131> THE PATH OF TZADDI

The arrangement is the same. The Letter TZADDI is substituted for that of QOPH in the S. E. On the Altar is the Tarot Key of THE STAR. Officers seated as before, each with a Cup of Water. Hegemon requires the Admission Badge of the Solid Pyramid of the Elements.

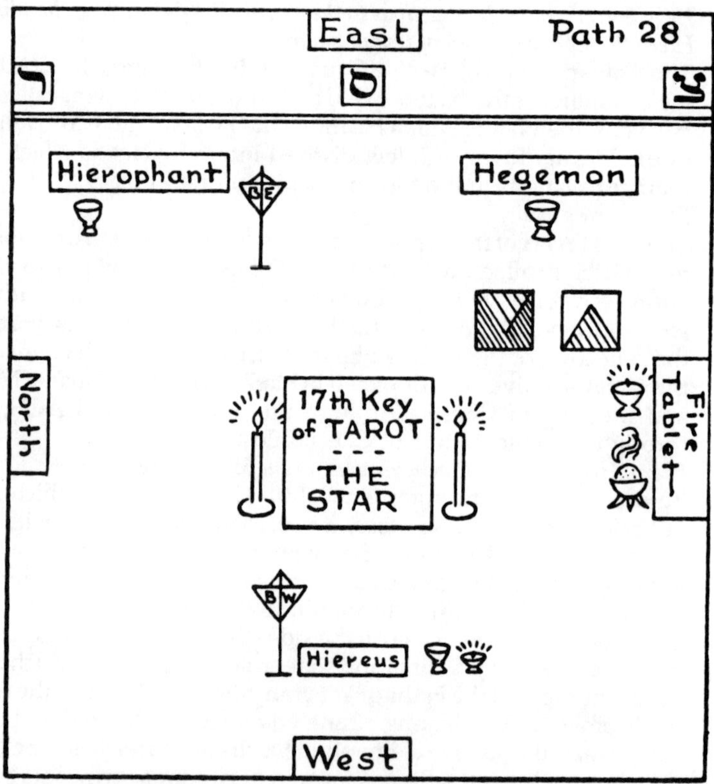

The Temple is symbolically in YESOD, whence the Candidate is taken by the Path of TZADDI to the Gate of NETZACH. Therefore the other paths symbolically in the East are those of RESH in the N. E., and SAMEKH in the East.

<132> *Hiero* Honoured Hegemon, you have my commands to present the Practicus with the necessary Admission Badge and to admit him.

Hegemon goes out, presents Practicus with the solid pyramid of the Elements, and admits him, saying:

Heg And ever forth from their Celestial Source, the Rivers of Eden flow.

Leads Practicus to the S. E. before Pillars.

Hiero Frater Monocris de Astris, the Path now open to you is the 28th leading from the ② = 9 of Theoricus to the ④ = 7 of Philosophus. Take in your right hand the solid pyramid of the Elements, and follow the Guide of the Path.

Hegemon and Practicus circumambulate the Hall once. As they approach Hiero, the second time, he rises Cup in hand. They halt.

The Priestess with the Mask of ISIS spake and said: I am the Rain of Heaven descending upon Earth, bearing with it the fructifying and germinating power. I am the plenteous Yielder of Harvest. I am the Cherisher of Life.

Hegemon leads Practicus to seat of Hiereus. He rises, Cup in hand. They halt.

Hiereus The Priestess with the Mask of NEPHTHYS spake and said: I am the Dew descending viewless and silent, gemming the Earth with countless diamonds of Dew, bearing down the influence from above in the solemn darkness of Night.

Hegemon leads Practicus to his own seat, takes Cup and says:

<133> *Heg* The Priestess with the Mask of ATHOR spake and said: I am the Ruler of Mist and Cloud wrapping the Earth, as it were, in a Garment, floating and hovering between Earth and Heaven. I am the Giver of the Dew-clad Night.

Replaces Cup and leads Practicus to a place West of the Altar, facing Hiero. and returns to place.

Hiero Where the Paternal Monad is, the Monad is enlarged and generateth two, and beside Him is seated the Duad and glittereth with Intellectual Sections. Also to govern all things and order everything not ordered. For in the whole Universe shineth the Triad over which the Monad ruleth. This Order is the beginning of all sections.

Hiereus For the Mind of the Father said that all things should be cut into Three, whose will assented and then all things were divided.

For the Mind of the Eternal Father said, Into Three, governing all things by Mind. And there appeared in it the Triad, Virtue, Wisdom and Multicient Truth. Thus floweth forth the form of the Triad, being Pre-existent, not the first Essence, but that whereby all things are measured.

Heg For thou must know that all things bow before the Three Supernals. The first Course is Sacred — but in the midst thereof another, the third aerial, which cherisheth Earth in Fire, and the Fountain of
<134> Fountains and of all Fountains — the Matrix containing All. Thence springeth forth abundantly the generation of multifarious Matter.

Hegemon conducts Practicus to the foot of Hiero's Throne and hands to Hiero the Solid Pyramid of the Elements.

Hiero This Pyramid is attributed to the Four Elements. On the four triangles are their Hebrew Names: Asch — Fire; Mayim — Water; Ruach — Air; Aretz — Earth. On the Apex is the word ETH composed of the first and last letters of the Alphabet and implying Essence. The square base represents the Material Universe and on it is the word OLAM meaning World.

Hiero puts Pyramid aside.

The 28th PATH of the Sepher Yetzirah which answereth unto the Letter TZADDI is called the Natural Intelligence — and it is so called because through it is consummated and perfected the Nature of every existing being under the Orb of the Sun. It is therefore the reflection of the Airy Sign Aquarius, the Water-bearer, unto which is attributed the Countenance of Man, the ADAM who restored the World.

Hiero, Hegemon, and Practicus come West of the Altar.

Before you upon the Altar is the 17th Key of TAROT which symbolically resumes these ideas.

The large STAR in the centre of the Heavens has seven principal and
<135> fourteen secondary rays and this represents the Heptad multiplied by the Triad. This yields 21 — the Number of the Divine Name EHEIEH which, as you already know, is attached to KETHER.

In the Egyptian sense, it is SIRIUS the Dog-Star, the Star of Isis-Sothis. Around it are the Stars of the Seven Planets each with its seven-fold counterchanged operation.

The nude female figure with the Star of the Heptagram on her brow is the synthesis of Isis, of Nephthys, and of Athor. She also represents the planet VENUS through whose sphere the influence of Chesed descends. She is Aima, Binah, Tebunah, the Great Supernal Mother — Aima Elohim, pouring upon the Earth the Waters of Creation which unite and form a River at her feet, the River going forth from the Supernal Eden which floweth and faileth not.

Note well, that in this Key she is completely unveiled while in the 21st Key she is only partially so.

The two Urns contain the influences from Chokmah and Binah. On the right springs the Tree of Life, and on the left the Tree of Knowledge of Good and of Evil whereon the Bird of Hermes alights, and therefore does this Key represent the restored World, after the formless and the Void and the Darkness, the New ADAM, the Countenance of the Man which falls in the Sign AQUARIUS. And therefore doth the astronomical ripple of this sign represent, as it
<136> were, Waves of Water — the ripples of that River going forth out of Eden — but, therefore also, is it justly attributed to Air and not unto Water because it is the Firmament dividing and containing the Water.

Hierophant returns to his place.

I have much pleasure in conferring upon you the Title of Lord of the 28th Path. You will now quit the Temple for a short time and on your return the Ceremony of your passage of the 27th PATH will take place.

Hegemon leads Practicus out.

<137>

THE 27TH PATH OF PEH

The Temple is symbolically in HOD, and the Paths in the East and S. E., leading from it, are those of Mem, Ayin, Peh, Resh, and Shin. Of these, PEH is shown in the South, before which now stand the Pillars. Hierophant returns to his Throne on the Dais, Hiereus with his Banner is seated before the Dais in the N. E., Hegemon in the S. E. The Officers are supplied with Red Lamps.

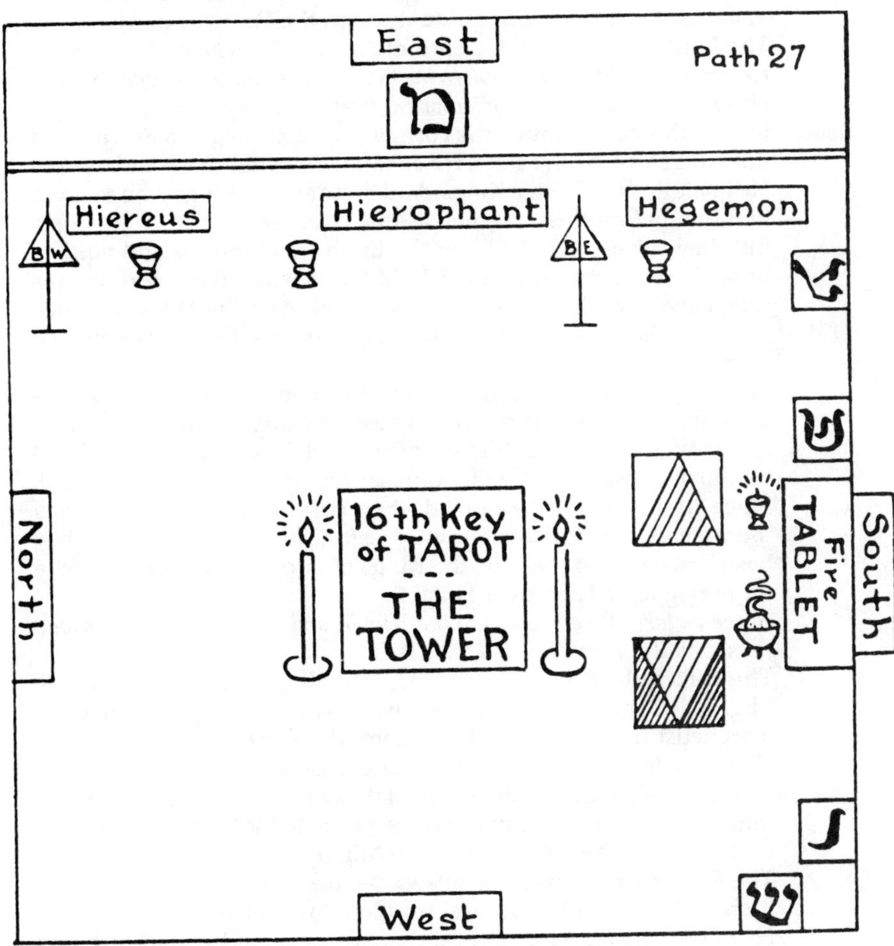

On the Altar is the Tarot Key of THE TOWER. The Admission Badge is the Calvary Cross of Ten Squares.

<138> *Hiero* Honoured Hegemon, you have my commands to present the Practicus with the necessary Admission Badge and to admit him.
Hegemon goes out, gives the Calvary Cross of Ten Squares to the Candidate and admits him saying:

Heg The River Kishon swept them away, that Ancient River, the River Kishon. O my Soul, thou hast trodden down strength.
Hegemon leads Practicus to the South, and places him before the Pillars.

Hiero *(knocks)* Frater Monocris de Astris, the Path now open to you is the 27th, which leads from the ③ = 8 Grade of Practicus to the ④ = 7 of Philosophus. Take in your right hand the Calvary Cross of Ten Squares and follow your guide through the Pathway of Mars.

Heg The Lord is a man of War; Lord of Armies is his Name!

Hegemon leads Practicus between the Pillars and round to Hierophant, halting at the foot of the Dais. Hierophant rises, red Lamp in hand.

Hiero Ere the Eternal instituted the Formation, Beginning and End existed not. Therefore, before Him, He expanded a certain Veil, and therein He instituted the Primal Kings. And these are the Kings who reigned in Edom before there reigned a King over Israel.

But they subsisted not. When the Earth was formless and void — behold this is the reign of EDOM. And when the Creation was established, lo, this is the reign of Israel. And the Wars of titanic
<139> forces in the Chaos of Creation, Lo, these are the Wars between them.

From a Light-bearer of unsupportable brightness, proceeded a radiating flame, hurling forth, like a vast and mighty Hammer, those sparks which were the Primal worlds. And these Sparks flamed and scintillated awhile, but being unbalanced, they were extinguished. Since lo, the Kings assembled, they passed away together, they themselves beheld, so they were astonished. They feared. They hasted away. And these be the Kings of Edom who reigned before there reigned a King over Israel.

Hegemon takes Practicus round the Temple, and halts before Hiereus who rises with Red Lamp in hand.

Hiereus The Dukes of Edom were amazed, trembling they took hold of the Mighty Moab, Lord, when Thou wentest out of SEIR, when Thou marchedst out of the Field of Edom, the Earth trembled and the Heavens dropped — the Clouds also dropped Water.

Curse ye MEROZ, said the Angel of the Lord — curse ye bitterly, the inhabitants thereof, because they came not to the help of the Lord — to the help of the Lord against the Mighty.

The River Kishon swept them away — that ancient River, the River Kishon. O my Soul, thou hast trodden down Strength!

He bowed the Heavens, also, and came down and the Darkness was under His Feet. At the brightness that was before Him the thick
<140> clouds passed — Hail-stones and flashings of Fire. The Lord thundered through the Heavens and the highest gave forth His Voice — Hail-stones and flashings of Fire. He sent out His Arrows and scattered them: He hurled forth His Lightnings and destroyed them.

Then the channels of the Waters were seen and the Foundations of the World were discovered. At Thy rebuke, O Lord — at the blast of the Breath of Thy Nostrils, the Voice of Thy Thunder was in the Heavens and Thy Lightnings lightened the World. The Earth trembled and shook. Thy way is in the Sea and Thy Path in the Great Waters and Thy Footsteps are not known.

Hegemon leads Practicus to her own seat before the Dais, takes Lamp and says:

Heg O Lord, I have heard Thy Speech and was afraid. The Voice of the Lord is upon the Waters. The God of Glory thundereth. The Lord is upon many Waters. The Voice of the Lord is powerful. The Voice of the Lord is full of Majesty. The Voice of the Lord breaketh the Cedars of Lebanon. The Voice of the Lord divideth the Flames of Fire. The Voice of the Lord shaketh the wilderness of Kadesh.

Hegemon places Practicus in a seat West of the Altar, facing Hiero; and takes the Calvary Cross. He returns to his place.

Hiero ELOAH came from Teman of EDOM and the Holy One from Mount Paran. His Glory covered the Heavens and the Earth was full of His
<141> praise. His brightness was as the Light. He had KARMAIM in His Hands and there was the hiding of His Power.

Before Him went the pestilence and Flaming Fire went forth at His Feet. He stood and measured the Earth. He beheld and drove asunder the Nations. And the Everlasting Mountains were scattered — and Perpetual Hills did bow. His ways are everlasting. I saw the tents of Cushan in affliction and the curtain of the Land of Midian did tremble.

Was the Lord displeased against the Rivers? Was Thy Wrath against the Sea that Thou didst ride upon Thy horses and Chariots of Salvation? Thou didst cleave asunder the Earth with the Rivers. The Mountains saw Thee and they trembled. The deluge of waters rolled by. The Deep uttered His voice and lifted up His hands on high. The SUN and the MOON stood still in their Habitations. At the Light of Thine arrows they went — at the shining of Thy Glittering Spear. Thou didst march through the Land in indignation. Thou didst thrash the Heathen in Thine Anger. Thou didst march through the Sea with Thy Horses — through the depth of the Mighty Waters.

Hegemon leads practicus to Hiero and gives Hiero the Calvary Cross.

The Calvary Cross of Ten Squares refers to the Ten Sephiroth in balanced disposition, before which the Formless and the Void rolled
<142> back. It is also the opened out form of the Double Cube and of the Altar of Incense.

Places Cross aside.

The 27th PATH of the Sepher Yetzirah which answereth unto PEH is called the Exciting Intelligence, and it is so called because by it is created the Intellect of all created Beings under the Highest Heaven, and the Excitement or Motion of them.

It is therefore the Reflection of the Sphere of Mars, and the Reciprocal Path connecting Netzach with Hod, Victory with Splendour. It is the lowermost of the three Reciprocal Paths.

Hiero, Heg, and Practicus come to the W. of Altar.

Hiero Before you upon the Altar is the 16th Key of TAROT, which symbolically resumes these ideas.

It represents a Tower struck by a Lightning Flash proceeding from a rayed circle and terminating in a triangle. It is the Tower of Babel struck by the Fire from Heaven. It is to be noted that the triangle at the end of the flash, issuing from the circle, forms exactly the astronomical symbol of Mars.

It is the Power of the Triad rushing down and destroying the Columns of Darkness. Three holes are rent in the walls, symbolising the establishment of the Triad therein and the Crown at the summit of the Tower is falling, as the Crowns of the Kings of Edom fell, who are also symbolised by the men falling headlong. On the right hand side
<143> of the Tower is LIGHT and the representation of the Tree of LIFE by ten circles this disposed.

On the left hand side is DARKNESS and eleven circles symbolising the QLIPPOTH.

Hierophant returns to his throne. Hegemon and Practicus remain West of Altar.

I have much pleasure in conferring upon you the Title of LORD OF THE 27TH PATH.

You will now quit the Temple for a short time and on your return, the Ceremony of your Reception into the ④ = [7] Grade of Philosophus will take place.

Hegemon leads Practicus out.

<144>

THE ENTRY INTO NETZACH
GRADE OF PHILOSOPHUS

The Pillars are placed on either side of the Altar, North, and South. On the Altar are the Cross and Triangle placed to represent the symbol of Sulphur. At each Angle of the Triangle a red lamp burns. East of the Altar, suspended from a banner pole, is the

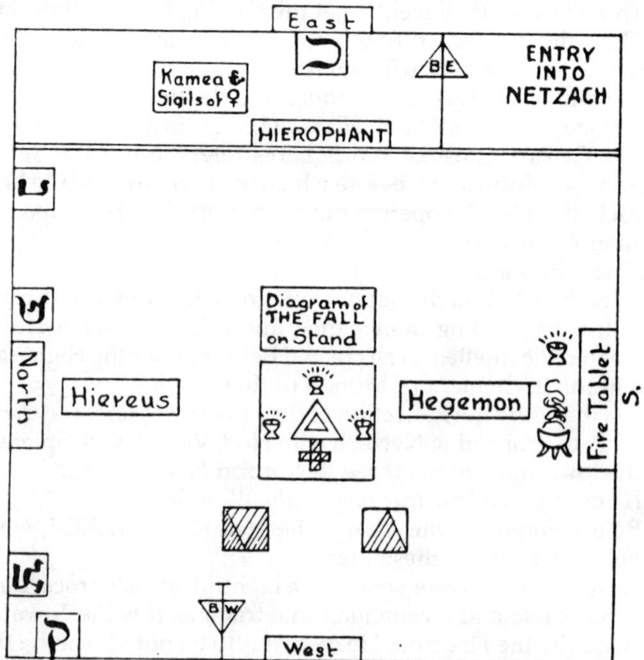

Diagram of THE FALL, facing West. The Temple is now symbolically in NETZACH so the Paths which enter it from the East and North are shown: E. CAPH; N. E.
<145> *corner NUN; N. PEH; N. W. TZADDI; N. W. corner QOPH. The symbol of VENUS on the Tree of Life is shown in the East. Hierophant is seated in the East; Hiereus and Hegemon North and South of the Altar, respectively, beside the Pillars. Hegemon requires the Sash of the Grade, and Badge of LAMEN of Hegemon.*

Hiero Honoured Hegemon, you have my commands to present the Practicus with the necessary Admission Badge and to admit him.

Hegemon instructs Practicus to knock, gives him Lamen, and admits him.

In the North West are the Portals of the 29th and 28th PATHS by which you have symbolically entered this Grade from the ① = [10] and the ② = [9] Grades respectively, while in the North is the Portal of the 27th PATH by which you have just passed from the Grade of Practicus.

Hegemon leads Practicus to Hiereus.

Hiereus By what symbol dost thou enter herein?

Heg By the peculiar Emblem of the Hegemon which is the Calvary Cross of Six Squares.

Hiereus This Cross embraces, as you see, Tiphareth, Netzach, Hod and Yesod, and rests upon Malkuth. Also, the Calvary Cross of Six Squares forms the Cube, and is thus referred to the Six Sephiroth of Microprosopus which are Chesed, Geburah, Tiphareth, Netzach, Hod and Yesod.

Hegemon faces Practicus to the Diagram at the Altar. Hiero comes West of Altar and points to Diagram. Hegemon resumes seat.

<146> *Hiero* This is the symbolic representation of THE FALL. For, the Great Goddess who, in the ③ = [8] Grade was supporting the Columns of the Sephiroth, in the sign of the ② = [9] Grade, being tempted by the Tree of Knowledge (whose branches indeed tend upward into the Seven Lower Sephiroth, but also tend downward unto the Kingdom of Shells) reached down unto the Qlippoth, and immediately the Columns were unsupported and the Sephirotic system was shattered, and with it fell ADAM, the MICROPROSOPUS.

Then arose the Great DRAGON with Seven Heads and Ten Horns, and the Garden was made desolate, and MALKUTH was cut off from the Sephiroth by his intersecting folds, and linked unto the Kingdom of Shells. And the Seven Lower Sephiroth were cut off from the Three Supernals in DAATH, at the feet of AIMA ELOHIM.

And on the Heads of the Dragon are the Names and Crowns of the Edomite Kings. And because in DAATH was the greatest rise of the Great Serpent of Evil, therefore is there, as it were, another Sephirah, making for the Infernal or Averse Sephiroth, Eleven instead of Ten.

And hence were the Rivers of Eden desecrated, and from the Mouth of the DRAGON rushed the Infernal Waters in DAATH. And this is LEVIATHAN, The Crooked Serpent.

But between the Devastated Garden and the Supernal Eden, YOD
<147> HE VAU HE ELOHIM placed the Letters of THE NAME and THE FLASHING SWORD that the uppermost part of the Tree of Life might not be involved in the Fall of Adam. And thence it was necessary that the SECOND ADAM should come to restore all things and that, as the First Adam had been extended on the Cross of the Celestial Rivers, so the SON should be crucified on the Cross of the Infernal Rivers of DAATH. Yet, to do this, he must descend unto the lowest first, even unto Malkuth and be born of her.

The ④ = [7] Grade of PHILOSOPHUS is referred unto the Sephirah NETZACH and the 27th, 28th, and 29th PATHS are bound thereto. The Sign of this Grade is given by raising the hands to the fore-head, and with the thumbs and index fingers forming a triangle, apex up thus .... This represents the element of FIRE to which this Grade is allotted, and also the Spirit which moved upon the Waters of Creation. The Grip or token is the general Grip of the First Order. The GRAND WORD is a Name of nine letters — YOD HE VAU HE TZABAOTH, which means Lord of Armies.

The Mystic Number is 28 and from it is formed the Pass Word KAPH CHETH, which should be lettered separately when given. It means Power.

Unto this Grade, and unto the Sephirah NETZACH, the Seventh Path of the Sepher Yetzirah is referred. It is called the Recondite
<148> Intelligence, and it is so called because it is the Refulgent Splendour of all the Intellectual Virtues which are perceived by the Eye of the Mind and by the Contemplation of Faith.

The distinguishing Badge of this Grade which you will now be entitled to wear, is the sash of a Practicus, with the addition of a bright green cross above the violet cross and the numbers ④ in a circle and [7] in a square on either side of its summit, and below the number 31, the numbers 27, 28, and 29 in bright green, between narrow bars of the same colour.

This Grade is especially referred to FIRE and therefore, the Great Watch-Tower or Terrestrial Tablet of the South forms one of its principal Emblems. It is known as the Fourth or Great Southern Quadrangle and is one of the Four Great Tablets delivered unto ENOCH by the Great Angel Ave. From it are drawn the Three Holy Secret Names of God OIP TEAA PEDOCE, which are borne upon the Banners of the South, and numberless Divine and Angelic Names which appertain unto the Element of Fire. The meanings of the other Tablets have already been explained to you.

The Triangle surmounting the Cross upon the Altar represents the Fire of the Spirit surmounting the Cross of Life and of the Waters of Edom. You will note that it thus forms the Alchemical Emblem of Sulphur. The Red Lamps at the angles of the Triangle are the Threefold form of Fire.

<149> *Hiero resumes his seat. Hegemon conducts Practicus to him.*
The Portals in the East and North East conduct to higher Grades. The others are those of Paths you have already traversed. This Grade is related to the Planet VENUS, Ruler in NETZACH. Its Symbol, when inscribed on the Tree of Life is shown in the East. It embraces the whole of the Sephiroth, and is therefore a fitting emblem of the Isis of Nature; hence, also, its circle is represented larger than that of Mercury.

Hegemon leads Philosophus to a seat West of the Altar, facing East, and removes the diagram of The Fall. He returns to his place.

I now congratulate you Honoured Frater, on having passed through the Ceremony of the ④ = 7⃞ Grade of Philosophus and in recognition thereof, I confer upon you the Mystic Title PHAROS ILLUMINANS, which means Illuminating Tower of Light, and I give you the symbol of ASCH which is the Hebrew Name for Fire.

And, as having attained at length to the highest Grade of the First Order, and being, as it were, the connecting link with the Second Order, I further confer upon you the title of respect "Honoured Frater" and I give you the further symbol of PHRATH or Euphrates, the Fourth River. *(knocks)* In the name of YOD HE VAU HE TZABAOTH, I now proclaim that you have been duly advanced to the ④ = 7⃞ Grade of Philosophus and that you are Lord of the 27th,
<150> 28th, and 29th PATHS.

Hiereus Honoured Frater, as a Member of this important Grade, you are eligible for the post of Hiereus when a vacancy occurs. You are furthermore expected, as having risen so high in the Order, to aid to your utmost the Members of the Second Order in the working of the Temple to which you are attached; to study thoroughly the Mysteries which have been unfolded to your view in your progress from the humble position of Neophyte, so that yours may not be the merely superficial knowledge which marks the conceited and ignorant man, but that you may really and thoroughly understand what you profess to know, and not by your ignorance and folly bring disgrace on that Order which has honoured you so far.

Your duty is also to supervise the studies of weaker and less advanced brethren, and to make yourself as far as possible an Ornament, alike to your Temple and to your Order.

CLOSING

Hiero *(knocks)* Assist me to close the Temple in the ④ = 7⃞ Grade of Philosophus. Honoured Hegemon, see that the Temple is properly guarded.

Heg Very Honoured Hierophant, the Temple is properly guarded.

Hiero Let us adore the Lord and King of Fire. *(knocks)*
All face East.

Hiero YOD HE VAU HE of Hosts, Mighty and Terrible! Commander of
<151> the Ethereal Armies art thou! Amen!
All salute. Hiero goes to Fire Tablet. Hiereus stands behind him S. W.,

Hegemon places Practicus in the North facing South, and goes S. E. Any members present should arrange themselves in balanced formation behind Hiereus and Hegemon.

Let us rehearse the Prayer of the Salamanders or Fire Spirits. *(knocks)*

Immortal, Eternal, Ineffable and Uncreated Father of all, borne upon the Chariot of Worlds which ever roll in ceaseless motion. Ruler over the Etherial Vastness where the Throne of Thy Power is raised, from the summit of which Thine Eyes behold all and Thy Pure and Holy Ears hear all — help us, thy children, whom Thou hast loved since the birth of the Ages of Time! Thy Majesty, Golden, Vast and Eternal, shineth above the Heaven of Stars. Above them art Thou exalted.

O Thou Flashing Fire, there Thou illuminatest all things with Thine Insupportable Glory, whence flow the Ceaseless Streams of Splendour which nourish Thine Infinite Spirit. This Infinite Spirit nourisheth all and maketh that inexhaustible Treasure of Generation which ever encompasseth Thee —replete with the numberless forms wherewith Thou hast filled it from the Beginning.

From this Spirit arise those most holy Kings who are around Thy
<152> Throne and who compose Thy Court.

O Universal Father, One and Alone! Father alike of Immortals and Mortals. Thou hast specially created Powers similar unto Thy Thought Eternal and unto Thy Venerable Essence. Thou hast established them above the Angels who announce Thy Will to the world.

Lastly, Thou hast created us as a third Order in our Elemental Empire.

There our continual exercise is to praise and to adore Thy Desires: there we ceaselessly burn with Eternal Aspirations unto Thee, O Father! O Mother of Mothers! O Archetype Eternal of Maternity and Love! O Son, the Flower of all Sons! Form of all Forms! Soul, Spirit, Harmony and Numeral of all things! Amen!

Hiero makes Banishing Circle and Pentagrams with sceptre before Tablet.

Depart ye in peace unto your habitations. May the blessing of YOD HE VAU HE TZABAOTH be upon ye! Be there peace between us and you, and be ye ready to come when ye are called.

Hiero returns to his place. The others follow. Hegemon leads Philosophus to his seat.

In the name of YOD HE VAU HE TZABAOTH, I declare this Temple closed in the ④ = [7] Grade of Philosophus.

Hiero ווו ווו ו
Hiereus ווו ווו ו
Heg ווו ווו ו

Hegemon conducts the Philosophus out.

BOOK THREE

RITUALS OF THE INNER ORDER, THE ROSEAE RUBAE ET AUREAE CRUCIS.

<155> RITUAL OF THE PORTAL OF THE VAULT OF THE ADEPTI

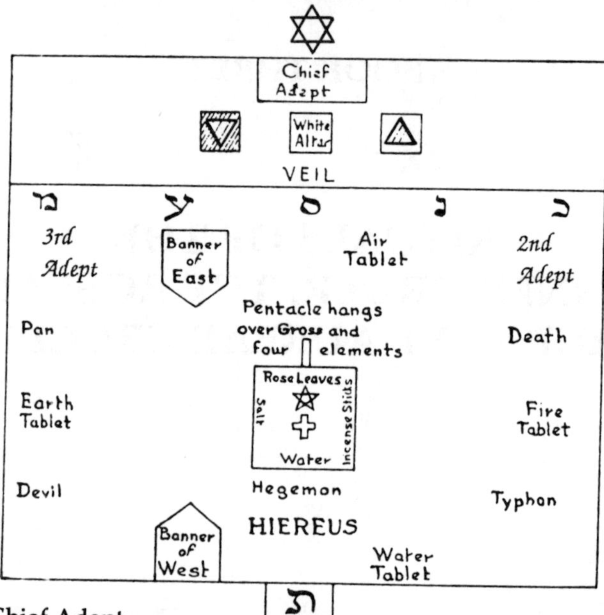

<156> Chief Adept—

White Cassock, Yellow Shoes, Red Cloak of Hierophant, Yellow and White Nemyss, Rose-Cross on Yellow Collar. Sceptre of five Elemental Colours surmounted by Pentagram, White Lamp and Brazier, Candle.

Second Adept—

White Cassock and Collar, Blue Shoes, Blue and Orange Cloak and Nemyss, Lamen of Red Triangle in Green Pentagram, Red Wand headed by Red Sulphur Symbol, Red Lamp and Incense Sticks.

Third Adept—

White Cassock, Blue Collar, and Red Shoes, Red and Green Nemyss and Cloak, Blue Wand headed by Blue Salt Symbol, Lamen of Blue Cup on Orange Octagram, Cup of Water.[1]

Hiereus—

Black Cassock, Black Collar, Black and White Nemyss, Red Shoes and Collar, Sword, Lamen of Four Colours of Malkuth with White Hexagram, Salt.

[1]The Wands of the Chief and Second Adepts are a "cut-out" pentagram, and a red Sulphur Symbol painted on a green oval, respectively. The Lamens of the Second and Third Adepts are simply cut out in the correct polygon form with the Red Triangle painted on the green Penta-*gon,* and the Blue-Cup painted on an orange lamen with eight sides.

The Hiereus Lamen is, in reality, a modification of the design on the Earth Pentacle. H.S.

Hegemon—

Black Cassock, White Cloak, Red Shoes, Yellow and Purple Nemyss, Mitre-headed Sceptre, Lamen of Red and Blue Hexagram on White Ground, Yellow Collar, Rose Leaves.

OPENING

Chief Adept is behind the Veil in the East, symbolically in Tiphareth—other Officers in their Sephirotic Stations — Third Adept in the North East,
<157> *Second Adept in the South East — Hiereus in West, Hegemon East of Altar.*[1]
The Hall is in Darkness, the Elemental Lamps unlit — no lights except those burning behind the Veil and shaded candles for Officers.

Any Members attending must give the Portal Signs on entering the Temple. Portal Members sit in the North — full ⑤ = [6] Members in the South.

2nd Ad. *(Knock. All rise.)* Very Honourable Fratres and Sorores, assist me to open the Portal of the Vault of the Adepti. Honourable Hiereus, see that the entrance is closed and guarded.

Hiereus Very Honourable Second Adept, the entrance is closed and guarded.

2nd Ad. Very Honourable Fratres and Sorores, in token of our search for the Light, give the Sign of the ⓪ = [0] Grade of Neophyte.

All turn East and stand in the Sign of the Enterer. From behind the Curtain, the Chief Adept's hand is stretched out, holding a white Lamp or Candle. Chief Adept unseen, gives the Sign of Silence—all repeat Sign as Light is withdrawn.

Ch. Ad. The Light shineth in Darkness, but the Darkness comprehendeth it not.

2nd Ad. The Dukes of Edom ruled in Chaos, Lords of unbalanced force. Honourable Hiereus, what is the Symbol upon the Altar?

Hiereus The Symbol of the equated forces of the Four Elements.

<158> *2nd Ad.* Banished be the Power of the Dukes of Edom, and let the Power of the Cross be established.[2]

Chief Adept signs Cross with lighted candle. Hiereus goes to East, begins Lesser Ban. Ritual of Pentagram. When he returns East all Officers and Members make Qabalistic cross, facing East and repeat words with him. Hiereus returns to place West and makes ① = [10] Sign.

Hegemon in the East makes ② = [9] Sign and knocks.

Third Adept in North makes ③ = [8] Sign and knocks.

[1]Note to the Opening Description.

Chief Adept	Tiphareth (behind the Veil)	Spirit
Second Adept	Netzach ④ = [7]	Fire
Third Adept	Hod ③ = [8]	Water
Hiereus	Malkuth (all give ⓪ = [0])	Earth
Hegemon	Yesod ② = [9]	Air

At this point in the Ceremony, the Spirit is about to descend onto its Throne—Chariot of the Elements. H.S.

[2]To really comprehend the Ritual of the Portal and the Ceremony ⑤ = [6] Grade of Adeptus Minor one should re-read Mathers Lecture "The Microcosm-Man" on p. 203 of Book One, especially the top half of p. 206, reflecting on the Elemental Attributions of IHVH, the Black Jehovah, represented by four of the officers of this Portal Ritual. Then, considering the change affected by the Descent of the Spirit into the Midst of the Elements, as represented by the Chief Adept in this Ritual, one must analyze FYING ROLL X, by Mathers, delivered Good Friday, March 31st, 1893, (as reprinted in *Astral Projection, Magic and Alchemy,* edited by Francis King). H.S.

Second Adept in the South makes ④ = [7] *Sign and knocks.*

Ch. Ad.
The Cross upon the Altar is also a Cross of corrosion, corruption, disintegration and death. Therefore, doth it fall in the Paths of Death and the Devil, unless in Hod, the Glory triumpheth over matter and the Corruptible putteth on Incorruption, thus attaining unto the beauty of Tiphareth; unless in Netzach, Death is swallowed up in Victory and the Transformer becometh the Transmuter into Pure Alchemic Gold. 'Except ye be born of Water and the Spirit, ye cannot enter the Kingdom of God.'
What then Very Honourable Third Adept, is the additional Mystic Title bestowed upon a Philosophus as a link with the Second Order?

3rd Ad. Phrath, the Fourth River of Eden.

Hiereus Tau.

Heg Resh.

3rd Ad. Peh.

<159> *Ch. Ad.* Very Honourable Second Adept, what may be added to this Word?

2nd Ad. Kaph *(knock)*

Hiereus Tau *(knock)*

Heg Resh *(knock)*

3rd Ad. Peh *(knock)*

Ch. Ad. The whole Word is Paroketh, which is the Veil of the Tabernacle.
All make Signs of Rending of the Veil.

Ch. Ad. *(knocks)* In and by that Word, I permit the Portal of the Vault of the Adepti to be opened.
Second and Third Adepts draw aside curtains revealing Chief Adept who rises with Pentacle and taper in left hand, Sceptre in right.
Let us establish the Dominion of the Mystic ETH over the Four Elements.
Chief Adept faces East. All face East. Chief Adept having descended from the Dais and taken his position in front of Air Tablet, Hegemon stands behind Chief bearing Rose Leaves. All make Qabalistic Cross. Hegemon places Rose Leaves before Air Tablet and stands in the ② = [9] *Sign. Chief lights the Lamps as he goes round. Chief Adept invokes Air and lights Lamp. Hegemon takes Rose Leaves to Altar and puts them on Air arm of Cross and remains East of Altar facing West.*
Chief Adept goes to South. Second Adept comes behind, places sticks of incense before Tablet and stands in ④ = [7] *Sign.*
Chief Adept invokes Fire and lights Lamp as before. Second Adept
<160> *takes incense to Altar and places it on Fire arm of the Cross and stands at the*
South of Altar looking North.
Chief Adept goes West lights Lamp. Third Adept stands behind him, places Cup before Tablet and stands in Sign of ③ = [8]. *Chief Adept invokes Water. Third Adept takes Cup to Altar, places it on Water arm of Cross and stands in Sign of* ③ = [8].
Chief Adept goes North. Lights Lamp, Hiereus stands behind him, places Salt before Tablet and stands in ① = [10] *Sign. Chief Adept invokes Earth.*

Hiereus takes Salt to the Altar, places it on Earth arm of Cross and stands at the North of Altar. Chief Adept completes circle in East, then circumambulates with Sol to West of Altar, having now lit all the Elemental Lamps.

In the Great Name YOD HE VAU HE.

All give ⓪ = [0] *Signs towards Altar, and then stand in Elemental Signs. Chief Adept makes Invoking Spirit Pentagrams with Deity Names EHEIEH and AGLA closing with the Qabbalistic Cross. He moves round the Altar to East, faces West lays Pentacle over Cross. Holds Candle and Wand on high.*

May the Cross of the Four Elements become truly purified and planted in Incorruption. Wherefore in the Name of YOD HE VAU HE and in the Concealed Name YEHESHUA, do I add the power of the Pentagram constituting the Glorified body of Osiris, the Sign of the Microcosmos.

<161> *All lights are turned up. Chief Adept lays Pentacle for a moment on Cross then hangs it on hook in centre of Hall, raises Sceptre and Candle on high, and invokes:*

OL SONUF VA-ORSAGI GOHO IADA BALATA. ELEXARPEH COMANANU TABITOM. ZODAKARA, EKA ZODAKARE OD ZODAMERANU. ODO KIKLE QAA PIAPE PIAMOEL OD VAOAN.

Chief Adept returns to Dais. Second and Third follow and stand by Pillars. Hiereus and Hegemon face East, North and South of Altar.

Let us adore the Lord and King of Hosts.
Holy art thou, Lord of the Universe.
Holy art Thou Whom Nature hath not formed;
Holy art Thou the Vast and the Mighty One,
Lord of the Light and of the Darkness.*

By the Word Paroketh and in the Sign of the Rending of the Veil, I declare that the Portal of the Vault of the Adepti has been opened.

Ch. Ad. וווו ו
2nd Ad. וווו ו
3rd Ad. וווו ו
Hiereus וווו ו
Heg וווו ו

He circumambulates once, then returns to seat. All take seats, after the Elements are replaced in Four Quarters by respective Officers.

<163> THE RITUAL OF THE CROSS AND FOUR ELEMENTS

Ch. Ad (Concealed behind the Veil):
The Portal symbolically opened for the Order, is yet closed to the unprepared Candidate.

*The prayer above, a key to the Neophyte Ritual, (which opens the Outer Order as the Portal Ritual opens the Second Order), is the happy song raised by the mystic-theurgist of the *POEMANDRES, Corpus Hermeticum,* Book One, verse thirty one. Greek text can be found in *Scotts Hermetica,* sympathetic explanation can be found in Mead's *Thrice-Greatest Hermes.* H.S.

Elemental Lamps are veiled. Temple in darkness save at East.

2nd Ad. V.H. Fratres and Sorores, our Honoured Frater........having been a member of the ④ = [7] Grade of Philosophus for the space of 7 months and having passed the five-fold examination prescribed for admission to the Second Order, has been duly approved.
I hold a Dispensation from the G. H. Chiefs of the Second Order to permit him to approach the Portal of the Vault of the Adepti.
V.H. 3rd Adept, see that he is duly prepared by wearing the Sash of the ④ = [7] Grade, admit him, having placed around his neck the Admission Badge, and having examined him in his knowledge of the Grip, Sign, Words, etc. of the ④ = [7] Grade and of the Word Phrath before you instruct him in the necessary knock.
Lights are extinguished. 2nd Ad. stands before the Veil. Hiereus and Heg. bar the way near the door. 3rd Adept, having prepared Phil. opens door showing Darkness but for faint Light in the East, and brings Phil, just within the door.

Heg. The Realm of Chaos and of Ancient Night, ere ever the Aeons were,
<164> when there was neither Heaven or Earth, nor was there any Sea, when naught was, save the Shape Unluminous, formless and void.

Hiereus To and fro in the Deeps, swayed the coils of the Dragon with 8 Heads and 11 Horns. Eleven were the curses of Mount Ebal, eleven the Rulers of the Qlippoth, and at their head were the Dual Contending Forces.[1]
Hiereus and Heg. lower weapons and step back.

2nd Ad. *(faces East)* Then breathed forth Tho-oth out of the Unutterable Abyss the Word! Then stood forth Tho-oth in the Sign of the Enterer, on the Threshold of the Hall of Time as Time was born of the Eternal. *(Gives* ⓪ = [0] *Sign)*........So stood Tho-oth in the Power of the Word, giving forth Light, while the Aeons that were unbegotten unfolded before him.[2]
Phil. directed to give ⓪ = [0] Sign.

2nd Ad. And Elohim said "Let there be Light".
The hand of the Ch. Ad. hands out the Candle. 2nd receives it and gives Sign of Silence. Phil. is directed to make Sign. 3rd Ad. leaves Phil. comes East. Takes Candle and returns with Sol. He holds Candle before Phil. and takes Banner of W. in left hand.

2nd Ad. Honoured Frater, what was the Title you received in the ④ = [7] Grade of Philosophus?

Phil. *(unprompted)* Pharos Illuminans.

[1]For the details of these forces in the Un-Luminous Void of the Dark Night of Time see the instructional paper issued to the Isis-Urania Temple on July 2, 1900, called "The Qlippoth of the Qabalah", (and reprinted in *The Sorcerer and His Apprentice*, by R.A. Gilbert). H.S.

[2]Here is a powerful key to the MAGICAL COSMOGONY of the Secret Tradition operating in the Darkness and Silence behind the Inner Order of the Golden Dawn. For insight into these matters, go to Book Five, page 150-151 of Vol. III, and study the Egyptian-Gnostic mythology behind the Opening Exordium and Particular Exordium of the Z-Documents. Then you can profit by pursuing Florence Farrs' (S.S.D.D.), book on *Egyptian Magic*, and from there to *The Gnostic Religion* by Hans Jonas. H.S.

3rd Ad. gives Phil. Candle and takes his station on the left hand of Phil.

2nd Ad. Honoured Frater Pharos Illuminans, we are here assembled to open for you the Portal of the Vault of the Adepti, which admits you to the
<165> Second Degree and brings you to the Threshold of the Inner or Second Order.

But because of the increased influence over the Members of the Order that such advancement necessarily confers, and because of the increased power for good or evil that will follow if, with steadfast will and aspiration, you take this step in essence as well as in form, it is needful that you take further pledges, which however, as in the previous Degree, contains nothing contrary to your civil, moral or religious duties. Are you willing to take these pledges?

Phil. I am willing.

2nd Ad. Then you will take in your right hand the Banner of the West *(3rd Ad. gives it to him)* and place your left hand in that of the Very Honoured 3rd Adept, who is the living Symbol of the Black Pillar which ruleth in the Outer Order, and touch the corresponding emblem, the Black Sash of restriction, on your breast, and thus bind yourself while raising the Light which you hold, in witness of your pledge.

Phil. raises right hand holding Banner and Light, while his left hand, held by 3rd Ad. touches Sash.

2nd Ad. Firstly, do you pledge yourself never to reveal the secrets and Mysteries of these Paths and of this Ceremony, either to the outer and uninitiated world, or to a Member of the 1st Order, save in full Temple and with due sanctions?

Phil. I do.

2nd Ad. Secondly, do you further solemnly promise to use whatever practical knowledge you may now, or at any future time possess, for a good end alone?

<166> *Phil.* I do.

2nd Ad. Thirdly, do you also promise to regard all the knowledge imparted to you as a trust, given into your hands, not for your selfish advantage, but for the service of all mankind, that the ancient tradition of Initiation be kept pure and undefiled, and the Light be not lost for those that seek it in this Path?

Phil. I do.

2nd Ad. And lastly, do you solemnly promise to exercise brotherly love, charity and forbearance towards the Members of the Order, neither slandering, back-biting nor reviling them, whether you have cause of the same or not, but uniting with them to form a fabric of mutual confidence and support; and do you further undertake, not to be a stirrer up of strife, of schism, or of opposition to the Chiefs, but rather to uphold their authority in all loyalty?

Phil. I do.

2nd Ad. Then, realising the Cross about your neck, you will lift up your right hand, holding the Banner and the Light and say: —

"I undertake to maintain the Veil between the First and the Second Orders, and may the Powers of the Elements bear witness to my pledges."

Done. Phil. repeating words as directed. 3rd Ad. leaves Phil. and returns to his place, having replaced Banner of West.

2nd Ad. The Symbol of the 1st Grade of Neophyte is ⓪ = [0]. To the first O is attached a Circle — to the second, a Square. The union of the circle and the square hath many meanings, of which one must be put
<167> before you, for this you must accomplish in your own person, ere you can advance further. For if in the Mystic sphere of Truth, the way of Initiation may be trodden alone, yet in another Sphere, it hath a three-fold aspect. Part that can be given to man from without — part that can be attained by man himself — part that can only come from the Divine. Now, in the Order, you were given intellectual teaching, and won your Grades in tests of what was taught. Here, you must prove that you have truly attained thus far of your own strength, and after, you may progress by the higher Soul within you.

Round your neck, you wear the Symbol of the Cross of Four Elements, equilibriated and equated. Establish it firmly in the Sphere of your own being and advance with courage.

Hiereus and Heg. bar the way as in ① = [10].

Hiereus. Give me the Signs and Words of the Grade of Zelator.

Done. Heg. returns to place.

Hiereus. Give me also the Grip of the First Order.

(Done)

He takes Phil, to N. directing him to take up Salt from before Earth Tablet. They face N. Hiereus makes + over Salt with Sword then stands in the ① = [10] Sign while Phil. circumambulates with Sol repeating Earth Names.

Phil. Adonai Ha Aretz. Emor Dial Hectega. Auriel. Ic Zod Heh Chal.

He returns to N. Hiereus makes Earth Pentagram over Salt. Phil. reveals Lamp. Hiereus takes Phil. to Altar and directs him to place Salt at N. side of Altar. Hiereus takes him to diagrams in West.

<168> *Hiereus.* The Cross of Four Triangles called the Maltese Cross, is a Symbol of the Four Elements in balanced disposition. It is here given in the colours of the King's scale, and is also assigned to the Four Sephiroth ruling the Grades of the Outer — Earth to Malkuth, Air to Yesod, Water to Hod and Fire to Netzach.

It is again, the Cross which heads the Praemonstrator's Wand, who represents the Sephira Chesed, the Fourth Sephirah. Four is also the number of Jupiter, whose Path unites Chesed to Netzach.

The Cross is therefore a fit Emblem for a Philosophus of the Grade of ④ = [7].

In this diagram are represented the Circle, the Point, the Line, the Cross, the Square and the Cube. For the Circle is the Abyss, the Nothingness, the AIN. The Point is Kether. Now, the Point has no dimension, but in moving, it traces the Line. This gives the first number — Unity — yet therein, lies duality unmanifest, for two Points mark its ends. The movement of the line maketh the Plane or Square thus: — *(indicates)*. The motion of the Point at angles to its first direction and intersecting it maketh the Cross. So therefore, are the square and the Cross but one Symbol, deriving from the Circle and the Point.

Below, is shown the Occult Symbol of Malkuth, the Tenth Sephirah. It is in Four parts, corresponding to the Maltese Cross. They are Fire of Earth, Water of Earth, Air of Earth, Earth of Earth, as is indicated by the Symbol. They correspond to the Four Grades of the First Order,
<169> which in one sense, quitteth not Malkuth, being the Grades of the Four Lowest Sephiroth of Malkuth in Assiah.* Upon them, is surcharged a white Hexagram in a Circle. The 6 and the 4 make 10, the number of Malkuth on the Tree. The Hexagram is also the Sign of the Macrocosm — of Tiphareth, and of the Six Upper Sephiroth, wherefore here it is white — Spirit ruling over matter. Six is a perfect number, for its whole equals the sum of its parts.

Six are the middle points of the planes bounding a cube, which derives from the square, and from the Cross, if the centre point moves thus *(indicates third direction)*.

In these numbers and figures are hid many revelations.

Remember that the whole number of Malkuth is 496 — which is again a perfect number. Malkuth must then be equated and perfected by the 6 ruling the 4: and the link between 6 and 4 is the number of the Pentagram.

2nd Ad. Having achieved the entry into Malkuth, it is needful that you should pass through the Path of Tau, the dark Path of the Astral Plane. Go, therefore, to the Tablet of the East.

Phil. goes to E. Hs. and Heg. bar the way, points of implements downwards and touching. Heg. demands ② = [9] Sign and Words. Hs. returns to *place. Heg. leads Phil. to Tablet, gives Phil. rose leaves, makes Cross over bowl and directs Phil. to circumambulate repeating Names. Heg. stands in* ② = [9] Sign while Phil, traverses Path of Tau in the Names of Shad-
<170> *dai El Chai, Raphael, ORO IBAH AOZPI and Bataivah. Phil. returns to E. Heg. makes invoking Pent. and directs Phil. to uncover Lamp. Heg. takes Phil. to the Altar and directs him to put Rose leaves at East side, then, standing East of the Altar in Yesod, Heg. shows Great Hermetic Arcanum.*

Heg. This Symbol represents the Great Hermetic Arcanum. The feet of the Figure rest upon the Earth and the Sea. In the Hand are represented the hot and moist natures, symbolised by the torch and the horn of water. These are further strengthened by the Solar and fiery Emblems of the King and Lion, and the Luna and watery emblems of the Queen and Dolphin. Above the Whole figure rise the wings of the aerial nature, the Reconciler between the Fire and the Water. Compare this Symbol with the Angel described in the 10th Chapter of the Apocalypse of St. John:—"And I saw another mighty Angel come down from Heaven clothed with a cloud; and a rainbow was

*This is an important point, often overlooked. In Book Five, p. 82 of Vol. III, we read: "The Temple, as arranged in the Neophyte Grade of the Order of the Golden Dawn in the Outer, is . . . in Malkuth in Assiah." This means the Temple in the ⓪ = [0] is the Bottom Five Sephiroth of the Tree of Life in the Sphere of Malkuth on the Material Plane. Consider this if you are quick to be proud. Without its tether-line . . . THE KITE FALLS! H.S.

upon his head, and his face as it were, the Sun, and his feet were as pillars of fire, and he had in his hand a little book open; and he set his right foot upon the Sea and his left foot upon the Earth, and he cried with a loud voice as when a lion roareth, *(the Green Lion, the Path of Leo above Tiphareth, referring to Teth)* and when he cried, seven thunders uttered their voices *(seven Aeons, represented under the regimen of the Planets)*. The Dragon issuing from the cave represents volcanic fires.

Heg. leads Phil. once round, and hands him over to Hiereus in the North and returns to place.

Hiereus. This is the Image of the Vision of Nebuchadnezzar, which was
<171> showed you in the passage of the 27th Path, leading to the ④ = [7] Grade of Philosophus. "Thou, O King, sawest and beheld a great image. This Great Image, whose brightness was excellent stood before thee and the form thereof was terrible. This Image's head was pure gold, his breast and his arms were silver, his belly and his thighs were brass, his legs of iron and his feet part of iron and part of clay. Thou sawest till that a stone was cut out without hands, which smote the Image upon its feet, which were part of iron and part of clay, and brake them to pieces. Then was the iron, the clay, the brass, the silver and the Gold broken to pieces together and became like the chaff of the summer threshing floors; and the wind carried them away and no place was found for them; and the stone that smote the Image became a great mountain and filled the whole earth. Thou, O King, art a King of Kings, for the God in heaven hath given unto thee *(makes Qabalistic Cross)* the Kingdom, the Power and the Glory! Thou art this head of Gold. *(to Phil.)* Thou art this head of Gold! Thy head represents in thee the dominion of the Divine ruling over the rest of the body. The Silver is the world of the heart, the brass is the material passion, the iron is the firm purpose, and the feet, part of iron and part of clay, are the mingled strength and infirmity of the natural man. And the Stone made without hands is the Eternal Stone of the Wise, which will become the Mountain of Initiation, whereby the whole Earth shall be filled with the knowledge of God.

Hiereus takes Phil. to second diagram.

<172> *Hiereus.* This Tablet shows the Symbolic manner in which certain names have been used by our ancient brethren. You will note that the initials of this sentence make the Latin word Vitriolum, Sulphuric acid. Furthermore, the words Vitriol, Sulphur, and Mercury each consist of seven letters answering to the alchemic powers of the seven Planets. The initials of the following sentence in Latin — (the subtle fluid, the Light of the Earth) make the word S. A. L. T. salt, and further, the four words of the sentence answer to the four Elements — Subtilis, Air; Aqua, Water; Lux, Fire; and Terra, Earth. And the four words united yield 20 letters, that is, the product of four, the number of the Elements, multiplied by Five, the number of the Pentagram. The words Fiat Lux, meaning "Let there be Light," consist of 7 letters. The letters of Fiat form the initials of Flatus, Air; Aqua,

Water; Ignis, Fire; and Terra, Earth. *(Heg. goes to South).* Which four names again yield 20 letters as in the previous case. And the word Lux is formed from the angles of the Cross, L V X.

He leads Phil. once round and then to Heg. who awaits them in the S.

Heg. The Seraphim in the vision of Isaiah are described as having six wings:—"With twain He covered his face, and with twain He covered his feet, and with twain he did fly." That is, his synthesis is to be found in the Hexagram and in the idea of the Seven, more especially dominating the planetary region. But the Kerubim of Ezekiel have each 4 faces — those of the Lion, the Bull, the Man and the Eagle
<173> counterchanged with each other by revolution, whence the symbolic forms of the wheels beside them, wherein was the Spirit; and with two of the wings they covered their bodies and two were stretched upwards one to another. So the synthesis of the Kerubim is found in the revolving Cross, in the Pentagram, and in the idea of one Spirit dominating the four Elements. But the Kerubim of St. John's vision in the Apocalypse are uncompounded, having single heads, but they have six wings and thus unite the powers of the seven with the four. And their cry is similar to that of the Seraphim of Isaiah: — "Holy, Holy, Holy".*

Heg. returns to place. 2nd and 3rd Ad. bar way in S. W. Ask for ③ = [8] *Words. 3rd Ad. comes forward and conducts Phil. to W. Gives Phil. cup of Water —directs Phil. to go round repeating the Words while he remains standing in the* ③ = [8] *Sign. Phil. returns to W. 3rd Ad. makes invoking Pent. of Water over Cup. Phil. removes shade from Light. 3rd Ad. takes him to Altar where he places cup in the W. 2nd Ad. and 3rd Ad. bar way and ask for* ④ = [7] *Words. 2nd Ad. comes forward and conducts Phil. to S. 3rd remaining at Altar in* ③ = [8] *Sign, while Hiereus and Heg. come to N. and*

*Note: The Four Kerubim, through their assignment to the four Archangels, are thus Four of the Seven in the Presence of the Lord. The Hebrew Qaballah, the Egyptian Gnostics and the Enochian System of John Dee each express in their own terms the recognition of the REALITY of these FOUR and the SEVEN:

	Qaballist	**Gnostic**	**Enochian**
	(The Book of Enoch: Ch. IX. v. I)	The Gnostic "Four Lights" *(Nag Hammadi)*	John Dee: God Names of the Quarters
The Four Arch-Angels	1 Michael	Armozel	Bataivah
	2 Uriel	Oroiael	Iczhikal
	3 Raphael	Daveithe	Raagiosl
	4 Gabriel	Eleleth	Edlprnaa
	"The Seven"	The Seven Thrones (Papyri Graecae Magicae)	John Dee: The Sons of Light
The Seven in the Presence	1 Uriel	Achlal	I
	2 Raphael	Lalaphenourphen	Ih
	3 Raguel	Baleeo	Ilr
	4 Michael	Bolbeo	Dmal
	5 Zerachiel	Bolbeoch	Heeoa
	6 Gabriel	Bolbesro	Beigia
	7 Remiel	Yyphtho	Stimcul

Note: These lists are meant only as a suggestion for inquiry. H.S.

E. of Altar and stand in Grade Signs. 2nd Ad. in S. gives Phil. incense, makes a Cross over it. Phil. walks round repeating ④ = [7] Words while 2nd Ad. stands in ④ = [7] Sign. Phil. returns S. removes shade. 2nd Ad. takes him to Altar, directs him to place Incense at S. He takes Cross from Phil.'s neck and places it in the midst of the Four Elements. Phil. is directed to stand W.
<174> *of Altar in ⓪ = [0] Sign, 3rd Ad. behind Phil. The four Officers in Grade Signs.*

Hiereus. From the centre outwards, so moveth the point as it traceth the line and the Cross. Equated and equilibrated lie here the Four Elements of the body of Osiris slain.

2nd Ad. May the corrosive Cross return upon itself, from without inward from the Four Quarters to the Center, and become by sacrifice and transmutation, an offering acceptable, a body glorified.

Chief Adept unseen sounds gongs once.

2nd Ad. *(to Phil.)* You will now quit the Temple for a short time, and on your return, the Ceremony of your advance will be proceeded with.

Phil. gives Sign of Silence and is led out by Hiereus.

<175> RITE of the PENTAGRAM and the FIVE PATHS.

Temple arranged as in Diagram. 2nd Ad. sits on Dais at S. E. 3rd Ad. sits on Dais to N. E. Altar in Yesod under hanging Pentagram. On it are the 4 Elemental Emblems — Incense, Cup, Rose leaves and Salt. In middle,

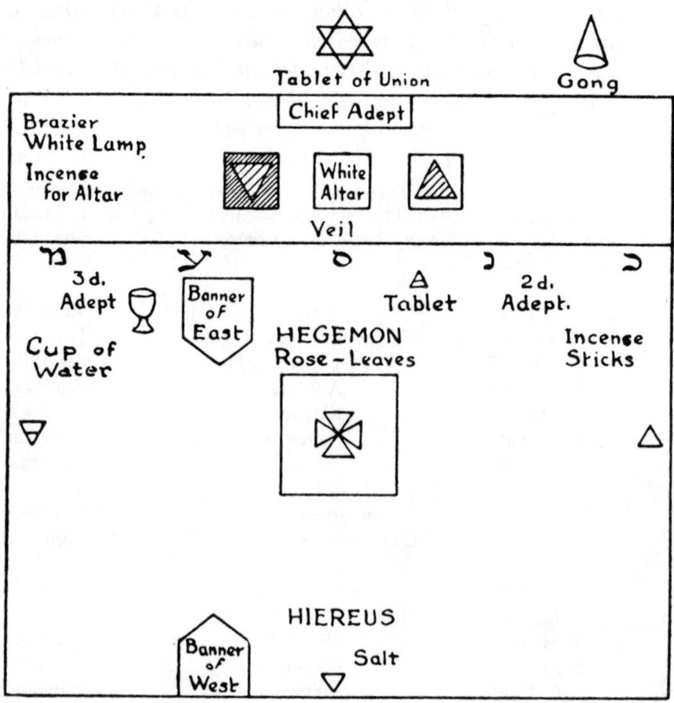

Greek Cross of 5 squares. Heg. W. of Altar facing W. Hs. in W. facing E. Admission Badge, Lamen of Hiereus. Temple lighted as at end of Part One.

<176> *2nd Ad.* ו

3rd Ad. ו

Heg. ו

Hiereus ו

Ch. Ad. parts curtain, makes Pent. with Torch. Knocks and withdraws.

2nd Ad. Hon. Hiereus, you have my permission to present the Philosophus with the necessary admission Badge. Instruct him in the proper alarm and admit him.

Hs. salutes, makes Qab. Cross and goes out. He gives Lamen to Phil. who knocks וווו ו. *Hegemon opens door. Phil. enters, gives Qab. Cross. Hegemon returns to place. Hs. takes Phil. to W. and points out Diagram of Malkuth.*

Hiereus Herein has been established the Equated Cross, which is ruler over the Kingdom of Matter. This Symbol may be found even upon the crowns of the Kings of this Earth.

Hands Phil. Tau Portal.

The Letter Tau leads from the Airy quarter of Malkuth into Yesod. Air is uppermost in the Symbol as in the Planet Earth where the atmosphere is furthest from the core. Moreover, the Letter Tau signifieth the Cross, the impact of Spirit upon matter. My Lamen is given you as your Badge, for I am the Ruler in Malkuth, and the Guardian against the underworld. I am also Lord of the Path Tau, the link between the first and second degrees, and also between the Outer and the Inner. This Path of Tau, dark and full of mystery, under the presidency of Saturn and the Tarot Key of The Universe,
<177> leads, as you have learned in the ② = [9] Grade, through the Astral Plane. Therefore, in the Ritual of the 32nd Path, you were passed by the Four Kerubic Stations, as a fore-shadowing of the Rites of the Cross, the full completion of the First Order which you have now accomplished.

Having traversed the Path of Tau, the darkness of the Astral Plane and of the Black Pillar, stand firm in Yesod, that the Black Pillar may become the White.

Hs. takes away Tau after leading Phil. to Heg. at Altar. Heg. rises but stands between Phil. and the Altar, so that Phil. does not too clearly apprehend the change of Symbols.

Heg. Before you, in the East, are the Five Portals of the 21st, 24th, 25th, 26th and 23rd Paths. Five will divide the Number of the Letter of each of them, as it will divide without remainder that of every Path from Yod 20th, to Tau, the 32nd. The Five Paths here visible are assigned to Mem, Water; Ayin, Capricornus, an Earthy Sign; Samekh, Sagittarius, a Fiery Sign; Nun, Scorpio, a Watery Sign, but in its highest aspect also a Ruler of Fire; and Kaph, Jupiter, which Planet is akin to Spirit, and rules especially Aspiration. Thus both in Number and in significance these Planets jointly set forth the eternal symbol of the Pentagram. This Symbol must now be established — wherefore advancing by the Kerubic Path of Aquarius approach the highest in Netzach.*

Heg. leads Phil. to foot of Dais to 2nd Ad. before Kaph and Nun.

<178> *2nd Ad.* Wherefore do you stand at the base of the White Pillar, being but Lord of the First Degree?

Phil. *(prompted)* I seek the Path of Kaph, the Path of Aspiration.

Hiereus *(knocks)* Beware. Temerity is not courage, Lord of the First Degree. Remember the warning of the Tower struck by Lightning that was revealed in the highest Path you have yet adventured. As a house built upon the Sand cannot endure, so without the strength of Geburah the Height of Chesed cannot be scaled. Stay, therefore, ere your limbs be broken upon the Wheel.

2nd Ad. The Portal of Kaph is barred, yet it is well to aspire, though it may be folly to attempt. This Path is governed by the Wheel of Life and Death, and hard it is to be freed from that Wheel.

Phil. *(prompted by Heg.)* Let me seek then the Path of Nun.

2nd Ad. It is open to you, unto the limit of your strength.

Heg. returns to Altar. 2nd Ad. guides Phil. to W. Hiereus bars way.

Hiereus In the Power of Typhon the Destroyer, and of Death the Transformer, stand. *(Knocks)*

2nd Ad. Thus far and no farther is it permitted to penetrate into the Path of Nun. The mysteries may now be partially be revealed unto you.

2nd Ad. takes Phil. to Tarot Key of Death.

*Note: The Outer Order of the Elemental Grades could be likened to the Four Elemental Quadangles of John Dee's Great Table of the Watchtowers. The Pentagram itself has its four lower points arranged in the same order as the Watch Towers with the Tablet of Union "Set Over it".

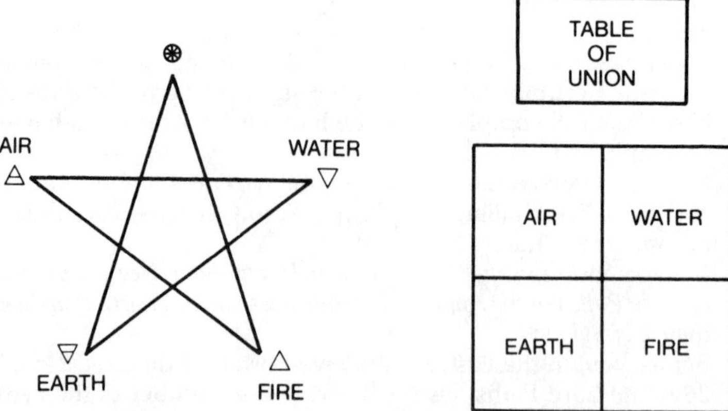

Here the Five Paths of Sameck, Mem, Kaph, Nun and Ayin are said to "... set forth the eternal Symbol of the Pentagram. Mem is Water, Ayin is Earth, and Sameck is Fire. But to which points and elements do we allocate Air and Spirit? The clues we are given is Jupiter's ruling of Aspiration, thus, *in this Context,* Air, and being told "Scorpio is a Watery Sign, but in its highest aspect also a Ruler of Fire ..." ... we caution to guess that Nun ought to be attributed to the upper point of the SPIRIT, in that it "unites Water and Fire," and mystical "Death" is the Gate to the Inner Order. H.S.

2nd Ad. The 13th Key of Tarot represents the figure of a Skeleton, upon
which some portions of flesh still remain. In a field he is reaping off
with the Scythe of Death the fresh vegetation which springs from
corrupting bodies buried therein — fragments of which — such as
<179> hands, heads and feet appear above the soil. Bones also are strewn
upon the surface. One of the heads wears a kingly crown; another is
apparently that of a person of little note, showing that death is the
equaliser of all conditions. The five extremities, the head, hands and
feet, allude to the powers of the number five, the Letter He, the Pentagram — the concealed Spirit of Life and the Four Elements — the
originator of all living form. The Sign of Scorpio especially alludes to
stagnant and foetid water — that property of the moist nature which
initiates putrefaction and decay. The eternal change from life into
death through death into life, is symbolised by the grass which
springs from and is nourished by putrifying and corrupting carcasses; the herbiage, in its turn affords food to animals and man,
which again when dead, nourisheth vegetable life and bring to
growth and perfection the living herbiage. This is further shown by
the figure itself putrifying and decaying as it reaps the grass of the
field. "As for man, his days are as grass, as a flower of the field, so he
flourisheth." The top of the scythe forms the Tau Cross of Life, showing that what destroys also renews.

The whole is a representation of the eternal transmutation of the life
of nature, which reforms all things into fresh images and similitudes.
This symbol represents the corrosive and destructive action of the
infernal Fire as opposed to the Celestial — the Dragon of the Waters,
the Typhon of the Egyptians, the Slayer of Osiris — which later yet
rises again in Horus. The Scorpio, Serpent of Evil, delineated before
<180> the figure of Death in the more ancient form of the Key, refers to the
mixed and transforming, therefore deceptive, nature of this emblem. Behind him, is the Symbol of the Nameless One, representing
the Seed and its germ, not yet differentiated into Life, therefore
incapable of definition. The Scorpion is the emblem of ruthless destruction; the Snake is the mixed and deceptive nature, serving alike
for good and evil; the Eagle is the higher and Divine Nature, yet to be
found herein, the Alchemical Eagle of distillation, the Renewer of
life. As it is said:—"Thy youth shall be renewed like the Eagles."
Great indeed, and many are the mysteries of this terrible Key.

2nd Ad. and Hiereus show Phil. the figure of Typhon.

Hiereus This drawing represents the symbolic figure of Typhon, the Destroyer. The eleven circles represent the eleven Averse Sephiroth. He stands upon Earth and Ocean, his head lost in the clouds, a colossal image of evil and destruction. The brow denotes the confusion of opposing Elemental Forces in the higher regions of the Air, and confusion of mind and madness in man. The eyes are the devouring flames of lust and violence — the breath is storm, devastation and rage, alike in the universe which is the greater world, and in Man who is the lesser. The arms and the hands are the swift executors of evil works, the bringers of pestilence and disease. The heart is malice and envy in man, the nourisher of evil in the atmosphere, which later are again symbolised by the numerous and twining serpents.

<181> *2nd Ad.* The 24th Path of Sepher Yetzirah to which the Tarot Key of Death is referred is the Imaginative Intelligence, and it is so called because it giveth form to all similitudes which are created in like manner similar to its harmonious elegances. For the outward form always follows the Hidden law, thus from Chaos is produced Harmony, just as a beautiful flower is produced from decaying matter. Return now to Yesod, for here no more may be spoken.

2nd Ad. returns to place. Phil. goes to Heg. near Altar.

Heg Approach now the station of Hod by the Path of Resh, the Sun.

Phil. approaches the 3rd Ad.

3rd Ad. Already the Sash of the Black Pillar is upon you — already you have passed the dark Path of Tau. What more do you seek of me, Lord of the 1st Degree?

Phil. (prompted by Heg.) I seek the Path of Mem, the Path of Sacrifice.

Heireus *(knocks)* Be warned, O, vainglorious one. Samson broke down the Two Pillars and perished. Having but one Pillar, can you bear up the might of Geburah, can you attain strength without the Life of Tiphareth?

3rd Ad. The Portal of Mem is barred. Yet it is well to be willing for the Sacrifice itself, if as yet, not fully prepared. For in the Path of Mem rules the Hanged Man, the power of the Great Waters. Can your tears prevail against the Tide of the Sea, your might against the waves of the storm, your love against the sorrows of all the world?

<182> *Phil. (prompted by Heg.)* Let me seek then the path of Ayin

3rd Ad. It is open to you to the limit of your strength.

Heg. returns to Altar. 3rd Ad. descends and leads Phil, with Sol to W. Hiereus going to N. bars their way.

Heireus *(knocks)* By the Power of Pan and the Goat of Mendes, stand.

3rd Ad. Thus far and no farther are you permitted to penetrate the Path of Ayin, whose mysteries may now be partially revealed to you. The 15th Key of the Tarot represents a goat-headed, satyr-like Demon whose legs are hairy—his feet and claws, standing upon a Cubical Altar. He has heavy bat-like wings. In his left hand, which points downwards, he holds a lighted torch, and in his right, which is elevated, a horn of water. The left hand points downwards to show that it is the infernal and burning, not the celestial and life-giving flame which is kindled in his torch—just as when the Sun is in Capricornus, to which cold and earthy Sign this Key corresponds, Solar light is at its weakest and the natures of cold and moisture triumph over heat and dryness. The cubical Altar represents the Universe — right and left of it, bound thereto by a cord attached to a circle which typifies the centre of the Earth, are two smaller demons, one male and one female. They hold a cord in their hands. The whole figure

shows the gross generative powers of nature on the material plane, and is analogous to the Pan of the Greeks and the Egyptian Goat of Mendes (the symbol of Khem). In certain aspects, this Key rep-
<183> resents the brutal forces of nature, which to the unbelieving man only obscure and do not reflect the luminous Countenance of God. It also alludes to the sexual powers of natural generation. Thus therefore the Key fitly balances the symbol of Death on the other side of the Tree of Life. Of the smaller demons, one points downwards and one upwards, answering to the positions of the hands of the central figure. Beneath his feet are Pentagrams on which he tramples (whence comes their title of Wizard's foot) and his head is covered with the evil and reversed Pentagram. As his hands bear the torch and the horn — the symbols of Fire and Water, so does his form unite the Earth in his hairy and bestial aspect, and the Air in his bat-like wings. Thus he represents the gross and materialised Elemental Forces of Nature; and the whole would be an evil symbol, were it not for the Pentagram of Light above his head which regulates and guides his movements. He is the eternal renewer of all the changing forms of Creation in conformity with the Law of the All-Powerful One (Blessed be He) which controlling law is typified by the controlling Pentagram of Light surmounting the whole. This Key is an emblem of tremendous force; many and universal are its mysteries.

Hiereus and 3rd Ad. go to diagram of Pan.

Hiereus This drawing represents the Symbolic figure of Pan, the Greek God of Nature. He stands upon the Cube of the Universe, holding in his right hand the pastoral staff of rural authority, and in his left the 7 reeded pipe symbolical of the harmony of the Planetary Spheres.
<184> The Nine Circles represent the Sephiroth with the exception of Kether, exactly those which are included in the symbol on the Tree of Life. The ruddy face is the heat of the Earth — the horns are the Rays — the body contains the Elements and the Cube is the firm basis. Observe that the higher part of the figure is human, growing more bestial as it nears the Earth.

3rd Ad. The 26th Path of the Sepher Yetzirah, to which the Tarot Key of the Devil is referred, is called the Renovating Intelligence, because, by it, God the Holy One reneweth all the changing forms which are renewed by the Creation of the World. Return again to Yesod, for here no more may be spoken.

3rd Ad. returns to place. Hs. to Altar. Heg. rises as Phil, comes to Altar. Hs. and Heg. stand on either side of Phil. W. of Altar, facing East.

Hiereus In guardianship and not in enmity, have I barred your venturing, O Philosophus. Now may it be revealed unto you how that in my Lamen of Office is hidden the Key which you seek. For the Triangle in the Circle is the High symbol of the Holy Trinity, and the first three Sephiroth and of Binah wherein is the Sphere of Saturn, Ruler of the Path Tau. Therefore do I wear it, and therefore, when you entered the Hall of the Neophytes in the ⓪ = [0], when first the

hood-wink was raised, you beheld before you the Sword that barred and the Symbol which overcometh the barrier. The Lamen in its more special attributions to the Hiereus, has the following meanings. In the circle are the Four Sephiroth, Tiphareth, Netzach, Hod and
<185> Yesod. The first three mark the angles of the Triangle inscribed within, while the sides are the Paths of Nun, Ayin and Peh, respectively. In the centre is marked the Letter Samekh indicating the 25th Path.

While the Wheel revolves, the hub is still. Seek ever then the centre, look from without to within. Behold the Key of your Path.

Puts Badge aside

Heg Five Paths are before you — four have you attempted and each was guarded by a symbol sinister and dread.

Remember that in the ① = [10] Grade it was told you, that above Malkuth were the Paths Qoph, Shin, Tau, — making Qesheth, the Bow of promise. From the many coloured Bow, is loosed in Yesod, the Arrow of Sagittarius — Samekh, soaring upward to cleave open the Veil unto the Sun in Tiphareth. Thus it is a fit symbol for hope and aspiration, for in the Sign Sagittarius, Jupiter, Ruler of Kaph is Lord. Thus, by this straight and narrow way only, is advance between the dangers that have threatened you, possible.

3rd Ad. descends to North side of Altar.

3rd Ad. But Sagittarius, the Archer, is a bi-corporate Sign — the Centaur, the Man and the Horse combined. Recall what was said unto thee in the passage of the 31st Path of Fire, leading unto the ③ = [8] Grade of Practicus: — "Also there is the vision of the fire flashing Courser of Light, or also a child borne aloft upon the shoulders of the Celestial
<186> Steed, fiery or clothed with gold, or naked and shooting from the bow, shafts of light, and standing on the shoulders of a horse. But, if thy meditation prolongeth itself thou shalt unite all these symbols in the form of a Lion." For thus wilt thou cleave upward by the Path of Sagittarius, through the Sixth Sephirah into the Path of Teth, answering to Leo, the Lion — the reconciling Path between Mercy and Severity, Chesed and Geburah, beneath whose centre hangs the glorious Sun of Tiphareth. Therefore, by the straight and narrow Path of Sagittarius, let the Philosophus advance, like the arrow from the centre of Qesheth, the Bow. And as this Sign of Sagittarius lieth between the Sign of Scorpio — Death and Capricornus the devil, so had Jesus to pass through the Wilderness, tempted by Satan.

2nd Ad. descends to South of the Altar.

2nd Ad. Before you, upon the Altar, lie the Four Emblems of your purified body, and over them is the Symbol of the Pentagram, while beneath in the midst is the five-squared Cross of the Four Elements and the Spirit within them. If you are willing, in service and in sacrifice to offer the purified powers of your body, bind about your neck the Cross, and stretch the Light *(gives Phil. light)* you carry over the Four Emblems in prayer and offering. *(Phil. does so.)*

All come East of the Altar. Phil. in middle with candle and Cross on neck. 2nd

Ad. right and 3rd Ad. left. Heg. and Hiereus behind. Each take Elemental Emblems — Hs. Salt, Heg. Rose-leaves, 2nd Ad. Incense, 3rd Ad. Water and Phil. Motto written on paper.

<187> *2nd Ad.* Honoured Philosophus, what was the additional title given you in the ④ = [7] as a link with the Second Order?

(All advance to Dais)

Phil. Phrath.

2nd Ad. O Hidden Warden of the Portal of the Vault, here is one who cometh in the Word Phrath.

Ch. Ad. *(knocks gong unseen)* If he would rend the Veil, let him complete the Word.

2nd Ad. Honoured Hiereus, what know you of the Word?

Hiereus Tau, the Letter of Saturn, ruling the Path of Malkuth to Yesod, linked to Earth.

2nd Ad. Honoured Hegemon, what know you of the Word?

Heg Resh, the Letter of Sol, of the Path joining Yesod to Hod, and it is also the Letter linked with rule over Air as the Sun ruleth the Air in Tiphareth.

Ch. Ad. Very Honoured 3rd Ad. what know you of the Word?

3rd Ad. Peh, the Letter of Mars, of the Path joining Hod to Netzach, which is also a Letter linked to Water, as Mars ruleth Water, and to Fire, as Mars ruleth Fire in Geburah.

2nd Ad. Mars in Peh, linketh the base of the Black Pillar to the Base of the White Pillar, and the converse of Mars is Jupiter — for Jupiter is Lord of Fire, but in Chesed he ruleth Water, balancing Mars in Geburah. Now, the Letter of Jupiter is Kaph, linking Netzach with Chesed; and Kaph continueth the Path Peh to Chesed, and is the highest Path now visible to you. It is the Path of Aspiration and its Planet Jupiter rules also in Sagittarius. Therefore, take the Light of the Highest for
<188> Guide, and thus do I reveal the Letter Kaph unto you and complete the Word: —

3rd Ad. Peh *(knocks, gives Sign of Water).*

Heg Resh *(knocks, gives Sign of Air).*

2nd Ad. Kaph *(knocks, gives Sign of Fire).*

Hiereus Tau *(knocks, gives Sign of Earth).*

All. Paroketh *(All make Qabalistic Cross saying the words).*

Phil. *(prompted by 3rd Ad.)* In the Word Paroketh, in the Power of the Cross and the Pentagram, I claim to behold the Portal of the Vault of the Adepti.

Ch. Ad. *(unseen, sounds gong)* It is the Word of the Veil, the Veil of the Tabernacle, of the Temple, before the Holy of Holies, the Veil which was rent asunder. It is the Veil of the Four Elements of the Body of Man, which was offered upon the Cross for the service of Man. *(Ch. Ad. stands)* In the Word Phrath, in the Spirit of service and sacrifice draw nigh.

2nd and 3rd Ads. stand at the Veil. 2nd shows Phil. opening Sign.

2nd Ad. This is the Sign of the rending of the Veil, and thus standing, you form the Tau Cross.

Phil. gives the Sign. 2nd and 3rd Ads draw back Veil, revealing Ch. Ad. who stands also in the Sign of Tau, with Sceptre and White Lamp. 2nd and 3rd Ads. and Phil. mount Dais. Phil. if able should stand in Sign during Offering Ritual. Lights turned up. Hs. and Heg. stand behind Phil, who is between the Pillars — 2nd Ad. South and 3rd Ad. North.

Ch. Ad. Freely and of full purpose and with understanding do you offer
<189> yourself upon the Altar of the Spirit?

Phil. I do.

As they say their Words, Hiereus and Heg. ascend Dais to drop their emblems into the brazier. Each officer makes his Grade Sign as he does so. Ch. Ad. makes appropriate Pent. holding up White Lamp. Phil. drops in Motto.

Hiereus In the Letter Tau. *(Salt)*
Ch. Ad. In the Letter Heh. *(Incense)*
Heg In the Letter Resh. *(Rose leaves)*
Ch. Ad. In the Letter Vau. *(Incense)*
3rd Ad. In the Letter Peh. *(Water)*
Ch. Ad. In the Letter Heh. *(Incense)*
2nd Ad. In the Letter Kaph. *(Incense sticks)*
Ch. Ad. In the Letter Yod. *(Incense)*
All. In the Letter Shin. *(Phil. drops in Motto)**

Ch. Ad. makes Spirit Pentagrams over the whole, then stretching out Sceptre touches Phil. on the breast.

Ch. Ad. May this offering be as the offering of Abel, which ascended unto God. *Phil. lowers his arms. Ch. Ad. sits down.*

Ch. Ad. Stretch out your left hand to touch the Black Pillar *(done)* the Pillar of the First Degree, wherein all was as yet in the darkness of the Path Tau. This was a period of restriction and of groping, as was shown by the black sash, the Sign of the First Degree. Among its symbols were the Cross, upon which meditate, that the mysteries of growth and change may become revealed.

Stretch out now your right hand to touch the White Pillar *(done)* the
<190> Pillar of the Second Degree, wherein is the Fire of the Path Samekh. Its token in our Order, is the White Sash. Standing thus you are in the point of equilibrium, Master of both, Lord of the Second Degree, Lord of the Paths of the Portal of the Vault of the Adepti — wherefore, in recognition of your achievement, I confer upon you the White Sash of Probation. *(3rd Ad. puts on white sash)*. The grip of this Degree is the Grip of the First Order, but given with the left hand, and represents the Sephira Chesed, and the White Pillar. The Sign is given thus: — *(gives it)* and symbolises the rending asunder of a curtain or veil. The answering Sign is given by the converse thus. *(gives*

*Here we have the Sacred Name of the Demi-Urge, I.H.V.H., and the Shin which transforms it into the Redeemed-One, Yeheshuah, mingled together with the letters of Paroketh, the Veil, i.e.:

P R K T H (Paroketh)
\+ I H Sh H (Jeheshuah, Jesus)

(Th.) *H.* (R.) *V.* (P.) *H.* (K.) *I.: Sh.*
(The order of Letters in Ritual) H.S.

it) The Pass-word is, as you have been told, Paroketh, which is the Veil of the Tabernacle, and is exchanged by letter thus: —

Ch. Ad. Peh.

Phil. *(prompted)* Resh.

Ch. Ad. Kaph.

Phil. Tau.

Ch. Ad. Further, I give you the Word ETH which crowns the Pyramid of the Four Elements in the ④ = [7] Grade, and is one symbol of the Spirit which converts the Cross into the Pentagram. Wherefore, above my Throne is this Tablet *(points to Tablet of Union)* which is called the Tablet of Union, and binds together the Four Tablets into one under the presidence of the Spirit.

Thus far by work of the intellect, and by aid of our Rites, have you come. Now must you labour to establish the Pentagram in yourself.

<191> That it be the Pentagram of Good, upright and balanced, not the evil and reversed Pentagram of the Goat of Mendes; to make yourself truly a Microcosm reflecting the Macrocosm whose symbolic Hexagram of Tiphareth presides above you.

This Degree is in one sense attributed to Yesod, base of the Path of probation, Sagittarius. In Yesod is the Sphere of Luna, who in her fullness reflects the Sun of Tiphareth. The number given to the Moon in the ② = [9] is Nine, but in a more esoteric sense the number of Luna is Five, the number of the Pentagram and the Microcosm.

Ch. Ad. rises with Sceptre and white lamp. 2nd Ad. places Tablet of Union on the Altar in readiness. Heg. places two forms of Temperance by Altar W. Ch. Ad. puts white lamp on Altar. Officers replace Elements before their respective Tablets, and return to form a Cross round the Altar.

Ch. Ad. This drawing represents the more ancient form of the 14th Key of Tarot, for which the later and more usual form of Temperance was soon substituted, as better representing the natural symbolism of the Path Sagittarius. The earlier figure was considered not so much a representation of this Path alone, as the synthesis of that and the others conjoined. The later figure, therefore, is better adapted to the more restricted meaning. The more ancient form shows a female figure crowned with the crown of five rays, symbolising the Five Principles of Nature, the concealed Spirit and the Four Elements of Earth, Air, Water and Fire. About her head is a halo of light. On her
<192> breast is the Sun of Tiphareth. The Five-rayed Crown further alludes to the Five Sephiroth Kether, Chokmah, Binah, Chesed and Geburah. Chained to her waist are a Lion and an Eagle, between which is a large cauldron whence arise steam and smoke. The Lion represents the Fire in Netzach — the Blood of the Lion, and the Eagle represents the Water in Hod, the Gluten of the Eagle — whose reconcilement is made by the Air in Yesod, uniting with the volatilised Water arising from the cauldron through the influence of the Fire beneath it. The chains which link the Lion and the Eagle to her waist, are symbolic of the Paths of Scorpio and Capricornus as

shown by the Scorpion and the Goat in the background. In her right hand, she bears the Torch of Solar Fire elevating and volatilising the Water in Hod by the fiery influence of Geburah, while with her left hand, she pours from a vase the Waters of Chesed to temperate and calm the Fires of Netzach. This later form is the usual figure of Temperance, symbolising in a more restricted form than the preceding, the peculiar properties of this Path. It represents an Angel with the Solar emblem of Tiphareth on her brow, and wings of the aerial and volatilising nature, pouring together the fluidic Fire and the fiery Water — thus combining, harmonising and temperating those opposing elements.

One foot rests on dry and volcanic land, in the background of which is a volcano whence issues an irruption. The other foot is in the water by whose border springs fresh vegetation, contrasting strongly with the arid and dry nature of the distant land. On her breast is a square,
<193> the emblem of rectitude. The whole figure is a representation of that straight and narrow way of which it is said "few there be that find it" which alone leads to the higher and glorified life. For to pursue that steady and tranquil mean between two opposing forces, is indeed difficult, and many are the temptations to turn aside either to the right or to the left — wherein, remember, are but to be found the menacing symbols of Death and the Devil.

The 25th Path of the Sepher Yetzirah to which the Tarot Key of Temperance is referred, is called the Intelligence of Probation, and it is so called because it is the primary temptation by which the Creator tries all righteous persons. That is, that in it, there is ever present the temptation to turn aside to the one hand or the other.

2nd and 3rd Ads. give Cup and red lamp to Phil. who holds them in form of Tau Cross.

Ch. Ad. Let this remind you once more, that only in and by the reconciliation of opposing forces is the Path-way made to true occult knowledge and practical power. Good alone is mighty and Truth alone shall prevail. Evil is but weakness and the power of evil magic exists but in the contest of unbalanced forces, which in the end, will destroy and ruin him who hath subjugated himself thereto. As it is said "Stoop not down, for a precipice lieth beneath the Earth — a descent of seven steps; and therein, is established the throne of an evil and fatal force. Stoop not down unto that dark and lurid world. Defile not thy brilliant flame with the earthy dross of matter. Stoop not down, for
<194> its splendour is but seeming, it is but the habitation of the Sons of the Unhappy."

2nd and 3rd Ads. take back red lamp and Cup and restore them to their Tablets. On the Altar is the White Lamp and the Tablets of Union. Phil. is seated West of Altar. 2nd and 3rd Ads. return to places. Hs. goes to N. Heg. to S. Ch. Ad. returns to Throne in E. takes up Banner of the East and Hierophant's Lamen.

Ch. Ad. Seeing that you are now Lord of the Paths of the Portal of the Vault of the Adepti, and are entered into the Second Degree, approaching the Second or Inner Order, it is fitting that you should have the knowledge of these emblems to complete as far as may be, your understanding of the Powers of the Officers of the First or Outer Order. Both refer in natural succession of numbers to the six following the five. Thus all progress is by steps, gradual and secure. The inner revelation may come suddenly to some, even in the twinkling of an eye or it may be after long waiting — a slow and gradual process from the beginning, yet ever the liquid must be prepared to the point of saturation.

The Hierophant's Lamen is a synthesis of Tiphareth, to which the Calvary Cross of six squares, forming the cube opened out, is fitly referred. The two colours, red and green, the most active and the most passive, whose conjunction points out the practical application of the knowledge of equilibrium, are symbolic of the reconciliation of the celestial essences of Fire and Water, for the reconciling yellow
<195> unites with blue in green, which is the complementary colour to red, and with red in orange which is the complementary colour to blue. The small inner circle placed upon the Cross alludes to the Rose that is conjoined therewith in the symbolism of the Rose and Cross of our Order.

The field of the Banner of the East is White, the colour of light and purity. As in the previous case, the Calvary Cross of six squares is the number six of Tiphareth, the yellow Cross of Solar Gold, and the cubical stone bearing in its centre the sacred Tau of Life, and having bound together upon it the form of the Macrocosmic Hexagram, the red triangle of Fire and the blue triangle of Water — the Ruach Elohim and the Waters of Creation. The six angles of the Hexagram described upon the Tree of Life will give the Planets referred to it as follows: Daath, Saturn; Chesed, Jupiter; Geburah, Mars; Netzach, Venus; Hod, Mercury; Yesod, Luna — while in the centre is the Sun of Tiphareth.

Upon my breast is a symbol, which, O Lord of the Paths of the Portal of the Adepti, is as yet unknown to you. It is no Symbol of the Order of the Stella Matutina, nor of the First or Outer Order, nor even of your Degree. It is the symbol of the Red Rose and the Cross of Gold, uniting the powers of the 4 and 5 and of the 6 within itself, but to learn its full meaning, it is needful that you be admitted to the fellowship of that other Order to which the Stella Matutina is one of the Veils. Of this matter, you have no right to speak to any below your degree.

Admission further can be earned no more by excellence in intellec-
<196> tual learning alone, though that also is required of you. In token that all true knowledge cometh of grace, not of right, such admission is granted, not on demand, but at the discretion of the Greatly Honoured Chiefs of the Second Order. Moreover, an interval of nine months must elapse before the Portal is again opened to you. Nine is the number of Luna in Yesod, nine lunar months are the period of gestation before birth; Five is the number of the Pentagram of the

Microcosm, the esoteric Luna number — the number of the Spirit and the Four Elements — of the Soul entering the body. Nine multiplied by five yields 45, the number of Yesod, and the supreme number of the Square of Saturn, as the Triad expanded into matter.

CLOSING

Ch. Ad. *(knocks)* Very Honoured Fratres and Sorores, assist me to close the Portal of the Vault of the Adepti. *All rise.*
Honoured Hiereus see that the entrance is properly guarded.

Hiereus Very Honoured Chief Adept, the entrance is properly guarded.

Ch. Ad. Very Honoured Fratres and Sorores, give the Signs of the Neophyte, Zelator, Theoricus, Practicus and Philosophus. Give the Sign of the Rending of the Veil. Give the Sign of the Closing of the Veil. Very Honoured 2nd Ad. what is the Word?

2nd Ad. Peh.

Ch. Ad. Resh.

2nd Ad. Kaph.

Ch. Ad. Tau.

<197> *2nd Ad.* The whole Word is Paroketh, which is the Veil of the Tabernacle.

Ch. Ad. In and by that Word, I declare the Portal of the Vault of the Adepti duly closed.

Ch. Ad. draws curtain. Officers take up their stations before Elemental Tablets. Ch. Ad. stands W. of the Altar, facing East. Phil. stands behind him.

Ch. Ad. In the Power of the Name Yod, Heh, Vau, Heh, and in the might of the concealed Name YEHESHUA, in the symbol of the Tablet of Union and by the Word Eth, Spirits of the Five Elements, adore your Creator.

At the word "depart," below each Officer simultaneously makes banishing Pentagram of his own Element before the Tablet, ending with Grade Sign.

Ch. Ad. Depart in peace unto your habitations. May there be peace between us and you, and be ye ready to come when you are called.

Ch. Ad. makes banishing Pent. of Spirit and gives LVX Signs. All face East and make Qab. Cross all saying together: —

All. Unto Thee Tetragrammaton, be ascribed Malkuth, Geburah, Gedulah, unto the Ages, AMEN.

Ch. Ad. וווו ו
3rd Ad. וווו ו
2nd Ad. וווו ו
Hiereus וווו ו
Heg וווו ו

<198>

CEREMONY

OF THE

⑤ = [6] GRADE OF ADEPTUS MINOR

OFFICERS REQUIRED:

Chief Adept—⑦ = [4], Merciful Exempt Adept.
Second Adept—⑥ = [5], Mighty Adeptus Major.
Third Adpt—⑤ = [6], Associate Adeptus Minor.
Candidate—Hodos Chamelionis.

These Officers should have attained at least these ranks and may be of higher Grade. Men and Women are equally eligible for any of these offices. The Ordinary members are entitled Very Honoured Fratres et Sorores.

This ceremony is divided into Three Points.

*ROBES:**

Chief Adept—Blue and purple, with winged Sphere.
2nd Adept—Red and Orange, with Phoenix.
3rd Adept—Yellow and Rose Pink, with Lotus.

All may wear yellow shoes or shoes to match robes. Candidates should have crossed Sashes, declaration, and recommendation signed by the two Chiefs. Admission Badges; Hiereus Lamen, Sword and Serpent.

LIST OF REQUIREMENTS:

Black Sash and White Sash for Candidates. Black Robe and Cords, Admission Badges. Attestation of Examinations and Recommendations.

<200> On Altar ¾ Cup of Wine, Candle, Crucifix, Chain, Dagger, Crook and Scourge. Incense. Cross.

Each Officer carries a Crux Ansata on his left wrist.

OPENING

Chief Adept Knocks. All rise.

Chief ו
Second ו
Third ו
Chief ו
Third ו

*Note, with regard to the Robes:
The Chief Adept, who had represented Tiphereth in the Portal Grade, in the Adeptus Minor Grade now represents Chesed (another good reason to attribute Kaph to AIR) and thus carries the Winged Sphere or Orb of Jupiter's Authority. The Second Adept who had represented Netzach, now represents the Fire of Geburah, and so bears the Phoenix Wand of the Seven Double Letters. The Third Adept who had represented the sphere of Hod, (Mercury being the "follower of the Sun"), now is given the Grade of Tiphareth. H.S.

<199>

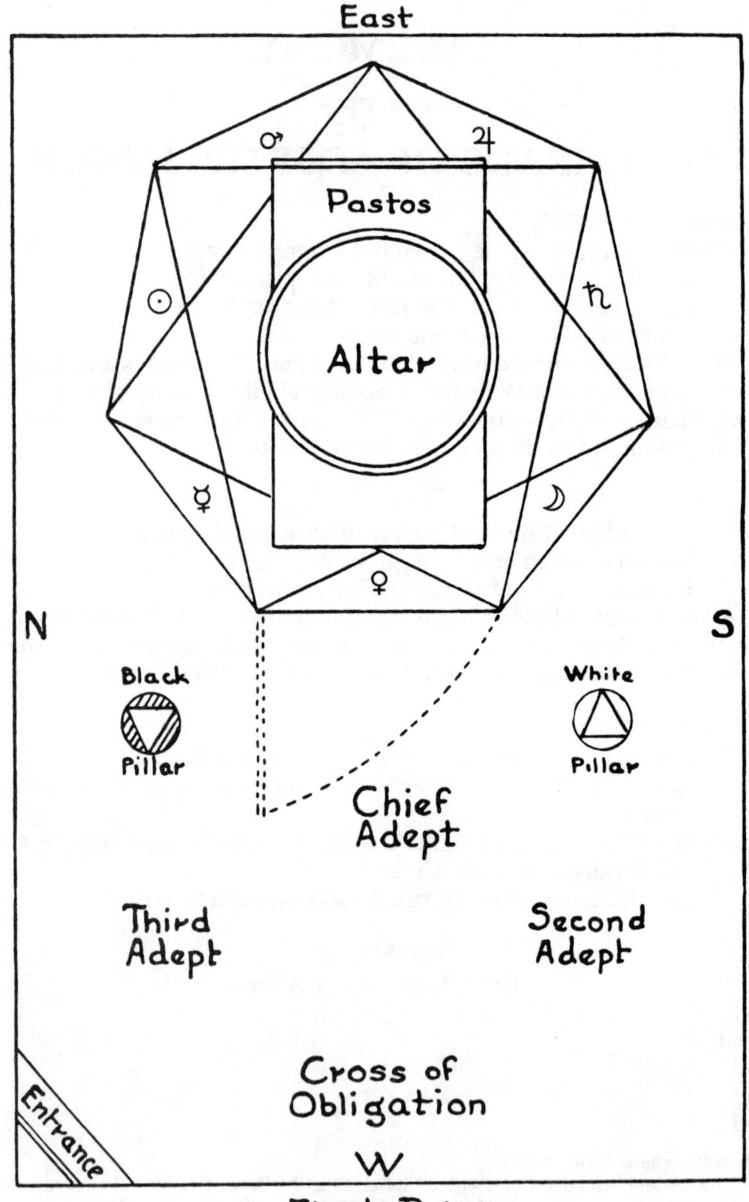
East
Pastos
Altar
N
S
Black
Pillar
White
Pillar
Chief
Adept
Third
Adept
Second
Adept
Cross of
Obligation
Entrance
W
First Point

Second ו

Chief Avete, Fratres et Sorores.

Second Roseae Rubeae.

Third Et Aureae Crucis.

Chief Very Honoured Fratres et Sorores, assist me to open the Tomb of the Adepti. Associate Adeptus Minor, see that the Portal is closed and guarded.

Third Adept does so and salutes.

Third Merciful Exempt Adept, the Portal of the Vault is closed and guarded.

Chief Mighty Adeptus Major, by what sign hast thou entered the Portal?

Second By the Sign of the Rending Asunder of the Veil. *(gives it)*

Chief Associate Adeptus Minor, by what sign hast thou closed the Portal.

Third By the Sign of the Closing of the Veil. *(gives it)*

Second Peh.

Third Resh.

Second Kaph.

Third Tau.*

<201> *Third* Which is the Veil of the Sanctum Sanctorum.

Second The Mystic Number of this Grade is 21.

Chief Associate Adeptus Minor, what is the Pass-Word formed therefrom?

Third Aleph.

Chief Heh.

Third Yod.

Chief Heh.

Third Eheieh.

Second The Tomb of the Adepti is the symbolic Burying Place of Christian Rosenkreutz, which he made to represent the Universe.

Third He is buried in the Centre of the Heptagonal Sides and beneath the Altar, his head being towards the East.

Second He is buried in the Centre because that is the point of balanced forces.

Third The Mystic Name of Christian Rosenkreutz signifies the Rose and Cross of Christ; the Fadeless Rose of Creation, the Immortal Cross of Light.

Second This place was entitled by our still more ancient Fratres and Sorores, the Tomb of Osiris Onnophris, the Justified One.

Third The shape of the Tomb is that of an equilateral Heptagon, a figure of Seven sides.

Second The Seven Sides allude to the Seven Lower Sephiroth, the seven Palaces, and the Seven Days of Creation. Seven is the height above. Seven is the depth beneath.

Third The Tomb is symbolically situated in the Centre of the Earth, in the

*P. R. K. Th.: Paroketh, the Veil between the Outer Order of the Golden Dawn and the Inner Order of the Red Rose and Gold Cross. H.S.

<202> Mountain of the Caverns, the Mystic Mountain of Abiegnus.

Third The meaning of this title of Abiegnus — Abi-Agnus, Lamb of the Father. It is by metathesis Abi-Genos, Born of the Father. Bia-Genos, Strength of our race, and the four words make the sentence: ABIEGNUS ABIAGNUS ABI-GENOS BIA-GENOS. "Mountain of the Lamb of the Father, and the Strength of our Race." I. A. O. YEHESHUA. Such are the words.

All salute with ⑤ = [6] Signs.

Chief Mighty Adeptus Major, what is the Key to this Tomb?

Second The Rose and the Cross, which resume the Life of Nature, and the powers hidden in the word I. N. R. I.

Third The Emblem which we bear in our left hands is a form of the Rose and the Cross, the ancient Crux Ansata, or Egyptian symbol of Life.

Second It represents the force of the Ten Sephiroth in Nature, divided into a Hexad and a Tetrad. The oval embraces the first Six Sephiroth, and the Tau Cross the lower Four answering to the Four Elements.

Chief Associate Adeptus Minor, what is the Emblem which I bear upon my breast?

Third The complete symbol of the Rose and Cross.

Chief Mighty Adeptus Major, what is its meaning?

Second It is the Key of Sigils and Rituals, and represents the force of the Twenty Two Letters in Nature, as divided into a Three, a Seven, and a Twelve. Many and great are its Mysteries.

Third I bear a simple Wand, having the colours of the Twelve Signs of the
<203> Zodiac between Light and Darkness, and surmounted by the Lotus Flower of Isis. It symbolises the development of Creation.

Second Mine is a Wand terminating in the Symbol of the Binary, and surmounted by the Tau Cross of Life, or the head of the Phoenix, sacred to Osiris. The Seven colours of the Rainbow between Light and Darkness are attributed to the Planets. It symbolises Rebirth and Resurrection from Death.

Chief My Wand is surmounted by the Winged Globe, around which the twin Serpents of Egypt twine. It symbolises the equilibriated force of the Spirit and the Four Elements beneath the everlasting wings of the Holy One.*

Associate Adeptus Minor, what are the words inscribed upon the Door of the Tomb? And how is it guarded?

Third Post Centum Viginti Annos Patebo. After one hundred and twenty years I shall open. The door is guarded by the Elemental Tablets and the Kerubic Emblems.

Chief To the 120 years are referred symbolically the five grades of the First Order, and to the revolution of the powers of the Pentagram. Also

*Note that the Rose and Cross (see pg. 56, Vol. III)., with its Flower of three circles of three, seven and twelve petals respectively comprises the three mother, seven double and twelve simple letters of the Hebrew Alphabet. Their Yetziric Attributions, in turn, expound the Chief Adept's Wand, the Phoenix Wand, and the Lotus Wands, being the Magical Weapons of Chesed, Geburah and Tiphareth respectively, just as the Fire Wand, Water Cup, Air Dagger and Earth Pentacle each establish the Magus in Netzach, Hod, Yesod and Malkuth. H.S.

the five preparatory examinations for this grade. It is written "His days shall be 120 years." and 120 divided by 5 equals 24, the number of hours in a day, and of the thrones of the Elders in the Apocalypse. Further, 120 equals the number of the Ten Sephiroth multiplied by
<204> that of the Zodiac, whose Key is the working of the Spirit and the Four Elements, typified in the Wand which I bear.

All face East. Chief Adept opens the Door wide, passes to East or head of Pastos of C. R. C., and faces West. Second enters and passes to South facing North. Third enters and passes to North facing South. Other members remain without, but Hodos may enter Vault to form fourth side in making Signs. The Three Officers raise their Wands to form pyramid above altar, Cruces touching below wands.

Chief Let us analyse the Key Word. I.
Second N.
Third R.
All I.
Chief YOD.
Second NUN.
Third RESH.
All YOD.
Chief Virgo, Isis, Mighty Mother
Second Scorpio, Apophis, Destroyer.
Third Sol, Osiris, Slain and Risen.
All Isis, Apophis, Osiris—I. A. O.

All separate Wands and Cruces, and give Sign of Cross.

All The Sign of Osiris Slain.
Chief L—The Sign of the Mourning of Isis. *(with bowed head)*
Second V—The Sign of Typhon and Apophis. *(with head erect)*
<205> *Third* X—The Sign of Osiris Risen. *(with head bowed)*
All L V X, the Light of the Cross. *(saluting Sign and head bowed)*

All quit Tomb and return to previous places.

Chief In the Grand Word YEHESHUA, by the Key-Word, I. N. R. I., and through the concealed Word LVX, I have opened the tomb of the Adepti.

All present give LVX Signs.

FIRST POINT

The Tomb is prepared as before, but closed, and curtains drawn. Chief Adept is not seen as such; Second Adept is Principal Officer, 3rd Associate Adept, Introducing Adept — Hodos Chamelionis.

Second Very Honoured Fratres et Sorores, our H. Frater......., Lord of the 24th, 25th, and 26th Paths of the Portal of the Vault of the Adepti, is a Candidate for admission to the Second Order, and is waiting without.

V. H. Frater Hodos Chamelionis, prepare the Aspirant and act as his introducer. Associate Adeptus Minor, guard the hither side of the Portal, and admit them in due form.

Aspirant is prepared by making him wear Portal Sash across that of the ④ =

[7]. *He carries Lamen of Hiereus, and Recommendation from the Chiefs of his Temple, a certificate of having passed the requisite examinations, and a written out speech.*

<206> *Third (opening door)* Whom bringest thou here with thee?

Aspirant (Loudly and firmly) Hear ye all that I, the Honoured Frater........ stand before you, being a member of the ④ = [7] Grade of the First Order, the Highest Grade of the Stella Matutina in the Outer, a Philosophus; one qualified to fill the important post of Hiereus in a Temple of the First Order, one who hath passed the five examinations prescribed between the First and Second Orders, and hath been declared Lord of the 24th, 25th, and 26th Paths in the Portal of the Adepti. I bear a written recommendation from the Chiefs of my Temple guaranteeing my qualifications, honour and fidelity; as also an attestation of my having passed the Pentagonal Examination. By virtue of these honours and dignities, I now come to demand my reception and acknowledgement as an Adeptus Minor of the ⑤ = [6] Grade of the Second Order.

Second O Aspirant! It is written that he who exalteth himself shall be abased, but that he who humbleth himself shall be exalted, and that blessed are the poor in spirit for theirs is the Kingdom of Heaven. It is not by proclamation of honours and dignities, great though they may be, that thou canst gain admission to the Tomb of the Adepti of the Rose of Ruby and the Cross of Gold, but only by that humility and purity of spirit that befitteth the aspirant unto higher things.

<207> Associate Adeptus Minor, bring unto me the recommendation and attestation which he beareth; and test thou his knowledge ere he be rejected for the sins of presumption and spiritual pride.

Third Thou knowest the arrangement of the Ten Sephiroth on the Tree of Life; now what symbolic weapon doth their natural succession form?

Aspirant answers unprompted.

Third And what symbolic creature is traced by the natural succession of the Paths?

Aspirant answers unprompted.

Second O Aspirant. Let this be a sign unto thee. For the Flaming Sword and the Serpent of Wisdom shall be the symbol which shall procure thee admission. Return thou then, and divest thyself of these ornaments. They are not humble enough to entitle thee to be received. V. H. Frater Hodos Chamelionis, clothe him in the black robe of mourning. Let his hands be bound behind his back, symbolic of the binding force of his obligations, and put a chain about his neck, the emblem of repentance and humility.

Hodos Mighty Adeptus Major, it shall be done.

Hodos Chamelionis salutes and retires with Aspirant, strips him of all ornaments, brings him back to door in plain black robe, roped and carrying diagram of Sword and Serpent. Gives one gentle knock. Third Adept opens door, saying.

Third By the aid of what symbol do ye seek admission?

Hodos *(shows diagram)* By the aid of the Flaming Sword, and the Serpent
<208> of Wisdom.

Third takes badge, admits them, and recloses door.

Second Whom bringest thou there?

Hodos Mighty Adeptus Major, I bring with me one who has passed the trial of humiliation, and who humbly desireth admission to the Tomb of the Mystical Mountain.

Second Let the Aspirant be assisted to kneel.

Aspirant is brought to curtained door of Tomb between Third Adept and Hodos Chamelionis. All face East, and kneel.

Second From Thine Hand, O Lord, cometh all good. The characters of Nature with Thy Fingers Thou hast traced; but none can read them unless he hath been taught in Thy school. Therefore, even as servants look unto the hands of their masters and handmaidens unto their mistresses, even so our eyes look unto Thee, for Thou alone art our help. O Lord our God, who should not extol Thee? Who should not praise Thee?

All is from Thee — All belongeth unto Thee. Either Thy Love or Thy Anger all must again re-enter. Nothing canst Thou lose, for all must tend unto Thy Honour and Majesty.

Thou art Lord alone, and there is none beside Thee. Thou dost what Thou wilt with Thy mighty Arm, and none can escape from Thee.

Thou alone helpest in their necessity the humble, the meek-hearted and the poor, who submit themselves unto Thee; and whosoever humbleth himself in dust and ashes before Thee, unto such an
<209> one Thou art propitious.

Who should not praise Thee, then, O Lord of the Universe, unto whom there is none like? Whose dwelling is in Heaven, and in every virtuous and God-fearing heart. O God the Vast One, Thou art in all things. O Nature, Thou Self from Nothing, for what else can I call Thee? In myself I am nothing. In Thee I am Self, and exist in Thy Selfhood from Nothing. Live Thou in me, and bring me unto that Self which is in Thee. Amen.

Let the hands of the Aspirant be unbound.

This is done, Aspirant remains kneeling. Officers rise.

Third Think not, O Aspirant, that the trial of humility through which thou hast passed, was ordained but to jest with thy feelings. Far from us be any such design. But it was intended to point out to thee that the truly wise man is but little in his own eyes, however great his attainments may appear to the ignorant, and that even the highest intellectual achievements are but as nothing in the sight of the Lord of the Universe, for He looketh at the heart. It is written: "When I consider the Heavens, the work of Thy fingers, the moon and stars which Thou hast ordained, what is man that Thou art mindful of him, or the son of man that thou visitest him?" And couldst thou even attain unto the height of a God upon this earth, how small and insignificant yet wouldst thou be in the presence of God the Vast One.

Second Rise, then, O Aspirant of the Rose of Ruby and the Cross of Gold.

<210> Rise, glorified by suffering. Rise, purified by humility.
Aspirant rises.

Second Despise not sadness, and hate not suffering, for they are the Initiators of the heart; and the black robe of mourning which thou wearest is at once the symbol of sorrow and of strength. Boast not thyself above thy brother if he hath fallen, for how knowest thou that thou couldst have withstood the same temptation. Slander not, and revile not. If thou canst not praise, do not condemn. When thou seest another in trouble in humiliation, even though he be thy enemy, remember the time of thy own humiliation when thou didst kneel before the door of the Tomb, clothed in the Robe of Mourning, with the Chain of Affliction about thy neck, and thy hands bound behind thy back, and rejoice not at his fall.

And in thine intercourse with the members of our Order, let thy hand given unto another be a sincere and genuine pledge of fraternity. Respect his or her secrets and feelings as thou wouldst respect thine own. Bear with one another and forgive one another, even as the Master hath said.

V. H. Frater Hodos Chamelionis, what is the symbolic age of the Aspirant?

Hodos His days are an hundred and twenty years.

Second It is written: "My Spirit shall not always strive with man, seeing that he also is flesh, yet his days shall be an hundred and twenty years."

<211> Associate Adeptus Minor, unto what do those 120 years of the Aspirant's symbolic age correspond?

Third To the Five Grades of the First Order through which it is necessary for the Aspirant to have passed before he can enter the Tomb of the Sacred Mountain. For the three months interval between the Grades of Practicus and Philosophus are the Regimen of the Elements; and the seven months between the Philosophus and the Portal symbolise the Regimen of the Planets; while the Elements and the Planets both work in the Zodiac; so that three plus seven multiplied by twelve yieldeth the number 120.

Second O Aspirant, ere thou canst enter the Tomb of the Adepti of the Rose of Ruby and the Cross of Gold, it is necessary to take a solemn Obligation of Secrecy, Fidelity, Fraternity, and Justice. But as in all the previous obligations, there is nothing contained therein contrary to thy civil, moral, or religious duties. Art thou willing to take such a pledge?

Aspirant I am.

Second Let the Aspirant be bound to the Cross of Suffering.

The Aspirant is led to the Cross, and his hands put through the running nooses and cords are bound about his waist and feet. Two Adepti stand on either side to support thim, and Third Adept takes his place ready to hand Cup and Dagger to Second Adept who stands in front of and facing Aspirant.

<212> *Second Adept holds out Rose Crucifix to Aspirant, saying:*

Second The Symbol of Suffering is the symbol of strength. Wherefore bound as thou art, strive to raise this holy symbol in thy hands, for he that will not strive shall not attain.

Aspirant takes Crucifix in both hands, the cords being allowed to run out long enough to allow him to do so.

Second I invoke Thee, the great avenging Angel HUA, in the divine name IAO, that Thou mayest invisibly place Thy hand upon the head of the Aspirant in attestation of his Obligation.

Second Adept raises his hands on high to invoke the force; then lowers them and takes crucifix which is replaced by Third Adept on Altar. Aspirant is now bound more firmly to the cross.

Second Repeat after me your sacramental Name, and say:

OBLIGATION

Kether I, (Christian Rosenkreutz), a member of the Body of Christ, do this day spiritually bind myself, even as I am now bound physically upon the Cross of Suffering.

Chokmah That I will to the utmost lead a pure and unselfish life, and will prove myself a faithful and devoted servant of this Order.

Binah That I will keep secret all things connected with the Order, and its Secret Knowledge, from the whole world, equally from him who is a member of the First Order of the Stella Matutina, as from an uniniti-
<213> ated person, and that I will maintain the Veil of strict secrecy between the First and Second Orders.

Chesed That I will uphold to the utmost the authority of the Chiefs of the Order, and that I will not initiate or advance any person in the First Order, either secretly or in open Temple, without due authorisation and permission; that I will neither recommend a Candidate for admission to the First Order without due judgment and assurance that he or she is worthy of so great confidence and honour, nor unduly press any person to become a candidate; and that I will superintend any examination of Members of lower Grades without fear or favour in any way, so that our high standard of knowledge be not lowered by my instrumentality; and I further undertake to see that the necessary interval of time between the Grades of Practicus and Philosophus and between the latter Grade and the Portal, be, when possible, maintained.

Geburah Furthermore, that I will perform all practical work connected with this Order in a place concealed and apart from the gaze of the outer and uninitiated world, and that I will not display our Magical Implements, nor reveal the use of the same, but will keep secret this Inner Rosicrucian Knowledge even as the same hath been kept secret through the ages; that I will not make any symbol or Talisman in the Flashing Colours for any uninitiated person without a special per-
<214> mission from the Chiefs of the Order. That I will only perform any practical magic before the uninitiated which is of a simple and already well-known nature; and that I will show them no secret mode of working whatsoever, keeping strictly concealed from them our modes of Tarot and other Divination, of Clairvoyance, of Astral

projection, of the Consecration of Talismans and Symbols, and the Rituals of the Pentagram and Hexagram, and most especially of the use and attribution of the Flashing Colours, and the Vibratory mode of pronouncing the Divine Names.

Tiphereth I further promise and swear that with the Divine Permission I will, from this day forward, apply myself to the Great Work — which is, to purify and exalt my Spiritual Nature so that with the Divine Aid I may at length attain to be more than human, and thus gradually raise and unite myself to my higher and Divine Genius, and that in this event I will not abuse the great power entrusted to me.

Netzach I furthermore solemnly pledge myself never to work at any important symbol without first invocating the highest Divine Names connected therewith, and especially not to debase my knowledge of Practical Magic to purposes of evil and self-seeking, and low material gain or pleasure, and if I do this, notwithstanding this my oath, I invoke the Avenging Angel HUA, that the evil and material may react on me.

Hod I further promise to support the admission of both sexes to our
<215> Order, on a perfect equality, and that I will always display brotherly love and forbearance towards the members of the whole Order, neither slandering nor evil-speaking, nor repeating nor tale-bearing, whereby strife and ill-feeling may be engendered.

Yesod I also undertake to work unassisted at the subjects prescribed for study in the various practical grades from Zelator Adeptus Minor to Adept Adeptus Minor, on pain of being degraded to that of Lord of the Paths of the Portal only.

Malkuth Finally, if in my travels I should meet a stranger who professes to be a member of the Rosicrucian Order, I will examine him with care before acknowledging him to be such.

Such are the words of this my Obligation as an Adeptus Minor, whereunto I pledge myself in the Presence of the Divine One, and of the Great Avenging Angel, HUA, and if I fail herein — may my Rose be disintegrated and my power in Magic cease.

Third hands Dagger to Second Adept and holds Cup conveniently for him. Second dips point of Dagger in Wine and makes Cross on Aspirant — on brow, feet, right hand and left hand, and heart, saying:

(for brow) There are Three that bear witness in Heaven; the Father, the Word, and the Holy Spirit, and these Three are One.

(for feet) There are Three that bear witness on Earth; the Spirit, the Water, and the Blood, and these Three agree in One.

<216> *(right Hand)* Except ye be born of Water and the Spirit, ye cannot enter the Kingdom of Heaven.

(left hand) If ye be crucified with Christ, ye shall also reign with Him.

(He marks heart in silence) Then says:

Second Let the Aspirant be released from the Cross of Suffering. It is written, that he who humbleth himself shall be exalted.

V. H. Frater Hodos Chamelionis, remove from the Aspirant the

Chain of Humility and the Robe of Mourning, and re-invest him with the Crossed Sashes.

This is done.

Third Know, then, O Aspirant, that the Mysteries of the Rose and the Cross have existed from time immemorial, and that the Rites were practised, and the Wisdom taught, in Egypt, Eleusis, Samothrace, Persia, Chaldea and India, and in far more ancient lands.

The story of the introduction of these mysteries into mediaeval Europe has thus been handed down to us.

In 1378 was born the Chief and Originator of our Fraternity in Europe. He was of noble German family, but poor, and in the fifth year of his age was placed in a cloister where he learned both Greek and Latin. While yet a youth he accompanied a certain brother P. A. L. on a pilgrimage to the Holy Land, but the latter, dying at Cyprus, he himself went to Damascus. There was then in Arabia a Temple of
<217> the Order which was called in the Hebrew tongue "Damkar" (דמכר), that is "The Blood of the Lamb." There he was duly initiated, and took the Mystic title Christian Rosenkreutz, or Christian of the Rosy Cross. He then so far improved his knowledge of the Arabian tongue that in the following year he translated the book *M* into Latin, which he afterwards brought back with him to Europe.

After three years he went on into Egypt, where there was another Temple of the Order. There he remained for a time still studying the mysteries of Nature. After this, he travelled by sea to the city of Fessa, where he was welcomed at the Temple there established, and he there obtained the knowledge and the acquaintance of the habitants of the Elements, who revealed unto him many of their secrets. Of the Fraternity he confessed that they had not retained their Wisdom in its primal purity, and that their Kabala was to a certain extent altered to their religion. Nevertheless, he learned much there. After a stay of two years he came to Spain, where he endeavoured to reform the errors of the learned according to the pure knowledge he had received. But it was to them a laughing matter, and they reviled and rejected him, even as the prophets of old were rejected. Thus also was he treated by those of his own and other nations when he showed them the errors that had crept into their religions. So, after five years residence in Germany, he initiated three of his former
<218> monastic brethren, Fratres G. W., I. A., and I. O., who had more knowledge than many others at that time. And by these four was made the foundation of the Fraternity in Europe.

These worked and studied at the writings and other knowledge which C. R. C. had brought with him, and by them was some of the Magical Language transcribed (which is that of the Elemental Tablets) and a Dictionary thereof made; and the Rituals and part of the Book *M* were transcribed.

For the True Order of the Rose Cross descendeth into the depths, and ascendeth into the heights — even unto the Throne of God Himself, and includeth even Archangels, Angels and Spirits.

These four Fratres also erected a building to serve for the Temple and Headquarters of their Order, and called it the Collegium ad Spiritum Sanctum, or the College of the Holy Spirit. This being now finished, and the work of establishing the Order extremely heavy, and because they devoted much time to the healing of those sick and possessed, who resorted to them, they initiated four others, viz: Fratres R. C. (the son of the deceased father's brother of C. R. C.), C. B. a skillful artist, G. C., and P. D., who was to be Cancellarius; all being Germans except I. A., and now eight in number. Their agreement was:

1. That none of them should profess any other thing, than but to cure the sick, and that freely.

2. That they should not be constrained to wear any distinctive dress,
<219> but therein follow the custom of the country.

3. That every year on the day of Corpus Christi, they should meet at the Collegium ad Spiritum Sanctum, or write the cause of absence.

4. Everyone should look for some worthy person of either sex, who after his decease might succeed him.

5. The word R.C. to be their mark, seal, and character.

The Fraternity to remain secret for one hundred years. Five of the Fratres were to travel in different countries, and two were to remain with Christian Rosenkreutz.

Second Frater I.O. was the first to die, and then in England where he had wrought many wonderful cures. He was an expert Kabbalist as his book *H* witnesseth. His death had been previously foretold him by C. R. C. But those who were later admitted were of the First Order, and knew not when C. R. died, and save what they learned from Frater A., the sucessor of D. of the Second Order and from their library after his death, knew little of the earlier and higher Members, and of the Founder, nor yet whether those of the Second Order were admitted to the Wisdom of the highest members. The discovery then of the Tomb wherein that highly illuminated Man of God, our Father C. R. C., was buried occurred as follows.

After Frater A. died in Gallia Narbonensi, there succeeded in his
<220> place Frater N.N. He, while repairing a part of the building of the College of the Holy Spirit, endeavoured to remove a brass memorial tablet which bore the names of certain brethren, and some other things. In this tablet was the head of a strong nail or bolt, so that when the tablet was forcibly wrenched away it pulled with it a large stone which thus partially uncovered a secret door, *(he draws back curtain, revealing door)*, upon which was inscribed in large letters "Post CXX Annos Patebo" — After an hundred and twenty years I shall open, with the year of our Lord under, 1484. Frater N.N., and those with him then cleared away the rest of the brickwork, but let it remain that night unopened as they wished first to consult the ROTA.

Third You will now quit the Portal for a short time, and on your return the Ceremony of Opening the Tomb will be proceeded with. Take with you this Wand and Crux Ansata, which will ensure your re-admission.

Aspirant goes out, carrying the Wand and Crux of Chief Adept.

SECOND POINT

Prepare Tomb as in diagram. Chief Adept lies in Pastos on his back to represent C. R. C. He is clothed in full Regalia; on his breast is the complete Symbol of the Rosy Cross suspended from the double Phoenix Collar. His arms are crossed on breast, and he holds Crook and Scourge; between them lies the
<222> *book T. Lid of Pastos closed and Circular Altar stands over it. Other Adepti outside Tomb as before. On the Altar are replaced Rose Cross, Cup of Wine, Chain and Dagger.*

Second Associate Adeptus Minor, let the Aspirant now be admitted.

Third Ad. opens the door, and admits Aspirant, who carries Wand and Crux of Chief. He is placed in front of and facing Vault Door.

Second Before the Door of the Tomb, as symbolic Guardians, are the Elemental Tablets, and the Kerubic Emblems, even as before the mystical Gate of Eden stood the watchful Kerubim, and the Sword of Flame. These Kerubic Emblem be the powers of the Angles of the Tablets. The Circle represents the four Angles bound together in each Tablet through the operation of the all-pervading Spirit, while the Cross within forms with its spokes the Wheels of Ezekiel's Vision; and therefore are the Cross and the Circle white to represent the purity of the Divine Spirit. And inasmuch as we do not find the Elements unmixed, but each bound together with each — so that in the Air we find not only that which is subtle and tenuous, but also the qualities of heat, moisture and dryness, bound together in that all-wandering Element; and further also that in Fire, Water and Earth we find the same mixture of Nature — therefore the Four Elements are bound to each Kerubic Emblem counterchanged with the colour of the Element wherein they operate; even as in the Vision of Ezekiel
<223> each Kerub had four faces and four wings. Forget not therefore that the Tablets and the Kerubim are the Guardians of the Tomb of the Adepti. Let thy tongue keep silence on our mysteries. Restrain even the thought of thy heart lest a bird of the air carry the matter.

Third Upon more closely examining the Door of the Tomb, you will perceive, even as Frater N. N., and those with him did perceive, that beneath the CXX in the inscription were placed the characters IX thus:

POST CXX ANNOS PATEBO
IX

being equivalent to Post Annos Lux Crucis Patebo — At the end of 120 years, I, the Light of the Cross, will disclose myself. For the letters forming LVX are made from the dismembered and conjoined angles of the Cross and 120 is the product of the numbers from 1 to 5, multiplied in regular progression, which number five is symbolised in the Cross with four extremities and one centre point.

Second On the following morning, Frater N. N. and his companions forced

<221>

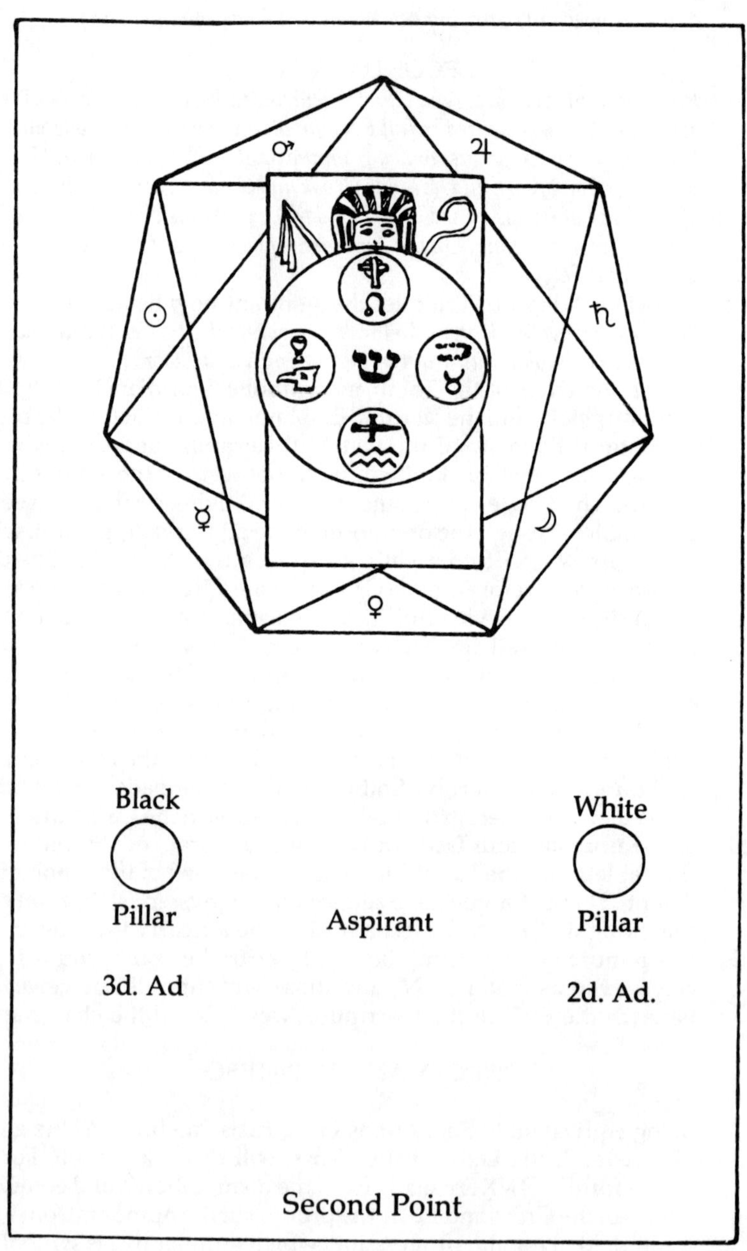
♂
♃
☉
♄
☿
☽
♀
ש
Black
Pillar
3d. Ad
Aspirant
White
Pillar
2d. Ad.
Second Point

open the door *(he opens it wide)* and there appeared to their sight a Tomb of Seven Sides and Seven Corners. Every side was five feet broad, and eight feet high, even as the same is faithfully represented before you.

Second Adept enters and passes by North to East of Vault, and turns to face West. Third Adept places Aspirant on North facing South, and takes his place at South facing North.

<224> *Second* Although in the Tomb the Sun does not shine, it is lit by the symbolic Rose of our Order in the centre of the first heptagonal ceiling. In the midst of the Tomb stands a circular Altar with these devices and descriptions on it:

A.G.R.C.—Ad Gloriam Roseae Crucis.
A.C.R.G.—Ad Crucis Roseae Gloriam.
Hoc Universal Compendium Unius Mihi Sepulchrum Feci—

Unto the Glory of the Rose Cross I have constructed this Tomb for myself as a Compendium of the Universal Unity.

Within the next circle is written:

Yeheshua Mihi Omnia—Yeheshua is all things to me.

In the centre are four figures of the Kerubim enclosed within circles surrounded by the following four inscriptions and each distinguished by one of the letters of the Tetragrammaton:—

Yod—Lion—Nequaquam Vacuum—
Nowhere a Void.
Heh—Eagle—Libertas Evangelii—
Liberty of the Gospel
Vau—Man—Dei Intacta Gloria—
Unsullied Glory of God.
Heh(f)—Ox—Legis Jugum—
Yoke of the Law.

and in the midst of all is Shin, the Letter of the Spirit forming thus the Divine Name Yeheshua, from the Tetragrammaton. Therefore, by God's Grace, having come thus far, let us kneel down together, and say:

<225> *All kneel, joining wands above Altar.*

Second Unto Thee, Sole Wise, Sole Mighty and Sole Eternal One, be praise and Glory forever, Who has permitted this Aspirant who now kneeleth before Thee to penetrate thus far into the Sanctuary of Thy Mysteries. Not unto us, but unto Thy Name be the Glory. Let the influence of Thy Divine Ones descend upon his head, and teach him the value of self-sacrifice, so that he shrink not in the hour of trial, but that thus his name may be written on high, and that his Genius may stand in the presence of the Holy Ones, in that hour when the Son of Man is invoked before the Lord of Spirits and His Name in the presence of the Ancient of Days.

It is written: "If any man will come after Me, let him take up his cross, and deny himself, and follow Me."

Third Adept hands Chain to Aspirant, and takes Wand and Cross from him.

Second Take therefore this Chain, O Aspirant, and place it about thy neck and say: I accept the Bonds of Suffering and Self-Sacrifice.

2nd and 3rd Adepts rise. Aspirant repeats words as directed.

Second Rise, then, my Frater, in the symbol of self-renunciation and extend thine arms in the form of a cross.

Aspirant rises, feet together, and arms extended.

Second Associate Adeptus Minor, take from the Altar the Dagger of Penance and the Cup of Tribulation, that I may confirm the vow of the
<226> Aspirant forever by marking him afresh with the Stigmata of the Cross.

Second takes Dagger from Third and marks Aspirant anew as at Obligation: brow, feet, right hand, left hand, and heart. Gives Dagger back to Third who replaces it on Altar, and then hands Aspirant the Rose Crucifix.

Second Take that symbol, raise it with both hands above thy head and say: "Thus will I uphold the Sign of Suffering and of Strength." And I heard the voice of the King of Earth cry aloud and say: "He that aideth me in my suffering, the same shall partake with me in my rising." Replace then, O Aspirant, that Cross upon the Altar, and say: "In and by that Sign, I demand that the Pastos of our founder be opened, for my victory is in the Cross of the Rose."

For it is written "If ye be crucified with Christ, ye shall also reign with Him."

Aspirant replaces Crucifix and repeats words as directed. Third gives him back Wand and Crux of Chief Adept. Second and Third Adepts move away Altar revealing upper part of Pastos. They open lid, disclosing Chief Adept within.

Third And the Light shineth in Darkness, and the darkness comprehendeth it not.

Second Touch with the head of thy Wand the Rose and Cross upon the breast of the Form before thee, and say: "Out of the darkness, let the light arise."

Done. Chief, without moving or opening his eyes, says:

<227> *Chief* Buried with that Light in a mystical death, rising again in a mystical resurrection, cleansed and purified through Him our Master, O Brother of the Cross and the Rose. Like Him, O Adepts of all ages, have ye toiled. Like Him have ye suffered tribulation. Poverty, torture and death have ye passed through. They have been but the purification of the Gold.

In the alembic of thine heart, through the athanor of affliction, seek thou the true stone of the Wise.

Aspirant gives Wand and Crux to Chief Adept who gives in exchange the Crook and Scourge.

Chief Quit then, this Tomb, O Aspirant, with thine arms crossed upon thy breast, bearing in thy right hand the Crook of Mercy and in thy left the Scourge of Severity, the emblems of those Eternal Forces betwixt which the equilibrium of the Universe dependeth; those forces whose reconcilation is the Key of Life, whose separation is evil and death. Therefore thou art inexcusable, whosoever thou art, that judgest another, for in that thou condemnest another, thou condemnest but thyself. Be thou therefore merciful, even as thy Father who is in Heaven is merciful. Remember that tremendous Obligation of rectitude and self-sacrifice which thou hast voluntarily taken upon thyself, and tremble thereat. And let the humble prayer of thy heart be: "God, be merciul to me a sinner, and keep me in the pathway of Truth."

Third Thus, then, did Frater N. N. and his companions, having moved
<228> aside the Circular Altar, and having raised the brazen plate or lid of the Pastos, discover the body of our Founder, with all the ornaments and insignia as here shown before you. Upon his breast was the Book *T*, a scroll explaining in full the mystic Tarot; at the end of which was written a brief paragraph concerning Christian Rosenkreutz, beneath which the earlier Fratres had inscribed their names. Following this came the names of the three Highest Chiefs of the Order, viz:

Frater Hugo Alverda, the Phrisian, in the 576th year of his age.
Frater Franciscus de Bry, the Gaul, in the 495th year of his age.
Frater Elman Zata, the Arab, in the 463rd year of his age.

Last of all was written: Ex Deo Nascimur; In Yeheshuah Morimur; Per Spiritum Sanctum Reviviscimus. "In God are we born, in Yeheshuah we die, through the Holy Spirit we rise again."

They re-close the Pastos, and replace Altar.

Second So, then, our Frater N. N. and his companions reclosed the Pastos for a time, set the Altar over it, shut the Door of the Tomb, and placed their seals upon it.

All quit the Vault. Aspirant carries Crook and Scourge; the door is closed, and Aspirant is led out of the Portal. The Tomb is then re-opened and Chief Adept released.

<229>

THIRD POINT

Tomb prepared as in diagram. Door not quite closed. In South East angle is diagram of Minutum Mundum; in N. E. that of Sword and Serpent. Due East, the Mountain. Altar as before with Crook and Scourge added later. Chief stands at East with arms extended. Pastos outside in Portal, head to the East. Lid laid side by side with space between. Second Adept seated at head, Third at Foot of Pastos. Aspirant is admitted, still carrying Crook and Scourge. 2nd and 3rd Adepts discard cloaks.

Second And lo, two Angels in White apparel sitting, the one at the head and the other at the foot, where the body of the Master had lain, who said: "Why seek ye the living among the dead?"

Chief I am the Resurrection and the Life. He that believeth in Me, though

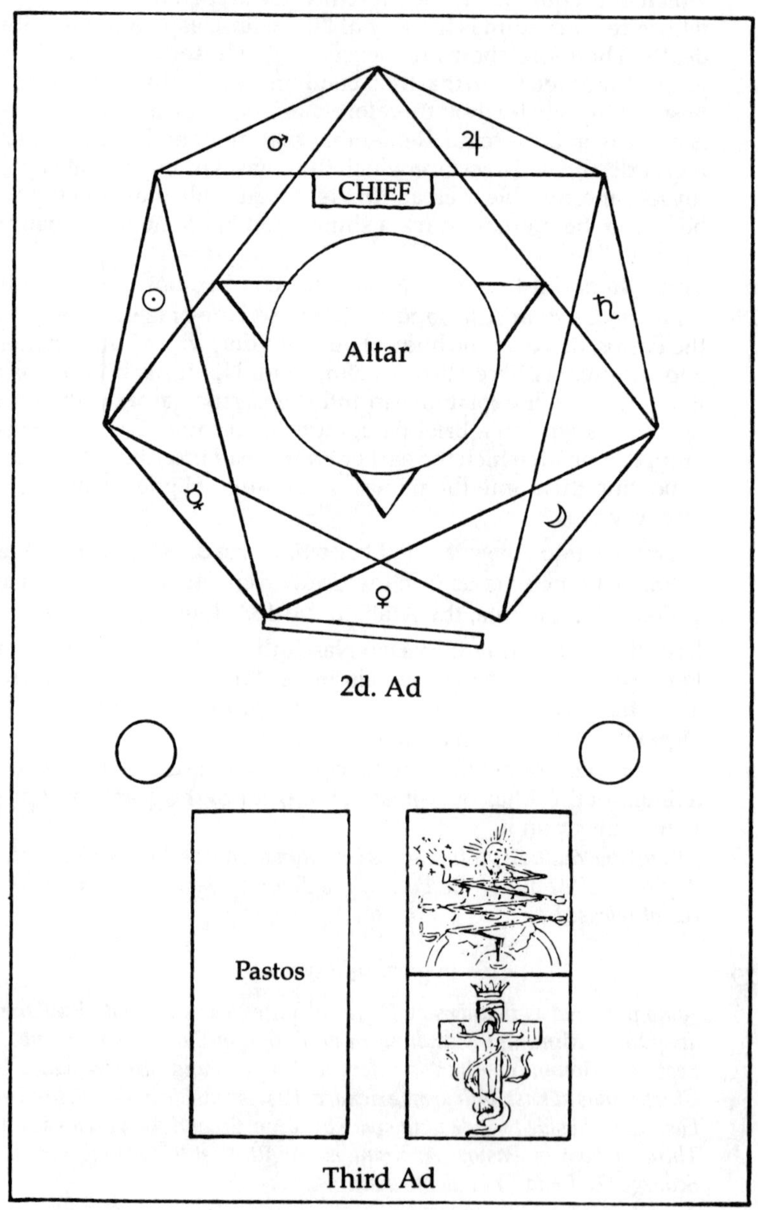
♂
♃
CHIEF
☉
♄
Altar
☿
☽
♀
2d. Ad
Pastos
Third Ad

Third Point

he were dead, yet shall he live. And whosoever liveth and believeth in Me, shall never die.

Second Behold the Image *(points to lower half of lid)* of the Justified One, crucified on the Infernal Rivers of DAATH, and thus rescuing Malkuth from the folds of the Red Dragon.

Third points to upper half of lid.

Third And being turned, I saw Seven Golden Light-bearers, and in the midst of the Lightbearers, One like unto the Ben Adam, clothed with a garment down to the feet, and girt with a Golden Girdle. His head and his hair were white as snow, and His eyes as flaming fire; His feet
<231> like unto fine brass, as if they burned in a furnace. And His voice as the sound of many waters. And He had in His right hand Seven Stars, and out of his mouth went the Sword of Flame, and his countenance was as the Sun in His Strength.

Chief I am the First and I am the Last. I am he that liveth and was dead, and behold! I am alive for evermore, and hold the keys of Death and of Hell.

Second He that hath an ear, let him hear what the Spirit saith unto the Assemblies.

Second and Third Adepts open Door of Tomb, and lead Aspirant in. They kneel down West of Altar with heads bent. Chief stands at East of Altar with arms extended.

Chief For I know that my Redeemer liveth, and that He shall stand at the latter day upon the earth. I am the Way, the Truth and the Life. No man cometh unto the Father but by me.

I am the purified. I have passed through the Gates of Darkness into Light. I have fought upon earth for Good. I have finished my Work. I have entered into the Invisible.

I am the Sun in his rising. I have passed through the hour of cloud and of night.

I am Amoun, the Concealed One, the Opener of the Day. I am Osiris Onnophris, the Justified One. I am the Lord of Life triumphant over Death. There is no part of me which is not of the Gods.

I am the Preparer of the Pathway, the Rescuer unto the Light; Out of
<232> the Darkness, let that Light arise.

Aspirant Before I was blind, but now I see.

Chief I am the Reconciler with the Ineffable. I am the Dweller of the Invisible.

Let the White Brilliance of the Spirit Divine descend.

Chief raises his hands invoking the Divine White Brilliance. There is a pause.

Chief *(to Aspirant)* Arise now as an Adeptus Minor of the Rose of Ruby and the Cross of Gold, in the sign of Osiris Slain.

All rise. Second and Third Adepts raise Aspirant, and extend his arms in a cross. They then recross his arms on his breast and turn him to face West. Chief advances within reach of Aspirant. Third Adept N. W. They both join wands over his head and Cruces a little lower.

All We receive thee as an Adeptus Minor in the Sign Rectitude and Self-

Sacrifice.

Still keeping Wands joined over the lower cruces, Chief touching base of brain, Second left temple, Third right temple.

Chief Be thy mind opened unto the higher.

Chief places Crux against spine between shoulder blades. Second Adept against left breast, Third against right breast.

Second Be thy heart a centre of Light.

Chief places Crux at the base of the spine. Second at left hip. Third at right hip.

Third Be thy body the Temple of the Rosy Cross.

Aspirant is faced to East, and Adepts return to former positions. Crook and
<233> *Scourge are laid on Altar over Dagger, crossing at yellow bands.*

Chief Repeat with us the following words which are the Signs of the Hidden Wisdom of our Order.

Aspirant is made to repeat each word after the Officer.

Chief I.

Second N.

Third R.

All I.

Chief Yod.

Second Nun.

Third Resh.

All Yod.

Chief Virgo, Isis, Mighty Mother.

Second Scorpio, Apophis, Destroyer.

Third Sol, Osiris, Slain and Risen.

All Isis, Apophis, Osiris, I. A. O.

All separate Wands and give the Sign of Osiris Slain.

All The Sign of Osiris Slain.

Chief L The Sign of the Mourning of Isis. *(with bowed head)*

Second V. The Sign of Typhon and Apophis *(head erect)*

All X. Isis, Apophis, Osiris, I.A.O.

They give the saluting Sign with heads bowed. A pause.

Chief The Mystic number of this Grade is 21, the Heptad multiplied by the Triad; and from it is derived the Password of this grade which is EHEIEH, which should be lettered separately when given thus, Aleph.

<234> *Aspirant* Heh.

Chief Yod.

Aspirant Heh.

Chief The Keyword is I. N. R. I. which is inscribed with its correspondences upon this complete symbol of the Rose and Cross which I bear upon my breast. These letters have been occasionally used as the initials of the following sentences: JESUS NAZARENUS REX JUDECORUM, whence it symbolises the Grand Word of this Grade which is YEHESHUA or the Hebrew Name of Jesus, formed of the Holy letter Shin, representing the Ruach Elohim, placed within the Centre of the Name Tetragrammaton. Also it has been interpreted as: Igne Natura Renovatur Integra; Igne Natura Renovando Integrat; Igne Nitrum Roris Invenitur; Intra Nobis Regnum Dei.

Chief *(indicating Diagram of the Minutum Mundum)* Behold the diagram Minutum Mundum sive Fundamental Coloris — the Small Universe or Foundation of Colour. Treasure it in thy heart, and mark it well, seeing that herein is the Key of Nature. It is, as thou seest, the diagram of the Sephiroth and the Paths, with the colours appropriately attributed thereto. See that thou reveal it not to the profane, for many and great are its mysteries.

Kether is the highest of all, and herein scintillates the Divine White Brilliance, concerning which it is not fitting that I should speak more fully. Chokmah is Grey, the mixture of colours. Binah is darkness,
<235> the absorption of colours. And thus is the Supernal Triad completed. In Kether is the root of the Golden Glory, and thence is the yellow reflected into Tiphareth. In Chokmah is the root of Blue, and this is reflected into Chesed; in Binah is the root of Red, and this is reflected into Geburah. And thus is the first reflected Triad completed. The beams of Chesed and Tiphareth meet in Netzach and yield Green. The beams of Geburah and Tiphareth meet in Hod and yield a tawny Orange. The beams of Chesed and Geburah fall in Yesod and yield Purple. And thus is the Third Triad completed. And from the rays of the Third Triad are these three colours shown in Malkuth, together with a fourth which is the synthesis. For from the Orange Tawny of Hod and the Greening Nature of Netzach is reflected a certain Greenish Citrine — Citron; from the Orange Tawny mixed with the Puce of Yesod proceedeth a red russet Brown —Russet; and from the Green and the Puce cometh a certain other darkening green — Olive. The synthesis of all these is blackness and bordereth on the Qlippoth.

But the colours of the 22 Paths are derived from and find their roots in those of the First Reflected Triad of the Sephiroth, the Three Supernals not otherwise entering into their composition, and thus are their positive colours found. Unto the Air is ascribed the Yellow colour of Tiphareth. Unto the Water is ascribed the blue Colour of
<236> Chesed. Unto the Fire is ascribed the Red Colour of Geburah. The Colours are to be found in Malkuth.

Those of the Planets are in the Rainbow scale; thus: Saturn —Indigo; Jupiter — Violet; Mars — Red; Sol — Orange; Mercury —Yellow; Venus — Green; Luna — Blue.

Unto the Signs of the Zodiac are ascribed the following: Aries — Scarlet; Taurus — Red-Orange; Gemini — Orange; Cancer — Amber; Leo — Greenish-Yellow; Virgo — Yellowish-Green; Libra — Emerald; Scorpio — Greenish-Blue; Sagittarius — Blue; Capricornus — Indigo; Aquarius — Purple; Pisces — Crimson. Further, thou wilt observe that the colours of the Paths and the Sephiroth form a mutual balance and harmony on the Tree. Colours are Forces, the Signatures of the Forces; and the Child of the Children of the Forces art thou. And therefore about the Throne of the Mighty One is a Rainbow of Glory, and at His Feet is the Crystal Sea. But there are many other attributions of colour also, seeing that the respective rays meet and blend with each other. And therefore do I greet thee with the Mystic Title of "Hodos Chamelionis", the Path of the Chamelion, the Path of Mixed Colours, and I give thee the Symbol of Hiddekel, the Third River which floweth towards the East of Assiah.

They return to Altar, and 2nd Adept indicates Crook and Scourge thereon.

Second The colours of the Crook and Scourge are taken from those of the
<237> Minutum Mundum Diagram, and they thus represent the just equilibrium between Mercy and Severity on the Tree of Life. The Crook therefore is divided into the colours symbolic of: Kether, Aleph, Chokmah, Taurus, Chesed, Leo, Tiphareth, Aries, Hod, Capricornus. And the Scourge into those symbolising: Netzach, Scorpio, Tiphareth, Gemini, Binah, Cancer, Geburah, Mem.

Third *(indicates Sword and Serpent)* The colours of the Minutum Mundum are also the key to those which compose the Admission Badge of the Sword and Serpent; and thus by their aid it may be the better examined and comprehended. The one is ascending, the other is descending; the one is fixed, the other is volatile; the one unites the Sephiroth, the other the Paths. Furthermore, in the Serpent of Wisdom is shown the ascending Spiral, and in the Sword the rush of the descending White Brilliance from beyond Kether, differentiated into various shades and colours, darkening more and more as they near Malkuth.

Chief *(indicates Diagram of Mountain)* This is the symbolic Mountain of God in the centre of the Universe, the sacred Rosicrucian Mountain of Initiation, the Mystic Mountain of Abiegnus. Below and around it are darkness and silence, and it is crowned with the Light ineffable. At its base is the Wall of Enclosure and Secrecy, whose sole Gateway, invisible to the profane, is formed of the Two Pillars of Hermes. The ascent of the Mountain is by the Spiral Path of the Serpent of
<238> Wisdom. Stumbling on between the Pillars is a blindfolded figure, representing the Neophyte, whose ignorance and worthlessness while only in that Grade is shown by the ⓪ = [0], and whose sole future claim to notice and recognition by the Order is the fact of his having entered the Pathway to the other Grades, until at length he attains to the summit.

I now proceed to instruct you in the mystic symbolism of the Tomb itself. Let the Altar be moved aside. *(Done)* It is divided into three parts — the Ceiling which is White; the Heptagonal Walls of seven Rainbow colours, and the Floor whose prevailing hue is black; thus showing the powers of the Heptad between the Light and the Darkness.

On the ceiling is a Triangle enclosing a Rose of 22 petals, within a Heptangle formed of a Heptagram reflected from the Seven Angles of the Wall. The Triangle represents the Three Supernal Sephiroth; the Heptagram, the Lower Seven; the Rose represents the 22 paths of the Serpent of Wisdom.

The Floor has upon it also the Symbol of a Triangle enclosed within a Heptagram, bearing the titles of the Averse and Evil Sephiroth of the Qlippoth, the Great Red Dragon of Seven Heads, and the inverted and evil triangle. And thus in the Tomb of the Adepti do we tread down the Evil Powers of the Red Dragon *(Chief Adept stamps thrice on diagram)* and so tread thou upon the evil powers of thy nature. For
<240> there is traced within the evil Triangle the Rescuing Symbol of the Golden Cross united to the Red Rose of Seven times Seven Petals. As it is written "He descendeth into Hell." But the whiteness above shines the brighter for the Blackness which is beneath, and thus mayest thou comprehend that the evil helpeth forward the Good. And between the Light and that Darkness vibrate the Colours of the Rainbow, whose crossed and reflected rays, under the Planetary Presidency are shewn forth in these Seven Walls. Remember that thou hast entered by the door of the Planet Venus, whose symbol includes the whole Ten Sephiroth of the Tree of Life. Each Wall of the

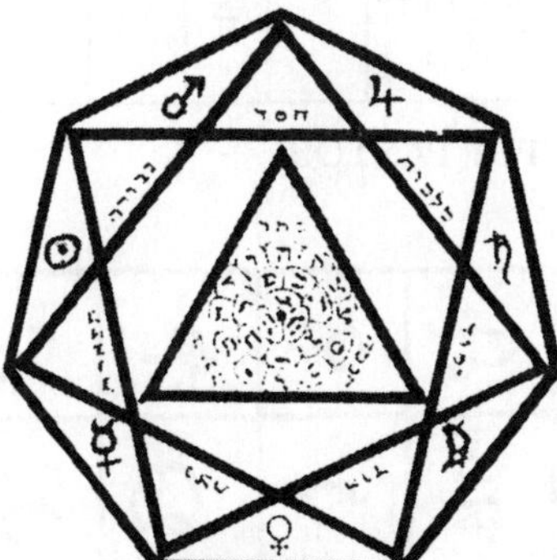

The Ceiling of the Vault

The Floor of the Vault

The Circular Altar

The Rose and Cross at the Head of Pastos (49 Petals)

White		
Scarlet	Vermilion	Red
Red-Orange		
Orange	Orange	
Amber		
Greenish-Yellow	Yellow	Yellow
Yellowish-Green		
Emerald	Green	
Green-Blue		
Blue	Blue	Blue
Indigo	Indigo	
Violet		
Crimson	Purple	
Black		

THE SIDE OF THE PASTOS

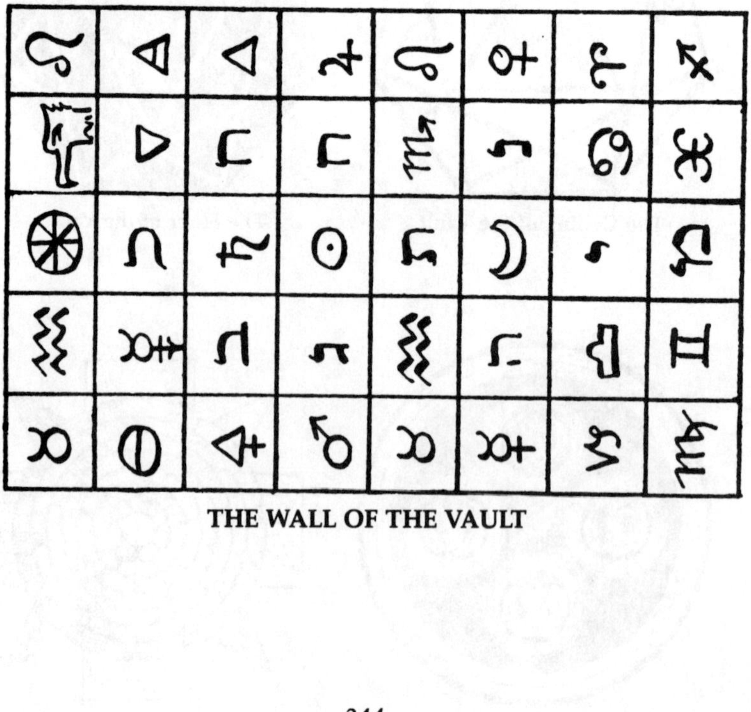

♉	♒	⊛	[illegible]	♌
⊖	☿	כ	🜄	🜁
🜍	ב	♄	ח	🜂
♂	ג	☉	ח	♃
♉	♒	ת	♏	♌
☿	ה	☽	נ	♀
♑	♎	י	♋	♈
♍	♊	מ	♓	♐

THE WALL OF THE VAULT

<241>

The Cross of Obligation

The Cross of Victory

The Foot of the Pastos

Tomb is said mystically to be in breadth five feet and in height eight feet, thus yielding forty squares, of which ten are marked and salient, representing the Ten Sephiroth in the form of the Tree of Life, acting throughout the Planet. The remaining squares represent the Kerubim and the Eternal Spirit, the Three Alchemic Principles, the Three Elements, the Seven Planets, and the Twelve Signs, all operating in and differentiating the rays of each planet. Note that in all, the Central upper square alone remains white and unchanged, representing the changeless Essence of the Divine Spirit, thus developing all from the One, through the Many under the government of One.

The colours of the varying squares may be either represented by the colour of the Planet and the colour of the Force therein mixed
<242> together, or by these colours being placed in juxtaposition, or in any other convenient manner; but the foundation of them all is the Minutum Mundum Diagram.

The symbolism of the Altar was briefly explained to you in the Second point. Upon the Altar stands a black Calvary cross, charged with a Rose of Five times Five petals, representing the interchanging energies of the Spirit and the Elements.

Chief leads Aspirant out of Tomb. Two Adepti replace Altar, and all resume their places as at beginning of Third Point.

Chief The head of the Pastos is white, charged with a golden Greek Cross and Red Rose of 49 Petals. The foot is black with a white Calvary Cross and Circle placed upon a pedestal of Two steps. On the sides are depicted the 22 Colours of the Paths, between Light and Darkness.

Aspirant is placed between Lid and Pastos. Chief stands facing him on opposite side of the Pastos.

Chief Frater *(vel Soror)* I now greet you with the grip of this Grade which is given thus. *(shows it)* The fingers of the right hand are held so as to form the letters L. V. X. The thumb and first fingers are stretched to form the letter L. The first and middle fingers are extended to suggest the V. The little finger is crossed over the third finger to make X. This may be done with both hands, and is always exchanged by placing the hands, with fingers thus arranged, over the wrist of the Frater
<243> or Soror being greeted.

You will note that this grip must never be exchanged except across the Pastos. You will also remember that you must observe strict silence in regard to the place where you received this rite.

It is well for you to understand that you are expected to promise that you will never tell anyone when, at what time, or where, of from whom you received this grip, or who was present at your initiation into this Order.

The Signs and Passwords you have already received. Finally, you must understand that you are never permitted to say to anyone not a member of this Order that you are a Rosicrucian. Let the Pastos be replaced within the Vault.

The Adepti replace Pastos as before, and all resume places as at opening of Ceremony.

CLOSING

Chief Adept knocks. All rise.

Chief *Knocks.*ו
Second *Knocks.*ו
Third *Knocks.*ו
Chief *Knocks.*ו
Third *Knocks.*ו
Second *Knocks.*ו
Second Roseae Rubeae.
Third Et Aureae Crucis.
Chief Very Honoured Fratres and Sorores, assist me to close the Tomb of the Adepti. Associate Adeptus Minor, how many Princes did Darius set over his Kingdom?
<244> *Third* It is written in the Book of Daniel that there were One Hundred and Twenty.
Chief Mighty Adeptus Major, how is that number formed?
Second By the continued multiplication of the first five numbers of the decimal scale.
Chief Post Centum Viginti Annos Patebo. Thus have I closed the Tomb of the Adepti in the Mystic Mountain of Abiegnus.
Chief Adept closes Door of Vault and draws Curtains.
Third Ex Deo Nascimur.
Second In Yeheshua Morimmur.
Chief Per Spiritum Sanctum Reviviscimus.

All present make LVX signs in silence. Aspirant signs Inner Roll and is led out. All disrobe and disperse. Aspirant should be directed to make Saluting Sign of ⑤ = 6 on entering and leaving.

<245>

CEREMONY
OF THE
EQUINOX

This Ceremony is held twice yearly: THE VERNAL EQUINOX about March 21st; The AUTUMNAL EQUINOX about September 21st.

Officers assemble and Robe. Chiefs seat themselves on the Dais. Members gowned and wearing their sashes enter and sit as far as possible by members of the same grade—Inner Members in the East, Philosophi in the South, Practici and Theorici in the West, Zelatores and Neophytes in the North. The Temple is Opened in the Neophyte Grade. All are seated.

Hiero (*knocks*) Fratres and Sorores of all Grades of the Stella Matutina in the . . . . . . Temple, let us celebrate the Festival of the VERNAL (Autumnal) EQUINOX.

All rise except Hierophant.

(*knocks*) Frater Kerux, proclaim the EQUINOX and announce that the Pass-word is abrogated.

Kerux passes to the North East, raises his Wand, and facing West, says:

Kerux In the Name of The Lord of the Universe, Who works in Silence and Whom naught but Silence can express, and by command of the Very
<246> Honoured Hierophant, I proclaim that the VERNAL (Autumnal) EQUINOX is here and that the Pass-word . . . . . . is abrogated.

Kerux returns to his place.

Members stand facing towards the Altar and follow the Officers in making the Signs towards it.

Hiero Let us consecrate according to ancient custom the return of the Equinox.

Hiero LIGHT

Hiereus DARKNESS

Hiero EAST

Hiereus WEST

Hiero AIR

Hiereus WATER

Heg (*knocks*) I am the Reconciler between them.

All make Neophyte Signs towards the Altar.

Dad HEAT

Stol COLD

Dad SOUTH

Stol NORTH

Dad FIRE

Stol EARTH

Heg (*knocks*) I am the Reconciler between them.

All make Signs towards the Altar.

Hiero ONE CREATOR
Dad ONE PRESERVER
Hiereus ONE DESTROYER
Stol ONE REDEEMER
Heg *(knocks)* One Reconciler between them.

All make Signs towards the Altar.

Hierophant goes to the West of the Altar and lays down his Sceptre, saying:

<247> *Hiero* With the Pass-word . . . . . . I lay down my Sceptre.

Hierophant takes the ROSE from the Altar and returns to his place.

Hiereus passes direct to the Altar and lays down his Sword, saying:

Hiereus With the Pass-word . . . . . . I lay down my Sword.

Hiereus takes the Cup of Wine and returns to place.

Hegemon comes direct to the East of the Altar and lays down Sceptre, saying:

Heg With the Password . . . . . . I lay down my Sceptre.

Hegemon remains standing East of the Altar.

Kerux comes direct to the Altar, hands his Lamp to Hegemon, and lays down his Wand, saying:

Kerux With the Pass-word . . . . . . I lay down my Lamp and Wand.

Kerux returns to his place. Hegemon also returns, taking Lamp of Kerux.

Stolistes comes round by East and South to West of Altar and puts down Cup, saying:

Stol With the Pass-word . . . . . . I lay down my Cup.

Stolistes takes the Paten of Bread and Salt and returns to place. Dadouchos comes direct to the Altar and lays down his Censer, saying:

Dad With the Pass-word . . . . . I lay down my Censer.

Dadouchos takes the Red Lamp from the Altar and returns with Sun to his place.

<248> *Sentinel comes by South to East of the Altar and puts down his Sword, saying:*

Sent With the Pass-word . . . . . . I lay down my Sword.

He returns by North and East to his place.

Kerux passes to the North East to begin his Circumambulation. As he reaches each Quarter, and the Prayer is said, Officers and Members face that Quarter and at the end of the Prayer, all make Signs towards the Quarter. Kerux moves to the East and halts before Hierophant, who, holding up the Rose, faces East. All face East.

Hiero Let us adore the Lord of the Universe.
Holy art Thou, Lord of the AIR, Who hast created the Firmament.

Hierophant makes a Cross in the Air with the Rose and salutes. All salute.

Kerux passes to the South and faces Dadouchos, who turns South holding up the Lamp. All face South.

Dad Let us adore the Lord of the Universe.
Holy art Thou, Lord of FIRE, wherein Thou hast shown forth the Throne of Thy Glory.

Dadouchos makes a Cross with the Lamp and salutes. All salute. Kerux passes to West and faces Hiereus, who turns West holding Cup on high. All face West.

Hiereus Let us adore the Lord of the Universe.
Holy art Thou, Lord of the WATERS, whereon Thy Spirit moved at the Beginning.

<249> *Hiereus makes a Cross with the Cup, and salutes. All salute. Kerux passes to the North and faces Stolistes, who turns North, holding Paten on high, and says:*

Stol Let us adore the Lord of the Universe.
Holy art Thou, Lord of the EARTH, which Thou hast made for Thy Foot-stool!

Stolistes makes a Cross with the Paten and salutes. All salute. Kerux passes round the Temple to his place. All face towards the Altar. Hegemon stands East of the Altar, facing West, and holding Kerux's Lamp on high, says:

Heg Let us adore the Lord of the Universe.
Holy art Thou, Who art in all things—in Whom are all things. If I climb up to Heaven, Thou art there and if I go down to Hell Thou art there also!
If I take the Wings of the Morning and flee unto the uttermost parts of the Sea,
Even there shall Thy hand lead me and Thy right hand shall hold me.
If I say, Peradventure the Darkness shall cover me, even the Night shall be turned Light unto Thee!
Thine is the AIR with its Movement!
Thine is the FIRE with its Flashing Flame!
Thine is the WATER with its Ebb and Flow!
Thine is the EARTH with its enduring Stability!

Hegemon makes a Cross over the Altar with the Lamp. All salute towards the Altar. Hegemon keeps the Lamp. All sit down.
Imperator rises and knocks, and says:

<250> *Imperator* By the Power and Authority vested in me, I confer the new Pass-word. It is . . . . . .

Hierophant, taking the Rose, quits his Throne, which is taken by Imperator. Hierophant then goes East of the Altar and lays down the Rose. He returns to the East and lays his Lamen and Cloak at the foot of the Throne, and takes his place in the East as a Member of the Temple. In the same manner, Hiereus puts down the Cup, Hegemon the Lamp of Kerux, Stolistes the Paten, Dadouchos the Red Lamp in turn, and lay their Lamens at the foot of the Throne and all are seated with Members of their own rank.
Praemonstrator rises to read out the names of the new Officers.

Praemonstrator The Officers appointed to do the Work of the Temple for the ensuing six months are . . . . . .

At the end, he says:

Praemonstrator The Brethren of the Outer Order will now retire for a season.

Kerux gathers up and leads out all who have not attained the White Sash.
There is a pause while the New Officers are provided with Nemysses and Lamen Collars.

Outer Order Members, taking Office, should take these things with them and clothe outside in readiness for their Installation by the New Hierophant now to be appointed.

All Inner Order Members now present assume their Rose-Crosses. Chief
<251> *takes his place on the Throne of East. Second on his left; Third on his right. Lesser Officers leave dais and take seats among other Members.*

Chief Peace Profound, my Brethren. *(he rises)*

Second Emanuel. *(he rises)*

Third God is with us. *(he rises)*

Chief In Nomine Dei viventis.

Second Et vivificantis.

Chief Qui vivit et regnet in saecula saeculorum.

Third Amen.

Chief Avete, Fratres et Sorores.

Second Rosae Rubae

Third Et Aureae Crucis.

Chief Very Honoured Fratres et Sorores, seeing that the things which are above do continually lift up unto their high estate the things which are below, and do thence return them after a certain great transfiguration, that the work of Wisdom may continue and that the Grace and Sanctification of the Holy and Glorious Zion may be communicated to the Zion which is on Earth, wherefore the worlds rejoice together and are fulfilled in all completion, I beseech you to join with me in my intention, and to ratify in your hearts, the solemn and sacramental words by which I assume this external and visible Temple of the Stella Matutina into the House not made by hands, builded of Lively Stones — the Company of the Adepts. And it is so assumed accordingly.

Second Cum Potestate et Gloria.

Third Amen!

<252> *The Chiefs are seated.*

Chief Fratres et Sorores of the Roseae Rubeae et Aureae Crucis. We know that the Mystic Temple, which was erected of old by Wisdom, as a Witness of the Mysteries which are above the Sphere of Knowledge, doth abide in the Supernal Triad — in the Understanding which transcends Reason, in the Wisdom which comes before Understanding and in the Crown which is the Light of the Supernals. We know that the Shekinah, the co-habiting Glory, dwelt in the Inner Sanctuary, but the first Creation was made void. The Holy Place was made waste and the Sons of the House of Wisdom were taken away into the captivity of the Senses. We have worshipped since then in a house made with hands, receiving a Sacramental Ministration by a derived Light in place of the Co-habiting Glory. And yet, amidst Signs and Symbols the Tokens of the Higher Presence have never been wanting in our hearts. By the Waters of Babylon we have sat down and wept, but we have ever remembered Zion, and that Memorial is a Witness testifying that we shall yet return with exultation into the House of our Father. As a Witness in the Temple of the

Heart, so in the Outer House of our Initiation, we have ever present certain Watchers from within, deputed by the Second Order to guard and lead the Lesser Mysteries of the Stella Matutina and those who advance therein, that they may be fitted in due course to participate in the Light which is beyond it. It is in virtue of this connect-
<253> ing link, this bond of consanguinity, that I have assumed the things which are without in the Temple of the Stella Matutina into the things which are within the company of the Second Order at this secret meeting held at the ...... Equinox for the solemn purpose of proclaiming a new Hierophant charged with the Rites of the Temple during the ensuing six months, being a part of the temporary period which intervenes between us and our rest.

Second Let us work, therefore, my Brethren and effect righteousness, because the Night cometh.

Third Wherein no man shall labour.

Chief *(rises)* Fratres and Sorores of the Roseae Rubeae et Aureae Crucis, by the power in me vested, I proceed to the installation and investiture of the Hierophant of the Stella Matutina Temple in the Order of the R. R. et A. C. in the Portal of the Vault of the Adepti.

Second *(rises)* Benedictus qui venit.

Third *(rises)* In Nomine Domini.

The Three Adepti give LVX signs, and seat themselves.

Chief Very Honoured Frater, at the discretion of the Chiefs of the Second Order you have been appointed to the Office of Hierophant of this Temple for the ensuing six months. Are you willing to assume its duties and responsibilities?

Hiero I am.

Chief Then I will thank you to advance to the East, giving the Grand Sign of the Order of the R. R. et A. C. *(done)*

<254> *Second* Benedictus Dominus deus Noster.

Third Qui dedit nobis hoc Signum *(touches Rose Cross on breast)*

Chief Very Honoured Frater ...... Standing in the Eastern place of the Temple, I will thank you to give me the secret word of the Order R. R. et A. C. *(done)*

Second Habes Verbum.

Third Et verbum caro factum est, et habitavit in nobis.

Chief *(rises)* Wherefore, Brethren, let us remember that when the Body is assumed by the Word, the Man becomes a living Soul. For which reason we persevere in the Pathway of the Cross as we look for the Assumption of the Rose. The Very Honoured Adeptus Secundus will now deliver the Charge before Installation. *(he sits down)*

Second *(rises)* The high Office to which you have been appointed by the decree of the Chiefs of the Second Order involves duties of a solemn kind and their proper fulfillment is a sacred responsibility which rests for a period upon you. While the rule of the Outer Order is more particularly committed to the Imperator, while the instruction of its members is entrusted to the Praemonstrator above all, and the general business of the Temple devolves especially upon the Can-

cellarius, amidst the distinction of these services there is still a common ground of interaction which must be maintained by a perfect adjustment to ensure the right conduct and harmony of the whole,
<255> In like manner, the Chief Officers of the Temple are distinct and yet allied; the perfection and beauty of its Ritual depends indeed upon the Hierophant as the Expounder of the Mysteries, but not on him alone. For all must work together to encompass the good of all. I invite you, therefore, not only to take counsel with the Chiefs of the Second Order on all important occasions and to maintain a regular communication with the Guardians of the Outer Temple, but to consult and assist the Lesser Officers so that these Rites which, under the Supreme Authority, are about to be placed in your hands, may, after your term of Office, be restored to the Chief Adept not merely intact in their working but showing an increased beauty and a greater Light of Symbolism. Thus and thus only will you give, when the time comes, a good account of your stewardship. Let me further remind you that the Guardians of the Outer Temple should at all times, in all things, command your respect as the Deputies of the Absolute Power which dwells behind the Veil, directing all things in the two Orders for the attainment of its Divine Ends. Let the memory of these objects abide with you, even as it abides in them and do you assist them in their labour so to direct the Temple that Peace may be maintained with Power.

He sits down. Chief rises.

Chief In the presence of this solemn Convocation of Adepti of the Second Order, seated in this assumed Temple, I again ask you whether you
<256> are prepared in your mind to accept the responsible Office to which you have been appointed?

Hiero I am.

Chief Then you will kneel down, repeat the Sacramental Name by which you are known in the Order and say after me:

I, Frater. . . . ., in the Name of the Lord of the Universe, and of that Eternal and Unchangeable Unity which I seek in common with my Brethren, do solemnly promise, that I will, to the utmost of my power, fulfill the high Office which has been imposed upon me, and by me accepted freely, for the good of the whole Order; that I will maintain the rites of the Order and observe the duties of my position with conscientiousness and loving care, not alone towards the Temple itself, but every individual Member; that I will co-operate with the Guardians of the Temple; that I will execute the decree of the Chiefs of the Second Order, acting with justice and without fear or favour in accordance with the dictates of my conscience. This I affirm by the Symbol worn upon the breast of the Officiating Adept.

Hiero is directed to stretch out his hand in the direction of the Rose-Cross on Chief Adept's breast.

Arise, Very honoured Frater and receive at my hand the highest Office I can bestow upon you in this Temple. By the Power in me

vested, I now appoint you Hierophant of the Stella Matutina Temple
<257> to work and confer the Grades of the Outer Order, under the dispensation of the Chiefs during the ensuing six months. May the Light which is behind the Veil shine through you from your Throne in the East on the Fratres and Sorores of the Order, and lead them to the Perfect Day.

Second When the Glory of this World passes.

Third And a Great Light shines over the Splendid Sea.

Chief invests Hierophant with Robes assisted by a server.

Chief I clothe you with the Robe of a Hierophant. Bear it unspotted, my brother, during the period of your office. Keep clean your heart beneath it, so shall it sanctify your flesh and prepare you for that great Day when you, who are now clothed by the Power of the Order, shall be unclothed from the body of your death. I invest you also with the Lamen of your Office; may the virtue which it typifies without, be present efficaciously within you, and after the term of your present dignity, may such virtue still maintain you in your search after the White Stone on which a New Name is written which no man knoweth save he who receiveth it. You will now pass to the symbolic Altar of the Universe and assume the Sceptre of the Hierophant.

Hiero goes to West of Altar, raises Sceptre in both hands and says:

Hiero By the Pass-word . . . . . . I claim my Sceptre.

He returns to East. Chief takes him by both hands and enthrones him with the grip of the Second Order.

<258> *Chief* By the Power in me vested, I install you Hierophant of the Stella Matutina Temple. May the steps of this Throne lead you to your proper place among the Seats of the Mighty which are above. *(He turns to Members)* Behold my Brethren, him who now stands amongst us, clothed with the attribute of lawful Revealer of the Mysteries for those whom we are leading towards the Light. You are the Adepti of those Mysteries and you can assist him to proclaim them, that those who are still without may be lead by loving hands to that which is within. Fratres and Sorores of the R. R. et A. C., I now invite you to join with me in a common act of prayer.

All face East.

We give Thee thanks, Supreme and Gracious God, for the manifestation of Thy Light which is vouchsafed to us, for that measure of knowledge which Thou hast revealed to us concerning Thy Mysteries, for those guiding Hands which raise the corner of the Veil and for the firm hope of a further Light beyond. Keep, we beseech Thee, this man our brother, in the Justice of Thy Ways, in the Spirit of Thy Great Council, that he may well and worthily direct those who have been called from the tribulation of the Darkness into the Light of this little Kingdom of Thy Love; and vouchsafe also, that going forward in love for Thee, through Him and with Him, they may pass from the Desire of Thy house into the Light of Thy Presence.

Second The Desire of Thy House hath eaten me up.

<259> *Third* I desire to be dissolved and to be with Thee.

Chief God save you, Fratres et Sorores. The work of the Light for which we have assumed this Temple has been accomplished faithfully, and the Temple has received its Hierophant. By the power in me vested, I now remit it into its due place in the Outer World taking with it the Graces and benedictions which at this time we have been permitted to bestow thereon. And it is so remitted accordingly. In Nomine Dei Viventis.

Second Et vivificantis.

Chief Qui vivit et regnet in saecula saeculorum.

Third Amen.

All Adepti give LVX Signs, and resume their proper places in the Temple. They remove Rose Crosses. Praemonstrator goes to the door, opens it and says:

Praem The Brethren of the Outer Order will resume their places in the Temple.

Done. Door closed. Chief rises, and says:

Chief Fratres et Sorores of the Order of the Stella Matutina behold your Hierophant, our Frater . . . . . . who has been regularly installed and enthroned, and by the power in me vested, I proclaim him the Revealer of Mysteries among you for the ensuing six months, being part of that temporal period through which we are conducted into Light. Very Honoured Frater, in the presence of the Children of your Temple, I call upon you to make your Confession.

<260> *Hiero (rising)* Fratres et Sorores of the Order, seeing that the whole intention of the Lower Mysteries, or of external initiation, is by the intervention of the Symbol, Ceremonial, and Sacrament, so to lead the Soul that it may be withdrawn from the attraction of matter and delivered from the absorption therein, whereby it walks in somnambulism, knowing not whence it cometh nor whither it goeth; and seeing also, that thus withdrawn, the Soul by true direction must be brought to study of Divine Things, that it may offer the only clean Oblation and acceptable sacrifice, which is Love expressed towards God, Man and the Universe; now, therefore, I confess and testify thereto, from my Throne in this Temple, and I promise, so far as in me lies, to lead you by the Rites of this Order, faithfully conserved, and exhibited with becoming reverence, that through such love and such sacrifice, you may be prepared in due time for the greater Mysteries, the Supreme and inward Initiation.

He sits down.

The installation of the Lesser Officers is now proceeded with.

Cloaks and Lamens are arranged at the foot of the Dais, ready for the Server to hand them to Hierophant. The Ceremony of Installation follows immediately the Confession of the Hierophant. The Outer Members are called
<261> *in by Praemonstrator and Kerux sees that all have places. Hierophant reads his Confession, then says:*

Hiero In virtue of the power to me committed, I proceed to invest my Officers.

Let the Hiereus come to the East.

Hiereus, standing in the East, is invested with the Cloak by the Server, who also clips the Lamen in place and Hierophant holds the Lamen while saying:

By the power to me committed, I ordain you Hiereus of this Temple for the ensuing six months, and I pray that from your Throne in the West, symbolising the failing light, you also, may lead the Fratres and Sorores of the Order, to the full Light in the end, and that you and they, in the midst of material gloom, will ever remember that the Divine Darkness is the same as the Divine Glory.

Hiereus passes to the East of the Altar and takes up the Sword, saying:

By the Pass-word . . . . . . I claim my Sword.

He goes to his Throne. When he is seated, Hierophant says:

Let the Hegemon come to the East.

Hegemon is given the Cloak and Lamen in the same way, and Hierophant, holding the Lamen, says:

By the power to me committed, I ordain you Hegemon of this Temple for the ensuing six months, and I pray that from between the Pillars, you may lead the Fratres and Sorores into the equilibrium of perfect reconciliation.

<262> *Hegemon goes to the East of the Altar, takes his Sceptre, and says:*

Heg By the Pass-word . . . . . . I claim my Sceptre.
(takes his place)

Hiero Let the Kerux come to the East.

Kerux and other Officers to follow are served with the Lamen which Hierophant holds while addressing them.

By the power to me committed, I ordain you Kerux of this Temple for the ensuing six months, to guard the inner side of the Portal, and to lead all Mystic Processions. I pray that you may ever go before us with the Torch of the Higher Luminaries, uttering the Watchwords of the Day. Thanks be to God, my brother, for the Admirable Light.

Kerux By the Pass-word . . . . . . I claim my Lamp and Wand.

Hiero Let the Stolistes come to the East.

By the power to me committed, I ordain you Stolistes of this Temple for the ensuing six months, to watch over the Cup of Clear Water, and to purify the Hall, the Brethren and the Candidate. May you also, in your own Soul, be sprinkled with Hyssop and be cleansed — may you be washed and made whiter than snow. Thanks be to God, my brother, for the living Water which purifies the whole Creation.

Stol By the Pass-word . . . . . . I claim my Cup.

Hiero Let the Dadouchos come to the East.

By the power to me committed, I ordain you Dadouchos of this Tem-
<263> ple for the ensuing six Months, to watch over the Fires of the Temple and to perform the Consecrations by Fire. Remember the sweet odour of the Greater Sanctuary, and the Savour of the Beauty of the House. Thanks be to God, my brother, for the true Incense which hallows our life.

Dad By the Pass-word . . . . . . I claim my Censer.

Hiero Let the Sentinel come to the East.
By the power to me committed, I ordain you Sentinel of this Temple for the ensuing six months. Be thou faithful, keep strict watch without, lest any Evil enter our Sacred Hall.

Sent By the Pass-word . . . . . . I claim my Sword.
Hierophant sits down. All are seated.
Kerux comes forward and arranges the Elements properly upon the Altar.
The Chiefs will now make any announcements.
The Hierophant can address the Temple.
When he has finished, he gives one knock and Kerux comes forward to begin the Closing, which is that of the Neophyte Grade.

<264> # THE CONSECRATION CEREMONY

OF THE

VAULT OF THE ADEPTI

With WATCH-TOWER CEREMONY

(To be used for a new Vault and on each day of Corpus Christi.)

Members assemble and wear Regalia. Three Chiefs robed and seated as in opening of ⑤ = [6]. Door of Vault closed; Pastos remains inside Vault, but Circular Altar is placed in the Outer Chamber, in the centre. Upon the Altar are the Cross, Cup, Dagger, and Chain as usual; also the crossed Scourge and Crook. Incense burning is also placed over Letter Shin. Water is placed in the Cup.

Chief Associate Adeptus Minor, see that the Portal of the Vault is closed and guarded. *(done)*

Chief advances to Altar, lifts his Wand on high, and says:

HEKAS HEKAS ESTE BEBELOI!

Associate Adeptus Minor, let the Chamber be purified by the Lesser Banishing Ritual of the Pentagram.

Returns to place. Third Adept performs Ritual with black end of Wand, holding it by the White band.

Mighty Adeptus Major, let the place be purified by the Lesser Banishing Ritual of the Hexagram.

<265> *Second Adept performs this with black end of Wand, holding it by the White band. He faces East, Qabalistic Cross, tracing the four forms from right to left, and saying at each quarter, ARARITA. On completing the Circle in the East, he gives the ⑤ = [6] Signs, and the analysis of the Keyword INRI.*

Chief Adept again advances to Altar without his Wand, taking Cross from Altar, goes to South, raises Cross above head and slowly circumambulates chamber with Sol, repeating:

And when, after all the phantoms are banished, thou shalt see that holy and Formless Fire, that Fire which darts and flashes through the hidden depths of the Universe, hear thou the Voice of Fire.

On reaching South, he faces South, and makes with the Cross the Invoking Pentagram of Fire, saying:

OIP TEAA PEDOCE. In the Names of Letters of the Great Southern Quadrangle, I invoke ye, ye Angels of the Watch Tower of the South.

Replaces Cross on Lion. Takes Cup, goes to West, sprinkles Water, and circumambulates with Sol, saying:

So therefore first the Priest who governeth the works of Fire must sprinkle with the Lustral Water of the Loud Resounding Sea.

On reaching West, he faces West, and makes the Invoking Pentagram of Water with Cup, saying:

EMPEH ARSEL GAIOL. In the Names and Letters of the Great West-
<266> ern Quadrangle, I invoke ye, ye Angels of the Watch Tower of the West.

Replaces Cup on Eagle's head. Takes Dagger and strikes forward with it;

then circumambulates with Sol, repeating:

Such a Fire existeth extending through the rushings of Air — or even a Fire formless whence cometh the Image of a Voice, or even a flashing Light, abounding, revolving, whirling forth, crying aloud.

On reaching East, he strikes forward with Dagger, makes invoking Air Pentagram, and repeats:

ORO IBAH AOZPI. In the Names and Letters of the Great Eastern Quadrangle, I invoke ye, ye Angels of the Watch Tower of the East.

Replaces Dagger on Aquarius. Takes Chain, goes to North, raises it on high, shakes thrice, circumambulates place with:

Stoop not down into the darkly splendid world wherein lieth continually a faithless depth, and Hades wrapped in gloom, delighting in unintelligible images, precipitous, winding — a black, ever-rolling Abyss, ever espousing a body, formless, unluminous and void.

Reaches North and facing It, shakes Chain thrice and describes the Invoking Earth Pentagram, saying:

EMOR DIAL HECTEGA. In the Names and Letters of the Great Northern Quadrangle, I invoke ye, ye Angels of the Watch Tower of the North.

<267> *Replaces Chain upon Taurus. Takes Incense, goes to West of Altar, faces East, raises it, and describes Equilibrium Spirit Pentagrams.*

EXARP BITOM. *(Active Pent.)* HCOMA NANTA. *(Passive Pent.)*

In the Names and Letters of the Mystical Tablet of Union, I invoke ye, ye Divine Forces of the Spirit of Life. I invoke ye, ye Angels of the Celestial Spheres whose dwelling is in the Invisible. Ye are the Guardians of the Gates of the Universe! Be ye also the Watchers of our Mystic Vault. Keep far removed the Evil; strengthen and inspire the Initiates, that so we may preserve unsullied this abode of the Mysteries of the Eternal Gods.

Let this place be pure and holy, so that we may enter in and become partakers of the Secrets of the Divine Light.

He replaces Incense upon Shin and resumes his place, saying:

The Sun daily returning, is the dispenser of Light to the Earth. Let us thrice complete the circle of this place, the abode of the Invisible Sun.

Chief leads, Second follows, then all the others, and Third last. They circumambulate thrice, saluting the East with ⑤ = [6] *Signs as they pass. Chief extends arms like Cross.*

Holy art Thou, Lord of the Universe.
Holy art Thou, Whom Nature hath not Formed.
Holy art Thou the Vast and the Mighty One.
Lord of the Light and the Darkness.

<268> *Chief Adept changes place with Third Adept. Third Adept as Hierophant Inductor performs the Ceremony of Opening of Portal. Any other Adept can take the place of Associate Officer in West.*

Third וווו ו. Very Honoured Fratres and Sorores, assist me to open the

Portal of the Vault of the Adepti. Give the Signs of a Neophyte, Zelator, Theoricus, Practicus, Philosophus. Very Honoured Associate Adept, what is the additional Mystic Title bestowed on a Philosophus as a link with the Second Order.

Assoc. Phrath.

Third To what does it allude?

Hodos To the Fourth River of Eden.

Third What is the Sign?

Hodos The Sign of the Rending Asunder of the Veil.

Third What is the Word?

Hodos Peh.

Third Resh.

Assoc Kaph.

Third Tau.

Hodos The whole word is PAROKETH, meaning the Veil of the Tabernacle.

Third In and by that Word, I declare the Portal of this Vault of the Adepts duly opened. *(makes Qabalistic Sign of Cross)* Unto Thee, O Tetragrammaton, be ascribed Malkuth, Geburah, and Gedulah *(crossing fingers)* unto the ages, Amen.

All make same Sign and say same words. Replace Altar within Vault, leave
<269> *Cross, Cup and Dagger in place outside for use in Obligation. Close door of Vault. Three Adepts take places and open in the ⑤ = 6 Grade. The Vault Door is thus opened and may so remain till close of Ceremony.*

Second ו

Third ו

Chief ו

Second ו

Chief Ave, Fratres et Sorores.

Second Roseae Rubeae.

Third Et Aureae Crucis.

Chief Very Honoured Fratres et Sorores, assist me to open the Vault of the Adepts. *(knocks)* Very Honoured Hodos Chamelionis, see that the Portal is closed and guarded.

Hodos *(having done so, saluting)* Merciful Exempt Adept, the Portal of the Vault is closed and guarded.

Chief Mighty Adeptus Major, by what Sign hast thou entered the Portal?

Third By the Sign of the closing of the Veil. *(gives it)*

Chief Associate Adeptus Minor, by what Sign hast thou closed the Portal?

Third By the Sign of the closing of the Veil. *(gives it)*

Second Peh.

Third Resh.

Second Kaph.

Third Tau.

Second PAROKETH.

Third Which is the Veil of the Sanctum Sanctorum.

<270> *Chief* Mighty Adeptus Major, what is the Mystic Number of this Grade?

Second Twenty one.

Chief What is the Pass-word formed therefrom?

Third Aleph.

Chief Heh.

Third Yod.

Chief Heh.

Third EHEIEH.

Chief Mighty Adeptus Major, what is the Vault of the Adepts?

Second The Symbolic burying place of our Founder Christian Rosenkreutz, which he made to represent the Universe.

Chief Associate Adeptus Minor, in what part of it is he buried?

Third In the centre of the Heptagonal sides and beneath the Altar, his head being towards the East.

Chief Mighty Adeptus Major, why in the centre?

Second Because that is the point of perfect equilibrium.

Chief Associate Adeptus Minor, what does the Mystic Name of our Founder signify?

Third The Rose and Cross of Christ; the Fadeless Rose of Creation — the Immortal Cross of Light.

Chief Mighty Adeptus Major, what was the Vault entitled by our more Ancient Fratres and Sorores?

Second The Tomb of Osiris Onnophris, the Justified One.

Chief Associate Adeptus Minor, of what shape was the Vault?

Third It is that of an equilateral heptagon or figure of seven sides.

<271> *Chief* Mighty Adeptus Major, unto what do these seven sides allude?

Second Seven are the lower Sephiroth, seven are the Palaces, seven are the days of the Creation; Seven in the Height above, Seven in the Depth below.

Chief Associate Adeptus Minor, where is this Vault symbolically situated?

Third In the centre of the Earth, in the Mountain of Caverns, the Mystic Mountain of Abiegnus.

Chief Mighty Adeptus Major, what is this Mystic Mountain of Abiegnus?

Second It is the Mountain of God in the Centre of the Universe, the Sacred Rosicrucian Mountain of Initiation.

Chief Associate Adeptus Minor, what is the meaning of this title Abiegnus?

Third It is Abi-agnus, Lamb of the Father. It is by metathesis Abi-Genos, born of the Father. Bia-Genos, Strength of our Race, and the Four words make the sentence, Mountain of the Lamb of the Father, and the strength of our race. IAO. Yeheshua. Such are the Words.

All salute with ⑤ = [6] *Signs.*

Chief Mighty Adeptus Major, what is the Key to this Vault?

Second The Rose and Cross which resume the Life of Nature and the Powers hidden in the word I N R I.

Chief Associate Adeptus Minor, what is the Emblem which we bear in our left hands?

Third It is a form of the Rose and Cross, the Ancient Crux Ansata or Egyptian symbol of Life.

<272> *Chief* Mighty Adeptus Major, what is its meaning?

Second It represents the force of the Ten Sephiroth in Nature, divided into a Hexad and a Tetrad. The oval embraces the first six Sephiroth and the Tau Cross the lower Four, answering to the four Elements.

Chief Associate Adeptus Minor, what is the Emblem which I bear upon my breast?

Third The complete symbol of the Rose and Cross.

Chief Mighty Adeptus Major, what is its meaning?

Second It is the Key of Sigils and of Rituals, and represents the force of the twenty two Letters in Nature, as divided into a three, a seven, and a twelve; many and great are its Mysteries.

Chief Associate Adeptus Minor, what is the Wand which thou bearest?

Third A simple Wand having the colours of the twelve Signs of the Zodiac between Light and Darkness, and surmounted by the Lotus Flower of Isis. It symbolises the development of Creation.

Chief Mighty Adeptus Major, thy Wand and its meaning?

Second A Wand terminating in the symbol of the Binary and surmounted by the Tau Cross of Life, or the Head of the Phoenix, sacred to Osiris. The seven colours between Light and Darkness are attributed to the Planets. It symbolises rebirth and resurrection from death.

Chief My Wand is surmounted by the Winged Globe, around which the twin Serpents of Egypt twine. It symbolises the equilibriated Force of the Spirit and the Four Elements beneath the everlasting Wings of
<273> the Holy One. Associate Adeptus Minor, what are the Words inscribed upon the door of the Vault, and how is it guarded?

Third "Post Centum Viginti Annos Patebo"—after one hundred and twenty years I shall open — and the door is guarded by the Elemental Tablets and by the Kerubic Emblems.

Chief The 120 years refer symbolically to the 5 Grades of the First Order and to the revolution of the Powers of the Pentagram; also to the five preparatory examinations for this Grade. It is written, "His days shall be 120 years" and 120 divided by 5 yields 24, the number of hours in a day and of the Thrones of the Elders in the Apocalypse. Further 120 equals the number of the Ten Sephiroth multiplied by that of the Zodiac, whose Key is the working of the Spirit and the Four Elements typified in the Wand which I bear.

Chief knocks. All face East. Chief Adept opens the Vault wide, enters, passes to the Eastern end, or place of the head of the Pastos or Coffin of C.R., and then faces West. Second enters and passes to South. Third to North. Other Members remain standing as before. The three Officers, each with a special Wand in his right hand and Crux Ansata in left, then stretch out their Wands to form a pyramid above the Altar and also the Cruces below.

Chief Let us analyse the Key-word. I.

Second N.
Third R.
All I.
Chief Yod.
<274> *Second* Nun.
Third Resh.
All Yod.
Chief Virgo. Isis. Mighty Mother.
Second Scorpio, Apophis, Destroyer.
Third Sol, Osiris, Slain and Risen.
All Isis, Apophis, Osiris, IAO.

All then simultaneously separate Wands and Cruces, and say:

All The Sign of Osiris Slain. *(gives it)*
Chief *(giving L Sign with bowed head)* L. The Sign of the Mourning of Isis.
Second *(giving V Sign with head erect)* V. The Sign of Typhon and Apophis.
Third *(with bowed head gives X Sign)* X. The Sign of Osiris Risen.

All together with the Saluting Sign and bowed head.

All L V X, LUX, the Light of the Cross.

All quit the Vault and return to previous places.

Chief In the Grand Word YEHESHUAH, by the Key-word I N R I, and through the concealed Word LVX, I have opened the Vault of the Adepts.

All give LVX Signs.

Second Let the Cross of the Obligation be set in its place.
Chief Upon this Cross of the Obligation, I, freely and unasked, on behalf of the Second Order, do hereby pledge myself for the due performance and fulfillment of the respective clauses of the Oath taken by each Member on the Cross of Suffering at his admission to the Grade of Adeptus Minor.
<275> *Second* It is written: "Whosoever shall be great among you shall be your minister, and whosoever of you will be the chiefest, shall be the servant of all." I therefore, on behalf of the Second Order, do require of you to divest yourself of your robes and insignia as a Chief Adept, to clothe yourself with the black robe of mourning, and to put the chain of humility about your neck.

Chief disrobes, puts on chain and is fastened to the Cross. Second recites Obligation adding after "do this day spiritually bind myself" the words "on behalf of the whole Second Order."

Chief *(while still bound)* I invoke Thee, the Great Avenging Angel HUA to confirm and strengthen all the Members of this Order during the ensuing Revolution of the Sun — to keep them steadfast in the Path of rectitude and self-sacrifice, and to confer upon them the Power of discernment, that they may choose between the evil and the good, and try all things of doubtful or fictitious seeming with sure knowledge and sound judgment.
Second Let the Chief Adept descend from the Cross of Suffering.

He is released and the Cross removed.

Second Merciful Exempt Adept, I, on behalf of the Second Order, request you to re-invest yourself with the insignia of your high office, which alone has entitled you to offer yourself unto the high powers as surety for the Order.

Chief Adept reclothes. Three Adepts enter the Vault — roll Altar aside, open
<276> *lid of Pastos, put Book "T" upon the table. Chief steps into the Pastos, and stands facing the door. The Three Adepts join Wands and Cruces.*

Chief I invoke Thee, HRU, the Great Angel who art set over the operations of this secret Wisdom, to strengthen and establish this Order in its search for the Mysteries of the Divine Light. Increase the Spiritual perception of the Members and enable them to rise beyond that lower self-hood which is nothing, unto that Highest Self-hood which is in God the Vast One.

The Three Adepts disjoin Wands, and lower them into the Pastos, joining them together at the black ends, directing them towards the centre of the floor. They hold Cruces as before.

And now, in the tremendous Name of Strength through sacrifice, YEHESHUA YEHOVASHA, I authorise and charge ye, ye Forces of Evil that be beneath the Universe, that, should a member of this Order, through will, forgetfulness, or weakness, act contrary to the obligation which he hath voluntarily taken upon himself at his admission, that ye manifest yourselves as his accusers to restrain and to warn, so that ye, even ye, may perform your part in the operations of the Great Work through the Order. Thus therefore, do I charge and authorise ye through YEHESHUA YEHOVASHAH, the name of Sacrifice.

Three Adepts disjoin Wands and Cruces. Chief steps out of Pastos.

Let the Pastos be placed without the Vault as in the third point of the
<277> Ceremony of Adeptus Minor.

Pastos is carried out into the outer chamber. Lid is removed and placed beside it. Chief stands between Pastos and Lid facing door of Vault, his arms crossed. Second stands at head of Pastos, and Third at foot. Other Adepts form a circle round, join Wands over head of Chief, then separate Wands from head and give Signs of ⑤ = 6 *Grade.*

(slowly and loudly) I am the Resurrection and the Life. He that believeth on Me, though he were dead, yet shall he live. And whosoever liveth and believeth on me shall never die. I am the First and I am the Last. I am he that liveth but was dead, and behold I am alive for evermore, and hold the Keys of Hell and of Death.

Chief quits Circle, Second follows, then the other Members, with Third last. All enter the Vault and proceed round the Altar with the Sun. Chief reads the sentences following and all halt in former positions, Chief in centre, others round.

For I know that my Redeemer liveth and that He shall stand at the latter day upon the Earth. I am the Way, the Truth and the Life. No man cometh unto the Father but by Me. I am purified. I have passed through the Gates of Darkness unto Light. I have fought upon Earth for good. I have finished my work. I have entered into the invisible. I

am the Sun in his rising. I have passed through the hour of Cloud
<278> and Night. I am AMOUN the Concealed One, the Opener of the day. I am OSIRIS ONNOPHRIS, the Justified One. I am the Lord of Life, triumphant over Death. There is no part of me that is not of the Gods. I am the Preparer of the Pathway, the Rescuer unto the Light! Out of the Darkness, let the Light arise.

At this point, the Chief Adept reaches the Centre point between Pastos and Lid. He faces towards Vault, other Adepts round him. They join Wands over his head. He raises his face and hands and continues:

I am the Reconciler with the Ineffable. I am the Dweller of the Invisible. Let the white Brilliance of the Divine Spirit descend.

Chief lowers face and hands. Other Adepts withdraw their Wands.

(raising his hand) In the Name and Power of the Divine Spirit, I invoke ye, ye Angels of the Watch-towers of the Universe. Guard this Vault during this revolution of the Solar Course. Keep far from it the evil and the uninitiated that they penetrate not into the abode of our mysteries, and inspire and sanctify all who enter this place with the illimitable Wisdom of the Light Divine!

Chief Adept gives Sign of ⑤ = 6. All others copy them and take their places as in the opening of the Vault.

Business to be conducted.

CLOSING

Pastos is replaced in Vault. Altar is put over it. Door open.

<279> *Chief* ו

Second ו

Chief ו

Second ו

Third ו

Chief Ave Fratres.

Second Roseae Rubeae.

Third et Aureae Crucis.

Chief Very Honoured Fratres and Sorores, assist me to close the Vault of the Adepts. Associate Adeptus Minor, how many Princes did Darius set over his Kingdom?

Third It is written in the Book of Daniel that they were 120.

Chief Mighty Adeptus Major, how is that Number found?

Second By the continal multiplication together of the first five numbers of the decimal scale.

Chief Post Centum Viginti Annos Patebo.

Thus have I closed the Vault of the Adepts in the Mystic Mountain of Abiegnus.

Third Ex Deo Nascimur.

Second In Yeheshuah Morimur.

Chief Per Sanctum Spiritum Reviviscimus.

All present give LVX Signs in Silence.

THE SYMBOLISM OF THE SEVEN SIDES

<280>

By G. H. FRATER, N.O.M.

Among those characteristics which are truly necessary in the pursuit of magical knowledge and power, there is hardly any one more essential than thoroughness. And there is no failing more common in modern life than superficiality.

There are many who, even in this grade which has been gained by serious study, after being charmed and instructed by first view of the Vault of Christian Rosencreutz, have made no attempt to study it as a new theme. There are many who have attended many ceremonial admissions and yet know nothing of the attribution of the seven sides, and nothing of the emblematic arrangement of the forty squares upon each side.

Some of you do not even know that Venus is in an astrological sense misplaced among the sides, and not two in five have been able to tell me why this is so, or what is the basis of the arrangement of the seven colors and forces. Many have told me which element out of the four is missing, and others have told me that the sign Leo occurs twice, but very few can tell me why the two forms of Leo are in different colours in each case, and only a few can tell me without hesitation which Three Sephiroth have no planet attached.

And yet even in the 1 = 10 grade you are told you must analyse and comprehend that Light or Knowledge, and not only take it on per-
<281> sonal authority. Let us then be Adepti in fact, and not only on the
surface; let our investigations be more than skin deep. That only which you can demonstrate is really known to you, and that only which is comprehended can fructify and become spiritual progress as distinguished from intellectual gain. Unless you can perceive with the soul as well as see with the eye your progress is but seeming, and you will continue to wander in the wilds of the unhappy.

Let your maxim be *Multum non multa* — Much, rather than many things. And tremble lest the Master find you wanting in those things you allow it to be supposed that you have become proficient in. Hypocrisy does not become the laity; it is a fatal flaw in the character of the occultist. You know it is not only the teacher in this Hall before whom you may be humiliated, but before your higher and divine Genius who can in no wise be deceived by outward seeming, but judgeth you by the heart, in that your spiritual heart is but the reflection of his brightness and the image of his person, even as Malkuth is the material image of Tiphareth, and Tiphareth the reflection of the crowned Wisdom of Kether, and the concealed One.

There is but a couple of pages in the 5-6 Ritual which refer to the symbolism of the seven sides of the Vault. Read them over carefully, and then let us study these things together. First, the seven sides as a group, and then the forty squares that are on each side.

The seven sides are all alike in size and shape and subdivision, and the forty squares on each side bear the same symbols. But the colouring is varied in the extreme, no two sides are alike in tint, and none of the squares
<282> are identical in colour excepting the single central upper square of each wall, that square bearing the Wheel of the Spirit. The Seven walls are under the planetary presidency, one side to each planet. The subsidiary squares represent the colouring of the combined forces of the planet; the symbol of each square is represented by the ground colour, while the symbol is in the colour contrasted or complementary to that of the ground.

Now these planetary sides are found to be in a special order, neither astronomical nor astrological. The common order of the succession of the planets is that defined by their relative distances from Earth, putting the Sun, however, in the Earth's place in the series thus: Saturn, Jupiter, Mars, Sun, Venus, Mercury, Moon. Saturn is farthest from the Earth, and the Earth is between Mars and Venus. Beginning with Saturn in the case of the Walls of the Vault, the order is Saturn, Jupiter, Mars, Sun, Mercury, Venus, Moon. Here Mercury and Venus are transposed.

But there is something more than this. For Saturn, the farthest off, is neither the door nor the East, nor anywhere else that is obviously intended. For it is the corner between the South and the South-West sides. Nor is Luna, at the other end of the scale, in any notable position on the old lines.

There is, then, a new key to their order to be found and used, and such as are very intuitive see it at a glance. The planets are in the order of the Rainbow colours, and in colours because this Adeptus Minor grade is the especial exponent of colours. You Adepti are in the Path of the Chamelion — Hodos Chamelionis.

<283> If now you take the planetary colours and affix the planets and arrange them in the order of the solar spectrum and then bend up the series into a ring and make the chain into a Heptagram, and turn the whole about until you get the two ends of the series to meet at the Eastern point, you will have this mysterium:

Violet—Jupiter. Indigo—Saturn. Blue—Moon.
Green—Venus. Yellow—Mercury. Orange—Sun.
Red—Mars.

Science teaches, and has rediscovered a great truth, that however valuable the seven colours of the prism may be, there are rays invisible and so not demonstrated here by space. Beyond the red end of the spectrum begins the violet, and these have a great chemical or Yetsiratic force. These forces, ever present and unseen, are represented by the Chief Adept standing erect at the Eastern angle, the most powerful person in the group, and delegate of the Chiefs of the Second Order, and through them of the mystic Third Order. He it is who has, symbolically, at any rate, passed from death unto life, and holds the Keys of all the creeds. And he it is who may place in our hands the Keys of the locked Palace of the King if we are able to make our knocking heard. Representing the East, coming from the East, he faces the Western world, bringing intuition with him; before him lies the symbolic body of our Master C.R.C., our grand exemplar and founder — or at other times, the empty pastos, from which he has arisen, the Chief Adept.

He has Mars and Geburah at his right hand, and Jupiter and Gedulah at his left hand. He faces Venus in the West, the Evening Star, which represents
the entry of the Candidate who has toiled all day until the evening.
<284> At even he enters the Western door of the planet Venus, that sole
planet unto whose symbol alone all the Sephiroth are conformed.
At "evening time there shall be light," the light of the mixed colours. So the newly admitted Adept comes in contact with totality of the planetary forces for the first time. A great opportunity opens before him; let him see well that he use it worthily. He enters through the green side of the vault. Green is the colour of growth; let him see that he grows.

Upon each side of the vault are forty squares, five vertical series and eight horizontal, the whole being symbolically 5′ x 8′. Now the published and printed *Fama Fraternatitas* says these forty feet were divided into ten squares. If you are mathematicians you would know that ten similar squares could not alone be placed in such an area and yet fill it. Ten squares alone to fill a rectangle could only be placed in an area of the shape 5′ x 6′. Hence in the *Fama,* ten squares are marked and salient" — they are the Sephiroth.

Besides the Ten Sephiroth, there are the following: There are the Four Kerubim, Three Alchemical Principles, Three Elements, Seven Planets, Twelve Zodiacal Signs, One Wheel of the Spirit — thus 40 in all. The Spirit Wheel is on every side and always in the centre, and is always depicted unchanged in black upon white.

Upon the side there are always the 4 Kerubic emblems — zodiacal, yet different, for the Eagle replaces Scorpio. (Scorpio has three forms, the Scorpion, the Eagle, and the Snake for the evil aspect.)

These Kerubim represent the letters of the name YHVH, and
<285> note that they are always arranged in the Hebrew order of the let-
ters. Yod for the Lion, Heh for the Eagle, Vau for the Man, Heh final for the Ox, the Tauric Earth.

Note that these four Zodiacal signs are not in their own colours, but as symbols of the elements have elementary colours. As Zodiacal signs, then, they are found to be compounds of the zodiacal and planet colours; but they are here as Kerubic emblems compounded of the Elemental colour and the Planetary colour of the side.

The Three Principles are composed of the colour of the Principles, and the colour of the Planet of any particular wall. Mercury being fundamentally blue, Sulphur red, and Salt yellow.

The Three Elements have fundamentally the usual three colours, Fire red, Water blue, Air yellow. Note that Earth is missing.

The Seven planets have their colours as are often stated, and note that each of the seven is set beside its appropriate Sephirah, so that there are three Sephiroth which have no Planet: Kether, Chokmah, and Malkuth.

The 12 Zodiacal Signs are the lower portion of the sides of the vertical column. The central one has none of the twelve; they are so allotted between the four remaining columns. Further note that they are only three ranks, the 5th, 7th, and 8th; none are in the 6th rank from above.

This arrangement then shows: Four Triplicities and three Quaternaries.

Observe well the arrangement; it is complex but not confused.

<286>	1. Kerubic.	Fixed.	Shining Rank.
	2. Cardinal.	Fiery.	Solar Rank.
	3. Common (mutable)	Airy.	Subtle Rank.

From above down, or in columns these are: Earthy Signs. Airy Signs. Watery Signs. Fiery Signs.

Rank 5. The Kerubic line shows the signs in the order of Tetragrammaton read in Hebrew.

Rank 7. The Cardinal line shows the signs from the right in the order of astronomical sequence of the solar course: vernal equinox, summer solstice, autumn equinox, winter solstice.

Rank 8. The common line shows the Signs again in a different position. Here the earliest in the year is Gemini on the left of Mem, and passing left to Virgo, you then go round to extreme right to Sagittarius, pass centrewards to Pisces close to Malkuth.

The colouring of each square is dual — a ground colour, and the colour of the emblem. The ground colour is a compound of the colour of the Planet of the side tinting the colour of the Force to which the Square is allotted.

Each side has the Square of its own planet in its own unmixed colour, and with this exception all the coloured grounds are compound. The emblem colour is always complementary to the ground colour.

The ritual of the Adeptus Minor gives the definite colours of each planet and sign which are to be used in this system. There are other allotments of colour to each of these symbols and forces, but these are retained as mysteries yet to be evolved and revealed when you have become familiar with the present simple and elementary system.

CONCERNING THE USE OF THE VAULT

<287>

By G. H. FRATER, F. R.

The Vault of the Adepti may be said to represent or symbolise various things; first of course, it is the symbolic burying place of our Founder C. R. C. It is also the mystic Cavern in the Sacred Mountain of Initiation. — Abiegnus; and therefore it is the Chamber of Initiation wherein, after passing through the preliminary training of the Outer, we are received into the Portal of the Vault of the Rose of Ruby and the Cross of Gold.

All who are eligible should use the Vault when it is in its place. When working it is well to be clothed in the White Robe and yellow sash, yellow slippers and yellow and white Nemyss on your head. Rose Cross should be upon the breast. Remember that within the Vault you never use a banishing Ritual. The chamber is highly charged by the Ceremonies which have been held there and the atmosphere thus created should not be disturbed.

At first I do not recommend you to fast as a preliminary. Though later on when you set yourselves to attain some definite point, this may be necessary. Being then clothed, and at peace, you enter the Vault, light the candle, and kindle either a pastile in the small censer or, if you prefer it, some incense in the larger one. Place a chair as near East as you can, and having shut the door stand in the East, facing West, the door by which you entered, the wall bearing the symbol of Venus. Now cross your hands upon your breast in
<288> the Sign of Osiris Arisen, breathe in a fourfold rhythm, regularly,
and compose your mind. Then being calm and collected, make the full L V X Signs, repeating the accompanying words, and endeavour to bring down the Divine White Brilliance. Having done this, seat yourself, and give yourself up to meditation, tranquil and without fear. At first try to feel, it may be, or to see the play of the colours as they pass and repass from side to side and from square to square. Then await with serene expectation what message may be vouchsafed to you. When you are used to the place it is well to extinguish the light, for the darker the material atmosphere the better it is. Before leaving the Vault make the L V X Signs, and quit it with arms crossed upon breast in the Sign of Osiris risen.

If you have elected to work in a group of two or three, proceed in the same manner, but take care to place yourselves in balanced disposition. Let me warn you never to argue, even in a friendly manner, while in the Vault. It may often happen that one of you sees more or less differently from the others. In this case make an audible note of the differences but do not go on to discuss it till you have ended the sitting, as any discussion is apt to disturb the delicate currents and so break the thread of your vision. It is permissible to take notes in writing during the sitting, but on the whole it is perhaps more satisfactory to impress everything clearly on your mind and write it down immediately afterward.

The next seven visits should be devoted to a careful study of each side of the Vault in turn, recalling all you know about each *before you begin,* and having your queries defined before you expect replies.

Another time, contemplate the roof, and if you feel strong
<289> enough, the floor. But it is best for you to have an advanced Adept with you for the latter. Again you may draw aside the Altar, lift the lid of the Pastos and contemplate the figure you may perceive lying within it. For this you should have a small candle lit on the Altar. Or you may lie down in the Pastos yourself and meditate there. Sometimes you may see the simulacrum of C. R. C. in the Pastos, or it may be your own Higher Self. In every case you should gain knowledge, power, and satisfaction. If you do not, you may be sure you are either acting from a wrong motive, or you are not physically strong enough, or your methods are at fault. No normal person in a good state of mind can possibly spend half an hour in this way without feeling better for it. But if you should happen to be out of harmony with your surroundings or at variance with your neighbours, leave there thy gift before the Altar, and go thy way, first be reconciled.

When more than one person enters the Vault they must all make the L V X Signs together.

THE THREE CHIEFS

By FRATER A. M. A. G.

The first Temple founded in England in 1887-88 under the governance of the Hermetic Order of the Golden Dawn was named very appropriately Isis-Urania. Isis-Urania is Venus, and she is the occult planet which represents the Genius of this Order — Venus, the Evening and the Morning Star, presaging the rising of the Sun of ineffable Light. Venus is also, as Isis, a symbol of the Qabalistic *Shekinah,* the Glory of the Presence Divine, the Holy Spirit. After the Revolt in the Order about 1900, the schismatic sect appropriated as the name of their Order, Stella Matutina, the Morning Star, thus continuing the significance of the enlightening function and purpose for which the Order was founded originally. For, if one may speak of the Order as having a specific purpose, then that sublime motive is to bring each man to the perfection of his own *Kether,* to the glory of his own higher Genius, to the splendour of the Golden Dawn arising within the heart of his soul. And its technique is always encompassed through the uplifting of the heart and mind by a theurgic invocation to Isis-Urania, the symbolic personification of the Sephiroth of the Supernal Light.

It is well known that Venus is a planet peculiarly associated with occult and mystical aspiration. In *The Secret Doctrine* we find Blavatsky stating that "Venus, or Lucifer, the planet, is the light-bearer of our Earth, in both
<291> a physical and mystical sense." And in quoting from the Stanzas of Dzyan, she presents the statement that "Thus Earth is the adopted child and younger brother of Venus." Hence a good deal of wisdom is concealed in the very choice of the name of the Order. To this we will have occasion to refer on a later page.

In the Ritual of the Grade of Adeptus Minor, the Third Adept, reading from the historical account of the origins of the Order, states that "The True Order of the Rose Cross ascendeth into the heights even unto the Throne of God himself." If the reader will well have studied the preliminary knowledge material of the Outer Order, he will remember it is said that the symbol of Venus — a true symbol of growth and development — embraces all the Ten Sephiroth of the Qabalistic Tree of Life. Since the Order is under the presidency of Venus, and in view of the above quotation, it would seem that the Order considered from a variety of viewpoints is allied to the Tree of Life, and vice-versa. Thus the system of grades, and the division of the organisation into Three Separate Orders — the Order of the Golden Dawn in the Outer, the Second Order of the R.R. et A.C., and the unnamed Third Order of Masters, whose Sephiroth obtain above the Abyss — is based upon a natural and a very recondite series of correspondences. "As above so below." So that as the Tree of Life consists of a glyph which represents not only a material physical universe but also a uranography of the invisible and spiritual world, so does the Order consist, in all actuality, of more than an external Order. Concealed within and behind the grade system, is the invisible Order, of true adepts, unknown and, in most cases, unnamed Masters.

At the close of the Second Point of the 5-6 Ceremony, there are
<292> named, without further reference, the Names and Ages of the "Three Highest Chiefs of the Order". These Chiefs are Hugo Alverda, whose age is given as 576, Franciscus, who died at the age of 495 years and Elman Zata, who died at the age of 463. In addition to these three there is Christian Rosencreutz the Founder who died at the age of 106 years.

These enormous ages, unbelievably long in the case of the three chiefs, imply — that is if we accept the history in its obvious and literal sense — that, as Adepts, they had discovered and employed the secret of the Elixir of Life, in order to prolong the period of their usefulness on Earth. And though they have died, that is discarded their purely physical instruments, it is not to be supposed they are cut off from our sphere of activity. Such is not the occult teaching. Apart from the probability that they may have since incarnated voluntarily once more on this plane to continue their work on behalf of mankind in their own silent ways, they would have become what are known in the East as Nirmanakayas. Speaking in *The Secret Doctrine* of one group of Adepts, Blavatsky gives a definition of Nirmanakayas which is distinctly worth quoting: "*Maruts* is, in occult parlance, one of the names given to those Egos of great Adepts who have passed away, and who are known also as *Nirmanakayas;* of those Egos for whom — since they are beyond illusion — there is no Devachan (heaven) and who, having either voluntarily renounced it for the good of mankind, or not yet reached Nirvana, remain invisible on Earth." Such must therefore be the nature of the divine guardians of our Order. A few lines following the above quotation in *The Secret Doctrine,*
<293> Madame Blavatsky further remarks "*Who* they are 'on earth' — every student of Occult science knows." Whether they do or not, at any rate, it is clear the Order has a little to say on this matter.

There is an enormous amount of significant material in *The Secret Doctrine* which should be very suggestive to the student of the magical wisdom. For *The Secret Doctrine* assists in the comprehension of the Order knowledge, and likewise the Order knowledge makes brilliantly clear what are otherwise highly obscure passages in that colossal monument of Blavatsky's erudition. The only one of these points that I wish to consider at the moment is this question of Adepts in relation to the Order. In the first half of Volume Two of *The Secret Doctrine,* there is a passage or two which I must quote: "Alone a handful of primitive men — in whom the spark of divine Wisdom burnt bright, and only strengthened in its intensity as it got dimmer and dimmer with every age in those who turned it to bad purposes — remained the elect custodians of the Mysteries revealed to mankind by the divine Teachers. There were those among them, who remained in their *Kumaric* (divine purity) condition from the beginning; and tradition whispers, what the secret teachings affirm, namely, that these Elect were the germ of a Hierarchy, *which never died since that period.*" The magical tradition has it too that the Three Chiefs and Christian Rosencreutz were of those who retained their

knowledge of their divine origins and spiritual nature, and they have been constantly with us. The student would be well-repaid to study what H. P. B. has to say in the first Volume of *The Secret Doctrine* about the stem and
<294> root of Initiators, that Mysterious Being who, born in the so-called
Third Race of our evolutionary era, is called "The Great Sacrifice" and "the tree from which in subsequent ages, all the great historically known Sages and Hierophants . . . have branched off." More cannot be quoted here, but it is all highly significant, and the employment of Order methods corroborates a great deal of what she wrote. But I do intend to quote from what she calls the Catechism of the Inner Schools, which deals still further with the theme of the Secret Chiefs of our Order, or the undying Adepts of all Ages. 'The inner man of the first . . . only changes his body from time to time; he is ever the same, knowing neither rest nor Nirvana, spurning Devachan and remaining constantly on Earth for the Salvation of mankind. . . . Out of the seven virgin-men *(Kumara)* four sacrificed themselves for the sins of the world and the instruction of the ignorant, to remain till the end of the present Manvantara. Though unseen they are ever present. When people say of one of them, 'He is dead', behold, he is alive and under another form. These are the Head, the Heart, the Soul, and the Seed of undying knowledge. Thou shalt never speak, O Lanoo, of these great ones before a multitude, mentioning them by their names. The wise alone will understand." Though I have little intention to speak of them more clearly, little harm can be done from what is already stated above, for the names used are clearly the pseudonyms or magical mottos of those great beings.

If however, we consider these Chiefs from a wholly different point of view, the results are not less suggestive. Some students of the Order
<295> have thought that these Three Chiefs may be considered as repre-
sentative of certain principles in Nature or Sephiroth of the Tree of Life, particularly as it is said that the Order of the Rose Cross (the Ankh or the Venus symbol) ascendeth unto the Throne of God himself. How may we discover, then, what principles are involved, and why? Two hints are given in the Adeptus Minor Ritual as to what procedure the student may follow in order to elucidate these obscure mysteries. Almost deliberately the ritual states, in the first place, that Damcar, whither our Father C. R. C. journeyed, may be transliterated into Hebrew, thus yielding דמכר, two words which, if translated mean the "Blood of the Lamb". The Lamb has always been a symbol of the Higher Ego. Secondly, there is the analysis of the Key-word I. N. R. I., whereby the English letters are transliterated into Hebrew, attributed to certain Yetziratic correspondences, Egyptian deities, signs and ideas. This must, then, be our technique with regard to this problem. The Qabalah is the means whereby we may unlock the closed doors of the veiled intimations which abound in the Order rituals.

Through the application of this technique to the Names and Ages of the Chiefs, one may reasonably conclude that, as the historical lection of the Third Adept showed, They represent the Triune Supernal Light, the Divine White Brilliance invoked in the Vault of the Adepti — the letter Shin extended, bursting through the balanced elemental powers of Tetragrammaton to confer the attainment of the Grade. If we transliterate the Names into Hebrew, first, of all, we have the following:—

<296> פראנכיסכם = 541 = 10 = 1 = Kether ☿
חוגע = 84 = 12 = 3 = Binah ⊖
חאלמאן = 776 = 20 = 2 = Chokmah 🜍

(It may be here remarked that the method of reducing numbers to units as shown above, while often called Theosophical addition, is actually the mode of working called *Aiq Beker,* or the Qabalah of Nine Chambers. This method of working was eliminated from the Order papers issued in one Temple by several high-grade initiates, whose natural stupidity was far in excess of their adeptship. By this method of *Aiq Beker,* the 22 letters and 5 finals of the Hebrew alphabet are grouped together by threes according to units, tens, and hundreds in nine divisions.)

Elman Zata is represented in the Rituals as being an Arab; that is his origins are in the South and East, representing heat and fire, and so the Alchemical Sulphur is a fit attribution. Sulphur is also an attribution of Chokmah, to which also the element of Fire is allocated. Hugo is called the Phrisian. If we refer this place to Frisia in Denmark, the North, then the Alchemical Salt is a proper reference — Binah, and the element of Water, the Great Salt Sea. Franciscus is the Gaul, which country is a point between the North and the South, a temporate zone. Hence, he is the reconciler between them, a mediator, surely the Alchemical Mercury. Thus from this point of view, the Gematria of the Names of the Three Chiefs, allies them with the Light of the Supernal Sephiroth, that Light which ascendeth into the heights, even unto the Throne of God himself.

Leaving, however, the Gematria of their individual Names for a moment, and proceeding to the Qabalah of the numbers of their
<297> Ages, an equally interesting and significant fact is revealed.

Hugo's age is given as 576, which reduces to 18=9.
Franciscus age is given as 495, which reduces to 18=9.
Elman's age is given as 463, which reduces to 13=4.

9 plus 9 plus 4, added together yield 22. 22 is the number of the letters of the Hebrew Alphabet, the totality of the Paths linking the Sephiroth on the Tree of Life. This number also represents, therefore, the Serpent of Wisdom which rises from Malkuth to Kether, the ascending Spiral, the path which the aspirant to the Great Order must tread. In short, the Chiefs represent the Path itself which is to be followed, even as They represent the goal which is at the end thereof. Each initiate, it is the universal tradition of the Mystic path, must not only tread the Way, but must *become,* even as did these Three Chiefs, that Path itself.

By referring the number 22 in a slightly different way to the Qabalah of Nine Chambers, we may obtain 220, which is the Gematria of Kor כר, the Lamb, Abi-Agnus, the Strength of our Race — also the initials of Christian Rosenkreutz. Moreover, 2 plus 2, equals 4, which is the number of *Daleth,* which means a door, referred to Venus, the symbolical figure which embraces the whole Tree of Life, revealing that compassion or love is that fiery

force which binds together through an orderly growth and progression the whole Sephirotic Scheme into a Unity. And Daleth and Venus are the attributions of that door into the Tomb of the Justified One, the Vault of the Adepti, even as the reciprocal Path of Venus, Daleth, on the Tree of Life, is the
Secret Gate which leads out from the Garden of Venus into the
<298> newer life, the Glory of the Boundless Light. The secret of that Gate
abides in the womb of the Great Mother, the intrinsic regenerating nature of the Empress of the Tarot — Isis-Urania.

Again, there are other considerations. At the end of the Order document on the symbolism of the neophyte grade there is the statement that "*Nephesch ha-Mesiach,* the Animal Soul of the Messiah" is "the Shekinah or Presence between the Kerubim." Note that the Shekinah represents, as I previously attempted to point out, Aima Elohim, the Supernal Sephiroth as a synthetic Unity, the Divine White Brilliance. Since this is spoken of as *between* the Kerubim, the Middle Pillar of the Tree, which is thus by definition the Path of the Redeemer or Messiah, the path of the Sushumna traversed by the Kundalini serpent is referred to. Now Messiah in Hebrew is spelt משיח and its Gematria is 358. There is another word in Hebrew having precisely the same enumeration, and that word is נחש, Nachash, meaning a Serpent. As we demonstrated above, the ascending Spiral is represented by the Serpent of Wisdom, which is the path of the 22 letters of the Alphabet — and to this Serpent are the ages of the Three Chiefs referred. Thus between the Serpent of Wisdom which represents the Way to the Crown, the Paths of the Tree of Life, and the Power of the Chiefs of the Order, there is seen a *gematria* connection. Interestingly enough, in all ancient systems, the Serpent is also the Tempter, Lucifer — and once again, Lucifer is Venus, the Redeemer.

Thus the Three Chiefs of the Order of the R. R. et A. C. are the symbolic
representatives of the Way to that Land which is beyond "honey,
<299> and spice and all perfection", the Way to the Light itself. But they are
also the Light at the end of the Way; they have *become* the divine attainment. How significant becomes the statement "I am the Way, the Truth and the Life. No man cometh unto the Father but by me."

There is one last correspondence before closing this paper. The symbolic drama of the Adeptus Minor Ritual has as its goal the union of the aspirant with the divine nature of Christian Rosencreutz. Theoretically, it is assumed that our Father C. R. C. is the type and symbol of spiritual attainment, a man who achieved union with his Higher and Divine Genius, and was brought to the Light of his Kether. He is portrayed as a living man, who symbolically died, and like Osiris of old, was glorified through trial, perfected through suffering, and rose again in a mystical resurrection. Now in the Ritual, he is referred to as "The Light of the Cross" and this latter is pictorially shown as "I, CXX", which is 120. The Light of the Cross, CXX, is of course the LVX, the Light of the Supernals. Now 120 reduces to 12, and it is interesting to note that 12 is also the numeration of the Great Angel HUA who is invoked to overshadow the Aspirant when he is bound to the Cross of Obligation. HUA is, in the Zohar, one of the mystical Titles of Kether, the Crown of the Tree. Analysis of the Name expands the idea considerably. The Name is composed of three letters, Heh, Vau, Aleph. Heh is 5 in number, the Pentagram which is

also the symbol of the microcosm. Vau is 6, the Hexagram, the symbol of the Macrocosm, the Greater World. Aleph is Unity. Thus the whole name symbolises the union of the microcosm with Macrocosm, and is a com-
<300> plete synthesis of the nature of the Adeptus Minor Grade itself, the accomplishment of the Great Work. So that the very expression of C. R. C. — 'I, the Light of the Cross" with the implication of its number, identifies him mystically with the Great Angel HUA. Both become therefore the symbolic representatives of the higher and divine Genius of the Candidate for initiation — giving us the rationale of dramatic ceremonial, that the depicting of the life of a revered personality who at one time in the past attained, may also induce within the heart and mind of the aspirant the overwhelming glory of that same attainment.

It becomes peculiarly significant to trace out, in this slight way, the unity and identical nature of all the symbols employed, and show how by analogous methods and meditation the whole of the Order teaching may be expanded into a profound and highly significant system.

(Note: Since there is no need for me to hide behind a cloak of anonymity, this essay was written by me soon after my advancement to the Adeptus Minor Grade. A. M. A. G. are the initials of the motto Ad Majorem Adonai Gloriam which I then employed.—I. R.)

End of Volume Two

VOLUME THREE

BOOK FOUR

PRIMARY TECHNIQUES

<9>

THE RITUAL
OF THE
PENTAGRAM

The Pentagram is a powerful symbol representing the operation of the Eternal Spirit and the Four Elements under the divine Presidency of the letters of the Name Yeheshuah. The elements themselves in the symbol of the Cross are governed by Yhvh. But the letter Shin, representing the *Ruach Elohim,* the Divine Spirit, being added thereto, the Name becometh Yeheshuah or Yehovashah — the latter when the letter Shin is placed between ruling Earth and the other three letters of Tetragrammaton.

From each re-entering angle of the Pentagram, therefore, issueth a ray, representing a radiation from the Divine. Therefore is it called the Flaming Pentagram, or Star of Great Light, in affirmation of the forces of Divine Light to be found therein.

Traced as a symbol of good, it should be placed with the single point upward, representing the rule of the Divine Spirit. For if thou shouldst write it with the two points upward, it is an evil symbol, affirming the empire of matter over that Divine Spirit which should govern it. *See that thou doest it not.*

Yet, if there may arise an absolute necessity for working or conversing with a Spirit of evil nature, and that to retain him before thee without tormenting him, thou hast to employ the symbol of the Pentagram reversed — (for, know thou well, thou canst have no right to injure or hurt even evil Spirits to gratify curiosity or caprice) — in such a case, thou shalt hold the blade of thy Magical Sword upon the single lowest point of the Penta-
<10> gram, until such time as thou shalt license him to depart. Also, revile
not evil spirits — but remember that the Archangel Michael of whom St. Jude speaketh, when contending with Satan, durst not bring a railing accusation against him but said 'The Lord rebuke thee'.

Now, if thou wilt draw the Pentagram to have by thee as a symbol, thou shalt make it of the colours already taught, upon a black ground. There shall be the sign of the Pentagram, the Wheel, the Lion, the Eagle, the Ox, and the Man, and each hath an angle assigned unto it for dominion. Hence ariseth the Supreme Ritual of the Pentagram, according to the angle from which the Pentagram is traced. The circle or Wheel answereth to the all-pervading Spirit: The laborious Ox is the symbol of Earth; the Lion is the vehemence of Fire; the Eagle, the Water flying aloft as with wings when she is vaporized by the force of heat: the Man is the Air, subtle and thoughtful, penetrating hidden things.

At all times complete the circle of the place before commencing an invokation. The currents leading from Fire to Air and from Earth to Water are those of Spirit — the mediation of the Active and Passive Elements. These two Spirit

Pentagrams should precede and close Invokations as the equilibrium of the Elements, and in establishing the harmony of their influence. In closing, these currents are reversed.

Diagram I

TABLET OF UNION NAMES

Active—Air	Exarp
Passive—Water	Hcoma
Passive—Earth	Nanta
Active—Fire	Bitom

<11>

Diagram 2

SPIRIT
INVOKING PENTAGRAMS

SPIRIT BANISHING

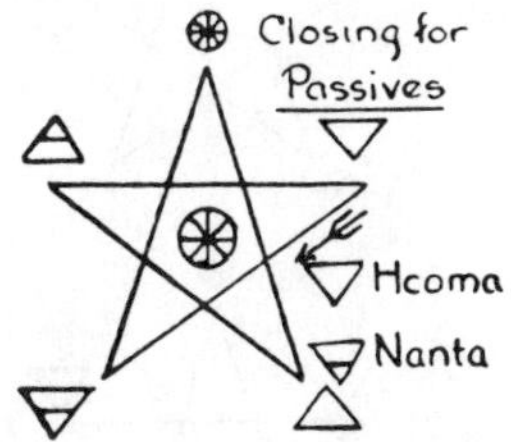

They are the invoking and banishing Pentagrams of the Spirit; the Sigil of the Wheel should be traced in their centre. In the invoking Pentagram of Earth the current descendeth from the Spirit to the Earth. In the Banishing Pentagram, the current is reversed. The Sigil of the Ox should be traced in the centre. These two Pentagrams are in general use for invokation or banishing, and their use is given to the Neophyte of the first Order of the Golden Dawn under the title of the Lesser Ritual of the Pentagram. This Lesser Ritual of the Pentagram is only of use in general and unimportant invokations. Its use is permitted to the Outer that Neophytes may have protection against opposing forces, and also that they may form some idea of how to attract and to come into communication with spiritual and invisible things. The Banishing Pentagram of Earth will also serve thee for a protection if thou trace it in the Air between thee and any opposing Astral force. In all cases of tracing a Pentagram, the angle should be carefully closed at the finishing point.

<12> The invoking Pentagram of Air commenceth from Water, and that of Water commenceth from the Angle of Air. Those of Fire and Earth begin from the angle of Spirit. The Kerubic sign of the Element is to be traced in the centre. The banishing Signs are the reversing of the current. But before all things, complete the circle of the place wherein thou workest, seeing that it is the key of the rest. Unless you want to limit or confine the force, make *not* a circle round each Pentagram, unless for the purpose of tracing the Pentagram truly. In concentrating however the force upon a symbol or Talisman, thou *shalt* make the circle with the Pentagram upon it so as to gather the force together thereon.

<13> *Diagram 3*

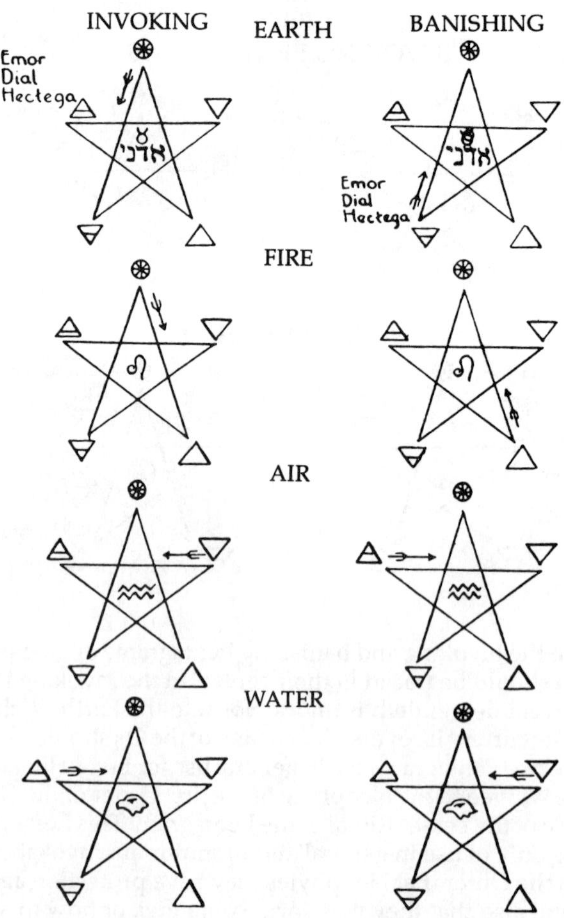

<14> **RULE: Invoke towards, and banish from, the point to which the Element is attributed.**

Air hath a watery symbol ♒, because it is the container of rain and moisture. Fire hath the form of the Lion-Serpent ♌. Water hath the alchemic Eagle of distillation [eagle symbol]. Earth hath the laborious ♉. Spirit is produced by the One operating in all things.

The elements vibrate between the Cardinal points for they have not an unchangeable abode therein, though they are allotted to the Four Quarters in their invokation in the Ceremonies of the First Order. This attribution is derived from the nature of the winds. For the Easterly wind is of the Nature of Air more especially. The South Wind bringeth into action the nature of Fire. West winds bring with them moisture and rain. North winds are cold and dry like Earth. The S. W. wind is violent and explosive — the mingling of the contrary elements of Fire and Water. The N. W. and S. W. winds are more harmonious, uniting the influence of the two active and passive elements.

Yet their natural position in the Zodiac is: Fire in the East, Earth in South, Air in West, and Water in the North. Therefore they vibrate: Air between West and East. Fire between East and South. Water between North and West. Earth between South and North.

Spirit also vibrateth between Height and Depth.

So that, if thou invokest, it is better to look towards the position of the winds, since the Earth, ever whirling on her poles, is more subject to their influence. But if thou wilt go in the Spirit Vision unto their abode, it is better for thee to take their position in the Zodiac.

Air and Water have much in common, and because one is the container of the other, therefore have their symbols been at all times transferred, and the Eagle assigned to Air and Aquarius to Water. Nevertheless, it is better that they should be attributed as before stated and for the foregoing reason is it that the invoking sign of the one and the banishing sign of the other counterchange in the Pentagram.

<15> When thou dealest with the Pentagram of the Spirit thou shalt give the saluting sign of the ⑤ = [6] Grade, and for the Earth the Sign of Zelator, and for Air that of Theoricus, and for Water that of Practicus, and for Fire, Philosophus.

If thou wilt use the Pentagram to invoke or banish the Zodiacal forces, thou shalt use the Pentagram of the Element unto which the Sign is referred, and trace in its centre the usual Sigil of the Sign thus:

Diagram 4

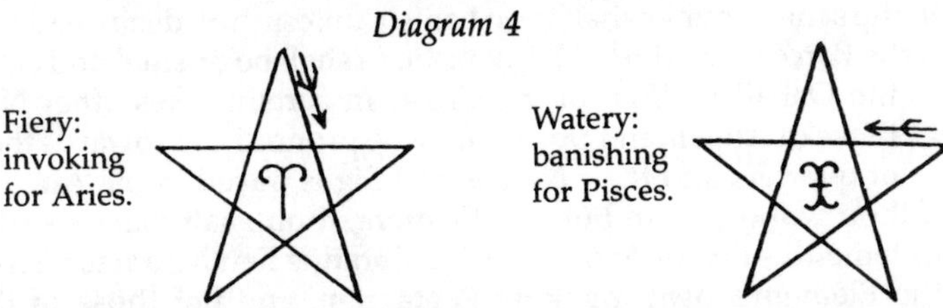

And whenever thou shalt trace a Sigil of any nature, thou *must* commence at the left hand of the Sigil or symbol following the course of the Sun.

Whenever thou invokest the forces of the Zodiacal Signs as distinct from the Elements, thou shalt erect an astrological scheme of the Heavens *for the time of working* so that thou mayest know toward what quarter or direction thou shouldst face in working. For the same Sign may be in the East at one time of the day and in the West at another.

Whenever thou shalt prepare to commence any magical work or operation, it will be advisable for thee to clear and consecrate the place by performing the Lesser Banishing Ritual of the Pentagram. In certain cases, especially when working by or with the forces of the Planets, it may be wise also to use the Lesser Banishing Ritual of the Hexagram.

In order that a *Force* and a *current* and a *colour* and a *sound* may be united together in the same symbol, unto each angle of the Pentagram certain Hebrew divine Names and Names from the Angelic Tablets are allotted.
<16> These are to be pronounced with the invoking and banishing Pentagrams as thou mayest see in the foregoing diagrams.

The attributions of the angles of the Pentagram is the key of its Ritual. Herein, during ordinary invokation without the use of the Tablets of the Elements, thou shalt pronounce the Divine Name Al with the Pentagram of Water, and Elohim with Fire, etc. But if thou art working with the Elemental or Enochian Tablets, thou shalt use the Divine Names in the Angelic language drawn therefrom. For Earth, Emor Dial Hectega, etc., and for Spirit the four words: Exarp in the East; Hcoma in the West; Nanta in the North; and Bitom in the South.

In the pronunciation of all these Names, thou shalt take a deep breath and vibrate them as much as possible inwardly with the outgoing breath, not necessarily loudly, but with vibration thus: A-a-a-el-ll. Or — Em-or-r. Di-a-ll Hec-te-e-g-ah. If thou wilt, thou mayest also trace the letters of Sigils of these Names in the Air.

To invoke the forces of the Four Elements at once, at the Four Quarters, commence at the East and there trace the equilibrating Pentagram of the Actives and the invoking Pentagram of Air and pronounce the proper Names. Then carry round the point of thy wand to the South and there trace the equilibrating Pentagram for Actives and the invoking Pentagram of Fire and pronounce the proper Names. Thence, pass to the West, trace the Equilibrating Pentagram for Passives and the Invoking Pentagram for Water and pronounce the proper Names; thence to the North, trace the equilibration of the Passives and the invoking Pentagram of Earth, pronounce the proper Names, and then complete the circle of the place.

In the same manner shalt thou banish, unless thou desirest to retain certain of the Forces for a time. All invokations shall be opened and closed with the Qabalistic Sign of the Cross. In certain cases other Names, as
<17> those of Angels and Spirits, may be pronounced towards their proper quarters and their Names and Sigils traced in the Air.

If thou workest with but one Element, thou shalt make — (if it be an active element as Fire or Air) — the equilibrating Pentagram for Actives only and the Element's own invoking Pentagram, and not those of the other Elements. If it be a passive Element — Earth or Water — thou shalt make the Equilibrating Pentagram of the passives only and the invoking Pentagram of the one Element at the Four Quarters. In closing and banishing follow the same law. Also, see that thou pronouncest the proper Names with the proper Pentagrams.

<18> # SUPREME INVOKING RITUAL

OF THE

PENTAGRAM

Diagram 5

Face East. Make Qabalistic Cross.

Make Equilibriated Active Pentagram of Spirit.

Vibrate **Exarp** in making Pentagram.

Vibrate **Eheieh** in making Wheel.

Finish with the ⑤ = [6] Signs.

Make the Invoking Pentagram of Air.

Vibrate **Oro Ibah Aozpi** in making Pentagram.

Vibrate **Yhvh** in making Aquarius.

Finish with the ② = [9] Sign.

Carry Point to South—

Make Equilibriated Active Pentagram of Spirit.

Vibrate **Bitom** in making Pentagram.

Vibrate **Eheieh** in making Wheel.

Give ⑤ = [6] Signs.

Make the Invoking Pentagram of Fire.

Vibrate **Oip Teaa Pedoce** in making Pentagram.

Vibrate **Elohim** in making Leo sigil.

Make the ④ = [7] Sign.

<19> *Carry Point to West—*

Make Equilibriated Passive Pentagram of Spirit.
Vibrate **Hcoma** in making Pentagram.
Vibrate **Agla** in making Wheel.
Give ⑤ = [6] Signs.

Make Invoking Pentagram of Water.
Vibrate **Empeh Arsel Gaiol** in making Pentagram.
Vibrate **Al** in making Eagle Head.
Give the ③ = [8] Sign.

Carry Point to North—

Make Equilibriated Passive Pentagram of Spirit.
Vibrate **Nanta** in making Pentagram.
Vibrate **Agla** in making Wheel.
Give ⑤ = [6] Sign.

Make Invoking Pentagram of Earth.
Vibrate **Emor Dial Hectega** in making Pentagram.
Vibrate **Adonai** in making Taurus.
Give ① = [10] Sign.

Finish in East as in Lesser Pentagram Ritual with the Four Archangels and Qabalistic Cross.

<20>

THE RITUAL
OF THE
HEXAGRAM

The Hexagram is a powerful symbol representing the operation of the Seven Planets under the presidency of the Sephiroth, and of the letters of the seven-lettered Name, Ararita. The Hexagram is sometimes called the Signet or Symbol of the Macrocosm, just as the Pentagram is called the Signet Star or Symbol of the Microcosm.

Ararita is a divine name of Seven letters formed of the Hebrew initials of the sentence:

"One is his beginning. One is his individuality. His permutation is one."

As in the case of the Pentagram, each re-entering angle of the Hexagram issueth a ray representing a radiation from the divine. Therefore it is called the Flaming Hexagram, or the six-rayed Signet Star. Usually, it is traced with the single point uppermost. It is not an evil symbol with the two points upward, and this is a point of difference from the Pentagram.

Now if thou dost draw the Hexagram to have by thee as a Symbol, thou shalt make it in the colours already taught and upon a black ground. These are the Planetary Powers allotted unto the Angles of the Hexagram.

		(King Scale)	*(Queen Scale)*
Unto the uppermost	♄	Indigo	Black
Unto the lowermost	☽	Blue	Puce
Unto the right hand upper	♃	Violet	Blue
Unto the right hand lower	♀	Green	Green
Unto the left hand upper	♂	Red	Red
Unto the left hand lower	☿	Yellow	Orange
In the centre is the fire of the Sun	☉	Orange	Golden

<21> The order of attribution is that of the Sephiroth on the Tree of Life. Hence ariseth the Supreme Ritual of the Hexagram according to the Angles from which it is traced.

The uppermost angle answereth also to *Daath* and the lowest to *Yesod,* and the other angles to the remaining angles of the Microprosopus. The Hexagram is composed of the two angles of Fire and Water, and is therefore *not* traced in one continuous line like the Pentagram, but by each Triangle separately. All the invoking Hexagrams follow the course of the Sun in their current, that is from left to right. But the *banishing* Hexagrams are traced from right to left from the same angle as their respective invoking Hexagrams *contrary* to the course of the Sun. The Hexagram of any particular Planet is traced in two Triangles, the first starting from the angle of the Planet, the second opposite to the commencing angle of the first. The Symbol of the Planet itself is then traced in the centre. Thus in the case of the invoking Hexagrams of Saturn, the first triangle is traced from the angle of Saturn, following the course of the Sun, the second triangle from the angle of the Moon.

(Only trace the central Planetary symbol in practice — the others are shown *only* for illustration.)

Diagram 6

But the invoking Hexagram of the Moon is first traced from the angle of the Moon, its second angle being traced from the triangle of Saturn.

The banishing Hexagram for Jupiter, for example, is traced from
<22> the same angle as the invoking Hexagram, and in the same order, but reversing the current's direction. In all cases the Symbol of the Planet should be traced in the centre.

But for the Sun *all* six invoking Hexagrams of the Planets should
<26> be traced in their regular planetary order and the symbol ☉ traced in the centre. And for his banishing hexagram also, all the six banishing hexagrams of the other Planets should be employed in their regular order, only that the symbol of the Sun should be traced therein.

Remember that the symbol of Luna varieth, and as ☽ in her increase she is favourable. But ☾ is not so favourable for good in her decrease. The symbol of Luna in the centre of the Hexagram should be traced ☽ if in her increase; by ☾ if in her decrease. Remember that ☾ represents restriction and is not so good a symbol as ☽, and at the full Moon exactly it is ○, but at new Moon a dark circle ●.

The last two forms of Luna are not good in many cases. If thou wilt invoke the Forces of the Head of the Dragon of the Moon thou shalt trace the lunar invoking Hexagram and write therein the symbol ☊, and for the tail ☋. These Forces of ☊ and ☋ are more easy to be invoked when either the Sun or the Moon is with them in the Zodiac in conjunction. In these invokations thou shalt pronounce the same Names and Letters as are given with the Lunar Hexagram. ☊ is of a benevolent character, and ☋ of a malefic, save in a very few matters. And be thou well wary of dealing with these forces of ☊ and ☋ or with those of Sol and Luna during the period of an eclipse; for they are the Powers of an eclipse. For an eclipse to take place both the Sun and Moon must be in conjunction with them in the Zodiac, these two luminaries being at the same time either in conjunction or opposition as regards each other.

Diagram 7

INVOKING
BANISHING
שדי אל חי
אראריתא
א
SHADDI EL CHAI

אלהים צבאות
אראריתא
ת
ELOHIM TZABAOTH

אל
אראריתא
ר
EL

<23>

Diagram 8

Invoking
Banishing
אלהים גבור
אראריתא
א
ELOHIM GIBOR
יהוה צבאות
אראריתא
YHVH TZABAOTH

<24>

Diagram 9

Invoking

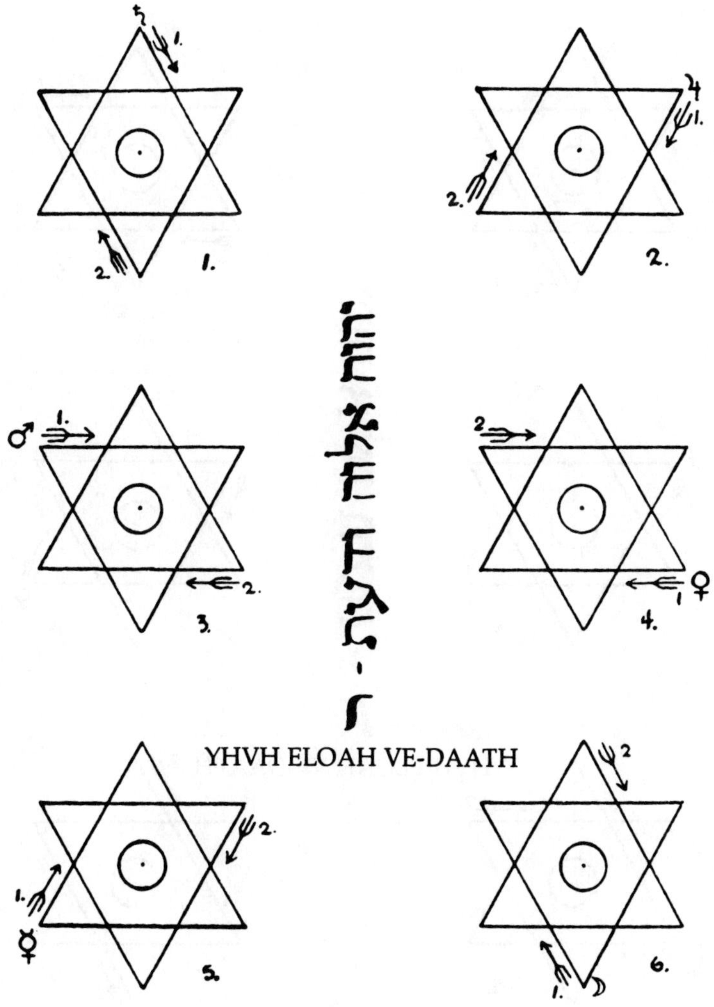

Six Invoking Hexagrams for Sol.

<25>

Diagram 10

Banishing

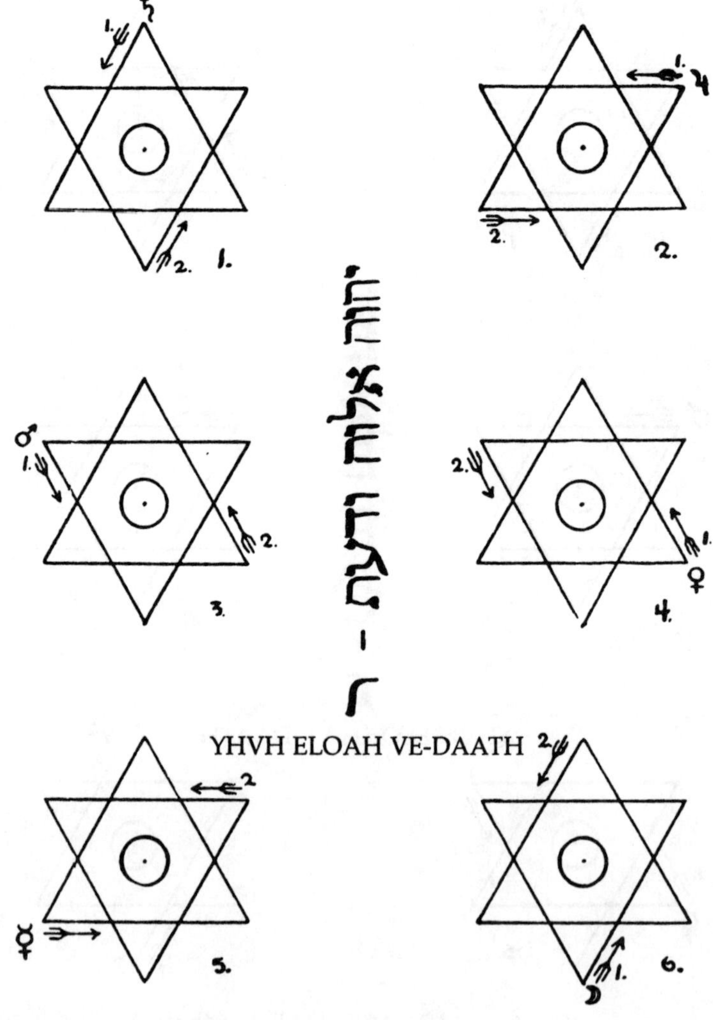

Six Banishing Hexagrams for Sol.

In all Rituals of the Hexagram as in those of the Pentagram, thou shalt complete the circle of the place. Thou shalt *not* trace an external circle round each Hexagram itself unless thou wishest to confine the force to one place — as in charging a Symbol of Talisman.

<27> From the attribution of the Planets, one to each angle of the Hexagram, shalt thou see the reason of the sympathy existing between each superior planet and one certain inferior Planet. That is, that to which it is exactly opposite in the Hexagram. And for this reason is it that the Triangle of their invoking and banishing Hexagrams counter-change. The superior Planets are Saturn, Jupiter, Mars. The inferior Planets are Venus, Mercury, Luna. And in the midst is placed the Fire of the Sun. Therefore the superior Saturn and the Inferior Luna are sympathetic, so are Jupiter and Mercury, Mars and Venus.

In the Supreme Ritual of the Hexagram the Signs of the ⑤ = [6] Grade are to be given, but not those of the Grades of the First Order, notwithstanding these latter are made use of in the Supreme Ritual of the Pentagram. And because the Hexagram is the Signet Star of the Macrocosm or Greater World, therefore is it to be employed in all invocations of the Forces of the Sephiroth: though the Signet Star of the Pentagram represents their operation in the Luna World, in the Elements and in Man.

If thou wilt deal with the Forces of the Supernal Triad of the Sephiroth, thou shalt make use of the Hexagrams of Saturn; for Chesed those of Jupiter, for Geburah those of Mars; for Tiphareth those of the Sun, and for Netzach those of Venus, and for Hod those of Mercury, and for Yesod and Malkuth those of the Moon.

Know also that the Sephiroth are not to be invoked on every slight occasion, but only with due care and solemnity. Above all, the forces of Kether and Chokmah demand the greatest purity and solemnity of heart and mind in him who would penetrate their mysteries. For such high knowledge is only to be obtained by him whose Genius can stand in the Presence of the Holy Ones. See that thou usest the Divine Names with all reverence and humility for cursed is he that taketh the Name of the Vast One in vain.

<28> When thou tracest the Symbol of a Planet in the centre of a Hexagram, thou shalt make the same of a proportionable size to the interior of the Hexagram, and thou shalt trace them from left to right generally following the course of the Sun as much as possible. Caput and Cauda Draconis may follow the general rule.

When thou shalt invoke either the Forces of one particular Planet or those of them all, thou shalt turn thyself towards the Quarter of the Zodiac where the Planet thou invokest then is. For owing both to their constant motion in the Zodiac and to the daily movement of the same, the position of a Planet is continually changing, and therefore it is necessary for thee in such a case to erect an Astrological Figure or Scheme of the position of the Planets in the heavens for the actual time of working, so that thou mayest see the direction of each Planet from thee. This is even more necessary when working with the Planets than with the signs of the Zodiac.

When thou shalt desire to purify or consecrate any place, thou shalt perform the Lesser Banishing Ritual of the Hexagram, either in conjunction with, or instead of that of the Pentagram, according to the circumstances of the case. For example, if thou hast been working on the plane of the Elements before, it will be well to perform the Lesser Ritual of the Pentagram before proceeding to work of a Planetary nature, so as thoroughly to clear the places of Forces which, although not hostile or evil of themselves, will yet not be in harmony with those of an altogether different Plane. And ever be sure that thou dost complete the circle of the place wherein thou workest.

THE FOUR FORMS

These are the four forms assumed by conjoining the two triangles of the Hexagram on which the Lesser Ritual of the Hexagram is based. The first form is:

Diagram 11

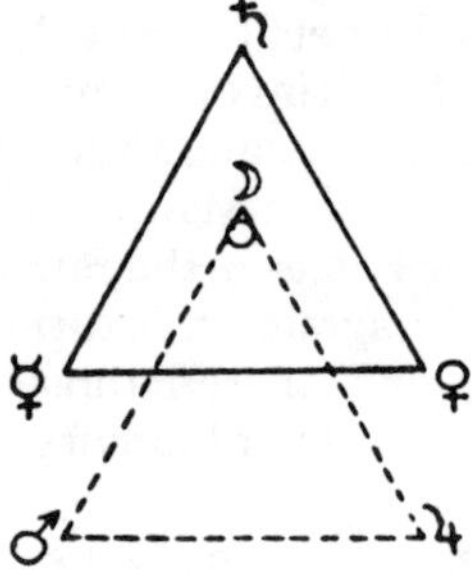

The angles are attributed as in the diagram. Its affinity is with the Eastern Quarter, the position of Fire in the Zodiac. (Note: To form these from the usual Hexagram, lower the inverted triangle, then reverse it by throwing the Lunar angle up to top from being lowest. Mars and Jupiter do not change sides.)

Diagram 12

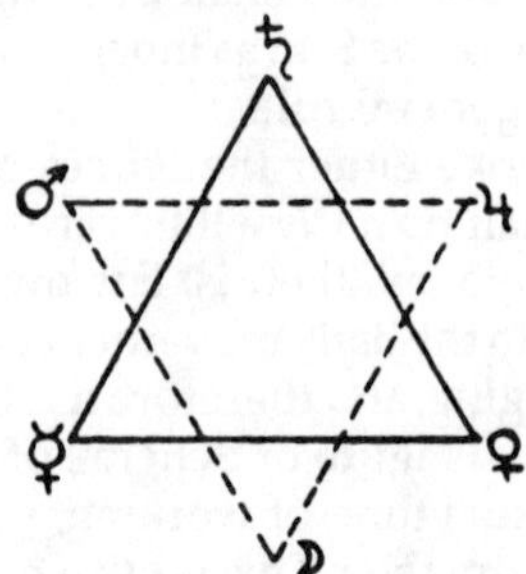

The second form is the ordinary Hexagram with the attribution of the angles as usual: the affinity being rather with the Southern Quarter, the position of Earth in the Zodiac, and of the Sun at his culmination at noon.

<30> The third form is:

Diagram 13

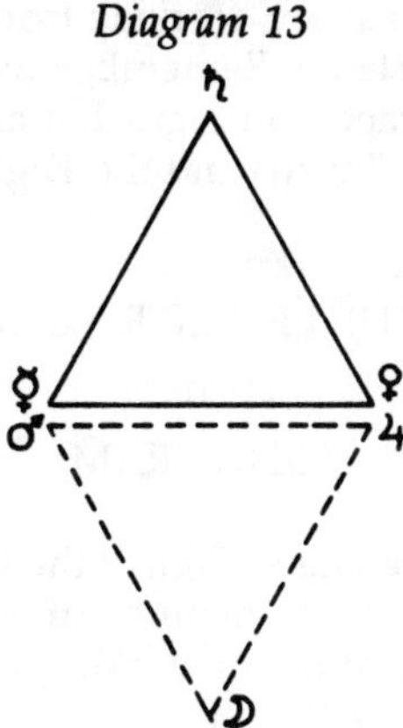

The angles are attributed as shown and its affinity is with the Western Quarter, the position of Air in the Zodiac.

The fourth form is

Diagram 14

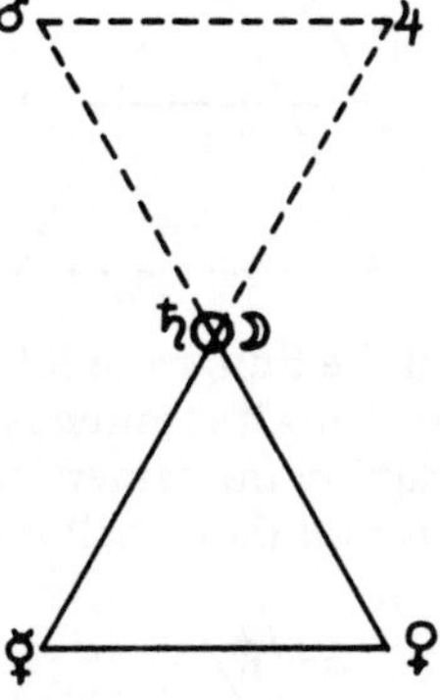

The angles are attributed as shown and its affinity is with the Northern Quarter, the position of Water in the Zodiac.

With each of these forms the Name Ararita is to be pronounced — seven letters.

<31> Also as in the preceding cases there will be seven modes of tracing each of these four forms, according to the particular Planet with those Forces thou art working at the time.

The Hexagrams of Saturn may be used in general and comparatively unimportant operations, even as the Pentagrams of Earth are used in the Lesser Ritual of the Pentagram. In these four forms of the Hexagram thou shalt trace them beginning at the angle of the Planet under whose regimen thou art working, following the course of the Sun to invoke, and reversing the course to banish. That is to say, working from left to right for the former and from right to left for the latter. Remember always that the symbols of the elements are not usually traced on Sigils but are replaced by the Kerubic Emblems of Aquarius, Leo, Taurus and the Eagle head.

<32>

THE LESSER RITUAL OF THE HEXAGRAM

Commence with the Qabalistic Sign of the Cross as in the Lesser Ritual of the Pentagram, and use what manner of Magical implement may be necessary according to the manner of working, either the Lotus Wand or the Magical Sword.

Stand facing East. If thou desirest to *invoke* thou shalt trace the figure thus:

Diagram 15

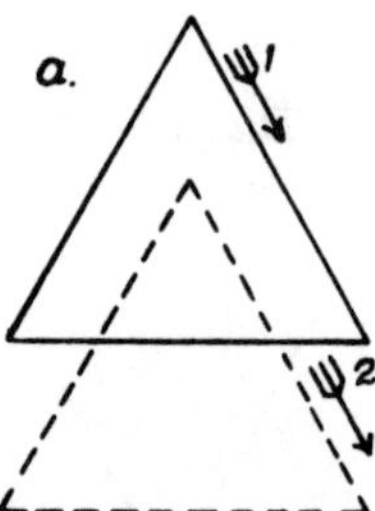

Following the course of the Sun, from left to right and thou shalt pronounce the name Ararita, vibrating it as much as possible with thy breath and bringing the point of the Magical Implement to the centre of the figure.

But if thou desirest to *banish* thou shalt trace it thus:

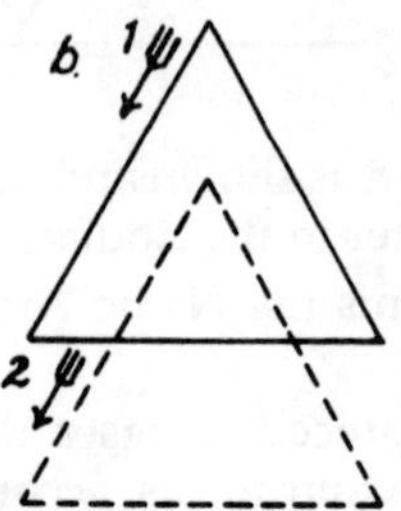

From right to left, and see that thou closest carefully the finishing angle of each triangle.

<33> Carry thy magical implement round to the South, and if thou desirest to *invoke* trace the figure thus:

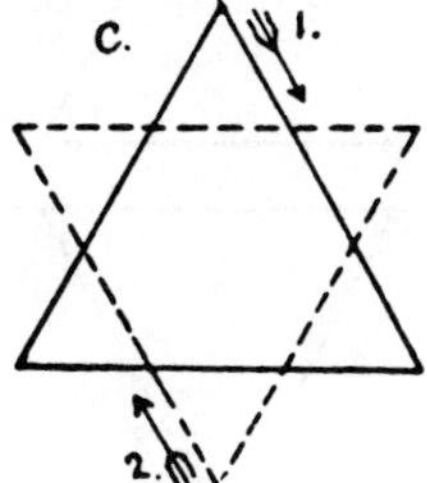

But if to *banish* then from left to right thus:

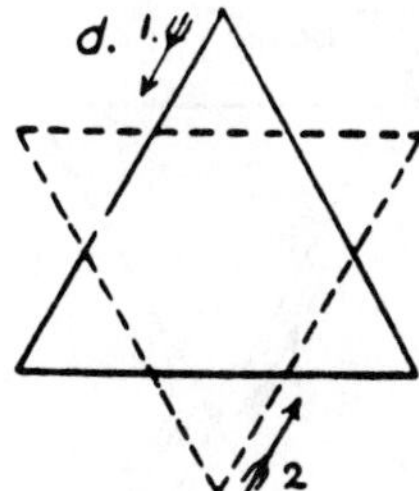

Bring as before the point of thy magical implement to the centre and pronounce the Name Ararita.

Pass to the West, and trace the figure for *invoking* thus:

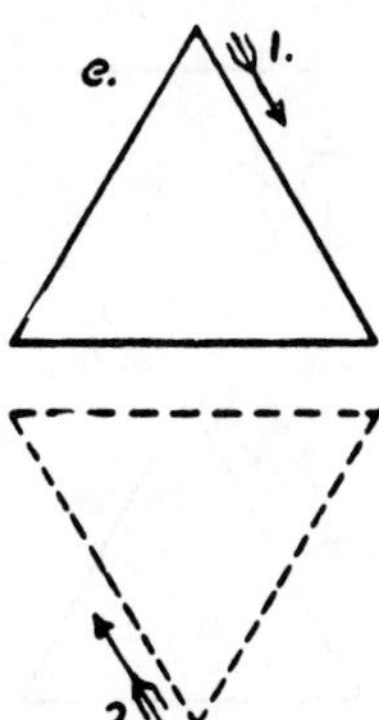

<34> *Banishing* thus:

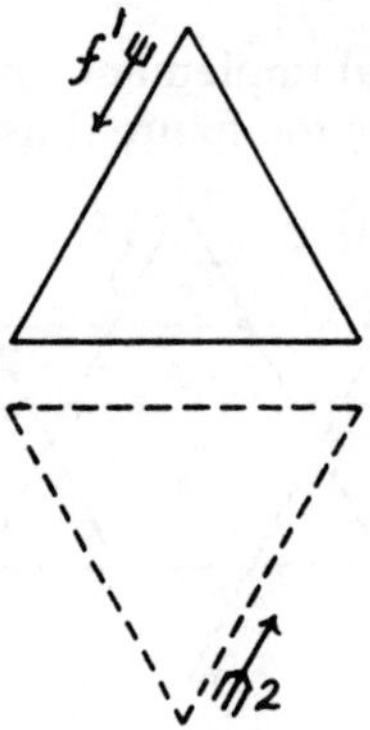

Then to the North, Invoking:

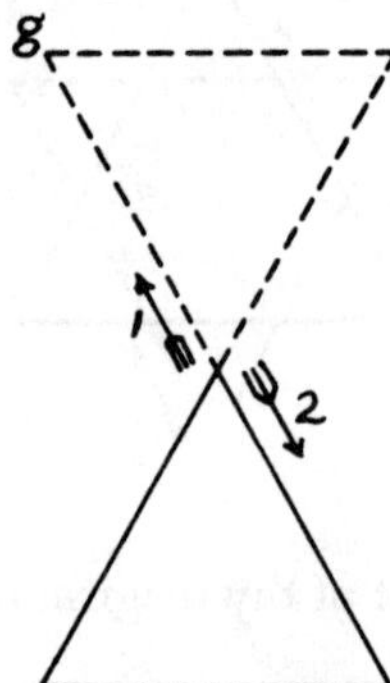

Banishing:

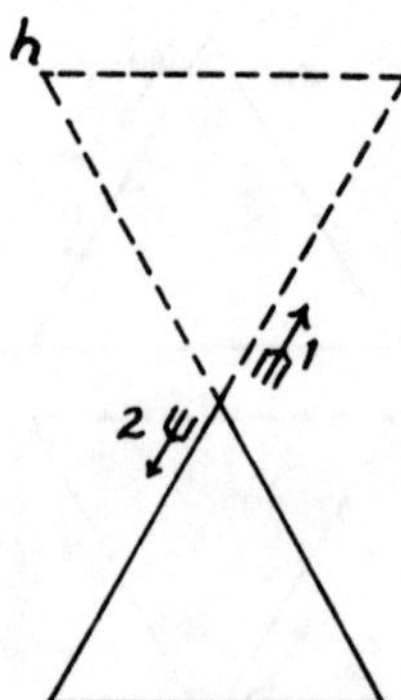

Then pass round again to the East so as to complete the circle of
<35> the place wherein thou standest, then give the LVX signs and repeat
the analysis of the Pass-word INRI of the ⑤ = [6] Grade.

ADDENDUM

Now in the Supreme Ritual of the Hexagram, when thou shalt wish to attract in addition to the forces of a Planet, those of a Sign of the Zodiac wherein he then is, thou shalt trace in the centre of the invoking Hexagram of the planet, the Symbol of that Sign of the Zodiac beneath his own; and if this be not sufficient, thou shalt also trace the invoking Pentagram of the Sign as it is directed in the ritual of the Pentagram.

In the tracing of the Hexagram of any Planet thou shalt pronounce therewith in a vibratory manner as before taught, both the Divine Name of the Sephirah which ruleth the Planet and the Seven-lettered Name Ararita, and also the particular letter of that Name which is referred to that particular Planet.

Now if thou shalt wish to invoke the forces of One particular Planet, thou shalt find in what Quarter of the heavens he will be situate at the time of working. Then thou shalt consecrate and guard the place wherein thou art by the Lesser Banishing Ritual of the Hexagram. Then thou shalt perform the Lesser Invoking Ritual of the Hexagram, yet tracing the four figures employed from the angle of the Planet required, seeing that for each Planet the mode of tracing varieth. If thou dealest with the Sun, thou shalt invoke by all six forms of the Figure and trace within them the Planet Symbol and pronounce the Name Ararita as has been taught.

Then shalt thou turn unto the quarter of the planet in the Heavens and shalt trace his invoking Hexagram and pronounce the proper Names, and
invoke what Angels and Forces of that Nature may be required, and
<36> trace their Sigils in the air.

When thou hast finished thy invocation thou shalt in most cases license them to depart and perform the Banishing Ritual of the Planet which shall be the converse of the invoking one. But in cases of charging a Tablet or Symbol or Talisman, thou shalt *not* perform the Banishing Symbols upon it which would have the effect of entirely de-charging it and reducing it to the condition it was in when first made — that is to say dead and lifeless.

If thou wishest to bring the Rays of all or several of the Planets into action at the same time, thou shalt discover their quarter in the Heavens for the time of working, and thou shalt trace the general Lesser Invoking Ritual of the Hexagram, but *not differentiated* for any particular Planet, and then thou shalt turn to the Quarters of the respective Planets and invoke their Forces as before laid down; and banish them when the invocation is finished, and conclude with the Lesser Banishing Ritual of the Hexagram. And ever remember to complete the circle of the place wherein thou workest, following the course of the sun.

<37>

DIAGRAM
OF THE
LOTUS WAND

Diagram 16

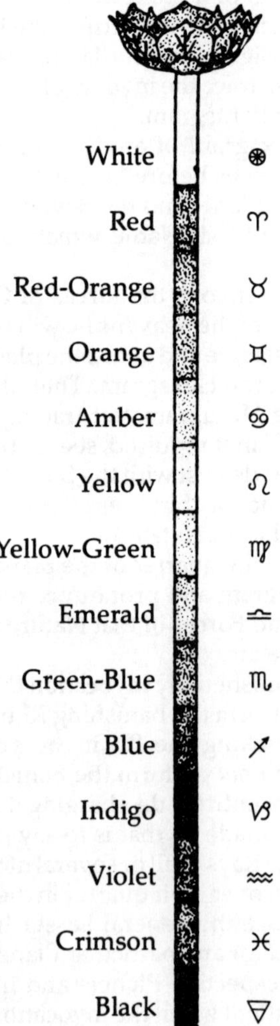

<38> *Diagram 17*

a.

Lotus Flower from above:
Centre: Orange or gold

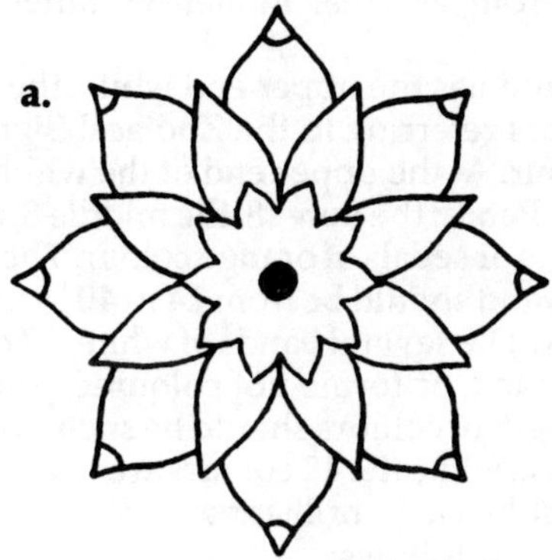

b.

Inmost Petals,
10 in number,
White both sides.

c.

Calyx, 4 Petals,
Coloured orange.

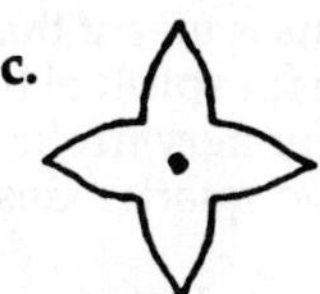

d.

Two whorls of 8 Petals, white inside and olive green outside, with 5 veins shown on the green.

<39>

THE LOTUS WAND

This is for general use in magical working. It is carried by the Z. A. M. at all meetings of the Second Order at which he has the right to be present. It is to be made by himself unassisted, and to be consecrated by himself alone. It is to be untouched by any other person, and kept wrapped in white silk or linen, free from external influences other than his own on the human plane.

The Wand has the upper end white, the lower black. Between these are the 12 colours referring to the Zodiacal Signs, in the positive or masculine scale of colour. At the upper end of the white is fixed a Lotus flower in three whorls of 26 Petals: the outer 8, the middle 8, and the innermost 10. The calyx has four lobes or sepals of orange colour. The flower centre is orange or gold. The Lotus Wand should be from 24 to 40 inches long, and of wood about half an inch thick. The several bands of white, 12 colours, and black may be painted or enamelled, or formed of coloured papers pasted on.

The length of colours should be such that the white is a little the longest, then the black, while the 12 colours are equal, and smaller than the black. The colours must be clear, brilliant and correct.

They are as follows:

White: Aries—red: Taurus—red-orange: Gemini—orange: Cancer—amber: Leo—lemon-yellow: Virgo—yellow-green: Libra—emerald: Scorpio—green-blue: Sagittarius—bright-blue: Capricornus—indigo: Aquarius—violet: Pisces—crimson: black.

The Lotus flower may be made of sheet metal or card board, in 3 whorls of 8, 8, and 10 petals, white internally and tips curved in a little, olive outside with 5 markings as shown in diagram. The centre is orange, or a brass bolt to keep all together will do.

<40> As a general rule, use the white end in invocation and the black end to banish. The white end may be used to banish by tracing a banishing symbol against an evil and opposing force which has resisted other efforts. By this is meant that by whatever band you are holding the Wand, whether white for spiritual things, by black for mundane, by blue for Sagittarius or by red for fiery triplicity, you are, when invoking, to direct the white extremity to the quarter desired. When banishing, point the black end to that quarter.

The Wand is never to be inverted, so that when very material forces are concerned, the black end may be the most suitable for invocation, but with the greatest caution.

In working on the plane of the Zodiac, hold the Wand by the Portion you refer to between the thumb and two fingers.

If a Planetary working be required, hold the Wand by the Portion representing the day or night House of the Planet, or else by the Sign in which the Planet is at the time.

♄	Day House—Capricorn	Night House—Aquarius
♃	Day House—Sagittarius	Night House—Pisces
♂	Day House—Aries	Night House—Scorpio
♀	Day House—Libra	Night House—Taurus
☿	Day House—Gemini	Night House—Virgo
Sol	☉ in Leo only	Luna ☽ in Cancer only

For example, if Venus be the Planet referred to, use in the day Libra, and in the night Taurus.

Should the action be with the Elements, one of the Signs of the Triplicity of the Elements should be held according to the nature of the Element intended to be invoked. Bear in mind that the Kerubic Emblem is the most powerful action of the Element in the triplicity. For example, Leo — Violent heat of summer. Aries — Beginning of warmth in spring. Sagittarius, waning of heat in autumn.

<41> *Hold the Wand by the white portion* for all Divine and Spiritual Matters or for the Sephirotic influences, and for the process of rising in the Planes.

Hold the Wand by the black part only for material and mundane matters.

The 10 upper and inner Petals refer to the Purity of the Ten Sephiroth. The middle 8 refer to the counter-charged natural and spiritual forces of Air and Fire. The lowest and outer 8 refer to the powers of Earth and Water. The centre and amber portion refers to the Spiritual Sun, while the outer calyx of 4 orange sepals shows the action of the Sun upon the life of things by differentiation.

The Wand should never be used inverted.

The Lotus Flower is not to be touched in working, but in Sephirotic and Spiritual Things, the Flower is to be inclined towards the forehead; and to rise in the Planes, the orange coloured centre is to be fully directed to the forehead.

CONSECRATION OF THE LOTUS WAND

1. *Provide a private room, white triangle, red cross of six squares. Incense, a rose, water in a vase, Lamp or vessel of Fire, Salt on a platter, and an astrological figure of the heavens for the time of consecration. If possible a set of astrological symbolic diagrams of the Twelve Signs should be set around the room. Have ready also the Ritual of the Pentagram, New Wand, white silk or linen wrapper, table with black cover for altar.*
2. *Find position of East.*
3. *Prepare an invocation of the Forces of the Signs of the Zodiac.*
4. *Place Altar in centre of room, cover it with black.*
5. *Arrange upon it, the cross and triangle. Incense and Rose in East above Cross and Triangle. Lamp in South. Cup in West. Salt in North.*
6. *Illumine Lamp.*

<42> 7. *Stand, holding new Wand at West of Altar, facing East.*

8. *Grasp Wand by black portion and say:*
9. Hekas! Hekas! Este Bebeloi.
10. *Perform Lesser Banishing Ritual of the Pentagram.*
11. *Purify room first with Water, then with Fire, as in the* ⓪ = [0] *Grade, repeating as you do so, these two passages from the Ritual of the 31st Path.*
    (with Water) So therefore, first, the Priest who governeth the works of Fire, must sprinkle with lustral water of the loud resounding sea.
    (with Fire) And when, after all the Phantoms are vanished, thou shalt see that Holy and Formless Fire, that Fire which darts and flashes through the hidden depths of the Universe, hear thou the Voice of Fire.

12. *Take up the Wand again, by white portion. Circumambulate the room three times and, at the end, repeat the adoration of the Lord of the Universe as in the Ritual of ⓪ = [0] Grade, saluting at each adoration with the Neophyte Sign, and at "Darkness" giving the Sign of Silence.*

    Holy art Thou, Lord of the Universe.
    Holy art Thou whom Nature hath not formed.
    Holy art Thou the Vast and the Mighty One.
    Lord of the Light and of the Darkness.

13. *Perform the Supreme Invoking Ritual of the Pentagram at the 4 Quarters of the Room, tracing the proper Pentagram at each quarter and pronouncing the appropriate Angelic and Divine Names, taking care to give Grade Sign appropriate to Element.*
14. *Stand then in the Eastern Quarter, facing East, hold Wand by white portion, give ⑤ = [6] Signs, look upward, hold Wand on high, and say:*

    O Harpocrates, Lord of Silence, Who art enthroned upon the Lotus.

    Twenty-Six are the Petals of the Lotus, Flower of thy Wand. O Lord of
<43> Creation, they are the Number of Thy Name.

    In the name of Yod He Vau He, let the Divine Light descend!

15. *Facing consecutively the quarter where each Sign is according to the Horary Figure for the time of working, repeat in each of the 12 directions the invocation which follows, using the appropriate Divine and Angelic Names and Letters for each specially. Begin with Aries, hold the Wand at the appropriate coloured Band, and in the left hand the Element, from off the Altar, which is referred to the particular Sign and say:*

    (This for Aries) The Heaven is above and the Earth is beneath. And betwixt the Light and the Darkness the colours vibrate. I supplicate the Powers and Forces governing the Nature, Place, and Authority of the Sign Aries, by the Majesty of the Divine Name Yod He Vau He, with which, in Earth life and language, I ascribe the letter Heh, to which is allotted the symbolic Tribe of Gad and over which is the Angel Melchidael, to bestow this present day and hour, and confirm their mystic and potent influence upon the Red Band of this Lotus Wand, which I hereby dedicate to purity and to Occult Work, and may its grasp strengthen me in the work of the character of Aries and his attributes.

    As this is recited, trace in the Air with the Lotus end, the invoking Pentagram of the Sign required, and hold the corresponding element from the altar in the left hand, while facing in each of the 12 Zodiacal directions.

16. *Lay Wand on the Altar, Lotus end towards the East.*
17. *Stand at West of Altar, face East, raise hands, and say:*

    O Isis! Great Goddess of the Forces of Nature, let Thine Influence
<45> descend and consecrate this Wand which I dedicate to Thee for the performance of the works of the Magic of Light.

18. *Wrap the Wand in silk or linen.*
19. *Purify the room by Water and by Fire as at first.*
20. *Perform reverse circumambulation.*
21. *Standing at West of Altar, face East, and recite:*

    In the Name of Yeheshuah, I now set free the Spirits that may have been imprisoned by this ceremony.

22. *Preferably, perform the Lesser Banishing Ritual of the Pentagram.*

<44> THE INVOCATION TO THE FORCES OF THE SIGNS OF THE ZODIAC

SIGN	PERMUTATION OF NAME				HEBREW LETTER	TRIBE OF ISRAEL	ANGEL	COLOUR
Aries	Yod	Heh	Vau	Heh	Heh	Gad	Melchidael	Red
Taurus	Yod	Heh	Heh	Vau	Vau	Ephraim	Asmodel	Red-Orange
Gemini	Yod	Vau	Heh	Heh	Zayin	Manasseh	Ambriel	Orange
Cancer	Heh	Vau	Heh	Yod	Cheth	Issachar	Muriel	Amber
Leo	Heh	Vau	Yod	Heh	Teth	Judah	Verchiel	Lemon-Yellow
Virgo	Heh	Heh	Vau	Yod	Yod	Naphthali	Hamaliel	Yellow-Green
Libra	Vau	Heh	Yod	Heh	Lamed	Asshur	Zuriel	Emerald
Scorpio	Vau	Heh	Heh	Yod	Nun	Dan	Barchiel	Green-blue
Sagittarius	Vau	Yod	Heh	Heh	Samech	Benjamin	Advachiel	Blue
Capricorn	Heh	Yod	Heh	Vau	Ayin	Zebulun	Hanael	Indigo
Aquarius	Heh	Yod	Vau	Heh	Tzaddi	Reuben	Cambriel	Violet
Pisces	Heh	Heh	Yod	Vau	Qoph	Simeon	Amnitziel	Crimson

<46> # THE RITUAL

OF THE

ROSE CROSS

1. Light a stick of Incense. Go to the South East corner of the room. Make a large cross and circle thus:

Diagram 18

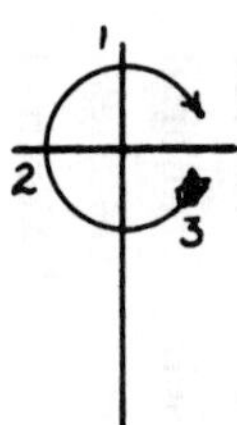

and holding the point of the incense in the centre vibrate the word Yeheshuah.

2. With arm outstretched on a level with the centre of the cross, and holding the incense stick, go to the South West corner and make a similar cross, repeating the Word.

3. Go to the North West Corner and repeat the cross and the Word.

4. Go to the North East Corner and repeat the cross and the Word.

5. Complete your circle by returning to the South East corner and bringing the point of the incense to the central point of the first cross which you should imagine astrally there.

6. Holding the stick on high, go to the centre of the room, walking diagonally across the room towards the North West corner. In the centre of the room, above your head, trace the cross and circle and vibrate the Name.

7. Holding the stick on high, go to the North West and bring the
<47> point of the stick down to the centre of the astral cross there.

8. Turn towards the South East and retrace your steps there, but now, holding the incense stick directed towards the floor. In the centre of the room, make the cross and circle towards the floor, as it were, under your feet, and vibrate the Name.

9. Complete this circle by returning to the South East and bringing the point of the stick again to the centre of the Cross, then move with arm outstretched to S.W. corner.

10. From the centre of this cross, and, raising stick before, walk diagonally across the room towards the North East corner. In the centre of the room, pick up again the cross above your head previously made, vibrating

<48> *Diagram 19*

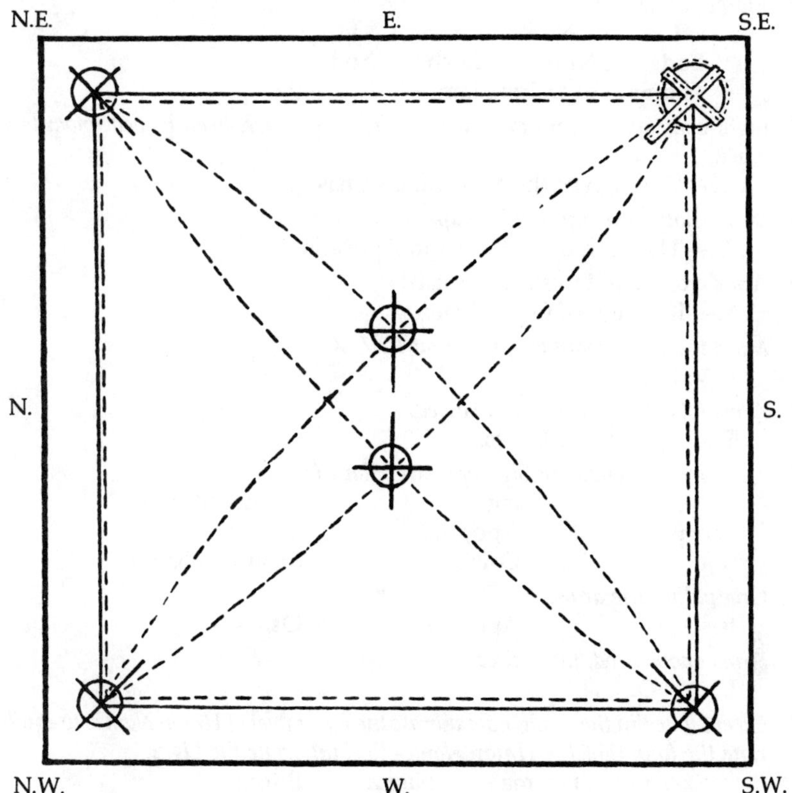

the Name. It is not necessary to make another cross.

11. Bring the stick to the centre of the North East cross and return to the South West, incense stick down, and pausing in the centre of the room to link up with the cross under your feet.

12. Return to the South West and rest the point of the incense a moment in the centre of the cross there. Holding the stick out, retrace your circle to the North West, link on to the N. W. Cross — proceed to the N. E. cross and complete your circle by returning to the S. E., and the centre of the first cross.

13. Retrace the Cross, but larger, and make a big circle, vibrating for the lower half Yeheshuah, and for the upper half Yehovashah.

14. Return to the centre of the room, and visualise the six crosses in a net-work round you. This ceremony can be concluded by the analysis of the Key-Word given as follows:

1. *Stand with arms outstretched in the form of a cross. Face East.*
2. *Vibrate these words:*

   I. N. R. I.
   Yod Nun Resh Yod
   The Sign of Osiris Slain.

3. *Right arm up, left arm extended out from shoulder, head bowed towards left hand.*

   L.—The Sign of the Mourning of Isis.

<49> 4. *Both arms up in a V shape.*

   V.—The Sign of Typhon and Apophis.

5. *Arms crossed on breast, head bowed.*

   X.—The Sign of Osiris Risen.

6. *Make the signs again as you repeat L. V. X.*

   L. V. X. Lux.

7. *Arms folded on breast, head bowed.*

   The Light of the Cross.

8. *Then arms extended in Sign of Osiris Slain (see 1).*

   Virgo Isis Mighty Mother
   Scorpio Apophis Destroyer
   Sol Osiris Slain and Risen

9. *Gradually raise arms.*

   Isis Apophis Osiris

10. *Arms above head, face raised.*

    I. A. O.

11. *Except when in the Vault, now vibrate the four tablet of Union Names to equilibriate the four Tablet of Union Names to equilibriate the Light.*

    Exarp Hcoma Nanta Bitom

12. *Aspire to the Light and draw it down over your head to your feet.*

    Let the Divine Light Descend.

(Note: For diagrams of these signs refer to pages 43 and 44 of Volume II.—I.R.)

THE USE OF THE ROSE CROSS RITUAL

1. It encloses the aura with a protection against outside influences. It is like a veil. The Pentagrams protect, but they also light up the astral and make entities aware of you. They are more positive for magical working. When much distracted, use the Pentagrams to banish and the Rose-cross to maintain peace.

2. It is a call to another mode of your consciousness and withdraws you from the physical. It is a good preparation for meditation and, combined with the Key-Word, a form of invocation of the Higher Wisdom which is
<50> helpful when solving problems or preparing for a difficult interview, or in order to be calm and strong to help another.

3. When you are quite familiar with the Ritual, but most certainly not before, it can be done in imagination while resting or lying down. Part of

yourself goes out, and you get all the sensation of walking around your own quiescent body. Used thus, with rhythmmic breathing, it will withdraw your mind from pain (if it be not too severe) and release you for sleep. You can do the analysis of the Key-Word standing behind your physical head, and you can call down the Divine White Brilliance, watching it flow over your body and smooth out the tangles in the etheric double, bringing peace and rest.

4. You can do the Ritual with intention to help others in pain or difficulty. For this purpose, you build up an astral image of the person, in the centre of the room, and call down the Light upon him, after surrounding him with the six crosses. When the ceremony is done, command the astral shape you have made to return to the person, bearing with it the peace of Yeheshuah.

5. It is a protection against psychic invasion from the thoughts of others or from disturbed psychic conditions, such as there might be in a place charged with fear, where terrible things had happened.

<51> THE COMPLETE SYMBOL OF THE ROSE CROSS

This symbol is to be worn suspended from a yellow collarette of silk, the motto of owner placed on the reverse side, with white sash, and is for general use in Magical working, to be worn at all meetings of Adepts.

It is to be made by each Adept alone, and consecrated by himself and never touched by any other person; and wrapped in white silk or linen when not in use.

It is a complete synthesis of the Masculine, Positive or Rainbow scale of Colour attributions, which is also called "The Scale of the King."

The four ends of the Cross belong to the four Elements, and are coloured accordingly. The white portion belongs to the Holy Spirit and the Planets.

The Twenty-two petals of the Rose refer to the twenty-two Paths. It is the Cross in Tiphareth, the receptacle and the centre of the Forces of the Sephiroth and the Paths.

The extreme centre of the Rose is white, the reflected Spiritual brightness of Kether, bearing upon it the Red Rose of Five Petals and the Golden Cross of Six Squares; four green Rays issuant around the Angles of the Cross, from which the Second Order takes its name. They are the Symbols of the Receiving Force.

Upon the white portion of the Symbol, below the Rose, is placed the Hexagram, with the Planets in the order which is the key of the Supreme Ritual of the Hexagram.

Around the Pentagrams, which are placed one upon each Elemental coloured arm, are drawn the symbols of the Spirit and the Four Elements, in the order which is the key to the Supreme Ritual of the Pentagram.

<52> Upon each of the floriated ends of the Cross are arranged the Three Alchemical Principles, but in a different order for each Element, and as showing their operation therein.

The upmost Arm of the Cross, allotted to Air, is of the yellow colour of Tiphareth. In it the flowing Philosophic Mercurial nature is chief and without hindrance to its mobility; hence the ever moving nature of Air. Its Sulphureous side is drawn from the part of Fire, whence its luminous and electrical qualities. Its Saline side is from the Water, whence result clouds and rain from the action of the Solar Forces.

The lowest Arm of the Cross, allotted to Earth, is of the four colours of Malkuth, the Earth being of the nature of a container and receiver of the other influences. The Citrine answers to its Airy part, the Olive to the Watery, the Russet to the Fire, and the black to the lowest part, Earth. Here also is the Mercurial part chief, but hindered by the compound nature whence its faculty becomes germinative rather than mobile, while the Sulphur and the Salt are respectively from the sides of Water and Fire, which almost neutralize their natural operation and bring about the fixedness and immobility of Earth.

The extremity allotted to Fire is of the scarlet colour of Geburah, and in it the Sulphureous nature is chief, whence its powers of heat and burning. The Salt is from the side of Earth, whence the necessity for a constant substantial pabulum whereon to act, and the Mercury is from the side of Air, whence the leaping, lambent motion of flame especially when acted upon by wind.

The extremity allotted to Water is of the blue colour of Chesed, and in it the Saline side is chief as exemplified in the salt water of the Ocean, to which all waters go; and from whence also is derived the nature of always preserving the horizontal line. The Mercurial part is from Earth, whence the weight
and force of its flux and reflux. Its Sulphuric part is from the Air
<53> whence the effect of waves and storms. So that the disposition of
these Three Principles forms the key of their Alchemic operation in the Elements.

The White rays issuing from behind the Rose at the inner angles between the Arms, are the Rays of the Divine Light issuing and corruscating from the Reflected Light of Kether in its centre; and the letters and symbols on them refer to the analysis of the Key Word of an Adeptus Minor, I. N. R. I. by which the opening of the Vault is accomplished.

The Twelve letters of the Twelve Petals follow the Order of the Signs of the Zodiac. Uppermost is Heh, the letter of Aries, followed by Vau, Zayin Cheth, Teth, Yod, while the letter of Libra, which is Lamed is lowermost. Ascending are Nun, Samekh, Ayin, Tzaddi, Qoph.

The Seven Double Letters of the middle row are allotted to the Planets in the order of their Exaltations, the planets being wanderers; the Stars are fixed with respect to the Earth. These letters are Peh, Resh, Beth, with Daleth exactly over Libra, followed by Gimel, Caph, Tau.

The Three Mother letters are allotted to the Elements and are so arranged that the Petal of Air should be beneath the Arm of the Cross allotted to Air, while those of Fire and Water are on counterchanged sides, so that the forces of the Arms of the Cross should not too much override the Planetary and Zodiacal forces in the Rose, which might otherwise be the case were the Petal of Fire placed on the same side as the Arm of Fire and that of Water on the side of Water.

(The Mode of Sigil Formation from the Rose Petals is taught in the supplement to this Ritual, reproduced in Book Seven in Volume Four.)

The back of the Cross bears inscriptions in Latin: "The Master Jesus Christ, God and Man," between four Maltese Crosses which represent the Four Pyramids of the Elements opened out.

This is placed at the upmost part because therein is affirmed a
<54> Descent of the Divine Force into Tiphareth, which is the central point
between Supernals and Inferiors.

But at the lowest part is written the motto of the Zelator Adeptus Minor, because therein is the affirmation of the elevation of the Human into the Divine. But this is impossible without the assistance of the Divine Spirit from Kether, whence the space above Malkuth is white upon the front aspect of the Cross, white being the Symbol of the Spiritual rescued from the

Material.

In the centre is written in Latin between the Symbols of the Alchemical Principles, of which the outermost is Sulphur, the Purgatorial Fire of Suffering and Self-Sacrifice, "Blessed be the Lord our God who hath given us the Symbol Signum." And this is a word of six letters, thus representing the six Creative Periods in the universe.

The Cross may be cut out of cardboard and the coloured portions may be painted or formed by pasting on portions of coloured papers of the required size and shape. The Colours must be correct, clear and brilliant. If they are not, the Symbol is useless either as a Symbol or Insignium. If this occurs the whole should be destroyed, for faulty colours or shapes in Divine Symbols are a degradation of Divine things and are practical blasphemy, because it is substituting the Evil and disorderly for the Good.

NOTES ON THE ROSE CROSS

It is unfortunate that I have not been able to reproduce the symbol in its colours as painted by the Adeptus Minor. Black and white give no indication of the beauty and impressive quality which this symbol possesses. The reader should therefore make one for himself and colour it according to these directions.

The upper arm, above the Rose, attributed to the Element of Air, is painted in bright yellow. Various lacquer enamels are now available, the
<55> use of which produces just the right kind of brilliance required for
these magical symbols and flashing Tablets. Over the yellow should be painted the symbols shown in its direct complement, pale mauve.

The right arm attributed to Water, is blue, and the symbols should be painted thereon in orange. It is difficult to describe the correct tone or depth of colour in these complementaries, but the student will know when he has hit upon the right hue for then the symbols will begin visibly to flash.

The left arm, the Fire arm, is red, and the symbols appear on it in bright emerald green. Beneath the Rose are two sections. The first is white, upon which a hexagram with planetary attributions is painted in black. Beneath this is the Earth section, which should be painted in the four colours of Malkuth: Citrine, Olive, Russet, and Black. Superimposed on this, the pentagram and symbols will be painted in white.

The Petals of the Rose wil be painted in the appropriate colours of the King Scale, and the Letters, on them, in the complementary colours, the Cross within is Gold, the barbs green, and the Rose red.—I.R.

<57>

CONSECRATION

OF THE

ROSE CROSS

CONSECRATION CEREMONY

1. *Arrange a central Altar draped in black.*
2. *Place on it the Triangle and Cross as in the* 0 = 0 *grade.*
3. *Place on it the Rose, Cup, Salt and Fire; but place Cup between Cross and Triangle*

Diagram 20

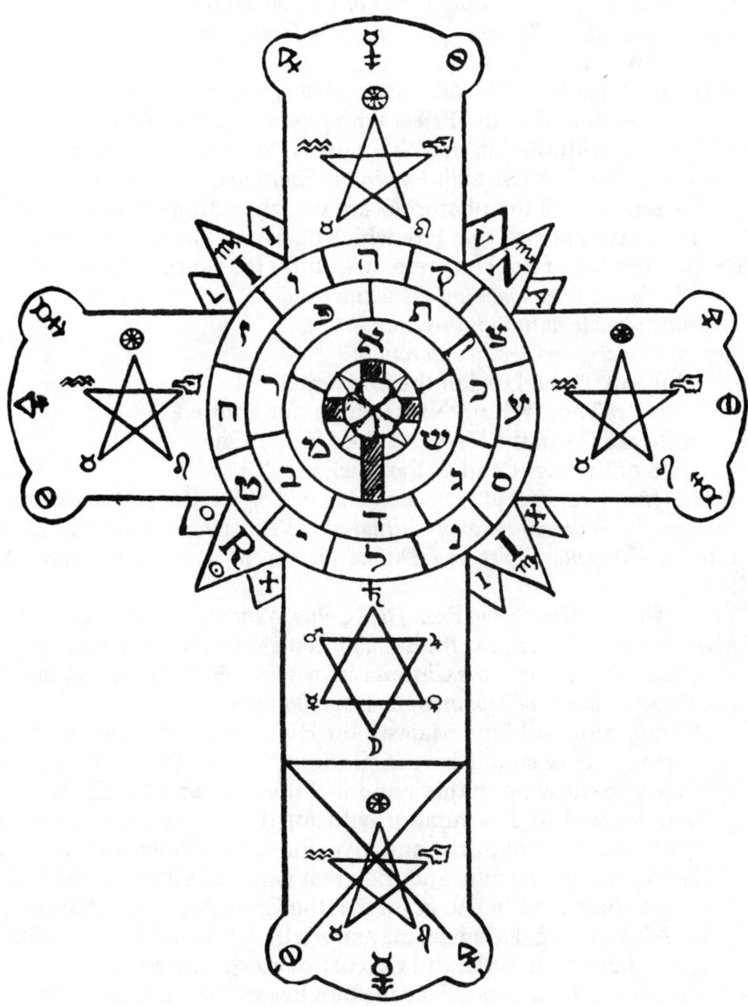

THE ROSE CROSS LAMEN

as in the ⓪ = [0]. *Rose and Incense East.*

4. *Place the new Rose Cross upon Triangle.*
6. *Take up Lotus Wand in right hand, (black band).*
7. *Repeat:* Hekas, Hekas, Esti Bebeloi!
8. *Perform the Lesser Banishing Ritual of the Pentagram.*
9. *Perform the Lesser Banishing Ritual of the Hexagram.*
10. *Deposit Wand upon the Altar.*
11. *Purify the Chamber with Water in the Four Quarters, repeating the Words:*
    "So therefore first the Priest who governeth the Works of Fire, shall sprinkle with the Lustral Water of the loud resounding Sea."
12. *Consecrate the Chamber with Fire in the Four Quarters, saying:*
    "When after all the phantoms are vanished, thou shalt see that Holy and Formless Fire, that Fire which darts and flashes through the hid-
    <58> den depths of the Universe, hear thou the voice of Fire."
13. *Take up thy wand by the white band.*
14. *Circumambulate with Sun three times.*
15. *Return to place, and repeat Adoration:*
    "Holy art Thou, Lord of the Universe!
    Holy art Thou Whom Nature hath not Formed.
    Holy art Thou, the Vast and the Mighty One.
    Lord of the Light and of the Darkness."

    Give Sign of Neophyte at each adoration, and Sign of Harpocrates at close.
16. *Perform the Supreme Invoking Ritual of the Pentagram at the four Quarters, using the Angelic Tablet and Divine Names, for each, with proper Grade Signs.*
17. *Stand West of Altar, facing East. Hold Lotus Wand by White band.*
18. *Make over the Rose Cross in the Air, with Lotus Wand, and as if standing on centre of Rose, the Symbol of the Circle and Cross thus* ⊕, *and invoke all the Divine and Angelic Names of Tiphareth by a special form:*

    "O Thou most sublime Majesty on High, who art at certain seasons worthily represented by the glorious Sun of Tiphareth, I beseech Thee to bestow upon this symbol of the Rose and the Cross, which I have formed to Thy honour, and for the furtherance of the Great Work, in a spirit of purity and love, the most excellent virtues, by the Divine Name of Yhvh, and the great name of Yhvh Eloah Ve Daath. Deign I beseech Thee to grant that the Great Archangel Raphael, and the Mighty Angel Michael may strengthen this emblem, and through the sphere of the splendid Orb of Shemesh may confer upon it such
    <59> Power and Virtue, as to lead me by it towards the solution of the Great Secret."

    (Alternative:)

    "O Thou Most Glorious Light which lightenest every man who cometh into the world. Thou who art in due season shadowed forth by Tiphareth, the Sun of Beauty, I implore Thee to direct Thy Light upon this symbol of the Rose and Cross which I have fashioned in Thine Honour and for the furtherance of the Great Work. By the Divine Name Yhvh, by Thy Name of Wisdom Yhvh Eloah Ve Daath, permit I beseech Thee Thy shining Archangel Raphael, and Thy Strong Angel Michael, so to influence this emblem that it may be mighty for all good so that through the glorious sphere of Shemesh they may bestow upon it such power that in wearing it, I may at length lose and so find myself in that Ineffable Light which I most humbly seek."

Raise the hands and eyes to heaven during the prayer, and lowering them as you finish it.

19. *Repeat these words from Genesis:*

 "And a River, Nahar, went forth out of Eden to water the Garden, and from thence it was parted and came into four heads."

20. *Describe over the white portion the Invoking Hexagrams of the Planets, as if standing upon it, repeating the necessary names, holding the Wand by the White part.*

21. *Describe Equilibriating Pentagrams of Spirit with words as laid down.*

 Eheieh *with* Exarp, Bitom.

 Hcoma, Nanta, *with* Aglah.

22. *Then over the four coloured arms in turn describe the Invoking Pentagrams of each Element, using words and Grade Signs, and repeating the verse of Gen,*
<60> II, 13,14,15, *referring to each, holding the wand by the part allotted to the Kerub Sign of the Element.*

23. *Over the Red Fire Arm read:*

 "And the Name of the First River is Pison, it is that which compasseth the whole land of Havilah, where there is gold. And the gold of that land is good. There is Bdellium and the Onyx stone."

 Making Invoking Fire Pentagram, holding Wand by Leo — lemon-yellow band, make sign of Philosophus, and vibrate Elohim, Oip Teaa Pedoce.

24. *Over Blue Water Arm, read:*

 "And the Name of the Second River is Gihon, the same as that which compasseth the whole land of Ethiopia."

 Make Invoking Water Pentagram, holding Wand by Scorpio band blue-green, and make Sign of Practicus, and say:

 El, Empeh Arsel Gaiol.

25. *Over Yellow Air Arm, read:*

 "And the Name of the Third River is Hiddekel, that is it which goeth forth to the East of Assyria."

 Make Invoking Air Pentagram, holding wand by Aquarius band, violet, make Sign of Theoricus, and say:

 Yhvh, Oro Ibah Aozpi.

26. *Over dark Earthy Arm read:*

 "And the Fourth River is Euphrates."

 Make Invoking Earth Pentagram, and hold wand by Taurus band, red-orange. Make Sign of Zelator, saying:

 Adonai, Emor Dial Hectaga.

27. *Lastly, holding wand again by White part, describe a circle from left to*
<61> *right over the outermost Twelve Petals of Rose, and pronounce the Name:* Adonai, *vibrating it as taught.*

28. *Describe similar Circle over Seven Middle Petals pronouncing the word:* Ararita.

29. *Describe Circle over Three Innermost Petals, saying:* Yhvh.

30. *Finally, trace a perpendicular line from top to bottom and say:* Eheieh.
31. *Trace a horizontal from left to right and say:* Elohim.
32. *Wrap up Rose Cross in white silk or linen.*
33. *Close the Ceremony by Purification by Water, and Consecration by Fire.*
34. *Reverse Circumambulation three times.*
35. *Stand at West of Altar, face East, and say:*

    "In the Name of Yeheshuah, I now set free any Spirits that may have been imprisoned by this ceremony."
36. *Perform the Lesser Banishing Ritual of the Pentagram.*

<62>

THE MAGIC SWORD

It is to be used in all cases where great force and strength are to be used and are required, but principally for banishing and for defence against evil forces. For this reason it is under the Presidency of Geburah and of Mars, whose Names and Forces are to be invoked at its consecration, which should take place in the day and hour of Mars, or else during the course of the Fiery Tattwa.

Any convenient sword may be adapted to this use, but the handle, hilt and guard must be such as to offer surfaces for inscriptions. It should be of medium length and weight.

The motto of the Adeptus should be engraved upon it, or upon the hilt in letters of emerald green, in addition to the mystic devices and names. The hilt, pommel and guard are to be coloured a flame red. The blade should be clean and bright. Pentagrams should be painted on salient portions, because this is the lineal figure of Geburah. The Divine and Angelic Names related to Geburah are then to be added in emerald, and also their Sigils taken from the Rose. The Sword must then be consecrated in due form.

Here again let the Zelator Adeptus Minor remember his Obligation never to use his knowledge of practical Magic for purposes of Evil, and let him be well assured that if he do this, notwithstanding his pledge, the evil he endeavours to bring about will re-act on himself. He will experience in his own person and affairs that very thing which he has endeavoured to bring about for another. So also may he perish and be blotted out from among us.

To obtain real force implanted in any magical weapon, by consecration, the Adept requires to be healthy, pure, strong in mind, free from anxi-
<63> ety and apart from disturbances. He requires also to have mastered the details of the ceremony and to be familiar with the proper pentagrams and other symbols.

CONSECRATION RITUAL OF SWORD

Prepare: Chamber, central Altar draped in Black, Red Cross and White Triangle, Rose and Incense, Cup and Water, Lamp, Plate and Salt. White Robe, Sash, Consecrated Rose Cross and Lotus Wand, New Sword, Red Cloak and Lamen. An Invocation to Mars and Geburah. An Astrological figure to show position of Mars at the time. In wording and formulating the Invocation to the Forces of Geburah, force and strength are to be specially requested.

1. *Place the Sword upon Altar, hilt to East near Incense, point to West near Water.*
2. *Take up Lotus Wand by Black part.*

3. *Stand at West of Altar, facing East.*
4. *Say:*

    Hekas Hekas Esti Bebeloi.

5. *Take up Cup and purify with Water sprinkling to E. S. W. N.*
6. *Saying:*

    And first the Priest who governeth the works of Fire must sprinkle with the Lustral Water of the loud resounding sea.

7. *Put down Cup on Altar.*
8. *Take up Incense and wave it as you pass round E. S. W. N.*
9. *Saying:*

    And when after all the Phantoms are vanished thou shalt see that holy and formless Fire, that Fire which darts and flashes through the hidden depths of the Universe, hear thou the voice of Fire.

10. *Put down Incense. Take up Wand.*

<64> 11. *Circumambulate with Sun three times, grasping Wand by white band. Return to West, face East, say Adoration:*

12. Holy art Thou Lord of the Universe.
    Holy art Thou Whom nature hath not Formed.
    Holy art Thou the Vast and Mighty One.
    Lord of the Light and of the Darkness.

13. *Perform Lesser Invoking Ritual of the Hexagram of Mars, holding Wand by White Band. Give* ⑤ = 6 *Signs and analyse Key-Word.*
14. *Return to West of Altar.*
15. *Turn to face the direction in which you have found Mars to be — standing so that the Altar is between yourself and Mars for convenience.*
16. *Describe in the Air the Invoking Pentagram of Sign Mars is in.*
17. *Describe Invoking Hexagram of Mars, saying:* Elohim Gibor. *Then, still holding Wand by White Band,*
18. *Recite your Invocation to the power of Geburah and the Forces of Mars, tracing the Sigil of each as you read it.*

    O Mighty Power who governeth Geburah, Thou strong and terrible Divine *Elohim Gibor,* I beseech Thee to bestow upon this Magic Sword Power and Might to slay the evil and weakness I may encounter. In the Fiery Sphere of *Madim,* may it be welded and tempered to unswerving strength and fidelity. May Thy Great Archangel *Kamael* bestow upon me courage wherewith to use it aright and may The Powerful Angels of the Order of *Seraphim* scorch with their flames the feebleness of purpose which would hinder my search for the True Light.

19. *Then trace in the Air, slowly, above Sword, and as if standing upon it, the Invoking Hexagram of Mars. Do this with the Lotus end, still holding the White Band.*
20. *Next trace over the Sword the letters of the names in the invocation and their several Sigils.*

<65> 21. *Put down Wand.*

22. *Take up Cup and purify new Sword with Water, making Cross upon it; put down Cup.*
23. *Take up Incense and wave it over new Sword.*

24. *Take up new Sword and with it perform the Lesser Invoking Ritual of the Hexagram and also trace the Invoking Hexagram of Mars, repeating* Ararita *and* Elohim Gibor.
25. *Lay down Sword.*
26. *With Cup purify Chamber as before.*
27. *With Incense purify as before.*
28. *Reverse circumambulation three times and say:*
29. In the Name of Yeheshuah, I now set free all Spirits that may have been imprisoned by this Ceremony.
30. *Perform with the Sword the Lesser Banishing Ritual of Hexagram.*
31. *Perform Lesser Banishing Ritual of Pentagram.*
32. *Conclude with Qabalistic Prayer.*
33. *Wrap up Sword, white or scarlet silk or linen. Henceforth no one else may touch it.*

<66>

THE FOUR ELEMENTAL WEAPONS

These are the Tarot Symbols of the letters of the Divine Name Yhvh, and of the elements, and have a certain bond and sympathy between them. So that even if only one is to be used the others should be also present, even as each of the Four Elemental Tablets is divided in itself unto Four Lesser Angles representing the other three Elements bound together therewith in the same Tablet. Therefore also let the Z. A. M. remember that when he works with these forces he is as it were dealing with the Forces of the Letters of the Divine Name.

Each Implement must be consecrated, and when this has been done, no one else must touch it.

THE WAND FOR FIRE

The staff of the Wand should be of wood, rounded and smooth and perforated from end to end. Within it should be placed a magnetised steel rod, just so long as to project 1/16 inch beyond each end of the wood. It is often convenient to form the Wand of cane which has a natural hollow through it. If of cane, there should be three natural lengths according to the knots, so that these knots may be placed similarly to the manner in the figure which is such as a turner would produce.

Eighteen inches is an extreme length; (Note: That of the present writer is about ten inches long.—I.R.) The magnet would be a strong one. One end of the wood should be cone-shaped. The North end of the magnet, known by its repelling the so-called North Pole of a compass needle, should be placed at the end of the Wand which is plain.

The whole is coloured flame Scarlet, and is divided into three parts
by yellow bands. The cone-shaped end has also painted upon its red
<68> surface three wavy flame-shaped Yods as ornaments, they are paint-
ed bright yellow.

The Divine and Angelic Names of the Element of Fire should then be written in bright green paint along the shaft and on the cone. Their Sigils should be added and the motto of the Adeptus.

The Wand must then be consecrated. It is for all workings of the nature of Fire and under the presidency of Yod and of the "Wand of the Tarot."

THE CUP FOR WATER

Any convenient glass Cup may be adapted for this use. The bowl should be somewhat the shape of a crocus flower, and must show eight petals. A smooth glass cup is preferable unless it have eight cuts or ridges. These eight

<67> *Diagram 21*

THE SWORD AND ELEMENTAL WEAPONS

petals must be coloured bright blue; neither too pale nor too dark. They must be edged with bright orange colour. The colours must be clear and correct. The petals may be formed by paint or by coloured paper pasted on the glass.

The proper Divine and Angelic Names are then to be written upon the petals in Orange colour together with their Sigils from the Rose; then add the Motto of Adeptus. The Cup must then be consecrated. It is to be used in all workings of the nature of Water, and under the presidency of the letter Heh, and the "Cup of the Tarot."

THE DAGGER FOR AIR

Any convenient dagger or knife or sword may be adapted to the use; the shorter it is, the better.

The hilt and pommel and guard are to be coloured in bright pure yellow. The Divine and Angelic Names should be written upon the yellow background in purple or violet, together with their Sigils from the Rose, and the motto of the Adeptus.

It is to be used in all work of the Airy Nature, and under the presidency of Vau, and the "Sword of the Tarot."

<69> Let there be no confusion between the Magical Sword and the Air Dagger. The Magical Sword is under Geburah and is for strength and defence. The Air Dagger is for Air, for Vau of Yhvh, and is to be used with the three other Elemental Implements. They belong to different planes and any substitution of one for the other is harmful.

THE PENTACLE FOR EARTH

The Pantacle or Pentacle should be formed of a round disc of wood, about 4½ inches in diameter, and from ½ inch to 1 inch in thickness; nicely polished, and truly circular, and of even thickness.

There should be a circular white border and a white Hexagram on each face of the Disc. The space within the white border should be divided into four compartments by two diameters at right angles. These four compartments are to be coloured: the upper, Citrine; right, Olive-green; left, Russet-brown; lowest, Black.

The Divine and Angelic Names should be written in black round the white border; each name followed by its Sigil taken from the Rose. The motto of the Adeptus to be added.

The Pentacle should be the same on both sides, and should be held in the hand with the citrine uppermost; unless there is any special reason for using one of the other compartments. And in this matter remember that Citrine is the Airy part of Earth; Russet the Fiery; Olive the Watery; Black the Earthy part of Earth.

The Pentacle must then be consecrated.

It is then to be used in all work of the nature of Earth, and is under the presidency of Heh final, and of the "Pentacle of the Tarot."

<70> # RITUAL OF CONSECRATION
OF THE
FOUR ELEMENTAL WEAPONS

Provide Altar, Lamp, Cup, Salt, Incense and Rose, White Triangle, and Red Cross.

Four new implements. Fire Wand, Air Dagger, Water Cup, and Earth Pentacle. Magical Sword, Rose Cross, Lotus Wand, White Sash.

Drape and arrange Altar as in ⓪ = [0] Repast. Put on White Robe, Sash, and Rose Cross. Light the Lamp, put Water in the Cup, kindle the Incense.

Select time for the Ceremony during the course of the appropriate Tattwas.

(Note: The Angelic Names used in these rituals are names from the Angelic or Enochian Tablets. This whole subject is elucidated in the final section of this set of volumes.—I. R.)

1. *Take up the Lotus Wand by the Black portion, and say:*

   Hekas Hekas Este Bebeloi.

   Put down the Wand and take up the Magic Sword.
2. *Perform the Lesser Banishing Ritual of the Pentagram. Pass to the East to begin. Use Magic Sword.*
3. *Lay down Sword, and purify with Water, saying:*

   "So therefore first the Priest who governeth the works of Fire must sprinkle with the Lustral Water of the loud-resounding Sea."
4. *Consecrate with Fire, saying:*

   "And when, after all the Phantoms are vanished, thou shalt see that Holy formless Fire, that Fire which darts and flashes through the hidden depths of the Universe, hear thou the Voice of Fire."

<71>

5. *Take up the Lotus Wand by White portion.*
6. *Circumambulate with the Sun three times.*
7. *Repeat the Adoration, salute with the ⓪ = [0] Sign each time.*

   "Holy art thou, Lord of the Universe.
   Holy art Thou, whom Nature hath not Formed.
   Holy art Thou, the Vast and the Mighty One.
   Lord of the Light and of the Darkness."
8. *Varying with each Implement on different days, or 20 minutes between each commencement, according to Tattwas, perform Supreme Invoking Ritual of the Pentagram of the particular elemental Implement with Lotus Wand, holding it by appropriate band of Kerubic Figure.*
9. *With the Lotus Wand in thy hand, and standing by the Altar and facing the Quarter of the Element whose Implement you are consecrating, describe in the Air over the Implement, as if standing upon it, the Invoking Pentagram of that Implement.*
10. *Invocate the Divine and Angelic Names already graven upon the Implement,*

making their letters and Sigils in the Air, over the Implement with the Lotus.

"O Thou, Who art from everlasting, Thou Who hast created all things, and doth clothe Thyself with the Forces of Nature as with a garment, by Thy Holy and Divine Name

For Pentacle	Adonai	אדני
For Dagger	Yhvh	יהוה
For Cup	El	אל
For Wand	Elohim	אלהים

whereby Thou art known especially in that quarter we name

For Pentacle and Earth	Tzaphon צפון	North
For Dagger and Air	Mizrach מזרח	East
For Cup and Water	Mearab מערב	West
For Wand and Fire	Darom דרום	South

<72> I beseech Thee to grant unto me strength and insight for my search after the Hidden Light and Wisdom.

I entreat Thee to cause Thy Wonderful Archangel

For Pentacle	Auriel	אוריאל	Who governeth the works of Earth
For Dagger	Raphiel	רפאל	Who governeth the works of Air
For Cup	Gabriel	גבריאל	Who governeth the works of Water
For Wand	Michael	מיכאל	Who governeth the works of Fire

to guide me in the Pathway; and furthermore to direct Thine Angel

For Pentacle	Phorlakh	פורלאך
For Dagger	Chassan	חשן
For Cup	Taliahad	טליהד
For Wand	Aral	אראל

To watch over my footsteps therein.

May the Ruler of *(name element)* the Powerful Prince

For Pentacle and Earth	Kerub	כרוב
For Dagger and Air	Ariel	אריאל
For Cup and Water	Tharsis	תרשים
For Wand and Fire	Seraph	שרף

by the gracious premission of the Infinite Supreme, increase and strengthen the hidden forces and occult virtues of this *(name implement)* so that I may be enabled with it to perform aright those Magical operations, for which it has been fashioned. For which purpose I now perform this mystic rite of Consecration in the Divine Presence of

For Pentacle	Adonai	אדני
For Dagger	Yhvh	יהוה
For Cup	El	אל
For Wand	Elohim	אלהים

<73> 11. *Lay aside the Lotus Wand.*

12. *Take up the Magic Sword, and read the Invocation to the King, tracing in the Air the Invoking Pentagram of the Element.*

"In the Three Great Secret Holy Names of God borne upon the Banners of the

For Pentacle and Earth	North	Emor Dial Hectega
For Dagger and Air	East	Oro Ibah Aozpi
For Cup and Water	West	Empeh Arsel Gaiol
For Wand and Fire	South	Oip Teaa Pedoce

I summon Thee, Thou Great King of the

For Pentacle	North	Ic Zod Heh Chal
For Dagger	East	Bataivah
For Cup	West	Ra Agiosel
For Wand	South	Edel Pernaa

to attend upon this Ceremony and by Thy presence increase its effect, whereby I do now consecrate this Magical *(name implement)*. Confer upon it the utmost occult might and virtue of which Thou mayest judge it to be capable in all works of the nature of *(name element)* so that in it I may find a strong defence and a powerful weapon wherewith to rule and direct the Spirits of the Elements."

13. *Still with the Sword, trace in the Air over the Implement the Hexagram of Saturn, and read the Invocation to the Six Seniors.*

"Ye Mighty Princes of the *(name Quadrangle)* Quadrangle, I invoke you who are known to me by the honourable title, and position of rank, of Seniors. Hear my petition, oh ye mighty Princes, the Six Seniors of the *(same point)* quarter of the Earth who bear the names of:

🜃 Laidrom Alphctga Aczinor Ahmlicv Lzinopo Liiansa
🜁 Habioro Ahaozpi Aaozaif Avtotar Htmorda Hipotga
🜄 Lsrahpm Slgaiol Saiinor Soniznt Laoaxrp Ligdisa
🜂 Aaetpoi Aapdoce Adoeoet Anodoin Alndvod Arinnap

and be this day present with me. Bestow upon this *(name weapon)* the
<74> Strength and purity whereof ye are Masters in the Elemental Forces which ye control; that its outward and material form may remain a true symbol of the inward and spiritual force."

14. *Then read the Invocations of the Angels governing the Four Lesser Angles. During each, make the Invoking Pentagram of the Element whose implement is being consecrated. Cup, Wand, Dagger, or Pentacle, according to which lesser angle is in Process, making the Pentagram in the air immediately over the Implement with the Sword.*

FIRE WAND

Lesser Angle of Fire. "Oh Thou Mighty Angel Bziza who art Ruler and President over the Four Angels of the Fiery Lesser Quadrangle of Fire, I invocate Thee to impress into this weapon the force and fiery energy of Thy Kingdom and Servants, that by it I may control them for all just and righteous purposes.

With the Sword, trace invoking Fire Pentagram with Lion Kerub.

Lesser Angle of Water: O Thou mighty Angel Banaa, Ruler and President over the Four Angels of Fluid Fire, I beseech Thee to impress into this weapon Thy Magic Power that by it I may control the Spirits who serve Thee for all just and righteous purposes.

With the Cup, trace invoking Fire Pentagram.

Lesser Angle of Air: Oh Thou Mighty Angel Bdopa, Ruler and President over the Four Angels and Governors of the subtle and aspiring Etheric Fire, I beseech Thee to bestow upon this weapon Thy strength and fiery steadfastness, that with it I may control the Spirits of Thy Realm for all just and righteous purposes.

Trace Invoking Fire Pentagram with the Dagger.

Lesser Angle of Earth: O Thou Mighty Angel Bpsac, who art Ruler and President over the Four Angels of the denser Fire of Earth, I beseech Thee
<75> to bestow upon this weapon Thy strength and fiery steadfastness that with it I may control the Spirits of Thy realm for all just and righteous purposes.

Trace Invoking Fire Pentagram with Pentacle.

WATER CUP

Lesser Angle of Fire: O Thou Powerful Angel Hnlrx, Thou who are Lord and Ruler over the Fiery Waters, I beseech Thee to endue this Cup with the Magic Powers of which Thou art Lord, that I may with its aid direct the Spirits who serve Thee in purity and singleness of aim.

With Wand trace invoking Water Pentagram with Eagle Kerub.

Lesser Angle of Water: O Thou Powerful Angel Htdim, Thou who art Lord and Ruler over the pure and fluid Element of Water, I beseech Thee to endue this Cup with the Magic Powers of which Thou art Lord, that I may with its aid direct the Spirits who serve Thee in purity and singleness of aim.

With Sword trace invoking Water Pentagram.

Lesser Angle of Air: O Thou Powerful Angel Htaad, Thou who art Lord and Ruler of the Etheric and Airy Qualities of Water, I beseech Thee to endue this Cup with the Magic Powers of which Thou art Lord, that I may with its aid direct the Spirits who serve Thee in purity and singleness of aim.

With Dagger trace invoking Water Pentagram.

Lesser Angle of Earth: O Thou Powerful Angel Hmagl, Thou who art Lord and Ruler of the more dense and solid qualities of Water, I beseech Thee to endue this Cup with the Magic Powers of which Thou art Lord, that with its aid I may direct the Spirits who serve Thee in purity and singleness of aim.

With Pentacle trace invoking Water Pentagram.

<76>

AIR DAGGER

Lesser Angle of Fire: O Thou Resplendent Angel Exgsd, Thou who governest the Fiery Realms of Air, I conjure Thee to confer upon this Dagger, Thy Mysterious and Magical Powers, that I thereby may control the Spirits who serve Thee for such purposes as be pure and upright.

With the Wand trace invoking Air Pentagram with Aquarius as Kerubic emblem.

Lesser Angle of Water: O Thou Resplendent Angel Eytpa, Thou who governest the Realms of Fluid Air, I conjure Thee to confer upon this Dagger, Thy Mysterious Powers that by its aid I may control the Spirits who serve Thee for such purposes as be pure and upright.

With the Cup trace invoking Air Pentagram.

Lesser Angle of Air: O Thou Resplendent Angel Erzla, Thou who rulest the Realms of Pure and Permeating Air, I conjure Thee to confer upon this Dagger the Magic Power of which Thou art Master, whereby I may control the Spirits who serve Thee, for such purposes as be pure and upright.

With the Sword trace invoking Air Pentagram.

Lesser Angle of Earth: O Thou Resplendent Angel Etnbr, Thou who rulest the Denser Realms of Air symbolised by the Lesser Angle of Earth, I conjure Thee to confer upon this Dagger the Magic Powers of which Thou art Master, whereby I may control the spirits who serve Thee, for such purposes as be pure and upright.

With the Pentacle trace invoking Air Pentagram.

EARTH PENTACLE

Lesser Angle of Fire: O Thou Glorious Angel Naaom, Thou who governest the Fiery essences of Earth, I invocate Thee to bestow upon this Pentacle the Magic Powers of which thou art Sovereign, that by its help I may
<77> govern the Spirits of Whom Thou art Lord, in all seriousness and steadfastness.

With Wand over Russet, trace invoking Earth Pentagram with Taurus Kerub.

Lesser Angle of Water: O Thou Glorious Angel Nphra, Thou who governest the moist and fluid essences of Earth, I invocate Thee to bestow upon this Pentacle the Magic Powers of which Thou art Sovereign that by its help I may govern the Spirits, of whom Thou art Lord, in all seriousness and steadfastness.

With Cup over Olive part, trace invoking Pentagram.

Lesser Angle of Air: O Thou Glorious Angel Nboza, Thou who governest the Airy and Delicate Essence of Earth, I invocate Thee to bestow upon this Pentacle the Magic Powers of which Thou art Master, that with its help I may govern the spirits of whom Thou art Lord, in all seriousness and steadfastness.

With Dagger over Citrine part, trace invoking Earth Pentagram.

Lesser Angle of Earth: O Thou Glorious Angel Nroam, Thou who governest the dense and solid Earth, I invocate Thee to bestow upon this Pentacle the Magic Powers of which Thou art Master, that with its help I may govern the spirits of whom Thou art Lord, in all seriousness and steadfastness.

With Sword over Black part, trace invoking Earth Pentagram.

15. *Then take up the newly consecrated Implement and perform with it the Supreme Invoking Ritual of the Pentagram of its Element in the Four Quarters, preceding each Pentagram with the Equilibriating Pentagram suitable, and reciting the*

Divine Name. Close with Qabalistic Cross and Prayer. When completed each Implement is to be wrapped in silk or linen, white, or suitable colour.

<78> 16. *Purify with water, repeating verse as in opening.*

17. *Consecrate with Fire, repeating the verse as in opening.*

18. *Reverse Circumambulation.*
19. *Stand at West of Altar, and say,*
    "In the name of Yeheshuah, I now set free any Spirits that may have been imprisoned by this ceremony."
20. *Perform the Lesser Banishing Ritual of Pentagram in 4 Quarters.*
21. *If preferred, the Supreme Banishing Ritual of Pentagram of special element, if one or two or three Implements have been consecrated and not all four at same ceremony.*

(Note: When tracing the Pentagrams over the Implement to be consecrated, remember that the same Pentagram is traced but each time with another of the weapons. In the consecration of the Cup, the Water Pentagram is the only one used, but it is traced using the Sword and the other implements. This is mentioned so that, for example, the student will not use different Pentagrams traced with different weapons when consecrating one implement.—*I. R.)*

BOOK FIVE

(Composed of Golden Dawn Official Documents Labelled Z.1., Z.2., and Z.3.)

<81> Z. 1

THE ENTERER OF THE THRESHOLD

The General Exordium

The Speech in the Silence:
The Words against the Son of Night:
The Voice of Thoth* before the Universe in the presence of the eternal Gods:
The Formulas of Knowledge:
The Wisdom of Breath:
The Radix of Vibration;
The Shaking of the Invisible:
The Rolling Asunder of the Darkness:
The Becoming Visible of Matter:
The Piercing of the Coils of the Stooping Dragon:
The Breaking forth of the Light:
All these are in the Knowledge of Tho-oth.

The Particular Exordium

At the Ending of the Night: At the Limits of the Light: Tho-oth stood before the Unborn Ones of Time!
Then was formulated the Universe:
Then came forth the Gods thereof:
The Aeons of the Bornless Beyond:
Then was the Voice vibrated:
Then was the Name declared.
At the Threshold of the Entrance,
Between the Universe and the Infinite,
In the Sign of the Enterer, stood Tho-oth,
As before him were the Aeons proclaimed.
<82> In Breath did he vibrate them:
In Symbols did he record them:
For betwixt the Light and the Darkness did he stand.

The complete explanation of the symbolism of, and the Formulae contained in, the $\textcircled{0} = \boxed{0}$ Grade of Neophyte of the Order of the Golden Dawn.

"Enterer of the Threshold" is the name of the $\textcircled{0} = \boxed{0}$ Grade of Neo-

*Note that there are Three basic forms of Thoth, . . . first, Thoth the Speaker of the Work (and Word) of the Universe. He thus stands at Kether, the Tree of Life being his Speech. The second is the Thoth we see in Hod, as messenger from beyond the Abyss, (there is a conscious play on words here). The third is the sexual or generative Moon God, who stands in Yesod, (the Sphere of the Moon), in the sign of the Enterer, leaning forward over the Thirty-Second Path, called, in the Tarot, "The Universe." H.S.

phyte. "The Hall of the Neophytes" is called "The Hall of the Dual Manifestation of Truth," that is of the Goddess *Thmaah,* whose name has three forms according to the nature of her operation. This is explained under the chapter concerning the Hegemon.

Of the Temple in Reference to the Sephiroth. The Temple, as arranged in the Neophyte Grade of the Order of the Golden Dawn in the Outer, is placed looking towards the Yh of Yhvh in Malkuth in Assiah. That is, as *Y* and *H* answer unto the Sephiroth Chokmah and Binah in the Tree, (and unto Abba and Aima, through whose knowledge alone that of Kether may be obtained) even so, the Sacred Rites of the Temple may gradually, and as it were, in spite of himself, lead the Neophyte unto the knowledge of his Higher Self. Like the other Sephiroth, Malkuth hath also its subsidiary Sephiroth and Paths. Of these Ten Sephiroth, the Temple as arranged in the Neophyte Grade, includeth only the four lower Sephiroth in the Tree of Life, viz: Malkuth, Yesod, Hod, and Netzach, and the *Outer* side of Paroketh, the Veil. Paroketh formeth the East of the Temple. First in importance cometh the symbolism of the East.

The Three Chiefs who govern and rule all things, the Viceroys in the Temple of the unknown Second Order beyond, are the reflections therein of the Powers of Chesed, Geburah and Tiphareth. They represent: the Imperator — Geburah and the Grade ⑥ = [5]: the Praemonstrator — Chesed and the Grade ⑦ = [4]: the Cancellarius — Tiphareth and the Grade ⑤ = [6].

<83> Now the Imperator governeth, because in Netzach, which is the highest Grade of the First Order, ④ = [7], is the Fire reflected from Geburah.* The Praemonstrator is Second, because in Hod, which is the next highest Grade, ③ = [8], is the Water reflected from Chesed. The Third is the Cancellarius, because in Yesod, ② = [9], is the Air reflected from Tiphareth. Thus the Order is governed by a Triad, one in intention but having different functions: the Imperator to command: the Praemonstrator to instruct: the Cancellarius to record.

The proper mantle of Office of the Imperator is the flame scarlet Robe of Fire and Severity, as on him do the energy and stability of the Temple depend: and if he has sub-Officers to assist him, they partake of his symbolism. His Mantle is the symbol of unflinching Authority, compelling the obedience of the Temple to *all commands* issued by the Second Order; and upon the left breast thereof, is the Cross and Triangle of the Golden Dawn, both white, representing the purification of the Temple in the Outer Order by Fire. He may wear a Lamen similar to that of Hierophant, of the same colours, but depending from a scarlet collar, and he may bear a Sword similar to that of Hiereus. His place in the Temple is at the extreme right of the Dais and at the Equinox he takes the Throne of Hierophant when that Office is vacated.

*Note: This reflection is passed from Geburah into the Imperator, Fire being the "Head" of the God-Name of Jehovah, i.e. Yod, Heh, Vau and Heh Final. Likewise, the Outer Order follows this Elemental Ordering, consisting of itself, the body of the Demiurge, with Netzach being the upper-most of the four elemental grades, corresponding to FIRE. This is clearly an intentional ritual ranking, as the new Philosophus is told at the conclusion of his or her initiation . . . "You are, as having risen so high in the Order, to . . . aid . . . the Members of the Second Order . . . also to supervise the studies of the . . . less advanced brethren, . . ." (Book Three, p. 150) H.S.

The proper Mantle of Office of the Praemonstrator is the bright blue Robe of Water, representing the reflection of the Wisdom and Knowledge of Chesed. His duty is that of Teacher and Instructor of the Temple, always limited by his Obligation to keep secret the Knowledge of the Second Order from the Outer Order. He superintends the working of the Outer Order, seeing that in it nothing be relaxed or profaned; and duly issues to the Temple any instruction regarding the Ritual received by him from the Greatly Honoured Chiefs of the Second Order. He is therefore to the Temple the Reflector of the Wisdom beyond. His sub-officers partake of his sym-
<84> bolism. The White Cross and Triangle on his left Breast on the Robe
represents the purification of the Outer Order by Water. He may wear a Lamen like that of Hierophant, but blue upon an orange field and depending from a collar of blue. He may bear a Sceptre surmounted by a Maltese Cross in the Elemental Colours.

The proper Mantle of Office of the Cancellarius is the yellow Robe of Air. Upon him depend the Records of the Temple, the order of its working, the arrangements of its Meetings and the circulation of its manuscripts. He is the Recorder and, more immediately than either of the preceding Chiefs, the Representative of the executive authority of the Second Order over the Outer. His duty is to see that in *no* case knowledge of a Grade be given to a Member who has not properly attained to it. He is the immediate circulator of all *communications* from the Second Order. His sub-officers partake of his symbolism. His White Cross and Triangle represent the purification of the Outer Order by Air. Cancellarius may wear a Lamen like that of Hierophant, but of yellow on a purple field, and depending from a purple Collar; and he may bear a Sceptre surmounted by a Hexagram of amber and gold.

The Sceptres of the Chiefs should be of the same colour as their Mantles, with a gold band to represent Tiphareth, being the first Grade of the Inner Order. The Sword of Imperator should have a plain scarlet hilt, with gold or brass mountings, while the Sceptre of Praemonstrator should be blue with a gold band. The proper seat of the Chiefs is beside the Hierophant, and if desired the Imperator and Cancellarius may be seated to the right and Praemonstrator and Immediate Past Hierophant to his left — the Calcellarius and Immediate Past Hierophant being nearest to the Hierophant on their respective sides. The Chiefs stand before the Veil in the East of the Temple, as the Representatives of the Inner Order and therefore no meeting can be held without one of them. Preferably all Three Chiefs should be present.
<85> The other Officers of the Temple exist only by their authority and
permission.

Because the East of the Temple is the outer side of Paroketh, all Members of the Second Order wear the *Crossed Sashes* of a Lord of the Paths of the Portal of the Vault only — no higher Grade being allowed to be shown in a Temple of the First Order. Members of the Second Order should be seated in the East of the Temple when practicable. Any Past Hierophant may wear a Mantle of a Hierophant and a Jewel of that Lamen, but not a large Collar Lamen. Immediate Past Hierophant may have a Sceptre of a Hierophant.

The Chiefs, or Members asked to represent them on the Dais, wear white gowns. The cords and tassels of all Mantles of Chiefs or Officers should be white to symbolise spiritual purity and influence of the Divine and Shining Light. Members of the Outer Order wear a black gown or tunic, with a Sash indicating their Grade across it. The Black Sash crosses from the left shoulder (from the side of the Black Pillar, as they first received it), and the White Sash from the Right shoulder.

Egyptian Head-Dresses, or Nemysses are worn by the Chiefs and Officers, those of the Chiefs being of the Colour of their Mantles striped with the complementary colour; those of the Officers being striped equally black and white. Members may wear similar nemysses in black and white or plain black squares of approved pattern.

The Key to the formation of the tunic and nemyss is the Crux Ansata for the nemyss makes the oval, and the arms and body of the tunic, the cross.

THE SYMBOLISM OF THE TEMPLE

The Bases of the two Pillars are respectively in Netzach and Hod; the White Pillar being in Netzach and the Black Pillar in Hod. They represent the Two Pillars of Mercy and Severity. The bases are cubical and black to
<86> represent the Earth Element in Malkuth. The columns are respectively black and white to represent the manifestation of the Eternal Balance of the Scales of Justice. Upon them should be represented in counterchanged colour any appropriate Egyptian designs, emblematic of the Soul.

The scarlet tetra-hedonal capitals represent the Fire of Test and Trial: and between the Pillars is the porchway of the Region Immeasurable. The twin lights which burn on their summits are "The Declarers of the Eternal Truth." The bases of the tetrahedra, being triangular, that on the white pillar points East, while that on the Black points West. They thus complete the Hexagram of Tiphareth — though separate, as is fitting in "The Hall of the Dual Manifestation of Truth."

The Altar, whose form is that of a double cube, is placed in the Eastern part of Malkuth, as far as the Neophyte is concerned. But to the Adeptus Minor, its blackness will veil on the East Citrine, on the South olive, on the North russet, while the West side alone, and the base, will be black, while the summit is of a brilliant whiteness.

The Symbols upon the Altar represent the Forces and Manifestation of the Divine Light, concentrated in the White Triangle of the Three Supernals as the synthesis; wherefore, upon this sacred and sublime Symbol, is the obligation of the Neophyte taken as calling therein to witness the Forces of the Divine Light.

The Red Cross of Tiphareth (to which the Grade of 5 = 6 is referred) is here placed above the White Triangle, not as dominating it, but as bringing it down and manifesting it unto the Outer Order; as though The Crucified One, having raised the symbol of self-sacrifice, had thus touched and brought into action in matter, the Divine Triad of Light.

Around the Cross are the Symbols of the Four Letters of the Name Jehovah — the Shin of Yeheshuah being only *implied* and not expressed in the Outer Order. At the East is the Mystical Rose, allied by its scent to
<87> the Element of Air. At the South is the Red Lamp, allied by its Flame

with the Element of Fire. At the West is the Cup of Wine, allied by its fluid form to the Element of Water. At the North are Bread and Salt, allied by their substance to the Element of Earth.

The Elements are placed upon the Altar according to the Winds.

"For Osiris on-Nophris who is found perfect before the Gods, hath said:
'These are the Elements of my Body,
Perfected through Suffering, Glorified through Trial.
For the scent of the Dying Rose is as the repressed Sigh of my suffering:
And the flame-red Fire as the Energy of mine Undaunted Will:
And the Cup of Wine is the pouring out of the Blood of my Heart:
Sacrificed unto Regeneration, unto the Newer Life:
And the bread and Salt are as the Foundations of my Body,
Which I destroy in order that they may be renewed.
For I am Osiris Triumphant, even Osiris on-Nophris, the Justified:
I am He who is clothed with the Body of Flesh,
Yet in whom is the Spirit of the Great Gods:
I am The Lord of Life, triumphant over Death.
He who partaketh with me shall arise with me:
I am the Manifestor in Matter of Those Whose Abode is the Invisible:
I am purified: I stand upon the Universe:
I am its Reconciler with the Eternal Gods:
I am the Perfector of Matter:
And without me, the Universe is not.' "

Technically, the Door is supposed to be situated behind the seat of Hiereus in the West; but it may be in any part of the Hall, seeing that the walls represent the Barrier to the Exterior. "The Gate of the Declarers of <88> Judgment" is its name — and its symbolic form is that of a straight and narrow Doorway, between two Mighty Pylons. "The Watcher against the Evil Ones" is the name of the Sentinel who guards it and his form is the symbolic one of Anubis.

THE STATIONS OF THE OFFICERS

The Hierophant is placed in the East of the Temple, on the outer side of the Veil Paroketh, to rule the Temple under the Presidency of the Chiefs. There he fills the place of a Lord of the Paths of the Portal of the Vault of the Adepts, acting as Inductor to the Sacred Mysteries. The Insignia and Symbols of Hierophant are:

The Throne of the East in the Path of Samekh, outside the Veil.
The Mantle (or Cloak. See pg. 111, Vol. III) of bright flame scarlet, bearing a white cross on the left breast.
The Lamen suspended from a white Collar.
The Crown-headed Sceptre.
The Banner of the East.

The position of the Throne on the Path Samekh is fitting for the Inductor to the Mysteries, as there being placed in that balanced and central position of that Path by which alone is safe entrance to the mystical knowledge of the Light in Tiphareth. Being placed before Paroketh at the point of its rending, it there marks the shining forth of the Light through the Veil; and that translation of the Three Supernals to the Outer Order, which is represented by the red Calvary Cross and the White Triangle upon the Altar. Thus the station of Hierophant's Throne, fitly represents the Rising of the Sun of Life and Light upon our Order.

The Robe of scarlet represents the flaming energy of the Divine Light, shining forth into infinite Worlds. Upon the left breast is a White Cross to represent purification unto the Light, and this Cross may be one of the following forms:—

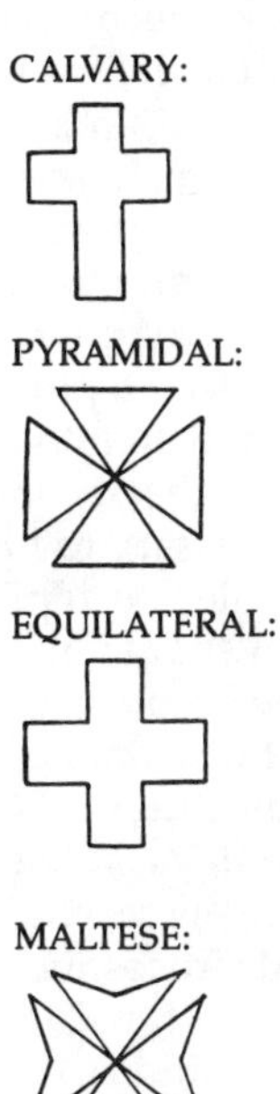

In which case it alludes ei-
<89> ther to the cross of six
squares of Tiphareth or to
the Cross of the Rivers.

The Cross of the Elements, to represent the descent of the Divine and Angelic Forces into the pyramid symbol.

A Cross of the Elements, symbolising their purification through the Light of the Four-lettered Name Yhvh in Tiphareth.

The Cross of Four arrowheads, representing the keen and swift impact of the Light, coming from behind the Veil, through the Elements symbolised by the arrow of Sagittarius in the Path Samekh.

It is indifferent which of the Crosses be employed, seeing that each represents the operation of the Light through the Veil.

The Sceptre represents the forces of the Middle Pillar. It is scarlet with
gold bands to represent the places of the Sephiroth Daath, Tiphareth
<90> and Yesod, the pommel being Malkuth. The shaft represents the
Paths Gimel, Samekh and Tau. The Grip by which it is wielded, is the
path Tau, representing the Universe governed by and attracting the forces of the Light. The Names of Sephiroth and Paths are not marked thereon, but the Hierophant Initiate of the Second Order should remember the sublimity of the symbolism while he wields it. It represents him as touching thereby the Divine Light of Kether and attracting it through the Middle Pillar to Malkuth. It is called "The Sceptre of Power" and invests him with the power of declar-

ing the Temple Open or Closed in any Grade, if time be short, and this is done by saying: "By the power in me vested by this Sceptre, I declare this Temple duly opened (or closed)."

This method of Opening and Closing "by Sceptre" should only be used in great emergency where time presses. It should not be used in a Ceremony Elemental Spirits have been invoked — especially not in the Closing.

The Lamen is partially explained in the Portal Ceremony thus: "The Hierophant's Lamen is a synthesis of Tiphareth, to which the Calvary cross of six squares, forming the cube opened out, is fitly referred. The two colours, red and green, the most active and the most passive, whose conjunction points out the practical application of the knowledge of equilibrium, are symbolic of the reconciliation of the celestial essences of Fire and Water. For the reconciling yellow unites with blue in green, which is the complementary colour to red, and with red in orange which is the complementary colour to blue. The small inner circle placed upon the Cross alludes to the Rose that is conjoined therewith in the symbolism of the Rose and Cross of our Order." But in addition to this, it represents the blazing light of the Fire of the Sun bringing into being the green vegetation of the otherwise barren Earth. And
also the power of self-sacrifice requisite in one who would essay to
<91> initiate into the Sacred Mysteries. So as the Sceptre represents the
Authority and Power of the Light, the Lamen affirms the qualifications necessary to him who wields it, and therefore is it suspended from a white collar, to represent the Purity of the White Brilliance from Kether. Hence it should always be worn by the Hierophant.

The Banner of the East is also partially explained in the Portal:—"The field of the Banner of the East is White, the colour of light and purity. As in the previous case, the Calvary Cross of six squares is the number of six of Tiphareth, the yellow Cross of Solar Gold, and the cubical stone, bearing in its centre the sacred Tau of Life, and having bound together upon it the form of the Macrocosmic Hexagram, the red triangle of Fire and the blue triangle of Water — the Ruach Elohim and the Waters of Creation."

In addition to this explanation, it affirms the Mode of Action employed by the Divine Light in its operation by the Forces of Nature. Upon it is the symbol of the Macrocosm so coloured as to affirm the action of the Fire of the Spirit through the Waters of Creation under the harmony of the Golden Cross of the Reconciler. Within the centre of the Hexagram is a Tau cross in White, to represent its action as a Triad; and the whole is placed on a white field representing the Ocean of the Ain Soph Aour. The Banner is suspended from a gold coloured bar by red cords, and the pole and base should be white. The base represents the purity of the foundation — the shaft, the Purified Will directed to the Higher. The golden cross-bar is that whereon the Manifested Law of Perfection rests; the Banner itself, the Perfect Law of the Universe, the red cords and tassels the Divine Self-renunciation, Whose trials and sufferings form, as it were, the Ornament of the Completed Work. The whole represents the ascent of the Initiate into Perfect Knowledge of the Light — therefore in the address of the Hiereus the Neophyte hears "Even
the Banner of the East sinks in Adoration before Him," as though that
<92> symbol, great and potent though it be, were yet but an inferior pre-

sentment of the Higher, fitted to our comprehension.

"Expounder of the Sacred Mysteries" is the name of the Hierophant, and he is "Osiris" (Aeshoorist) in the Nether World. (St added as a suffix to a name indicates the influence from Kether.)

The Station of Hiereus is at the extreme West of the Temple and in the lowest point of Malkuth where he is enthroned in its darkest part, in the quarter represented black in the Minutum Mundum Diagram. Representing a Terrible and Avenging God at the Confines of Matter, at the borders of the Qlippoth, he is enthroned upon Matter and robed in Darkness, and about his feet are Thunder and Lightning — the impact of the Paths of Shin and Qoph — Fire and Water, terminating respectively in the russet and olive quarters of Malkuth. There, therefore, is he placed as a mighty and avenging Guardian to the Sacred Mysteries. The Symbols and Insignia of Hiereus are:

The Throne of the West in the Black of Malkuth, where it borders on the Kingdom of Shells,
The Black Robe of Darkness, bearing a white cross on the left breast;
The Sword of Strength and Severity;
The Lamen suspended from a Scarlet Collar.
The Banner of the West.

The position of the Throne of the West at the limits of Malkuth is fitting for the Avenger of the Gods, for he is placed there in eternal affirmation against the Evil Ones — "Hitherto shall ye come and no further." The Throne is also placed there as a seat of witness and of punishment decreed against Evil.

The Robe or Mantle is of Darkness, threatening and terrible to the Outer, as concealing an avenging Force ever ready to break forth against the Evil Ones. On the left breast is a white Cross to represent the Purification
<93> of Matter unto the Light. The Sword represents the Forces of the Pillar of Severity as a whole, but the places of the Sephiroth are not necessarily indicated thereon. The guard is Hod and may be of brass; the Grip is the Path of Shin and may be of scarlet, and the pommel, Malkuth, may be black. The grip by which it is wielded, being the Path Shin, represents the Universe governed by the flaming force of Severity, and represents the Hiereus as wielding the Forces of Divine Severity. "The Sword of Vengeance" is its name.

The Lamen is partially explained in the Portal thus: "The Outer Circle includes the four Sephiroth, Tiphareth, Netzach, Hod, and Yesod, of which the first three mark the angles of the triangle inscribed within, while the connecting Paths Nun, Ayin, and Peh form its sides. In the extreme centre is the Path Samekh through which is the passage for the Rending of the Veil. It is therefore a fitting Lamen for Hiereus as representing the connecting Link between the First and Second Orders, while the white triangle established in the surrounding Darkness is circumscribed in its turn by the Circle of Light." In addition to this explanation, the Lamen represents "The Light that shineth in Darkness though the Darkness comprehendeth it not." It affirms the possibility of the Redemption from Evil and even that of Evil itself, through self-sacrifice. It is suspended from a scarlet Collar as representing its dependence on the Force of Divine Severity over-awing the evil. It is a symbol of tremendous Strength and Fortitude, and is a synthesis of the Office of Hiereus as regards the Temple, as opposed to his Office as regards the outer world. For these reasons it should always be worn by Hiereus.

The Banner of the West completes the symbols of Hiereus. It is thus explained in the Zelator Grade: "The White Triangle refers to the three Paths connecting Malkuth with the other Sephiroth; while the red cross is the Hidden Knowledge of the Divine Nature which is to be obtained through their aid. The Cross and Triangle together represent Life and Light." In
<94> addition to this explanation from the Zelator Grade, it represents
eternally the possibility of Rescuing the Evil; but in it the Tiphareth cross is placed *within* the White Triangle of the Supernals as thereby representing that Sacrifice as made only unto the Higher. The red Cross may be bordered with gold in this instance, to represent the Perfect Metal obtained in and through the Darkness of Putrefaction. Black is its field which thus represents the Darkness and Ignorance of the Outer, while the White Triangle is again the Light which shineth in the Darkness but which is not comprehended thereby. Therefore is the Banner of the West the symbol of Twilight — as it were the equation of Light and Darkness. The pole and the base are black, to represent that even in the Depths of Evil can that symbol stand. The cord is black, but the transverse bar and the lance-point may be golden or brass and the tassles scarlet as in the case of the Banner of the East, and for the same reasons.

The Banner of the West, *when it changes its position in the Temple,* represents that which bars and threatens, and demands fresh sacrifice ere the Path leading to the Higher be attained.*

"Avenger of the Gods" is the name of Hiereus, and he is "Horus in the Abode of Blindness unto, and Ignorance of, the Higher." Hoor is his name.

The Station of Hegemon is between the Two Pillars whose bases are in Netzach and Hod, at the intersection of the Paths Peh and Samekh, in the symbolic Gateway of Occult Science — as it were, at the Beam of the Balance, at the Equilibrium of the Scales of Justice; at the point of intersection of the Lowest Reciprocal Path with that of Samekh, which forms a part of the Middle Pillar. She is placed there as the Guardian of the Threshold of Entrance and the Preparer of the Way for the Enterer — therefore the Recon-
<95> ciler between Light and Darkness, and the Mediator between the
Stations of Hierophant and Hiereus. The Symbols and Insignia of Hegemon are:

The Robe of Pure Whiteness, bearing on the left breast a Red Cross.
The Mitre Headed Sceptre.
The Lamen suspended from a Black Collar.

The Robe represents the Spiritual Purity which is required in the Aspirant to the Mysteries and without which qualification none can pass between the Eternal Pillars. It represents the Divine Light which is attracted thereby and brought to the aid of the Candidate. It symbolises the Self-

*The White Triangle is the Supernals which lay beyond the Abyss from which No-One returns, because the only entry to resurrection is Death . . . without compromise or abridgement. The East is our Horizon. The West, the Horizon of the Gods Gone Utterly Beyond. All that *can* die, *must* die before the eternal can be expressed. H.S.

Sacrifice that is offered for another to aid him in the attainment of the Light. It also signifies the atonement of error, the Preparer of the Pathway unto the Divine. Upon the left Breast is a Cross, usually the Calvary form, of red to represent the energy of the lower Will, purified and subjected to that which is Higher — and thus is the Office of Hegemon especially that of the Reconciler.

The Mitre-Headed Sceptre is the distinctive ensign of Office of Hegemon. On the Tree of Life it represents the forces of the Pillar of Mercy. It should be of scarlet with gold bands and pommel. The bands represent the places of the Sephiroth Chesed and Netzach — the shaft being formed by the Paths Vau and Kaph, the grip by which it is wielded being the Path Qoph, while the pommel is Malkuth. The Mitre is gold with red mountings and each point terminates in a ball. The mitre is charged with a red calvary cross of Six squares. This Mitre represents the Wisdom of Chokmah as a duplicated aspect of Kether, attracted by the symbol of self-sacrifice. The Sceptre is wielded by the forces of Flux and Reflux, shown by the grip being referred to the Path Qoph, and it represents the attraction into the Universe of the Forces of Divine Mercy. The Sephiroth and Paths are marked only as bands, and owing to its meaning, should be carried by Hegemon in all conduct-
<96> ing of the Candidate, as representing to the latter the attraction of the Forces of his Higher Self. It is called "The Sceptre of Wisdom."

The Lamen is explained in part in the Grade of Philosophus thus: "The peculiar emblem of the Hegemon is the Calvary Cross of Six Squares within a Circle. This Cross embraces Tiphareth, Netzach, Hod and Yesod, and rests upon Malkuth. Also the Calvary Cross of Six Squares forms the cube and is thus referred to the Six Sephiroth of Microprosopus which are Chesed, Geburah, Tiphareth, Netzach, Hod and Yesod."

In addition to this explanation, it represents the black Calvary Cross of Suffering as the Initiator by Trial and Self-Abnegation, and the Opener of the Way into the Comprehension of the Forces of the Divine Light. It is therefore suspended from a black Collar to show that Suffering is the Purgation of Evil.

"Before the Face of the Gods in the Place of the Threshold" is the name of Hegemon, and she is the Goddess Thma-Ae-St having the following Coptic forms:

Thma-Ae-St — This as regards the Middle Pillar and the influence from Kether.

Thma-aesh — This more Fiery as regards her influence with respect to the Pillar of Severity.

Thmaa-ett — This more Fluidic with regard to her influence with respect to the Pillar of Mercy.

She is the Wielder of the Sceptre of Dual Wisdom from Chokmah and therefore is the Mitre head split in two and not closed, to indicate the Dual Manifestation of Wisdom and Truth: even as the Hall of the Neophytes is called "the Hall of the Dual Manifestation of the Goddess of Truth."

The Three Inferior Officers do not wear Mantles, but only Lamens suspended from black Collars. The designs are in white on a black field to show that they are Administrators of the Forces of Light acting through the Darkness, under the Presidency of the Superior Officers.

<97> The Lamen of Kerux, is thus explained in the Grade of Theoricus: "The Tree of Life and the Three Mother Letters are the Keys wherewith to unlock the Caduceus of Hermes. The upper point of the Wand rests on Kether and the Wings stretch out to Chokmah and Binah, thus comprehending the Three Supernal Sephiroth. The lower seven are embraced by the Serpents whose heads fall on Chesed and Geburah. They are the twin Serpents of Egypt and the currents of Astral Light. Furthermore, the Wings and the top of the Wand form the letter Shin, the symbol of Fire; the Heads and upper halves of the Serpents form Aleph the symbol of Air; while their tails enclose Mem, the symbol of Water — the Fire of Life above, the Waters of Creation below, and the Air symbol vibrating between them."

In addition to this, the Caduceus of Kerux represents the balanced forces of Eternal Light working invisibly in the Darkness — even as the Light borne before the hood-winked Candidate at his Initiation, is symbolic of the Light which guides him in the darkness of the world though he sees it not nor knows it. This Caduceus is the Rod of Hermes, containing invisible and unsuspected forces, the rules of whose administration may be revealed through meditation. It is the outer form of the Wand surmounted by the Winged Globe below which the Twin Serpents are shown — the Wand of the Chief Adept in the ⑤ = [6] Grade.

The Lamen of Stolistes is thus explained in the Grade of Practicus: "The Cup of Stolistes partakes in part of the symbolism of the Laver of Moses and the Sea of Solomon. On the Tree of Life it embraces nine of the Sephiroth exclusive of Kether. Yesod and Malkuth form the triangle below, the former apex, the latter the base. Like the Caduceus, it further represents the three Elements of Water, Air, and Fire. The crescent is the Water which is above the Firmament; the circle is the Firmament, and the triangle is the consuming Fire below, which is opposed to the Celestial Fire symbolised by the upper part of the Caduceus."

<98> In addition to this explanation, the Cup represents the Receptacle and Collector of the more Fluidic Forces of the Light, and is the symbol of an inexhaustible Bowl of Libation from which Reservoir the Adept may draw the Reserved Forces of the Light — which matter again calls for meditation.

The Lamen of Dadouchos is thus explained in the Grade of Zelator: "The Hermetic Cross, which is also known as Fylfot, Hammer of Thor, and Swastika, is formed of 17 squares taken from a square of 25 lesser squares. These 17 fitly represent the Sun, the Four Elements and, the Twelve Signs of the Zodiac."

In addition to this, the Lamen has a more extended meaning. The Hermetic Cross, the Bolt of Whirling Flame, which is represented by the cross of Four Axes whose heads may be either double of single and turned in either direction, is a symbol of terrific Strength, and represents the Fire of the Spirit, cleaving its way in all directions through the Darkness of Matter. Therefore is it borne on the Lamen of Dadouchos whose office is that of Purification and Consecration by Fire, and from it also may be drawn by meditation several formulae of strength.

The Kerux is the principal form of Anubis, as the Sentinel is the subsidiary form.

Kerux is *Ano-Oobist Empe-Eeb-Te*—"Anubis of the East."

Sentinel is *Ano-Oobi Em-Pemen-Te*—"Anubis of the West."

The Kerux is the Herald, the Guardian and Watcher *within* the Temple, as Sentinel is the Watcher *Without* — and therefore is his charge the proper disposition of the furniture and stations of the Temple. He is also the Proclaimer. His peculiar ensigns of Office are:

The Red Lamp to signify the Hidden Fire over which he watches.

The Magic Staff of Power to represent a Ray of the Divine Light which kindles the Hidden Fire.

<99> Two Potions whereby to produce the effect of Blood.

He is the Guardian of the Inner side of the Portal — the sleepless Watcher of the Gods and the Preparer of the Pathway to Divine Wisdom. "Watcher for the Gods" is the name of Kerux, and he is Ano-Oobist, the Herald before them.

The Stolistes is stationed in the Northern Part of the Hall to the North-West of the Black Pillar whose base is in Hod, and is there as the Affirmer of the powers of Moisture, Water, reflected through the Tree into Hod. The Cup is the Receptacle of this, filled from Hod so as to transmit its forces into Malkuth, restoring and purifying the vital forces therein by Cold and Moisture. "Goddess of the Scale of the Balance at the Black Pillar" is the name of Stolistes and she is "The Light Shining through the Waters upon Earth," Aura-Mo-Ooth, and there is a connection between her and the Aurim or Urim of the Hebrews.

The Dadouchos is stationed towards the midst of the Southern part of the Hall, to the South-West of the White Pillar whose base is in Netzach and is there as the Affirmer of the Powers of Fire, reflected down the Tree to Netzach. The Censer is the Receptacle thereof — the transmitter of the Fires of Netzach to Malkuth, restoring and purifying the vital force therein by Heat and Dryness. "Goddess of the Scale of the Balance at the White Pillar" is the name of Dadouchos and she is "Perfection through Fire manifesting on Earth." Thaum-Aesch-Nia-eth, and there is a connection between her and the Thummim of the Hebrews.

The Stolistes has the care of the Robes and Insignia of the Temple as symbolising by their cleansing and purification the Purging away of the Evil of Malkuth by the Waters of the Spirit.

The Dadouchos has charge of all lights, fires and incense, as representing the purifying and purging of Malkuth by Fire and the Light of the Spirit. These Officers also purify the Temple, the Members and the Candidate by Water and by Fire, as it is written: "I indeed baptise you with Water,
<100> but One shall come after me who shall baptise ye with the Holy Ghost and with Fire."

This completes the names and titles of the Officers of a Temple and they are Seven in number and may all be taken by a Frater or Soror. As they represent powers and not persons, the feminine form of the Greek names is not usually used, for the powers are positive (male) or negative (female) according to the God-form used. Thus Hierophant, Hiereus, and Kerux are more natural offices for Fratres, while Hegemon, Stolistes and Dadouchos are more natural for Sorores —but the office itself carries no implication of sex and sometimes the psychic balance of a ceremony may be better maintained when a Frater is Hegemon and a Soror Hierophant.

The Hierophant must be of the ⑤ = 6 Grade and a Zelator Adeptus Minor. The Hiereus must be at least Philosophus, and the Hegemon at least Practicus, and preferably Philosophus. Kerux must be at least Theoricus while Stolistes and Dadouchos must be Zelator — a Neophyte being qualified only for Sentinel.* In case the feminine forms of the names of the Officers should wish to be known, they are as follows:

V. H. Hierophant or V. H. Hierophantria
H. Hiereus or H. Hiereia
H. Hegemon or H. Hegemone
Kerux or Kerukaina
Stolistes or Stolistria
Dadouchos or Dadouche
Sentinel or Phulax

OF THE THREE CHIEFS

The Three Chiefs are in the Temple and rule it, yet they are not comprehended in, nor understood by, the Outer Order. They represent, as it were, *Veiled Divinities* sending a form to sit before the Veil Paroketh, and, like
the Veils of Isis and Nephthys, impenetrable save to the Initiate. The
<101> synthesis of the Three Chiefs may be said to be in the form of Tho-
oth Who cometh from behind the Veil at the point of its Rending. Yet
separately, they may be thus referred:

The Imperator, from his relation to Geburah, may be referred to the Goddess Nephthys,

The Praemonstrator, from his relation to Chesed, may be referred to the Goddess Isis,

The Cancellarius, from his property of Recorder, may be referred to the God Thoth:

No ceremony of the Outer Order may take place without a Chief — preferably the Three Chiefs or their Vice-gerants present — and on account of the *Stations* on the Dais, it is well to have these stations filled by an Adept, should a Chief be absent. These Stations and those of the Officers are called the Visible Stations of the Gods, and descriptions of the forms which an Adept Officer builds up as a focus of force are given in another paper.

THE INVISIBLE STATIONS

These are:

1. The Stations of the Kerubim.

*Note that: Stolistes and Dadouchos are offices in the Neophyte and Zelator rituals, but in no higher elemental ritual. Kerux is an office in the Neophyte, Zelator and Theoricus rituals, but in no higher elemental ritual. Hierophant, Hiereus and Hegemon are the only initiating officers in the Practicus and Philosophus rituals. From these observations, in the light of the above instructions, we feel that an office does not appear above the grade that is grade appropriate for the office as defined. Since the Sentinel is an office only open to a Neophyte, we believe that it should only appear in the Neophyte ritual and not in any of the elemental grades. G.W.

2. The Stations of the Children of Horus.
3. The Stations of the Evil One.
4. The Station of Harpocrates.
5. The Stations of Isis, Nephthys, Aroueris.

1. *The Kerubim:* The Stations of the Man, the Lion, the Bull, and the Eagle are at the Four Cardinal Points without the Hall, as invisible Guardians of the limits of the Temple. They are placed according to the winds — beyond the Stations of Hierophant, Dadouchos, Hiereus, and Stolistes — and in this order do their symbols appear in all Warrants of Temples.

The Kerub of Air formulates behind the Throne of Hierophant. She has a young girl's countenance and form, with large and shadowing wings; and she is a power of the Great Goddess Hathor who unites the powers of Isis and Nephthys. To the Sign Aquarius is she referred as a correlative,
<102> which represents Springs of Water breaking upon Earth; though as
a Zodiacal Sign it is referred to Air, the container of Rain. The Egyptian name of the Sign Aquarius is Phritithi.

Note: "Thou shalt not confound the Kerubim with their Signs of the Zodiac, notwithstanding that the latter be under the Presidency of the former, seeing that the Kerub representeth a far more Sublime Potency, yet acting by a harmonious sympathy through the particular Sign allotted unto their correspondence."

The Kerub of Fire has the face and form of a Lion with large and clashing wings. He formulates behind the Throne of Dadouchos and he is a power of the Great Goddess Tharpesh or Tharpheshest, the latter syllable being nearly Pasht. The action of the Lion Kerub is through the Flaming Fire of Leo of which the Egyptian name is Labo-Ae.

The Kerub of Water has the face and form of a Great Eagle with large and glistening wings and he formulates behind the throne of Hiereus. He is a power of the Great God Thoomoo, and his operation is by the Sign of Scorpio, which is called in Egyptian Szlae-Ee. (Note: In Egyptological works the name of this God is Tum or Tmu.—I. R.)

The Kerub of Earth has the face and form of a Bull with heavy and darkening wings. He formulates behind the Throne of Stolistes and he is a power of the Great God Ahaphshi and his operation is by the Sign Taurus called Ta-Aur in Egyptian.

2. The Children of Horus: Between the Invisible Stations of the Kerubim are those of the Four Vice-gerants of the Elements and they are situated at the Four Corners of the Temple, at the places marked by the Four Rivers of Eden in the Warrant; for the body of a Warrant, authorising the formation and establishment of a Temple, represents the Temple itself — of which the Guardians are the Kerubim and the Vice-gerents in the places of the Rivers.

Ameshet (man-headed) is placed in the North East, between
<103> *the Man and the Bull. Ameshet or Amesheth. (The spelling is Coptic
and differs according to the force intended to be invoked by the letters.)

Tou-mathaph, jackal-headed, is placed in the South East between the

*(Note: In making up the 2nd Edition, page 103 of Vol. III and page 103 of Vol IV were accidentally transposed. The proper location is now restored in this 5th Edition.) C.L.W.

Man and the Lion. Toumathph or Tmoumathv.

Ahephi, Ape-faced, is placed in the South West between the Lion and the Eagle. Ahephi or Ahaphix.

Kabexnuv, Hawk-faced, is placed in the North-West, between the Eagle and the Bull. Kabexnuv or Dabexnjemouv.

3. The Station of the Evil One. This station is in the place of Yesod and is called the Station of the Evil One, the Slayer of Osiris. He is the Tempter, Accuser, and Punisher of the Brethren and in Egypt is represented mostly with the head of a Water-Dragon, the body of a Lion or leopard, and the hind-parts of a Water-horse. He is the Administrator of the power of the Evil Triad:

The Stooping Dragon, Apophrassz.
The Slayer of Osiris—Szathan Toophon.
The brutal power of Demonic Force—Bessz.

The Synthesis of this Evil Triad "The Mouth of the Power of Destruction" is called Ommoo-Szathan.

4. The Station of Harpocrates. The Invisible Station of Harpocrates is in the Path of Samekh, between the Station of Hegemon and the Invisible Station of the Evil Triad. Harpocrates is the God of Silence and Mystery, whose Name is the Word of this Grade of Neophyte. He is the younger brother of Horus, Hoor-Po-Krattist.

5. The Stations of Isis and Nephthys. The Stations of Isis and Nephthys are respectively at the Places of the Pillars in Netzach and Hod, and these Great Goddesses are not otherwise shown in the Grade, save in
<104> connection with the Praemonstrator and Imperator, as operating through the Hierophant, seeing that Isis corresponds to the Pillar of Mercy and Nephthys to that of Severity; and therefore the positions of the Pillars or Obelisks are but, as it were, the Places of their feet.

The Station of Aroueris. The Invisible Station of Aroueris (Horus the Elder) is beside the Hierophant as though representing the power of Osiris to the Outer Order — for while the Hierophant is an Adeptus, he is shown only as Lord of the Paths of the Portal — so that, when the Hierophant moves from the Throne of the East, he is no longer Osiris but Aroueris. Yet when the Hierophant is on the Dais the Station of Aroueris is that of the Immediate Past Hierophant who sits on the Hierophant's left. Aroo-ouerist.

This ends the Constitutory Symbolism of a Temple in the ⓪ = ⓪ Grade of Neophyte. Should a Member have occasion to quit his place, he shall do it moving with the course of the Sun; and as he passes the place of Hierophant, he shall salute with the Sign. And when he enters or quits the Temple, he shall salute the Hierophant's Throne when within the Portal.

<105>

THE SYMBOLISM OF THE OPENING OF THE ⓪ = ⓪ GRADE OF NEOPHYTE

The Opening Ceremony begins with the Cry of the "Watcher Within" who should come to the right front of Hierophant and raise his Wand. This

Symbol of the Ray of the Divine Light from the White Triangle of the Three Supernals thus descends into the Darkness and warns the Evil and uninitiated to retire, so that the White Triangle may be formulated upon the Altar through the combined effect of the formulae of the Opening Ceremony.

Having done this, he sees that the Entrance is properly guarded. And then the Hierophant calls to the Hiereus to test the members by the Signs, the knowledge of which shows that they, though in the Land of Blindness and Ignorance, have yet seen that Triangle of Divine Light from the Three Supernals formulated in Darkness. It is then noted that the names of the three chief Officers begin with the Letter of Breath the Coptic ϩ . In the name of Osiris the ϩ is mute, and silent, and concealed, as it were, by 'H' the Eta. In the name Horus, it is manifest and violently aspirated, while in the name Thmaest, it is partly one and partly the other, for it is compounded with the Letter 'T' in Θ.

(H "Ae" is attributed to Chesed — ϩ to Aries, and Θ to Earth and Saturn. This is intended to affirm the Unknown Life, which is Inspired from the Beyond, sent out to Aries, the commencement of the Spring of the year, the Life which after being Inspired, is breathed forth again; and also the *possible use* of that Breath, between the Inspiration and the Expiration, in the combination between it and the Forces of the Microcosm.)

<106> The whole is a rehearsal of the properties of the reflection of the Element *Air* down through the Middle Pillar of the Sephiroth, representing the reflection of the Air from Kether, through Tiphareth to Yesod, and even to the Citrine part of Malkuth. For the subtle Aether is, in Kether, inspired from the Divine Light beyond; thence reflected into Tiphareth, wherein it is combined with the Reflexes from the Alchemical Principles in that great Receptacle of the Forces of the Tree. In Yesod, it affirms the foundation of a formula and from Malkuth it is breathed forth or reflected back.

And this formula the Adept can use. Standing in his Sphere of Sensation he can, by his knowledge of the Sacred Rites, raise himself unto the contemplation of Yechidah and from thence aspire (in the sense of Adspire, *i.e.,* to attract *towards* you in breathing) downwards into himself the Lower Genius as though temporarily to inhabit himself as its Temple.

Another formula of Vibration is here hidden. Let the Adept, standing upright, his arms stretched out in the form of a Calvary Cross, vibrate a Divine Name, bringing with the formulation thereof a deep inspiration into his lungs. Let him retain the breath, mentally pronouncing the Name in his *Heart,* so as to combine it with the forces he desires to awake thereby; thence sending it downwards through his body past Yesod, but not resting there, but taking his physical life for a material basis, send it on into his feet. There he shall again momentarily formulate the Name — then, bringing it rushing upwards into the lungs, thence shall he breathe it forth strongly, while vibrating that Divine Name. He will send his breath steadily forward into the Universe so as to awake the corresponding forces of the Name in the Outer World. Standing with arms out in the form of a Cross, when the breath has been imaginatively sent to the feet and back, bring the arms forward in "The

Sign of the Enterer" while vibrating the Name out into the Universe. On completing this, make the "Sign of Silence" and remain still, contemplating the Force you have invoked.

<107> This is the secret traditional mode of pronouncing the Divine Names by vibration, *but let the Adept beware that he applies it only to the Divine Names of the Gods.* If he does this thing ignorantly in working with Elemental or Demonic Names, he may bring into himself terrible forces of Evil and Obsession. The Method described is called "The Vibratory Formula of the Middle Pillar."

After noting the Names of the Three Chief Officers, comes the recapitulation of the Stations and duties of the Officers, thus occultly affirming the establishment of the Temple so that the Divine Light may shine into the Darkness. Then follows the purification and consecration of the Hall by Water and by Fire, thus marking the limitation of the Four Cardinal Points at the Four Quarters, and the Equation of the Elements. This is the Baptism of the Place and, as it were, the Preparation of a fitting Shrine for the Forces of the Divine Light. While all this goes forward, especially after the Hierophant's "for by Names and Images are all powers awakened and reawakened," the Officers become clothed in their God-forms and the Invisible Stations awake.

The Procession of Officers is then formed in the North in readiness for the "Mystic Circumambulation in the Path of Light" (that is to say, none of the partakers is hood-winked). It is formed in the North, beginning from the Station of Stolistes, the symbol of the Waters of Creation attracting the Divine Spirit, and therefore alluding to the Creation of the World by the Spirit and the Waters. The Mystic Reverse Circumambulation forms its Procession in the South, beginning from the Station of Dadouchos, as symbolic of the Ending and Judgment of the World by Fire. But also, the Mystic Circumambulation commences by the Paths of Shin and Resh, as though bringing into action the Solar Fire; while the Reverse Circumambulation commences beside those of Qoph and Tzaddi as though bringing the Watery Reflux into action.

<108> The Order of the Mystic Circumambulation. First comes Anubis, the Watcher within; next Thmaest, the Goddess of the Hall of Truth; then Horus; then the Goddesses of the Scales of the Balance, then Members, if the Hall be large enough, and at the end the Watcher Without, Sentinel. It is as though a gigantic Wheel were revolving, as it is said: "One Wheel upon Earth beside the Kerub." The Name of the Sphere of the Primum Mobile, Rashith ha-Gilgalim, signifies the heads or beginnings of Whirling Motions or Revolutions. Of this Wheel in the Mystic Circumambulation, the ascending side begins from below the Pillar of Nephthys, and the descending side from below the Pillar of Isis; but in the Reverse Circumambulation, the contrary.

Now the nave or axis of this Wheel is about the Invisible Station of Harpocrates — as though that God, in the Sign of Silence were there placed affirming the Concealment of that Central Atom of the Wheel, which alone revolves not.

The Mystic Circumambulation is called symbolic of the Rise of Light and

from it is drawn another formula for the circulation of the breath. It is the formula of the Four Revolutions of the Breath (not, of course, of the actual air inspired, but of the subtle Aethers which may be drawn thence and of which it is the Vehicle — the aethers which awaken centres in the subtle body through the formula). This formula should be preceded by that of the Middle Pillar, described previously. By this method, having invoked the Power you wish to awaken in yourself, and contemplated it, begin its circumambulation thus: Fill the lungs and imagine the Name vibrating in the contained Air. Imagine this vibration going down the left leg to the sole of the left foot — thence passing over to the sole of the right foot — up the right leg to the lungs again, whence it is out-breathed. Do this four times to the rhythm of the Four-
fold breath. (Note: In this connection read very carefully the section
<109> in Volume 4, entitled *The Four Serpent Formulae of the Four Aces* of the
Tarot. Some hint may be there gleaned of the relation of the breath to the Macrocosmic forces.—I.R.)

The Object of the Mystic Circumambulation is to attract and make the connection between the Divine Light above and the Temple. Therefore the Hierophant does not quit his post to take part therein, but remains there to attract by his Sceptre the Light from beyond the Veil. Each member in passing gives the Sign of the Enterer, thus projecting the Light forward on his Path from East to West, as he receives it from the Hierophant's Throne. Horus passes only *once,* for he is the Son of Osiris and inherits the Light by birthright from him. Therefore he goes at once to his station to *fix* the Light there. Thmaest, the Goddess of Truth, passes *twice* because her rule is of the Balance of the Two Scales, and she retires to her Station between the Pillars there to complete the reflex of the Middle Column. The Watcher Within and the rest circumambulate *thrice* as affirming the completion of the Reflection of the Perfecting of the White Triangle of the Three Supernals upon the Altar.

Then follows the Adoration of God, the Vast One, the Lord of the Universe — at which again all give the Sign of the Enterer, the Sign of the Projection of the Force of the Light. Then only does the Watcher declare that the Sun has arisen and that the Light shineth in Darkness. Now comes the *Battery* of the ⓪ = ⃞0 Grade — the single knock of Hierophant repeated by Hiereus and Hegemon. This affirms the establishment of the White Triangle and therefore the Completion of the Opening Ceremony. The Mystic Words "Khabs Am Pekht" which accompany the knocks seal the image of the Light. Their significance implies, by various Qabalistic methods of analysis, as well as by a certain reading of the Coptic and Egyptian hieroglyphics, "Light in Extension" or "May Light be extended in Abundance upon you."
<110> Konx Om Pax is the Greek corrupted pronunciation of this, put here to link it with its right origin.

The Grade of Neophyte has O or the Circle for its Number, as if hiding all things under the negative symbol. This is placed within a circle and a square connected by equal lines, as if affirming the hidden quality of their origin in Kether where all things are One, and the consequent Universal application of the Secret Formulae.

<110> *Diagram 22*

WANDS OF THE CHIEFS ON DAIS

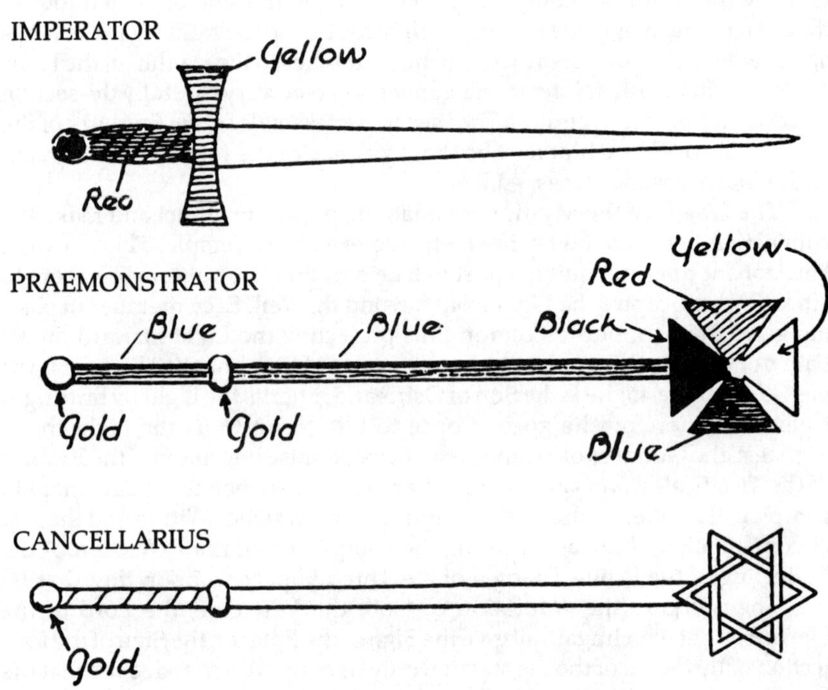

<111> *Diagram 23*

HIEROPHANT'S CLOAK AND WAND

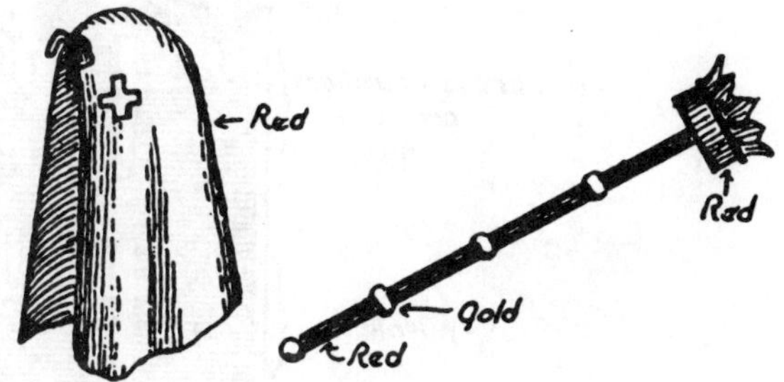

HEGEMON'S CLOAK AND WAND

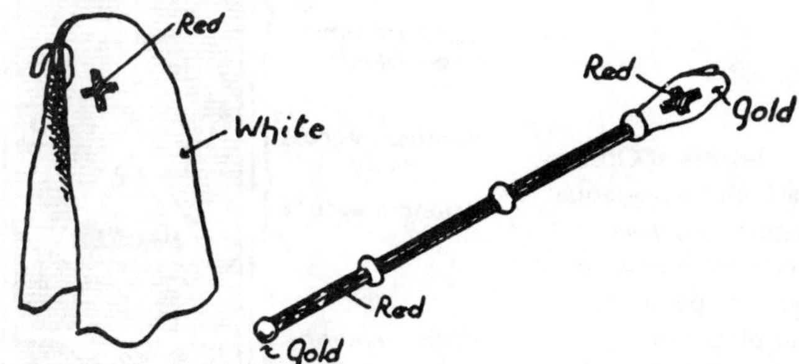

CLOAK AND SWORD OF HIEREUS

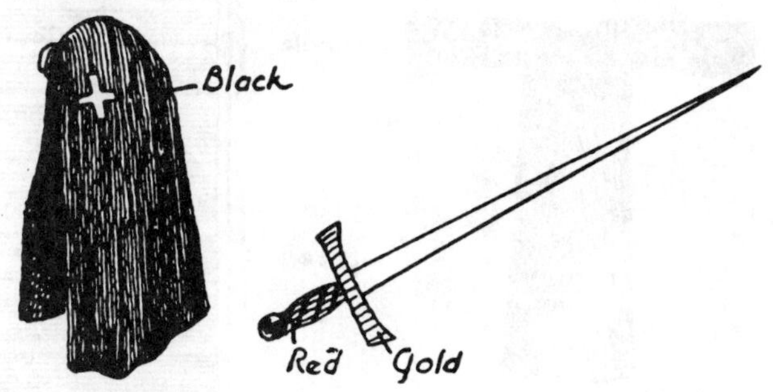

Diagram 24

SASH OF GRADES

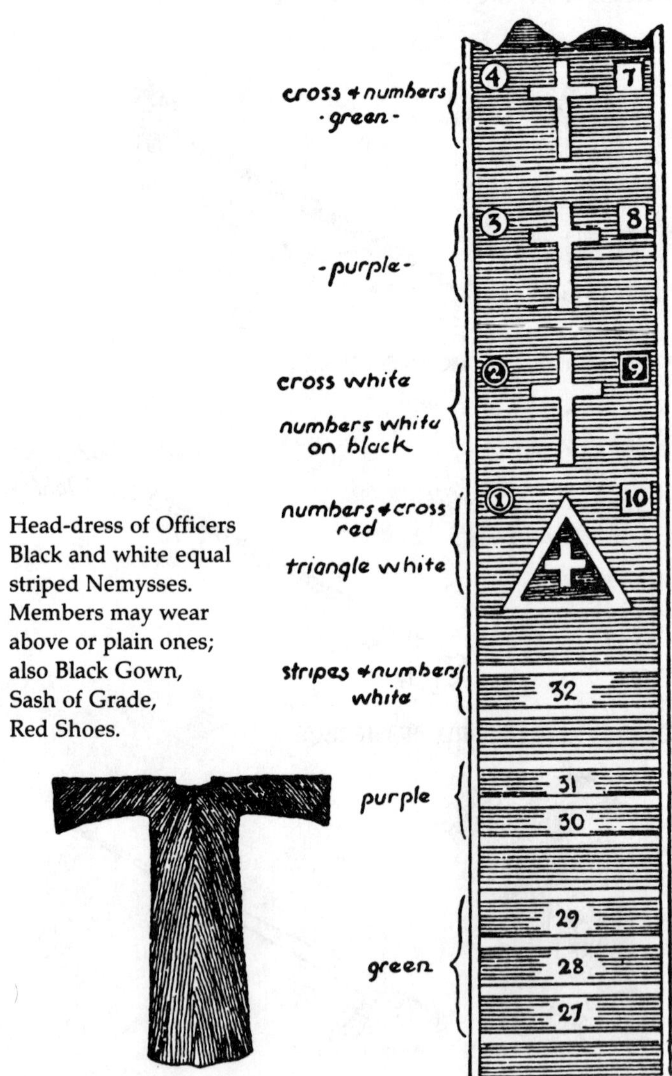
cross + numbers
· green ·
4
7
- purple -
3
8
cross white
numbers white
on black
2
9
numbers + cross
red
triangle white
1
10
stripes + numbers
white
32
purple
31
30
green
29
28
27
Head-dress of Officers
Black and white equal
striped Nemysses.
Members may wear
above or plain ones;
also Black Gown,
Sash of Grade,
Red Shoes.

<113>

Diagram 25

OFFICERS' LAMENS

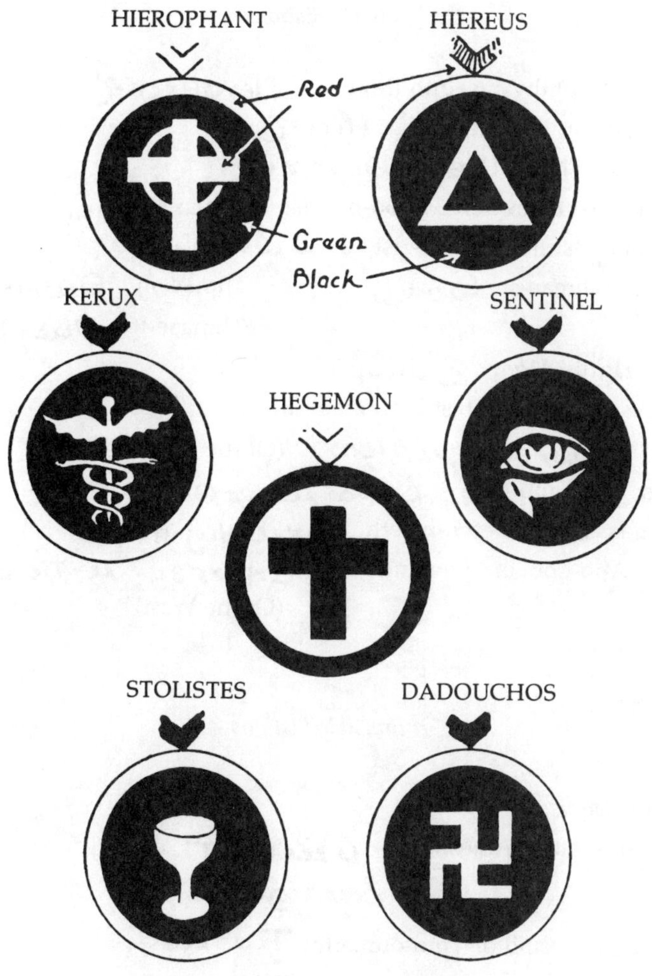

<114> COPTIC NAMES OF THE CHIEFS AND OFFICERS

Visible Stations

Imperator: Nephthys: Neoph-tho-osest Ⲛⲉⲩⲫⲑⲟⲩⲥⲉ-ⲋ
Praemonstrator: Isis: Ae-isest Ⲏⲓⲥⲉ-ⲋ
Cancellarius: Thoth: Tho-ooth Ⲑⲱⲟⲩⲑ
Past Hierophant: Aroueris: Aroo-ouerist Ⲁⲣⲱⲟⲩⲉⲣⲓ-ⲋ
Hierophant: Osiris: Ae-shoo-rist Ⲏϣⲱⲱⲣⲓ-ⲋ
Hegemon: Thmae-st Ⲑⲙⲁⲏⲋ Thmae-sh Ⲑⲙⲁⲏ-ϣ
Thmaae-tt Ⲑⲙⲁ-ϯ
Hiereus: Horus: Hoor Ϩⲱⲱⲣ
Kerux: Anubis: Ano-oobist-em-Pe-eeb-tte
Ⲁⲛⲱⲟⲩⲃⲓ-ⲋ ⲙ-Ⲡⲉⲓⲟϯ (Of the East)
Stolistes: Aur-a-mo-ooth Ⲁⲟⲩⲣⲁ-ⲙⲱⲟⲩⲑ
Dadouchos: Thaum-aesch-niaeth Ⲑⲁⲩⲙ-Ⲏϣ-Ⲛⲓⲏⲑ
Sentinel: Ano-oobi em-Pementte Ⲁⲛⲱⲟⲩⲃⲓ- ⲙ-Ⲡⲉⲓⲟϯ
(Of the West)

Invisible Stations

Children of Horus:

N.E.—Ameshett or Amesheth Ⲁⲙⲉϣⲉⲧ
or Ⲁⲙⲉϣⲉⲑ

S.E.—Tto-oumathph or Tmo-oumathv Ⲧⲱⲟⲩⲙⲁⲑϥ
or Ⲧⲱⲟⲩⲙⲁⲑϥ

N.W.—Kabexnuv or Dabexnjemouv Ⲕⲁⲃⲉⲝⲛⲟⲩϥ
or Ⲕⲁⲃⲉⲝⲛϫⲉⲙⲟⲩϥ

S.W.—Ahephi or Ahaphix Ⲁϩⲉⲫⲓ
or Ⲁϩⲁⲡϩⲓⲝ

<115> *Kerubim:*

Kerub			*Sign*	
Ahathoor	ἀϩαθωωρ	Phritithi	φριτιθι	♒
Tharpesh	θαρφε-ϣ	Labo-ae	λαβω-η	♌
Tho-oom Mo-oo	θωουμ-μωου	Szlae-ee	Cληι	♏
Ahapshi	ἀϩαπϣι	Ta-aur	Τοουρ	♉

Tharpesh can also be spelt Tharpeshest

Cardinal Points:

North ______________________ Anmehitt Νμεϩιτ
South ______________________ Phraestt Φρηστ
East ______________________ E-eebtt Ειοτ
West ______________________ Emantt Εμντ

Harpocrates: Ho-or-Po-Kratt-I St ϩωωρ-πο-κρατι-ϭ

Evil Persona

Apophra-i Ssz	ἀποφρασσ	Stooping Dragon
Szathan-Toophon	σαθαν-τουφων	Slayer of Osiris
Bessz	Βεσσ	Brutal Power of Demonic Force
Ommoo Szathan	Ομμου-σαθαν	Power of the Mouth of the Power of Destruction

<116>

THE EGYPTIAN GOD-FORMS
OF THE
NEOPHYTE GRADE

The stations of the God-forms used in our symbolism come under two heads:

1. Visible Stations.
2. Invisible Stations.

The Visible Stations are the places of the Officers, each of whom has a special astral shape suitable to the forces he represents.

On the dais are places for the Three Chiefs, the Past Hierophant and the Hierophant. The order in which they sit (as you face East) is:

Imperator—Nephthys
Cancellarius—Thoth
Hierophant—Osiris
Past Hiero.—Aroueris
Praemonstrator—Isis

The names below are those of the God-forms they represent. The following are the descriptions of the God-forms of the seven Officers of the Neophyte Grade.

Hierophant: Osiris in the Netherland. Expounder of the Mysteries in the Hall of the Dual Manifestation of the Goddess of Truth.

Hierophant is represented by two God-forms, the Passive and active aspects of Osiris. Seated on the Dais as Hierophant, he is clothed in the God-form of Osiris. He wears the tall white crown of the South flanked by feathers striped white and blue. His face is green, the eyes blue, and from his chin hangs the royal beard of authority and judgment, blue in colour and gold tipped. He wears a collar in bands of red, blue, yellow, and black —
<117> and on his back is a bundle strapped across his chest by scarlet
bands. He is in mummy wrappings to the feet, but his hands are free to hold a golden Phoenix Wand, a Blue Crook and Red Scourge. The hands are green. His feet rest on a pavement of black and white.

The God-form of Osiris never moves from the Dais. When the Hierophant has to move from the Dais, he is covered by the form of Osiris in action — Aroueris, which is built up by the Past Hierophant, seated on Hierophant's left. If no one is seated as Past Hierophant, then inner Members help the Hierophant to formulate the second God-form.

Aroueris, Horus the Elder, is very lively to look upon — like pure flames. He wears the Double Crown of Egypt, the cone shaped crown in red inside the white crown of the North, with a white plume. His nemyss is purple banded with gold at the edges. His face and body are translucent scarlet. He has green eyes and wears a purple beard of authority. He wears a yellow tunic with a waist cloth of yellow striped with purple, from which depends a lion's tail. In common with all Egyptian Gods, he has a white linen kilt showing like an apron under the coloured waist cloth. His armlets and anklets are of gold. He carries in his right hand, a blue Phoenix Wand and in his left, a blue Ankh. He stands on a pavement of purple and gold.

Hiereus: Horus in the Abode of Blindness unto and Ignorance of the Higher. Avenger of the Gods.

He wears the Double Crown of the South and North, red and white, over a nemyss of scarlet banded with emerald green. His face is that of a lively hawk — tawny and black with bright piercing eyes, his throat is white. His body, like that of Aroueris, is entirely scarlet. He wears collar, armlets, and anklets of emerald; a waist cloth of emerald striped red, from which depends a lion's tail and he carries in his right hand an Emerald Phoenix Wand, and in his left a blue Ankh. He stands on a pavement of emerald and scarlet.

<118> *Hegemon:* Thmaa-Est "Before the Face of the Gods in the Place of the Threshold."

Thmaa-est wears a black nemyss bound at the brow with a purple band from which rises, in front, a tall ostrich feather of green striped with red in equal bands. She wears a banded collar of red, yellow, blue and black. Her tunic is emerald green reaching to the feet where it is banded to match the collar. She has purple and green shoulder straps and a purple girdle also bordered in the colours mentioned above. Her face and body are natural colour—*i.e.,* a light Egyptian red-brown. She wears armlets of emerald and red, and carries a combined form of Lotus and Phoenix Wand. It has an orange flower — a blue stem, and ends in an orange Sign of the Binary. In her left hand she carries a blue Ankh, and she stands on a pavement of yellow and purple, bordered with blocks of red, blue, yellow, black, in succession.

Kerux: Anubis of the East. Watcher of the Gods.

Anubis has the head of a black jackal, very alert, pointed ears well pricked up. His nemyss is purple banded with white; he wears a collar of yellow and purple bands, and a tunic of yellow flecked with tufts of black hair. His body is red. His waist cloth is yellow striped with purple and from it hangs a lion's tail. His ornaments are purple and gold; his Phoenix Wand and Ankh, blue. He stands on a pavement of purple and yellow.

Stolistes: Auramo-ooth. "The Light shining through the Waters upon Earth." "Goddess of the Scales of the Balance at the Black Pillar."

Auramo-ooth is mainly in blue. Her face and body are natural. She wears a blue Crown of the North from which springs a delicate gold plume, over a Vulture head-dress of orange and blue. Her collar is orange and blue, she carries a blue Ankh and a Lotus Wand, having an orange lotus on a green stem. Her plain blue tunic reaches to the feet. She stands on black.

<119> *Dadouchos:* Thaum-Aesch-Niaeth. "Perfection through Fire manifesting on Earth." "Goddess of the Scales of the Balance at the White Pillar."

Thaum-aesch is mainly in red. Her face and body are natural. She wears a red Crown of the South, flanked by two feathers in green barred black, over a vulture head-dress in red and green. Her collar is red and green and she carries a green Ankh and a Lotus Wand with a red flower and a green stem. Her simple red tunic reaches to the feet and she stands on black.

Sentinel: Anubis of the West.

His form is the same as that of Kerux but his nemyss, ornaments, and dress are black and white. He has a lion's tail and carries a black Phoenix Wand and Ankh. He stand on black.

(Note: If the reader, who is interested, will consult some such text as *The Gods of the Egyptians* by Sir E. Wallis Budge, he will find pictures of the gods referred to. He would be well-advised to make his own tracings or drawings of them with colour as directed by these instructions.—I.R.)

THE THREE CHIEFS

Imperator: Nephthys

Nephthys has a face and body of translucent gold. She is crowned with a Cap over a vulture head-dress of black and white, the vulture head being red. Her collar and ornaments are black and white, and she wears a black robe to the feet. It is bordered in black and white. She carries a blue Ankh and a Lotus Wand with a green flower and a blue stem. She stands on black and white pavement.

Praemonstrator: Isis.

Isis has a face and body of translucent gold. She is crowned with a Throne over a vulture head-dress of blue and orange. The vulture
<120> head is red. Her robe is of blue bordered with gold. Her ornaments
are blue and orange, and she carries a blue Ankh and a Lotus wand with a green flower and a blue stem. She stands on blue and orange.

Cancellarius: Tho-oth.

The God-form of Thoth is built up by the Cancellarius or the officer seated on the right of Hierophant. This is his visible station, but during a Neophyte Grade, he also has an invisible station in the East while the Obligation takes place.

He has an Ibis head, black beak and white throat. His nemyss is yellow bordered with mauve. His collar yellow with a middle band of squares in mauve and green. His tunic is mauve with yellow stripes, and he has a lion's tail. His limbs are natural colour, his ornaments are red and green. He carries a blue Ankh, and a stylus and writing tablet. He stands on mauve and yellow.

THE INVISIBLE STATIONS

These fall naturally into four groups given below in order of their importance.

1. Stations in the Path Samekh in the Middle Pillar — Hathor — Harparkrat — Evil Persona.
2. Kerubim.
3. Children of Horus.
4. The Forty-Two Assessors.

1. *Hathor:* This Great Goddess formulates behind Hierophant in the East. Her face and limbs are of translucent gold. She wears a scarlet Sun Disc, resting between black horns from the back of which rise two feathers in white, barred blue. She has a black nemyss — a collar of blue, red, blue; and blue bands which support her robe of orange, bordered with blue and red.

Her ornaments are blue and orange. She carries a blue Ankh and a Lotus Wand with a green flower and a blue stem. She stands on black bordered with blue.

<121> *Harparkrat:* He formulates in the centre of the Hall between Hegemon and the Altar, where he sits or stands on a Lotus, facing East. His face and body are translucent emerald green. He has blue eyes, and a curl of blue hair, denoting youth, comes round his face on the right side. He wears the double crown, red and white. His collar is yellow and blue; his waist cloth is yellow and blue with a mauve girdle, whence depends a lion's tail. His Lotus has leaves alternately blue and yellow, and rests on a pavement of mauve and orange. He has no insignia. His left forefinger is on his lips.

Omoo-Sathan. Typhon, Apophis, Set. The Evil Persona is a composite figure of the powers arising from the Qlippoth. It rises from the base of the Altar standing East of the Altar facing West, in the Sign of Typhon. He is black, and has an animal, somewhat lizard-like, head, a black body, and tail, and he stands on black. His nemyss is of olive green decorated with russet, his collar of russet and citrine. He has a white apron and a waist cloth of dull red striped with russet. He has no ornaments.

2. *The Kerubim. The Kerub of Air* is formed behind Hathor and she is a power of Hathor, and has the same general colouring. She has a young girl's countenance and behind her are spread large and shadowing wings.

The Kerub of Fire is in the South beyond the seat of Dadouchos. It is a power of the Great Goddess Tharpesh, and has the face and form of a Lion with large and clashing wings. The colouring is very lively and flashing Leo green with ruby and flame-blue and Emerald green.

The Kerub of Water is formed behind Hiereus and is a power of the Great God Toum or Tmu. It has the face and form of a great Eagle with large and glistening wings. The colours are mostly blue and orange with some green.

<122> *The Kerub of Earth* is in the North behind the Seat of Stolistes. It is a power of the Great God Ahapshi and has the face and form of a Bull with heavy darkening wings, and the colours are black, green, red, with some white.

These forms are not described in detail. We are to imagine them there as great stabilising forces whose forms vary according to circumstances.

3. *The Children of Horus.* These have their invisible stations in the corners of the Hall. They are the guardians of the viscera of the human being — every part of whom comes up for judgment in its right time and place.

Ameshet: The man-faced is in the North East. He has a blue nemyss banded with red, blue and black. His face is red and he has a black ceremonial beard. Round the shoulders of his white mummy shape are bands of red, blue and black, three times repeated. He stands on red, blue and black with a border of green, white and yellow.

Tmoomathaph, the Jackal-faced, is in the South East. He has a black face with yellow linings to his pointed ears. He wears a blue nemyss with borders of black, yellow and blue — the same colours appearing threefold at his shoulders. He has a white mummy shape and stands on blue, yellow and black, with a border of green, yellow, mauve.

Kabexnuv: The Hawk-faced, is in the North West. He has a black and tawny face, and a nemyss of black bordered with red, yellow, black. The same colours appear three fold, at his shoulders. He has a white mummy shape and stands on red, yellow, and black with a border of green, mauve, white.

Ahepi: The Ape-faced, is in the South West. He has a blue nemyss bordered with red, blue and yellow bands. These colours appear on his
<123> shoulders in the same order. His face is red; and he stands on red,
blue, and yellow, with a border of green, orange, and mauve.

Note: Tmoomathaph is sometimes written Duamutef. Kabexnuv is sometimes written Qebhsenef. Ahephi is sometimes written Hapi. Ameshet is sometimes written Mesti.

4. *The Forty-Two Assessors.* These are not described at all save to say that they make the Sign of the Enterer as the Candidate is passed by them. They are Witnesses in the Judgment Hall of Osiris.

<124>

THE CANOPIC GODS

THE SYMBOLISM OF THE FOUR GENII OF THE HALL OF THE NEOPHYTES

By G. H. FRATRE *Sub Spe*

In a Temple of the Grade of Neophyte, the Four Gods, Ameshet, Ahephi, Tmoumathaph, Kabexnuf, said also to be Vice-gerants of the Elements, and answering to the Rivers of Eden as drawn in the Warrant of the Temple, are said to rule in the four Corners of the Hall between the Stations of the Kerubim.

In Egyptian Mythology, these Gods are also said to be the Children of Horus, and to partake of his symbology. If now, we regard the Neophyte Ceremony as representing the entrance into a new life, Regeneration —Mors Janua Vitae — the Egyptian symbology wherein that idea was so clearly and exactly worked out becomes important. Bear in mind that a new life means a new plane or a higher world, a passing, say, from the Kether of Assiah to the Malkuth of Yetzirah.

Now as behind Kether depend the Veils of the Negative Existence: Ain, Ain Soph and Ain Soph Aour, so through Negative Existence must pass the Soul that goes from Assiah to Yetzirah, or vice-versa. This process is illustrated by the Neophyte Ceremony as described in Z-3., and as seen by the clairvoyant eye. In Egyptian mythology, the Dead, when the Ceremonies are complete, the Soul weighed and passed, the Body mummied and preserved from corruption, became one with Osiris, and is called an Osirian. Hence, the Hierophant, who represents Osiris when the Candidate is placed in the North, speaks to him in the character of his Higher Soul — "The Voice of my undying and Secret Soul said unto me" etc.

Osiris, however, is a mummied form, and the body of the Egyptian dead was mummied at this part of the Ceremony. Let us now consider the

<125> nature of the body which is mummied. The body itself may be considered as a vehicle whereby the life forces act, and the medium whereby these life-forces act is what are termed the Vital organs. Withdraw or destroy any of these, and the life ceases to function in that body. Not less important, then, than the body itself, the vehicle of the Soul, are the Organs, the media for the action of organic life, and it is equally important to preserve these from corruption, yet not together with the body. For as the body of Osiris was broken up, so must the body of the Osirian be divided. This is the meaning of the viscera being preserved apart from the body.

The death and resurrection of Christ has other symbology and the teachings belong to a higher Grade. Let none therefore object that His Body was laid in the Tomb entire. (The Body of Osiris was first laid in the Chest or Pastos whole. The division into 14 parts was subsequent. N. B. 1 plus 4 = 5, the five wounds.) For even as Yod Heh Vav Heh must be known before Yod Heh Shin Vav Heh can be comprehended, and as Moses must precede Christ, so must the Mysteries of Osiris first be known.

Now the Guardian of the Hall and of the Neophytes against the Qlippoth (whose Kether is Thaumiel, the Dual or Two-headed One, the Demons of Corruption and disintegration) is the Hiereus or Horus, and to the Children of Horus, who partake of his symbology, are the viscera committed, to guard them against the demons of disintegration and corruption. As the elements and the forces of the Elements are to the world, so are the vital organs and the Life which animates them to the human body. Appropriately, then, are the vital organs and the life which animates them, placed under the charge of the Vice-gerents of the Elements, the Children of Horus, the Great Gods Ameshet, Ahephi, Tmoumathaph and Kabexnuf, who regulate their functions in material life, and guard them after so-called death, when the man that was has become an Osirian.

Consider then, what are these vital organs and their functions.
<126> Broadly they may be divided into the alimentary system and the circulatory system, for in this classification we take no account of the brain or reproductive organs which belong to another classification, and are not Elemental nor concerned in the maintenance of the life of the material body.

Each of these divisions may be further divided into that which divides or distributes to the body — that which is needed for life, and that which casts out from the body and renders to the Qlippoth that which is unnecessary or pernicious. From this arises a four-fold division as in the following diagram:

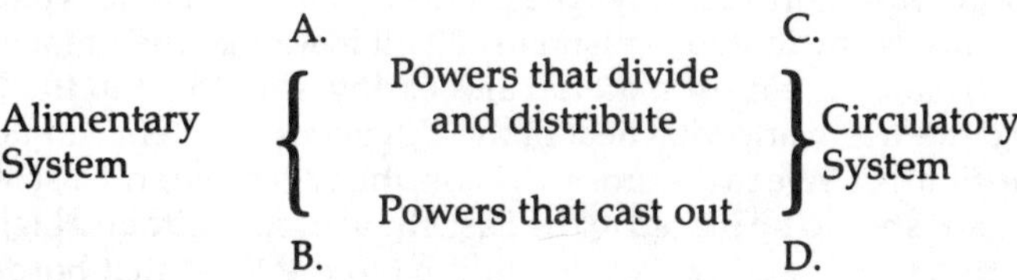

With this Key, the division becomes easy, for in the Alimentary System, the stomach and the upper intestines divide the food taken into the system by a process called digestion, and by assimilation retain what is necessary. This therefore is "A" in the diagram. But the lower intestines receive and cast out that which is rejected, these therefore will be represented by "B". In the circulatory system, the heart is the organ which distributes the blood which it receives washed and purified by the lungs. Hence the lungs and heart are represented by "C". The matter rejected from the circulatory system is rejected and cast forth by the liver and gall-bladder, which therefore will be represented by "D".

Now as to the treatment of these vital organs in the process of mummification. Seeing that during life they were under the guardianship of the Great Gods mentioned, so in death they were dedicated each to one
<127> of these, who were the four Genii of the Under-world, or the Lesser Gods of the Dead.

These vital organs then, being taken out and separately embalmed, were placed in egg-shaped receptacles, symbolic of Akasa, under the care of Canopus, the Pilot of Menelaus, and the God of the Waters of Creation, the Eternal Source of Being, whose symbol was a jar; and under the especial protection of that one of the Genii of the Underworld or Vice-gerents of the Elements to whom that particular organ was dedicated. Hence each egg-shaped package was enclosed in a jar whose lid was shaped like the head of that especial God.

Now Ameshet was also termed "The Carpenter" for he it is who by the medium of his organ, the Stomach, frames the rough materials and builds up the structure of the body; to him the Stomach and Upper Intestines were dedicated (A).

Ahephi was also termed "The Digger" or "Burier" for he puts out of sight or removes that which is useless or offensive in the body, and to him the Lower Intestines or Bowels were dedicated (B).

Tmoumathph was also called "The Cutter" or "Divider" for he divides and distributes the blood bearing with it the Prana and the Subtle Ether by the Holy Science of Breath brought into the body, and to him were the lungs or heart dedicated (C).

Kabexnuf was termed "The Bleeder" for as a stream of blood is drawn from the body, so is a stream of impurity drawn from the blood, and cast out into the draught by the action of the Liver and Gall-Bladder, and to him therefore, these organs were dedicated (D).

These jars were called Canopic Jars and were disposed in a certain order round the Mummy. Consider now, the points of the compass to which they would naturally be attributed. Reason itself will insist that the organs of the Alimentary System, the most material and earthy, should be in the North, and the warm and vital heat of the Circulatory System should be to
<128> the South, while in the cross division, the Receptive and distributive organs should be placed to the East, the source of Life and Light, and the organs that purify and cast out should be to the West that borders on the Qlippoth.

This gives us the following arrangement:

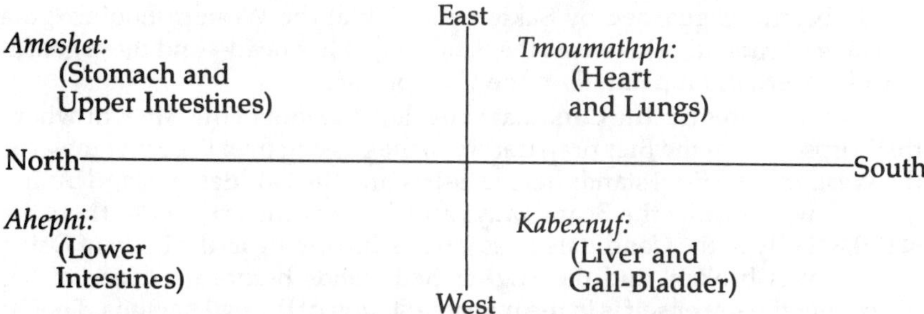

Yet this arrangement, would, as it were, symbolise the entire separation of the Alimentary System and the Circulatory System, which is contrary to Nature, for they continually counter-change, and thus arises Life. Wherefore in the Hall of the Two Truths, the portions of Ahephi and Kabexnuf are reversed, and the order becomes.

East—Ameshet. South—Tmoumathph
North—Kabexnuf West—Ahephi

Now these, being thus arranged, do partake of the symbology of the elements to which they belong. For Ameshet being to the East, the quarter of Air, has the head of a Man. Tmoumathph, to the South, has the head of a Jackal who is the purveyor of the Lion, (for these are the Vice-Gerents of the Elements, while the Kerubim are the Lords thereof); so Tmoumathph is properly a jackal. Kabexnuf in the West, in the region of Water, has the form of a Hawk, the subordinate form to the Alchemic Eagle of Distillation, and the form also, of Horus, the Hiereus, beside whom is his station, and of whose symbology he partakes.

<129> Ahephi in the North, has the head of an Ape. The symbology of the Ape in Ancient Egypt is very complex. Here it may be taken that while Apis, the Bull, represents the Divine Strength of the Eternal Gods, the Ape represents the Elemental Strength which is far inferior and blended with cunning. Ahephi, however, has other symbology and other attributes. For by reason of the fertilising qualities of the Nile and of the fact that what is brought down by the Nile as refuse from the Land of the Sacred Lakes is, to Egypt, its life and the source of its fertility, so there arises a correspondence between the Nile and the lower intestines, and both are under the care of Ahephi (Hapi) who thus was worshipped as Nilus, and in this connection he has for his symbol, a head-dress of Lotus Flowers.

Now, further, the Alimentary System is under the special guardianship of Isis and Nephthys. Isis who conquers by the power of Wisdom and the forces of Nature, guards Ameshet. And Nephthys who hides that which is secret, guards Ahephi — whence also, until recent days, in the fulness of Time, the sacred sources of Ahephi, the Nile, were kept secret from the whole world.

Tmoumathph is under the guardianship of Neith, the Dawn. This is the Celestial Space, who makes the Morning to pass and awakes the Light of a Golden Dawn in the Heart of Him whom the Eternal Gods shall choose, by the Sacred Science of the Breath.

Kabexnuf is guarded by Sakhet, the Sun at the Western Equinox, the Opening of Amenti, who wears the Scorpion on her head—and these guardianships were often painted on the Canopic jars.

When, therefore, the Candidate kneels at the foot of the Altar, or where the Corpse lies on the Bier preparatory to the passing over the River towards the West, and the Soul stands before Osiris, and the Goddesses stand by and watch while the Beam sways and the decision is taken — then, the
<130> body of the Candidate is, as it were, broken up as the body of Osiris
was broken, and the Higher Self stands before the place of the pillars, but the lower self is in the invisible station of the evil persona. Then is the Candidate nigh unto death, for then, symbolically, his Spirit passes through the Veils of the Negative Existence, passing from the Kether of Assiah to the Malkuth of Yetzirah. Therefore, unless the Genii of the Underworld were then present and directing their forces on the vital organs, he must inevitably die.

Let their symbols then be represented in all operations and formulae drawn from the symbolism of the Hall of the Two Truths, for they are of the utmost importance, but as their stations are Invisible, so shall their symbols be astral and not material.

Thus shall perfect health of body be preserved, which is of utmost importance in all magical working, and thus shall the lessons of the Hall of the Neophytes be duly carried out in our daily life.

<131> Z. 3

THE SYMBOLISM
OF THE
ADMISSION OF THE CANDIDATE

THE ADMISSION OF THE CANDIDATE

The Candidate is waiting without the Portal under the care of the Sentinel — "The Watcher Without" — that is, under the care of the form of Anubis of the West symbolically that he may keep off the "Dog-Faced Demons," the opposers of Anubis, who rise from the confines where matter ends, to deceive and drag down the Soul. The Ritual of the 31st Path says: "Since ever dragging down the Soul and leading it from sacred things, from the confines of matter arise the terrible Dog-Faced Demons never showing a true image unto mortal gaze."

The Hierophant gives a single knock to announce the just commencement of a vibration in the Sphere of Sensation of the Candidate. He then states that he holds the Dispensation from the G. H. Chiefs of the Second Order, to affirm that the effect of the ensuing Ceremony upon the Candidate is only authorised by the Higher Powers for the purpose of Initiation which shall ultimately lead to the knowledge of his Higher Self. He is admitted to the Grade of Neophyte which has no number, concealing the commencement of all things under the similitude of no thing.

The Hegemon, the representative of the Goddess of Truth and Justice, is consequently sent to superintend the preparation, symbolising that it is the Presider of Equilibrium who is to administrate the process of Initiation, by the commencement of the forces of equilibrium in the Candidate himself, through the symbols of rectitude and self-control. But the actual
<132> preparation of the Candidate should be performed by the Sentinel — the "Watcher Without" — to show that this preparation must be accomplished before the establishment of equilibrium can occur. Therefore, does the Hegemon superintend the preparation rather than perform it actually. *A Triple Cord* is bound round the body of the Neophyte, symbolising the binding and restriction of the lower nature. It is triple in reference to the White Triangle of the Three Supernals. Then, also, are the eyes bandaged to symbolise that the light of the material world is but darkness and illusion compared with the radiance of the Divine Light. The preparation also represents a certain temporary binding and restriction of the natural body.

The Hierophant, being a Member of the Second Order and therefore initiated into the Secret Knowledge of the symbolism, shall, together with any Officers and Members also of the Inner Order, remember what tremendous Gods and Goddesses they represent — the Divine Forces of the Eternal in the administration of the Universe. The Ritual should be read in a loud, clear, stern and solemn voice so as to impress the Candidate with the solemnity of the occasion. In this, there should be no foolish nervousness or hesitation, but the Ritual as performed by an initiated Hierophant should become in his hands something more than this.

Thus should he act. Let him remember what particular God he represents. Exalting his mind unto the contemplation thereof, let him think of himself as a vast figure, standing or moving in the likeness of that God, colossal, his head lost in the clouds, with the light flashing round it from the head-dress of the God — his feet resting upon Earth in darkness, thunder and rolling clouds, and his form wrapped in flashes of lightning — the while vibrating the Name of the God. Thus standing, let him endeavour to hear the voice of the God whom he represents and of the God-Forms of the other officers as previously explained.

<133> Let him speak, then, not as if unto an assembly of mortals but as to an assembly of Gods. Let his voice be so directed as to roll through the Universe to the utmost confines of space. Let the Candidate represent unto him, as it were, a world whom he is beginning to lead unto the knowledge of its governing Angel. As it is written "The lightning lighteneth out of the East and shineth even unto the West, even so, shall the coming of the Son of Man be."

The Candidate during the Ceremony is addressed as Child of Earth, as representing the earthly or terrestrial nature of man — he who comes forward from the darkness of Malkuth to endeavour to regain the knowledge of the light. This is what is meant by the speech of the Hegemon, because the Path of the Initiate is but darkness and foolishness to the natural man. The single knock given by the Hegemon without the door represents the consenting will of the natural man to receive the force formulated by the Hierophant, and is answered by the Kerux within as if a witness were confirming the same. This being done, the Kerux, as a witness, demands authority from the Hierophant to admit the Candidate into the Hall of Truth and Justice. The Hierophant, in granting the permission, seals the Candidate with a new name given to the physical body of the outward man, but signifying the aspirations of his Soul. As a consequence of the affirmation of the Motto as the Name of the Candidate in the hall of Truth, Osiris as once sends forward the Goddess of the Scales of the Balance to baptise him with Water and the companion Goddess to consecrate him with Fire. As it is written "Unless a man be born of Water and of the Spirit, he shall in no wise enter the Kingdom of Heaven."

The Kerux instantly bars the Candidate's passage to mark that though he has been admitted, the natural man of unpurified desires cannot be a dweller in the Hall of Truth. The Goddesses of the Scales immediately purify and consecrate him, which operation calls into action the forces of the
<134> Pillars in his own sphere of sensation. This is the first of four consecrations because when the Pillars of the Tree are projected onto the Sphere of Sensation there are four pillars, of which the Middle Pillar is the axis. (Note: This idea is elaborated more clearly and at greater length in the Astronomical View of the Tarot, in Book Eight, Volume 4.—I. R.)

At this point of the Ceremony, the astral appearance of the Candidate is that of a form wrapped in darkness as if extinguished thereby, and having unto his right and unto his left the faint semblance of the Two Great Pillars of

Fire and of Cloud, whence issue faint rays into the Darkness which covers him. Immediately above his sphere of sensation there will appear a ray of bright light as if preparing to penetrate the darkness covering him. The result of this will be that the Candidate, during the whole of the ceremony of Admission, will usually appear to be somewhat automatic and vague.

The reception and consecration take place symbolically in the darkest part of Malkuth. The moment this is finished, the Candidate is conducted to the foot of the Altar, that is under the citrine part of Malkuth which receives the impact of the Middle Column. Now, the Hegemon throughout the Ceremony acts as guide, prompter and answerer for the Candidate. His office toward the Candidate is analogous to that of his Higher Soul — wherefore also, the Hegemon holds in his hand the mitre-headed sceptre to attract, since it is the sceptre of Wisdom, the Higher Self of the Candidate.

At this momemt, as the Candidate stands before the Altar, as the simulacrum of the Higher Self is attracted, so also arises the form of the Accuser in the place of the Evil Triad. This similarly attracts the simulacrum of the Evil Persona of the Candidate — and were it not for the power of the 42 lettered name in the Palaces of Yetzirah (the Gods of which name are usually called the "Great Assessors of Judgment") the actual evil Persona would at once formulate and be able to obsess the Ruach of the Candidate. For, seeing that at this time, the simulacrum of the Higher Soul is attracting the
<135> Neschamah of the Candidate, the human will is not as powerful in the Ruach for the moment, because the Aspirant of the Mysteries is now, as it were, divided. That is, his Neschamah is directed to the contemplation of his Higher Self attracted by the Hegemon. His natural body is bound and blinded, his Ruach threatened by the simulacrum of the Evil Persona attracted by Omoo-Szathan, and a species of shadow of himself thrown forward to the place of the Pillars, where the Scales of Judgment are set. At the same time that the first consecration establishes a semblance of the Pillars to his right and left, it also has drawn forth from him a semblance of himself to the place vacated by the Hegemon between the Pillars. (That is, the ceremony induces a species of schizophrenia so that the initiation may be effected. But see Jung's Commentary to *The Secret of the Golden Flower*, and also my book on alchemy *The Philosopher's Stone.*—I. R.)

Here then stands the shadow of the Candidate while the Scales of the Balance oscillate unseen. Unseen also and colossal, there is imaged before him Tho-oth, as Mettatron, in the Sign of the Enterer of the Threshold, ready, according to the decision of the human will, to permit or withhold the descent of the Lower Genius of the Candidate.

Meanwhile, the Great Assessors of Judgment examine into the truth of the accusations formulated by the Evil and averse antithesis. The Assessors of Judgment come not under the head of invisible stations, but during the Obligation and circumambulation of the Candidate, until he is brought to the Light, they hover immediately about the limits of the Temple and their evil antithesis immediately below. Therefore, when the Candidate stands before the Altar before the Obligation, is the decision actually taken by the human will of the Candidate. Rarely in his life has he been nearer death, seeing that he is, as it were, disintegrated into his component parts. The process of sym-

bolic judgment takes place during the speech of the Hierophant to
<136> the Candidate, the answer of the Hegemon and his consent to take
the Obligation.

The moment the Candidate thus consents, the Hierophant advances between the Pillars as if to assert that the Judgment is concluded. He advances by the invisible station of Harpocrates to that of the Evil Triad, which he symbolically treads down, so that as Aroueris he stands upon the opposer. He then comes to the East of the Altar, interposing between the place of the Evil Triad and the Candidate. At the same time, the Hiereus advances on the Candidate's left, the Hegemon on his right, thus formulating about him the symbol of the Higher Triad before he places his hand upon the symbol of the Three Supernals upon the Altar. Again, before doing so, he has been bidden to kneel in adoration of that symbol, as if the natural man abrogated his will before that of the Divine Consciousness.

As he kneels in the presence of the Triad of Aroueris, Thmaa-est and Horus, he places his left hand in that of his Initiator as affirming his passive reception of the Ritual, but his right hand is on the white triangle as symbolising his active aspiration towards his Higher Self. His head is bowed as representing the Voluntary submission of the human will to the Divine — and for this latter reason he repeats in the Obligation his name in the outer world.

The Hierophant gives one knock, affirming that the submission unto the higher is perfect. Only at this moment, does the invisible and colossal figure of Tho-oth cease to be in the Sign of the Enterer and give the Sign of Silence, permitting the first real descent of the Genius of the Candidate, who descends to the invisible station of Harpocrates as a witness of the Obligation.

The Hiereus and the Hierophant return to their Thrones, and therefore it is not Aroueris, but Osiris himself that addresses the speech to the Candidate — "The Voice of my Higher Self," etc., which confirms the link
established between the Neschamah and the Genius by formulat-
<137> ing the conception thereof into the Ruach. For this, Osiris speaks in
the character of the Higher Soul, the symbolic form of which is standing between the columns before him. The affirmation of the Higher Soul as the God of the man does not mean that this is the only God, but rather that it is the only presentment of him which the natural man can grasp at all. Neither is it just to say that the Higher Soul is one with God, seeing that the part is by no means the whole, nor can the whole be accurately and sufficiently described as an assemblage of parts. Let not the reverence for the God of thy self cause thee by a misconception to lose thy reverence for the Gods who live for ever — the Aeons of Infinite Years. Herein is a great error and one which may, in its ultimatum bring about the fall of the Genius, a sin which entails none the less terrible consequences because it is a sign of the higher plane where the choice is not between good and evil but between the higher and the lower forms of good.

Therefore is the Mystic Circumambulation in the Path of Darkness led by the Kerux with the symbolic light, as formulating that the Higher Soul is not the *only* Divine Light but rather a spark from the Ineffable Flame — and the Kerux, in his turn, is but the Watcher of the Gods. After the Kerux comes the Hegemon, the translator of the Higher Self, leading the Candidate; and then come the Goddesses of the Scales of the Balance, the Stolistes and the Dadouchos. They move once round; the formation in darkness of the Binah angle of the White Triangle of the Three Supernals. The Hierophant knocks once as they pass him in affirmation of Mercy — the Hiereus in affirmation of Severity; and the invisible Assessors each give the Sign of the Enterer as the Candidate passes on his way. At the second passing of the Hierophant, the knock affirms the commencement of the angle of Chokmah.

The Kerux bars the Candidate's approach to the West to mark that the natural man cannot obtain the understanding of even the Son of Osiris unless by purification and equilibrium. Again is the Candidate
<138> purified and consecrated, the Pillars about his Sphere of Sensation
being rendered more manifest. After this second consecration, the Candidate is allowed to approach the place of "The Twilight of the Gods" and for a brief space the hood-wink is slipped up, to present a glimpse, but a glimpse only, of the Beyond. In the challenge of the Hiereus to know the Name is signified the knowledge of the formula. For if the formula of Horus be not with the Candidate, that of Osiris cannot be grasped. But to the Candidate the power of Horus as yet can only appear as a terrible and incomprehensible force — "The Force of the Avenger of the Gods", whence the speech of the Hegemon for him. The Candidate cannot as yet comprehend that before Mildness can be exercised rightly, the forces of Severity and Mercy must be known and wielded, but to accomplish this the greatest courage and energy is required and not hysterical weakness and absence of resolution in action. Hence in the answer of the Hiereus is an affirmation of the necessity of courage and of the danger of fear, and he gives one knock to seal the vibration of that force imaged in the Candidate's sphere of sensation.

The next barring and consecration of the Candidate is an extension of the previous one and the commencement of the formulation of the angle of Kether. The hood-wink is again slipped up giving a still further glimpse of the nature of the Divine Light, though to the mind of the Candidate, an imperfect one. Therefore it is to him, as expressed in the answer of the Hegemon, a light dimly seen through the Darkness, yet heralding a Glory beyond. The speech of the Hierophant formulates the forces of the hidden central pillar. After this, the Candidate passes to the Altar of the Universe, which receives the influences of the three Pillars, as though then the Ray from the Divine would descend into the darkness of the mind, for then, but not till then, is he fitted to realise what are the first things necessary to the "Search for the Shining Light."

<139> The Hierophant now leaves his Throne and passes between
the Pillars, either halting there during the prayer or halting at the places of Harpocrates, or that of the Evil Triad, or East of the Altar. It does not particularly matter which, but one of them may seem more appropriate to a particular candidate than another and the Hierophant will usually find that he halts at the right place instinctively.

The Hiereus stands on the left of the Candidate, the Hegemon on his right, thus forming the Triad of the Supernals. The Kerux, Stolistes and

Dadouchos represent an inferior and supporting Triad behind him as if they affirmed that he has passed the Judgment of the Balance. It is best, though not absolutely necessary, that the Hierophant and the Hiereus should hold their Banners. In any case, it should be done astrally.

The Higher Self of the Candidate will be formulated in the invisible station of Harpocrates behind the Hierophant, who in his present position is Aroueris. The Hierophant gives a single knock to seal the matter and then invokes the Lord of the Universe. Then only is the hood-wink removed definitely.

The Hierophant, Hiereus, and Hegemon join sceptres and sword above the Candidate's head, thus formulating the Supernal Triad, and assert his reception into the Order. They recite the mystic words to seal the current of the Flowing Light.

The Higher Self remains in the station of Harpocrates, and at this point, the spirit-vision should see a gleaming white triangle formulated over the Candidate's head.

The Hierophant now calls forward the Kerux, cautioning the Candidate that the Light has preceded him without his knowledge. It represents to him here, a vague formulation of ideas which as yet he can neither grasp nor analyse. This Light is not a symbol of his Higher Self, but a Ray from the Gods to lead him thereto.

Only after having thus been brought to the Light is the Can-
<140> didate led to the East of the Altar — the place of the station of the Evil
Triad — to affirm that with this Light he will be able to cast out and trample on his own Evil Persona which, when it has been put in its place, will then become a support to him. It is to the Hiereus, "The Avenger of the Gods" therefore, that the duty of entrusting the Candidate with the secret signs, etc., is delegated. It is he who places him for the first time between the Pillars and superintends his final consecration — thus bringing the peculiar force in matter of the Hiereus to the aid of the Candidate, so that he may more safely and resolutely combat the temptations of the Evil Persona.

The Hierophant has returned to his Throne while the Hegemon holds the insignia of the Hiereus while he confers the Signs, etc. She thus affirms the necessity of the force represented by the Hiereus to the Candidate.

The Hierophant on the Throne, the Hiereus East of the Black Pillar and the Hegemon East of the White Pillar again form a Triad which here represents the reflection of the Three Supernals. The Higher Soul is formulated between the Pillars in the Place of Equilibrium. The Candidate is in the place of the Evil Triad and the Hiereus now advances to the place of Harpocrates between the Pillars to give the words.

After the giving of the words and signs, the Hiereus draws the Candidate forward between the Pillars and for the second time in the Ceremony, the Higher Soul stands near and ready to touch him. The Hiereus returns to his place East of the Black Pillar so that the Three Chief Officers may formulate and draw down to the Candidate, by their insignia, and the influence of their symbols, the forces of the Supernal Triad. It is important, therefore, that at this point, they should be in these places.

The Candidate now stands between the Pillars, bound with a rope like

the mummied form of Osiris, between Isis and Nephthys. The final Consecration now takes place by the Goddesses of the Scales of the
<141> Balance. The Candidate stands for the first time during the Ceremony at the point representing the equilibrium of the balance. Meanwhile, the Kerux goes to the North, ready for the circumambulation so as to link that with the final Consecration of the Candidate. The final Consecration is also demanded by the Hiereus — Horus, the powerful Avenger of Osiris, as still menacing the Evil Persona of the Candidate. Its effect is to seal finally, in balanced formation, the Four Pillars in the Sphere of Sensation of the Candidate. This does not imply that they were not naturally there before. But in the natural man, the symbols are unbalanced in strength — some being weaker and some stronger. The effect of the Ceremony is to strengthen the weak, to purify the strong, and so begin to equilibriate them and at the same time make a link between them and the corresponding forces of the Macrocosm.

This being done, the Hierophant commands the removal of the Rope which has hitherto been purposely retained, symbolically to restrain the actions of the natural man, whose temptation is towards the Evil Persona.

The Four Pillars being thus firmly established, the Candidate is invested with the Badge of the White Triangle of the Three Supernals formulating in Darkness. Now, also, the Higher Self is enabled in reality to form a link with him, if the human will of the natural man be *in reality* consenting thereto. The free-will of the natural man is never obsessed either by the Higher Soul or by the Ceremony, *but, the will consenting, the whole of the Ceremony is directed to strengthening its action.* As the badge is placed upon him, it is as if the two Great Goddesses, Isis and Nephthys, stretched forth their wings over Osiris to restore him again to life.

The Mystic Circumambulation follows in the Path of Light to represent the rising of Light in the Candidate, through the operation of self-sacrifice. As he passes the Hierophant's throne the red Calvary Cross is astrally formed above the astral White Triangle on his fore-head, so that so long as
<142> he belongs to the Order, he may bear that potent and sublime symbol as a link with his Higher Self and as an aid in searching out the forces of the Divine Light — if he will.

The Higher Soul or Genius now returns to the invisible station of Harpocrates, the place of the hidden Centre, yet continuing to retain the link formed with the Candidate. The address of the Hierophant is intended simply to effect the distinct formulation of the symbols of the ⓪ = [0] Grade of Neophyte in the Candidate, and it is therefore only when this is finished that the Watcher Anubis announces that the Candidate has been duly admitted as an initiated Neophyte.

The Hiereus is charged with a warning address as again confirming the will of the Candidate and addressing a final menace to the Evil Persona. The Hierophant then states clearly what the Candidate must begin to study. He affirms that the symbols must be equilibriated in the sphere of sensation before a link can be formulated between them and the Forces of the Macrocosm. The necessity of examination is insisted upon so that this may be completely done.

The Kerux then pours out the two fluids to make the semblance of blood. This is to fix in the Candidate's sphere the symbols of the forces of transmutation in Nature and also to make an astral link between these and the Candidate's physical life, as a guard of the secrecy of the Mysteries. This particular form of transmutation is used as showing the effect of a mixture of forces as producing a third appearance totally different from them. The red colour is symbolic of the blood of the Candidate. In the Ancient Mysteries, the Candidate's blood was actually drawn at this time and preserved as an avenging link in case of his proving unworthy. Our transmutation effects the matter quite as well, seeing that the astral link is formly established.

The final speech of the Hierophant is further intended besides its apparent meaning, to affirm that a person only partially initiated is neither fitted to teach nor to instruct even the outer and more ignorant in Sub-
<143> lime Knowledge. He is certain, through misunderstanding the principles, to formulate error instead of truth.

CLOSING

The greater part of the closing ceremony is explained by the opening. The Reverse Circumambulation, however, is intended to formulate the withdrawal of the Light of the Supernal Triad from the Altar, so that it may not be profaned by abiding without due guard. Not that the Divine Light would suffer thereby, but because it might initiate an Avenging Current if profaned. This is what is implied by the Law of Moses in the prohibition about offering unconsecrated Fire either before or within the Veil of the Tabernacle. As a vibratory formula, the reverse Circumambulation represents the reversal of the current and the restoration of the Operator to his ordinary condition.

The Mystic Repast then follows. It is a communion in the Body of Osiris. Its Mystic Name is "The Formula of the Justified One," and it is sufficiently explained in the section concerning the Altar.

The Kerux, in finishing, inverts the Cup, as the Watcher of the God, to show that the symbols of self-sacrifice and of regeneration are accomplished. The proclamation is confirmed by the Hierophant and the Chief Officers giving the three strokes, emblematic of the Mystic Triad, and they repeat the Mystic Words.

The Hierophant, in his final speech, seals the link first formulated between the Members and the Supernal Triad for each one present that it may prove to him or her, a guide for the ultimate attainment of the Supreme Initiation — if he will.

THE SYMBOLISM AND MEANING OF THE STEP, SIGNS, GRIP OR TOKEN AND THE WORDS

They have this three-fold interpretation:

1. Apparent meaning.
2. Spiritual or mystical reference.
3. Practical application.

<144> Each is therefore considered under three heads.

The Step. (1) The foot is advanced about six inches representing the foot on the side of *Chesed* put forward and taking a hesitating step in darkness — the left foot, to represent the power of Isis or the beginning of action rather than Nephthys as the end thereof. The term 6 inches is employed here only to render it more intelligible to English Initiates. It means a convenient measure of 6, and preferably 6 times the measure of the Phalanx of the thumb — Spirit and Will.

2. It symbolises the beginning of the stamping down of the Evil Persona. The foot is advanced 6 metrical distances answering to the number 6 of *Tiphareth* — Osiris — alluding therefore to the self-sacrifice necessary to accomplish this.

3. It represents the practical application of the beginning of a magical force. Let the Adept, in using the Sign of the Enterer, give the step as he commences the Sign and let him imagine himself colossal, clothed with the form of the God or Goddess appropriate to the work — his head reaching to the clouds — his feet resting upon Earth. And let him take the step as if he stamped upon the Earth and the Earth quaked and rocked beneath him. As it is said "Clouds and Darkness are round about Him — lightnings and thunders the habitation of His feet." Its secret name is "The Step of the Avenger."

THE SALUTING SIGN

1. That of groping forward in search of truth.

2. It represents the involution and bringing forward of the Light into the material to aid the will of the Candidate in his search for and aspiration towards the Higher.

3. Standing as before described, in the form of the God, and elevating the mind to the contemplation of *Kether,* take the step like a stroke with the foot, bring the arms up above the head as if touching the Kether, and
<145> as the step is completed bring the hands over the head forwards.
Thrust them out direct from the level of the eyes horizontally — arms extended, fingers straight, palms downwards, the hands directed towards the object it is wished to charge or to affect. At the same time, sink the head till the eyes look exactly between the thumbs. In this way, the rays from the eyes, from each finger and from the thumbs, must all converge upon the object attacked. If any of them disperse, it is a weakness.

Thus performed, this Sign is a symbol of tremendous attacking force and of projection of will power, and it should be employed in all cases where force of attack is required — especially in charging of Talismans and the like. Generally, it is best to have the thumbs and all the fingers extended — but if a particular effect is desired, you may extend only the fingers appropriate thereto, keeping the rest folded back in the hand. Herewith also, may be combined the attribution of the Planets to the head: (Mars to the right nostril, Mercury to the Mouth, etc., as explained in the Microcosm Lecture), sending at the same time an imaginary ray of colour of the Planet desired from the part of the head attributed to it. But, when finished, be careful to withdraw the rays again or they will remain like so many outlets of astral force and thus exhaust you. The best way to protect yourself against this is to give the Sign of Silence immediately. For the first Sign should always be answered by the second. The secret names of the Saluting Signs are "The Attacking Sign" or

"The Sign of the Enterer of the Threshold."

THE SIGN OF SILENCE

1. This is simply that of secrecy regarding the Mysteries.
2. It is the affirmation of the station of Harpocrates, wherein the Higher Soul of the Candidate is formulated in part of the admission Cere-
<146> mony. It is the symbol of the Centre and of the "Voice of the Silence" which answers in secret the thought of the heart.
3. The Sign of Silence withdraws the force put out by the Sign of the Enterer. Take upon thyself as before taught the colossal form of the God Harpocrates. Bring the left foot sharply back, both heels together — beat the ground once with the left foot as it is placed beside the right. Bring the left hand to the mouth and touch the centre of the lower lip with the left forefinger. Close the other fingers and thumb, and drop the right hand to the side. Imagine that a watery vapor encircles and encloses you. This is the reflux of the current.

This Sign is also used as a Protection against attack. The Sign represents a concentration of astral light about the person. Having given the Sign as above, it is a protection against all attack and danger of obsession. To make it yet stronger, the form of the God should be taken. If Spiritual force is required, formulate as if standing on a Lotus or rising from it. For force in contemplation and meditation, formulate as if seated upon a Lotus. But for more material force, as if standing upon a Dragon or a Serpent like some statues of Harpocrates. As a defence and protection, the Sign is as strong as the Banishing Pentagram, though of a different nature. And as the Sign of the Enterer represents attack, so does this sign represent defence thereto, as a shield is a defence against the Sword. From this Sign is a formula of invisibility derived. (See Ritual in Part Six.—I. R.)

The Secret Names of this Sign are: "The Sign of the God of Silence" or the "Sign of Defence or Protection." It may be performed with any finger of either hand, but it is most protective when the left forefinger is used, the Water of Chesed, for the fingers of the right hand represent more violent action, and those of the left more watery action. (If you have not a convenient implement, a Sigil or a Pentagram may be traced with any finger of any hand according to the correspondence required.)

<147> It may here be remarked that the so-called Christian Sign of Benediction, consisting of the thumb and first two fingers only, projected, is the affirmation of Osiris, Isis and Nephthys — or Spirit, Fire, and Water.

With regard to taking on mentally the forms of the Gods, it may here be noted that the process is of great assistance and use in all magical working, whether of invocation or of evocation, contemplation, meditation, skrying in the spirit vision, alchemy, etc. For the forms of the Gods do here represent a certain symbolic material action of the Divine Forces.

THE GRIP AND THE PASSWORD

1. The steps are taken and the Grip exchanged simultaneously. They mean seeking guidance in the darkness and silence of the Mysteries.

2. It shows that a steady and resolute will, acting in union with good, will accomplish what it desires, no matter how often it fail at first. It inculcates the necessity for harmony and brotherly love — of doing away with pettiness and of too much self-concentration — for allowances for the weaknesses of others within limits — of shunning resolutely anything in the nature of slander. So that in the grip of the Neophyte the Initiates meet hand to hand and foot to foot in the true greeting of a brother or sister, and not in the veiled hostility of an enemy. For, in the working of the Inner, where all invoke the same forces in the same manner, he or she becomes unsympathetic with the rest, separates himself or herself from them, and though he weaken the combination of working, yet he still more certainly attracts upon himself a reflex current from the Avengers of Evil.

The Name of the God of Silence which is the Grand Word of this Grade also represents the silence of the Sacred Mysteries to be observed towards the Outer Order. It shows also the necessity for respect towards the
<148> secrets of any Frater or Soror committed to your care, not endeavouring to search them out for purposes of curiosity nor repeating them when discovered, nor in any way referring to them so as to wound the other, nor in any way employing them as a means of causing humiliation, but to keep them as a sacred trust and not to be deflected by them from acting justly and harmoniously together.

3. In any magical ceremony, or other working, if more than one member be taking part, all present, putting themselves into the form of the God as taught, should exchange Sign, Grip and Words, so as to establish a current of harmony and the affirmation of a mutual direction of will towards the same object.

THE PASSWORD

1. Merely to guard the Secrets of the Order against any Members resigned or not working; hence changed each Equinox.

2. It is an affirmation of the different spiritual as well as the different physical constitutions of the Candidates — that all natures cannot be the same without evil and injury resulting thereby — but that each nature should be brought to its own Kether — the best of its kind. This too, may be done in all things. It is the basis of Alchemy.

3. It should be pronounced as if attracting the Solar Force — the Light of Nature, during the 6 months following the Equinox at which it is issued, as a link with the Solar Force, between that and the Order. This password, therefore, may also be used in a magical ceremony as attracting the support of the Light of Nature acting upon natural forces.

THE CEREMONY OF THE EQUINOX

The whole formulae of the Ceremony of the Equinox are intended to create a magical link between the Sun, as the Light of Nature, and the Order; and it should be celebrated within 48 hours at least of the Sun's actual entry into Aries or Libra. The single knock given by the Hierophant
<149> heralds the initiation of a fresh current. The Password, as already explained, is the symbol of the connecting link of the purpose of the

ceremony and therefore, before beginning fresh operation to attract a fresh current, the Kerux proclaims that the former password is abrogated. In the whole Ceremony, save at the exchange of Insignia, the Hierophant, Hiereus, Hegemon, Stolistes and Dadouchos remain in their places — the Kerux, or Watcher of the Gods being the only one who moves.

First comes the establishment of a vertical current in the direction of the middle column by the exchange of words between the Hierophant and the Hiereus, while the Hegemon, who is in the whole Ceremony of the Equinox the important Officer, by reason of his insignia, seals and arrests the current in the centre by a single knock and the words "I am the Reconciler between them." Then follows the cross current established between the Stolistes and Dadouchos — again fixed and sealed by the Hegemon, thus symbolising the equilateral cross of the Elements (of which the centre would naturally be about the invisible station of Harpocrates) but is arrested by the Hegemon between the Columns. The cross currents are thus thrown into the image of the Calvary Cross of the Rivers to ally it with the symbolism of Tiphareth and of the Sephiroth.

Then the Hierophant, Dadouchos, Hiereus and Stolistes formulate a circle enclosing the symbol, which is again sealed by the Hegemon. Then the Officers, being careful to follow the course of the Sun deposit in turn, their Insignia upon the Altar, taking therefrom instead the mystical symbols of the Body of Osiris corresponding to their Cardinal Points. The Hegemon takes the Lamp of Kerux. The Kerux then circumambulates, halting at the Cardinal Points and facing them, representing the course of the Sun through the Zodiac in order to attract the Solar Ray, but under the control of its Superior, the Light of Osiris, and the adorations are performed at the Stations of the Kerubim to mark the limits of the Circle.

<150> This time, it is with the Lamp of the Watcher of the Gods and with the Sign of the Calvary Cross of Tiphareth that the Hegemon seals in the centre the Solar Light. The formal assertion of the entry of a new current of Light is proclaimed, and the Mystic Words are recited to close the ceremony.

From this Ceremony there are many practical formulae derivable which will be easily comprehended by the Z. A. M. who has mastered the whole of this lecture. Only let him remember that the formulae of the Ceremony of the Equinox represents *the sudden attraction and sealing of a Force in Nature then in operation* — rather than a continuous and graduated ceremony to build up the same. Consequently also, it is well to use the password then in being as an adjunct to the other Names employed in magical ceremonies as bringing into operation the link with the Solar Light.

NOTES ON THE OPENING EXORDIUM OF "Z"

The Great Tho-oth is the highest aspect of the Hermes of the most ancient Egyptian Mysteries, and corresponds almost to the Great Angel Metatron. It is the Archangel of Kether in the Briatic World. The Mercury of the Romans must not be confused with this Great Hermes.*

The doctrines of Gnosticism and of Valentinus approached those of the pure Qabalah. In them we find Speech and Silence. Across the Abyss of Silence comes the Primal Speech. The Divine Ones here referred to are the Aeons in the Atziluthic World. These formulae of knowledge are designed in terms cognizable to us in the lower world.

Eheieh — implicit and explicit sound. "Every being pronounces all its existence, the Name of the Lord of Life, by inspiration and expiration."

Macroprosopus is Aima and Abba, Mother — Father. The two nostrils pass up and down the two breaths, as through the two Great Pillars. These throw all things into vibration; compare the Rashith ha-Gilgalim.
<151> Piercing of the Dragon's Coils suggests the freeing of Malkuth, which is also referred to as the Washing of the Garments of the Queen, the Inferior Mother. Then comes the Breaking Forth of the Light. Over Malkuth as Guardians are Metatron and Sandalphon as the Two Pillars, and Nephesch ha-Messiah, the animal soul of Messiah, the Shekinah or Presence between the Kerubim.

THE PARTICULAR EXORDIUM

The Bornless Ones of Time referred to are those corruscations of the Divine Light which are above Kether of Atziluth. In such Supernal Realms, the Ain Soph, though negative to us, is there intensely positive. Thence came forth the Gods, the Voice, the Aeons, and the Name.

The Egyptian Gods are generally most differentiated by their Crowns: Amen-Ra by the high feathers, Mo-ooth (Maut) has the same headdress as Horus. She corresponds to Aima Elohim. The high Hermes-Tho-oth has the same headdress as Amoun Kneph, the Sacred Spirit. Remember that Tho-oth, Truth, has two aspects — the higher and the lower. The higher is Absolute, the lower is suitable to human comprehension. To tell the higher form of a truth to one who cannot understand it is to lie to him because, though correctly formulated, it will not be correctly received.

The Forms of Thmaah. There are four forms of spelling for the Goddess Thma-Est whereby she is attributable to the Four Letters of the Name, and therewith to the Elements and the Tree.

Water. Binah. Heh. Thma-oe-Tt	Fire. Chokmah. Yod. Thma-oe-Sh
Air. Tiphareth. Vau. Thm-a-oe-St	Earth. Malkuth. Heh. (final) Thm-a-Oe

(The Middle Pillar)

In the Equinox Ceremony, the Hegemon is Air, Spirit, and the principal officer. She reconciles from East to West, and from North to South, and in a circular formulae.

*Note: Mathers' instinct was far more true than the scholars of his era. In *3 Enoch,* (the Hebrew Enoch), we have that matrix where Gnostic Cosomogony fused with Jewish Enochian and Throne and Chariot Mysticism. Here Metatron served the Great God of the Jews, as "Little I.A.O." did the Gnostic Transcendant Deity. Another title of Metatron, (whose *secret* Name was Michael), was Johoel, or YAH-God, also called "Little Jaho". For this See *Jewish Gnosticism, Merkabah Mysticism and Talmudic Tradition* by Gershom G. Scholem, as well as *Language and Gnosis* by J. Michael La Fargue, and especially the eye-opening *The Lion Becomes Man, (the Gnostic Leontomorphic Creator),* by Howard M. Jackson. H.S.

<152> Z. 2

THE FORMULAE OF THE MAGIC OF LIGHT

AN INTRODUCTION TO THE PRACTICAL WORKING OF THE Z. 2 FORMULAE

By G. H. FRATER S. R. M. D.

In the Ritual of the Enterer are shadowed forth symbolically, the beginning of certain of the Formulae of the Magic of Light. For this Ritual betokeneth a certain Person, Substance or Thing, which is taken from the dark World of Matter, to be brought under the operation of the Divine Formulae of the Magic of Light.*

Also herein are contained the commencements of all formulas of Evocation, the development of which is further shown in the Inner Knowledge of the succeeding grades of the Outer Order. In the true knowledge of the application of the Symbolism of the "Enterer" lies the entrance to the knowledge of Practical Magic: and therefore are all the Formulae drawn from the Ritual classed under Five several heads, according unto the Letters of the name Yeheshuah.

For to the Letter Yod י and the element of Fire belong the works of Ceremonial Magic, as the evocations of the Spirits of the Elements, etc.

Unto the First Heh ה the consecration and charging of Telesmata, and the production of Natural Phenomena, as storms, earthquakes, etc.

Unto the Great Holy Letter Shin ש are allotted Three classes of works: spiritual development, transformations and invisibility.

Unto the Letter Vau ו Divination in all its branches; and the art of making the Link between the subject of the work and the process of divination.

And to the Final Heh ה the works and operations of the Art of Alchemy, the order of its processes and Transmutation.

<153>

FOREWORD

By FRATER A. M. A. G.

This document, which was presented to advanced members of the Zelator Adeptus Minor grade, lists under the name of the Pentagrammaton several modes of magical working. It comprises, altogether, seven formulae. For the first five of these, I have provided herewith examples of the appropriate kind of Ritual in order to enable the reader or student to form some notion of their nature. They are not produced here that they may be slavishly

*Note: Here we have the heart of the Golden Dawn's Magic of Light. Just as the profane Ego, the "Person" of the Neophyte is bound by oath of submission and faith to the current invested in the Golden Dawn in the neophyte Ritual, so too, every semi-autonomous process, conscious and unconscious, dwelling with that ego in the Kingdom of the Mind must likewise be initiated as a Neophyte in the Golden Dawn. At every conceivable level of your personality, the little whirling wheels of the Cross-Flux of the Elemental Forces represented by I. H. V. H. must each come to view themselves as the vehicles for the Spirit represented by Shin, thus transforming the whole person, atom by atom, into Yeheshuah!

In Tibet, Padmasambhava converted all the Bon spirits to Buddhism. Transcendant realities know no Sect. H.S.

followed, since they are purely personal productions. My motive in including them is only to assist the student as showing him a completed type of ceremony. The formula for Spiritual Development so-called, is represented by two distinct rituals each quite different in structure, yet equally efficacious in its own especial way. The Bornless Ritual, the second of the two, was reproduced in rudimentary form in my *Tree of Life.* Because of the excellent dovetailing of certain Order formulae and speeches with the barbarous words of the older Ritual, rendering it in practice a magnificent and inspiring ceremony, I have decided to republish it here so that interested students may observe how older fragments may be treated.

So far as the writer is concerned, the section on Divination never acquired much meaning, but it was thought advisable to retain it in the event that significance may be seen in it by others. As an example of the first stages of that mode of operation, there is given an experience recorded many years ago by G. H. Frater Sub Spe, and to some it may prove suggestive. The section on Alchemy remains quite obscure since the subject does not interest me; and I regret that I have not been able to acquire a record of an operation based on it. (N. B. Since this was written, my book entitled *The*
<154> *Philosopher's Stone* has been published. It is a fairly protracted survey and analysis of alchemical ideology.—I. R.)

The Requiem Ritual is an original contribution, though based on fundamental formulae, and I hope it will be found useful.

So far as the first sections on actual Ceremonial Magic are concerned a few remarks may seem appropriate. Let it be noted first of all that a formal Circle and Triangle are required only in that type of operation called Evocation. It is preferable to paint the circle and divine names on the floor or on canvas, or on a neutral coloured sheet of linoleum so that the circle and names appear brilliant and clear cut. But for convenience' sake, and for quicker working, it is useful to lay out a circle in coloured tapes. The colour naturally will depend on the nature of the ceremony. At the appropriate angles of quarters of this taped circle, pentacles or flashing Tablets of the requisite Divine Names or symbols may be placed.

The other ceremonies, Consecration and Invisibility for example, require no such device, for the performance of the Banishing Rituals of the Pentagram and Hexagram followed by the Consecrations — either as in the Neophyte Ceremony or as in the Opening by Watch-Tower — clears a space for working which is amply protected. This procedure suffices for most operations, though in Evocation the greatest precautions and protections are necessary, and these are afforded by the presence of the Circle and Divine Names.

A great deal of attention should be paid to that part of the ceremony demanding the Invocation of the Higher. Success herein spells success for the entire ceremony. That is, there should be a clear consciousness of the presence of the divine force coursing through the operator. He should become aware of the awakening of a titanic force within him. It is an unmistakable sensation. So strong and powerful can this become, that at times it may almost seem to be a physical one. If this Invocation is slurred over or
<155> inconsequentially performed, then a great deal of power must be

expended unnecessarily on the remaining parts of the ritual in order to redeem the entire operation from failure. And the operation would suffer from the disadvantage of having been effected by the human part of the magician, instead of by his own Higher Genius. If the Vibratory formula of the Middle Pillar is very powerfully employed, using the name appropriate to the operation on hand, and if the force thus invoked is distributed throughout the Sphere of Sensation by the formulae of the Mystic Circumambulation — both of which are fully described in Z. 1, Book Five —then the chances of success are great. It is imperative to stress this point for it is my belief that the greater number of the cases of failure in, let us say, evocation are due solely to hastening past this important stage to the actual and stated purpose of the ceremony. This haste causes failure. Failure brings about disappointment in the formula as a whole. This is why so little work has been done on this particular system of Magic.

In passing, may I say that before the Vibratory Formula of the Middle Pillar can be at all successfully employed, the student should have put in a great deal of work on the exercise called the Formulation of the Middle Pillar. This exercise, described in the Portal paper reprinted in Part One and at great length in my book *The Middle Pillar,* awakens the magical centres in the psycho-spiritual make-up of the student. Needless to say, that without the power derived, directly or indirectly, from these Sephirotic centres of chakras, there can be no successful Magic. When a certain amount of success has been obtained in this formulation, then the vibratory formula should be assiduously practised. Its results are salutary — and quite apart from the spiritual and psychic effect, which is that to be aimed at, its reaction incidentally on the physical health and vitality is so marked as almost to be miraculous.

The two important adjuncts to success in Ceremonial Magic
<156> are briefly the God-form and the Vibration of the Divine Name. The
assumption of the appropriate form of the Egyptian God — or the Telesmatic Image especially built up by the imagination based upon the signification of the letters of the Name — and the powerful vibration of the Name itself by the Vibratory Formula of the Middle Pillar are bound, if all other conditions are complied with, to yield salutary results. The symbolic God-form held firmly in the imagination, the Name vibrated with great force — then the subsequent invocations, and the gradual materialisation or other manifestation of the force, require practically no effort. The most frequent mistake, and of course a natural one, is to concentrate upon the stated purpose of the operation.

The type of Invocation of the Higher employed in most of the ceremonies shown here has no authority obtaining within the Order. It is fundamentally the result of my own spiritual bias. The Higher invocations more usually employed within the Order approximate to the nature of ordinary prayers. These, for many reasons into which I do not wish to enter, do not please me.

The procedure delineated above should of course be followed in all other types of ceremonial — for the consecration of Flashing Tablets and Talismans; and especially in operations striving towards invisibility or transformation is the successful invocation of the divine force necessary.

One final word as to these ceremonies. The student is not to assume that these operations in themselves are important. That is, from the spiritual point of view, the fact that the Magician can attain invisibility or effect a transformation or a materialisation is relatively unimportant. What does matter however, is that these operations comprise a discipline and a type of training which is almost indispensable in the serious labours of spiritual development. The student who has struggled with these formulae, and who has kept his aspiration to the divine keen and untarnished, has a disciplined and a powerful instrument at his command.

<157> *Index for general reference to the Enterer Ceremony of the ⓪ = 0 Grade*

1. A—The Ceremony itself. The place of the Temple.
2. B—The Hierophant.
3. C—The Officers.
4. D—The Candidate.
5. E—The Ceremony of Opening.
6. F—Hierophant states that he has received a Dispensation from Second Order, and commands Hegemon to prepare Candidate. Candidate prepared. Speech of Hegemon.
7. G—Admission of Candidate. First barring by Kerux. First baptism of the Candidate with Water and Fire.
8. H—The Candidate is conducted to the foot of the Altar. Hierophant asks "Wherefore hast thou come, etc." Candidate replies "I seek the hidden Light, etc."
9. I—Candidate is asked whether he is willing to take the Obligation. He assents; and is instructed now to kneel at the Altar.
10. J—Administration of the Obligation, and raising the Neophyte from the kneeling position.
11. K—Candidate is placed in the North. Oration of the Hierophant, "The Voice of my Higher Self, etc." Hierophant commands the mystic circumambulation in the Path of Darkness.
12. L—Procession. Candidate barred in South. Second Baptism of Water and Fire. Speech of Hegemon. Allowing the Candidate to proceed.
13. M—Hoodwink slipped up. Challenge of Hiereus. Speech of Hegemon. Speech of Hiereus. Candidate re-veiled and passed on.
14. N—Circumambulation. Barred in North. Third Baptism. Speech
<158> of Hegemon allowing Candidate to approach unto the Gate of the East.
15. O—Hoodwink slipped up for the second time. Hierophant challenges. Hegemon answers for Candidate. Speech of Hierophant. Candidate passes on.
16. P—Candidate led to West of Altar. Hierophant advances by the Path of Samekh. Officers form the Triangle. Prayer of Hierophant.
17. Q—Candidate rises. Hierophant addresses him, "Long hast thou dwelt in darkness. Quit the Night and seek the Day." Hoodwink finally removed. Sceptres and Swords joined. "We receive thee, etc." Then

the Mystic Words.

18. R—Hierophant indicates Lamp of Kerux. He commands that the Candidate be conducted to the East of the Altar. He orders Hiereus to bestow signs, etc. Hiereus places Candidate between Pillars. Signs and words. He orders the fourth and final consecration to take place.
19. S—Hegemon removes rope and invests Candidate with his Insignia. Hiereus then ordains the Mystic Circumambulation in the Path of Light.
20. T—Hierophant lectures on the Symbols. Proclamation by Kerux.
21. U—Hierophant commands Hiereus to address Candidate.
22. V—Hierophant addresses Neophyte on subject of study.
23. W—Blood produced. Speech of Kerux. Hiereus' final caution.
24. X—The closing takes place.

<159> I. י

EVOCATION

A—The Magic Circle.

B—The Magician, wearing the Great Lamen of the Hierophant; and his scarlet Robe. A Pentacle, whereon is engraved the Sigil of the Spirit to be invoked, has painted on the back of it the circle and cross as shown on the Hierophant's Lamen.

C—The Names and Formulae to be employed.

D—The Symbol of the whole evocation.

E—The Construction of the circle and the placing of all the symbols, etc., employed, in the places properly allotted to them; so as to represent the interior of a G. D. Temple in the Enterer, and the purification and consecration of the actual piece of ground or place, selected for the performance of the Evocation.

F—The Invocation of the Higher Powers. Pentacle formed of three concentric bands, name and sigil therein, in proper colours, is to be bound thrice with a cord, and shrouded in black, thus bringing into action a Blind Force to be further directed or differentiated in the Process of the Ceremony. Announcement aloud of the Object of the working; naming the Spirit or Spirits, which it is desired to evoke. This is pronounced standing in the Centre of the Circle and turning towards the quarter from which the Spirit will come.

G—The Name and Sigil of the Spirit, wrapped in a black cloth, or covering, is now placed within the circle, at the point corresponding to the West, representing the Candidate. The consecration of Baptism by water and fire of the Sigil then takes place, and the proclamation in a loud and firm voice of the spirit (or spirits) to be evoked.

H—The veiled Sigil is now to be placed at the foot of the Altar. The
<160> Magician then calls aloud the Name of the Spirit, summoning him to appear, stating for what purpose the spirit is evoked: what is desired in the operation; why the evocation is performed at this time, and

finally solemnly affirming that the Spirit *shall* be evoked by the Ceremony.

I—Announcement aloud that all is prepared for the commencement of the actual Evocation. If it be a good spirit the Sigil is now to be placed *within* the White Triangle on the Altar, the Magician places his left hand upon it, raises in his right hand the magical Implement employed (usually the Sword) erect; and commences the Evocation of the Spirit N., to visible appearance. The Magician stands in the Place of the Hierophant during the Obligation, irrespective of the particular quarter of the Spirit.

But if the nature of that Spirit be evil, then the Sigil must be placed *without* and to the West of the White Triangle and the Magician shall be careful to keep the point of the Magical Sword upon the centre of the Sigil.

J—Now let the Magician imagine himself as clothed *outwardly* with the semblance of the form of the Spirit to be evoked, and in this let him be careful *not to identify himself* with the spirit, which would be dangerous; but only to formulate a species of mask, worn for the time being. And if he knows not the symbolic form of the Spirit, then let him assume the form of an Angel belonging unto the same class of operation, this form being assumed. Then let him pronounce aloud, with a firm and solemn voice, a convenient and potent oration and exorcism of the Spirit unto visible appearance.

At the conclusion of this exorcism, taking the covered sigil in his left hand, let him smite it thrice with the flat blade of the Magic
<161> Sword. Then let him raise on high his arms to their utmost stretch, holding in his left hand the veiled sigil, and in his right the Sword of Art erect. At the same time stamping thrice upon the ground with his right foot.

K—The veiled and corded sigil is then to be placed in the Northern part of the Hall at the edge of the Circle, and the Magician employs the oration of the Hierophant, from the throne of the East, modifying it slightly, as follows: "The voice of the Exorcism said unto me, Let me shroud myself in darkness, peradventure thus may I manifest myself in Light, etc." The Magician then proclaims aloud that the Mystic Circumambulation will take place.

L—The Magician takes up the Sigil in his left hand and circumambulates the Magic Circle once, then passes to the South and halts. He stands (having placed the sigil on the ground) between it and the West, and repeats the oration of the Kerux. And again consecrates it with Water and Fire. Then takes it in his hand, facing westward, saying, "Creature of . . . ., twice consecrate, thou mayest approach the gate of the West."

M—The Magician now moves to the West of the Magical Circle, holds the Sigil in his left hand and the sword in his right, faces South West, and again astrally masks himself with the form of the Spirit, and for the first time partially opens the covering of the Sigil, without however entirely removing it. He then smites it once with the flat blade of the

sword, saying, in a loud, clear, and firm voice: "Thou canst not pass from concealment unto Manifestation, save by the virtue of the Name Elohim. Before all things are the Chaos and the Darkness, and the Gates of the Land of Night. I am He Whose Name is darkness. I am the Great One of the Path of the Shades. I am the Exorcist in the midst
<162> of the Exorcism. Appear thou therefore without fear before me, so pass thou on." He then reveils the Sigil.

N—Take the Sigil to the North, circumambulating first, halt, place Sigil on the ground, stand between it and the East, repeat the oration of the Kerux, again consecrate with Fire and Water. Then take it up, face North, and say "Creature of . . . . . . thrice consecrate, thou mayest approach the Gate of the East."

O—Repeat Section M in North East. Magician then passes to East, takes up Sigil in left and Sword in right hand. Assumes the Mask of the Spirit form, smites the Sigil with the Lotus Wand or Sword, and says, "Thou canst not pass from concealment unto manifestation save by virtue of the name YHVH. After the Formless and the Void and the Darkness, then cometh the knowledge of the Light. I am that Light which riseth in the Darkness. I am the Exorcist in the midst of the exorcism. Appear thou therefore in visible form before me, for I am the Wielder of the Forces of the Balance. Thou hast known me now, so pass thou on to the Cubical Altar of the Universe!"

P—He then recovers Sigil and passes to Altar, laying it thereon as before shown. He then passes to the East of the Altar, holding the sigil and sword as already explained. Then doth he rehearse a most potent Conjuration and invocation of the Spirit unto visible appearance, using and reiterating all the Divine, Angelic, and Magical Names appropriate to this end, neither omitting the signs, seals, sigils, lineal figures, signatures and the like from that conjuration.

Q—The Magician now elevates the covered Sigil towards heaven, removes the veil entirely, leaving it yet corded, crying with a loud voice, "Creature of . . . . . . long hast thou dwelt in darkness. Quit the Night and
<163> seek the Day." He then replaces it upon the Altar, holds the Magical Sword erect above it, the pommel immediately above the centre thereof, and says, "By all the names, Powers, and Rites already rehearsed, I conjure thee thus unto visible appearance." Then the Mystic Words.

R—Saith the Magician, "As Light hidden in the Darkness can manifest therefrom, *so shalt thou* become manifest from concealment unto manifestation."

He then takes up the Sigil, stands to East of Altar, and faces West. He shall then rehearse a long conjuration to the powers and spirits immediately superior unto that one which he seeks to invoke, *that they shall force him to manifest himself unto visible appearance.*

He then places the Sigil between the Pillars, himself at the East facing West, then in the Sign of the Enterer doth he direct the whole current of his will upon the Sigil. Thus he continueth until such time as he shall perceive his Will power to be weakening, when he protects himself from the reflex of the current by the sign of silence, and drops his hands. He now looks towards the Quarter that the Spirit is to appear in, and he should now see the first signs of his visible manifestation. If he be not thus faintly visible, let the Magician repeat the conjuration of the Superiors of the Spirit, from the place of the Throne in the East. And this conjuration may be repeated thrice, each time ending with a new projection of Will in the sign of the Enterer, etc. But if at the third time of repetition he appeareth not, then be it known that there is an error in the working.

So let the Master of Evocations replace the Sigil upon the Altar, holding the Sword as usual: and thus doing, let him address a hum-
<164> ble prayer unto the Great Gods of Heaven to grant unto him the force necessary to correctly complete that evocation. He is then to take back the Sigil to between the Pillars, and repeat the former processes, when assuredly that Spirit will begin to manifest, but in a misty and ill-defined form.

(But if, as is probable, the Operator be naturally inclined unto evocation, then might that Spirit perchance manifest earlier in the Ceremony than this. Still, the Ceremony is to be performed up to this point, whether he be there or no.)

Now as soon as the Magician shall see the visible manifestation of that Spirit's presence, he shall quit the station of the Hierophant, and consecrate afresh with Water and with Fire, the Sigil of the evoked spirit.

S—Now doth the Master of Evocations remove from the Sigil the restricting cord, and holding the freed Sigil in his left hand, he smites it with the flat blade of his sword, exclaiming, "By and in the Names of...... I do invoke upon thee the power of perfect manifestation unto visible appearance." He then circumambulates the circle thrice holding the sigil in his Right hand.

T—The Magician, standing in the place of the Hierophant, but turning towards the place of the Spirit, and fixing his attention thereon, now reads a potent Invocation of the Spirit unto visible appearance, having previously placed the sigil on the ground, within the circle, at the quarter where the Spirit appears.

This Invocation should be of some length; and should rehearse and reiterate the Divine and other Names consonant with the working.

That Spirit should now become fully and clearly visible, and should be able to speak with a direct voice, if consonant with his
<165> nature. The Magician then proclaims aloud that the Spirit N. hath been duly and properly evoked in accordance with the sacred Rites.

U—The Magician now addresses an Invocation unto the Lords of the plane of the Spirit to compel him to perform that which the Magician shall demand of him.

V—The Magician carefully formulates his demands, questions, etc., and writes down any of the answers that may be advisable. The Master of

Evocations now addresses a Conjuration unto the Spirit evoked, binding him to hurt or injure naught connected with him, or his assistants, or the place. And that he deceive in nothing, and that he fail not to perform that which he hath been commanded.

W—He then dismisses that Spirit by any suitable form, such as those used in the higher grades of the Outer. And if he will not go, then shall the Magician compel him by forces contrary to his nature. But he must allow a few minutes for the Spirit to dematerialise the body in which he hath manifested, for he will become less and less material by degrees. And note well that the Magician (or his companions if he have any) shall never quit the circle during the process of evocation, or afterwards, till the Spirit hath quite vanished.

Seeing that in some cases, and with some constitutions, there may be danger arising from the Astral conditions, and currents established, and without the actual intention of the Spirit to harm, although if of a low nature, he would probably endeavour to do so. Therefore, before the commencement of the Evocation, let the operator assure himself that everything which may be necessary, be properly arranged within the circle.

But if it be actually necessary to interrupt the Process, then let him stop at that point, veil and re-cord the Sigil if it have been unbound or uncovered, recite a License to Depart or a Banishing Formula, and per-
<166> form the Lesser Banishing Rituals both of the Pentagram and Hexagram. Thus only may he in comparative safety quit the circle.

Note—Get the Spirit into a White Triangle outside the midheaven, then shall he speak the truth of necessity.

II. ה

CONSECRATION OF TALISMANS

A—The place where the operation is done.

B—The Magical Operator.

C—The Forces of Nature employed and attracted.

D—The Telesma or material basis.

E—In Telesmata, the selection of the Matter to form the Telesma; the preparation and arrangement of the place. The drawing and forming of the body of the Telesma. In Natural Phenomena the preparation of the operation; the formation of the Circle, and the selection of the material basis, such as a piece of Earth, a cup of Water, a Flame of Fire, a Pentacle, or the like.

F—The invocation of the highest divine forces, winding a black cord round the Telesma or material basis, covering the same with a black veil, and initiating the blind force therein. Naming aloud the *Nature* of the Telesma or Operation.

G—The Telesma or material Basis is now placed towards the West, and duly consecrated with Water and Fire. The purpose of the operation, and the effect intended to be produced is then to be rehearsed in a loud and clear voice.

H—Placing the Talisman or material basis at the foot of the Altar, state aloud the object to be attained, solemnly asserting that it will be attained, and the reason thereof.

I—Announcement aloud that all is prepared and in readiness, either for charging the Telesma, or for the Commencement of the Operation
<167> to induce the natural Phenomena. Place a good Telesma or Material Basis within the White Triangle on the Altar. Place bad to the West of same, holding the sword erect in the right hand for a good purpose, or its point upon the centre of the Triangle for evil.

J—Now follows the performance of an Invocation to attract the desired spirit to the Telesma or material basis, describing in the air above it the lineal figures and sigils, etc., with the appropriate instrument. Then, taking up the Telesma in the left hand, let him smite it thrice with the flat of the blade of the Sword of Art. Then raise it in the left hand (holding erect and aloft the Sword in the right hand stamping thrice upon the Earth with the right foot).

K—The Talisman or Material basis is to be placed towards the North, and the Operator repeats the Oration of the Hierophant to the candidate. "The voice of the Exorcism said unto me, Let me shroud myself in darkness, peradventure thus shall I manifest myself in light. I am the only being in an abyss of Darkness. From the Darkness came I forth ere my birth, from the silence of a primal sleep. And the Voice of Ages answered unto my soul, Creature of Talismans, the Light shineth in the darkness, but the darkness comprehendeth it not. Let the Mystic Circumambulation take place in the path of Darkness with the symbolic light of Occult Science to lead the way."

L—Then, taking up the Light (not from the Altar) in right hand, circumambulate. Now take up Telesmata or M. B., carry it round the circle, place it on the ground due South, then bar it, purify and consecrate with Water and Fire afresh, lift it with left hand, turn and facing
<168> West, say, "Creature of Talismans, twice consecrate, thou mayest approach the gate of the West."

M—He now passes to the West with Telesmata in left hand, faces S.E., partly unveils Telesmata, smites it once with the flat blade of the Sword, and pronounces, "Thou canst not pass from concealment unto manifestation, save by virtue of the name *Elohim.* Before all things are the Chaos and the Darkness, and the gates of the land of Night. I am He whose Name is Darkness. I am the great One of the Paths of the Shades. I am the Exorcist in the midst of the Exorcism. Take on therefore manifestation without fear before me, for I am he in whom fear is Not. Thou hast known me so pass thou on." This being done, he replaces the veil.

N—Then pass round the Circle with Telesmata, halt due North, place Talisman on ground, bar, purify, and consecrate again with Water and with Fire, and say, "Creature of Talismans, thrice consecrate, thou mayest approach the Gate of the East." (Hold Talisman aloft.)

O—Hold Telesmata in left hand, Lotus Wand in right, assume Hierophant's form. Partly unveil Talisman, smite with flat of sword, and say, "Thou canst not pass from concealment unto manifestation save by virtue of the name YHVH. After the formless and the Void and the Darkness, then cometh the knowledge of the Light. I am that Light which riseth in darkness. I am the Exorcist in the midst of the Exorcism. Take on therefore manifestation before me, for I am the wielder of the forces of the Balance. Thou hast known me now so pass thou on unto the Cubical Altar of the Universe."

P—He then recovers Talisman or M. B., passes on to the Altar, laying it thereon as before shewn. He then passes to East of Altar, hold left
<169> hand over Talisman, and sword over it erect. Then doth he rehearse a most potent conjuration and invocation of that Spirit to render irresistible this Telesmata or M. B., or to render manifest this natural phenomenon of . . . . . ., using and reiterating all the Divine, Angelic, and Magical Names appropriate to this end, neither omitting the signs, seals, sigils, lineal figures, signatures, and the like from that conjuration.

Q—The Magician now elevates the covered Telesma or Material Basis towards Heaven, then removes the Veil entirely, yet leaving it corded, crying with a loud voice. "Creature of Talismans, (or M. B.), long hast thou dwelt in darkness. Quit the Night and seek the Day."

He then replaces it in the Altar, holds the Magical Sword erect above it, the Pommel immediately above the centre thereof, and says, "By all the Names, Powers, and rites already rehearsed, I conjure upon thee power and might irresistible." Then say the Mystic Words, Khabs Am Pekht, etc.

R—Saith the Magician, "As the Light hidden in darkness can manifest therefrom, so shalt thou become irresistible." He then takes up the Telesmata, or the M. B., stands to East of the Altar, and faces West. Then shall he rehearse a long conjuration to the Powers and Spirits immediately superior unto that one which he seeks to invoke, to make the Telesmata powerful. Then he places the Talisman or M. B. between the Pillars, himself at the East, facing West, then in the Sign of the Enterer, doth he project the whole current of his Will upon the Talisman. Thus he continueth until such time as he shall perceive his will power weakening, when he protects himself by the Sign of
<170> Silence, and then drops his hands. He now looks toward the Talisman, and a flashing Light or Glory should be seen playing and flickering on the Talisman or M. B., and in the Natural Phenomena a slight commencement of the Phenomena should be waited for. If this does not occur, let the Magician repeat the Conjuration of the Superiors from the place of the Throne of the East.

And this conjuration may be repeated thrice, each time ending with a new projection of Will in the Sign of the Enterer, etc. But if at the third time of repetition the Talisman or M. B. does not flash, then be it known that there is an error in the working. So let the Master of Evocations replace the Talisman or M. B., upon the Altar holding the Sword as usual, and thus doing, let him address an humble prayer unto the Great Gods of Heaven to grant unto him the force necessary to correctly complete the work. He is then to take back the Talisman, to between the Pillars, and repeat the former process, when assuredly the Light will flash.

Now as soon as the Magician shall see the Light, he shall quit the station of the Hierophant and consecrate afresh with water and with fire.

S—This being done, let the Talisman or M. B. have the cord removed and smite it with the Sword and proclaim "By and in the Names of . . . . ., I invoke upon thee the power of . . . . . ." He then circumambulates thrice, holding the Talisman or M. B. in his right hand.

T—Then the Magician, standing in the place of the Hierophant, but fixing his gaze upon the Talisman or M.B. which should be placed on the ground within the Circle, should now read a potent invocation of some length, rehearsing and reiterating the Divine and other
<171> Names consonant with the working. The Talisman should now flash visibly, or the Natural Phenomena should definitely commence.

Then let the Magician proclaim aloud that the Talisman has been duly and properly charged, or the Natural Phenomena induced.

U—The Magician now addresses an Invocation unto the Lords of the plane of the Spirit to compel him to perform that which the Magician requires.

V—The Operator now carefully formulates his demands, stating clearly what the Talisman is intended to do, or what Natural Phenomena he seeks to produce.

W—The Master of Evocations now addresses a conjuration unto the Spirit, binding him to hurt or injure naught connected with him, or his assistants, or the place. He then dismisses the Spirits in the name of Jehovashah and Jeheshua, but wrap up Talisman first, and no Banishing Ritual shall be performed, so as not to discharge it, and in the case of Natural Phenomena it will usually be best to state what duration is required. And the Material Basis should be preserved wrapped in white linen or silk all the time that the Phenomena is intended to act.

And when it is time for it to cease, the M. B. — if water, is to be poured away; if Earth, ground to powder and scattered abroad; if a hard substance as a metal, it must be decharged, banished and thrown aside; if a flame of fire, it shall be extinguished; or if a vial containing air, it shall be opened and after that well rinsed out with pure water.

III. ש
א — INVISIBILITY

A—The Shroud of Concealment.
B—The Magician.
C—The Guards of Concealment.
<172> D—The Astral Light to be moulded into the Shroud.
E—The Equation of the Symbols in the Sphere of Sensation.

F—The Invocation of the Higher; the placing of a Barrier without the Astral Form; the Clothing of the same with obscurity through the proper invocation.

G—Formulating clearly the idea of becoming Invisible. The formulating of the exact distance at which the shroud should surround the Physical Body. The consecration with Water and Fire, so that their vapour may begin to form a basis for the shroud.

H—The beginning to formulate mentally a shroud of concealment about the operator. The affirmation aloud of the reason and object of the working.

I—Announcement that all is ready for the commencement of the operation. Operator stands in the place of the Hierophant at this stage, placing his left hand in the centre of the white triangle and holding in his right the Lotus Wand by the black end, in readiness to concentrate around him the shroud of Darkness and Mystery.

(N. B. In this operation as in the two others under the dominion of Shin, a Pentacle or Telesma suitable to the matter in hand, *may* be made use of, which is then treated as is directed for Telesmata.)

J—The Operator now recites an Exorcism of a Shroud of Darkness to surround him and render him invisible, and, holding the Wand by the black end, let him, turning round thrice completely, formulate a triple circle around him, saying, "In the Name of the Lord of the Universe, etc., I conjure thee, O Shroud of Darkness and of Mystery, that thou encirclest me so that I may become invisible, so that seeing me, men see me not, neither understand, but that they may see the thing that
<173> they see not, and comprehend not the thing that they behold! So mote it be."

K—Now move to the North, face East, and say, "I have set my feet in the North, and have said 'I will shroud myself in Mystery and concealment." Then repeat the Oration, "The Voice of my Higher Soul, etc.," and then command the Mystic Circumambulation.

L—Move round as usual to the South, Halt formulating thyself as shrouded in darkness, on the right hand the Pillar of Fire, and on the left the Pillar of Cloud, but reaching from Darkness to the Glory of the Heavens.

M—Now move from between the Pillars thou hast formulated to the West, face West, and say, "Invisible I cannot pass by the Gate of the Invisible save by the virtue of the name of 'Darkness.' " Then formulating forcibly about thee the shroud of Darkness, say, "Darkness is my Name, and concealment. I am the Great One Invisible of the Paths of the Shades. I am without fear, though veiled in Darkness, for within me, though unseen, is the Magic of Light."

N—Repeat process in L.

O—Repeat process in M but say, "I am Light shrouded in darkness. I am the wielder of the forces of the balance."

P—Now, concentrating mentally about thee the Shroud of Concealment, pass to the West of the Altar in the place of the Neophyte, face East, remain standing, and rehearse a conjuration by suitable Names for the formulating of a shroud of Invisibility around and about Thee.

Q—Now address the Shroud of Darkness, thus: "Shroud of Concealment.
Long hast thou dwelt concealed. Quit the Light, that thou mayest conceal me before men." Then carefully formulate the shroud of con-
<174> cealment around thee and say, "I receive thee as a covering and as a
guard." Then the Mystic Words.

R—Still formulating the shroud, say, "Before all Magical manifestation cometh the knowledge of the hidden light." Then move to the pillars and give the signs and steps, words, etc. With the Sign of the Enterer, project now thy whole will in one great effort to realise thyself actually fading out, and becoming invisible to mortal eyes; and in doing this must thou obtain the effect of thy physical body actually gradually becoming partially invisible to thy natural eyes, as though a veil or cloud were formulating between it and thee (and be very careful not to lose thy self-control at this point.) But also at this point is there a certain Divine Exstasis and an exaltation desirable, for herein is a sensation of an exalted strength.

S—Again formulate the shroud as concealing thee and enveloping thee, and thus wrapped up therein, circumambulate the circle thrice.

T—Intensely formulating the Shroud, stand at the East and proclaim, "Thus have I formulated unto myself a shroud of Darkness and of Mystery, as a concealment and guard."

U—Now rehearse an invocation of all the Divine Names of Binah, that thou mayest retain the Shroud of Darkness under thy own proper control and guidance.

V—State clearly to the shroud what it is thy desire to perform therewith.

W—Having obtained the desired effect, and gone about invisible, it is required that thou shouldst conjure the Powers of the Light to act against that shroud of Darkness and Mystery so as to disintegrate it, lest any force seek to use it as a medium for an obsession, etc.
Therefore rehearse a conjuration as aforesaid, and then open the
<175> shroud and come forth out of the midst thereof, and then disin-
tegrate that shroud, by the use of a conjuration to the forces of Binah to disintegrate and scatter the particles thereof, but affirming that they shall again be readily attracted at thy command.

But on no account must that shroud of awful Mystery be left without such disintegration, seeing that it would speedily attract an occupant which would become a terrible vampire praying upon him who had called it into being.

And after frequent rehearsals of this operation, the thing may almost be done "per Motem."

מ TRANSFORMATIONS

A—The Astral Form.

B—The Magician.

C—The Forces used to alter the Form.

D—The Form to be taken.

E—The Equation of the Symbolism in the Sphere of Sensation.

F—Invocation of the Higher. The definition of the Form required as a delineation of blind forces, and the awakening of the same by its proper formulation.

G—Formulating clearly to the mind the Form intended to be taken. The Restriction and Definition of this as a clear form and the actual baptism by Water and by Fire with the Order Name of the Adept.

H—The Actual Invocation aloud of the form desired to be assumed to formulate before you, the statement of the Desire of the Operator and the reason thereof.

I—Announcement aloud that all is now ready fo the operation of the Transformation of the Astral Body. The Magician mentally places the form as nearly as circumstances permit in the position of the Enterer,
<176> himself taking the place of the Hierophant, holding his Wand by the black portion ready to commence the Oration aloud.

J—Let him now repeat a powerful exorcism of the shape into which he desires to transform himself, using the Names, etc., belonging to the Plane, Planet, or other Eidolon, most in harmony with the shape desired. Then holding the Wand by the black End, and directing the flower over the head of the form, let him say, "In the name of the Lord of the Universe, Arise before me, O Form of . . . . ., into which I have elected to transform myself. So that seeing me men may see the thing that they see not, and comprehend not the thing they behold."

K—The Magician saith, "Pass toward the North, shrouded in darkness, O Form of . . . . ., into which I have elected to transform myself." Then let him repeat the usual Oration from the Throne of the East. Then command the Mystic circumambulation.

L—Now bring the Form around to the South, arrest it, and formulate it there, standing between two great Pillars of Fire and Cloud. Purify it with Water and by Fire, by placing these elements on either side of the Form.

M—Passes to West, face South East, formulate the form before thee, this time endeavouring to render it physically visible. Repeat speeches of Hiereus and Hegemon.

N—Same as L.

O—Same as M.

P—Pass to the East of Altar, formulating the Form as near in the position of the Neophyte as may be. Now address a solemn invocation and conjuration by Divine, Names etc., appropriate to render the form fitting for thy Transformation therein.

Q—Remain East of Altar, address the Form "Child of Earth, etc.," endeavouring now to see it physically. Then at the words, "we receive Thee,
<177> etc." he draws the form towards him so as to envelop him, being careful at the same time to invoke the Divine Light by the rehearsal of the Mystic Words.

R—Still keeping himself in the form of the Magician say, "Before all Magical Manifestation cometh the knowledge of the Divine Light." He then moves to the Pillars and gives Signs, etc., endeavouring with the whole force of his Will to feel himself *actually* and *physically* in the shape of the Form desired. And at this point he must see as if in a cloudy and misty manner the outline of the form enshrouding him, though not yet completely and wholly visible. When this occurs, but not before, let him formulate himself as standing between the two vast Pillars of Fire and Cloud.

S—He now again endeavours to formulate the Form as if visibly enshrouding him; and still, astrally, retaining the form, he thrice circumambulates the place of working.

T—Standing at the East, let him thoroughly formulate the shape, which should now appear manifest, and as if enshrouding him, even to his own vision; and then let him proclaim aloud, "Thus have I formulated unto myself this Transformation."

U—Let him now invoke all the Superior Names, etc., of the Plane appropriate to the Form that he may retain it under his proper control and guidance.

V—He states clearly to the Form what he intends to do with it.

W—Similar to this W section of Invisibility, save that the conjurations, etc., are to be made to the appropriate plane of the form instead of to Binah.

<178> ## ש SPIRITUAL DEVELOPMENT

A—The Sphere of Sensation.

B—The Augoeides.

C—The Sephiroth, etc. employed.

D—The Aspirant, or Natural Man.

E—The Equilibration of the Symbols.

F—The Invocation of the Higher. The limiting and controlling of the lower and the closing of the material senses, to awaken the spiritual.

G—Attempting to make the Natural Man grasp the Higher by first limiting the extent to which mere Intellect can help him herein; then by purification of his thoughts and desires. In doing this let him formulate himself as standing between the Pillars of Fire and Cloud.

H—The Aspiration of the whole Natural Man towards the Higher Self, and a prayer for Light and guidance through his Higher Self, addressed to the Lord of the Universe.

I—The Aspirant affirms aloud his earnest prayer to obtain Divine Guidance, kneels at the West of the Altar; in the position of the Candidate in the Enterer, and at the same time astrally projects his consciousness to the East of the Altar, and turns, facing his body, to the West, holding astrally his own left hand with his astral left. And he raises his Astral right hand holding the presentment of his Lotus Wand by the White portion thereof, and raised in the Air erect.

J—Let the aspirant now slowly recite an oration unto the Gods and unto the Higher Self (as that of the Second Adept in the entering of the Vault) but as if with his Astral Consciousness, which is projected to the East of the Altar.

(Note: If at this point the Aspirant should feel a sensation as of faintness coming on, let him at once withdraw the projected Astral and properly master himself before proceeding any further.)

<179> Now let the Aspirant, concentrating all his intelligence in his body, lay the blade of his Sword thrice on the Daath point of his neck, and pronounce with his whole will, the words "So help me, the Lord of the Universe and my own higher soul."

Let him then rise, facing East, and stand for a few moments in silence, raising his left hand open, and his right holding the Sword of Art, to their full length above his head; his head thrown back, his eyes lifted upwards. Thus standing let him aspire with his whole will towards his best and highest Ideal of the Divine.

K—Then let the Aspirant pass unto the North, and facing East solemnly repeat the Oration of the Hierophant, as before endeavouring to project the speaking conscious self to the place of the Hierophant (in this case to the Throne of the East.) Then let him slowly mentally formulate before him the Eidolon of a Great Angel Torch-bearer, standing before Him as if to lead and light the way.

L—Following it, let the Aspirant circumambulate, and pass to South, then let him halt, and aspire with his whole will, first to the Mercy side of the Divine Ideal, and then to the Severity thereof. And then let him imagine himself as standing between two great Pillars of Fire and Cloud, whose bases indeed are buried in black ever rolling clouds of darkness, which symbolises the chaos of the World of Assiah, but whose summits are lost in glorious light undying, penetrating unto the White Glory of the Throne of the Ancient of Days.

M—Now doth the Aspirant move unto the West, faces S. E., and repeats alike the speeches of Hiereus and Hegemon.

<180> N—After another circumambulation, the Adept aspirant halts at the South and repeats the meditation in L.

O—And so he passes unto the East, and repeats alike the words of the Hierophant and the Hegemon.

P—And so let him pass to the West of the Altar, ever led by the Angel Torchbearer. And he projects his Astral, and he implants therein his consciousness, and his body kneels what time his soul passes between the Pillars. And he prayeth the Great Prayer of the Hierophant.

Q—And now doth the Aspirant's Soul re-enter unto his gross-form; and he dreams in Divine Exstasis of the Glory Ineffable which is in the Bornless beyond; and so meditating doth he arise, and lifts to the Heavens, his hands, and his eyes, and his hopes, and concentrating his Will on the Glory, low murmurs he the Mystic Words of Power.

R—So also doth he presently repeat the words of the Hierophant concerning the Lamp of the Kerux, and so also passeth he by the East of the Altar unto between the Pillars; and standing between them (or formulating them if they be not there as it appears unto him) so raises he his heart unto the Highest Faith, and so he meditates upon the highest Godhead he can dream of. Then let him grope with his hands in the darkness of his ignorance, and in the Enterer sign invoke the Power that it remove the darkness from his spiritual vision. So let him then endeavour to behold before him in the Place of the Throne of the East, a certain light or Dim glory, which shapeth itself into a Form.

(Note: And this can be beholden only by the mental vision. Yet, owing unto the spiritual exaltation of the Adept, it may sometimes appear as if he beheld it with mortal eye.)

<181> Then let him withdraw awhile from such contemplation and formulate for his equilibriation once more the Pillars of the Temple of Heaven.

S—And so again doth he aspire to see the Glory conforming — and when this is accomplished, he thrice circumambulates, reverently saluting with the Enterer the Place of Glory.

T—Now let the Aspirant stand opposite unto the Place of that Light, and let him make deep meditation and contemplation thereon. Presently also imagining it to enshroud and envelope him, and again endeavouring to identify himself with its glory. So let him exalt himself in the likeness or eidolon of a colossal Being, and endeavour to realise that this is the only True Self, and that the Natural Man is as it were the base and throne thereof, and let him do this with due and meet reverence and awe.

And therefore he shall presently proclaim aloud "Thus at length have I been permitted to begin to comprehend the form of my Higher Self."

U—Now doth the aspirant make entreaty of that Augoeides to render comprehensible what things may be necessary for his instruction and comprehension.

V—And he consults It in any matter he may have especially sought for guidance from the Beyond.

W—And lastly, let the Aspirant endeavour to formulate a link between the Glory and his self-hood; and let him renew his obligation of purity of mind before it, avoiding in this any tendency to fanaticism or spiritual pride.

(And let the Adept remember that this process here set forth is on no account to be applied to endeavouring to come in contact with the higher soul of Another. Else thus assuredly will he be led into error, hallucination, or even madness.)

<182>

IV. ו

DIVINATION

A—The Form of Divination.

B—The Diviner.

C—The Forces acting in the Divination.

D—The subject of the Divination.

E—The preparation of all things necessary, and the right understanding of the process so as to formulate a connecting-link between the process employed and the Macrocosm.

F—The Invocation of the Higher; arrangement of the scheme of divination and initiation of the forces thereof.

G—The first entry into the matter. First assertion of limits and correspondences: beginning of the working.

H—The actual and careful formulation of the question demanded; and consideration of all its correspondences and their classifications.

I—Announcement aloud that all the correspondences taken are correct and perfect; the Diviner places his hand upon the instrument of Divination; standing at the East of the Altar, he prepares to invoke the forces required in the Divination.

J—Solemn invocation of the necessary spiritual forces to aid the Diviner in the Divination. Then let him say, "Arise before me clear as a mirror, O magical vision requisite for the accomplishment of this divination."

K—Accurately define the term of the question; putting down clearly in writing what is already *known,* what is *suspected* or *implied,* and what is sought to be known. And see that thou verify in the beginning of the judgment that part which is already known.

L—Next let the Diviner formulate clearly under two groups or heads (a) the arguments for, (b) the arguments against, the success of the subject
<183> of one divination, so as to be able to draw a preliminary conclusion therefrom on either side.

M—First formulation of a conclusive judgment from the premises already obtained.

N—Same as section L.

O—Formulation of a second judgment, this time of the further developments arising from those indicated in the previous process of judgment, which was a preliminary to this operation.

P—The comparison of the first preliminary judgment with one second judgment developing therefrom, so as to enable the Diviner to form an idea of the probable action of forces beyond the actual plane, by the invocation of an angelic figure consonant to the process. And in this matter take care not to mislead thy judgment through the action of thine own preconceived ideas; but only relying, after due tests, on the indication afforded thee by the angelic form. And know, unless the form be of an angelic nature its indication will not be reliable, seeing, that if it be an elemental, it will be below the plane desired.

Q—The Diviner now completely and thoroughly formulates his whole judgment as well for the immediate future as for the development thereof, taking into account the knowledge and indications given him by the angelic form.

R—Having this result before him, let the Diviner now formulate a fresh divination process, based on the conclusions at which he has arrived, so as to form a basis for a further working.

S—Formulates the sides for and against for a fresh judgment, and deduces conclusion from fresh operation.

T—The Diviner then compares carefully the whole judgment and decisions arrived at with their conclusions, and delivers now plainly a succinct and consecutive judgment thereon.

<184> U—The Diviner gives advice to the Consultant as to what use he

shall make of the judgment.

V—The Diviner formulates clearly with what forces it may be necessary to work in order to combat the Evil, or fix the Good, promised by the Divination.

W—Lastly, remember that unto thee a divination shall be as a sacred work of the Divine Magic of Light, and not to be performed to pander unto thy curiosity regarding the secrets of another, and if by this means thou shalt arrive at a knowledge of another's secrets, thou shalt respect and not betray them.

V ח
ALCHEMY

A—The Curcurbite or the Alembic.

B—The Alchemist.

C—The processes and forces employed.

D—The matter to be transmuted.

E—The selection of the Matter to be transmuted, and the formation, cleansing and disposing of all the necessary vessels, materials, etc., for the working of the process.

F—General Invocation of the Higher Forces to Action. Placing of the Matter within the curcurbite or philosophic egg, and invocation of a blind force to action therein, in darkness and silence.

G—The beginning of the actual process. The regulation and restriction of the proper degree of Heat and Moisture to be employed in the working. First evocation followed by first distillation.

H—The taking up of the residuum which remaineth after the distillation from the curcurbite or alembic; the grinding thereof to form a powder in a mortar. This powder is then to be placed again in the curcurbite. The fluid already distilled is to be poured again upon it. The curcurbite or philosophic egg is to be closed.

<185> I—The curcurbite or Egg Philosophic being hermetically sealed, the Alchemist announces aloud that all is prepared for the invocation of the forces necessary to accomplish the work. The Matter is then to be placed upon an Altar with the elements and four weapons thereon; upon the white triangle and upon a flashing Tablet of a general nature, in harmony with the matter selected for the working. Standing now in the place of the Hierophant at the East of the Altar, the Alchemist should place his left hand upon the top of the curcurbite, raise his right hand holding the Lotus Wand by the Aries band (for in Aries is the beginning of the life of the year), ready to commence the general invocation of the forces of the Divine Light to operate in the work.

J—The pronouncing aloud of the Invocation of the requisite general forces, answering to the class of alchemical work to be performed. The conjuring of the necessary Forces to act in the curcurbite for the work required. The tracing in the air above it with appropriate weapon the necessary lineal figures, signs, sigils and the like. Then let the Alchemist say: "So help me the Lord of the Universe and my own Higher Soul." Then let him raise the curcurbite in the air with both hands, saying: "Arise herein to action, O ye forces of the Light

Divine."

K—Now let the matter putrefy in the Balneum Mariae in a very gentle heat, until darkness beginneth to supervene; and even until it becometh entirely black. If from its nature the mixture will not admit of entire blackness, examine it astrally till there is the astral appearance of the thickest possible darkness, and thou mayest also evoke an elemental form to tell thee if the blackness be sufficient. But be thou sure that in this latter thou art not deceived, seeing that the nature of such an
<186> elemental will be deceptive from the nature of the symbol of Darkness, wherefore ask thou of him nothing *further* concerning the working at this stage but only concerning the blackness, and this can be further tested by the elemental itself, which should be either black or clad in an intensely black robe. (Note, for this evocation, use the names, etc., of Saturn.)

When the mixture be sufficiently black, then take the curcurbite out of the Balneum Mariae and place it to the North of the Altar and perform over it a solemn invocation of the forces of Saturn to act therein; holding the wand by the black band, then say: "The voice of the Alchemist" etc. The curcurbite is then to be unstopped and the Alembic Head fitted on for purposes of distillation. (Note: In all such invocations a flashing tablet should be used whereon to stand the curcurbite. Also certain of the processes may take weeks, or even months to obtain the necessary force, and this will depend on the Alchemist rather than on the matter.)

L—Then let the Alchemist distil with a gentle heat until nothing remaineth to come over. Let him then take out the residuum and grind it into a powder; replace this powder in the curcurbite, and pour again upon it the fluid previously distilled.

The curcurbite is then to be placed again in a Balneum Mariae in a gentle heat. When it seems fairly re-dissolved (irrespective of colour) let it be taken out of the bath. It is now to undergo another magical ceremony.

M—Now place the curcurbite to the West of the Altar, holding the Lotus Wand by the black end, perform a magical invocation of the Moon in her decrease and of Cauda Draconis. The curcurbite is then to be exposed to the moonlight (she being in her decrease) for nine con-
<187> secutive nights, commencing at full moon. The Alembic Head is then to be fitted on.

N—Repeat process set forth in section L.

O—The curcurbite is to be placed to the East of the Altar, and the Alchemist performs an invocation of the Moon in her increase, and of Caput Draconis (holding Lotus Wand by white end) to act upon the matter. The curcurbite is now to be exposed for nine consecutive nights (ending with the Full Moon) to the Moon's rays. (In this, as in all similar exposures, it matters not if such nights be overclouded, so long as the vessel be placed in such a position as to receive the direct rays did the cloud withdraw.)

P—The curcurbite is again to be placed on the white triangle upon the Altar. The Alchemist performs an invocation of the forces of the Sun to act in the curcurbite. It is then to be exposed to the rays of the sun for twelve hours each day; from 8:30 a.m. to 8:30 p.m. (This should be done preferably when the sun is strongly posited in the Zodiac, but it can be done at some other times, though *never* when he is in Scorpio, Libra, Capricornus, or Aquarius).

Q—The curcurbite is again placed upon the white triangle upon the altar. The Alchemist repeats the words: "Child of Earth, long hast thou dwelt, etc." then holding above it the Lotus Wand by the white end, he says: "I formulate in thee the invoked forces of Light," and repeats the mystic words. At this point keen and bright flashes of light should appear in the curcurbite, and the mixture itself (as far as its nature will permit) should be clear. Now invoke an Elemental from the curcurbite consonant to the Nature of the Mixture, and judge by the nature of the colour of its robes and their brilliancy whether the matter has attained to the right condition. But if the flashes do *not* appear, and if
<188> the robes of the elemental be not brilliant and flashing, then let the curcurbite stand within the white triangle for seven days; having on the right hand of the Apex of the triangle a flashing tablet of the Sun, and in the left one of the Moon. Let it not be moved or disturbed all those seven days; but not in the dark, save at night. Then let the operation as aforementioned be repeated over the curcurbite, and this process may be repeated altogether three times if the flashing light cometh not. For without this latter the work would be useless. But if after three repetitions it still appear not, it is a sign that there hath been an error in the working, such being either in the disposition of the Alchemist or in the management of the curcurbite. Wherefore let the lunar and the solar invocations and exposures be repeated, when without doubt, if these be done with care (and more especially those of Caput Draconis and Cauda Draconis with those of the Moon as taught, for these have great force materially) then without doubt shall that flashing light manifest itself in the curcurbite.

R—Holding the Lotus Wand by the white end, the Alchemist now draws over the curcurbite the symbol of the Flaming Sword as if descending into the mixture. Then let him place the curcurbite to the East of the Altar. The Alchemist stands between the pillars, and performs a solemn invocation of the forces of Mars to act therein. The curcurbite is then to be placed between the Pillars (or the drawn symbols of these same) for seven days, upon a flashing tablet of Mars. After this period, fit on the Alembic Head, and distil first in Balneum Mariae, then in Balneum Arenae till what time the mixture be all distilled over.

S—Now let the Alchemist take the fluid of the distillate and let him
<189> perform over it an invocation of the forces of Mercury to act in the clear fluid, so as to formulate therein the alchemic Mercury, even the Mercury of the philosophers. (The residuum or the dead head is not to be worked with at present, but is to be set apart for future use.) After the invocation of the Alchemic Mercury a certain brilliance should manifest itself in the whole fluid, that is to say, it should not only be clear, but also brilliant and flashing. Now expose it in an her-

metic receiver for seven days to the light of the Sun; at the end of which time there should be distinct flashes of light therein. (Or an egg philosophic may be used; but the receiver of the alembic if close stopped will answer this purpose.)

T—Now the residuum or Dead Head is to be taken out of the curcurbite, ground small and replaced. An invocation of the Forces of Jupiter is then to be performed over that powder. It is then to be kept in the dark standing upon a flashing Tablet of Jupiter for seven days. At the end of this time there should be a slight flashing about it, but if this come not yet, repeat this operation up to three times, when a faint flashing of Light is *certain* to come.

U—A flashing Tablet of each of the four Elements is now to be placed upon an altar as shown in the figure, and thereon are also to be placed the magical elemental weapons, as is also clearly indicated. The receiver containing the distillate is now to be placed between the Air and Water Tablets, and the curcurbite with the Dead Head between the Fire and Earth Tablets. Now let the Alchemist perform an invocation using especially the Supreme Ritual of the Pentagram, and the lesser magical implement appropriate. First, of the forces of Fire to act in the curcurbite on the dead head. Second of those of Water to act on the
<190> distillate. Third, of the forces of the Spirit to act in both (using the white end of Lotus Wand). Fourth, of those of the Air to act on the distillate; and lastly, those of the Earth to act on the Dead Head. Let the Curcurbite and the receiver stand thus for five consecutive days, at the end of which time there should be flashes manifest in both mixtures. And these flashes should be lightly Coloured.

Diagram 25

V—The Alchemist, still keeping the vessels in the same relative positions, but removing the Tablets of the elements from the Altar, then substitutes one of Kether. This must be white with golden charges, and is to be placed on or within the white triangle between the vessels. He then addresses a most solemn invocation to the forces of Kether; to render the result of the working that which he shall desire, and making over each vessel the symbol of the Flaming Sword.

<191> This is the most important of all the Invocations. It will only succeed if the Alchemist keepeth himself closely allied unto his Higher Self during the working of the invocation and of making the Tablet. And at the end of it, if it have been successful, a keen and translucent flash will take the place of the slightly coloured flashes in the receiver of the curcurbite; so that the fluid should sparkle as a diamond, whilst the powder in the curcurbite shall slightly gleam.

W—The distilled liquid is now to be poured from the receiver upon the residuum of the Dead Head in the curcurbite, and the mixture at first will appear cloudy. It is now to be exposed to the Sun for ten days consecutively (ten is Tiphareth translating the influence of Kether.) It is then again to be placed upon the white triangle upon the Altar, upon a flashing Tablet of Venus, with a solemn invocation of Venus to act therein. Let it remain thus for seven days, at the end of which time see what forms and colour and appearance the Liquor hath taken, for there should now arise a certain softer flash in the liquid, and an elemental may be evoked to test the condition. When this softer flash is manifest, place the curcurbite into the Balneum Mariae to digest with a very gentle heat for seven days. Place it then in the Balneum Mariae to distil, beginning with a gentle, and ending with a strong heat. Distil thus till nothing more will come over, even with a most violent heat. Preserve the fluid in a closely stoppered vial, it is an Elixir for use according to the substance from which it was prepared. If from a thing medicinal, a medicine; if from a metal, for the purifying of metals; and herein shalt thou use thy judgment. The residuum thou shalt place without powdering into a crucible, well sealed and luted.

And thou shalt place the same in thine Athanor, bringing it first to a
<192> red, and then to a white heat, and this thou shalt do seven times in
seven consecutive days, taking out the crucible each day as soon as thou hast brought it to the highest possible heat, and allowing it to cool gradually.

And the preferable time for this working should be in the heat of the day. On the seventh day of this operation thou shalt open the crucible and thou shalt behold what *Form* and *Colour* thy Caput Mortuum hath taken.

It will be like either a precious stone or a glittering powder. And this stone or powder shall be of Magical Virtue in accordance with its nature.

Finished is that which is written concerning the Formulae of the Magic of Light.

(Note: Instances of Rituals based upon these formulae will be found in the next section, Book Six.—I.R.)

BOOK SIX

(Rituals based upon the Golden Dawn Formulae of Z.3 in Book Five.)

CEREMONIAL MAGIC

<195>

EVOCATION

The Temple is arranged as in the Neophyte Grade. There is a circle about ten feet in diameter, formed by coloured tapes. Pantacles, bearing the divine Names, are placed at the four quarters on the rim of the circle. Adonai Ha-Aretz, Adonai Melekh, and Agla are written in Hebrew lettering; and Emor Dial Hectega, in Enochian characters, on the Pantacles. About a foot outside the Circle, and towards the North is a Triangle formed by white tapes. The letters of Nephesch Ha-Messiach in Hebrew are written about its angles. In the Triangle is a Pantacle bearing the Sigil of Axir, based upon the letters of the Rose. The same Sigil is painted on the back of the Hierophant's Lamen worn by the Magus, and it is also painted on another Pantacle which is carried by the Magus, later to be veiled, and bound; it is upon this latter that he works.

A heavy-bodied incense should be used, and copiously. Dittany of Crete is probably the best — or any other fairly stable and harmonious incense.

When all is ready, announce from the Altar, holding the Lotus Wand

Hekas, Hekas este Bebeloi

Then, taking the Sword, perform the Lesser Banishing Rituals of the Pentagram and Hexagram, closing with the L.V.X. Signs.

Pass to Altar without either Wand or Sword, take up the Fire Wand, go South, raise Fire Wand above head, attract the Light and circumambulate slowly with the Sun, saying:

And when, after all the phantoms have vanished, thou shalt see that holy and formless fire, that fire which darts and flashes through the hidden depths of the universe, hear thou the voice of Fire.

On reaching the South, face the quarter, trace Fire Pentagram, with Leo in centre, and say:

<196> Oip Teaa Pedoce. In the names and letters of the Great Southern Quadrangle, I invoke ye, ye Angels of the Watch-tower of the South.

Replace Wand. Take Cup to West, sprinkle Water, raise Cup, circumambulate with Sol, saying:

So therefore first the priest who governeth the works of Fire must sprinkle with the lustral water of the loud resounding sea.

On reaching the west, face West, sprinkle Water, and make with the Cup the Pentagram of Water, Eagle Kerub in centre.

Empeh Arsel Gaiol. In the names and letters of the Great Western Quadrangle, I invoke ye, ye Angels of the watch-tower of the West.

Replace, Cup, take dagger, past to East, face East, and strike air thrice, circumambulate, saying:

Such a Fire existeth, extending through the rushings of Air. Or even a Fire formless whence cometh the image of a voice. Or even a flashing Light, abounding, revolving, whirling forth, crying aloud.

Reaching East, face East, strike Air with dagger, and make Invoking Air Pentagram with Aquarius in centre, and say:

Oro Ibah Aozpi. In the names and letters of the Great Eastern Quadrangle, I invoke ye, ye Angels of the Watch-tower of the East.

Replace Dagger. Take Pantacle, go North, face North, circumambulate, after shaking Pantacle thrice.

Stoop not down into the darkly splendid world wherein continually lieth a faithless depth and Hades wrapped in gloom, delighting in unintelligible images, precipitous, winding; a black ever-rolling abyss ever espousing a body unluminous, formless and void.

Reaching North, shake Pantacle, make Earth Pentagram, with Taurus in centre, and say:

Emor Dial Hectega. In the names and letters of the Great Northern Quadrangle, I invoke ye, ye angels of the Watch-tower of the North.

<197> *Replace Pantacle. Go West of Altar, face East, raise the Censer and describe invoking Pentagrams of Spirit both Active and Passive, saying:*

Exarp. Bitom. Nanta. Hcoma. In the names and letters of the mystical Tablet of Union, I invoke ye, ye divine forces of the Spirit of Life.

Replace Censer. Make the Portal Sign of the Rending of the Veil.

I invoke ye, ye Angels of the celestial spheres whose dwelling is in the invisible. Ye are the guardians of the Gates of the Universe, be ye also the guardians of this mystic sphere. Keep far removed the evil and the unbalanced. Strengthen and inspire me so that I may preserve unsullied this abode of the mysteries of the Eternal Gods. Let my sphere be pure and holy so that I may enter in and become a partaker of the secrets of the Light Divine.

Circumambulate three times to draw down the Light. Return to altar, face East, and utter the Adoration:

Holy Art Thou Lord of the Universe.
Holy Art Thou, Whom Nature hath not Formed.
Holy Art Thou, the Vast and the Mighty One.
Lord of the Light and of the Darkness.*

Pause. Then take up the Lotus Wand, and pass between the Pillars. Make the Zelator Sign, and say:

Let us adore the Lord and King of Earth. Adonai Ha-Aretz. Adonai Melekh. Unto thee *(make the Qabalistic Cross)* be the Kingdom, the Power, and the Glory.

<198> Malkuth, Geburah, Gedulah, Amen. *(Trace the Cross and Circle in air with Wand.)* The Rose of Sharon and the Lily of the Valley. Amen.

Pass round the Temple to the Earth Tablet in the North. Make the Invoking Pentagrams of Spirit, Active and Passive, and the Invoking Earth Penta-

*Hereafter, this form of opening the Temple, up to the Adoration, will be referred to as the *Formula of Opening by Watchtower.* It is an ideal method of preparing any chamber for practical work, and even as a complete ceremony by itself has much to commend its very frequent use. As preparation for serious meditation, for skrying, for difficult magical works, it is as fine a preliminary as could be wished for.

gram with Taurus symbol in centre.

And the Elohim said: Let us make Adam in our own Image after our likeness, and let them have dominion over all the earth. In the name of Adonai Melekh, and in the name of the Bride and Queen of the Kingdom, Spirits of Earth, adore Adonai.

Trace Taurus Kerub in Air; also Sigil of Auriel.

In the name of Auriel, the Great Archangel of Earth, and by the Sign of the head of the Ox, Spirits of Earth, adore Adonai.

Make Cross in Air.

In the names and letters of the Great Northern Quadrangle, spirits of Earth, adore Adonai.

Hold Wand on high.

In the Three Great Secret Names of God borne upon the Banners of the North, Emor Dial Hectega, and in the name of Ic Zod Heh Chal, Great King of the North, Spirits of Earth, adore Adonai.

Go to East to commence the Supreme Invoking Ritual of the Earth Pentagram, beginning and closing with the Qabalistic Cross. Then return to North, and vibrate very powerfully the Enochian Key.

Sapah Zimii duiv, od noas ta Qanis Adroch, dorphal coasg od faonts piripsol ta blior. Casarm am pizi nazarth af, od dlugar zizop zlida caosgi tol torgi, od z chis e siasch l ta vi u, od iaod thild ds hubar *peoal,* soba cormfa chis ta la, vls, od q cocasb. Eca niis od darbs qaas. F etharzi od blior. Ia-ial ed nas cicles. Bagle? Ge-iad I L.

Go to the South of the Altar, and face the North. Draw the Hebrew letters of
<199> *Adonai Ha-Aretz in the Air before you. Also the Sigil. Then imagine both in the heart. Vibrate the name several times by the Vibratory Formula of the Middle Pillar until the whole body throbs and pulses with the divine power.*

Adonai Ha-Aretz. O Thou who art the King of Earth, taking the earth for thy footstool, I invoke Thee and adore Thee. Dwell thou within my heart, I beseech thee, to awaken that which shall prove a true channel for the working of thy divine power. May this ceremony for the Evocation of the Earth Angel Axir which I am about to perform, be a focus for the ray of thy illuminating power. To the end that I may use this consecration to progress further in the Great Work, and thereby help others who may come within my sphere of influence.

Trace the Earth Pentagram and in it the Sigil and Hebrew Letters of Auriel. Picture the Name in the lungs, and vibrate it several times by the vibratory formula, circulating the force thereafter.

Grant unto me the presence and power of thy Archangel Auriel who governeth the spirits of Earth, that he may guide me in my quest for the hidden stone.

Trace the Sigil and letters of Phorlach in the air. Then in the heart, and vibrate.

Direct thy Angel Phorlach to watch over my footsteps in this Path of Light. O thou mighty Angel of Earth, I conjure thee by the divine Names that thou

*For these, and the other Enochian Rituals, their translations, and directions for use, see Volume 4.

permeate my mind now in this Temple, to aid me with thy power, that I may truly evoke to visible manifestation the Angel Axir of the Lesser Angle of Earth of the Northern Quadrangle.

Trace the Sigil and letters of Kerub and vibrate.

May the ruler of Earth, by the permission of Adonai Melekh, extend his power so that, divinely, I may be aided to perform aright this magical evocation and bring it to successful culmination, even as Malkuth is the throne of the Ten Sephiroth.

<200> *Pause. Contemplate the Kether above the head, and endeavour to bring down its light.*

In the names of Sandalphon, Metatron and Nephesch Ha-Messiach, the three Kerubim ruling over Malkuth, and by the power of the choir of Angels who art set over the governance of the Kingdom, *(Trace Sigils of all these Names and vibrate very powerfully)*, the Aschim, the holy Souls of Fire, let it be known that I, Ad Majorem Adonai Gloriam,* Neophyte of the golden Dawn, and Frater R. R. et A. C. have summoned the powers of Earth to my presence. Let there be formed a true and potent link between my human soul on the one hand, and all those divine powers of Malkuth which receive the influx from on high. To this end, I propose to evoke unto physical manifestation, the Great Angel Axir of the Third Lesser Angle of the Watch-tower of the North in the name of Adonai Ha-Aretz and by the divine aid of Emor Dial Hectega.

Bind and veil Sigil with white cord and black cloth. Place it without the Circle at the West, and say:

Hail unto ye, Lords of the Land of Life, hear ye these my words for I am made as ye are, who are the formers of the soul. With the divine aid, I now purpose to call forth this day and hour from the dark depths of my sphere of sensation the Angel Axir of the Lesser Earthy Angle of the Northern Quadrangle, whose magical seal I now bind with this triple cord of bondage, and shroud in the black darkness of concealment. Even as I have bound about this Sigil this cord so let Axir be bound in his abode and habitation, that he move not therefrom save to manifest unto the Light before me. Even as with this veil of black I shroud the Light of Day from this Sigil, so do I render him in his place, blind and dumb, that he may in no wise move except unto manifestation and appearance before me. And the reason of this my working is to obtain from that Angel the true knowledge of Earth, how I may securely fix within my being the secret philosophical stone of creation whereon is a hidden
<201> name inscribed. To this end, I implore the divine assistance in the names of Adonai Ha-Aretz, Auriel, Phorlach; Emor Dial Hectega, and Ic Zod Heh Chal.

Draw the Pantacle into the circle with the point of Sword.

Creature of Sigils, enter thou within this sacred Circle that the Angel Axir may pass from concealment unto manifestation.

Consecrate immediately with Fire and with Water at the West of the Circle.

Creature of Sigils, purified and made consecrate, enter thou the Pathway of Evil.

Hold Sigil aloft and move in a N. E. direction. Stop at the N. E. of Altar, strike Sigil with flat of sword, saying:

*Regardie's magical name. The student, obviously, should substitute his/her own. C.L.W.

The great Angel Samael spake and said. I am the Prince of Darkness and of Night. The foolish and rebellious gaze upon the face of the created world, finding therein naught but terror and obscurity. To them it is the terror of darkness, and they are but as drunken men stumbling in the darkness. Return, thou creature of Sigils; not as yet canst thou pass by.

Return to West. Then move S. E. Strike Sigil as before.

The great Angel Metatron spake and said. I am the Angel of the Presence Divine. The wise gaze upon the created world and behold therein the dazzling image of the Creator. O creature of Sigils, not as yet canst thine eyes behold that dazzling image of Adonai. Return. Thou canst not pass by.

Return with Sigil to West, and this time go straight forward to the Altar. Smite upraised Sigil with the flat of sword.

The great Angel Sandalphon spake and said. I am the Reconciler for Earth, and the Celestial Soul therein. Form is invisible alike in darkness and in blinding light. I am the angel of Paphro-Osoronnophris — and I
<202> prepare the way to manifestation unto the Light. Prepare thou, therefore, to manifest thyself unto visible appearance.

Place Sigil at foot of Altar, and say:

O thou mighty and powerful Angel Axir, I bind and conjure thee in the name of Sandalphon who thus prepares the way for thee, that thou appear in visible form before me in the triangle without this Circle of Art. In the name of Emor Dial Hectega, I command that thou shalt speedily come hither from thy darkened abodes in the land of Ophir, to appear before me in a physical form. And I further command, by all the names divine, that thou teach me how best the great creative work may be pursued, and how I may find the hidden stone of the wise whereby I may fix within a purified body my Higher Self. And, in this hall of the Dual manifestation of Truth, in the presence of Adonai Ha-Aretz and all the powers of Malkuth, I invocate and charge thee, that even as within me is concealed the knowledge of the magic of the light divine, so *shalt* thou pass from concealment unto manifestation visibly in this triangle placed without this Circle of Art.

Place Sigil on Altar on the White Triangle. Stand East, face West, place left hand on Sigil, hold Sword aloft, and over it trace appropriate Sigils of the Names as they are rehearsed.

O Invisible King, who taking the Earth for foundation, didst hollow its depth to fill them with thy almighty power. Thou whose name shaketh the Arches of the World, thou who causest the seven metals to flow in the veins of the rocks, King of the seven lights, rewarder of the subterranean workers, lead us into the desirable air and into the realm of Splendour. We watch and we labour unceasingly. We seek and we hope, by the twelve stones of the holy City, by the buried talismans, by the axis of the lodestone which passes through the centre of the Earth. Adonai. Adonai. Adonai. *(Vibrate by formula of the Middle Pillar and circumambulate it.)* Have pity upon those who suffer, expand our hearts, unbind and upraise our minds, enlarge our natures!
<203> O Stability and Motion! O Darkness veiled in brilliance! O Day clothed in Night! O Master Who never dost withold the wages of thy workmen! O Silver and Harmonious diamond! Thou who wearest the heavens on thy finger like a ring of sapphire! Thou who hidest beneath the earth

in the kingdom of gems, the marvellous seed of the stars. Live, reign and be thou the eternal dispenser of the Treasures whereof thou hast made us the wardens.

Trace Invoking Earth Pentagram over Sigil, and say:

In the three great Secret Holy Names of God borne upon the banners of the North, Emor Dial Hectega *(Vibrate by the Middle Pillar and circumambulate)* I invoke thee, Thou great King of the North, Ic Zod Heh Chal *(trace a whirl with sword over Sigil)* to be present here by me this day, and to grant Thy protection and power unto me, to enable me to evoke Axir, an Angel subservient to the lesser Angle of Earth of the Northern Quadrangle, unto visible manifestation.

Trace Saturn Hexagram over Sigil, but using the Taurus Symbol of the Kerub.

I invocate ye, ye great princes of the Northern Quadrangle, who are known by the title and honourable office of Seniors. Hear ye my petition, ye celestial Seniors who rule over the Earth in the North Quadrangle, and who bear the names of Laidrom, Alhectega, Aczinor, Ahmbicv, Lzinopo, Liiansa. Be this day present with me, so that the Angel Axir may be caused to manifest physically unto me in this Temple, to the end that he may teach me the creative art, and how I may divinely fix the Higher Self within a purified body, and how I may find the hidden stone of the philosophers, that stone whereon is a new name written.

O thou Angel, Axir, subservient in the Lesser Angle of Earth, in the Great Northern Quadrangle, I do invocate and conjure Thee, being armed with divine power. By the name of Ic Zod Heh Chal and by the spirit
<204> name of Nanta, I conjure thee. By the name of Cabalpt and Arbiz the
holy names of God, and by the name of Nroam that great Archangel who governeth thy lesser Angle of the Watch-tower situate in the North, and by Taxir, the Angel who is thy immediate superior, I do invoke Thee, and by invocating, do conjure thee. And being armed with the power of Adonai, I do strongly command Thee by Him who spake and it was done, and unto whom all creatures of the earth are obedient. And I, being made after the image of the Elohim, and endued therefore with the power of the Holy Spirit, created also unto divine will, do evoke thee by the name of Adonai Ha-Aretz. *(vibrate by the Middle Pillar and circumambulate)*. I conjure thee in the name of Adonai Melekh, *(Vibrate by Middle Pillar, etc.)* The Lord and King of the Earth. And I conjure ye powerfully by the three holy Archangels of the Kingdom: Metatron, Sandalphon, and Nephesch Ha-Messiach, and by those powerful Souls of Fire, the Aschim. And I command thy manifestation in the name and power of Auriel the Great Archangel of Earth. By these names do I evoke and conjure thee that thou dost forthwith leave thine abodes in the kingdom of Earth and appear unto me here, visibly and in material form before me in the magical triangle without this circle, in fair shape and true. And by all these divine Names do I command and conjure thee to manifest thyself.

Wherefore come now, thou Angel Axir. Come! Manifest thyself in visible and material form before me, and without delay, from wherever thou mayest be, and make true and faithful answer unto those things I shall have cause to demand of thee. Come thou peaceably, visibly, and affably, and without delay, manifesting that which I desire. Come, I command ye, by all the holy names, by the Archangels above thy kingdom, and by the rulers of thy realm. Come, Axir, come!

Take up Sigil, smite it thrice with Sword. Rise it in left hand, stamping thrice
<205> *with right foot. Place veiled Sigil in North, and say, as though from the throne of the East.*

The Voice of the Exorcist said unto me. Let me shroud myself in darkness, peradventure thus may I manifest myself in Light. I am the only being in an abyss of darkness. From the darkness came I forth ere my birth, from the darkness of a primal sleep. And the Voice of the Exorcist said unto me, "Creature of Sigils, the Light shineth in darkness, but the darkness comprehendeth it not."

Pick up Sigil in left hand and circumambulate once, attracting the Light. Pass to South, and bar Sigil with the Sword.

Unpurified and Unconsecrate, thou mayest not approach the gate of the West.

Purify with Water and consecrate with Fire, as in Neophyte ceremony. Then lift Sigil aloft, and say:

Creature of Sigils, twice consecrate and twice purified, thou mayest approach the gate of the West.

Pass to West with Sigil in left hand. Partially unveil it, and assume the astral mask of Axir. Smite the Sigil once with flat of blade, and say:

Thou canst not pass from concealment unto manifestation, save by virtue of the name Elohim. Before all things are the Chaos, the Darkness and the Gates of the Land of Night. I am He whose Name is Darkness. I am the Great One of the Paths of the Shades. I am the Exorcist in the midst of the Exorcism. Appear thou therefore without fear before me. For I am he in whom fear is not. Thou hast known me now, so pass thou on.

Reveil the Sigil. Circumambulate once more attracting the Light. Then halt at the North. Place Sigil on the ground, purify and consecrate it as before, then pass to the East. Partially unveil the Sigil, smite it once with the flat of sword, and assume the astral mask of the Spirit.

Thou canst not pass from concealment unto manifestation, save by virtue of the name Yhvh. After the Formless and the Void and the Darkness,
<206> then cometh the knowledge of the Light. I am that Light which riseth in Darkness. I am the Exorcist in the midst of the Exorcism. Appear thou therefore in visible form before me, for I am the wielder of the forces of the balance. Thou hast known me now, so pass thou on to the cubical altar of the universe.

Recover Sigil, and return to Altar. Stand at East, face West. Sword is held in right hand over Sigil, left hand is placed flat over Sigil on the White Triangle. Invoke powerfully, and re-trace all Sigils and Pentagrams as may be required.

Thou who art the Lord and King of Malkuth, having taken the Earth for thy footstool, Adonai Ha-Aretz and Adonai Melekh, grant unto me the power and help of the Great Archangel Auriel that he may command unto my assistance the Angel Phorlach and his Ruler Kerub, that they working through me may cause to appear visibly and physically before me in this Temple the

Angel Axir of the Third Lesser Angle of the Great Northern Quadrangle. Cause him to come swiftly from his abode in the darkling splendours of the hidden Earth to manifest himself in the triangle without this circle.

Emor Dial Hectega, thou secret of secrets in the vast kingdom of Earth, grant unto me the presence and power of Ic Zod Heh Chal, the mighty King of the North, that he may aid and guard me in this work of Art. *(Trace Saturn Hexagram.)* O ye six mighty Angelical Seniors who keep watch over the Northern Quadrangle, I invoke ye by your names: Laidrom, Alhectega, Aczinor, Ahmbicv, Lzinopo, Liiansa, that ye be present this day with me. Bestow upon me the firmness and stability whereof ye are masters in the element of Aretz, that I may evoke unto visible appearance in the triangle at the North of this Circle the Earthy Angel Axir from the Third Lesser Angle of the Northern Quadrangle.

Thahaaothe, thou great Governor of the northern Watch-
<207> tower, I do invoke thee to send hither the Angel Axir that in accordance with these sacred rites he may manifest unto me. Let him be for me a solid and tangible link, true and perfect, with all the powers of stability, majesty, and sanctity which rise rank upon rank from the feet of Malkuth even unto the throne of Aimah Elohim. To the end that the Wisdom and Light of the Divine Ones may descend upon my head; and through this creature of Evocations, manifest unto me the perfect purity and the unsullied vision and perfect consecration of the hidden philosophical stone. That by its assistance I may ever pursue the Great work in the pathway of Light, and thus be the better able to help and teach my fellow men.

Therefore in the name of Cabalpt, I invoke thee, Axir. In the name of Arbiz, I powerfully command thy presence and physical manifestation before me. Come forth! Come forth! Manifest thou in visible form before me, O Angel Axir. I conjure thee anew. Accept of me these magical sacrifices which I have prepared to give thee body and form. Herein are the magical elements of the Holy Kingdom, the foundation and throne of the Tree of Life. For these rose petals are the symbols of the gentle breezes wafting through the land of Ophir. And this oil is the fire thereof which shall accomplish thy salvation. This wine is the symbol of the waters which are, as it were, the blood of the earth, the water of thy purification. This bread and salt are types of Earth, thy body which I destroy by fire that it may be renewed in manifestation before me. And the fire which consumes all is the magical flame of my will and the power of these ineffable and sacred rites.

As each element is mentioned cast it on the charcoal block or the censer.

Come, therefore, Axir. Manifest thyself in power and presence, in comely and pleasing form, before me in the triangle placed without my magic circle. I command ye by all the names of God whose footstool is the realm of thy abode. For the Spirit of the Godhead is within me, and above me
<208> flames the glory of Adonai, and my feet are planted firmly by the might of Emor Dial Hectega. Come, therefore, come!

Elevate covered sigil. Remove the black cloth, leaving the cord on, and say:

Creature of Earth, long hast thou dwelt in darkness. Quit the night and seek the Day.

Replace Sigil on Altar, hold Sword above it, and say:

By all the names, powers and rites already rehearsed. I conjure thee unto visible appearance.

Khabs Am Pekht. Konx Om Pax. Light in Extension. As the Light hidden in Darkness can manifest therefore, so *shalt* thou become manifest from concealment unto manifestation.

Hold Sigil in left hand, standing East of Altar, face West, and recite the long conjuration as follows:

Taxir, thou Angel of God, in the name of Emor Dial Hectega, and by the very powerful names of Cabalpt and Arbiz, I conjure thee to send unto me this Angel Axir. Do thou cause him to manifest before me without this circle of Art. Taxir, in the name of Adonai Ha-Aretz, send thou unto me in a form material and visible this Angel Axir. In the name of the Great Archangel of Earth, Auriel *(vibrate the name and trace Sigils)* send thou unto me in material form the Angel Axir. In the name of Ic Zod Heh Chal, I command thee to come unto me, thou Angel Axir. By the power of Thahaaothe, come unto me in visible form. In the divine names Nroam and Roam who are thy immediate superiors, come unto me thou Angel Axir. O Taxir, Taxir, thou mighty Angel of the Earth Angle of the Northern Quadrangle, in all the mighty names and seals and symbols here employed and displayed, I conjure thee in the name of the Highest, to cause this Spirit Axir to make a visible manifestation before me in the great triangle without this circle of art.

Take up Sigil. Place it between Pillars. Stand at the East before it and
<209> *charge with the Will powerfully in the Sign of the Enterer. Protect with the Sign of Silence. Manifestation should begin in the North. If not, repeat the invocation to Taxir in the East until it has been said three times, and then charge with will as before. If at the third invocation and charging no manifestation commences, replace the Sigil on Altar, and address a prayer to the Gods.*

O ye great Lords of the holy Kingdom which is the throne of the Holy Spirit, ye Spirits of life who preside over the weighing of souls in the place of judgment before Aeshoorist, Lord of Life Triumphant over death. Give me your hands, for I am made as ye, who are the formers of the soul. Give me your hands and your magic power, that I may have breathed into my spirit the power and might irresistible to compel this Angel Axir, of the Northern Quadrangle of Earth, to appear before me, that I may accomplish this evocation of Magical art, according to all my words and aspirations. In myself, O Adonai, I am nothing. In thee, thou great Lord of Malkuth whose footstool is the earth, I am Self and exist in the Spirit of the Mighty to Eternity. O Thoth, who makest victorious the word of Osiris against his foes, make thou the words of me, who also am Aeshoorist, triumphant and victorious over this Angel Axir, and thus rooted in a true foundation.

Return to Pillars and charge. If manifestation commences consecrate Temple and Sigil anew with Fire and Water. This done, remove the cord, and hold Sigil aloft, saying:

By and in the name of Adonai Ha-Aretz and Adonai Melekh, I do conjure upon thee the power of perfect manifestation unto visible appearance.

Smite the Sigil with flat of blade, and circumambulate thrice with Sigil aloft in right hand. Go to East, after having placed Sigil on the ground at the quarter where the Spirit manifests, and utter a potent invocation to visible appearance.

<210> Behold, thou great and mighty Angel Axir I have conjured thee hither at this time to demand of thee certain matters relative to the secret magical knowledge which shall be conveyed to me through thee from thy lord Emor Dial Hectega. But prior to my further proceeding, it is necessary that thou assume a shape and form distinctly material and visible. Therefore in order that thou mayest appear more fully tangible, know then that I am possessed of the means, rites, and powers of evoking thee. Thus do I rehearse before thee yet again the mighty words, names and Sigils of great Efficacy. Wherefore, make haste, thou mighty Angel Axir, and appear visibly before me in the triangle without this Circle of Art.

Burn large quantities of heavy incense at this juncture. Then repeat the long invocation beginning on pages 203-204. If necessary repeat it. Trace all seals, symbols, and sigils anew. Pass to between the Pillars, holding Sword and say:

Hear me, ye Guardians of the Tenth Sephirah, Malkuth. Hear Me, ye immortal powers of the Magic of Light, that this Angel Axir hath been duly and properly evoked in accordance with the sacred rites.

O ye great Lords of the Royal Kingdom, ye powers of Malkuth which receives the wisdom and power of the Ten Sephiroth, ye I invoke and conjure. Cause this mighty Angel Axir to perform all my demands; manifest ye through him the majesty and radiance of your presence, the divinity of your knowledge that I may be led one step nearer the fulfillment of the Great Work, that I may be taught how to purify my earthly self, and fix therein the glory of my higher and divine genius, and how I may find the hidden stone whereon the new spiritual name shall be written. And that in so doing, the being of this Angel Axir may become more glorified and enlightened, and more responsive to the influx of that Divine Spirit which abides eternally in the heart of God and Man.

Turn now to the triangle and address Axir.

<211> O thou mighty Angel, I do command and conjure thee not in my name but by the majesty of Adonai Ha-Aretz and Emor Dial Hectega, the Lord and King of Earth, and ruler over Malkuth, that thou formulate between thy kingdom and my soul a true and potent link. That thou teach me the mystery of the earthly self of man, and how it may be made creative. Teach me in what manner it may be purified, and fix therein the hidden stone of the Philosophers, that stone whereon is written the new name of redemption. And finally swear thou by the mighty magic Seal which in my hand I hold that thou wilt always speedily appear before me, coming whensoever I call thee by word or will, or by a magical ceremony. To the end that thou mayest be a perpetual link of communication between the Lords of Malkuth and my human soul therein.

When all is fulfilled and prior to his banishing, say:

Inasmuch as thou hast obeyed my wish, I now conjure thee, Axir, that thou hereafter harm me not, nor this place, my companions, or aught pertaining unto me, that thou faithfully perform all these things as thou hast sworn by the names of God, and that thou deceive in naught. Therefore do I burn, and feel thou, these grateful odours of the incense of my magic art which are agreeable unto thee.

Burn much incense. Also perform the L.V.X. Signs and draw down the Light on the manifestation.

And now I say unto thee, Axir, depart in peace in the name of Adonai Ha-Aretz unto thine abodes and habitations. Let there ever be peace between me and you, and be thou ready to come when thou art called. May the blessing and light of Yeheshuah the Redeemer be with thee, and inspire thee, and lead thee unto the ways of everlasting peace.

Pause for a few minutes. Reverse Circumambulation. Reconsecration of Temple with Fire and Water. Then powerful banishing rituals of Pentagram and Hexagram.

<212>

CONSECRATION CEREMONY FOR JUPITER TALISMAN

Temple furniture arranged as for the Grade of Neophyte. Banishing Rituals of both Pentagram and Hexagram. Open the Temple by the Ceremony of the Watch-towers. After Adoration, perform the Invoking Hexagram Ritual of the Supernals, using Eheieh and Ararita. Employ the Vibratory Formula of the Middle Pillar to invoke Kether, and do not proceed until the sensation of the divine force is present in every vein and nerve. Then contemplate the higher and divine Genius, and utter the following prayer.

Unto Thee Sole Wise, Sole Eternal, and Sole Merciful One, be the praise and glory for ever. Who hath permitted me, who now standeth humbly before Thee, to enter thus far into the sanctuary of thy mystery. Not unto me, Adonai, but unto thy name be the glory. Let the influence of thy divine ones descend upon my head, and teach me the value of self-sacrifice so that I shrink not in the hour of trial. But that thus my name may be written on high, and my Genius stand in the presence of the Holy One. In that hour when the Son of Man is invoked before the Lord of Spirits and his Name before the Ancient of Days.

Pause. Then formulate Pillars. Stand between them and make Sign of Practicus.

Let us adore the Lord and King of Water. Holy art thou Lord of the Mighty Waters, whereon thy spirit moved in the beginning. Elohim Tzabaoth. Glory be unto thee Ruach Elohim whose spirit hovered over the Waters of Creation.

Go to the West. Before the Water Tablet make Active and Passive Spirit Pentagrams and Invoking Water Pentagram with Eagle Kerub in the Centre, using Lotus Wand.

And the Elohim said, Let us make Adam in our own image, after our
<213> likeness, and let him have dominion. In the name Al strong and
mighty, Spirits of Water, adore your creator.

Sign the Eagle Kerub with Water Cup.

In the Sign of the Head of the Eagle, and in the name of Gabriel, Great Archangel of Water, Spirits of Water, adore your Creator.

Make Cross with Cup.

In the names and letters of the Great Western Quadrangle, Spirits of Water, adore your creator.

Hold Lotus Wand on high.

In the Three great secret holy Names of God borne upon the banners of the West, Empeh Arsel Gaiol, and in the name of Ra-Agiosel, Great King of the West, Spirits of Water, adore your creator.

Still facing West, vibrate very powerfully the Fourth Enochian key invoking the line Hcoma from the Tablet of Union. Formulate an astral banner of the East surrounding one.

In the name of Elohim Tzabaoth and in the name of Al, I command ye, O ye dwellers in the realm of Water that ye fashion for me a magical base in the Astral Light wherein I may invoke the divine forces to charge this Talisman of Tzedek.

Go East, to begin the Supreme Invoking Ritual of the Jupiter Hexagram. Precede with Qabalistic Cross, closing with Key-word. Return to Altar, so that the latter is between the operator and the previously ascertained position of Jupiter. The Magus should wear, in addition to his Rose Cross lamen, a seal of Jupiter in proper colours.

O thou Divine One who dwellest in the Majesty and Love of Chesed, the Fourth Sephirah; Al, source of the River Gihon, Lord of Fire, look upon me I beseech thee as I perform this consecration ceremony. Let a ray from thy perfection descend upon me, to awaken within my being that which shall prove a channel for the working of thine abundant power. May this Jupiter
<214> talisman which I have made be a focus of thy light and life and love so that it may awaken within my soul a clear vision and a stronger aspiration to the Light.

Draw the letters Al in Hebrew, and its Sigil, in the heart, and vibrate it several times. Trace Sigil and Letters in the Air first.

Grant unto me thou great and merciful King of Chesed, the presence and power of thy holy Archangel Tzadkiel that he may aid me with his power.

Draw the Invoking Hexagram of Jupiter and in it the Sigil of Tzadkiel. Vibrate the name strongly.

O ye brilliant Ones of Chesed, I conjure ye by the mighty name of Al strong and mighty, and by the name of Tsadkiel whose throne and seat ye are. Chashmalim, come unto me now. Manifest yourselves through me, and fill my sphere with your magic power to accomplish this work of art.

Draw the Sigil of Chashmalim, and vibrate the name.

Command unto me the presence of Sachiel, the Angel of Jupiter, and his Intelligence, Yohphiel, that they may consecrate this most powerful symbol. Yohphiel *(Vibrate several times)* I conjure ye potently to make manifest your presence within my soul that this talisman of Jupiter may be charged. Come, now, O all ye powers and forces of the realm of Chesed, obey ye now the name of Al, the divine ruler of your kingdom, and Tzadkiel, your Archangelic ruler and the mighty powers of the Brilliant Ones of Tzedek.

Place Talisman outside the circle, to West, and then draw it within with the point of Sword.

Creature of Talismans. Enter thou within this sacred circle that thou mayest become a dwelling place of Yohphiel, the Intelligence of Jupiter, a body for the manifestation of the majesty of Chesed.

The Talisman, which previously had been wrapped in black cloth, and bound thrice with cord, should be purified with water and consecrated with fire.

In the Name of Al, I proclaim, all ye powers and forces now invoked
<215> that I, Ad Majorem Adonai Gloriam*, Neophyte of the Stella Ma-

* The student should substitute his/her own magical name.

tutina, and Frater R. R. et A. C. have invoked ye in order to form a true and potent link between my human soul and that spirit of abundance and love and graciousness summed up in the name of Chesed. To this end I have formed and perfected a Talisman bearing upon one side the Sigil of Yohphiel the Intelligence of Tzedek, and the geomantic symbols and sigils pertaining to Jupiter. On the other side is a Seal referred to Jupiter, represented in flashing colours. This is now covered with a black veil, and bound thrice with a cord, so that Yohphiel shall not see the light not move until he manifest unto me. I proclaim that this Talisman *shall* be charged by the Intelligence Yohphiel, in order that spiritual vision may be mine, and that it may assist me to overcome all obstacles of both a spiritual and a material nature so that I may be enabled to perform the Great Work.

Pick up the Talisman and place it at foot of Altar.

I, Frater Ad Majorem Adonai Gloriam,* do solemnly pledge myself in the name of Al, to consecrate in due ceremonial form this Jupiter Talisman. And I assert that with divine aid I shall invoke the Intelligence Yohphiel from his abode in Tzedek that life and power may be imparted to this Talisman. To the end that I may be assisted to perform the Great Work, and that I may be the better able to assist my fellow men. May the powers of Chesed witness this my solemn pledge.

Place Talisman on the white triangle on Altar. Stand West of Altar, face East.

Ye powers of Chesed which I have invoked to this Temple, know that all is now in readiness to consecrate this Talisman. Aid me with your power that I may cause the great Angel Yohphiel to give life and strength to this creature of Talismans in the name of Al Ab.

Go to East of Altar, face West. Place left hand on Talisman, and hold Sword erect over it, and say, making over the talisman such lineal figures, seals, sigils and letters as may be named.

Abba, Father of all fathers, thee I invoke by thy name Al. Descend, I
<216> beseech Thee, through my being to manifest unto me the wisdom
and love and that prodigality of spirit which are the characteristics of Tzedek. So that in the enhancement of my true spiritual nature I may continually aspire unto thy glory and grace. Grant unto me the power and help of thy great Archangel Tzadkiel who is the righteousness of thy sphere. Tzadkiel, command I beseech thee to my assistance thy Brilliant Ones, the Chashmalim, that they may bind into this Talisman the magnificence and mercy of Tzedek and all the powers of Chesed. Chashmalim, O ye Brilliant Ones of Jupiter, assist me in this my invocation of Sachiel. Sachiel, Thou great Angel of Tzedek ruling therein by the virtue of Al Ab, whose name thou must obey, and in the name of Tzadkiel, your most potent Archangel, I command ye to send hither thine Intelligence, the Angel Yohphiel that he may concentrate and bind into this Talisman his life and power. In taking it for his body, let him thereby form a true and wonderful link for me with all those powers of love and wisdom, grace, abundance and benignity which rise rank upon rank to the feet of the Holy Spirit. O ye divine powers of Chesed, manifest yourselves through this intelligence Yohphiel, to show forth the majesty of your realm, the love and the magnificence of your Godhead, so that through

* The student should substitute his/her own magical name.

this creature of Talismans I may ever pursue the Great Work and assist in the initiation of my fellow men. And in so doing, grant that unto Yohphiel who shall charge this Talisman, shall be given a great reward in that day when the crown of the glory of my Genius shall be placed upon my head, and that his nature may become more illumined and glorified, more capable of receiving that divine influx which abides in the heart of God and Man.

Lift Talisman in left hand, smite it thrice with Sword, and raise both it and sword aloft, stamping three times. Then take the Talisman to North, and repeat:

The Voice of the Exorcism said unto me: Let me shroud myself in
<217> darkness, peradventure thus shall I manifest myself in light. I am the
only being in an Abyss of Darkness. From the Darkness came I forth ere my birth, from the silence of a primal sleep. And the voice of Ages answered unto my Soul, Creature of Talismans, the Light shineth in the darkness, but the darkness comprehendeth it not. Let the mystic circumambulation take place.

Take the Talisman, and circumambulate. After going round once, stop in the South, and place it on ground.

Unpurified and unconsecrated, thou canst not enter the gate of the West.

Purify the Talisman with Water and consecrate with Fire. Lift it with left hand, face towards West, and say:

Creature of Talismans, twice purified and twice consecrated, thou mayest approach the gateway of the West.

Pass to West with Talisman in left hand. Partly unveil it, smite it once with Sword, and say:

Thou canst not pass from concealment unto manifestation, save by virtue of the name Elohim. Before all things are the Chaos and the Darkness and the gates of the land of Night. I am He whose name is darkness. I am the great One of the Path of the Shades. I am the Exorcist in the midst of the Exorcism. Take on therefore manifestation before me without fear. For I am he in whom fear is not. Thou hast known me, so pass thou on.

Reveil Talisman, and carry it once more round the Circle. Then halt in the North, place it on ground. Bar, purify, and consecrate as before, and after so doing, pass towards the East. Strike it, after unveiling it partly, and say:

Thou canst not pass from concealment unto manifestation save by virtue of the name Yhvh. After the formless and the Void and the Darkness, then cometh the knowledge of the Light. I am that Light which ariseth in dark-
<218> ness. I am the Exorcist in the midst of the Exorcism. Take on there-
fore manifestation before me for I am the wielder of the forces of the Balance. Thou hast known me now. Pass Thou on unto the cubical altar of the Universe.

Reveil the Talisman, pass to Altar, place it on white triangle, and stand East, facing West, with left hand on Talisman, and sword held over it with right hand. Retrace all Sigils, etc.

Thou Intelligence of Tzedek named Yohphiel, I invoke thee in the divine name of Al. O Thou, who art the father of all things, source of the mighty waters, lord of fire, thou whose heart is mercy, and whose being love, lift me up, I beseech thee, and manifest through me thy power and grace and thy generosity of spirit. Grant unto me the mighty power and help of the Archangel Tzadkiel who rules over the divine realm of Chesed, that he may command to my assistance the Choir of Angels, those Brilliant Ones, the Chashmalim, that they may consecrate with power this Talisman which lieth before thee. O ye brilliant Ones of Jupiter, command unto me the Angel of Tzedek, Sachiel, that he may cause Yohphiel, his intelligence, to come unto me. Yohphiel, thou great Angel of Jupiter thou divine Intelligence of Tzedek, I invoke thee by the knowledge of thy name. I call thee by thy Sigil, and the symbol of Jupiter which I bear upon my breast. Come unto me now, I conjure thee to give me of thy substance so that this creature of Talismans may have power and life and love to make a divine link with all those powers of love and majesty and graciousness summed up in the holy name of Chesed. I invoke thee powerfully by the name of Al *(vibrate by formula of Middle Pillar and mystical circumambulation)*. Thus do I potently conjure and exorcise thee, to charge this talisman, thou Intelligence Yohphiel.

Lift the Talisman, remove the veil, leaving the cord underneath, and cry:

<219> Creature of Talismans, long hast thou dwelt in darkness. Quit the night and seek the day.

Replace it on the Triangle upon Altar, hold the pommel of the Sword immediately over it, and say:

By all the names, powers, and rites already rehearsed, I conjure upon thee power and might irresistible. Khabs Am Pekht, Konx om Pax, Light in extension. As the Light hidden in darkness can manifest therefrom, so shalt thou become irresistible.

Pause and then invoke Amoun as follows, also using the Amoun God-form:

O Thou the concealed One, the Opener of the Day, Thee, Thee do I invoke. Amoun *(vibrate by Middle Pillar)*. O thou Circle of stars whereof my Genius is but the younger brother, marvel beyond imagination, soul of Eternity before whom time is ashamed, the Ruach bewildered, and the Neschamah dark, not unto thy majesty may I attain unless thine image be love. Therefore by seed and root, and by bud and leaf, and by flower and fruit of my entire being, do I invoke thee, whose name and power is love. *(Assume God-form of Amoun.)* O secret of secrets that art hidden in the being of all that lives, lord secret and most holy — source of light, source of life, source of love, source of liberty, be thou ever constant and mighty within me that I may forever remain in thine abundant joy, Amoun *(Vibrate and circumambulate by Middle Pillar)*, thou Father of all the great Gods above, whose name is strength, whose being is love, whose nature is benign, thee do I invoke. Amoun. Mighty, merciful, magnificent, thee do I invoke. Thou whose Sephirah is Chesed, whose lordship is the realm of whirling fire and raging storm, thee, thee do I invoke. O thou whose head is of amethystine blue, whose heart is pitiful, and whose judgment just, where the Rose Dawn shines out amid the gold, thee do I invoke.

O Amoun *(vibratory formula of Middle Pillar)* before thee have I covered my face. Arise, great King, arise and shine in me, for I have hidden
<220> myself and stand humbly before the glory of thy face. In the chariot of life eternal is thy seat, and thy steeds course the firmament of Nu.

Behold! Thou didst lift up thy voice, and the hills were shaken! Thou didst cry aloud, and the everlasting hills did bow. O my father, my father; the chariots of Israel and the horsemen thereof. The sound of thy voice was freedom. Thy lightnings were kindled and lighted. Thy thunder was heard on the deep. The stars with thy fear shook and whitened, while the voice of the Lord was uplifted. The wilderness also obeys. For the flames of thy fire are rifted, and the waves of the Sea know thy ways. They did hear thee, the cedars of Lebanon; and the desert of Kadesh hath known. O Amoun *(vibratory formula)* thou Spirit of Illimitable Light and Life and Love. Thou with the plume and the Wand, is thy path in the Waters? The marvellous deeps of the Sea? To that abyss of waters do I raise my soul to receive thy truth. Amoun; *(Vibratory formula)* I invoke thee; exalt my soul to the feet of thy glory. Hear me and manifest in splendour to him who worships at thy throne.

(Pause, while circumambulating the force within.) This is the Lord of the Gods! This is the Lord of the Universe! This is He whom the Winds fear. This is He, who having made voice by his commandment is Lord of all things, King, ruler, and helper. I am He, the Bornless Spirit having sight in the feet, strong and immortal fire. I am he the Truth. I am he who hate that evil should be wrought in the world. I am he that lighteneth and thundereth. I am he from whom is the shower of the life of Earth. I am He whose mouth ever flameth. I am He, the begetter and manifester unto the Light. I am He, the Grace of the World, the Heart girt with the Serpent is my name. I am the Sun in his rising passed through the hour of cloud and of Night. I am Amoun the concealed One, the Opener of the Day. I am Osiris Onnophris the Justified One, Lord of
Light, triumphant over death. There is no part of me which is not of
<221> the Gods. I am the Preparer of the Pathway, the Rescuer unto the
Light. Let the white brilliance of the divine spirit descend.

Therefore with the light of the Godhead above and within me do I invoke Tzadkiel, the Archangel of Chesed, to command unto me the Chashmalim, the brilliant Ones of Tzedek. Come unto me, ye brilliant ones, that the Angel of Jupiter, Sachiel, may cause his Intelligence, Yohphiel, to make powerful this consecrated Telesmata. Cause him to take this for his body that a true and sacred link may be formulated between the Spirit of the Godhead in Chesed and the human soul of the exorcist.

Lift the Talisman and place it between Pillars. Go East, face West, and in the Sign of the Enterer project the whole current of will upon the talisman. Protect with the Sign of Harpocrates. A light should play about the talisman. If not repeat the above invocation from the Throne of the East. As soon as the Light is seen, quit the East and repurify and reconsecrate the Talisman with water and fire.

This done, remove the cord from talisman, lift it high, and smite it three times with sword, and proclaim:

By and in the names of Amoun the concealed One, and Al strong and mighty I invoke upon thee the power of Jupiter, bestower and receiver.

Circumambulate three times with Talisman in right hand. Return to the Throne of the East, place the Talisman upon the ground between the Pillars, and repeat the invocation on page 215. Alternate it with this conjuration.

I heard the voice of the Holy One proclaim, "Thou art my Son. This day have I begotten thee. Thou shalt rule the nations with a rod of iron. Thou shalt break them in pieces as a potter's vessel." Let therefore the elements obey the voice of Yhvh. O ye spirits of flashing fire, and air, Spirits of water and earth,
even ye legions of demons who dwell in the land of twilight, recog-
<222> nise in me your master, and in this creature of Talismans one whom
ye are powerless to hurt or touch. Turn ye, O ye creatures of night and the darkness; come and obey my will; serve and fear me. I bind even ye to help me in the works of the magic of light. I bind ye by the curse of Elohim Gibor and by the power of Kamael, and by the overwhelming powers of Geburah. By the awful curse of Paschal, and the Fire of the letter Shin. I summon and command ye all to do my will in the cause of this magical art, to the glory of the ineffable name. Look ye now upon this Jupiter Talisman and tremble, for the powers of the divine ones are in it. Look ye now upon the Exorcist, for the crown of the Godhead is over him. Empty are your places in the world above. Your habitations are beneath my feet. Elohim, let there be unto the void restriction! Yeheshuah, where are now their Gods?

O my Father, I saw Thee when thou camest forth from Edom, when Thou wentest out of the field of Seir. Why were Thy garments red, O mighty one? What were the sounds that behind thee rose from hell? A crying and a groaning, a wail as of pain! For the power of the mighty ones is shattered. Red are Thy robes, my Father, for their blood is spilt. Broken is the strength of hell. Fallen are its walls of adamant; heaped in ruins are its walls of deception. I came—and the Lord smote the warriors of ignorance. I came—and the thrones of the Ghogiel were empty. I came, and around me hovered the Auphanim, with Ratziel at their head, the Lord of Knowledge. O my Father, there are the wheels of thy chariot. Al Ab blessed be thy name. Broken is thy strength O concealer, and fallen are the powers wherein ye have trusted. Shaken are your fenced cities to their unseen foundations.

He shall hide me under the shadow of his wings. His truth shall be for ever more in the name of this Creature of Talismans, because I have called upon
the most High, even Amoun have I called my habitation. I shall
<223> tread upon the lion and adder. The young lion and dragon shall I
trample under foot, because he hath set his love upon me. He will set me upon high, for I am He even as He is in me. Lift up your heads, O ye gates. Be ye opened, ye everlasting doors, that the King of Glory may come in. *(Make over Talisman the Sign of the Rending of the Veil, and say)* Let the white brilliance of the divine Spirit descend upon this creature of Talismans, to fill it with the glory of thy majesty, that for ever it may be unto me an aid to aspire to the Great Work.

Draw Flaming Sword over Talisman and say:

Glory be unto thee, Lord of the Land of Life, for thy splendour flows out rejoicing, even unto the ends of the earth.

Take up talisman, pass to between Pillars, formulate an astral Banner of the East about it, and say:

Behold ye powers and forces of Chesed which I have invoked. Take witness that I have duly consecrated this Creature of Talismans with the aid of Yohphiel, the intelligence of Tzedek, that it may aid me to overcome all spiritual and material obstacles, and by the exaltation of my higher nature assist me in my Path to the Light Divine.

Wrap Talisman in silk or linen, put it away, and announce:

In the name of Yeheshuah the redeemer, I do now suffer all spirits bound by this ceremony, no longer needed in the service of this Telesmata, to depart in peace unto their places. May the blessing of Yeheshuah Yehovashah be with you now and forever more, and let there be peace between me and you.

APPENDIX TO THE JUPITER TALISMAN RITUAL

The foregoing is a fairly good example of a Ritual for the Consecration of a Talisman employing the formulae of the Neophyte Ceremony described in the document Z.2. Properly performed, it takes about one and a half
<224> hours. There is a slight variation of this which can be employed, using the formula of the Rite of the Kerubic Stations from the Theoricus grade ceremony. If this is added, and the student should certainly experiment with its employment since it produces an astonishingly powerful effect, the total time taken by the ceremony will be around two hours. The result of this addition is to build up more deliberately an astral body of incarnation for the invoked spiritual force.

The best place for the insertion of this phase of the ceremony is after the three circumambulations, when the operator has projected the entire force of his will upon the talisman which is placed between the two Pillars. In this instance, the following appendix is added to page 221, just prior to the invocation repeated from page 215. I will repeat part of the rubric.

Circumambulate three times with Talisman in right hand. Return to the Throne of the East, and holding the Talisman aloft, proclaim:

Behold the Exorcist in the midst of the Exorcism. And the power of the Exorcist said unto the Talisman, Let us enter the presence of the Ancient of Days. Arise, and come with me.

Still holding Talisman aloft, attract the light as you pass between the Pillars. Circumambulate, saying:

Amoun the Concealed One spake and said: I am the Secret of Secrets hidden in the heart of all things. I am the Grace of the majesty divine. I am the Lord of perfected work.

Having circumambulated once, stop in the East, face East, saying:

Before thou canst be a means for the manifestation of the divine light thy body must be formed from the swift-flowing air.

Place Talisman before the Air Tablet, and make round it the invoking circle and Pentagram of Active Spirit with Wheel, and Air Pentagram with Aquarius Kerub:

<225> In the name of Yhvh, and in the name of Shaddai El Chai, and in the name of Raphael, your archangel, Spirits of Air, ye I command. Bind unto this Creature of Talismans the substance of your element of Air. *(Make Cross.)* In the Three Great Secret Holy Names of God borne upon the banners of the East: Oro Ibah Aozpi, Spirits of Air, give unto me the substance of your realm that it may be mine for ever, binding it unto this Creature of Talismans which I have created. *(Make Invoking Circle)* In the name of Bataivah, Great King of the East, Spirits of Air, concentrate upon this creature of Talis-

mans the substance of your realm, so that the all-potent forces may descend and dwell therein as in a perfect body of manifestation. To the end that this Creature of Talismans may perform that for which it has been created. Creature of Talismans, I have bound unto thee the Air of life, that thy body may be truly formed. So pass we on.

Take up Talisman in left hand, pass round again endeavouring to formulate about it a sphere of light. Say:

Yohphiel spake unto the Exorcist: I am the aspiration to the throne of Chesed. I am the Intelligence of the Sphere of Tzedek. I have entered the presence of the Majesty divine through the power of the Mighty Name.

Having gone completely round, stop before Fire Tablet in South.

Before thy body can be filled with the glory of the Divine Ones in Wisdom, it must be potent with the Fire of life.

Place Talisman before Fire Tablet, make about it the invoking Circle and Pentagram of Actives, and Fire Pentagram with Leo Kerub in centre, invoking:

In the name of Elohim and in the name of Yhvh Tzaboath, and by the name of Michael, your Ruler, Spirits of Fire, ye I command. Bind into this creature of Talismans the substance of your fiery realm. *(Make Cross)* In the
<226> Three great Secret Holy Names of God borne upon the banners of
the South: Oip Teaa Pedoce, Spirits of Fire, give unto me of the substance of your realm that it may be mine for ever. Bind it unto this Creature of Talismans which I have created. *(Invoking Circle.)* In the name of Edelpernaa, Great King of the South, Spirits of Fire, ye I command. Concentrate upon this Talisman the substance of your realm, so that the all-potent forces descending may impart unto it a tireless strength, and an all prevailing energy. So that unto me it may be a Talisman ever helping me to aspire unto the Divine with the extended flame of an all-penetrant vision. Creature of Talismans, thou hast the fire of life. So pass we on.

Take up Talismans, and pass round completely, holding the Talisman aloft, and attracting the Light.

I have passed through the Gates of Wisdom and come unto the palace of Peace. Give me your hands, O ye Lords of Truth, for I am made as ye. Ye are the teachers of the soul.

Go to West, face quarter, place Talisman before Water Tablet, saying:

Before thou canst have a body fitted for the incarnation of the divine, thou must receive the water, the blood, and the tears for the remission of sins.

Make Invoking Circle and Pentagram of Passives, with Wheel; and Invoking Water Pentagram with Eagle Kerub.

In the name of Al mighty and powerful, and in the name of Elohim Tzabaoth, and by the name of your Archangel Gabriel, Spirits of Water ye I command. Infuse ye into this Creature of Talismans the substance of the Waters. *(Make Cross.)* In the Three Great Secret Holy Names of God borne upon the banners of the West: Empeh Arsel Gaiol, Spirits of Water, ye I command. Give unto me of the substance of your realm that it may be mine forever. Bind it unto this Creature of Talismans which I have created. *(Make Invoking*
<227> *Circle.)* In the name of Ra-agiosel, great King of the West, spirits of
Water ye I command. Concentrate upon this creature of Talismans

the substance of your realm so that it may have a body firm and substantial, manifesting unto me as a solid in the Astral Light that through it the powers of Tzedek may manifest unto me. Creature of Talismans I have bound unto thee the Water. So pass we on.

Take up Talisman, raise it aloft again attracting the Light, circumambulate, saying:

O Lord of the Universe, thou art in all things, and thy name is in all things. Before thee the shadows of the Night roll back and the darkness hasteth away.

Pass on to North. Face Earth Tablet, and say:

Creature of Talismans, before the mercy of Chesed can manifest in thy being, the elements of thy body must have an enduring stability.

Place talisman before Earth Tablet, make invoking Circle round it and Pentagram of Passive Spirit with Wheel, and Invoking Earth Pentagram with Taurus Kerub, saying:

In the name of Adonai Ha-Aretz and Adonai Melekh, Spirits of Earth adore your creator. In the name of the Bride and the Queen of the Kingdom, and by the name of your Archangel Auriel, Spirits of Earth ye are mine to command. Bind unto this creature of talismans the substance of your realm. *(Make Cross.)* In the Three Great Secret Holy Names of God borne upon the banners of the North: Emor Dial Hectega, Spirits of Earth give unto me of the substance of your realm that it may be mine for ever. Bind it unto this creature of Talismans which I have created. *(Make Invoking Circle.)* In the name of Ic Zod Heh Chal, great king of the North, Spirits of Earth, concentrate unto this creature of Talismans the substance of your realm, that the all-potent forces may descend and rest upon it, even the grace and mercy of Tzedek. Creature of Talismans, I have bound unto thee the element of enduring stability. So pass we on.

<228> *Take up Talisman, and pass between Pillars. Place it on the ground between them, and strongly formulate around it sphere of sensation.*

Creature of Talismans, that the power of Amoun the concealed One may manifest through thee, I give thy body the soul of Spirit.

Make Passive and Active Spirit Pentagrams. Also the Rose Cross Symbol. Vibrate powerfully the Enochian Exhortation used in the Portal Ceremony.

In the name of Eheieh and Agla, and by all the names and letters of the Mystical Tablet of Union, I command ye, O ye forces of Eth. I invoke ye, ye Angels of the Celestial Sphere, whose dwelling is in the invisible, to give me of your light for ever. Bind unto this Creature of Talismans the ethereal splendour of your realm so that it may become a living creature, well fitted to receive the incarnation of the divine. Give it life and energy, I beseech thee, so that always it may manifest unto me the glorious quality of Chesed.

Make the Sign of the Rending of the Veil. Then repeat the invocation on page 215, beginning:

Abba, Father of all fathers, thee I invoke by Thy Name Al, etc.

<229>

INVISIBILITY

Temple as in ⓪ = 0 Grade. Banish thoroughly with Lesser Ritual of the Pentagram and Hexagram, using Qabalistic Cross and Key-word. Purify with Fire and Water. Circumambulate three times. Return to Altar for Adoration.

Or open by the Formula of the Watch-Towers.

Invoke the forces of the Tablet of Union by means of Supreme Ritual of Pentagram, with Active and Passive Spirit, with Eheieh and Agla. Return to Altar, and recite the following Enochian Spirit Invocation:

Ol Sonuf Vaorsag Goho Iad Balt, Lonsh Calz Vonpho. Sobra Z-ol Ror I Ta Nazps, od Graa Ta Malprg. Ds Hol-q Qaa Nothoa Zimz, Od Commah Ta Nobloh Zien. Soba Thil Gnonp Prge Aldi. Ds Vrbs Oboleh G Rsam. Casarm Ohorela Taba Pir Ds Zonrensg Cab Erm Iadnah. Pilah Farsm Znrza Adna Gono Iadpil. Ds Hom Od Toh. Soba Ipam Lu Ipamis. Ds Loholo Vep Zomd Poamal Od Bogpa Aai Ta Piape Piaomel Od Vaoan. Zacare Eca Od Zamran. Odo Cicle Qaa. Zorge Lap Zirdo Noco Mad. Hoath Iaida.

Adgt Vpaah Zong Om Faaip Sald, Vi-i-vl, Sobam Ialprg Izazaz Pi Adph, Casarma Abramg Ta Talho Paracleda, Q Ta Lorslq Turbs Ooge Baltoh. Givi Chis Lusdi Orri, Od Micalp Chis Bia Ozongon. Lap Noan Trof Cors Ta Ge O Q Manin Iaidon. Torzu Gohe L. Zacar Eca Ca Noquod. Zamran Micalzo Od Ozazm Vrelp. Lap Zir Io-Iiad.

Pause and feel the invoked force.

In the name of Yeheshuah, Yehovashah, I invoke the power of the Recording Angel. I adjure thee, O Light invisible, intangible, wherein all thoughts and deeds of all men are written. I adjure Thee by Thoth, Lord of Wisdom and Magic who is thy Lord and God. By all the symbols and words of power; by the light of my Godhead in thy midst. By Harpocrates, Lord of
<230> Silence and of Strength, the God of this mine Operation, that thou leave Thine abodes and habitations to concentrate about me, invisible, intangible, as a shroud of darkness, a formula of defence; that I may become invisible, so that seeing me men see not, not understand the thing that they behold.

Go to East and perform invoking Hexagram Ritual of Binah, tracing Saturn Hexagram with Yhvh Elohim and Ararita. Close with I.N.R.I. Return to Altar.

Lady of Darkness who dwellest in the Night to which no man can approach, wherein is Mystery and Depth unthinkable and awful silence. I beseech Thee in thy name Shekinah and Aimah Elohim, to grant thine aid unto the highest aspirations of my Soul, and clothe me about with thine ineffable mystery. I implore Thee to grant unto me the presence of Thy Archangel Tzaphqiel, the great Prince of Spiritual initiation through suffering, and of spiritual strife against evil, to formulate about me a shroud of concealment. O ye strong and mighty ones of the Sphere of Shabbathai, ye Aralim, I conjure ye by the Mighty name of Yhvh Elohim, the divine ruler of Binah, and by the name of Tzaphqiel, your Archangel. Aid me with your power, in your office to place a veil between me and all things belonging to the outer and material world. Clothe me with a veil woven from that silent darkness which surrounds your abode of eternal rest in the sphere of Shabbathai.

Pause.

Come unto me, O Thmaah. Goddess of Truth and Justice, who presidest over the Eternal balance in this Hall of Dual Manifestation of Truth. Auramooth, come unto me, thou Lady of the Purifying Waters of Life. Thaum-aesh-Neith, Come unto me, Lady of the Consuming Fire, purify me and consecrate me who am Aeshoorist, the Justified One, Lord of Life, triumphant over death.

Upon my brow are arrayed the twelve stars of light. Wisdom and
<231> understanding are balanced in my Neschamah. Geburah and
power on my right hand, and the thunderbolts of Mars! Chesed on my left hand and the sweet fountains of magnificence. In my heart is Yeheshuah, the Reconciler, who is the symbol of golden harmony. My two thighs are as mighty pillars on the right and on the left supporting me; Splendour and Victory, for they cross with the currents reflected from the supernal light. I am established as an eternal Rock of Righteousness, for Yesod is the foundation of the Righteous. The sphere of my Nephesch, and the seven palaces of Malkuth are cleansed and consecrated, balanced and pure, in the might of Thy Name, Adonai, to whom be Malkuth, Gedulah, Geburah, the Rose of Sharon and the Lily of the Valley.

Vibrate the names in the following invocation by the formula of the Middle Pillar, and circulate it through the body. Proceed slowly to make certain the power is invoked.

Hoor-po-krat-ist, Thou Lord of the Silence. Hoor-po-krat-ist, Lord of the Sacred Lotus. O Thou Hoor-po-krat-ist *(pause a moment or two to contemplate the force invoked)* Thou that standest in victory on the heads of the infernal dwellers of the waters wherefrom all things were created. Thee, Thee I invoke, by the name of Eheieh and the power of Agla.

O Thou divine Babe in the Egg of Blue, Lord of defence and silence, Thou that bearest the Rose and Cross of Life and Light! Thee, thee I invoke for my exaltation to that Light.

Behold! It is written: I am a circle on whose hands stands the twelvefold kingdom of my godhead. I am the Alpha and the Omega, the first and the last, for my life is as the circle of infinite heaven. I change, but death does not come nigh me. O ye divine birds of Resurrection who are the hope of men's mortality, come unto me and aid me. Depart from me, ye workers of evil before the light of Aeshoorist.

Behold! He is in me and I in him. Mine is the Lotus, as I rise as Har-
<232> pocrates from the firmament of waters. My throne is set on high. My
light is as that of Ra in the firmament of Nu. I am the centre and the shrine, the silence and the eternal light of Godhead. Beneath my feet they rage in dumb impotence. For I am Hoor-po-krat-ist, the Lotus-throned Lord

of Silence. Were I to say, Come up upon the mountains, the celestial waters would flow at my word, and the celestial fires would surge forth in torrents fierce of flame. For I am Ra enshrouded, Khephra unmanifest to man. I embody my father Hoor, the might of the avenging God, and my mother Isis, eternal wisdom veiled in eternal beauty and love.

Therefore I way unto Thee, bring me unto thine abode in the Silence unutterable, all-Wisdom, all-light, all-power. Hoor-po-krat-ist, Thou nameless child of Eternity. Bring me to Thee, that I may be defended in this work of art. Thou, the Centre and the Silence; Light shrouded in darkness is thy name. The Celestial Fire is thy father. Thy mother the heavenly sea. Thou, the Air of Life, art the harmony of all, and Lord against the face of the dwellers within the waters! Bring me, I say, bring me to thine abode of everlasting silence, that I may awake to the glory of my godhead, that I may go invisible, so that every spirit created, and every soul of man and beast, and everything of sight and sense, and every spell and scourge of God, may see me *not* nor understand!

And now, in the name of Elohim, let there be unto the void a restriction! Yeheshuah, where are now their Gods. Oh my father, my father; there are the wheels of thy chariot! Lift up your heads, O ye Gates! Be ye opened, ye everlasting doors, that the King of Glory and of Silence and of Night may come in!

Thus do I formulate a barrier without mine astral form that it may be unto me a wall and as a fortress, and as a sure defence. And I now declare that it *is* so formulated, to be a basis and receptacle for the Shroud of Darkness, the Egg of Blue with which I shall presently girdle myself.

<233> *Trace Active and Passive Spirit Pentagrams and vibrate the Enochian invocation of Portal Grade.*

And unto ye, O ye forces of the Spirit of Life whose dwelling is in the invisible, do I now address my will. In the great names of your ruling Angels Elexarph, Comananu, Tabitom, and by all the names and letters of the holy Tablet of Union, by the mighty names of God: Eheieh, Agla, Yhvh Elohim, and by the Great Lord of Silence, Hoor-po-krat-ist, by your deep purple darkness, and by the white and brilliant light of the Crown above my head, do I conjure ye. Collect yourselves about me, and clothe this my astral form with an egg of blue, a shroud of darkness. Gather yourselves, ye flakes of Astral Light, and shroud my form in your substantial night. Clothe me and hide me but at my control. Darken man's eyes that he see me not. Gather at my word divine, for ye are the watchers, and my soul is the shrine.

Invoke the highest by Qabalistic Cross and I.N.R.I. Formulate the black egg around you, the idea of becoming invisible. Imagine the results of success, then say:

Let the shroud of concealment encircle me at a distance of eighteen inches from the physical body.

Let the Egg be consecrated with fire and water.

Place fire and water on either side of you.

O Auramo-oth and Thaum-Aesh-Neith, ye Goddesses of the scales of the Balance, I invoke and beseech you, that the vapours of this magical water and this consecrating fire be as a basis on the material plane for the formation of this shroud of Art.

Formulate mentally the shroud.

I, A.M.A.G., Frater of the Order of the G. D. and a ⑤ = 6 of the R.R. et A.C., a Lord of the Paths in the Portal of the Vault of the Adepti, do hereby formulate to myself the blue-black egg of Harpocrates as a shroud of concealment that I
may attain unto knowledge and power for the accomplishment of
<234> the Great Work, and to use the same in the service of the Eternal
Gods, that I may pass unseen among men to execute the will of my Genius. And I bind and obligate myself, even as I was bound to the Cross of Obligation, and do spiritually swear and affirm that I will use this power to a good purpose only, to help me eventually to aid and serve my fellow man. And I declare that with the divine Aid in this Operation I *shall* succeed, that the Shroud *shall* conceal me alike from men and spirits, that it shall be under my control, ready to disperse and to re-form at my command. And I declare that all is now ready for the due fulfillment of this ceremony of the Magic of Light.

Go to East of Altar, facing West, left hand on triangle, right hand holding black band of Lotus Wand upright.

Come unto me, O shroud of darkness and of night, by the power of the name Yeheshuah, Yehovashah. Formulate about me, thou divine egg of the darkness of spirit. I conjure ye, O particles of astral darkness, that ye enfold me as a guard and shroud of utter silence and of mystery in and by the name Eheieh, and the name Agla, the names of the centre of infinite Light. In and by the name Exarp. In and by the name Hcoma. In and by the name Nanta. In and by the name Bitom, those holy names of the sacred Tablet of Union. In the name of Yhvh Elohim which rules the divine darkness. In and by the name of Hoor-po-krat-ist, I conjure and invoke this shroud of concealment. By your deep purple darkness, and by the white brilliance of the Genius about and within me, I invoke ye and conjure ye. I exorcise ye potently. I command and constrain ye. I compel ye to absolute, instant, and complete obedience, and that without deception or delay. For the Light of my Genius is upon me, and I have made Yhvh my hope. Gather, ye flakes of Astral Light, to shroud my form in your substantial night. Clothe me and hide me in an egg of blue.
Darken man's eyes, and blind him in his soul, so that he see me not.
<235> Gather, O gather at my word divine, for ye are the Watchers, my soul
the shrine.

Turn around three times. Resume former position and say:

In the name of the Lord of the Universe, and by the power of my Augoeides, and by the aspiration of thine own higher Soul. O shroud of darkness and of mystery, I conjure Thee, that thou encirclest me, so that I may become invisible. So that seeing me men may see me not, neither understand. But that they may see the thing that they see not, and comprehend not the thing that they behold. So mote it be!

Pass to North, face East, and say:

I have set my feet in the North, and have said: I will shroud myself in mystery and concealment. The Voice of my Higher Soul said unto me, Let me enter the path of darkness, peradventure thus may I attain the Light. I am the only being in an Abyss of Darkness; from the Darkness came I forth ere my birth, from the silence of a primal sleep. And the Voice of Darkness answered unto my soul, I am He that formulates in darkness, the light that shineth in darkness, but the darkness comprehendeth it not. Let the Mystic Circumambulation take place in the Place of Darkness.

Go round, knock when passing East and West and East again. Pass to the South, halt, formulate the Pillars of Fire and Cloud, reaching from darkness to the Heavens. Formulate shroud between them, and pass to the West.

Invisible, I cannot pass by the Gate of the Invisible save by virtue of the Name of darkness.

Formulate forcibly the egg of dark blue-black.

Darkness is my Name, and Concealment. I am the Great One Invisible of the Paths of the Shades. I am without fear, though veiled in darkness, for within me, though unseen, is the Magic of the Light divine.

Go round, knock as before, halt in North, formulate Pillars, and the blue-black egg between them. Then pass to East.

<236> Invisible, I cannot pass by the Gate of the Invisible, save by virtue of the Name of Light

Formulate shroud forcibly.

I am Light shrouded in darkness. I am the wielder of the forces of the balance.

Concentrate shroud mentally. Go West of the Altar, remain standing, and say:

O thou divine egg of the creative darkness of Spirit, formulate thou about me. I command thee by the name of Yeheshuah. Come unto me, Shroud of darkness and of night. I conjure ye, O particles of spiritual darkness, that ye enfold me as an unseen guard and as a shroud of utter silence and of mystery. In and by the names Eheieh, Agla, and Yhvh Elohim, I conjure thee. In and by the holy names Exarp, Bitom, Hcoma, Nanta, I invoke thee. In and by the names Elexarpeh, Comananu, Tabitom, I constrain thee. By the name of Hoor-po-krat-ist I invoke this shroud of concealment. By the deep purple darkness of the eternal Spirit of Life, and by the white brilliance of the Genius within me, I invoke ye and conjure ye to absolute and instant obedience, without deception or delay. For the Crown of my Father is upon me, and in Yhvh is my trust. Gather, ye flakes of astral Light, and shroud my form in your substantial night. Clothe me, and hide me in an egg of blue, so that seeing me, men may see me *not,* neither understand. But that they may see the thing that they see not, and comprehend not the thing that they behold. For ye are the Watchers, my soul the shrine.

Egg of divine darkness, shroud of concealment, long hast thou dwelt concealed. Quit the Light, that thou mayest conceal me before men!

Carefully formulate shroud about you.

I receive Thee as a covering and a guard. Khabs Am Pekht. Konx Om Pax. Light in Extension.

Before all magical manifestation cometh the knowledge of the hidden Light.

Go to the Pillars. Face West and give the Signs, steps, words, etc., and with
<237> *the Sign of the Enterer project your whole Will so as to realize the self fading out. The effect should be that the physical body will become gradually and partially invisible, as though a veil or cloud were coming between it and*

Thee. Divine ecstasy may follow, but guard against loss of self-control. Make Sign of Silence forcibly, and vibrate with power the name Hoor-po-krat-ist.

Reformulate shroud, and circumambulate thrice. Intensely formulate Shroud, stand at East, and say:

Thus have I formulated unto myself this shroud of Darkness and of Mystery as a concealment and a guard.

Supernal Splendour which shinest in the sphere of Binah, Yhvh Elohim, Aima, Shekinah, Lady of Darkness and of Mystery, Thou High Priestess of the Concealed Silver Star, Divine Light that rulest in thine own deep darkness. Come unto me, and dwell within my heart, that I also may have power and control, even I, over this shroud of Darkness and of Mystery. And now I conjure thee, O shroud of Darkness and of Mystery, that thou conceal me from the eyes of all men, from all things of sight and sense, in this my present purpose, which is to remain invisible for the space of one hour, and to receive therein the holy mysteries of the Lord of Silence enthroned upon his Lotus, Hoor-po-krat-ist.

When it is wished to banish the shroud, make very forcibly the Qabalistic Cross, to bring down the Light, and then analyse the Key-Word, invoking the Divine White Brilliance. Then say:

In the name of Yhvh Elohim, I invoke thee, who art clothed with the Sun, who standest upon the Moon, and art crowned with the crown of twelve stars. Aima Elohim, Shekinah, Who art Darkness illuminated by the Light divine,
send me thine Archangel Tzaphkiel, and thy legions of Aralim, the
<238> mighty Angels of the sphere of Shabbathai, that I may disintegrate
and scatter this shroud of darkness and of mystery, for its work is ended for the hour.

I conjure Thee, O shroud of darkness and of Mystery, which has well served my purpose, that thou now depart unto thine ancient ways. But be ye, whether by a word or will, or by this great invocation of your powers, ready to come quickly and forcibly to my behest, again to shroud me from the eyes of men. And now I say unto ye, Depart ye in peace, with the blessing of God the Vast and Shrouded One, and be ye very ready to come when ye are called!

Lesser Banishing Ritual of Pentagram and Hexagram. Stand in Astral Banner of East.

<239>

TRANSFORMATION

Open the Temple arranged as for 0 = 0 by usual banishings, and the Ceremony of the Watchtowers.

After the Adoration, face East, and invoke the name Eheieh by the vibratory and circumambulation formula of the Middle Pillar. Do not proceed until the physical sensation of the invoked force is experienced. Then contemplate the higher genius for some little while. Lift both hands on high.

In the divine name Iao, I invoke Thee thou great and holy Angel Hua. Lay thy hand invisibly upon my head in attestation of this my solemn aspiration to the Light. Aid and guard me I beseech thee, and confirm me in this path of truth and rectitude, for the glory of the ineffable name.

Lower arms, and quietly utter:

Unto Thee sole Wise, sole Eternal and sole Merciful One, be the praise and glory for ever, who hath permitted me, who now standeth humbly before thee, to enter thus far into the sanctuary of thy mystery. Not unto me, Adonai, but unto Thy Name be the glory. Let the influence of thy divine ones descend upon my head, and teach me the value of self-sacrifice so that I shrink not in the hour of trial, but that thus my name may be written on high and my genius shand in the presence of the Holy One. In that hour when the Son of Man is invoked before the Lord of Spirits and his Name before the ancient of Days.

Formulate the Pillars, and make 2 = 9 Sign, between them.

Let us adore the Lord and King of Air.

Go forward to Air Tablet. Make Active and Passive Spirit Pentagrams, and Invoking Air Pentagram with Aquarius.

And the Elohim said, "Let us make Adam in our own image, after
<240> our likeness, and let them have dominion over the fowl of the air."

In the name Yhvh and in the name Shaddai El Chai, Spirits of Air, adore your creator!

Make the Aquarius Kerub before Tablet with Air Dagger.

In the Sign of the Head of the Man, and by the name of Raphael Great Archangel of Air, Spirits of Air adore your creator.

Make Cross with Rose or the Censer.

In the names and letters of the Great Eastern Quadrangle, Spirits of Air adore your creator.

Hold Lotus Wand on high.

In the three great secret holy names of God borne upon the banners of the East, Oro Ibah Aozpi, Spirits of Air, adore your creator.

Trace whorl in front of Air Tablet, with Lotus Wand.

In the name of Bataivah, Great King of the East, Spirits of Air adore your creator.

Still facing East, vibrate powerfully the Third Enochian Key invoking the line Exarp from the Tablet of Union. Then formulate an astral Banner of the East about one.

In the name of Shaddai El Chai, and in the name of Yhvh, I command ye, ye dwellers in the realms of Air, that ye fashion for me a powerful magical base in the Astral Light whereon I may build a true body of transformation.

Perform Supreme Invoking Ritual of the Luna Hexagram, Precede with Qabalistic Cross, closing with Key-word. Return to Altar, face East, and say:

Crowned with star-light, and clothed with the Sun, I invoke Thee who art the ultimate root of all things, for thy righteousness and love are the foundations of the universe. Look upon me as I perform this ceremony, and, I beseech thee, let a ray of thy power descend here and now to awaken within my soul
that power which shall prove a true channel for the working of the
<241> divine strength. May this ceremony to form a body of Transforma-
tion of the holy goddess Isis, enable me to progress in the Great Work, clarifying my spiritual vision, and illuminating me so that I may be the better able to help my fellow men.

Draw the name Shaddai El Chai and Sigil in heart, while facing East, and vibrate it several times by the vibratory formula of the Middle Pillar. Then trace Sigil and Hebrew letters of the Name in the Air with the Lotus Wand.

Grant unto me the presence, I beseech Thee, of thy Great Archangel of the sphere of Yesod, that he may aid me at this time, even Gabriel, the Archangel of strength and power.

Draw the Invoking Hexagram of Luna and in it the Sigil and letters of Gabriel. Vibrate it similarly several times.

O ye mighty ones of the sphere of Yesod, I invoke ye by the mighty name of Shaddai El Chai, whose seat and throne ye are, and by the name of Gabriel, your Archangel. Come unto me now, and let the magical force of Yesod flow through me so that I may accomplish this work of transformation.

Draw Sigil of Kerubim in the Hexagram. Pause for some while, formulating the God-form of Isis.

In the name of Shaddai El Chai, I proclaim all ye powers and forces of Yesod, that I, *Ad Majorem Adonai Gloriam,** Neophyte of the Golden Dawn, and a Frater Roseae Rubeae et Aureae Crucis, have summoned ye to my presence for the forming of a true and potent link between my human soul in Malkuth and the great goddess Isis, whose true abode is in the Supernals, yet reflected in Yesod, the eternal foundation of all things. To this end I now formulate a magical image of Isis in the Astral Light, so that by its assumption and with the divine aid I may be transformed from corruption into incorruption, and putting aside mortality become divinity itself through the descent of that
Supernal Light which cometh with healing in its wings. And I
<242> solemnly pledge myself to use this body of Transformation of the
goddess Isis, for the forwarding of the highest aspirations of my soul, and for the pursuit of the Great Work, that it may in very truth become a

* The student should substitute his/her own magical name.

perfect body of transmutation. Formulate before me now in the evoked elements of Air, O ye powers of Yesod, a true and tangible form of Isis, that through its assumption, my own inner being may be wholly dissolved as though eaten up by the Airs of the Spirit, and transformed into a divine transfiguration. To the end that by the descent of the Shekinah and my assumption into the Holy Spirit, I may become the embodiment of the true Magic of Light, and acquire more perfect knowledge to help my fellow men.

And I now declare that all is in readiness for this magical operation, devoted to the formulation of a body of transformation of the Goddess Isis.

Pass to the West of the Temple with Fire and Water, and place them either side of the formulation of Isis, saying:

O form of Isis I formulate thee in the name *Ad Majorem Adonai Gloriam,** that thou mayest become a living body for the manifestation of the wisdom of God-head. And in the holy names of the Goddesses of the Scales of the balance, I purify thee with water and consecrate thee with fire, that from the vapours of these elements a basis may be formed for thee in the Astral Light.

Pass to the East of the Altar, facing West. In the West, kneeling at the altar where in the Neophyte ceremony the newly-admitted aspirant would be, formulate the god-form of Isis. Imagine that your left hand holds the left hand of the form. Hold the black section of the Lotus Wand in the right hand, tracing over the form such letters, sigils, and lineal figures as may occur in the following Oration.

In the divine name Shaddai El Chai, I invoke Thee, thou great goddess of Nature who clothest thyself with the forces of life as with a garment.
<243> O thou who art Isis, the High Priestess of the Silver Star, the perfect purity and illumination of the divine Presence of the Supernal Light, whose sphere is Yesod reflecting the Light and Air from the Crown. Lift me up, I beseech thee, through the path of Tau, and manifest unto me a body of transformation, showing forth thy love and power and stability. Grant unto me the mighty power and help of the Archangel Gabriel who rules over the fundamental strength of Yesod, that he may command to my assistance the Choir of Angels the Kerubim that they may formulate with power this form of Isis. Let them give life and vitality unto this form of transmutation before me. Let them bind therein the reflection of the Light of the Supernals so that by my assumption of it, the body of transformation may become a solid link, tangible and unbreakable with all those powers of love and understanding which rise rank upon rank to the feet of the Holy Spirit. Grant that the Wisdom and Light of the Divine Ones may descend and through this form, manifest unto me the true holiness and unsullied vision of the Light.

Vibrate and circumambulate Isis by the vibratory formula of the Middle Pillar. Holding Lotus Wand by black end, directing flower over the head of form, say:

In the name of the Lord of the Universe, arise before me, O form of Isis unto which I have elected to tranform myself, so that seeing me, men may see the thing they see not, and comprehend not the divine form that they see.

*The student should substitute his/her own magical name.

Leave Altar, and move slowly towards the North.

Pass towards the North shrouded in darkness, O form of Isis into which I have elected to transform myself. The Voice of the Transformer said: Let me enter the path of darkness, peradventure thus may I manifest the Light. I am the only being in an abyss of darkness, from the darkness came I forth ere my birth, from the silence of a primal sleep. And the Voice of the
<244> Transformation said unto me, Child of Earth, the light shineth in
darkness, but the darkness comprehendeth it not. Let the Mystic circumambulation take place.

Pass round once leaving the form. Formulate it in the South between two Pillars, and place Fire and Water on either side. Pass to West, endeavouring to visualize the form strongly.

Thou canst not pass from concealment unto manifestation save by virtue of the name of Elohim. Before all things are the chaos, the darkness, and the gates of the land of Night. I am He whose name is darkness. I am the great one of the Paths of the Shades. I am the transformer in the midst of the transformation. Formulate thou without fear before me as a firm body of transformation, for I am he in whom fear is not. Thou hast known me, O thou form of Isis, pass thou on.

Pass round once. Bring it to North, between Pillars, and place Fire and Water on either side. Then go East, visualising Isis.

Thou canst not pass from concealment unto manifestation save by virtue of the name Yhvh. After the formless, the void and the darkness, then cometh the knowledge of the Light. I am that Light arising in Darkness. I am the Transformer in the midst of the transformation. Manifest thou therefore as a tangible body of transformation, for I am the Wielder of the Forces of the Balance. Thou hast known me now, O form of Isis, so pass thou on unto the cubical altar of the Universe.

Pass to East of Altar, formulating Isis as standing West in the place of the Candidate.

And I beheld a great wonder in Heaven. A woman clothed with the Sun, with the Moon at her feet, and on her head was the diadem of the Twelve Stars. O thou Queen of Love and Mercy, thou crowned with the Throne, horned as the Moon, whose countenance is mild and glowing, hear me, O Isis, hear and save. Isis *(vibrate by Middle Pillar.)* Thou who art in matter manifest, Mother, Queen, and Daughter of the Justified One, thee, thee do I invoke. O
<245> Virgin Glory of the Godhead unspeakable, immortal Queen of the
Gods, I invoke Thee. Isis *(circumambulate within).* By this Lotus, the sacred flower of thy Life, I invoke thee, I who dwell in the vast hall of living death, crying as thy child Horus towards the Golden Dawn. Isis *(vibrate)* Bid me awake, O mother, from the darkness of this earthy tomb, that I may as the living Osiris speak back to thee. O Isis, thou form of the Holy Spirit, from the marble halls of life, the immeasurable deep of Yesod, the sea of the sacred love, I invoke thee. Isis, *(circumambulate within)* descend from thy Palace of the Stars.

O Mother. O Archetype Eternal of Maternity and Love. O Mother, the flower of all Mothers, whose voice all Amenti hears. Speak unto me and manifest about me that I may rise from the chaos, from the world of shapeless and illusory forms, of dead men's husks, and unsubstantial things. O Isis, great queen of Heaven, supernal splendour which dwellest in that Light to which no man approach, wherein is Mystery and awful silence, come unto me, and make open the gates of bliss. Hail unto Thee, O thou mighty mother. Isis, unveil thou, O Soul of Nature, giving life and energy to the Universe. From thee all things do proceed. Unto Thee all must return. Thou springest from the Sun of splendour, shrouded from all. Lead me to the truth, bright maiden of the Night, and guide me in all my wanderings in darkness, as I travel upwards and onwards to the Light of the Eternal Crown. Come forth, O gracious Mother. Come unto me and dwell within my heart, Thou who art crowned with Starlight, who shineth amongst the Lords of Truth; whose place is in the abode of the Light of Heaven. Isis *(vibrate and circumambulate.)*

Now address the body of Isis as though it were physically visible before you at the Altar.

Child of Earth, long hast thou dwelt in Darkness. Quit the Night and seek the Day.

<246> *Draw the form towards you, so that it envelopes you.*

I receive thee as a true body of Isis, a body of transformation. Khabs Am Pekht. Konx om Pax. Light in Extension.

Analyse Key-word and make the L.V.X. Signs.

Before all magical manifestation cometh the knowledge of the Light divine.

Move forward to the Pillars, face West. Endeavour to feel the form of Isis as almost physical. Then make the 0 = 0 *Signs powerfully, and to feel actually in the shape desired. The form should seem as a cloud of mist enveloping you, but not yet wholly visible. When this occurs, but not before, formulate the Pillars standing on either side. If not, repeat the conjuration, and then return to Pillars. Circumambulate the Temple three times, completely enshrouded by form. Then say:*

Thus have I formulated unto myself this transformation.

Still in the East, utter the following conjuration.

Shaddai El Chai, almighty and ever living One, blessed be thy Name, ever magnified in the life of all. *(Vibrate the Name by the Middle Pillar, and mystic circumambulation.)* Grant unto me the power and presence of the Archangel of Yesod, Gabriel, who rules over the Kerubim, that they may vitalise and make strong this form of the God-head, so that it may be moulded as upon a firm and stable foundation, and inspired as a living body of Isis. Grant also unto me that this form of Isis which I have formulated may remain clear and strong so long as I shall have need of it, and that I may retain it under proper control and guidance until it shall have accomplished the work of transformation.

Return to Altar, addressing the form.

O thou form of Isis, which I have created to envelope and transform me, be thou in truth open to the divine Presence, the Understanding and
<247> Love of the Supernals. Be thou open to the wisdom and glory of the Goddess Isis so that thou mayest be a living Soul within me, and to prove my transfiguration, a body and soul of Resurrection. For the desire of the heavenly house hath eaten me up, and I desire to be with thee, O Isis.

Implant within me the seeds of Love and Understanding, so that I may prosper in the Great Work, and assist others to its glory.

Before leaving the Temple with the god-form, say:

In the name of Yeheshuah, the Redeemer, I do now suffer all Spirits who may have been bound by this ceremony, and who are not now needed in the work of transformation, to depart unto their abodes and habitations, with the blessing of Yhvh.

Having obtained the desired effect, and when the form no longer is needed, return to Temple, and shatter the form with the conjuration.

In and by the name Shaddai El Chai, with the Aid of Gabriel, Great Archangel of Yesod, and the Kerubim, I do now banish the powers of Yesod, and all the Spirits of Air from this form. Disintegrate it, I command ye, by all the divine names, and depart ye in peace unto your habitations, and let there ever be peace between me and you. Dissipate every vestige of this form, and let its elements return into their component parts. I now cast it forth. Let it cease to be.

In the name Shaddai El Chai, I now declare this Temple closed.

Perform the Banishing Rituals of Pentagram and Hexagram.

<248>

SPIRITUAL DEVELOPMENT

Hekas Hekas Este Bebeloi.

Face East, make Qabalistic Cross, and perform the Lesser Banishing ritual of the Pentagram, with the black end of the Lotus Wand, holding it by the white band. Then perform the Lesser Banishing Ritual of the Hexagram.

Make the full LVX Signs.

Advance to Altar without Wand and take therefrom the Fire Wand. Face South, raise the Wand above thy head, and slowly circumambulate with Sol, saying:

And when, after all the phantoms have vanished, thou shalt see that holy and formless Fire, that Fire which darts and flashes through the hidden depths of the universe, hear thou the Voice of Fire.

On reaching South, making the invoking Fire Pentagram and say:

Oip Teaa Pedoce. In the Names and Letters of the Great Southern Quadrangle, I invoke ye, ye Angels of the Watch-tower of the South.

Replace Wand on Altar, take Cup and go West. Sprinkle to West and circumambulate Temple with Sol, saying:

So therefore, first, the Priest who governeth the works of Fire must sprinkle with the Lustral Water of the Loud Resounding Sea.

On reaching West sprinkle with Water, make Invoking Water Pentagram and the Sign of Eagle's head, and say:

Empeh Arsel Gaiol. In the Names and Letters of the Great western Quadrangle, I invoke ye, ye Angels of the Watch-tower of the West.

Replace Cup, take Dagger, strike towards East, and circumambulate with Sol, saying:

Such a Fire existeth, extending through the rushings of Air, or even
<249> a Fire Formless, whence cometh the image of a Voice; or even a
Flashing Light, abounding, revolving, whirling forth, crying aloud.

On reaching East, strike forward with Dagger, and make invoking Air Pentagram, saying:

Oro Ibah Aozpi. In the Names and Letters of the Great Eastern Quadrangle, I invoke ye, ye Angels of the Watch-tower of the East.

Replace Dagger. Take Pentacle, go North, shake thrice, and circumambulate with Sol, saying:

Stoop not down into the darkly splendid world wherein lieth continually a faithless depth and Hades wrapped in gloom, delighting in unintelligible images, precipitous, winding; a black, ever-rolling abyss, ever espousing a body, unluminous, formless and void.

Reaching the North. Shake Pentacle thrice and with it make Invoking Earth

Pentagram, saying:

Emor Dial Hectega. In the Names and Letters of the Great Northern Quadrangle I invoke ye, ye Angels of the Watch-tower of the North.

Replace Pentacle. Take Incense, go West of Altar, Face East, raise it, describing Active equilibriating Spirit Pentagram, saying:

Exarp Bitom

Describe Passive Equilibriating Spirit Pentagram, saying:

Hcoma Nanta. In the Names and Letters of the Mystical Tablet of Union, I invoke ye, Angels of the celestial Spheres, whose dwelling is in the Invisible. Ye are the Guardians of the Gates of the Universe; be ye also the Watchers of my Mystic Sphere. Remove and banish far the evil; strengthen and inspire me that I may preserve unsullied this my body, as the abode of the Mysteries of the Eternal Gods. Let my sphere be pure and holy so that I may be able to enter into the centre of my being, and become a partaker of the secrets of the Divine Light.

Pass to the North. Take Lotus Wand and say:

<250> The visible Sun is the dispenser of Light to the Earth. Let me therefore form a vortex in this chamber that the Invisible Sun of the Spirit may shine thereinto from above.

Circumambulate with Sol thrice, saluting with ⑤ = 6 Signs as you pass the East. Go West of Altar, face East, and extend arms in the form of a cross, say:

Holy art Thou Lord of the Universe.
Holy art Thou whom Nature hath not Formed.
Holy art Thou the Vast and the Mighty One.
Lord of the Light and the Darkness.

Take Lotus Wand by White Band, perform Invoking Hexagram Ritual of the Supernals, and Pentagram Ritual of Spirit, and say:

Supernal Splendour which dwellest in the Light to which no man can approach, wherein is Mystery, and Depth unthinkable, and awful Silence. I beseech Thee, who art Shekinah and Aimah Elohim, to look upon me in this Ceremony which I perform to Thine Honour and for my own Spiritual development. Grant thine aid unto the highest aspirations of my Soul, in thy Divine Name Yhvh Elohim, by which Thou dost reveal thyself as the perfection of creation, and the Light of the World to come.

I implore Thee to grant unto me the presence of Thy Archangel Tzaphqiel. *(Trace Sigils as required and vibrate powerfully.)* O Tzaphqiel, Thou Prince of Spiritual Initiation through suffering, and of spiritual strife against evil, aid me I beseech Thee to conquer the evil that is in me, by the binding and controlling of my mortal parts and passions.

O ye strong and mighty ones of the sphere of Shabbathai, O ye Aralim, Aralim, I conjure ye by the mighty name of Yhvh Elohim, the divine ruler of your realm, and by the name of Tzaphqiel, your Archangel. Aid me with your power, in your office to place a veil between me and all things
<251> belonging to the outer and lower world. Let it be a veil woven from that silent darkness which surrounds your abode of eternal rest in the sphere of Shabbathai, that in this chamber of the Divine Mystery, I may hear nothing that comes not from on high, and see naught that may distract

my vision from the Glory of the eternal Crown. That I may behold only the holy vision that descends from that Divine Brilliance, the scintillation and corruscation of the Divine Glory. That Divine Brilliance, that Light which lighteth the universe, that Light which surpasseth the Glory of the Sun, beside which the Light of mortals is but darkness. That in the closing of my physical senses to the vibrations of the outer and the lower, I may learn to awaken those spiritual faculties by which I may attain at length to perfect union with divine and unalterable being.

Consider the Divine ideal, and say slowly:

From Thine hands, O Lord, cometh all good. From Thine hands flow down all grace and blessing. The characters of Nature with Thy finger Thou hast traced, but none can read them unless he hath been in thy school. Therefore, even as servants look unto the hands of their masters and handmaidens unto their mistresses, even so do our eyes look up unto Thee, for Thou alone art our help, O Lord of the Universe. All is from Thee, all belongeth unto Thee. Either Thy love or Thine Anger all must again re-enter. Nothing canst thou lose, for all must tend to Thine honour and majesty. Thou art Lord alone, and there is none beside Thee. Thou doest what Thou wilt with Thy Mighty Arm and none can escape from Thee. Thou alone helpest in their necessity the humble and meek-hearted and poor who submit themselves unto Thee; and whosoever humbleth himself in dust and ashes before Thee, unto such a one art Thou propitious. Who should not praise Thee, O Lord of the Universe, unto whom there is none like, whose dwelling is in the Heavens and in every virtuous and god-fearing heart.

<252> O God, the Vast One, Thou art in all things. O Nature, Thou Self from nothing, for what else can I call Thee. In myself, I am nothing, in Thee I am Self, and exist in Thy Selfhood from Nothing. Live Thou in me and bring me unto that Self which is in Thee, Amen.

I desire the attainment of the knowledge and conversation of my higher and Divine Genius, the summum bonum, true wisdom and perfect happiness, the power of the great transformation.

Kneel West of the Altar, and say, whilst aspiring strongly:

In the divine name IAO I invoke Thee, Thou Great Avenging Angel Hua, to confirm and strengthen me in the path of the Light. O messenger of the beloved One, let thy shadow be over me. Thy name is death, it may be, or shame or love. So thou bringest me tidings of the beloved one I shall not ask thy name. Keep me steadfast in the path of rectitude and self-sacrifice. Confer upon me the power of discernment that I may choose between the evil and the good, and try all things of doubtful and fictitious seeming with sure knowledge and sound judgment.

Rise, project the Astral to the East of the Altar. Hold the Lotus Wand in the right hand, turn, face your body, take the left hand in the left hand of the Astral, and in both astral and physical say:

Eheieh. Eheieh. Eheieh. Eheieh. *(Vibrate and circumambulate by Formula of the Middle Pillar.)* Thou who dwellest in the Boundless Light, in whom only is Being, who alone can say I Am, Beginner of movement, bestower of the gift of life in all things, Thou who fillest the limitless universe with Thy essence, grant unto me the presence of the Prince of Countenances, the great Angel

Metatron, He who bringeth others before the face of God. Let him lead me in my aspirations after that divine and only selfhood which is in Thee, that I may be enabled so to live that by the absolute control and purification of
<253> my natural body and soul, I having no other desire, may become a fit
dwelling for my higher Genius. For the desire of Thy house O Adonai hath eaten me up, and I desire to be dissolved and be with Thee. May my human nature, becoming as the perfect Malkuth, the resplendent intelligence, be thus exalted above every head and sit on the throne of Binah, and being clothed with the Sun, illuminate the darkness of my mortal body. Cause the Divine influx to descend from that great Archangel Metatron, to rend away the veils of darkness from my mortal vision, that I may know Thee, Adonai, the only true Self, and Yeheshuah Yehovashah, Thy perfect Messenger, the Guardian Angel in me, my only hope of attainment to the eternal Glory.

Place aside the astral Lotus. Return into the physical body, place Sword on neck, and say:

So help me, the Lord of the Universe and my Higher Soul.

Rise, holding Sword in right hand. Raise both arms on high. Contemplate with imagination and aspire unto the Ideal, and say:

I invoke Thee, Hru, thou great Angel who art set over the operations of this Secret Wisdom. Strengthen and establish me in my search for the Mysteries of the Divine Light. Increase my spiritual perception and assist me to rise beyond that lower selfhood which is nothing unto the highest selfhood which is in God the Vast One.

Pass to the North. Project the Astral to the throne of the Hierophant in the East, and facing your body, say:

The voice of my Higher Self said unto me "Let me enter the Path of Light, peradventure I may be prepared to dwell there. I am the only being in this glory of the Ineffable. From the divine Brilliance came I forth at my birth, from the splendour of the infinite Light."

Return to body. Circumambulate with Sol, saying, while drawing down the
<254> *divine brilliance into the vortex, having formulated an Angel Torch-bearer*
who lights and leads the way:

I am Osiris, the Sun veiled by night, united to the Higher by purification, perfected through suffering, glorified through trial. I have come where the Great Gods are, through the power of the Mighty Name. Yhvh. Tzaphqiel.

Then pass round again following the Angelic Kerux.

I have passed through the Gates of the Firmament. Give me your hands, O ye Lords of Truth, for I am made as ye. Hail unto ye, for ye are the formers of the Soul. Yod He. Ratziel.

Pass on and halt in South. Formulate the Two Pillars, and aspire to the Genius. Pass to the West, and say:

Before all things are the Chaos, the Darkness and the Gates of the Land of Night. Therefore in the place of the Guardian of the Gate of the West, I tread Thee down beneath my feet, O form of darkness and of fear. For fear is failure, and except I be without fear, I cannot cast out the evil ones into the Earth. I have conquered Thee, so I pass on.

Go round, saying:

O Lord of the Universe, Thou art above all things, and Thy Name is in all things, and before Thee the shadows of the Night roll back and the darkness hasteth away. Eheieh. Metatron.

Thus have I formulated the white Triangle of the Light Divine that, rising and expanding, may shine within my heart, a centre of the Supernal splendour.

Stop in the North, form the Pillars, aspire. Pass East, say:

After the formless and the void and the Darkness, then cometh the knowledge of the Light. So in the place of the Guardian of the Gate of the East, I draw thee into my heart, O vision of the Rising Sun. Thou dwellest in the place of the balance of the forces, where alone is perfect justice.
<255> Unbalanced mercy is but weakness, and unbalanced severity is
cruelty and oppression. Therefore, in the name of the Motionless Heart, I pass on unto that great Altar whereon is sacrificed the body of my higher Genius.

Pass to Cauldron on the Altar. Stand at East of Altar, facing West, and as you read, place the ingredients into the Cauldron.

O Adonai, thou mighty and secret Soul that is my link with the infinite Spirit, I beseech Thee in the name of Eheieh and in the tremendous Name of strength through sacrifice Yeheshuah Yehovashah, that thou manifest in me. Manifest thou unto me, I beseech Thee my Angel, for my assistance in the Great Work so that I, even I, may go forward from that lower selfhood which is in me, unto that highest selfhood which is in God the Vast One. That thou mayest be able to manifest thyself unto me, in me, and by a material manifestation I do here offer unto Thee the elements of the Body of Aeshoorist upon the place of Foundation.

For Osiris Onnophris hath said, These are the elements of my Body perfected through suffering and glorified by trial. For the scent of the dying rose is as the suppressed sigh of my suffering. And the flame red fire as the strength of mine undaunted will. The Cup of Wine is as the pouring forth of the blood of my heart, sacrificed unto regeneration, unto the newer life. And the bread and salt is as the foundation of my body which I destroy in order that it may be renewed.

Wherefore behold! Into this brazen cauldron I cast this Wine, this Bread and Salt, and finally this Rose, that their essences may be volatilised by the Fire which is beneath. Accept now these elements thus volatised by the Fire, and from them form a body by me and in me, that thou my Genius, the spirit of my soul, mayest manifest thyself physically unto me, for my assistance in the Great Work.

Pass West of Altar. Kneel, project Astral to Pillars, say:

<256> Father of all Beings, and of the Spaces, I invoke Thee and I adore
Thee. Look with favour upon my higher aspirations, and grant unto me that my Genius may manifest unto me, and in me, and through me, with a physical manifestation. Khabs Am Pekht. Konx Om Pax. Light in Extension.

Return to body. Rise and go East of Altar, face East.

And now, in the tremendous name of strength through suffering, Yeheshuah Yehovashah, do I crush ye down, O ye forces of evil that be beneath the universe in me, and thus do I transmute ye, that ye also may become a base and a foundation unto my higher Soul, that my Genius may manifest unto me physically, in me and by me, and thus also ye shall help forward the Great Work.

Pass forward to between the Pillars. Arms in the form of a Cross, attracting Genius from above, and say:

O Mighty Being, the locks of whose head are formed from the divine white Brilliance of the eternal Crown, Who art clothed with the Garment of purity, and girt with the golden Girdle of the Sun of Beauty, in whose right hand are grasped with an absolute rule the Seven mighty Archangels who govern the seven states of mortal man, grant unto me the power, I beseech Thee, to rise above the planetary darkness wherein I must live, here on Earth, until my regeneration is accomplished. Out of the darkness may Light arise for me. O Thou, from whose mouth cometh the sword of flame, rend I beseech Thee with that Sword the veils of darkness which hide from my spirit's vision, that Golden Light wherein Osiris dwells, that I being thus enabled to enter the secret chamber of my own Soul, may behold the Glory of the Eternal Crown, and beholding that great Light be willing to forego all that Earth can offer, that I may attain unto that Supernal and only Self, united in the glory of Ain Soph Aour. Let me dwell in that land which far-off travellers call Naught.
<257> O land beyond honey and spice and all perfections. I will dwell therein with my Lord Adonai for ever.

Visualise and attract Genius from above by aspiration. Vibrate the name Eheieh by the formula of the Middle Pillar, and circumambulate, and strive by all the power of the human will to exalt yourself unto the genius. Then circumambulate three times. Then return to Pillars, face East, and invoke:

I am the Resurrection and the Life. He that believeth on me, though he were dead, yet shall he live; and whomsoever liveth and believeth on me shall never die. I am the First and the Last. I am He that liveth and was dead, and behold I am alive for evermore, and hold the keys of Hell and of Death. For I know that my Redeemer liveth and that He shall stand at the latter day upon the Earth. I am the Way, the Truth, and the Life. No man cometh unto the Father but by me. I am the Purified. I have passed through the Gates of Darkness unto Light. I have fought upon Earth for good, and have finished my work. I have entered into the invisible.

Circumambulate slowly once with Sol, saying as you pass round:

I am the Sun in his rising, passed through the hour of cloud and of Night. I am Amoun the concealed One, the Opener of the Day. I am Osiris Onnophris, the Justified One, Lord of Life, triumphant over death. There is no part of me that is not of the Gods. I am the Preparer of the Pathway, the Rescuer unto the Light. Out of the darkness, let the Light arise.

At this point, reach the pillars again, and facing East, raise hands and eyes, and say:

I am the Reconciler with the Ineffable. I am the Dweller of the Invisible. Let the White Brilliance of the Divine Spirit descend.

In the Name and Power of that Divine Spirit, I invoke Thee, O my divine Genius that thou manifest Thyself to me and in me, to help me to
<258> purify my lower self, to teach me and assist me to unite myself unto

thee in divine perfection, so that I also may be built into the living rock, a pillar of the Temple of my God. That I may no more come out to dwell on Earth as mortal man, but that I may be as Osiris going forth to seek and to save the lost ones of the race of Man.

After contemplating.

Thus at length have I been enabled to begin to comprehend the form of my Higher Self.

Return to West of Altar, facing East.

And now in the Name and Power of the Divine Spirit, I invoke ye, ye Angels of the Watch-towers of the Universe, and charge ye to guard this my sphere. Keep far from me the evil and the unbalanced, that they penetrate not into my abode of the Mysteries. Inspire and sanctify me that I may enter in to the centre of my being, and there receive the illimitable wisdom of the light divine.

Give the Signs of the ⑤ = [6].

Close by purifying with water and consecrating with Fire. Reverse circumambulation, adoration to East, and say:

Nothing now remains but to partake of the sacred repast composed of the elements of the body of Osiris. For Osiris Onnophris hath said: These are the elements of my Body, perfected through suffering, glorified by trial. The scent of the dying Rose is as the suppressed sigh of my suffering. And the flame red fire as the strength of mine undaunted will. And the Cup of Wine is as the pouring forth of the blood of my heart, sacrificed unto regeneration, unto the newer life. And the bread and salt is as the foundation of my body which I destroy that it may be renewed.

Take Elements astrally. Then say:

In the name of Yhshvh the Redeemer, I now set free any spirits that may have been imprisoned by this ceremony.

Conclude with L V X Signs.

<259> THE BORNLESS RITUAL FOR THE INVOCATION OF THE HIGHER GENIUS

Temple arranged with Banners of East and West, Four Enochian Tablets, with a Tablet of Union on altar with the elements arranged over it. Cross and triangle in centre. The whole ritual to be performed either with the Hierophant's Sceptre or Lotus Wand. Z. A. M. to be clothed in white, wearing yellow slippers, white sash and consecrated Rose Cross.

Standing West of Altar, face East, and cry:

Hekas Hekas Este Bebeloi.

Purify the Temple with Water as in the 0 = 0 *Grade.*

Consecrate the Temple with Fire, saying appropriate versicles.

Holding Lotus Wand by White band, circumambulate Temple three times.

Standing West of Altar, face East for Adoration:

Holy art Thou Lord of the Universe.
Holy art Thou Whom Nature hath not formed.
Holy art Thou the Vast and the Mighty One.
Lord of the Light and of the Darkness.

Still facing East, perform the Qabalistic Cross, formulating Kether very strongly above one's head, equilibriating it in the form of a cross. Then, aspiring to the higher Genius, say:

Thee I invoke the Bornless One.
Thee that didst create the Earth and the Heavens.
Thee that didst create the Night and the Day.
Thee that didst create the Darkness and the Light.
Thou art Osorronophris, whom no man hath seen at any time.
Thou art Iabas. Thou art Iapos.
Thou hast distinguished between the Just and the Unjust.
<260> Thou didst make the female and the male.
Thou didst produce the Seed and the fruit.
Thou didst form men to love one another and to hate one another.

I am *(here insert sacramental name and Grade)* of the Order of the R.R. et A.C., thy Prophet unto whom Thou didst commit Thy Mysteries, the ceremonies of the Magic of Light. Thou didst produce the moist and the dry and that which nourisheth all created things. Hear me Thou. For I am the Angel of Paphro Osorronophris. This is Thy true Name, handed down to the Prophets of the Sun.

Pause a while to formulate about you the Banner of the East. Then make Rose Cross over Altar, vibrating Yhshvh by the Formula of the Middle Pillar.

Still facing East, but expanding the astral form to the limit of one's power, say:

The Voice of my Higher Self said unto me, "Let me enter the Path of Dark ness, and peradventure there shall I find the Light. I am the only being in an Abyss of Darkness; from an Abyss of Darkness came I forth ere my birth, from the silence of a Primal Sleep. And the Voice of Ages answered unto my Soul: "I am He who formulates in Darkness, the Light that shineth in Darkness, yet the Darkness comprehendeth it not."

Pass by North to the East of Temple. Face quarter, and trace the Spirit Pentagram of Actives and Invoking Pentagram of Air using names as in the Supreme Ritual of Pentagram. At the same time, imagine yourself clothed with the colossal form of the God Aroueris, and that the words of the Invocation travel out infinitely to the ends of the quarter. Also imagine that the elements evoked by the pentagrams surge through the God-form, eliminating all impurities.

Hear me: Ar; Thiao; Rheibet; Atheleberseth; A; Blatha; Abeu; Ebeu; Phi; Thitasoe; Ib; Thiao. Hear me, and make all Spirits subject unto me,
<261> so that every Spirit of the Firmament and of the Ether, upon the Earth
and under the Earth, on dry land and in the Water, of Whirling Air, and of Rushing Fire, and every Spell and Scourge of God the Vast One may be obedient unto me.

Make one complete circumambulation deosil, to formulate the Angle of Kether in the Supernal Triangle of the Genius. Pass to the South, assume the astral God-form of Horus, and that as the invocation proceeds the Fire purges you of all blemish. Use Spirit Pentagram of Actives and Invoking Pentagram of Fire.

I invoke Thee, the Terrible and Invisible God Who dwellest in the void place of the Spirit. Aragogorobrao. Sothou. Modorio. Phalarthao. Doo. Ape. The Bornless One. Hear me and make all Spirits subject unto me, so that every Spirit of the firmament and of the Ether, upon the Earth and under the Earth, on dry land and in the Water, of Whirling Air and of Rushing Fire, and every spell and scourge of God may be made obedient unto me.

Make one complete circumambulation to formulate the Angle of Chokmah. Pass to West, assume form of the Goddess Isis, and imagine after invocation that the element flows in waves through you. Make Passive Pentagram of Spirit and Invoking Pentagram of Water.

Hear me: Roubriao. Mariodam. Balbnabaoth. Assalonai. Aphnaio. I. Thoteth. Abrasar. Aeoou. Ischure, Mighty and Bornless One.

Hear me, and make all spirits subject unto me, so that every Spirit of the firmament and of the Ether, upon the Earth and under the Earth, on dry land and in the Water, of Whirling Air, and of Rushing Fire, and every spell and scourge of God may be made obedient unto me.

Circumambulate again, forming the Binah angle. Pass to North, assume
<262> *God-form of Nephthys, and after invocation imagine that the Earth cleanses*
you. Make passive Pentagram of Spirit, and Invoking Pentagram of Earth.

I invoke Thee. Ma. Barraio. Ioel. Kotha. Athorebalo. Abraoth. Hear me, and make all spirits subject unto me, so that every spirit of the firmament and of the Ether, upon the Earth and under the Earth, on dry land and in the Water, of Whirling Air, and of Rushing Fire, and every spell and scourge of God may be made obedient unto me.

Go direct to East without circumambulation. Perform Qabalistic Cross.

Atoh, Malkuth, ve Geburah, ve Gedulah, le Olam, Amen. Before me Raphael, Behind me Gabriel, on my Right Hand Michael, on my left hand Auriel. Before me flames the Pentagram, and behind me shines the six rayed Star. Atoh, Malkuth, ve Geburah, ve Gedulah, le Olahm, Amen.

Pass to the West of Altar, and face East. Imagine yourself as clothed in the God-form of Thoth. Make the Sign of the Rending of the Veil, and use the Exhortation of the Portal:

Ol Sonuf Vaorsagi Goho Iad Balata. Elexarpeh. Comananu. Tabitom. Zodacara Eka Zodacare Od Zodameranu. Odo Kikale Qaa, Piape Piamoel Od Vaoanu.

Make the Invoking Pentagram of Spirit Active over the Altar, vibrating: Exarp, Bitom, and Eheieh, and say:

Hear me: Aoth. Abaoth. Basum. Isak. Sabaoth. Isa! This is the Lord of the Gods. This is the Lord of the Universe. This is He whom the Winds Fear. This is He, who having made voice by his commandment is Lord of all things, King, Ruler and Helper.

Hear me, and make all spirits subject unto me, so that every spirit of the Firmament and of the Ether, upon the Earth and under the Earth, on dry land, and in the Water, of Whirling Air, and of Rushing Fire, and every
<263> spell and scourge of God may be made obedient unto me.

Pass to the East. Pause, then make the Passive Spirit Pentagram, with Hcoma, Nanta, and Agla. While vibrating the following words, let the Z.A.M. imagine that, standing between the Pillars, he is formulated as a black Egg of Akasa, and that from the dark centre of that Egg, its Tiphareth, extends upwards into the heights an astral semblance of his Wand. As each word is vibrated let this Sceptre shoot higher and higher towards the Kether of the Universe. The conception should be of the formation of an astral Middle Pillar, down the centre of which the Divine White Brilliance may descend.

Hear me, Ieou. Pur. Iou. Pur. Iaeo. Ioou. Abrasar. Sabriam. Do. Uu. Adonai. Ede. Edu. Angelos Ton Theon. Anlala Lai. Gaia. Ape. Diathana Thorun.

Above the Lotus of the Sceptre, the Z.A.M. should now see the Divine White Brilliance clearly, formulated as a flashing angelic figure descending upon the black egg. Say:

He comes in the Power of the Light.
He comes in the Light of Wisdom.
He comes in the Mercy of the Light.
The Light hath healing in its wings.

Aspring, and imagining the while that the Flower at the top of the Wand grows and opens wider that the Genius may enter, make LVX Signs in Silence, and say very slowly:

I am the Resurrection and the Life. He that believeth in me, though he were dead, yet shall he live. And whosoever liveth and believeth in Me, shall never die. I am the First and I am the Last. I am He that liveth and was dead, and behold, I am alive for evermore, and hold the Keys of Hell and of Death. For I know that my Redeemer liveth and that he shall stand at the latter day

upon the Earth. I am the Way, the Truth, and the Life. No man com-
<264> eth unto the Father but by Me. I am the Purified. I have passed
through the Gates of Darkness unto Light. I have fought upon Earth
for good, and have now finished my work. I have entered into the invisible.

I am the Sun in his rising, passed through the hour of cloud and of night. I am Amoun, the concealed one, the Opener of the Day. I am Osiris Onnophris, the Justified One, Lord of Life triumphant over death. There is no part of me that is not of the gods. I am the preparer of the Pathway, the Rescuer unto the Light

Now let the Z.A.M. formulate the descent of the Light into the Flower. Then pause, and say this prayer:

Unto Thee, Sole Wise, Sole Mighty, and Sole Eternal One, be praise and glory forever, who hath permitted me, who now kneeleth humbly before Thee, to penetrate thus far into the Sanctuary of Thy Mysteries. Not unto me, but unto Thy Name be the Glory. Let the influence of Thy Divine Ones descend upon my head, and teach me the value of self-sacrifice, so that I shrink not in the hour of trial, but that my name may be written on high, and that my Genius may stand in the presence of the Holy Ones, in that hour when the Son of man is invoked before the Lord of Spirits and his Name in the presence of the Ancient of Days.

After this prayer, circumambulate three times, and then formulate the flashing descent of the Supernal Light down the Astral shaft into the Tiphareth centre, and that the Black Egg surrounding the Z.A.M. gradually becomes illumined, until it changes into white.

Out of the Darkness, let that Light arise. Before I was blind, but now I see. I am the Dweller in the Invisible, the Reconciler with the Ineffable.

Let the Z.A.M. make the L.V.X. Signs as described in the Rose Cross Ritual, so that as he makes, finally, the X Sign, he calls down the Light.

<265> Let the White Brilliance of the Divine Spirit Descend.

When the Z.A.M. has felt the Brilliance, and perceived the radiance of the Egg, let him withdraw the Shaft into his heart, and say:

I am He, the Bornless Spirit, having Sight in the Feet, Strong, and the Immortal Fire. I am He, the Truth.

I am He who Hate that Evil should be wrought in the world.

I am He that Lighteneth and thundereth.

I am He from whom is the shower of the Life of Earth.

I am He, whose mouth ever flameth.

I am he, the Begetter and Manifester unto the Light.

I am He, the Grace of the World.

The Heart Girt with a Serpent is my Name.

Come Thou forth and follow me and make all spirits subject unto me so that every spirit of the firmament and of the Ether, upon the Earth and under the Earth, on dry land, and in the Water of whirling Air, and of rushing Fire, and every spell and scourge of God the Vast One may be made obedient unto me. Iao. Sabao. Such are the Words.

After contemplating that glory for some while go to West of Altar and face East.

Be my mind open to the Higher.
Be my heart a centre of the Light.
Be my body a Temple of the Rose Cross.

Then banish by Pentagram Ritual or:

"In the name of Yhshvh, I now set free any spirits that may have been imprisoned by this ceremony."

<266>

REQUIEM

Arrangement of the Temple as in Neophyte Grade. Opening by Watchtower Ceremony. Circumambulation thrice, and then the Adoration.

Go to the East. Lotus Wand, held by white band, and perform the Invoking Ritual of the Supernals by the Hexagram. Trace Sigils in the air as they are vibrated.

Supernal Splendour which dwellest in the Light to which no man can approach, wherein is Mystery and depth Unthinkable, and awful Silence. I beseech Thee who art Shekinah and Aimah Elohim, to look down upon me in this Ceremony which I perform to thine honour, and for the assistance of those who have passed through the veil. Grant thine aid unto the highest aspirations of my Soul, in thy Divine Name Yhvh Elohim by which thou dost reveal thyself as the perfection of Creation and the Light of the World to Come.

I implore thee to grant unto me the presence of thine Archangel Tzaphqiel. O Tzaphqiel, thou prince of spiritual initiation through suffering and of strife against evil, aid me I beseech thee to transcend the evil that is in me, so that I may be enabled to perform a higher and diviner work.

O ye strong and mighty ones of the sphere of Shabbathai, O ye Aralim, Aralim, I conjure ye by the mighty name of Yhvh Elohim, the divine ruler of your realm, and by the name of Tzaphqiel, your Archangel. Aid me with your power, in your office to place a veil between me and all things belonging to the outer and lower world. Let it be a veil woven from that silent darkness which surrounds your abode of eternal rest, that in this chamber of the divine mystery, I may hear nothing that comes not from on high, and see naught that may distract my vision from the ineffable glory of the Supernals. Grant unto me, I beseech thee, the power of the spirit to bring the brilliance of the eternal splendour to one who has now entered the invisible. Lift me, I
<267> beseech thee, lift me up so that I may be made a divine messenger
bearing the peace and harmony of higher spheres to . . . . . . whose death to this earthly plane we do now commemorate. Wherever he may now be, and on whatever plane he may now pursue his ideal, let him be blessed with a diviner rest and an utter cessation from strife.

Trace Saturn Hexagram with Sigil in centre.

Term of all that liveth, whose name is Death and inscrutable, be thou favourable unto us in thine hour. And unto him, from whose mortal eyes the veil of physical life hath fallen, grant that there may be the accomplishment of his True Will. Should he will absorption in the Infinite, or to be united with his chosen and preferred, or to be in contemplation, or to be at peace, or to achieve the labour and heroism of incarnation on this planet or another, or in any star, or aught else, unto him may there be granted the accomplishment of his true will.

Go to Altar, visualise deceased at the East facing West, and invoke:

I invoke thee by the divine name IAO, thou great Angel Hru, who art set over the operations of this Secret Wisdom. Strengthen and establish . . . . . . in his search for the divine Light. Increase his spiritual perception so that he may accomplish his True Will, and that thus he may be enabled to rise beyond that lower self-hood which became as nothing unto that highest self-hood which is the Clear Light of the Spirit.

Go to East of Altar. Make Rose Cross over the Elements vibrating the Enochian Spirit invokation. Make Qabalistic Cross.

For Osiris Onnophris who is found perfect before the Gods hath said: These are the elements of my Body perfected through suffering, glorified through trial. The scent of the dying Rose is as the repressed sigh of my Suffering. And the flame-red Fire as the energy of mine undaunted Will. And the Cup of Wine is the pouring out of the blood of my heart, sacrificed unto
<268> Regeneration, unto the newer life. And the bread and salt are as the foundations of my body, which I destroy in order that they may be renewed.

For I am Osiris Triumphant. Even Osiris Onnophris the Justified One. I am He who is clothed with the body of flesh yet in whom flames the spirit of the eternal Gods. I am the Lord of Life. I am triumphant over Death, and whosoever partaketh with me shall with me arise. I am the manifester in Matter of Those whose abode is the Invisible. I am the purified. I stand upon the Universe. I am its Reconciler with the eternal Gods. I am the Perfector of Matter, and without me the universe is not.

Pause for a moment or two, visualising Kether as a brilliance above the head.

Buried with that Light in a mystical death, rising again in a mystical resurrection, cleansed and purified through him our Master, O thou dweller of the invisible. Like him, thou pilgrim of the ages, hast thou toiled. Like him hast thou suffered tribulation. Poverty, torture, and death hast thou passed through. They have been but the purification of the gold. In the alembic of thine heart, through the Athanor of Affliction, seek thou the true Stone of the Wise.

Pass from the Altar to the East.

Come in peace, O beautiful and divine one, to a body glorified and perfected. Herald of the Gods, knowing his speech among the living! Pass thou through every region of the invisible unto the place wherein thy Genius dwelleth, because thou comest in peace, provided with thy wealth. Dwell thou in that sacred land that far-off travellers call naught. O land beyond honey and spice and all perfection! Dwell therein with thy Lord Adonai for ever.

Turn and look westwards, raising eyes.

O Lord of the Universe, the vast and the mighty one, ruler of the light and the darkness, we adore thee and we invoke thee, Look thou with favour
<269> upon this pilgrim who is now before thee, and grant thine aid unto the highest aspirations of his soul, to the glory of the ineffable

Name.

Slowly walk to the altar, visualising the brilliance descend upon the image of the deceased in the place of the Neophyte.

I come in the power of the Light. I come in the light of Wisdom. I come in the mercy of the Light, the Light hath healing in its wings. *(name deceased)* I tell thee that as the light can manifest from the darkness so by these rites shall the Light descend unto thee. Long hast thou dwelt in darkness. Quit the darkness and seek the Light.

Return to between the Pillars, and visualise the descent of the brilliance above.

I am the resurrection and the life. Whosoever believeth on me though he were dead, yet shall he live, and whosoever liveth and believeth on me shall never die. I am the First, and the Last. I am he that liveth and was dead, and behold I am alive for evermore, and hold the keys of hell and of death. For I know that my Redeemer liveth, and that he shall stand at the latter day upon the Earth. I am the Way, the Truth and the Life. No man cometh unto the Father but by me. I am the Purified. I have passed through the Gates of Darkness unto Light. I have fought upon Earth for good, and have finished my work. I have entered into the invisible.

Vibrate Yeheshuah by the vibratory formula of the Middle Pillar. Also the mystical circumambulation. Then, walk round slowly whilst saying:

I am the Sun in his rising, passed through the hour of cloud and of night. I am Amoun the concealed one, the Opener of the day. I am Osiris Onnophris the Justified One, Lord of Life triumphant over death. There is no part of me which is not of the Gods. I am the preparer of the pathway, the rescuer unto the Light. Out of the darkness, let the Light arise.

Pass between the Pillars, face East.

I am the reconciler with the Ineffable, the dweller of the invisible.
<270> Let the white brilliance of the divine spirit descend.

Visualise the deceased now standing well in front in the East, and address him thus:

...... whoever thou art in reality, and wheresoever thou now mayest be, by the power of the Spirit devolving upon me by this ceremony, I do project unto thee this ray of the divine white Brilliance that it may bring thee peace and happiness and rest.

Make the Sign of the Enterer three times to project the Light.

Be thy mind open unto the higher. Be thy heart a centre of the Light. Be thy body, whatsoever its nature, a Temple of the holy Spirit.

Pause. Make Qabalistic Cross.

Unto thee, sole Wise, sole Eternal and Sole Merciful One be the praise and the glory forever, who has permitted ......, who now standeth invisibly and humbly before thee to enter thus far into the sanctuary of thy mystery. Not unto us but unto thy name be the glory. Let the influence of thy divine ones descend upon his head, and teach him the value of self-sacrifice so that he shrink not in the hour of trial. But that thus his name may be written upon high and his Genius stand in the presence of the holy Ones in that hour when the Son of Man is invoked before the Lord of Spirits and his name in the presence of the Ancient of Days.

Go to Altar.

And now in the name and power of the Divine Spirit, I invoke ye, ye Angels of the Watchtowers of the Universe, and charge ye by the divine names Yeheshuah Yehovashah to guard this sphere of . . . . . . Keep far from him all evil and the unbalanced that they penetrate not into his spiritual abode. Inspire and sanctify him so that he may enter in to the centre of his being and there receive the vision of the Clear Light, and thus accomplish his True Will.

Pause for some while for meditation. Then close by usual formulae.

<271> PRACTICAL Z. PREPARATION FOR DIVINATION

By G. H. FRATER *Sub Spe*

The Preparation for Divination — Opening Ceremony of ⓪ = [0] *The Temple is the Aura or Sphere of Sensation. The Hierophant is the Diviner, the positive active will which manipulates and controls all the other bodily functions, and all the forces operating in the Aura.*

Sitting in as comfortable position as possible, close the eyes, and begin to fix attention on the Pole Star and circumpolar constellations, endeavouring to visit each prominent star and then to pass from one to another. Then, in the same way to visit the South Polar constellations. Then to be conscious of both simultaneously as one might be of head and feet. In this way the astral grew gradually colossal, and the sensation arose of being outside of, and in fact *containing* the whole starry universe. The earth had become a mere insignificant speck. The sense of human form was wholly lost, but there was a sense of up and down, and of the pole of a spherical aura. Endeavoured to place this so as to correspond with the centre of Draco, the Kether of the Starry Sphere. This caused a more definite idea of the sphere and of the Sephiroth and Paths therein, and the belt of the Zodiac coloured of a hollow sphere or magic circle, wherein a blinding white light was in the place of Kether, and thick darkness on Malkuth. Stood immediately in front of Kether and realised that the blackness of Malkuth guarded the sphere from evil and sub-human forces, the Qlippoth, or on this spiritual plane, the bondage to the material. Endeavoured to formulate this Black Darkness into a giant Guardian, realising also that it was my own negative will saying "Thus far, and no further."

<272> In front of this Guardian which I perceived, was the reflection of my own material universe, *i.e.*, everything I was or could possibly be conscious of in the body, "All thoughts, all passions, all delights — whatsoever stirs this mortal frame," but only the reflection thereof as in a mirror, and having therefore no power to move the spiritual consciousness. The form was a square of earth cast in the form of a double cube answering to the Tenth Sephirah, for every possible thought or emotion of the body, however lofty, was represented there, even to the highest spiritual aspirations, all dominated by the white triangle of the Triune God and the Red Cross of self-sacrifice.

I then realised that even the reflection of my own universe, including my very thoughts and aspirations in the body, stood without a colossal portal of a Temple, my Spiritual Will being within, and the shadowy Portal grew up between the perceiving consciousness and the perceived Universe. Two vast pillars of positive and negative, the eternal contraries, were the Gateway; and the pure white of equilibrium and eternal silence was between them. My spiritual conscious Will now advanced as it were below the centre of its sphere, near to that point of equilibrium so as to survey through the portal of the Pillars the reflection of my own universe.

Fixing myself there as immovable — because eternally right, being dominated only by the forces of the Eternal God, my lower nature lay before me as it were, mapped out. In front the Great Portal shutting out all that had not attained to, and retained, perfect equilibrium, beyond and as far distant from the point of equilibrium as my own consciousness, was my evil self, the root of all evil. And I was now conscious in that past which was the root of all good. And thus again an equilibrium was preserved between the Pillars. At
an equal distance again beyond this evil self, were the reflection of
<273> the perceived universe, formulated as the cubical altar whereon
were the symbols of the elements and the triangle and cross, and beyond this the dark and threatening black figure of the Great Guardian of the West. Furthermore, from my right hand came the cool influence of moisture, from my left the warmth of fire, and from the moist warmth at the point of equilibrium sprang the idea of generation, birth, growth and development which forces were directed upon the Cubical Altar, bringing the forces of Life into my universe.

Yet — all this was *myself.* I realised that far beyond the possibilities of bodily thought there were in myself forces, powers and knowledge far transcending all that the body can ever perceive or imagine in its loftiest flights. In this manner I was able to order and direct the forces of the intellectual brain — the Kerux, Anubis, the "Watcher without" being the conscious intellectual brain which thinks and acts in the material body.

The Watcher within, the higher intuitive intellect whose workings are mostly unconscious to the material man. Recognising now the importance of maintaining this exalted attitude and preventing the entrance of any material and mundane thoughts, my spiritual will ordered the logical intellect, by will-force rather than definite thought, to clear the Temple, and the intellect bearing a ray of white light from the supreme and lighted by the lamp of wisdom commanded all material things to stand aloof. Then and not till then the Spiritual Will which now seemed to be *myself,* began to function. It initiated a current of force and commanded the higher intuitional intellect to see that the sphere was properly closed against material thoughts. This was accomplished by a communication between the intuitional intelligence and the physical logical brain, the latter keeping guard over the material body (by this time almost forgotten, its cerebrations having become unconscious).

<274> The Spiritual Will now directs the Guardian of the West to make
sure that all forces operating are forces of good, and in obedience to the Spiritual Will, whose controlling force is the ineffable Power of God Himself. This is done by every force treading down the evil, and invoking and bringing forward the light into the material. The sensation here should be that every force in the sphere of sensation is in unity and affirming the Will of God.

A certain equilibrium having thus been established the whole sphere of Sensation should be vitalised by the vibratory formula of the Middle Pillar.

The sensation is that the consciousness which is in the spiritual will draws in a deep inspiration of divine power from the supreme hierarchy, and by an effort of Will sends it down to the Guardian of the west, whence it rushes forth in strength and power, vitalising the Genius of equilibrium between the Pillars, and thence the whole sphere. The attention is then fixed on each force in turn, now alive and clothed with a definite symbolic form. In this it is desirable to use the forms of the Gods of Egypt, so as to avoid the chance of illusion through memory creeping in by the appearance of the human officers one is accustomed to see. Each of this considered in detail assumes a symbolic form. Note, that as the present purpose is to examine the reflection of some earthly event or force, the symbology is particularly regarded with reference thereto. Thus the Hiereus specially guards against the intrusion of any material wish or thought or emotion which might disturb the perfect calm of the divining mind. The Dadouchos is not alone the power of heat and dryness but of energy, fire, passion, impetuous zeal; and Stolistes is not alone cold or moisture, but pleasure, love, luxury, etc. In fact the forces of Wands and Cups. The fiery zeal prepares the way for the prayer which rises from the soul like incense, this prayer being related also to the suffering which is the purification by Fire.
<275> The receptive and negative forces of the Cup are those which
develop the perception of the symbology of the various forces. The intuitive intellect (Anubis, the Watcher within) regulates the imaginative forming of the sphere of sensation itself — guides the formulated movements thereof — keeps alive the light of occult science and grasps the ray of Divine Wisdom. So the genius of equilibrium, Thmaah, must introduce the question to be investigated, for unless this be done by perfect equilibrium no good result can be attained.

I now felt every force moved by my own higher intuition, directed by the Spiritual Will. All thoughts of earth were lost altogether, and only the great forces were perceived, which *might* produce a material result, but that result was not perceptible. Unless this result is attained at this stage, I have found it useless to go further. I next endeavoured to mark the limits of the sphere of sensation by the consecrations of fire and water. Now a complete establishment of calm and passive equilibrium in the Sphere was required, and the formulation of a vortex, to draw in the highest spiritual influences. I therefore, directed as in the ⓪ = 0, the circumambulation of these mighty forces, as it were, a great wheel which set revolving, whose centre was the point of silence, the Throne of Harpacrat. The whole sphere then adored the Lord of the Universe.

At this stage I found that I could formulate the figure of a terrestrial globe in the place of the Altar, and fixing the attention on any point of the surface, get a mental picture of what was transpiring there, recognising at the same time that it took place by the action and reaction of the great forces which moved by the Will of God and were therefore in all things perfectly good. This rendered impossible any feeling of joy or sorrow at any event, any hope or any fear, any affection for any individual, or any antipathy. The
<276> desire to know became simply a desire to be associated in the
knowledge of God and therefore so far united to Him.

Unless this stage is reached at this point, earthly thoughts have intruded, the Temple has not been properly cleansed and guarded, and according to my experience no true results can be expected. If this result is attained the process may then be sealed, and the divination may proceed.

End of Volume Three

VOLUME FOUR

BOOK SEVEN
CLAIRVOYANCE, TALISMANS, SIGILS

<11> CLAIRVOYANCE

(Note: this paper is compiled from several unofficial documents which were not sufficiently interesting to publish in unabridged form by themselves. Also several pieces of oral instruction are here included. I have kept rigidly to the technique as taught and practised in the Order—I.R.)

"The subject of clairvoyance must always be in the highest degree interesting to all who are aspiring after Adeptship even in its lowest grades... We frequently meet with two opposite attitudes towards the subject, both in the outer world and amongst our junior members. Both these attitudes are hindrances to its proper study, and therefore I shall preface my remarks by a few words concerning each of them.

"The first is fear of clairvoyance. And the second is a disproportionate estimate of its value.

"Both of these attitudes arise from a misunderstanding of its true character. People imagine that somehow the power of clairvoyance is obtained secondhand from the powers of evil; or that its exercise will bring those who practice it under their influence. Or, on the other hand, they imagine that the power of clairvoyance will save them a great deal of trouble, and give them a short and easy path to the information and guidance they desire. In fact, that these may almost be attained at will. Nay more, would such a power not fully satisfy that curiosity which is one of the pitfalls of the superficial student?

"The properly trained clairvoyant need have no fear that he will thereby expose himself to the powers of evil. It is the *untrained natural* clair-
<12> voyant who is in danger. Training will give him knowledge, discipline and protection, such as will protect him from the onslaught of the averse powers.

"On the other hand, let him who desires to save himself trouble and to gain knowledge to which he has no claim, be very well assured that only 'in the sweat of his brow' can he obtain this power and exercise it in security. And that he who seeks to gratify his curiosity will either be mortified by disappointment or distressed by discoveries he would much prefer not to have made. Trained, humble, and reverent clairvoyance is a great gift, opening up new worlds and deeper truths, lifting us out of ourselves into the great inpouring and outpouring of the heart of God." (G. H. Fratre F.R.'s notes.)

The earliest experiments in clairvoyance as taught by the Order are with the Tattwa symbols. These, with their traditional names, significances, symbols and colours are:

Akasa—Ether or Spirit.	Symbol: black or indigo egg.
Vayu—Air.	Symbol: a sky-blue disc or circle.
Tejas—Fire.	Symbol: Red equilateral triangle.
Apas—Water.	Symbol: a silver crescent.
Prithivi—Earth.	Symbol: a yellow square or cube.

In brief, the traditional occult concept of the Tattwa is that of a vital current of ether or force—the Hindu Pranas—which issues in a steady stream from the Sun. That stream is five-fold, and flows around our earth, vitalising its astral substance or its sphere of Sensation. In short, they are the currents of sub-planes of the Astral Light. The theory has it that the Element of Akasa is strongest at dawn, when the Sun rises, and its power continues for the space of two hours, when its force subsides and glides into Vayu, Air.

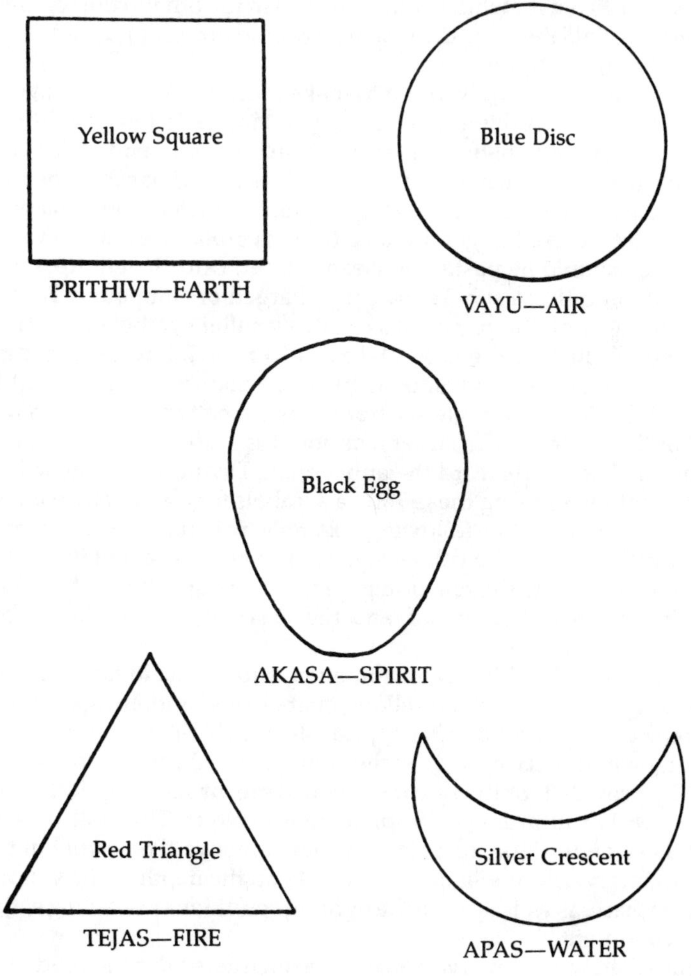

TATTWA SYMBOLS

This also persists or is in course for the same period. Each Tattwa or
<13> current of force is believed to exist strongly for this length of time,
each merging at the end into the succeeding Tattwa in the order given above. After the current of Prithivi is exhausted, the cycle recommences with Akasa, and continues in the same order again and for the same periods.

As no element on our plane can exist in an unmixed form, but
<14> contains within itself the constituents of all the others, or possesses
several grades or planes of its own substance, so each Tattwa is subdivided into five divisions, currents or planes. Akasa of Akasa, Spirit of Spirit, would be the most Tenuous and purest form of that element, the integral nature of Spirit—its highest essence. Vayu of Akasa would refer to its airy quality; Tejas of Akasa to its fiery and dynamic aspect; Apas of Akasa, its fluidic and watery phase, while Prithivi of Akasa, its most terrestrial phase, or that aspect of its power which more nearly than the others contacts the earth. The same five-fold division, in the same five-fold order, applies equally to the other elements.

The student is strongly urged to make these symbols, and have a set of them with him for working. The primary or simple Tattwa should be made about two or two and a half inches in height. It is recommended that coloured papers be used rather than water colours, since the brilliance of the former is much greater than the latter. The lacquer paints which are now easily obtainable may also be used to good effect. If the symbols are cut from coloured papers, they should be pasted on clean unused cards length upwards. The method of indicating a sub-Tattwa, or a charged or compound Tattwa, is to paint or paste upon the principal symbol a smaller symbol of the charge or sub-element. Thus, in the case of Tejas of Prithivi, Fire of Earth, Prithivi which is the major symbol should be made about two and a half inches square, whilst the red triangle, each angle about half an inch long, should be pasted in the centre of the larger symbol. It is a useful preliminary also to write on the back of the card the appropriate Divine and Angelic Names.

The method of using these Tattwa symbols for clairvoyance is a simple one. My remarks in the following example will refer to the element of Prithivi, Earth, the yellow square, and what is said of this will apply
<15> equally well to the remaining symbols. Though the method is simple,
it is far from fool-proof, and the description of it should be read several times.

The student should be calm and quiet, and, sitting in his chair, take the card bearing the symbol of the yellow square in his hand, and gaze intently at it for about twenty seconds. Quickly transferring his attention from the symbol to any white surface, such as the ceiling, or a sheet of paper at his side especially provided for the purpose, he will see, by reflex optical action, the same shape but in a direct complementary colour. This will be a sort of luminous lavender-blue, or pale translucent mauve. The actual tint of this complementary colour will depend wholly on the depth of the yellow used in the first place, as well as upon the lighting conditions prevailing at the time of the experiment.

Immediately this mauve square is seen, the student should close his eyes, and endeavour to visualize in imagination this mauve square as standing before him. This clearly perceived by the mind's eye, let the student at once imagine that it enlarges itself, becoming an object large enough for him to pass through. The next step is to imagine that he is actually passing through this square, as though it were a door. The best method of doing this is to employ the Neophyte sign, the Sign of the Enterer, which is that of "groping for light." It is essentially a projecting sign, and the effect should be of having projected himself through this door or gateway. It is recommended that the student rise to his feet at this juncture and, still visualizing the enlarged square with closed eyes of course, perform this Sign of Horus physically, and believing himself through it, sit down ready to commence the vision.

One of the other instructions puts it thus: "First meditate on the element selected, soak yourself in it till, if it be Fire, you feel hot; if Water, wet, and so on, all the time co-ordinating the symbol with your sensations. Then, laying aside the symbol, and closing your eyes, endeavour to project and
<16> enlarge that symbol before you, regarding it as a gateway through
which you are to pass . . . Deliberately will to pass through the gateway. Let him imagine that he can hear it close behind him."

Yet another version, this time written by D.D.C.F. says: "Keep up the design, form and colour in the Akasic Aura, as clearly as they appeared in material form to the outward seeing. Transfer the vital effort from the optic nerve to the mental perception, or thought-seeing as distinct from the seeing with the eye. Let one form of apprehension glide on into the other. Produce the reality of the dream vision by positive will in the waking state . . . Then maintaining your abstraction from your surroundings, still concentrated upon the symbol and its correlated ideas, you are to seek a perception of a scene or panorama or view of the plane. This may also be brought on by a sense of tearing open, as a curtain is drawn aside, and seeing the 'within' of the symbol before you."

The principal idea is to imagine the symbol, in its complementary colour, as a door and to pass through it. Having imagined that there has been a passing through the door, and clearly realising, in this instance, the mauve Square *behind* him, the seer should make an effort to look about him. Let him endeavour to see objects, entities, or some sort of landscape. Most always these take the form of pale stilled pictures, seen as it were with the mind, or the eye of imagination. Hillocks, meadows, rocks, vast brown boulders may be seen, and what is most important, there should be a strong sense of being *within* the element; the seer should understand, as he has never quite realised before, the true nature, the 'feel' of Earth.

Before aught else occurs, the Divine Names appropriate to that element should now be vibrated, beginning with the Deity Name. The student should vibrate each slowly and audibly several times. Thus, he would vibrate *Adonai Ha-Aretz,* three or four times, then the name of *Auriel* the Archangel of
<17> Earth, followed by the name of *Phorlakh* the Angel of Earth. These will
usually suffice though the Hebrew name of the element and cardinal quarter may also be employed. Various changes may now be perceived to occur to the landscape; it will become alive, vivified and dynamic, and the sense of the element should become even more clearly and vividly defined.

Also a being may appear, one whose characteristics pertain to the element of Earth, and his garments, their colours, and his other ornaments should be in the appropriate colours. Under *no* circumstances should the Seer wander from his doorway *alone;* he should always wait until one of these elemental beings or "guides" appears, and he should continue vibrating the names until one does appear, or until he obtains the sense that one is present. Sometimes, and with some students, there is no clear vision of these occurrences or beings, but only a sense or intuition or powerful instinct that such and such a thing is happening, and that such a type of being has appeared. This often is more trustworthy than the use of sight or other sense.

The guide having made his appearance, he is to be tested by every means at the Seer's disposal. First of all, it is well to assume the Sign of the Grade to which that element is referred. In this instance, the Sign of the Zelator should be made, by *physically* as well as astrally raising the right arm to an angle of forty-five degrees. The guide should answer this with the same Sign or another which is unmistakeable proof that he belongs to the element and has been *sent* to act as guide. If there is deception, these signs will cause him distress, or at once the vision will break up, or the false guide will disappear. He should also be asked clearly and deliberately whether he comes to act as guide in the name of the appropriate Deity Name. If all this strikes the Seer as satisfactory, and his doubts settled, let him follow the guide to wherever he is being led, carefully noting whither he goes, and asking questions about the element or whatever he sees.

<18> A very important thing is here to be noted. On these subtler planes, or within the realms of these symbols, form takes on symbolic implication which we, on earth, have obscured if not lost. It is only human beings who swathe themselves in garments whose shape and colour bear no relation to their true character. "Even on our own plane, the clothing of animals is pregnant with meaning, and on the astral plane this is far more emphatically the case. An elemental may, for some purpose of its own, masquerade for a time in alien garb, but we are given a certain definite procedure to follow in dealing with them."

The Signs of the elemental Grades, the vibration of divine and angelic names, and the tracing of appropriate pentagrams are symbols which powerfully affect these elemental inhabitants of the astral, and prevent or disclose deception. It is but rarely that there will be necessity to resort to anything so drastic as the Pentagrams in these tattwa visions, for the vibration of the Hebrew name either of the element, or of the Archangel will restore order and harmony. The true form, colour, clothing, even adornments such as jewels and embroideries are consonant to the element and character of the beings under discussion. And unless they are, the Seer may be sure he is being imposed on, and should act accordingly — at once. In a short while, after only a few astral experiences, these symbolic ideas will have been sufficiently familiar to the student to enable him at once to detect error or imposition.

In the event of employing a charged or compound Tattwa such as let us assume, Fire of Earth, indicated by a Red Triangle within a larger Yellow square, it may happen that the seer may find himself being escorted from one guide to another, and passed from one plane to another. The same test

should be applied, and not the slightest loophole should be left for the entry of even the smallest incongruous item. The divine names of the secondary
Tattwa should be vibrated, and the grade Sign attributed to it should
<19> be assumed. Only when fully satisfied, and he must never permit
himself to be easily satisfied, should the Seer proceed. If the first guide be left behind, he must be accorded courtesy of farewell. "*Always* treat these beings with courtesy and in accord with their rank. Pay deference to the superior orders, the Archangels, Angels and Rulers. To those of lower rank, bear yourself as an equal; and to those lower still, as to servants whom you treat politely, but do not allow familiarity. Elementals pure and simple, such as fairies, gnomes and so on, must be treated with firmness and decision, as they are often mischievous and irresponsible, even though free from malice." It is also said to be a good practice, since form is symbolic in these regions, to imagine yourself as large as possible, always taller than the being confronting you; and under every circumstance maintain self-control and fearless demeanour.

At first, and for the first half-a-dozen experiments, the student should be content with the simple observation of the landscape and, if possible, the type of guide who appears in answer to the Names. At the beginning it is more important to acquire facility in passing through these symbolic doors than in acquiring impressive visions. The Seer will find himself on the right track if he is content, for quite some little time, with a glimpse of a hill, a cave, an underground hall, or an Angel of the Element, and so on, returning after the brief visit. With facility acquired, he may stay in the vision for a longer period, which should be relatively full of incident and action, and should impart no little knowledge.

The method of leaving the Tattwa and returning to Earth is the precise reversal of the initial process. After thanking the guide and bidding him farewell, the Seer should retrace his footsteps to the symbolic Door — the purple or lavender-blue square. It is insisted that this return should be made as definite as possible. That is, there should be no sudden departure
from the place and finding oneself back in one's normal state of mind.
<20> The Seer will be wise if he carefully follows the passage he has
walked through, even if it has been a very long way, the reason being that it is well to keep the two states of consciousness, the two planes, quite distinct from one another. There should be no merging of the elemental plane into the plane of everyday consciousness, and the best way of ensuring this is to make both coming and going follow a definite and distinct technique. After having found your way back to the door, you pass through it, again with the Sign of the Enterer, and return to your body. At once stand up, and make physically and firmly the Sign of Silence, raising the left forefinger to the lips, and stamping with the right foot. Always note that the first Sign of the Enterer is answered and followed by the Sign of Silence.

It is not well to repeat these experiments too frequently at first; some advise an interval of several days between them, for the first few months of one's efforts in this direction. But when performed, the seer should make every effort to avoid self-delusion and deception. He should be alert the whole time, and never embark on these experiments when tired or not physically well. At the least threat of incoherence, or the entry of incongruous symbols or elements into the vision, the names, signs, and symbols should be repeated. Thus and thus alone may he hope to avoid delusion. These planes are a source of untold danger to whosoever is not able to take them with the proverbial grain of salt. Flattery, which is one of the most frequent types of delusion encountered, and the most common source of trouble, should be avoided like the plague. Madness lies that way and I cannot stress too strongly that vanity should be wholly discarded, and flattery eschewed.

During his adventures, the Seer should endeavour to describe carefully and in full detail the landscape of the vision. He should discover if possible the special attributes and nature of that plane, the type of its in-
<21> habitants —spiritual, elemental and so on; the plants, animals and minerals which would correspond to its nature; the operation of its influence upon Man, animals, plants and minerals here.

The process of working by placing the symbol upon the forehead, instead of imaginatively passing through it, is not a good practice. S.R.M.D. claims that it is liable to derange the brain-circulation and cause mental illusions and disturbance, headache and nervous exhaustion. It is also necessary to avoid self-hypnotism, for this would dispose towards mediumship and make the Seer the playground of forces. The Seer at all costs must control, and not permit himself to be controlled. If in danger at any time, or should he feel that he cannot accommodate the forces of the vision to his will, or that his self-control is breaking, he should resort to the vibration of the Names, and then retire from the vision.

By continuing these practices for a long period of time, the inner clairvoyance will develop, and with perseverance the visions will grow from vague indeterminate pictures, hardly distinguishable from imaginative concepts, to vivid powerful experiences. But even when these do occur he should under no circumstances accept them on their face value or neglect his tests, for the whole astral plane, apparently, seeks to delude the Seer and if he opens himself, by neglecting the tests, he is lost. With considerable practice, too, the symbols may be discarded for they will not be required to give entrance to the planes, though for the beginner *no* attempt should be made to work without the use of the actual material symbol. It will be found wisest to keep as much to the physical plane as possible, by employing the physical symbols, and by making the appropriate signs and steps with the physical body, as well as by speaking audibly and describing the vision as it proceeds.

When the student has become fairly proficient with the use of simple Tattwas, he should experiment with the compound Tattwas, and not
<22> be satisfied with his ability to skry until he is perfectly familiar with every part of the planes represented by those symbols. Then he can devise further experiments with other symbols. The use of the element Akasa, the indigo egg, was in the Order usually postponed until entry had been obtained into the Second Order. The reason for this was that no traditional Names are provided for use with this symbol as with the other four, and the student must discover or devise his own. As has already been

described at length the entrance into these subtle planes is obtained by means of the Divine Names; the rule being to invoke the highest Names known by the Seer. Any student who has studied the Adeptus Minor Ceremony, and the Ritual of the Pentagram will realise what Names are required for use with this symbol of Akasa. *Eheieh, Agla, Yeheshuah,* and *Eth* will be the general Names for the simple Tattwa, and the compound or charged Akasa cards will demand the use of the Names from the Enochian Tablet of Union.

It will be found a good plan to prepare cards of the Geomantic symbols painted in their appropriate colours, for these make perfect "doors" through which the Seer can pass. And while these symbols are also attributed to the elements, the vision acquired from the Geomantic symbols using the names of the appropriate Rulers and genii will be quite distinct in character from those of the Tattwa cards. The Hebrew letters, the Tarot cards and Sigils, the planetary and zodiacal Signs, and Sigils of every description may be used to yield the symbolic door to a subtle plane. A vast new field of knowledge is thus opened up. The names appropriate to each of these symbols are given in these papers, which should be carefully studied by the student. And he should remember that the formula of the employment of the divine Names and signs applies equally to these other symbols as they did to the Tattwa cards.

There was a good deal of glib parlance within the Order as to
<23> "astral vision" and "etheric vision." The former was described as the
ordinary Tattwa vision, in which objects and landscapes, though vivid and alive, are yet "flat" as though reflected on a mirror, rather like a cinematograph film. "In this form of descrying, note that you see objects reversed, as to right and left, for which suitable allowance must be made." The use of the phrase "mirror-like vision" is actually a very adequate description. Yet this is capable, as development proceeds, of merging into another type of vision — a full-blooded clairvoyance, in which things and people are seen in three dimensions, and as though the seer were not merely watching the scene, but were actually in it. Some explained that as "etheric vision" although the actual Order documents describe this as the clairvoyance ensuing from astral projection. Greatly Honoured Fratre D.D.C.F. states: "If instead of this simple vision a ray of yourself is sent out and actually goes to the place (astral projection) there is not necessarily the sense of reversal of objects... Scenes, things, instead of being like pictures, have the third dimension, solidity; they stand out like bas-relief, then haut-relief, then you see as from a balloon, as it is said, by a bird's-eye view. You feel to go to the place, to descend upon it, to step out upon the scene, and to be an actor there." The same rules laid down for the simpler method of skrying should be followed here, and always the highest divine names should be used, and constant tests applied. The paper which follows this, dealing with Skrying and Astral Projection by V.N.R. will explain the process a little more fully by means of setting forth an example of its working.

Another technique, making use of this faculty, was described in a paper recording a lecture by Fratre Sub Spe. The idea was to re-read the rituals, and then endeavour to re-tread the Paths astrally. One example given, was that

the Seer should formulate in imagination a vast pylon, and within its gates he should visualise the Hebrew Letter Tau, the 32nd Path. This should
<24> be preceded by a study of the Ritual of the Theoricus Grade, es-
pecially of the Rite of the Kerubic Stations. Then, imagining himself passing through this Letter Tau, and entering the Pylon, he should proceed to make the appropriate Pentagrams and Hexagrams, and vibrating the Divine Names appropriate to that plane. The resulting vision should be similar to the passage of the Path in the ceremony, but whereas this latter was purely symbolic, the former may be real and dynamic, and may develop into an initiation in the true sense of the word. The same technique may be applied to every Path and to every Sephirah.

Developing still further from this, there is another practice which passes beyond mere clairvoyance, though making use of it. This is called Rising on the Planes, and is a spiritual process after spiritual conceptions and higher aims. "By concentration and contemplation of the divine, you formulate a Tree of Life passing from you to the spiritual realms above and beyond yourself. Picture to yourself that you stand in Malkuth, then by the use of the Divine Names and aspiration, you strive upwards by the Path of Tau towards Yesod, neglecting the crossing rays which attract you as you pass up. Look upwards to the Divine Light shining downward from Kether upon you. From Yesod, leads upward the Path of Samekh, Temperance; the Arrow, cleaving upwards, leads the way to Tiphareth, the great central Sun." D.D.C.F. also suggests that, having risen to Tiphareth, the Adept skryer should formulate to himself that he is bound to a Cross, exactly as occurred in the Adeptus Minor Ceremony, and by invoking the Great Angel HUA beseech help and guidance in the pathway of Light. By this method, he may more easily ascend the planes which lead to the glory of the Crown. Thus formulating in the imagination the different parts of the Tree of Life, and vibrating the God-names appropriate to the Sephiroth or Paths, the Seer may find him-
<25> self, if his aspiration is sincere and keen, rising towards the Spiritual
Light, bathed in that golden glory of effulgence which is continuously shed from above.

Though it may seem rather out of place to quote Aleister Crowley here, yet he has written things in his *Magick* on this subject that are so very important that I am impelled to quote them here for the benefit of the student. The important drill practises, in his belief, are:

"1. The fortification of the Body of Light by the constant use of rituals, by the assumption of God-forms, and by the right use of the Eucharist.

"2. The purification and consecration and exaltation of that Body by the use of rituals of invocation.

"3. The education of that body by experience. It must learn to travel on every plane; to break down every obstacle which may confront it."

In a footnote to the above, he has appended a footnote which I reproduce herewith:

"The Aspirant should remember that he is a Microcosm. 'Universus sum et Nihil universi a me alienum puto' should be his motto. He should make it his daily practice to travel on the Astral Plane, taking in turn each of the most synthetic sections, the Sephiroth and the Paths. These being thoroughly understood, and an Angel in each pledged to guard or to guide him at need, he should start on a new series of expeditions to explore the subordinate sections of each. He may then practice Rising on the Planes from these spheres, one after the other in rotation. When he is *thoroughly* conversant with the various methods of meeting unexpected emergencies, he may proceed to investigate the regions of the Qlippoth and the Demonic Forces. It should be his aim to obtain a comprehensive knowledge of the entire Astral Plane, with impartial love of truth for its own sake; just as a child learns the geography of the whole planet though he may have no intention of ever leaving his native land."

The clairvoyance thus obtained may be used to watch the prog-
<26> ress of Ceremonies, when it becomes a highly useful gift, sometimes
a necessity; and also in observing what occurs astrally when certain Sigils or Pentagrams are traced or Names vibrated.

There are several methods of testing and protection, in addition to those already mentioned. The supreme method of protection — though it is infinitely more than technical means of banishing — is through the assumption of the God form Harpocrates. The astral image should be formulated either as rising from a Lotus, or else standing erect over two crocodiles. Little need be said about this technique; it is adequately described elsewhere, in Z.1. Incidentally, this is an excellent preparation for meditation or vision, to formulate the form about and around one, and to identify oneself with it.

In the event, during any vision, that the Seer is approached by entities, as to whose integrity or true character he has some doubts, the simplest form of testing is to formulate between the Seer and the approaching entity the Banner of the West. As described in the document about the symbolism of the Neophyte Ceremony, this Banner is that which bars and threatens. It is one of the insignia of the Hiereus, whose throne is in the West of the Temple, and his office is that of "Avenger of the Gods," so situated as to represent a seat of witness and of punishment decreed against evil. And all his insignia partake of this symbolism. Thus, should the being be of an evil nature — "thus far and no farther" is the message indicated to it by the Banner. The interposition of the Banner would be immediately efficacious, by causing it to disappear instantaneously. If, however, the entity is well-intentioned and not evil, no harm will have been done by that formulation. No balanced force, no power of good, will object or resent legitimate forms of testing its integrity.

Since, likewise, the Banner of the East, one of the insignia of the Hierophant in the East of the Temple, "represents the ascent of the Initiate
<27> unto perfect knowledge of the light," it may assist to formulate this
Banner about his own being. The Central Cross of the banner will suggest his own form with outstretched arms — a true calvary cross. About him, the Seer will visualise vividly the interlaced red and blue triangles of the Tiphareth hexagram, at the same time imagining that the white triangle of the Supernals has descended into his heart. The alternate and occasionally simultaneous use of these Banners is a powerful means of banishing the evil, and invoking balanced power to one's aid. In the rubrics of certain rituals, the injunction occurs to formulate this Banner about talismans or flashing Tablets that are being consecrated, as this process assists the descent or the incar-

nation of the Light, or the invoked force, into the symbol.

The employment of the Rose-Cross together with the vibration of the Pentagrammaton, YHShVH is likewise another method of ensuring protection and of banishing evil. Usually, as previously stated, any threat of danger on the elemental planes represented by the Tattwa symbols may be met simply by the vibration of the appropriate divine names, and, though very rarely necessary, by the banishing Pentagrams traced in the air. The Rose Cross and the Pentagrammaton will apply more to planes above or more powerful than those of the Tattwas. Experience combined with a sound instinct will dictate to the Seer when such symbols should be used. He will find it occasionally of great assistance to commence his experiments by the preliminary use of the Banishing Rituals and by burning some incense.

In the Outer Order of the Stella Matutina, or the Golden Dawn, formal dress for this type of work as for Temple ceremonies consisted of a black gown, red slippers, and a black and white nemyss; the sash of the grade could also be worn. In the Order of the R.R. et A.C., it was customary to wear a white gown, yellow or gold slippers, a nemyss of white and yellow stripes,
<28> and the Rose-Cross lamen on one's breast. The Lotus Wand should
be employed and held in the hand whilst skrying, and the Four Elemental Weapons — Fire Wand, Water Cup, Air Dagger, and Earth Pentacle, should be placed before one. If there is a small table convenient, this should be covered with a black cloth, and the implements grouped on this as upon the Altar, while the Cross and Triangle of the Order should be put in the centre. Sometimes, a sympathetic projection into the elements may be encompassed by the preliminary use of the appropriate Prayer of the Elements provided in the grade rituals.

<29> OF SKRYING AND TRAVELLING IN THE SPIRIT-VISION

By V. H. SOROR, V.N.R.

Having acquired the general rules, it is probable that the student will discover for himself particular methods more or less suited to his own particular temperament. But it may prove useful to some for me to write in some detail the mode of skrying and of astral projection which I have proved likely to bring successful results, and which by reasons of its continual tests would tend to lessen the many chances of illusion. Before proceeding further it may be well to refer to the Microcosm Lecture (in Volume One) regarding the theory of skrying and astral projection.

The rules for skrying and astral projection being almost similar, the two subjects can be studied together, the one being taken as the complement of the other.

You can commence the operation "skrying" simply. That is to say, not projecting the astral beyond the sphere of Sensation into the Macrocosmos, but retaining it and perceiving some scene in the Universe reflected in the symbol which you hold, this latter being to you as a mirror which shall reflect to you some scenes not within your range of sight. And secondly, you can continue the operation by using the same symbol, and by passing through it project yourself to the scene in question, which before you had only perceived as a reflection. The latter process will probably appear more vivid to the perception that the prior one, just as in material vision one is less
<30> likely to be deceived by going to a place and actually examining it, than by obtaining knowledge of it from a mere reflection in a mirror.

For example, in the room in which I am now, I see reflected in a mirror a portion of the garden. I obtain an impression of all within my range of sight, but not nearly so powerful a one as when I step out into the garden to the spot in question, and examine all the objects therein, feel the atmosphere, touch the ground, smell the flowers, etc.

But it is well to practise both methods. The latter will probably be found to be more instructive, though far more fatiguing, since you will, when projecting the astral, have to supply it with much vitality, drawn mostly from the Nephesch.

In both skrying and astral projection, then, the key of success would appear to be, alternately to employ Intuition and Reason, firstly by permitting each thought-picture to impress itself on the brain in the manner comprehended generally by the word 'inspiration,' followed by the reason applying its knowledge of correspondences to an affirmation or correction of the same.

You must be prepared to receive impressions of scenes, forms and sounds as vivid thought forms. "Thought forms" I use for want of a better word. There are distinctly in these experiences, things heard, things felt as well as things seen, which would prove that the qualities that we are here using are really the sublimated senses. That the faculty of clairvoyance, etc. exists is easily provable after a little patient exercise with one of the first methods given unto us for the practice of skrying.

Take the Tattwa cards, and from them choose one at random, without looking to see what symbol it may represent, and lay it down on a table face downwards. Then try mentally to discover the symbol. To do this make your mind a blank as much as possible (yet always keeping control over the same) chasing therefrom, for the time being, the reasoning element,
<31> memory, etc. You will find that after a few moments of gazing attentively at the back of the card, that it will seem as though the thought form of the Tattwa appeared to enter the mind suddenly, and later, when more practised, it will probably appear to you as if the Tattwa symbol were trying to precipitate itself materially through the back of the card. (1) But sometimes, especially if the cards have been long kept together in the pack in the same order, we may find that the back of the card in question is charged astrally *not* with the symbol upon its face, but with that upon the card whose face has been next its back in the order of the pack.

Some may find it easier to turn the card over astrally, that is in imagination, and in imagination endeavour to perceive what flashes into the mind at that moment.

As it is with the Tattwas that our first experiences are made, I will choose one to illustrate the following rules, preferably one that shall be in harmony with the time that I commence my working. (2).

RULES FOR SKRYING

Work if possible in an especially prepared magical room, S. M. altar in the centre, on which stand the four elements and the Cross and Triangle, incense burning, lamp lighted, water in the cup, (3), bread and salt. As well as these, place on the Altar your four magical implements. Clothe yourself in your White Robe, and ⑤ = 6 sash, wearing on breast your Rose-Cross.

Have by you your Sword and Lotus Wand. Sit at the side of the Altar facing the Quarter of the Element, Planet or Sign with which you are working. Should any other Frater or Soror be with you, arrange that they shall sit in balanced disposition (5) around the Altar. That is, if the forces with which you work be in the West, your place is East of the Altar facing West across it. Should it be inconvenient for you to have your own consecrated room, or to have all or any of your implements for your experiment, do your utmost to imagine them as astrally existing about you, and in any case in astral
<32> projection wear the garments and insignia astrally all through the experience. In fact, after constant, most constant, practice you will not probably find the absolute physical so necessary. Yet remember, that though the material in magical working is the least important of the planes in one sense, yet in another it is of the utmost importance for it crystallises the astral plane and completes it. And also have before you the exact correspondences

of certain universal formulae (for in the aforesaid insignia and implements you hold a perfect representation of the Universe (6), the contemplation of which should in itself tend to prevent your mind dwelling on irrelevant subjects, but on the contrary compel your attention to the sublime studies of the mysteries of the Macrocosm.) Also do these Insignia, which have been consecrated, give you a certain power through their having attracted rays of force from the Infinite Invisible more or less potent in proportion to your development.

The importance of using the implements on every occasion would appear to be great. For the implement assists the invoking of a ceremony, and the latter should help the implement, and therefore every voyage, for example, to the realms of Fire or Water should add a flame to the Wand and moisture to the Cup.

Next purify the room with Fire and Water and the Lesser Banishing Ritual of the Pentagram. Imagine that we have chosen as a Tattwa, Apas-Prithivi. For this symbol naturally, use the correspondences of Water and Earth, but bear in mind that the World of Water is here chiefly expressed, the Earth being secondary. Therefore in this particular example, it is well to use principally the Cup, the Pentacle only in a minor sense. To imply this, use the Cup to make even many of the Earth symbols, and only occasionally employ the Pentacle in working the particular symbol.

<33> In this suppositious case of , thoroughly to fill your Sphere with the idea of this Tattwa, draw with the Cup around your Room the Greater Invoking Ritual of the Pentagram both of Water and of Earth. Then return to your seat, and for Process One, Skrying, do the following. Place the Tattwa card before you on the Altar, take the Cup in the right hand and the Pentacle in the left, and look at the symbol long and steadily until you can perceive it clearly as a thought vision when you shut your eyes. Vibrate the Names of Water and of Earth (Empeh Arsel, etc.) and try to realise the mental union more and more. It may help you to perceive it as a large crescent made of blue or silvery water containing a cube of yellow sand. Continue trying to acquire a keen perception of the Tattwa until the Element and its shape and its qualities shall seem to have become a part of you, and you should then begin to feel as though you were one with that particular Element, completely bathed in it, and as if all other Elements were non-existent. If this be correctly done, you will find that the thought of any other Element than the one with which you are working will be distinctly distasteful to you.

Having succeeded in obtaining the thought vision of the symbol, continue vibrating the Divine Names with the idea well fixed in your mind of calling before you on the card a brain picture of some scene or landscape. This, when it first appears, will probably be vague, but continue to realise it more and more of whatever nature (imagination or memory, etc., (8), you may believe it to be — remembering that this is a passive state of the mind, and not yet is the time to test or reason (9). Only when the thought picture shall have become sufficiently tangible and vivid, and you find that you are beginning to lose the sense of confusion and vagueness should you begin to apply tests. Before this period, all reasoning, all doubting, is destructive to the experiment.

In all probability, the thought picture may become so clear to
<34> you (though this may be a matter of time and much practice) that it
will seem as though the picture were trying to precipitate through the symbol. In such a case as this there can be no difficulty, for the vision will be nearly as clear to the perception as a material one might be. But you can arrive at a great deal by merely receiving the impression of the landscape as a thought. For example, I perceive appearing an expanse of sea, a slight strip of land — high grey rocks or boulders rising out of the sea. To the left a long gallery of cliffs jutting out some distance into the sea (10). This appears sufficiently vivid, so I begin my tests. I suspect my memory chiefly, so I draw in front of the picture on the card, with the Lotus Wand, a large TAU in light. Then, believing that I may have constructed the scene in imagination, I now formulate on the card a large Caph. In this case, neither of these symbols banish or dim the scene in any way, so I continue. (But if the scene vanishes or changes or becomes blurred, it is well to banish with a Pentagram whatever may remain on the card, and simply recommence the process at the point where you are endeavouring to attract a picture on the card.)

I now draw over the picture with the Cup the water Pentagram, and with the Pentacle the Earth Pentagram (11) using the correct vibration. This intensifies the picture, and I now perceive flung into it many figures, principally of the Water spirit type. On gazing further, and repeating the vibration, I perceive a much larger figure than the elementals, overshadowing them, clothed in blue and white, with some glimmering of silver. To obtain detail I must work for some time longer, and must continue invoking with my water and earth Symbols, and look and test alternately.

Believing that sufficient has been herein explained to enable a student to understand the general method of this process of skrying, I will proceed
further to the rules for astral projection, but be it remembered that it
<35> is possible to carry this vision very far indeed, and that the student
should by no means stop where I have done.

ASTRAL PROJECTION

(12). Therefore you will follow the rules given in the preceding pages for Skrying, until the point where the symbol of the Tattwa has become perfectly vivid to the perception and when you feel as though you were almost one with the Element. You may modify the earlier stages of the working by so enlarging the symbol astrally that the human being can pass through it. When very vivid, and not until then, *pass, spring or fly through it,* and do not begin to reason till you find yourself in some place or landscape (13). And as before, only test when the landscape shall have become a tangible and somewhat complete picture. If you have made your mind a blank as much as possible, the first idea that enters your mind (that is to say vividly) after you have traversed the symbol should be a correct correspondence of the Tattwa in question.

Having already, by the process of skrying, obtained a vision of , in this particular case I will use the same symbol, on which I still perceive the reflected picture, and will leap through it, and go astrally to the scene in question. I therefore astrally fly or leap through it.

My first impression is to find myself standing on a boulder slightly out at sea, which I had noted as an important point in the picture. I realise that I am standing clothed in my ⑤ = [6] insignia and white robe, on this rock, facing the shore. Turning to the right I am conscious of the gallery of cliffs, and to the left and back of me the sea, everywhere.

(On the planes, it would appear well to act exactly as one would in a physical experience or a landscape, realising each step as one goes, *not trying to look on both sides at once or at the back of one's head,* but turning first to
<36> the right hand and examining that, and then to the left, then turning
right around, and so on. It is better as much as possible to remain in one spot (until very experienced) to avoid reflexes. In fact, the more practically the experiences are worked, the more chance of success.)

I have an impression that the air is very cold. I stoop down and feel the rock, which I find is of a coral nature. I have already tested this vision in process One (skrying), but it is well to repeat the same, to see if I am sufficiently in touch with the landscape. I therefore trace with my astral Lotus Wand the symbols I evoked before, the TAU and the CAPH, in white light, making them very forcibly. In fact, I do not cease tracing them until I actually perceive them as vividly as I do the landscape. Seeing that the scene does not vanish or become dim (14) I now with my Astral Cup and Pentacle, draw in Light very large Water and Earth Pentagrams, standing on the sea. These, even more than the former symbols should be continued and accentuated until they become to the impression of the mind as living entities as the landscape itself. If these latter be correctly drawn and sufficiently realised, there will be little chance of illusion during the rest of the experience.

The drawing of these Pentagrams standing above the sea appears at once to increase the vitality of the scene, for the rather intangible Elementals and Angelic Being that I had perceived in the reflected picture became more and more real to the impression.

Had I commenced at once with astral projection without the introduction of my Skrying experience, I should have had probably to evoke these figures. In such a case, using the Invoking Pentagrams of Water, I should continue vibrating the Deity Names, etc. of these Elements (employing as well as the names before mentioned, those of the Angels and Rulers, such names as Tharsis, Kerub, etc., being very potent) and would call upon a force
<37> by right of these names and symbols to manifest, and I should con-
tinue this process until some forms appeared.

After careful examination, by first receiving the impression and then testing it, I can describe the following. The Angelic being, feminine in type, pale brown hair and light grey-eyes, is draped in blue and white, draperies heavy in nature, and wears a crown formed of crescents. She holds in the left hand a curious cup, heavy, and with a squarish base, and in the right a wand with a symbol much much like the positive element of Water.

The Elementals vary in type, the majority being of the mermaid and merman nature, but again many tending to the Earth and Air nature.

Turning to the Angelic Being, I make the ⑤ = [6] Signs and LVX Signs, and to the Elementals the ③ = [8] and ① = [10] Signs, and by right of these (that is to say by the knowledge of the central spirit, and, in their instance of that of water and earth) I ask to have explained some of the secrets of the working of the plane of [symbol]

The Angel having answered my signs by similar ones, gives the impression that she is willing to instruct me. (This can enter the mind as an extraneous thought, or may be heard (15) clairaudiently.) She shows how even the work on this particular spot is varied, and according to the types of the Elementals is the labour allotted. Some of the Elementals tending to the gnome type are digging in the cliffs, with spiky instruments, and boring holes therein, thereby permitting the water to enter freely. (This may explain the spongy rather than broken aspect of the rock). The mermaid and merman Elementals, which are in the large majority, I think, receive some of the dust, which they carry into the sea. (Some of this may go to form islands.) Others also are bringing earth and weeds and such-like from the depths, also
<38> probably to form land. There are also figures holding funnel-like
Cups who rise from the sea, and having drawn air into them, dive again, carrying that element into the sea. (16)

It can be understood how these investigations can be carried to very great detail, but to be as brief as possible I ask if I may be shown the effect of this Ray of [symbol] on the Universe generally and on this Planet in particular.

I understand that the effect of the Ray is generating and fructifying generally, and on the whole beneficient, though everything would depend on the Force with which it was united. Its correlative would be thick rich water, containing such substance. I ask for its influence on the Earth. (To do this I can show as a thought-picture this planet of ours, with its continents, seas, etc., drawn thereon, and pray this Angel to send a ray first to one spot and then to another.) In answer I perceive the ray falling right through the water of the Earth, as if the affinity lay with all land under water. "The Lifter of Earth in the Waters is its Name" does the Angel say. Nearly all vegetation attracts this ray, but very especially water plants, most of all those growing under water. The Zoophyte only partially attracts it, this latter seeming rather largely composed of some active element, Fire, I think. Among animals the Ray appears to fall on the seal and hippopotamus, and has a general affinity for most amphibious animals. With fish, the link seems to be small, a tortoise, a frog, and a snail are shown me, and *some* water-fowl of the duck type, very few actual birds, a sea fowl to an extent.

Falling on man, on the savage it would appear to be beneficial to health generally, to give a feeling of well-being, and would also govern to some extent generation. Its tendency would be to accentuate sensuality and laziness. On the intellectual man it increases intuition, with some desire
<39> to clothe idea with form, therefore the first vague development of
form in the mind of the artist. (As before remarked, these experiences can be carried very far indeed, but as this experience has already become rather voluminous I will cease at this point — believing that sufficient is here expressed to suggest the manner of working these astral experiences generally.)

I salute therefore the Angel with the LVX Signs and the Elementals by the ③ = [8] and ① = [10] Signs, and banish astrally the Pentagram and other symbols that I have traced upon the scene. The more powerfully the symbols have been evoked, the more powerfully should they be banished.

If you should be feeling a sensation of fatigue, as I before mentioned, make towards the symbols the sign of the Enterer indrawing their vitality into yourself again by the sign of Harpocrates. Then return by the way in which you came, that is through the symbol, and back into your room. (17) Once in your room, perform the Banishing Ritual of the Pentagrams (Supreme) that you have evoked; supposing a scene to remain on the symbol of the Tattwa banish that also. When you have had considerable practise it is probable that such detailed care as is herein indicated will not be necessary. Should the operation be too complicated to accomplish at one sitting it would be possible to divide it into parts. It is certain that you will find that you have practised your spritual vision and acquired more knowledge in one experience carefully worked and tested than in a hundred careless and vague experiments which simply strengthen mental deception.

NOTES

1. This experiment is very good for the practice of Spiritual Sight, and in this manner you can easily prove correctness of vision. Also for this kind of simple experience you need not prepare yourself spiritually to such
<40> an extent as with further working, so that you can have your cards if you wish continually with you, and practise with them when you will, at odd moments.

2. To find Tattwa when in course, note time of sunrise. Akasa always begins with sunrise and lasts 24 minutes, followed by Vayu 24 minutes, Tejas 24 minutes, Apas 24 minutes, Prithivi 24 minutes.

3. Placed at junction of Cross and Triangle, the incense, lamp etc., should be at angles of arms of Cross.

4. All ⑤ = 6 members who are Zel. Ad. Min. have the right to wear the white robe and yellow girdle of the 3rd Adept, but not his cloak or Nemyss.

5. If 2 persons, one should be opposite the other.
If 3 persons, form a triangle.
If 4 persons, form a square.
If 5 persons, a pentagram, etc.

6. The G. D., Altar, the most synthetical of the symbols. Material universe ruled by the Spirit and Four Elements. The Rose-Cross contains the affirmation of the principal divisions of the Universe, synthetical like the Altar, but particular in the sense that it is attributed to the Sephirah Tiphareth, the central Sun, and is therefore the symbol for the Microcosm — Man, the Adept, he to whom perfection of the Microcosm means a certain conscious union with the Macrocosm.

The white robe and yellow girdle imply Purity — Kether, Harmony — Gold, Tiphareth. Lotus Wand — Mercy. Sword — Severity.

7. Imagination (eidolon) means the faculty of building an Image. The imagination of the artist must lie in the power, which he possesses more or less in proportion to his sincerity, and his intuition, of perceiving forces in the Macrocosm, and allying or attuning himself thereto, his talents naturally and

his artificial training permitting him to formulate images which shall express those forces.

<41> 8. During this process, it is more than likely that you will be believing that the picture is one of memory, of imagination, of construction, etc. All these qualities being analogous to the faculty that you are employing, and the probability of their arising at this moment will be great.

9. Let it be remembered that this can only be a *part* of the plane of the Symbol expressed by (i.e., The compound Tattwa you are working. C.L.W.)

10. Employ the "Lords who Wander" (the 7 Planets), the planetary Tarot trumps, as important test symbols.

For Memory	♄	ת	Lord of the Night of Time.
For Construction	♃	כ	
For Anger, Impatience	♂	פ	
For Vanity	☉	ר	
For Pleasure	♀	ד	
For Imagination	☿	ב	
For Wandering Thoughts	☽	ג	

11. Use occasionally the Pentacle, so as not to ignore to too great an extent the part that Earth plays herein.

12. In the case of starting the entire experience with Astral Projection only, you will understand that you ignore the portion of the process which attracts the picture to the card, but simply go forward through the symbol when once the latter is realised.

13. If working with correct correspondences, you are bound to arrive at some place answering to the same, if you project your astral sufficiently.

14. If after these repeated tests the Vision becomes diminished or changes very much, banish with the Astral implement, and return in the way you came, through the symbol, and start again freshly. If you feel you have expended too much force in the symbols which you traced in the scenes, redraw some of the force spent into yourself again by the formula of the
<42> signs of Horus and Harpocrates. Extend towards the symbols in the sign of Hoor, redrawing them into yourself by the sign of Hoorpokraat.

15. Sometimes it seems as though one had to find the words to translate the impression; sometimes the words appear to be found already, for one believes that one has heard them.

16. The symbol shows the potency of the whorl-formation.

17. Some students, I believe, have great difficulty in returning. In such a case one can do so gradually by first flying into space, thinking of this Planet, fixing the thoughts on the particular country, then on the particular spot therein, then on the House, and lastly on the room and entering therein. But in most cases this would be unnecessarily complicated.

<43> TATTWA VISIONS

Here follow two Tattwa visions by Soror Vestigia. These are provided as simple examples of the technique, and the procedure to be followed. The first of them is the fiery sub-element of Earth, Tejas of Prithivi.

Vestigia states that she found herself, after going through the imagined symbols, "in a volcanic district. No fire is to be seen, but the type of land is volcanic. Hill and mountains, hot air, and sunny light. Using a Pentacle, and calling on the Earth Names, I see before me a species of Angelic King Elemental. On testing him, I find that he gives me the Neophyte Saluting Sign, and the Philosophus (Fire) Sign. He bows low to the symbols that I give him, and says that he is willing to show me some of the working of the plane. He has a beautiful face, somewhat of the Fire type, yet sweet in expression. He wears a Golden Crown, and a fiery red cloak, opening on to a yellow tunic, over which being a shirt of mail. In his right hand he bears a wand, the lower end or handle being shaped somewhat as the Pentacle implement, and the staff and upper end being as the Fire Wand. In his left hand (but this I do not clearly see) he bears a Fire Wand; I think that the right hand points upwards and the left downwards, and is a symbol to invoke forces. Little figures of the gnome type come at his call. When commanded some broke the rocky parts of the Mountain with pick-axes which they carry. Others appear to dig in the ground. In breaking off these rocky pieces, there fall away little bits of bright metal or copper. Some of these Gnomes collected the bits of metal and carried them away in little wallets slung by a baldrick from their shoulders. We followed them and came to some mountainous peaks.
<44> From these peaks issued some large and fierce, some hardly perceivable, fires. Into cauldrons or bowls placed above these fires, the collected pieces of metal were placed. I was told that this was a lengthy process, but asked that I might see the result of what appeared to be a gradual melting of this metal. I was then shown some bowls containing liquid gold, but not I imagine, very pure metal. I again followed my guide, the Angelic King Elemental Ruler, who gave me his name as Atapa, and followed by some gnomes bearing the bowl of liquid gold, we came, after passing through many subterranean passages cut in the mountains, to a huge cavern of immense breadth and height. It was like a Palace cut out of the rock. We passed through rudely cut passages, until we reached a large central hall, at the end of which was a Dais on which were seated the King and Queen, the courtier gnomes standing around. "This Hall seemed lighted by torches, and at intervals were roughly cut pillars. The Gnomes who accompanied us presented to the King and Queen their gold. These latter commanded their attendants to remove this to another apartment. I asked the King and Queen for a further explanation, and they appointing substitutes in their absence, retire to an inner chamber which appeared more elevated than the rest. The architecture here seemed to be of a different kind. This small hall had several sides, each with a door, draped by a curtain. In the center of the Hall was a large tripod receiver containing some of the liquid gold such as that we had brought with us. The King and Queen who before had worn the colours of Earth now donned, he the red, and she the white garments. They then with their Earth-Fire Wands invoked and joined their wands over the Tripod. There appeared in the air above, a figure such as Atapa, he who had brought me here. He, extending his wand, and invoking, caused to appear from each

door a figure of a planetary or zodiacal nature. These each in turn held out his wand over the gold, using some sigil which I can but dimly follow.
<45> The gold each time appearing to undergo a change. When these last figures have retired again behind the curtains, the King and Queen used a species of ladle and compressed together the gold, making it into solid shapes and placing one of these at each of the curtained doors. Some gold still remained in the bowl. The King and Queen departed, and it seemed to me that I saw a figure again appear from behind each curtain and draw away the pieces of gold."

The second one I shall quote is a vision of Spirit of Water, Akasa of Apas, also by Vestigia.

"A wide expanse of water with many reflections of bright light, and occasionally glimpses of rainbow colours appearing (perhaps symbolising the beginning of formation in Water). When divine and other names were pronounced, elementals of the mermaid and merman type appear, but few of other elemental forms. These water forms are extremely changeable, one moment appearing as solid mermaids and mermen, the next melting into foam.

"Raising myself by means of the highest symbols I have been taught, and vibrating the names of Water, I rose until the Water vanished, and instead I beheld a mighty world or globe, with its dimensions and divisions of Gods, Angels, elementals, demons—the whole universe of Water (like the tablet ruled by EMPEH ARSEL GAIOL), I called on this latter name, and the Universe seemed to vivify more and more. I then called on HCOMA, and there appeared standing before me a mighty Archangel (with four wings) robed in glistening white, and crowned. In one hand, the right, he held a species of trident, and in the left a Cup filled to the brim with an essence which appeared to be derived from above. This essence, brimming over, poured down below on either side. From the overflowing or overrunning of this Cup, which derives its essence from Atziluth, apparently the cup being in Briah, the World of Yetzirah obtains its moisture. It is there differentiated into its various operative forces.

"These operative forces are represented by Angels each with
<46> their respective office in the world of moisture. These forces working in Yetsirah, when descending and mingling with the Kether of Assiah, are initiating the force of that which we as human beings call Moisture."

<47> M.

THE VISION OF THE UNIVERSAL MERCURY

"We stood upon a dark and rocky cliff that overhung the restless seas. In the sky above us was a certain glorious sun, encircled by that brilliant rainbow, which they of the Path of the Chamelion know.

"I beheld, until the heavens opened, and a form like unto the Mercury of the Greeks (1) descended, flashing like the lightning; and he hovered between the sky and the sea. In his hand was the staff (2) wherewith the eyes of mortals are closed in sleep, and wherewith he also, at will, re-awakeneth the sleeper; and terribly did the globe at its summit dart forth rays. And he bare a scroll whereon was written:

Lumen est in Deo,
Lux in homine factum,
Sive Sol,
Sive Luna,
Sive Stelloc errantes,
Omnia in Lux,
Lux in Lumine
Lumen in Centrum,
Centrum in Circulo,
Circulum ex Nihilo,
Quid scis, id eris. (3)
F.I.A.T. (4)
E.S.T. (5)
E.S.T.O. (6)
E.R.I.T. (7)
In fidelitate et veritate universas ab aeternitate. (8)
Nunc Hora.
Nunc Dies.
<48> Nunc Annus,
Nunc Saeculum,
Omnia sunt Unum,
et Omnia in Omnibus.
A.E.T.E.R.N.I.T.A.S. (9)

Then Hermes cried aloud, and said:

"I am Hermes Mercurius, the Son of God, the messenger uniting Superiors and Inferiors. I exist not without them, and their union is in me. I bathe in the Ocean. I fill the expanse of Air. I penetrate the depths beneath."

And the Frater who was with me, said unto me:

"Thus is the Balance of Nature maintained, for this Mercury is the beginning of all movement. This He, (10) this She, this IT, is in all things, but hath wings which thou canst not constrain. For when thou sayest 'He is here' he is not here, for by that time he is already away, for he is Eternal Motion and Vibration."

Nevertheless in Mercury must thou seek all things. Therefore not without reason did our Ancient Fratres say that the Great Work was to "Fix the Volatile." There is but one place where he can be fixed, and that is the Centre, a centre exact. "Centrum in trigono centri." (11) The Centre in the triangle of the Centre.

If thine own soul be baseless how wilt thou find a standing point whence to fix the soul of the Universe?

"Christus de Christi,
Mercury de Mercurio,
Per viam crucis,
Per vitam Lucis
Deus te Adjutabitur!" (12)

<49>

TRANSLATION OF AND NOTES ON DOCUMENT M

By G. H. FRATER, S.R.M.D.

1. Hermes is Greek, Mercury is Roman.

2. Compare with v. 47 ODYSSEY: "Him promptly obeyed the active destroyer of Argus. Forth sped he, and under his feet he bound his ambrosial sandals. Then, taking his staff wherewith he the eyes of mortals closeth at will, and the sleeper at will reawakens."

3. Translation: The Light is in God, the LVX hath been made into Man. Whether Sun, or Moon, or Wandering Stars, all are in Lux, the Lux in the Light, the Light in the Centre, the Centre in the Circle, the Circle from the Nothingness (Negative or Ain אין) What thou mayest be (i.e. what thou hast in thyself, the capability of being) that shalt thou be (or become).

4. Flatus. Ignis. Aqua. Terra. (Air. Fire. Water. Earth.)

5. Ether. Sal. Terrae. (Ether, the Salt of the Earth.)

6. Ether. Subtilis. Totius. Orbis. (The subtle Ether of the whole universe.)

7. Ether. Ruens. In. Terra. (The Ether rushing into the Earth.)

8. Let it be (or become). It is. Be it so. It shall be (or endure). In Universal faithfulness and truth from eternity. Now an hour, Now a day, Now a year, Now an age, all things are One, and All in All. ETERNITY.

9. These ten letters are Notaricons of: Ab Kether. Ex Chokmah. Tu Binah. Ex Chesed. Regina Geburah. Nunc Tiphareth. In Netzach. Totius Hod. Ad Yesod. Saeculorum Malkuth. (From the Crown, out of Wisdom—Thou, O Understanding art Mercy, Queen of Severity. Now the perfect Beauty, in the Victory, of all Splendour, for the Foundation, of the Ages of the Universe.)

10. Probably alludes to the Three Principles.

11. This was, I believe, but am not certain, the motto of our Frater Count Adrian a Meynsicht, otherwise known as Henricus Madathanus.

<50> 12. The Christ from the Christ. The Mercury from the Mercury, Through the Path of the Cross, Through the life of the Light, God shall be Thy Help.

(Note: An illustration accompanying this manuscript depicted a conventional nude figure of Mercury, winged helmet and sandals, diving into the sea. In the right hand was the Caduceus, and the left bore a scroll showing the words described in the text.—I.R.)

<51> # TALISMANS

THE FORMATION OF TALISMANS AND FLASHING TABLETS

A TALISMAN is a magical figure charged with the force which it is intended to represent. In the construction of a Talisman, care should be taken to make it, as far as is possible, so to represent the Universal Forces that it should be in exact harmony with those you wish to attract, and the more exact the symbolism, the more easy it is to attract the force — other things coinciding, such as consecration at the right time, etc.

A SYMBOL should also be correct in its symbolism, but it is not necessarily the same as a Talisman.

A FLASHING TABLET is one made in the complementary colours. A flashing colour, then, is the complementary colour which, if joined to the original, enables it to attract, to a certain extent, the Akasic current from the atmosphere, and to a certain extent from yourself, thus forming a vortex which can attract its flashing light from the atmosphere. Therefore, to make anything of this description which shall be really operative, so does it proportionately tire you.

The complementary colours are:

White	complementary to Black and Grey
Red	complementary to Green
Blue	complementary to Orange
Yellow	complementary to Violet
Olive	complementary to Violet
Blue Green	complementary to Red-Orange
Violet	complementary to Citrine
Reddish Orange	complementary to Green Blue
Deep Amber	complementary to Indigo
Lemon Yellow	complementary to Red Violet
Yellow Green	complementary to Crimson

<52> The other complementaries of other mixed colours can easily be found from this scale.

Coming now to the nature and method of formation of the Talisman, the first thing to be remembered is that it is not always a just and right thing to form a Talisman with the idea of completely changing the current of another person's Karma. In any case you could only do this in a certain sense. It will be remembered that the words of the CHRIST which preceded His cures were "Thy sins be forgiven thee," which meant that the Karmic action was exhausted. Only an Adept who is of the nature of a God can have the power, even if he have the right, to take upon himself the Karma of another. That is to say, that if you endeavour to change completely, (I am not now speaking of adapting and making the best of a person's Karma), the life current, you must be of so great a force that you can take this Karma from them by right of the Divine Power to which you have attained — in which case you will only do it in so far as it does not hinder their spiritual development.

If, however, this is attempted on a lower plane, it will usually be found that what you are endeavouring to bring about is in direct opposition to the Karma of the person concerned. It will not work the required effect and will probably bring a current of exhaustion and trouble on yourself. Without doing much good you will have attracted his own Karma into your own atmosphere and, in fact, brought it on yourself.

These remarks only apply to an attempted radical change in the Karma of another, which is a thing you have no right to do until you have attained the highest adeptship.

The formation or adaptation of Talismans in ordinary matters should be employed with great discernment. What may assist in material things is often a hindrance spiritually, seeing that for a force to work, it must attract
<53> elemental forces of the proper description, which may thus, to an
extent, endanger your spiritual nature.

Also, in making Talismans for a person, you must endeavour to isolate yourself entirely from him. You must banish from your mind any feeling of love or hate, irritation, etc., for all these feelings operate against your power.

It is but rarely that a Talisman for the love of a person is a right and justifiable thing to construct. Pure love links us to the nature of the Gods. There is a perfect love between the Angels and the gods because there is perfect harmony among them, but that is not the lower and earthly love. Thus a Talisman made for terrestrial love would be sealed with the impress of your own weakness, and even if successful, would react on you in other ways. The only way in which real power can be gained, is by transcending the material plane and trying to link yourself to your Divine and Higher Soul. That is why trouble is so great an initiator, because trouble brings you nearer spiritual things when material things fail.

Therefore, a Talisman as a rule is better made for one in whom you have no interest. In the work of actual consecration, it is always a good thing to purify the room and use the Banishing Ritual of the Pentagram. All these are aids which the Adept, when sufficiently advanced, will know when to use and when not to do so. It is better, if possible, to finish a Talisman at one sitting, because it is begun under certain conditions and it may be difficult to put yourself in the same frame of mind at another time.

Another point that beginners are apt to run away with, is that Talismans can be made wholesale. Suppose a dozen Talismans were made to do good to as many different people, a ray from yourself must charge each Talisman. You have sent out a sort of spiral from your aura which goes on to the Talisman and attracts a like force from the atmosphere — that is, if you have learned to excite the like force in yourself at the moment of consecra-
<54> tion. So that, in the case supposed, you would have a dozen links con-
necting with you, like so many wires in a telegraph office, and whenever the force which any of these Talismans was designed to combat becomes too strong for the force centred therein, there is an instantaneous

communication with you — so that the loss of force to which you would be continually liable might be such as to deplete you of vitality and cause you to faint.

In cases where Talismans and symbols have done their work, they should be carefully de-charged, and then destroyed. If this is not done, and you take a symbol, say of water, still charged and throw it into the fire to get rid of it, you are inflicting intense torment on the Elemental you have attracted, and it will re-act on you sooner or later. Also, if you throw away a still charged Talisman, thus desecrating it, it will become the property of other things, which, through it, will be enabled to get at you. It is for these reasons that the Talisman should be de-charged with the Pentagram and Hexagram according as it partakes of the planetary or zodiacal nature — and these remarks apply equally to Flashing Tablets.

If a Talisman is given to a person who goes away, and does not return it, you can render it inoperative by invoking it astrally and then de-charging it with great care and force.

A FLASHING TABLET should be carefully made charged, and consecrated, and then each morning the Adeptus should sit before it and practise clairvoyance, endeavouring to go through it to the plane it represents, and then to invoke the power and ask for strength to accomplish the matter desired, which will be granted if it be a lawful and laudable operation.

Any Flashing Tablet of two colours should be as nearly balanced in proportion of the extent of colour as possible — the ground one colour, and the charge another. There is also a mode in which three colours can be
<55> used in a planetary talisman. This is done by placing the seven
colours on the Heptagram, and drawing two lines to the points exactly opposite, which will thus yield two flashing colours. This properly drawn, will give the effect of a flashing light playing on the symbol, partly visible physically and partly clairvoyantly, i.e., if properly charged. An advanced Adept should be able to charge his Tablet to a certain extent as he constructs it.

The radical colour of the Planet is symbolical. But a Talisman for harmony of idea say, could be well represented by the TIPHARETH of VENUS — a beautiful yellow-green, and so on.

The Lion Kerub of VENUS would represent spiritual fire and thus symbolises the inspiration of the poet — the colour being a soft and beautiful pearl grey, and the charges should be white. The Watery part of Venus would represent the reflective faculty and answer to spiritual beauty, colour a bluish-green. The Vault contains a perfect scale of Talismans of every description of Planet, and shows how a planetary man will look at everything according to the colour of his aura, due to the planet under which he is born. The real Adept comes forth from the sides to the centre. He is no longer under the dominion of the Stars.

Having made a Magical Talisman, you should use some form of charging and consecrating it, which is suitable to the operation. There are certain words and Letters which are to be invoked in the charging of a Tablet, the Letters governing the Sign under which the operation falls, together with the Planet associated therewith (if a planetary Talisman). Thus in Elemental operations, you take the Letters of the appropriate zodiacal triplicity, adding AL thereto, thus forming an Angelic Name which is the expression of the force. Hebrew Names as a rule, represent the operation of certain general forces, while the names on the Enochian or Angelical Tablets represent a species of more particular ideas. Both classes of Names should be used in these operations.

<56> After preparing the room in the way laid down for the consecration of lesser magical implements, supposing this to be an Elemental Talisman, first formulate towards the Four Quarters the Supreme Ritual of the Pentagram as taught. Then invoke the Divine Names, turning towards the quarter of the Element.

Let the Adeptus then, being seated or standing before the Tablet, and looking in the requisite direction of the force which he wishes to invoke, take several deep inspirations, close the eyes, and holding the breath, mentally pronounce the letters of the Forces invoked. Let this be done several times, as if you breathed upon the Tablet pronouncing them in the vibratory manner. Then, rising, make the sign of the Rose and Cross over the Tablet, and repeating the requisite formula, first describe round the Talisman, a circle, with the appropriate magical implement, and then make the invoking Pentagrams five times over it, as if the Pentagrams stood upright upon it, repeating the letters of the Triplicity involved with AL added. Then solemnly read any invocation required, making the proper sigils from the Rose as you pronounce the Names.

The first operation is to initiate a whorl from yourself. The second, to attract the force in the atmosphere into the vortex you have formed.

Then read the Elemental Prayer as in the Rituals, and close with the Signs of the circle and the cross (that is the Rose-Cross) after performing the necessary Banishing.

Be careful, however, not to banish over the newly consecrated Talisman, as that would simply decharge it again and render it useless. Before Banishing, you should wrap the charged Talisman in clean white silk or linen.

<57>

SIGILS

In the Opening Ceremony of the grade of ⑤ = 6 Adeptus Minor, the Complete Symbol of the Rose and Cross is called the "Key of Sigils and of Rituals," and it is further said that it represents the Forces of the 22 Letters in Nature, as divided into a Three, a Seven, and a Twelve. (See Diagram 20, Pg. 56 of Vol. III)

The inner Three Petals of the Rose symbolise the active Elements of Air, Fire, and Water, operating in the Earth, which is as it were the recipient of them, their container and ground of operation. They are coloured, as are all the other petals, according to the hues of the Rainbow in the masculine (positive) scale. The seven next Petals answer to the Letters of the Seven Planets, and the Twelve Outer to the Twelve Signs of the Zodiac.

Now if thou wilt trace the Sigil of any word or name either in the Air, or written upon paper, thou shalt commence with a circle at the point of the initial letter on the Rose, and draw with thy magical weapon a line from this circle unto the place of the next letter of the name. Continue this, until thou hast finished the word which the letters compose. If two letters of the same sort, such as two Beths or Gimels, come together, thou shalt represent the same by a crook or wave in the line at that point.

And if there be a letter, as Resh in Metatron, through which the line passeth to another letter and which yet formeth part of the name, thou shalt make a noose in the line at that point thus: ____O____ to mark the same. If thou art drawing the Sigil thou mayest work it in the respective colours of the letters and add these together to form a synthesis of colour. Thus the Sigil of Metatron shall be: blue, greenish-yellow, orange, red-orange, and greenish-blue: the synthesis will be a reddish-citron.

<58>

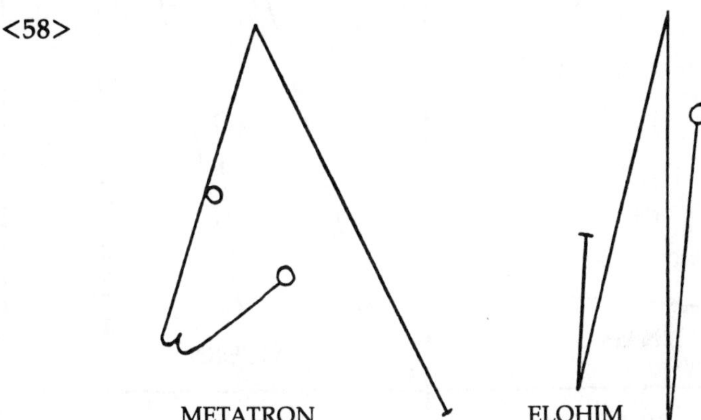

(Note: If the reader will draw a Rose, copied from the complete symbol of the Rose-Cross, about three-and-a-half to four inches in diameter, and trace the above Sigils on a piece of fairly transparent paper placed over the Rose, he will learn for himself how these Sigils are drawn. He should experiment tracing half a dozen or so of these.—I.R.)

Now we will trace, for example, the Sigils of the Forces under Binah, the Third Sephirah. Incidentally, the Sigils for the plane of a Sephirah are always worked out on this system in this order:

First. Sigil of the Sephirah—Binah.

Second. Sigil of the Divine Name, representing the force of the Sephirah in the World of Atziluth. For Binah, YHVH ELOHIM.

Third. The Sigil of the Archangel, representing the force of the Sephirah in Briah—Tzaphqiel.

Fourth. Sigil of the Choir of Angels, representing the force of the Sephirah in Yetzirah—Aralim.

Fifth. The Sigil of the Sphere of the Planet representing the force of the Sephirah in Assiah—Shabbathai.

Finally, the Sigils of any other names whose numbers have some relation to the powers of the Sephirah or its Planet.

<60> Yet these latter (the Sigils of the Intelligence and Spirit) are more usually taken from the Magical Kamea or Square of the Planets according to a slightly different system as will be shown hereafter.

<59>

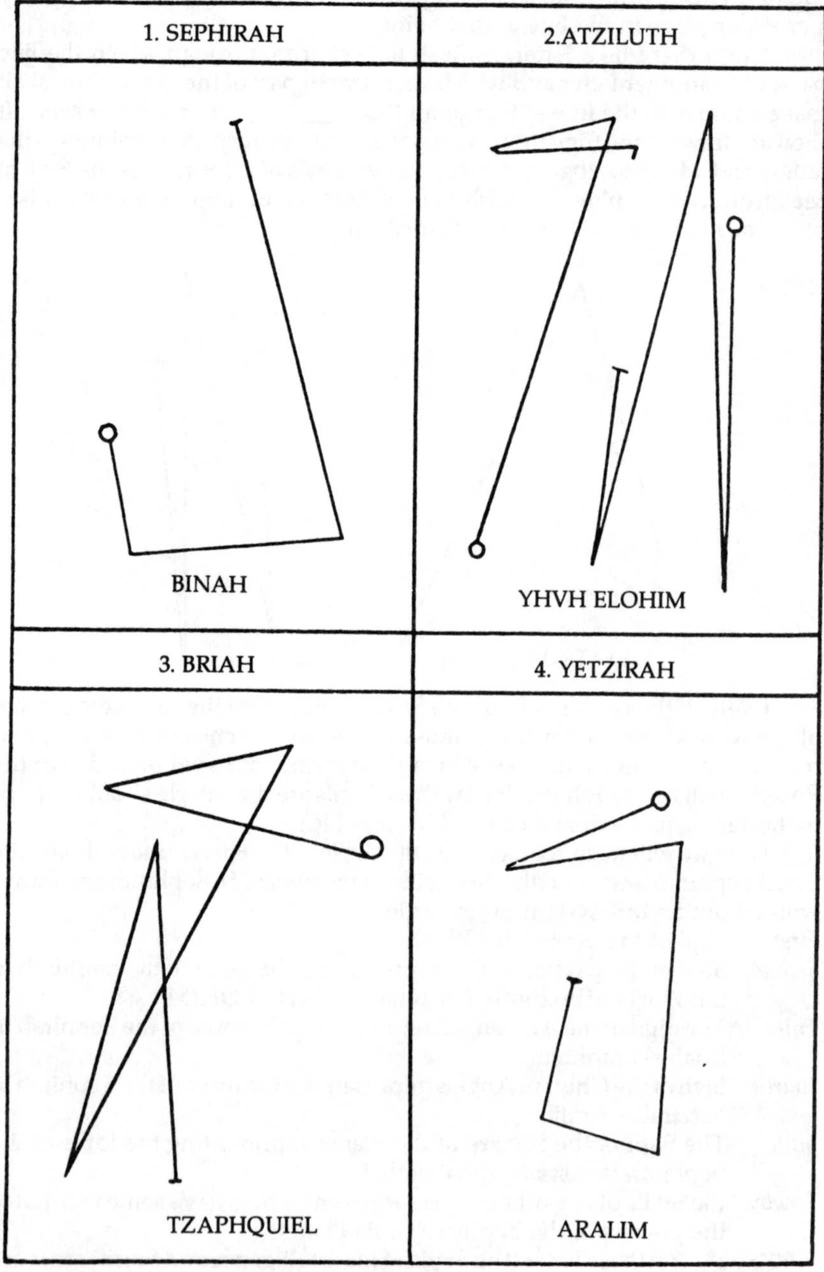
1. SEPHIRAH
2.ATZILUTH
BINAH
YHVH ELOHIM
3. BRIAH
4. YETZIRAH
TZAPHQUIEL
ARALIM

<60>

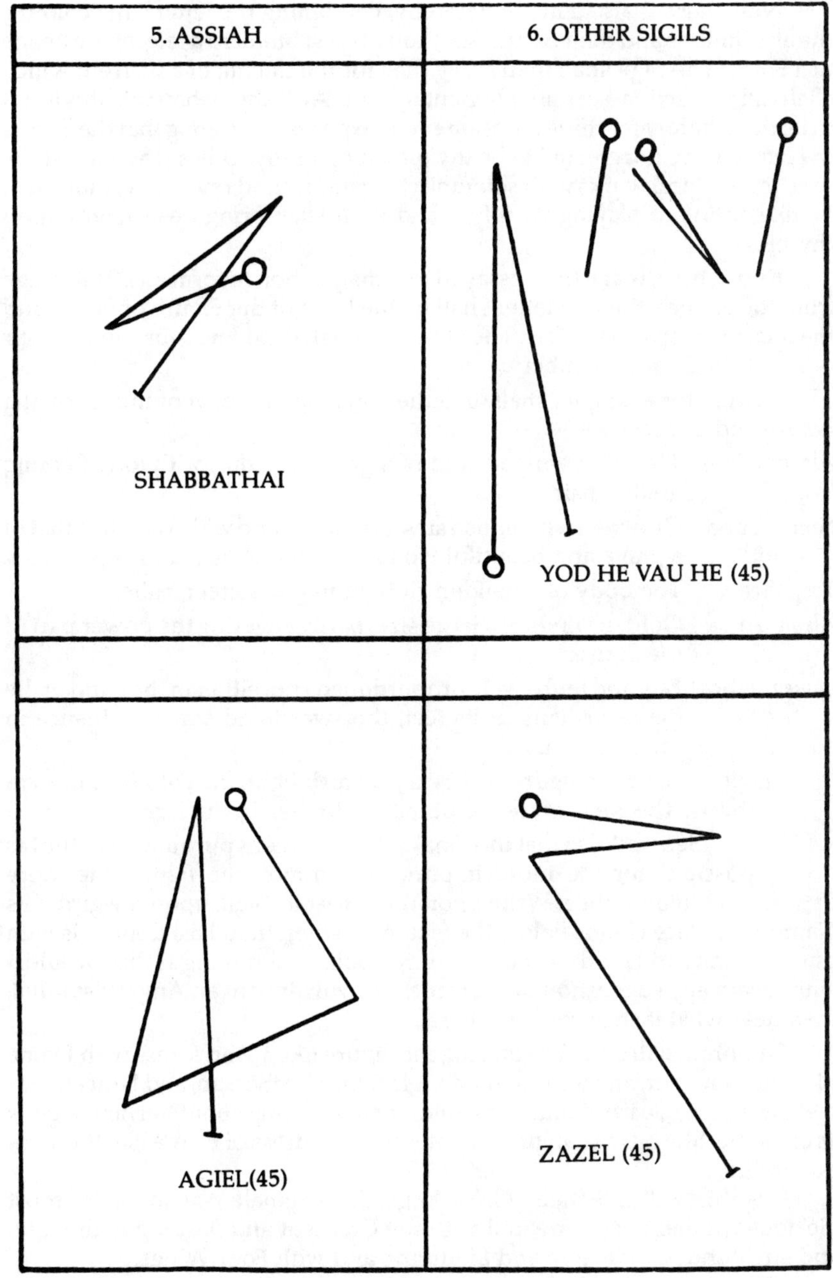
5. ASSIAH
6. OTHER SIGILS
SHABBATHAI
YOD HE VAU HE (45)
AGIEL(45)
ZAZEL (45)

<61> TELESMATIC FIGURES

Now there is also a mode whereby, combining the letters, the colours, the attributions and their Synthesis, thou mayest build up a telesmatic Image of a Force. The Sigil shall then serve thee for the tracing of a Current which shall call into action a certain Elemental Force. And know thou that this is not to be done lightly for thine amusement or experiment, seeing that the Forces of Nature were not created to be thy plaything or toy. Unless thou doest thy practical magical works with solemnity, ceremony and reverence, thou shalt be like an infant playing with fire, and thou shalt bring destruction upon thyself.

Know, then, that if thou essay in the imagination to form an astral image from the Names, the first letter shall be the head of the Figure or Form, and the final letter shall be its feet. The other letters shall be, and represent in their order, its body and members.

AGIEL, for example, shall give thee an Angelic Form of the following nature and appearance:

Aleph, Air. The head winged, and of a golden colour, with long floating golden hair.

Gimel, Luna. Crowned with bluish silver crescent, and with a face like that of a grave and beautiful woman, with a bluish halo.

Yod, Virgo. The body of a maiden clothed in grass green robe.

Aleph, Air. Golden wings of a large size, partly covering the power part of the figure.

Lamed, Libra. Feet and limbs well-proportioned and, either in the hand of the figure or lying at its feet, the sword and scales of Justice in bright green.

Playing round the figure will be a greenish light, the colour of its synthesis. The Keys of the Tarot may help thee in the form.

<62> See well also that thou makest the Image as pure and beautiful as possible, for the more impure or common the figure, the more dangerous is it unto thee. Write upon the breast its Sigil, upon the girdle its Name, and place clouds below the feet. And when thou hast done this with due solemnity and rigid correctness of symbolism, shunning as thou wouldst shun death any suggestion of coarseness or vulgarity in an Angelic symbol, then hear what it shall say unto thee.

Seraphim will give thee an Angelic Figure like a Warrioress with Flame playing about her, and a countenance glorious like the Sun, and beneath her feet the stormy Sea and thunder clouds, and lightning about her, and a glow as of Flame. She has a triangular helmet or head-dress of Flame like the symbol of Fire.

Graphiel will give thee a Great Angel like a Female Warrior with a most glorious countenance, crowned with the Crescent and flashing with Light, and surrounded by Flame and Lightning and with Four Wings.

The termination EL *always* gives to Angelic Forms the Wings and Symbols of Justice. The ending YAH will make the Figures like enthroned Kings or Queens, and with flaming glory at their feet.

THE VIBRATORY MODE
OF
PRONOUNCING THE DIVINE NAMES

In vibrating the Divine Names, the Operator should first of all rise as high as possible towards the idea of the Divine White Brilliance in KETHER — keeping the mind raised to the plane of loftiest aspiration. Unless this is done, it is dangerous to vibrate only with the astral forces, because the vibration attracts a certain force to the operator, and the nature of the force attracted rests largely on the condition of mind in which the operator is.

The ordinary mode of vibrating is as follows: Take a deep and
<63> full inspiration and concentrate your consciousness in your heart, which answers to Tiphareth. (Having first, as already said, ascended to your Kether, you should endeavour to bring down the white Brilliance into your heart, prior to centering your consciousness there.)

Then formulate the letters of the Name required in your heart, in white, and feel them written there. Be sure to formulate the letters in brilliant white light, not merely in dull whiteness as the colour of the Apas Tattwa. Then, emitting the breath, slowly pronounce the Letters so that the sound vibrates within you, and imagine that the breath, while quitting the body, swells you so as to fill up space. Pronounce the Name as if you were vibrating it through the whole Universe, and as if it did not stop until it reached the further limits.

All practical occult work which is of any use, tires the operator or withdraws some magnetism, and therefore, if you wish to do anything that is at all important, you must be in perfect magnetic and nervous condition, or else you will do evil instead of good.

When you are using a Name and drawing a Sigil from the Rose, you must remember that the Sephirah to which the Rose and Cross are referred, is Tiphareth, whose position answers to the position of the heart, as if the Rose were therein. It is not always necessary to formulate before you in space the telesmatic angelic figure of the Name. As a general rule, pronounce the Name as many times as there are letters in it.

<64> FURTHER ON TELESMATIC FIGURES

As before taught the Names of all Angels and Angelic Forces terminate, with few exceptions, in either AL or YAH. The Divine Name AL belongs to Chesed and it represents a good, powerful, and mighty force, but of somewhat milder operation than the Name YAH. Since not only the Angels but even devils are said to draw their force and power directly from the prolific source of the divine energies, therefore frequently to the names of evil spirits, is AL added. The Name YAH is added to the name of an Angel or Spirit who exercises only a good and somewhat beneficent office.

This being understood, these two terminations being rather in the nature of incidental attributions than of essential distinction, they need not be taken too much notice of in the construction of a telesmatic image.

In building up such an image, you can either imagine it astrally before you, or paint the actual resemblance. Care should however be taken to pronounce the Divine Names belonging to the world under which the telesmatic image under course of construction would fall. Thus to ATZILUTH are allotted Deific Names. To BRIAH, Archangelic and so on. It is also useful to employ the Sephirotic Names which are comprised in the special world to which the Telesmatic Image is allotted.

It is well to note that the four Worlds themselves formulate the Law involved in the building up or expression of any material thing. The world of ATZILUTH is purely archetypal and primordial, and to it, as before said, Deific Names are applied. BRIAH is creative and originative, and to it certain Great Gods called Archangels are allotted. YETZIRAH is formative and Angelic Orders are allotted thereunto. ASSIAH which is the material world consists of the great Kingdoms of the Elementals, human beings, and
<65> in some cases of the Qlippoth — though these latter really occupy the planes below Assiah.

From these remarks it will be seen that a Telesmatic Image can hardly apply to Atziluth; that to Briah it can only do so in a restricted sense. Thus a Telesmatic Image belonging to that world would have to be represented with a kind of concealed head, possessing a form shadowy and barely indicated. Telesmatic Images, then, really belong to YETZIRAH. Therefore it would be impossible to employ the telesmatic image of a Divine Name in Atziluth, for it would not represent that in the world of Atziluth, but rather its correlation in Yetzirah. In Assiah you would get Elemental forms.

The sex of the figure depends upon the predominance of the masculine or the feminine in the whole of the Letters together, but a jumble of the sexes should be avoided in the same form. The image built up should be divided into as many parts as there are letters, commencing at the upper part and so on in order. In addition to this method of determining the sex of the Telesmatic Image of a Name, certain Names are inherently masculine, others feminine, and some epicene, irrespective of the mere testimony of the Letters.

SANDALPHON, for instance is thus analysed:

SAMEKH	Male	PEH	Female
NUN	Male	VAU	Male
DALETH	Female	NUN	Male
LAMED	Female		

Therefore masculine predominates, and if it were an ordinary Name you would make a masculine Form out of it. But as this Name is especially applied to the feminine Kerub, it is an exception to the rule; it is an Archangelic Name, belonging to the Briatic World and not merely an Angelic Name relating to Yetzirah. SANDALPHON is also called *Yetzer*, meaning "left," and its letters are: female, female and male, so that, in this case, it may be any of these.

<66> The Seven Letters composing the Name SANDALPHON are thus adapted to the Telesmatic Image.

SAMEKH	Head. Would represent a beautiful and active face rather thin than fat.
NUN	Neck, would be admirably full.

DALETH Shoulders of a beautiful woman.
LAMED Heart and chest, the latter perfectly proportioned.
PEH Hips strong and full.
VAU Legs massive.
NUN Feet sinewy and perhaps winged.

If it be desired to build up an elemental form out of this Name a very peculiar figure would result.

SAMEKH	Head fierce, but rather beautiful.	Blue
NUN	Neck with eagle's wings from behind.	Blue-green
DALETH	Shoulders feminine, rather beautiful.	Green-blue
LAMED	Chest of a woman.	Emerald
PEH	Strong and shaggy hips and thighs.	Red
VAU	Legs of a Bull.	Red-orange
NUN (final)	Feet of an Eagle.	Green-blue

This it will be seen, is almost a synthetical Kerubic Figure. This figure may be represented, as it were, with its feet on the Earth, and its head in the clouds. The colours in the scale of the King would synthesize as a delicate and sparkling green.

The uncovered parts of the body would be blue, the countenance belonging to Sagittarius would be almost that of a horse. The whole form would be like that of a goddess between ATHOR and NEITH holding a bow and arrows, that is if represented as an Egyptian symbol.

If again, we endeavour to translate this Name into symbols on a
<67> Tattwic Plane, we get the following:

SAMEKH comes under FIRE
NUN comes under WATER
DALETH comes under WATER OF EARTH
LAMED comes under AIR
PEH comes under FIRE
NUN comes under WATER.

These would be synthesized thus: A silver crescent on a red triangle placed over a yellow square. All three would be charged and enclosed within a large silver crescent.

Now, taking an example, the Telesmatic Image appertaining to the Letter ALEPH. This on the Briatic Plane, would be rather masculine than feminine and would be resumed by a spiritual figure hardly visible at all, the head-dress winged, the body cloud-veiled and wrapped in mist, as if clouds were rolling over and obscuring the outline, and scarcely permitting the legs and feet to be seen. It represents the Spirit of Ether. In the Yetziratic World, it would be like a Warrior with winged helmet, the face angelic but rather fierce, the body and arms mailed and bearing a child — the legs and feet with mailed buskins and wings attached to them.

In ASSIAH, this same letter ALEPH is terrific energy and represents, as it were, mad force (the shape of the Letter is almost that of a Swastika). On the human plane, it would represent a person who was a lunatic and at times given to frightful fits of mania. Translated to the elemental plane, it would represent a form whose body fluctuated between a man and an animal, and

indeed, the Assiatic form would be a most evil type with a force something like that compounded of that of a bird and that of a demon — an altogether horrible result. The Letter ALEPH represents spirituality in high things, but when translated to the plane contiguous to or below Assiah is usually
<68> something horrible and unbalanced, because it is so opposed to mat-
ter that the moment it is involved therein, there is no harmony between them.

Radiating forces of Divine Light, otherwise called Angelic Forms, have not gender in the grosser acceptation of the term, though they can be classed according to the masculine and feminine sides. As, for example, in the human figure, sex is not so strongly marked in the upper part, the head, as in the body, while yet the countenance can be distinctly classed as of a masculine or a feminine type. So, also, on quitting the material plane, sex becomes less marked, or rather appreciable in a different manner, though the distinction of masculine or feminine is retained. And herein is the great error of the Phallic Religions — that they have transferred the material and gross side of sex to Divine and Angelic planes, not understanding that it is the lower that is derived from the higher by correlation in material development, and not the higher from the lower. Gender, in the usual meaning of the term, belongs to the Elemental Spirits, Kerubic Forms, Fays, Planetary Spirits and Olympic Spirits — also to the Qlippoth in its most exaggerated and bestial aspects, and this is a ratio increasing in proportion to the depths of their descent. Also, in certain of the evil Elemental Spirits, it would be exaggerated and repulsive.

But, in the higher and angelic natures, gender is correlated by forms, either steady and firm, or rushing. Firmness like that of a rock or pillar is the nature of the feminine; restlessness and movement, that of the Masculine. Therefore, let this be clearly understood in ascribing gender to angelic forms and images. Our tradition classes all forces under the heads of vehement and rushing force, and firm and steady force. Therefore a figure representing the former would be a masculine and that representing the latter, a feminine form.

But for convenience in the formation of Telesmatic images of ordinary occult names and words, the letters are arranged in masculine and feminine classification. This classification is not intended to affirm that the let-
<69> ters have not in themselves both natures (seeing that in each letter as in each Sephirah is hidden the dual nature of masculine and feminine) but shows more their *tendency* as regards the distinction of force beforementioned.

Those, then, are rather masculine than feminine to which are allotted forces more rapid in action. And those, again, are rather feminine than masculine which represent a force more firm and steady whence all letters whose sound is prolonged as if moving forward are rather masculine than feminine. Certain others are epicene, yet incline rather to one nature than to another.

TELESMATIC ATTRIBUTIONS
OF THE
LETTERS OF THE HEBREW ALPHABET

ALEPH. Spiritual. Wings generally, epicene, rather male than female, rather thin type.

BETH. Active and slight. Male.

GIMEL. Grey, beautiful yet changeful. Feminine, rather full face and body.

DALETH. Very beautiful and attractive. Feminine. Rather full face and body.

HEH. Fierce, strong, rather fiery; feminine.

VAU. Steady and strong. Rather heavy and clumsy, masculine.

ZAYIN. Thin, intelligent, masculine.

CHETH. Full face, not much expression, feminine.

TETH. Rather strong and fiery. Feminine.

YOD. Very white and rather delicate. Feminine.

CAPH. Big and strong, masculine.

LAMED. Well-proportioned; feminine.

MEM. Reflective, dream-like; epicene, but female rather than male.

NUN. Square determined face, masculine, rather dark.

SAMEKH. Thin rather expressive face; masculine.

<70> AYIN. Rather mechanical, masculine.

PEH. Fierce, strong, resolute, feminine.

TZADDI. Thoughtful, intellectual, feminine.

QOPH. Rather full face, masculine.

RESH. Proud and dominant, masculine.

SHIN. Fierce, active, epicene, rather male than female.

TAU. Dark, grey, epicene; male rather than female.

(These genders are only given as a convenient guide.)

SUMMARY

In the vibration of Names concentrate first upon the highest aspirations and upon the whiteness of Kether. Astral vibrations and material alone are dangerous. Concentrate upon your Tiphareth, the centre about the heart, and draw down into it the White Rays from above. Formulate the letters in White Light in your heart. Inspire deeply, and then pronounce the Letters of the Name, vibrating each through your whole system — as if setting into vibration the Air before you, and as if that vibration spread out into space.

The Whiteness should be brilliant.

The Sigils are drawn from the lettering of the Rose upon the Cross, (See pg. 56, Vol. III) and these are in Tiphareth, which corresponds to the heart. Draw them as if the Rose were in your heart.

In vibrating any Name, pronounce it as many times as it has letters. This is the Invoking Whirl.

Example: The Vibration of Adonai Ha-Aretz.

Perform the banishing Ceremony of the Pentagram in the four quarters of your room, preceded by the Qabalistic Cross. Then in each quarter perform the Signs of the Adeptus Minor, saying IAO and LVX, making the symbol of the Rose-Cross as taught in the paper describing the Rose-Cross Ritual in Volume III. (Pages 46-50, Vol. III)

Pass to the centre of the Room, and face East. Then formulate before you in brilliant white flashings the Letters of the name in a Cross — i.e.
<71> both perpendicularly and horizontally as a picture before you extrinsically:

א
ד
א ד נ י נ ה א ר ץ
י
ה
א
ר
ץ

Formulate the perception of Kether above you, and draw down the White Light about this cross. Then, taking a deep inspiration, pronounce and vibrate the Letters of the Name. Flashing brilliant White Light should hover round them. This is the *Expanding Whirl* in the Aura.

Having gained the whiteness, then form the Telesmatic Image, not in your heart but before you, extending it and encouraging the ideal figure to expand and fill the Universe. Then immerse yourself in its rays — and absorbing, also be absorbed by, the brightness of that Light, until your Aura radiates with its brightness.

These, then, are two processes: The INVOKING WHIRL related to the Heart. The EXPANDING WHIRL related to the Aura.

ADNI makes the figure from head to waist; HA ARTZ from waist to feet. the whole Name is related to Malkuth, Matter, and Zelatorship.

ALEPH. Winged, white, brilliant, radiant Crown.

DALETH. Head and neck of woman, beautiful but firm, hair long, dark and waving.

NUN. Arms bare, strong, extended as a cross. In the right hand are ears of corn, and in the left a golden Cup. Large dark spreading wings.

YOD. Deep yellow-green robe covering a strong chest on
<72> which is a square lamen of gold with a scarlet Greek Cross — in the angles four smaller red crosses.

In addition a broad gold belt on which ADONAI HA ARETZ is written in Theban or Hebrew characters.

The feet are shown in flesh colour with golden sandals. Long yellow green drapery rayed with olive reaches to the feet. Beneath are black lurid clouds with patches of colour. Around the figure are lightning flashes, red. The crown radiates White Light. A Sword is girt at the side of the figure.

FURTHER CONCERNING THE FORMATION OF TELESMATIC IMAGES

(Note: This is a precis of the document numbered "M" — Lecture on the Lineal Forms of the Names of the Sephiroth.—I.R.)

Translate the letters of the Name of each Sephirah into the numerical equivalents which will be yielded by reference to the Qabalah of Nine Chambers. If these letters and numbers are again translated into their Yetziratic attributions and combined with the lineal figures represented by the numbers, an analysis of the name is obtained compounded of two scales of interpretation.

For instance, in the case of Kether, the letters are Kaph, Tau, Resh. Caph is referred in the Sepher Yetzirah to Jupiter, Tau to Saturn, and Resh to the Sun. Again, the lineal figure of Caph, which reduces to the number 2 by Aiq Bkr or the Qabalah of Nine Chambers, will be the Cross. Tau reduces to 4, whose lineal figure is the square. Resh reduces also to 2, symbolised likewise by the Cross. There are three letters in the name Kether — which itself, as a whole, may be symbolised by a triangle. If the above symbolic lineal figures are placed within the lineal figure of the whole Name, the Triangle, "a
species of Hieroglyphic form of each Sephirah will result. This may
<73> again be represented by a cognate Angelic form, as taught in the For-
mation of Sigils from the Rose." The Yetziratic attributions will yield the information as to what colours, symbols, etc. are to be used in formulating the Image.

The same principle applies to the remaining Sephirotic names.

<74>

TALISMANS AND SIGILS

There are innumerable methods of forming Sigils for use in connection with Talismans and their construction. One method, using the Rose of the Zelator Adeptus Minor, has previously been described. In the Order this was the method most often used. Herein, will be found methods of forming talismanic emblems and sigils from the Kameas of the Planets, or their Magical Squares, and also from the Geomantic points and symbols.

So far as the Geomantic symbols are concerned, the student will do well to become acquainted with the instruction on Geomancy in the section on Divination. (Pg. 112-136, Vol. IV) After having become fully acquainted with the names of the symbols, and their forms, as well as having obtained some experience of divination by that method, let him note that geomantic sigils or Talismanic emblems, as they are sometimes called, are formed from the Geomantic figures by drawing various lines from point to point. These characters are then attributed to their ruling planets and ideas. The simplest form of each will be found on page 75.

Innumerable more sigils, and a host of other designs may be formed from the fundamental Geomantic symbols. As many as ten or a dozen different emblems may be derived from two or three of the symbols. If the student uses a little ingenuity and imagination in this matter, he will discover quite a lot as to the nature and import of Sigils. The significance of the emblems may be divined, from one point of view, by employing them as "doors" through which to skry in the spirit-vision. More can be learned this way concerning the real implication of Sigils than almost by any other method.

<75>

Puer 	Amissio 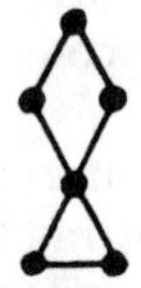	Albus 	Populus 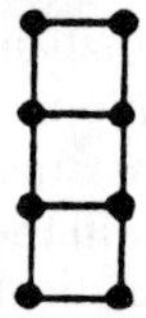
Via 	Fort. Maj. 	Fort. Min. 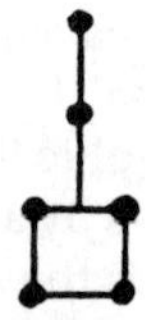	Puella 
Rubeus 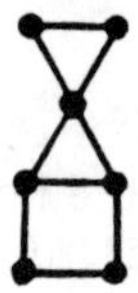	Acquisitio 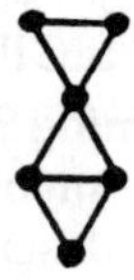	Carcer 	Trist. 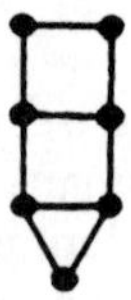
Laetitia 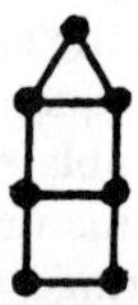	Conjunctio 	Caput Drac. 	Cauda Drac. 

The signatures and Seals of the Angels and Genii who rule over each of the symbols may be found in the full instruction on Geomancy. Those seals and sigils are highly important, and some place should be found for them on the Talisman.

The student should make a number of experiments drawing
<76> harmonious and balanced talismans, even when it is not his intention to use and consecrate them. After drawing a half a dozen rough sketches, he will almost as though by accident stumble upon the "knack" or drawing the "right" kind of talisman. In the *Key of King Solomon,* translated by McGregor Mathers, may be found samples of about forty different types of

talismans, attributed to the Planets. These should be consulted, for they will convey quite a little as to how symbols should be drawn. But they should not be followed or copied. Talismans should be personal things, made for personal ends, and based upon individual needs and conceptions.

<77> The following important characters—letters of the Angelic or Enochian Alphabet—are attributed to the Seven Rulers in the Twelve Signs and the Sixteen Figures in Geomancy.

Signifies Muriel and *Populus,* a figure of Chasmodai or Luna in Cancer increasing.

Signifies Muriel and *Via,* a figure of Chasmodai and Luna in Cancer decreasing.

Signifies Verchiel or *Fortuna Major,* a figure of Sorath or the Sun in Northern declination.

Signifies Verchiel or *Fortuna Minor,* a figure of Sorath or the Sun in Southern declination.

Signifies Hamaliel or *Conjunctio,* a figure of Taphthartharath or Mercury in Virgo.

Signifies Zuriel or *Puella,* a figure of Kedemel or Venus in Libra.

Signifies Barchiel or *Rubeus,* a figure of Bartzabel or Mars in Scorpio.

Signifies Advachiel or *Acquisitio,* a figure of Hismael or Jupiter in Sagittarius.

Signifies Hanael or *Carcer,* a figure of Zazel or Saturn in Capricorn.

Signifies Cambriel or *Tristitia,* a figure of Zazel or Saturn in Aquarius.

Signifies Amnitzel or *Laetitia,* a figure of Hismael or Jupiter in Pisces.

Signifies Zazel and Bartzabel in all their ideals, being *Cauda Draconis.*

Signifies Hismael and Kedemel in all their ideas, being a figure of *Caput Draconis.*

Signified Melchidael or *Puer,* a figure of Bartzabel or Mars in Aries.

Signifies Asmodel and *Amissio,* a figure of Kedemel or Venus in Taurus.

Signifies Ambriel or *Albus,* a figure of Taphthartharath or Mercury in Gemini.

A mode of using the Talismanic forms drawn from the Geomantic Figures is to take those yielded by the Figures under the
<78> Planet required and to place them at opposite ends of a wheel of eight radii as shown below. A versicle suitable to the matter may then be written within the double circle. Occasionally, a square of any convenient

number of compartments may be substituted for the wheel or one form may be used for the obverse and the other for the reverse of the Talisman.

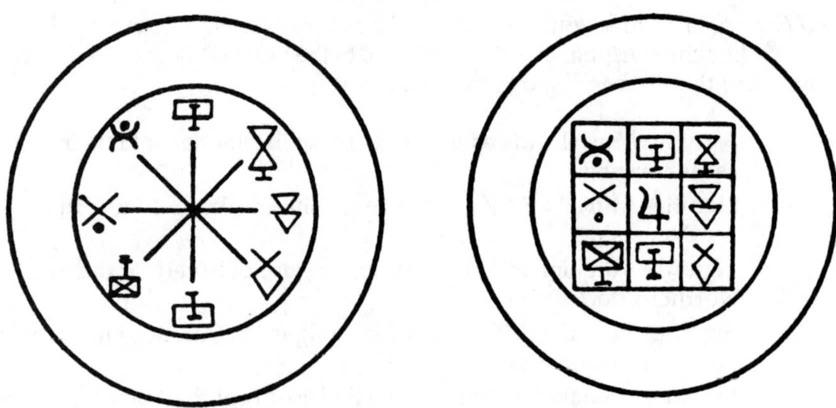

Sigils of the Planetary Squares

Another very important mode of forming Sigils anciently was through the medium of the Kameas of the Planets, or the Magical squares. Magical squares are arrangements of numbers so arranged as to yield the same number when added horizontally, vertically, or diagonally. Also the sum of the total of all the numbers in the square is a number of special significance to the planet to which that square is referred.

The method of forming Sigils from these is very simple. The knowledge of how this was done, however, had, during the time of my membership in the Order, completely faded from memory, and none of the members or the Chiefs of the Temple could give any information. Yet this was the principal method employed by the traditional authorities in obtaining Sigils. The method of using the Rose-Cross is an anachronism, and while in certain instances it is very useful or perhaps the most *convenient* mode, it has no root in antiquity. Not only had the knowledge of Sigils from the Kameas faded from the Order, but the Chiefs even eliminated the magical squares from the knowledge lectures. It was claimed that a number of mistakes had
<79> crept into the numbers on the squares. Had they known it, the
method and the correct form of the Squares were in certain books and manuscripts in the British Museum. None of them, however, made the least attempt to recover the true or accurate form of the Kameas.

The sole requisite to tracing Sigils of the Planetary names formed from the Kameas is *Aiq Beker,* or the Qabalah of Nine Chambers. (Incidentally, this too was eliminated from the knowledge lectures.) By this method, the letters of the Hebrew Alphabet are grouped together according to the similarity of their numbers. Thus in one Chamber, Gimel, Lamed and Shin are placed;

their numbers are similar—3, 30, and 300. The same rule applies to the others. The name of the method obtains from the letters placed in the first two chambers. In the first chamber are Aleph, Yod, and Qoph, whose numbers are 1, 10, and 100, while in the second chamber are Beth, Caph, Resh—2, 20, and 200—thus Aiq Bkr. The usual form is given below; while there is another method of using the same grouping of letters and numbers but placing them in chambers referred to the Sephiroth.

300	30	3	200	20	2	100	10	1
ש	ל	ג	ר	כ	ב	ק	י	א
600	60	6	500	50	5	400	40	4
ם	ס	ו	ך	נ	ה	ת	מ	ד
900	90	9	800	80	8	700	70	7
ץ	צ	ט	ף	פ	ח	ן	ע	ז

Now in order to find the Sigil of a Name by using the Kamea, it is necessary to reduce those letters and their numbers to tens or units by means of the above quoted scheme. For example, in the case, say, of *Zazel,* the Spirit of Saturn, the letters are Zayin 7, Aleph 1, Zayin 7, and Lamed 30. The only letter which requires reduction in this instance will be Lamed which reduces to 3. The next step is to trace a line on the square following the succes-
<80> sion of numbers. Thus, in the name of *Zazel,* the line will follow the numbers 7, 1, return to 7 again, and then to 3. A little circle should be placed on the first letter of the Sigil to show where the name begins.

The so-called Seal or Sigil of the Planet is a symmetrical design so arranged that its lines pass through every number on the square. The Seal thus becomes an epitome or synthesis of the Kamea.

Below are given the Kameas of the seven planets together with the traditional Seals of their Planets, Intelligences, and Spirits. The student will do well to attempt to work these out himself. I shall give one more example of a more difficult kind, in order that no misunderstanding may exist about the method of Sigil formation.

The name *Taphthartharath* is the Spirit of Mercury, and his Sigil would be traced upon the magical Square having 64 squares, 8 on each side. The attribution of Squares to planets follows the attribution of the Sephiroth on the Tree of Life; thus Mercury is referred to the eighth Sephirah HOD. Now *Taphthartharath* is composed of seven letters, Tau 400, Peh 80, Tau 400, Resh 200, Tau 400, Resh 200, and Tau 400. This will reduce by *Aiq Beker* to 40, 8, 40, 20, 40, 20, 40. A continuous line will be traced beginning with a circle in the square of 40, and moving to each of the numbers quoted. All the other Sigils follow this same rule.

There are also appended the Sigils and attributions of the Olympic Planetary Spirits. Nothing was known in the Order about them, and they too were extirpated from the papers. More information may be found in the *Hep tameron* of Pietro de Abano. These Sigils should be used for skrying as a means of acquiring knowledge as to their nature, using the appropriate planetary divine Names.

<81>

KAMEA OF SATURN

4	9	2
3	5	7
8	1	6

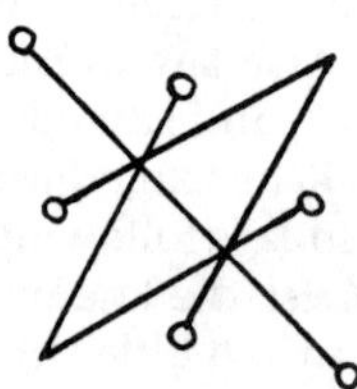

Seal of the Planet

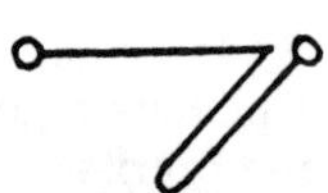

Spirit: ZAZEL

Intelligence: AGIEL

KAMEA OF JUPITER

4	14	15	1
9	7	6	12
5	11	10	8
16	2	3	13

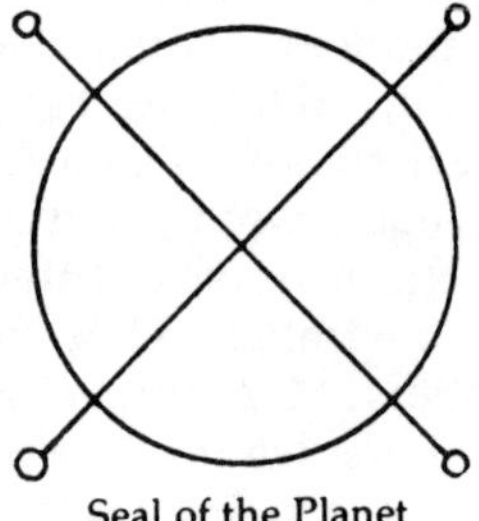

Seal of the Planet

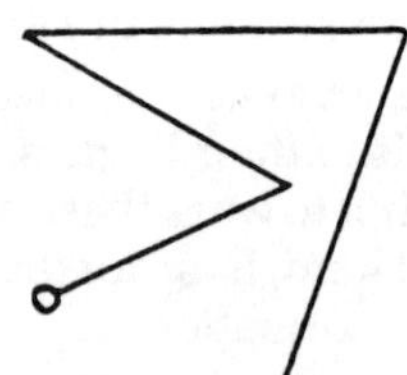

Spirit: HISMAEL

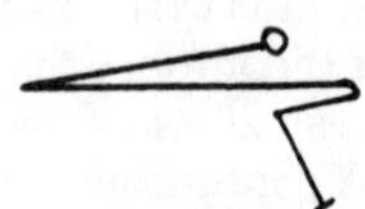

Intelligence: YOPHIEL

<82>

KAMEA OF MARS

11	24	7	20	3
4	12	25	8	16
17	5	13	21	9
10	18	1.	14	22
23	6	19	2	15

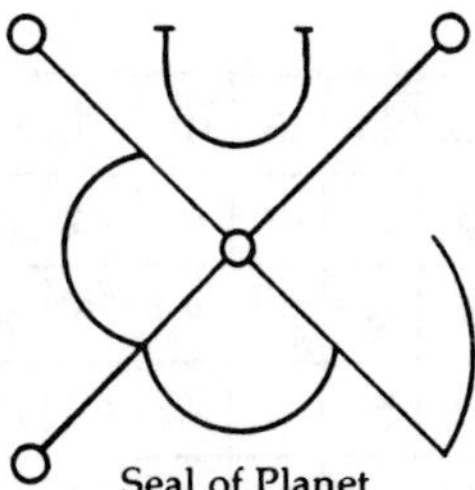
Seal of Planet

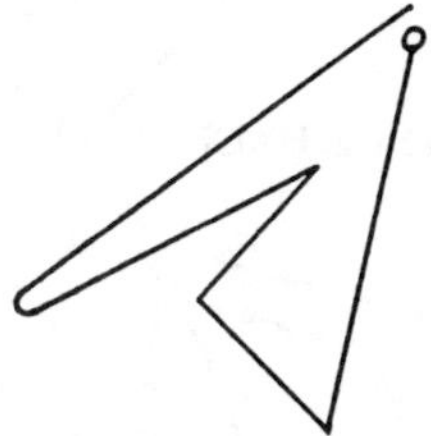
Intelligence: GRAPHIEL

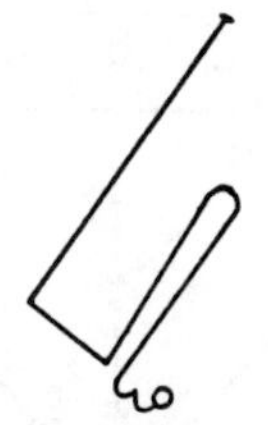
Spirit: BARTZABEL

<83>

KAMEA OF SOL

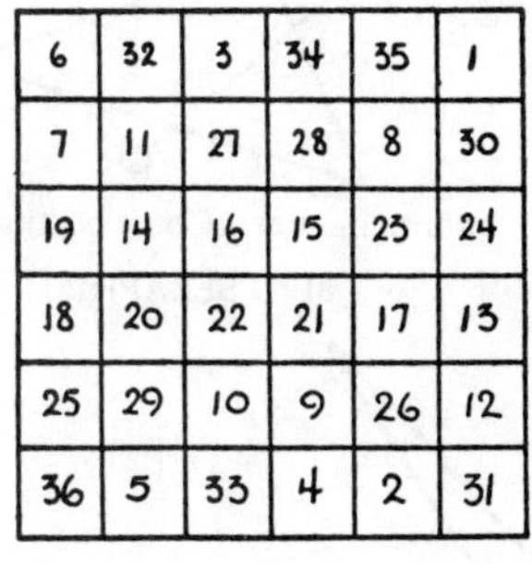

6	32	3	34	35	1
7	11	27	28	8	30
19	14	16	15	23	24
18	20	22	21	17	13
25	29	10	9	26	12
36	5	33	4	2	31

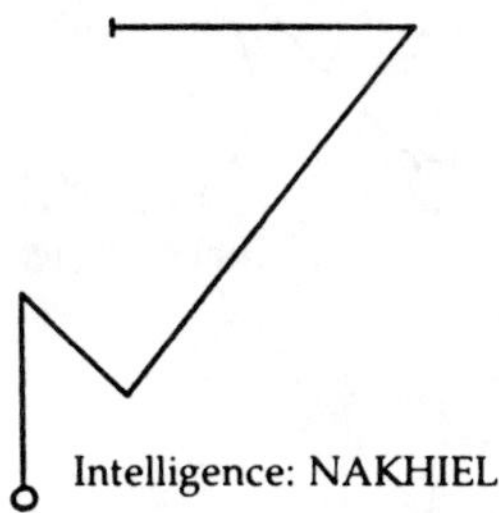
Intelligence: NAKHIEL

Seal of Planet

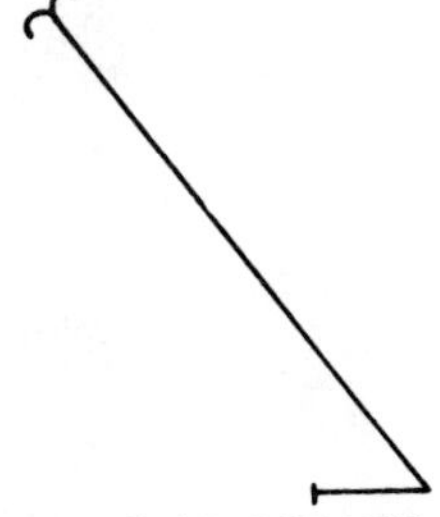
Spirit: SORATH

<84>

KAMEA OF VENUS

22	47	16	41	10	35	4
5	23	43	17	42	11	29
30	6	24	49	18	36	12
13	31	7	25	43	19	37
38	14	32	1	26	44	20
21	39	8	33	2	27	45
46	15	40	9	34	3	28

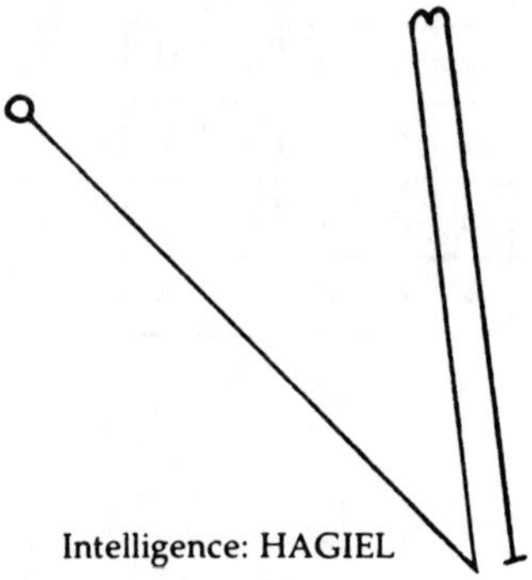

Intelligence: HAGIEL

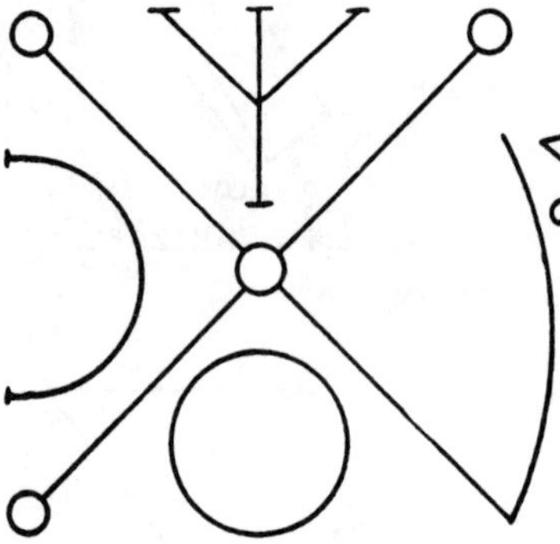

Seal of Planet

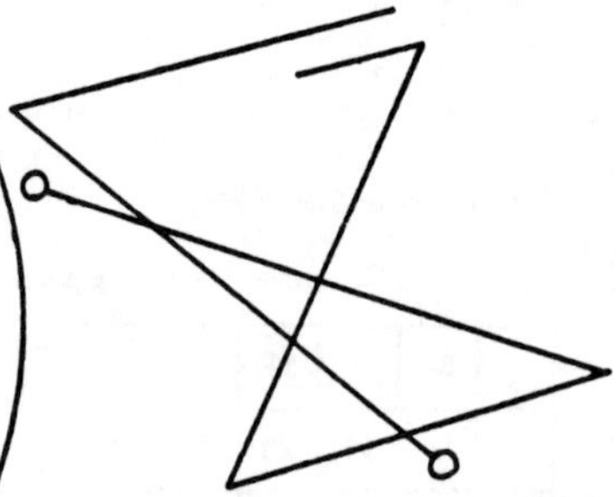

Intelligence: (Choir of Angels)
BENI SERAPHIM

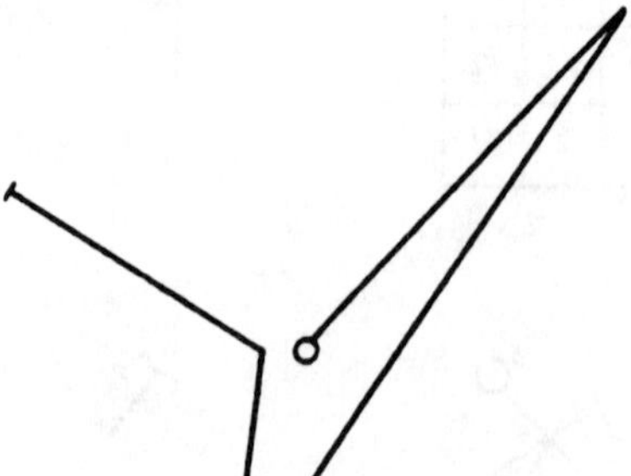

Spirit: KEDEMEL

<85>

KAMEA OF MERCURY

8	58	59	5	4	62	63	1
49	15	14	52	53	11	10	56
41	23	22	44	45	19	18	48
32	34	35	29	28	38	39	25
40	26	27	37	36	30	31	33
17	47	46	20	21	43	42	24
9	55	54	12	13	51	50	16
64	2	3	61	60	6	7	57

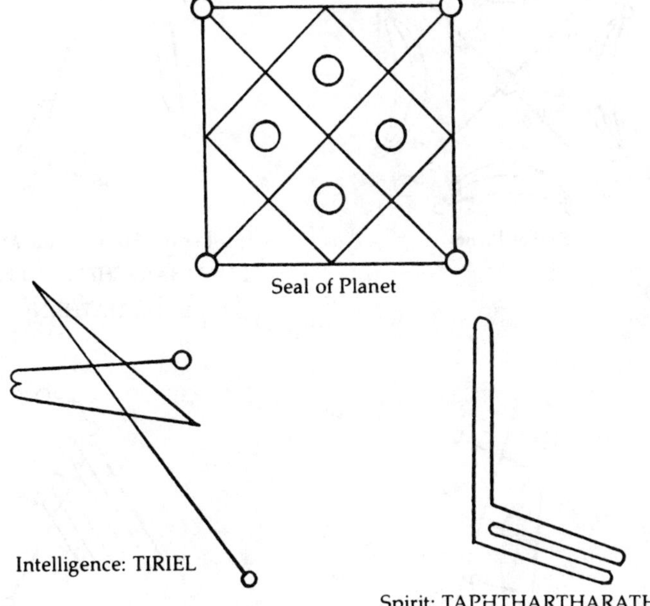

Seal of Planet

Intelligence: TIRIEL

Spirit: TAPHTHARTHARATH

<86>

KAMEA OF LUNA

37	78	29	70	21	62	13	54	5
6	38	79	30	71	22	63	14	46
47	7	39	80	31	72	23	55	15
16	48	8	40	81	32	64	24	56
57	17	49	9	41	73	33	65	25
26	58	18	50	1	42	74	34	66
67	27	59	10	51	2	43	75	35
36	68	19	60	11	52	3	44	76
77	28	69	20	61	12	53	4	45

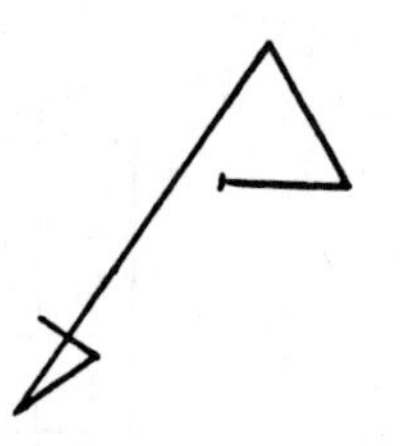

Spirit: CHASHMODAI

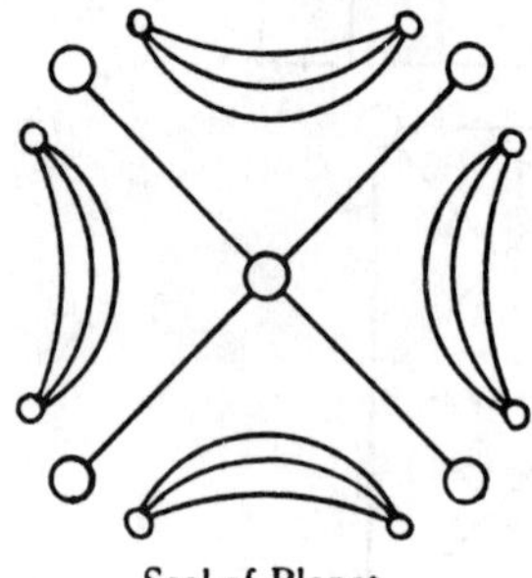

Seal of Planet

Spirit of the Spirits of the Moon: SHAD BARSCHEMOTH HA-SCHARTATHAN

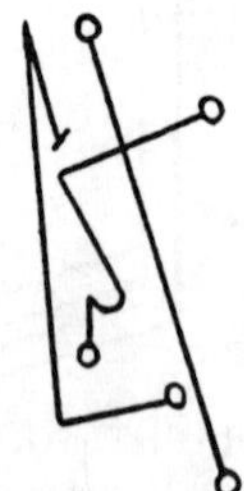

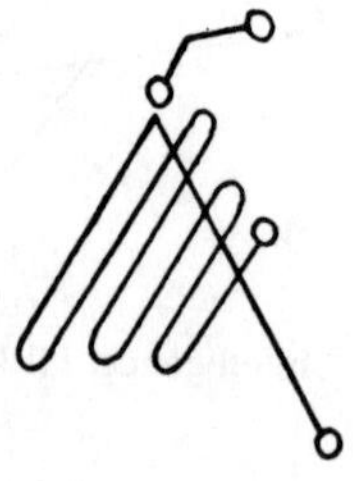

Intelligence of the Intelligences of the Moon: MALCAH BETARSHISIM VE-AD RUACHOTH HA-SCHECHALIM

<87> NAMES AND SIGILS OF OLYMPIC PLANETARY SPIRITS

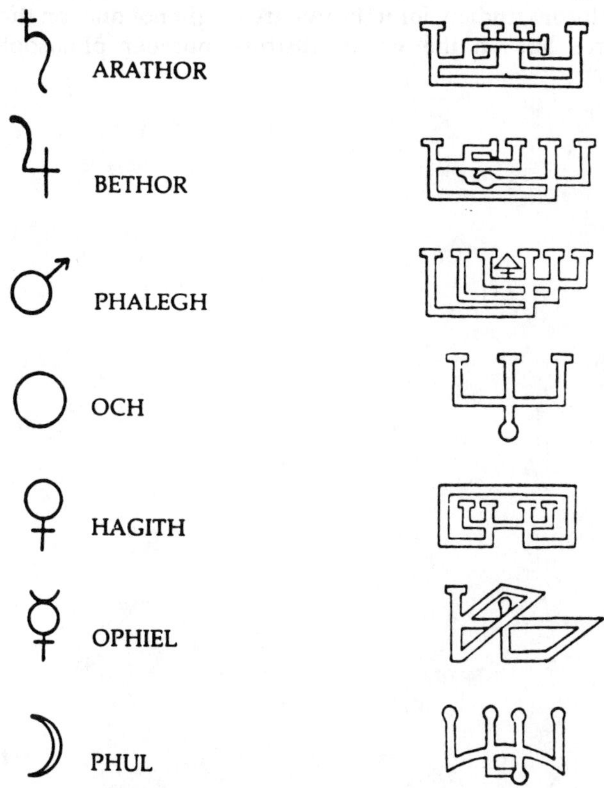

So far as concerns the foregoing Sigils, tradition has it that the Spirits are evil, the Intelligences good. The Seals and Names of the Intelligences should be used on all Talismans for a good effect. Those of the Spirits of the Planets serve for evil, and should therefore *not* be used in any operation of a beneficial kind. The tradition however implies usually by an evil force, such as the Spirits of the planets, a *blind force,* which contrary to popular notion
<88> can be used to good and beneficial ends when employed *under* the
presidency of their immediate superiors, the good Intelligences. Thus to make use of, when it is absolutely necessary to do so, the Sigils of the Spirits, the Seals and Names of the Intelligences should be inscribed on the same Talisman as well.

In addition to the Seals, Sigils and Emblems, it is customary to inscribe on Talismans and Pentacles the appropriate lineal figures. In the formation of a magical Talisman or Pentacle, consider first of all under what Planet, Sign, or Element the matter falls. The next step is to collect all the Names of the Sephirah to which it is attributed, as well as those of its Archangels, Angels, Intelligences, etc. Also the Seals, Sigils, Numbers, Lineal Figures, Geomantic characters, etc., thereto belonging. Then, with all this material before you, classify and arrange.

The following notes are an abridged version of "Polygons and Polygrams" a highly illuminating document circulated in the Outer Order. It should be closely studied, for it throws great light not only on the matter of lineal figures but on the whole abstruse number philosophy of the Qabalah.

<89> POLYGONS AND POLYGRAMS*

The Point within the Circle represents the operation of Kether in general, and *the Cross within the Circle* that of Chokmah, for therein are the roots of Wisdom. In using these lineal figures in the formation of Talismans under the Sephiroth, remember that:

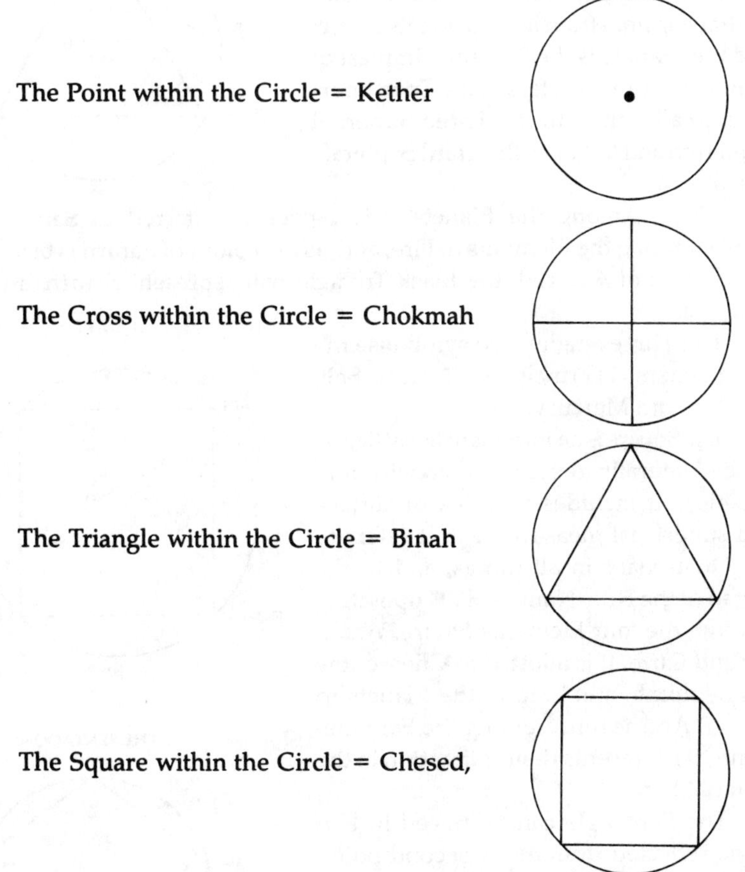

The Point within the Circle = Kether
The Cross within the Circle = Chokmah
The Triangle within the Circle = Binah
The Square within the Circle = Chesed,

*Much further discussion of this subject area may be found in *The New Magus* by Donald Tyson, Llewellyn, 1987.

and that the remaining Sephiroth should have the double, treble or quadruple forms of their lineal figures bound together in their Talismans. For example, in the Heptangle for Netzach, the Heptagon and the two forms of the Heptagram should be united in the same Talisman, the extremities of the angles coinciding.

The Endekangle is attributed to the Qlippoth, the Dodekangle to Zodiacal Forces in Malkuth. Kether hath the Primum Mobile, Chokmah the Sphere of the Zodiac in command, and Malkuth that of the elements.

And many other meanings are bound together in the lineal figures besides those which are given in this book. Two or more different lineal figures may be bound together in the same Talisman.

THE TRIANGLE

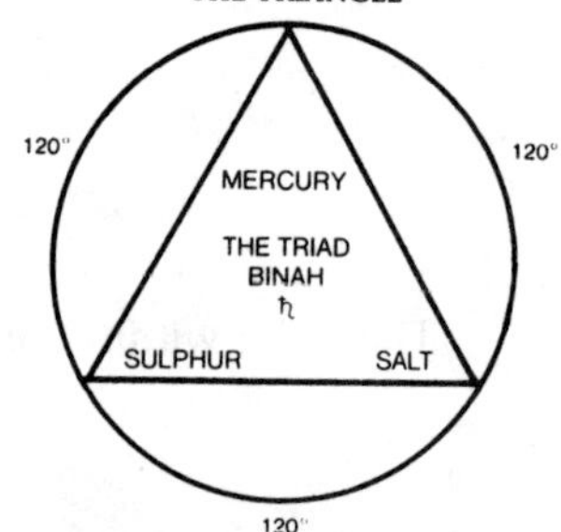

The Triangle is the only lineal figure into which all surfaces can be reduced, for every Polygon can be divided into triangles by drawing lines from its angles to its centre; and the triangle is the first and simplest of all lineal figures. It refers to the Triad operating in all things, to the Three Supernal Sephiroth and to Binah, the Third Sephirah, in particular.

Among the Planets it is especially referred to Saturn, and
<90> among the Elements to Fire, and, as the colour of Saturn is black, and
that of Fire red, the black Triangle will represent Saturn, and the red, Fire.

SQUARE

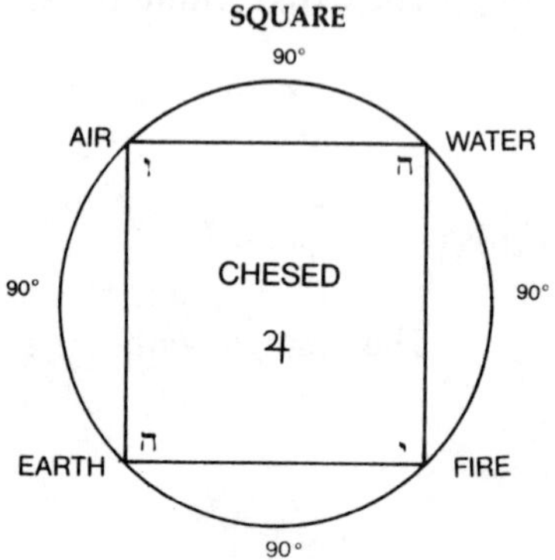

The Three Angles also symbolise the three alchemical Principles of Nature: Salt, Sulphur and Mercury.

The Square is an important lineal figure, which naturally represents stability and equation. It includes the idea of surface and superficial measurement. It refers to the Quaternary in all things, and to the Tetrad of the Holy Name YHVH operating through the four Elements of Fire, Water, Air and Earth. It is allotted to Chesed, the 4th Sephirah, and among the Planets to Jupiter. And as representing the Four elements, it represents their ultimation in the Material Form.

THE PENTAGON

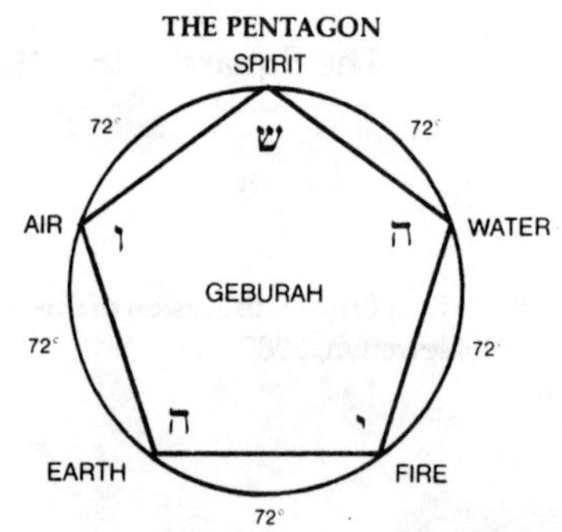

The Pentangle can be traced in two ways: reflected from every second point, when it is called the pentagon; and reflected from every third point when it is called the Pentagram. The Pentangle as a whole is referred to the Fifth Sephirah, Geburah.

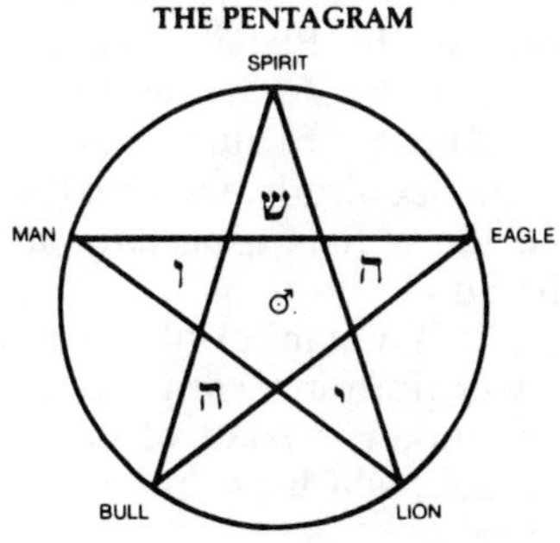

The Pentagon naturally represents the power of the Pentad, operating in Nature by the *dispersal* of the Spirit and the four Elements through it.

The Pentagram with a single point upwards is called the "Sign of the Microcosm," and is a good symbol, representing man with his arms and legs extended adoring his Creator, and especially the dominion of the Spirit over the four Elements, and consequently of reason over matter.

But with the single point downwards it is a very evil symbol. The Head of the Goat, or Demon's Head, representing the abasement of reason beneath the blind forces of matter, the elevation of anarchy above order, and of conflicting forces driven by chance above God.

It represents the concentrated force of the Spirit and the four Elements governed by the five letters of the Name of the Restorer of all things YHSHVH, and it is especially attributed to the Planet Mars. It also shows the Kerubim and the Wheel of the Spirit.

<91> It is a symbol of tremendous force, and of HEH, the letter of the Great Supernal Mother AIMA.

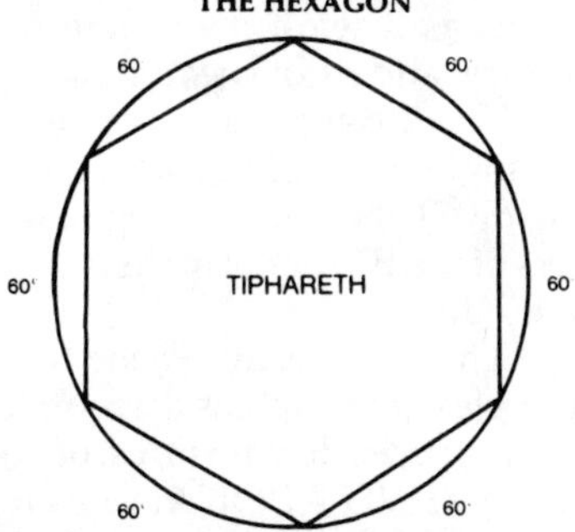

The Hexangle can be traced in two ways as a complete symbol: viz, reflected from every 2nd point, when it is called the Hexagon, and reflected from every 3rd point when it is called the Hexagram. The Hexangle as a whole is referred to the 6th Sephirah Tiphareth. The Hexangle naturally represents the powers of the Hexad operating in Nature, by the dispersal of the rays of the Planets, and of the Zodiac emanating from the Sun. The number of degrees of a great circle cut off between its angles is sixty, forming the astrological sextile aspect, powerful for good. It is not so consonant to the Sun nature as the Hexagram, and remember thou, that *the 'Gon signifieth dispersion, distribution, and radiation of a force; but the 'Gram concentration.* Hence use thou the 'Gon for spreading, and the 'Gram for concentration and sealing; and when there is need, thou canst compare, interpose and combine them; but the 'Gon *initiateth the whirl.*

The Hexagram with a single point uppermost is called the "Sign of the Macro-cosm," or greater world, because its six angles fitly represent the six days or periods of Creation evolved from the manifestation of the Triune; while its synthesis forms the seventh day, a period of rest, summed up in the hexagonal centre.

THE HEXAGRAM

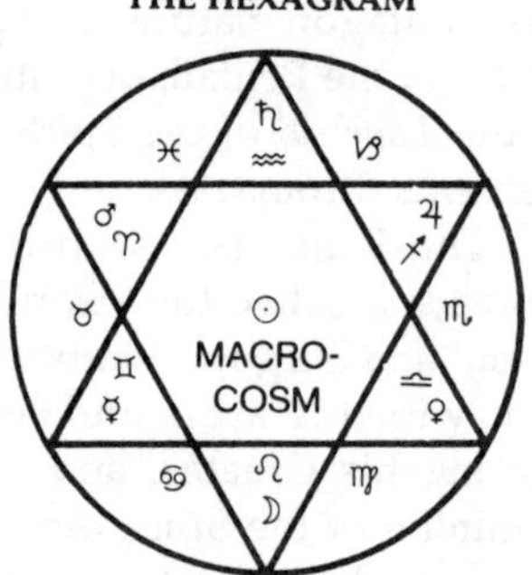

It represents especially the concentrated force of the Planets, acting through the Signs of the Zodiac, and thus sealing the Astral Image of Nature under the presidency of the Sephiroth; and also the 7 Palaces of the same. It is especially attributable to the Sun.

It is a symbol of great strength and power, forming with the Cross and the Pentagram, a triad of potent and good symbols, which are in harmony with each other.

The Heptangle (*Figure A)* as a whole is referred to the 7th Sephirah, Netzach.

The Heptagon naturally represents the dispersal of the powers
<92> of the seven planets through the week, and through the year. It alludes to the power of the Septenary acting through all things, as exemplified by the seven colours of the rainbow.

The Heptagram *(Figure B)* reflected from every 3rd point yieldeth 7 triangles at the apices thereof; fitly representing the Triad operating in each Planet, and the Planets themselves in the week and the year.

The Heptagram is the Star of Venus, and is especially applicable to her nature.

And as the Heptagram is the lineal figure of the Seven Planets, so is Venus as it were their Gate or entrance, the fitting symbol of the Isis of Nature, and of the seven lower Sephiroth of the Bride.

The Octangle as a whole is referred to the Eighth Sephirah, Hod. The Octangle naturally represents the power of the Ogdoad, and the Octagon *(Figure C)* showeth the Ogdoad operating in Nature by the dispersal of the rays of the Elements in their dual aspect under the presidency of the 8 letters of the name.

The Octagram *(Figure D)* reflected from every 3rd point yielded 8 triangles at the apices thereof; fitly representing the Triad operating in each element in its dual form, i.e. of Positive and Negative, under the powers of the Name YHVH ADONAI or as it is written bound together IAHDONHI.

This Octagram *(Figure E)* reflected from every fourth point is the Star of Mercury, and is especially applicable to his nature.

It is further a potent symbol, representing the binding together of the concentrated Positive and Negative Forces of the Elements under the Name of IAHDONHI.

And forget not that ADONAI is the key of YHVH.

The Enneangle *(Figure F)* as a whole is referred to the 9th Sephirah Yesod. It naturally representeth the power of the Ennead, and the Enneagon showeth the Ennead operating in Nature by the dispersal of the rays of the seven Planets and of the Head and Tail of the Dragon of the Moon.

<93> The Enneagram reflected from every 3rd point representeth the Triple Ternary operating both in the 7 Planets with the Caput and Cauda Craconis of the Moon, and with the Alchemical principles counterchanged and interwoven *(Figure G)*

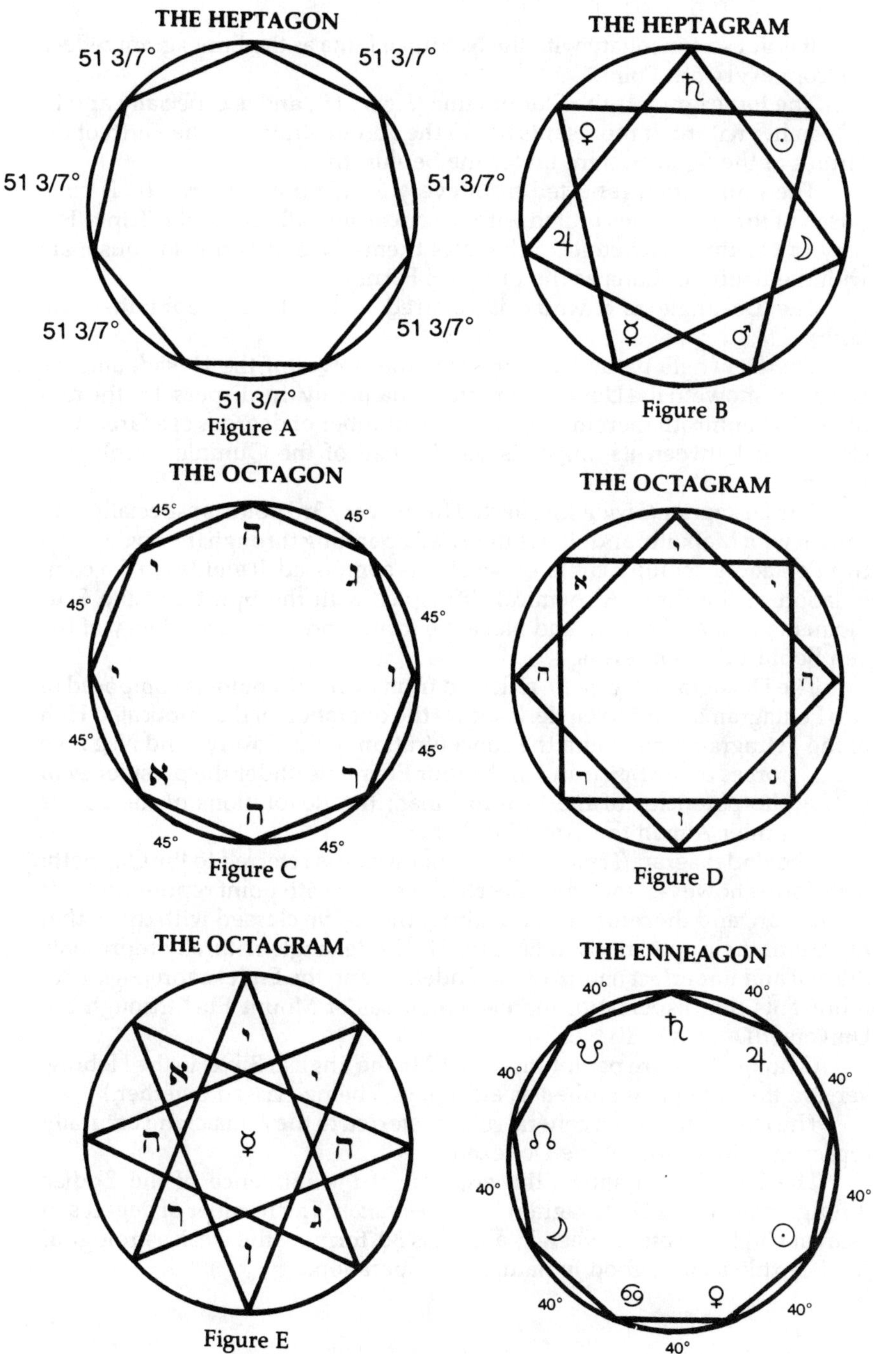

Figure A

Figure B

Figure C

Figure D

Figure E

Figure F

It is not so consonant with the Nature of Luna as the Enneagram reflected from every 5th Point.

The Enneagram is the Star of Luna *(Figure H)*, and is especially applicable to her nature. It represents her as the administratrix to the Earth of the virtues of the Solar System under the Sephiroth.

The Enneagram reflected from every fourth point *(Figure I)* is composed of three triangles united within a circle, and alludes to the Triple Ternary of the three alchemical principles themselves. It is not so consonant with the nature of Luna as the previous Form.

The Dekangle as a whole is referred to the Tenth Sephirah—Malkuth.

The Dekangle naturally represents the power of the Dekad, and the Dekagon showeth the Dekad operating in nature by the dispersal of the rays of the 10 Sephiroth therein *(Figure J)*. The number of degrees of a Great Circle cut off between its angles is 36, the half of the Quintile astrological aspect.

The Dekagram*(Figure K)*reflected from every 3rd point is especially consonant with Malkuth, and shows the Triad operating through the angle of the two Pentagons within a circle, of which it is composed. It alludes to the combination of the three Alchemical Principles with the Spirit and the Four Elements in their Positive and Negative form, under the presidency of the Ten Sephiroth themselves.

The Dekagram *(Figure L)* reflected from every 5th point is composed of two Pentagrams within a circle. It shows the operation of the duplicated Heh of the Tetragrammaton, and the concentration of the Positive and Negative
forces of the Spirit and of the four Elements under the presidency of
<94> the potencies of the Five in Binah; the Revolutions of the Forces
under Aimah the Great Mother.

The Endekagram*(Figure M)*as a general rule is referred to the Qlippoth: of its forms however, the one reflected from every 4th point represents their restriction, and therefore it is not altogether to be classed with those that represent their operations in Nature. The Endekangle naturally represents the evil and imperfect nature of the Endekad, and the Endekagon *(Figure N)* represents the dispersal of the eleven curses of Mount Ebal through the Universe (Deut. XXVII).

(Though they are paraphrased as 12 in the English Bible, in the Hebrew version they are paragraphed as eleven, two being classed together.)

The Dodekangle as a general rule is referred to the Zodiac, and naturally represents the power of the Dodekad.

The Dodekagon shows the *dispersal* of the influence of the Zodiac through nature, the Dodekagram its *concentration.* The number of degrees of a Great Circle cut off between its angles is 30, forming the weak astrological semi-Sextile aspect, good in nature and operation.

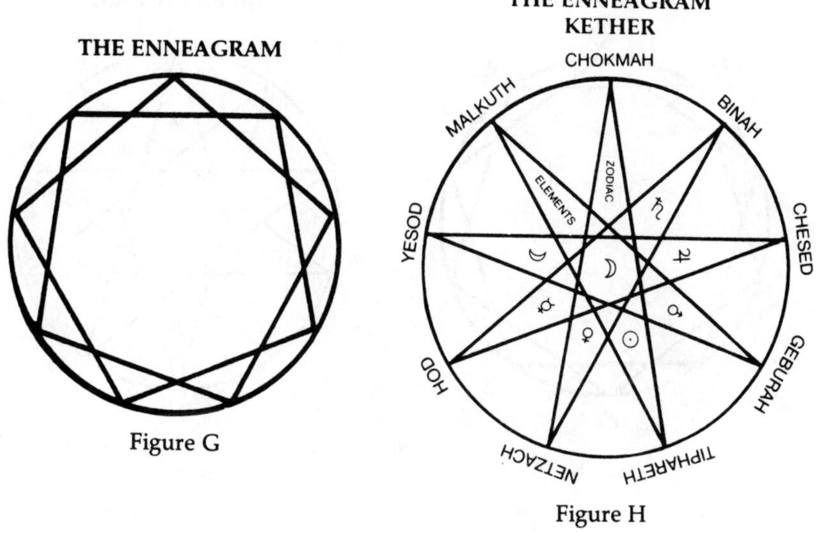

Figure G

Figure H

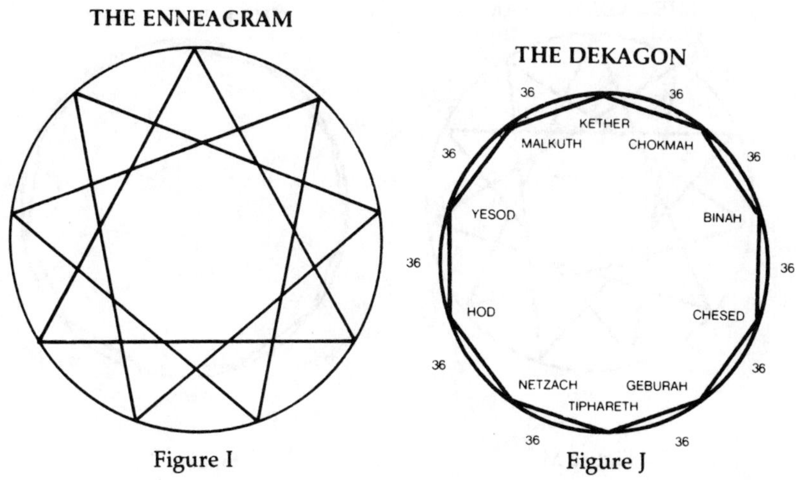

Figure I

Figure J

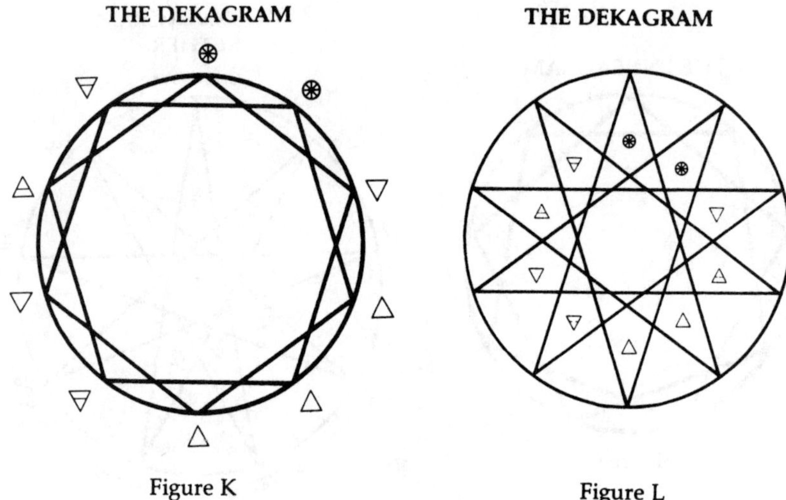

Figure K

Figure L

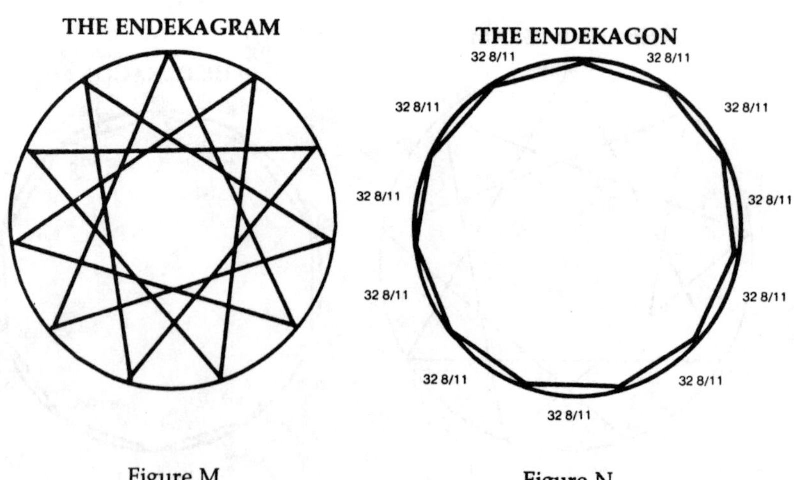

Figure M

Figure N

THE DODEKAGON

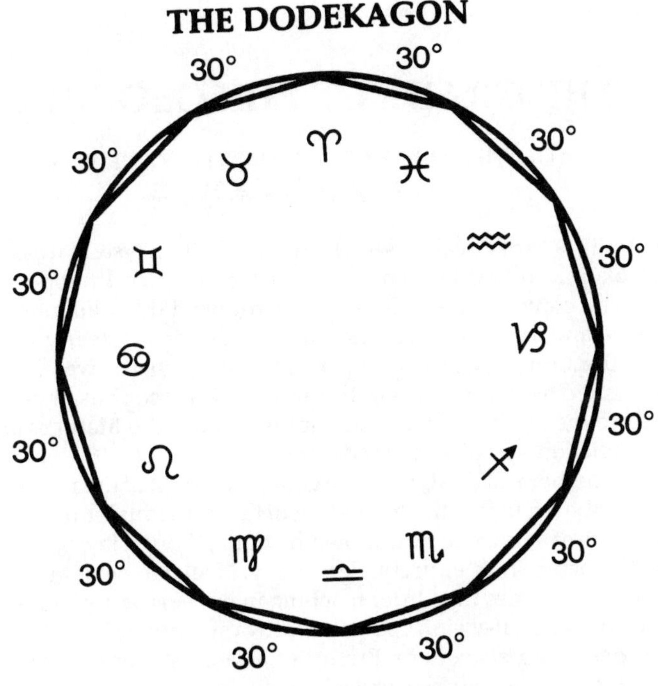

THE DODEKAGRAM

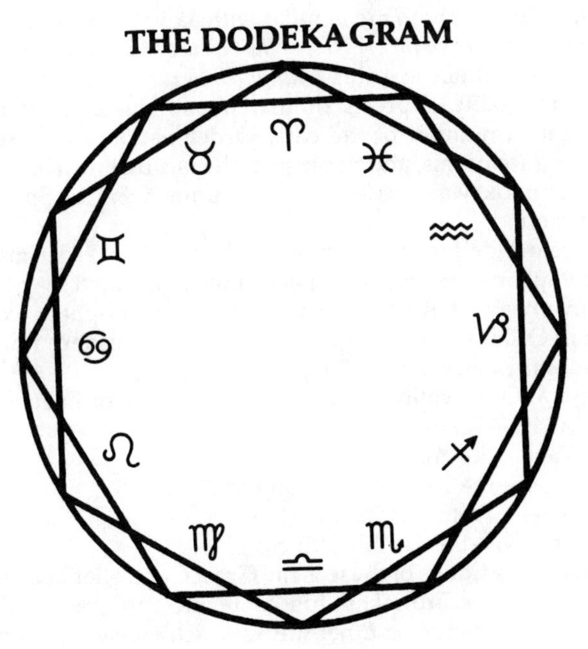

<95> THE GRADE OF PHILOSOPHUS

ADDITIONAL LECTURE ON THE TATTWAS OF THE EASTERN SCHOOL

(Note: This paper dealing with the Hindu Tattwa system was withdrawn from circulation in that branch of the Order of which I happened to be a member. The copy from which I have reproduced the following was properly labelled and dated August, 1894, and is therefore as clearly authoritative as any of the Order papers could be, indicating that it was formally and officially issued to all members of the grade of Philosophus. It has also been conveyed to me that the American temples, under the Mathers and Brodie Innes jurisdiction, circulated this document.

As to whether it accords with the general content of the rest of the Order system must be left to the discrimination of the individual student. That it has several points of value will be doubted by none, though few will care to subscribe to the paper in its entirety. Personally, I feel it to be definitely an alien system, which touches the Order teaching in but very few places. The mode of skrying in the Spirit-vision using the Tattwa symbols is sound enough, and has been described elsewhere. But other aspects suggest that the two systems are not likely to mix particularly well.

Some students who are familiar with early Theosophical literature will recall a book *Nature's Finer Forces, or the Science of Breath,* by Rama Prasad, and it may occur to them that this *Additional Lecture on the Tattwas of the Eastern School* is in reality a precis of that book. This has been observed by quite a number of the early Order people, and I understand that
<96> because of this, and because of the fact that no acknowledgement of
the book was made in the document, Fratre Sub Spe withdrew the document.

I have decided to issue it here, with the other Order manuscripts, as it may convey for some minds a special message which may be absent in the others. In any event, it seems to me that I have no right to extirpate from an account of Order teaching a paper which was considered highly important by some of the early Order Adepti.—I.R.)

General Observation. There are five Tattwas or Principles:

1. Akasa—Ether.
2. Vayu—the Aerial principle.
3. Tejas—the Principle of Light and Heat.
4. Apas—Watery Principle.
5. Prithivi—the Earthly Principle.

But the first Cause of these is the Great Controller of all things, the One Light, the Formless. From Him first came into appearance Ether; thence the Air, the motion producing Ether waves which causes Light and Heat, and so on in the above order.

The Yogi comes to know the principle of these five Tattwas, their Sukshma Sharira, but how? Further on you will see how. The Astrologer who has no knowledge of the Swara is as worthless as a man without a wife. It is the soul itself; it is the Swara, the Great Controller of all, who creates, preserves, and destroys, and causes whatsoever is in this World. Experience and Tradition both say no knowledge is more precious than this knowledge of the Swara. None else lays bare the workings of the machinery of this world, or the secret workings of this world.

By the power of Swara may be destroyed an enemy. Power, wealth, and pleasure, all these can be commanded by Swara. The beginner in our
<97> Science must be pure and calm in mind and in thought, virtuous in
actions, and having unmixed faith in his spiritual teacher. He must be strong in his determination, and grateful.

Swara in the Body. Ten manifestations of this Swara are in the body. But before the Neophyte is told this, he must gain a thorough knowledge of the nervous system. This is very important, and according to his knowledge of this science, the Neophyte gains success. To give a rough outline of the parts we have chiefly to deal with in our endeavour to explain the elementary treatise: There are ten principal nerves, this includes the tubes, etc. It is in the ten manifestations of Swara that the ten so-called Vayus move. We mean by this ten forces which perform ten different functions. The three most important nerves are the following, as the beginner has only to deal with these:

1. Ida—the left bronchus.
2. Pingala—the right bronchus.
3. Sushumna—in the middle.

The ten Vayus are:

1. Prana, in the breast.
2. Apana, about the excretory organs.
3. Samana, in the navel.
4. Undana, middle of the throat.
5. Vyana, pervading the whole body.
6. Kurmana, the eyes, helping them open.
7. Kirkala, in the stomach, producing hunger.
8. Nag, whence comes vomiting.
9. Devadatta, causes yawning.
10. Dhananjaya, that which doth not leave the body after death.

These ten vayus, or forces, have their play in the ten principal nerves, not one in each. They are the regulators of the body of man. If they go on working properly, a man remains perfectly healthy; if not, different kinds of diseases spring up.

<98> A Yogi keeps them always working, and consequently diseases
never come to him. The key to all these nerves lies in the working of the Prana Vayu, or vital principle drawing the air through the Ida, the Pingala, and the Sushumna. When the Air is drawn through the Ida it is felt coming out or going in through the left nostril. When through the Pingala, in the right nostril. When through the Sushumna it is felt through both nostrils simultaneously. The air is drawn or felt through either or both of the nostrils at certain appointed times. Whenever in any given time, the Breath goes in and

comes out of the wrong nostril it is a sure sign some sort of disease is coming on.

The Ida is sometimes called the Chandra Nadi, or the Moon Nerve. The Pingala, the Surya Nadi or Sun nerve. These are called, the former, the Chandra Swara and the latter the Surya Swara.

The reason is that when the breath is in the Ida it gives coolness to the body, and that when in the Pingala it gives heat to the body. The Ancient Magi used to say the place of the Moon in the human body was in Ida, and the Sun in Pingala.

The Course of the Breath. The Lunar month, it is well known, is divided into two parts, the fortnight of the Waxing and the fortnight of the Waning. On the first fortnight, or the Bright Fortnight, just at Sunrise of the first day the Breath must come into the left nostril and must be so for three days successively. At the beginning of the 4th day the Breath must come through the right nostril and must do so for the three succeeding days, when again the 7th day must begin with the Moon breath, and so on in the same order. Thus wc have said that such and such days begin with such and such a breath.

But how long is our breath to remain in one nostril? For five Gharis, or 2 hours. Thus when the first day of the Bright fortnight begins with the Moon Breath, after five Gharis, the Sun Breath must set in, and this again
<99> must change into the Moon Breath after the same interval of time. So on for every day.

Again, the first day of the dark fortnight must begin with the Sun Breath, and proceed in the same way, changing after five Gharis and the three succeeding days. It will be seen that all the days of the month have been divided into the Ida and the Pingala. In the Sushamna, the Swara flows only when it changes, either in its natural course or in certain other conditions to be afterwards mentioned. This is the course of Nature. But a Yogi commands Nature. He turns everything into his own way. Rules for this will be given in the proper place.

COURSE OF THE TATTWAS

For five Gharis, as we have above said, the breath flows through our nostrils. In these 5 Gharis, or two hour periods, the Tattwas have their course. In the first we have Akasa, in the second Vayu, in the third Tejas, in the fourth Apas, in the fifth Prithivi. Thus in one night and day, or 60 Gharis, we have twelve courses of these 5 Tattwas each remaining one Ghari and returning again in two hours. There are again further five subdivisions of each Tattwa in a Ghari. Thus, Akawa is subdivided into Akas-Akasa; Akas-Vayu; Akas-Tejas; Akas-Apas; Alas-Prithivi — and similarly with the other four.

How to know which of the Tattwas is at a certain time in course, not merely by a mathematical calculation but with the certainty of an eye witness, is of the greatest importance in the practical part of this science. We shall come to it further on.

The Ida. When the Breath is in Ida, that is in the left Nostril: then only is it well to perform the following actions. Stable works such as erecting a building, or the construction of a well or tank, going on a distant journey, entering a new house, collection of things, giving gifts, marriage, making jewels or

clothes, taking medicines and tonics, seeing a superior or master for
<100> any purpose of trade, amassing of wealth, sowing of seed in a field,
negotiations, commencement of trade, seeing of friends, works of charity and faith, going home, buying of animals, doing work for the benefit of others, placing money on security, singing, dancing, taking up abode in any village or city, drinking or making water at the time of sorrow, pain, fever, etc. All these acts should be done when the Swara is in Ida. It must however be kept in mind that the Tattwas Vayu and Tejas are to be excluded from these actions, likewise Akasa.

During the Tattwas Prithivi and Apas only, are these actions to be done. In a fever, the Yogi keeps his Chandra Swara going, and brings the Apas or Water Tattwa in course, so the fever is all over in a very short time. How mastery is gained over the Tattwas will come further on.

The Pingala. In the Surya Swara only, are the following actions to be done: Reading and teaching hard and difficult subjects of knowledge, sexual intercourse, shipping, hunting, mounting a hill or fort, riding a donkey, camel or horse, swimming over a powerful stream or river, writing, painting, buying and selling, fighting with swords or hands, seeing a king, bathing, eating, shaving, bleeding, sleeping — and such like. All these secure success and health, as the case may be, if done in the Surya Swara.

The Sushumna. When the Breath comes out of both nostrils at the same time, it is flowing in the Sushamna. Nothing ought to be done under these conditions, for everything turns out badly. The same is the case when the Breath is now in one and now in the other nostril. When this is the case, sit down and meditate upon or over the Sacred Hansa. This joining of the Breath is the only time for Sandha, meditation.

NOTE. Zanoni secured success in gaming for Cetosa and overcame the effects of the poisoned wine of the Prince di D__________ as follows. In the
first place, he changed his breath to the right nostril, and threw an
<101> envelope of the Akasa Tattwa over his antagonist, who consequent-
ly became all empty, the money in gaming flowing towards the Surya Swara. In the latter case he brought the Water, Apas, Tattwa into course, directed it with the full force of his trained will towards the poisoned wine, and consequently the burning heat of the poison was counteracted for a very long time, and before it could recover strength enough to act on the system, it was there no longer. S. R. M. D.

THE TATTWAS

To each of the five Tattwas a special colour has been assigned. Akasa—Black; dark; or no colour really. Vayu—Green (blue by some). Tejas—Red. Apas, White or really all colours. Prithivi—Yellow. It is by these colours that a practical man finds on the spur of the moment which Tattwa is at the time in course. Besides, these Tattwas have different shapes and tastes. These figures are seen by taking a bright mirror and letting the breath fall upon it, as it comes out of the Nose. The divided part takes one of the following forms according to the Tattwa then in course. Prithivi—a figure having four Angles. Apas, a half moon, or crescent. Tejas, triangular. Vayu, spherical. Akasa, oval like a human ear. To sum up their qualities:

Prithivi—moves always in the middle of the Paths of Air and Water. Apas—downwards, straight through the nose. Tejas—upwards. Vayu—obliquely towards the right or left arm, as the case may be. Akasa—transversely always.

Tattwa	Colour	Form	Taste	Distance of Breath below Nose	Natural Principle
Prithivi	Yellow	Having 4 Angles	Sweet	12 fingers	Bulky
Apas	White or all colours	Half Moon	Astringent	16 fingers	Cold
Vayu	Green or Blue	Sphere	Acid	8 fingers	Always in motion
Tejas	Red	Triangle	Hot tastes such as pepper, etc.	4 fingers	Hot
Akasa	Black, Dark, or no colour	Human ear, oval, egg	Bitter	Upwards	Universally pervading

<102> Tests of the Tattwas. For practice, let a man take five little bullets or counters coloured: red, yellow, green or blue, white or silver, and black. And place or carry them in his pocket. Now let him close his eyes and take one of them out of his pocket. The colour of the bullet will be that of the Tattwa then in course. Whilst still keeping the eyes closed, let him see if the colour of the bullet floats before them.

He must not suppose he will be correct all at once. By and by the confusion will disappear, and colours well-defined, staying for the proper length of time, will begin to come before him, and the colour of the bullet will be the same as that seen before his eyes. And then he will have gained the power of knowing which of the Tattwas is in course, and can at pleasure find them.

There is a particular method of concentrating the mind and practising with the eyes for this purpose, which will come with practise.

Let him ask any of his friends to imagine one of the five colours, say a flower. He will only have to shut his eyes to find the Tattwa then in course, and he can astonish his friends by naming the colour. Again, if a man sitting amongst his friends finds the Vayu Tattwa set in, let him be sure that those of his friends who are in perfect health and in a normal state both of body and mind, wish to go away. Let him ask them to say frankly, and they will answer "yes."

In what way other Tattwas affect both the body and mind of man will be stated in another place. Some higher secrets are purposely reserved for those who safely and honestly pass the elementary stage. When the man has reached the stage of finding at will any of the Tattwas, let him not imagine he has become perfect.

If he goes on practising, his inward sight becomes keener, and he will recognise the five subdivisions of the Tattwas. On and on let him go with his meditation, and innumerable shades of color will be recognised according to
the different proportions of the Tattwas. Whilst during these inter-
<103> vals he is trying to distinguish between the different shades of the
colours, his work will be for a time very tedious. We say tedious at

(Note: In making up the 2nd Edition, page 103 of Vol. III and page 103 of Vol. IV were accidentally transposed. The proper location is now restored in this 5th Edition.) C.L.W.

first, because when the thousand shades of colour become fixed and defined in his eyes by perseverance and practice, he will have before his eyes, an everchanging prospect of colour of the most beautiful shades, and this for a time will be sufficient food for his mind.

To avoid the tediousness, let him meditate upon his breath, as is laid down in the chapter of meditation of the Tattwas.

Action to be done during the different Tattwas. Actions of a sedate and stable nature are those of the sort enumerated under the Chandra Swara, to be done when Prithivi the Earthy Principle is in course. Those of a fleeting nature, which are to be done and gone through very soon are to be done during Apas. Actions of a hard nature, those in which a man has to make violent struggle to hold his own, are to be done during Tejas. If a Yogi wishes to kill a man he must try to do so with the Vayu Tattwa. In the Akasa, nothing should be done but meditation, as works begun during this always end badly. Works of the above nature only prosper in the Tattwas specified; and those whose actions prosper may see this by experiment.

MEDITATION AND MASTERY OVER THE TATTWAS

We have previously given summary rules for distinguishing the various colours of the different Tattwas which are of great use to the beginner. But now we are going to explain the final method of mastering the Tattwas, and of practising. This is a secret which was only imparted to the most promising Adepts of Yoga. But a short practise will fully show the important results to be gained by this practice.

The student will by degrees become able to look into futurity at will, and have all the visible world before his eyes, and he will be able to command Nature.

During the day, when the sky is clear, let him once or twice for
<104> about an hour or two withdraw his mind from all external things; and sitting on an easy chair, let him fix his eyes on any particular part of the blue sky, and go on looking at it without allowing them to twinkle. At first he will see the waves of the water, this is the watery vapour in the atmosphere which surrounds the whole world. Some days later, as the eyes become practised, he will see different sorts of buildings and so on in the air, and many other wonderful things as well. When the Neophyte reaches this stage of practise, he is sure of gaining success.

After this he will see different sorts of mixed colours of Tattwas in the sky, which will after a constant and resolute practice show themselves in their proper and respective colours.

To test the truth of this, the neophyte during the practice should occasionally close his eyes and compare the colour floating in the sky with that which he sees inwardly. When both are the same the operation is right. Other tests we have given before, and other wonders resulting from this will of themselves present themselves to the Yogi. This practice is to be done in the daytime.

For the night, let the student rise about two o'clock in the morning, when everything is calm, when there is no noise, and when the cold light of the stars breathe holiness, and a calm rapture enters into the soul of man. Let him wash his hands, feet, the crown of his head, and the nape of his neck with cold water. Let him put his shin bones on the ground, and let the back of his thighs touch his calves, and let him put his hands upon his knees, the fingers pointing towards the body. Let him now fix his eyes on the tip of his nose. To avoid this tediousness, he must always, especially during the meditation, meditate upon his breath, coming in and going out.

Besides the above, this has many other advantages given elsewhere. It may here be said that by constant practice of this meditation over his breath, the man is to develop two distinct syllables in his thought. It is evi-
<105> dent that when a man draws his breath in, a sound is produced
which is imitated in Han. When out, the sound Sa. By constant practice, the going in and coming out of the breath is so much connected with these sounds that without any effort the mind understands Han-sa with the production of these sounds. Thus we see that one full breath makes Han-Sa, this is the Name of the Ruler of the Universe, together with his powers. They are exerted in the working out of natural phenomena. At this stage of perfection, the Yogi should commence as follows:

Getting up at two or three in the morning, and washing himself in the aforementioned manner, let him know and fix his mind upon the Tattwa then in course. If the Tattwa in course be then Prithivi, let him think of it as something having 4 angles, a good yellow colour, sweet smelling, small in body, and taking away all diseases. Let him at the same time repeat the word LAM. It is very easy to imagine such a thing.

If it be the Apas Tattwa, let him imagine something of the shape and brightness of the half moon, putting down heat and thirst, and that he is immersed in the ocean of Water. Let him at that time repeat the word VAM.

If the Tattwa be Tejas, let him imagine it as something triangular in shape, shedding a red glare, consuming food and drink, burning away everything, and thus making itself unbearable. At the same time let him repeat RAM.

If the Tattwa be Vayu, let him imagine it as something of a spherical shape, of a colour Green, or Blue, like the green leaves of a tree after rain, and carrying him with a mighty power away from the ground and flying in space like the birds. And let him repeat the syllable PAM.

If the Tattwa be Akasa, let him imagine it as having no shape but giving forth a brilliant light, and let him repeat the syllable HAM.

<106> By diligent practice, these syllables uttered by the tongue of a
Yogi become inseparable from the Tattwas. When he repeats any of these, the special Tattwa appears with as much force as he may will, and thus it is that a Yogi can cause whatever he likes, lightning, rain, wind, and so forth.

CURE OF DISEASES

Every disease causes the breath to flow out of the wrong nostril, and the wrong Tattwa to come into course. When the breath therefore is restored to the proper nostril, and the proper Tattwa has been brought into course, let not anyone expect that all that is necessary has been done. If the disease be obstinate and the attack a very violent one, the man will have to persevere in battle a very long time before he conquers.

If a beginner cannot succeed very soon, let him aid the power of his breath by a suitable medicine, and Swara will be restored very soon.

It may be noticed that the Chandra Swara is generally the best for all diseases. Its flow is an indication of the soundness of Health. In cold, cough, and other diseases, this breath ought to flow.

Of the Tattwas as well as of the Swaras, no one causes pain if it goes on properly. In this state it ought not generally to be meddled with. But when anyone gains an undue predominance and causes diseases, it ought to be at once changed. Experience shows that the Apas and the Prithivi Tattwas are the only ones generally good for health, and indeed, the fact that during the course of the Apas Tattwa the breath is felt 16 fingers breadth below the nose, and during the Prithivi 12 fingers, argues at those times a more sound and powerful working of the functions of the body, than when it is felt only 8, or 4, or no finger-breadth below the nose.

Akasa therefore is the worst for health, and in a state of ill-health, a man will generally find in course, either Akasa, Vayu, or Tejas.

<107> Let him therefore, when need be, proceed in the following manner. After having changed his Breath, from the wrong nostril to the proper one, generally the Left, and pressing the opposite side by a cushion so that it may not change again, let the man sit on an easy chair and bind his left thigh a little above the knee joint with his handkerchief. In a short time, whose length, varies inversely as the deficiency of practice, and directly as the violence of the disease, he will perceive that the Tattwa changes to the one immediately below it and so on; and then the next, and so forth. If he be an acute observer of the conditions of his body, he will perceive that slowly his mind is becoming more and more easy. Let him tighten his bandage still more if need be. When at last he reaches the Prithivi Tattwa, he will find in the state of his health a great change for the better. Let him preserve in this state, or, still better, the Apas Tattwa for some time, and return to it occasionally for some days, even after the attacks of the disease have ceased. He will no doubt be cured.

FORECAST OF FUTURITY

Although a Yogi obtains the power of knowing everything that is, has been, or is to be, beyond the reach of the senses, yet generally he becomes indifferent to such knowledge, forgetting himself, as he does, in his eternal presence before the Light which breathes beauty into all we see in the world. We shall therefore represent him here revealing if not all his knowledge of Futurity, only on questions being put to him by others. But our Neophytes may as well put the questions themselves, and then answer them according to the laws here laid down.

When a man comes and says to the Yogi that he has a question to ask, let him:

(a) see which of the Tattwas is in course. If the Tattwa be Prithivi, the question is about some root, something belonging to the vegetable
<108> kingdom, or something in which the Earthy nature is predominant.

(b) If it be Apas, it is about some Life, birth, death, etc.

(c) If Tejas, the question is of metals, gain or loss, etc.

(d) If Akasa, he means to ask nothing.

(e) If Vayu, about some journey.

These are but elementary things. The practical Yogi who can distinguish between the mixture of the Tattwas can name the particular things.

Now let him see through which of his nostrils the Breath is flowing, which is the fortnight then in course of passing, which the days, and what direction of himself, the enquirer.

If the breath comes through the Left nostril, to secure complete success in the work which makes the subject of the question, and which will be of the sort specified under Ida, he must have the following coincidences: The fortnight must be bright, that is of the Waxing Moon; the day must be even, 2, 4, 6, and so on; the direction must be East or North. If these things coincide the man will get what he wants.

Again, if the Surya and Swara coincide with the dark fortnight, the day odd, the direction South and West, the same result may be predicted but not so thoroughly. The action will be of the sort prescribed under Pingala.

According as any of these do not coincide, will the success be more or less imperfect. It must be remembered that the breath at the time must not be flowing through the wrong nostril. This has many bad consequences; we only just touch the subject.

Of the Wrong Swara. If at the commencement of the day the wrong Swara arises, the Lunar for the Solar, and vice versa, a man may expect something wrong. If it happens the first day, there is sure to be some sort
<109> of mental uneasiness. If the second, some loss of wealth. If the third,
a journey will come. If the fourth, some dear object will be destroyed. If the fifth, loss of kingdom. If the sixth, loss of everything. If the seventh, illness and pain sure to come. If the eighth, death.

If the Sun breath flows in the morning and at noon and the Moon in the evening, a sad discomfiture will be the result, the reverse being a sign of Victory.

If a man, going to travel, raises his foot which coincides in direction with the empty nostril at the time being, he will not get what he desires from his travels.

BOOK EIGHT

DIVINATION

<112>

GEOMANCY

CHAPTER ONE

The figures of Geomancy consist of various groupings of odd and even points in 4 lines. Of these the greatest possible number of combinations is 16. Therefore these sixteen combinations of odd and even points arranged on four lines are the sixteen figures of Geomancy. These are again classed under the heads of the Elements, the Signs of the Zodiac, and the Planets ruling these. Two figures are attributed to each of the Seven Planets, while the remainder are attributed to Caput and Cauda Draconis—the Head and Tail of the Dragon, or the North and South Nodes of the Moon. Furthermore, to each Planet and Sign certain ruling Genii are attributed, as shown on pages 114 and 115.

CHAPTER TWO

Roughly speaking, the mode of obtaining the first four Geomantic figures, from which the remainder of the Divination is calculated, is by marking down at random on paper with a pencil held by a loosely tensed hand 16 lines of points or dashes, without counting the number placed in each line during the operation. And all the time thinking fixedly of the subject of the demand. When the 16 lines are completed, the number of points in each line should be added up, and if the result be odd a single point or cross should be
made in the first of the three compartments to the right of the paper.
<113> If even, two points or crosses. These 16 lines will then yield four
Geomantic figures. The results, odd and/or even, of lines 1 to 4 inclusive comprise the first figure. Of lines 5 to 8 the second figure; of lines 9 to 12 the third; of lines 13 to 16, the 4th figure, as shown in the diagram on page 114.

The symbol of a Pentagram either within or without a circumscribed circle should be made at the top of the paper on which the dashes are made. The paper itself should be perfectly clean and should have never been previously used for any other purpose. If a circle be used with the Pentagram, it should be drawn before the latter is described. The Pentagram should always be of the "invoking" type, as described in the Pentagram Ritual. Since the Pentagram concerns the element of Earth, it should therefore be drawn beginning at the top descending to the lower left hand point, carefully closing the angle at the finish. Within the centre of the Pentagram, the Sigil of the "Ruler" to which the matter of the question specially refers, should be placed.

If the question be of the Nature of Saturn, such as agriculture, sorrow, death, etc., the Sigil of Zazel should be placed in the Pentagram. If of Jupiter, concerning good fortune, feasting, church preferment, etc., the Sigil of Hismael. If of Mars, war, fighting, victory, etc., the Sigil of Bartzabel. If of the Sun, power, magistracy, success, etc., the Sigil of Sorath. If of Venus, love, music, pleasure, etc., the Sigil of Kedemel. If of Mercury, such as science, learning, knavery, etc., the Sigil of Taphthartharath, etc. If of travelling, fishing, etc., under Luna, then the Sigil of Chasmodai. In the diagram appended the Sigil of Hismael is employed.

During the marking down of the points, the attention should be fixed upon the Sigil within the Pentagram, and the mind should carefully consider the question proposed. (Note: A common practice is to repeat audibly the name of the Ruler as though to invoke him, followed by a short sentence concerning the matter of divination.—I. R.) The hand should not be moved from the paper until the 16 lines of points are complete. A pencil is therefore preferable to a pen for this purpose—unless, of course, a very reliable fountain pen is employed. It is practically more convenient to draw or rule four lines across the paper beforehand to mark off the space for such four lines composing a Geomantic Figure as shown on the previous page. The first four Geomantic figures formed directly from the 16 lines of points are called The Four Mothers. It is from them that the remaining figures necessary to complete the Geomantic scheme of direction are derived.

These should now be placed in a row from right to left, for the greater convenience of the necessary calculations — though much practice may render this unnecessary. The first figure will be attributed to the South, the Second to the East, the Third to the North, and the Fourth to the West.

<116>

EXAMPLE
PLAN OF GEOMANTIC DIVINATION

15 points	odd	*	
15 points	odd	*	Fortuna Minor
16 points	even	* *	
14 points	even	* *	
15 points	odd	*	
16 points	even	* *	Amissio
15 points	odd	*	
14 points	even	* *	
12 points	even	* *	
6 points	even	* *	Fortuna Major
9 points	odd	*	
7 points	odd	*	
10 points	even	* *	
11 points	odd	*	Rubeus
10 points	even	* *	
10 points	even	* *	

<114> GEOMANTIC

Sigil of Ruler	Name of Ruler	Planet which rules Answer		Sign of Zodiac	
	Bartzabel	Mars	♂	♈	Aries
	Kedemel	Venus	♀	♉	Taurus
	Taphthartharath	Mercury	☿	♊	Gemini
	Chasmodai	Luna	☽	♋	Cancer
	Sorath	Sol	☉	♌	Leo
	Taphthartharath	Mercury	☿	♍	Virgo
	Kedemel	Venus	♀	♎	Libra
	Bartzabel	Mars	♂	♏	Scorpio
	Hismael	Jupiter	♃	♐	Sagittarius
	Zazel	Saturn	♄	♑	Capricorn
	Zazel	Saturn	♄	♒	Aquarius
	Hismael	Jupiter	♃	♓	Pisces
	Zazel and Bartzabel	Saturn and Mars	♄ ♂	☋	Cauda Draconis
	Hismael and Kedemel	Venus and Jupiter	♀ ♃	☊	Caput Draconis
	Sorath	Sol	☉	♌	Leo
	Chasmodai	Luna	☽	♋	Cancer

(Note: When attributing the above Geomantic figures to the Tree of Life, the two Saturnian figures represent the Three Supernals. The Planetary

<115> ATTRIBUTIONS

Element	Geomantic Figure	Name and Meaning of Figure
Fire	* * * * *	PUER (a boy, yellow, beardless.)
Earth	* * * * * *	AMISSIO (loss, comprehended without.)
Air	* * * * * * *	ALBUS (white, fair.)
Water	* * * * * * * *	POPULUS (People, congregation.)
Fire	* * * * * *	FORTUNA MAJOR (Greater fortune and aid; safeguard, entering.)
Earth	* * * * * *	CONJUNCTO (Assembly, conjunction.)
Air	* * * * *	PUELLA (a girl, beautiful.)
Water	* * * * * * *	RUBEUS (red, reddish.)
Fire	* * * * * *	ACQUISITIO (obtaining, comprehended within.)
Earth	* * * * * *	CARCER (a Prison; bound.)
Air	* * * * * * *	TRISTITIA (sadness, dammed, cross.)
Water	* * * * * * *	LAETITIA (joy, laughing, healthy, bearded.)
Fire	* * * * *	CAUDA (the lower threshold, going out.) DRACONIS
Earth	* * * * *	CAPUT (Heart, upper threshold; entering.) DRACONIS
Fire	* * * * * *	FORTUNA MINOR (Lesser fortune; and aid; safeguard going out.)
Water	* * * *	VIA (way, journey.)

figures are placed on the appropriate Sephiroth, while the Caput and Cauda Draconis signify Malkuth.—I.R.)

The Four Mothers

4th West	3rd North	2nd East	1st South
* *	* *	*	*
*	* *	* *	*
* *	*	*	* *
* *	*	* *	* *
Rubeus	Fort. Major	Amissio	Fort. Minor.

From these Four Mothers, four resulting figures called the *Four Daughters* are now to be derived, thus: The uppermost points of the First Mother will be the uppermost points of the First Daughter. The corresponding, that is the first line of, points of the Second Mother will be the second points of the First Daughter. The same line of points of the Third Mother will constitute the third points of the First Daughter. The same point of the Fourth Mother will be the fourth point of the First Daughter. The same rule applies to all the figures. The second line of points of the four Mother figures will
<118> comprise the Second Daughter. The third line of points of the Four Mothers will comprise the Third Daughter, and the fourth line of points of the Four Mothers will comprise the Fourth Daughter.

	Mothers: 4th	3rd	2nd	1st
First Daughter, 4 uppermost points	* *	* *	*	*
Second Daughter, 4 next points	*	* *	* *	*
Third Daughter, 4 next points	* *	*	*	* *
Fourth Daughter, 4 last points	* *	*	* *	* *
	Rubeus	Fort Major	Amissio	Fort. Minor.

Applying the above rule throughout, the following will represent the Four Daughters:

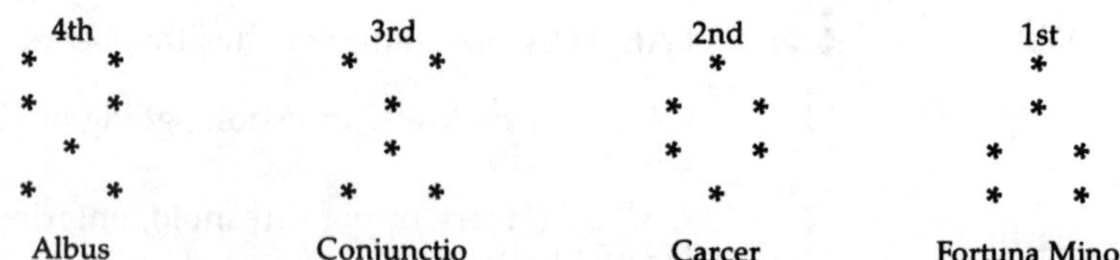

These, again for the convenience of the beginner, are now to be placed on the left hand of the Four Mothers in a single line from right to left.

Four Daughters: 8th	7th	6th	5th	Four Mothers: 4th	3rd	2nd	1st
* *	* *	*	*	* *	* *	*	*
* *	*	* *	*	*	* *	* *	*
*	*	* *	* *	* *	*	*	* *
* *	* *	*	* *	* *	*	* *	* *
Albus	Conjunctio	Carcer	Fort. Minor	Rubeus	Fort. Major	Amissio	Fort. Minor

From these eight figures, four others are now to be calculated
<119> which may be called the *Four Resultants,* or the Four Nephews. These will be the 9th, 10th, 11th, and 12th figures of the whole scheme. The Ninth figure is formed from the points of the first and second figures compared together. The Tenth from the 3rd and 4th figures; the 11th from the 5th and 6th figures, the 12th from the 7th and 8th figures. The rule is to compare or add together the points of the corresponding lines. If, for instance, the first line of the First Mother consists of one point, and the first line of the Second Mother also consists of one point, these two are added together, and since they are an even number two points are marked down for the first line of the Resultant. If the added points are odd, only one point is marked for the resulting figure. The Ninth figure is thus formed:

2nd Fig.	1st Fig.			
*	*	Uppermost	points added equals 2:-	* *
* *	*	Second	points added equals 3:-	*
*	* *	Third	points added equals 3:-	*
* *	* *	Lowest	points added equals 4:-	* *
				Conjunctio

The other Resultants are calculated in precisely the same way:

Four Daughters					Four Mothers		
8th	7th	6th	5th	4th	3rd	2nd	1st
* *	* *	*	*	* *	* *	*	*
* *	*	* *	*	*	* *	* *	*
*	*	* *	* *	* *	*	*	* *
* *	* *	*	* *	* *	*	* *	* *
Albus	Conjunctio	Carcer	Fort. Minor	Rubeus	Fort. Major	Amissio	Fort. Minor

In this way are yielded the four Resultants:

12th	11th	10th	9th
* *	* *	* *	* *
*	*	*	*
* *	* *	*	*
* *	*	*	* *
Rubeus	Acquisitio	Caput Drac.	Conjunctio

And thus the Twelve Principal Figures of the Geomantic
<120> scheme of Divination are completed. These again correspond to the 12 Astrological Houses of Heaven, with which they will later on be compared.

CHAPTER THREE

For the greater assistance of the Diviner in forming a judgment upon the general condition of the scheme of 12 figures thus far obtained, it is usual to deduce from them three other subsidiary figures. These three are of less importance than the twelve previous figures, and are not to be considered at all in the light of component figures of the scheme, but only as aids to the general judgment. These other figures are known as the Right Witness, Left

Witness, and the Judge.

The two witnesses are without significance in the divination, except as they are the roots from which the figure known as the Judge is derived. The Right Witness is formed from the 9th and 10th figures by comparing the points in the manner before shown in the formation of the Resultants. That is the corresponding lines of points in the two figures are compared together, and the addition, whether odd or even, comprises the points of the Witness. The Left Witness represents the combination in a similar manner of the 11th and 12th figures. The Judge again is formed in precisely the same way from the Two Witnesses, and is therefore a synthesis of the whole figure. If he be good, the figure is good and the judgment will be favourable; and vice versa. From the nature of the formation of the 15th figure, the Judge, it should always consist of an even number of points, and never of odd. That is, in adding together the four lines of points comprising the Judge, the result should be an even number. For if the Judge were a figure of odd points it would show that a mistake had been made somewhere in the calculations.

The Reconciler is a 16th figure sometimes used for adding the Judgment by combining the Judge with the Figure in the Particular House signifying
the thing demanded. Thus, in the preceding scheme, the Judge
<121> formed is Populus, and the Second Figure, being Amissio, their
combination also yields Amissio.

In order to discover where ⊕ The Part of Fortune will fall, add together all the points of the first twelve figures. Divide that number by twelve, and place the Part of Fortune with the figure answering to the remainder. If there is no remainder it will fall on the 12th figure. The Part of Fortune is a symbol of ready money, money in cash belonging to the Querent, and is of the greatest importance in all questions of money.

CHAPTER FOUR

The following is the signification of the 12 Houses of Heaven, in brief:

First House
(Ascendant) Life, health, querent, etc.
Second House Money, property, personal worth.
Third House Brothers, sisters, news, short journeys, etc.
Fourth House Father, landed property, inheritance.
The grave, the end of the matter.
Fifth House Children, pleasure, feasts, speculation.
Sixth House Servants, sickness, uncles and aunts, small animals.
Seventh House Love, marriage, husband or wife. Partnerships and associations, public enemies, law suits.
Eighth House Deaths, wills, legacies; pain, anxiety. Estate of deceased.
Ninth House Long journeys, voyages. Science, religion, art, visions, and divinations.
Tenth House Mother. Rank and honour, trade or profession, authority, employment, and worldly position generally.
Eleventh House Friends, hopes and wishes.
<122> Twelfth House Sorrows, fears, punishments, enemies in secret,
institutions, unseen dangers, restriction.

The Twelve Figures of the geomantic Scheme as previously calculated are to be thus attributed to a map of the Twelve Houses of Heaven, and are placed therein.

The First figure goes with the Tenth House.
The Second figure goes with the First House.
The Third figure goes with the Fourth House.
The Fourth figure goes with the Seventh House.
The Fifth figure goes with the Eleventh House.
The Sixth figure goes with the Second House.
The Seventh figure goes with the Fifth House.
The Eighth figure goes with the Eighth House.
The Ninth figure goes with the Twelfth House.
The Tenth figure goes with the Third House.
The Eleventh figure goes with the Sixth House.
The Twelfth figure goes with the Ninth House.

Thus the figures derived by the calculations provided in the example given previously would occupy a Geomantic map as follows:

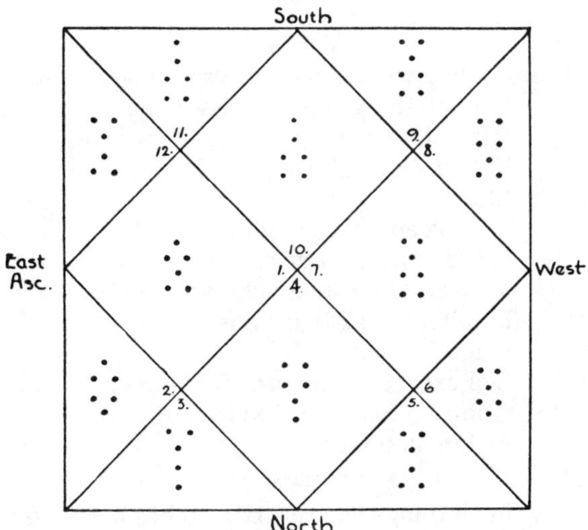

CHAPTER FIVE

(Note: I here omit a series of interpretations based upon the use of the Two Witnesses and the Judge. I have found these most untrustworthy, giving answers in utter contradiction to the proper divination worked out by the readings which follow. The mediaeval origin of the present omission is clearly shown, and is not a credit to the system. The following facts, which should be very carefully studied, will provide the fundamental authoritative data to enable the student to divine correctly.—I. R.).

Herein follows a set of general Tables of the Sixteen figures in the Twelve Houses for the better convenience of forming a general judgment of the Scheme. Under the head of each figure separately is given its general effect in whatever House of the Map of the Heavens it may be located.

Thus, by taking the House signifying the end or result of the
<124> matter, the Fourth House, etc., and by noting what figures fall therein, the student may find by these tables the general effect in that position.

ACQUISITIO

Generally good for profit and gain.

Ascendant	Happy, success in all things.
Second House	Very prosperous.
Third House	Favour and riches.
Fourth House	Good fortune and success.
Fifth House	Good success.
Sixth House	Good—especially if it agree with the 5th.
Seventh House	Reasonably good.
Eighth House	Rather good, but not very. The sick shall die.
Ninth House	Good in all demands.
Tenth House	Good in suits. Very prosperous.
Eleventh House	Good in all.
Twelfth House	Evil, pain and loss.

AMISSIO

Good for loss of substance and sometimes for love; but *very bad* for gain.

Ascendant	Ill in all things but for prisoners.
Second House	Very ill for money, but good for love.
Third House	Ill end—except for quarrels.
Fourth House	Ill in all.
Fifth House	Evil except for agriculture.
Sixth House	Rather evil for love.
Seventh House	Very good for love, otherwise evil.
Eighth House	Excellent in all questions.
Ninth House	Evil in all things.
Tenth House	Evil except for favour with women.
Eleventh House	Good for love, otherwise bad.
Twelfth House	Evil in all things.

<125> FORTUNA MAJOR

Good for gain in all things where a person has hopes to win.

Ascendant	Good save in secrecy.
Second House	Good except in sad things.
Third House	Good in all.
Fourth House	Good in all, but melancholy.
Fifth House	Very good in all things.
Sixth House	Very good except for debauchery.
Seventh House	Good in all.
Eighth House	Moderately good.
Ninth House	Very good.
Tenth House	Exceedingly good. Go to superiors.
Eleventh House	Very good.
Twelfth House	Good in all.

FORTUNA MINOR

Good in any matter in which a person wishes to proceed quickly.

Ascendant	Speed in victory and in love, but choleric.
Second House	Very good.
Third House	Good—but wrathful.
Fourth House	Haste; rather evil except for peace.
Fifth House	Good in all things.
Sixth House	Medium in all.
Seventh House	Evil except for war or love.
Eighth House	Evil generally.
Ninth House	Good, but choleric.
Tenth House	Good, except for peace.
Eleventh House	Good, especially for love.
Twelfth House	Good, except for alteration, or for suing another.

<126> LAETITIA

Good for joy, present or to come.

Ascendant	Good, except in war.
Second House	Sickly.
Third House	Ill.
Fourth House	Mainly good.
Fifth House	Excellently good.
Sixth House	Evil generally.
Seventh House	Indifferent.
Eighth House	Evil generally.
Ninth House	Very good.
Tenth House	Good, rather in war than in peace.
Eleventh House	Good in all.
Twelfth House	Evil generally.

TRISTITIA

Evil in almost all things.

Ascendant	Medium, but good for treasure and fortifying.
Second House	Medium, but good to fortify.
Third House	Evil in all.
Fourth House	Evil in all.
Fifth House	Very evil.
Sixth House	Evil, except for debauchery.
Seventh House	Evil for inheritance and magic only.
Eighth House	Evil, but in secrecy good.
Ninth House	Evil except for magic.
Tenth House	Evil except for fortifications.
Eleventh House	Evil in all.
Twelfth House	Evil. But good for magic and treasure.

<127> PUELLA

Good in all demands, especially in those relating to women.

Ascendant	Good except in war.

Second House	Very good.
Third House	Good.
Fourth House	Indifferent.
Fifth House	Very good, but notice the aspects.
Sixth House	Good, but especially so for debauchery.
Seventh House	Good except for war.
Eighth House	Good.
Ninth House	Good for music. Otherwise only medium.
Tenth House	Good for peace.
Eleventh House	Good, and love of ladies.
Twelfth House	Good in all.

PUER

Evil in most demands, except in those relating to War or Love.

Ascendant	Indifferent. Best in War.
Second House	Good, but with trouble.
Third House	Good fortune.
Fourth House	Evil, except in War and love.
Fifth House	Medium good.
Sixth House	Medium.
Seventh House	Evil, save in War.
Eighth House	Evil, save for love.
Ninth House	Evil except for War.
Tenth House	Rather evil. But good for love and War. Most other things medium.
Eleventh House	Medium; good favour.
Twelfth House	Very good in all.

<128>

RUBEUS

Evil in all that is good and Good in all that is evil.

Ascendant	Destroy the figure if it falls here! It makes the judgment worthless.
Second House	Evil in all demands.
Third House	Evil except to let blood.
Fourth House	Evil except in War and Fire.
Fifth House	Evil save for love, and sowing seed.
Sixth House	Evil except for blood-letting.
Seventh House	Evil except for war and fire.
Eighth House	Evil.
Ninth House	Very evil.
Tenth House	Dissolute. Love, fire.
Eleventh House	Evil, except to let blood.
Twelfth House	Evil in all things.

ALBUS

Good for profit and for entering into a place or undertaking.

Ascendant	Good for marriage. Mercurial. Peace.
Second House	Good in all.

Third House	Very good.
Fourth House	Very good except in War.
Fifth House	Good.
Sixth House	Good in all things.
Seventh House	Good except for War.
Eighth House	Good.
Ninth House	A messenger brings a letter.
Tenth House	Excellent in all.
Eleventh House	Very good.
Twelfth House	Marvellously good.

<129>

CONJUNCTIO

Good with good, or evil with evil. Recovery of things lost.

Ascendant	Good with good, evil with evil.
Second House	Commonly good.
Third House	Good fortune.
Fourth House	Good save for health; see the 8th.
Fifth House	Medium.
Sixth House	Good for immorality only.
Seventh House	Rather good.
Eighth House	Evil; death.
Ninth House	Medium good.
Tenth House	For love, good. For sickness, evil.
Eleventh House	Good in all.
Twelfth House	Medium. Bad for prisoners.

CARCER

Generally evil. Delay, binding, bar, restriction.

Ascendant	Evil except to fortify a place.
Second House	Good in Saturnine questions; else evil.
Third House	Evil.
Fourth House	Good only for melancholy.
Fifth House	Receive a letter within three days. Evil.
Sixth House	Very evil.
Seventh House	Evil.
Eighth House	Very evil.
Ninth House	Evil in all.
Tenth House	Evil save for hidden treasure.
Eleventh House	Much anxiety.
Twelfth House	Rather good.

<130>

CAPUT DRACONIS

Good with good; evil with evil. Gives a good issue for gain.

Ascendant	Good in all things.
Second House	Good.
Third House	Very good.
Fourth House	Good save in war.
Fifth House	Very good.

Sixth House	Good for immorality only.
Seventh House	Good especially for peace.
Eighth House	Good.
Ninth House	Very good.
Tenth House	Good in all.
Eleventh House	Good for the church and ecclesiastical gain.
Twelfth House	Not very good.

CAUDA DRACONIS

Good with evil, and evil with good. Good for loss, and for passing out of an affair.

Ascendant	Destroy figure if it falls here! Makes judgment worthless.
Second House	Very evil.
Third House	Evil in all.
Fourth House	Good especially for conclusion of the matter.
Fifth House	Very evil.
Sixth House	Rather good.
Seventh House	Evil, war, and fire.
Eighth House	No good, except for magic.
Ninth House	Good for science only. Bad for journeys. Robbery.
Tenth House	Evil save in works of fire.
Eleventh House	Evil save for favours.
Twelfth House	Rather good.

<131>

VIA

Injurious to the goodness of other figures generally, but good for journeys and voyages.

Ascendant	Evil except for prison.
Second House	Indifferent.
Third House	Very good in all.
Fourth House	Good in all save love.
Fifth House	Voyages good.
Sixth House	Evil.
Seventh House	Rather good, especially for voyages.
Eighth House	Evil.
Ninth House	Indifferent. Good for journeys.
Tenth House	Good.
Eleventh House	Very good.
Twelfth House	Excellent

POPULUS

Sometimes good and sometimes bad; good with good, and evil with evil.

Ascendant	Good for marriage.
Second House	Medium good.
Third House	Rather good than bad.
Fourth House	Good in all but love.

Fifth House Good in most things.
Sixth House Good.
Seventh House In war good; else medium.
Eighth House Evil.
Ninth House Look for letters.
Tenth House Good.
Eleventh House Good in all.
Twelfth House Very evil.

<132>

CHAPTER SIX

By essential dignity is meant the strength of a Figure when found in a particular House. A figure is, therefore, *strongest* when in what is called its house, *very strong* when in its exaltation, *strong* in its Triplicity, *very weak* in its Fall; *weakest* of all in its detriment. A figure is in its fall when in a House opposite to that of its exaltation, and in its *detriment* when opposite to its own house.

The Geomantic figures, being attributed to the Planets and Signs, are dignified according to the rules which obtain in Astrology.* That is to say they follow the dignities of their Ruling Planets, considering the Twelve Houses of the scheme as answering to the Twelve Signs. Thus, the Ascendant or First House answers to Aries, the Second House to Taurus, the Third House to Gemini, and so on to the Twelfth answering to Pisces. Therefore the figures of Mars will be strong in the First House, but weak in the Seventh House, and so forth.

Name of Sign	Ruler	Element	Exaltation	Fall	Detriment	Strong
Aries	Mars	Fire	Sun	Saturn	Venus	Jupiter
Taurus	Venus	Earth	Luna	—	Mars	Jupiter
Gemini	Mercury	Air	—	—	Jupiter	Saturn
Cancer	Luna	Water	Jupiter	Mars	Saturn	Mercury
Leo	Sol	Fire	—	—	Saturn	Mars
Virgo	Mercury	Earth	Mercury	Venus	Jupiter	Saturn
Libra	Venus	Air	Saturn	Sol	Mars	Jupiter
Scorpio	Mars	Water	—	Luna	Venus	Sun
Sagittarius	Jupiter	Fire	—	—	Mercury	Venus
Capricorn	Saturn	Earth	Mars	Jupiter	Luna	Mercury
Aquarius	Saturn	Air	—	—	Sol	—
Pisces	Jupiter	Water	Venus	Mercury	Mercury	—

Caput Draconis is strong in the dignities of Jupiter and Venus.

Cauda Draconis is strong in the dignities of Saturn and Mars.

<133>

CHAPTER SEVEN

Remember always that if the figures Rubeus or Cauda Draconis fall in the Ascendant, or first house, the figure is not fit for Judgment and should be destroyed without consideration. Another figure for the question should not be erected before at least two hours have elapsed.

*Note: These geomantic rules are those of *classical* astrology. Thus, the recently discovered planets Uranus, Neptune, Pluto, Chiron, etc. should not be substituted for the classical rulerships. C.L.W.

Your figure being thoroughly arranged as on a Map of the heavens, as previously shown, note first to what House the demand belongs. Then look for the Witnesses and the Judge, as to whether the latter is favourable or otherwise, and in what particular way. Put this down.

Note next what Figure falls in the House required. Also whether it passes or springs — that is whether it is also present in any other House or Houses. These should also be considered — as for example in a question of money stolen, if the figure in the second House be also found in the sixth House, it might also show that the thief was a servant in the house.

Then look in the Table of Figures in the Houses and see what the Figure signifies in the special House under consideration. Put this down also. Then look in the Table for the strength of the figures in that House. Following this, apply the astrological rule of aspects between houses, noting what houses are Sextile, Quintile, Square, Trine, etc. Write the "Good" one side and the "Evil" on the other, noting also whether these figures also are "strong" or "weak," "friendly" or "unfriendly" in nature to the figure in the House required. Note that in looking up the aspects between houses, there are two directions, Dexter and Sinister. The Dexter aspect is that which is *contrary* to the natural succession of the houses; the Sinister is the reverse. The Dexter aspect is more powerful than the Sinister.

Then add the meaning of the figure in the Fourth House, which will
signify the end of the matter. It may also assist you to form a Recon-
<134> ciler Figure from the Figure in the house required and the Judge,
noting what figure results and whether it harmonises with either or
both by nature. Now consider all you have written down, and according to the balance of "good" and "evil" therein form your final judgment.

Consider also in "money" matters where the Part of Fortune falls.

For example, let us consider the figure previously set up and form a judgment for "Loss of money in business" therefrom.

Populus is the Judge, and we find that in questions of money, which concern the Second House, it signifies "medium good." The question as a whole is of the nature of the Second House, where we find Carcer. We then discover that Carcer here is "evil," as showing obstacles and delays. The Part of Fortune is in the Ascendant with Amissio, signifying loss through Querent's own mistake, and loss through Querent's self.

The figure of Amissio springs into no other house, therefore this does not affect the question. "Carcer" in the Second House is neither "strong" nor "weak"; its strength for evil is medium. The figures Sextile and Trine of the Second are Conjunctio, Fortuna Major, Fortuna Minor, and Acquisitio, all "good" figures, helping the matter and "friendly" in nature. This signifies well intentioned help of friends. The figures square and opposition of the Second are Fortuna Minor, Conjunctio, Albus which are not hostile to Carcer, therefore showing "opposition not great."

The figure in the Fourth House is Fortuna Major which shows a good end but with anxiety. Let us now form a Reconciler between the figure of the Second House which is Carcer and the Judge, Populus, which produces Carcer again, a sympathetic figure, but denoting delay — delay, but helping the Querent's wishes. Now let us add all these together:

1. Medium
2. Evil and Obstacles, delay.

<135> 3. Loss through querent's self.

4. Strength for evil, medium only.
5. Well-intentioned aid of friends.
6. Not much opposition from enemies.
7. Ending—good; but with anxiety.
8. Delay, but helping Querent's wishes.

And we can formulate the final judgment:

That the Querent's loss in business has been principally owing to his own mismanagement. That he will have a long and hard struggle, but will meet with help from friends. That his obstacles will gradually give way, and that after much anxiety he will eventually recoup himself for his former losses.

SUMMARY OF STAGES IN GEOMANTIC DIVINATION:

1. If Rubeus or Cauda Draconis in Ascendant destroy the figure.
2. Note the House to which the question belongs. See if the figure there springs into another house.
3. Form the Judge from the two witnesses.
4. Part of Fortune—that is, if money question.
5. See if Figure in House concerned is "strong" or "weak." If it pass or spring into any other house.
6. See figures Sextile and Trine, Square and Opposition.
7. Friendly or unfriendly.
8. Note the figure in Fourth House, signifying the end or outcome.
9. Form a Reconciler from Judge and the figure in House to which the demand appertains.

(Note: Although this whole instruction of Geomancy describes the process as being performed throughout on paper with a pencil, yet it should be remembered that this description is but a makeshift for the convenience of the unenterprising student. By definition, Geomancy is a scheme of divination by and through the Element of Earth. Therefore the student with initiative, to whom this method appeals, should act accordingly.

<136> Let him therefore prepare a quantity of clean and dry black earth — or desert sand, if possible, but not that taken from the sea-shore — and also a tray or wooden box which is to be reserved solely for the purpose of housing this consecrated earth. The outside of the box might be decorated with sigils or symbolic paintings in harmony with the general idea, and painted in the four Malkuth colours. A small slender wand, pointed to make clean sharp holes or markings, should be prepared since it will be with this instrument that the sixteen lines of dots or holes in the earth will be made. When all has been duly prepared, the box of Earth should be given a ceremonial consecration; the student who has studied the general formulae of consecration will know exactly what should be done.

In actual divinatory practice, the invoking Earth Pentagram enclosing the Sigil, and the sixteen rows of dots from which the Four Mothers will be formed, can be quickly marked on the Earth with this special wand or pointer. Then, for convenience' sake, the student can transfer these four primary figures to paper, calculate the remaining eight figures to be placed on the Map and proceed to judgment exactly as this instruction lays down. Experience shows that the actual use of Earth as a means of forming the fundamental magical link between the initiated diviner and the Geomantic divinatory Genii is psychologically more valid and effectual than with paper and pencil, besides yielding far more satisfactory results.—I. R.).

<*137*>

BOOK "T" — THE TAROT

(Comprising Manuscripts N, O, P, Q, R, and an Unlettered T.A.M. Instruction.)

"What thou seest write in a Book, and send it unto the Seven Abodes that are in Assiah."

"And I saw in the right hand of Him that sat upon the Throne a book sealed with Seven Seals." "And I saw a strong Angel proclaiming with a loud voice, "Who is worthy to open the Books and to loose the seals thereof?' "

<138>

H. R. U.

THE GREAT ANGEL IS SET OVER THE OPERATION OF THE SECRET WISDOM

THE TITLES OF THE TAROT SYMBOLS

1. Ace of Wands is called the Root of the Powers of Fire.
2. Ace of Swords is called the Root of the Powers of Air.
3. Ace of Pentacles is called the Root of the powers of Earth.
4. Ace of Cups is called the Root of the Powers of Water.
5. The Knight of Wands is called the Lord of Flame and Lightning. The King of the Spirits of Fire.
6. The Queen of Wands is The Queen of the Thrones of Flames.
7. The King of Wands is The Prince of the Chariot of Fire.

<139>

8. The Knave of Wands is The Princess of the Shining Flame, and The Rose of the Palace of Fire.
9. The Knight of Cups is The Lord of the Waves and the Waters, and The King of the Hosts of the Sea.
10. The Queen of Cups is The Queen of the Thrones of the Waters.
11. The King of Cups is The Prince of the Chariot of the Waters.
12. The Knave of Cups is The Princess of the Waters and the Lotus.
13. The Knight of Swords is The Lord of the Wind and the Breezes, The Lord of the Spirits of the Air.
14. The Queen of Swords is The Queen of the Thrones of the Air.
15. The King of Swords is The Prince of the Chariots of the Wind.
16. The Knave of Swords is The Princess of the rushing Winds, The Lotus of the Palace of Air.
17. The Knight of Pentacles is The Lord of the Wide and Fertile land, King of the Spirits of the Earth.
18. The Queen of Pentacles is The Queen of the Thrones of Earth.
19. The King of Pentacles is The Prince of the Chariot of Earth.
20. The Knave of Pentacles is The Princess of the Echoing Hills, The Rose of the Palace of Earth.

No.	Card	Lord of	Decan	In
21	5 of Wands	Strife	♄	♌
22	6 of Wands	Victory	♃	♌
23	7 of Wands	Valour	♂	♌
24	8 of Pentacles	Prudence	☉	♍
25	9 of Pentacles	Material Gain	♀	♍
26	10 of Pentacles	Wealth	☿	♍
27	2 of Swords	Peace Restored	☽	♎
28	3 of Swords	Sorrow	♄	♎
29	4 of Swords	Rest from strife	♃	♎
30	5 of Cups	Loss in Pleasure	♂	♏
<140>				
31	6 of Cups	Pleasure	☉	♏
32	7 of Cups	Illusionary success	♀	♏
33	8 of Wands	Swiftness	☿	♐
34	9 of Wands	Great Strength	☽	♐
35	10 of Wands	Oppression	♄	♐
36	2 of Pentacles	Harmonious Change	♃	♑
37	3 of Pentacles	Material Works	♂	♑
38	4 of Pentacles	Earthy Power	☉	♑
39	5 of Swords	Defeat	☿	♒
40	6 of Swords	Earned Success	☿	♒
41	7 of Swords	Unstable Effort	☽	♒
42	8 of Cups	Abandoned Success	♄	♓
43	9 of Cups	Material Happiness	♃	♓
44	10 of Cups	Perpetual Success	♂	♓
45	2 of Wands	Dominion	♂	♈
46	3 of Wands	Established Strength	☉	♈
47	4 of Wands	Perfected Work	♀	♈
48	5 of Pentacles	Material Trouble	☿	♉
49	6 of Pentacles	Material Success	☽	♉
50	7 of Pentacles	Success Unfulfilled	♄	♉
51	8 of Swords	Shortened Force	♃	♊
52	9 of Swords	Despair and Cruelty	♂	♊
53	10 of Swords	Ruin	☉	♊
54	2 of Cups	Love	♀	♋
55	3 of Cups	Abundance	☿	♋
56	4 of Cups	Blended Pleasure	☽	♋

No.	Card	22 Keys of the Book	Letter	Attribution
57	Fool	The Spirit of Ether.	א	△
58	Magician	The Magus of Power.	ב	☿
59	High Priestess	The Priestess of the Silver Star.	ג	☽
60	Empress	Daughter of the Mighty Ones.	ד	♀
61	Emperor	Son of the Morning, chief among the Mighty.	ה	♈
62	Hierophant	Magus of the Eternal Gods.	ו	♉
63 <141>	Lovers	Children of the Voice Divine, The Oracles of the Mighty Gods.	ז	♊
64	Chariot	Child of the Power of the Waters, Lord of the Triumph of Light.	ח	♋
65	Fortitude	Daughter of the Flaming Sword, Leader of the Lion.	ט	♌
66	Hermit	The Magus of the Voice of Light, The Prophet of the Gods.	י	♍
67	Wheel of Fortune	The Lord of the Forces of Life.	כ	♃
68	Justice	Daughter of the Lord of Truth, The Holder of the Balances.	ל	♎
69	Hanged Man	The Spirit of the Mighty Waters.	מ	△
70	Death	The Child of the Great Transformers, Lord of the Gates of Death.	נ	♏
71	Temperance	Daughter of the Reconcilers, The Bringer Forth of Life.	ס	♐
72	Devil	Lord of the Gates of Matter, Child of the Forces of Time.	ע	♑
73	Blasted Tower	Lord of the Hosts of the Mighty.	פ	♂
74	The Star	Daughter of the Firmament, Dweller between the Waters.	צ	♒
75	The Moon	Ruler of Flux and Reflux, Child of the Sons of the Mighty.	ק	♓
76	The Sun	Lord of the Fire of the World.	ר	☉
77	Judgment	The Spirit of the Primal Fire.	ש	△
78	Universe	The Great One of the Night of Time.	ת	♄

<142> THE DESCRIPTIONS OF THE 78 TAROT SYMBOLS TOGETHER WITH THEIR MEANINGS

OF THE ACES

First in order and appearance are the four Aces, representing the force of the Spirit acting in, and binding together the four scales of each element and answering to the Dominion of the Letters of the Name in the *Kether* of each. They represent the Radical or Root-Force. The Four Aces are said to be placed on the North Pole of the Universe, wherein they revolve, governing its revolution, and ruling as the connecting link between Yetsirah and the Material Plane of Universe.

I. The Root of the Powers of Fire.

ACE OF WANDS

A white radiating angelic Hand issuing from Clouds and grasping a heavy Club which has three branches in the colours and with the Sigils of the

Scales. The right and left hand branches end respectively in three Flames and the centre one in four Flames, thus yielding Ten the number of the Sephiroth. Two and Twenty leaping Flames or Yods surround it, answering to the Paths of these. Three fall below the right branch for Aleph, Mem and Shin. Seven above the central branch for the double letters. And between it and that on the right, twelve — six above and six below — about the left hand Branch. The whole is a great and Flaming Torch. It symbolises Force, Strength, Rush, Vigour, Energy, and it governs according to its nature various works and questions. It implies natural as opposed to Invoked Force.

<143> *II. The Root of the Powers of the Waters.*

ACE OF CUPS OR CHALICES

A Radiant white Angelic Hand issuing from clouds and supporting on the palm thereof a Cup, resembling that of the Stolistes. From it rises a fountain of clear and glistening Water; and spray falling on all sides into clear calm water below, in which grow Lotus and water lilies. The great letter Heh of the Supernal Mother is traced in the spray of the Fountain. It symbolises Fertility, Productiveness, Beauty, Pleasure, Happiness, etc.

III. The Root of the Powers of Air.

ACE OF SWORDS

A white radiating Angelic Hand, issuing from clouds, and grasping the hilt of a Sword, which supports a white radiant celestial Crown from which depend, on the right, the olive branch of Peace, and on the left, the palm branch of Suffering. Six Vaus fall from its point.

It symbolises *invoked* as contrasted with natural Force; for it is the Invocation of the Sword. Raised upward, it invokes the Divine Crown of Spiritual Brightness. But reversed it is the invocation of demoniac force, and becomes a fearfully evil symbol. It represents therefore very great power for good or evil, but *invoked.* And it also represents whirling force, and strength through trouble. It is the affirmation of Justice, upholding Divine authority; and it may become the Sword of Wrath, Punishment and Affliction.

IV. The Root Powers of the Earth.

ACE OF PENTACLES

A white radiant Angelic Hand, holding a branch of a rose Tree, whereon is a large Pentacle, formed of five concentric circles. The innermost Circle is white, charged with a red Greek cross. From this white centre 12
<144> rays, also white, issue. These terminate at the circumference, making the whole something like an astrological figure of the Heavens.

It is surmounted by a small circle, above which is a large Maltese Cross, and with two white wings; four roses and two buds are shewn. The hand issueth from the clouds as in the other three cases. It representeth materiality in all senses, good and evil, and is therefore in a sense illusionary. It shows Material gain, Labour, Power, Wealth, etc.

The Sixteen Court or Royal Cards.

THE FOUR KINGS

The Four Kings or Figures mounted on Steeds represent the *Yod* forces of the Name in each suit, the Radix, Father, and commencement of Material Forces. A Force in which all the others are implied and of which they form the development and completion. A force swift and violent in action, but whose effect soon passes away, and therefore symbolised by a figure on a steed riding swiftly, and clothed in complete armour.

Therefore is the knowledge of the scale of the King so necessary for the commencement of all magical working.

THE FOUR QUEENS

Are seated upon Thrones, representing the Forces of *Heh* of the Name in each suit, the Mother, and bringer forth of material Force, a Force which develops, and realises the Force of the King. A force steady and unshaken, but not rapid though enduring. It is therefore symbolised by a figure seated upon a Throne but also clothed in armour.

THE FOUR PRINCES

These Princes are figures seated in Chariots, and thus borne forward. They represent the *Vau* Forces of the Name in each suit; the Mighty son of the King, and the Queen, who realises the Influence of both scales of Force. A prince, the son of a King and Queen, yet a Prince of Princes, and a
<145> King of Kings. An Emperor, whose effect is at once rapid (though not so swift as that of a king) and enduring (though not as steadfast as that of a Queen). It is therefore symbolised by a figure borne in a chariot, and clothed with armour. Yet is his power illusionary, unless set in motion by his Father and Mother.

THE FOUR PRINCESSES

Are the Knaves of the Tarot Pack. The Four Princesses or Figures of Amazons standing firmly by themselves, neither riding upon Horses, nor seated upon Thrones, nor borne on Chariots. They represent the forces of *Heh* final of the Name in each suit, completing the influences of the other scales. The mighty and potent daughter of a King and Queen: a Princess powerful and terrible. A Queen of Queens, an Empress, whose effect combines those of the King, Queen and Prince. At once violent and permanent, she is therefore symbolised by a figure standing firmly by itself, only partially draped and having but little armour. Yet her power existeth not save by reason of the others, and then indeed it is mighty and terrible materially, and is the Throne of the Forces of the Spirit. Woe unto whomsoever shall make war upon her when thus established!

The Sphere of Influence of the Court Cards of the Tarot Pack.

The Princesses rule over the Four Parts of the Celestial Heavens which lie around the North Pole, and above the respective Kerubic Signs of the Zodiac, and they form the Thrones of the Powers of the Four Aces.

The Twelve Cards, 4 Kings, 4 Queens, and 4 Princes, rule the Dominions of the Celestial Heavens between the realm of the Four Princesses and the

Zodiac, as is hereafter shewn. And they, as it were, link together the signs.

<146> WANDS

V. The Lord of the Flame and the Lightning.

King of the Spirits of Fire.

KNIGHT OF WANDS

A winged Warrior riding upon a black Horse with flaming mane and tail. The Horse itself is not winged. The Rider wears a winged Helmet (like an old Scandinavian and Gaulish Helmet) with a royal Crown. A corselet of scale-mail and buskins of the same, and a flowing scarlet mantle. Above his Helmet, upon his cuirass, and on his shoulder pieces and buskins he bears, as a crest, a winged black Horse's head. He grasps a Club with flaming ends, somewhat similar to that in the symbol of the Ace of Wands, but not so heavy, and also the Sigil of his scale is shewn.

Beneath the rushing feet of his steed are waving flames of Fire. He is active, generous, fierce, sudden and impetuous. If ill-dignified he is evil-minded, cruel, bigoted, brutal. He rules the celestial Heavens from above the 20th degree of Scorpio to the First two Decans of Sagittarius and this includes a part of the constellation Hercule (who also carries a club).

Fire of Fire. King of the Salamanders.

VI. Queen of the Thrones of Flame.

QUEEN OF WANDS

A crowned Queen with long red-golden hair, seated upon a Throne, with steady Flames beneath. She wears a corselet and buskins of scale mail, which latter her robe discloses. Her arms are almost bare. On cuirass and buskins are leopards' heads winged. The same symbol surmounteth her crown. At her side is a couchant leopard on which her hands rest. She bears a long Wand with a very heavy conical head. The face is beautiful and resolute.

Adaptability, steady force applied to an object. Steady rule;
<147> great attractive power, power of command, yet liked notwithstanding. Kind and generous when not opposed. If ill-dignified: obstinate, revengeful, domineering, tyrannical and apt to turn suddenly against another without a cause. She rules the Heavens from above the last Decan of Pisces to above the twentieth degree of Aries, including a part of Andromeda.

Water of Fire. Queen of the Salamanders or Salamandrines.

VII. The Prince of the Chariot of Fire.

KING OF WANDS

A Kingly figure with a golden winged Crown, seated on a Chariot. He has large white wings. One wheel of his chariot is shewn. He wears corselet and buskin of scale armour, decorated with winged Lions' heads, which symbol also surmounts his crown. His chariot is drawn by a lion. His arms are bare, save for the shoulder pieces of the corselet, and he bears a torch or fire-wand, somewhat similar to that of the Z. A. M. Beneath the Chariot are flames, some waved, some salient.

Swift, strong, hasty, rather violent, yet just and generous, noble and scorning meanness. If ill-dignified: cruel intolerant, prejudiced, and ill-natured. He rules the Heavens from above the last decan of Cancer to the 2nd decan of Leo. Hence he includes most of Leo Minor.

Air of Fire. Prince and Emperor of Salamanders.

VIII. Princess of the Shining Flame.

The Rose of the Palace of Fire.

KNAVE OF WANDS

A very strong and beautiful woman, with flowing red-golden hair, attired like an Amazon. Her shoulders, arms, bosoms and knees are bare. She wears a short kilt, reaching to the knees. Round her waist is a broad belt of scale mail, narrow at the side, broad in the front and back, and having a winged tiger's head in front. She wears a Corinthian shaped Helmet, and crown, with a long plume. It also is surmounted by a tiger's head, and the same symbol forms the buckle of her scale-mail buskins.

<148> A mantle lined with Tiger's skin falls back from her shoulders. Her right hand rests on a small golden or brazen Altar, ornamented with Ram's heads, and with Flames of Fire leaping from it. Her left hand leans on a long and heavy club, swelling at the lower end, where the sigil is placed. It has flames of fire leaping from it the whole way down, but the flames are ascending. This Club or torch is much longer than that carried by the King or Queen. Beneath her firmly placed feet are leaping Flames of Fire.

Brilliance, courage, beauty, force, sudden in anger, or love, desire of power, enthusiasm, revenge.

Ill-dignified: superficial, theatrical, cruel, unstable, domineering. She rules the heavens over one quadrant of the portion round the North Pole.

Earth of Fire. Princess and Empress of the Salamanders. Throne of the Ace of Wands.

CUPS

IX. Lord of the Waves and the Waters.

King of the Hosts of the Sea.

KNIGHT OF CUPS

A beautiful youthful winged Warrior, with flying hair, riding upon a white Horse, which latter is not winged. His general equipment is similar to that of the Knight of Wands, but upon his helmet cuirass and buskins is a peacock with opened wings. He holds a Cup in his hand, bearing the sigil of the Scale. Beneath his horses' feet is the sea. From the cup issues a crab.

Graceful, poetic, venusian, indolent, but enthusiastic if roused. Ill-dignified, he is sensual, idle, and untruthful. He rules the heavens from above 20° of Aquarius to 20° Pisces including the greater part of Pegasus.

Fire of Water. King of Undines and of Nymphs.

X. Queen of the Thrones of the Waters.

QUEEN OF CUPS

A very beautiful fair woman like a crowned Queen, seated
<149> upon a Throne, beneath which is flowing water, wherein Lotuses are seen. Her general dress is similar to that of the Queen of Wands, but upon her Crown, Cuirass and Buskins is seen an Ibis with opened wings, and beside her is the same Bird, whereon her hand rests. She holds a Cup, wherefrom a crayfish issues. Her face is dreamy. She holds a Lotus in the hand upon the Ibis.

She is imaginative, poetic, kind, yet not willing to take much trouble for another. Coquettish, good-natured, underneath a dreamy appearance. Imagination stronger than feeling. Very much affected by other influences, and therefore more dependent upon good or ill-dignity than upon most other symbols. She rules from 20° Gemini to 20° Cancer.

Water of Water. Queen of Nymphs and Undines.

XI. Prince of the Chariot of the Waters.

KING OF CUPS

A winged Kingly figure with a winged crown, seated in a chariot drawn by an Eagle. On the wheel is the symbol of a Scorpion. The Eagle is borne as a crest upon his crown, cuirass and buskins. General attire like King of Wands. Beneath his chariot is the calm and stagnant water of a Lake. His scale armour resembles feathers more than scales. He holds in one hand a Lotus, and the other a Cup, charged with the Sigil of his scale. A serpent issues from the Cup, and has its head tending down to the waters of the Lake.

He is subtle, violent, crafty and artistic. A fierce nature with calm exterior. Powerful for good or evil, but more attracted by the evil, if allied with apparent Power or Wisdom. If ill-dignified, he is intensely evil and merciless. He rules from 20° of Libra to 20° Scorpio.

Air of Water. Prince and Emperor of Nymphs and Undines.

XII. Princess of the Waters and Lotus of the Palace of the Floods.

KNAVE OF CUPS

<150> A beautiful Amazon-like figure, softer in nature than the Princess of Wands. Her attire is similar. She stands on a sea with foaming spray. Away to her right is a Dolphin. She wears as a crest on her Helmet, belt and buskins, a Swan with opening wings. She bears in one hand a Lotus, and in the other an open Cup from which a Turtle issues. Her mantle is lined with swans-down, and is of thin floating material.

Sweetness, poetry, gentleness, and kindness. Imagination, dreamy, at times indolent, yet courageous if roused. Ill-dignified, she is selfish and luxurious. She rules a quadrant of the Heavens around Kether.

Earth of Water. Princess and Empress of Nymphs and Undines. Throne of the Ace of Cups.

SWORDS

XIII. Lord of the Winds and Breezes.
King of the Spirit of Air.

KNIGHT OF SWORDS

A winged Warrior with crowned and winged Helmet, mounted upon a brown Steed, his general equipment is as that of the Knight of Wands, but he wears as a crest a winged six-pointed star, similar to those represented on the heads of Castor and Pollux, the Dioscuri, the Twins—Gemini (a part of which constellation is included in his rule). He holds a drawn sword with the Sigil of his Scale upon its pommel. Beneath his Horse's feet are dark, driving, stratus clouds.

He is active, clever, subtle, fierce, delicate, courageous, skillful, but inclined to domineer. Also to over-value small things, unless well-dginified. Ill-dignified: deceitful, tyrannical and crafty. Rules from 20° Taurus to 20° Gemini.

Fire of Air. King of Sylphs and Sylphides.

XIV. Queen of the Thrones of Air.

QUEEN OF SWORDS

A graceful woman with curly waving hair, like a Queen seated
<151> upon a Throne, and crowned. Beneath the Throne are grey cumu-
lous clouds. Her general attire is similar to that of the Queen of Wands. But she wears as a crest a winged child's head (like the head of an infantile Kerub, seen sculptored on tombs.) A drawn sword in one hand, and in the other a large bearded newly-severed head of a man.

Intensely perceptive, keen observation, subtle, quick, confident, often perseveringly accurate in superficial things, graceful, fond of dancing and balancing. Ill-dignified: cruel, sly, deceitful, unreliable, though with a good exterior. Rules from 20° Virgo to 20° of Libra.

Water of Air. Queen of the Sylphs and Sylphides.

XV. Prince of the Chariots of the Winds.

KING OF SWORDS

A Winged King with a winged Crown, seated in a chariot drawn by Arch Fays, archons, or Arch Fairies, represented as winged youths very slightly draped, with butterfly wings, heads encircled with a fillet with Pentagrams thereon, and holding wands surmounted by Pentagram-shaped stars. The same butterfly wings are on their feet and fillet. General equipment is that of the King of Wands, but he bears as a crest, a winged Angelic Head, with a Pentagram on the Brow. Beneath the chariot are grey rain clouds or nimbi. His hair long and waving in serpentine whirls, and whorl figures compose the scales of his armour. A drawn sword in one hand, a sickle in the other. With the sword he rules, with the sickle he slays.

Full of ideas and thoughts and designs, distrustful, suspicious, firm in friendship and enmity, careful, slow, over-cautious. Symbolises Alpha and Omega, the Giver of Death, who slays as fast as he creates. Ill-dignified: harsh, malicious, plotting, obstinate, yet hesitating and unreliable. Ruler from 20° Capricorn to 20° Aquarius.

Air of Air. Prince and Emperor of Sylphs and Sylphides.

<152> *XVI. Princess of the Rushing Winds.*
Lotus of the Palace of Air.

KNAVE OF SWORDS

An Amazon figure with waving hair, slighter than the Rose of the Palace of Fire (Knave of Wands). Her attire is similar. The feet seem springy, giving the idea of swiftness. Weight changing from one foot to another, and body swinging round. She resembles a mixture of Minerva and Diana, her mantle resembles the Aegis of Minerva. She wears as a crest the head of Medusa with Serpent hair. She holds a sword in one hand and the other rests upon a small silver altar with grey smoke (no fire) ascending from it. Beneath her feet are white cirrus clouds.

Wisdom, strength, acuteness, subtleness in material things, grace and dexterity. If ill-dignified, she is frivolous and cunning. She rules a quadrant of the Heavens around Kether.

Earth of Air. Princess and Empress of the Sylphs and Sylphides. Throne of the Ace of Swords.

PENTACLES

XVII. Lord of the Wild and Fertile Land.
King of the Spirits of Earth.

KNIGHT OF PENTACLES

A dark winged Warrior with winged and crowned helmet; mounted on a light brown horse. Equipment as of the Knight of Wands. The winged head of a stag or antelope as a crest. Beneath the horse's feet is fertile land, with ripened corn. In one hand he bears a sceptre surmounted with a hexagram, in the other a pentacle like a Z. A. M.'s.

Unless very well dignified, he is heavy, dull, and material. Laborious, clever and patient in material matters. If ill-dignified he is avaricious, grasping, dull, jealous, not very courageous, unless assisted by other symbols. Rules from above 20° of Leo to 20° of Virgo.

Fire of Earth. King of the Gnomes.

<153> *XVIII. Queen of the Thrones of Earth.*

QUEEN OF PENTACLES

A woman of beautiful face with dark hair, seated upon a throne, beneath which is dark sandy earth. One side of her face is dark, the other light, and her symbolism is best represented in profile. Her attire is similar to that of the Queen of Wands. But she bears a winged goat's head as a crest. A goat is by her side. In one hand she bears a sceptre surmounted by a cube, and in the other an orb of gold.

She is impetuous, kind, timid, rather charming, great-hearted, intelligent, melancholy, truthful, yet of many moods. Ill-dignified, she is undecided, capricious, foolish, changeable. Rules from 20° Sagittarius to 20° Capricorn.

Water of Earth. Queen of Gnomes.

XIX. Prince of the Chariot of Earth.

KING OF PENTACLES

A winged kingly figure seated in a chariot drawn by a bull. He bears as a crest the symbol of the head of a winged bull. Beneath the chariot is land with many flowers. In one hand he bears an orb of gold held downwards, and in the other a sceptre surmounted by an orb and cross.

Increase of matter, increase of good and evil, solidifies, practically applies things, steady, reliable. If ill-dignified, animal, material, stupid. In either slow to anger, but furious if roused. Rules from 20° Aries to 20° of Taurus.

Air of Earth, Prince and Emperor of the Gnomes.

XX. Princess of the Echoing Hills.
Rose of the Palace of Earth.

KNAVE OF PENTACLES

A strong and beautiful Amazon figure with red brown hair, standing on grass and flowers. A grove of trees near her. Her form suggests Here, Ceres, and Proserpine. She bears a winged ram's head as a crest, and wears
<154> a mantle of sheep's skin. In one hand she carries a sceptre with a circular disc, in the other a pentacle similar to that of the Ace of Pentacles.

She is generous, kind, diligent, benevolent, careful, courageous, preserving, pitiful. If ill-dignified, she is wasteful and prodigal. Rules over one Quadrant of the Heavens around the North Pole of the Ecliptic.

Earth of Earth. Princess and Empress of the Gnomes. Throne of the Ace of Pentacles.

<156> THE THIRTY-SIX DECANS

Here follow the descriptions of the smaller cards of the 4 Suits, thirty-six in number, answering unto the 36 Decans of the Zodiac.

There being 36 Decanates and only seven Planets, it follows that one of the latter must rule over one more decanate than the others. This is the Planet Mars which is allotted the last decan of Pisces and first of Aries, because the long cold of the winter requires a great energy to overcome it and initiate spring.

The beginning of the decanates is from the Royal King Star of the Heart of the Lion, the great star Cor Leonis, and therefore is the first decanate that of Saturn in Leo.

Here follow the general meanings of the small cards of the Suits, as classified under the Nine Sephiroth below Kether.

CHOKMAH

The Four Deuces symbolise the Powers of the King and Queen; first uniting and initiating the Force, but before the Prince and Princess are thoroughly brought into action. Therefore do they generally imply the initiation and fecundation of a thing.

<155> Herein are resumed the special characteristics of the 4 Court Cards of the suit:

Suit	Card	Crest	Symbols	Hair	Eyes
	King	Winged black horse's head	Black horse, waving flames. Club. Scarlet gold cloak.	Red-gold	Grey or Hazel
	Queen	Winged leopard	Leopard. Steady flames. Wand with heavy head or end.	Red-gold	Blue or Brown
Wands	Prince or Knight	Winged lion's head	Wand and salient flames. Fire wand of Z. A. M.	Yellow	Blue Grey
	Princess or Prince	Tiger's head	Tiger, leaping flames. Gold Altar, long club, largest at bottom.	Red-gold	Blue
	King	Peacock with open wings	White horse, crab issuing from cup. Sea.	Fair	Blue
	Queen	Ibis	Crayfish is issuing from River.	Gold-brown	Blue
Cups	Prince	Eagle	Scorpion, Eagle-serpent is issuing from lake.	Brown	Grey or Brown
	Princess	Swan	Dolphin, Lotus. Sea with spray, turtle from cup.	Brown	Blue or Brown
	King	Winged Hexagram	Winged brown horse, driving clouds, drawn Sword.	Dark Brown	Dark
	Queen	Winged Child's head	Head of man severed. Cumulous Clouds. Drawn sword.	Grey	Light Brown
Swords	Prince	Winged Angel's head	Arch-Fairies winged. Clouds. Nimbi. Drawn Swords.	Dark	Dark
	Princess	Medusa's head	Silver Altar. Smoke. Cirrus Clouds. Drawn sword.	Light Brown	Blue
	King	Winged stag's head	Light brown horse. Ripe corn land. Sceptre with Hexagram as Z. A. M.	Dark	Dark
Penta-cles	Queen	Winged goat's head	Barren land. Face light one side only. Sceptre with orb of gold.	Dark	Dark
	Prince	Winged bull's head	Flowery land. Bull; sceptre with orb and cross. Orb held downwards.	Dark Brown	Dark
	Princess	Winged ram's head	Grass. Flowers, grove of trees. Sceptre with disk. Pent. as all.	Rich Brown	Dark

BINAH

The Four Threes, generally, represent the realisation of action owing to the Prince being produced. The central symbol on each card. Action definitely commenced for good or evil.

CHESED

The Four Fours. Perfection, realisation, completion, making a matter settled and fixed.

GEBURAH

The Four Fives. Opposition, strife and struggle; war, obstacle to the thing in hand. Ultimate success or failure is otherwise shown.

TIPHARETH

The Four Sixes. Definite accomplishment, and carrying out of a matter.

<157> NETZACH

The Four Sevens. Generally shows a force, transcending the material plane, and is like unto a crown which is indeed powerful but requireth one capable of wearing it. The sevens then show a possible result which is dependent on the action then taken. They depend much on the symbols that accompany them.

HOD

The Fours Eights. Generally show solitary success; i.e., success in the matter for the time being, but not leading to much result apart from the thing itself.

YESOD

The Four Nines. Generally they show very great fundamental force. Executive power, because they rest on a firm basis, powerful for good or evil.

MALKUTH

The Four Tens. Generally show fixed culminated completed Force, whether good or evil. The matter thoroughly and definitely determined. Similar to the force of the Nines, but ultimating it, and carrying it out.

These are the meanings in the most general sense.

<158> Here follow the more particular descriptions and meanings.

Decan cards are always modified by the other symbols with which they are in contact.

Saturn in Leo, 1°—10°. XXI. The Lord of Strife.

5 OF WANDS

Two white radiant angelic hands issuing from clouds right and left of the centre of the card. They are clasped together as in the grip of the first Order, and they hold at the same time by their centres Five Wands, or torches, which are similar to the wand of a Z. A. M. Four Wands cross each other, but the Fifth is upright in the centre. Flames leap from the point of junction. Above the central Wand is the symbol Saturn and below it that of Leo representing the Decanate.

Violent strife and contest, boldness, rashness, cruelty, violence, lust and desire, prodigality and generosity, depending on well or ill dignified.

Geburah of Yod. (Quarrelling and fighting.) This decan hath its beginning from the Royal Star of Leo, and unto it are allotted the two Great Angels of the Schemhamephoresch, Vahaviah and Yelayel. (Note: the Hebrew spellings of these Angelic Names are provided in Volume One, with the preliminary knowledge material.—I.R.)

Jupiter in Leo, 10°—20°. XXII. Lord of Victory.

6 OF WANDS

Two hands in grip, as in the last, holding six Wands crossed, 3 and 3, Flames issuing from the point of junction. Above and below are two short wands with flames issuing from a cloud at the lower part of the card, surmounted respectively by the symbols of Jupiter and Leo, representing the Decanate.

Victory after strife, success through energy and industry, love, pleasure gained by labour, carefulness, sociability and avoiding of strife, yet victory therein. Also insolence, pride of riches and success, etc. The whole depending on dignity.

<159> Tiphareth of Yod. (Gain.) Hereunto are allotted the Great Angels from the Schemhamephoresch, Saitel and Olmiah.

Mars in Leo, 20°—30°. XXIII. Lord of Valour.

7 OF WANDS

Two hands holding by grip, as before, 6 Wands, three crossed by three, a third hand issuing from a cloud at the lower part of the card holding an upright wand, which passes between the others. Flames leap from the point of junction. Above and below the central wand are the symbols Mars and Leo, representing the Decan.

Possible victory, depending upon the energy and courage exercised; valour, opposition, obstacles, difficulties, yet courage to meet them, quarrelling, ignorance, pretence, wrangling and threatening, also victory in small and unimportant things, and influence over subordinate. Depending on dignity as usual.

Netzach of Yod. (Opposition yet courage.) Herein rule the two great Angels Mahashiah and Lelahel.

Sun in Virgo, 1°—10°. XXIV. Lord of Prudence.

8 OF PENTACLES

A white radiating Angelic hand issuing from a cloud and grasping a branch of a rose tree, with four white roses thereon which touch only the four lowermost pentacles. No rosebuds seen, but only leaves touch the four uppermost disks. All the Pentacles are similar to that of the Ace, but without the Maltese cross and wings. These are arranged as the figure Populus:

* *
* *
* *
* *

Above and below them are the symbols Sol and Virgo for the Decan.

Over-careful in small things at the expense of the great.
<160> "Penny-wise and pound-foolish." Gain of ready money in small
sums. Mean, avariciousness. Industrious, cultivation of land, hoarding, lacking in enterprise.

Hod of Heh. (Skill, prudence, cunning.) There rule those mighty angels Akaiah and Kehethel.

Venus in Virgo, 10° to 20°. XXV. Lord of Material Gain.

9 OF PENTACLES

A white radiating angelic hand as before holding a Rose branch with nine white roses, each of which touches a Pentacle arranged thus:

* *
* *
*
* *
* *

and then are more buds arranged on the branches as well as flowers. Venus and Virgo above and below.

Complete realisation of material gain, inheritance, covetousness, treasuring of goods and sometimes theft, and knavery. All according to dignity.

Yesod of Heh. (Inheritance, much increase of goods.) Herein rule the might angels Hazayel, and Aldiah.

Mercury in Virgo, 20°—30°. XXVI. Lord of Wealth.

10 OF PENTACLES

An angelic hand holding a branch by the lower extremity, whose roses touch all the pentacles. No buds however are shown. The symbols of Mercury and Virgo are above and below Pentacles thus:

* *
*
* *
* *
*
* *

Completion of material gain and fortune, but nothing beyond. As it
were, at the very pinnacle of success. Old age, slothfulness, great
<161> wealth, yet sometimes loss in part, and later heaviness, dullness of
mind, yet clever and prosperous in money transactions.

Malkuth of Heh. (Riches and wealth.) Herein rule the Angels Hihaayah and Laviah.

Moon in Libra, 1°—10°. XXVII. Lord of Peace Restored.

2 OF SWORDS

Two crossed swords, like the air dagger of Z. A. M., each held by a white radiating angelic hand. Upon the point where the two cross is a rose of five petals, emitting white Rays, and top and bottom of card are two small daggers, supporting respectively the symbols of Luna (in horizontal position) and Libra, representing the Decan.

Contradictory characteristics in the same nature. Strength through suffering. Pleasure after pain. Sacrifice and trouble yet strength arising therefrom symbolised by the position of the rose, as though the pain itself had brought forth the beauty. Peace restored, truce, arrangement of differences, justice. Truth and untruth. Sorrow and sympathy for those in trouble, aid to the weak and oppressed, unselfishness. Also an inclination to repetition of affronts if once pardoned, of asking questions of little moment, want of tact, often doing injury when meaning well. Talkative.

Chokmah of Vav. (Quarrels made up, but still some tension in relationships. Actions sometimes selfish and sometimes unselfish.) Herein rule the great Angels, Yezalel and Mebahel.

Saturn in Libra, 10°—20°. XXVIII. Lord of Sorrow.

3 OF SWORDS

Three white radiating angelic hands issuing from clouds and holding three swords upright (as if the central sword had struck apart from the two others which were crossed in the preceding symbol.) The central sword cuts asunder the Rose of Five Petals (which in the preceding symbol
<162> grew at the junction of the swords), its petals are falling, and no
white rays issue from it. Above and below the central Sword are the symbols of Saturn and Libra, referring to the Decanate.

Disruption, interruption, separation, quarrelling, sowing of discord and strife, mischief-making, sorrow, tears, yet mirth in evil pleasures, singing, faithfulness in promises, honesty in money transactions, selfish and dissipated, yet sometimes generous, deceitful in words and repetition. The whole according to dignity.

Binah of Vau. (Unhappiness, sorrow, tears.) Therein rule the Angels Harayel and Hoqmiah.

Jupiter in Libra, 20°—30°. XXXIX. The Lord of Rest from Strife.

4 OF SWORDS

The white angelic radiating hands, each holding two swords, which four cross in the centre. The rose of five petals with white radiations is reinstated on the point of intersection. Above and below, on the points of two small daggers are the symbols of Jupiter and Libra representing the Decan.

Rest from sorrow, yet after and through it. Peace from and after War. Relaxation of anxiety. Quietness, rest, ease and plenty, yet after struggle. Goods of this life, abundance. Modified by the dignity as in the other cases.

Chesed of Vav. (Convalescence, recovery from sickness, change for the better.) Herein rule Laviah and Kelial.

Mars in Scorpio, 1°—10°. XXX. Lord of Loss in Pleasure.

5 OF CUPS OR CHALICES

A white radiating angelic hand as before holding Lotuses or water lilies of which the flowers are falling right and left. Leaves only and no buds surmount them. These lotus stems ascend between the cups in the manner of a fountain, but no water flows therefrom, neither is there water in any
<163> of the Cups, which are somewhat of the shape of the magical implement of the Z. A. M. Above and below are the symbols of Mars and Scorpio, representing the Decan.

Death or end of pleasures. Disappointment. Sorrow and loss in those things from which pleasure is expected. Sadness, deceit, treachery, ill-will, detraction, charity and kindness ill-requited. All kinds of anxieties and troubles from unexpected and unsuspected sources.

Geburah of Heh. (Disappointments in love, marriage broken off, unkindness from a friend, loss of friendship.) Therein rule Livoyah and Pehilyah.

Sun in Scorpio, 10°—20°. XXXI. Lord of Pleasure.

6 OF CUPS

An angelic hand as before, holds a group of stems of Lotuses or water lilies from which six flowers bend, one over each cup. From these flowers a white glistening water flows into the cup as from a fountain, but they are not yet full. Above and below are the symbols of Sun and Scorpio, representing the Decanate.

Commencement of steady increase, gain and pleasure, but commencement only. Also affront, defective knowledge, and in some instances, contention and strife, arising from unwarranted self-assertion and vanity. Sometimes thankless and presumptuous. Sometimes amiable and patient, according to dignity.

Tiphareth of Heh. (Beginning of wish, happiness, success or enjoyment.) Therein rule Nelokhiel and Yeyayel.

Venus in Scorpio, 20°—30°. XXXII. Lord of Illusionary Success.

7 OF CUPS

The Seven of Cups are thus arranged:

V V V
V
V V V

A hand as usual holds the lotus stems which arise from the central
<164> lower cup. The hand is above this cup and below the middle one.

With the exception of the central lower cup, each is overhung by a lotus flower, but no water falls from them into cups which are quite empty. Above and below are the symbols of the Decanate, Venus and Scorpio.

Possibly victory, but neutralized by the supineness of the person. Illusionary success. Deception in the moment of apparent victory. Lying error, promises unfulfilled. Drunkenness, wrath, vanity, lust, fornication, violence against women. Selfish dissipation. Deception in love and friendship. Often success gained, but not followed up. Modified by dignity.

Netzach of Heh. (Lying. Promises unfulfilled. Illusion. Error. Deception, slight success at outset, but want of energy to retain it.) Therein rules Melchel and Chahaviah.

Mercury in Sagittarius, 1°—10°. XXXIII. The Lord of Swiftness.

8 OF WANDS

Four white Angelic Hands radiating: (two proceeding from each side) issuing from clouds, clasped in two pairs in the centre with the grip of First Order. They hold 8 wands crossed four and four. Flames issue from the point of junction. Surmounting two small wands with flames issuing down them. Placed in the centre at top and bottom of card are the symbols of Mercury and Sagittarius, representing the Decan.

Too much force applied too suddenly. Very rapid rush, but too quickly passed and expended. Violent but not lasting. Swiftness. Rapidity. Courage, boldness, confidence, freedom, warfare. Violence, love of open air, field sports, garden, meadows. Generous, subtle, eloquent, yet somewhat untrustworthy. Rapacious, insolent, oppressive. Theft and robbery, according to dignity.

Hod of Yod. (Hasty communication and messages. Swiftness.) Therein rule Nithahiah and Haayah.

Moon in Sagittarius, 10°—20°. XXXIV. The Lord of Great Strength.

<165> 9 OF WANDS

Four Hands as in the previous symbol holding eight wands crossed four and four, but a fifth hand at the foot of the card holds another wand upright, which traverses the point of junction with the others. Flames leap therefrom. Above and below the symbols Luna (depicted horizontally) and Sagittarius.

Tremendous and steady force that cannot be shaken. Herculean strength, yet sometimes scientifically applied. Great success, but with strife and energy. Victory preceded by apprehension and fear. Health good and recovery, yet doubt. Generous, questioning and curious, fond of external appearances, intractable, obstinate.

Yesod of Yod. (Strength, power, health. Recovery from sickness.) Herein rule Yirthiel and Sahiah.

Saturn in Sagittarius, 20°—30°. XXXV. The Lord of Oppression.

10 OF WANDS

Four hands upholding 8 wands crossed as before. A fifth hand at foot of card holding two wands upright which traverse the junction of the others. Above and below the symbols Saturn and Sagittarius. Flames issue therefrom.

Cruel and overbearing force and energy, but applied only to selfish and material ends. Sometimes shows failure in a matter, and the opposition too strong to be controlled arising from the person's too great selfishness at the beginning. Ill-will, levity, lying, malice, slander, envy, obstinacy, swiftness in evil, if ill-dignified. Also generosity, self-sacrifice, and disinterestedness when well-dignified.

Malkuth of Yod. (Cruelty, malice, revenge and injustice.) Therein rule Reyayel and Avamel.

Jupiter in Capricorn, 1°—10°. XXXVI. Lord of Harmonious Change.

<166> 2 OF PENTACLES

Two wheels, discs or Pentacles similar to that of the Ace. They are united by a green and gold Serpent, bound about them like a figure of Eight. It holds its tail in its mouth. A white radiant angelic hand (grasps the centre or) holds the whole. No roses enter into this card. Above and below are the symbols Jupiter and Capricorn. It is a rovolving symbol.

The harmony of change. Alternation of gain and loss, weakness and strength, ever varying occupation, wandering, discontented with any fixed condition of things; now elated, now melancholy, industrious yet unreliable, fortunate through prudence of management, yet sometimes unaccountably foolish. Alternately talkative and suspicious. Kind yet wavering and inconsistent. Fortunate in journeying. Argumentative.

Chokmah of Heh final. (Pleasant change, visit to friends.) Herein rule Lekabel and Veshiriah.

Mars in Capricorn, 10°—20°. XXXVI. The Lord of Material Works.

3 OF PENTACLES

A white rayed angelic hand as before, holding a branch of a rose-tree, of which two white rose-buds touch and surmount the topmost pentacle. The latter are arranged in a Triangle thus:

```
  *
*   *
```

Above and below are symbols of Mars and Capricorn. Working and constructive force, building up, erection, creation, realisation, and increase of material things, gain in commercial transactions, rank, increase of substance, influence, cleverness in business, selfishness, commencement of matter to be established later. Narrow and prejudiced, keen in matter of gain.
<167> Modified by dignity. Sometimes given to seeking after the impossible.

Binah of Heh final. (Business, paid employment, commercial transactions.) Therein rule Yechavah and Lehachiah.

Sun in Capricorn, 20°—30°. XXXVIII. The Lord of Earthly Power.

4 OF PENTACLES

A hand holding a branch of a rose-tree, but without flowers or buds, save that in the centre is one fully blown white rose. Four pentacles thus, with Sun and Capricorn above and below:

```
*   *
*   *
```

Assured material gain, success, rank, dominion, earthly power completed, but leading to nothing beyond. Prejudiced, covetous, suspicious, careful and orderly, but discontented. Little enterprise or originality. Altered by dignity as usual.

Chesed of Heh final. (Gain of money or influence. A present.) Therein rule Keveqiah and Mendial.

Venus in Aquarius, 1°—10°. XXXIX. The Lord of Defeat.

5 OF SWORDS

Two rayed hands each holding two swords nearly upright, but falling apart from each other, right and left of card. A third hand holds a sword upright in centre as if it had disunited them. The petals of the rose (which in the four of Swords had been re-instated in the centre) are torn asunder and falling. Above and below the symbols of Venus and Aquarius.

Contest finished, and decided against the person, failure, defeat, anxiety, trouble, poverty, avarice. Grieving after gain, laborious, unresting, loss and vileness of nature. Malicious, slandering, lying, spiteful and
<168> tale-bearing. A busybody and separator of friends, hating to see peace and love between others. Cruel yet cowardly, thankless, and unreliable. Clever and quick in thought and speech. Feelings of pity easily roused but unenduring. As dignity.

Geburah of Vav. (Defeat, loss, malice, spite, slander, evil-speaking.) Herein rule Aniel and Chaamiah.

Mercury in Aquarius, 10°—20°. XL. The Lord of Earned Success.

6 OF SWORDS

Two hands as before, each holding three swords which cross in centre. Rose re-established hereon. Mercury and Aquarius above and below, supported on the points of two short daggers or swords.

Success after anxiety and trouble. Selfishness, beauty, conceit, but sometimes modesty therewith, dominion, patience, labour, etc., according to dignity.

Tiphareth of Vav. (Labour, work, journey by water.) Herein rule Rehaayal and Yeyeziel.

Moon in Aquarius, 20°—30°. XLI. The Lord of Unstable Effort.

7 OF SWORDS

Two hands as before, each holding swords. A third hand holds a single sword in the centre. The points of all the swords do just touch one another, the central sword not altogether dividing them. The rose of the previous symbols of this suit is held by the hand which holds the central Sword, as if the Victory were in its disposal. Above and below Luna and Aquarius. (In the small cards, the Lunar Decans are always represented by a crescent on its back.)

Partial success, yielding when victory is within grasp, as if the last reserves of strength were used up. Inclination to lose when on the point of gaining through not continuing the effort. Love of abundance, fascinated by display, given to compliment, affronts and insolences, and to detect and spy

on another. Inclined to betray confidences, not always intentional.
<169> Rather vacillating and unreliable, according to dignity as usual.

Netzach of Vav. (Journey by land, in character untrustworthy.) Herein rule Michael and Hahihel.

Saturn in Pisces, 1°—10°. XLII. The Lord of Abandoned Success.

8 OF CUPS

A hand holding a group of stems of Lotuses or water lilies. There are only two flowers shown which bend over the two centre cups pouring into them a white water. The Cups are not yet filled.

Y Y Y
Y Y
Y Y Y

The three upper cups are empty. At top and bottom Saturn and Pisces.

Temporary success, but without further result. Things thrown aside as soon as gained. No lasting even in the matter in hand. Indolence in success. Journeying from place to place. Misery and repining without cause. Seeking after riches. Instability according to dignity.

Hod of Heh. (Success abandoned, decline of interest in anything.) Herein rule Vavaliah and Yelahiah.

Jupiter in Pisces, 10°—20°. XLIII. The Lord of Material Happiness.

9 OF CUPS

Hand from cloud holding Lotuses or water lilies, one flower of which overhangs each cup, and from which water pours.

Y Y Y
Y Y Y
Y Y Y

All the cups are full and running over. Above and below are the symbols of Jupiter and Pisces representing the Decan.

Complete and perfect realisation of pleasure and happiness
<170> almost perfect. Self-praise, vanity, conceit,much talking of self, yet
kind and lovable, and may be self-denying therewith. Highminded, not easily satisfied with small and limited ideas. Apt to be maligned through too much self-assumption. A good, generous, but, maybe, foolish nature.

Yesod of Heh. (Complete success, pleasure, happiness, wish fulfilled.) Therein rule Saliah and Aariel.

Mars in Pisces, 20°—30°. XLIV. The Lord of Perfected Success.

10 OF CUPS

Hand holding bunch of Lotuses or water-lilies whose flowers pour a pure white water into *all* the cups, which *all run over.*

Y Y Y
Y Y Y
Y Y Y

The top cup is held sideways by a hand and pours water into top left hand cup. A single lotus flower surmounts top cup and is the source of the water that fills it. Above and below Mars and Pisces.

Permanent and lasting success, happiness because inspired from above. Not sensual as Nine of Cups, "The Lord of Material Happiness," yet almost more truly happy. Pleasure, dissipation, debauchery. Pity, quietness, peace-making. Kindness, generosity, wantonness, waste, etc., according to dignity.

Malkuth of Heh. (Matters definitely arranged as wished, complete good fortune.) Herein rule Aasliah and Mihal.

Mars in Aries, 1°—10°. XLV. The Lord of Dominion.

2 OF WANDS

Hand grasping two Wands crossed. Flames issue from the point of junction. On two small wands, above and below, with flames issuing from them, are Mars and Aries.

<171> Strength, Dominion, harmony of rule and justice. Boldness, courage, fierceness, shamelessness, revenge, resolution, generous, proud, sensitive, ambitious, refined, restless, turbulent, sagacious withal, yet unforgiving and obstinate, according to dignity.

Chokmah of Yod. (Influence over others. Authority, power, dominion.) Rule therein Vehooel and Deneyal.

Sun in Aries, 10°—20°. XLVI. The Lord of Established Strength.

3 OF WANDS

Hand issuing from clouds holds three wands in centre. Two crossed and one upright. Flames from point of junction. Above and below Sun and Aries.

Established force and strength. Realisation of hope. Completion of labour, success of the struggle. Pride, nobility, wealth, power, conceit. Rude self assumption and insolence. Generosity, obstinacy according to dignity.

Binah of Yod. (Pride, arrogance and self-assertion.) Herein rule Hechashiah and Aamamiah.

Venus in Aries, 20°—30°. XLVII. Lord of Perfected Work.

4 OF WANDS

Two hands as before, issuing from clouds each side of card, and clasped in centre with First Order grip, holding four wands crossed. Flames issue at point of junction. Above and below on two small flaming wands are Venus and Aries, representing the Decan.

Perfection, a completion of a thing built up with trouble and labour. Rest after labour. Subtlety, cleverness, beauty, mirth, success in completion. Reasoning faculty, conclusions drawn from previous knowledge. Unreadiness, unreliable, and unsteady, through over anxiety and hurriedness of action. Graceful in manners. At times insincere, etc.

Chesed of Yod. (Settlement, arrangement, completion.) Herein rule Nanael and Nithal.

<172> *Mercury in Taurus, 1°—10°. XLVIII. Lord of Material Trouble.*

5 OF PENTACLES

Hand holding a branch of White Rose Tree, from which roses are falling, leaving no buds behind. Five pentacles similar to Ace. Mercury and Taurus for Decan.

Loss of money or position. Trouble about material things. Toil, labour, land cultivation, building, knowledge and acuteness of earthly things, poverty, carefulness. Kindness, sometimes money regained after severe toil and labour. Unimaginative, harsh, stern, determined, obstinate.

Geburah of Heh final. (Loss of profession, loss of money, monetary anxiety.) Therein rule Mabahiah and Pooyal.

Moon in Taurus, 10°—20°. XLIX. Lord of Material Success.

6 OF PENTACLES

Hand holding a rose branch with white roses and buds, each of which touch a pentacle, arranged thus:

```
* *
* *
* *
```

Above and below Luna and Taurus represent the Decanate.

Success and gain in material undertakings, power, influence, rank, nobility, rule over the people. Fortunate, successful, just and liberal. If ill-dignified, may be purse-proud, insolent from success, or prodigal.

Tiphareth of Heh final. (Success in material things. Prosperity in business.) Herein rule Nemamiah and Yeyelal.

Saturn in Taurus, 20°—30°. L. The Lord of Success Unfulfilled.

7 OF PENTACLES

<173> Hand from a cloud holding rose branch of seven pentacles thus arranged:

```
*   *
  *
*   *
*   *
```

Only five of which overhang but do not touch the five upper pentacles. No other buds shown, and none are near or touch the two lower pentacles. Above and below Saturn and Taurus.

Promises of success unfulfilled. (Shown in the symbolism of the rosebuds, which do not as it were come to anything.) Loss of apparently promising fortune. Hopes deceived and crushed. Disappointment. Misery, slavery, necessity and baseness. A cultivator of land, and yet is loser thereby. Sometimes it denotes slight and isolated gains with no fruits resulting therefrom, and of no further account, though seeming to promise well. According to dignity.

Netzach of Heh. (Unprofitable speculation and employment. Little gain for much labour.) Therein rule Herochiel and Mitzrael.

Jupiter in Gemini, 1°—10°. LI. Lord of Shortened Force.

8 OF SWORDS

Four hands as usual, each holding two swords, points upwards, touching near top of card, two hands lower on left, two on right of card. The rose of other sword symbols re-established in centre. Above and below Jupiter and Gemini.

Too much force applied to small things, too much attention to detail, at expense of principle and more important points. Ill-dignified, these qualities produce malice, pettiness, and domineering qualities. Patience in detail of study, great ease in some things, counterbalanced by equal disorder in others. Impulsive, equally fond of giving or receiving money, or presents.
Generous, clever, acute, selfish, and without strong feeling of affec-
<174> tion. Admires wisdom, yet applies it to small and unworthy ob-
jects.

Hod of Vav. (Narrow, restricted, petty, a prison.) Herein rule Vemibael and Yehohel.

Mars in Gemini, 10°—20°. LII. The Lord of Despair and Cruelty.

9 OF SWORDS

Four hands (somewhat as in preceding symbol) hold eight swords upright but with the points falling away from each other. A fifth hand holds a ninth sword upright in the centre, as if it had disunited them, and struck them asunder. No rose at all is shown (as if it were not merely cut in pieces but completely and definitely destroyed). Above and below Mars and Gemini.

Despair, cruelty, pitilessness, malice, suffering, want, loss, misery. Burden, oppression, labour, subtlety and craft, lying, dishonesty, slander. Yet also obedience, faithfulness, patience, unselfishness, etc., according to dignity.

Yesod of Vav. Therein rule Aaneval and Mochayel.

Sun in Gemini, 20°—30°. LIII. Lord of Ruin.

10 OF SWORDS

Four hands (as in previous symbol) hold eight swords with points falling away from each other. Two hands hold two swords crossed in the centre (as if their junction had disunited the others). No rose, flower or bud is shown. Above and below Sun and Gemini.

(Almost a worse symbol than Nine of Swords.) Undisciplined warring force, complete disruption and failure. Ruin of all plans and projects. Disdain, insolence and impertinence, yet mirth and jolly therewith. A Marplot, loving to overthrow the happiness of others, a repeater of things, given to much unprofitable speech, and of many words, yet clever, acute, and eloquent, etc., depending on dignity.

Malkuth of Vav. (Ruin, death, defeat, disruption.) Herein rule Dambayah and Menqal.

<175> *Venus in Cancer, 1°—10°. LIV. Lord of Love.*

2 OF CUPS

Hand at lower part from cloud holds lotuses. A Lotus flower rises above water, which occupies the lowest part of card, and rises above the hand holding the Lotus. From this Lotus flower a stem rises, terminating nearly at the top of the card in another Lotus or water-lily flower, from which a white water gushes like a fountain. Crossed on the stem just beneath are two Dolphins, gold and silver; on to which the water falls and from which it pours in full streams, like jets of gold and silver, into two cups, which in their turn overflow, flooding the lower part of the card. Above and below Venus and Cancer.

Harmony of masculine and feminine united. Harmony, pleasure, mirth, subtlety, sometimes folly, dissipation, waste, and silly action, according to dignity.

Chokmah of Heh. (Marriage, home, pleasure.) Herein rule Ayoel and Chabooyah.

Mercury in Cancer, 10°—20°. LV. Lord of Abundance.

3 OF CUPS

Hand as before holds group of Lotuses or Water-lilies, from which two flowers rise on either side of, and overhanging the top cup, pouring into it the white water. Flowers in the same way pour water into the lower cups. All the cups overflow, the topmost into the two others, and these upon the lower part of the card. Above and below Mercury and Cancer.

Y

Y Y

Abundance, plenty, success, pleasure, sensuality, passive success, good luck and fortune. Love, gladness, kindness and bounty. According to dignity.

Binah of Heh. (Plenty, hospitality, eating and drinking, pleasure, dancing, new clothes, merriment.) Herein rule Rahael and Yebomayah.

<176> *Moon in Cancer, 20°—30°. LVI. The Lord of Blended Pleasure.*

4 OF CUPS

Four cups, the two upper overflow into the two lower, which do not overflow. A hand grasps a bunch of lotuses from which ascends a stem bearing one flower at the top of the card, from which water issues into two top cups. From the centre two leaves pass right and left, making as it were a cross between the four cups. Luna and Cancer above and below.

Success or pleasure, approaching their end. A stationary period in happiness which may or may not continue. It does not show marriage and love so much as the previous symbol. It is too passive a symbol to represent perfectly complete happiness. Swiftness, hunting and pursuing. Acquisition by contention; injustice sometimes. Some drawbacks to pleasure implied.

Chesed of Heh. (Receiving pleasure, but some slight discomfort and anxieties, therewith. Blended pleasure and success.) Therein rule Hayayel and Mevamayah.

NOTE

Here finishes the description of the 36 smaller cards, referring to the 36

Decanates of the Zodiac. Although the Angels of the Schem ha-Mephoresch have been linked with the Decanates, yet their dominion is far more exalted, extended, and important than this would at first sight seem to imply. In all of this I have not only transcribed the symbolism, but have tested, studied, compared, and examined it both clairvoyantly and in other ways. The result of these has been to show me how *absolutely* correct the symbolism of the Book T is, and how exactly it represents the occult Forces of the Universe.

S. RIOGHAIL MA DHREAM.

<177>

TAROT DIVINATION

This form is especially applicable to Divination concerning the ordinary material events of daily life.

It is a mode of placing the cards based upon the scheme of the dominion of the Tarot Symbols. The more rigidly correct and in harmony with the scheme of the Universe is any form of Divination, so much the more is it likely to yield a correct and reliable answer to the enquirer. For then and then only is there a firm link, and bond of union, established between it and the Occult forces of Nature. The moment the correct correspondence of the Symbols employed ceases to be observed, the link between them and the inner Occult forces is strained, and in some cases broken. For this cause, therefore, is it that the same mode of Divination will sometimes yield a true and sometimes false answer, and at other times a partly true and partly false; because the correspondences are either not rigidly observed or else made use of by an ignorant and uninitiated person.

Therefore the Diviner should enter upon the Divination with a mind clear and unprejudiced, neither disturbed by anger, fear, nor love, and with a sound knowledge of the correspondences of the symbols which he employs. Also he should be able to employ his clairvoyant and intuitive faculties therein when necessary and should avoid as much as possible a warped or strained decision. Also it is not well to divine *repeatedly* concerning the same matter; and the Diviner should also recognise that even the material occult forces do not act as the instruments of a blind fatality, but rather in accordance with the will of the more spiritual powers which are behind them.

Also it may be well for the Diviner to put on his insignia, and make over
the pack any invoking hexagram or Pentagram, either with the hand
<178> alone, or with convenient magical instruments. And it may also be
advisable in some instances to invoke an elemental force consonant
with the matter, to aid in the divination.

And let it not be forgotten that in working with the lesser magical implements all the four should be at hand, even though only one be actually employed. For if this be not done, it will give undue force to the suit corresponding to the Element invoked, and instead of being an aid in the matter, it will be a hindrance to correct reading.

(A formula which may be found useful to assist concentration, and to formulate a link between the Diviner and the intelligences referred to the Tarot, is to take the pack in the left hand, and with the right hand hold the Wand or any lesser instrument. Then say: "In the divine name IAO, I invoke Thee thou Great Angel HRU who art set over the operations of this Secret

Wisdom. Lay thine hand invisibly on these consecrated cards of art, that thereby I may obtain true knowledge of hidden things, to the glory of the ineffable Name. Amen."—I.R.)

THE OPENING OF THE KEY

The mode of performing the Divination called "The Opening of the Key" is by five consecutive operations of laying out the cards, they having been previously well shuffled, and, in addition in the first and fourth cases, having been cut as well, and in a certain manner. These five operations answer respectively, the first to the Dominion of the Four Princesses under the presidency of the Four Aces; the Second to that of the Kings, Queens and Princes, referred to the Twelve Houses; the Third to that of the Twelve Keys attributed to the Signs; the Fourth to that of the smaller cards answering to the 36 Decanates; and the Fifth and last to the rule of the Sephiroth in the Celestial Heavens.

<179> These are five distinct operations, consecutively executed from the mode of Operation called the "Opening of the Key," which, as has been before said, is especially applicable to the daily events of life. The first of these methods shows the opening of the matter as it then stands. The 2nd, 3rd, 4th, its consecutive development, and the 5th its termination.

Before commencing the Divination, one of the sixteen court cards should be selected to represent the significator of the enquirer, and should answer as nearly to his description.

WANDS generally—very fair-haired and red-haired persons with fair complexion.
CUPS generally—moderately fair persons.
SWORDS—generally—dark persons.
PENTACLES generally—very dark persons.
KINGS—Generally men.
QUEENS—Generally women.
PRINCES (KNIGHTS)—Generally young men.
PRINCESSES (KNAVES)—Generally young women.

Of these the Queens and Princes in reading the cards during the processes almost always represent persons connected with a matter under consideration. The Kings, if looking *against* the direction of the reading, or if meeting it, represent the coming of a person or event, or phase of an event, but if looking *with* the direction of the reading represent the departure of a person or the going off or wane of some event.

The Princesses (Knaves) if looking *with* the direction of the reading, represent general opinion in harmony with, and approving the matter; but if looking *against* the direction of the reading the reverse.

If the Diviner be performing the Divination for a person at a distance and of whose general description he is ignorant, he can select the significator by cutting the pack, and taking one of the court cards of that suit, cut to
<180> represent him of course earnestly thinking of the person at the time.

It is usually much better for the *Enquirer* to shuffle or cut the cards himself; but if the Diviner should have to do this himself, he must, while doing so, earnestly think of the person enquiring, or concerning whom the Divination is performed. In all cases of shuffling and cutting, the person doing so should *think earnestly* of the matter in hand. In cutting, if a false cut be made, that is to say if one or more cards should drop in the process, the cards should be at once reshuffled, and again cut clearly, otherwise it is probable that the answer will be unreliable.

(Note: If the matter be important, he should wait twelve hours before reshuffling.)

In the laying out of the Cards, if any are inverted, they must remain so and must not be turned round, as that would alter the direction in which they would be looking. A card has the same meaning and forces, whether right or inverted, so that no particular attention need be paid to the circumstances.

The *order* of the cards as laid down must also *not* be interfered with. In the reading of the cards when laid out, the Significator of the Enquirer is *the starting point,* and reading proceeds by counting over certain cards *in the direction* in which the face of the Court card chosen as Significator of the Enquirer is turned.

The mode of counting is as follows, recognising the card from which one starts as the No. 1.

From every Ace—Five cards (spirit and four elements).
Princess (Knave)—Seven cards (seven palaces of Malkuth).
King, Queen, Prince—Four cards, (letters of Tetragrammaton).
Smaller cards—Its own number (a Sephirah).
Key of *Aleph Mem Shin*—Three cards (number of the Mother letters).
<181> Key of duplicated letters—Nine cards (number of planets and Caput and Cauda Draconis).
Key of single letters Twelve (number of signs).

The counting is continued till one alights on a card which has already been read.

Thus, in the following example, we will suppose that the significator is the *Queen of Cups,* and that she is looking to the left. We should read as follows: Queen of Cups—a fair woman; counting four, we come to Five of Pentacles, i.e. "Loss of money" and as it has on one side the Moon and on the other a card of Pentacles, it shows that it is through deception in business matters,) we then count 5, the number of the card, from the 5 of Pentacles, which falls on the 6 of Cups "Success." But as this has on one side the Foolish Man, and on the other the Ace of Wands, this will not be great owing to unwise conduct. Then we count six from the 6 of Cups, still going in the same direction which brings us to the Queen of Cups, a card we have already read, so we finish there.

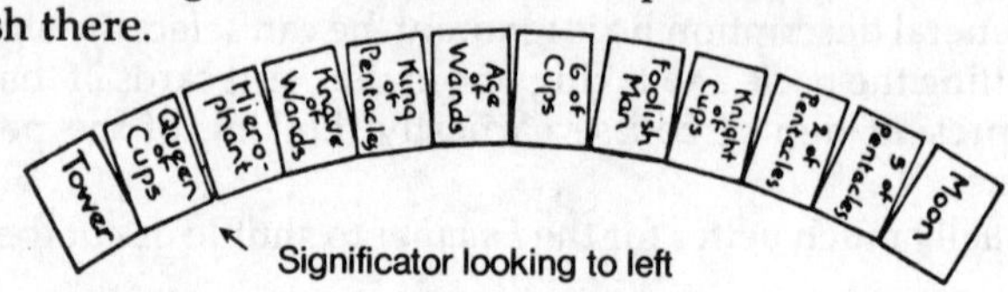

Significator looking to left

SIGNIFICATOR—QUEEN OF CUPS

Thus the reading will be "A rather fair woman has lost money through some cheating in business, and though she is again beginning to succeed, this success is liable to be damaged by unwise conduct on her part for which she will have herself to thank.

If the significator were the Knave of Wands, and (looking towards the right) we should count seven to the 2 of Pentacles, then two from that to the 5 of Pentacles; then five from that to the Hierophant, twelve from that to the Queen of Cups, four from that to the King of Pentacles; then four to
<182> the Foolish Man, and thence three to the 2 of Pentacles, where we
stop, having read that card already. "A young woman is just making a change in her business, which brings her loss of money through some deceit on the part of a fair woman, and a dark man whose foolish advice has led to the change." The cards would then be paired two by two, from opposite ends as hereafter shown: thus: Moon and Tower, "The deceit is discovered." 5 of Pentacles and Queen of Cups, "on the part of this person who has brought about her loss." 2 of Pentacles and Hierophant, "by advising the change." Knight of Cups and Knave of Wands, "for the young woman meets an older man," King of Pentacles and Fool "who counteract the foolish advice of the dark man." Ace of Wands and 6 of Cups "and she in consequence succeeds better, but only by the dint of energy and hard work."

The scheme of Divination called "The Opening of the Key" is worked out in the following manner. I adjoin an example carried carefully through the five stages for the instruction of the Z.A.M. The complete pack of 78 cards is employed.

FIRST OPERATION

Representing the Opening of the Question

The significator being chosen, the enquirer shuffles the cards, thinking earnestly of the matter under consideration. He then places the cards in a single packet on the table before him, face downwards. This represents the Name YHVH, which is now to be separated unto the component letters. He therefore is to cut the pack as nearly in the middle as his eye can direct, and to face the uppermost portion to the right of the lowermost; the former will represent YH and the latter VH (final). He again is to cut the packet to the right hand into two parts, as nearly in the centre as he can, and place the uppermost part to the right again. This will represent Y and the lower part the remaining H. He is now to cut the packet to the left, its uppermost
<183> part will represent V and its lower part H (final). So that he will now
have four packets nearly equal in size, answering from right to left to the name YHVH—יהוה under the presidency of the Four Princesses (knaves) and through them to the four radical forces (Aces). These four packets are then turned face upwards without altering their relative position, and the meaning of their four bottom cards thus shown *may* be read as an indication of the matter. Each packet is now examined to find in which the Significator of the Enquirer is, being careful not to alter the order of the Cards. The packet containing the Significator is retained for reading, and the others are put aside and not used in this particular reading (operation). Carefully note to

which of the Four letters the packet containing the significator of the Enquirer corresponds. If to Y and Wands, energy and strife. If to H and Cups, pleasure. If to V and Swords, sickness and trouble. If to H final and Pentacles, business and money. The packet containing the significator is now spread out face upwards in the form of a horseshoe (count in the way the Significator looks) and its meaning is read in the manner previously described. First by counting to certain cards until one is alighted upon which has been previously read; and then by pairing them together in succession from opposite ends of the horseshoe. (You do not miss the significator.)

Before commencing counting from the Significator, the Diviner should first notice what suit predominates in the number of cards. In this a majority of Wands would signify energy, quarrelling, opposition. Of Cups, pleasure and merriment. Of Swords, trouble and sadness, sometimes sickness and death. Of Pentacles, business, money, possession, etc. Also if in the cards laid out there should be either three or four cards of a sort, such as 3 Aces, 4 Fives, etc., their meaning should be noted according to the table hereafter given. A majority of the *Keys* shows forces beyond one's control.

<184>

EXAMPLE

Supposing that a young man asks the question "Shall I succeed in my present affairs?" His complexion is fair, and his hair light brown. The Diviner therefore takes the Prince of Cups for Significator.* (Had he been an older man he would have selected the King of the same suit instead) and requests Enquirer to carefully shuffle the pack and place it face downwards on the table before him. He then instructs him to cut the pack as nearly in the centre as possible, and to place the uppermost half well to the right, and then to cut each of the packets as nearly in the centre as possible, putting each uppermost half to the right of and beside the lower half, thus yielding four packets of nearly equal dimensions.

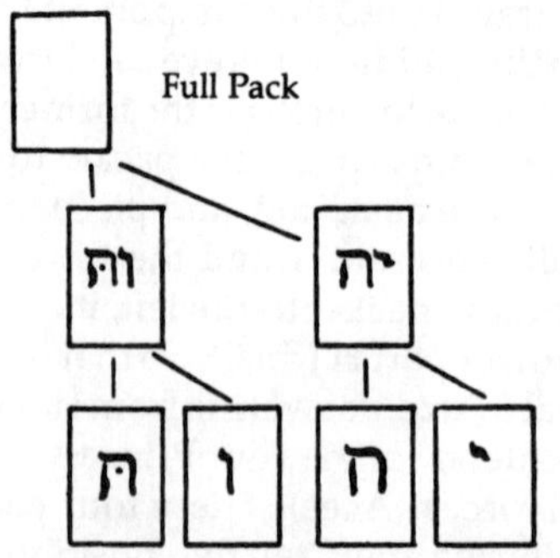

Whoever cuts, cuts to his own right

These four packets are now turned face upwards and we find them thus placed as regards the four bottom cards.

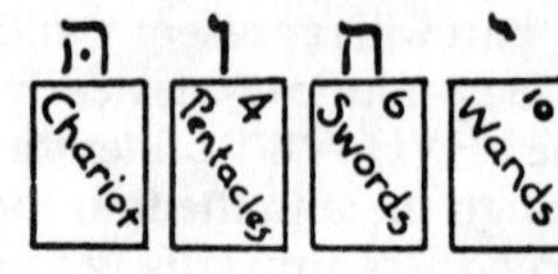

*I've left this as it was in the original to illustrate the process, but the reader will soon discover that the example, and the illustration, that follows does indeed use the King of Cups, and not the Prince, as the Significator. C.L.W.

Here the 10 of Wands is strong, being in the place of Yod which governs Wands—Fire. The Six of Swords is moderately strong, being in the place of Heh which rules Cups—Water, which is not a hostile and contrary element to Air; the 4 of Pentacles is weak because it is in the place of Vau which rules the contrary element to Earth, viz. Air; and the Chariot—Cancer, a watery sign is fairly strong, being in the place of Heh final, which rules Earth, a friendly element to Water.

The Diviner then reads these 4 Cards as a preliminary thus: "The
Enquirer works very hard and gains but little money, yet matters are
<185> beginning to improve." Because the 10 of Wands shows cruelty,
harshness, etc. 6 of Swords, labour and work. 4 of Pentacles, gain of
money, and the Chariot, success.

The Diviner then examines the Four Packets to find in which one the Significator is. It proves to be in the one of which the 6 of Swords is the bottom card. This is in the place answering to the letter Heh, which represents pleasure and rules Cups. This is so far a good omen, as it shows society and merriment. This pack of cards is retained for reading, the others are put aside as not bearing on the question. Let us suppose that this packet consists of 20 cards, and that they are in the following order. The Diviner spreads them out in the form of a horseshoe:

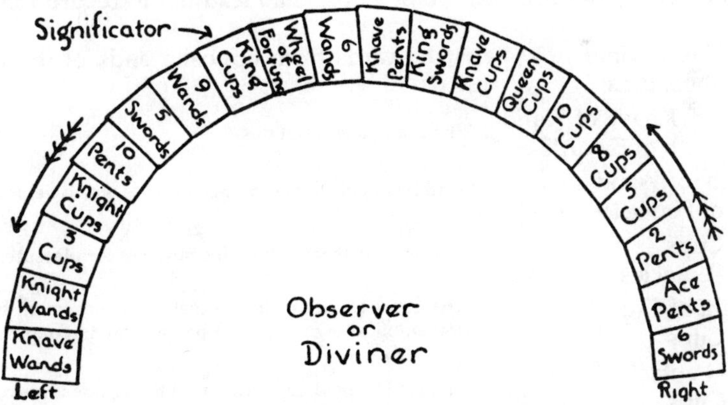

The suit of Cups is distinctly in the majority—pleasure, visiting friends, love-making, etc. There are 3 Knaves which indicates Society of the young. From which the Diviner reads that the Enquirer is fond of young people and of flirting, etc. There being no other set of 3 or 4 cards of a sort, the Diviner proceeds to read by counting from the Significator, whose face is turned towards the 9 of Wands.

The counting therefore proceeds in the direction of the arrow, thus: 4 from the King of Cups, 10 of Pentacles. 10 from this, 8 of Cups. 8 from this,
Wheel of Fortune. 9 from this, Knave of Wands, 7 from this, 10 of
<186> Cups. 10 from this, 5 of Wands. 5 from this, Knight of Wands. 4 from
this, Ace of Pentacles. 5 from this, 10 of Cups. And as this card has
already been taken, this form of reading finishes here.

In this reading as hereafter explained, each card is modified by the card in either side of it; if it be an end card, such as the 6 of Swords, in this case it is modified not only by the card next to it, Ace of Pentacles, but also by the card at the opposite end, Knave of Wands.

If these cards are of a contrary element to the card itself, they very much weaken and neutralize its force, but if the contrary element is only in one card, and the other is of a connecting nature, it does not much matter. This is explained later among the tabluated rules. The King of Cups is between the 9 of Wands and the Wheel of Fortune, both of which cards are of a fiery nature, and therefore contrary to Cups which is Water, and therefore it shows that the Enquirer is rather lacking in perseverance and energy. 10 of Pentacles, "His business will begin to prosper," 8 of Cups, "but yet he will lose interest in it, owing to his love of pleasure and society" (shown by 8 of Cups having the suit on each side of it). Wheel of Fortune, "and through his fortune changing for the better." Knave of Wands (Knight of Wands on one side and 6 of Swords on the other), "He yet is anxious through falling in love with a graceful and sprightly girl with chestnut hair and fair complexion whom he has recently met" (shown by Knight of Wands turned contrary to the course of the reading). 10 of Cups, "His suit is at first favourably received," 5 of Swords, "but some slanderous reports and mischief making" (not altogether without foundation) "come to her knowledge." Ace of Pentacles, "though his increasing prosperity in business," 10 of Cups, "had lead her to regard him with favour."

The Diviner now pairs the cards from opposite ends of the horseshoe, thus:

<187> Knave of Wands 6 of Swords	"She is anxious about this."
Knight of Wands Ace of Pentacles	"And he begins to neglect his business which yet is fairly good.
3 of Cups 2 of Pentacles	"And instead throws aside his business for pleasures.
Knight of Cups 5 of Cups	"The consequence of this is that the engagement between them is broken off, shown by knight being turned in opposite direction.
10 of Pentacles 8 of Cups	"Still his business does fairly well though he is losing interest in it.
5 of Swords 10 of Cups	"The matter is the subject of much gossip.
9 of Wands Queen of Cups	(These two cards of contrary suits and therefore of little importance.) "Among their acquaintances."
King of Cups Knave of Cups	"He moreover, begins to pay attention to another girl of not quite so fair complexion.
Wheel of Fortune King of Swords	"who, however, prefers a dark man, who is much admired by the fair sex (shown by his being next two Knaves and a Queen.)
6 of Wands Knave of Pentacles	"But he has already gained the affections of a girl with dark brown eyes and hair." (This description is obtained by mixing the effect of the Wands with Pentacles.)

This concludes the reading in the First Operation, which may be thus resumed:

"The enquirer is a fair young man who works very hard, and has hitherto gained but little money, yet matters are beginning to improve. He is fond of society, and of visiting friends. He is rather lacking in per-
<188> severance and energy, though notwithstanding this, his business and money transactions will begin to prosper. But yet he will lose interest in it owing to his love of pleasure and society, and though his fortune is changing for the better he has yet much anxiety through falling in love with a graceful and sprightly girl with chestnut hair and fair complexion whom he has recently met. His suit is at first favourably received, but some slanderous tales and mischief-making not altogether without foundation, come to her knowledge, though his increasing prosperity in business has led her to regard him with favour. She is made anxious by this, and he begins to neglect his business which yet is fairly good, and instead abandons it for pleasure and merry-making."

"The consequence of this is that the engagement is broken off. Still his business does fairly well though he has lost interest in it. The whole affair is the subject of much gossip among their mutual acquaintances. (One of the chief mischief-makers is a fair middle-aged woman shown by the Queen of Cups.) He, however, soon begins to pay attention to another girl of not quite so fair a complexion. She, however, prefers a dark young man who is much admired generally by the fair sex, but he has already gained the affection of a young woman with dark brown hair and blue eyes."

SECOND OPERATION

(Representing the development of the Matter.)

The Enquirer again carefully shuffles the cards, and places the Pack on the table face downwards, but is *not* to cut them. The Diviner now takes the Pack and deals it round card by card in 12 Packets face downwards in rotation as in the following diagram: (Deal and read in order of Houses against the direction of the Sun.) So that the first packet answering to the Ascendant will consist of the 1st, 13th, 25th, 37th, 49th, 61st, 73rd cards, as shown, and so on.

This Operation is under the presidency of the Court Cards,
<189> whose dominion in the Celestial Heavens falls immediately between that of the 4 Knaves and that of the Keys answering to the 12 Signs of the Zodiac. It represents the 12 Astrological Houses of Heaven, as shown. Without altering the relative order of the packets, or of the cards in the packets, the Diviner examines each in succession, till he finds the one which contains the Significator. This he retains for reading, noting carefully to which astrological house it corresponds and gathers up the other packets, and puts them aside, as they are not of any further use in this operation.

As before, the Diviner reads the packet containing the Significator, by spreading them out in the form of a horseshoe, first reading by counting the cards in order from the Significator in the direction in which the face of the figure on the card is turned, and next by pairing the cards together from the opposite ends of the horseshoe. It is hardly likely that in so small a packet there will be either 3 or 4 cards of a sort, but if there be, the Diviner takes note of the same, and also observes which suit predominates. I now continue the

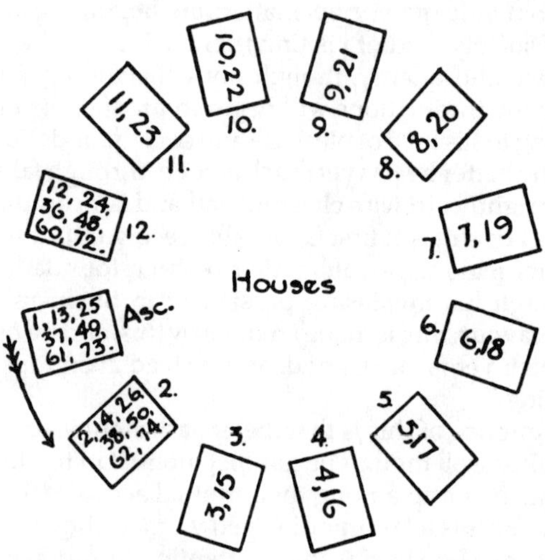

examples commenced in the previous operation. I must here ob-
<190> serve that the example is purely of my own invention, and of course
is not contained in the Book T, wherein only the mode of working is
given. I have purposely taken a commonplace, trivial, and material question for elucidation. (S.R.M.D.)

EXAMPLE
(Cont.)

We will suppose the Enquirer to have duly and carefully shuffled the Cards, thinking of his affairs, and that the Diviner has dealt them round into 12 packets as above shown. The packet containing the Significator is located in the Ascendant, and it contains the following cards in the order given.

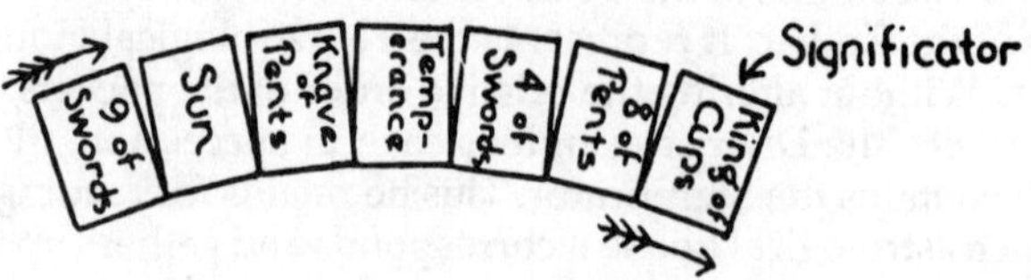

This mode of reading shows that as the Significator is in the Ascendant it will principally relate to the Enquirer's manner of living at this point.

The Significator is in this case right way up, whereas in the previous reading it was inverted and is looking towards the 9 of Swords, which direction therefore the reading proceeds, counting thus: 4 from King of Cups—Knave of Pentacles; 7 from this—Sun; 9 from this—Knave of Pentacles; 7 from this—Sun; where the reading ends.

King of Cups

Knave of Pentacles — "The Enquirer is unhappy" (looking to 9 of Swords) "and makes the acquaintance of the girl with the dark hair and blue eyes with whom the dark young man (his rival) is in love. (She is artistic and well-mannered, and hopes to carry out her wishes, i.e. to marry the dark man with whom the fair girl, to whom the Enquirer has transferred his affection, is now in love.) For she is beginning to be apprehensive regarding her success, and is jealous in consequence."

<191> Pairing the cards from opposite ends of the horseshoe the Diviner proceeds:

King of Cups
9 of Swords — "The Enquirer is anxious, and his health begins to suffer,

8 of Pentacles
Sun — "but hopes ultimately to succeed through skillful action in the matter."

4 of Swords
Knave of Pentacles — "He therefore endeavours to make a friend of the dark girl

Temperance — as he expects to realize his wishes by his means in the end." (This is shown by the card being single in the end.)

THIRD OPERATION

(Continuing the Development of the Question)

The Enquirer again carefully shuffles the cards, while thinking earnestly of her affairs. The pack is not cut. The Diviner deals out the cards into 12 Packets in precisely the same manner as in the Second Operation. Only instead of being referred to the 12 Astrological Houses, these 12 Packets are under the presidency of the 12 Keys of the Tarot attributed to the 12 Signs of the Zodiac. The first packet, Emperor—Aries, the 2nd, Hierophant—Taurus, the 3rd, Lovers—Gemini, and so on. As before the Diviner selects the packet which contains the Significator for reading, and rejects the rest. He notes also the meaning of the Key answering to the Sign of the Zodiac, under which the Packet falls. He spreads the cards out in the form of a horseshoe, exactly as before. I now continue the example before commenced.

EXAMPLE

We will suppose that the Packet containing the King of Cups is that whose position answers to the Hierophant—Taurus and that it consists of the following cards, arranged as in the diagram on page 192.

The Hierophant and the majority of the cards in this packet
<192> being Keys alike show that the forces at present at work are ceasing to be under the control of the Enquirer. The reading proceeds according to the usual order of counting, as follows: King of Cups, 2 of Wands. Magician—Queen of Wands; Universe—Tower; 2 of Wands again. It

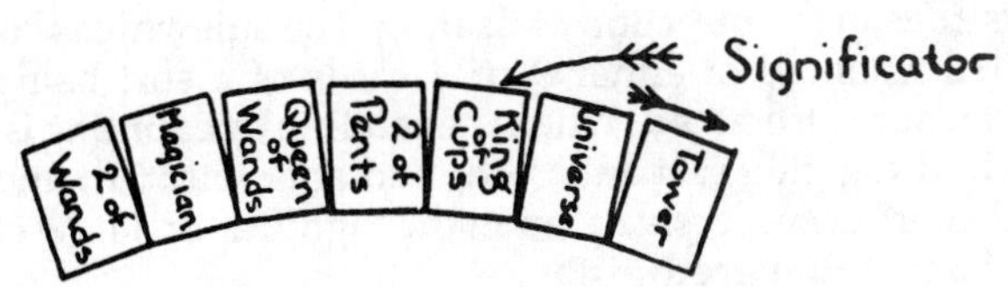

may be mentioned that supposing a packet to consist of six cards, and the Significator to be a Knave, or counting 7 from it, it would come back to the Knave again, this would show that the Enquirer would act according to his own ideas in this point of the question, and would not let his line of action be influenced by the opinion of others. (The reading would then proceed by the pairing of the cards as usual:)

King of Cups 2 of Wands	"Though anxious concerning several matters, he (the Enquirer) is beginning to succeed better by this line of action
Magician Queen of Wands	"which seems to be quite the best. But the older woman (who previously made mischief and was represented by the Queen of Cups in the 1st Operation) who is artful and a gossip
Universe—Tower 2 of Wands	"again injures the matter because she wishes to get an influence over the Enquirer herself."

Pairing the cards, the Diviner proceeds:

2 of Wands Tower	"Her influence cunningly exercised, brings about a complete disruption of the whole matter.
Universe Magician	"The entire matter becomes invested with trickery and glamour
Queen of Wands King of Cups	"as she herself pays him a good deal of attention and sympathy
2 of Pentacles	"which furthers her plans by bringing about a friendship between them."

<193>

FOURTH OPERATION

(The further development of the Question)

As before the Enquirer is instructed to shuffle the pack and place it on the table but not to *cut* it.

The Diviner takes the Pack, turns it face upwards, and goes through it, being careful not to disarrange the order of the cards, till he finds the Significator; at this point he cuts the Pack, that is to say, he takes the Significator and the cards which had been beneath it and places them on the top of the remainder, turning the whole face downwards again, ready for dealing out. (Very careful here: S.A.)

The consequence of this Operation is that the Significator becomes the top card in the pack (bottom, really; face on table.) The Diviner takes off the Significator, places it face upwards on the middle of the table and then the following 36 Decanates—36 cards out in the form of a circle round it, face upwards, answering to the 36 Decanates of the Zodiac, and showing the further development of the Question. These are dealt round in the order and direction of dealing as the 12 packets in the two previous operations.

The reading proceeds by the same law of counting, but instead of counting from the Significator itself, it begins from the first card of the 36, and always goes in the direction of dealing. The suit which is in the majority and the circumstances of either 3 or 4 cards of a sort being found in the 36 Decanates are also noted. When the reading by counting is finished the cards are paired together: 1st and 36th; 2nd and 35th; 3rd and 34th; and so on, placed in order successively upon the Significator. I now continue the example before commenced:

EXAMPLE

We will suppose the Enquirer to have shuffled the pack, and that the Diviner takes it in his hands, and in turning it up finds the bottom card to be Temperance. On going through it he comes to the Significator, thus:

<194>

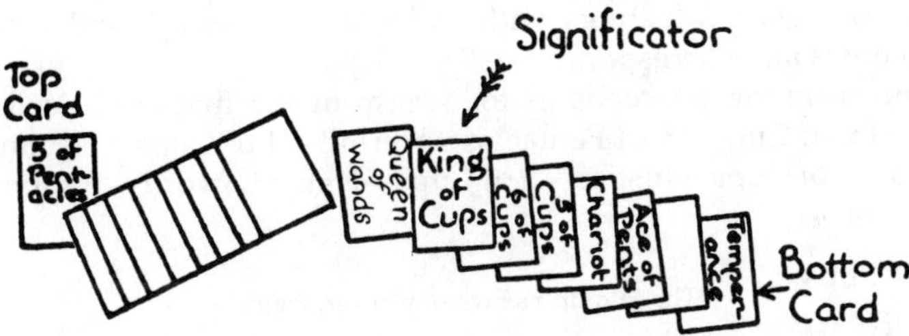

He therefore takes the cards from King of Cups to Temperance included and places them above (or behind, *S.A.)* the 5 of Pentacles, being careful not to disturb their relative order. This has really the effect of cutting the pack between the Queen of Wands and the King of Cups and of course when he

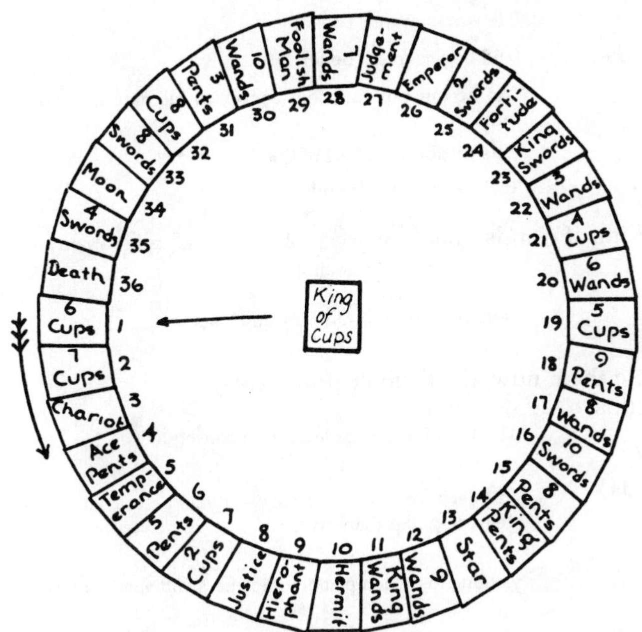

again turns them face downwards ready for dealing, the King of Cups will necessarily be the top card and the Queen of Wands the bottom card; Temperance being immediately above the 5 of Pentacles, the *former* top
<195> card. The Diviner takes the top card, the Significator and places it face upwards in the centre, and then deals round in succession 36 cards, face upwards in the order shown in the Diagram on page 194.

Let us suppose them to be thus arranged. The reading always proceeds in the same direction as the dealing in this form of operation, commencing the counting from the 1st card dealt.

We here find 12 out of the 22 keys; 7 of Wands; 7 of Cups; 5 of Swords; 6 of Pentacles; total 37 including Significator. The preponderance of the Keys represent "Influences beyond the control of the Enquirer." There are four Princes (Kings)—"Meetings with influential persons," and four Eights, "Much news and correspondence."

The counting proceeds as follows from the first card dealt. King of Cups—Six of Cups—5 of Pentacles—Hermit—4 of Cups—Fortitude—4 of Swords—7 of Cups—Justice—5 of Cups—King of Swords—Emperor—6 of Cups again.

King of Cups
6 of Cups — "The Enquirer's love of pleasure-going

5 of Pentacles — "brings about loss of money and business

Hermit — "and he is forced to be more prudent,

4 of Cups — "and not go into the society of others so much, which has already brought him anxiety" (shown by 4 Cups between 2 Wands, contrary element weakening effect on this card.)

Fortitude — "He works more closely,

4 of Swords — "and begins to get better.

7 of Cups — "Yet he has not sufficient energy in his nature to stick to work for long."

Justice — "The retributive effect of this is

5 of Cups — "that he loses his friends."

<196> King of Wands — "And his former rival who, though rather a vain man, is energetic and hard working

Emperor
6 of Cups — "replaces him in popularity and esteem."

Pairing them now, the Diviner proceeds:

King of Cups
Death
6 of Cups — "The Enquirer loses pleasure in consequence

4 of Swords
7 of Cups — "and becomes less energetic even than before, and more anxious for pleasure-going than ever,

Moon
Chariot — "yielding to the temptation of idleness and vanity by means of fraud.

8 of Swords
Ace of Pentacles — "He embezzles the money of his employer, and sees prison staring him in the face."

8 of Cups
Temperance — "The result of this is the loss of good name

3 of Pentacles
5 of Pentacles — "and of his situation of trust.

10 of Wands 2 of Cups	"His former friends and admirers turn a cold shoulder to him.
Foolish Man Justice	"And the result of his folly is that he is arrested and brought before a court of law.
7 of Wands Hierophant	"The decision is adverse
Judgment Hermit	"and judgment very justly given against him.
Emperor King of Wands	"But his employer, though stern, is a kind-hearted man, and
2 of Swords 9 of Wands	"offers to take him back and overlook the past
<197> Star Fortitude	"As he hopes this will have proved a lesson to him,
King of Swords King of Pentacles	"and points out to him that his former rival,
3 of Wands 8 of Pentacles	"though perhaps vain, was yet a hard-working and good man of business."
4 of Cups 10 of Swords	"The Enquirer in consequence of this determines to completely give up his former mode of life which had brought him to the brink of ruin, and becomes a steady man.
8 of Wands 6 of Wands	"After this he suddenly receives a hasty message which gives him much pleasure,
5 of Cups 9 of Pentacles	"stating that owing to the loss of a relative he is the inheritor of a legacy."

This concludes the Fourth Operation.

It is always necessary for the Diviner to employ his intuition in reading, and sometimes he may have to clairvoyantly "go through" a card of doubtful signification. Thus in the reading just given it is only the circumstance of the Moon, Chariot, 8 of Swords, Ace of Pentacles being followed by other comformative cards which justifies such an evil meaning of them.

FIFTH OPERATION

(Conclusion of the Matter)

The cards are to be again carefully shuffled by the Enquirer but NOT cut. The Diviner then takes the Pack, and deals it card by card in rotation into ten answering to the Tree of Life. This refers to the rule of the 10 Sephiroth in the Celestial Heavens. This being done, the Diviner selects the packet containing the Significator for reading, noting carefully under which Sephirah it falls, and taking this as a *general* indication in the matter. This packet is then spread out in a horseshoe form, and read in the usual way, counting from
<198> the Significator and this time in the direction in which the face of the
figure looks. The cards are finally paired together as in the previous Operation. This completes the Mode of Divination called "The Opening of the Key." I now give the conclusion of the example.

EXAMPLE

We will suppose that the cards have been shuffled and dealt in the following manner into 10 Packets answering to the Sephiroth in the Tree of Life:

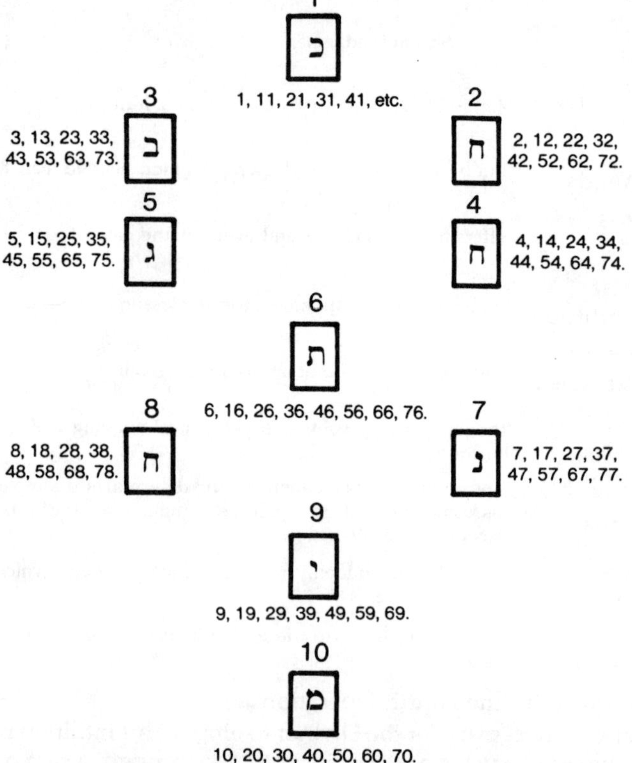

The packet containing the Significator falls under Binah, containing the 3, 13, 23, 33, 43, 53, 63, and 73rd cards dealt. This is an argument of sadness and trial. The cards are spread as follows:

<199>

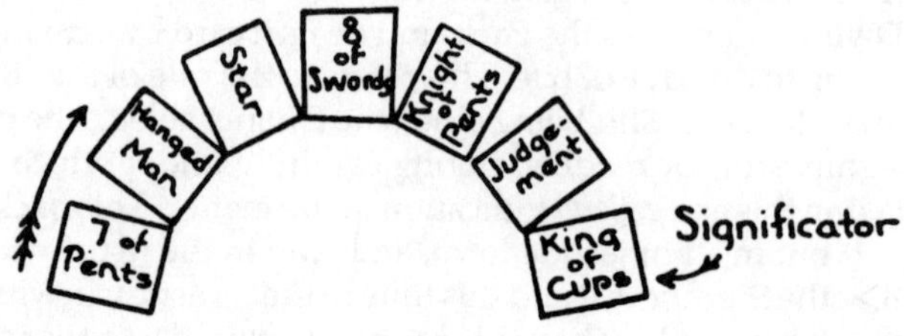

The counting proceeds as follows: King of Cups—Star—Judgment—King of Cups again. Evil cards are in the majority, another argument of loss and trouble.

King of Cups Star Judgment	"He has hopes of thus re-establishing his fortunes and that a favourable result will ensue for him."

The diviner then pairs them thus:

King of Cups 7 of Pentacles	"He plunges therefore into speculation by which he loses heavily (7 Pents. is near Hanged Man.)
Knave of Cups Hanged Man	"and his love affair comes to nothing.
Star Judgment	"All his expectations are disappointed
Knight of Pentacles 8 of Swords	"and his life for a time is arduous, petty, and uninteresting"

(The coming of trouble is here shown by the Knight of Pentacles looking *against* the direction of the reading. If it were turned the other way it would show that his troubles were quitting him and that matters would improve.) This completes the operation, and shows the general development and result of the question.

<200> TABULATED RULES

1. *Shuffling, Cutting, Dealing and Examining.*

In shuffling, the mind of the Enquirer should be earnestly fixed on the matter concerning which he desires information. If any cards fall in the process, they should be taken up without being noticed and the shuffling resumed. The shuffling being concluded, and the pack placed upon the table, if any cards fall to the ground, or become turned in a different direction, the shuffling should be done again.

A cut should be clean and decided. If any cards fall from the hand in the performance, the operation of shuffling should be repeated before they are again cut. In dealing, care should be taken not to invert the cards, and their relative order should be strictly observed. In examining a pack of cards, their relative order should be rigidly maintained, as without care in this respect, one may be easily pushed under or over another, which would of course have the effect of completely altering the counting in the Reading.

2. *Of the Selection of the Significator, and of the Complexion assigned to the Court Cards.*

Wands generally—fair and red-haired person.
Cups generally—moderately fair.
Swords generally—moderately dark.
Pentacles generally—very dark.
The Kings—Men.
Queens—Women.
Princes—Young Men.
Princesses (Knaves)—Young women.

Therefore the Significators are to be thus selected. For example, a dark complexioned middle-aged man, King of Pentacles. A fair young woman, Princess (Knave) of Cups, etc.

In the actual reading of the cards, these descriptions can be
<201> modified by those which are on either side of them, thus: The
Queen of Cups, which indicates a fair woman with golden brown hair, if between cards of the suits of Swords and Pentacles, would show a woman with rather dark brown hair and dark eyes. As before stated, the Princes and Queens almost invariably represent actual men and women connected with the subject in hand. But the Kings sometimes represent either the coming on or going off of a matter; arrival, or departure, according to the way in which they face. While the Princesses (Knaves) show opinions, thoughts, or ideas, either in harmony with or opposed to the subject.

3. *Of the General signification of the Majority of a particular suit and of the particular signification of either 3 or 4 cards of a sort in a reading:*

A majority of Wands—Energy, quarrelling, opposition.

A majority of Cups—Pleasure and merriment.

A majority of Swords—Trouble and sadness, sometimes sickness and even death.

A majority of Pentacles—business, money, possessions, etc.

A majority of Keys—Forces of considerable strength, but beyond the Enquirer's control.

A majority of Court Cards—Society, meeting with many persons.

A majority of Aces—Strength generally; the aces are always strong cards.

4 Aces—Great power and Force.

3 Aces—Riches and Success.

4 Kings—Great swiftness and rapidity.

3 Kings—unexpected meetings.

Kings generally show news.

4 Queens generally—Authority and influence.

3 Queens generally—Powerful and influential friends.

4 Princes or Knights—Meetings with the great.

3 Princes or Knights—Rank and honour.

4 Princesses (Knaves)—New ideas and plans.

3 Princesses (Knaves)—Society of the young.

4 Tens generally—Anxiety and responsibility.

<202> 3 Tens generally—Buying, selling, commercial transactions.

4 Nines generally—Added responsibility.

3 Nines generally—Much correspondence.

4 Eights generally—Much news.

3 Eights generally—Much journeying.

4 Sevens generally—Disappointments.

3 Sevens generally—Treaties and compacts.

4 Sixes generally—Pleasure.

3 Sixes generally—Gain and Success.

4 Fives generally—Order, regularity.

3 Fives generally—Quarrels, fights.

4 Fours generally—Rest and Peace.
3 Fours generally—Industry.
4 Threes generally—Resolution and determination.
3 Threes generally—Deceit.
4 Deuces generally—Conference and conversations.
3 Deuces generally—Reorganization and recommencement of a thing.
The Keys are *not* noticed as above, by threes and fours.

4. *Extra, and brief meaning of the 36 smaller cards.*

WANDS

Deuce—Influence over another. Dominion.
Three—Pride and arrogance. Power sometimes.
Four—Settlement. Arrangement completed.
Five—Quarrelling. Fighting.
Six—Gain and success.
Seven—Opposition; sometimes courage therewith.
Eight—A hasty communication, letter or message. Swiftness.
Nine—Strength. Power. Health. Energy.
Ten—Cruelty and malice towards others. Overbearing strength. Revenge. Injustice.

CUPS

Deuce—Marriage, love, pleasure. Warm friendship.
<203> Three—Plenty. Hospitality, eating, drinking. Pleasure, dancing, new clothes and merriment.
Four—receiving pleasures or kindness from others, yet some discomfort therewith.
Five—Disappointment in love. Marriage broken off, etc. Unkindness from friends. (Whether deserved or NOT is shown by the cards with it, or counting from or to it.) Loss of friendship.
Six—Wish, happiness, success, enjoyment.
Seven—Lying, deceit, promises unfulfilled, illusion, deception. Error, slight success, but not enough energy to retain it.
Eight—Success abandoned, decline of interest in a thing. Ennui.
Nine—Complete success. Pleasure and happiness. Wishes fulfilled.
Ten—Matters definitely arranged and settled in accordance with one's wishes. Complete good-fortune.

SWORDS

Deuce—Quarrel made up, and arranged. Peace restored, yet some tension in relations.
Three—Unhappiness, sorrow, tears.
Four—Convalescence, recovery from sickness, change for the better.
Five—Defeat, loss, malice. Slander, evil-speaking.
Six—Labour, work; journey, probably by water. (Shown by cards near by.)
Seven—In character untrustworthy, vacillation. Journey probably by land (shown by cards near, etc.)
Eight—Narrow or restricted. Petty. A prison.

Nine—Illness. Suffering. Malice. Cruelty. Pain.
Ten—Ruin. Death. Failure. Disaster.

PENTACLES

Deuce—Pleasant change. Visit to friends, etc.
Three—Business, paid employment. Commercial transactions.
Four—Gain of money and influence. A present.
<204> Five—Loss of profession. Loss of money. Monetary anxiety.
Six—Success in material things; prosperity in business.
Seven—Unprofitable speculations, employments; also honorary work undertaken for the love of it, and without desire of reward.
Eight—Skill, prudence, also artfulness, and cunning. (Depends on cards with it.)
Nine—Inheritance. Much increase of money.
Ten—Riches and wealth.

5. *Brief Meanings of the 22 Keys.*

0. *Foolish Man.* Idea, thought, spirituality, that which endeavours to rise above the material. (That is, if the subject which is enquired about be spiritual.) But if the Divination be regarding a material event of ordinary life, this card is not good, and shows folly, stupidity, eccentricity, and even mania, unless with very good cards indeed. It is too ideal and unstable to be generally good in material things.

1. *Magician or Juggler.* Skill, wisdom, adaptation. Craft, cunning, etc., always depending on its dignity. Sometimes Occult Wisdom.

2. *High Priestess.* Change, alteration, Increase and Decrease. Fluctuation (whether for good or evil is again shown by cards connected with it.) Compare with Death and Moon.

3. *Empress.* Beauty, happiness, pleasure, success, also luxury and sometimes dissipation, but only if with very evil cards.

4. *Emperor.* War, conquest, victory, strife, ambition.

5. *Hierophant.* Divine Wisdom. Manifestation. Explanation. Teaching. Differing from, though resembling in some respects, the meaning of The Magician, The Prophet, and The Lovers. Occult Wisdom.

6. *The Lovers.* Inspiration (passive and in some cases mediumistic, thus differing from that of the Hierophant and Magician and Prophet.) Motive, power, and action, arising from Inspiration and Impulse.

<205> 7. *The Chariot.* Triumph. Victory. Health. Success though sometimes not stable and enduring.

8. *Justice.* Eternal Justice and Balance. Strength and Force, but arrested as in the act of Judgment. Compare with 11—Fortitude. Also in combination with other cards, legal proceedings, a court of law, a trial at law, etc.

9. *The Hermit, or Prophet.* Wisdom sought for and obtained from above. Divine Inspiration (but active as opposed to that of the Lovers). In the mystical titles, this with the Hierophant and the Magician are the 3 Magi.

10. *Wheel of Fortune.* Good fortune and happiness (within bounds), but sometimes also a species of intoxication with success, if the cards near it bear this out.

11. *Fortitude. (At one time 8 Justice and 11 Fortitude were transposed.)* Cour-

age, Strength, Fortitude. Power not arrested as in the act of Judgment, but passing on to further action, sometimes obstinacy, etc. Compare with 8—Justice.

12. *Hanged Man or Drowned Man.* Enforced sacrifice. Punishment, Loss. Fatal and not voluntary. Suffering generally.

13. *Death.* Time. Ages. Transformation. Change involuntary as opposed to The Moon, XIX. Sometimes death and destruction, but rarely the latter, and the former only if it is borne out by the cards with it. Compare also with High Priestess.

14. *Temperance.* Combination of Forces. Realisation. Action (material). Effect either for good or evil.

15. *Devil.* Materiality. Material Force. Material temptation; sometimes obsession, especially if associated with the Lovers.

16. *Tower.* Ambition, fighting, war, courage. Compare with Emperor. In certain combinations, destruction, danger, fall, ruin.

17. *Star.* Hope, faith, unexpected help. But sometimes also dreaminess, deceived hope, etc.

<206> 18. *Moon.* Dissatisfaction, voluntary change (as opposed to 13—Death). Error, lying, falsity, deception. (The whole according whether the card is well or ill-dignified, and on which it much depends.)

19. *Sun.* Glory, Gain, Riches. Sometimes also arrogance. Display, Vanity, but only when with very evil cards.

20. *Judgment.* Final decision. Judgment. Sentence. Determination of a matter without appeal on its plane.

21. *Universe.* The matter itself. Synthesis. World. Kingdom. Usually denotes the actual subject of the question, and therefore depends entirely on the accompanying cards.

6. *On the Signification of the Cards.*

A card is strong or weak, well-dignified or ill-dignified, according to the cards which are next to it on either side. Cards of the same suit on either side strengthen it greatly either for good or evil, according to their nature. Cards of the suits answering to its contrary element, on either side, *weaken* it greatly for good or evil. Air and Earth are contraries as also are Fire and Water. Air is friendly with Water and Fire, and Fire with Air and Earth.

If a card of the suit of Wands falls between a Cup and a Sword, the Sword modifies and connects the Wand with the Cup, so that it is not weakened by its vicinity, but is modified by the influence of both cards; therefore fairly strong. But if a card pass between two which are naturally contrary, it is not affected by either much, as a Wand between a Sword and a Pentacle which latter, being Air and Earth, are contrary and therefore weaken each other.

Here the question being of the Wand, this card is not to be noticed as forming a link between the Sword and Pentacle.

<207>

A FEW EXAMPLES GIVEN BY S.R.M.D.

9 Sw.	10 Sw.	5 Sw.	Very strong and potent in action. Very evil.
10 W.	10 Sw.	2 W.	Not quite so strong. Ruin checked and perhaps overcome.

6 C.	10 Sw.	10 C.	Rather good than otherwise. It is bounty overcoming loss, like a piquant sauce which adds to pleasure.
9 P.	10 Sw.	10 C.	Very weak, slight loss in material things, but more anxiety than actual loss.
5 Sw.	2 W.	9 Sw.	Moderately strong. Rashness which brings evil in its train. Evil.
9 P.	2 W.	6 P.	Fairly strong. Good. Considerable gain and victory.
10 C.	2 W.	6 C.	Weak, evil. Victory which is perverted by debauchery and evil living. But other cards may mitigate the judgment.
9 Sw.	10 C.	5 Sw.	Medium strong. Evil. Sorrow arising from pleasure and through one's own pleasures.
9 P.	10 C.	6 P.	Perfect success and happiness.
10 W.	10 C.	5 Sw.	Rather evil. Pleasure that when obtained is not worth the trouble one has had in obtaining it.
10 Sw.	6 C.	9 P.	Fairly strong and good. The Sw. and P. being opposite elements counteract each other. Therefore is it as if they were not there.
10 Sw.	6 C.	10 W.	Fairly good. Some trouble, but trouble which is overcome. If If 6 C. were a bad card the evil would carry the day.
9 Sw.	Death	3 Sw.	Death accompanied by much pain and misery.
9 W.	9 Sw.	High Priestess	Recovery from sickness.
6 Sw.	Q. W.	King P.	An active woman, courageous and reliable with dark chestnut hair, and open fearless expression.
7 C.	King C.	5 Sw.	A rather fair man but very deceitful and malicious.

7. *On pairing the Cards together in reading.*

On pairing the cards each is to be taken as of equal force with
<208> the other. If of opposite elements they mutually weaken each other.

If at the end of the pairing of the cards in a packet, one card remains over, it signifies the partial result of that particular part of the Divination only. If an evil card and the others good, it would modify the good.

If it be the Significator of the Enquirer, or of another person, it would show that matters would much depend on the line of action taken by the person represented. The reason of this importance of the single card is, that it is alone, and not modified. If two cards are at the end instead of a single one, they are not of so much importance.

8. *On the Exercise of Clairvoyance and Intuition.*

The Diviner should, in describing any person from a Significator in the actual reading, endeavour, by Clairvoyance and using the card in question as a symbol, to see the person implied using the rules to aid, and restrict, his vision. In describing an event from the cards in the reading, he should employ his intuition in the same manner. Personal descriptions are modified by the cards next them; e.g., the Knave of Wands represents usually a very fair girl, but if between cards of the suit of Pentacles, she might be even quite dark, though the Wands would still give a certain *brightness* to hair, eyes, and complexion.

9. *On counting in the Reading.*

In all cases of counting from the card last touched, the card itself is 1, that next it is 2, and so on.

From every Ace—5 is counted.
From every Princess (Knave)—7 is counted.
From every other Court card—4 is counted.
From every small card—the number of its pips.
From every Key answering to an Element—3 is counted.
From every Key answering to a Sign—12 is counted.
From every Key answering to a Planet—9 is counted.

<209> Unofficial

THE TAROT TRUMPS

By G. H. Soror, Q.L.

The cards of the Lesser Arcana present to us the vibrations of Number, Colour and Element—that is, the plane on which number and colour function. Thus, in the Ten of Pentacles we have the number Ten and tertiary colours, citrine, olive, and russet, working in Malkuth, the material plane. Whereas in the Ten of Wands we have the number Ten and the tertiaries working in pure energy. In these cards, the Sephirah is indicated by the colouring of the clouds; the plane by the colouring of the symbols

The four honours of each suit taken in their most abstract sense may be interpreted as:

Potential Power .... The King
Brooding Power .... The Queen
Power in action .... The Prince
Reception and Transmission .... The Princess

All these cards are coloured according to their elements plus the Sephirah to which they are attributed. With the Greater Arcana, the Trumps, however, we are given the Keys to divine manifestation, each one an individual force to be considered independently. It must never be forgotten that the Trumps are, intrinsically, glyphs of cosmic not human forces.

0. *The Foolish Man.* This card as usually presented shows a man in motley striding along, heedless of the dog which tears his garments and threatens to attack him. In this is seen only the lower aspect of the card, giving no hint to the Divine Folly of which St. Paul speaks. But in the Order pack, an effort is made to reveal the deeper meaning. A naked child stands beneath a rose-tree bearing yellow roses—the golden Rose of Joy as well as the
<210> Rose of Silence. While reaching up to the Roses, he yet holds in
leash a grey wolf, worldly wisdom held in check by perfect innocence. The colours are pale yellow, pale blue, greenish yellow—suggestive of the early dawn of a spring day.

I. The Magician. It represents the union and balance of the elemental powers controlled by mind. The Adept dedicating the minor implements on the Altar. The paths of Beth and Mercury link Kether the Crown with Binah, the Aimah Elohim. The Magician, therefore, is reflected in the Intellect which stores and gathers up knowledge and pours it into the House of Life, Binah. The number of the Path, 12, suggests the synthesis of the Zodiac, as Mercury is the synthesis of the planets. The colours yellow, violet, grey and indigo, point to the mysterious astral light surrounding the great Adept. It is a card linked with the name Tahuti and Hermes as the previous one is with Krishna and Harparkrat or Dionysius.

II. The High Priestess. The High Priestess rules the long path uniting

Kether to Tiphareth, crossing the reciprocal Paths of Venus and Leo. She is the great feminine force controlling the very source of life, gathering into herself all the energising forces and holding them in solution until the time of release. Her colours, pale blue, deepening into sky blue, silvery white, and silver, relieved by touches of orange and flame, carry out these ideas.

III. The Empress. She is an aspect of Isis; the creative and positive side of Nature is suggested here. The Egyptian trilogy, Isis, Hathor and Nephthys, symbolised by the crescent, full moon, and gibbous moon are represented in the Tarot by the High Priestess, Hathor. The Empress, Isis, takes either the crescent moon or Venus as her symbol. Justice, Nephthys, takes the gibbous moon.

Isis and Venus gives the aspect of Love, while Hathor is rather the Mystic, the full moon reflecting the Sun of Tiphareth while in Yesod, transmitting the rays of the Sun in her path Gimel. In interpreting a practical
<211> Tarot it is often admissable to regard the Empress as standing for Occultism. The High Priestess for religion, the Church as distinguished from the Order.

The Empress, whose letter is Daleth, is the Door of the inner mysteries, as Venus is the door of the Vault. Her colours are emerald, sky-blue, blue-green and cerise or rose-pink.

IV. The Emperor. Here we have the great energising forces as indicated by the varying shades of red. It may be noted here that the red paths remain red in all planes, varying only in shade. Thus Aries, the Emperor, the Pioneer, the General, is blood and deep crimson, red, pure vermillion or flowing fiery red. He is *Ho Nike,* the Conqueror, hot, passionate, impetuous, the apotheosis of Mars, whether in love or in war. He is the positive masculine as the Empress is the positive feminine.

V. Hierophant. The High Priest is the counterpart of the High Priestess. As Aries is the house of Mars and the exaltation of the Sun, so Taurus is the house of Venus and the exaltation of the Moon. He is the reflective or mystical aspect of the masculine. He is the thinker as the Emperor is the doer.

His colours unlike those of the Emperor, vary considerably. Red, orange, maroon, deep brown, and chestnut brown, suggest veiled thought, interior power, endurance, contemplation and reconciliation. This card frequently indicates the hidden guardianship of the Masters.

VI. The Lovers. The impact of inspiration on intuition, resulting in illumination and liberation—the sword striking off the fetters of habit and materialism, Perseus rescuing Andromeda from the Dragon of fear and the waters of Stagnation. (Note: Incidentally note that this is the design of the Order card. Andromeda is shown manacled to a rock, the dragon rising from the waters at her feet. Perseus is depicted flying through the air to her assistance, with unsheathed sword. The design is wholly different from that of the Waite pack.—I.R.)

<212> The colours are orange, violet, purplish grey and pearl grey.

The flashing colour of orange gives deep vivid blue while the flashing colour for violet is golden yellow. The flashing colours may always be introduced if they bring out the essential colour meaning more clearly. In practise this card usually signifies sympathetic understanding.

VII. The Chariot. Here we have a symbol of the spirit of man controlling the lower principles, soul and body, and thus passing triumphantly through the astral plane, rising above the clouds of illusion and penetrating to the higher spheres.

The colours amber, silver-grey, blue-grey, and the deep blue violet of the night sky elucidate this symbol. It is the sublimation of the Psyche.

VIII. Strength. This also represents the mastery of the lower by the higher. But in this case it is the soul which holds in check the passions, although her feet are still planted on earth, and the dark veil still floats about her head and clings around her. The colours, pale greenish yellow, black, yellowish grey and reddish amber, suggest the steadfast endurance and fortitude required, but the deep red rose which is the flashing colour to the greenish yellow, gives the motive power.

IX. The Hermit. Prudence. These three trumps should be collated in studying them for they represent the three stages of initiation. The man wrapped in hood and mantle, and carrying a lantern to illuminate the Path and a staff to support his footsteps, He is the eternal seeker, the Pilgrim soul. His hood and mantle are the brown of earth, and above him is the night-sky. But the delicate yellow-greens and bluish greens of spring are about him, and spring is in his heart.

X. *Wheel of Fortune.* In the Etz Chayim, or the Tree of Life, the Wheel is placed on the Pillar of Mercy, where it forms the principal column linking Netzach to Chesed, Victory to Mercy. It is the revolution of experience and progress, the steps of the Zodiac, the revolving staircase, held in
<213> place by the counterchanging influence of Light and Darkness,
Time and Eternity—presided over by the Plutonian cynocephalus below, and the Sphinx of Egypt above, the eternal Riddle which can only be solved when we attain liberation. The basic colours of this Trump are blue, violet, deep purple, and blue irradiated by yellow. But the zodiacal spokes of the wheel should be in the colours of the spectrum, while the Ape is in those of Malkuth, and the Sphinx in the primary colours and black.

XI. Justice. Nephthys, the third aspect of Luna, the twin sister of Isis. Justice as distinguished from love. Her emblems are the Sword and the Scales. Like her sister, she is clothed in green, but in a sharper colder green than the pure emerald of Isis. Her subsidiary colours are blue, blue-green, pale green. It is only by utilising the flashing colours that we can find the hidden warmth and steadfastness.

XII. The Hanged Man. An elusive, because a profoundly significant symbol. It is sacrifice — the submergence of the higher in the lower in order to sublimate the lower. It is the descent of the Spirit into Matter, the incarnation of God in man, the submission to the bonds of matter that the material may be transcended and transmuted. The colours are deep blue, white and black intermingled but not merged, olive, green and greenish fawn.

XIII. Death. The sign of transmutation and disintegration. The skeleton which alone survives the destructive power of time, may be regarded as the foundation upon which the structure is built, the type which persists through the permutations of Time and Space, adaptable to the requirements of evolution and yet radically unchanged; the transmuting power of Nature working from below upwards, as the Hanged Man is the transmuting power of the spirit working from above downwards. The colours are blue-green, both dark and pale, the two dominant colours of the visible world, and the flashing colours of orange and red-orange.

<214> *XIV. Temperance.* This is the equilibrium not of the balance of Libra but of the impetus of the Arrow, Sagittarius, which cleaves its way through the air by the force imparted to it by the taut string of the Bow. It requires the counterchanged forces of Fire and Water, Shin and Qoph, held by the restraining power of Saturn, and concentrated by the energies of Mars to initiate this impetus. All these are summed up in the symbolism of the figure standing between Earth and Water, holding the two amphorae with their streams of living water, and with the volcano in the background. The colours are bright-blue, blue-grey, slate-blue, and lilac-grey.

XV. The Devil. This card should be studied in conjunction with No. 13. They are the two great controlling forces of the Universe, the centrifugal and the centripetal, destructive and reproductive, dynamic and static. The lower nature of man fears and hates the transmuting process; hence the chains binding the lesser figures and the bestial forms of their lower limbs. Yet this very fear of change and disintegration is necessary to stabilise the life-force and preserve continuity. The colours are indigo, livid brown, golden brown and grey.

XVI. The Tower. As always red remains persistent throughout the four planes, although modified in tone. Thus we find vivid scarlet shading into deep sombre red and vermillion shot with amber. The contrasting shades of green serve to throw the red into relief. The tremendous destructive influence of the lightning, rending asunder established forms to make way for new forms to emerge, revolution as distinguished from transmutation or sublimation, the destructive as opposed to the conservative, energy attacking inertia, the impetuous ejection of those who would enclose themselves in the walls of ease and tradition.

XVII. The Star. This shows the seven-pointed Star of Venus shining above the Waters of Aquarius, the guiding force of love in all its forms and aspects, illuminates the soul during her immersion in Humanity, so
<215> that the bonds of Saturn are dissolved in the purified Waters of Bap-
tism. The dove of the Spirit hovers above the Tree of Knowledge giving the promise of ultimate attainment — and on the other side gleams of the Tree of Life.

Pale colours suggest dawn and the morning Star — amethyst, pale grey, fawn, dove colour and white, with the pale yellow of the Star.

XVIII. The Moon. Here also is a river but it is the troubled waters of Night, wherein is to be described a crayfish, counterpart of the Scarabeus. From the water's edge winds the dark path of toil, effort and possible failure. It is guarded by the threatening watchdogs, seeking to intimidate the wayfarers, while in the distance the barren hills are surmounted by the frowning fortresses still further guarding the way to attainment. It is the path of blood and tears in which fear, weakness, and fluctuation must be overcome. The colours are dark crimson, reddish brown, brownish crimson and plum colours — but their sombre hues are lightened by the translucent faint greens and yellows to be found in their counterparts.

XIX. The Sun. The Watery Paths of trial and probation are counterbalanced by the fiery paths of Temptation, Judgment, and Decision. In violent contrast to the sombre colouring of Aquarius and Pisces, we are confronted by the flaring hues of the Sun and Fire. The too-aspiring Icarus may find his waxen wings of Ambition and Curiosity shrivelled and melted by the fiery rays of the Sun and the heat of Fire, but approached with humility and reverence, the Sun becomes the beneficient source of life.

Protected by an enclosing wall, standing by the Waters of repentance, the Pilgrim may submit himself humbly but without fear to the searching Light and absorb warmth and vitality from it for the struggle before him. The colours are clear-orange, golden-yellow, amber shot with red, and the contrasting blue and purple.

<216> *XX. The Last Judgment.* The three trumps attributed to the Elemental Paths are perhaps the most difficult to understand. They represent the action of forces exterior to the experience of humanity, not the influence of environment but the impact of the Supernals upon the sublunary.

In the Air we have pure spirit holding in leash the lust of the flesh. In water, the sublimating power of sacrifice. Here in Fire, we are shown the cosmic forces concentrating on the pilgrim from all sides. Judgment is pronounced upon him. He is not the judge nor does decision rest in his hands. Lazarus cannot emerge from the Sepulchre until the voice cries out, "Come forth!" Nor can he cast aside the conflicting grave-clothes until the command, "Loose him!" is given. Man of himself is helpless. The impulse to ascend must come from above, but by its power he may transcend the sepulchre of environment and cast aside the trammels of desire. Here once more, the fiery energy of red burns through the planes. Fiery scarlet, glowing crimson, burning red are emphasized by the passive greens.

XXI. The Universe. Observe that this represents not the World but the Universe. It should be remembered that to the ancients, Saturn represented the confines of the Solar system. They had no means of measuring either Uranus or Neptune. To them, therefore, Saturn passing through the spiral path of the Zodiac, marked at its cardinal points by the symbols of the Kerubim forming the Cross, was a comprehensive glyph of the whole.

Thus, in this card we afind a synthesis of the whole Taro or Rota. The central figure should be taken as Hathor, Athor, or Ator, rather than Isis, thus indicating the hidden anagram which may perhaps be translated thus: ORAT — man prays. ATOR — to the Great Mother. TARO — who turns. ROTA — the wheel of Life and Death.

The colours like those of the Wheel of Fortune include the
<217> colours of the Spectrum and those of the elements, but they are
placed against the indigo and black of a Saturn, with the white gleam of the Stars shining in the darkness and the misty figure of the Aimah Elohim in the midst. In the practical Tarot, this card is taken to signify the matter in hand, that is the subject of any question that has been asked.

Having now revised the 22 Atous or Trumps in succession, it will be wise for the Student to reverse the process and seek to follow the Path of the Pilgrim from below upwards, thus seeking to comprehend the interior process of Initiation and Illumination. It is a process in which the whole Universe does not disdain to take part, for Man is himself the Microcosm of the Macrocosm and the Child of the Gods. And again, the Macrocosm must itself be undergoing a corresponding process in which the experience not only of humanity but of each individual must be an integral part. The fragments are gathered up into the baskets, that nothing may be lost; and from the feeding of the multitude there remains not less but more than the unbroken bread and fish — fit emblems of Earth and Water.

Cease not to seek day and night the Purifying Mysteries.

(Note: This paper on the Trumps is not an official document. It should be conceived rather in the nature of a so-called Side Lecture or Flying Roll. That is not to say that it is unimportant, or that there is little of interest therein. On the contrary, certain aspects of this interpretation are not without high significance. Moreover, it should be carefully studied as well as the preceding official Tarot instructions in conjunction with the description of certain of the Trumps in the grade rituals of the First Order.—I.R.)

<218>

THE TREE OF LIFE AS PROJECTED IN A SOLID SPHERE

NOTE BY S.R.M.D.

The Planets' sphere which illustrates this manuscript, a part of the Z.A.M.'s Abstract of the Tarot, has been drawn by S.R.M.D. as instructed. It represents the Heavens polarized on the plane of the Ecliptic, *not* on the plane of the Equator of our Earth, so that its North Pole is the veritable North Pole of our Heavens and not merely that part of them to which the North Pole of our Earth now points.

Another very important difference is that, throughout the true Tarot, the teaching assigns the commencing Point of the Zodiac to the bright Star "Regulus" which is in Leo. And it measures Right Ascension and Longitude from that point, and not from a suppositious point divided by the Equinox and *called* the 0° of Aries (though in reality now far removed from the constellation of that name), which has been adopted by modern or western astronomy and astrology.

By this now usual way of reckoning, and the Precession of the Equinoxes, it has gradually come to pass that the signs (or divisions, each of 30°, of the Zodiac) no longer coincide with the constellations of the same name, and each decade of years shows them slowly but surely receding.

But the Tarot method of reckoning from the star named Regulus has, it will be seen, the effect of making the Signs and the Constellations coincide.

"Regulus" is also named Cor Leonis — "The Heart of the Lion." "Regulus" means "Star of the Prince." "Regulus" coincides with the position of the
"heart" in the figure of Leo upon the Star Maps.
<219> (Note: The principia or fundamental ideas of this astronomical
view of the Tarot may be found, as least in its essential form, in the astronomical writings of Claudius Ptolemy of Alexandria. Naturally, this reference only concerns the signs, constellations and other astronomical divisions noted. The expansion of this scheme, and its allocation to other forms of universal symbolism, such as the Tarot cards, Hebrew letters, and Enochian Tablets, has its roots in the synthetic genius of the Golden Dawn. The idea of projecting the Tree of Life into a solid sphere, having application
among other things to the starry heavens and the constellations,
<220> certainly is peculiar to this system alone. Most of the fundamentals
inhering in the other aspects of the Golden Dawn teaching may be found in exoteric occult literature of past centuries. But, as again I must insist, the peculiar practical application of them as exemplified in the Golden Dawn routine can nowhere else be found, save, of course, in other authentic esoteric systems. The student is urged to study this whole section very thoroughly; it is well worth it. In the early days of the Order there was a

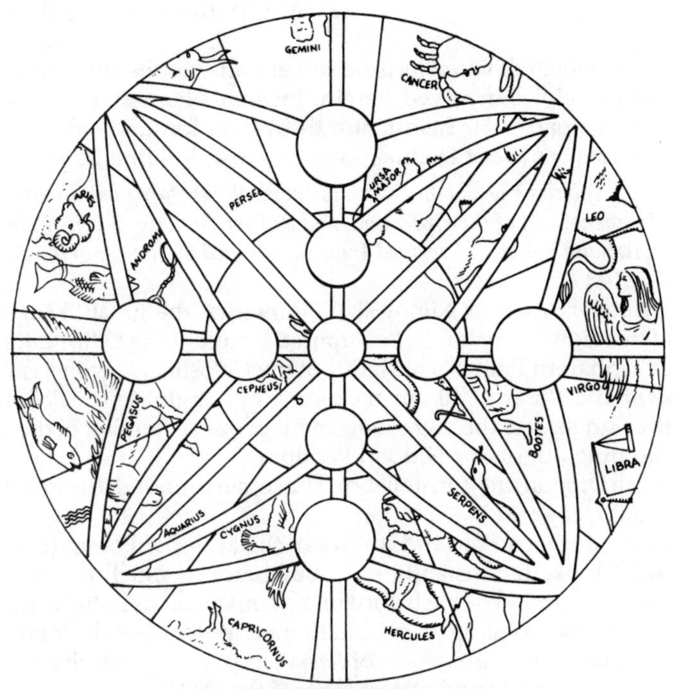

NORTHERN HEMISPHERE

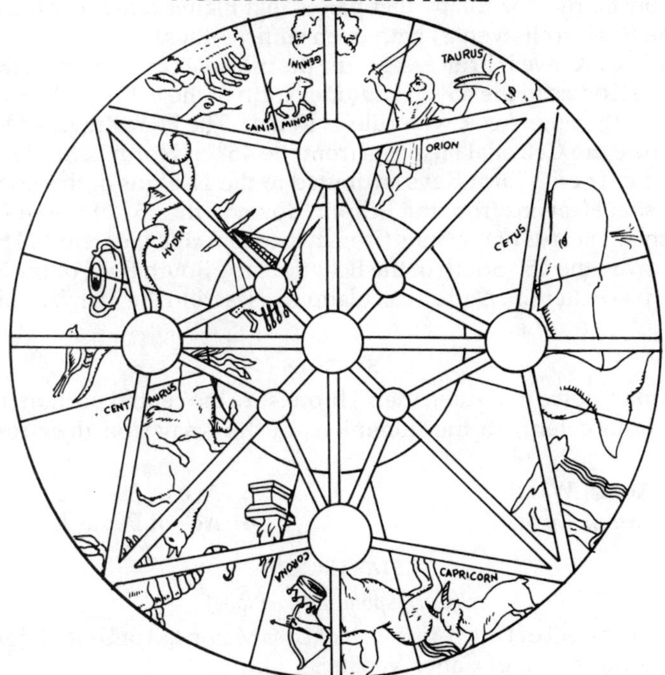

SOUTHERN HEMISPHERE

special group which devoted its time and energies to the study and application of the principles involved herein. Incidentally, may I point out how much light this particular instruction throws on innumerable passages in Blavatsky's *Secret Doctrine*—especially in Volume II.—I.R.)

<221> *Tabular View of the Dominion of the Symbols of Book T in the Celestial Heavens, and of the Operation, and Rule of The Tree of Life in the same as Projected on a Solid Sphere. (Abridged Treatise arranged for the use of the Z.A.M.'s in Anglia by S.R.M.D.)*

The Zelator Adeptus Minor shall know that the great "King Star" or "Heart of the Lion," which is in Leo upon the path of the Ecliptic and one of the "Four Tiphareth Points" (see later) of the Celestial Heavens, is the commencement and Ruler of all our reckoning of Longitude (or Ecliptic). The Path of the Sun itself is the commencement of our reckoning of the Latitude in the searching out of our Hidden Wisdom.

Also the Dragon, the constellation Draco, surroundeth the Pole *Kether* of our Celestial Heavens.

But the Northern Pole and Kether of the Material Planet (even of our Erthe, earth) looketh constantly unto Binah, for as much as she is under sorrow and suffering. When, oh Lord of the Universe, shall she turn from her evil ways so that she shall again behold Kether? Wherefore she is now a place of trial. For each thing in this world of Assiah looketh towards that which is its Natural Governor, and to what part of the Celestial Heavens the Kether of a Planet constantly looketh, by that part is that Planet ruled. For in all things shine the Sephiroth even as hath been sufficiently said.

The Four Knaves (Princesses) rule the celestial Heavens from the North Pole of the Zodiac to the 45° of Latitude North of the Ecliptic. They form the Thrones of the Four Aces, who rule in Kether. The Four Kings, 4 Queens, 4 Princes rule the Celestial Heavens from the 45° of North Latitude down to the Ecliptic. The 12 Tarot Keys attributed to the 12 Signs of the Zodiac rule the Celestial Heavens from the Ecliptic, down to the 45° of South Latitude. The 36 smaller cards of the Suits (from two to ten) rule the Celestial Heavens from the 45° South of the Ecliptic to the South Pole, or the Malkuth
<222> place therein. And all calculation arises from the Star "Regulus," the 0° of our Leo.

SYMBOLS

These Four revolve in Kether, their Thrones are the central portion (of 45° of Longitude in extent) in the dominions of the Knaves of their respective suits.

1. Ace of Wands
2. Ace of Cups
3. Ace of Swords
4. Ace of Pentacles

STAR GROUPS

(Corresponding to above)

1. A part of the tail of Draco, fore-feet of Ursa Major, tail of Ursa Major, and of the Northern dog of Canes Venatici.
2. Head of Draco, body and legs of Hercules.
3. Body of Draco. Right arm of Cepheus, head and body of Lacerta. Body

of Cygnus.

4. Body of Draco. Legs of Cepheus. Tail of Ursa Minor, and the Pole Star. Legs of Cassiopeia. Head and neck of Camelopardus.

8. *Princess (Knave) of Wands.* Rules from North Pole to 45° and from 0° of Cancer to 30° of Virgo, the end of Virgo. The Throne of the Ace of Wands extends 45° from 22°-30′ of Cancer to 7°-30′ of Virgo within the limits of 45° Latitude.

Star groups corresponding to above. Tail of Draco. Head and forepart of Ursa Minor, left arm and part of head and chest of Bootes. The greater part of the Northernmost dog of Canes Venatici. Tail and back of Ursa Major, (ancient Italian name was *Septemtriones,* the 7 Ploughing Oxen). This includes the celebrated Seven stars of the constellation called "Charles Wain" by the English; "Seven Rishis" by the Hindus, and in the Egyptian Book of the Dead,
Ch. XVII, "The Seven bright ones who follow their Lord, the Thigh
<223> of the northern Heaven." (Note: In the Zodiac of Denderah, and in
the Tablet of Edfu, that Ursa Major is represented as the thigh of an Ox.—S.R.M.D.)

12. *Princess (Knave) of Cups.* Rules from North Pole to 45° of Latitude and from 0° of Libra to 30° of Sagittarius in Longitude. The Throne of the Ace embraces from 22°-30′ of Libra to 7°-30′ of Sagittarius within the above limits of Latitude.

Star Group. Head of Draco. Left arm, body and legs of Hercules, part of head, right shoulder and club of Bootes.

16. *Princess (Knave) of Swords.* Rules from North Pole to 45° Latitude and from 0° of Capricorn to 30° of Pisces Longtiude. The Throne of the Ace extends from 22°-30′ of Capricorn to 7°-30′ of Pisces as before.

Star Group. Body of Draco, part of Lyra. Head, body and right arm of Cepheus, the King and Father of Andromeda, the whole of Cygnus, head and body of Lacerta, back and part of head of Vulpecula the Fox.

20. *Princess (Knave) of Pentacles.* Rules from North Pole to 45° Latitude, and from 0° of Aries to 30° of Gemini Longitude. The Throne of the Ace embraces from 22°-30′ of Aries to 7°-30′ of Gemini within the Latitude as above.

Star Group. Body of Draco, legs and part of right arm, and Sceptre of Cepheus, tail and hind quarters of Ursa Minor, with the Pole Star of our Earth, head and neck of Camelopardalis (Giraffe), body and right arm, throne and legs of Cassiopeia, the Queen of Cepheus and Mother of Andromeda, head of Ursa Major.

7. *Prince of Wands.* Rules from Ecliptic to 45° North Latitude and from 20° Cancer to 20° Leo in Longitude.

Star Group. Head, body, and tail of Leo, body and tail of Leo Minor, hind quarters and legs of Ursa Major, head and fore-quarters of Southern dog of Canes Venatici.

King of Pentacles. Rules from Ecliptic to 45° North Latitude and from 20° of Leo to 20° of Virgo.

<224> *Star Group.* Head and body of Virgo, left arm of Bootes, hair of
Berenice. Body and hind quarters of Southern dog of Canes Venatici, hind feet of Northern dog of Canes Venatici.

14. *Queen of Swords.* Rules from Ecliptic to 45° and from 20° of Virgo to 20° of Libra.

Star Group. Right leg of Virgo, body and right arm, and right leg of Bootes. Beam and part of Scales of Libra.

11. *Prince of Cups.* Rules from Ecliptic to 45° and from 20° of Libra to 20° to Scorpio.

Star Group. Part of Scales of Libra, left claws of Scorpio, body and legs of Ophiuchus, the holder of the Serpent. Front half of Serpent's head, right arm and club of Hercules.

5. *The King of Wands.* Rules from Ecliptic to 45° North Latitude and from 20° of Scorpio to 20° of Sagittarius.

Star Group. Top of head and bow of Sagittarius, head and right arm of Ophiuchus, near half of Serpent.

18. *Queen of Pentacles.* Rules from Ecliptic to 45° North Latitude and from 20° of Sagittarius to 20° of Capricorn.

Star Group. Top of head, neck and horns of Capricorn, left hand of Aquarius, the man who carries the Water, the whole of Aquila, the Eagle, the greater part of Delphinus, whole of Sagitta, the Arrow, forefeet and body of Vulpecula the Fox, and the tail of the Cygnet which he seizes.

15. *Prince of Swords.* Rules from Ecliptic to 45° North Latitude, and from 20° of Capricorn to 20° of Aquarius.

Star Group. Tail of Capricornus, head and body of Aquarius, head and forelegs of Pegasus, the winged horse who sprang from the blood of Medusa, near the sources of the ocean, the whole of Equuleus, the lesser horse, part of head of Dolphin, tail and hind quarters of Vulpecula, part of wing of Cygnus, the swan, part of head of Pisces.

<225> 9. *King of Cups.* Rules from Ecliptic to 45° of North Latitude and from 20° of Aquarius to 20° of Pisces.

Star Group. Body and tail of one of the Pisces, and part of the band. Body and wings of Pegasus, head and arms of Andromeda, chained to the rock-tail of Lacerta.

6. *Queen of Wands.* Rules from Ecliptic to 45° North Latitude and from 20° of Pisces to 20° of Aries.

Star Group. The other Fish and part of Band of Pisces, head and back of Aries, body and legs of Andromeda, the Triangle, hand left arm of Cassiopeia, the winged instep of Aries.

19. *Prince of Pentacles.* Rules from Ecliptic to 45° North Latitude and from 20° of Aries to 20° of Taurus.

Star Group. Tail of Aries, one horn and shoulder and back of Taurus, whole of Perseus, and the head of Medusa, hind quarters and legs of Camelopardalis, left leg of Auriga, Charioteer, and part of Capella, the she-goat which bears kids in her arms.

13. *King of Swords.* Rules from Ecliptic to 45° North Latitude from 20° of Taurus to 20° Gemini in Longitude.

Star Group. Head and body of Castor, one of the Gemini, greater part of Auriga and Capella, head and forepart of Lynx, forefeet of Camelopardalis.

10. *Queen of Cups.* Rules from Ecliptic to 45° North Latitude, and from 20° Gemini to 20° of Cancer in Longitude.

Star Group. Head and body of Pollux, the other of the Gemini; greater part of Cancer, crab; face of Leo; head and face of Ursa Major.

THE FOLLOWING TWELVE KEYS GOVERN
THE CELESTIAL HEAVENS
FROM THE ECLIPTIC TO 45° OF SOUTH LATITUDE

65. *Fortitude.* Rules the whole of Leo, from the point of Regulus or Cor Leonis.

Stars. The fore-legs and hind-feet of Leo, greater part of the Sextans and of Crater, the cups, part of the body of Hydra, the great Water ser-
<226> pent, greater part of Antlia Pneumatica, the air Pump, greater part of Pyxis Nautica, a small part of the ship Argo.

66. *Hermit or Prophet.* Rules the whole of Virgo.

Stars. Left arm, hand, and arm of Virgo, and her ear of Corn; part of the body of Hydra, Corvus, the Crow, part of Crater, tail and right hand of Centaurus, the man-horse, small part of Air-Pump and of Argo.

68. *Justice.* Rules the whole of Libra.

Stars. Part of the South Scale of Libra, tail of Hydra, head, body, arms and forefeet of Centaurus. Legs, body and tail of Lupus, the Wolf which he is killing. Right claw of Scorpio.

70. *Death.* Rules the whole of Scorpio.

Stars. Body and Tail of Scorpio, head and neck of Lupus, Whole of Ara—Altar, two feet of Ophiuchus, point of arrow of Sagittarius, part of Norma, Mason's square.

71. *Temperance.* Rules the whole of Sagittarius.

Stars The whole of Sagittarius, the Archer, except right hind leg, the tail, the crown of the head, extreme points of Bow and Arrow, Corona Australis, Telescope, Pavo—Peacock.

72. *The Devil.* Rules the whole of Capricorn.

Stars. Whole lower half of Capricornus, the he-Goat, part of Piscis Australis, Southern Fish, Microscope, Part of Grus, the Crane. Part of Indus.

74. *The Star.* Rules the whole of Aquarius.

Stars. Legs of Aquarius, and the issuant water head of Piscis Australis, part of Grus, part of Phoenix, part of apparatus Sculptorum, part of Cetus.

75. *The Moon.* Rules the whole of Pisces.

Stars. The connecting band of Pisces, the body of Cetus, the sea Monster to which Andromeda was exposed, part of Apparatus Sculptoris. Part of Phoenix, part of Fornax.

61. *The Emperor.* Rules the whole of Aries.

Stars. Legs of Aries, part of body of Taurus, head and fore-part of Cetus, part of Fornax and of Eridanus.

62. *The Hierophant.* Rules the whole of Taurus.

<227> *Stars.* Head and forepart of Taurus the Bull. The Bull sent by Neptune to frighten the horses of Sol and those of the Hippolytus. The greater part of Orion the Giant, and hunter. The beginning of the River Eridanus into which Phaeton was hurled when attempting to drive the horses of the Sun, greater part of Lepus, the Hare.

63. *The Lovers.* Rule the whole of Gemini.

Stars. Legs of Castor and Pollux, the Gemini, Canis Minor, a small part of Cancer. The whole of Monoceros, the Unicorn, except the hind-quarters. Head and forepart of Canis Major, the greater Dog.

64. *The Chariot.* Rules the whole of Cancer up to Regulus in Leo.

Stars. One claw and part of the body of Cancer, forepaws of Leo, head and part of Hydra, part of Sextans, part of Pyxis Nautica, hind legs and tail of Monoceros, part of the mast, rigging, and prow of the ship Argo.

Note: The Keys answering unto the Seven Lords who wander (planets) and the Three Spirits (the elements) are not assigned any fixed dominion. The following 36 small cards (2's to 10's) rule the decans of the signs in the Celestial Heavens and their Dominion extendeth from 45° South of the Ecliptic unto Malkuth at the Southern Pole.

21	5 of Wands	0°-10° of	♌	♄	Part of Argo, part of Piscis Volans.
22	6 of Wands	10°-20° of		♃	Part of Argo, part of Piscis Volans.
23	7 of Wands	20°-30° of		♂	Part of Argo, part of Piscis Volans.
24	8 of Pentacles	0°-10° of	♍	☉	Part of Argo, part of Piscis Volans.
25	9 of Pentacles	10°-20° of		♀	Hind feet of Centaurus, part of Piscis Volans.
26	10 of Pentacles	20°-30° of		☿	Hind legs of Centaurus, pt. Chameleon.
27	2 of Swords	0°-10° of	♎	☽	Hind legs of Centaurus, pt. Crux, pt. Musca and Chameleon.
28	3 of Swords	10°-20° of		♄	Pt. of Crux, Musca and Chameleon.
29	4 of Swords	20°-30° of		♃	Pt. of Musca, Circinus, Compasses, and Chameleon.

<228>

30	5 of Cups	0°-10° of	♏	♂	Pt. Circinus, Chameleon and of Triangulum Australe.
31	6 of Cups	10°-20° of		☉	Pt. Triangulum Australe, Apus the Swallow and Octans.
32	7 of Cups	20°-30° of		♀	Part of Pavo, Apus, Octans.
33	8 of Wands	0°-10° of	♐	☿	Part of Pavo, Apus, Octans.
34	9 of Wands	10°-20° of		☽	Part of Pavo, Apus, Octans.
35	10 of Wands	20°-30° of		♄	Pt. of Pavo, Pt. Hydra, watersnake.
36	2 of Pentacles	0°-10° of	♑	♃	Part of Pavo, Part of Hydra.
37	3 of Pentacles	10°-20° of		♂	Part of Toucan, Part of Hydra.
38	4 of Pentacles	20°-30° of		☉	Part of Toucan, Part of Phoenix.
39	5 of Swords	0°-10° of	♒	♀	Part Phoenix, end of Eridanus.
40	6 of Swords	10°-20° of		☿	Parts Hydrus, Reticulum Rhomboidalis.
41	7 of Swords	20°-30° of		☽	Parts Phoenix, Hydra, Reticulum and Eridanus.
42	8 of Cups	0°-10° of	♓	♄	Part Phoenix, Eridanus, Reticulum.
43	9 of Cups	10°-20° of		♃	Part Phoenix, Eridanus, Reticulum.
44	10 of Cups	20°-30° of		♂	Part Phoenix, Dorado, Reticulum.
45	2 of Wands	0°-10° of	♈	♂	Part Phoenix and Dorado.
46	3 of Wands	10°-20° of		☉	Part Caelum Sculptoris and Dorado.
47	4 of Wands	20°-30° of		♀	Part Caelum Sculptoris (Engravers Burin).

48	5 of Pentacles	0°-10° of ♉	☿	Part Eridanus, Columba Noae, Dorado, Equuleus, Pictoris.
49	6 of Pentacles	10°-20° of	☽	Forepart of Lepus, Tail and Wing of Columba, part of Equuleus.
50	7 of Pentacles	20°-30° of	♄	Part Equuleus and Lepus, body of Columba.
51	8 of Swords	0°-10° of ♊	♃	Feet of Canis Major, Prow Argo, part Equuleus Pictoris.
52	9 of Swords	10°-20° of	♂	Legs of Canis Major. Part of Prow of Argo.
53	10 of Swords	20°-30° of	☉	Hind quarters of Canis Major, part of Prow of Argo.
54	2 of Cups	0°-10° of ♋	♀	Prow Argo. Tail Canis Major.
55	3 of Cups	10°-20° of	♀	Prow of Argo.
56	4 of Cups	20°-30° of	☽	Prow of Argo.

(Note: That while the greater number of the Northern Constellations are connected with classical mythology, the titles of many of the Southern Constellations, and especially of those near the South Pole, are of more
<229> or less recent nomenclature, and bear witness to absence of reference to Occult Knowledge; such names for instance as Reticulum, and Caelum Scluptoris, Octans, etc.—S.R.M.D.

RECAPITULATION

In the dominion of the various forces, the rule of each may be divided into three portions. The centre is the most pronounced in its accord with the nature of its Ruler, and the two outer portions are tinged with the nature of the Ruler of the dominion bordering thereon. For example, in the case of Leo, the Dominion of Fortitude, the central 10 degrees will have most of this nature. For the beginning ten degrees are tinged with the nature of Cancer, and the last ten degrees with the nature of Virgo, the nature of Leo however predominating the mixture.

The whole Heavens then, are thus divided into Four Great Belts or Zones:

The Uppermost being the Dominion of the Knaves like a Cross within a Circle.

The Second Belt under the Dominion of the other Court cards represents a Belt of Influence descending vertically.

The Third Belt under the Dominion of the 12 Keys related to the Signs of the Zodiac, represents a Belt of Influence acting horizontally. This Zone in union with the second Belt will therefore yield a great Zone of 12 Crosses encircling the heavens.

The Fourth Belt consists of 36 Decans under the Dominion of the 36 small cards of the four suits, the numbers 2—10 of each suit. In each of these sets of 3 parts of a Sign, the central one will be more pronounced in effect than the lateral parts.

Therefore the 3 Decanates of each of the Signs will be sym-
<230> bolised by a triangle. Thus are yielded twelve Triangles surrounding the lower heavens, and therefore there will ultimate twelve

Crosses surmounting 12 Triangles surrounding the heavens. In other words, the symbol of the G.D. in the Outer, 12 times repeated.

Influence of the 12 Court Cards

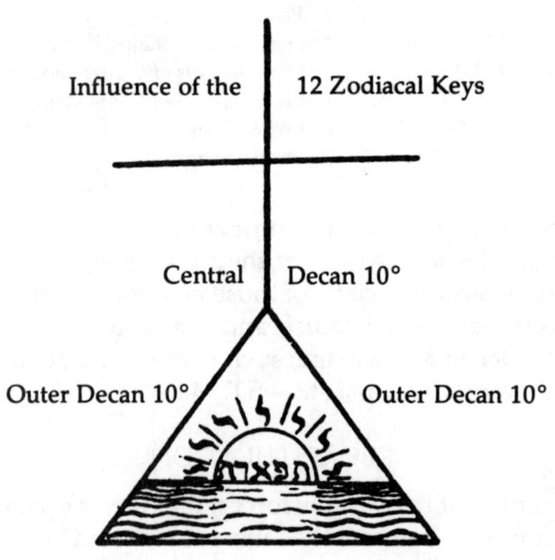

Hidden Sun of Tiphareth operating and rising above the Waters of Space

And the central Rising Sun will represent the hidden influence of Tiphareth in the centre of the Sphere, as will be hereafter explained, rising above the waters of Space (the ethereal expanse of the Sky called by the Egyptians "The Waters of Nu which are the parents of the Gods," The Shoreless Ocean of Space).

But in the Golden Dawn initiation, the Cross surmounting the Triangle is preferably represented by a Calvary Cross of 6 Squares, as still more allied to Tiphareth.

<231>

OF THE OPERATION AND RULE OF THE TREE OF LIFE IN THE CELESTIAL HEAVENS PROJECTED AS IF IN A SOLID SPHERE

When the Tree of Life is considered not as being a plane but as a solid figure, and when it is projected *in* the Sphere, the North Pole of the Sphere will coincide with Kether, and the South Pole with Malkuth.

And as we have before sufficiently learned the Ten Sephiroth are repeated not alone, in each whole figure, but also in the parts therefore, so that every material thing created, will have its own Sephiroth and Paths.

Now as the North Pole corresponds with *Kether,* and the South Pole corresponds with *Malkuth,* the central Pillar of the Sephirotic Tree will form the invisible Axis of the Sphere, the Central point coinciding with Tiphareth. This latter Sephirah together with that of Yesod will be completely hidden from view, so that Tiphareth will be the exact centre of the Sphere.

Also the Sephiroth Chokmah, Binah, Chesed, Geburah, Netzach and Hod will be duplicated. As also the Paths, Aleph, Beth, Gimel, Vau, Cheth, Caph, Mem, Qoph, and Shin, and so many of the others will be even quadrupled. But although Tiphareth and Yesod will be concealed, there will be four especial points where the influence of each will be indicated.

As projected in the before-described Celestial Sphere, *Kether* will govern a Radius of 10° around the North Pole, thus embracing the whole body of the Constellation Draco.

Chokmah will be on the 60° North Latitude; embracing a radius of 10°, the right foot of Hercules; the left arm, hand, and part of head of Bootes. Also on the other side of the Heavens, a radius of 10° including the head and shoulders of Cephus, and the head of Lacerta.

Binah, has a similar radius and is posited on the same parallel of
<232> Latitudes, and includes the pole Star of the Earth, the head of Camelopardelus, the tip of the tail of Draco; also Lyra and left knee of Hercules in the opposite side of the Heavens.

Chesed with a similar radius, and posited in the 30° of North Latitude, will include part of Coma Berenices, of Bootes, and of Virgo, and parts of Andromeda and of Pegasus.

And so with the other Sephiroth of the outer Pillars, each being 30° distant from the line of the Sephiroth above and below it, and having a radius of 10°.

The central line of the Two Pillars of Mercy and Severity will respectively traverse, that of Mercy the 15° of Virgo and 15° of Pisces; that of Severity the 15° of Gemini and the 15° of Sagittarius. The four Yesod points will be on the line of the 60° of South Latitude, and at similar Zodiacal points. From which circumstances the path of Influence or nature of the Sun will be along the line of the Ecliptic, coinciding with Tiphareth, and that of the Moon will be on the 60° of South Latitude answering to the Yesod points on that line.

<236>

THE LAW OF THE CONVOLUTED REVOLUTION OF THE FORCES SYMBOLISED BY THE FOUR ACES ROUND THE NORTHERN POLE

(Note: Though this is not official to the grade of Zelator Adeptus Minor, nor included within the general Tarot instructions usually issued, it is manifestly written by Greatly Honoured Frater S.R.M.D. Some students consider it a highly important piece of work, claiming that it was part of the study prescribed for the Theoricus Adeptus Minor. Clearly, it requires further teaching thoroughly to be understood, but students who have a good working knowledge of Astrology, as well as an understanding of the theory of the Tattwa tides or currents, will find that this document throws much light on

<233>

S.A.'s KEY PLAN OF SEPHIROTH

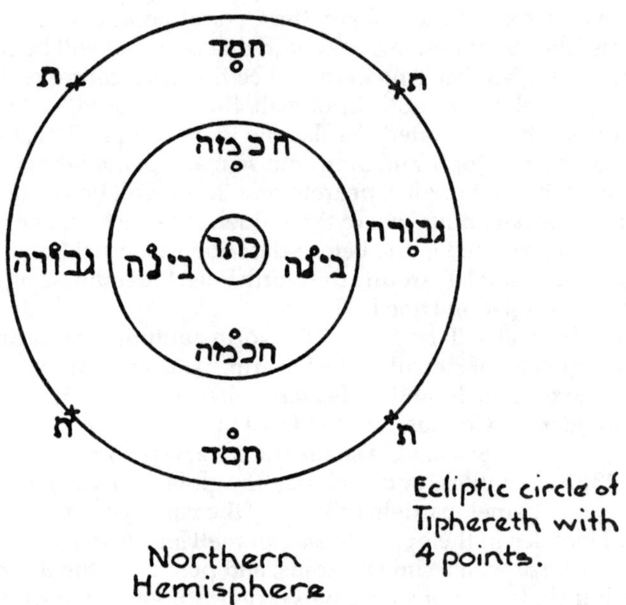

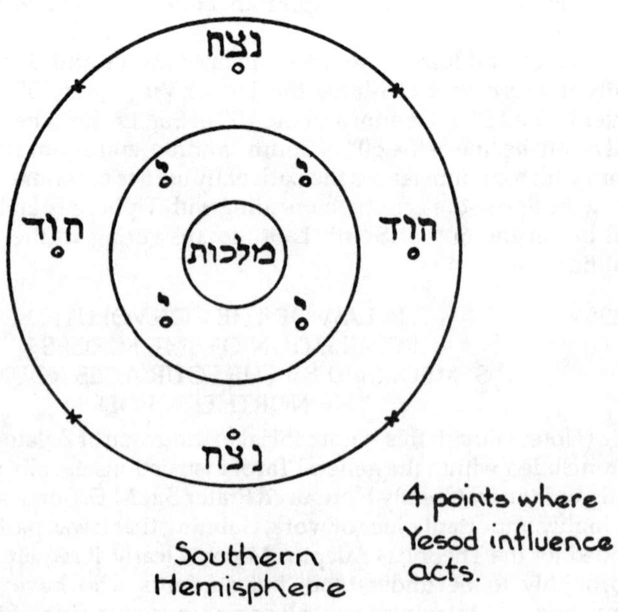

<234>

S.A.'s KEY PLAN OF THE PATHS

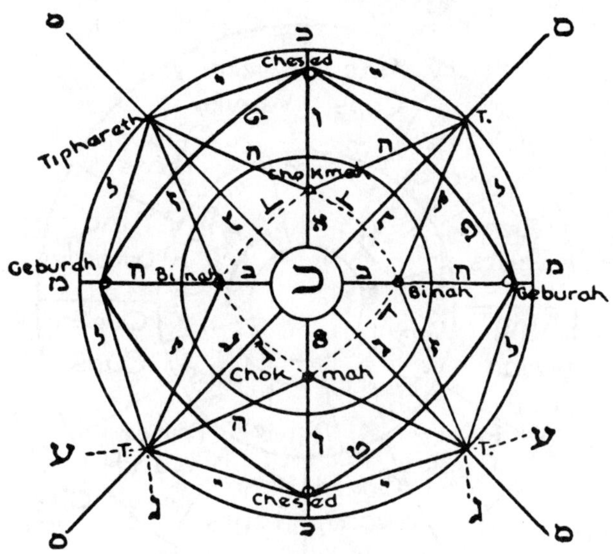

Northern Hemisphere

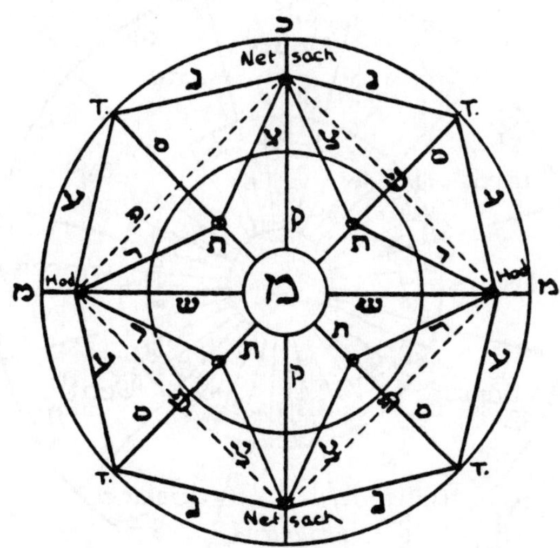

Southern Hemisphere

<235>

S.A.'s KEY PLAN OF THE TAROT

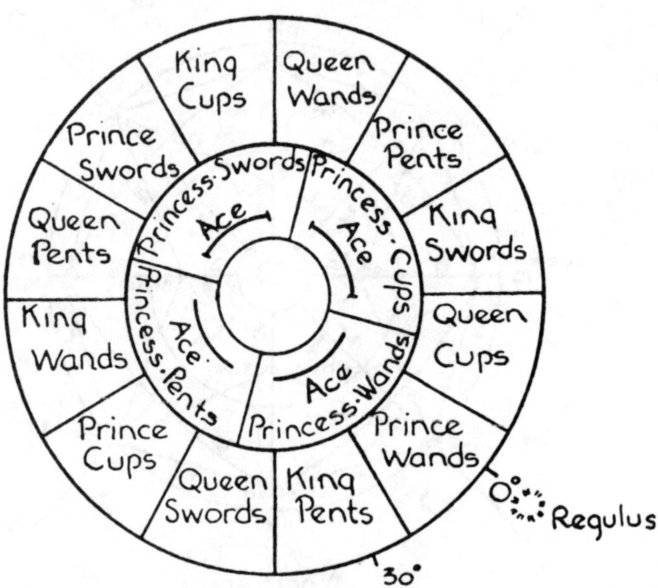

Northern Hemisphere

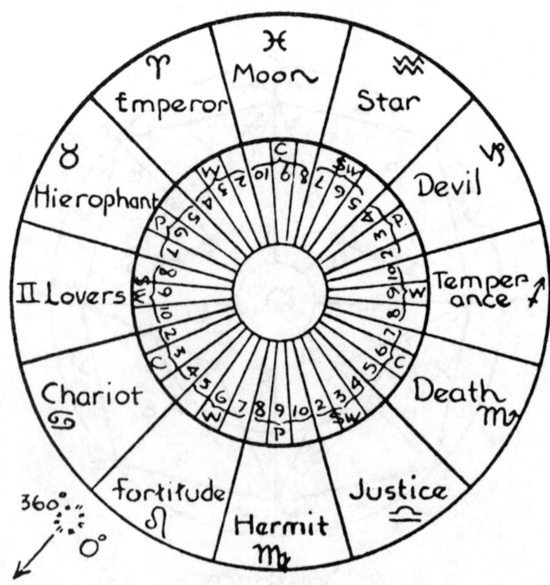

Southern Hemisphere

the esoteric system of Astrological divination.—I.R.)

In the Book "T," it is written: "Also the Dragon (i.e. Draco, the constellation at the Northern pole of the Heavens) surroundeth the Pole Kether of the Celestial Heavens." It is further laid down that the Four Aces, (symbolised by the Princesses and Amazons), rule the Celestial Heavens from the Northern Pole of the Zodiac unto the 45th Degree of Latitude North of the Ecliptic, and from the Thrones of the Four Aces which rule in Kether.

And again it is stated that:

The Throne of the Ace of Cups............The head of Draco
The Throne of the Ace of Swords............Fore part of body
The Throne of the Ace of Pentacles............Hind part of body
The Throne of the Ace of Wands............Tail of Draco

Regard thou then the form of this Constellation of the Dragon. It is convoluted in the four places answering unto the rule of the Aces.

Head, First convolution............Ace of Cups
Second convolution............Ace of Swords
Third convolution............Ace of Pentacles
<237> Fourth convolution............Ace of Wands

And this convoluted course will represent the Law of the Aces.

Now in the Four Faces of YHVH, Fire and Water be contrary, and also Earth and Air be contrary. And the throne of the Element will attract and seize, as it were, the Force of that element, so that herein be the Forces of Antipathy and of Sympathy, or what are known chemically as attraction and repulsion.

Recall also the allotment of the Triplicities:

Aries, Leo, Sagittarius = Fire = Wands of the Tarot.
Cancer, Scorpio, Pisces = Water = Cups of the Tarot.
Gemini, Libra, Aquarius = Air = Swords of the Tarot.
Taurus, Virgo, Capricorn = Earth = Pentacles of the Tarot.

Now, the order of the Princesses, and consequently of the Thrones, is formed from right to left thus:

Heh (final)	Vau	Heh	Yod
Princess	Princess	Princess	Princess
of	of	of	of
Pentacles	Swords	Cups	Wands
Taurus	Aquarius	Scorpio	Leo
Earth	Air	Water	Fire

While that of the Aces is formed from left to right, though their motion is from right to left:

Yod	Heh	Vau	Heh (final)
Ace	Ace	Ace	Ace
of	of	of	of
Wands	Cups	Swords	Pentacles

This, then will be the order of their movement. Let us first suppose the aces on the following stations:

Station 2	Station 1	Station 12	Station 11
Ace of	Ace of	Ace of	Ace of
Wands	Cups	Swords	Pentacles

Now the Station 2 is the Throne of the Ace of Wands, while the movement of the Aces is steadily from right to left in the direction of the numbering of the stations. In the ordinary course the Ace of Wands would pass to Station 3; the Ace of Cups to Station 2; the Ace of Swords to Station 1; the Ace of Pentacles to Station 12.

<238> But the Station 2, being the Throne of the Ace of Wands, attracts and arrests the movement of that Force so that instead of passing into Station 3, it remains on Station 2 until the other Aces have passed over it in turn.

Ace of Wands remains on Station 2,
Ace of Cups passes also on to Station 2,
Ace of Swords passes on to Station 1,
Ace of Pentacles passes on to Station 12.

Again,

Ace of Cups passes to Station 3,
Ace of Wands remains at Station 2,
Ace of Swords passes also on to Station 2,
Ace of Pentacles passes also on to Station 1.

Again,

Ace of Cups passes on to Station 4,
Ace of Swords passes on to Station 3,
Ace of Wands remains at Station 2,
Ace of Pentacles passes also on to Station 2.

Again,

Ace of Cups passes to Station 5,
Ace of Swords passes to Station 4,
Ace of Pentacles passes on to Station 3,
Ace of Wands still remains on Station 2.

But Station 5 is the Throne of the Ace of Cups. Therefore it attracts and arrests that Force, in the same manner that the Throne of the Ace of Wands acted previously in attracting and arresting the Ace of Wands, the result of which has been to make that Force which previously was leading become the last of the Four.

Again,

Ace of Cups remains on Station 5,
Ace of Swords passes also on to Station 5,
Ace of Pentacles passes also on to Station 4,
Ace of Wands, now at last passes into Station 3.

For it has now become the last of the Four, and the Ace of Cups has commenced to act through its Throne,and the Ace of Pentacles, moving
<239> to Station 4, a hiatus would occur in the movement of the Aces, if the Ace of Wands did not move forward to Station 3, and also there is the attraction of the motion of those Aces in front of it. Wherefore all these Forces combining, at length cause it to move forward.

The movement then continues, thus:

The Ace of Swords passes on to Station 6,
The Ace of Cups remains on Station 5,

The Ace of Pentacles passes also on to Station 5,
The Ace of Wands passes also on to Station 4.
Again,
The Ace of Swords passes on to Station 7,
The Ace of Pentacles passes on to Station 6,
The Ace of Cups still remains on Station 5,
The Ace of Wands passes also on to Station 5.
Again,
The Ace of Swords passes on to Station 8, its Throne,
The Ace of Pentacles passes on to Station 7,
The Ace of Wands passes on to Station 6,
The Ace of Cups still remains on Station 5.
Again,
The Ace of Swords remains on Station 8,
The Ace of Pentacles passes also on to Station 8,
The Ace of Wands passes on to Station 7,
The Ace of Cups now at length passes on to Station 6, and so on.

The movement of the Aces will be very similar to the convolutions of Draco thus:

The Course of the Aces:

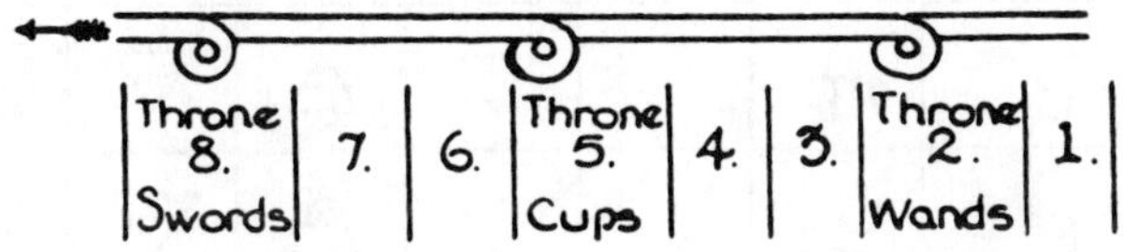

And will imply a much more sustained exercise of force through the Thrones than elsewhere. So that the generic effect of the Thrones will be that of the seasons, while the other stations will give the variations thereof in
<241> accordance with their natures and with the order of the movement of the aces in them.

And as Kether acted directly upon Tiphareth which is, as it were, the centre and focus of the Sephiroth when projected in a sphere, so do the Aces act upon the Sun as the centre and focus of the Solar System. So that the Sun, according to his position with regard to the Equinox and the Earth's surface will translate the effect of the seasons, he being the translator of the force of heat thereto, whether the then position of the Equinoctial points coincide with what we call 0° Aries, and 0° Libra (reckoning from Regulus) or not. So that his effect North of the Equator shall produce when just leaving the Equinoctial point, the effect of Aries, whether he be with that constellation actually in the heavens or not.

Conversely also, for the South of the Equator (as in the country of Australia) his quitting the Equinoctial point southward will translate the same effect of Aries.

But this rule shall not for one moment affirm that Aries and Libra are identical in nature. Nor that the Zodiac proper is inoperative. Nor that the nature of the Sun is not modified by the constellation in which he is. But only that the direct effect of the physical impact of his rays falling upon a cer-

<240> Table showing the Order of the Passage of the 4 Aces, above the Signs, in the dominion of the Princesses.

	Sign	Throne of	First in order	Second in Order	Third in Order	Fourth in Order
Moveable	♈		🜃	🜂	🜄	🜁
Fixed	♉	Ace of Pentacles	🜃	🜂	🜄	🜁
Common	♊		🜂	🜄	🜁	🜃
M.	♋		🜂	🜄	🜁	🜃
F.	♌	Ace of Wands	🜂	🜄	🜁	🜃
C.	♍		🜄	🜁	🜃	🜂
M.	♎		🜄	🜁	🜃	🜂
F.	♏	Ace of Cups	🜄	🜁	🜃	🜂
C.	♐		🜁	🜃	🜂	🜄
M.	♑		🜁	🜃	🜂	🜄
F.	♒	Ace of Swords	🜁	🜃	🜂	🜄
C.	♓		🜃	🜂	🜄	🜁

tain portion of the earth's surface, will be in proportion to the duration of their action, in the excitement they produce in the terrestrial forces.

And now as the Forces symbolized by these Aces, pass in succession over these stations, so will they awake certain terrestrial action, according unto the sign of the division of the Zodiac above which they pass in the domain of the Knaves of Princesses, and according unto the nature thereof. Nevertheless, the force roused by the Ace when on its Throne will be of longer duration than at other points.

And hence it is that the Signs of the Zodiac be divided into
<242> Fixed or Kerubic, Moveable or changing, and common or fluctuat-
ing, according unto the nature of the power which can be awakened therein. And again, these will be varied according unto their Elements, for the Elements have a various classification.

NOTE BY S.R.M.D.

I think it is here advisable to transcribe the following from Cornelius Agrippa:

"Of The Four Elements and Their Natural Qualities:

"It is necessary that we should know and understand the nature and quality of the Four Elements, in order to our being perfect in the principles and groundwork of our studies in the Talismanic or Magical Art.

"Therefore, there are four Elements, the original grounds of all corporeal things, viz.: Earth, Air, Fire, and Water, of which elements all inferior bodies are compounded, not by way of being heaped up together, but by transmutation and union; and when they are destroyed, they are resolved into elements.

"But there are none of the sensible elements that are pure. But they are more or less mixed, and apt to be changed the one into the other, even as earth being moistened and dissolved becomes water, but the same being made thick and hard becomes earth again, and being evaporated through heat it passes into air, and that being kindled into fire; and this being extinguished into air again; but being cooled after burning becomes water again, or else stone or sulphur, and this is clearly demonstrated by lightning.

"Now every one of these Elements has two specific qualities: the former whereof it retains as proper to itself; in the other as a mean, it agrees with that which comes directly after it. For Fire is hot and dry; Water cold and moist; and Air hot and moist; and so in this manner, the Elements, according to two contrary qualities are opposite one to the other, as Fire to Water, and Earth to Air.

"Likewise the Elements are contrary one to the other on another account. Two are heavy, as Earth and Water; and the others are light, as
<244> Fire and Air. Therefore the stoics called the former 'passives,' but
the latter 'actives.' And Plato distinguishes them after another manner, and assigns to each of them three qualities, viz.: To the Fire brightness, thinness and motion. To the Earth, darkness, thickness, and quietness. And according to these qualities the Elements of Fire and Earth are contrary. Now

the other Elements borrow their qualities from these, so that the Air receives two qualities from the Fire, thinness and motion, and from the Earth one, darkness. In like manner, Water receives two qualities from the Earth, darkness and thickness; and from the Fire one, motion. But Fire is twice as thin as Air, thrice more moveable, and four times lighter. The Air is twice more bright, thrice more thin, and four times more moveable than Water. Therefore, as Fire is to Air, so is Air to Water, and Water to Earth. And again, as the Earth is to the Water, so is Water to Air, and Air to Fire. And this is the root and foundation of all bodies, natures, and wonderful works. And he who can know and thoroughly understand these qualities of the Elements and their mixtures shall bring to pass wonderful and astonishing things in Magic.

"Now each of these Elements has a threefold consideration, so that the number of four may make up the number of twelve; and by passing by the number of seven into ten, there may be a progress to the Supreme Unity upon which all virtue and wonderful things do depend. *Of the first Order,* are the pure Elements, which are neither compounded, changed, nor mixed, but are incorruptible and not of which but *through* which the virtues of all natural things are brought forth to act. No man is fully able to declare their Virtues, because they can do all things upon all things. He who remains ignorant of

---

<243>

TABLE SHOWING QUALITIES OF ELEMENTS

△ Heat, dryness, excessive lightness, brilliance, excessive subtlety, motion rapid.

▽ Cold, moisture, weight, obscurity, solidity, motion.

🜁 Heat, moisture, lightness, slight obscurity, subtlety, excessive motion.

🜃 Cold, dryness, excessive weight, excessive obscurity, excessive solidity, rest.

TABLE SHOWING THE QUALITIES OF THE ELEMENTS WHEN MIXED IN PAIRS

△ & ▽ Slight weight, some subtlety, intense and rapid motion.

△ & 🜁 Great heat, intense lightness, slight brilliance, intense subtlety, intense motion.

△ & 🜃 Great dryness, slight obscurity.

▽ & 🜁 Great moisture, intense motion.

▽ & 🜃 Great cold, intense weight, intense obscurity, intense solidity.

🜁 & 🜃 Some weight, intense obscurity, little solidity, little motion.

---

these, shall never be able to bring to pass any wonderful matter.

"Of the *second order* are Elements that are compounded, changeable and impure, yet such as may, by art, be reduced to their pure simplicity,
<245> whose virtue, when they are thus reduced, doth above all things, perfect all occult and common operations of Nature; and these are the foundations of the whole of natural Magic.

"Of the *third Order* are those elements which originally and of themselves are not elements, but are twice compounded, various, and changeable unto another. These are the infallible medium, and are called the Middle Nature, or *Soul of the Middle Nature;* very few there are that understand the deep mysteries thereof. In them is, by means of certain numbers, degrees and orders, the perfection of every effect in what thing soever, whether *natural,* celestial, or *super*-celestial. They are full of wonders and mysteries, and are operative in Magic, natural or divine. For, from these, through them, proceeds the binding, loosing, and transmutation of all things — the knowledge and foretelling of things to come, also the expelling of evil and the gaining of Good Spirits. Let no one, therefore, without these three sorts of Elements, and the true knowledge thereof, be confident that he can work anything in the occult science of Magic and Nature.

"But whosoever shall know how to reduce those of one order into another, impure into pure, compounded into simple, and shall understand distinctly the *nature, virtue,* and *power* of them, into number, degrees and order, without dividing the substance, he shall easily attain to the knowledge and perfect operation of all natural things, and celestial secrets likewise; and this is the perfection of the Qabalah, which teaches all these before mentioned; and by a perfect knowledge thereof, we perform many rare and wonderful experiments. In the original and exemplary world all things are all in all. So also in this corporeal world. And the elements are not only in these inferior things; but are in the Heavens, in stars, in devils, in angels, and likewise in God Himself, the maker and original example of all things.

"Now it must be understood that in these inferior bodies the
<246> elements are gross and corruptible, but in the heavens they are, with their natures and virtues, after a celestial and more excellent manner than in sublunary things. For the firmness of the celestial Earth is there without the grossness of Water, and the agility of Air without exceeding its bounds. The heat of Fire without burning, only shining, giving light and life to all things by its celestial heat."

End of transcription.

Now the successive effect of the passage of the Aces over the Stations above the place of a Sign in the excitement of the Forces of that Sign may be readily calculated by the tables of the qualities of the elements simple and mixed, always being careful to take also into account the effect of the Throne upon the Season as well, and the nature of the Sign.

It is said that Kether is in Malkuth, and again, that Malkuth is in Kether but after another manner.

For downwards through the Four Worlds the Malkuth of the less material will be linked unto the Kether of the more material. From the Synthesis of the Ten corruscations of the AOUR (Light) proceedeth the influence unto EHEIEH, the Kether of Atziluth. And the connecting thread of the AIN SOPH is extended through the worlds of the Ten Sephiroth and is in every direction. As the Ten Sephiroth operate in each Sephiroth, so will there be a KETHER in every MALKUTH, and Malkuth in every Kether. Thus:

ADONAI MELEKH will be the MALKUTH of ATZILUTH,
METATRON will be the KETHER of BRIAH.
SANDALPHON
METRATON will be the MALKUTH of BRIAH.
NEPHESCH ha-MESSIAH
CHAIOTH ha QADESH will be the KETHER of YETZIRAH.
ASCHIM will be the MALKUTH of YETZIRAH.
<247> RASHITH ha GILGALIM, the KETHER of ASSIAH.
CHOLEM YESODOTH, the MALKUTH of ASSIAH.
THAUMIEL, the KETHER of the QLIPPOTH.

The symbol of the connection between MALKUTH of YETZIRAH and KETHER of ASSIAH will be of a form somewhat resembling that of an hour glass. The thread of the AIN SOPH before alluded to, traversing the centre thereof, and forming the AIN SOPH connection between the Worlds:

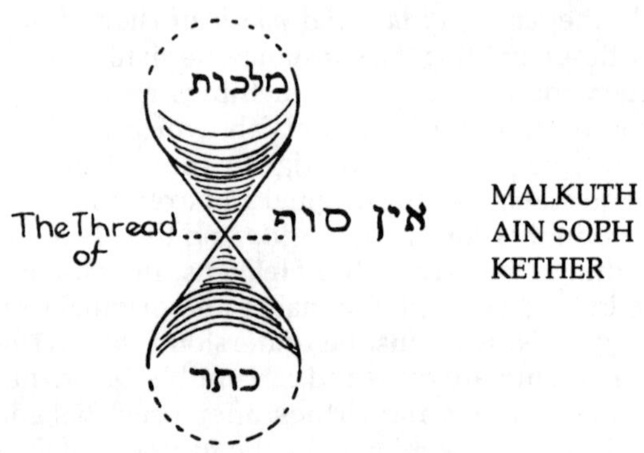

So that the symbol of the connection between the two planes is this. And also the modus operandi of the translation of force from one plane into another is in this, and hence doth the title of the Sphere of Kether of Assiah signify the commencement of a whirling motion.

Now also, in the diagram of Minutum Mundum, there be four colours attributed unto Malkuth. Citrine, russet, olive, and black. And if we consider them as in a vertical sphere, we shall find citrine uppermost and horizontal, russet and olive midmost and vertical, black lowermost and horizontal.

And again, these four represent in a manner the operation of the four elements in Malkuth; for example:

Citrine—Air of Earth   Russet—Fire of Earth
Olive—Water of Earth   Black—Earth of Earth

<248> From the diagram of the hour glass symbol it will be manifest

then that MALKUTH of YETZIRAH will be the transmitter of the Yetziratic forces unto KETHER of ASSIAH, and that the latter will be the recipient thereof, and that the Hour-glass symbol or double cone, will be the translator from the one plane unto the other. Here, therefore, let us consider the Yetziratic nomenclature of the *Tenth Path* answering unto Malkuth, and of the *First Path* answering unto Kether.

The Tenth Path: It is called the Resplendent Intelligence and it is so-called because it is exalted above every head, and sitteth on the Throne of Binah, and it illuminateth the splendour of all the Lights, and it causeth the current of Influence to flow from the Prince of Countenances, i.e. Metatron.

The First Path: It is called the Wonderful or Hidden Intelligence (The Highest Crown) for it is the Light to cause to understand the Primordial without commencement, and it is the Primal Glory, for nothing created is worthy to follow out its essence.

Whence it is plain that MALKUTH is, as it were, the collector together and synthesis of all the forces in its plane or world. While KETHER being superior unto all else in its plane or world, will be the recipient and arranger of the forces from the plane beyond, so as to distribute them unto its subordinate Sephiroth in a duly ordered manner.

And therefore any force of the multitudinous and innumerable forces in Malkuth may act through the upper cone of the hourglass symbol, and by means of the lower one translate its operation into KETHER below, but its mode of transmission will be through the cones by the thread of the Ain Soph, or of the Unformulated.

So that in the transmission of force between two worlds the Formulate must first become Unformulate, ere it can *reformulate* in new con-
<249> ditions. For it must be plain that a force *formulated* in one world, if translated into another will be *unformulated,* according to the laws of a plane different in nature. Even as water in its fluid state will be subject to different laws to those governing it when in the conditions of either ice of steam.

And as before said, there being in the Minutum Mundum diagram four chief elemental divisions of the Sephirah MALKUTH, each of these will have its correlative formula of transmission unto the succeeding Kether. Hence also in the Order Tarot teaching is there the Dominion of the four Knaves or Princesses of the Tarot pack around the North Pole. Why then is it that it is the Four Amazons or Knaves, answering unto the final Heh of YHVH, that are here placed, rather than the Four Kings, Queens or Princes, or one of each nature?

We are taught that these are the Vice Regents of the name in the Four Worlds, and that they are thus attributed among the Sephiroth.

Yod	Heh	Vau	Heh (final)
Chokmah	Binah	Tiphareth	Malkuth
King	Queen	Prince	Princess

Now as Kether of Assiah is to *receive* from Malkuth of Yetzirah, it is necessary that in and about Kether there should be a force which partaketh of the *nature* of Malkuth, though more subtle and refined in nature. And there-

fore is it that the final Heh, or Princess force, have their dominion placed about Kether. They are so placed that they may attract from the Malkuth of the Higher and form the basis of action for the Aces. So that a refined matter may attract its like, and the spiritual forces may not lose themselves in the void, to produce but a mistaken and whirling destruction for want of a settled basis. And herein is the mutual formula in all things, of a *spirit* and of a *body,* seeing that each supplies unto each that wherein the other is lack-
<250> ing, yet herein also must there be a certain condition, otherwise the
harmony will not be perfect. For unless the *body* be refined in nature, it will hinder the action of a *spirit* cognate unto it. And unless the *spirit* be willing to ally itself unto the body, the latter will be injured thereby and each will mutually react on the other.

Diagram showing the convoluted transmission of the 4 forces from Malkuth to Kether.

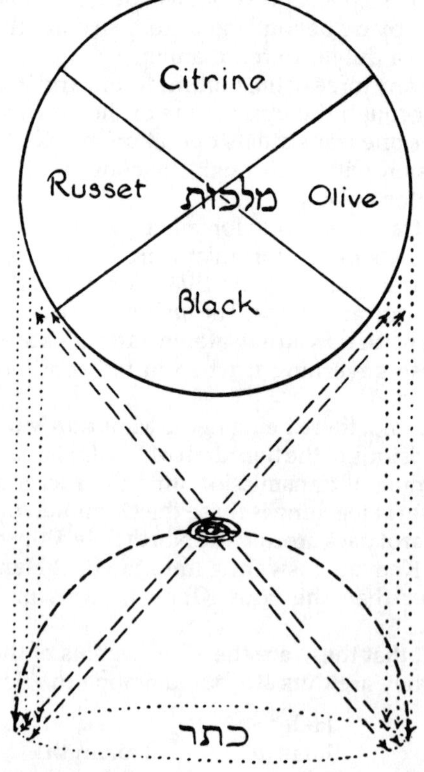

Dotted lines show the natural lines at transmission of the Forces, were both Sephiroth in the same World. Lines of dashes show the mode in which these lines are caught and convoluted by the Hour-Glass symbol

Therefore, also, let the Adeptus Minor understand that there
<251> may be fault of the *spirit* as well as of the *body,* and that there is little
difference between the material and sensuous person, and the envious, malicious and self-righteous person — save that from their being more subtle and less evident, the sins of the latter are more insidious than those of the former, though both are alike evil. But it is as necessary to govern the Spirit as to refine the body, and of what use is it to weaken the body by abstinence, if at the same time uncharitableness and spiritual pride are encouraged! It is simply translating one sin into another.

And therefore are the final Heh forces so necessary in Kether, as it is said in the Tenth Path of the Sepher Yetzirah: "It is so called because it is exalted above every head, and sitteth on the Throne of Binah." Now, in the Tree, the two Sephiroth, Chokmah and Binah, are referred unto the Briatic World which is also called the Throne or vehicle, that is of the Atzilutic World unto which latter Kether is referred on the Tree. And referring unto the dominions of the Four Princesses, thou shalt find that in the sphere they include Chokmah and Binah as well as Kether.

Now there will be, not one, but four formulae of the application of the Four Forces of Malkuth, unto the revolution of the Aces in Kether, and these acting not singly but simultaneously and with a different degree of force.

Were Malkuth or Kether in the same plane or world the transmission of these forces from the one unto the other would proceed *more or less in direct lines.* In this case, *seeing that Malkuth and Kether be in different planes or worlds,* the lines of transmission of these forces are caught up and whirled about by the *upper cone* of the hour glass symbol into the *vortex* where through passeth the thread of the *unformulated,* i.e. the Ain Soph. Thence they are projected in a whirling convolution (yet according unto their nature) through the lower cone of the hourglass symbol unto Kether.

Whence it resulteth that these formulae are of the nature of the
<252> Dragon, that is to say, moving in convolutions, and hence they are
called the *Dragon or Serpent Formulae.*

Now imagining MALKUTH of Yetzirah to be in a vertical position above Kether of Assiah, it will be plain that the whole of the black part of Malkuth will be towards Kether, but only a portion of the russet and olive parts, and that the citrine parts will be entirely removed and on the further side. Wherefore the natural operation of these four forces towards Kether will be: black, rather horizontal than vertical, and acting fully. Citrine rather horizontal than vertical but acting at the edge of the circumference of Kether, and slightly rather than strongly. Russet and olive rather vertical than horizontal, and acting moderately.

<253> Now these four formulae will imply four simultaneous move-
ments in the revolution of the forces symbolised by the four aces round the Northern Pole.

The *first* and *most forcible* in its immediate action will be that answering unto the Earth of Malkuth of Yetzirah, transmitting unto Kether of Assiah, and following the convolutions of the Constellation Draco. It is called the *Direct* or *Creeping Formula* and for this reason the Dragon may be wingless and footed as regards its symbolic representation. This formula has been thor-

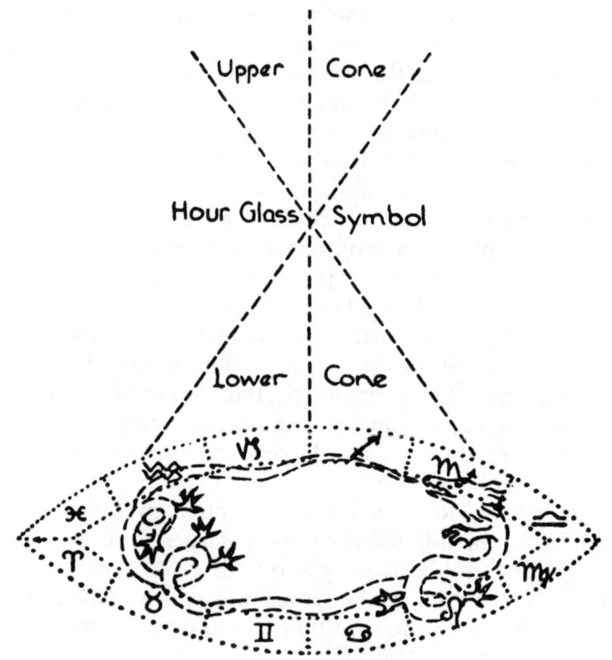

DIRECT OR CREEPING FORMULA

oughly explained in the beginning of this section on the revolution of the Aces. In the expressions Earth of Malkuth, etc., it should be remembered that these do not imply pure but mixed elemental natures, seeing that Malkuth receiveth the ultimate effect of all the forces in the Tree of Life, even as the colours which be attributed thereto be not primaries, but tertiaries. Therefore each element in Malkuth will be counterchanged with others, even as the Kerubim in the Kerubim in the Vision of Ezekiel have each, not one but four heads and counterchanged.

The *second* and *least forcible* in its immediate action will be the Dragon formula answering unto the Air of Malkuth of Yetzirah, transmitting unto Kether of Assiah, and following the convolutions of four serpents upon the four triplicities of the elements in the Zodiac or more properly speaking, upon the stations in the Dominions of the Princesses above them. (Now also the Throne in each Dominion is marked in the Book T as embracing more than a third of each dominion, because of the enduring effect of its force.) This formula is also called the *looped* or *Flying Formula,* and hence the serpents may be represented footless, but winged. Its action is more round the circumference at its edge, than that of the other formulae. This formula of operations will be readily understood on reference to the diagram thereof, but more especially from the four diagrams showing the change of order and course of the aces. In this formula the heads of the four serpents will be above the four cardinal signs.

<254> The *Third Dragon Formula, moderately forcible* in its immediate action, is that answering unto the Fire of Malkuth of Yetzirah, Transmitting unto Kether of Assiah, and following the law of the attraction and repulsion of the elements of the triplicities of the Zodiac. This is also called the *Leaping* or *Darting Formula,* and its serpents may be represented both footed and winged — footed to represent the attraction of the elements, winged to represent the repulsion by the contrary elements. This formula is more vertical in action, while the preceding two are more horizontal as

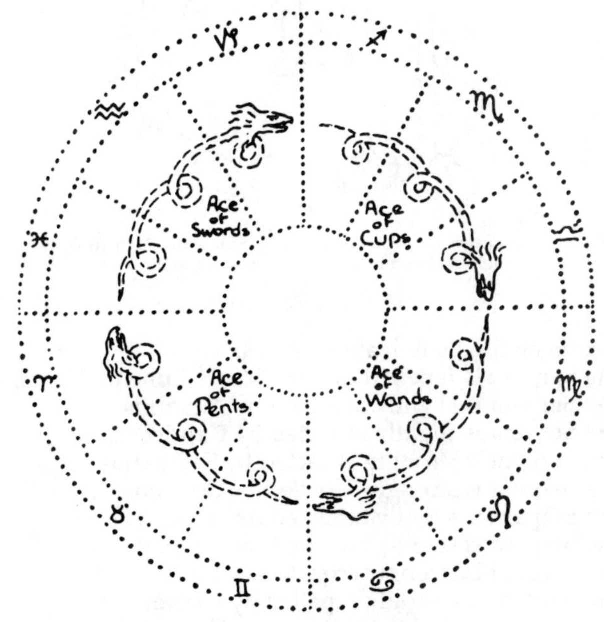

LOOPED OR FLYING FORMULA

before shown. This formula will be readily understood from the four diagrams thereof and also from those showing the change of order in the course of the Aces. As before the heads of the serpents rest upon the Stations above the Cardinal Signs.

The explanation of the course of one of the four serpents will be
<255> sufficient to explain the whole. Let us take that of Fire:

Fire is strongly attracted by the Station above Fire,
Fire is strongly repelled by the Station above Water,
Fire is slightly attracted by the Station above Air,
Fire is slightly repelled by the Station above Earth.

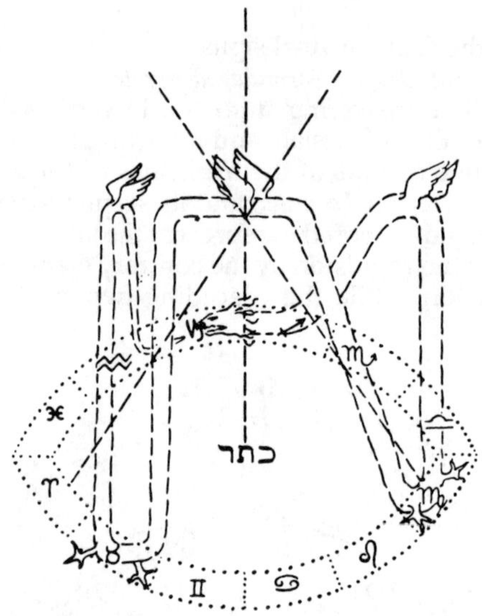

(The attraction and repulsion of the Serpent of the Earth Triplicity only, is shown in this diagram to avoid confusion.)

LEAPING FORMULA

The Head rests on the Station above Aries.
The Serpent is repelled into the lower Cone by Pisces,
The Serpent is slightly attracted by Aquarius,
The Serpent is slightly attracted by Capricorn,
<256> The Serpent is strongly attracted by Sagittarius,
The Serpent is strongly repelled by Scorpio,
The Serpent is slightly attracted by Libra,
The Serpent is slightly attracted by Virgo,
The Serpent is strongly attracted by Leo,
The Serpent is strongly repelled by Cancer.
The Serpent is slightly attracted by Gemini and Taurus.

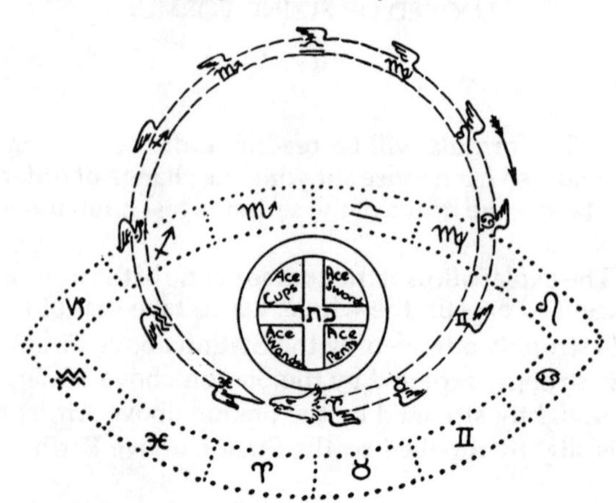

The tail is strongly attracted by Aries, where it is united with the head again. (The course of the Four Serpents is shown in four different diagrams to avoid confusion.)

REVOLVING OR FLOWING FORMULA

The *Fourth Dragon Formula* and *moderately forcible,* is that answering unto the Water of MALKUTH of Yetzirah, transmitting into the Kether of Assiah, and following the Law of the Zodiacal succession of the Signs in gradual Order. This is also called the *Revolving* or *Flowing Formula,* and its serpent may be represented neither winged nor footed, but with fins to sym-
<257> bolise its flowing movement. This formula will be more vertical in
action, and can be readily understood from the diagram thereof, and from those showing the change of order in the course of the Aces.

This formula may be best symbolically represented by the four Aces revolving as in a smaller wheel upon a great circle whose body is composed of the powers of the twelve Signs, so that this latter in its turn revolves upon the stations above the Zodiac. The effect of the revolution of the Wheel of the Aces will be to excite by the Ace of Wands the Fiery Signs, by the Ace of Cups the Watery Signs, by the Ace of Swords the Airy Signs, and by the Ace of Pentacles the Earthy Signs. Yet through the forces of the revolution of the Serpent as well, the forces of the Aces will be in their turn modified by the zodiacal natures in the body of the Serpent.

And as before said the action of these formulae will be simultaneous though differing in degree, and of them all that first explained which followeth the convolutions of the Constellation Draco is the strongest in operation. And it is to be noted that in two of these formulae, the heads of the Serpents are with the Order of the Signs, and in the other two against the natural order of succession of them in the Zodiac.

Also the action of the Spirit of Malkuth of Yetzirah transmitting unto Kether of Assiah will equal that of continued vibratory rays, acting from the centre to the circumference, and thus bringing into action the force from the "Thread of the Unformulate" MEZLA.

Recall that which is written in the Chapter of the Chariot—(Ezekiel, 1. 45.)

"And I beheld, and lo! a tempestuous whirlwind came out from the North, a mighty cloud, and a fire violently whirling upon itself, and a splendour revolving upon itself, and from the midmost as an eye of brightness from the midst of the fire. And from the midmost the forms of the Four Chaioth."

BOOK NINE

THE ANGELIC TABLETS

<260>

INTRODUCTION
TO THE
ENOCHIAN SYSTEM
By FRATRE AD MAJOREM ADONAI GLORIAM

To the First Order of the Golden Dawn little was said of the Angelic Tablets or Watch Towers. They were mentioned in the Grade Rituals but their subject matter did not enter into the Knowledge Lectures directly. But the detailed study of the Tablets and the method of using them with the Enochian invocations for skrying in the Spirit-Vision formed a definite part of the course of work prescribed for the Adeptus Minor of the R.R. et A.C., though I have never met anybody who had done it with any degree of thoroughness.[1]

There was a considerable mass of detailed and highly complex instruction on this subject, contained in a number of documents. There are in my possession manuscripts totalling at least 70,000 words, besides some large charts, diagrams and coloured boards. Therefore it has been found necessary to provide a paper which attempts to cover the whole ground in logical sequence giving quotations where necessary from the original documents of G.H. Frater D.D.C.F. This probably will be of more general use than reproducing the whole rather disconnected mass of Enochian literature, which in many cases is simply a development of the fundamentals, and thus can be worked up by each individual reader who studies this book.

<261> At the outset, let it be said that a good deal of systematic study will be required to appreciate the value and subtle significance of this system. It is one of the most amazing magical schemes that I have ever encountered, since it provides a thorough-going and comprehensive synthesis of the entire magical system of the Golden Dawn. Every important item of knowledge and practice found itself incorporated within the scope of these Angelic Tablets. Every worth-while technical form of Magical procedure and all branches of ritualistic work find themselves represented in a single noble system.[2]

[1] Israel Regardie was a member of the Hermes Lodge for only a brief time in the 1930's, his main magical tutelege being with Crowley years *prior* to his admission to the G.D. The Hermes Lodge, founded by Dr. R. W. Felkin as an offshoot of his Amoun Temple of the Stella Matutina was a third generation G.D. temple which likely never inherited much of the oral materials and private papers of the original Mathers-Farr-Yeats Golden Dawn. Mathers continued to expand the original G.D. into the Second Order. At the time, Felkin didn't wholeheartedly embrace this newer growth of Mathers even after their reapproachment and reconciliation. Brodie-Innes and Berridge were in closer contact. H.S.

[2] It is noteworthy that the Enochian Words of Power were utilized in the original Cipher Manuscripts, Folios 24, 30, 34, and 38, and thus pre-date Mathers' work on the rituals in 1887. Folio 55 with the Tablet of Union in English *is* a later addition, but not these! H.S.

Therefore, because it is a synthetic amalgamation of all the Order Work, the student will find it necessary and imperative to have made himself thoroughly familiar with all the other items of knowledge taught by the Golden Dawn. He must know his Tarot and Geomantic attributions so well that the names, symbols and ideas are all at his finger tips — this, naturally, in addition to the basic knowledge items of the Hebrew Alphabet, Tree of Life, and the Qabalah generally. The formulae of practical Magic derived from the Z documents, dealing with the symbolism of the Candidate, the Temple, and the Ceremony of the Neophyte Grade, will require to be not only memorised and known, but understood. The student will need to be perfectly acquainted with the Pentagram and Hexagram Rituals, the formulae of the Consecration Ceremonies, the general art of invocation, and formulating Telesmatic images, and drawing Sigils. The Tablets are excellent instances of Talismans and Flashing Tablets.

D. D. C. F. says in his *Notanda* to the Book of the Concourse of the Forces, that "the tablets of Enoch require in truth many years of study, and will repay such an expenditure of time and energy. The knowledge embodied in this manuscript is very superficial and elementary, and entirely fails to do justice to the Enochian scheme. You must take it as only a feeble attempt to
<262> provide what is seen at first glance, by the intellect, and as having no
relation to the world of Spiritual truth which the Tablets enshrine and which a high Adept can make them give out."

Very little is known about the origin of these Tablets and the invocations that accompany their use. Practically nothing was said in the Order which explained this matter, though in the Adepus Minor Ritual it is said that Christian Rosenkreutz and his immediate colleagues, whose supposed date is *circa* 1400 A.D., transcribed some "of the magical language, which is that of the Elemental Tablets." So far as we are able to make out, however, the System originated by means of the ceremonial skrying of Dr. John Dee and Sir Edward Kelly towards the close of the 16th century. The original diaries of Dr. John Dee, recording the development of the system, may be found in Sloane Manuscripts 3189-3191 in the British Museum. But this stands out very clearly, that in these diaries is a rudimentary scheme which bears only the most distant relation to the extraordinarily developed system in use by the Order. Whoever was responsible for the Order scheme of the Angelic Tablets — whether it was Mathers and Westcott or the German Rosicrucian Adepts from whom the former are supposed to have obtained their knowledge — was possessed of an ingenuity and an understanding of Magic such as never was in the possession either of Dee or Kelly.*

*This paragraph is repeatedly quoted without due credit. (Unfortunately, it is also mis-information, and no credit to the late Israel Regardie.) First, the original system of Dee and Kelly was vastly more sophisticated than even the Golden Dawn version, but it had not been pulled together at that time, so Regardie had insufficient materials at hand to form his judgement. Second, the Golden Dawn reduces all occult symbology to an "Elemental-Bias", and then combines elemental attributions quite mechanically to constitute everything into what they took of the Dee System. *This is valid and powerful!* H.S.

Some of the Order clairvoyants have claimed that Dee and Kelly in some way obtained access to the construction of the Enochian system whilst they were in Central Europe. It is claimed that numerous Rosicrucian centres existed in Germany, Austria, and Bohemia, and both Dee and Kelly were received therein. Whilst this may be a plausible theory, there is not the least vestige of objective evidence for this assumption. Still others have believed that it represents a revival of certain species of Atlantean Magic, though those
<263> who press this theory do not explain the Dee diaries, not his account of the method he and Edward Kelly employed to acquire the roots of this system.

Roughly, the facts which are concerned with the origins of the system are these. Over one hundred large squares filled with letters were obtained by Dee and Kelly in a manner which we cannot quite determine. When working, Dee, for example, would have before him on a writing table one or more of these Tables, as a rule 49″ x 49″, some full while others were lettered only on alternate squares. Then Sir Edward Kelly would sit down at what they called the Holy Table on which were various magical pentacles, and which also rested on wax seals. On this Table was a large Crystal or Shewstone, in which, after a while, he reported to see an Angel who would point with a wand to letters on certain charts in succession. Kelly would thereupon report to Dee that the Angel pointed, for example, to column 4, rank 29, of one of the many charts, and so on, apparently not mentioning the letter, which Dee would then find on the table before him and write it down. When the Angel had finished his instruction, the message — when it concerned certain of the major invocations or Calls — was rewritten backwards. It had been dictated the wrong way round by the Angel since it was considered too dangerous to communicate in a straightforward manner, each word being so powerful a conjuration that its direct pronunciation or dictation would have evoked powers and forces not desired at that moment.

Regardless of their origin, these Tablets and the whole Enochian system do represent realities of the inner planes. Their value is undoubted, as only a little study and application prove. Whilst it may seem, at first sight, that their governance is solely in the world of the elementals, that is the Astral plane, there is much to indicate that they extend to planes which are spiritual and divine in nature. In any event the magical conception of the Elements is rather different from that which obtains in most so-called occult philosophies.

<264> Perhaps a word or two of caution might be added. Undoubtedly prudence is required in this matter. It is a very powerful system, and if used carelessly and indiscriminately will bring about disaster and spiritual disintegration. The warnings given in connection with the Invocations are not to be regarded as conventions or as platitudinous moralisings. They represent a knowledge of true facts, and the student will do well to take cognisance thereof. Let him study the theory first of all, so that he has a thorough knowledge of the construction of the squares and pyramids. This must be so ingrained within his mind, that a glance at the Tablets will automatically start an associative current which will bring up without delay the attributions of any given letter or square which strikes the eye. Only

when this has been accomplished, dare he venture to the actual use of the Pyramids with the God-forms, or to the employment of the Invocations in ceremonial.

At this juncture, also, let me record one or two facts about the Angelic language in which the invocations are couched. The Outer Order rituals state, when the Tablets are pointed out in the Temple to the Candidate, that they are written "in what our tradition calls the Angelic Secret Language." The Tablets in use in the Temples, as well as those reproduced herein, are lettered in English. These, however, are a translation or, more accurately, a transliteration of characters belonging to the Enochian Alphabet. These letters will be found reproduced on a later page. It is said that these Letters are not simple in character, but partake of the nature of Sigils. In the section on Talismans, it will have been noticed that certain Geomantic emblems and Astrological symbols are referred to these letters.

This Angelic Secret Language, whatever its origin, is a true language. It has, quite clearly, a syntax and grammar of its own, and the invocations in that language are not mere strings of words, but sentences which can be translated, not simply transliterated into English. For instance, the Invo-
<265> cation of the three Archangels ruling over the Spirit Tablet, em-
ployed in the opening of the Portal Grade reads: "Ol Sonuf Vaorsagi Goho Iada Balata. Lexarph, Comanan, Tabitom. Zodakara, eka; zodakare od zodamran. Odo kikle qaa, piape piaomoel od vaoan." This, translated, means "I will reign over you, saith the God of Justice. Lexarph, Comanan, Tabitom, move, therefore. Show yourselves forth and appear. Declare unto us the mysteries of your creation, the balance of righteousness and truth."

In a First Order side-lecture issued to newly-initiated Zelatores by G. H. Fratre Sub Spe, there is this note on the Enochian system and language which might be worth reproducing:

"One more point is shown you in this first part of the 1 = 10 Grade, and that is the Great Terrestrial Watch-Tower or Tablet of the North. At present it will probably be to all of you who are here present, with the exception of those who have passed into the Second Order, an absolute sea of mystery. It appears a curious arrangement of squares and letters in different colours, and perhaps you may wonder to see English and not Hebrew letters upon it, seeing that it is one of the most ancient symbols in the world. I may tell you, without betraying any knowledge which is beyond you, that these letters are transliterated for convenience. I do not think there is any one present, except myself, who could read the original language in which they are written. But I may tell you that it is a great curiosity merely from the linguistic point of view, because that language and those characters in which it is written, are a perfect language which can be translated, and yet there is no record, so far as I am aware that that language was ever spoken, or those characters were ever used by mortal man. Now that Muller and other great philologists have said that it is impossible that any human being should invent a language, here is a language which has existed for as far back as we are
<266> able to trace. We find traces of it on rock-cut pillars and on temples,
apparently as old as the world. We find traces of it in the sacred mysteries of some of the oldest religions in the world, but we find no trace of it

ever having been used as a living language, and we hold the tradition that it is the Angelic secret language. Only one instance of this I may perhaps be allowed to give. The high priest of Jupiter in the earliest days of Rome was called Flamen *Dialis,* and you will find that the most learned are utterly ignorant as to whence came the word *Dialis.* They will tell you that it is ancient Etruscan, but beyond that they can tell you nothing. It is not the genitive of any known nominative. On that Tablet (Earth) you will see that the second of the Three Holy Secret Names of God is *Dial."*

Although no philologist, and without the least scientific knowledge of comparative languages, yet I have found the study of this Angelical or Enochian language an absorbing interest. Going through the invocations with the intention of compiling a dictionary of the extant words has convinced me personally that we have here fragmentary pieces of a very ancient tongue — a language which is far older even than the Sanskrit. It must have been a living tongue at one time, though many thousands of years ago, and it may therefore be claimed for Enochian that the fragments we do have are in the oldest language of which we have any knowledge. In short, though as pure speculation, it is believed that the language in which these invocations are written are remnants of the tongue of the age-old Atlanteans. True, there are no means for the time being of proving this speculation, or of bringing forward the least convincing item of corroboration other than that it is an instinctive or intuitive conviction. In the quotation rendered above, Fratre Sub Spe does give one example of an Enochian word appearing in antiquity, and this to some may prove suggestive. If only we knew it, there probably are hordes of words similar to the case quoted, and these may come to light when expert attention is given to the subject.

<267> Since writing the above, another instance of an Enochian word has come to my attention. Reading Charles Johnson's translation of, and Theosophical commentary upon, the great Upanishads of India, I find reference to a certain character of legend, Uma Haimavati. The Kena Upanishad speaks of her as the daughter of the Snowy Mountain, and she is, interprets Mr. Johnson, a symbol of the hidden Wisdom personified as the child of the Himalaya who reveals the Eternal. And Charles Johnson then proceeds, "Curiously, while the inner significance of the name of this woman greatly radiant is lost in Sanskrit, *it must have been clear in the older tongue which lies behind Sanskrit;* for it remains in the group of younger Aryan tongues called Slavonic. Here, the root *Um* is the common word for intelligence."

The italics marked in Johnson's commentary are mine. This point must strongly be indicated, for the significance of that word Um is retained, not alone in the Slavonic as shown by Mr. Johnson, but also in the Enochian or Angelical language. For example, in the Second Enochian Key, used to invoke the Angels of the Spirit Tablet, and in the Sixteenth Key we find the word "OM" translated by "Understand." (Let me remark here too, that the translation of the words in the Enochian invocations came from the same occult or angelic source as the invocations themselves, and were not made by either Dee or Kelly.) Again, in the Fifteenth Key, we find the English version of the Call "O thou . . . who knowest" as equivalent to "Ils . . . ds *omax."* While in the Call of the Thirty Aethers, "Oma" is rendered as "understanding."

Thus there is every indication to believe that if there was a language "which lies behind Sanskrit" as supposed by Mr. Charles Johnson and of course by many others, which according to the philosophy of the Ancient Wisdom is that of Atlantis, then the Enochian or Angelical language bears several strong points of resemblance to it.

<268> Yet, the puzzle is this. Prior to the previously described ceremonial skrying of Dr. Dee and Sir Edward Kelly towards the close of the 16th century there is absolutely no trace of any part of the Enochian magical system or Angelical language in Europe. There are innumerable ancient and mediaeval records of so-called "barbarous names of evocation," many of them being assembled apparently in sentences and runes, etc. But none of these latter have the coherence which the Enochian language *does* have, nor do they betray traces of grammar and syntax which are clearly indicated in the Angelical Keys. In some incomprehensible manner, this pair of psychics must have stumbled on a thread which unfolded, perhaps from their own subconscious memory of former lives, parts of this strange tongue of a bygone age. Stumbled, I use advisedly, for a close perusal of their diaries both published and unpublished reveals nothing to indicate that Dee or Kelly had anything but the remotest idea of what it was that they were recording so carefully. The way they have recorded the invocations, as shown in Sloane mss 3191 in the British Museum, indicates they had never studied its intricacies or grammar, and thus many words became jumbled and joined together. Only a little study of the Calls is necessary to reveal their mistakes, and to restore what is clearly the original arrangement of words. For instance, the word "L" or "EL" meaning "The first" or "One" is invariably joined on to the succeeding word in the Dee version; there is no necessity for this.

It is clear that the Angelical language was not in the possession of a possessive case, and thus we find several instances of the English translation, where the possessive case is used, not tallying exactly with the Enochian. We find "Lonshi Tox" translated by "His Power" when strictly it ought to be, if the words are literally to be translated "The power of him." and "Elzap Tilb" is rendered "Her course" instead of "The course of her." I mention this simply to show that the language is a real one, and not a mere jumble of
<269> unmeaning words to which an arbitrary translation was given. With the publication of the invocations here, I hope that serious experienced philologists will devote some attention to this matter so that we can thrash out once and for all, on the objective plane, the true nature of the language and the vertical source of its origins.

It is said in the ⑤ = [6] Ritual that some of the early Fratres of the Order compiled a dictionary of this language. At any rate, such is not in existence now, though the writer, using the Angelical Calls, has compiled a dictionary of the extant Enochian words. Unfortunately, it is not possible to include this dictionary with the present account of Order Teaching.

Incidentally, for practical purposes, the language is pronounced by taking each letter separately, whenever a lack of vowels renders it necessary. But, with a little practice, the pronounciation will come instinctively when the student wants it. "Z" is always pronounced "Zod" with a long "o."[1]

My last word is an insistence upon the necessity for a thorough grasp of the preliminary part. It should be read again and again, so that the student actually absorbs the material, rather than learns it by a feat of memory or conscious intellection. It may take some months this way, but once it has made it a part of his mode of thinking, so that it has been assimilated into the very structure of his brain, the real significance and meaning of the system will begin to dawn on him.

I. Regardie

<274>

THE BOOK OF THE CONCOURSE OF THE FORCES

PART ONE

The Enochian Tablets are four in number, each referred to one of the elements of Earth, Air, Fire and Water. In addition to these four there is another smaller Tablet, which is called The Tablet of Union, referred to the element of Ether or Spirit. Its function, as its name implies, is to unite and bind together the four elemental Tablets. For purposes of study the four Elemental Tablets or Watch-Towers are arranged as are the elements in the Pentagram, although the order is rather different:[2]

1. Air Tablet	2. Water Tablet
3. Earth Tablet	4. Fire Tablet

To each Tablet are referred innumerable attributions, which will be dealt with in the course of this paper, the principal elementary ones being those of colour. Certain squares on each Tablet were painted in the colour of the Element, according to the King Scale, whilst others were left wholly or partly white. Thus in each Tablet there are four principal types of square. There are those of:

1. The Great Cross of 36 squares, lettered in black on white, stretching through the entire Tablet.
2. The Sephirotic Calvary Crosses, lettered also in black on white, in the four corners on the Tablets.
3. The Kerubic Squares, which are always in the elemental colour of the Tablet, and are the four squares immediately above each Sephirotic Cross.

<275>

4. The Servient Squares, always in the colour of the Tablet, and consist of the 16 squares of each lesser angle beneath each Sephirotic Cross.

[1] Unfortunately, Israel Regardie overlooked *Spirits and Apparations*, Dee's published journals where pronunciation keys are given. Regardie's rendering of the Calls blurs pronunciation aids and Enochian spellings, a misguidance he inherited. H.S.

[2] These match the lower four points of the Pentagram. H.S.

<270>

THE FIRST WATCHTOWER *OR THE* GREAT EASTERN QUADRANGLE OF AIR

r	Z	i	l	a	f	A	^{y}u	t	l_{i}	p	a
a	r	d	Z	a	i	d	p	a	L	a	m
C	z	o	n	s	a	r	o	$_{v}Y$	a	u	b
T	o	i	T	t	^{z}x	o	P	a	c	o	C
S	i	g	a	s	o	^{n}m	r	b	z	n	h
f	m	o	n	d	a	T	d	i	a	r	l_{i}
o	r	o	i	b	a	h	a	o	z	p	i
^{t}c	N	a	b	^{r}a	V	i	x	g	a	^{s}z	d
O	i	i	i	t	T	p	a	l	O	a	i
A	b	a	m	o	o	o	a	C	^{u}v	c	a
N	a	o	c	O	T	t	n	p	r	^{u}a	T
o	c	a	n	m	a	g	o	t	r	o	i
S	h	i	a	l	r	a	p	m	z	o	x

THE SECOND WATCHTOWER
OR THE
GREAT WESTERN QUADRANGLE OF WATER

T	a	O	A	d	^{u}V	p	t	D	n	i	m
a_{o}	a	b_{l}	c	o	o	r	o	m	e	b	b
T	^{o}a	g	c	o	n	x_{z}	m_{i}	^{a}nu	l	G	m
n	h	o	d	D	i	a	i	l_{a}	a	o	c
f_{p}	a	t_{c}	A	x	i	V_{o}	V	s	P	x_{s}	$^{yl}N_{h}$
S	a	a	i	^{z}x	a	a	r	V	r	L^{c}	i
m	p	h	a	r	s	l	g	a	i	o	l
M	a	m	g	l	o	i	n	L	i	r	x
o	l	a	a	D	n_{a}	g	a	T	a	p	a
p	a	L	c	o	i	d	x	P	a	c	n
n	d	a	z	N	^{z}x	i	V	a	a	s	a
r_{i}	i	d	P	o	n	s	d	A	s	p	i
x	r	^{i}r	n	h	t	a	r	n_{a}	d	i	L

THE THIRD WATCHTOWER
OR THE
GREAT NORTHERN QUADRANGLE OF EARTH

b	O	a	Z	a	R	o	p	h	a	R	a
u V	N	n	a	x	o	P	S	o	n	d	n
a	i	g	r	a	n	o	a o	m	a	g	g
o	r	p	m	n	i	n	g	b	e	a	l
r	s	O	n	i	z	i	r	l	e	m	u
i	z	i	n	r	C	z	i	a	M	h	l
M	O	r	d	i	a	l	h	C	t	G	a
R o	C O	a c	n a	c nm	h c	i h	ia bt	s a	o s	m o	t m
A	r	b	i	z	m	i	i l	l	p	i	z
O	p	a	n	a	l B	a	m	S	m	a	T L
d	O	l	o	P F	l	n	i	a	n	b	a
r	x	p	a	o	c	s	i	z	i	x	p
a	x	t	i	r	V	a	s	t	r	i	m

<273>

THE FOURTH WATCHTOWER
OR THE
GREAT SOUTHERN QUADRANGLE OF FIRE

d	o	n	p	a	T	d	a	n	V	a	a
o	l	o	a	G	e	o	o	b	a	u v	a i
O	P	a	m	n	o	v o	G	m n	d	n	m
a	p b	l	s	T	e	c d	e	c	a	o	p
s	c	m	i	o	a	n	A	m	l	o	x
V	a	r	s	G	d	L	b v	r	i	a	p
o	i	P	t	e	a	a	p	D	o	c	e
P	s	u v	a	c	n	r	Z	i	r	z	a
S	i	o	d	a	o	i	n	r	z	f	m
d	a	l b	t	T	d	n	a	d	i	r	e
d	i	x	o	m	o	n	s	i	o	s	p
O	o	D	p	z	i	A	p	a	n	l	i
r	g	o	a	n	n	O p	A	C	r	a	r

The Kerubic and Servient squares on each Tablet are coloured in the elemental colour, with the letters drawn thereon in the complementary colour, thus:

AIR TABLET painted in Yellow. Lettering on Air quarter Mauve.
WATER TABLET painted in Blue. Lettering on Water quarter Orange.
EARTH TABLET painted in Black. Lettering on Earth quarter Green.
FIRE TABLET painted in Red. Lettering on Fire quarter Green.

The lettering on the other three Angles follows the element. Thus, to consider the Fire Tablet as an example, the colouring of each Angle of the Tablet will be:

1.
Lesser Angle
of AIR
Yellow Letters
on Red

2.
Lesser Angle
of WATER
Blue Letters
on Red

3.
Lesser Angle
of EARTH
Black Letters
on Red

4.
Lesser Angle
of FIRE
Green Letters
on Red

The TABLET OF UNION, which is attributed to Spirit, the fifth point of the Pentagram, is a small Tablet of twenty squares, five letters wide, four deep. Its letters are painted on a white ground:

EXARP, attributed to Air, is painted in yellow letters. 1st line.
HCOMA, attributed to Water, is painted in blue letters. 2nd line.
NANTA, attributed to Earth, is painted in black letters. 3rd line.
<276>
BITOM, attributed to Fire, is painted in red letters. 4th line.

Each of these twenty squares is attributed in part to Spirit, and its letters are used in combination with those on the Elemental Tablets in the formation of certain Names.

The most important item on each Angelic Tablet is the Great Cross whose shaft descends from the top to bottom and whose bar crosses the Tablet in the centre. This Cross comprises 36 squares, and has a double vertical line which is called *Linea Dei Patris Filiique,* the Line of God, the Father and the Son, and *Linea Spiritus Sancti,* the Line of the Holy Spirit, crossing this horizontally, and containing one rank of letters. The *Linea Spiritus Sancti* is always the seventh line or rank of letters from the top, while the two vertical columns of the *Linea Dei Patris Filiique* are always the sixth and seventh columns counting from either right or left.

From this Great Cross, various Angelic and Divine Names are produced, which are of supreme importance. First of all there are the "Three Great Secret Holy Names of God" which are found in the Linea Spiritus Sancti. This line comprises twelve letters, which are divided into names of three, four, and five letters reading from left to right. Thus in the Air Tablet, you will find ORO IBAH AOZPI; in the Water Tablet: MPH ARSL GAIOL; in the Earth Tablet: MOR DIAL HCTGA, and in the Fire Tablet; OIP TEAA PDOCE.

These Three Secret Holy Names of God are the major names of the Tablets. These Names are conceived to be borne as ensigns upon the Banners of the Great King of each quarter. The Name of the Great King is always a name of eight letters and comprises a spiral or whirl in the centre of the Great Cross. Thus in the Air Tablet, the Great King is BATAIVAH. It is produced:

<277>

And so for the other three Angelic Tablets. The King is a very powerful force, and since it initiates the whirl it is to be invoked with due care.

The next series of important names obtained from the Great Cross are the Six Seniors. Their names begin from the sixth and seventh squares of the Linea Spiritus Sancti, including these squares, and read *outwards* along the three lines of the Cross to the edge of the Tablet. Each is a name of seven letters. In the case of the Air Tablet, the Six Seniors are:

HABIORO

AAOXAIF

HTMORDA

AHAOZPI

AVTOTAR

HIPOTGA

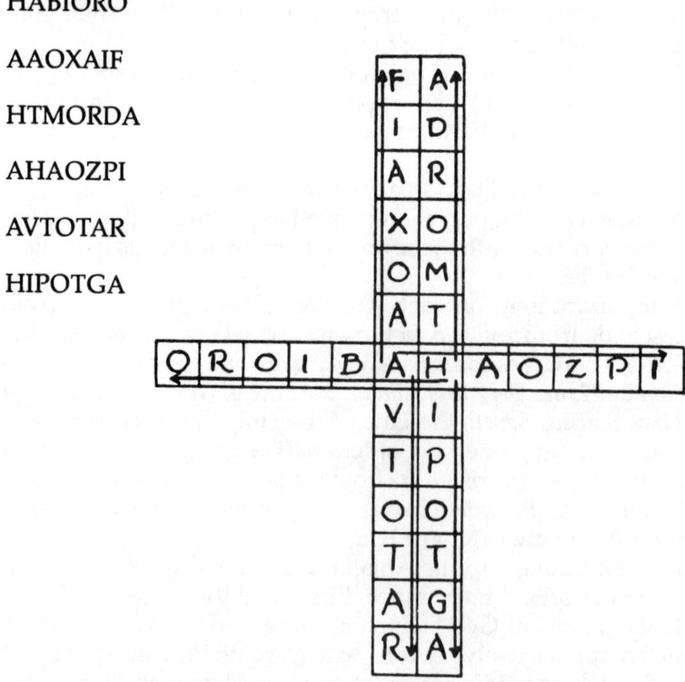

(Note the overlapping of letters in the central squares). The Eight-
<278> lettered Name of the King, and the six Names of seven letters each of

the Seniors, are invoked by means of the Hexagram. They are attributed to the Sun and Planets, and are on a different and higher plane than are the elemental names. The attribution to the points of the Hexagram is:

The King is attributed to the Sun, and the six Solar Hexagrams invoke him. The Senior formed on the left hand of the Linea Spiritus Sancti is attributed to Mars; that on the right hand to Venus. The Name of the Senior formed by the letters in the upper half of the Linea Dei Patris (which is the *left* descending column of the Cross, as the *right* column is the Linea Dei Filiique) is attributed to Jupiter, and the lower half to Mercury. The Senior formed by the letters on the upper half of the Linea Dei Filiique is referred to Luna, whilst the Name formed by the letters in the lower half is referred to Saturn.

These rules apply to each of the Four Tablets and are constant and invariable throughout. These three sets of names — the Holy Names of God, the Name of the King, and the Names of the Six Seniors, are all taken from the Great Central Cross. Their Names are always painted in black letters on a white ground.

We must now refer to the lesser Angles of each Tablet. The order given to the arrangement of the Four Tablets also applies to the structure of each individual Tablet, for each is shown together with its appropriate sub-elements. The Great Cross is the mechanism which divides the Tablet and separates (and binds together) the four sub-elements or Lesser Angles, as they are called, from the other.

In the centre of each Lesser Angle will be seen a Cross of Ten squares. This is called the Sephirotic Calvary Cross. From the letters arranged on this Cross are taken two divine names which call forth and control the angels and spirits of the Lesser Angle, and their names are used in a preliminary invocation when working magically with a square of a lesser angle. From
<279> the vertical line of the Sephirotic Cross, reading from above downwards, comes a Deity Name of six letters. Thus, in the Air Lesser Angle of the Air Tablet, we find, in the white descending line of the Cross, the name IDOIGO. It is with this name that the Angels and Spirits of the Lesser Angle are to be called. From the cross-bar, reading from left to right, comes the deity name of five letters, ARDZA, which is used to command those Angels called by the first name. Thus in every Sephirotic Cross in every Lesser Angle, we obtain two divine names. One on the descending shaft, always of six letters, and one on the cross-bar, reading from left to right, of five letters. These names must be read in these prescribed directions, for if they are reversed, they call forth evil forces. Like the Names from the Great Cross, these Names on the Sephirotic Cross are painted in black letters on white. But unlike the former, these latter are employed with the Pentagram.

We now come to the coloured squares grouped above and below the Sephirotic Cross in each of the Lesser Angles. The most important of these are the four *above* the cross-bar of the Sephirotic Cross — called the Kerubic Squares. From these four squares are derived four names of four letters each. Thus, for the top rank of the Airy Angle of the Air Tablet, we have:

R Z (I) L A

Note that the white square in the centre, belongs to the Sephirotic Cross and is not included in the names derived from the Kerubic Squares. From these four letters we obtain four names, thus: RZLA. ZLAR. LARZ. ARZL.

These Four Names, the Names of the Four Kerubic Angels of the Lesser Angle, rule the servient squares below the Sephirotic Cross, and of the four, the first is the most powerful as the others are derived therefrom. By prefixing to these four names a letter from the appropriate line of the Tablet of Union, we obtain even more powerful names, archangelic in char-
<280> acter. Thus for the Kerubic Rank of the Air Lesser Angle of the Air Tablet, which we are using as our example, the letter "E" of the word "EXARP" on the Tablet of Union is prefixed. This produces ERZLA. EZLAR. ELARZ. EARZL.

The rule is that the *first letter* of the appropriate line of the Tablet of Union is prefixed only to the Names formed from the Kerubic Squares. In the Airy Angle of the Water Tablet, the principle Kerubic Name is TAAD. The name formed by the addition of the appropriate letter from the Tablet of Union is HTAAD: and so on. As an example of this method applied to the remaining servient squares of the Air Angle of the Air Tablet, we find:

X is added to the 16 servient squares of the angle of AIR.
A is added to the 16 servient squares of the angle of WATER.
R is added to the 16 servient squares of the angle of EARTH.
P is added to the 16 servient squares of the angle of FIRE.

Hence EXARP will be used entirely on the Air Tablet, and is never used on the other three Tablets. The First letter applies to the Kerubic Squares of each of the four Lesser Angles, whilst the remaining four letters apply to the sixteen servient squares of those Angles as shown above. The other names of the Tablet of Union are attributed similarly to Water, Earth, and Fire. As an example, I give below Names formed from the Lesser Angle of Fire in the Water Tablet:

N	L	I	R	X
A	T	A	P	A
X	P	A	C	N
V	A	A	S	A
D	A	S	P	I
R	N	D	I	L

HNLRX	HLRXN	HRXNL	HXNLR.
AXPCN	APCNX	ACNXP	ANXPC.
AVASA	AASAV	ASAVA	AAVAS.
ADAPI	AAPID	APIDA	AIDAP.
ARNIL	ANILR	AILRN	ALRNI.

<281> The ritual for the consecration of the Four Elemental Weapons gives excellent examples of the spirit or archangelic names formed from the Kerubic Squares by the addition of letters from the Tablet of Union.

The attribution of the Name Yod He Vau He.

This Name is the key to the whole of the Enochian attributions of the squares to the Elements: The letters are thus referred:

י	YOD	FIRE	WANDS
ה	HE	WATER	CUPS
ו	VAU	AIR	SWORDS
ה	(final) HE	EARTH	PENTACLES

The letters of the great name attributed to the Four Tablets in order together:

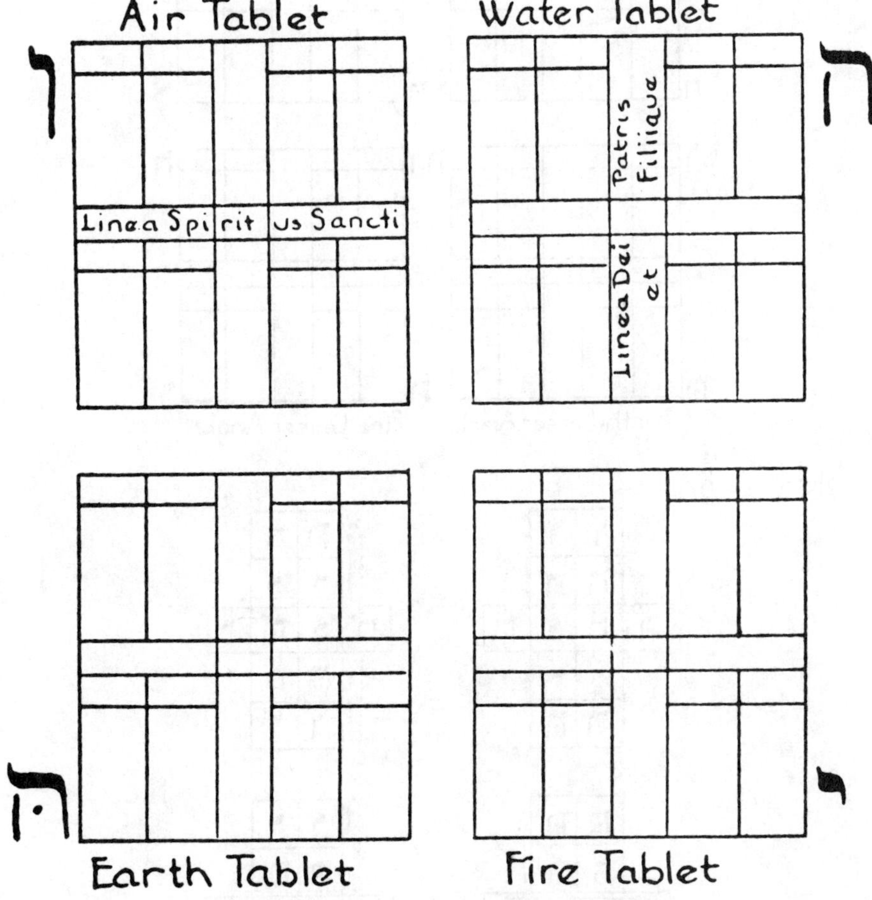

Not only are the Letters of Tetragrammaton attributed to the Tablets themselves, and to the Lesser Angles of the Tablets, but they are so arranged that even the Squares of the Tablets come under the jurisdiction and governance of the letters. So far as concerns the Great Cross, the method for attributing to it the letters of the Name is to divide each vertical and horizontal line into groups of three adjoining squares. Against the *top* left hand corner of the Great Cross, and on the *left* of its horizontal shaft, put the letter of the name for the Element of the Tablet, thus VAU for the Air Tablet, Yod for the Fire Tablet, etc.

<282> *The letters of the great name attributed to each corner of the separate Tablets:*

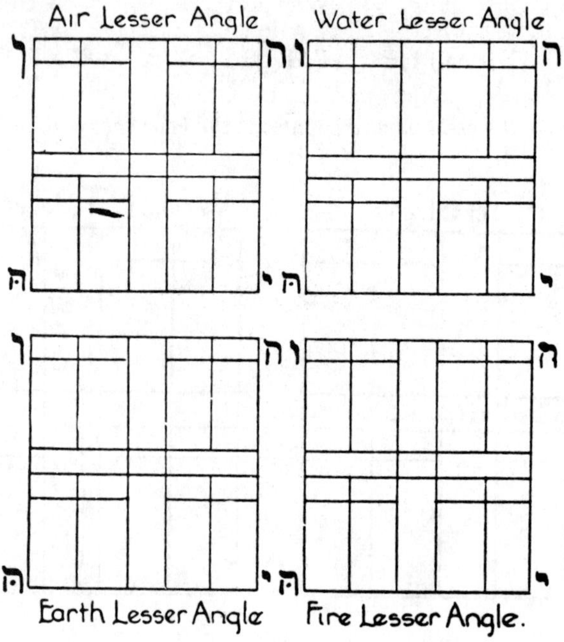

<283>

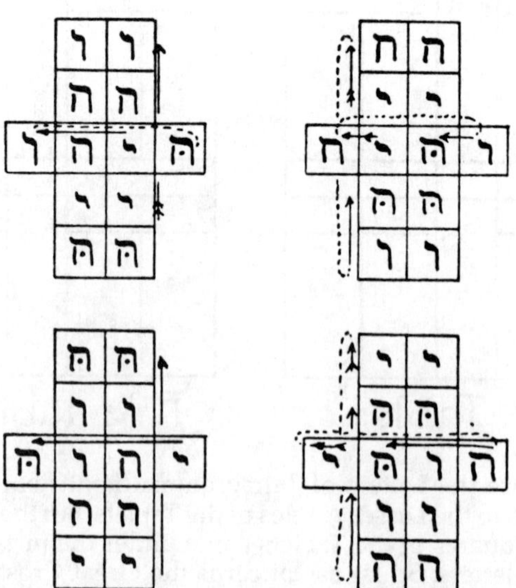

Each square of the above diagram represents *three squares* on the Tablets. This attribution is perfectly simple if it be remembered that the letter consonant to the Tablet always comes to the *top* and *left*.

The arrows show the direction in which the Name is to be read.

The Sephirotic Crosses in the Lesser Angles have as the student will already have noted, ten Squares, each of which is referred to one of the Sephiroth of the Tree of Life. The Sephirotic Cross therefore represents the Sephiroth modified by the letter of the lesser angle. Thus Kether in the Airy Lesser Angle is the *Kether* of *Vau.* In the Watery Lesser Angle, it is the *Kether* of *Heh,* and so on. The letters, in this case, as elsewhere explained, refer to the four Worlds.

Referring to the other squares of the lesser angles, in the Kerubic Rank the *outside* square is always attributed to the letter corresponding to the Element of the Lesser Angle. In the Tablets of Air and Water, the Name reads right to left in the two upper quarters; in the two lower quarters it reads from left to right. In the Tablets of Earth and Fire, left to right in the upper,
<284> but in the two lower quarters form right to left. Thus in the Four Tablets, the Name reads:

AIR ←

VHYH (f)	YH(f) VH
H(f) YHV	HVH(f) Y

WATER ←

VHYH(f)	YH(f) VH
H(f) YHV	HVH(f) Y

→ EARTH →

VH(f) YH	VH(f) YH
H(f) VHY	H(f) VHY

←

→ FIRE →

VH(f) YH	VH(f) YH
H(f) VHY	H(f) VHY

←

Though the last two groups of the name are the same, this does not indicate that the squares are identical. Their elemental composition differs enormously in each lesser angle, as a little later will be seen.

The Servient Squares beneath the Calvary Cross may be considered as of four vertical columns of four squares each, or, looking at it from a different angle, of four horizontal ranks also of four squares each. In attributing the letters of Tetragrammaton to these Servient Squares, the rule is that they follow the attributions of the Kerubic Squares. The columns (that is reading from above downwards) follow the order of the Kerubic Squares above, and this order is invariably followed *downwards* for the ranks, reading from right to left. Thus in the Air Lesser Angle of the Air Tablet, the Kerubic Rank has attribution to the Name:

VAU HEH YOD HEH (Final)

Therefore applying the above rule, the Servient squares beneath the Sephirotic Cross follow:

	VAU	HEH	YOD	HEH (Final)
(Final) HEH	*	*	*	*
YOD	*	*	*	*
HEH	*	*	*	*
VAU	*	*	*	*

From this example, it will be clearly indicated that each square has a double attribution to the letters of Tetragrammaton, none being the same since a
column and a rank differ. Thus, Column VAU rank YOD does not
<285> coincide in nature with Column YOD rank VAU.

We must now approach the reason for this complex series of references of the letters of the Tetragrammaton to the squares. According to these attributions, so are certain Astrological, Tarot, Geomantic and Hebrew symbols referred to the Squares.

It will be remembered that in attributing the letters of the Name to the Great Cross, we subdivided the latter into groups or blocks of three squares each. Every block was attributed to some one letter of Tetragrammaton. Now the Signs of the Zodiac are to be attributed to the Great Cross, and each of those twelve Signs is to be referred to three squares constituting one group or block. The order of their attribution is governed by the letters of the Great Name already referred to the arms of the Great Cross. For instance, Fiery Signs (Aries, Leo, and Sagittarius) are attributed to YOD. Watery Signs (Cancer, Scorpio, and Pisces) are attributed to HEH. Airy Signs (Gemini, Libra, Aquarius) are attributed to VAU. Earthy Signs (Taurus, Virgo, and Capricorn) are attributed to HEH final.

Thus each group of three squares, constituting a single unit, is attributed to one sign of the Zodiac, depending upon the letter of the Name referred to that group. Each Zodiacal Sign, being divisible into three Decanates, or divisions of ten degrees, it follows that each of three Decanates of the Sign may be referred to one of the squares in any group of three squares. The Sign refers to the group, the Decan refers to one square of that group.

The rule governing the attributions of the Twelve Signs to the Great Cross is: the Four Kerubic or Fixed Signs (Taurus, Leo, Scorpio, and Aquarius) are referred to the squares of the Linea Spiritus Sancti. The Four Cardinal Signs (Aries, Cancer, Libra, Capricorn) are referred to the left side of
the Linea Dei Patris Filiique, and the Four Mutable Signs (Gemini,
<286> Virgo, Sagittarius and Pisces) to the right side of the Linea Dei
Patris Filiique.

The decanate system as employed by the Order will be found in the part of this book dealing with the significance of the Tarot Cards. They begin with the attribution of the first decanate of Aries to the planet Mars, and ending with the last decanate of Pisces also ruled by Mars. The order of planets for the decanates follows the order of Sephiroth on the Tree of Life: Saturn, Jupiter, Mars, Sol, Venus, Mercury, and Luna.

There are 36 small cards of the Tarot, as explained in the appropriate documents, attributed to the decanates of the Twelve Signs. Therefore to each of the decanate squares on the Great Cross will be attributed one of the small cards of the Tarot. 2, 3, and 4, of each of the four Suits of Tarot are referred to Cardinal Signs. 5, 6, 7 to the Kerubic or Fixed Signs; and 8, 9, and 10 to the Mutable Signs. Thus in the Air Tablet, the Great Cross shows the Tarot and decanate attributions as shown.

<287> THE GREAT CROSS OF THE AIR TABLET
SHOWING TAROT AND DECANATE ATTRIBUTIONS

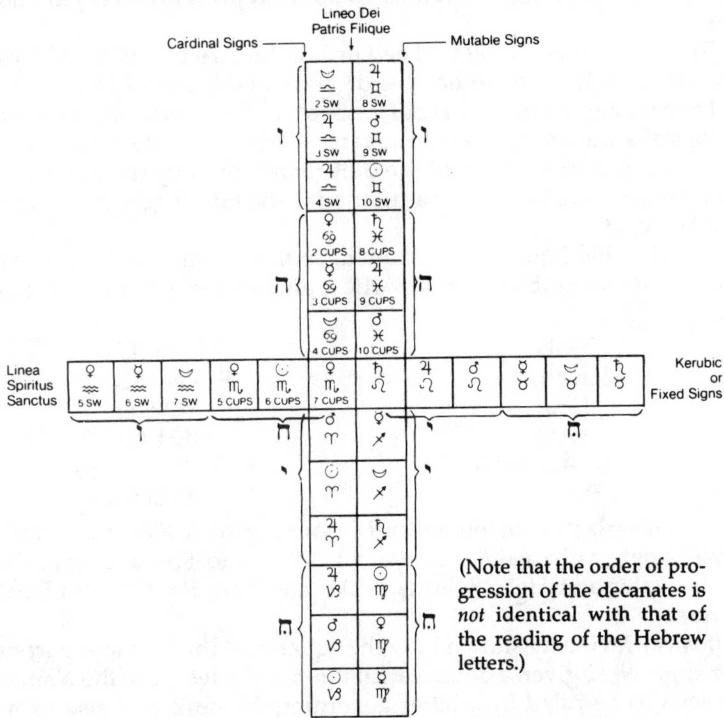

(Note that the order of progression of the decanates is *not* identical with that of the reading of the Hebrew letters.)

The attribution of the Sephiroth to the ten squares of the Sephirotic Cross is shown on the Admission Badge to the 27th Path of Peh, and reproduced in one of the Knowledge Lectures. The planetary attributions to the Sephirotic Cross as used in the Enochian system are rather different from those used on the Tree of Life. But the system that is here employed is constant, and applies to each of the sixteen Sephirotic Crosses on the four Tablets.

In this mode of attributing the planets to the Sephiroth on the Calvary Cross of the Lesser Angles, Saturn is excluded, and Jupiter and the Tarot Trump, the Wheel of Fortune is attributed to Kether. The title of this card is "The Lord of the Forces of Life," and Kether is the origin and source of Life.

To Chokmah is attributed Mercury, the Tarot Key, The Ma-
<288> gician, "The Magus of Power" seeing that Chokmah is the distributor of the power from Kether, even as Mercury is the messenger of Jupiter of classical mythology.

To Binah is referred the Moon, and the Tarot Key, "The Priestess of the Silver Star," even as Binah is the completer of the Triad of the Supernals, and as it were High Priestess to the Inferior Sephiroth. (Compare also, says S.R.M.D., the position of the Path of Gimel in the Tree of Life.)

To Chesed, Venus, and the Key of The Empress, "The Daughter of the Mighty Ones." Chesed is, as it were, the first of the Inferiors below Binah, and the Path of Venus is thus reciprocal between Chokmah and Binah, forming, as it were, the base of the Triangle of the Supernals.

To Geburah, Mars, and the Tarot Key, The Blasted Tower, "The Lord of the Hosts of the Mighty," even as Geburah represents strength and fiery power.

To Tiphareth is the Sun, "The Lord of the Fire of the World," even as Tiphareth is, as it were the heart and centre of the Sun of Life.

The remaining four squares of the Sephirotic Cross have no planetary or astrological attributions. The ten squares of the Sephirotic Cross also stand for the Ace and small cards of the Suit represented by the Element of the Lesser Angle. Thus Wands are attributed to the Fire Angle, Pentacles to the Earth Angle, etc.

The Kerubic Squares are allotted, as their name implies, to the four Kerubim whose emblems follow the order of the letters of Tetragrammaton:

YOD	HEH
Lion—Leo	Eagle—Scorpio
King	Queen
VAU	HEH (final)
Man—Aquarius	Bull—Taurus
Prince	Princess

These last are of the suit corresponding to the Element of the Lesser
<289> Angle as explained above, viz: Wands to Fire and Yod; Cups to
Water and Heh; Swords to Air and Vau; Pentacles to Earth and Heh final.

It was previously shown how the squares of the Servient part of each lesser angle were given a double attribution to the letters of the Name. They were seen to be ruled by a letter governing the rank, and also by a letter governing the column. In order to work out the astrological attributions of this allocation, note that the columns go by the triplicity of the Kerubic Square at the top, the ranks by quality. By this method there results a highly intricate and ingenious subdivision of elements in the sub-elements of the Lesser Angles.

YOD and Fire are referred to the Cardinal Signs, ♈ ♋ ♎ ♑.
HEH and Water are referred to the Kerubic or Fixed Signs, ♉ ♌ ♏ ♒.
VAU and Air are referred to the Mutable Signs, ♊ ♍ ♐ ♓.
HEH final and Earth are referred to the Elements, △ ▽ 🜁 🜃.

As to the reasons of this latter attribution, S.R.M.D. says that the Four Cardinal Signs are called the most fiery because most solar in nature. That is, the Equinoxes and Solstices occur when the Sun is in these signs. The Kerubic or Fixed Signs are considered watery because they are the most shining and glittering in nature. The remaining four Mutable signs are called the most Airy because they are the most subtle in nature. While the four elements are the most Earthy because their operation is mainly terrestrial. Incidentally, instead of the usual Earth symbol, the planet Saturn is used in the Enochian system, because, to quote S.R.M.D. "though one of the seven
Lords who wander (planets), Saturn is yet here classed with those
<290> who abide because he is the heaviest of the seven and thus formeth a
link between the Wanderers and Abiders."

The following diagram shows how any Lesser Angle may be worked out using the above rules:

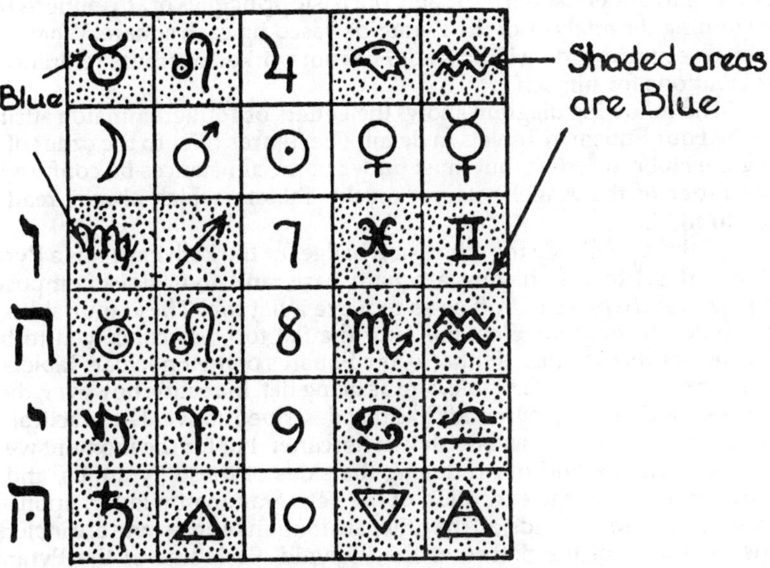

EARTH ANGLE OF WATER TABLET

One final set of attributions concerns the Tablet of Union, which is referred to Spirit. It is employed, as before shown, in binding together the Tablets, and in building up Angelic Names. Its attributions are to the Four Aces of the Elements and to the Court Cards. The Aces represent the root force, and the essential spiritual noumenon of the element. The Court Cards are the vice-gerents of the root force in the element.

	☸	🜁	🜄	🜃	🜂
🜁	ACE SWORDS	PRINCE SWORDS	QUEEN SWORDS	PRINCESS SWORDS	KING SWORDS
🜄	ACE CUPS	PRINCE CUPS	QUEEN CUPS	PRINCESS CUPS	KING CUPS
🜃	ACE PENTS	PRINCE PENTS	QUEEN PENTS	PRINCESS PENTS	KING PENTS
🜂	ACE WANDS	PRINCE WANDS	QUEEN WANDS	PRINCESS WANDS	KING WANDS

<291> The foregoing methods of attributing the Enochian squares should be completely grasped before proceeding further. It is imperative to understand thoroughly the basic principles of attributions before beginning the analysis of the Pyramids based on each square. What follows will have little meaning if the reader has not worked out these references and attributions for himself.

The following diagram shows the Letters of Tetragrammaton attributed to the Four Enochian Tablets in detail. The figures refer to the order of reading the Hebrew letters, but must under no circumstances be confused with the order of the Angelic names on the Tablets, which always read from left to right.

In the 4=7 Grade the admission badge for the 28th Path was a Pyramid. It was described as having a square base, and four sides composed of equilateral triangles cut off so as to leave a flat top. These four sides were attributed to the four Elements, and the flat top was conceived to be the throne of Eth, the Spirit. Hithcrto, the Squares of the Enochian Tablets have been treated as a single whole, and as being flat. In reality, however, they are represented as being pyramids like that described above. The practical magical significance of this will be shown hereafter, but for the moment we must consider the method of producing the sides of these Pyramids, and their attributions. With the exception of the Tetragrammaton letter, upon which everything else depends, all the other attributions appear and are included in the definition of the nature of the Pyramid. Each side of the Pyramid is coloured according to its own appropriate element, or left white for Spirit. It by no means follows for example that a square from the Airy Angle of Air will build up a completely yellow pyramid. But every square of the Air Tablet, in every angle, has at least one Airy yellow side to its pyramid. Every square of

<292>

KEY OF ATTRIBUTIONS

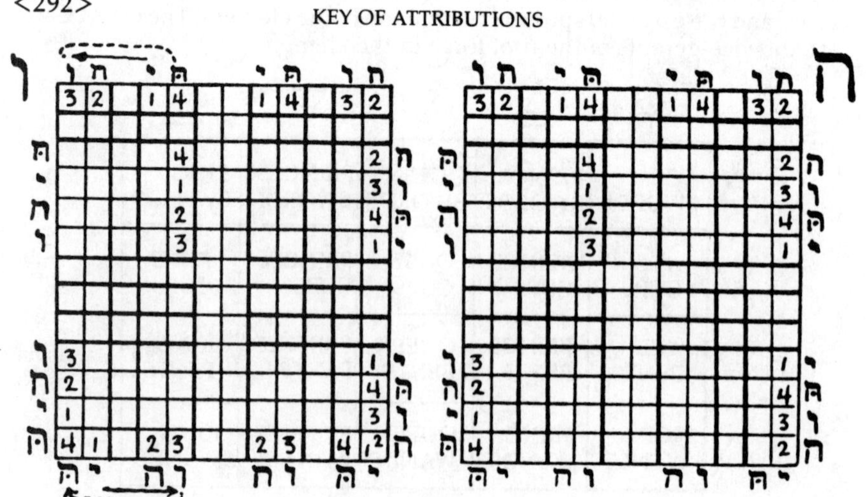

ATTRIBUTION
OF THE
GREAT NAME TO
THE FOUR LESSER ANGLES

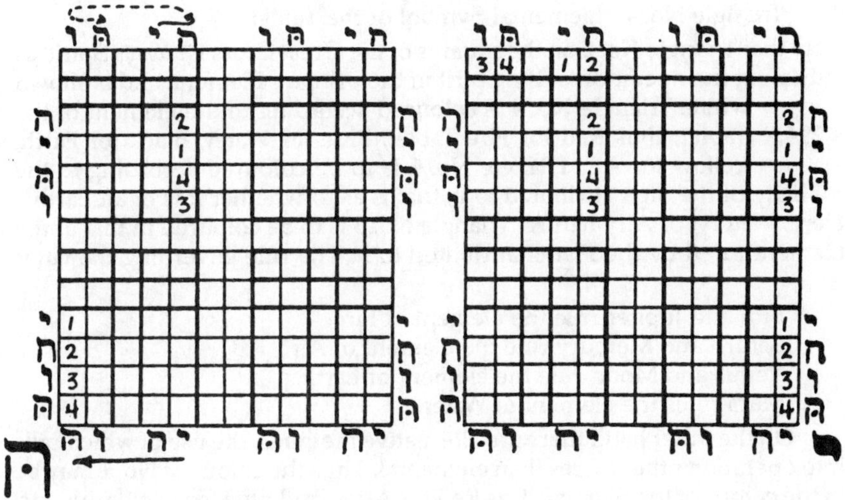

<293> the Airy Angle of all four Tablets has at least one Airy side.

On a flat surface, the Pyramid is represented by dividing the Square into four triangles, leaving a small square in the centre to mark the flat top. On this, if desired, the appropriate Enochian letter may be placed. The following will be the standard of reference, so that later should mention be made of Triangle No. 2, the following diagram will show its position.

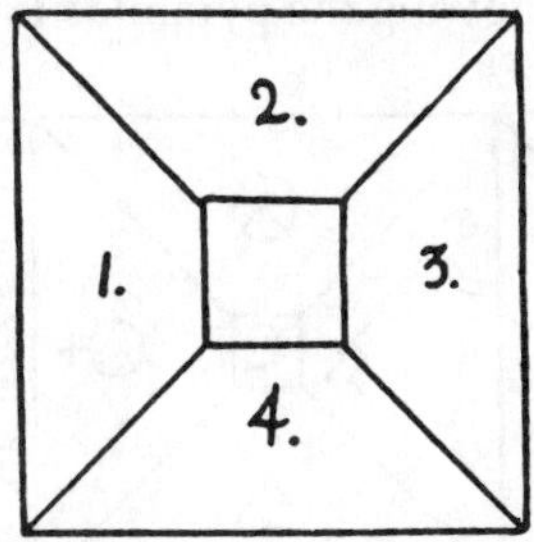

The Pyramid is supposed to be in position on the Tablet, so that Triangle No. 2 points to the top of the Tablet. To work out the pyramid of any square completely, it is necessary to know the attributions of the Four Triangles and the element of each. Since every Tablet comprises four distinct divisions, each of these must be considered separately as each produces a different type of pyramid. The rules for analysing the pyramid based on the squares will be concisely put thus:

Great Cross.

Triangle No. 1. Sign of Zodiac, small card of Tarot.
Triangle No. 2. Spirit.
Triangle No. 3. Planet of Decan.
Triangle No. 4. Elemental Symbol of the Tablet.

Note that Triangle No. 2 on the squares of the Great Cross is *always* Spirit, as indicating the operation of the Spirit in the primary Element, and is shown white. Triangle No. 4 is coloured according to the element of the
<294> Tablet; thus Red for Fire Tablet, Blue for Water, Black for Earth,
Yellow for Air. Triangle No. 1 is to be coloured according to the triplicity of the Sign attributed to it, that is as to whether it is of an Earthy, Fiery, Watery, or Airy nature. Triangle No. 3 is to be coloured in that of the Element ruled by the Planet attributed to it. The rule governing the latter is:

Sun and Jupiter rule the element of Fire.
Saturn and Mercury rule the element of Air.
Venus and Moon rule the element of Earth.
Mars rules the element of Water.

On the other hand there are alternative methods, the use of which calls into operation other forces than elemental. Thus the colour of No. 1 may be in the colour of the Sign itself, as Red for Aries, and Blue for Sagittarius, etc. Triangle No. 3 may also be coloured in the colour of the Planet itself, Orange for the Sun, Green for Venus, etc. If these latter are used, planetary and zodiacal forces would be inferred in lieu of purely elemental ones. The former, however, may be found to be the most practicable for most circumstances.

The method of applying these rules to the Great Cross may be seen in the following, consisting of the three left hand squares of the Linea Spiritus Sancti of the Air Tablet, showing the pyramids formed from the squares of the letters ORO:

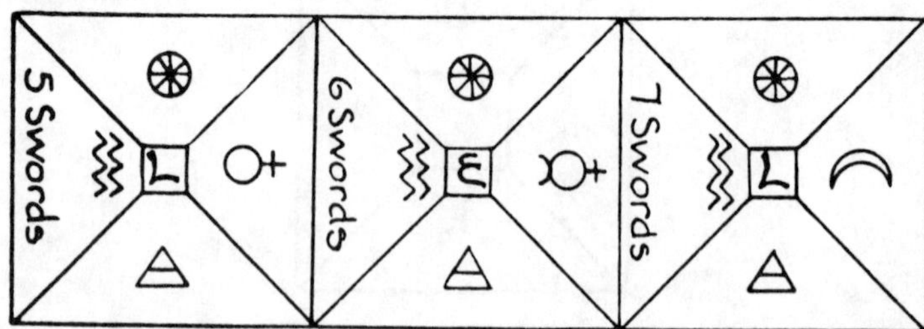

Sephirotic Cross.

Triangle No. 1. Elemental Emblem of Tablet.
Triangle No. 2. Emblem of Spirit.
Triangle No. 3. Elemental Emblem of Lesser Angle.
<295> Triangle No. 4. Sephirah. Letter of Tetragrammaton. Tarot Card.

Colouring: No. 1, Colour of the Element of Tablet. 2, Always white. 3, Elemental colour of Lesser Angle. 4, Either white for Spirit, or in colour of Sephirah.

Kerubic Squares of the Lesser Angles.

Triangle No. 1. Tarot Card of Lesser Angle.
Triangle No. 2. Elemental Emblem of Tablet.
Triangle No. 3. Kerubic symbol answering to letter of Name.
Triangle No. 4. Elemental Emblem of Lesser Angle.

No. 1 will agree with the colouring of No. 3 always. That is, the colour will be that of the element of the Court card corresponding to the Kerub. No. 2 shows the elemental colour of Tablet. No. 4, elemental colour of the Lesser Angle.

Servient Squares.

Triangle No. 1. Element of Great Tablet with astrological attribution.
Triangle No. 2. Elemental Emblem of letter ruling the *Column* with Tarot Trump.
Triangle No. 3. Elemental Emblem of Lesser Angle with Geomantic figure.
Triangle No. 4. Elemental Emblem of Letter ruling *Rank* with Hebrew of Letter corresponding to Tarot Trump in Triangle No. 2.

The colouring of these triangles is the simplest because it follows its elemental emblem. It has not been mentioned before, but it is the rule, when drawing or painting these pyramids and triangles, to paint the symbols on the appropriate sides in complementary colours. Thus, to take Triangle No. 1 of a servient square in the Water Angle of Water, the colour will be Blue to refer to the element of the Tablet as a whole, while the appropriate astrological attribution will be painted on it in Orange. This rule applies to all the squares.

<296> The method sounds highly complex, but in practice it is much easier than it sounds. In fact, it takes far less time to work out a square than to describe the method.

Tablet of Union.

Triangle No. 1. Element of Column. (Spirit in first column).
Triangles No. 2 and No. 4. Always Spirit.
Triangle No. 3. Element of rank.

The colours of each of the Triangles are clearly indicated.

I append below examples of the above, so that there may be no difficulty

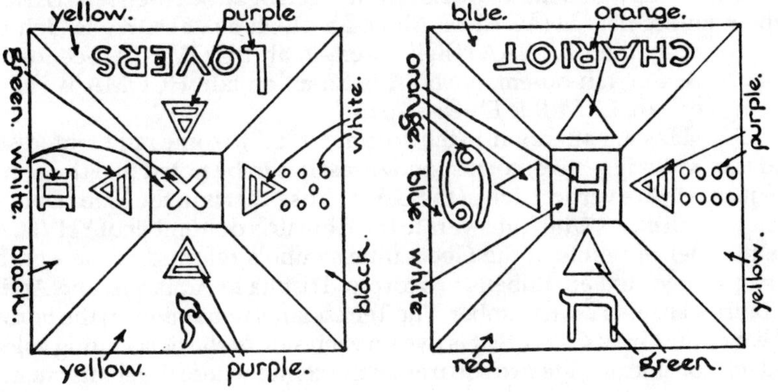

at all in understanding how this procedure obtains. Consider the Earth Lesser Angle of the Earth Tablet; the servient square in Rank VAU and Column VAU. The column is ruled by Vau, attributed to Air, therefore the Astrological symbol will be an Airy Sign. The Rank is ruled by VAU therefore the symbol will be Mutable Air, Gemini.

The Tarot Key for Gemini is The Lovers. The Hebrew Letter attributed to it is Zayin. The Geomantic attribution is Albus.

Take the Water Tablet, Air Angle, Column Heh, Rank Yod. The
<297> Column is ruled by Heh which is attributed to Water. Therefore the
astrological symbol will be a watery Sign.

The Rank is ruled by Yod, therefore the symbol will be Cardinal or Fiery Water—Cancer.

The Tarot Key for Cancer is The Chariot.
The Hebrew Letter for Cancer is Cheth.
The Geomantic attribution is Populus.

The following is by S.R.M.D. "Briefly, regarding the pronunciation of the Angelical Language, thou shalt pronounce the consonants with the vowel following in the nomenclature of the same letter in the Hebrew Alphabet. For example, in Beth, the vowel following 'B' is 'e' pronounced AY. Therefore, if 'B' in an Angelic Name precede another as in 'Sobha,' thou mayest pronounce it 'Sobeh-hah.' 'G' may be either Gimel or Jimel (as the Arabs do call it) following whether it be hard or soft. This is the ancient Egyptian use, whereof the Hebrew is but a copy, and that many times a faulty copy, save in the Divine and Mystical Names, and some other things.

"Also 'Y' and 'I' are similar, also 'V' and 'U,' depending whether the use intended be vowel or consonant. 'X' is the ancient Egyptian power of Samekh; but there be some ordinary Hebrew Names wherein 'X' is made Tzaddi."

From one ritual written by S.A., we find the following given as to the pronunciation of Names.

"In pronouncing the Names, take each letter separately. M is pronounced Em; N is pronounced En (also Nu, since in Hebrew the vowel following the equivalent letter Nun is 'u'); A is Ah; P is Peh; S is Ess; D is Deh.

"NRFM is pronounced En-Ra-Ef-Em or En-Ar-Ef-Em. ZIZA is pronounced Zod-ee-zod-ah. ADRE is Ah-deh-reh or Ah-deh-er-reh. TAASD is Teh-ah-ah-ess-deh. AIAOAI is Ah-ee-ah-oh-ah-ee. BDOPA is Beh-deh-
oh-peh-ah. BANAA is Beh-ah-en-ah-ah. BITOM is Beh-ee-to-em or
<300> Beh-ee-teh-oo-em. NANTA is En-ah-en-tah. HCOMA is Heh-co-
em-ah. EXARP is Eh-ex-ar-peh."

S.R.M.D. calls attention, in the document "S," to some rather interesting, that is to say, suggestive, correspondences. It is to be noted that the number of squares in the vertical line of the Great Cross, that is in the Linea Dei Patris Filiique, will be 26, which answers to the Gematria or number of YHVH. Also the number of points in the Geomantic symbols referred to the Kerubim, Fortuna Major to Leo, Rubeus to Scorpio, Tristitia to Aquarius, and Amissio to Taurus, are also 26 in number. The Ten squares remaining on the horizontal bar of the Great Cross, that is five on each side of the descending column, and not considering the two squares on the centre where the shafts cross, will

NOTES TO THE BOOK OF THE CONCOURSE OF THE FORCES

The following Table of Attributions, repeated though it is for the most part from earlier knowledge which should be familiar, may be useful for reference in working out the Squares.

Col.	Rank	Letter	Tarot Trump	Symbol	Geomantic Fig.
ו	הּ	א	Fool	🜁	Fort. Min.
S.C.	Chokmah	ב	Magician	☿	—
S.C.	Binah	ג	High Priestess	☾	—
S.C.	Chesed	ד	Empress	♀	—
י	י	ה	Emperor	♈	Puer
הּ	ה	ו	Hierophant	♉	Amissio
ו	ו	ז	Lovers	♊	Albus
ה	י	ח	Chariot	♋	Populus
י	ה	ט	Strength	♌	Fort. Maj.
הּ	ו	י	Hermit	♍	Conjunctio
S.C.	Kether	כ	Wheel of Fortune	♃	—
ו	י	ל	Justice	♎	Puella
ה	הּ	מ	Hanged Man	🜄	Via
ה	ה	נ	Death	♏	Rubeus
י	ו	ס	Temperance	♐	Acquisitio
הּ	י	ע	Devil	♑	Carcer
S.C.	Geburah	פ	Tower	♂	—
ו	ה	צ	Star	♒	Tristitia
ה	ו	ק	Moon	♓	Laetitia
S.C.	Tiphareth	ר	Sun	☉	—
י	הּ	ש	Last Judgment	🜂	Cauda Drac.
הּ	הּ	ת	Universe	♄ (🜃)	Caput Drac.

"S.C." stands for Sephirotic Cross.

<299> THE FOLLOWING IS THE ENOCHIAN ALPHABET (this sometimes, though wrongly, was called Theban) TOGETHER WITH THE ENGLISH EQUIVALENTS OF ITS LETTERS, AND THE ENOCHIAN TITLES

Enochian	Title	English
	Pe	B.
	Veh	C or K.
	Ged	G.
	Gal	D.
	Orth	F.
	Un	A.
	Graph	E.
	Tal	M.
	Gon	I, Y, or J.
	Na-hath	H.
	Ur	L.
	Mals	P.
	Ger	Q.
	Drun	N.
	Pal	X.
	Med	O.
	Don	R.
	Ceph	Z.
	Vau	U, V, W.
	Fam	S.
	Gisa	T.

refer to the Ten Sephiroth. And the first three letters of those squares will symbolise the triad of the Supernals operating through the Quadrangle.

Looking at the horizontal line again, and considering its full quota of twelve squares, instead of as ten as before, then since they are divided into a 3, a 4, and a 5, — as in OIP TEAA PDOCE — they may be said to symbolise the Triad of the Supernals, the Tetrad of the Elements, and the Pentagram. Again, in the commencing Triad of the Linea Spiritus Sancti of each Tablet, it may be said that:

ORO will be symbolical of the Voice of the Man Kerub.
MPH will be symbolical of the Cry of the Eagle Kerub.
MOR will be symbolical of the Low of the Bull Kerub.
OIP will be symbolical of the Roar of the Lion Kerub.

There are various ways of looking at the Pyramids prior to undertaking the practical work of using them as the symbol for skrying in the spirit-vision. S.R.M.D. suggests a useful mode of meditation which elaborates in a most illuminating way the ordinary attributions. He says: "Thou mayest regard
the upper triangle (No. 2) as representing a Force acting *downwards.*
<301> The lower triangle (No. 4) as a force striving *upwards.* The left hand
Triangle (No. 1) as acting *horizontally* from *left* to *right,* and the right
hand Triangle (No. 3) as a force acting from *right* to *left.* While the centre will be the common force. Thus:

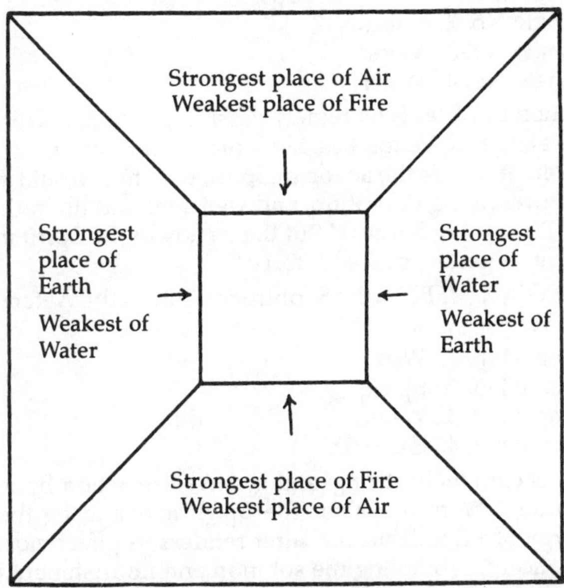

"Spirit is strong in any position. Remember that Fire acteth most strongly upwards, Air downwards, Water from right to left horizontally, and Earth from left to right. And in those Tablet Squares according to their positions in the Great Tablet. And thus canst thou apply thy reason unto the elucidation of the effect of the four forces thus rushing together."

Though this may sound wholly incomprehensible at first, a little reflection on the nature of the movement of these forces yields a wealth of idea. S.R.M.D. provides a few examples at hazard of this analysis, and I quote them as follows:

"*The Square of 'A' of Exarp* in the Tablet of Union.

Triangle No. 2. Queen of Swords.
Triangle No. 2. Spirit.
<302> Triangle No. 3. Air.
Triangle No. 4. Spirit.

"Nearly all the squares of this Tablet represent some combined effect of Light and Life. Here Spirit acts both downwards and upwards. Air is not very strong in action when it is here placed; and the Queen of Swords represents the moist force of Air, *Heh* of *Vau.* Therefore, if one could attribute a *direct* material action unto the Squares of the Tablet of Union, the terrestrial effect would be that of a moist and gentle, scarcely moving, breeze; with a soft vibrating Light playing through it, like the most gentle sheet-lightning in summer."

It will aid the reader considerably if, when meditating upon these examples, he draws the Pyramid with the triangles so that he can refer to it at a moment's notice.

"*The Square 'H' of 'MPH'* in the Great Cross of the Water Tablet.

Triangle No. 1. Seven of Cups. ♏
Triangle No. 2. Spirit.
Triangle No. 3. Venus.
Triangle No. 4. Water.

"Here the action of Water is extremely passive, Scorpio, representing especially Still Water, and Venus has her quiet action still more intensified. Therefore, were it not for the action of Spirit, the effect would be rather evil than good, representing deception, and well summed up in the 7 of Cups. 'The Lord of Illusionary Success.' But the Action of the Spirit makes it mild and beneficent. A gentle, peaceful, force."

"*The Square of 'O' of 'OMEBB'* in the Sephirotic Cross of the Water Lesser Angle of the Water Tablet.

Triangle No. 1. Water.
Triangle No. 2. Spirit.
Triangle No. 3. Water.
Triangle No. 4. Geburah.

"Here Water is extremely strong, and is stirred to action by the energy of
Geburah. Were it not for the Spirit it would be the destroying
<303> energy of a flood, but the latter renders its effect more gentle and
beneficent, promoting the solution and nourishment of matter."

"*The Square of 'M' of 'AISMT,'* a Kerubic Square of the Fiery Lesser Angle of the Earth Tablet.

Triangle No. 1. Queen of Wands.
Triangle No. 2. Earth.
Triangle No. 3. Eagle Kerub. Water.
Triangle No. 4. Fire.

"Here Earth acting downwards and Fire upwards, the effect would be volcanic. The water is as strongly placed as the Fire, rendering it explosive, though helping to stifle the Fire by its union with the Earth. The Queen of Wands equals the Water of Fire, *Heh* of *Yod*, reconciling these two elements. Therefore the whole effect would be to produce a moist generating heat, like that of a conservatory, or rather of a hot-house. A force intensely excitant and generative and productive. The earth force of the tropics.

"*The Servient Square 'R' of 'BRAP'* in the Watery Lesser Angle of the Fire Tablet.

Triangle No. 1. Virgo. Fire.
Triangle No. 2. Earth.
Triangle No. 3. Water. Conjunctio.
Triangle No. 4. Air.

"Here Water is in the strongest place, but otherwise the Force of the Square is somewhat different to the former, from the influence of Air in the lowest triangle. The effect will then be that somewhat of lands — fertile indeed, but ultimating its harvest, and therefore not nearly as excitantly generative as in the former square. And the land of Virgo as usually described will be a very fair representation thereof."

The following statements concerning aspects of the philosophy underlying the Enochian Tablets are also written by G. H. Fratre S.R.M.D. Some of them are very profound and the student will do well if he gives them a good deal of attention — especially in connection with the idea of the projection of the Tree of Life into a solid sphere and forming Five Pillars.

<304> This part of the Enochian teaching is taken from a manuscript entitled "X. The Book of the Concourse of the Forces. Binding together the Powers of the Squares in the Terrestrial Quadrangles of Enoch."

"Each of these Terrestrial Tablets of the Elements is divided into 4 Lesser Angles by the Great Central Cross which cometh forth as from the Gate of the Watch Tower of the Element itself. The Horizontal Line of each of these Three Great Crosses is named 'Linea Spiritus Sancti.' The Perpendicular is called 'Linea Dei,' the Line of God the Father and Son, the 'Patris Filiique,' Macroprosopus and Microprosopus combined. For these 4 Vertical lines resemble 4 mighty Pillars each divided into twain by a light line shewing this forth; The Father Himself, in the absence of the line. And in its presence shewing the Son.

"As aforesaid the central points of these 4 Great Crosses do shew in the Celestial Heavens, and do correspond unto the 4 Tiphareth points referred to in the Book of the Astronomic view of the Tarot. Naturally then the Linea Spiritus Sancti coincides with the Zodiacal Belt wherein is the Path of the Sun who is the administrant of The Spirit of Life, and "The Lord of the Fire of the World." The Four Linea S. S. then form the complete circle of the Ecliptic, a circle at the centre of the Zodiacal circle.

"It is demonstrated in the Tarot manuscripts that when the 10 Sephiroth in their grouping which is called the Tree of Life are projected in a Sphere (Kether coinciding with the North Pole, Malkuth coinciding with the South Pole, the Pillar of Mildness with the Axis) then the Pillars of Severity and of

Mercy are quadrupled, i.e. there are five Pillars instead of three Pillars.

"The same scheme is therefore applicable to the Celestial Heavens, and the mode of the governance of these Tablets in the Heavens is also set forth in the Tarot manuscripts. But as before and as there is said, the rule of
<305> these Four Tablets, Terrestrial as well as in the Heavens, is in the Spaces between the 4 Pillars. That is, between the double Pillars of Severity and Mercy. In these vast spaces at the ends of the Universe are these Tablets placed as Watch-Towers, and therein is their dominion limited on either side by the Sephirotic Pillars, and having the great central cross of each Tablet coinciding with one of the 4 Tiphareth points in the Celestial Heavens. Therefore even in the small squares into which each Tablet is divided, each represents a vast area of dominion, having the correlation thereof in the Universe, in the Planets, in our Earth, in the Fixed Stars, and even in Man, in animals, vegetables, and minerals.

"Therefore do the 4 Perpendicular or Vertical Lines of the 4 Crosses represent 4 Great Currents of Force passing between North above and South below, intersecting the Tiphareth points and thus affirming the existence of the Hidden Central Pillar of the Tree of Life forming the Axis of the Sphere of the Celestial Heavens.

"Therefore are these Lines which are vertical called 'Linea Dei Patris Filiique,' as manifesting that Central Column wherein are Kether and Tiphareth, Macroprosopus and Microprosopus.

"The Calvary Cross of 10 Squares which are in each of the 4 Lesser Angles of each Tablet are attributed unto the action of the Spirit through the 10 Sephiroth herein. This Cross of 10 Squares is the admission badge of the 27th Path leading unto the Grade of Philosophus, the only Grade of the First Order in which all the Tablets are shewn. It represents the Sephiroth in balanced disposition, before which the Formless and Void roll back. It is the form of the opened out double cube and altar of incense. Therefore it is placed to rule each of the Lesser Angles of each Tablet.

"A knowledge of these tablets will then, if complete, afford an
<306> understanding of the Laws which govern the whole creation. The dominion of the Tablet of Union is above that of the 4 Terrestrial Tablets and towards the North of the Universe.

"Of the letters on the Tablets, some be written as capitals. These are the initial letters of certain Angels' names drawn forth by another method, not now explained, and the offices of these do not concern a Z.A.M. Some squares have more than one letter. In these cases, either letter characterises the Square. The higher one is preferable. The lower is weaker. If two letters are side by side, the presumption is in favour of equality. Where two letters are in one square, the best plan is to employ both. But one alone may be used with effect.

"Of the difference between these Mystical Names of the Angels of the Tablets and the Hebrew Names such as Kerub, Auriel, and Michael, etc. Those Hebrew Angel Names which have been taught unto the First Order are rather general than particular, attending especially to an office or rule whereunto such an Angel is allotted. As it is written: 'One Angel does not undertake two messages.' For these mighty Angels do rather shew forth their power in the

governance of the 4 Great Sephirotic Columns as aforesaid, viz: the double columns of Severity and Mercy when projected in a sphere, and this also is under the Presidency of the Sephiroth. But the Names of the Angels of the Enochian Tablets do rather express *particular* adaptations of Forces shewing forth all variations and diverse combinations of those which are in the other case manifested in a more *general* way."

It will be found written in the *Clavicula Tabularum Enochi:* "Now we are to understand that there are Four Angel-Overseers . . . Each one of these Angels is a mighty Prince, a Mighty Angel of the Lord and they are of Him. They are as chief Watchmen and Overseers, set over several and respective
<307> parts of the World, viz: East, West, North, South, as under the
Almighty, their Governor, Protector, Defender. And the seals and authority of whom are confirmed in the beginning of the World. To whom belong Four Characters, being tokens of the Son of God, by whom all things are made in the creation, and are the natural marks of his Holiness."

Now thou shalt observe that in the Book of the Concourse of the Forces, a sign is annexed unto each of the Four Tablets of the Elements. That is, unto the Tablet of Air, a symbol of a T having four Yods above it.

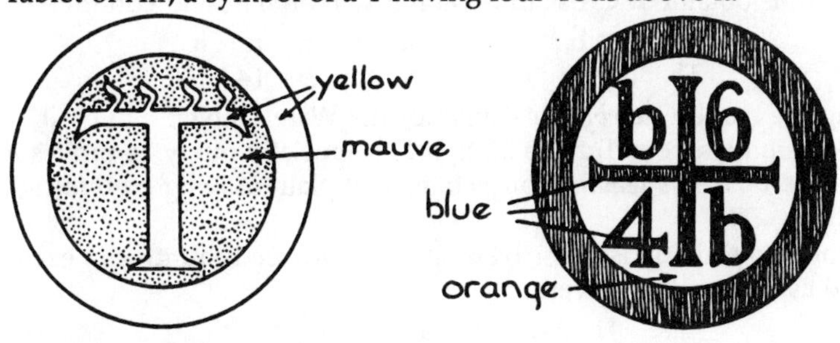

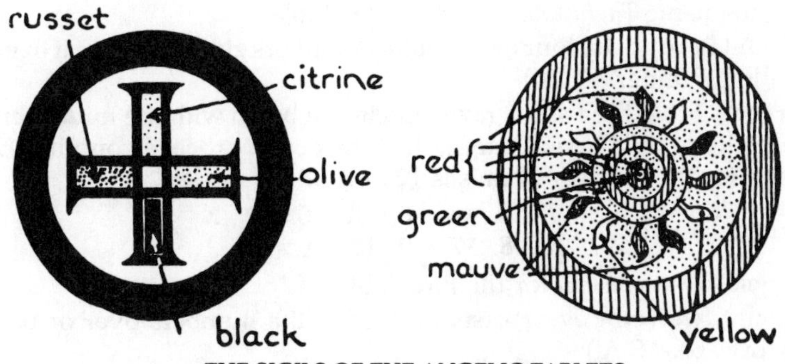

THE SIGILS OF THE ANGELIC TABLETS

Unto the Tablet of Water a Cross Potent, having two letters b. b. a figure 4 and a figure 6 in the angles thereof.

Unto the Tablet of Earth, a simple Cross potent without additions.

Unto the Fire Tablet there is a circle having twelve rays. These
<308> be the sacred seals or characters alluded to in the preceding quota-
tion. Thou shalt know that these four seals be taken from the *Sigillum Dei AEmeth,* after and according unto a certain guidance of letters which is there set forth. This "Liber AEmeth sive Sigillum Dei" that is the Book of

Truth, or the Seal of God, entereth not into the knowledge of a Zelator Adeptus Minor.

From these Four Sigils there are Four names drawn forth. From the Tau with Four Yods or $\overset{4}{\text{T}}$ of the Sigillum Ameth, T and 4 other letters are obtained, counting by the rule of 4 (from the $\overset{4}{\text{T}}$ which is found at the top of the circle of letters and numbers on the Sigillum Dei Ameth), thus:

4.22. 20.18. l. og.
T h a o 8

This yields the name *Tahaoelog* for the Air Tablet.

(The Fourth square each time from the last will show the letter and figure given. You are not to count, say, 22 or 20 or 18, but 4 only.—N.O.M.)

From b.4. 6.b. grouped about a cross, note that T equals t, (the Cross equals th), is obtained: Cross to h, then b.4., then 6.b., and continue 6:

4. 22. b. y. 6. 6. a. t. n. n.
Th h 4 14 b A 5 9 14

yielding the name *Thahebyobeaatanun* for the Water Tablet.

(Four moves from T gives 22.h. b.4. is specially put. y.14 moves to 22 from t. Then 6.b. is special. From 6.b. it is all plain moving by 6 to right.—N.O.M.)

From the plain Cross, which equals Th 4, proceed counting in each case forward as by numbers given:

4. 22. 11. a. o. t. h.
Th h a 5 10 11

yielding the name *Thahaaothe* for the Earth Tablet.

(Count here not by four or six, but by numbers given. To right if over, to left if under.—S.A.)

<309> From the twelve rayed circle, we begin with the middle circle on the Sigillum, the Greek Omega, the long o, and proceed counting 12 in each case, for the number of rays is 12 around the circle:

6. 12. o. o. o. h. 6. t. n.
W. h. 8. 17. 20. 12. A. 9.

which yields *Ohooohaatan* for the Fire Tablet.

(Count twelve in every case, neglecting the numbers over or under, always forward.—S.A.)

These Names are not to be lightly pronounced.

(Note: Some remark obviously is required for the above. First, the *Sigillum Dei Ameth* is part of the very complex system worked out by Dee and Kelly. No mention of it is made in any of the official Order teaching for the grade of Z.A.M. other than the above. I have, through meditative and British Museum research, obtained a good deal of information about this Sigillum and associated "Enochiana," but have decided to withhold publication for the time being since this volume is intended to reproduce veridical Order teaching and not the result of personal research. The Names yielded by the analysis of the Sigils are to be considered as the Elemental Kings of the entire Tablet. There should be no confusion between the nature and function of the King whose name is derived from the whorl in the centre of the Great Cross, and the elemental King whose name is implicit in the sigil. The King of the Quarter bearing the Banners of the Names of God is planetary in nature, representing rather the operation of the divine spirit through the Element and its four sub-elements. Whereas, the King whose name is derived from the Sigil is a powerful elemental force. His operation is essentially elemental, and his nature is elemental, and he does not represent in any way the operation of the Spirit. That is not to say that he is an evil force. On the contrary; but it is purely and intrinsically an elemental force and as such should be handled by invocation with great care.—I. R.)

<310>

PART TWO
THE CONCOURSE OF THE FORCES

The Keys of the Governance and Combinations of the Squares of the Tablets. They are the Sphynx and the Pyramid of Egypt; that is, the combination of the Kerubs being the Sphynx. The combination of the Elements being the Pyramid.

Now learn a mystery of the Wisdom of Egypt: "When the Sphynx and the Pyramid are united, thou hast the formulae of the magic of Nature."

"These are the keys of the wisdom of all Time; and its beginning — who knoweth it? In their keeping are the sacred mysteries and the knowledge of Magic and all the Gods."

In the Ritual of the 32nd Path leading unto the Theoricus Grade, it is thus written: "The Sphynx of Egypt spake and said: I am the synthesis of the Elemental Forces. I am also the symbol of Man. I am Life. I am Death. I am the Child of the Night of Time."

The solid Pyramid of the Elements again is the Admission Badge of the 28th Path leading to the Philosophus Grade. It is attributed to the Four Elements. Therefore on its base is the word *Olahm,* meaning World, and upon its sides are the names of the Elements: *Aesh, Ruach, Mayim, Aretz* or *Ophir.* Yet the Apex is not allowed to remain vacant, nor quite acute in shape, but is cut off and so a small square is formed at the Apex, and the Letters *Eth,* meaning Essence are placed therein.

This small square maketh of the pyramid a certain Throne or shrine. On
this throne a certain ruling force is seated. Within the Throne is a
<311> sacred symbol. Place then within each Pyramid its appropriate
sphynx, and the image of its God above. Take thou each Pyramid as the *key* of the nature of each Tablet Square. The Sphynx of each will vary in form according to the proportion of the elements comprising the Square. The God of Egypt, whose image is to be placed above each Pyramid, shall represent the force ruling under the direction of the Great Angel of the

Square. (That is, under the Name formed by the addition of a letter from the Tablet of Union.—I.R.). This God shall be the symbol of the *power* of the Light acting therein, as the Angel shall be the *descent* of that Light itself. The Angelic Name may be typified by the correspondences of the four Letters of the Angel's name, adding AL to the Name — the letters of the Name standing for head, bust, arms, body, and lower limbs, etc., as taught in the instruction on Telesmatic Images. Place the name in Theban or Enochian letters on the girdle.

The four forms of the Sphynx are:

The Bull	Wingless
The Eagle or Hawk	Winged
Angel or Man	Winged
Lion	Wingless

This variation as to wings is another reason why, in grouping the Tablets and the lesser angles of the same, the two forms of Air and Water are placed above the two Tablets of Earth and Fire.

From the pyramid of the square, the symbolic form of each Sphynx is formed thus: The upmost of the four Triangles (Triangle No. 2.) sheweth the head and neck, and in the case of the Angel or Eagle, it shows whether wings are to be added to the form of the Sphynx. The two triangles right and left (Triangles No. 1 and 3) show the body with the arms or Fore-limbs here also. If Angel or Eagle there are Wings added unto the representation of the Figure. The lowest triangle (No. 4.) adds the lower limbs, and the tail of the Bull, Eagle and Lion.

<312> When Air and Fire predominate there is a male tendency. When Water and Earth, the type tendeth to female.

It is to be understood that what is here written regarding the Sphynx of the Pyramid and the God of Egypt ruling above is applicable especially unto the 16 squares of the Servient Angels in each lesser angle.

Concerning the Skrying of the Squares Servient in the Spirit Vision. Have in readiness the necessary implements and insignia; also let the Zelator Adeptus Minor have before him the symbol of the Pyramid of the square. Rehearse the Angelic calls appropriate thereunto and, having invoked the appropriate names governing the Plane and division thereof in question. Let the Z.A.M. imagine unto himself that he is enclosed within that Pyramid. Or let him believe that he is voluntarily standing within an atmosphere corresponding unto that symbolised by the Pyramid of the Square, whether of Heat or Moisture, of Cold or Dryness, or of combinations of these.

Let him then endeavour to follow the Ray therefrom unto the limits of the Macrocosmic world and to find himself in a scene corresponding unto the nature of the Pyramid Square. That is, either of landscape, or clouds, or water, or fire, or ether, vapour, or mist, or raying light, or a combination or combinations of these, according unto the nature of the Plane.

For the Pyramids of the Squares are not solid pyramids of brick or stone built by the hand of man. But rather the symbolical representation of the elemental formula governing the plane of that particular sphere.

Having arrived at the plane required, let the Z.A.M. invoke the God of

Egypt who ruleth above the Pyramid by the power of the Angel of the Sphere — the name formed by adding the appropriate Tablet of Union letter to the Angel's name. At the same time, vibrate the Egyptian (Coptic) Name of the God or Goddess, whereby he shall perceive before him the colossal
<313> symbolic form of the God or Goddess. Let him again use the Angelic formulae, and test it by the power of symbols and signs. If it abide these tests, thus showing it is a true image, then let him request it to make manifest before him the Sphynx of its power.

This shall also appear in a colossal figure and shape, and should be tested by the proper formula. He shall continue his invocations until he can behold it clearly, even invoking the Angel of the plane by the superior Names, and by the God of Egypt. Also let him vibrate the name of the Angel, invoking it by its own name, and by the knowledge of its symbolic (telesmatic) image, the Sphynx and by the name of the God of Egypt, and by his own particular symbolic form, according to the formula of the Square. Thus therefore in this manner only — if thou wishest to escape from delusion — shalt thou be able to discern truly, by skrying, the nature of the plane and of its operation. Standing before the Sphynx, and saluting it with the proper signs, and invoking the God of Egypt by his proper and true names, thou shalt ask by the virtue and power of those symbols and names for the knowledge of the operations and influences of that plane. Thou shalt ask concerning the special attributes of that vast portion of the confines of the universe included in that sphere, its varying nature, its elemental nature; its inhabitants, elemental and spiritual etc.; the operation of its rays through the Greater World, that is, the Universe; of its influence upon this particular planet, upon animals, plants, minerals, and lastly upon man the Microcosm.

And when thou shalt have obtained all this reflect that even then it is but a small part of the knowledge of the Wisdom of the Formulae contained in the plane — even of that one square.

NOTES BY FRATRE S.R.M.D.

For quick working, make sixteen plain triangles; 4 red, 4 blue, 4 yellow, and 4 black.

Make also Kerubic Figures. A red lion, a black bull, blue eagles,
<314> yellow angel. (Note: These should be made all about the same height and width, so that when they are cut, the separate pieces may be pieced together — as in a jigsaw puzzle — in different combinations, without there being too great a discrepancy in size.—I. R.). Divide each into three; the centre piece being halved by a horizontal cut. From these make composite sphynxes to lay under the pyramid. (Note: the Sphynx in this instance becomes a synthetic kerubic figure. Thus you can make a Sphynx with the head of a Lion, the shoulders and wings of an Eagle, the body of a Man, and the hind-legs and tail of a Bull, etc.—I.R.).

Make small Egyptian Gods to place above the Pyramid. (Note: When drawing these God forms if a little tongue is left at the bottom of the cardboard on which the form is painted, that tongue can be fitted very easily into a slot of about the same size at the top or throne of the Pyramid.—I.R.).

Make a shallow inverted Pyramid of card-board. Fill the sides as required with the coloured triangles to represent the several squares. Let the Pyramid be shallow enough to show all four sides at once.

These be the Gods of Egypt who rule above the Pyramids of the sixteen servient Angels and squares of each Lesser Angle. In the middle of each pyramid is the sphynx of its power. Revere then the sacred symbols of the Gods, for they are the Word manifested in the Voice of Nature.

These be the Elohim of the Forces of the Eternal, and before their faces the forces of Nature are prostrate.

(Note: It is perhaps hardly necessary to suggest to the student that he should not attempt to employ the Sphynx and God-form formula with the Pyramid until he has had much experience in ordinary Tattwa vision. When he has become perfectly acquainted with the nature of the subtle planes, and has learned to apply the simple forms of tests, so that he is quick to detect imposition or deception, then he may skry in the planes symbolized by the Pyramids.—I.R.)

<318> In order to show something of the nature of these Enochian pyramids as revealed by skrying therein with the spirit-vision, I have thought it advisable to include here two or three examples of simple visions obtained by members of the old Order. These are provided only as instances of the procedure and results to be obtained. Under no circumstances should the student permit his own skrying researches to be influences and moulded by these visions. He must not attempt to make his own accounts of the nature of the Pyramids accord with those given here. The technique alone should be noted, and the manner of applying tests — but nothing further than that should be used in actual practice.

1. "A vision of the 'N' square in the Airy Lesser Angle of the Water Tablet. The full name is nhdD, and the Pyramid God is Ahephi.

"Having recited the 4th and 10th Enochian Calls, and invoked the Angelic Names of the Tablet of Water, and the Airy Angle, I was carried up by the gentle moving waves of warm moist Air, through which I could see bright blue sky with greyish white clouds moving across rapidly. I rose in the Air till I found myself on a vast sandy plain, on the right little vegetation, on the left a broad river with trees and grass on its banks. A cool breeze was blowing from the river across the plain, and seemed to refresh the green after the heat of the day.

"I called on Ahephi to appear and the form gradually filled the place till the scene disappeared altogether. Tested by the letters, it grew immensely larger, and seemed to have a yellow and blue striped Nemyss, whitish wrappings, with broad blue bands round it, and a greenish yellow light shown about it. I gave the L.V.X. signs and asked to be shown the Sphynx of its power. This gradually appeared through the yellow light behind the God-form, human head, very fair and bright face, wings, yellow and blue nemyss, claws of Eagle extended in front, and hind-legs and tail of a lion in reclining position.

<319> "On asking for the action of the force of the Square, was shown a bubble of Water into which Air was continually pouring, and expanding it till it burst and disappeared, the energy seeming then to pass

<315>

No.	Elements	Coptic	⓪ = [0]
1	SPIRIT: or one triangle of each element	Hϣωωpι(ϵ) OSIRIS	Hierophant on throne
2	WATER: or 3 out of 4 Water	Hιcε(ϵ) ISIS	Praemonstrator
3	EARTH: or 3 out of 4 Earth	Nεrφθεε(ϵ) NEPHTHYS	Imperator
4	FIRE: or 3 out of 4 Fire	Zωωp HORUS	Hiereus
5	AIR: or 3 out of 4 Air	Apнωrεpι(ϵ) AROUERIS	Past Hierophant Hiero. off Throne
6	2 WATER 2 EARTH	ATHOR Azaθωωp	Invisible Station Kerub of East
7	2 FIRE 2 WATER	SOTHIS ϣHωεr	Invisible Station Kerub of West
8	2 AIR 2 WATER	HARPOCRATES Zωωpποκpat(ϵ)	Invisible Station between Altar and Hegemon
9	2 FIRE 2 EARTH	APIS Azaπϣι	Invisible Station Kerub of North
10	2 AIR 2 EARTH	ANUBIS Anωrβι	Kerux
11	2 FIRE 2 AIR	PASHT (Sekhet θapφεϣ	Invisible Station Kerub of South
12	FIRE WATER EARTH	AMESHET Amεϣεt	Invisible Station N.E. Child of Horus
13	FIRE WATER AIR	AHEPHI Azεφi	Invisible Station S.W. Child of Horus
14	EARTH WATER AIR	TMOUMATHPH ϯmτmaθφ	Invisible Station S.E. Child of Horus
15	EARTH AIR FIRE	KABEXNUV Kaβεξnry	Invisible Station N.W. Child of Horus

"ST" or ϵ added to a Coptic deity name represents a more spiritual force since ϵ is attributed to Kether.

<316>

1.
2.
3.
4.
7.
6.
5.
Color Key
Blue
Green
Yellow
Orange
Red
Purple
White and black
are as shown on
on the sketches.

<317>

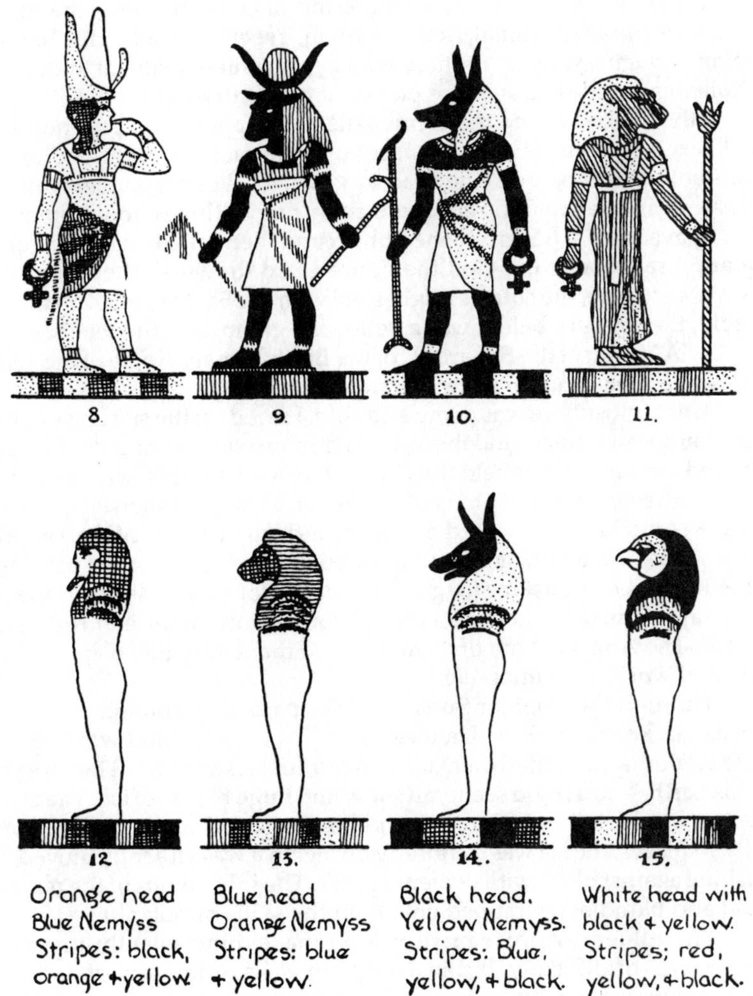
8.
9.
10.
11.
12
13.
14.
15.
Orange head
Blue Nemyss
Stripes: black,
orange + yellow.
Blue head
Orange Nemyss
Stripes: blue
+ yellow.
Black head.
Yellow Nemyss.
Stripes: Blue,
yellow, + black.
White head with
black + yellow.
Stripes; red,
yellow, + black.

into other forms and come under the rule of another square. It seemed a transitory action, more the initiator of fresh conditions than an end in itself. I asked its effect on the earth, and was taken to the scene I had left, and saw again how the moist breeze from the river gave fresh life to the vegetation which had flagged during the day. Asking its effect on the animal world, I was shown a Deer standing by a lake. A current of force passing over it, seemed to bring the dawn of reason and glimmering of consciousness, the first conscious stirrings of an animal. Acting on man, it seemed to affect the brain, producing a vague waving motion which prevented fixity of thought and definiteness of idea, loss of the power of concentration.

"I then asked to see the elementals of the plane, and saw numbers of small-sized human figures, fair, active expression on face, bodies rather solid-looking compared to the head, large wings like dragon flies which were iridescent and seemed to reflect the colouring of things about them.

"I gave the 5 = 6 Signs to the Sphinx and then called on the Angel of the Square. I saw above the God the figure I had drawn — the Wings on the Crown were blue, the cuirass bright steel with the Eagle symbol on the breast in gold, the drapery below was a yellowish green, and the feet bare."

2. "A Vision of the Square "1" of the Earthy Lesser Angle of the Tablet of Air. Name lSha. Anoubi is the Pyramid God.

"This atmosphere was damp and cold. I stood on the summit of a mountain, cloud-enwrapped, and there, having rehearsed the Angelical Calls, and vibrated the names, I beheld the colossal form of Anubis, who, after a time, shewed me the Sphinx of his Power. This again shewed me a mighty
<320> Angel who answered my signs, and when in that of the Theoricus I saw that a brilliant ray descended into the outstretched palm of each of her hands. On my asking for guidance and information, she gave me one of these rays, which I beheld as a crystal cord whose other end rested in the Eternal. The Angel led me first among the Ethers, and after a space I beheld stars and worlds innumerable.

"Through the brighter Suns, particles passed — coming out the other side as blackened cinders. Then came forth a mighty hand which gathered these cinders and welded them into a mass, lifeless and vast. Then we passed to this Earth — to a frigid scene, all snow and huge blocks of ice. The cold was intense, but I felt it not. Here were polar bears, and seals, as also many sea gulls. In places, the ice was stationery but again it was violently moved, block crashing against block with deafening roar. The inhabitants of the place were small and bloodless, wrapped chiefly in the skins of polar bears.

"The influence of this square on Man, makes him violently impetuous in the absence of difficulty, but instantly hopeless in the face of an obstacle, abandoning at once every project. The Elementals are demure, bird-like creatures with semi-human faces. The spiritual beings are beautiful diaphanous Angels, light brown in colour, with sweet serious faces. They were all much occupied when I saw them. Some had silver in their left hands and mercury in their right, which they would put into a golden vessel together, whence immediately a pale gold coloured flame which ever increased in size, spreading out through the Worlds. Others bearing the legend 'Solve et Coagula' woven into their belts, mixed water and the principle of cold which

they bore in a pair of scales, and the union was the ice of the region we were in. I was wondering whether all this had any counterpart in human nature, and its possibilities of development when I saw two types. One an ancient man toiling along most painfully and the other a child skipping
<321> along light-heartedly. As they faded there rose between them a
radiant figure clad in gold, bearing on her brow the sign Libra in living emerald. Then I understood that only in and by the reconciliation of these two forces, the fixed and the volatile is 'the pathway of true equilibrium' found. On asking for plants I was shown mushrooms, which seemed to be particularly consonant to this square."

3. "A vision of the square 'C' in the Watery Lesser Angle of the Air Tablet. Name: CPao. Hoorpokrati, the Pyramid God.

"Read the 3rd and 7th Calls. Vibrated Oro Ibah Aozpi, Bataivah, the Angel CPao. The Egyptian God is Hoorpokrati.

"Found myself in the air in the midst of whirling clouds. Travelled on by the above names. Saw the Angel of colossal size clothed in white. Tested with a letter Tau and Beth placed over the form, but there was no change, so removed those letters. Clouds seemed to be floating around the Angel. Saluted with LVX Signs and asked to see Egyptian God, who appeared equally colossal while the Angel floated up above his head. Tested as before.

"Vibrated Hoorpokrati second time, saluted as before, and asked to see the Sphinx, both Angel and Harpocrates returning the saluting sign. Sphinx then appeared with Eagle head, lower part human, on one side Eagle's wings, the other side human arms. Tested and saluted as before. The Sphinx was of colossal size.

"Now I vibrated all the names repeatedly, and asked to see the meaning of the Square. I was told that it was the astral region of storm and rain clouds with wind. I saw elementals in grey or pearly robes floating on the white fleecy clouds. (Note: I get them greyer and less defined.—D.D.C.F.) On dark thunder clouds were forms in dark lurid grey raiment, bearing thunderbolts like the images attributed to Zeus; many eagle-headed forms among them. Presently I saw one with a Crown. I asked him to show me, and he took me by the hand and we traversed an enormous distance
<322> beyond the Earth which became invisible. Then we soared upwards
still in the midst of the same surroundings, till I saw the Sun of that region, shining brightly, but clouds frequently drifting across it, while the clouds were now below us but only partially so. He told me that the nature of this Square was to supply the forces on the Astral Plane which generate wind, rain, clouds, and storm on the natural plane. That these occurred throughout the Universe but with different effect. That on our evil planet the effect was sometimes disastrous, being perverted from their original intention by our evil sphere. But on other higher planes the effect was always beneficial, clearing away that which had fulfilled its purpose and replacing it by fresh influence. The region attributed to this Square seemed simply limitless. We traversed an enormous distance, yet seemed no nearer the end. So he brought me back again. Then I thanked him and saluted him, and descended to the former plane. There I thanked and saluted the Angel Hoorpokrati,

and the Sphinx. So I returned home, dimly seeing my natural body before re-entering it."

<323> FURTHER RULES FOR PRACTICE

By G. H. FRATRE *Sapere Aude*

1. Prepare for private use Four Tablets with correct lettering as given in the Official Lecture; and a Tablet of Union.
2. Make the Four Tablets coloured as brilliantly and as flashingly as possible, and in exact proportion. This should be done with coloured papers. They may be done in water-colours, but this is not so good. (Enamel or Lacquer paints are best.—I.R.)
3. The Four minor Implements are to be used with the Enochian Tablets. A small Altar should be arranged in the room at the time of working. It should be draped with a black cloth, with a lighted candle by the wand, incense burning by the dagger, gold and silver or bread and salt with the Pentacle, and Water in the Cup.
4. Use the Ritual of the Hexagram for the Invocation of the King and the Six Seniors.
5. Use the Ritual of the Pentagram for the Spirit and the Four Elements.
6. The Calvary Cross Names call forth with a word of Six Letters and command with a word of Five. They rule the Lesser Angles in which they are situated, and should be used in the preliminary invocation.
7. The Six Seniors and Kings are on a higher plane and should be invoked with the Hexagram Ritual. The Names of the Six Seniors are each of Seven letters, that of the King Eight.
8. The Deity Names consist of a Name of Three letters, Four letters and Five letters, respectively, corresponding to the Supernal Triad, IAO.
   Also to the triad of YHVH, Yeheshuah, Yehovashah.

<324> 9. The Name of the King and the Letters from the centres of the Great Central Crosses initiate the Whirl, and should not be used by those who do not understand its action.

10. Remember that the East is attributed to Air, South to Fire, West to Water, North to Earth, when you *summon* Spirits or Forces. When, however, you go to *seek* Spirits or Forces on their own planes, the attribution of the elements to the Cardinal points is as in the Zodiac, as follows: East to Fire, South to Earth, West to Air, North to Water.
11. Bearing this in mind, place yourself (imaginatively) in the centre of a hollow cube, standing in the centre of the Tablet of Union between the O of HCOMA and the second N of NANTA:

E X A R P
H C O M A
x
N A N T A
B I T O M

Now imagine the Four Elemental Tablets standing round you like the four walls of a room, that is, at the four cardinal points. This is subjective working.

12. Another method is to imagine a moonstone spheroid, containing the Universe, yourself standing as it were, at first, in the centre, and the Tablet of Union at the North and South Poles. At the same time divide the surface into four quarters, and imagine yourself outside the spheroid. This is objective working.
13. These Tablets can be applied to the Universe, to the Solar System, to the Earth, or to Man himself. "As above, so below."

14. Perhaps the most convenient method for a beginner to
<325> adopt is to apply this scheme to the Earth, treating the Three
Deity names as the Three Signs of the Zodiac in one quarter. For example, take the Fire Tablet and place OIP on the Sign Leo, TEAA in Virgo, and PDOCE in Libra. And so on with the other God Names, treating the Kerubic Sign as the *point de depart,* one quarter of a house in Astrology being roughly equal to the square of each letter.

Each of these spaces, under these circumstances, would appear to be governed by a heroic figure of, say, twelve feet high, not winged. But the Spirit Names and the names above the Calvary Cross, even on the Earth plane, bring forth figures of tremendous size and beauty, which could easily lift a human being in the palm of the hand. From the fiery Lesser Angle of Fire, I have seen AZODIZOD, the figure being fiery red with flaming wings and hair of emerald green. ZODAZODEE, black and white, flashing and flaming. EEZODAHZOD, blue and orange, with a mist of flame about him. ZODEEZODAH, orange, with hazy gold wings like gold gauze, and nets of gold around him.

Having selected one of the above methods, let the Zelator Adeptus Minor perform the Lesser Banishing Rituals with the Sword. Invoke, with the minor implement, the Element required.

Our example being the Square of OMDI, a watery and earthy square in the Lesser Angle of Earth in the Great Southern Quadrangle or Fire Tablet, we take the Fire Wand. In the four quarters we invoke, with the equilibriating Pentagram for Actives, and the Fire Pentagram, using only the Tablet Names: "EDELPERNAA, (the Great King of the South). VOLEXDO and SIODA, (the two Deity Names on the Sephirotic Calvary Cross). I command ye in the Divine Name OIP TEAA PEDOCE and BITOM that the Angel who governs the Watery and Earthy square of OMDI shall obey my behest and submit to me when I utter the holy name OOMDI (pronounced Oh-Oh-Meh-Deh-ee)."

<326> Having repeated this Invocation in the Four Quarters, turn to
the East if you wish to go to the plane, or to the South if you wish to invoke the Spirits to come to you. Look at the painted Tablet which you have prepared until you can carry it in your mind, then close the eyes and vibrate the name OMDI and OOMDI until your whole body trembles and you almost feel a sensation of burning.

(The items which follow are quite open to discussion and are simply my own personal experience.—S.A.) Then pass through the Tablets and try to see some sort of landscape. My experience of this particular plane was a dull red crumbling earth. I first found myself in a Cave. As a symbol I was told that this Square of OMDI was like the roots of a tiger lily; the Square MDIO to the right, representing the Life working in it. The square IOMD to the left, represented the sap flowing through the stalk and the leaves, as it were; the Square DIOM to the left of that, the orange flower with the black spots upon it, fitly representing Air, Fire and Earth — yellow, red and black.

Afterwards I invoked the King and Six Seniors to explain the general bearings of the Quadrangle. After passing through several fiery planes, each of them of greater whiteness and brilliance than the last, I seemed to be stationed on a high tower situated in the centre of the Quadrangle between the two a's in the centre of the Great Cross, and I was told by the Six Seniors that they were partly representative of the planets, but that their Names should really be read in a circle, in a way we should be taught later, etc.

Final note. From the lectures circulated among the Adepti, (S.A. here refers to certain statements made in the *Clavicula Tabularum Enochi* which is here omitted.—I.R.), I have gathered that the Angels placed over the Kerubic Squares of the Lesser Angles of the Great Quadrangle have the following properties:

<327> *Air Angle.* "Knitting together and destruction." Centrifugal and centripetal forces. Expansive and contractive, etc.

Water Angle. "Moving from place to place." Motion, vibration, changing of forms.

Earth Angle. "Mechanical crafts." Creative or productive of results on the material plane.

Fire Angle. "Secrets of Humanity." Controlling human nature, clear vision, etc.

And that the Subservient Angels of these Angles, that is the Angels of the sixteen servient squares under the Sephirotic Cross, rule:

Air Angle. "Elixirs." Purification from illusions, diseases, sins, etc. by sublimination.

Water Angle. "Metals." the right methods of polarising the Soul so as to attract the LVX.

Earth Angle. "Stones." The fixing of the Higher Self in the purified body.

Fire Angle. "Transmutations." The consecration of the body and the transmutation brought about by consecration.

(It is to be noted that the Lesser Angles in each Quadrangle have identical properites and qualities differing only according to the primary Element of the Tablet in which they are situated. That is, the Lesser Angle of Air in the Air Quadrangle will be very similar in nature to the Lesser Angle of Air in the Water Tablet, or the Earth and Fire Tablets; and that the only difference between them will be in the nature of their particular Quadrangle. The Lesser Angle of Air is said to be concerned with "physic" or healing. The use of the Lesser Angle of Air in the Fire Tablet would have to be for quite different objects and purposes than for example the Air Lesser Angle of the Earth Tablet. And so for the other Lesser Angles in the primary Elements.—I.R.)

<328>

PART THREE

THE CONCOURSE OF THE FORCES

THE FORTY-EIGHT ANGELICAL KEYS OR CALLS

These Calls or Keys which follow are only to be made use of with the greatest care and solemnity; especially if they be pronounced in the Angelical Language as given. Anyone profaning them by using them with an impure mind, and without a due knowledge of their attribution and application, shall be liable to bring serious spiritual and physical harm unto himself.

The first Nineteen Calls or Keys, of which 18 alone are expressed, are attributed unto, and to be used with, The Tablet of Union and the Four other Terrestrial Enochian Tablets.

The first Key hath no number and cannot be expressed, seeing that it is of the God-Head. And therefore it hath the number of O with us, though in the Angelic Orders it is called First. Therefore, their Second Key is with us the First.

Unto the Tablet of Union are attributed Six Calls, of which the First is the highest and above the other five. The remaining Twelve Calls, together with Four of those belonging unto the Tablet of Union, are allotted unto the Four Tablets of the Elements.

The First Key governeth generally, that is as a whole, the Tablet of Union. It is to be used first in all invocations of the Angels of that
<329> Tablet but *not* at all in the invocations of the Angels of the other four Tablets.

The Second Key is to be used as an invocation of the Angels of the Letters E.H.N.B. representing the especial governance of the Spirit in the Tablet of Union. It is also to precede in the second place all invocations of the Angels of that Tablet. Like the First Key it is not to be employed in the invocations of the Angels of the four other Tablets.

(The Numbers such as 456 and 6739, etc. which occur in some of the Calls contain mysteries which are not here to be explained.)

The next Four Keys or Calls are used both in the Invocations of the Angels of the Tablet of Union, and in those of the Angels of the Four Terrestrial Tablets as well. Thus:

The Third Key is to be used for the invocation of the Angels of the letters of the line EXARP, for those of the Air Tablet as a whole, and for the Lesser Angle of this Tablet which is that of the Element itself — Air of Air.

The Fourth Key is to be used for the Invocation of the Angels of the letters of the line HCOMA, for those of the Water Tablet as a whole, and for the Lesser Angle of this Tablet — Water of Water.

The Fifth Key is to be used for the Invocation of the Angels of the letters of the line NANTA, for those of the Tablet of Earth as a whole, and for the Lesser Angle of this Tablet — Earth of Earth.

The Sixth Key is to be used for the Invocation of the Angels of the letters of the line BITOM, for those of the Tablet of Fire as a whole, and for the Lesser Angle of this Tablet — Fire of Fire.

This finishes the employment of the Keys of the Tablet of Union. The remaining Twelve Keys refer to the remaining Lesser Angles of the Four Terrestrial Tablets, as hereafter set forth in the following Table.

<330>

KEY No. of	FIRST WORDS	GOVERNMENT
1st	I reign over you, saith the God of Justice.	Tablet of Union as a whole.
2nd	Can the Wings of the Winds understand your Voices of Wonder.	E.H.N.B.
3rd	Behold, saith your God, I am a Circle, on whose hands stand Twelve Kingdoms.	EXARP and Tablet of Air. IDOIGO and Air of Air.
4th	I have set my feet in the South and have looked about me, saying:	HCOMA and Tablet of Water. NELAPR and Water of Water.
5th	The Mighty Sounds have entered into the Third Angle.	NANTA and Tablet of Earth. CABALPT and Earth of Earth.
6th	The Spirits of the Fourth Angle are Nine, mighty in the Firmament of Waters.	BITOM and Tablet of Fire. RZIONR and Fire of Fire.
7th	The East is a House of Virgins singing praises amongst the Flames of First Glory.	Water of Air LILACZA.
8th	The mid-day, the First, is as the Third Heaven made of Hyacinthine Pillars.	Earth of Air AIAOAI.
9th	A mighty Guard of Fire with two-edged Swords Flaming:	Fire of Air. AOUVRRZ.
10th	The Thunders of Judgment and Wrath are numbered, and are harboured in the North in the likeness of an Oak.	Air of Water OBLGOTCA.
11th	The Mighty Seats groaned aloud and there were five thunders which flew into the East.	Earth of Water MALADI.
12th	O you that reign in the South and are 28, the Lanterns of Sorrow.	Fire of Water IAAASD.
13th	O you Swords of the South which have 42 eyes to stir up the Wrath of Sin.	Air of Earth ANGPOI.
14th	O you Sons of Fury, the Children of the Just which sit upon 24 seats.	Water of Earth ANAEEM.
15th	O Thou, the Governor of the First Flame, under whose wings are 6739 which weave.	Fire of Earth OSPMNIR.
16th	O Thou, Second Flame, the House of Justice, which hast thy Beginnings in Glory.	Air of Fire NOALMR.
17th	O Thou Third Flame, whose wings are thorns to stir up vexation:	Water of Fire VADALI
18th	O Thou mighty Light, and burning flame of comfort.	Earth of Fire UVOLBXDO

<331> Wherefore, unto the Tablet of AIR are attributed the 3rd, 7th, 8th, and 9th KEYS. Unto the Tablet of WATER, the 4th, 10th, 11th, and 12th KEYS. Unto the Tablet of EARTH, the 5th, 13th, 14th, and 15th KEYS. And unto the Tablet of FIRE, the 6th, 16th, and 17th and 18th KEYS.

So that, to invoke, for example, the Angels of the line NANTA of the Tablet of Union, thou shalt first read the First and Second Keys, and then the Fifth Key, and then employ the necessary Names.

And to invoke the Angels of the Lesser Angle IDOIGO, Air Angle of the Tablet of Air, thou shalt read the Third Key only, and then employ the necessary Names.

But to invoke the Angels of the Lesser Angle VADALI, Water Angle of the Tablet of FIRE, thou shalt first read the Sixth Key, and then the 17th Key, and after that use the necessary Names. Whereas, for the Angle of FIRE OF FIRE therein, the Sixth Key alone would suffice, as also for the King and Angelical Seniors of that Tablet.

And so of the other Angles of the other Tablets, these rules shall suffice.

Now, though these CALLS are thus to be employed to aid thee in the Skrying of the Tablets in the Spirit Vision, and in magical working therewith,
yet shalt thou know that they be allotted unto a much higher plane
<332> than the operation of the Tablets in the Assiatic World. And, there-
fore, are they thus employed in bringing the Higher Light and the All-Potent Forces into action herein; and so also, are they not to be profaned, or used lightly with an impure or frivolous mind as before said.

Also these CALLS may be employed in the invocation of the Chiefs of the Elementals according to the title of the Book T associated therewith. And in this case, it will be well to employ the names of the Archangels Michael, Raphael, etc., and their inferiors. And thou shalt understand that these Hebrew names are more *general* as representing *Offices;* while those of the Angelic Tablets are more *particular* as representing *Natures.*

The Calls or Keys of the Thirty Aethers be all one in form, only that the particular name of the Aether in question is employed, such as ARN, ZAA, etc.

<333>

THE FIRST KEY

[1]I reign over you	[2]Saith the God of Justice	[3]In power exalted above
[1]*Ol Sonf Vorsag*	[2]*Goho Iad Balt*	[3]*Lonsh*
[1]The Firmament of Wrath:	[2]In Whose Hands	[3]The Sun is as a sword
[1]*Calz Vonpho*	[2]*Sobra Z-Ol*	[3]*Ror I Ta Nazps*
[1]And the Moon	[2]As a thorough-thrusting fire:	[3]Who measureth
[1]*Od Graa*	[2]*Ta Malprg*	[3]*Ds Hol-Q*
[1]Your garments in the midst of my vestures		[2]And trussed you together
[1]*Qaa Nothoa Zimz*		[2]*Od Commah*
[1]As the palms of my hands:	[2]Whose seat	[3]I garnished with the fire
[1]*Ta Nobloh Zien*	[2]*Soba Thil*	[3]*Gnonp Prge*
[1]Of gathering:	[2]Who beautified	[3]Your garments with admiration:
[1]*Aldi*	[2]*Ds Vrbs*	[3]*Oboleh G Rsam*
[1]To Whom I made a law	[2]To govern the Holy Ones:	[3]Who delivered you
[1]*Casarm Ohorela*	[2]*Taba Pir*	[3]*Ds Zonrensg*

[1]A rod [2]With the Ark of Knowledge. [3]Moreover Ye lifted up Your
[1]*Cab* [2]*Erm Iadnah* [3]*Pilah Farzm*

[1]Voices and sware [2]Obedience and faith [3]To Him [4]That liveth and
[1]*Znrza* [2]*Adna Gono* [3]*Iadpil* [4]*Ds Hom Od*

[1]Triumpheth: [2]Whose beginning is not [3]Nor end cannot be: [4]Which
[1]*Toh* [2]*Soba Ipam* [3]*Lu Ipamis* [4]*Ds*

[1]Shineth as a flame in the midst of your palace [2]And reigneth
[1]*Loholo* Vep Zomd Poamal* [2]*Od Bogpa*

[1]Amongst you as the balance [2]Of righteousness and truth. [3]Move
[1]*Aai Ta Piap* [2]*Piamol Od Vaoan* [3]*Zacare*

[1]Therefore and show yourselves: [2]Open the mysteries of your
[1]*(e) Ca Od Zamran* [2]*Odo Cicle*

[1]Creation. [2]Be friendly unto me [3]For I am [4]The servant of the same
[1]*Qaa* [2]*Zorge* [3]*Lap Zirdo* [4]*Noco*

[1]Your God, [2]The true worshipper of [3]The Highest.
[1]*Mad* [2]*Hoath* [3]*Iaida.*

TABLET OF UNION.

*(Or *Sobolo;* I am not certain which.)

TABLET OF UNION

E	X	A	R	P
H	C	O	M	A
N	A	N	T	A
B	I	T	O	M

<334>

THE SECOND KEY

[1]Can the Wings of the Winds [2]Understand your voices of wonder
[1]*Adgt Vpaah Zong* [2]*Om Faaip Sald*

[1]O You the Second of the First [2]Whom the burning flames [3]Have framed
[1]*Vi-I-V L* [2]*Sobam Ial-Prg* [3]*I-Za-Zaz*

[1]Within the depth of my jaws: [2]Whom [3]I have prepared as cups for a
[1]*Pi-Adph* [2]*Casarma* [3]*Abramg Ta Talho*

[1]Wedding [2]Or as the flowers in their beauty [3]For the Chamber of the
[1]*Paracleda* [2]*Q Ta Lorslq Turbs* [3]*Ooge*

[1]Righteous. [2]Stronger are your feet [3]Than the barren stone [4]And
[1]*Baltoh* [2]*Givi Chis Lusd* [3]*Orri* [4]*Od*

[1]Mightier [2]Are your voices than the Manifold Winds. [3]For ye are
[1]*Micalp* [2]*Chis Bia Ozongon* [3]*Lap*

[1]Become [2]A building such as [3]Is not save in the mind of the
[1]*Noan* [2]*Trof Cors Ta* [3]*Ge O Q Manin*

[1]All-Powerful. [2]Arise, [3]Saith the First. [4]Move, [5]Therefore, [6]Unto
[1]*Ia-Idon* [2]*Torzu* [3]*Gohe L* [4]*Zacar* [5]*(E) Ca* [6]*C*

[1]Thy servants. [2]Show yourselves [3]In power and make me [4]A strong seer
[1]*Noqod* [2]*Zamran* [3]*Micalzo Od Ozazm* [4]*Vrelp*

[1]Of things, for I am of Him [2]That liveth forever.
[1]*Lap Zir* [2]*Io-Iad.*

Rules Letters E. H. N. B. of Tablet of Union

THE THIRD KEY

[1]Behold [2]Saith your God. [3]I am a Circle [4]On Whose Hands stand Twelve
[1]*Micma* [2]*Goho Mad* [3]*Zir Comselha* [4]*Zien Biah Os*

[1]Kingdoms. [2]Six are the Seats of Living Breath, [3]The rest are as
[1]*Londoh* [2]*Norz Chis Othil Gigipah* [3]*Vnd-L Chis ta*

[1]Sharp Sickles [2]Or the Horns of Death, [3]Wherein the creatures of Earth

[1]Pu-Im [2]Q Mospleh Teloch [3]Qui-I-N Toltorg

[1]Are and are not [2]Except Mine own Hands [3]Which also sleep [4]And shall rise.

[1]Chis I Chis-Ge [2]In Ozien [3]Ds T Brgdo [4]Od Torzul.

[1]In the first I made you [2]Stewards and placed [3]You in seats Twelve of

[1]I Li E Ol [2]Balzarg Od Aala [3]Thiln Os

[1]Government, [2]Giving unto [3]Every one of you [4]Power successively [5]Over

[1]Netaab [2]Dluga Vonsarg [3]Lonsa [4]Cap-Mi Ali [5]Vors

[1]Four Five and Six, [2]The True Ages of Time: [3]To the intent that from

[1]CLA [2]Homil Cocasb [3]Fafen

<335> [1]The Highest Vessels [2]And [3]The corners of [4]Your governments

[1]Izizop [2]Od [3]Miinoag [4]De Gnetaab

[1]Ye might work My power: [2]Pouring down [3]The Fires of Life and Increase

[1]Vaun [2]Na-Na-E-El Panpir [4]Malpirg

[1]Continually upon the Earth. [2]Thus ye are become [3]The Skirts of

[1]Pild Caosg [2]Noan [3]Vnalah

[1]Justice and Truth. [2]In the Name of the Same [3]Your God [4]Lift up, [5]I say

[1]Balt Od Vaoan. [2]Do-O-I-A p [3]Mad [4]Goholor [5]Gohus

[1]Yourselves. [2]Behold His mercies [3]Flourish [4]And His Name is become

[1]Amiran [2]Micma Iehusoz [3]Ca-Cacom [4]Od Do-O-A-In Noar

[1]Mighty [2]Amongst us, [3]In Whom we say: [4]Move, [5]Descend and

[1]Mica-Olz [2]A-Ai-Om [3]Casarmg Gohia [4]Zacar [5]Vniglag Od

[1]Apply yourselves unto us, [2]As unto the Partakers of [3]The Secret Wisdom of

[1]Im-Va-Mar Pugo [2]Plapli [3]Ananael

[1]Your Creation.

[1]Qa-A-An.

EXARP, AIR.

THE FOURTH KEY

[1]I have set [2]My feet in [3]The South [4]And have looked about me [5]Saying:

[1]Othil [2]Lusdi [3]Babage [4]Od Dorpha [5]Gohol

[1]Are not [2]The Thunders of Increase [3]Numbered [4]Thirty-three

[1]G-Chis-Ge [2]Avavago [3]Cormp [4]P D

[1]Which reign [2]In the Second Angle? [3]Under Whom [4]I have placed

[1]Ds Sonf [2]Vi-Vi-Iv [3]Casarmi [4]Oali

[1]Nine Six Three Nine [2]Whom None [3]Hath yet numbered but One:

[1]MAPM [2]Sobam Ag [3]Cormpo Crp L

[1]In Whom [2]The Second Beginning of things [3]Are and wax strong,

[1]Casarmg [2]Cro-Od-Zi [3]Chis Od Vgeg

[1]Which also successively [2]Are the [3]Numbers of Time [4]And their powers

[1]Ds T Capimali [2]Chis [3]Capimaon [4]Od Lonshin

[1]Are as the first [2]4 5 6. [3]Arise [4]Ye Sons of pleasure [5]And visit the Earth:

[1]Chis Ta L-O [2]CLA [3]Torzu [4]Nor-Quasahi [5]Od F Caosga

[1]For I am the Lord [2]Your God [3]Which is [4]And liveth for ever.

[1]Bagle Zire [2]Mad [3]Ds I [4]Od Apila.

[1]In the Name of the Creator, [2]Move and [3]Show yourselves

[1]Do-O-A-Ip Qaal [2]Zacar Od [3]Zamran

[1]As pleasant deliverers [2]That you may praise Him [3]Amongst

[1]Obelisong [2]Rest-El [3]Aaf

<336> [1]The Sons of Men.

[1]Nor-Molap.

HCOMA, Water.

THE FIFTH KEY

[1]The Mighty Sounds [2]Have entered [3]Into the Third Angle [4]And

[1]Sapah [2]Zimii [3]D U-I-V [4]Od

[1]Are become [2]As Olives [3]In the Olive Mount [4]Looking with gladness

[1]Noas [2]Ta Qanis [3]Adroch [4]Dorphal

[1]Upon the Earth [2]And [3]Dwelling in [4]The brightness of the Heavens

[1]Caosg [2]Od [3]Faonts [4]Piripsol

[1]As continual comforters. [2]Unto whom [3]I fastened [4]Pillars of Gladness
[1]Ta Blior [2]Casarm [3]A-M-Ipzi [4]Nazarth

[1]19 [2]And gave them [3]Vessels [4]To water the Earth [5]With all her creatures:
[1]AF [2]Od Dlugar [3]Zizop [4]Zlida Caosgi [5]Tol Torgi

[1]And [2]They are the [3]Brothers [4]Of the first [5]And the Second
[1]Od [2]Z Chis [3]E Siasch [4]L [5]Ta-Vi-U

[1]And the beginning of their own [2]Seats [3]Which are garnished with
[1]Od Iaod [2]Thild [3]Ds

[1]Continual Burning Lamps [2]6, 9, 6, 3, 6 [3]Whose numbers
[1]Hubar [2]P E O A L [3]Soba Cormfa

[1]Are as the First, [2]The Ends, [3]And the Content [4]Of Time
[1]Chis Ta La [2]Vls [3]Od Q- [4]Cocasb

[1]Therefore come ye [2]And obey your creation. [3]Visit us [4]In peace
[1](E) Ca Niis [2]Od Darbs Qaas [3]F [4]Etharzi

[1]And comfort. [2]Conclude us [3]Receivers of [4]Your Mysteries. [5]For why?
[1]Od Bliora [2]Ia-Ial [3]Ed-Nas [4]Cicles [5]Bagle

[1]Our Lord and Master is the All One!
[1]Ge-Iad I L

NANTA, Earth.

THE SIXTH KEY

[1]The Spirits of [2]The Fourth Angle [3]Are Nine, [4]Mighty in the Firmament
[1]Gah [2]S Diu [3]Chis Em [4]Micalzo Pil-

[1]Of waters: [2]Whom the First hath planted [3]A Torment to the Wicked
[1]Zin [2]Sobam El Harg [3]Mir Babalon

[1]And [2]A Garland to the Righteous: [3]Giving unto them Fiery Darts
[1]Od [2]Obloc Samvelg [3]Dlugar Malprg

[1]To Vanne [2]The Earth, [3]And [4]7, 6, 9, 9 [5]Continual Workmen
[1]Ar [2]Caosgi [3]Od [4]A C A M [5]Canal

<337> [1]Whose courses visit [2]With comfort [3]The Earth, [4]And are in government
[1]Sobol Zar F [2]Bliard [3]Caosgi [4]Od Chisa Netaab

[1]And continuance as [2]The Second [3]And the Third. [4]Wherefore,
[1]Od Miam Ta [2]Viv [3]Od D [4]Darsar

[1]Hearken unto my voice. [2]I have talked of you [3]And I move you
[1]Solpeth Bi-En [2]B-Ri-Ta [3]Od Zacam

[1]In power and presence: [2]Whose [3]Works [4]Shall be a Song of Honour
[1]G-Macalza [2]Sobol [3]Ath [4]Trian Lu-Ia He

[1]And the praise of your God. [2]In your creation.
[1]Od Ecrin Mad [2]Qaa-On.

[1]BITOM, Fire.

THE SEVENTH KEY

[1]The East [2]Is a House of Virgins [3]Singing praises [4]Amongst the Flames
[1]Raas [2]I Salman Paradiz [3]Oe-Crimi [4]Aao Ial-

[1]Of First glory, [2]Wherein [3]The Lord hath opened His mouth [4]And they are
[1]Pir-Gah [2]Qui-In [3]Enay Butmon [4]Od I*

[1]Become [2]8 [3]Living Dwellings [4]In whom [5]The Strength of Man
[1]Noas [2]NI [3]Paradial [4]Casarmg [5]Vgear

[1]Rejoiceth [2]And [3]They are apparelled with [4]Ornaments of brightness
[1]Chirlan [2]Od [3]Zonac [4]Luciftian

[1]Such as work [2]Wonders on all Creatures. [3]Whose Kingdoms [4]And
[1]Cors Ta Vaul [2]Zirn Tol Hami [3]Sobol Ondoh [4]Od

[1]Continuance [2]Are as [3]The Third [4]And Fourth, [5]Strong Towers [6]And
[1]Miam [2]Chis Ta [3]D [4]Od Es [5]V-Ma-Dea [6]Od

[1]Places of Comfort, [2]The Seat of Mercy [3]And Continuance.
[1]Pi-Bliar [2]Othil Rit [3]Od Miam

[1]O ye Servants of Mercy [2]Move, [3]Appear, [4]Sing praises [5]Unto the Creator!
[1]C-Noqol Rit [2]Zacar [3]Zamran [4]Oe-Crimi [5]Qaada.

[1]And be mighty [2]Amongst us! [3]For to [4]This Remembrance
[1]Od O-Micaolz [2]Aaiom [3]Bagle [4]Papnor

[1]Is given power, [2]And our strength [3]Waxeth strong [4]In Our Comforter!
[1]I Dlugam Lonshi [2]Od Vmplif [3]V-Ge-Gi [4]Bigliad

Water of AIR.

(*Note: IALPRG "Burning Flames" in the Second Call.—I.R.)

THE EIGHTH KEY

[1]The Mid-Day, [2]The First, [3]Is as the Third Heaven [4]Made of Hyacinthine
[1]Bazm [2]Elo [3]I Ta Piripson [4]Oln Nazavabh

<338> [1]Pillars [2]26 [3]In whom the Elders [4]Are become strong, [5]Which I have
[2]OX [3]Casarmg Vran [4]Chis Vgeg [5]Ds

[1]Prepared [2]For My own Righteousness [3]Saith the Lord, [4]Whose long
[1]Abramg [2]Baltoha [3]Goho Iad [4]Soba

[1]Continuance [2]Shall be as Buckles [3]To the Stooping Dragon [4]And like
[1]Mian [2]Trian Ta Lolcis [3]Abai-Vovin [4]Od

[1]Unto the Harvest of a Widow. [2]How many [3]Are there [4]Which remain in
[1]Aziagiar Rior [2]Irgil [3]Chis Da [4]Ds Pa-Aox

[1]The glory [2]Of the Earth, [3]Which are, [4]And shall not see [5]Death until
[1]Busd [2]Caosgo [3]Ds Chis [4]Od Ip Uran [5]Teloch Cacrg

[1]This House [2]Fall, [3]And the Dragon sink? [4]Come away!
[1]Oi Salman [2]Loncho [3]Od Vovina Carbaf [4]Niiso

[1]For the Thunders [2]Have spoken! [3]Come away! [4]For the Crown of the
[1]Bagle Avavago [2]Gohon [3]Niiso [4]Bagle Momao

[1]Temple [2]And the Robe [3]of Him [4]That Is [5]Was [6]And Shall Be Crowned
[1]Siaion [2]Od Mabza [3]Iad [4]O I [5]As [6]Momar

[1]Are Divided. [2]Come! [3]Appear unto [4]The Terror of [5]The Earth
[1]Poilp [2]Niis [3]Zamran [4]Ciaofi [5]Caosgo

[1]And unto our Comfort [2]And [3]Of such as are prepared.
[1]Od Bliors [2]Od [3]Corsi Ta Abramig.

Earth of AIR.

THE NINTH KEY

[1]A Mighty [2]Guard [3]Of Fire with Two-edged Swords [4]Flaming,
[1]Micaolz [2]Bransg [3]Prgel Napea [4]Ialpor

[1]Which have [2]Vials [3]Eight [4]Of Wrath [5]For two times and a half,
[1]Ds Brin [2]Efafafe [3]P [4]Vonpho [5]Olani Od Obza

[1]Whose Wings are of [2]Wormwood [3]And of the Marrow [4]Of Salt,
[1]Sobol Vpaah Chis [2]Tatan [3]Od Tranan [4]Balie

[1]Have settled [2]Their feet in the [3]West [4]And are measured
[1]Alar [2]Lusda [3]Soboln [4]Od Chis Holq

[1]With their Ministers [2]9996. [3]These gather up [4]The moss of the Earth
[1]C Noqodi [2]CIAL [3]Vnal Aldon [4]Mom Caosgo

[1]As the rich man [2]Doth his treasure. [3]Cursed [4]Are they whose
[1]Ta Las Ollor [2]Gnay Limlal [3]Amma [4]Chis Sobca

[1]Iniquities they are. [2]In their eyes are millstones [3]Greater than the Earth,
[1]Madrid Z Chis [2]Ooanoan Chis Aviny [3]Drilpi Caosgin

[1]And from their mouths run seas of blood. [2]Their heads [3]Are covered
[1]Od Butmoni Parm Zumvi Cnila [2]Dazis [3]Ethamza

<339> [1]With diamonds [2]And upon their hands [3]Are [4]Marble sleeves.
[1]Childao [2]Od Mirc Ozol [3]Chis [4]Pidiai Collal.

[1]Happy is he on whom [2]They frown not. [3]For why?
[1]Vlcinina Sobam [2]Vcim [3]Bagle?

[1]The God of Righteousness [2]Rejoiceth in them. [3]Come away! [4]And not
[1]Iad Baltoh [2]Chirlan Par. [3]Niiso [4]Od Ip

[1]Your Vials [2]For the time is [3]Such as requireth comfort.
[1]Efafafe [2]Bagle A Cocasb I [3]Cors Ta Vnig Blior.

Fire of AIR.

THE TENTH KEY

[1]The Thunders of Judgment and Wrath [2]Are Numbered [3]And
[1]Coraxo [2]Chis Cormp [3]Od

[1]Are harboured [2]In the North in the likeness [3]Of an Oak [4]Whose branches
[1]*Blans* [2]*Lucal Aziazor* [3]*Paeb* [4]*Sobol Ilonon*
[1]Are [2]22 [3]Nests [4]Of Lamentation [5]And Weeping, [6]Laid up for the Earth,
[1]*Chis* [2]*OP* [3]*Virq* [4]*Eophan* [5]*Od Raclir* [6]*Maasi Bagle Caosgi,*
[1]Which burn night [2]And day: [3]And vomit out [4]The Heads of Scorpions
[1]*Ds Ialpon Dosig* [2]*Od Basgim,* [3]*Od Oxex* [4]*Dazis Siatris*
[1]And Live Sulphur, [2]Mingled with Poison. [3]These be [4]The Thunders
[1]*Od Salbrox,* [2]*Cinxir Faboan* [3]*Unal Chis* [4]*Const*
[1]That [2]5678 [3]Times [4](in ye 24th part) of a moment roar
[1]*Ds* [2]*DAOX* [3]*Cocasg* [4]*Ol Oanio Yorb*
[1]With an hundred mighty earthquakes [2]And a thousand times
[1]*Vohim Gizyax* [2]*Od Matb Cocasg*
[1]As many surges [2]Which rest not [3]Neither [4]Know any [5]Echoing
[1]*Plosi Molvi* [2]*Ds Page Ip* [3]*Larag* [4]*Om Droln* [5]*Matorb*
[1]Time herein. [2]One rock [3]Bringeth forth a thousand [4]Even as
[1]*Cocasb Emna* [2]*L Patralx* [3]*Yolci Matb* [4]*Nomig*
[1]The heart of man doth his thoughts. [2]Woe! [3]Woe! Woe! Woe!
[1]*Monons Olora Gnay Angelard* [2]*Ohio* [3]*Ohio Ohio Ohio*
[1]Woe! Woe! [2]Yea Woe! [3]Be to the Earth, [4]For her iniquity [5]Is, [6]Was,
[1]*Ohio Ohio* [2]*Noib Ohio* [3]*Caosgon* [4]*Bagle Madrid* [5]*I* [6]*Zir*
[1]And shall be great. [2]Come away! [3]But not your mighty sounds.
[1]*Od Chiso Drilpa* [2]*Niiso* [3]*Crip Ip Nidali.*
Air of WATER.

THE ELEVENTH KEY

[1]The Mighty seat [2]Groaned aloud [3]And there were [4]Five [5]Thunders
[1]*Oxiayal* [2]*Holdo* [3]*Od Zirom* [4]*O* [5]*Coraxo*
<340> [1]Which [2]Flew [3]Into the East, [4]And the Eagle spake, [5]And cried with a loud
[1]*Ds* [2]*Zildar* [3]*Raasy* [4]*Od Vabzir Camliax* [5]*Od Bahal*
[1]Voice: [2]Come away! [3]And they gathered themselves together and
[2]*Niiso* 3
[1]Became [2]The House of Death, [3]Of whom it is measured, [4]And it is as
[2]*Salman Teloch* [3]*Casarman Holq* [4]*Od T I Ta*
[1]They whose Number is 31. [2]Come away! [3]For I have prepared for you
[1]*Z Soba Cormf I GA* [2]*Niiso* [3]*Bagle Abramg*
[1]A place. [2]Move therefore [3]And show yourselves. [4]Open the Mysteries
[1]*Noncp* [2]*Zacar (E) Ca* [3]*Od Zamran* [4]*Odo Cicle*
[1]Of your creation! [2]Be friendly unto me [3]For I am the servant of
[1]*Qaa* [2]*Zorge* [3]*Lap Zirdo Noco*
[1]The same your God, [2]The true worshipper of the Highest.
[1]*Mad* [2]*Hoath Iaida.*
Earth of WATER.

THE TWELTH KEY

[1]O You that reign in the South [2]And are [3]28 [4]The Lanterns of Sorrow,
[1]*Nonci Ds Sonf Babage* [2]*Od Chis* [3]*OB* [4]*Hubardo Tibibp*
[1]Bind up your girdles [2]And visit us! [3]Bring down your Train [4]3663.
[1]*Allar Atraah* [2]*Od Ef* [3]*Drix Fafen* [4]*MIAN*
[1]That the Lord may be magnified, [2]Whose Name amongst you [3]Is Wrath.
[1]*Ar Enay Ovof* [2]*Sobol Ooain* [3]*I Vonph*
[1]Move, [2]I say, [3]And show yourselves. [4]Open the Mysteries of your
[1]*Zacar* [2]*Gohus* [3]*Od Zamran* [4]*Odo Cicle*
[1]Creation. [2]Be friendly unto me! [3]For I am the servant [4]Of the same
[1]*Qaa* [2]*Zorge* [3]*Lap Zirdo Noco*
[1]Your God, [2]The true worshipper of the Highest.
[1]*Mad* [2]*Hoath Iaida.*
Fire of WATER.

THE THIRTEENTH KEY

[1]O You Swords of [2]The South [3]Which have [4]42 [5]Eyes to stir up the Wrath
[1]*Napeai* [2]*Babage* [3]*Ds Brin* [4]*V X* [5]*Ooaona Lring Vonph*

[1]Of Sin: [2]Making men drunken, [3]Which are empty. [4]Behold the Promise of
[1]*Doalim* [3]*Eolis Ollog Orsba* [2]*Ds Chis Affa* [4]*Micma Isro*
[1]God and His power, [2]Which is called amongst you a Bitter Sting!
[1]*Mad Od Lonshi Tox** [2]*Ds I Vmd Aai Grosb*
[1]Move [2]And [3]Show yourselves. [4]Open the Mysteries of [5]Your Creation.
[1]*Zacar* [2]*Od* [3]*Zamran* [4]*Odo Cicle* [5]*Qaa*
<341> [1]Be friendly unto me! [2]For I am the servant of [3]The same your God,
[1]*Zorge* [2]*Lap Zirdo Noco* [3]*Mad*
[1]The true worshipper [2]Of the Highest.
[1]*Hoath* [2]*Iaida.*
Air of EARTH.

* "Lonshi Tox" means "The power of Him."

THE FOURTEENTH KEY

[1]O You Sons of Fury, [2]The Children of the Just, [3]Which sit upon [4]24
[1]*Noromi Baghie* [2]*Pashs Oiad* [3]*Ds Trint Mirc* [4]*OL*
[1]Seats, [2]Vexing all creatures [3]Of the Earth [4]With age, [5]Which have under
[1]*Thil* [2]*Dods Tol Hami* [3]*Caosgi* [4]*Homin* [5]*Dr Brin Oroch*
You [1]1636. [2]Behold the Voice of God! [3]The Promise of Him Who is
[1]*QUAR* [2]*Micma Bialo Iad* [3]*Isro Tox Ds I*
[1]Called amongst you [2]Fury or Extreme Justice. [3]Move and show your-
[1]*Vmd Aai* [2]*Baltim* [3]*Zacar Od Zamran*
[1]selves. [2]Open the Mysteries of [3]Your Creation. [4]Be friendly unto me.
[2]*Odo Cicle* [3]*Qaa* [4]*Zorge*
[1]For I am [2]The servant of the same your God, [3]The true worshipper of
[1]*Lap Zirdo* [2]*Noco Mad* [3]*Hoath*
The Highest.
[1]*Iaida.*
Water of EARTH.

THE FIFTEENTH KEY

[1]O Thou, [2]The Governor of the First Flame, [3]Under Whose Wings [4]Are
[1]*Ils* [2]*Tabaan L Ial-Prt* [3]*Casarman Vpaahi* [4]*Chis*
[1]6739 [2]Which weave [3]The Earth with dryness: [4]Which knowest the great
[1]*DARG* [2]*Ds Oado* [3]*Caosgi Orscor* [4]*Ds Omax*
[1]Name Righteousness [2]And the Seal of Honour! [3]Move and show
[1]*Baeouib* [2]*Od Emetgis Iaiadix* [3]*Zacar Od Zamran*
[1]Yourselves! [2]Open the Mysteries of your Creation. [3]Be friendly unto me.
[2]*Odo Cicle Qaa* [3]*Zorge*
[1]For I am [2]The servant of the same your God, [3]The true worshipper of
[1]*Lap Zirdo* [2]*Noco Mad* [3]*Hoath*
[1]The Highest.
[1]*Iaida.*
Fire of EARTH.

THE SIXTEENTH KEY

[1]O Thou of the Second Flame, [2]The House of Justice, [3]Who hast Thy
[1]*Ils Viv Ialprt* [2]*Salman Balt* [3]*Ds A*
<342> [1]Beginning in Glory, [2]And shalt comfort the Just, [3]Who walkest on
[1]*Cro-Odzi Busd* [2]*Od Bliorax Balit* [3]*Ds Insi*
[1]The Earth with Feet [2]8763, [3]Which understand and separate creatures.
[1]*Caosgi Lusdan* [2]*EMOD* [3]*Ds Om Od Tliob*
[1]Great art Thou [2]In the God of Conquest. [3]Move and show yourselves!
[1]*Drilpa Geh Ils* [2]*Mad Zilodarp* [3]*Zacar Od Zamran*
[1]Open the Mysteries of [2]Your Creation. [3]Be friendly unto Me! [4]For
[1]*Odo Cicle* [2]*Qaa* [3]*Zorge* [4]*Lap*
[1]I am the servant of [2]The same your God: [3]The true worshipper of
[1]*Zirdo Noco* [2]*Mad* [3]*Hoath*
[1]The Highest.
[1]*Iaida.*
Air of FIRE.

THE SEVENTEENTH KEY

[1]O Thou Third Flame [2]Whose Wings are Thorns [3]To stir up vexation:
[1]*Ils D Ialpirt* [2]*Soba Vpaah Chis Nanba* [3]*Zixlay Dodseh*
[1]And Who hast [2]7336 [3]Living Lamps [4]Going before Thee:
[1]*Od Ds Brint* [2]*TAXS* [3]*Hubardo* [4]*Tastax Ilsi*
[1]Whose God is Wrath [2]In Anger. [3]Gird up Thy Loins [4]And hearken.
[1]*Soba Iad I Vonpho* [2]*Vnph* [3]*Aldon Dax Il* [4]*Od Toatar.*
[1]Move and show yourselves. [2]Open the Mysteries of [3]Your Creation.
[1]*Zacar Od Zamran* [2]*Odo Cicle* [3]*Qaa*
[1]Be friendly unto me. [2]For I am [3]The Servant of [4]The same your God:
[1]*Zorge* [2]*Lap Zirdo* [3]*Noco* [4]*Mad*
[1]The true worshipper of [2]The Highest.
[1]*Hoath* [2]*Iaida.*
Water of FIRE.

THE EIGHTEENTH KEY

[1]O Thou [2]Mighty Light [3]And Burning Flame of [4]Comfort which openest
[1]*Ils* [2]*Micaolz Olprt* [3]*Od Ialprt* [4]*Bliors Ds Odo*
[1]The Glory of God [2]Unto the Centre of the Earth, [3]In Whom the [4]6332
[1]*Busdir Oiad* [2]*Ovoars Caosgo* [3]*Casarmg* [4]*ERAN*
[1]Secrets [2]Of Truth have their abiding, [3]Which is called [4]In Thy Kingdom
[1]*Laiad* [2]*Brints Cafafam* [3]*Ds I Vmd* [4]*Aqlo Adohi*
[1]Joy [2]And not to be measured. [3]Be Thou a Window of Comfort unto me.
[1]*Moz* [2]*Od Ma-Of-Fas* [3]*Bolp Como Bliort Pambt*
[1]Move and show yourselves. [2]Open the Mysteries of [3]Your Creation.
[1]*Zacar Od Zamran* [2]*Odo Cicle* [3]*Qaa*
<343> [1]Be friendly unto me, [2]For I am the servant of [3]The same your God,
[1]*Zorge* [2]*Lap Zirdo Noco* [3]*Mad*
[1]The true worshipper of [2]The Highest.
[1]*Hoath* [2]*Iaida.*
Earth of FIRE.

These first eighteen CALLS are in reality nineteen — that is nineteen in the Celestial Orders, but with us, that First Table hath no CALL and can have no CALL seeing it is of the GOD-HEAD.

Thus, then, with us it hath the number of "0", though with them, that of "1" (even as the first Key of the Tarot is numbered "0"); and therefore, that which is with us the eighteenth KEY, is with them the nineteenth.

After these first eighteen, follow the CALLS and KEYS of the AIRES or 30 AETHERS, which are the same in substance, though varied by the NAME belonging thereto.

1. LIL	11. ICH	21. ASP
2. ARN	12. LOE	22. LIN
3. ZOM	13. ZIM	23. TOR
4. PAZ	14. VTA	24. NIA
5. LIT	15. OXO	25. VTI
6. MAZ	16. LEA	26. DES
7. DEO	17. TAN	27. ZAA
8. ZID	18. ZEN	28. BAG
9. ZIP	19. POP	29. RII
10. ZAX	20. CHR	30. TEX

THE CALL
OF THE
THIRTY AETHYRS

[1]The Heavens which dwell in [2]The First Aire [3]Are Mighty in the
[1]Madriaax Ds Praf *[2]LIL* *[3]Chis Micaolz*

[1]Parts of the Earth [2]And execute the Judgment of the highest! Unto
[1]Saanir Caosgo *[2]Od Fisis Balzizras Iaida*

<344> [1]You it is said: [2]Behold the Face of your God, [3]The Beginning of
[1]Nonca Gohulim *[2]Micma Adoian Mad* *[3]Iaod*

[1]Comfort, [2]Whose Eyes are the Brightness of the Heavens, [3]Which
[1]Bliorb *[2]Soba Ooaona Chis Luciftias Piripsol* *[3]Ds*

[1]Provided [2]You for the Government of Earth [3]And her Unspeakable
[1]Abraassa *[2]Noncf Netaaib Caosgi* *[3]Od Tilb Adphaht*

[1]Variety, [2]Furnishing you with a Power Understanding [3]To dispose all
[1]Damploz *[2]Tooat Noncf G Micalz Oma* *[3]Lrasd Tol*

[1]Things according to [2]The Providence of Him [3]That sitteth on the Holy
[1]Glo Marb *[2]Yarry* *[3]Idoigo*

[1]Throne: [2]And rose up in the Beginning saying: [3]The Earth
[2]Od Torzulp Iaodaf Gohol *[3]Caosga*

[1]Let her be governed [2]By her parts and let there be [3]Division in her
[1]Tabaord *[2]Saanir Od Christeos* *[3]Yrpoil Tiobl*

[1]That the glory of her [2]May be always drunken [3]And vexed in itself.
[1]Busdir Tilb *[2]Noaln Paid Orsba* *[3]Od Dodrmni Zylna.*

[1]Her course let it round (or run) [2]With the Heavens, and as
[1]Elzap Tilb Parm *[2]Gi Piripsax, Od Ta*

[1]An handmaid let her serve them. [2]One season, let it confound another
[1]Qurlst Booapis *[2]L Nibm Ovcho Symp*

[1]And let there be no creature [2]Upon or within her [3]One and the same.
[1]Od Christeos Ag Toltorn *[2]Mirc Q Tiobl* *[3]L El*

[1]All her members [2]Let them differ in their qualities, [3]And let there be
[1]Tol Paombd *[2]Dilzmo As Pian* *[3]Od Christeos*

[1]No one creature equal with another. [2]The reasonable creatures of
[1]Ag L Toltorn Parach Asymp *[2]Cordziz*

[1]The Earth, or Man, [2]Let them vex and weed out one another: [3]And
* *[2]Dodpal Od Fifalz L Smnad* *[3]Od*

[1]Their dwelling places [2]Let them forget their names. [3]The work of Man
[1]Fargt *[2]Bams Omaoas* *[3]Conisbra*

[1]And his pomp [2]Let them be defaced. [3]His buildings, let them become
[1]Od Avavox *[2]Tonug* *[3]Orsca Tbl Noasmi*

[1]Caves [2]For the beasts of the field! [3]Confound her understanding with
[1]Tabges *[2]Levithmong* *[3]Unchi Omp Tibl*

[1]Darkness. [2]For why? [3]It repenteth Me that I have made Man.
[1]Ors *[2]Bagle* *[3]Moooah Ol Cordziz.*

[1]One while let her be known, [2]And another while a stranger. [3]Because
[1]L Capimao Ixomaxip *[2]Od Cacocasb Gosaa* *[3]Baglen*

<345> [1]She is the bed of an harlot, [2]And the dwelling place of [3]Him that is
[1]Pii Tianta A Babalond, *[2]Od Faorgt* *[3]Teloc Vo-*

[1]Fallen.
[1]Vim.

[1]O Ye Heavens, Arise! [2]The Lower Heavens beneath you,
[1]Madriiax Torzu *[2]Oadriax Orocha*

[1]Let them serve you! [2]Govern those that govern. [3]Cast down such as
[1]Aboapri *[2]Tabaori Priaz Ar Tabas* *[3]Adrpan Cors Ta*

[1]Fall. [2]Bring forth with those that increase, [3]And destroy the rotten.
[1]Dobix *[2]Iolcam Priazi Ar Coazior* *[3]Od Quasb Qting.*

[1]No place let it remain in one number. [2]Add and diminish until
[1]Ripir Paaoxt Sa La Cor *[2]Vml Od Prdzar Cacrg*

[1]The Stars be numbered.
[1]Aoiveae Cormpt.

*To clarify—there is no text missing at this point. C.L.W.

[1]Arise! Move!
[1]*Torzu Zacar*
[1]Which He hath sworn
[1]*Ds Surzas*
[1]Your Creation
[1]*Qaa*

[2]And appear before
[2]*Od Zamran Aspt*
[2]Unto us in His Justice.
[2]*Tia Baltan.*
[2]And make us Partakers of
[2]*Od Ozozma Plapli*

[3]The Covenant of His Mouth
[3]*Sibsi Butmona*
[3]Open the Mysteries of
[3]*Odo Cicle*
[3]The Undefiled Knowledge.
[3]*Iadnamad.*

Note: In Equinox Volume 5, Aleister Crowley has published a series of visions, using the Calls of the Thirty Aethyrs in order to investigate and thus ascertain the nature of these Aethyrs. Further Enochian studies may be found in *Mysteria Magica* (Volume 3 of The Magical Philosophy) by Denning and Phillips, Llewellyn, 1986 and in *Enochian Magic: A Practical Manual,* Llewellyn, 1985, and in *An Advanced Guide to Enochian Magick,* Llewellyn, 1987—both by Gerald J. Schueler.

C.L.W.

<346> PART FOUR

THE CONCOURSE OF THE FORCES

ENOCHIAN OR ROSICRUCIAN CHESS

This is one of the sub-divisions of the Angelic system of Tablets about which, sad to say, very little can be said. No one in the Order, or my Temple, seemed to know anything about it. Whether this same condition applies to the other Temples is hard to say, though, from conversation with certain of the Adepti of those Temples, I gather the same conditions there prevailed. Nothing that was of practical value, as throwing any light on the nature and function of the game, was thrown on the subject by any of the Order members within the sphere of my acquaintance. It is probable that the knowledge of this system died with the early members.* All that I ever heard were fulsome praises of its remarkable divinatory capacity, together with quite a few amusing comments by those who manifestly knew nothing about it, though no precise indication was conveyed as to its procedure. On two of three occasions I have asked Adepti of the rank of ⑦ = [4] to play a game with me using my chess pieces and boards though each politely backed out of the invitation. Also the unmounted state of the Order chess-pieces was a clear indication that they had never and could never have been employed — like other aspects of the Order teaching. And the actual documents on the subject that were shown to me were vague and obviously incomplete, giving no
indication as to the true nature of this matter. No doubt it was in-
<347> tended, by those who wrote the papers and devised the system, that
the Adept should apply his own ingenuity to the bare-bones provided of the game, and formulate from that skeleton outline, as from the Enochian Tablets themselves, a complete system of initiation, and a profound magical philosophy. It is not therefore my intention to say very much about Rosicrucian chess, although it can be stated that the perspicacious student will divine ideas of great import and discover a depth of magical significance hidden under the cloak of an apparently trivial game.

However, the student who has mastered the foregoing sections of the Book of the Concourse of the Forces will no doubt be able to divine the relationship existing between the profundities of the Enochian Tablets and this chess-game. It will have been necessary as a preliminary step to have

*Keep in mind how *late* Israel Regardie became involved in active Temple work. Also keep in mind how brief his stay was: he left the Stella Matutina while still a fledgling Adeptus Minor. Crowley, Dion Fortune, and Israel Regardie, the three people who revealed most of what the general public knows of the Golden Dawn shared a common experience: all three demitted from the Order due to personality conflicts shortly after receiving their Adeptus Minor grade . . . the one in which the elemental self was to be sacrificed for the good of the Higher Self. H.S.

become perfectly familiar with the attributions of the Squares, so that any pyramid can be built up instantaneously in the imagination too. By this, I mean, that while playing a chess-game, the movement of a piece from one square to another should provide much material for thought, for the squares on the boards, as on the Tablets, may be formulated as Pyramids. Some experience, also, in employing the Pyramids for skrying in the Spirit-Vision will be required before any real appreciation of Enochan chess can be acquired.

In this game, the pieces are Egyptian god-forms, and the boards are certain adaptations of the Enochian Tablets. The Tablet of Union, however, is not used. Tablets are reproduced as Chess-boards minus the Great Central Cross, the Sephirotic Cross, and the Kerubic Squares over the Calvary Cross in each Lesser Angle. This leaves only the Servient squares in each of the Four Lesser Angles — sixteen in number, which gives us sixty-four squares per board — the number of squares in the ordinary chess-board.

One of the papers written by Greatly Honoured Fratre N.O.M.,
<348> gives a short history of Chess as it was derived from the Indian
Chaturanga, the Persian Shatranju, and the Arabic Chess. But since it contains very little that is of any practical import, I have thought better not to include it.

A few words now as to the nature of the Boards. The Boards consist of the purely elemental part of each Tablet. There is nothing in the symbolic structure of the Board to suggest the operation of the Spirit in any of its aspects through the Elements. This operation of the Spirit and its potencies, however, is indicated not by the squares, but by the pieces and their movements over the board.

To be of any real magical value, the board should be a sort of Talisman or Flashing Tablet. That is, it should be fully painted, showing all the triangles of the Pyramids as brightly and as flashingly as possible. The little flat squares shown at the summit of the Pyramid, indicating the throne of the god-form, are not necessary on these boards. The triangles are completely formed, and the resulting pyramidal shape is not truncated. The four Angles of each Tablet will thus stand out quite brightly, since the elemental colour of the quarter will show its nature, even though the triangles of yellow, blue, black and red will jostle each other cheek by jowl. When fully painted, the board is most impressive as a flashing Tablet. The student may know he has done his work properly when there appear white flashings at the angles of the squares. This is important, for the object of a Flashing Tablet is to attract an appropriate type of force. And if these chess-boards are made as Flashing Tablets, they will automatically attract force and their utilisation will become the more significant. In brief, each square is, as it were, the name and symbolic address of a different Angelic force. The flashing squares will attract the commencement of the operation of that type of Angelic power, and the movement of the Chess God-forms over the squares may produce even
brighter flashes and indicate the operation of the divine forces
<349> therein. With these hints the student is left to work this out for
himself.

There will be, in short, four different Boards. Each is representative of one of the Four Quadrangles or Watch-towers of the Elements, and the Angelic Names on the latter will be implied on the Boards even although no letters or Names are painted on them. The use of any of the four Boards will depend upon particular purposes, and the attributions of Elements as in the diverse schemes of Divination will determine which of the four boards must be used at any given time. In Tarot, the Element of Air, the Sword suit, indicates Sickness and Sorrow and unhappiness generally. Hence, in Enochian chess, for divining for some such question as touches upon trouble or unhappiness the Air Board would be employed. The Fire Board will represent the Tarot suit of Wands, implying swiftness, energy, activity. The Water Board indicates the Tarot suit of Cups of pleasure, happiness, merry-making, and marriage. The Earth Board will refer to all material plane matters of money, work, employment, occupation, and so forth.

The Four Boards of the Rosicrucian game, although different, nevertheless agree in certain particulars. In each board it is convenient to speak of the arrangement of the Lesser Angles as an Upper and Lower Rank — Air and Water forming the Upper Rank, and Earth and Fire the Lower.

It is evident that the columns of the one Rank are continuous with those of the other; and in this continuity a certain regular rule is observable. Every column of eight squares commencing in the Upper Rank is continued below by a column of the opposite Element.

Thus the Fiery columns below invariably stand on the Watery columns; the Watery on the Fiery; the Airy on the Earthy; and the Earthy on the Airy.

A different arrangement of the horizontal Files or Ranks of Squares is observable, and there is a difference in the Upper and Lower Tablets.

<350> In the Upper Tablets the Kerubic Rank of squares is continuous with the Elemental Rank; and the Cardinal is continuous with the Common sign Rank, whereas in the lower Tablets of Earth and Fire the various Ranks — Kerubic, Cardinal, etc., are continuous right across the board.

The pieces employed are, as previously remarked, Egyptian God-forms. A full set of chess-pieces numbers twenty men and sixteen pawns. (Note the possible relationship of the thirty-six pieces to the thirty-six decanate cards of the Tarot.) The game is played by four players, representing the Four Lesser Angles of the Board, thus giving each player one set of five pieces and four pawns. The five pieces represent the operation of the Spirit and Four Elemental Rulers — the Five points of the Pentagram, the five letters of YHShVH, and the Tarot Ace and Court Cards. The pawns are their servants or vice-gerents. Strictly to be in order, each of the twenty principal pieces represents a different God-form, thus:

Fire set.

King—Kneph
Knight—Ra
Queen—Sati-Ashtoreth
Bishop—Toum
Castle—Anouke

Air set.

King—Socharis
Knight—Seb
Queen—Knousou Pekht
Bishop—Shu Zoan
Castle—Tharpeshest

Water set.

King—Ptah
Knight—Sebek
Queen—Thouerist
Bishop—Hapimon
Castle—Shooeu-tha-ist

<351> *Earth set.*

King—Osiris
Knight—Horus
Queen—Isis
Bishop—Aroueris
Castle—Nephthys.

However, this tends to confusion, creating in practice far too complex a game. It will be found that four sets of the same five god-forms will suffice. There are only five major god-forms, the others being variations or different aspects of those types. These are:

Osiris, bearing crook, scourge, Phoenix wand. He is represented as sitting on a throne, silent unmoving. He is the *King* and represents Spirit, the operation of the Great Cross in the Tablets. He corresponds to the Ace in Tarot, the root-force of any element.

Horus, a God with Hawk's head, double mitre, and standing upright, as though to stride forward. He is the *Knight* of Enochian Chess and represents the operation of the ten-squared Sephirotic Cross in the Fire Angle of any Tablet or Board, and corresponds to the King in the Tarot, the figure astride a horse.

Isis, an enthroned Goddess with a Throne symbol mounted on the vulture head-dress. In Rosicrucian Chess, Isis is the *Queen,* and represents the operation of the Sephirotic Cross in the Water Angle of any Tablet. She corresponds to the Tarot Queen who is shown seated on a throne.

Aroueris, a human shaped God, with a double mitre. He is the *Bishop* in Enochian chess, and his form is that of a standing figure, to indicate his swift action. He represents the operation of the Sephirotic Cross in the Airy Angle of any Tablet, and represents the Prince or Knight of the Tarot — the figure driving a chariot.

Nephthys, a Goddess with an Altar or Crescent symbol above the vulture head-dress. She is the *Castle* or *Rook* of the Chess game. This piece is always represented as somewhat larger than the others, and is
<352> enclosed within a rectangular frame, within which she is enthroned. Her office is the representation of the operation of the Sephirotic Cross in the Earth Angle of any Tablet, and represents the Princess or Knave of the Tarot — the Amazon figure who stands alone.

These are the five principal forms used for each of the four angles of the

Board. Some difference should be made in the tone of the colouring of the front or face of the piece to indicate its angle on the board. Coloured bands may suffice for this purpose. Moreover the back of the piece — for it is customary to use flat pieces, not round as in ordinary chess — should be painted in the appropriate colour of the element it represents so as to avoid confusion in the recognition of its power. Thus the back of the King, as Osiris form, should be painted white to represent Spirit, and this rule applies to all four Kings in the four Angles. The Knight, Horus, should be coloured red. The Queen, Isis, should be blue; the Bishop, Aroueris, yellow, and the Castle, Nephthys, should be black and set in a large frame. Each piece should be cut about three inches high.

For practical use, these pieces should be mounted on square wooden bases, and those bases painted in different colours. It will be by the bases that their place on the board may be recognised. For example, there are four sets of Chess pieces to be set out in the four corners of the board. Each piece is more or less like its corresponding piece in some one of the other corners. The pieces placed in the Air quarter of the board, therefore, will be mounted on yellow bases. Those in the Water Angle will have blue bases. The pieces in the Earth Angle will have black bases, and those in the Fire quarter will have red bases. Thus, as in the Four Angelic Tablets, there results a minute subdivision of the sub-elements of the Tablet. There will be an Osiris piece, a King with a white back, on a yellow base, indicating that he is a King belonging to the Air Angle. He represents the sub-element of Spirit of Air,
<353> the most spiritual and subtle phase of that element, the Tarot Ace of
Swords. A King with a blue base indicates his place in the Watery Angle. A Queen, an Isis figure with a blue back, set on a red base, shows that she is the Queen of the Fire Angle, representing the Watery Aspect of the Fire sub-element of any Tablet, the Queen of Wands. A Bishop, yellow backed, mounted on a black base, shows that he belongs to the Earth Angle, as against a Bishop with a yellow base whose place is in the Air Angle and who, therefore, corresponds to the Prince of Swords in the Tarot pack. And so for the rest.

With but one or two slight exceptions, the pieces move exactly as do the corresponding pieces in Chess. The Queen here does not have the full liberty of the board as she does normally, nor is she the most powerful piece on the board. Here she can only move to every third square. This she can make in any direction, horizontally, vertically, or diagonally — but only three squares at any time. She can leap over intervening squares, and take pieces on the third square from wherever she stands. The other exception is that no Castling is permitted.

The Pawns in this Enochian Chess represent the God-forms of the four sons of Horus, the Canopic Gods. Their attributions are:

Fire. Kabexnuv, mummy-shaped, hawk-headed, the Knight's pawn.
Water. Tmoumathph, mummy-shaped, dog's head, Queen's pawn.
Air. Ahephi, mummy-shaped, ape-headed, the Bishop's pawn.
Earth. Ameshet, mummy-shaped, human-headed, the Castle's pawn.

The same rule for colouring the other pieces applies to the pawns. Their

backs should be painted in the colour of the piece they serve. Thus the back of the Knight's pawn will be painted the colour of the Knight, red. The base will be coloured according to the Lesser Angle in which it is placed. So that in each of the Four Angles you will have four pawns on bases in the
<354> colour of its sub-element. The Airy Angle, for example, will have
four pawns mounted on yellow bases. Those pawns will have four different coloured backs to indicate the piece, and therefore the element, which they represent and serve.

The pawn moves only one square at a time, and not two for the first move as in modern chess. The rule of *en passant* does not apply here, although the regular method of taking with pawn, via the diagonal, either to right or left, holds equally well.

It will be noted that the King has no pawn. Since he is Osiris, the other four pieces and their pawns are his personal servants and vice-gerents. His place on the board is *always* on the corner of the Lesser Angle, where the corresponding Letters of Tetragrammaton would be placed on the Angelic Tablets. On the four corners of the board as a whole, therefore, will be found the Four Kings. Identical in every way, they yet differ in the colour of their bases, the colour of the Angle which they rule. Some variation might be made as to the posture of the God. For instance, the Fire King could be cut as a standing figure, the Water King sitting, and so forth. Let it be noted that on the corner squares, two pieces will always be found. The king and the piece corresponding to the Letter of the Angle will occupy the same square.

A piece or pawn threatening, that is giving check, to the corner square also checks the King as well as whatever other piece happens to be upon that square.

In setting up the pieces for play, the rule of Tetragrammaton on the Kerubic Square of the Tablets, has application. That is, the order in which the letters of the Name YHVH are placed on the uppermost squares of the Servient Squares of any Lesser Angle, as reflected from the Kerubic Squares above, also govern the placing of the pieces. The Bishop will be placed on the Vau Square, the Queen on the Heh Square, the Castle on the Heh final Square, etc. The student who has thoroughly assimilated the prin-
<355> ciples involved in the attributions of the Enochian Tablets will find
all this perfectly straightforward, and experience no difficulty herein.

With regard to this injunction to set out the pieces on the board following the prime player's setting, whose chessmen are arranged according to the order of Kerubs, note that the remaining three sets of pieces are arranged, on any board, exactly in that order regardless of the order of Kerubs in their Angle. That is to say, if the prime player chooses an Earth of Water setting, his pieces will be set out: King and Castle on the corner square, then follow the Knight, Queen, and Bishop. The other three sets of Air, Water and Fire pieces on that board, are set out precisely in that order, either horizontally or vertically as the case may be.

It thus follows that there may result sixteen possible arrangements of pieces. That is, since there are four Kerubic ranks on each board, and there being four separate boards, the chess-pieces may be arranged on the board in sixteen different settings. The reason for any particular setting — if divination is the motive for play — must depend on the prime player's synthetic grasp of the Order teaching. Let him remember that there are sixteen figures of Geomancy, each with a special and specific divinatory value. It should be remembered that these Geomantic figures are each under the influence of a Zodiacal genius and a planetary ruler. Not only so, but each is attributed to a Hebrew letter, therefore to a corresponding Tarot Trump, with its allocation to a sign and a constellation in the heavens with all the hierarchical ideas that the latter implies. Thus the playing of this game resumes the whole philosophy of Magic.

The prime player must be guided in his selection of boards not only by choice of element as previously described, but by any one of these sixteen root significations of Geomancy. For each one of these sixteen figures may be applied to the sixteen Lesser Angles of the Enochian Tablets and
<356> chess-boards. So that each angle comes under the operation of a
Geomantic ruler and genius, and under the dominion of that por-

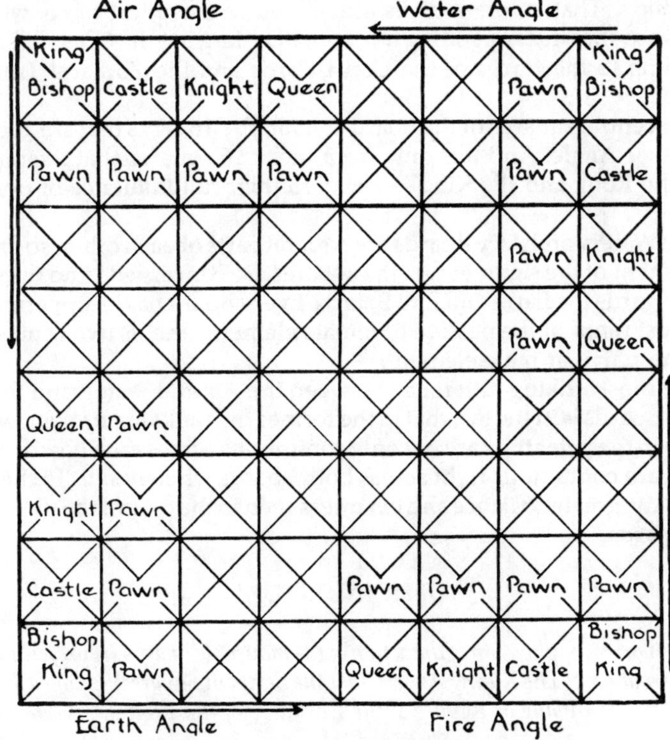

SETTING OF THE ENOCHIAN CHESS-MEN
FOLLOWING THE AIR ANGLE OF THE FIRE TABLET
(The arrows indicate direction of play)

tion of the starry heavens corresponding to its Tarot trump. The method of attributing the figures to the Angles is identical with the process described for the squares of both columns and ranks in the Lesser Angles. Thus the Airy

Lesser Angle of the Air Chess-board would be Mutable (Airy) Air, referred to the Zodiacal sign Gemini, and hence to the Geomantic figure of
<357> Albus, which is a mercurial figure under the presidency of Taph-
thartharath. The Watery Angle of the Air Tablet would be Kerubic or Fixed (Watery) Air, which is the Sign Aquarius, and the Geomantic figure of Tristitia, attributed also to Saturn, and the ruler over it is Zazel. The Earthy Angles of the Air Tablet, is elemental Air, referred to the Geomantic figure of Fortuna Minor, also a solar or Leo figure, ruled by Sorath. The fiery Angle is Cardinal Air, the Zodiacal Sign of Libra, and Puella would be the Geomantic figure, with a Venusian nature, ruled by Kedemel.

The same principle is involved in allocating the Geomantic figures to the other Tablets and angles. The magical and divinatory value of the Geomantic figures must therefore decide the choice of Chess-boards and Lesser Angle settings.

The yellow and red men are so placed that they advance to the attack of the black and the blue respectively by the *columns;* while the latter advance by the *ranks.* That is, the Actives are shown as a vertical force, while the Passives are shown as operating horizontally, shewing the Cross of Life, corresponding to the forces of the Court Cards and the Zodiacal Trumps in the Tarot.

The central squares of the board contain the 16 signs that are allotted to each Lesser Angle. And it is only from these 16 squares that the pieces — except the Rook and the King — develop their full influence or defensive force.

The Watery and Airy Boards are counterparts of each other, so far as the arrangement of the signs, etc., of the squares are concerned. And the same is true as regards the Earth and Fire Boards. Every Board has its uppermost and lowermost ranks of the passive or female element; and its two central ranks are of the active or male element.

The most striking difference between the Air and Water, and the Earth and Fire Boards is in the fact that in the former the ranks are broken; whereas in the latter they are not only continuous across each board, but they
<358> are continuous right across both boards when *in situ.* To this is due
the greater balance and evenness seen in the play of the pieces in the lower boards.

<359> OFFICIAL RITUAL

The correct application of the action of the moveable images (representing the motion of The Ruling Angels over the Servient Squares) is called The Playe or Raying of the Chequers of the Tablets.

By G. H. FRATRE D.D.C.F.

Of the Chess King and the Tarot Ace. The move of this piece is one square every way, and answereth to the action of the Spirit. Wherever it goeth, it commenceth and initiateth a fresh current, whence it is represented by the motion of only *one* square in *any* direction and there staying for this purpose before moving onward. So that his action is not hurried, but represents a balanced movement. Yet in his beginning of action is he at first a mute force, as though throned upon the water; as in the end of his action he is a life manifested and throned upon the earth. And herein is a mystery of the Lord Aeshoori (Osiris) when enthroned between Isis and Nephthys, thus representing the beginning and end of the action of Him in whom end and beginning are not, but rather concealment and then manifestation. Herein is a great mystery of life, for His Thrones are not in the two active elements, seeing that these latter are his horse and chariot of transition in the passage from concealment into manifestation. This piece, then, is the symboliser of the action of the potencies of the crosses on the Servient Squares.

Of the Chess Knight, the Tarot King. The move of this piece is three squares cornerwise every way (as in ordinary chess) and representeth the leaping action of the flickering flame. Wherefore also is he not stopped in his course by a piece or an intervening square, even as Fire seizing on a matter
<360> speedily rendereth it transparent. This piece representeth the action of Fire as the Revealer of the Strength of the Spirit, even as Hoor is the avenger of Aeshoori. It is a force potent and terrible, the King in the elemental operations.

Thus it openeth the locked doors of matter and sheweth forth the treasure hidden therein. Therefore hath all life its beginnings in a Fire Celestial. And the number of squares covered by the move of the Knight in the midst of the Board (reckoning from the Square on which he standeth, but not including it) is 16 squares, of which 8 are checked, and 8 are passed over.

Of the Chess Queen, The Tarot Queen. The move of this piece is unto every third square from her (reckoning the square whereon she standeth as the first) as well cornerwise, as well perpendicular, as horizontal. Thus again covering 16 squares out of a square of 25 squares, of which 8 are threatened, and 8 are passed over. But she threateneth *not* a piece upon the intervening square of her move. And her movement is as that of the waves of the sea, and (like the Knight) she is not hindered in her motion by a piece on an intervening square. This piece representeth the undulating action of water and of the sea, and she is ascribed unto the Great Goddess Isis, who is the Cherisher of Life.

The Chess Bishop or Fool, the Tarot Prince. The move of this piece is *any* number of squares cornerwise (that is only on the diagonal) in any direction even unto the limits of the Tablet. He representeth the keen and swift wind, and he is ascribed unto the God Aroueris. He *is* stopped by any piece in his way, even as the wind is stopped by a material barrier. He representeth the swift vehicle of the Spirit.

The Chess Castle or Rook, the Tarot Princess or Knave. The move of this piece representeth the ponderous and formidable force of earth and its motion is *any* number of squares in a square direction, perpendicular or horizontal (but not cornerwise) even unto the limits of the board.
<361> It is ascribed unto Nephthys the Goddess. It representeth the completed action of the Spirit in matter. Therefore is its movement square, and also stopped by intervening pieces, yet powerful from the length and breadth of its range.

The Pawns. The four pawns represent certain forces formed by the conjunction of the Spirit with each of the four elements severally, and they are severally ascribed unto Ameshet, Ahephi, Tmoumathph, and Kabexnuv, who stand before the face of Aeshoori. And their movement is but one square forward, perpendicular, and they threaten one square forward diagonal on each side, thus formulating the symbol of the Triangle, for they each represent a mixture of three elements under the presidency of the Spirit. Therefore, each is, as it were the servant of the God or Goddess, before whom he standeth. Yet, they be all, in a manner, alike in their action, although their Lords be different. Each is the servant of the God or Goddess whose element is expressed in his symbol, without its contrary.

In each set of three elements, taken together, two must be contrary. Wherefore, for example, Ameshet, who represents Water, Fire, and Earth, is the servant of Nephthys, whose element Earth is expressed in this attribution without the contrary of Air.

Ahephi, who represents Air, Fire, and Water, is the servant of Aroueris, whose attribution is Air.

Tmoumathph, who represents Water, Air, and Earth, is the Servant of Isis, whose attribution is Water.

Kabexnuv, who represents Fire, Air, and Earth, is the servant of Horus, whose attribution is Fire.

One of the rules concerning the Pawns in actual play is that should one reach the 8th square of its column, it may be exchanged for the piece of which it is vice-gerent. That is, as in ordinary chess, a pawn which reaches the eighth square may be exchanged for any piece the player desires — but in Enochian chess the exchange is limited by the elemental attributions of the
<362> pieces. So that were an Ahephi pawn the servant of Aroueris, to survive the battle of the entire game and win through to the top of the board, it could be exchanged for a Bishop, even though the Bishop were untaken and still on the board. And so with the others.

The opening of chess play is known under the technical title of "Awakening the Abodes." As already stated the game is set for four players, each of whom works the pieces at each of the four angles, playing in rotation. Should the game be used for the purposes of divination, the first player would be the querent, the one asking the question, or the person representing the matter about which information is required. This first player chooses which angle of the board he will play from, bearing in mind the divinatory qualities of the elements as set forth in the documents on Geomancy and Tarot.

The major difference between Enochian chess and the modern game is that in the former, when using it for divinatory purposes, the moves are decided by the throwing of a dice. Depending upon the number disclosed by the dice, so must a certain piece be moved, for the numbers are attributed to pieces. The actual details of the move — that is whether to right or left, backward or forward, to take an opponent or to press forward — are quite obviously left to the personal ingenium and divining mind of the player. The dice only determines specifically that such and such a piece shall be played.

The Prime Mover, or the owner of the Ptah piece, plays first, and his first move is to be decided by the throw of the dice to indicate which piece or pawn he must first play. Each player follows in rotation, deosil, that is round the board with the sun from the prime player. First the prime player moves, and if his setting is Air, then follow the Water pieces, the Fire pieces, the Earth pieces, and then back again to the Air who is the prime mover.

<363> The actual attributions of the numbers on the dice to the Enochian chess-pieces are as follows:

If the player throws:

1. He moves a King or any Pawn.
2. He moves a Knight.
3. He moves a Bishop.
4. He moves a Queen.
5. He moves a Castle.
6. He moves a Pawn.

At the first move of the game, if the dice cast throws up 1, it clearly cannot apply to the King, for this piece cannot move at all until the pawns have been cleared before him. In that event, a pawn would require to be moved.

The reason for the attribution of the numbers on the dice above shown to the chess-pieces are fairly simple. The explanation must be sought in the numbers and powers of the squares on the Sephirotic crosses. On the ten-squared cross, Kether, the Crown, is the first square, which is a fairly sound attribution to the King, who is Osiris, Spirit — the Number 1. Number 2 on the Cross is Chokmah, the Yod of Tetragrammaton, Abba, and therefore the Knight is appropriate. 3 is Binah, to which is referred in the Enochian attributions, the High Priestess card of the Tarot. The mitre of the High Priestess determines the selection of the Bishop. 4 is Chesed, to which is attributed the Tarot trump The Empress, who is the chess Queen. and 5 is the Castle, referred to Geburah, and the Tarot card The Tower struck by lightning. The remaining number 6 refers to the movement of any pawn, one square.

It is not always necessary to use four players. Two individuals may play, each operating two lesser angles and two sets of pieces. Fire and Air would be pitted against Water and Earth. If this is done, then the two sets of elemental pieces of any player must be regarded as a single unit in practice. That is to say if the first player whose pieces are the allies of Fire and Air, checks the Earth King, the second player must not continue the movements of
<364> the Water pieces, which are his allies, until he has moved the Earth
King out of check by any of the usual technical forms of chess. The reader who understands and appreciates ordinary chess manouevring will appreciate what is expected of him in the course of play.

When the so-called "stale-mate" occurs, which is when a player has no piece or pawn that he can move without incurring check, that is the King not being in check but so placed that he could not move without getting in to check, the result is that the player whose King is affected loses his turn until his state of "stale-mate" is removed.

For the purposes of Divination, an additional piece was employed. This was called the Ptah. Any book dealing with the Egyptian God-forms will describe the form in question. A small figure of this should be made, and on the

board it will represent the question or matter of divination. The mode of employing it is simple. It has no power at all, and is not actually used in the play. It is only used by the first player to be set on any square in the Lesser Angle from which he begins his play. Any square, that is, except the one on which the King first stands. The King must reach, in the course of the game, this square on which the Ptah is set and remain there for one round of the game undistrubed — that is without moving therefrom — and unchecked. A knowledge of the nature of the Pyramids with their elemental composition, and some knowledge of the Angelic forces represented by those squares and Pyramids, will decide the player as to what square shall be selected for the placing of the Ptah. If the divinatory question concerns the fiery Lesser Angle of the Element of Earth, a question involving Capricornus and the figure Carcer ruled by Zazel, then the Ptah probably should be placed upon a square of the Angle which is of the nature of Cardinal Earth, as rep-
<365> resenting the Yod type of Earth, or on Elemental Fire, that is the Heh (final) type of Fire. The ingenium of the interested student will guide his judgment herein.

NOTES CONCERNING THE BOARDS AND THE PLAY GENERALLY

Every Lesser Angle throughout the Tablets has a diagonal line of four squares starting from its prime square; which are allotted respectively to Aries, Gemini, Scorpio and Earth. From these four squares the Bishops can move one square into a square of Libra, Sagittarius, Taurus or Water, these completing the series of squares in that Lesser Angle in which a Bishop can move. Let us call this the Aries System of diagonal squares.

This diagonal is crossed by another which in the Airy and Watery boards is composed of Cancer, Leo, Virgo and Air Squares, having as subsidiaries, squares of Aquarius, Pisces, Capricorn and Fire. In the Earthy and Fiery board the second series of Four form the diagonal, and the first the subsidiaries. Let us call this the Cancer series.

If we now examine the Boards we shall see that the Aries system of any Lesser Angle is joined diagonally to the Aries system of the other three Lesser Angles; and that the Cancer also is similarly joined to every other Cancer system. So that we have two systems of squares; viz: the Aries and the Cancer; of the whole, each containing four squares allotted to every sign it contains. This resembles the black and white systems of squares of the ordinary board; and it is as if we allotted the White to Aries, and the black to Cancer.

When beginning a game see to which system the Ptah square belongs. Because if it be a square of the Aries system the attack of the opposing Queens is insignificant, while that of the Bishops is strong. In such a case the number of pieces is 6; 2 Bishops, 2 Knights and 2 Rooks. That is, in these matters the Airy attack is strong, and the Watery weak.

<366> If the Ptah be on a square of the Cancer System, one opposing Queen directly attacks this Square, but the Bishops do not. In this case the number of attacking pieces is 5; one Queen, 2 Knights, and 2 Rooks. That is, in these matters the Airy attack is insignificant, while the Watery

is strong.

If an opposing Queen can attack the Ptah, the defence should note well which Queen it is and should remember that this fact greatly enhances her power. He should thereupon not hesitate to exchange what might otherwise be considered a more powerful piece for her. She should certainly be exchanged for a Bishop, and probably also for a Knight.

The YHVH order of the pieces corresponds with their respective offensive and defensive Powers.

Yod. Knight. The most offensive piece.
Heh. Queen. More offensive than defensive.
Vau. Bishop. More defensive than offensive.
Heh (final) Rook. Most defensive. That is in a general sense.

Because, according to the circumstances of the actual play, every piece is able to assume both roles of attacking or defending.

Note that, as in ordinary chess, opposing Kings may not occupy contiguous squares. There must always be one square between them. This, however, does not apply to the Kings who are allies. That is, if Fire and Air are allies, then the Kings of these elements may approach each other and occupy contiguous squares. Naturally they do not check each other.

When a King has once been moved from the corner square which he occupied with another piece at the beginning of the game neither he nor that piece can be moved back again to that square unless it be vacant.

If the Prime Player's King is checked and he cannot move it, his game is arrested and his pieces cannot move until the pieces of his ally can release his King. That is to say that his pieces remain *in situ* but having during
<367> that time of check no power of action and can neither attack nor threaten; they only block the squares occupied. If the allied King can be check-mated, his partner continues to play and to seek to release him. When both Kings are checkmated, the game is at an end, and the partners checkmated have lost the game. The game is also lost by the first player, when though neither he or his ally is checkmated, the enemies hold such a position that the Prime Player cannot possibly attain the Ptah square.

The Knights or Fiery forces of the Elements meet and clash violently in all parts, and are strong in attack against every thing and everywhere. Their moves, like Fire, pass unarrested through the other elements in irregular courses like the lambent flame, leaping both diagonally and square-wise at every move. They contain the potential forces of the other pieces. Their force is similar to the Tarot *King,* and to Chokmah. They are the *Abba* forces, and with the Queens represent the Briatic forces of the scheme.

The Queens or Watery forces of the Elements never clash with one another, but ever undulate onwards, each in its own course unaffected by opposing or crossing waves. But the Watery forces only move in their respective pre-ordained courses; they cannot leave their limits and enter upon the domain of others. Water, like Fire, is unarrested and undulating, and like Air and Earth it can act diagonally or square-wise, containing the potential force of Air and Earth. They are the Queen of the Tarot, and Binah. They are the *Aimah,* and are of Briah.

The Bishops are subtle and sharp, Airy in quality, moving rapidly, but easily arrested in their course. They clash not with opposing bishops, and the friendly Airs support each other in attack and defence. Where the active Airs whirl the passives cannot come. They are the forces of the Princes, and of Yetzirah, the *Son.*

The Rooks are the heavy resisting powers of the Princess, the Earth by nature, mighty indeed in action when preceded by the action of the
<368> other three. That is, when in any matter the forces of Fire, Water, and
Air have been absorbed and equilibriated, i.e. removed from the board, the mighty powers of the castles come into play. But woe to him who too early calls these ponderous forces forth.

The Rook moves through columns as through ranks. She is able, therefore, to reach every square on the board, and is very powerful. But her movement is very ponderous, and it is a piece that is not moved many times in a game unless the forces of the other Elements have been absorbed in its working out. While the Aleph, Mem, and Shin forces are in full operation the Rook is easily attacked and with difficulty defended, unless she remain quiet, and act as a firm basis of support and defence to the side. If she, however, makes the mistake of entering early into action she is nearly sure to fall a prey to the more subtle forces whose proper sphere is attacked.

If the more subtle forces do not bring about a solution of the question, and the matter has to be fought out to the bitter end, that is, if the Yetziratic and Briatic forces are absorbed and balanced in the matter, then do the ponderous forces of Assiah, the Princess, engage in powerful combat.

End of Volume Four
Completing the Work

EPILOGUE

In 1903 the Golden Dawn was disbanded in a flurry of scandal and its sundry Adepts left to form their own tribes leaving the Order to die.

But did it? Like an oak, shattered by the storm, which scatters wide its acorns, The Hermetic Order of the Golden Dawn bequeathed a body of Knowledge, teachings and information to the ensuing generations. This became the root of the modern Neo-Pagan movement, which is the fastest growing religion in this country, according to the Institute for the Study of American Religion. In the last twenty years we have seen a vast and varied resurgence in the study of the Occult and Magickal Arts. Whole new realms of thought and consciousness have been opened, new arts and veins of creativity have been tapped. Many of these we can trace back to that not so old and yet ancient school called the Golden Dawn.

To understand the place of the Golden Dawn today, we must first examine its original purpose and intent. Immediately upon gazing into the system we see that its initiatory rituals served primarily to teach a philosophy and doctrine of Magickal thought. Each ritual presented the candidate, within the confines of a highly charged magickal space, a huge parcel of information to be assimilated before the next initiation. Other groups, such as Aleister Crowley's O.T.O., are not teaching orders and so many turn to the G.D. to found their practice within a coherent system.

Besides the communication, there is the transmission of the Magickal current. Magickly, according to the "Z" papers, the initiations served to imprint the energies of the system into the aura of the candidate. Together, the initiations attempted to build the Qabalistic microcosm called the Tree of Life into the soul of the Candidate. The intent was to both evolve the subject soul and to provide an artifice whereby the soul could articulate its will.

As a system of thought the Golden Dawn brought together and energized the sundry branches of Hermetic and Magickal Practice. For the first time since perhaps the ancient Egyptians, the divergent streams of magickal energy like daemonology,* astrology and tarot were fused together in a single coherent albeit unwieldy system.

For the Adepts the system was a vessel and vehicle for Magickal Power. The Golden Dawn as RR et AC functioned as framework within which to operate as a group. From this platform the adventurous could set out to explore new magicks while at the same time the mage could plot the course of her development by analogy to the Qabalistic Tree of Life. The value of this last to the aspirant is incalculable. By means of reference to the phases of consciousness and the symbols attributed to them the mage could always determine "where she is" and thus never be lost, a most horrible fate.

Today, however, this system functions exponentially, and it provides a baseline of information and technique for reference. All too often at the Neo-Pagan Festivals one overhears hushed whispers, "Well, in the G.D. they . . ."

*Not "demonology" in the common usage of evil spirits; rather *daemonology* concerns supernatural beings (including even The Holy Guardian Angel) intermediate between humanity and God. C.L.W.

We hear in the opening of the hall of the Neophytes "by names and images are all powers awakened and reawakened". Dion Fortune rightly notes that these thought-forms or structures of mind are vessels of power and the means of communication with the powers. As these structures endure beyond the minds of their creators they are available to those who use the names and images as published in such a work as this. In fact these natural forces, anthropomorphised into entities, are accessed by the newcomer through a relatively minute amount of concentration for these symbols were sturdily formulated by the founders of the system.

This ease of application is a major attraction to the users of the Golden Dawn system of magick. The energies that would have otherwise been necessary to make contact with spiritual powers could then be used towards creative application of the essences invoked.

Today, the task of the practitioner is to induce, through the rites and formulae, the transcendental spirit of the Order into the pre-created forms, thereby reincarnating the "soul of the Mysteries" essential to the reflowering of the Order.

The study of Magick leads one into harmony with Nature and the Universe at large. A major factor in the development of the Neo-Pagan movement was a growing concern with the environment and its abuse. Magick in the form of Wicca or the Craft formed the spiritual link whereby this awareness could express itself. The G.D. provided much of the technology.

It is interesting to note that an Adept of the G.D., J.W. Brodie-Innes, traveled extensively in the British Isles to study Witchcraft. Now the Witches study his Order in the learning of their Craft.

The elemental arrangements and attributions employed by the modern Witches often have their root in the G.D. The very concept of the Circle and the Guardians at the Four Quarters was not extant in the older family traditions at least until after the demise of the G.D.

The G.D. has been a fountain head of inspiration for the new Pagans. One beautiful example of use of G.D. technology in a new and creative manner is a variant on the Lotus Wand seen at an East coast festival. That pagan had formed a staff topped by a crystal ball. The shaft was painted in the traditional rainbow attributed by the Golden Dawn to the Zodiac and the Sigils of the Signs were painted in their flashing colors.

There is at least one group that being unable to decide upon a pantheon from any specific culture, chose to use the G.D. system of Enochiana to found their tradition upon. The G.D. practice was chosen over the others as being clearer, more easily worked and more highly developed.

Another line of development in the modern Craft, is called Traditionalist Wicca, (not to be confused with the Family Traditions). Upon realising that the inordinate amount of Enochiana and G.D. styled techniques was not a later accretion as previously thought, its adherents researched still deeper into the origins of their *Book of Shadows* or Grimoire. They concluded that the originator of their readition either had access to G.D. material before their popular publication or had been a member.

Thelema is another thriving avenue of thought that must be examined in the light of the Golden Dawn. Without a thorough knowledge of Golden Dawn symbolism and ritual the *Book of the Law, Liber AL,* is either impenetrable or ridiculous. The formula of "Ra-hoor-Khuit hath taken his seat in the East at the Equinox of the Gods" (AL. I, 49) only becomes meaningful within the context of the Golden Dawn Equinox ceremony.

The system of magick and philosophy founded by Aleister Crowley and developed further by many others is deeply indebted to the Golden Dawn. The primary rituals for daily practice in Thelemic Magick, "The Star Ruby," "V. vel Reguli" and the like, are patterned after the G.D. Lesser Banishing Ritual of the Pentagram, the

Greater Pentagram ritual and others. Their practice without previous mastery of the G.D. forms is difficult if not fruitless.

Thelema, as a semi-organised collective of the Magick Users, goes to great lengths to include the structure of the G.D. in the A ∴ A ∴ (see *Magick in Theory & Practice)*. The grade structure employed is practically identical, although augmented with yoga and a different separation of learning tasks. However, the states of magickal consciousness as symbolised by the grades are the same. Crowley used the space in the RR et AC mythos of the Third order to "slot in" his conception of the A ∴ A ∴. Nonetheless it was built firmly upon the foundation of the Golden Dawn and evolved further by his successors in that light.

Before one can fully appreciate the subtlety of the magicks of Will and Love it is necessary to have a firm grounding in magickal technology. No organized body of magickal practice is more geared to the neophyte than that of the Golden Dawn. Only Franz Bardon comes near in completeness and many find his works impenetrable and filled with blinds.

In many ways the G.D. practices and exercises are like the "forms" of Tai Chi and other martial arts. As the student masters the outer forms the inner energy and understanding blossoms within her. This is one meaning behind the aphorism "the rituals shall be half known and half concealed . . ." (AL. I, 34.)

This factor of having to master the forms before they are truly useful has been pointed to as evidence that the system is contrived. This and the aparently unsupportable overlays of one subsystem on top of another that Mathers and Crowley et al built into the attributional tables makes the totality insusceptible to rational analysis. Yet the fact that the Adept, after long practice, can make the system "work" demands that we ask how and sends us on that quest called "Initiation". A glance at the gymnast gracefully and easily executing maneuvers that would injure or kill the average person provides a fit analogy to the spiritual gymnastics of the adept and her required training period.

In the midst of the modern search for initiation into this Magick of Light it would serve the student well to examine the Alternative Health Community. Here she would find a faint but clear echo of the healing work reputed among the Adepts of the G.D. Israel Regardie speaks of the processes of healing through the use of the Middle Pillar. How similar to this are the practices of Shiatsu and Polarity Therapy! In all of these forms the Healer uses her own energies to readjust the flow of vital energies in the client.

The ability to channel energy, call it Light, chi, magnetism or whatever, is essential to the practice of Ceremonial Magick. This is the same force that forms the Pentagrams and sigils drawn in the rituals. Having developed these methods and technologies to a peak within the magickal substratum of Western culture, it is interesting and gratifying to see analogies of Golden Dawn technologies coming into general use.

Since the early part of this century we have learned much about ourselves and the Universe we live in. Many new paradigms for viewing the world and many new technologies for manipulating it have been discovered. Today we have the phenomenal tools that Information Theory provides to examine how the varied aspects of this System called the Golden Dawn hold together.

Jungian psychology would work hand in hand with the Magickal images to access levels of consciousness previously untapped with so much precision, as the G.D attributions provide keys telling the researcher what to expect and how to interpret the results.

Whole system or Gestalt psychology enables the magicker to see the many spirits and voices as parts of the self and yet the magickal technologies provide a means for articulating the interactions in a powerful and meaningful way.

These are ways the magickal worldview of the G.D. could be explored in the field of psychology, and yet the Hermetic Science also delved into the physics of nature. Now that the scientists have caught up with the ancient Hermetic philosophers in noting that the observer affects the observed (see Heisenberg's Uncertainty Principle, Bohr's Copenhagen Interpretation, and Schrödinger's Cat) it is now possible to correlate the teachings of ancient wisdoms, if we have the courage to see them clearly.

One profitable vein of research is in R. Buckminster Fuller's Synergetic Geometries which link the patterns of thought to the interpatternings of the stars and subatomic particles. This is clearly a not so faint echo of the axiom "As above, so below."

Another is in reexamining the ancient Egyptian teaching as brought to light by the researches of R.A. Schwaller de Lubicz connecting consciousness and matter in hieroglyphic expression. We may find the eternal wisdom of the ancient sages etched in stone and built into their architecture helpful in understanding humanity as part and not separate from Nature.

Things have changed a great deal from the days of Mathers, Crowley and Regardie. The New Pagans have sprung into being, and after two decades are beginning to mature. As we approach the 100th anniversary of the founding of the Golden Dawn, it is being reexamined by young thinkers with an eye to revamping it in light of the discoveries of the last 80 years since it "collapsed".

Or did it collapse? Perhaps it is better to remember that the Golden Dawn System of Magick is not a Book but is a living, growing, self-rectifying organism that will endure unto the end for in the end there is naught to endure.

April, 1986
Sam Webster
Albuquerque,
New Mexico

INDEX

- A -

A (in Bornless Ritual), 443 (III, 260)
A., Frater, 232 (II, 219)
A Document—*see* Adeptus Minor, curriculum
A to Z Horoscope Maker and Delineator (Llewellyn George), 5
A.A. (Argentum Astrum), ix, 10, 699
A.C.R.G., 235 (II, 224)
A.G.R.C., 235 (II, 224)
A.M.A.G. = Ad Majorem Adonai Gloriam (Israel Regardie), 272, 277, 405, 426 (II, 290, 300; III, 200, 233)
Aaetpoi, 325 (III, 73)
Aamamiah, 86, 561 (I, 171; IV, 171)
Aaneval, 86, 563 (I, 171; IV, 174)
Aaozaif, 325, 636 (III, 73; IV, 277)
Aapdoce, 325 (III, 73)
Aapid, 638 (IV, 280)
Aariel, 86, 560 (I, 174; IV, 170)
Aasav, 638 (IV, 280)
Aasliah, 86, 561 (I, 174; IV, 170)
Aatik Yomin, 77 (I, 153)
Aavas, 638 (IV, 280)
Abandoned Success, The Lord of—*see* Eights (Tarot), Cups
Abaoth, 444 (III, 262)
Abba, 72, 77-8, 100 (I, 141, 153-5, 205-6)
  Chokmah, 331, 693, 695 (III, 82; IV, 363, 367)
  consecration of talisman, 415, 422 (III, 215, 228)
  Enochian chess knight, 693, 695 (IV, 363, 367)
  Macroprosopus, 375 (III, 150)
  Yod, 331, 693, 695 (III, 82; IV, 363, 367)
  see also Supernal Father
Abel, 215 (II, 189)
Abeu, 443 (III, 260)
Abi-Agnus, 224, 261, 275 (II, 202, 271, 297)
Abiegnus, Mount, 224, 247, 261, 265, 270 (II, 202, 244, 271, 279, 287)
  drawing, 237, 242 (II, 229, 237-8)
Abramelin, The Sacred Magic of (trans. MacGregor Mathers), 8, 11, 16 (I, 18)
Abraoth, 443 (III, 262)
Abrasar, 443, 444 (III, 261, 263)
Abundance, Lord of—*see* Threes (Tarot), Cups
acacia tree, 58 (I, 115)
Aces (Tarot), 78, 347, 540, 542-3 (I, 154; III, 108-9; IV, 138, 142-4)
  celestial sphere, 596-7, 616 (IV, 222, 249)
    Draco, 607, 609 (IV, 236-7, 239)
    North Pole, 92, 603, 607-11, 613, 617, 618, 619, 621 (I, 184; IV, 236-41, 246, 251, 253, 254, 257)
Aces (Tarot) (continued):
  celestial sphere (continued):
    Sun, 609 (IV, 241)
  Cups, 543 (IV, 143)
  divination, 567, 568, 569 (IV, 178, 180, 183)
  divinatory meaning, 582 (IV, 201)
  Enochian:
    chess, 685, 686 (IV, 350, 351)
      kings, 696, 690 (IV, 351, 359)
    tablets:
      Sephirotic Calvary Crosses, 644 (IV, 288)
      Tablet of Union, 645 (IV, 290)
  Kether, 596 (IV, 221, 222)
  Pentacles, 543 (IV, 143-4)
    divination example, 571, 572, 577, 578, 579 (IV, 185, 186, 187, 194, 196, 197)
  Spirit and four elements, 568 (IV, 180)
  Swords, 543 (IV, 143)
    Enochian chess Air king, 687 (IV, 353)
  Tetragrammaton, 607 (IV, 237)
  Wands, 542-3 (IV, 142)
    divination example, 568, 569 (IV, 181, 182)
Achlal, 207n
Acnxp, 638 (IV, 280)
Acquisitio, 494, 495, 527, 529, 532, 539 (IV, 75, 77, 115, 119, 124, 134)
  see also geomancy, figures
active elements—*see* elements, active
Aczinor, 325, 407, 409 (III, 73, 203, 206)
Ad Crucis Roseae Gloriam, 235 (II, 224)
Ad Gloriam Roseae Crucis, 235 (II, 224)
Ad Majorem Adonai Gloriam (Israel Regardie), 405, 414, 415, 430, 431, 624 (III, 200, 215, 241, 242, 260)
  see also A.M.A.G.; Regardie, Israel
Adapi, 638 (IV, 280)
Adam, 155, 167, 404, 413, 429 (II, 71, 94; III, 198, 212, 239)
  altar diagram, The Fall, 33, 76, 193-4 (I, 59, 150-51; II, 146-7)
  altar diagram, The Garden of Eden, 33, 74, 177-8 (I, 58, 145; II, 115)
  Aquarius, 188 (II, 134, 135)
  lid of Pastos, 35 (I, 63)
  White Pillar, 61, 162 (I, 122; II, 85)
adder, 419 (III, 223)
"Additional Lecture on the Tattwas of the Eastern School," 514-22 (IV, 95-109)
Adept Adeptus Minor, 230 (II, 215)
Adept, Associate, in Vault consecration ceremony, 258, 260 (II, 264, 268)
  (not to be confused with Associate Adeptus Minor; *see* Adept, Third)

Adept, Chief—*see* Chief Adept
Adept, Second:
  Adeptus Minor ritual, 221-30 *passim*, 232-40 *passim*, 242, 247 (II, 198-216 *passim*, 219-33 *passim*, 236, 237, 242, 243, 244)
    Adeptus Major grade required for office, 221 (II, 198)
    Geburah and Fire, 221n
    Phoenix Wand, 221, 224 (II, 198, 203)
    robe, 221 (II, 198)
    spiritual development ritual, speech used in, 391 III, 178)
  Equinox ceremony, 251-5 *passim* (II, 251, 253, 254, 255, 257, 258, 259)
      Phoenix Wand, 258 (II, 265)
  Portal ritual, 198-205 *passim*, 207-12 *passim*, 214-8 *passim*, 220 (II, 156-67 *passim*, 169, 173-81 *passim*, 186-9 *passim*, 191, 193, 194, 196, 197)
    garments and implements, 198 (II, 156)
    Netzach and Fire, 199n
  Vault consecration ceremony, 258-65 *passim* (II, 265, 267, 269-79 *passim*)
Adept, Third:
  Adeptus Minor ritual, 221-9 *passim*, 231-40 *passim*, 242, 247, 272, 274 (II, 198-209 *passim*, 211, 212, 216, 217, 218, 220-3 *passim*, 225-33 *passim*, 237, 243, 244, 291, 295)
    Adeptus Minor grade required for office, 221 (II, 198)
    robe, 221 (II, 198)
    Tiphareth, 221n
  Equinox ceremony, 251, 252, 254, 255 (II, 251, 253, 254, 257, 259)
  Portal ritual, 198-204 *passim*, 207, 208, 209, 212-6 *passim*, 218, 220 (II, 155, 156, 158-61 *passim*, 163-6 *passim*, 173-6 *passim*, 181-90 *passim*, 193, 194, 197)
    Black Pillar, 203 (II, 165)
    garments and implements, 198 (II, 156)
    Hod and Water, 199n, 221n
  Vault consecration ceremony, 258-65 *passim* (II, 264, 267, 268-74 *passim*, 276-9 *passim*)
Adeptus Exemptus, 21 (I, 30)
  Chief Adept, 221 (II, 198)
  Praemonstator, 331 (III, 82)
Adeptus Major, 21 (I, 30)
  Enochian chess, 683 (IV, 346)
  Imperator, 331 (III, 82)
  Second Adept, 221 (II, 198)
Adeptus Major, Mighty—*see* Adept, Second
Adeptus Minor, xviii, 3, 9, 13, 21, 24, 277 (I, 30, 36; II, 300)
  Adept Adeptus Minor, 230 (II, 215)
  Cancellarius, 331 (III, 82)
  Crowley, Fortune, and Regardie, 683n
Adeptus Minor (continued):
  curriculum, 40, 42-3, 47 (I, 76, 81-4, 94-5)
  Enochian, 624 (IV, 260)
  grip, 246 (II, 242-3)
  Mystic Number, 240 (II, 233)
  Obligation, 10, 14, 37, 42, 43, 106, 229-30, 237, 317 (I, 68, 81, 84, 85, 215; II, 212-5, 227; III, 62)
    Vault consecration ceremony, 263 (II, 275)
  password, 240 (II, 233-4)
  ritual, 11, 23, 28, 29, 35-9, 42, 199n, 221-247, 266, 269, 274, 276, 426, 463, 464, 482, 625, 629 (I, 36, 47, 49, 63-74, 81; II, 198-244, 281, 286, 295, 299; III, 233; IV, 22, 24, 57, 262, 269)
    "Concerning the Use of the Vault," 270-1 (II, 287-9)
    closing, 247 (II, 243-4)
    obligation, 229-30 (II, 212-5)
    opening, 221-5 (II, 200-5)
    First Point, 225-33 (II, 205-21)
      trial of humility, 226-7 (II, 206-9)
    Second Point, 233-7 (II, 221-8)
    temple arrangement, 222, 238 (II, 199, 230)
      Vault, 234 (II, 221)
    Third Point, 237-46 (II, 229-43)
    "Three Chiefs, The," 272-7 (II, 290-300)
  signs—*see* L.V.X., signs
  "Task Undertaken by the Adeptus Minor," 106-8 (217-20)
  Theoricus Adeptus Minor, 44, 603 (I, 87; IV, 236)
  Third Adept, grade required for, 221 (II, 198)
  Tiphareth, 35, 333 (I, 65; III, 86)
  Zelator Adeptus Minor, 42, 43, 230 (I, 82, 84; II, 215)
    Bornless Ritual, 442, 444, 445 (III, 259, 263, 264, 265)
    elemental weapons, 320 (III, 66)
      Tarot, 545-6, 549, 551, 552, 555, 556 (IV, 147, 152, 155, 158, 161, 163)
    Enochian system, 656, 658 (IV, 306, 308, 309)
      skrying, 660, 669 (IV, 312, 325)
    Equinox formula, 374 (III, 149)
    Hierophant, grade required for, 342 (III, 100)
    Lotus Wand, 302 (III, 39)
    Neophyte formula, 376 (III, 153)
    Rose-Cross lamen, 311, 493 (III, 54; IV, 74)
    Sword, 317 (III, 62)
    Tarot, 594, 596, 603 (IV, 218, 221, 236)
      divination, 569 (IV, 182)
Adeptus Minor, Associate—*see* Adept, Third

Administrative Intelligence, 159 (II, 78)
admission badges, 39, 45, 70-1, 79 (I, 74, 90, 136-8, 156-8)
  Adeptus Minor, 221, 226-7 (II, 198, 207-8)
    see also Sword and Serpent
  elemental grades, 139
  meditation, 87, 88 (I, 175, 176-7)
  Paths:
    27th Path, 79, 189, 190, 191, 643, 656 (I, 156-7; II, 137-8, 140, 141-2; IV, 287, 305)
      see also cross, Calvary, Ten squares
    28th Path, 79, 186, 187, 646, 659 (I, 156; II, 131, 132, 134; IV, 291, 310)
    see also Pyramid of the Elements
    29th Path, 79, 183, 184, 185 (I, 156; II, 125, 126, 129)
      see also cross, Calvary, Twelve squares
    30th Path, 70, 173-4, 175 (I, 137; II, 106, 107, 109)
      see also cross, Greek
    31st Path, 70, 168-72 *passim* (I, 137; II, 95, 96-104 *passim*)
      see also Pyramid of Fire
    32nd Path, 70, 155-9 *passim* (I, 136-7; II, 70-8 *passim*)
      see also cross, Greek solid cubical
  Philosophus, 79, 139, 193 (I, 157; II, 145)
    see also cross, Calvary, Six squares
  Portal, 202, 209 (II, 163, 176)
  Practicus, 70-1, 176-7 (I, 137-8; II, 112-3)
    see also Cup of Stolistes
  Theoricus, 68, 139, 155, 161, 162, 176, 177 (I, 131; II, 70, 82-3, 83-4, 112, 113)
    see also caduceus
  Zelator, 68, 139, 142, 144, 148 (I, 131; II, 45, 49, 57)
    see also cross, Fylfot
Adoeoet, 325 (III, 73)
Adonai, 143-7 *passim*, 152, 153 (II, 46-55 *passim*, 65-8 *passim*)
  Bornless Ritual, 444, 448 (III, 263, 268)
  consecrations:
    Pentacle, 324 (III, 72, 72)
    Rose-Cross, 315 (III, 60, 61)
    talisman, 413 (III, 212)
  evocation, 404, 406, 407, 409, 410 (III, 198, 201, 202, 204, 208, 209)
  higher self, 14
  invisibility ritual, 424 (III, 231)
  pentagram rituals, 53, 281, 282, 286 (I, 106; III, 10, 13, 19)
  spiritual development ritual, 438, 439, 440 (III, 253, 255, 257)
  transformation ritual, 429 (III, 239)
  YHVH, 508 (IV, 92)
Adonai ha-Aretz, 62, 64, 80, 98 (I, 123, 126, 158, 198)
Adoni ha-Aretz (continued):
  consecration of talisman, 422 (III, 227)
  evocation ritual, 402-8 *passim*, 410, 411, 412 (III, 195, 197, 199-202 *passim*, 204, 206, 208, 209, 210)
  Portal ritual, 204 (II, 167)
  Tattwa vision, 459 (IV, 16)
  telesmatic image, 492 (IV, 71-2)
  Theoricus ritual, 156 (II, 73)
  vibration, 491 (IV, 70)
  Zelator ritual, 143, 147, 152 (II, 46, 48, 55, 66)
Adonai Melekh:
  consecration of talisman, 422 (III, 227)
  evocation ritual, 402-5 *passim*, 407, 408, 410 (III, 195, 197, 198, 199, 204, 206, 209)
  Malkuth of Atziluth, 614 (IV, 246)
  Zelator ritual, 143, 151, 152, 153 (II, 46, 47, 64, 66, 68)
Adoration:
  ("Holy art Thou..."), 4
    astral/cosmic Neophyte temple in Sphere of Sensation, 453 (III, 275)
    Bornless Ritual, 442 (III, 259)
    consecration rituals:
      elemental weapons, 323 (III, 71)
      Lotus Wand, 304 (III, 42)
      Rose-Cross, 314 (III, 58)
      Sword, 318 (III, 64)
      talisman, 413 (III, 212)
    invisibility ritual, 423 (III, 229)
    Neophyte ritual, 117, 120, 131-2, 347 (II, 11, 18, 41; III, 109)
    Opening by Watchtower:
      evocation, 403 (III, 197)
      spiritual development ritual, 436 (III, 249)
      Vault consecration, 259 (II, 267)
    Portal ritual, 206 (I, 161)
    requiem ceremony, 447 (III, 266)
    transformation ritual, 429 (III, 239)
  elemental grade rituals, 137
    Philosophus, 182-3 (II, 123-4)
    Practicus, 167-8 (II, 94-5)
    Theoricus, 155-6 (II, 71-2)
    Zelator, 142-3 (II, 46-8)
  Equinox ceremony, 249-50 (II, 248-9)
Adre, 650 (IV, 297)
Advachiel, 86, 305 (I, 173; III, 44)
  Enochian letter, geomantic figure, Zodiac, 495 (IV, 77)
Advanced Guide to Enochian Magick, An, (Gerald J. Schueler), 682n
Ae-isest, 352 (III, 114)
    see also Isis
Aeons, 330, 375 (III, 81, 150, 151)
Aeoou, 443 (III, 261)

Aeshoori, 691, 692 (IV, 359, 360, 361)
  see also Osiris
Aeshoorist (Ae-shoo-rist), 337, 352, 410, 424, 439 (III, 92, 114, 209, 230, 231, 235)
  see also Osiris
AETERNITAS (Ab Kether Ex Chokmah Tu Binah Ex Chesed Regina Geburah. Nunc Tiphareth In Netzach Totius Hod Ad Yesod Saeculorum Malkuth.), 477, 478 (IV, 48, 49)
Aethers—*see* Enochian, Aethers
Agiel, 65 (I, 127)
  sigil, 485, 498 (IV, 60, 81)
  telesmatic image, 486 (IV, 61)
Agla (Aglah):
  Bornless Ritual, 444 (III, 263)
  consecration of talisman, 422 (III, 228)
  evocation, 402 (III, 195)
  invisibility ritual, 423-7 *passim* (III, 229, 231, 233, 234, 235)
  passive pentagram of Spirit, 201, 315 (I, 160; III, 59)
  pentagram rituals, 53, 281-6 (I, 106; III, 11, 19)
  Tattwa vision, 463 (IV, 22)
Agrippa, Henry Cornelius, 9
  "Of the Four Elements and Their Natural Qualities," 611-3 (IV, 242-6)
Ahaozpi, 325, 636 (III, 73; IV, 277)
Ahaphix, 344, 352 (III, 103, 114)
Ahaphshi, 343, 353 (III, 102, 115)
Ahathoor, 353 (III, 115)
  see also Hathoor
Ahephi (Ahepi), 344, 352, 358, 359 (III, 103, 114, 124, 125)
  description, 358 (III, 122-3)
  Enochian:
    chess pawn, 687, 692 (IV, 353, 361)
    pyramids, 663 (IV, 315)
      skrying, 662 (IV, 318)
  illustration, 665 (IV, 317)
  lower intestines or bowels, 360, 361 (III, 127, 128)
  Nephthys, 361 (III, 129)
  Nile, 361 (III, 129)
  North, 361 (III, 129)
  Southwest, 344, 352, 358, 663 (III, 103, 114, 122; IV, 315)
  West, 361 (III, 128)
  see also Hapi
Ahmlicv, 325, 407, 409 (III, 73, 203, 206)
Aiaoai, 650, 672 (IV, 297, 330)
Aidap, 638 (IV, 280)
Ailrn, 638 (IV, 280)
Aima, 72, 77-8, 100, 428 (I, 141, 153-5, 205-6; III, 237)
  Binah, 331, 510 (III, 82; IV, 93-4)
  Enochian chess queen, 695 (IV, 367)
  Heh of YHVH, 331 (III, 82)
Aima (continued):
  Macroprosopus, 375 (III, 150)
  pentagram, 507 (IV, 91)
  The Star, 188 (II, 135)
  see also Supernal Mother
Aima Elohim (Aimah Elohim), 73, 76, 117, 197, 276 (I, 144, 150; II, 113-4, 146, 298)
  evocation, 409 (III, 207)
  invisibility ritual, 423, 428 (III, 230, 237)
  Mo-ooth, 375 (III, 151)
  requiem ceremony, 447 (III, 266)
  spiritual development ritual, 436 (III, 250)
  Tarot:
    The Magician, 588 (IV, 210)
    The Star, 188 (II, 135)
    The Universe, 592 (IV, 217)
Ain, 77, 358, 478 (I, 153; III, 124; IV, 49)
  circle, 204 (II, 168)
Ain Soph, 77, 358, 375, 614, 615, 617 (I, 153; III, 124, 151; IV, 246, 247, 248, 251)
Ain Soph Aour, 18, 77, 358, 440 (I, 23, 153; III, 124, 256)
  Banner of the East, 336 (III, 91)
Aiq Beker, 275, 493, 496-7 (II, 296, 297; IV, 72, 79-80)
Air, xxiii, 8, 514 (IV, 95)
  of Air:
    King (Prince) of Swords, 549 (IV, 151)
    see also Air, Enochian tablet, Air angle
  alchemical operation, 398 (III, 190)
  Ahephi, 687, 692 (IV, 353, 361)
  Aleph, 157, 159 (II, 75, 77)
  Ameshet, 361 (III, 128)
  birds, 109 (I, 222)
  breath, 345 (III, 105-6)
  caduceus, 162, 340 (II, 84; III, 97)
  Cancellarius, 332 (III, 84)
  consecration of talisman, 420, 421 (III, 225)
  Cup of Stolistes, 340 (III, 97)
  Dagger—*see* Dagger, elemental weapon (Air)
  divine name, archangel, angel, ruler, king, etc., 80 (I, 158)
  of Earth:
    King (Prince) of Pentacles, 550 (IV, 153)
    Malkuth, 209, 614, 618 (II, 176; IV,, 247, 253)
    Rose-Cross lamen, 310 (III, 52)
    see also Air, Enochian tablets
  elemental prayer, 164-5 (II, 89-90)
  elements, contains characteristics of other, 233 (II, 222)
  Enochian chess:
    bishop, 691, 695-6 (IV, 360,367)
    boards, 694 (IV, 365)
  Enochian tablets or Watchtowers:
    Air angle, 641 (IV, 283)

Air (continued):
Enochian tablets or Watchtowers (continued):
Air angle (continued):
angels, 670 (IV, 327)
Earth tablet, 327, 670 (III, 77; IV, 327)
call (thirteenth), 672, 679 (IV, 330, 341)
Enochian chess pawns, 688 (IV, 354)
Fire tablet, 326, 670 (III, 74; IV, 327)
call (sixteenth), 672, 679 (IV, 330, 342)
pyramids, 646-7 (IV, 291, 293)
Water tablet, 326, 638, 649, 650, 670 (III, 75; IV, 280, 296-7, 327)
call (tenth), 662, 672, 678 (IV, 318, 330, 339)
skrying, 662, 666 (IV, 318-9)
Air tablet, 636 (IV, 276, 277)
Air angle, 327, 637-8, 641, 670 (III, 76; IV, 279-80, 284, 327)
call (third), 671, 673 (IV, 329, 330, 331)
Enochian chess, 689-90 (IV, 356)
bishop, 686 (IV, 351)
pyramids, 646 (IV, 291)
archangels of angles, 326-7 (III, 76)
calls, 671, 673, 675 (IV, 329-30, 331, 335)
consecration of Dagger, 323, 325, 326-7 (III, 70, 73-4, 76)
consecration of talisman, 420 (III, 224)
Earth angle, 666 (IV, 319)
call (eighth), 672, 677 (IV, 330, 338)
Enochian chess, 690 (IV, 357)
Fire angle:
call (ninth), 672, 677 (IV, 330, 339)
Enochian chess, 690 (IV, 357)
illustration, 631 (IV, 270)
Opening by Watchtower:
evocation, 403 (III, 196)
spiritual development ritual, 435 (III, 249)
Vault consecration, 259 (II, 266)
Portal ritual, 198, 200, 205 (II, 155, 159, 169, 170)
pyramids, 646, 648 (IV, 291, 294)
Tarot, 642-3 (IV, 286-7)
Theoricus ritual, 156, 163-4 (II, 72, 87)
transformation ritual, 429 (III, 239, 240)
Vau, 639 (IV, 281, 282)
Water angle, 667 (IV, 321)
call (seventh), 672, 677 (IV, 330, 337)
Enochian chess, 690 (IV, 357)
Zodiac, decanates, 642-3 (IV, 286-7)
pyramids, 646-7, 649, 650, 654, 655 (IV, 291, 293, 296, 302, 303)
see also Enochian tablets; Oro Ibah Aozpi
finger, little, 100 (I, 204)
of Fire:

Air (of Fire) (continued):
King (Prince) of Wands, 546 (IV, 147)
Rose-Cross lamen, 311 (III, 52)
see also Air, Enochian tablets
Hegemon, 199n, 375 (III, 151)
hexagram, 295 (III, 30)
Hiddikel, 73, 177 (I, 145; II, 114)
Kaph, 221n
Kerub, 343, 357 (III, 101-2, 121)
see also Aquarius; Kerubim; man (Kerub)
Light, translator of, 101-2, 104 (I, 206-7, 211)
lungs, 100 (I, 205)
material basis, 387 (III, 171)
Mercury, 648 (IV, 294)
microcosm, 100, 101, 102, 104 (I, 204-7 *passim*, 211)
Middle Pillar, 345 (III, 106)
pentagram, 282, 284, 285 (III, 12, 13, 15, 18)
Bornless Ritual, 443 (III, 260)
consecration of dagger, 326-7 (III, 76)
consecration of Rose-Cross, 315 (60)
consecration of talisman, 420 (III, 224)
Opening by Watchtower:
evocation ritual, 403 (III, 196)
spiritual development ritual, 435 (III, 248)
Vault consecration, 259 (II, 266)
Portal ritual, 205 (II, 170)
Theoricus ritual, 155, 165 (II, 71, 90)
transformation ritual, 429 (III, 239)
pentagram, point of, 280, 281, 282 (III, 10-13 *passim*)
reconciler among Heavens, Water, and Earth, 151 (II, 64)
Resh, linked to by Tiphareth and Sun, 215 (II, 187)
Root of the Powers of—see Aces (Tarot), Swords
rose, 333, 334 (III, 86-7)
Rose-Cross lamen, 310-13 *passim* (III, 52-6 *passim*)
Air arm of cross and colors, 310, 312 (III, 52, 54-5)
consecration, 315 (III, 60)
alchemical principles and other elements in Air, 310 (III, 52)
location of petal (Aleph), 311 (III, 53)
Saturn, 648 (IV, 294)
symbol:
Enochian pyramids, 649, 650 (IV, 296)
pentagram rituals, 283 (III, 14)
used in spelling divine names, 83 (I, 166)
Tarot:
The Devil, 213 (II, 183)
The Fool, 71, 72, 542, 592 (I, 139, 141; IV, 140, 216)
Swords, 685 (IV, 349)
see also Tarot, suits

Air (Tarot) (continued):
Temperance, 217 (II, 192)
telesmatic image, 486, (IV, 61)
Theoricus grade, 29, 30, 155, 163, (I, 50, 52; (II, 71, 87)
ritual, 157 (II, 75)
Thm-a-oe-St, 375 (III, 151)
Tiphareth, 331 (III, 83)
transformation ritual, 429, 430, 431, 434 (III, 239, 240, 242, 247)
Vau, 639, 644 (IV, 281, 282, 289)
see also YHVH, elements
Vayu, 457 (IV, 12, 13)
telesmatic images, 489 (IV, 67)
of Water:
Air angle of Water tablet, 326, 638, 649, 650 (III, 75; IV, 280, 296-7)
King (Prince) of Cups, 547 (IV, 149)
Rose-Cross lamen, 311 (III, 52-3)
see also Air, Enochian tablets
Yesod, 20, 21, 331 (I, 27, 30; III, 83)
Zodiac:
air signs, 50, 68 (I, 100, 133)
Enochian:
chess, 690 (IV, 356)
tablets, 650 (IV, 296)
mutable signs, 644, 650 (IV, 289, 296)
see also elements
Aires—see Enochian, Aethers
Aismt, 654-5 (V, 303)
Akaiah, 86, 554 (I, 172; IV, 160)
Akasa, 457, 458, 462, 463, 514, 516-22 *passim* (IV, 12, 13, 14, 22, 96, 99, 100, 101, 103, 105, 106, 108)
Akas-Akasa, 516 (IV, 99)
Akasa of Apas, 476 (IV, 45-6)
Bornless Ritual, 443, 444, 445 (III, 263, 264, 265)
Canopic jars, 360 (III, 127)
Ham, 520 (IV, 105)
Portal grade, 35 (I, 65)
Akasic current, 479 (IV, 81)
Al, 97, 167 (I, 194-5; II, 94)
consecration of Jupiter talisman, 413-8 *passim*, 421, 422 (II, 213, 214, 215, 218, 221, 226, 228)
pentagram rituals, 284, 286 (III, 16, 19)
suffix, 660 (IV, 311)
see also El
Al Ab, 415, 419 (III, 215, 216, 222)
Al Chai, 98 (I, 197)
Albertus, Frater, *The Alchemist's Handbook,* 6
Albuquerque, 700
Albus, 494, 495, 527, 528, 529, 534-5, 538 (IV, 75, 77, 115, 118, 119, 128, 134)
Enochian:
chess, 690 (IV, 356-7)
pyramids, 649, 650 (IV, 296)
Albus (continued):
see also geomancy, figures
Alchemist's Handbook, The (Frater Albertus), 6
alchemy, xxi-xxii, xxv, 5-6, 15, 23, 25-6, 38 (I, 15, 35, 39-41, 71)
astrological symbols of planets, 83 (I, 165)
Elixir of Life, 111, 273 (I, 227; II, 292)
First Matter, 19, 33, 395, 396 (I, 25, 60; III, 184-7 passim)
god-forms, 372 (III, 147)
Heh final of Yeheshuah, 376, 395 (III, 152, 184)
I.N.R.I., 11
metals, 60, 399 (I, 119; III, 191)
Neophyte formula, 377, 395-9 (III, 153, 184-92)
password, 373 (III, 148)
philosopher's stone, xxii, 25, 28 (I, 38, 40, 47)
see also Stone of the Wise
Philosopher's Stone, The (Israel Regardie), 365, 377 (III, 135, 153-4)
principles (Mercury, Salt, and Sulphur):
dekagram, 510 (IV, 93)
enneagram, 508, 510 (IV, 93)
Pillars, capitals, 55 (I, 110)
Rose-Cross lamen, 310-11, 312 (III, 52-3, 54)
symbols, 60 (I, 119)
Tiphareth, 345 (II, 106)
triangle, 506 (IV, 90)
Vault symbolism, 246, 268 (II, 240, 284, 285)
solve et coagula, 32, 666 (I, 56-7; IV, 320)
Synesius, 28 (I, 47)
terms, 60-1, 84 (I, 119-21, 167-8)
Tree of Life, 82 (I, 163)
Triumphal Chariot of Antimony (Basil Valentine), 1
Vaughan, Thomas , 33, 39 (I, 60, 73)
Coelum Terrae, 19 (I, 25)
see also alembic; athanor; Balneum Arenae; Balneum Mariae; crucible; curcurbite; Dead Head; distillation; eagle; gold; lion; Mercury; mortar; philosophic egg; putrefaction; residuum; Salt; Sulphur
Aldiah, 86, 554 (I, 172; IV, 160)
alembic, 36, 84, 236, 395, 398, 448 (I, 67, 167; II, 227; III, 184, 189, 268)
head, 396, 397 (III, 186, 187, 188)
Aleph, 8, 151, 276, 277 (II, 64, 299)
Air, 157, 159 (II, 75, 77)
invisibility ritual, 387 (III, 171)
caduceus, 162, 340 (II, 84; III, 97)
crook, 242 (II, 237)
with hexagrams, as a letter of the name Ararita:
Mars, 290 (III, 23)

Air (with hexagrams) (continued):
Moon, 289 (III, 22)
Saturn, 288 (III, 21)
telesmatic image, 486, 489-90, 491, 492 (IV, 61, 67-8, 69, 71)
see also Hebrew alphabet
Alexandria, 594 (IV, 219)
Alhectega, 407, 409 (III, 203, 206)
see also Alphctga
alimentary system:
Children of Horus, 359-61 (III, 126-9)
Alndvod, 325 (III, 73)
Alpha and Omega, 424, 548 (III, 231; IV, 151)
alphabet—*see* Hebrew alphabet
Alphctga, 325 (III, 73)
see also Alhectega
Alrnl, 638 (IV, 280)
altar, 28, 333-4 (I, 46; III, 86-7)
alchemy, 395-9 *passim* (III, 185-90 *passim*)
diagram, 398 (III, 190)
Altar of Burnt Offering, 61, 149 (I, 121; II, 59)
Altar of Incense, 61, 151, 656 (I, 121; II, 63-4; IV, 305)
Calvary cross, 79, 191 (I, 157; II, 142)
Mother letters, 67 (I, 130)
Altar of the Spirit, 216 (II, 189)
astral/cosmic Neophyte temple in Sphere of Sensation, 451, 452, 453 (III, 272, 273, 275)
Bornless Ritual, 442, 445 (III, 259, 260, 265)
Circular Altar, 271 (II, 289)
Adeptus Minor ritual, 221, 222, 223, 229, 233-43 *passim*, 246 (II, 199, 200, 201, 212, 220-33 *passim*, 236, 238, 240, 242)
Vault consecration ceremony, 258, 260, 268, 275 (II, 264-268 *passim*, 275)
consecration of talismans, 385, 386, 414-7 *passim* (III, 166-70 *passim*, 213, 215, 218, 219)
divination, 394 (III, 182)
Equinox ceremony, 248, 249, 250, 254, 256 (II, 246-50 *passim*, 257, 258, 261)
evocation, 380, 382, 383, 402-6 *passim*, 408, 410 (III, 159, 162, 163, 195, 197, 198, 201, 202, 206, 208, 209)
invisibility ritual, 388, 423, 426, 427 (III, 173, 229, 230, 234, 236)
Neophyte ritual:
the ritual itself, 116, 117, 119, 121, 122, 125, 128, 132, 133 (II, 11, 12, 13, 15, 19, 21, 27, 28, 33, 42)
disussion, 114, 333-4, 365, 366, 367, 368, 370, 379, 380 (III, 86, 87, 134, 136, 139, 140, 143, 157, 158)
Nephthys, headdress, 686 (IV, 351)
Altar (continued):
requiem ceremony, 448, 450 (III, 267, 268, 270)
skrying (Enochian), 668 (IV, 323)
spiritual development ritual, 391, 392, 435, 436, 437, 439, 441 (III, 178, 180, 248, 249, 250, 252, 255, 256, 258)
Tarot:
The Devil, 212 (II, 182)
Knaves (Princesses), 546, 549, 551 (IV, 148, 152, 155)
The Magician, 588 (IV, 210)
Tattwa vision, 466 (IV, 28)
Theoricus ritual, 160 (II, 81)
transformation ritual, 390, 430-3 *passim* (III, 176, 240, 242-7 *passim*)
altar diagrams, 31, 35, plates f. 118 (I, 54, 63, plates f. 146 & 152)
The Fall, 32, 33, 76, plate f. 118 (I, 57, 59-60, 150-1, plate f. 152)
The Flaming Sword of the Kerubim, 141, 145, 147, 154, 161, 162 (II, 44, 52, 55, 56, 69, 82, 83, 85)
The Garden of Eden, 32-3, 73-4, plate f. 118, 176, 177-8 (I, 57-9, 144-5, plate f. 146, 112, 113-5)
The Serpent on the Tree of Life, 61-3, 161, 162-3 (I, 121-3; II, 82, 84-5)
see also diagrams
Alternative Health Community, 699
Alverda, Hugo, 237, 273 (II, 228, 292)
Salt, Binah, Water, 275 (II, 296)
"Amazing Grace," hymn, quoted, 239, 445 (II, 232; III, 264)
Amazons (Knaves of Tarot), 544, 546, 547, 549, 550, 607, 615, 686 (IV, 145, 147, 150, 152, 153, 236, 249, 351)
Ambriel, 86, 305 (I, 171; III, 44)
Enochian letter, geomantic figure, Zodiac, 495 (IV, 77)
Amen-Ra, 375 (III, 151)
Amentet, 56, 57 (I, 111, 113)
Amenti, 362, 432 (III, 129, 245)
Ameshet (Ameshett, Amesheth), 343, 352, 358, 359 (III, 102-3, 114, 124, 125)
description, 357 (III, 122)
East, Air, 361 (III, 128)
Enochian:
chess pawn, 687, 692 (IV, 353, 361)
pyramids, 663 (IV, 315)
illustration, 665 (IV, 317)
Isis, 361 (III, 129)
Nephthys, 691 (IV, 361)
Northeast, 343, 352, 357, 663 (III, 102-3, 114, 122; IV, 317)
stomach, 360, 361 (III, 127, 128)
see also Mesti
Amissio, 494, 495, 525, 527, 528, 529, 532,

Amisso (continued):
538, 539 (IV, 75, 77, 115-9 *passim*, 124, 134)
Enochian pyramids, 650 (IV, 300)
see also geomancy, figures
Amnitziel, 86, 305 (I, 174; III, 44)
Enochian letter, geomantic figure, Zodiac, 495 (IV, 77)
Amoun, 239, 265 (II, 231, 278)
Bornless Ritual, 445 (III, 264)
consecration of Jupiter talisman, 417-20 *passim*, 422 (III, 219-22 *passim*, 224, 228)
requiem ceremony, 448 (III, 269)
spiritual development ritual, 440 (III, 257)
Amoun Kneph, 375 (III, 151)
Amoun Temple, 624n
Anael, 172 (II, 104)
Anaeem, 672 (IV, 330)
analysis of keyword—*see* keyword analysis
analytical psychology, 92, 699 (I, 185)
see also Jung, Carl Gustav
anatomy, 5, 88 (I, 177)
Ancient of Days, 57, 77, 177, 235 (I, 114, 153; II, 114, 225)
Bornless Ritual, 445 (III, 264)
consecration of talisman, 413, 420 (III, 212, 224)
transformation ritual, 429 (III, 239)
Pillars, tops of, 392 (III, 179)
requiem ceremony, 449 (III, 270)
Andromeda, 589, 597, 599 (IV, 211, 223, 226)
constellation, 545, 595, 598 (IV, 146, 219, 225)
Chesed, 603 (IV, 231)
angel:
assumption of form, 381 (III, 160)
divination, 394 (III, 188)
see also HRU
Enochian calls, 626 (IV, 263)
head (as crest), 548, 551 (IV, 151, 155)
angel torch-bearer (angelic Kerux), 392, 438 (III, 179, 180, 254)
angelic choirs or hosts, 61, 64, 96-8 (I, 122, 126, 193-8)
altar diagram, The Serpent on the Tree of Life, 62, 162 (I, 123; II, 84)
"Angelic King Elemental Ruler," 475 (IV, 43-4)
Angelos Ton Theon, 444 (III, 263)
angels, 45, 67 (I, 89, 139)
angelic choir of Yesod, 98 (I, 197)
astral projection, 471, 472 (III, 36, 37)
elements, 80 (I, 158-9)
Enochian—*see* Enochian, angels
geomantic figures, 493 (IV, 75)
planets, 65 (I, 127)
Seven-Branched Candlestick, 150 (II, 62)
sigils, 483, 484 (IV, 58, 59)
Tattwa vision, 460, 465, 470, 476 (IV, 18, 25, 34, 45-6)
angels (continued):
telesmatic images, 490 (IV, 68)
true order of the Rose Cross, 231 (II, 218)
Zodiac, 85-6, 305 (I, 170-4; III, 44)
decanates, 85-6, 553-65 *passim* (I, 170-4; IV, 158-76 *passim*)
triplicities, 482 (III, 55, 56)
Angpoi, 672 (IV, 330)
Ani, 114
Aniel, 86, 559 (I, 174; IV, 168)
Anilr, 638 (IV, 280)
anima, xvii, 19, 35 (I, 25, 64)
animals, 109-10 (I, 222-5)
consciousness, 666 (IV, 320)
ankh, 274, 333, 354, 355, 356 (II, 295; III, 85, 117-20 *passim*)
Adeptus Minor ritual, 221, 224, 225, 233, 236, 239, 240, 245 (II, 200, 202, 204, 222, 225, 226, 227, 232, 241)
Vault consecration ceremony, 262, 263, 264 (II, 271-2, 273, 274, 276)
Anlala Lai, 444 (III, 263)
Anmehitt, 353 (III, 115)
Ano-Oobist, 341 (III, 99)
see also Anubis
Ano-Oobist Em-Pemen-Te (Ano-Oobi em-Pementte), 341, 352 (III, 98, 114)
Ano-Oobist Empe-Eeb-Te (Ano-oobist-em-Pe-eeb-tte), 341, 352 (III, 98, 114)
Anodoin, 325 (III, 73)
Anoubi—*see* Anubis
Anouke, 685 (IV, 350)
antelope, 549 (IV, 152)
anthropology, 22 (I, 31-3)
Antimony, Triumphal Chariot of (Basil Valentine), 1
Antlia Pneumatica, 599 (IV, 226)
Anubis, 57, 58, 157, 184 (I, 113, 115-6; II, 74, 127)
astral/cosmic Neophyte temple in Sphere of Sensation, 452, 453 (III, 273, 275)
description, 355, 356 (III, 118, 119)
Enochian pyramids, 663 (IV, 315)
skrying, 666 (IV, 319)
illustration, 665 (IV, 317)
Kerux, 341, 346, 347, 352, 355, 356, 369, 663 (III, 98, 108, 109, 114, 118, 119, 142; IV, 315)
The Moon, 185 (II, 130)
Sentinel, 334, 341, 352, 356, 363 (III, 88, 98, 114, 119, 131)
Anupassana, MaDhyan, x, xi, xxv
"The Basic Structure of the Grade Ceremonies," 137-40
"Introduction to the Elemental Grade Ceremonies," 135-7
"Introduction to the Neophyte Ceremony," 114-5
Anxpc, 638 (IV, 280)

Aoth, 444 (III, 262)
Aour, 614 (IV, 246)
  see also Ain Soph Aour
Aouvrrz, 672 (IV, 330)
Apana, 515 (IV, 97)
Apas, 457, 487, 514, 516-22 *passim* (IV, 12, 13, 63, 96, 99, 100, 101, 103, 105-8 *passim*)
  Apas of Akasa, 458, 516 (IV, 14, 99)
  Vam, 520 (IV, 105)
Apcnx, 638 (IV, 280)
ape:
  Ahepi, 344, 358, 361, 687 (III, 103, 122, 129; IV, 353)
  The Wheel of Fortune, 590 (IV, 213)
Ape, 443, 444 (III, 261, 263)
apes, 110 (223-4)
Aphnaio, 443 (III, 261)
Apida, 638 (IV, 280)
Apis, 361 (III, 129)
  Enochian pyramids, 663 (IV, 315)
  illustration, 665 (IV, 317)
  Kerub of North, 663 (IV, 315)
Apocalypse of St. John:
  Bride of the, 159 (II, 79)
  Holy City, 150 (II, 61)
  Kerubim, 207 (II, 173)
  River of the, 74, 177 (I, 145; II, 115)
  Seven Churches in Asia (Assiah), 159 (II, 79)
    Seven-Branched Candlestick, 150 (II, 62)
  Thrones of the Elders, 225, 242 (II, 203, 273)
  Woman of the, 73, 177 (I, 144; II, 114)
    The Moon, 185 (II, 130)
  see also Revelation, The
Apophis, 12-3, 357 (III, 121)
  see also keyword analysis; Set; Typhon
Apophrassz (Apophra-i-Ssz), 344, 353 (III, 103, 115)
Apostles, 150 (II, 61)
Apparatus Sculptoris, 599 (IV, 226)
Apponyi, Count, 17 (I, 19-20)
Apus, 600 (IV, 228)
Aquarius:
  Air sign rather than Water, 188, 283, 343 (II, 135; III, 14, 101-2)
  alchemy, 397 (III, 187)
  Circular Altar, 259 (II, 266)
    see also altar, Circular Altar; man (kerub)
  divine and angelic names, 86 (I, 174)
  divine name, Hebrew letter, Tribe of Israel, angel, and color, 305 (III, 44)
  Enochian:
    chess, 690, 694 (IV, 357, 365)
    pyramids, 648 (IV, 294)
  Kerub of Air, 343 (III, 101-2)
    see also Kerubim; man (Kerub)
  Lotus Wand, 302, 305, 315 (III, 39, 40, 44, 60)
Aquarius (continued):
  Phritithi, 343, 353 (III, 102, 115)
  star map, 595 (IV, 219)
  symbol, 50, 61, 156, 157, 283, 326-7, 403, 420, 429 (I, 99, 120; II, 72, 75; III, 14, 76, 196, 224, 239, 240)
    hexagram rituals, 296 (III, 31)
  Tarot:
    King (Prince) of Cups, 598 (IV, 225)
    Knight (King) of Cups, 546 (IV, 148)
    Queen of Pentacles, 598 (IV, 224)
    The Star, 71, 73, 188, 542, 591, 592, 599 (I, 139, 143; II, 135; IV, 141, 214, 215, 226)
    Swords:
      Ace, 607, 610 (IV, 237, 240)
      Five, Six, & Seven, 541, 559 (IV, 140, 167-8)
      King (Prince), 549, 598 (IV, 151, 224)
  Tristitia, 650 (IV, 300)
  28th Path, 182, 188 (II, 123, 134)
  see also Paths; Zodiac
Aquila, 598 (IV, 224)
Ar, 443 (III, 260)
Ara, 599 (IV, 226)
Arabia, 231, 275 (II, 216, 296)
Arabic, 231, 650 (II, 217; IV, 297)
Aragogorobrao, 443 (III, 261)
Aral, 80, 172 (I, 159; II, 105)
  consecration of Fire Wand, 324 (III, 72)
Aralim, 62, 64, 97 (I, 123, 126, 194)
  invisibility ritual, 424, 428 (III, 230, 237)
  requiem ceremony, 447 (III, 266)
  sigil, 483, 484 (IV, 58, 59)
  spiritual development ritual, 436 (III, 250)
Ararita, 258, 287, 289, 290, 295, 296, 297, 299 (II, 265; III, 20, 22, 23, 30, 32, 33, 35)
  consecration:
    Rose-Cross, 315 (III, 61)
    Sword, 319 (III, 65)
    talisman, 413 (III, 212)
  invisibility ritual, 423 (III, 230)
  planets, letters assigned to, 289-92, 299 (III, 22-5, 35)
Arbiz, 407, 409, 410 (III, 204, 207, 208)
archangels, xxiii, 40, 45, 207n (I, 76, 89)
  angelic choir of Hod, 98 (I, 196)
  cardinal points and elements, 54, 80 (I, 107, 158-9)
    Table of Shewbread diagram, 150 (II, 61)
  Enochian, 325-7 (III, 74-7)
  pentagram rituals, 54, 286 (I, 107; III, 19)
  Sephiroth, 61, 64, 96-98 (I, 122, 126, 193-8)
    altar diagram, The Serpent on the Tree of Life, 62, 162 (I, 123; II, 84)
  sigils, 483, 484 (IV, 58, 59)
  skrying, 468, 469, 473 (III, 31, 33, 40)
  spiritual development ritual, 440 (III, 256)

Archangels (continued):
Tattwa vision, 460, 461, 476 (IV, 18, 19, 45)
true order of the Rose Cross, 231 (II, 218)
Zodiac, 85-86 (I, 170-4)
geomantic figures, 495 (IV, 77)
arch fairies, 548 (IV, 151)
arch-fays, 109, 548 (I, 223; IV, 151)
archons, 548 (IV, 151)
Ardza, 637 (IV, 279)
Aretz, 80 (I, 158)
evocation, 408 (III, 206)
Pyramid of the Elements, 187 (II, 143)
Zelator grade, 151, 152 (II, 64, 65)
see also Earth
Argo, 599, 600, 601 (IV, 226, 227, 228)
see also Pyxis Nautica
Argus, 478 (IV, 49)
Ariel, 80 (I, 158)
consecration of Dagger, 324 (III, 72)
Aries:
alchemy, 395 (III, 185)
crook, 242 (II, 237)
divine and angelic names, 86 (I, 171)
divine name, Hebrew letter, Tribe of Israel, angel, and color, 304, 305 (III, 43, 44)
Enochian chess boards, 694 (IV, 365)
first point of, 594, 609 (IV, 218, 241)
Hori (Coptic letter), 345 (III, 105)
Mars, 495, 642 (IV, 77, 286)
pentagram, 283 (III, 15)
Rose-Cross lamen, 311 (III, 53)
star map, 595 (IV, 219)
symbol used in spelling divine names, 83 (I, 166)
Tarot:
The Emperor, 71, 72, 542, 575, 589, 599 (I, 139, 141; IV, 140, 191, 211, 226)
King (Prince) of Pentacles, 550, 598 (IV, 153, 225)
Knave (Princess) of Pentacles, 597 (IV, 223)
Wands:
Queen, 545, 598 (IV, 147, 225)
Two, 541, 550, 561 (IV, 140, 156, 170)
Three and Four, 541, 561 (IV, 140, 171)
see also Zodiac
Aries Press, ix, x
Arik Anpin, 77 (I, 153)
Arinnap, 325 (III, 73)
Arizona:
Flagstaff, xxiv
Sedona, xxii
Ark of the Covenant, 161 (II, 83)
see also Kerubim, on Ark of the Convenant
Armozel, 207n
ARN, 673, 680 (IV, 332, 343)
Arnil, 638 (IV, 280)
Aroo-ouerist, 344, 352 (III, 104m 114)
Aroueris, 343, 344, 352, 355, 366, 368, 473 (III, 101, 104, 114, 116, 117, 136, 139, 260)
Ahephi, 692 (IV, 361, 362)
description, 354 (III, 117)
Enochian:
chess bishop, 686, 687, 691 (IV, 351-2, 360)
pyramids, 663 (IV, 315)
Hierophant, 344, 354, 366, 663 (III, 104, 117, 136; IV, 315)
illustration, 664 (IV, 316)
Past Hierophant, 344, 352, 354 (III, 104, 114, 116)
see also Horus
Arrow, Path of the, 95, 591 (I, 191; IV, 214)
Art of True Healing, The (Israel Regardie) 3, 41, 92 (I, 80, 185)
Aryan languages, 628 (IV, 267)
Arzl, 638 (IV, 279)
Asava, 638 (IV, 280)
Ascendant—*see* astrology, geomancy, Ascendant
Asch, 80, 172 (I, 159; II, 103)
Philosophus grade, 195 (II, 149)
Pyramid of the Elements, 187 (II, 143)
Ashad Tree, 57 (I, 113)
Ashim (Aschim), 62, 64, 98 (I, 123, 126, 196)
evocation ritual, 405, 407 (III, 200, 204)
Malkuth of Yetzirah, 614 (IV, 246)
Ashkenazic, 52n (I, 104n)
Ashur, 152 (II, 65)
Asmodel, 86, 305 (I, 171; III, 44)
Enochian letter, geomantic figure, Zodiac, 495 (IV, 77)
aspects—*see* astrology, aspects
Aspirant:
Adeptus Minor ritual, 225-40 *passim*, 246, 247 (II, 199-211 *passim*, 219-31 *passim*, 238, 239, 240, 244)
Neophyte ritual—*see* candidate
Assalonai, 443 (III, 261)
Assessors—*see* Forty-two Judges of the Dead
Asshur, 305 (III, 44)
Assiah, 11, 63, 73, 596 (I, 125, 144; IV, 221)
Enochian:
chess, 696 (IV, 368)
tablets, 673 (IV, 332)
Heavens of, 63 (I, 125)
human being microcosm of macrocosm of Assiah, 106 (I, 215)
Kether of, 358, 362, 476, 614, 615, 617, 618, 619, 621 (III, 124, 130; IV, 46, 247, 248, 249, 252, 253, 254, 256, 257)
Malkuth of Assiah:
Cholem Yesodoth, 614 (IV, 247)
Neophyte temple, 331 (III, 82)

Assiah (continued):
  Malkuth of Assiah (continued):
    Outer Order rituals, 115, 205 (II, 168-9)
  Pillars, bases of, 392 (III, 179)
  Seven Palaces, 82, 103, 159 (I, 164, 209; II, 79)
    Seven-Branched Candlestick, 150 (II, 62)
  Seven Churches, 159 (II, 79)
    Seven-Branched Candlestick, 150 (II, 62)
  sigils, 483, 484, 485 (IV, 58, 59, 60)
  Supernals in, 100 (I, 203)
  telesmatic images, 488, 489, 490 (IV, 64, 65, 67)
Associate Adept—*see* Adept, Associate
Associate Adeptus Minor—*see* Adept, Third
Assyria, 315 (III, 60)
Astral Fire, 70, 171 (I, 137; II, 103)
  Anael, 172 (II, 104)
  Axiokersa, 170 (II, 100)
astral form or body:
  consecration of talisman, 420 (III, 224)
  invisibility ritual, 388, 425 (III, 172, 232, 233)
  transformation ritual, 389 (III, 175)
astral image, 463 (IV, 26)
Astral Light, xxiii, 55, 162, 340 (I, 109; II, 84; III, 97)
  Anael, 172 (II, 104)
  consecration of talisman, 414, 422 (III, 213, 227)
  invisibility ritual, 387, 426, 427 (III, 172, 234, 236)
  The Magician, 588 (IV, 210)
  Tattwa vision, 457 (IV, 12)
  transformation ritual, 430, 431 (III, 240, 241, 242)
Astral Plane, xxi, 67, 155, 159, 468 (I, 130; II, 71, 79; IV, 32)
  The Chariot, 590 (IV, 212)
  Enochian, 626 (IV, 263)
    skrying, 667 (IV, 332)
  Tattwa vision, 460, 462 (IV, 18, 21)
  32nd Path, 209 (II, 177)
  Yesod, 20 (I, 27)
astral performance of rituals:
  grade rituals, 463-4 (IV, 23)
  Lesser Banishing Ritual of the Pentagram, 54-55 (I, 108-9)
  Ritual of the Rose-Cross, 308-9 (III, 50)
astral projection, 9, 108, 463-5, 467, 468, 470-4 (I, 220-21; IV, 23-5, 29, 30, 31-32, 34, 35-49)
  Adeptus Minor Obligation, 229-30 (II, 214)
  protection, 465-6 (IV, 27)
  return, 473, 474 (IV, 39, 42)
  spiritual development ritual, 391, 392, 477, 478, 479 (III, 178, 179, 180, 252, 253, 255, 256)
astral projection (continued):
  testing, 463, 465 (IV, 23, 26)
    see also skrying; Tattwa vision
Astral Projection, Magic and Alchemy (Francis King), 199n
astral travel—*see* astral projection
astral vision—*see* skrying; Tattwa vision
astrology, 5, 10, 12, 41, 43, 87, 91, 603, 607, 697
  (I, 78, 83, 175, 182-3; IV, 236)
  aspects:
    geomancy, 538, 539 (IV, 133, 134, 135)
    polygons, 507, 510 (IV, 91, 93, 94)
  charts for time of working:
    consecration of Lotus Wand, 303, 304 (III, 41, 43)
    consecration of Sword, 317 (III, 63)
    hexagrams, 293 (III, 28)
    pentagrams, 283-4 (III, 15)
  Collecting Intelligence, 175 (II, 110)
  dignities, 537 (IV, 132)
  geomancy:
  Ascendent, 530-9 *passim* (IV, 121, 123-35 *passim*)
  houses, 529-39 (IV, 120-35)
  planets, symbols, 83 (I, 165)
  Sphere of Sensation and natal horoscope, 100 (I, 204)
  Tarot:
    attributions, 541-2 (IV, 139-41)
    divination:
      Ascendant, 573, 574 (IV, 188, 189, 190)
      houses, 573, 575 (IV, 188, 189, 191)
  Tattwas, 515 (IV, 96)
  see also Zodiac
Astrology (Louis MacNiece), 10
Astrology of Personality (Dane Rudhyar), 5
Atapa, 475 (IV, 44)
athanor, 36, 84, 151, 236, 399, 448
  (I, 67, 167; II, 64, 227; III, 191, 268)
Atheleberseth, 443 (III, 260)
Athor, 151, 187, 489 (II, 64, 133; IV, 66)
  Enochian pyramids, 663 (IV, 315)
  illustration, 664 (IV, 316)
  Kerub of East, 663 (IV, 315)
  Tarot:
    The Star, 188 (II, 135)
    The Universe, 592 (IV, 216)
  see also Hathor
Athorebalo, 443 (III, 262)
Atlantis:
  language, 628, 629 (IV, 266, 267)
  magic, 626 (IV, 262-3)
Atlas, 163 (II, 86)
Ator, 592 (IV, 216)
Atous—*see* Tarot, trumps
Atziluth, 63 (I, 125)
  Aeons, 375 (III, 150)
  Kether, 617 (IV, 251)

Atziluth (continued):
Kether of, 375 (III, 151)
Eheieh, 614 (IV, 246)
King scale of color, 95 (I, 192)
Malkuth of, Adonai Melekh, 614 (IV, 246)
sigils, 483, 484 (IV, 58, 59)
Tattwa vision, 476 (IV, 45)
telesmatic images, 488 (IV, 64, 65)
Yechidah, 105-6 (I, 214-5)
Aub, 172 (II, 103)
Aud, 172 (II, 103)
Augoeides, 32, 42, 426 (I, 58, 80; III, 235)
Aum, 68 (I, 133)
Auphanim, 62, 64, 96 (I, 123, 126, 194)
consecration of talisman, 419 (III, 222)
Aur, 172 (II, 103)
aura, 92, 308, 481, 697 (I, 184-5; III, 49; IV, 55)
control of, 87, 88-90 (I, 175, 177-80)
Neophyte temple in, 451-4 (III, 271-6)
Tattwa vision, 459 (IV, 16)
Tree of Life in, 3, 87, 90-1 (I, 175, 180-2)
vibration of divine names, 492 (IV, 71)
see also Middle Pillar ritual; Sphere of Sensation
Aura-Mo-Ooth (Aur-a-mo-oth, Auramooth, Auramo-ooth), 341, 352, 424, 425 (III, 99, 114, 230, 233)
description, 355 (III, 118)
Auriel, 80, 143, 204, 656 (I, 158; II, 47, 167; IV, 306)
consecration of Pentacle, 324 (III, 72)
consecration of talisman, 422 (III, 227)
evocation ritual, 404, 405, 407, 408, 410 (III, 198, 199, 201, 204, 206, 208)
Lesser Banishing Ritual of the Pentagram, 54, 444 (I, 107; III, 262)
Tattwa vision, 459 (IV, 16-7)
Auriga, 598 (IV, 225)
Aurim, 341 (III, 99)
Australia, xxii, 609 (IV, 241)
aborigines, 22 (I, 31)
Austria, 626 (IV, 262)
automatic consciousness—*see* Yesod, in microcosm
Avamel, 86, 558 (I, 173; IV, 165)
Avasa, 638 (IV, 280)
Ave, 148, 156, 164, 167, 178, 182, 194 (II, 56, 72, 87, 94, 116, 124, 148)
Avenger of the Gods—*see* Hiereus
Averse Sephiroth, 177, 193 (II, 114, 146)
drawing of Typhon, 211 (I, 180)
Avtotar, 325, 636 (III, 73; IV, 277)
"Awakening the Abodes," 692 (IV, 362)
Axieros, 174 (II, 107, 108)
Fire triangle, apex, 169 (II, 97)
Judgment, 172 (II, 104)
speech, 169-70 (II, 97-99)
Axiokersa, 169, 174 (II, 97, 104)
Axiokersa (continued):
Fire triangle, left basal angle, 170 (II, 99)
Judgment, 172 (II, 104)
speech, 170-1 (II, 100-1)
Axiokersos, 174 (II, 108)
Fire triangle, right basal angle, 170 (II, 100)
Judgment, 172 (II, 104)
speech, 170 (II, 99-100)
Axir, evocation of, 402-12 (III, 195-211)
Axpcn, 638 (IV, 280)
Ayin:
Capricorn, 305 (III, 44)
26th Path (Capricorn, The Devil):
Earth, 209, 210n (II, 177)
Hiereus's lamen, 214, 337 (II, 185; III, 93)
Philosophus ritual, 188 (II, 137)
Portal ritual, 198, 200, 209, 212-3 (II, 155, 158, 177, 182-4)
Practicus ritual, 176, 179 (II, 112, 117)
Temperance, 217-8 (II, 192)
see also Capricorn; Devil; Hebrew alphabet; Paths
Ayoel, 86, 564 (I, 172; IV, 175)
Aziz (Azodizod), 668 (IV, 325)
Azoth, 77 (I, 153)

- B -

B Document, 42 (I, 81, 82)
see also "The Ritual of the Pentagram," 280-6 (III, 9-19)
Babel, 191 (II, 142)
Babylon, Waters of, 251 (II, 252)
badges—*see* admission badges; lamens; sash
Bai, 56 (I, 111)
Balbnabaoth, 443 (III, 261)
Baleeo, 207n
balneum arenae, 84, 397 (I, 167; III, 188)
balneum mariae, 84, 396, 397, 399 (I, 167; III, 185, 186, 188, 191)
Banaa, 326, 650 (III, 74; IV, 297)
Banishing Ritual of the Pentagram—*see* Lesser Banishing Ritual of the Pentagram
banishing rituals never used in Vault, 270 (II, 287)
Banner of the East, 11, 46, plate f. 118, 334, 336-7 (I, frontis., 90; III, 88, 91-2)
Bornless Ritual, 442 (III, 259, 260)
consecration of talisman, 414, 419 (III, 213, 223)
invisibility ritual, 428 (III, 237)
Neophyte ritual, 116, 119, 120, 125, 127, 131, 132, 368 (II, 11, 16, 17, 27, 32, 40, 41; III, 139)
Philosophus ritual, 181, 186, 189, 192 (II, 121-2, 131, 137, 144)
Portal ritual, 198, 208, 218 (II, 155, 175, 194)

Banner of the East (continued):
Portal ritual (continued):
symbolism explained, 219 (II, 195)
Practicus ritual, 166, 173, 176 (II, 92, 106, 112)
skrying, 465 (IV, 26-7)
Theoricus ritual, 154, 157, 159, 161 (II, 69, 70, 74, 78, 82)
transformation ritual, 430 (III, 240)
Zelator ritual, 141 (II, 48)
Banner of the West, 46, plate f. 118, 337, 338 (I, frontis., 90; III, 92, 93-4)
Bornless Ritual, 442 (III, 259)
Neophyte ritual, 116, 119, 120, 125, 126, 368 (II, 11, 16, 17, 28, 30; III, 139)
Philosophus ritual, 181, 186, 188-9, 192 (II, 121-2, 131, 137, 144)
Portal ritual, 198, 202, 203, 204, 208 (II, 155, 164, 165, 166, 175)
Practicus ritual, 166, 173, 176 (II, 92, 106, 112)
skrying, 465 (IV, 26, 27)
Theoricus ritual, 154, 157, 158, 159, 161 (II, 69, 70, 75-78 *passim*, 82)
Zelator ritual, 141, 147, 148 (II, 44, 56, 58)
Banners of:
the East, 156, 164, 420, 429, 430 (II, 72, 87; III, 225, 240, 241)
the North, 143, 148, 422 (II, 48, 56; III, 227)
the South, 182, 194, 421 (II, 124, 148; III, 226)
the West, 167-8, 178, 421 (II, 94, 116; III, 226)
baptism:
Temple, 346 (III, 107)
Waters of, 591 (IV, 215)
barbarous names of evocation, 171, 377, 629 (II, 102; III, 153; IV, 268)
Barchiel, 86, 305 (I, 173; III, 44)
Enochian letter, geomantic figure, Zodiac, 495 (IV, 77)
Bardon, Franz, 699
Barraio, 443 (III, 262)
Barrett, Francis, *The Magus,* 9
Bartzabel, 65 (I, 127)
Enochian letters, geomantic figures, Zodiac, 495 (IV, 77)
geomancy, 524, 526 (IV, 113, 114)
sigil, 499, 526 (IV, 82, 114)
Basum, 444 (III, 262)
Bataivah, 156, 205, 207n, 325, 420, 430, 636 (II, 72, 170; III, 73, 225, 240; IV, 276-7)
skrying, 667 (IV, 321)
Bdopa, 326, 650 (II, 74); IV, 297)
beasts—*see* animals
Beauty—*see* Tiphareth
Before the Face of the Gods in the Place of the Threshold, 339, 355 (III, 96, 118)
behaviorism, xviii
Beigia, 207n
belts: Knaves (Princesses) of Tarot, 546, 547 (IV, 147, 150)
benediction, sign of, 372 (III, 147)
Beni Elohim, 62, 64, 98 (I, 123, 126, 196)
Beni Seraphim, sigil, 500 (IV, 84)
Benjamin, 305 (III, 44)
Bennett, Arnold, 16 (I, 18)
Berridge, Edmund William, 624n
Bessz, 344, 353 (III, 103, 115)
Beth:
Enochian:
pronunciation, 650 (IV, 297)
skrying, 667 (IV, 321)
imagination, 474 (IV, 41)
The Magician, 588 (IV, 210)
see also Hebrew alphabet
Bible, 31, 33 (I, 54, 59)
New Testament, 83 (I, 165-6)
see also Apocalypse; Chronicles; Daniel; Deuteronomy; Ezekiel; Exodus; Genesis; Habakkuk; Job; John; Judges; Kings; Matthew; Psalms; Revelation
Binah, 19, 21, 33-4, 61, 96-7 (I, 24, 25, 30, 60, 121, 194, 195)
Aima, 77-8, 331, 510 (I, 154-5; III, 82, 93)
Alverda, Hugo, 275 (II, 296)
Bornless Ritual, 443 (III, 261)
Briah, 617 (IV, 251)
caduceus, 162, 340 (II, 84; III, 97)
celestial sphere, 596, 603 (IV, 221, 231-2)
Daath, 179 (II, 117)
divine name, archangel, and angelic choir, 62, 64, 96-7 (I, 123, 126, 194)
Heh, 331, 615 (III, 82; IV, 249)
Hiereus's badge, 213 (II, 184)
invisibility ritual, 389, 423, 424, 428 (III, 174, 175, 230, 237)
Malkuth, throne of, 615, 617 (IV, 248, 251)
microcosm, 100-4 *passim* (I, 203-12 *passim*)
right side of brain or head, 100 (I, 203)
Moon, 643 (IV, 288)
Neschamah, 67 (I, 129)
Neophyte ritual, 367 (III, 137)
Neophyte temple, 331 (III, 82)
scourge, 242 (II, 237)
sigils, 483, 484 (IV, 58, 59)
spiritual development ritual, 438 (III, 253)
Tarot:
divination, 580 (IV, 198)
High Priestess, 643, 693 (IV, 288, 363)
Judgment, 172 (II, 104)
Knaves (Princesses), 617 (IV, 251)
The Magician, 588 (IV, 210)
Queens, 615 (IV, 249)
The Star, 188 (II, 135)
Temperance, 217 (II, 192)
Threes, 78, 552 (I, 156; IV, 156)

Binah (continued):
Tarot (threes) (continued):
Cups, 564 (IV, 175)
Pentacles, 558 (IV, 167)
Swords, 555 (IV, 162)
Wands, 561 (IV, 171)
Thmae-oe-Tt, 375 (III, 151)
transformation ritual, 391 (III, 177)
triangle, 505, 506 (IV, 89)
see also Sephiroth; Tree of Life
birds, 109 (I, 222)
bishop, Enochian chess—*see* Enochian, chess, pieces
Bitom:
Enochian call (sixth), 672, 676 (IV, 329, 330, 337)
pronunciation, 650 (IV, 297, 300)
skrying, 669 (IV, 325)
see also Exarp, Hcoma, Nanta, Bitom; key-word analysis; Opening by Watchtower
black:
altar, 333 (III, 86)
Malkuth, 614, 616, 617 (IV, 247, 250, 251)
station of Hiereus, 337 (III, 92)
Pentacle, 322 (III, 69)
Black Dragon, 60, 61, 151 (I, 120, 121; II, 64)
Black Jehovah, 199n
black magic, xvii
Black Pillar—*see* Pillars
black robe—*see* Robe of Mourning
Blackden, Marcus Worsley:
M.W.T. = Ma Wahanu Thesi, 56 (I, 111-2)
Blackwood, Algernon, ix
blasphemy, 76 (I, 149)
Blasted Tower—*see* Tower, The
Blatha, 443 (III, 260)
Blavatsky, H. P., xix, 33, 34, 272, 273, 274 (I, 59, 61; II, 290, 292, 293, 294)
Catechism of the Inner Schools, 274 (II, 294)
The Secret Doctrine, 32, 272, 273, 274, 596 (I, 57; II, 290-1, 292-3, 294; IV, 220)
The Stanzas of Dzyan, 272 (II, 192)
Blended Pleasure, The Lord of—*see* Fours (Tarot), Cups
blindfold—*see* hoodwink
blood:
Osiris, 334, 439, 441 (III, 87, 255, 258)
Spirit, 101 (I, 205)
Blood of the Lamb, 274 (II, 295)
Blood of the Lion, 217 (II, 192)
blue shoes—*see* shoes, blue
Boaz, 81 (I, 161-2)
Bodhisatva Sila Sutra, 27 (I, 45)
body and spirit, 616-7 (IV, 249-51)
Body of Light, 41, 464 (I, 79; IV, 25)
Bohemia, 626 (IV, 262)
Bohr, Niels, xviii, 700
Bolbeo, Bolbeoch, and Bolbesto, 207n
Bon spirits, 376n
Book H, 232 (II, 219)
Book M, 231 (II, 217, 218)
Book of the Coming Forth by Day—see Book of the Dead, Egyptian
"Book of the Concourse of the Forces, The," 625, 630-96 (IV, 261, 274-368)
"Binding together the Powers of the Squares in the Terrestrial Quadrangles of Enoch," 655-7 (IV, 304-6)
Book of the Dead:
Egyptian, 55-9, 114-5, 128 (I, 110-7; II, 34)
Adeptus Minor ritual, 239 (II, 231)
Bornless Ritual, 445 (III, 264)
spiritual development ritual, 440 (III, 257)
requiem ceremony, 449 (III, 269)
Ursa Major, 597 (IV, 222-3)
Vault consecration ceremony, 264-5 (II, 277-8)
Tibetan, 21 (I, 29)
Book of Enoch, 207n
Book of the Law, 698, 699
"Book of the Path of the Chameleon," 2, 95-9 (I, 191-202)
see also Hodos Chamelionis; Minutum Mundum; Path of the Chameleon
Book of Shadows, 698
Book T, 15, 233, 237, 264, 540, 565, 574, 596, 607, 618, 673 (I, 14; II, 222, 228, 276; IV, 137, 176, 190, 221, 236, 253, 332)
"Book 'T'—The Tarot," 540-65 (IV, 137-76)
Bootes, 596, 597, 598 (IV, 219, 222, 223, 224)
Chesed and Chokmah, 603 (IV, 231)
Bornless Ones of Time, 330, 375 (III, 81, 151)
Bornless Ritual, 377, 442-6 (III, 153, 259-65)
quoted in consecration of talisman, 418 (III, 220)
bow, 591 (IV, 214)
see also Qesheth
bowels:
Ahephi, 360 (III, 127)
Bpsac, 326 (III, 74-5)
Bradford, U.K., 18 (I, 22)
Brap, 655 (IV, 303)
brass:
alchemy, 60 (I, 119)
Image of the Vision of Nebuchadnezzar, 206 (II, 171)
serpent, 83 (I, 166)
bread and salt:
altar (Earth), 334 (III, 87)
Equinox ceremony, 249, 250 (II, 247, 249, 250)
evocation, 409 (III, 207)
requiem ceremony, 448 (III, 268)

bread and salt (continued):
evocation, 409 (III, 207)
requiem ceremony, 448 (III, 268)
skrying, 468, 668 (IV, 31, 323)
spiritual development ritual, 439, 441 (III, 255, 258)
breath, 345, 346-7, 360, 361 (III, 105-6, 108-9, 127, 129)
Coptic letter Hori, 345 (III, 105)
letter H, 118 (II, 14)
Nature's Finer Forces, or the Science of Breath (Rama Prasad), 514 (IV, 95)
breathing, 88, 90, 309, 515-6, 519-22 *passim* (I, 178-9; III, 50; IV, 98-9, 103-8 *passim*)
see also Moon Breath; pranayama; Sun Breath
Brenner, Charles, *An Elementary Textbook of Psychoanalysis,* 5
Briah, 63 (I, 124)
Chiah and Neschamah of microcosm, 105 (I, 214)
Chokmah and Binah, 617 (IV, 251)
Enochian chess, 695, 696 (IV, 367, 368)
Kether of, Metatron, 374, 614 (III, 150; IV, 246)
see also archangels; Metatron
Malkuth of, 614 (IV, 246)
Queen scale of color, 95 (I, 192)
sigils, 483, 484 (IV, 58, 59)
Tattwa vision, 476 (IV, 45)
telesmatic images, 488, 489 (IV, 64, 65, 67)
Bride, 60, 72, 77 (I, 120, 141, 155)
see also Kalah
Bride of the Apocalypse, 159 (II, 79)
Bringer Forth of Life, The—*see* Temperance
British Museum, 44, 496, 625, 629, 658 (I, 85: IV, 79, 262, 268, 309)
Brodie-Innes, John William, (Sub Spe), 377, 514, 624n, 698 (III, 153; IV, 95, 96)
"The Canopic Gods," 358-62 (III, 124-30)
Enochian, 627-8 (IV, 265-6)
Pathworking, 463-4 (IV, 23)
"Practical Z. Preparation for Divination," 451-4 (III, 271-6)
The Brotherhood of the Rosy Cross (A. E. Waite), 18 (I, 22)
Bry, Franciscus de—*see* de Bry, Franciscus
Buddha, 26 (I, 41)
Buddhism, Tibetan, 21, 376n (I, 29)
Budge, E. Wallis, *The Gods of the Egyptians,* 356 (III, 119)
Builders of the Adytum, xix
bull:
kerub, 46, 61, 158, 343, 357 (I, 90, 120; II, 77; III, 101, 102, 122)
King (Prince) of Pentacles, 550, 551 (IV, 153, 155)
Mor, 653 (IV, 300)
Taurus, 63 (I, 124)
bull (continued):
see also Kerubim; ox; Taurus
Bulwer-Lytton, *Zanoni,* 517 (IV, 100)
buskins: Tarot court cards, 545, 546, 547 (IV, 146-50 *passim*)
butterfly wings: figures on King (Prince) of Swords, 548 (IV, 151)
Bziza, 325 (III, 74)

- C -

C Document, 42 (I, 82)
see "The Ritual of the Hexagram," 287-99 (III, 20-36)
C.B., Frater, 232 (II, 218)
cabala—*see* Qabalah
Cabalpt, 407, 409, 410, 672 (III, 204, 207, 208; IV, 330)
caduceus, 68, 139, 155, 161, 162, 176, 177, 340, 478 (I, 131; II, 70, 82-3, 83-4, 112, 113; III, 97; IV, 50)
illustrations, 68, 351 (I, 131; III, 113)
see also lamen, Kerux
Caelum Sculptoris (Caelum; "Coelum Sculptori"), 600, 601 (IV, 228, 229)
California:
Los Angeles, xix, xxi, xxv, 2
San Francisco, xix
Studio City, xx
Call of the Thirty Aethers—*see* Enochian, calls
Calvary cross—*see* cross, Calvary
Cambriel, 86, 305 (I, 174; III, 44)
Enochian letter, geomantic figure, Zodiac, 495 (IV, 77)
Camelopardalis (Camelopardus), 597, 598 (IV, 222, 223, 225)
Binah, 603 (IV, 232)
Cancellarius:
Frater P.D., 232 (II, 218)
function and duties, 252-3, 332 (II, 254; III, 84)
mantle and lamen, 332 (III, 84)
Neophyte ritual, 116-7, 132, 331-2 (II, 11-2, 42; III, 82-4)
sceptre, 332 (III, 84)
illustration, 348 (III, 110)
Thoth, 342, 352, 354, 356 (III, 101, 114, 116, 120)
Cancer, 175-6 (II, 111)
divine and angelic names, 86 (I, 172)
divine name, Hebrew letter, Tribe of Israel, angel, and color, 305 (III, 44)
Enochian:
chess boards, 694 (IV, 365, 366)
letters and geomantic figures, 495 (IV, 77)
pyramids, 649, 650 (IV, 296, 297)
Leo, 601 (IV, 229)
Moon, 495 (IV, 77)
scourge, 242 (II, 237)

Cancer (continued):
star map, 595 (IV, 219)
Tarot:
The Chariot, 71, 72, 542, 574, 600 (I, 139, 142; IV, 141, 184, 227)
Cups:
Queen, 547, 599 (IV, 149, 225)
Two, Three, and Four, 541, 563-4 (IV, 140, 175-6)
King (Prince) of Wands, 546, 597 (IV, 147, 223)
Knave (Princess) of Wands, 597 (IV, 222)
The Lovers, 600 (IV, 227)
The Moon, 185 (II, 130)
see also Zodiac
candidate:
Enochian tablets, 627 (IV, 264)
Neophyte formula:
evocation, 380 (III, 159)
invisibility ritual, 388 (III, 173)
requiem ceremony, 449 (III, 269)
spiritual development ritual, 391 (III, 178)
transformation, 390, 431, 433 (III, 176, 242, 244)
Neophyte ritual, 121-9 *passim*, 363-70 *passim*, 379-80, 697 (II, 19-36 *passim*; III, 131-42 *passim*, 157-8)
astral appearance, 364-5, 368 (III, 134, 139)
probable behavior, 365 (III, 134)
"The Symbolism of the Admission of the Candidate," 363-75 (III, 131-51)
Enochian system, 624 (IV, 260)
see also Kasmillos; Neophyte
candle:
Adeptus Minor ritual, 221 (II, 200)
Portal ritual, 199-203 *passim* (II, 157-64 *passim*)
skrying (Enochian), 668 (IV, 323)
Candlestick, Seven-Branched, 150-1 (II, 62-3)
Canes Venatici, 596, 597 (IV, 222, 223, 224)
Canis Major, 600, 601 (IV, 227, 228)
Canis Minor, 595, 600 (IV, 220, 227)
"Canopic Gods, The," 358-62 (III, 124-30)
see also Horus, children of
Canopic jars, 360, 362 (II, 127-8, 129)
Canopus, 360 (III, 127)
Canticles, Queen of the, 159 (II, 79)
Capella, 598 (IV, 225)
Caph—*see* Kaph
Capricorn (Capricornus), 62 (I, 124)
alchemy, 397 (III, 187)
crook, 242 (II, 237)
divine and angelic names, 86 (I, 174)
divine name, Hebrew letter, Tribe of Israel, angel, and color, 305 (III, 44)
Enochian:
chess:
boards, 694 (IV, 365)
divination, 694 (IV, 364)
Capricorn (continued):
Enochian (continued):
letter and geomantic figure, 495 (IV, 77)
Saturn, 495 (IV, 77)
star map, 595 (IV, 219, 220)
Tarot:
The Devil, 71, 73, 212, 542, 599 (I, 139, 143; II, 182; IV, 141, 226)
King (Prince) of Swords, 549, 598 (IV, 151, 224)
Pentacles:
Queen, 549, 598 (IV, 153, 224)
Two, Three, and Four, 541, 558 (IV, 140, 165-7)
26th Path, 214 (II, 186)
Yod of Earth, 694 (IV, 364-5)
see also Zodiac; Paths
Caput Draconis, 51, 524, 526, 537 (I, 100; IV, 112, 114, 132)
alchemy, 396, 397 (III, 187, 188)
geomantic figure, 494, 495, 527, 529, 535-6 (IV, 75, 77, 115, 119, 130)
hexagram, 288, 293 (III, 26, 28)
Tarot divination, 568 (IV, 181)
see also geomancy, figures
Caput Mortuum, 399 (III, 192)
see also Dead Head
Carcer, 495, 527, 528, 529, 535, 538 (IV, 77, 115, 118, 119, 129, 134)
Enochian chess divination, 694 (IV, 364)
see also geomancy, figures
cardinal points, xxiii, 80 (I, 158-9)
consecration of talismans, 482 (IV, 56)
Coptic names, 353 (III, 115)
Equinox ceremony, 248, 374 (II, 246; III, 149)
evocation ritual, 402 (III, 195)
hexagram rituals, 294-8 (III, 29-34)
Kerubim, 343 (III, 101)
Neophyte ritual, 346 (III, 107)
see also Neophyte ritual
pentagram rituals, 53-4, 283, 285-6 (I, 106-7; III, 14, 18-19)
temple, 333-4 (III, 85-7)
The Universe, 592 (IV, 216)
see also East; elements; North; South; West
cardinal signs—*see* Zodiac
Case, Paul Foster, xix
The True and Invisible Rosicrucian Order, xxv
Cassiel, 65 (I, 127)
Cassiopeia, 597, 598 (IV, 222, 223, 225)
castle, Enochian chess—*see* Enochian, chess, pieces
Castor and Pollux, 548, 598, 599, 600 (IV, 150, 225, 227)
Catechism of the Inner Schools, 274 (II, 294)

Cauda Draconis, 51, 524, 526, 537 (I, 100; IV, 112, 114, 132)
  alchemy, 396, 397 (III, 186, 188)
  geomantic figure, 494, 495, 527, 536, 537, 539 (IV, 75, 77, 115, 130, 133, 135)
  hexagram, 288, 293 (III, 26, 28)
  Tarot divination, 568 (IV, 181)
  see also geomancy, figures
cauldron, in spiritual development ritual, 439 (III, 255)
Cedars of Lebanon, 191, 418 (II, 140; III, 220)
celestial longitude, 594, 596 (IV, 218, 221)
censer:
  Dadouches, 341 (III, 99)
    Equinox ceremony, 249 (II, 247)
    transmits Fires of Netzach to Malkuth, 341 (III, 99)
  evocation, 403, 409 (III, 197, 207)
  transformation ritual, 429 (III, 240)
centaur, 214 (II, 186)
Centaurus, 595, 599, 600 (IV, 220, 226, 227)
Centrum in Trigono Centri (Adrian a Meynsicht), 477, 478 (IV, 48, 49)
Centuries of Meditation (Thomas Traherne), 25 (I, 39-40)
Ceph, 495 (IV, 77)
  see also Enochian, letters
Cepheus, 595, 596, 597 (IV, 219, 222, 223)
  Chokmah, 603 (IV, 231)
ceremonial magic, 377, 378 (III, 154, 155-6)
  Yod of Yeheshuah, 376 (III, 152)
  see also evocation
ceremonial method, 23, 27-39, 277 (I, 34, 44-74; II, 300)
Ceremonial Magic (Israel Regardie), xviii
ceremonies—*see* rituals
"Ceremony of Advancement in the Path of TAU," 156-60 (II, 72-81)
Ceremony of the Equinox—*see* Equinox, Ceremony of the
Ceremony of Initiation, The (W. L. Wilmshurst), 9
Ceres, 172, 550 (II, 104; IV, 153)
Cerviel, 97 (I, 196)
Cetosa, 517 (IV, 100)
Cetus, 595, 599 (IV, 220, 226)
Chaamiah, 86, 559 (I, 174; IV, 168)
Chabooyah, 86, 564 (I, 172; IV, 175)
Chahaviah, 86, 557 (I, 173; IV, 164)
Chain of Humility:
  Adeptus Minor ritual, 221, 228, 231, 233, 236 (II, 200, 210, 216, 222, 225)
  Vault consecration ceremony, 258, 259, 263 (II, 264, 266, 267, 275)
Chaioth ha-Qadesh, 96, 621 (I, 193; IV, 257)
  Kether of Yetzirah, 614 (IV, 246)
  see also Chayoth ha-Qadesh
Chaldea, 231 (II, 216)
Chaldean Oracles, 31 (I, 53-4)
Chaldean Oracles (continued):
  consecration rituals:
    elemental weapons, 323, 328 (III, 70, 78)
    Lotus Wand, 303, 304 (III, 42, 45)
    Rose-Cross, 314, 316 (III, 57-8, 61)
    Sword, 318, 319 (III, 63, 65)
  Opening by Watchtower:
    evocation ritual, 402-3 (III, 195-6)
    spiritual development ritual, 435 (III, 248-9)
    Vault Consecration, 258-9 (II, 265-6)
  Portal ritual, 218 (II, 193-4)
  Practicus ritual, 33, 169-71, 174, 363 (I, 59: II, 97-103, 107-8; III, 131)
Chaldee, 51, 152 (I, 101; II, 65)
chakras, xxi, 378 (III, 155)
Chamaeleon (Chameleon), constellation, 600 (IV, 227, 228)
Chameleon, Path of the—*see* Hodos Chamelionis; Minitum Mundum; Path of the Chameleon
Chandra Nadi, 516 (IV, 98)
  see also Ida; Moon nerve
Chandra Swari, 516, 517, 519, 520 (IV, 98, 100, 103, 106)
Chanokh, 106-7 (I, 217)
  see also Enoch
Chariot, The, 590 (IV, 212)
  divination:
    example, 570, 571, 577, 588, 589 (IV, 184, 185, 194, 196, 197)
    meaning, 584 (IV, 205)
  Enochian pyramids, 649, 650 (IV, 296, 297)
  see also Tarot, trumps
chariots: Kings (Princes) of Tarot, 544, 545, 547, 548, 550, 686 (IV, 144, 145, 145, 149, 151, 153, 351)
Charles' Wain, 597 (IV, 222)
  see also Ursa Major
Chashmalim, 62, 64, 97 (I, 123, 126, 195)
consecration of Jupiter talisman, 414, 415, 417, 418 (III, 214, 216, 218, 221)
Chasmodai (Chashmodai):
  Enochian letters, geomantic figures, Zodiac, 495 (IV, 77)
  geomancy, 524, 526 (IV, 113, 114)
  sigil, 502, 526 (IV, 86, 114)
Chassan, 80, 324 (I, 158; III, 72)
Chaturanga, 687 (IV, 348)
Chayoth ha-Qadesh, 62, 64, 96 (I, 123, 126, 193)
Chemical Change, demonstration in Neophyte ritual, 117, 117n, 130, 341, 370, 380 (II, 11, 38; III, 99, 142, 158)
Chesed, 19, 21, 97, 98 (I, 26, 30, 194-5, 196)
  caduceus, 162, 340 (II, 84; III, 97)
  Calvary cross of six squares, 193 (II, 145)
  celestial sphere, 603 (IV, 232)
  Chief Adept in Adeptus Minor ritual, 221n

Chesed (continued):
consecration of Jupiter talisman, 414, 415, 417, 418, 419, 421, 422 (III, 213-6 *passim*, 218, 219, 221, 223, 225, 227, 228)
crook, 242 (II, 237)
divine name, archangel, and angelic choir, 62, 64, 97 (I, 123, 126, 194-5)
El (Al), 62, 64, 97, 487 (I, 123, 126, 194-5; IV, 64)
Enochian chess queen, 693 (IV, 363)
The Flaming Sword of the Kerubim, 145 (II, 52)
Geburah, 210 (II, 178)
reconciled with by serpent, 83 (I, 165)
Gihon, 73, 177 (I, 145; II, 114)
grip of Portal grade, 216 (II, 190)
Hegemon's lamen, 339 (III, 96)
Hegemon's sceptre, 339 (III, 95, 96)
Heta (Coptic letter), 345 (III, 105)
hexagram, 218, 293 (II, 195; III, 27)
Jupiter, 218 (II, 195)
balanced by Mars in Geburah, 215 (II, 187)
left arm of Adam, 74, 178 (I, 145; II, 115)
Lotus Wand, 474 (IV, 41)
microcosm, 100, 103 (I, 204, 209)
invisibility ritual, 424 (III, 231)
left arm, 100 (I, 204)
Nephesch, 103 (I, 209)
Paths:
19th Path, 214 (II, 186)
21st Path, 215 (II, 187)
29th Path, 185 (II, 129)
Praemonstrator, 204, 331, 332, 342 (II, 168; III, 82, 83, 101)
Sign of Silence, 371 (III, 146)
square, 505, 506 (IV, 89, 90)
step, 371 (III, 144)
Tarot:
The Empress, 643, 693 (IV, 288, 363)
Fours, 552 (IV, 156)
Cups, 564 (IV, 176)
Pentacles, 559 (IV, 167)
Swords, 555 (IV, 162)
Wands, 561 (IV, 171)
The Star, 188 (II, 135)
Temperance, 217, 218 (II, 192)
The Universe, 160 (II, 70)
The Wheel of Fortune, 590 (IV, 212)
Vault symbolism, 268 (II, 283)
Venus, 643 (IV, 288)
wand of Chief Adept, 224n
Water, 84, 215, 311 (I, 168; II, 187; III, 52)
see also Sephiroth
Chester Cathedral, Dean of, *Psycho-Synthesis*, 88 (I, 178)
Cheth:
Cancer, 305 (III, 44)
Enochian pyramids, 649, 650 (IV, 296, 297)
see also Hebrew alphabet
chi, 699
Chiah, 67, 105 (I, 129, 213-4)
Briah of microcosm, 105 (I, 214)
chess, 687, 688, 692, 693, 695 (IV, 353, 354, 362, 364, 366)
checkmate, 695 (IV, 367)
en passant, 688 (IV, 354)
Enochian or Rosicrucian—*see* Enochian, chess
history, 687 (IV, 348)
stalemate, 693 (IV, 364)
Chief Adept:
Adeptus Minor ritual, 221-5 *passim*, 236-43 *passim*, 246, 247, 267 (II, 198-205 *passim*, 226-38 *passim*, 240, 242, 243, 244, 283)
Adeptus Exemptus grade required for office, 221 (I, 198)
represents Chesed, 221n
robe, 221 (II, 198)
Winged-Sphere Wand, 221, 224, 233, 236, 340 (II, 198, 203, 222, 225, 226, 227; III, 97)
Equinox ceremony, 251-5 *passim* (II, 250-9 *passim*)
Portal ritual, 198-202 *passim*, 208, 209, 215-20 *passim* (II, 155-61 *passim*, 163, 164, 174, 175, 176, 187-97 *passim*)
garments and implements, 198 (II, 156)
sceptre, 198, 200, 201, 216, 217 (II, 155, 159, 160, 161, 188-91 *passim*)
Tiphareth and Spirit, 199n, 221n
Vault consecration ceremony, 258-65 *passim* (II, 264-79 *passim*)
Chief Among the Mighty—*see* Emperor, The
Chiefs, Secret—*see* Secret Chiefs
Chiefs, Three—*see* Three Chiefs
Child of the Forces of Time-*see* Devil, The, (Tarot)
Child of the Great Transformers, The—*see* Death (Tarot)
Child of the Power of the Waters—*see* Chariot, The
Child of the Sons of the Mighty—*see* Moon, The, (Tarot)
Children of Horus—*see* Horus, Children of
Children of the Voice Divine—*see* Lovers, The
child's head (as crest), 548, 551 (IV, 151, 155)
Chiron, 537n
chiropractic, xxi
Chokmah, 19, 21, 33-34, 96, 97 (I, 24, 25, 30, 60, 193-4)
Abba, 77-8, 331, 693, 695 (I, 154-5; III, 82; IV, 363, 367)
Bornless Ritual, 443 (III, 261)
Briah, 617 (IV, 251)
caduceus, 162, 340 (II, 84; III, 97)

Chokmah (continued):
celestial sphere, 603 (IV, 231)
Chiah, 67 (I, 129)
crook, 242 (II, 237)
cross in circle, 505 (IV, 89)
Daath, 179 (II, 117)
divine name, archangel, and angelic choir, 62, 64, 96 (I, 123, 126, 193-4)
Enochian chess knight, 693, 695 (IV, 363, 367)
Hegemon's sceptre, 339 (III, 95)
hexagram, 293 (III, 27)
Mazloth (Masloth), 63, 96 (I, 125, 194)
see also Chokmah, Zodiac, Sphere of the
Mercury, 643 (IV, 287)
microcosm, 100-4 *passim*, (I, 203-12 *passim*)
left side of brain or head, 100 (I, 203)
Neophyte ritual, 367 (III, 137)
Neophyte temple, 331 (III, 82)
no planet attributed, 268 (II, 286)
Tarot:
Knights (Kings), 615 (IV, 249)
Knaves (Princesses), 617 (IV, 251)
The Magician, 643 (IV, 287-8)
The Star, 188 (II, 135)
Temperance, 217 (II, 192)
Twos, 78-9, 550 (I, 156; IV, 156)
Cups, 564 (IV, 175)
Pentacles, 558 (IV, 166)
Swords, 555 (IV, 161)
Wands, 561 (IV, 171)
Thma-oe-Sh, 375 (III, 151)
Yod, 615, 693, 695 (IV, 249, 363, 367)
Zata, Elman, 275 (II, 296)
Zodiac, Sphere of the, 19, 63, 506 (I, 25, 125; IV, 89)
see also Chokmah, Masloth
see also Sephiroth
Cholem Yesodoth, 63n, 98 (I, 125, 198)
Malkuth of Assiah, 614 (IV, 247)
Christ, xxv, 36, 56, 80, 83, 150, 223, 229, 230, 236, 311, 359, 477, 478, 479 (I, 68, 111, 160, 166; II, 61, 201, 212, 216, 226; III, 53, 125; IV, 48, 50, 52)
see also Jesus
Christian sign of benediction, 372 (III, 147)
Chronicles, II, 3:17—81 (I, 162)
Churches, Seven—*see* Seven Churches in Asia
cipher manuscripts, 17, 18, 624n (I, 20, 22)
Circinus, 600 (IV, 227, 228)
circle:
Ace of Pentacles, 543 (IV, 143)
Ain, 204 (II, 168)
astrological symbols of planets, 83 (I, 165)
consecration of talisman, 416 (III, 217)
cross within, Chokmah, 505 (IV, 89)
Cup of Stolistes, 177, 340 (II, 113; III, 97)
circle (continued):
Enochian:
Fire sigil, 657, 658 (IV, 307-8, 309)
tablets, 233 (II, 223)
geomancy, 524, 525, 539 (IV, 113, 116, 136)
hexagram, 293 (III, 26)
Hiereus's lamen, 213 (II, 184)
Neophyte, 347 (III, 110)
pentagram, 282 (III, 12)
point within, Kether, 505 (IV, 89)
protective, 280, 282, 293, 294, 299, 698 (III, 10, 12, 26, 28, 36)
evocation, 377, 380, 381, 384, 402, 405, 406, 407, 409, 410, 411 (III, 154, 159, 161, 165, 195, 200, 201, 202, 204, 206, 207, 208, 210)
production of natural phenomena, 384, 385 (III, 166, 168)
square within, Chesed, 505 (IV, 89)
triangle within, Binah, 505 (IV, 89)
Vayu, 457 (IV, 12, 13)
Circular Altar—*see* altar
circulatory system, 359-61 (III, 125-8)
circumambulation, 28, 346-7, 378 (I, 46; III, 107-9, 155)
astral/cosmic Neophyte temple in Sphere of Sensation, 453 (III, 275)
Bornless Ritual, 442-5 *passim* (III, 259, 261, 262, 264, 266, 269)
consecration of talismans, 385, 387, 416, 417, 418, 420, 421, 422 (III, 167, 170, 217-21 *passim*, 224-7 *passim*)
Equinox ceremony, 249, 374 (II, 248; III, 149)
evocation, 381, 382, 383, 402, 403, 406, 407, 408, 410, 412 (III, 161, 162, 164, 195, 196, 197, 202-5 *passim*, 209, 211)
invisibility ritual, 388, 389, 423, 427, 428 (III, 173, 174, 229, 235, 237)
Opening by Watchtower, 259, 403 (II, 267; III, 197)
requiem ceremony, 447, 449 (III, 266, 269)
spiritual development ritual, 392, 393, 435-8 *passim*, 440, 441 (III, 178, 180, 181, 248, 249, 250, 252, 253-4, 257, 258)
transformation ritual, 390, 391, 429, 431, 432, 433 (III, 176, 177, 239, 243-6 *passim*)
see also Neophyte ritual
citrine, 98, 241, 310 (I, 197; II, 235; III, 52)
altar (East side), 333 (III, 86)
Malkuth, 345, 614, 616, 617 (III, 106; IV, 247, 250, 251)
pentacle, 322 (III, 69)
clairaudience, 472, 474 (IV, 37, 42)
clairvoyance, 9, 40, 41, 44, 109, 456-66, 468, 481 (I, 76, 78, 87, 221; IV, 11-28, 30, 54)
Adeptus Minor Obligation, 229 (II, 214)

clairvoyance (continued):
Tarot divination, 566, 579, 586-7 (IV, 178, 197, 208)
Clavicula Tabularum Enochi, 43-4, 657, 670 (I, 84, 85; IV, 306-7, 326)
clay, in Image of the Vision of Nebuchadnezzar, 206 (II, 171)
Clendenning, Logan, *The Human Body,* 5
cloaks, 117n
Cancellarius, 332 (III, 84)
Hegemon, 119, 338-9 (II, 15-6; III, 95)
Hiereus, 119, 337 (II, 16; III, 92-3)
Hierophant, 119, 250, 334, 335 (II, 16, 250; III, 88)
evocation, 380 (III, 159)
illustrations, 349 (III, 111)
Imperator, 331 (III, 83)
Past Hierophant, 332 (III, 85)
Praemonstrator, 332, (III, 83)
Closing of the Veil, 216-7, 223, 260 (II, 190, 200, 269)
closing pentagrams of Spirit—*see* Spirit, pentagrams, closing
clouds, Tarot:
court cards, Swords, 548, 549, 551 (IV, 150, 151, 152, 155)
numbered cards, 552, 553, 555, 557, 561 (IV, 158, 159, 161, 164, 171)
Coelum Sculptori—*see* Caelum Sculptoris
Coelum Terrae (Thomas Vaughan), 19 (I, 25)
Collecting Intelligence, 175 (II, 109-10)
collective unconscious, xviii, 20 (I, 28)
Collegium ad Spiritum Sanctum, 232 (II, 218, 219, 220)
see also Sanctus Spiritus
Collins, Mabel, *Light On The Path,* xx-xxi
colors and color scales, 95-99 (I, 191-202)
complimentary colors, 479 (IV, 51)
Columba, 600 (IV, 228)
Coma Berenices (Hair of Berenice), 597 (IV, 224)
Chesed, 603 (IV, 232)
Comananu—*see* Elexarpeh, Comananu, Tabitom
"Concerning the Use of the Vault," 270-1 (II, 287-9)
"Concerning the Microcosms of Macrocosm," 109-10 (I, 222-5)
confession of Hierophant, 255 (II, 260)
Conjunctio, 494, 495, 527, 528, 529, 535, 538 (IV, 75, 77, 115, 118, 118, 119, 129, 134)
Enochian pyramids, 655 (IV, 303)
see also geomancy, figures
conjunction, 539 (IV, 136)
see also astrology, aspects
consecration, 42 (I, 82)
body, 670 (IV, 327)
elemental weapons—*see* weapons, magical, elemental, consecration
consecration (continued):
Flashing Tablets, 481 (IV, 54, 55)
Lotus Wand, 303-5 (III, 41-5)
Rose-Cross lamen, 312-6 (III, 57-61)
Sword, 317-9 (III, 63-5)
talismans, 377, 378, 384-7, 465, 480, 481-2 (III, 154, 156, 166-71; IV, 27, 53, 55-6)
Heh of Yeheshuah, 376, 384 (III, 152, 166)
consecration and purification:
astral/cosmic Neophyte temple in Sphere of Sensation, 453 (III, 275)
Body of Light, 464 (IV, 25)
Bornless Ritual, 442 (III, 259)
consecration of talismans, 384, 385, 386, 387, 414, 416, 418 (III, 166, 167, 168, 170, 214, 217, 221)
evocation, 380, 381, 382, 383, 405, 408, 410, 412 (III, 159, 161, 162, 164, 201, 205, 209, 211)
by Fire and Water, 28 (I, 47)
invisibility ritual, 388, 423, 425 (III, 172, 229, 233)
skrying, 469 (IV, 32)
spiritual development ritual, 441 (III, 258)
temple, 377 (III, 154)
see also individual rituals
transformation ritual, 390, 431 (III, 175, 176, 242)
see also Neophyte ritual
Consecration Ceremony of the Vault of the Adepti, 258-65 (II, 264-78)
closing 265 (II, 278-9)
Opening by Watchtower, 258-9 (II, 264-7)
constellations, 451, 594-621, 689 (III, 271; IV, 218-57, 355)
Copenhagen Interpretation, 700
copper, alchemy, 60 (I, 119)
Coptic, 42, 345, 347 (I, 82; III, 105, 109)
names of Egyptian gods, 352-3, 661 (III, 114-5; IV, 312)
-*st* suffix, 337 (III, 92)
"Coptic Names of the Chiefs and Officers," 352-3 (III, 114-5)
Cor Leonis, 550, 594, 599 (IV, 156, 218, 225)
see also Regulus
cord (or rope), 28, 117, 121, 127, 363, 368-9, 380 (I, 46; II, 12, 19-20, 31; III, 132, 140, 158)
explained, 128 (II, 32-3)
consecration of talismans, 384, 386, 387, 414, 415, 417, 418 (III, 166, 169, 170, 214, 215, 218, 221)
evocation, 380-4 *passim*, 405, 409, 410 (III, 159, 161-5 *passim*, 200, 208, 209)
Corona Australis, 595, 599 (IV, 220, 226)
Corporeal Intelligence, 185 (II, 129)
Corpus Christi, 232, 258 (II, 219, 264)
corselets: court cards of Tarot, 545 (IV, 146)

Corvus, 599 (IV, 226)
Coster, Geraldine, *Psychoanlysis for Normal People,* 88 (I, 178)
court cards (Tarot)—*see* Tarot, court cards
Cpao, 667 (IV, 321)
crab, 546, 551 (IV, 148, 155)
Crater, 599 (IV, 225, 226)
crayfish:
  The Moon, 185, 591 (II, 130; IV, 215)
  Queen of Cups, 547, 551 (IV, 149, 155)
Creeping Formula, 617-8 (IV, 253)
crescent:
  Apas, 457, 469 (IV, 12, 13, 33)
    telesmatic images, 489 (IV, 67)
  astrological symbols of planets, 83 (I, 165)
  Cup of Stolistes, 177, 340 (II, 113; III, 97)
  Isis, Lunar crown, 159 (II, 79)
  Nephthys, headdress, 686 (IV, 351)
  Pisces, 185 (II, 130)
  telesmatic images, 486 (IV, 61, 62)
crests: court cards of Tarot, 545-50 *passim* (IV, 146-53 *passim*)
crocodile, 465 (IV, 26)
crocus, 320 (III, 68)
crook and scourge:
  Adeptus Minor ritual, 221, 233, 234, 236-7, 240, 242 (II, 200, 220, 221, 227, 228, 229, 232-3, 236-7)
  Osiris, 354, 686 (III, 117; IV, 351)
  Vault consecration ceremony, 258 (II, 264)
cross, 13, 39, 204-5, 508 (I, 74; II, 168; IV, 91)
  admission badges, 87, 88, 139 (I, 175, 176-7)
    see also admission badges
  Adeptus Minor ritual, 37-8, 221 (I, 70; II, 200)
  Banner of the West, 338 (III, 93)
  Calvary:
    Six squares, 79, 139, 193 (I, 157; II, 145)
      Banner of the East, 218, 465 (II, 195; IV, 27)
      Hegemon's lamen, 339 (III, 96)
      Hierophant's cloak, 335 (III, 88-9)
      Hierophant's lamen, 218 (II, 195)
      Tiphareth, 335, 336, 374, 602 (III, 88-9, 90, 91, 150; IV, 230)
    Ten squares, 79, 189, 190, 191, 656 (I, 156-7; II, 137-8, 140, 141-2; IV, 305)
      Sephirotic—*see* Enochian tablets, Sephirotic Calvary Crosses
    Twelve squares, 79, 183, 184, 185 (I, 156; II, 125, 126, 129)
    with triangle (Golden Dawn symbol), 28, 31, 333, 335 (I, 46, 54; III, 86, 88)
      alchemy, 398 (III, 190)
      astral/cosmic Neophyte temple in Sphere of Sensation, 451, 452 (III, 272, 273)
      astral projection, 466 (IV, 28)
cross (continued):
  Calvary (continued):
    with triangle (continued):
      Bornless Ritual, 442 (III, 259)
      Cancellarius, 332 (III, 84)
      consecration rituals:
        elemental weapons, 323 (III, 70)
        Lotus Wand, 303 (III, 41)
        Rose-Cross, 312, 314 (III, 57)
        Sword, 317 (III, 63)
      decanates of Zodiac, 601-2 (IV, 229-30)
      Imperator, 321 (III, 83)
      Neophyte ritual, 116-7, 366, 369, 370 (II, 11-2; III, 136, 141, 143)
        explained, 128 (II, 33-4)
      Philosophus ritual, 192, 184 (II, 144, 148)
      Practicus ritual, 178 (II, 117)
      Praemonstrator, 332 (III, 84)
      skrying, 468, 473 (IV, 31, 40)
      Theoricus ritual, 162 (II, 85)
      Zelator ritual, 147 (II, 56)
    vibratory formula, position of Adept, 345 (III, 106)
  circle, Chokmah, 505 (IV, 89)
  Cross of Obligation = Cross of Suffering, 228, 229, 231, 263, 276, 426 (II, 211, 212, 216, 274, 275, 299; III, 234)
    Hegemon's lamen, 339 (III, 96)
  crux ansata—*see* ankh
  cubical—*see* cross, Greek solid cubical
  elements, 208, 214, 280, 374 (II, 174, 186; III, 9, 149)
    see also various types of crosses
    see also elements
  Enochian:
    sigils, 657, 658 (IV, 307, 308)
    see also Enochian tablets
  five squares, 214 (II, 186)
  Fylfot, 68, 139, 142, 144, 148, 340 (I, 131; II, 45, 49, 57; III, 98)
  Great—*see* Enochian tablets, Great Cross
  Greek, 70, 173-4, 175, 208-9, 492 (I, 137; II, 106, 107, 109, 175; IV, 72)
    Ace of Pentacles, 543 (IV, 143)
    Hierophant's cloak, 335 (II, 89)
  Greek solid cubical, 70, 155-9 *passim* (I, 136-7; II, 70-8 *passim*)
  Hebrew letters, formed of, 492 (IV, 70-1)
  Hegemon's cloak, 338, 339 (III, 95)
  Hegemon's sceptre, 339 (III, 95)
  Hiereus's cloak, 337 (III, 92-3)
  Hierophant's cloak, 334-5 (III, 88-9)
  LVX formed by angles, 233 (II, 223)
  Maltese—*see* Maltese cross
  of Obligation, 222, 245 (II, 199, 241)
  planets, symbols, 83 (I, 165)
  Portal ritual, 198-201 *passim* (II, 155-61 *passim*)

cross (continued):
Portal ritual (continued):
neck of Philosophus, 203, 204, 208 (II, 166, 167, 173)
Rivers of Eden, 74, 76, 79, 177 (I, 145, 151, 156; II, 115)
Rose-Cross lamen, 310 (III, 51)
sash, 216 (II, 189)
illustration, 350 (III, 112)
Sephiroth, lineal figures, 493 (IV, 72)
Spirit, converted into pentagram by, 217 (II, 190)
Tarot:
Judgment, 172 (II, 104)
The Universe, 592 (IV, 216)
Tau—*see* Tau cross
Vault consecration ceremony, 258, 260 (II, 264, 265, 269)
of Victory, 245 (II, 241)
Wheels of Ezekiel's vision, 233 (II, 222)
see also qabalistic cross; Rose-Cross
crow, 84 (I, 167)
Crowley, Aleister, ix, xviii, xix, xxii, xxiv, 1, 9, 10-1, 624n, 682n, 683n, 697-700 *passim*
A.A., ix, 10, 32 (I, 56)
The Book of the Law, 698, 699
The Equinox, ix, 1, 7, 8, 682n
The Holy Books of Thelema, xxi
Magick in Theory and Practice, 464 (IV, 25)
O.T.O., 697
Thelema, 698, 699
Crown:
Egyptian:
Crown of the North, 355 (III, 118)
Crown of the South, 354, 355 (III, 116, 119)
Double Crown, 354, 355, 357 (III, 117, 121)
Lunar crown of Isis, 159 (II, 79)
Tarot:
Ace of Swords, 543 (IV, 143)
Tower, 192 (II, 142)
of twelve stars, 73 (I, 144)
see also Kether
crowns: court cards of Tarot, 545, 546, 547 (IV, 146-9 *passim*)
crucible, 151, 399 (II, 64; III, 191, 192)
crucifix, in Adeptus Minor ritual, 221, 228-9, 236 (II, 200, 212, 226)
Crux, 600 (IV, 227)
crux ansata—*see* ankh
cucurbite, 84 (I, 167)
cuirass: court cards of Tarot, 545, 546, 547 (IV, 146, 148, 149)
Cup, 334 (III, 87)
astral/cosmic Neophyte temple in Sphere of Sensation, 453 (III, 275)
Cup (continued):
consecration rituals:
Lotus Wand, 303 (III, 41)
Rose-Cross, 312 (III, 57)
Sword, 317, 318, 319 (III, 63, 65)
talismans, 413 (III, 213)
cross and triangle, 178 (II, 116)
Cup of Stolistes, 70-1, 176-7 (I, 137-8; II, 112-3)
Ace of Cups, 543 (IV, 143)
Equinox ceremony, 249 (II, 247)
illustrations, 71, 351 (I, 138; III, 113)
see also lamen, Stolistes
Cup of Tribulation (in Adeptus Minor ritual), 221, 228, 230, 233, 236 (II, 200, 211, 215, 222, 225)
elemental weapon (Water), 47, 320, 322 (I, 94; III, 68)
astral projection, 471 (IV, 36)
consecration, 323-5, 326, 327-8 (III, 70-4, 75, 77-8)
consecration of elemental weapons, 323 (III, 70)
Five of Cups, 556 (IV, 163)
Hod, 224n
illustration, 321 (III, 67)
Opening by Watchtower:
evocation ritual, 402 (III, 196)
spiritual development ritual, 435 (III, 248)
Vault consecration, 258 (II, 265-6)
skrying, 468, 469, 470, 473 (IV, 31-4 *passim*, 40)
spiritual development ritual, 435, 439, 441 (III, 248, 255, 258)
Tarot suit, 322 (III, 68)
Vault consecration, 258, 260 (II, 264, 265-6, 269)
Equinox ceremony, 249, 250 (II, 247-50 *passim*)
Neophyte ritual, 117, 121, 127, 132, 370 (II, 12, 19, 32, 41, 42, 43; III, 143)
Stolistes, 120, 121, 124, 125, 127 (II, 17, 20, 26, 31)
Philosophus ritual, 181, 184, 186, 187 (II, 121-2, 127, 128, 131, 132, 133)
Portal ritual, 198, 200, 207, 208, 218 (II, 156, 160, 173, 175, 193, 194)
Practicus ritual, 166, 167, 176 (II, 92-97 *passim*, 112)
production of natural phenomena, 384 (III, 166)
requiem ceremony, 448 (III, 267)
Tattwa vision, 476 (IV, 45)
Theoricus ritual, 154-60 *passim* (II, 69-80 *passim*)
see also weapons, magical, elemental
Waters of Hod transmitted to Malkuth by, 341 (III, 99)

Cups (Tarot suit)
court cards, 546-7 (IV, 148-50)
divinatory meaning, 582, 583 (IV, 201, 202-3)
Enochian chess, 685 (IV, 349)
numbered cards, 556-7, 560-1, 563-4 (IV, 162-4, 167-9, 175-6)
see also individual cards [e.g., Eights (Tarot), Cups]
see also Tarot
curcurbite, 395-9 *passim* (III, 184-91 *passim*)
Cushan, 191 (II, 141)
Cygnus, 595, 596-7, 598 (IV, 219, 222, 223, 224)
cynocpehalus, 590 (IV, 213)
Cyprus, 231 (II, 216)

- D -

D Document, 42 (I, 82)
see "The Lotus Wand," 300-5 (III, 37-44)
D., Frater, 232 (II, 219)
D.D.C.F. = Deo Duce Comite Ferro (MacGregor Mathers), 16-7, 45, 463, 464, 624, 625, 667, 690 (I, 19, 89; IV, 23, 24, 260, 261, 321, 359)
Daath, 33-34 (I, 59-62)
Chokmah and Binah, conjunction of, 179 (II, 117)
dragon, eighth head, 76 (I, 151)
Eden, rivers of, 73-4, 76, 177 (I, 144-5, 150; II, 114)
The Fall diagram, 193, 194 (II, 146-7)
The Flaming Sword of the Kerubim, 145 (II, 52)
hexagram, 218, 287 (II, 195; III, 21)
Hierophant's sceptre, 335 (III, 89)
Infernal Rivers, 239 (II, 229)
Mercury, on symbol of, 71, 179 (I, 138; II, 117)
microcosm, 102, 103, 105-6 (I, 208, 209, 210, 214)
neck, 392 (III, 179)
Saturn, 218 (II, 195)
Dabexnjemouv, 344, 352 (III, 103, 114)
see also Kabexnuv
Dadouches, 81, 340, 341, 342 (I, 161; III, 98, 99-100)
astral/cosmic Neophyte temple in Sphere of Sensation, 453 (III, 274)
duties, 341 (III, 99-100)
elemental grade ceremonies, 137
Equinox ceremony, 248, 249, 250, 256, 374 (II, 246, 247, 248, 250, 262-3; III, 149)
lamen, 340 (III, 98)
illustration, 351 (III, 113)
see also Fylfot cross
Dadouches (continued):
Neophyte ritual, 116-22 *passim*, 124, 125, 127, 131, 132, 364, 367, 368, 369 (II, 11, 12, 14-5, 17, 20, 21, 22, 25, 26, 27, 31, 40, 42; III, 133, 137, 139, 140-1)
explains duties, 118-9 (II, 14)
station, 129, 341 (II, 35; III, 99)
Kerub of Fire, 343, 357 (III, 101, 102, 121)
Mystic Reverse Circumambulation begins at, 346 (III, 107)
Thaum-aesch-niaeth, 341, 352, 355 (III, 99, 114, 119)
woman, office more natural for, 341 (III, 100)
Zelator grade required for, 137, 342 (III, 100)
Zelator ritual, 141, 142, 143, 145, 148, 149, 152 (II, 44-48 *passim*, 51, 58, 59, 67)
daemonology, 697
Dagger:
Dagger of Penance (in Adeptus Minor ritual), 221, 228, 230, 233, 236, 240 (II, 200, 211, 215, 222, 225, 226, 233)
elemental weapon (Air), 47, 322 (I, 94; III, 68-9)
consecration, 323-5, 326-7 (III, 70-4, 76, 77-8)
illustration, 321 (III, 67)
Opening by Watchtower:
evocation ritual, 402, 403 (III, 196)
spiritual development ritual, 435 (III, 248, 249)
Vault consecration, 259 (III, 266)
transformation ritual, 429 (III, 240)
Two of Swords, 555 (IV, 161)
Vault consecration, 258, 259, 260 (II, 264, 266, 269)
Yesod, 224n
Lesser Banishing Ritual of the Pentagram, 53 (I, 106)
see also weapons, magical, elemental
Daleth, 275-6 (II, 297)
The Empress, 589 (IV, 211)
pleasure, 474 (IV, 41)
Rose-Cross lamen, 311 (III, 53)
telesmatic image, 489, 491, 492 (IV, 66, 67, 69, 71)
see also Hebrew alphabet
Damascus, 14, 231 (I, 13; II, 216)
Dambayah, 86, 563 (I, 171; IV, 174)
Damcar (Damkar), 231, 274 (II, 217, 295)
Dan, 305 (III, 44)
Daniel, 247, 265 (II, 244, 279)
2:31-38—206 (II, 171)
Darius, 247, 265 (II, 243, 279)
Dark Night of the Soul, 33 (I, 60)
Darom (South), 80, 324 (I, 159; III, 71)

Darting Formula, 619-20 (IV, 254-5)
Data of the History of the Rosicrucians (William Wynn Westcott), 16 (I, 16-7)
Daughter of the Firmament—*see* Star, The
Daughter of the Flaming Sword—*see* Strength
Daughter of the Lord of Truth—*see* Justice
Daughter of the Mighty Ones—*see* Empress, The
Daughter of the Reconcilers—*see* Temperance
Daughters, Four—*see* Four Daughters
Daveithe, 207n
Davidson, Harriet Miller, "The Tarot Trumps," 588-93 (IV, 209-17)
Da Vinci, Leonardo, xxii
Dead Head, 397, 398, 399 (III, 189, 190, 191)
  see also Caput Mortuum; residuum
Dean of Chester Cathedral—*see* Chester Cathedral, Dean of
death, 111 (I, 227)
Death (Tarot), 95, 198, 210-11, 212, 214, 218, 590-1 (I, 191; II, 155, 178-80, 181, 186, 193; IV, 213)
  divination:
    example, 577, 578, 586 (IV, 194, 196, 207)
    meaning, 585 (IV, 205)
  see also Tarot, trumps
de Abano, Pietro, *Heptameron,* 497 (IV, 80)
de Bry, Franciscus, 237, 273 (II, 228, 292)
  Mercury, Kether, 275 (II, 296)
decanates of Zodiac, 149 (II, 60)
  angels, 85-86 (I, 170-74)
  Enochian:
    chess, 685 (IV, 350)
    tablets, 642-3 (IV, 285-7)
      pyramids, 648 (IV, 293, 294)
  Tarot, 541, 550, 564-5, 600 (IV, 139-40, 156, 176, 227)
    divination, 567, 576 (IV, 178, 193)
    The Sun, 175 (II, 110)
  triangles, 601-2 (IV, 229-30)
  see also Zodiac
Dee, John, 207n, 210n, 625-6, 628, 629, 658 (IV, 262-3, 267, 268, 309)
  Spirits and Apparations, 630n
  see also Enochian
Defeat, The Lord of—*see* Fives (Tarot), Swords
Dei Intacta Gloria, 235 (II, 224)
deity names—*see* divine names
Dekad, dekagon, dekangle, 510, 511 (IV, 93)
dekagram, 510, 512 (IV, 93)
Delphinus, 598 (IV, 224)
de Lubicz, R. A. Schwaller, 700
demonology, 697n
demons, 419 (III, 221)
  The Devil (Tarot), 212-3 (II, 182-3)
  dog-faced, 171, 363 (II, 102; III, 131)
  see also Qlippoth
Denderah, Zodiac of, 597 (IV, 222)
Deneyal, 86, 561 (I, 171; IV, 171)
Denmark, 275 (II, 296)
Denning, Melita, and Osborne Phillips, *Mysteria Magica,* 682n
Despair and Cruelty, The Lord of—*see* Nines (Tarot), Swords
detriment—*see* astrology, dignities
deuces—*see* Twos
Deuternomy 27—510 (IV, 94)
Devachan, 273, 274 (II, 292, 294)
Devadatta, 515 (IV, 97)
Devil, The, (Tarot), 95, 198, 212-3, 214, 218, 591 (I, 191; II, 155, 182-3, 184, 186, 193; IV, 214)
  divinatory meaning, 585 (IV, 205)
  see also Tarot, trumps
Dhananjaya, 515 (IV, 97)
Dharma, xxi
Dharmakaya, 21 (I, 29)
diagrams:
  Seven-Branched Candlestick, 150-1 (II, 62-3)
  The Table of Shew Bread, 67, 148, 149-50 (I, 130; II, 58, 60-1)
  see also altar diagrams
Dial, Dialis, 628 (IV, 266)
Diana, 549 (IV, 152)
diary, magical, x, xix-xx, xxiii
Diathana Thorun, 444 (III, 263)
dice in Enochian chess, 692-3 (IV, 363-3)
dignities—*see* astrology, dignities
Diom, 670 (IV, 326)
Dionysius, 588 (IV, 210)
Dioscuri, 548 (IV, 150)
Direct or Creeping Formula, 617-8 (IV, 253)
distillation, distillate, 395-9 *passim* (III, 184, 186, 188-91 *passim*)
Dittany of Crete, 402 (III, 195)
divination, 5, 9, 39, 40, 41, 87, 91 (I, 75, 76-7, 82, 175, 182-3)
  Adeptus Minor Obligation, 229 (II, 214)
  Enochian chess, 685, 689, 692, 693-4, 696 (IV, 349, 355, 362, 364, 368)
  geomancy, 524-39 (IV, 112-36)
  Neophyte formula, 377, 393-5 (III, 153, 182-4)
  "Practical Z. Preparation for Divination," 451-4 (III, 271-6)
  Tarot, 566-87 (IV, 177-208)
  Vau of Yeheshuah, 376, 393 (III, 152, 182)
  see also astrology; geomancy; Tarot
divine consciousness—*see* Yechidah
divine names, 45, 61, 64, 90, 96-8 (I, 89, 122, 126, 180-1, 193-8)
  Adeptus Minor Obligation, 230 (II, 215)
  altar diagram, The Serpent on the Tree of Life, 62, 162 (I, 123; II, 84)
  astral projection, 466, 471 (IV, 27, 36)
  consecration of talismans, 386, 387, 482

divine names (continued):
consecration of talismans (continued): (III, 169, 170-71; IV, 56)
elements, 80 (I, 158-9)
evocation, 383, 402 (III, 164, 195)
hexagram rituals, 293, 299 (III, 27, 35)
invisibility ritual, 389 (III, 174)
protection, 377 (III, 154)
sigils, 483, 484, 485 (IV, 58, 59, 60)
Supreme Invoking Ritual of the Pentagram in consecration of elemental weapons, 327-8 (III, 77)
skrying, 464, 469, 497 (IV, 24, 33, 80)
Tattwa vision, 458-61 *passim*, 463 (IV, 14, 16-9 *passim*, 22, 23)
telesmatic images, 487-8 (IV, 64, 65)
transformation ritual, 390 (III, 176)
vibration, 345-6, 378, 487, 491 (III, 106-7, 156; IV, 62-3, 70)
see also Enochian tablets, Three Great Secret Holy Names of God
Djin (King of Fire), 80 (I, 159)
Dmal, 207n
Dodekad, 510 (IV, 94)
dodekagon, 510 (IV, 94)
dodekangle, 506, 510, 513 (IV, 89, 94)
dog:
The Fool, 588 (IV, 209)
Toumathph, 687 (IV, 353)
dog-faced demons—*see* demons, dog-faced
dogs: The Moon, 591 (IV, 215)
dolphin:
Great Hermetic Arcanum, 205 (II, 170)
Princess of Cups, 547, 551 (IV, 150, 155)
Two of Cups, 564 (IV, 175)
Dominion, The Lord of—*see* Twos (Tarot), Wands
Dominions or Dominations, 97 (I, 195)
Do, 444 (III, 263)
Don, 495, 548 (IV, 77, 294)
see also Enochian, letters
Doo, 443 (III, 261)
doors:
astral, 463 (IV, 22)
temple—*see* temple, door
Dorado, 600, 601 (IV, 228)
Double Crown of Egypt, 354, 355, 357 (III, 117, 121)
double letters—*see* Hebrew alphabet, double letters
dove, 591 (IV, 215)
Draco:
Binah, 603 (IV, 232)
Dragon or Serpent Formula, 617, 621 (IV, 253, 257)
Kether, 451, 596, 603, 607 (III, 271; IV, 221, 231, 236)
Tarot, 596-7 (IV, 222, 223)
Draco (Tarot) (continued):
Aces, 607, 609, 617 (IV, 236-7, 239, 251)
dragon, 202, 330, 419 (I, 164; III, 81, 223)
Black, 60, 61, 151 (I, 120, 121; II, 64)
Draco, 596 (IV, 221)
The Fall diagram, 76 193-4 (I, 150-1; II, 146)
Garden of Eden diagram, 33, 35, 73 (I, 59-60, 63, 144)
Great Hermetic Arcanum, 206 (II, 170)
Harpocrates, 372 (III, 146)
Red, 12, 37, 76, 177, 239 (I, 70, 150; II, 114, 229)
Vault symbolism, 243 (II, 238)
Stooping, 330, 344, 353 (III, 81, 103, 115)
Tarot:
Death, 211 (II, 179)
The Lovers, 589 (IV, 211)
Water-Dragon, 344 (III, 103)
see also serpent
Dragon or Serpent Formula, 617-21 (IV, 251-7)
drawings—*see* diagrams
dreams:
interpretation, xxv
remembering, 94 (I, 188-9)
Drowned Man—*see* Hanged Man, The
Drun, 495 (IV, 77)
see also Enochian, letters
drunkeness, 104-5 (211-3)
Duamutef, 358 (III, 123)
see also Toumathph
Dukes of Edom, 190, 199 (II, 139, 157, 158)
Teman, 191 (II, 140)
see also Edom
Dunne, John William, *An Experiment with Time,* 20 (I, 28)
Dweller Between the Waters—*see* Star, The
Dzyan, The Stanzas of, 272 (II, 192)

- E -

E Document, 43 (I, 83)
see "The Complete Symbol of the Rose Cross," 310-6 (III, 51-61)
E.H.N.B. (Exarp Hcoma Nanta Bitom), 671, 672, 674 (IV, 329, 330, 334)
eagle:
alchemy, 84, 283, 361 (I, 167; III, 14, 128)
Enochian pyramids, 654-5 (IV, 303)
skrying, 666, 667 (IV, 320, 321)
Gluten of, 217 (II, 192)
Kerub, 46, 61, 158, 343, 357 (I, 90, 120; II, 76-77; III, 101, 102, 121)
Circular Altar, 235, 243, 259 (II, 224, 240, 266)
see also altar, Circular Altar
see also Kerubim; Scorpio

eagle (continued):
King (Prince) of Cups, 547, 551 (IV, 149, 155)
Mph, 653 (IV, 300)
Scorpio, 268 (II, 284)
symbol, 61, 158, 167 (I, 120; II, 77, 94)
consecration of Jupiter talisman, 413, 421 (III, 212, 213, 226)
hexagram rituals, 296 (III, 31)
Opening by Watchtower:
evocation ritual, 402 (III, 196)
spiritual development ritual, 435 (III, 248)
pentagram rituals, 280, 283, 286 (III, 10, 14, 19)
consecration of Cup, 325 (III, 75)
Tarot:
Death, 211 (II, 180)
Temperance, 217 (II, 192)
Vault symbolism, 268 (II, 284)
Earned Success, The Lord of—*see* Sixes (Tarot), Swords
Earth (element), xxiii
of Air:
Knave (Princess) of Swords, 549 (IV, 152)
Rose-Cross lamen, 310 (III, 52)
alchemical operation, 398 (III, 190)
Ameshet, 687, 642 (IV, 353, 361)
bread and fish, 583 (IV, 217)
bread and salt, 334 (III, 87)
consecration of talisman, 422 (III, 227)
creeping things and insects, 109 (I, 222)
divine name, archangel, angel, ruler, king, etc., 80 (I, 158)
of Earth:
Knave (Princess) of Pentacles, 550 (IV, 154)
Malkuth, 614 (IV, 247)
Rose-Cross lamen, 310 (III, 52)
see also Earth, Enochian tablet, Earth angle
elemental prayer, 142-3, 406-7 (II, 46-8; III, 202-3)
Enochian chess:
boards, 694 (IV, 365)
castle, 691, 696 (IV, 360, 367-8)
Enochian tablets or Watchtowers:
Earth angle:
Air tablet, 666 (IV, 319)
call (eighth), 672, 677 (IV, 330, 338)
Enochian chess, 690 (IV, 357)
angels, 670 (IV, 327)
Enochian chess castle, 686 (IV, 352)
Fire tablet, 669 (IV, 325)
call (eighteenth), 672, 680 (IV, 330, 343)
Earth (continued):
Enochian Tablets or Watchtowers (continued):
Earth Angle (continued):
Water tablet, 645 (IV, 290)
call (eleventh), 672, 678 (IV, 330, 340)
Earth tablet:
Air angle, 327, 670 (III, 77; IV, 327)
call (thirteenth), 672, 679 (IV, 330, 341)
archangels of angles, 327 (III, 76-7)
calls, 672, 673, 676 (IV, 329, 330, 331, 336)
consecration of talisman, 422 (III, 227)
Earth angle, 405, 407, 409, 410, 649-50 (III, 199, 200, 203, 204, 206, 208, 209, 296)
call (fifth), 672 (IV, 329, 330)
evocation, 403, 404, 405, 407, 409, 410 (III, 196, 198, 199, 200, 203, 204, 206-9 *passim*)
Fire angle, 654-5 (IV, 303)
call (fifteenth), 672, 679 (IV, 330, 341)
chess divination, 694 (IV, 364)
Heh final, 639 (IV, 281)
illustration, 633 (IV, 272)
Opening by Watchtower:
evocation, 403 (III, 196)
spiritual development ritual, 436 (III, 249)
Vault consecration, 259 (II, 266)
Water angle, call (fourteenth), 672, 679 (IV, 330, 341)
Zelator ritual, 141, 143, 147-8, 163, 627, 628 (II, 44, 47, 56, 87; IV, 265, 266)
pyramids, 649, 654-5 (IV, 296, 303)
see also Enochian, tablets
evocation ritual, 405, 409 (III, 200, 207)
finger, ring, 100 (I, 204)
of Fire:
Knave (Princess) of Wands, 546 (IV, 148)
Rose-Cross lamen, 311 (III, 52)
Fire, produced by, 151 (II, 64)
geomancy, 539 (IV, 135-6)
Heh and elements, 644 (IV, 289)
see also YHVH, elements
hexagram, 294-5 (III, 29)
Hiereus in Portal ritual, 199n
human digestive organs, 101 (I, 206)
Kerub, 343, 357 (III, 102, 122)
see also bull; Kerubim; ox; Taurus
Lotus Wand, 300 (III, 37)
Malkuth, 20, 21, 29, 215 (I, 27, 30, 48; II, 187)
of Yetzirah, 617, 618 (IV, 253)
material basis, 384, 387 (III, 166, 171)

Earth (continued):
Moon, 648 (IV, 294)
Nephesch, 103 (I, 210)
Pan drawing, 213 (II, 184)
Pentacle—*see* Pentacle, elemental weapon (Earth)
pentagram, 282, 284, 286, 296 (III, 12, 13, 16, 19, 32)
astral projection, 471 (IV, 36)
Bornless Ritual, 443 (III, 262)
consecrations:
Pentacle, 327 (III, 77)
talisman, 422 (III, 227)
Rose-Cross, 315 (III, 60)
evocation, 403-4, 407 (III, 196, 198-9, 203)
geomancy, 524, 539 (IV, 113, 136)
Opening by Watchtower:
evocation, 403 (III, 196)
spiritual development ritual, 435-6 (III, 249)
Vault consecration, 259 (II, 266)
skrying, 470 (IV, 34)
Zelator ritual, 143, 153 (II, 47, 68)
pentagram, point of, 280, 281, 282 (III, 10, 11, 13)
Phrath, 73, 177 (I, 145; II, 114)
Pillars, bases of, 333 (III, 86)
prayer—*see* Earth, elemental prayer
Prithivi, 457, 459, 460 (IV, 12, 13, 16, 17)
Root of the Powers of—*see* Aces (Tarot), Pentacles
Rose-Cross lamen, 310-13 (III, 52, 55, 56)
alchemical principles and other elements in Earth, 310-11 (III, 52)
Earth arm of cross and colors, 310-11, 312 (III, 52, 55)
consecration, 315 (III, 60)
Saturn, 644 (IV, 289-90)
serpent, 520 (IV, 255)
signs (astrology), 50, 63 (I, 100, 124)
Supreme Invoking Ritual of the Pentagram, 469 (IV, 33)
symbol, 50, 283 (I, 99; III, 14)
Tarot:
The Devil, 213 (II, 183)
The Moon, 185 (II, 130)
Theoricus ritual, 158-9 (II, 77-8)
Theta (Coptic letter), 345 (III, 105)
Thm-a-Oe, 375 (III, 151)
Venus, 648 (IV, 294)
of Water:
Knave (Princess) of Cups, 547 (IV, 150)
Rose-Cross lamen, 311 (III, 52)
Tattwa, 469 (IV, 32)
see also Earth, Enochian tablets
Yod, 694 (IV, 364-5)
Zelator grade, 28-30, 147 (I, 48-51; II, 56)
see also elements

Earth (planet):
Enochian tablets, 656 (IV, 305)
Hierophant's lamen, 336 (III, 90)
North Pole of celestial sphere, 594, 596 (IV, 218, 221)
Tomb of Christian Rosenkreutz, 223 (II, 201)
Earth Fire Wand, 475 (IV, 43, 44)
Earthy Power, The Lord of—*see* Fours (Tarot), Pentacles
Earzl, 638 (IV, 280)
East, xxiii, 80 (I, 158)
alchemical operation, 395, 396, 397 (III, 185, 187, 188)
altar, citrine side, 333 (III, 86)
altar in Eastern part of Malkuth, 333 (III, 86)
Ameshet, 361 (III, 128)
Banner of the—*see* Banner of the East
Bornless Ritual, 442-5 *passim* (III, 259-63 *passim*, 265)
canopic jars, 360-1 (III, 128)
consecration of talismans, 382, 414, 415, 416, 418, 420 (III, 162, 163, 213, 215, 217, 218, 221, 224, 225)
divination, 394 (III, 182)
E-eebtt, 353 (III, 115)
evocation, 385, 386, 402, 403, 404, 406, 408, 410, 411 (III, 168, 169, 196, 197, 198, 202, 205, 206, 208, 209)
hexagram rituals, 294, 296, 299 (III, 29, 32, 34-5)
Hierophant's station—*see* Throne of the East
invisibility ritual, 388, 389, 423, 426, 427, 428 (III, 173, 174, 230, 234, 235, 237)
Neophyte temple, 331, 332, (III, 82, 85)
see also Neophyte ritual, cardinal points and other directions
pentagram rituals, 53-54, 285 (I, 106-7; III, 18)
Pillar, White, base, 333 (III, 86)
requiem ceremony, 447, 448, 449 (III, 266-70 *passim*)
rose on altar (Air), 333 (III, 86)
spiritual development ritual, 391, 392, 435-41 *passim* (III, 178, 179, 180, 248, 249, 252-8 *passim*)
Throne of the—*see* Throne of the East
transformation ritual, 390, 391, 429-33 *passim* (III, 176, 177, 239-42 *passim*, 244, 246)
Vault symbolism, 267 (II, 283)
see also cardinal points
Ebal, Mount, 202, 510 (II, 164; IV, 94)
Ebeu, 443 (III, 260)
Ecliptic, 92, 594, 596, 603, 607 (I, 184; IV, 218, 221, 232, 236)
Enochian tablets, 655 (IV, 304)

Ecliptic (continued):
Tarot 597-9 (IV, 223-5)
Eda, 444 (III, 263)
Edelperna (Edlprnaa), 182, (II, 124)
consecration of Fire Wand, 325 (III, 73)
consecration of talisman, 421 (III, 226)
skrying, 669 (IV, 325)
Eden—*see* Garden of Eden
Edfu, 597 (IV, 222)
Edinburgh, 18 (I, 22)
Edinger, E. F., *Ego and Archetype*, xvii-xviii, xxv
Edlprna, 297n
Edlprnaa—*see* Edelperna
Edom, 190-1, 193, 419 (II, 138-41, 146; III, 222)
Dukes, 76, 190, 199 (I, 151; II, 139, 157, 158)
Kings, 76, 190 (I, 151; II, 138-9)
The Tower, 192 (II, 142)
Waters of, 194 (II, 148)
Edu, 444 (III, 263)
E-eebtt, 353 (III, 115)
Eeezodahzod—*see* Izaz
egg:
black (Akasa), 443, 444, 445, 457, 462 (III, 263, 264, 265; IV, 12, 13, 22)
blue (or black), 424-7 *passim* (III, 231-6 *passim*)
philosophic, 84, 395, 398 (I, 167; III, 184, 185, 189)
ego, xvii, 20, 34 (I, 26, 61)
Ruach, 33 (I, 58)
Ego and Archetype (E. F. Edinger), xvii-xviii, xxv
Egypt, 231, 697, 700 (II, 216, 217)
Alexandria, 594 (IV, 219)
Denderah, 597 (IV, 222)
Edfu, 597 (IV, 222)
Egyptian Magic (Florence Farr), 202n
Nile, 57 (I, 114)
Sakara, 55 (I, 111)
serpents, on caduceus, 162, 340 (II, 84; III, 97)
serpents, on Winged-Sphere Wand, 224, 252 (II, 203, 272)
sphinx—*see* sphinx
Thebes, 55-6 (I, 111)
see also Book of the Dead, Egyptian
Egyptian:
gods and god-forms, 43, 114-5, 274, 371, 372, 373, 375 (I, 84; II, 295; III, 144, 146, 147, 148, 151)
astral/cosmic Neophyte temple in Sphere of Sensation, 453 (III, 274)
astral projection, 464, 465 (IV, 25, 26)
Bornless Ritual, 443, 444 (III, 260, 261, 262)
ceremonial magic, 378 (III, 155-6)
consecration of talisman, 417 (III, 219)
Egyptian (continued):
gods and god-forms (continued):
elements, 663 (IV, 315)
Enochian:
chess, 684, 685-6, 687 (IV, 347, 348, 350-1, 352, 353)
pyramids, 627, 659-66 (IV, 264, 311-7, 319)
illustrations, 664-5 (IV, 316-7)
making figures, 661-2 (IV, 313-4)
Neophyte ritual, 114-5, 342-4, 352-62 (III, 100-4, 114-30)
"The Egyptian God-Forms of the Neophyte Grade," 354-62 (III, 116-30)
transformation ritual (Isis), 429-34 (III, 239-47)
head-dress—*see* nemyss
hieroglyphics, 347 (III, 109)
language, 650 (IV, 297)
magic, 16 (I, 16)
mysteries, 374 (III, 150)
Eheieh, 62, 64, 96, 188 (I, 123, 126, 193; II, 135)
with active pentagrams of Spirit, 201, 315 (I, 160; III, 59)
Bornless Ritual, 444 (III, 262)
consecration of Rose-Cross, 315, 316 (III, 59, 61)
consecration of talisman, 413, 422 (III, 212, 228)
invisibility ritual, 423-7 *passim* (III, 229, 231, 233, 234, 235)
Kether of Atziluth, 614 (IV, 246)
pentagram rituals, 53, 281, 285 (I, 106; III, 11, 18)
Portal ritual, 223, 240 (II, 201, 233-4)
sound, 375 (III, 150)
spelled with symbols of Yetziratic attributions of letters, 83 (I, 166)
spiritual development ritual, 437, 439, 440 (III, 250, 252, 254, 255, 257)
Tattwa vision, 463 (IV, 22)
transformation ritual, 429 (III, 239)
Vault consecration ceremony, 261 (II, 270)
Yechidah, 105 (I, 214)
Eights (Tarot), 552 (IV, 157)
Cups, 560 (IV, 169)
divination example, 571, 572, 577, 578 (IV, 185, 186, 187, 184, 196)
divinatory meaning, 578, 582 (IV, 195, 202)
Pentacles, 553-4 (IV, 159-60)
divination example, 574, 575, 577, 579 (IV, 190, 191, 194, 197)
Swords, 563 (173-4)
divination example, 577-81 *passim* (IV, 194, 196, 197, 199)
Wands, 557 (IV, 164)
divination example, 577, 579 (IV, 194, 197)
see also Tarot, numbered cards

Einstein, Albert, xviii
El, 62, 64, 97 (I, 123, 126, 194-5)
consecration of Cup, 324 (III, 71, 72)
consecration of Rose-Cross, 315 (III, 60)
pentagram rituals, 281, 284, 286 (III, 10, 16, 19)
with hexagram of Jupiter, 289 (III, 22)
suffix, 486, 487, 660 (IV, 62, 64, 311)
Elarz, 638 (IV, 280)
Elders, Thrones of the, 225, 242 (II, 203, 273)
Eleleth, 207n
"Elemental Grade Ceremonies, Introduction to" (Anupassana), 135-40
elemental grades, 28-34, 36 (I, 47-63, 66)
Enochian tablets and points of pentagram, 210n
Malkuth of Assiah, 115, 205 (II, 168-9)
rituals, 114-86 (II, 11-152)
basic structure, 137-40
closing, 140
Enochian tablets, 627 (IV, 264)
initiation, 139
opening, 137-9
Tarot trumps, 593 (IV, 217)
signs—*see* signs
Elemental Kings—*see* Enochian tablets, Kings, Elemental Kings
elemental prayers, 140
Air, 164-5 (II, 89-90)
astral projection, 466 (IV, 28)
consecration of talismans, 482 (IV, 56)
all elemental spirits, 220 (II, 197)
Equinox ceremony, 249-50 (II, 248-9)
Earth, 142-3, 406-7 (II, 46-8; III, 202-3)
Fire, 196 (II, 151-2)
Water, 179-80 (II, 119-20)
elemental weapons—*see* weapons, magical
elementals, 30, 60-1, 67, 80, 109, 110, 159, 160, 336 (I, 52, 120, 130, 158-9, 223, 225; II, 79, 80-81; III, 90)
astral projection, 470, 471, 472 (IV, 34, 36, 37-8)
Christian Rosenkreutz, 231 (II, 217)
chiefs, 673 (IV, 332)
control of, 75-6 (I, 148-9)
Enochian, 626 (IV, 263)
skrying, 666, 667 (IV, 320, 321)
evocation, 376 (III, 152)
alchemy, 396, 397, 399 (III, 185-6, 187-8, 189)
talismans, 481 (IV, 54)
Tattwa vision, 460, 461 (IV, 18, 19)
telesmatic images, 488, 490 (IV, 64, 65, 68)
see also gnomes; salamanders; sylphs; undines
An Elementary Textbook of Psychoanalysis (Charles Brenner), 5
elements, xxv, 20, 30, 45, 61, 63, 151 (I, 26, 52, 89, 120, 125; II,64)
elements (continued):
active and passive, 281, 611 (III, 10; IV, 244)
Enochian chess, 690 (IV, 357)
Agrippa, "Of the Four Elements and Their Natural Qualities," 611-3 (IV, 242-6)
alchemical operation, 398, 399 (III, 189, 190)
altar, 333-4, 442, 451 (III, 87, 259, 273)
skrying, 468 (IV, 31)
ankh, 225, 262 (II, 205, 272)
Bornless Ritual, 442, 443 (III, 259, 260)
cardinal points, 283, 668 (III, 14; IV, 324)
color scales, 95 (I, 192)
consecration of talisman, 419 (III, 221)
cross, 75, 208, 214, 280, 335, 374 (I, 148; II, 174, 186; III, 9, 89, 149)
cubical cross, 159 (II, 78)
Cup of Stolistes, 71, 177 (I, 138; II, 113)
dekagram, 510, 512 (IV, 93)
Egyptian gods and sphinxes, 663 (IV, 315)
elemental grade rituals, named in, 137
elemental weapons, 320 (III, 66)
see also weapons, magical
enneagram, 511
Enochian system, 626 (IV, 263)
chess, 684, 685, 689, 692, 696 (IV, 348, 349, 355, 361, 368)
Heh and Earth, 644 (IV, 289)
tablets, 648, 649 (IV, 294-5)
Lesser Angles, 645, 648, 649 (IV, 290, 294-5)
Linea Spritus Sancti, 653 (IV, 300)
pyramids, 646, 648, 651, 653 (IV, 291, 293-4, 298, 301)
Tablet of Union, 645, 649 (IV, 290, 296)
see also Enochian tablets, elements and YHVH
Equinox ceremony, 248-50 (II, 246-9)
FIAT = Flatis Aqua Ignus Terra, 206-7 (II, 172)
fingers of hand, 100 (I, 204)
Fylfot cross, 68, 148, 340 (I, 131; II, 57; III, 98)
geomantic figures, 463, 524, 537 (IV, 22, 112, 132)
Greek cross, 70, 175 (I, 137; II, 109)
Hebrew names, divine names, archangels, angels, rulers, kings, etc., 80 (I, 158-9)
hexagrams, 294-6 (III, 28-31)
Horus, Children of, 343, 358 (III, 102, 124)
human body, 100-101, 151, 215, 359 (I, 204-5; II, 64, 188; III, 125)
I.N.R.I. attribution, 12
Kerubim, 160 (II, 80)
Lotus Wand to invoke or banish, 303 (III, 40)
Malkuth, 98, 506, 618 (I, 198; IV, 89, 253)

elements (continued):
Maltese cross, 204 (II, 168)
Mother letters, 311 (III, 53)
Mystical Repast, 132, 370 (II, 41; III, 143)
Neophyte temple, 346 (III, 107)
octagon, 508, 509 (IV, 92)
orders, 612-3 (IV, 244-5)
Pan drawing, 213 (II, 184)
pentagon, 506, 507 (IV, 90)
pentagram, 507 (IV, 90)
points, 36, 210n, 214, 220, 310 (I, 66; II, 186, 196; III, 51)
rituals, 280, 293, 668 (III, 9, 27; IV, 323)
Portal ritual, 200-1 (II, 159-60)
Pyramid of the Elements, 79, 187, 659 (I, 156; II, 134; IV, 310, 311)
see also Enochian tablets, pyramids
qualities, 50, 611-2 (I, 99; IV, 243-4)
Regimen of the Elements, 228 (II, 211)
requiem ceremony, 448 (III, 267)
Rose-Cross lamen, 310, 482 (II, 51, 52; IV, 57)
SALT = Subtilis Aqua Lux Terra, 206 (II, 172)
spiritual development ritual, 439, 441 (III, 255, 258)
square, 506 (IV, 90)
symbols and qualities, 50 (I, 99)
talismans, 419, 481-2 (III, 221; IV, 55-6)
Tarot:
Aces, 542 (IV, 142)
attributions, 71, 72-3 (I, 139, 141-3)
divination, 568 (IV, 180)
Knaves (Princesses), 607 (IV, 237)
suits, 607. 639 (IV, 237, 281)
trumps, 600 (IV, 227)
Judgment, 172 (II, 105)
The Sun, 175 (II, 110-111)
Temperance, 217 (II, 192)
The Universe, 592 (IV, 217)
Tattwas, 457, 463, 469 (IV, 12, 22, 33)
Tetragrammaton—*see* YHVH, elements
32nd Path, 155, 159 (II, 71, 79)
Tree of Life, 84 (I, 168-9)
Vault symbolism, 246, 268 (II, 240, 284, 285)
Winged-Sphere Wand, 224, 262 (II, 203, 272)
YHVH—*see* YHVH, elements
Zodiac, 607, 611 (IV, 237, 242)
see also Air; Earth; Fire; Spirit; Water; YHVH
Eleusinian mysteries, 128 (II, 34)
Eleusis, 231 (II, 216)
Elexarpeh, Comananu, Tabitom (Lexarph, Comanan, Tabitom), 425, 427, 444, 627 (III, 233, 236, 262; IV, 265)
Elixir of Life, 111, 273 (I, 227; II, 292)
elixirs, 670 (IV, 327)
Elman—*see* Zata, Elman
Eloah, 178, 191 (II, 115-6; 140)
Elohim, 155, 167, 177, 182, 202 (II, 71, 94, 114, 123, 164)
Abba and Aima, 77 (I, 153)
angelic choir, 62, 64, 97 (I, 123, 126, 196)
consecration:
Fire Wand, 324 (III, 71, 72)
Rose-Cross, 315, 316 (III, 60, 61)
talismans, 385, 413, 416, 419, 421 (III, 168, 212, 217, 222, 225)
Egyptian gods, 662 (IV, 314)
evocation, 382, 404, 407, 408 (III, 161, 198, 204, 205)
God, 73, 143 (I, 144; II, 47)
human Tetragrammaton, 103 (I, 210)
invisibility ritual, 425 (III, 232)
pentagram rituals, 281, 284, 285 (III, 10, 16, 18)
Seven-Branched Candlestick, 150 (II, 62)
sigil, 483 (IV, 58)
spelled with symbols of Yetziratic attributions of letters, 83 (I, 166)
transformation ritual, 429, 432 (III, 239, 244)
Elohim Gibor, 62, 64, 97 (I, 123, 126, 195)
consecration of Sword, 318, 319 (III, 64, 65)
consecration of talisman, 419 (III, 222)
with hexagram of Mars, 290 (III, 23)
Elohim Tzabaoth, 62, 64, 80, 98, 167, 178, 179, 180, 183 (I, 123, 126, 159, 196; II, 94, 115, 118, 120, 125)
consecration of talisman, 413, 414, 421 (III, 212, 212, 213, 226)
with hexagram of Mercury, 289 (III, 22)
Emantt, 353 (III, 115)
Emanuel, 251 (II, 251)
Emerald Tablet, 128 (II, 23)
see also Hermes Trismegistus
Emor Dial Hectega (Mor Dial Hctga), 143, 148, 281, 282, 284, 286, 315, 635 (II, 48, 56; III, 10, 13, 16, 19, 60; IV, 276)
consecration of Pentacle, 325 (III, 73)
consecration of talisman, 422 (III, 227)
evocation ritual, 402-7 *passim*, 409, 410, 411 (III, 195, 196, 198, 200-3 passim, 206, 208, 210, 211)
Opening by Watchtower:
evocation ritual, 403 (III, 196)
spiritual development ritual, 436 (III, 249)
Vault consecration, 259 (II, 266)
Empeh Arsel Gaiol (Mph Arsl Gaiol), 167-8, 178, 281, 286, 315, 635 (II, 94, 116; III, 10, 19, 60; IV, 276)
consecration of Cup, 325 (III, 73)
consecration of talisman, 413, 421 (III, 213, 226)
Opening by Watchtower:
evocation ritual, 402 (III, 196)
spiritual development ritual, 435 (III, 248)

Empeh Arsel Gaiol (continued):
Opening by Watchtower (continued):
Vault consecration, 258 (II, 265)
skrying, 469 (IV, 33)
Tattwa vision, 476 (IV, 45)
Emperor = King (Prince) of Tarot, 544 (IV, 145)
Emperor, The, 589 (IV, 211)
divination:
example, 575, 577, 578, 579 (IV, 191, 194, 195, 196)
meaning, 584 (IV, 204)
see also Tarot, trumps
Empress = Knave (Princess) of Tarot, 544 (IV, 145)
Empress, The, 276, 589 (II, 298; IV, 210-11)
Chesed, 643, 693 (IV, 288, 363)
divinatory meaning, 584 (IV, 204)
Enochian chess queen, 693 (IV, 363)
Isis, 589, 590 (IV, 210, 213)
see also Tarot, trumps
en passant, 688 (IV, 354)
endekangle, 506, 510 (IV, 89, 94)
Endekad, 510 (IV, 94)
endekagon, endekagram, 510, 512 (IV, 94)
England, 232 (II, 219)
Bradford, 18 (I, 22)
Glastonbury, xxiv
London, xxiv, 18 (I, 22)
Warburg Institute, xxi
Weston-super-Mare, 18 (I, 22)
Ennead, 508 (IV, 92)
enneagram, 70, 508-11 *passim* (I, 136; IV, 92-3)
enneangle, 508, 509, 510 (IV, 92-3)
Enoch, 106-7, 156, 164, 167, 178, 182, 194, 625 (I, 217; II, 72, 87, 94, 116, 124, 148; IV, 261)
Book of, 207n, 375n
Enochian, xxiv, 10, 35-6, 43, 44, 698 (I, 65-6, 83, 84, 85)
Aethers, 680 (IV, 343)
alphabet, 652 (IV, 299)
see also Enochian, letters
angels, 441, 450, 482, 635-6, 656-7, 660, 661, 666, 667, 669, 670 , 671, 672 (III, 258, 270; IV, 55, 276-7, 306-7, 311, 312, 313, 319-22 *passim*, 325, 326, 327, 328-9)
see also Opening by Watchtower
archangels—*see* Enochian tablets, archangels of angles
"Book of the Concourse of the Forces," 625, 630-96 (IV, 625, 630-96)
calls (keys), 624-9 *passim*, 666, 671-82 (IV, 260, 262-5 *passim*, 267, 268, 269, 319, 328-45)
Call of the Thirty Aethers, 629, 673, 681-2 (IV, 267, 332, 343-5)

Enochian (continued):
calls (continued):
list, 672 (IV, 330)
numbered calls:
First, 423, 671, 673-4 (III, 229; IV, 328, 329, 331, 333)
true first call unexpressed and unnumbered, 671, 680 (IV, 328, 343)
Second, 628, 671, 673, 674 (IV, 267, 328, 329, 331, 334)
Third, 430, 667, 671, 673, 674-5 (III, 240; IV, 321, 329, 331, 334-5)
Fourth, 413, 662, 671, 675 (III, 213; IV, 318, 329, 335-6)
Fifth, 404, 672, 673, 675-6 (III, 198; IV, 329, 331, 336)
Sixth, 672, 673, 676 (IV, 329, 331, 336-7)
Seventh, 667, 676-7 (IV, 321, 337)
Eighth, 677 (IV, 337-8)
Ninth, 677 (IV, 338-9)
Tenth, 663, 677-8 (IV, 318, 339)
Eleventh, 678 (IV, 339-40)
Twelfth, 678 (IV, 340)
Thirteenth, 678-9 (IV, 340-1)
Fourteenth, 679 (IV, 341)
Fifteenth, 628, 679 (IV, 267, 341)
Sixteenth, 628, 679 (IV, 267, 341-2)
Seventeenth, 673, 680 (IV, 331, 342)
Eighteenth, 680 (IV, 342-3)
numbers, 671 (IV, 329)
skrying, 660, 662 (IV, 312, 318)
chess, 43, 683-96 (I, 83, 84; IV, 346-68)
boards, 684-90 *passim*, 694 (IV, 347-50, 352, 355-8, 365)
checkmate, 695 (IV, 367)
divination, 685, 689, 692, 693-4, 696 (IV, 349, 355, 362, 364, 368)
geomantic figures, 689-90 (IV, 355-7)
moves, 690-6 *passim* (IV, 359-61, 364, 365, 366, 367)
pawns, 685, 687-8, 691-3 (IV, 350, 353-4, 361-3)
colors, 687-8 (IV, 353-4)
on eighth rank, 692 (IV, 362)
pieces, 684-91, 693-6 (IV, 347, 348, 350-7, 359-68)
colors, 687 (IV, 352-3)
movement, 690-1 (IV, 357, 359-60)
placement (YHVH), 695 (IV, 366)
play, 692-3, 694-6 (IV, 362-4, 366-8)
opening, 692 (IV, 362)
Ptah, 692, 693-4, 695 (IV, 362, 364-7 *passim*)
stalemate, 693 (IV, 364)
dictionary, 628, 629 (IV, 266, 269)
original Rosicrucians, 231, 625, 629 (II, 218; IV, 262, 269)
divine names and the Sons of Light, 207n

Enochian (continued):
"Introduction to the Enochian System," 624-30 (IV, 260-73)
language, 625, 627-30 (IV, 262, 264-9)
pronunciation, 629-30, 650, 669 (IV, 269, 297, 300, 325)
letters, 402, 627 (III, 195; IV, 264)
geomantic and Zodiacal attributions, 495, 627 (IV, 77, 264)
pyramids, 647, 648, 660 (IV, 293, 294, 311)
tablets, 656 (IV, 306)
see also Enochian, alphabet
pentagram rituals, 284 (III, 15-16)
see also individual names
Enochian Magic, An Advanced Guide to (Gerald J. Schueler), 682n
Enochian Magic: A Practical Manual (Gerald J. Schueler), 682n
Enochian tablets (Watchtowers), 44, 46, 198, 220, 624, 625, 626, 630-59, 668, 669, 671, 672, 673, 683, 684, 688, 689 (I, 87, 90; II, 155, 197; IV, 260-4 *passim*, 270-309, 323, 324, 326, 328, 329, 331, 346, 347, 354-5)
Air—*see* Air, Enochian tablet
angels—*see* Enochian, angels
archangels of angles, 325-7 (III, 74-7)
Bornless Ritual, 442 (III, 259)
celestial sphere, 594, 655-7 (IV, 219, 304-6)
colors, 630, 635 (IV, 274, 275)
consecration of Rose-Cross, 314 (III, 58)
Earth—*see* Earth (element), Enochian tablet
elemental grade rituals, 137-8
elemental weapons, 320, 323 (III, 66, 70)
elements and YHVH, 638-9 (IV, 281-2)
Enochian chess boards, 685, 687 (IV, 349, 352)
Fire—*see* Fire, Enochian tablet
geomantic figures, 642 (IV, 285)
god names—*see* Enochian tablets, Three Great Secret Holy Names of God
Great Cross, 630, 635, 637, 639, 668, 670 (IV, 274, 276, 278, 281, 324, 326)
celestial sphere, 655, 657 (IV, 304, 306)
Enochian chess, 684 (IV, 347)
Kings, 636, 659 (IV, 276-7, 309)
Osiris, 686 (IV, 351)
pyramids, 648 (IV, 293-4)
YHVH, 639, 640, 642-3 (IV, 282, 283, 285)
Zodiac, 642-3 (IV, 285-6)
guardians of tomb of Christian Rosenkreutz, 224, 233, 242 (II, 203, 222-3, 272)
Hebrew letters, 642 (IV, 285)
illustrations, 631-4 (IV, 270-3)
Kerubic squares, 630, 635, 637-8, 670 (IV, 274, 275, 279-81, 326)
Enochian chess, 684 (IV, 347)

Enochian Tablets (Watchtowers) (continued):
Kerubic squares (continued):
pyramids, 649 (IV, 295)
Tarot suits, 644 (IV, 288-9)
YHVH, 641, 644 (IV, 283-4, 288)
Enochian chess, 688 (IV, 354)
Kings, 636, 637, 668, 670, 671 (IV, 276, 277-8, 323, 324, 326, 331)
Elemental Kings, 659 (IV, 309)
Enochian chess, 685 (IV, 350)
Lesser Angles, 637, 668, 669, 670 (IV, 278-9, 323, 325, 326, 327)
angels, 670 (IV, 327)
calls, 671, 672 (IV, 329)
celestial sphere, 656 (IV, 305)
Egyptian gods, 662 (IV, 314)
Enochian chess, 684-90 *passim*, 693, 693 (IV, 347-50 *passim*, 352-7 *passim*, 364, 365)
grouping according to sphinxes, 660 (IV, 311)
planets, signs, and elements, 645 (IV, 290)
Tarot suits, 644 (IV, 288)
YHVH, 640-1 (IV, 282-3)
Linea Dei Patris Filiique, 635, 638, 639 (IV, 276, 278, 281)
celestial sphere, 655, 656 (IV, 304, 305)
Tarot (numbered cards), 642-3 (IV, 285-6)
YHVH (gematria), 650 (IV, 300)
Zodiac, cardinal and mutable signs, 642-3 (IV, 285)
Linea Spiritus Sancti, 635, 636, 638, 639 (IV, 276, 277, 278, 281)
celestial sphere, 655 (IV, 304)
elements, 653 (IV, 300)
pentagram, 653 (IV, 300)
Sephiroth, 650, 653 (IV, 300)
Tarot (Fives, Sixes, and Sevens), 642-3 (IV, 285)
Zodiac, 669 (IV, 325)
fixed signs, 642-3 (IV, 285)
names drawn from, 482, 635-6, 673, 685 (IV, 55, 276-7, 332, 349)
Opening by Watchtower:
evocation, 402-3 (III, 196)
spiritual development ritual, 435-6 (III, 248-9)
Vault consecration, 258-9 (II, 265-7)
pentagram rituals, 284 (III, 16)
points of pentagram and elemental grades, 210n
Portal ritual, 200, 220 (II, 159-60, 197)
pyramids, 626, 627, 646-50, 653-5, 684 (IV, 264, 291-7, 300-3, 347, 348)
Egyptian gods, 659-66 (IV, 311-17, 319)
Enochian chess, 694 (IV, 364)
making, 661-2 (IV, 313-4)

Enochian Tablets (Watchtowers) (continued):
pyramids (continued):
skrying, 659-70 (IV, 310-27)
sphinxes, 659-2, 666 (IV, 311-4, 318-9)
seniors, 325, 636, 637, 668, 670, 673 (III, 73-4; IV, 277, 278, 323, 326, 331)
planets, 670 (IV, 326)
Sephirotic Calvary Crosses, 630, 637, 638, 668, 670 (IV, 274, 275, 278-9, 323, 327)
celestial sphere, 656 (IV, 305)
Enochian chess, 684, 693 (IV, 347, 363)
Horus, 686 (IV, 351)
planets, 643-4 (IV, 287-8)
pyramids, 648, 654 (IV, 294-5, 302)
Tarot, 644 (IV, 288)
Tree of Life, 641, 643 (IV, 283, 287)
Zodiac, 644 (IV, 288)
servient squares, 630, 635, 638 (IV, 275, 279)
angels, 660, 666, 670 (IV, 312, 319, 327)
Egyptian gods, 662 (IV, 314)
Enochian chess, 684, 690, 691 (IV, 347, 359)
pyramids, 649 (IV, 295)
skrying, 660-70 (IV, 312-27)
YHVH, 641-2, 644 (IV, 284-5, 289)
Enochian chess, 688 (IV, 354)
Zodiac, 644 (IV, 289)
sigils, 657-9 (IV, 307-9)
names drawn from, 658, 659 (IV, 308, 309)
spiritual development ritual, 435-6, 441 (III, 248-9, 258)
Tablet of Union—*see* Tablet of Union
Tarot, 642 (IV, 285, 286)
Three Great Secret Holy Names of God, 635-6, 637, 668, 669 (IV, 276, 278, 323, 325)
Zodiac, 669 (IV, 325)
Water—*see* Water, Enochian tablet
YHVH, 638-9, 642, 646-7, 651 (IV, 281-2, 285, 291-2, 298)
Zodiac, 642 (IV, 285)
Enterer, Ritual of the—*see* Neophyte ritual
Enterer, Sign of the—*see* signs, Neophyte, Enterer
"Enterer of the Threshold, The," (Document Z.1), 330-62 (III, 81-130)
Entry into Netzach, 192-5 (II, 144-50)
Ephraim, 305 (III, 44)
equilibrating pentagrams of Spirit—*see* Spirit, pentagrams, equilibrating
equinox:
first point of Aries, 609 (IV, 241)
Sakhet, 362 (III, 129)
Equinox, The, ix, 1, 7, 8, 682n
Equinox, Ceremony of the, 26, 248-57, 373-4, 698 (I, 41-2; II, 245-63; III, 148-50)
adoration, 249-50 (II, 248-9)
announcement of new officers, 250 (II, 250)
circumambulation by Kerux, 249, 374 (II, 248; III, 149)
closing, 257 (II, 263)
Hierophant installed, 253-4 (II, 255-8)
lesser officers installed, 255-7 (II, 260-263)
opening, 248 (II, 245)
Outer Order leaves, 250-51 (II, 250)
Outer Order returns, 255 (II, 259)
equinoxes, precession, 10, 594 (IV, 218)
Equuleus, 598, 601 (IV, 224, 228)
Equuleus Pictoris (Pictor), 601 (IV, 228)
Eridanus, 599, 600, 601 (IV, 226, 227, 228)
errors in ceremonies, 135
Erzla, 327, 638 (III, 76; IV, 280)
Esau, 76 (I, 151)
Essence, 77, 79 (I, 153, 156)
Established Strength, The Lord of—*see* Threes (Tarot), Wands
Eta, 345 (III, 105)
see also Heta
Eth, 200 (II, 159)
consecration of talisman, 422 (III, 228)
Enochian pyramids, 646, 659 (IV, 291, 310)
Portal ritual, 217, 220 (II, 190, 197)
Pyramid of the Elements, 79, 187, 217 (I, 156; II, 134, 190)
Tattwa vision, 463 (IV, 22)
see also Spirit
Ether:
Akasa, 514 (IV, 96)
Portal grade, 35 (I, 65)
Spirit of the, 489 (IV, 67)
etheric vision, 463 (IV, 22-3)
Ethiopia, 315 (III, 60)
Etnbr, 327 (III, 76)
Etruscan, 628 (IV, 266)
Etz Chayim, 590 (IV, 212)
see also Tree of Life
eucharist, 464 (IV, 25)
see also Mystical Repast
Evans-Wentz, W. Y., *Tibetan Book of the Dead,* 21 (I, 29)
Eve:
altar diagram, The Fall, 33, 76, 193 (I, 59, 150; II, 146)
altar diagram, The Garden of Eden, 33, 74, 178 (I, 58, 145; II, 115)
Black Pillar, 63, 162 (I, 123; II, 85)
Euphrates, 415 (III, 60)
see also Phrath
evil, 107, 337 (I, 217-8; III, 93)
pathway of, 146 (II, 52-3)
Evil One, 343, 344 (III, 101, 103)
Evil Persona, 106, 107, 353, 356, 365 (I, 215-6, 217-8; III, 115, 120, 134-5)
description, 357 (III, 121)
Neophyte, 368, 369 (III, 140, 141, 142)

Evil Persona (continued):
step, 371 (III, 144)
evil spirits, 280 (III, 9)
evocation, 381 (III, 160)
Evil Triad, 114, 115, 365, 366, 367, 368 (III, 134, 136, 139, 140)
evocation, 48 (I, 96)
alchemy, 395, 396, 397 (III, 184, 185, 191)
astral projection, 471 (IV, 36)
Neophyte formula, 376, 377, 378, 380-4, 402-12 (III, 152, 154, 155, 159-66, 195-211)
Yod of Yeheshuah, 376, 380 (III, 152, 159)
Ex Deo Nascimur, 237, 247, 265 (II, 228, 244, 279)
Exacting Intelligence, 191 (II, 142)
exaltation—*see* astrology, dignities
Exarp, 638 (IV, 280)
pronunciation, 650 (IV, 300)
pyramids, 654 (IV, 301)
transformation ritual, 430 (III, 240)
Exarp, Hcoma, Nanta, Bitom, 635 (IV, 275-6)
Bornless Ritual, 444 (III, 262-3)
consecration of Rose-Cross, 315 (III, 59)
invisibility ritual, 426, 427 (III, 234, 236)
Opening by Watchtower:
evocation, 403 (III, 197)
spiritual development ritual, 436 (III, 249)
Vault consecration, 259 (II, 267)
pentagram ritual, 281, 284, 285-6 (III, 10, 11, 16, 18-19)
pronunciation, 650 (IV, 297, 300)
Rose-Cross ritual, 308 (III, 49)
see also keyword analysis; Opening by
Exempt Adept—*see* Adeptus Exemptus
Exempt Adept, Merciful—*see* Chief Adept
Exgsd, 326 (III, 76)
Exodus, 85 (I, 170)
Exordium, General, 330, 374-5 (III, 81, 150-1)
Exordium, Particular, 330, 375 (III, 81-2, 151)
Experiment with Time, An (John William Dunne), 20 (I, 28)
Expounder of the Sacred Mysteries, 337, 354 (III, 92, 116)
exstasis, 389, 392 (III, 174, 180)
The Eye in the Triangle (Israel Regardie), xx, 1
Eytpa, 327 (III, 76)
Ezekiel, 145, 233, 618 (II, 52, 222, 253)
Ezekiel 1:45—621 (IV, 257)
Kerubim, 207, 233 (II, 172-3, 222-3)
Ezlar, 638 (IV, 280)

- F -

F Document, 43 (I, 83)
see also Rose-Cross, lamen, sigils
F.R. = Finem Respice (R. W. Felkin), 17-8, 456 (I, 21; IV, 12)
"Concerning the Use of the Vault," 270-1 (II, 287-9)
fairies, 461 (IV, 19)
fall—*see* astrology, dignities
Fall, The, 12, 33 (I, 60)
altar diagram, 32, 33, 76, plate f. 118, 192-4, 195 (I, 57, 59-60, 150-1, plate f. 152; II, 144, 145-7, 149)
Fam, 495 (IV, 77)
see also Enochian, letters
Fama Fraternitatis, viii, 14-5, 37, 268 (I, 13-5, 69-70; II, 284)
fan, in Theoricus ritual, 154-60 *passim* (II, 69-80 *passim*)
Farr, Florence, ix, 624n
Egyptian Magic, 202n
S.S.D.D. = Sapientia Sapienti Dono Data, 56 (I, 111-2)
fasting, 270 (II, 287)
Father—*see* Supernal Father
fays, 109, 490 (I, 222; IV, 68)
fear is failure, 74, 124 (I, 147; II, 26)
Felkin, R. W., xxii, 17-8, 624n (I, 21-2)
"Concerning the Use of the Vault," 270-1 (II, 287-9)
F.R. = Finem Respice, 17-8, 456 (I, 21; IV, 12)
Tattwa vision, 456 (IV, 11-2)
Felkin, R. W., Mrs.—*see* Davidson, Harriet Miller
feminine forms of names of officers, 341 (III, 100)
Fessa, 231 (II, 217)
Fez, Morocco, 14 (I, 13)
FIAT = Flatus Ignis Aqua Terra, 206-7, 477, 478 (II, 172; IV, 47, 49)
Fiery Serpents, 83 (I, 165)
Judgment, 172 (II, 104)
Fiji, xxii
fingers of hand, elemental attributions, 100 (I, 204)
Fire, xix, xxiii, 8
of Air:
Knight (King) of Swords, 548 (IV, 150)
Rose-Cross lamen, 310 (III, 52)
alchemical operation, 398 (III, 189)
Astral Fire, 70, 170, 171, 172 (I, 137; II, 100, 103, 104)
Banner of the East, 335 (III, 91)
caduceus, 162, 340 (II, 83; III, 97)
censer transmits Fires of Netzach to Malkuth, 341 (III, 99)
ceremonial magic, 376 (III, 152)
circumambulation, 346 (III, 107)
consecration by, 28 (I, 47)
consecration of talisman, 414, 419, 420 (III, 213, 222, 225, 226)

Fire (continued):
Cup of Stolistes, 71, 177, 340 (I, 138; II, 113; III, 97)
Dadouches, station of, 341 (III, 99)
divine name, archangel, angel, ruler, king, etc., 80 (I, 159)
of Earth:
Knight (King) of Pentacles, 549 (IV, 152)
Malkuth, 614 (IV, 247)
Rose-Cross lamen, 311 (III, 52)
Tattwas, 458, 460 (IV, 14, 18)
Enochian chess:
boards, 694 (IV, 365)
knight, 691 (IV, 359-60)
Enochian tablets or Watchtowers:
Fire angle:
Air tablet:
call (ninth), 672, 677 (IV, 330, 339)
Enochian chess, 690 (IV, 357)
angels, 670 (IV, 327)
Earth tablet, 654-5 (IV, 303)
call (fifteenth), 672, 679 (IV, 330, 341)
Enochian chess divination, 694 (IV, 364)
Enochian chess knight, 686 (IV, 351)
Water tablet, 638 (IV, 280)
call (twelfth), 672, 678 (IV, 330, 340)
Fire tablet, 181, 182, 183, 186, 194, 195, 669 (II, 121, 124, 125, 131, 148, 155; IV, 325)
Air angle, 326, 670 (III, 74; IV, 327)
call (sixteenth), 672, 679 (IV, 330, 342)
archangels of angles, 325-6 (III, 74-5)
calls, 672, 673 (IV, 329, 330, 331)
colors, 635 (IV, 275)
consecration of talisman, 420 (III, 225)
Earth angle, 669 (IV, 325)
call (eighteenth), 672, 680 (IV, 330, 343)
Fire angle, 669 (IV, 325)
call (sixth), 672, 673 (IV, 329, 330, 331)
illustration, 634 (IV, 273)
Opening by Watchtower:
evocation, 402 (III, 196)
spiritual development ritual, 435 (III, 248)
Vault consecration, 258 (II, 265)
Philosophus ritual, 181, 182, 183, 186, 194, 195 (II, 121, 124, 125, 131, 148, 155)
Water angle, 655 (IV, 303)
call (seventeenth), 672, 680 (IV, 330, 342)
Yod, 639 (IV, 281)
pyramids, 649, 654-5 (IV, 296, 303)
see also Enochian tablets

Fire (continued):
evocation, 409 (III, 207)
finger, middle, 100 (I, 204)
of Fire: Knight (King) of Wands, 545 (IV, 146)
Fylfot cross, 340 (III, 98)
Geburah, reflected from in Netzach, 331 (III. 83)
heart, 101 (I, 205)
Heh, 694 (IV, 365)
hexagram, 294, 336 (III, 29, 91)
Hierophant's lamen, 218, 336 (II, 194; III, 90)
Jupiter, 215, 648 (II, 187; IV, 294)
Kabexnuv, 687, 692 (IV, 353, 361)
Kabiri, 169-71, 172 (II, 97-101, 104)
Kerub, 343, 357 (III, 102, 121)
see also Kerubim; Leo; lion
lamp, red, (on altar), 334 (III, 87)
Latent Heat, 70, 172 (I, 137; II, 103, 105)
Malkuth of Yetzirah, 619 (IV, 254)
Mars, 215, 644 (II, 187; IV, 288)
material basis, 384, 387 (II, 166, 171)
Netzach, 20, 21, 31 (I, 26-7, 30, 55)
reflected in from Geburah, 331 (III, 83)
Paths:
25th Path, 216 (II, 190)
31st Path, 167, 169, 214 (II, 93, 97, 185)
Malkuth, russet quarter, 337 (III, 92)
Peh, 215 (II, 187)
pentagram, 282-5 *passim* (III, 12, 13, 15, 16, 18)
Bornless Ritual, 443 (III, 261)
consecrations:
Fire Wand, 325, 326 (III, 74, 75)
Rose-Cross, 315 (III, 60)
talisman, 420 (III, 225)
Opening by Watchtower:
evocation ritual, 402 (III, 195)
spiritual development ritual, 435 (III, 248)
Vault consecration, 258 (II, 265)
Philosophus ritual, 182, 196 (II, 123, 152)
skrying, 669 (IV, 325)
pentagram, point of, 280, 281, 282 (III, 10, 11, 13)
Philosophus grade, 29, 31, 182, 194 (I, 50, 54; II, 123, 147, 148)
Pillars, capitals, 333 (III, 86)
Pison, 73, 177 (I, 144; II, 114)
Practicus grade, 31, 33 (I, 53, 59)
produced other elements, 151 (II, 64)
Pyramid of Fire, 70, 169-72 *passim* (I, 137; II, 95, 96-104 *passim*)
quadrupeds, 109 (I, 222)
requiem ceremony, 448 (III, 267)
Root of the Powers of—*see* Aces (Tarot), Wands

Fire (continued):
Rose-Cross lamen, 310-13 (III, 52-3, 55, 56)
alchemical principles and other elements in Fire, 311 (III, 52)
Fire arm of cross and colors, 311, 312 (III, 52, 55)
consecration, 315 (II, 60)
location of petal (Shin), 311 (III, 53)
Second Adept in Portal ritual, 199n, 221n
serpent, 619 (IV, 254-5)
Solar Fire, 70, 169, 171, 172 (I, 137; II, 99, 103, 104)
circumambulation, 346 (III, 107)
spiritual development ritual, 439, 441 (III, 255, 258)
Sun, 175, 648 (II, 109; IV, 294)
symbol:
part of hexagram, 287 (III, 21)
pentagram rituals, 283 (III, 14)
used in spelling divine names, 83 (I, 166)
see also Fire, triangle
Tarot:
Death, 211 (II, 179)
The Devil, 213 (II, 183)
Judgment, 71, 73, 172, 542, 592 (I, 139, 143; II, 104; IV, 141, 216)
The Sun, 592 (IV, 215)
Temperance, 217, 218, 591 (II, 192; IV, 214)
The Tower, 644 (IV, 288)
Tejas, 317, 457, 489 (III, 62; IV, 12, 13, 67)
tetrahedron—*see* Pyramid of Fire
Theoricus ritual, 158 (II, 75-76)
Thma-oe-Sh, 375 (III, 151)
triangle, 80, 172, 506 (I, 160; II, 105; IV, 90)
telesmatic images, 486 (IV, 62)
triangle, solid—*see* Pyramid of Fire
Volcanic Fire, 70, 170, 171, 172 (I, 137; II, 99, 103, 104)
Wand—*see* Wand, elemental weapon (Fire)
of Water:
Knight (King) of Cups, 546 (IV, 148)
see also Fire, Enochian tablets
Yod, 644 (IV, 289)
see also YHVH, elements
Zata, Elman, 275 (II, 296)
Zodiac:
cardinal signs, 644, 650 (IV, 289, 297)
fire signs, 50, 80 (I, 100, 160)
see also Dadouches; elements
Firmament, circle on Cup of Stolistes, 71, 177, 340 (I, 138; II, 113; III, 97)
First Matter, 19, 33, 395, 396 (I, 25, 60; III, 184-7 *passim*)
First Order—*see* Outer Order; Stella Matutina
Firth, Violet, *The Machinery of the Mind,* 88 (I, 178)
see also Fortune, Dion
fish, 109 (I, 222)
Fives (Tarot), 552 (IV, 156)
Cups, 556 (IV, 162-3)
divination example, 571, 572, 577, 578, 579 (IV, 185, 187, 194, 195, 197)
divinatory meaning, 582 (IV, 202)
Pentacles, 562 (IV, 172)
divination example, 568, 569, 577, 578 (IV, 181, 194, 195, 196)
Swords, 559 (IV, 167-8)
divination example, 571, 572, 585, 586 (IV, 186, 186, 187, 207)
Enochian pyramids, 648 (IV, 294)
Wands, 552-3 (IV, 158)
see also Tarot, numbered cards
fixed signs—*see* Zodiac
Flagstaff, Arizona, xxiv
Flamen Dialis, 628 (IV, 266)
flames on numbered cards of Tarot, Wands, 523, 537, 561 (IV, 158, 159, 164, 165, 170, 171)
Flaming Sword, 61-2, 76, 226, 440 (I, 122-3, 150; II, 206, 256)
see also Flashing Sword
Flaming Sword of the Kerubim, The, 141, 145, 147, 154, 161, 162 (II, 44, 52, 55, 56, 69, 82, 83, 85)
Flashing Colors, 229, 230, 312, 415, 698 (II, 213, 214; III, 55, 215)
Tarot trumps, 589, 590 (IV, 212, 213)
Flashing Sword, 194 (II, 147)
alchemical operation, 397, 399 (III, 188, 190)
consecration of talisman, 419 (III, 223)
see also Flaming Sword
Flashing Tablets, 377, 378, 479, 481 (III, 154, 156; IV, 51, 54, 55)
alchemical operation, 395-9 *passim* (III, 185, 186, 188-91 *passim*)
Banner of the East, 465 (IV, 27)
consecration, 481 (IV, 54, 55)
Enochian:
chess boards, 687 (IV, 348)
tablets, 46, 625 (I, 90; IV, 261)
flowers: court cards of Pentacles, 550, 551 (IV, 153, 155)
Flowing Formula, 621 (IV, 256-7)
Flying Formula, 618-9 (IV, 253-4)
Flying Roll X (MacGregor Mathers), 199n
Fool, The, 588 (IV, 209-10)
divination:
example, 568, 569, 577, 579 (IV, 181, 182, 194, 196)
meaning, 584 (IV, 204)
zero, 680 (IV, 343)
see also Tarot, trumps

Fool (bishop)—*see* Enochian, chess, pieces
Foolish Man, The—*see* Fool, The
Fordham, Michael, xix
formula:
Ceremony of the Equinox, 374 (III, 150)
Neophyte ritual, 376-450 (III, 152-270)
Rite of the Kerubic Stations, 420-2 (III, 224-8)
"Formulae of the Magic of Light, The," (Document Z.2), 376-400 (III, 152-92)
see also Neophyte, formula
Fornax, 599 (IV, 226)
Fortitude—*see* Strength
Fortuna Major, 494, 495, 525, 527, 528, 529, 532, 538 (IV, 75, 77, 115-9 *passim*, 125, 134, 135)
Enochian pyramids, 650 (IV, 300)
see also geomancy, figures
Fortuna Minor, 494, 495, 525, 527, 529, 533, 538, 539 (IV, 75, 77, 115-9 *passim*, 125, 134, 135)
Enochian chess, 690 (IV, 357)
see also geomancy, figures
Fortune, Dion, ix, xxiv, 683n, 698
Society of the Inner Light, ix
see also Firth, Violet
Fortune, The Wheel of—*see* Wheel of Fortune, The
forty squares, Vault symbolism, 266, 267, 268 (II, 280, 281, 284, 285)
Forty-two Judges of the Dead, 58, 115, 356, 358, 365, 367 (I, 115; III, 120, 123, 134, 135, 137)
Forty-two lettered name of God, 365 (III, 104)
Foundation—*see* Yesod
Four Daughters, 528, 529 (IV, 117-8, 119)
see also geomancy
"Four Lights," 207n
Four Mothers, 525, 528, 529, 539 (IV, 113, 117-8, 119, 136)
see also geomancy
Four Nephews, 529 (IV, 119)
see also geomancy
Four Resultants, 529 (IV, 119)
see also geomancy
"Four Serpent Formulae of the Four Aces, The," 347 (III, 108-9)
Four Worlds—*see* Worlds, Four
Fours (Tarot), 552 (IV, 156)
Cups, 564 (IV, 176)
divination example, 577, 578, 579 (IV, 194, 195, 197)
divinatory meaning, 583 (IV, 202)
Pentacles, 558-9 (IV, 167)
divination example, 570, 571 (IV, 184, 185)
Swords, 555 (IV, 162)
divination example, 574, 575, 577, 578 (IV, 190, 191, 194, 195, 196)
Fours (Tarot) (continued):
Wands, 561 (IV, 171)
see also Tarot, numbered cards
Franciscus—*see* de Bry, Franciscus
framework (psychotherapy), xxv
Frazer, Sir J. G., 22 (I, 31-2)
The Golden Bough, 36 (I, 67-8)
free association, xxiv-xxv
Freemasonry and the Ancient Gods (J. S. M. Ward), 11-2
Freemasons, 9, 17-8 (I, 19-22)
Masonic Encyclopedia, 15 (I, 16)
Freudian psychoanalysis, xxi, xxiv
Frisia, 275 (II, 296)
Fuller, R. Buckminster, 700
Fuller, J.F.C., 1
Function of the Orgasm, The (Wilhelm Reich), 5
Fylfot cross, 68, 139, 142, 144, 148, 340 (I, 131; II, 45, 49, 57; III, 98)
see also lamen, Dadouches

- G -

G Document, 42 (I, 82)
see "The Magic Sword" and "The Four Elemental Weapons," 317-28 (III, 62-78)
G.C., Frater, 232 (II, 218)
G.W., Frater, 231 (II, 218)
Gabriel:
angel of the Moon, 65, 207n (I, 127)
archangel of Water, 80, 167, 207n (I, 159; II, 94)
consecration of Cup, 324 (III, 72)
consecration of Jupiter talisman, 413, 421 (III, 213, 226)
Lesser Banishing Ritual of the Pentagram, 54, 444 (I, 107; III, 262)
archangel of Yesod, 62, 64, 98 (I, 123, 126, 197)
transformation ritual, 430, 431, 433, 434 (III, 241, 243, 246, 247)
Gad, 304, 305 (III, 43, 44)
Gaia, 444 (III, 263)
gall bladder, 360, 361 (III, 126, 127, 128)
Galla Narbonensi, 232 (II, 219)
Garden of Eden, 12, 27 (I, 45)
altar diagram, 32-3, 73-4, plate f. 118, 176, 177-8 (I, 57-9, 144-5, plate f. 146, 112, 113-5)
elemental grade rituals, 139
gate guarded by Kerubim, 233 (II, 222)
see also above altar diagram
Hegemon, represented by station of, 160 (II, 81)
rivers of Eden, 73-4, 76, 177, 186, 193 (I, 144-5, 151; II, 114, 132, 146)
Calvary cross, 79, 162, 172, 185, 335, 374 (I, 156; II, 85, 104, 129; III, 89, 149)

Garden of Eden (continued):
  rivers of Eden (continued):
    Horus, Children of, 343, 358 (III, 102, 124)
    Rose-Cross, 315 (III, 60)
  Supernal, 188, 194 (II, 135, 146)
  32nd Path, Passing the Gates of, 159 (II, 79)
  see also Fall; Flaming Sword of the Kerubim
Garden of Pomegranates, The (Israel Regardie), 2, 52n (I, 104n)
Garstin, J. Langford, 1
Gaul, 275 (II, 296)
Geburah, 19, 21, 97, 98 (I, 26, 30, 195, 196)
  caduceus, 162, 340 (II, 83; III, 97)
  Calvary cross of six squares, 193 (II, 145)
  Chesed, 210 (II, 178)
  Enochian:
    chess castle, 693 (IV, 364)
    pyramids, 654 (IV, 302)
  Fire, 84, 311 (I, 168; III, 52)
  Flaming Sword of the Kerubim diagram, 145 (II, 52)
  divine name, archangel, and angelic choir, 62, 64, 97 (I, 123, 126, 195)
  Hegemon's lamen, 339 (III, 96)
  hexagram, 218, 293 (II, 195; III, 27)
  Imperator, 342 (III, 101)
  Malkuth, connected to through Hod and 31st Path, 172 (II, 103)
    consecration of talisman, 419 (III, 222)
  Mars, 218 (II, 195)
    balanced by Jupiter in Chesed, 215 (II, 187)
  microcosm, 100, 103 (I, 204, 209)
    invisibility ritual, 424 (III, 231)
    right arm, 100 (I, 204)
  Nephesch, 103 (I, 209)
  19th Path, 214 (II, 186)
  pentangle, 506 (IV, 90)
  Phoenix Wand, 224n
  Pison, 73, 177 (I, 144; II, 114)
  Portal ritual, 212 (II, 181)
  qabalistic cross, 53, 403, 444 (I, 106; III, 197, 262)
  reconciled with Chesed by serpent, 83 (I, 165)
  right arm of Adam, 74, 178 (I, 145; II, 115)
  scourge, 242 (II, 237)
  Second Adept in Portal ritual, 199n, 221n
  Sword, 317, 322, 468 (III, 62, 69; IV, 31)
    consecration, 318 (III, 63, 64)
  Tarot:
    Fives, 552 (IV, 156)
      Cups, 556 (IV, 163)
      Pentacles, 562 (IV, 172)
      Swords, 559 (IV, 168)
      Wands, 553 (IV, 158)
    Temperance, 217, 218 (II, 192)
    The Tower, 693 (IV, 364)
Geburah (continued):
  Tarot (continued):
    The Universe, 160 (II, 70)
  Vault symbolism, 268 (II, 283)
  see also Sephiroth
Ged, 495 (IV, 77)
  see also Enochian, letters
Gedulah, 424 (III, 231)
  qabalistic cross, 53, 403, 444 (I, 106; III, 197, 262)
  see also Chesed
Gehenna, in Theoricus ritual, 160 (II, 81)
gematria, xviii, 275-6 (II, 296-8)
  Adonai = L.V.X., 14
  YHVH on Enochian tablets, 650 (IV, 300)
  see also numbers
Gemini:
  divine and angelic names, 86 (I, 171)
  divine name, Hebrew letter, Tribe of Israel, angel, and color, 305 (III, 44)
  Enochian:
    chess, 690, 694 (IV, 356, 365)
    letter and geomantic figure, 495 (IV, 77)
    pyramids, 649, 650 (IV, 296)
  Mercury, 495 (IV, 77)
  Pillar of Severity, 603 (IV, 232)
  scourge, 242 (II, 237)
  star map, 595 (IV, 219, 220)
  Tarot:
    Knave (Princess) of Pentacles, 597 (IV, 223)
    The Lovers, 71, 72, 542, 575, 600 (I, 139, 142; IV, 140, 191, 227)
    Queen of Cups, 547, 599 (IV, 149, 225)
    The Sun, 175 (II, 111)
    Swords:
      Eight, Nine, and Ten, 541, 563 (IV, 140, 173-4)
      Knight (King), 548, 598 (IV, 150, 225)
  Vault symbolism, 269 (II, 286)
  see also Castor and Pollux; Zodiac
General Exordium, 330, 374-5 (III, 81, 150-1)
general semantics, 6
Genesis:
  2:10-14—315 (III, 59-60)
  2:20—109 (I, 222)
  5:24—106-7 (I, 217)
  6:3—228 (II, 210)
genii, 109, 463 (I, 223; IV, 22)
geomancy, 493, 524, 539 (IV, 75, 112, 136)
"Genii of the Hall of the Neophytes, The Symbolism of the Four," 358-62 (III, 124-30)
geomancy, 6, 10, 39, 40-1, 43, 44, 81, 493, 524-39 (I, 75, 76-8, 83, 87, 183; IV, 74, 112-36)
  Enochian system, 624 (IV, 260)
    chess divination, 692 (IV, 362)
  figures:
    elements:
      skrying, 463 (IV, 22)

geomancy (continued):
figures (continued):
Enochian:
chess, 689-90 (IV, 355-7)
gematria, 650 (IV, 300)
letters, 495, 627 (IV, 77, 264)
tablets, 642 (IV, 285)
pyramids, 649, 651 (IV, 295, 298)
sigils and talismans, 493-6 (IV, 73-8)
doors, 493 (IV, 74)
Zodiac, 69, 415, 495, 524, 526, 537, 689 (I, 135; III, 215; IV, 77, 112, 114, 132, 355)
George, Llewellyn, *A to Z Horoscope Maker and Delineator,* 5
Germany, 14, 231, 626 (I, 13; II, 217; IV, 262)
Nuremberg, 17 (I, 19, 21)
Gestalt psychology, 699
Gharis, 516 (IV, 98, 99)
Ghob, 80 (I, 158)
Ghogiel, 82, 419 (I, 163; III, 222)
Gihon, 73, 177, 315, 414 (I, 145; II, 114; III, 60, 213)
Gilbert, R. A., editor, *The Sorcerer and His Apprentice,* 202n
Gimel:
Enochian pronunciation, 650 (IV, 297)
The High Priestess, 335, 589 (III, 90; IV, 210)
telesmatic image, 486 (IV, 61)
13th Path (Moon, The High Priestess):
Binah, 643 (IV, 288)
Hierophant's sceptre, 335 (III, 90)
wandering thoughts, 474 (IV, 41)
see also Hebrew alphabet
Gisa, 495 (IV, 77)
see also Enochian, letters
Glastonbury, xxiv
Gluten of Eagle, 217 (II, 192)
gnomes, 30, 80, 160 (I, 52, 158; II, 80)
astral projection, 472 (IV, 37)
King of the—*see* Knights (Kings), Pentacles
prayer, 152-3, 406-7 (II, 67-8; III, 202-3)
Prince and Emperor of the—*see* Kings (Princes), Pentacles
Princess and Empress of the—*see* Knaves (Princesses), Pentacles
Tattwa vision, 461, 475 (IV, 19, 43-4)
Queen of—*see* Queens, Pentacles
see also elementals
Gnostic archangels, 207n
The Gnostic Religion (Hans Jonas), 13
Gnosticism, 4, 12, 375 (III, 150)
goat:
Capricorn, 62 (I, 124)
inverted pentagram, 507 (IV, 90)
Temperance, 218 (II, 192)
Queen of Pentacles, 549, 551 (IV, 153, 155)
Goat of Mendes, 212, 213, 217 (II, 182, 191)
god-forms:
assumption of, 371, 372, 373, 378, 443, 444 (III, 144-5, 148, 155-6, 260, 261, 262)
skrying, 464, 465 (IV, 25, 26)
see also Egyptian gods and god-forms
god names—*see* divine names
Goddesses of the Scale of the Balance, 341, 355, 364, 367, 369, 425, 431 (III, 99, 118, 133, 137, 140-1, 233, 242)
Gods of the Egyptians, The (E. Wallis Budge), 356 (III, 119)
gold:
alchemy, 60, 61, 236 (I, 119, 120, 121; II, 227)
circle and Sun, 83 (I, 165)
Image of the Vision of Nebuchadnezzar, 206 (II, 171)
Pison, 73, 177 (I, 144; II, 114)
skrying, 666 (IV, 320)
Golden Dawn, Hermetic Order of the, 697
Amoun Temple, 624n
cipher manuscripts, 17, 18, 624n (I, 20, 22)
demographics, 16 (I, 17)
Hermes Lodge, 624n
history, 15-8 (I, 16-22)
History Lecture, 15-6, 43 (I, 16, 84)
Isis-Urania Temple, ix, 16, 17, 202n, 272 (I, 17, 21; II, 290)
secrecy, 16, 22 (I, 18, 33)
Tree of Life, 272-3 (II, 291)
Gon, 495 (IV, 77)
see also Enochian, letters
good, pathway of, 146 (II, 52-3)
Gospel According to John, 12
Grace—*see* Chesed
grades, xix, 18, 21, 27-39, 44, 45, 699 (I, 23, 30, 44-74, 86-7, 88)
five grades of Outer Order referred to symbolically by 120 years, 224 (II, 202)
see also elemental grades
"Grade of Philsophus, The: Additional Lecture on the Tattwas of the Eastern School," 514-22 (IV, 95-109)
grade signs—*see* signs
Graph, 495 (IV, 77)
see also Enochian, letters
Graphiel, 65 (I, 127)
sigil, 499 (IV, 82)
telesmatic image, 486 (IV, 62)
Great Cross—*see* Enochian tablets, Great Cross
Great Hermetic Arcanum, 205 (II, 170)
Great Mother—*see* Mother
Great One of the Night of Time, The—*see* Universe, The
Great Strength, The Lord of—*see* Nines (Tarot), Wands

Greater Arcana—*see* Tarot, trumps
Greater Key of Solomon, The (trans. MacGregor Mathers), 8, 16, 493 (I, 18; IV, 76)
Greatness (Gedulah)—*see* Chesed
Greek cross—*see* cross, Greek
Green Lion, 60 (I, 120)
  Great Hermetic Arcanum, 206 (II, 170)
grip:
  Adeptus Minor, 246 (II, 242-3)
  First Order, 204 (II, 167)
    Neophyte, 126-7, 144, 372-3 (II, 30, 49; III, 147-8)
    Philosophus, 194 (II, 147)
    Practicus, 178, 183 (II, 115, 125)
    Tarot, 552, 553, 557, 561 (IV, 158, 159, 164, 171)
    Theoricus, 163, 168 (II, 86, 96)
    Zelator, 147, 156 (II, 55, 73)
  Portal, 216 (II, 190)
  Second Order, in Equinox ceremony, 254 (II, 257)
groups, xxiv, 23 (I, 34)
  see also orders
group work, ix, xviii-xix, 1
Grus, 599 (IV, 226)
guardians:
  astral/cosmic Neophyte temple in Sphere of Sensation, 451 (III, 271-2)
  circle, 698
    see also archangels, Lesser Banishing Ritual of the Pentagram
guides, in Tattwa vision, 460, 461 (IV, 17, 18, 19)

- H -

H, the letter, symbolic of breath, 118 (II, 14)
H, Book, 232 (II, 219)
H Document, 43-4 (I, 83, 85)
  see also Clavicula Tabularum Enochi
Haayah, 86, 557 (I, 173; IV, 164)
Habakkuk, third chapter quoted in ritual, 191 (II, 140-1)
Habioro, 325, 636 (III, 73; IV, 277)
Hagiel, 65 (I, 127)
  sigil, 500 (IV, 84)
Hahihel, 86, 560 (I, 174; IV, 169)
Hair of Berenice—*see* Coma Berenices
Ham, 520 (IV, 105)
Hamaliel, 86, 305 (I, 172; III, 44)
  Enochian letter, geomantic figure, Zodiac, 495 (IV, 77)
Hanael:
  angel of Venus, 65 (I, 127)
    see also Haniel
  archangel of Capricorn, 86, 305 (I, 174; III, 44)
    Enochian letter, geomantic figure, Zodiac, 495 (IV, 77)
hands on numbered cards of Tarot, 553-64 *passim* (IV, 158-76 *passim*)
Hanged Man, The, 212, 590 (I, 181; IV, 213)
  divination:
    example, 580, 581 (IV, 199)
    meaning, 585 (IV, 205)
  see also Tarot, trumps
Hanial, 97 (I, 196)
  see also Haniel
Haniel, 62, 64 (I, 123, 126)
Han, 520 (IV, 105)
Hansa, 517 (IV, 100)
Hapi, 358, 361 (III, 123, 129)
  see also Ahephi
Hapimon, 686 (IV, 350)
Harayel, 86, 555 (I, 173; IV, 162)
Harmonious Change, Lord of—*see* Twos (Tarot), Pentacles
Harmony—*see* Tiphareth
Harpocrates (Harpacrat, Harparkrat, Har-Par-Krat, Hoorpokrati, Hoor-po-krat-ist, Hoor-Po-Krattist, Ho-or-Po-Kratt-I St), 127, 304, 343, 344, 353, 356, 453 (II, 30; III, 42, 101, 103, 115, 120, 275)
  description, 357 (III, 121)
  Enochian:
    pyramids, 663 (IV, 315)
    skrying, 667 (IV, 321, 322)
  The Fool, 588 (IV, 210)
  god-form in astral projection, 465 (IV, 26)
  illustration, 665 (IV, 317)
  invisibility ritual, 423, 424-8 *passim*, 426 (III, 230, 231-4 *passim*, 233, 236, 237)
  sign of—*see* signs, Silence
  station, invisible, 346, 366, 367, 368, 369 (III, 108, 136, 139, 140, 142)
  see also Hoor-Po-Krattist
Harrison, Jane E., 22 (I, 31-2)
Hartmann, Franz, *In the Pronaos of the Temple,* 14 (I, 13)
Hathor, 343 (III, 101)
  description, 456-7 (III, 120)
  Kerub of Air behind, 357 (III, 121)
  Tarot:
    The High Priestess, 589 (IV, 210)
    The Universe, 592 (IV, 216)
  see also Athor
Havilah, 315 (III, 60)
hawk, 58 (I, 115)
  Horus, 686 (IV, 351)
  Kabexnuv, 344, 358, 361, 687 (III, 103, 122, 128; IV, 353)
Hayakawa, S. I., *Language in Action,* 6
Hayayel, 86, 564 (I, 172; IV, 176)
Hazayel, 86, 554 (I, 172; IV, 160)
Hcoma:
  consecration of talisman, 414 (III, 213)
  Enochian calls, 672, 672, 675 (IV, 329, 330, 336)

Hcoma (continued):
pronunciation, 650 (IV, 300)
Tattwa vision, 476 (IV, 45)
see also Exarp, Hcoma, Nanta, Bitom; keyword analysis; Opening by Watchtower
He (Hebrew letter)—*see* Heh
head:
apertures, planetary attributions, 103 (I, 210)
Tarot—*see* angel's head; child's head; horse, head; lion, head; man's head; ram's head
healing, 15, 91, 232, 520-1, 699 (I, 15, 182; II, 218; IV, 106-7)
Air angle of Enochian tablets, 670 (IV, 327)
heart, 360, 361 (III, 126-9 *passim*)
Heart Girt with a Serpent, 445 (III, 265)
heavenly spheres—*see* spheres, heavenly or planetary; planets
Heavens of Assiah, 63 (I, 125)
Hebrew:
Ashkenazic, 52n (I, 104n)
Egyptian language, 650 (IV, 297)
letters, 402, 404, 414, 430, 431 (III, 195, 198, 199, 214, 241, 242)
celestial sphere, 594 (IV, 219)
doors, 463 (III, 22)
Enochian:
chess, 689 (IV, 355)
tablets, 627, 642 (IV, 265, 285)
pyramids, 651 (IV, 298)
vibration, 487, 491 (IV, 63, 70)
see also Hebrew alphabet
names, 39, 482 (I, 74; IV, 55)
Enochian names, 656-7, 673 (IV, 306, 332)
pronunciation, 52n (I, 104n)
Sephardic, 52n (I, 104n)
transliteration into, 274 (II, 295)
writing by attributions, 83 (I, 166)
Hebrew alphabet, xxii-xxiii, 45, 51, 52, 150, 275, 276 (I, 89, 101, 102-3; II, 61, 296, 298)
double letters, 67, 150, 311 (I, 129; II, 62; III, 53)
Enochian, 624 (IV, 260)
pronunciation, 650 (IV, 297)
finals, 51 (I, 101)
Greek cubical cross, 70, 159 (I, 136-7; II, 78)
I.N.R.I. attribution, 12
Mother letters, 8, 55, 67, 151, 158n (I, 110, 129; II, 64)
Ace of Wands, 543 (IV, 142)
caduceus, 162 (II, 83)
Enochian chess, 696 (IV, 368)
Rose-Cross lamen, 311 (III, 53)
trumps, 568 (IV, 180)
Paths, 162 (II, 84)
planets, 71, 150 (I, 139; II, 62)
Rose-Cross, 224, 262, 482 (II, 202, 272; IV, 57)
Hebrew alphabet (continued):
single letters, 67, 311 (I, 129; III, 53)
Tarot and Zodiac attributions, 71, 542 (I, 139; IV, 140-1)
telesmatic images, 491 (IV, 69-70)
see also individual letters
see also Paths
Hecate, 169, 170, 171 (II, 98, 100, 102)
Hechashiah, 86, 561 (I, 171; IV, 171)
Heeoa, 207n
Hegemon, 27, 338-9, 342 (I, 45; III, 94-6, 100)
badge—*see* Hegemon, lamen
cloak, 119, 338-9 (II, 15-6; III, 95)
illustration, 349 (III, 111)
elemental grade rituals, 137, 139
Equinox ceremony, 248, 249, 250, 256, 374, 375 (II, 246, 247, 249, 250, 261-2; III, 149, 150, 151)
Harparkrat, between Hegemon and altar, 357 (III, 121)
insignia and symbols, 338-9 (III, 94-6)
lamen—*see* lamen, Hegemon
mediator between stations of Hierophant and Hiereus, 338 (III, 95)
Neophyte formula, speeches used in:
spiritual development ritual, 392 (III, 179, 180)
transformation ritual, 390 (III, 176)
Neophyte ritual, 166-22 *passim*, 124-7 *passim*, 131, 132, 133, 331, 347, 363-8 *passim*, 379-80 (II, 11, 12, 14-22 *passim*, 24-32 *passim*, 39, 40, 42, 43; III, 82, 109, 131-40 *passim*, 157-8)
explains station, duties, cloak, sceptre, 119 (II, 15-16)
station explained by Hierophant, 129 (II, 35)
Philosophus ritual, 181-93 *passim*, 195, 196 (II, 121-34 *passim*, 136-45 *passim*, 149-52 *passim*)
Portal ritual, 198-202 *passim*, 204-10 *passim*, 212-8 *passim*, 220 (II, 155-9 *passim*, 161, 163, 164, 167, 169, 170, 172, 173, 175-8 *passim*, 181, 182, 184-9 *passim*, 191, 194, 197)
garments and implements, 199 (I, 156)
Practicus grade required for, 342 (III, 100)
Practicus ritual, 166-80 *passim* (II, 92-7 *passim*, 199, 100, 101, 103-13 *passim*, 117, 118, 120)
sceptre—*see* sceptre, Hegemon
station, 119, 129, 338 (II, 15, 35; III, 94-5)
Theoricus ritual, 154-65 *passim* (II, 69, 71-78 *passim*, 81-4 *passim*, 187, 188, 191)
station represents Garden of Eden, 160 (II, 80)
Thmae-st, Thmae-sh, Thmaae-tt (Thmaa-Est), 339, 352, 355 (III, 96, 114, 118)
wand—*see* sceptre, Hegemon

Hegemon (continued):
woman, office more natural for, 342 (III, 100)
Zelator ritual, 141-50 *passim*, 152, 153 (II, 44-50 *passim*, 53, 54, 56, 58, 60, 61, 62, 67, 68)
Heh:
alchemy, 376, 395 (III, 152, 184)
Aries, 304, 305 (III, 43, 44)
Binah, 331, 615 (III, 82; IV, 249)
Circular Altar, 235 (II, 224)
consecration, 376, 384 (III, 152, 166)
Cup, 322 (III, 68)
dekagram, 510 (IV, 93)
Earth, 644 (IV, 289)
see also YHVH, elements
elements, 644 (IV, 289)
Enochian:
chess queen and castle, 695 (IV, 366)
pyramids, 650 (IV, 296)
Fire, 694 (IV, 365)
Great Mother, 150 (II, 61)
Kether, 617, 641 (IV, 251, 282)
natural phenomena, production of, 376 (III, 152)
Pentacle, 322 (III, 69)
pentagram, 276-7, 507 (II, 299; IV, 91)
Rose-Cross lamen, 311 (III, 53)
Tarot:
Ace of Cups, 543 (IV, 143)
Death, 211 (II, 179)
Queens and Knaves (Princesses), 544, 615, 616 (IV, 144, 145, 249)
Thma-oe-Tt and Thm-a-Oe, 375 (III, 151)
of Vau, 654 (IV, 302)
Water, 644 (IV, 288)
see also YHVH, elements
of Yod, 655 (IV, 303)
Zodiac:
fixed signs, 644 (IV, 288)
see also Hebrew alphabet
Heisenberg's Uncertainty Principle, 700
Heka, 159 (II, 77)
Hekas! Hekas! Este Bebeloi!:
Bornless Ritual, 442 (III, 259)
consecration rituals:
elemental weapons, 323 (III, 70)
Lotus Wand, 303 (III, 42)
Rose-Cross, 214 (III, 57)
Sword, 318 (III, 63)
Vault, 258 (II, 264)
Neophyte ritual, 118, 131 (II, 13, 39)
Opening by Watchtower:
evocation ritual, 402 (III, 195)
spiritual development ritual, 435 (III, 248)
Vault consecration, 258 (II, 264)
helmets: court cards of Tarot, 545-9 *passim* IV, 146, 148, 150, 152)
Heptad, 188, 240, 262 (II, 135, 233, 272)
Hepstad (continued):
Vault symbolism, 242 (II, 238)
heptagon, 506, 508, 509 (IV, 89, 91-2)
heptagram, 70, 506, 508, 509 (I, 136; IV, 89, 92)
Seven-Branched Candlestick, 150 (II, 62)
talismans, 481 (IV, 55)
Tarot:
The Star, 188 (II, 135)
The Universe, 160 (II, 80)
Tomb of Christian Rosenkreutz, 223 (II, 201)
Vault symbolism, 223, 242, 243, 266, 267 (II, 201, 238, 240, 283)
Heptameron (Pietro de Abano), 497 (IV, 80)
heptangle, 506, 508 (IV, 89, 91)
Vault symbolism, 242 (II, 238)
Here (Hera), 550 (IV, 153)
Hercules, 163 (II, 86)
constellation, 545, 595-8 *passim* (IV, 146, 219, 222, 223, 224)
Binah, 603 (IV, 232)
Chokmah, 603 (IV, 231)
hermaphroditical brass, 82 (I, 163)
Hermes, 477, 478 (IV, 48, 49)
bird of, 188 (II, 135)
caduceus, 162, 340, 478 (II, 83; III, 97; IV, 50)
see also caduceus
The Magician, 588 (IV, 210)
Pillars of—*see* Pillars
Thoth, 374-5 (III, 150)
Hermes Lodge, 624n
Hermes Mercurius, 477 (IV, 48)
Hermes Trismegistus, 17, 95 (I, 19, 191)
Emerald Tablet, 128 (II, 23)
Poemandres, Corpus Hermeticum, Book One, 201n
Scotts Hermetica, 201n
Thrice-Greatest Hermes (G. R. S. Mead), 201n
Hermes Tho-oth, 375 (III, 151)
Hermes Vision, 43, 44, 476-8 (I, 84, 85; IV, 47-50)
Hermetic Order of the Golden Dawn—*see* Golden Dawn
Hermit, The, xx, 590 (IV, 212)
divination:
example, 577, 578, 579 (IV, 194, 195, 196)
meaning, 584 (IV, 205)
see also Tarot, trumps
Herochiel, 86, 562 (I, 171; IV, 173)
Hesur, 158 (II, 77)
Heta (Coptic letter), 345 (III, 105)
Hexad, 185, 507 (II, 129; IV, 91)
hexagon, 507 (IV, 91)
hexagram, 7, 70, 205, 207, 507-8 (I, 136; II, 169, 172; IV, 91)
Banner of the East, 218, 336 (II, 195; III, 91)

hexagram (continued):
Enochian King and Seniors, 637 (IV, 278)
four forms, 294-6 (III, 28-31)
Jupiter, 414 (III, 214)
macrocosm, 277, 507 (II, 299; IV, 91)
Mars, 318, 319 (III, 64, 65)
Moon, 430 (III, 241)
officers, formed by:
elemental grade rituals, 137
Neophyte ritual, 122, 125 (II, 22, 28)
Pentacle, 322 (III, 69)
Pillars, formed by bases of, 333 (III, 86)
planetary attribution of points, 287, 312 (III, 20-21, 55)
planets, 287-93, 299 (III, 20-8, 35-36)
consecration of Rose-Cross, 315 (III, 59)
ritual, 42, 43, 48, 287-99 (I, 81, 84, 95; III, 20-36)
Adeptus Minor Obligation, 230 (II, 214)
Enochian system, 624 (IV, 260)
skrying, 668 (IV, 323)
Lesser Banishing Ritual of the Hexagram, 258, 284, 293-4, 299, 314, 318 (II, 264-5; III, 15, 28, 35, 36, 57, 65)
astral projection, 466 (IV, 27)
ceremonial magic, 377 (III, 154)
consecration of talisman, 413 (III, 212)
evocation, 384, 402, 412 (III, 166, 195, 211)
invisibility ritual, 423, 428 (III, 229, 238)
skrying, 669 (IV, 325)
spiritual development ritual, 435 (III, 248)
transformation ritual, 434 (III, 247)
Lesser Invoking Ritual of the Hexagram, 299 (III, 35-6)
Mars, 318, 319 (III, 64, 65)
Saturn, 423 (III, 230)
Supernals, 413, 447 (III, 212, 266)
Lesser Ritual of the Hexagram, 296-9 (III, 32-5)
Supreme Invoking Ritual of the Hexagram:
Jupiter, 414 (III, 213)
Moon, 430 (III, 240)
Supernals, 436 (III, 250)
Supreme Ritual of the Hexagram, 287, 293, 299, 310 (III, 21, 27, 35, 51)
Rose-Cross lamen, 310 (II, 51)
Saturn:
consecration of elemental weapons, 325 (III, 73)
evocation, 407, 409 (III, 203, 206)
requiem ceremony, 447 (III, 267)
sceptre of Cancellarius, 332 (III, 84)
skrying, 464 (IV, 24)
spiritual consciousness, 103 (I, 209-10)
Sun, 508 (IV, 91)
talismans, discharging, 481 (IV, 54)

hexagram (continued):
Tarot:
divination, 566 (IV, 177-8)
Knight (King) of Pentacles, 549, 551 (IV, 152, 155)
Knight (King) of Swords, 548, 551 (IV, 150, 155)
Tiphareth, 84, 205, 217, 465 (I, 168; II, 169, 191; IV, 27)
tracing, 287-8 (III, 21)
Vau, 277 (II, 299)
Zodiac, signs of, 299 (III, 35)
hexangle, 507 (IV, 91)
Hiddikel, 73, 177, 242, 315 (I, 145; II, 114, 236; III, 60)
Hiereus, 81, 337-8, 341-2 (I, 162; III, 92-4, 100)
astral/cosmic Neophyte temple in Sphere of Sensation, 453 (III, 274)
badge—*see* Hiereus, lamen
cloak, 119, 337 (II, 16; III, 92-3)
illustration, 349 (III, 111)
elemental grade rituals, 137, 139
Equinox ceremony, 248, 249, 250, 256, 374 (II, 246-50 *passim*, 261; III, 149)
installed, 256 (II, 261)
lays down sword, 249 (II, 247)
lays down lamen, 250 (II, 250)
Horus, 338, 352, 355, 359, 361, 366, 367, 369, 663 (III, 94, 114, 117, 125, 128, 136, 138, 141; IV, 315)
insignia and symbols, 337-8 (III, 92-4)
see also Banner of the West
Kerub of Water behind, 357 (III, 121)
lamen—*see* lamen, Hiereus
man, office more natural for, 341-2 (III, 100)
Neophyte formula, speeches used in:
spiritual development ritual, 392 (III, 179, 180)
transformation ritual, 390 (III, 176)
Neophyte ritual, 116-27 *passim*, 129-32 *passim*, 336, 345, 366-9 *passim*, 379-80 (II, 11-19 *passim*, 22, 24-32 *passim*, 36-37, 39, 40, 42, 43; III, 91, 105, 109, 136-42 *passim*, 157-8)
explains station, duties, cloak, sword, banner, 119 (II, 16)
station explained by Hierophant, 129 (II, 35)
Philosophus grade required for, 195, 226, 342 (II, 150, 206; III, 100)
Philosophus ritual, 181-4 *passim*, 196-90 *passim*, 192, 193, 195, 196 (II, 121-5 *passim*, 127, 131, 132, 133, 137, 139, 140, 144, 145, 150, 151, 152)
Portal ritual, 198-202 *passim*, 204-16 *passim*, 218, 220 (II, 155-61 *passim*, 163, 164, 167-78 *passim*, 180-9 *passim*, 194, 196, 197)

Hiereus (continued):
Portal ritual (continued):
garments and implements, 198 (II, 156)
Practicus ritual, 166, 167, 168, 170, 173, 174, 176-80 *passim* (II, 92, 93, 95, 96, 99, 100, 106, 107, 108, 112-8 *passim*, 120)
station (Throne of the West), 119, 123, 129, 337 (II, 16, 24, 35; III, 92)
Kerub of Water, 343 (III, 101, 102)
near door of temple, 334 (III, 87)
sword—*see* Sword, Hiereus
Theoricus ritual, 154-8 *passim*, 161, 162, 164, 165 (II, 69-73 *passim*, 75, 76, 77, 82, 83, 84, 89, 91)
Zelator ritual, 141, 142, 143, 146-53 *passim* (II, 44, 45, 47, 48, 52, 53, 54, 56, 58, 59, 60, 62, 63, 67, 68)
Hierophant, xviii, xxi, xxii, 23, 26, 27, 29, 38, 42, 334-7, 341-2 (I, 35, 42, 45-6, 49, 70, 82; III, 88-92, 100)
Aroueris, 344, 354, 366, 663 (III, 104, 117, 136; IV, 315)
cloak, 119, 250, 334, 335 (II, 16, 250; III, 88)
evocation, 380 (III, 159)
illustration, 349 (III, 111)
elemental grade rituals, 137-40 *passim*
Equinox ceremony, 248-57 *passim*, 374 (II, 245-8 *passim*, 250, 253, 256, 257, 258, 260-3 *passim*; III, 49)
confession , 255 (II, 260)
installed, 253-4 (II, 255-8)
lays down cloak and lamen, 250 (II, 250)
oath, 253 (II, 256)
insignia and symbols, 334-7 (III, 88-92)
see also Banner of the East
Hathor, behind, 356 (III, 120)
Isis and Nephthys, 344 (III, 104)
lamen—*see* lamen, Hierophant
man, office more natural for, 341-2 (III, 100)
Neophyte formula, pattern for magician:
alchemical operation, 395 (III, 185)
consecration of talismans, 385, 387 (III, 167, 168, 170)
divination, 451 (III, 271)
evocation, 381, 383 (III, 160, 161, 164)
invisibility ritual, 388 (III, 172)
spiritual development ritual, 392, 438 (III, 179, 180, 253)
transformation ritual, 390 (III, 176)
Neophyte ritual, 116-33 *passim*, 344-7 *passim*, 363-4, 366-70 *passim*, 379-80 (II, 11-29 *passim*, 31-43 *passim*; III, 105, 107, 109, 131-3, 135-42 *passim*, 157-8)
performance, assumption of god-form, 363-4 (III, 132-3)
Osiris, 114, 337, 344, 352, 354, 358, 364, 366, 663 (III, 92, 104, 114, 116-7, 124, 132-3, 136-7; IV, 315)
Hierophant (continued):
Past Hierophant:
Aroueris, 344, 352, 354, 663 (III, 104, 114, 116; IV, 315)
lamen, mantle, sceptre, 332 (III, 85)
Neophyte ritual, 116-7, 132, 332 (II, 11-12, 42; III, 84, 85)
Philosophus ritual, 181-96 *passim* (II, 121-52 *passim*)
Practicus ritual, 166-9 *passim*, 171-80 *passim* (92-9 *passim*, 101-13 *passim*, 116-20 *passim*)
sceptre—*see* sceptre, Hierophant
station:
Kerub of Air, 343 (III, 101)
see also Throne of the East
Theoricus ritual, 154-7 *passim*, 159-65 *passim* (II, 69-75 *passim*, 78-90 *passim*)
Thoth, seated on right of, 356 (III, 120)
wand—*see* sceptre, Hierophant
Zelator ritual, 141-9 *passim*, 151, 152, 153 (II, 44-59 *passim*, 63-8 *passim*)
Zelator Adeptus Minor grade required for, 342 (III, 100)
Hierophant, The, (Tarot), 589 (IV, 211)
divination:
example, 568, 569, 575, 577, 579 (IV, 181, 192, 191, 194, 196)
meaning, 584 (IV, 204)
see also Tarot, trumps
High Priestess, The, 558-9 (IV, 210)
Binah, 643, 693 (IV, 288, 363)
divination:
example, 586 (IV, 207)
meaning, 584 (IV, 204)
Hathor, 589 (IV, 210)
see also Tarot, trumps
Hihaayah, 86, 554 (I, 172; IV, 161)
Himalayas, 628 (IV, 267)
Hinduism, 20 (I, 27)
Hindus, 597 (IV, 222)
Hipotga, 325, 636 (III, 73; IV, 277)
Hippolytus, 600 (IV, 227)
Hismael, 65 (I, 127)
Enochian letters, geomantic figures, Zodiac, 495 (IV, 77)
geomancy, 524, 526 (IV, 113, 114)
sigil, 498 (IV, 81)
geomancy, 524, 525, 526 (IV, 113, 114, 116)
History Lecture, 15-6, 43 (I, 16, 84)
Hlrxn, 638 (IV, 280)
Hmagl, 326 (III, 75)
Hnlrx, 326, 638 (III, 75; IV, 280)
Ho Nike, 589 (IV, 211)
Hoc Universal Compendium Unius Mihi Sepulchrum Feci, 235 (II, 224)
Hockley, Frederick, 15, 17 (I, 16, 20)
Hod, 20, 21, 98 (I, 27, 30, 196, 197, 198)

Hod (continued):
Calvary cross of six squares, 193 (II, 145)
Chesed, Water from reflected in Hod, 331 (III, 83)
crook, 242 (II, 237)
cup (Water), 224n
Cup transmits Waters of Hod to Malkuth, 341 (III, 99)
divine name, archangel, and angelic choir, 62, 64 (I, 123, 126)
Hegemon's lamen, 79, 339 (I, 157; III, 96)
hexagram, 218, 293 (II, 195; III, 27)
Hiereus's lamen, 213, 337 (II, 184; III, 93)
Hiereus's sword, 337 (III, 93)
Maltese cross, 204 (II, 168)
Mercury, 218 (II, 195)
magic square, 497 (IV, 80)
microcosm, 102, 103 (I, 207, 209)
invisibility ritual, 424 (III, 231)
right leg, 102 (I, 207)
Neophyte temple, 331 (III, 82)
Nephesch, 103 (I, 209)
Nephthys, station of, 344 (III, 103)
octangle, 508 (IV, 92)
Paths:
from/to, 73, 76 (I, 144, 150)
27th Path, 31, 191, 215 (I, 55; II, 142, 187)
30th Path, 175, 215 (II, 110, 187)
31st Path, 172 (II, 103)
see also Paths; Tarot
Philosophus ritual, temple in, 188 (II, 137)
Pillar, Black, base of, 333, 338 (III, 85, 94)
station of Stolistes, 341 (III, 99)
Portal ritual, 200, 212 (II, 158, 181)
Practicus, 30, 73, 331 (I, 53, 144; III, 83)
temple in, 176-9 (II, 112-8)
Tarot:
Eights, 552 (IV, 157)
Cups, 560 (IV, 169)
Pentacles, 554 (IV, 160)
Swords, 563 (IV, 174)
Wands, 557 (IV, 164)
Temperance, 217, 218 (II, 192)
Third Adept in Portal ritual, 199n, 221n
Thoth, 330n
triangle on altar, angle of, 162 (II, 85)
Water from Chesed reflected in Hod, 331, 341 (III, 83, 99)
see also Sephiroth
Hodos Chamelionis, 43, 242 (I, 84; II, 236)
officer in Adeptus Minor ritual, 221, 225-8 *passim*, 230, 231 (II, 198, 205, 207, 208, 210, 216)
officer in Vault Consecration ceremony, 260 (II, 268, 269)
see also Minutum Mundum; Path of the Chameleon
Holder of the Balances, The—*see* Justice
"Holy art Thou, Lord of the Universe!"—see adoration
Holy Books of Thelema, The (Aleister Crowley), xxi
Holy City, 150 (II, 61)
Holy Guardian Angel, xx, xxiv, 11, 12, 697n
Holy Kabbalah, The (A. E. Waite), 44 (I, 87)
Holy Living Creatures, 96 (I, 193)
see also Chayoth ha-Qadesh
Holy of Holies, 215 (II, 188)
Holy Spirit, 29, 272, 407, 410, 431, 432, 635 (I, 49; II, 290; III, 204, 209, 242, 243, 245; IV, 276)
Holy Table (Dee and Kelly), 626 (IV, 263)
hood and mantle: The Hermit, 590 (IV, 212)
hoodwink, 117, 121, 124 (II, 12, 19-20, 26)
Neophyte ritual, 213-4, 353, 367, 368, 379 (II, 184; III, 132, 138, 139, 157, 158)
explained, 128 (II, 30)
removed, 125, 379 (II, 28, 158)
Philosophus ritual, 182 (II, 125, 126)
Practicus ritual, 168 (II, 95, 96)
Theoricus ritual, 156, 157 (II, 73, 74)
Zelator ritual, 142, 144, 145 (II, 45, 49, 50)
Hoor, 338, 352, 425 (III, 94, 114, 232)
Enochian chess knight, 691 (IV, 360)
see also Horus
Hoor-Po-Krattist (Hoorpokrati, Hoor-po-krat-ist, Ho-or-Po-Kratt-I St)—*see* Harpocrates
Hoqmiah, 86, 555 (I, 173; IV, 162)
Hori (Coptic letter), 345 (III, 105)
Hormaku, 157 (II, 75)
Horniman, Annie, ix
horse, 214 (II, 185)
head (crest), 545, 551 (IV, 146, 155)
see also water-horse
horses, Knights (Kings) of Tarot, 544, 545, 546, 548, 549, 551 (IV, 144, 145, 146, 148, 150, 152, 155)
Horus, 57 (I, 114)
Bornless Ritual, 443 (III, 261)
Children of, 114, 343-4, 352, 356, 357-62 (III, 101, 102-3, 114, 120, 122-30)
Enochian:
chess pawns, 687, 692 (IV, 353, 361)
pyramids, 663 (IV, 315)
illustration, 665 (IV, 317)
see also Ahephi; Ameshet; Kabexnuv; Toumathph
circumambulation, 346, 347 (III, 108, 109)
description, 355 (III, 117)
Enochian:
chess knight, 686, 687, 691 (IV, 351, 352, 360)
pyramids, 663 (IV, 315)
Fire, 692 (IV, 361)
Harpocrates, 344 (III, 103)

Horus (continued):
Hiereus, 338, 352, 355, 359, 361, 366, 367, 369, 663 (III, 94, 114, 117, 125, 128, 136, 138, 141; IV, 315)
Hori (Coptic letter), 345 (III, 105)
Horus the Elder (Aroueris), 344, 354 (III, 104, 117)
illustration, 664 (IV, 316)
Kabexnuv, 692 (IV, 361)
Mo-ooth, head-dress same as, 375 (III, 151)
Osiris, son of, 347 (III, 109)
sign of—*see* signs, Neophyte, Enterer
sons of—*see* Horus, Children of
Tarot:
Death, 211 (II, 179)
Judgment, 172 (II, 105)
transformation ritual, 432 (III, 245)
Water, 184 (II, 127)
hours—*see* planetary hours
houses—*see* astrology
Hru (HRU, H.R.U.), 264, 438, 448, 540, 566 (II, 276; III, 253, 267; IV, 138, 178)
Hrxnl, 638 (IV, 280)
Htaad, 326, 638 (III, 75; IV, 280)
Htdim, 326 (III, 75)
Htmorda, 325, 636 (III, 73; IV, 277)
Hua, 37, 229, 220, 263, 276, 277, 429, 437, 464 (I, 68; II, 212, 215, 275, 299, 300; III, 239, 252; IV, 24)
Hugo—*see* Alverda, Hugo
Human Body, The (Logan Clendenning), 5
humility, trial of, 226-7 (II, 206-9)
Hxnlr, 638 (IV, 280)
Hydra, 595, 599, 600 (IV, 220, 225-8 *passim*)
Hydrus, 600 (IV, 228)

– I –

I (in Bornless Ritual), 443 (III, 261)
I (Enochian Son of Light), 207n
I.A., Frater, 231 (II, 218)
Iaaasd, 672 (IV, 330)
IAO (Iao), 12, 37, 224, 229, 261, 375n (I, 68; II, 202, 212, 271)
Bornless Ritual, 445 (III, 265)
requiem ceremony, 448 (III, 267)
skrying (Enochian), 668 (IV, 323)
spiritual development ritual, 437 (III, 252)
Tarot divination, 566 (IV, 178)
transformation ritual, 429 (III, 239)
see also keyword analysis
I.N.R.I., xviii, 11-4, 224, 225, 240-1, 262, 263, 274 (II, 202, 205, 234, 271, 274, 295)
Rose-Cross lamen, 311 (III, 53)
see also keyword analysis
I.O., Frater, 231, 232 (II, 218, 219)
"I come in the power of the Light," 5, 27, 125, 449 (I, 45; II, 27; III, 269)
Iabas, 442 (III, 259)
Iaeo, 444 (III, 263)
Iahdonhi, 508 (IV, 92)
Iapos, 442 (III, 259)
Ib, 443 (III, 260)
ibis:
Queen of Cups, 547, 551 (IV, 149, 155)
Thoth, 356 (III, 120)
Ic Zod Heh Chal (Ikzhikal), 143, 204 (II, 48, 167)
consecration of Pentacle, 325 (III, 73)
consecration of talisman, 422 (III, 227)
evocation, 404, 405, 407, 409, 410 (III, 198, 201, 203, 206, 208)
Icarus, 592 (IV, 215)
Iczhhca, 207n
Ida, 515, 516, 522 (IV, 97-100 *passim*, 108)
Idoigo, 637, 672, 673 (IV, 279, 330, 331)
Ieou, 444 (III, 263)
Igne Natura Renovatur Integra or Igne Natura Renovando
Integrat, 241 (II, 234)
Igne Nitrum Roris Invenitur, 241 (II, 234)
Ih, 207n
IHVH—*see* YHVH
Ikzhikal—*see* Ic Zod Heh Chal
Illusionary Success, Lord of—*see* Sevens (Tarot), Cups
Ilr, 207n
Image of the Vision of Nebuchadnezzar, 206 (II, 170-1)
Imaginative Intelligence, 212 (II, 181)
Imperator:
Equinox ceremony, 250 (II, 249-50)
function and duties, 252, 331 (II, 254; III, 83)
lamen and cloak, 331 (III, 83)
Geburah, 342 (III, 101)
Nephthys, 342, 344, 352, 354, 356, 663 (III, 101, 104, 114, 116, 119; IV, 315)
Neophyte ritual, 116-7, 132, 331-2 (II, 11-2, 42; III, 82-4)
sword, 331, 332 (III, 83, 84)
illustration, 348 (III, 110)
In Nomine Dei viventis, 251, 255 (II, 251, 259)
In the Pronaos of the Temple (Franz Hartmann), 14 (I, 13)
incense:
Adeptus Minor ritual, 221 (II, 200)
astral projection, 466 (IV, 27)
consecration rituals:
elemental weapons, 323 (III, 70)
Lotus Wand, 303 (III, 41)
Rose-Cross, 314 (III, 57)
Sword, 317, 318, 319 (III, 63, 65)
Vault, 258, 259 (II, 264, 267)
evocation, 402, 411, 412 (III, 195, 210, 211)
Ritual of the Rose-Cross, 306, 307 (III, 46, 47, 48)

incense (continued):
skrying, 468, 473, 668 (IV, 31, 40, 323)
spiritual development ritual, 436 (III, 249)
sticks, Portal ritual, 198, 200, 208, 216 (II, 155, 173, 175, 189)
"Index for general reference to the Enterer [Neophyte] Ceremony," 379-80 (III, 157-8)
India, 231, 628 (II, 216; IV, 267)
individual work—*see* solitary work
Indus (constellation), 599 (IV, 226)
Infernal Palaces, Seven, 177 (II, 114)
Infernal Rivers of Daath, 239 (II, 229)
Infernal Sephiroth—*see* Averse Sephiroth
Information Theory, 699
infrared, 267 (II, 283)
"Inheritor of a Dying World," xvii, 121 (II, 20)
initiation, xvii, xix, xx, 4, 9, 18, 21-3, 27-39, 57-9, 363, 365, 697, 699 (I, 23, 30-5, 44-74, 114-7; III, 131, 135)
Pathworking, 463 (IV, 22)
self-initiation, 45 (I, 88)
Inner Light, Society of the, ix
Inner Order, xviii, xxiv, xxv, 36, 41, 41-2, 195 (I, 66, 79, 80; II, 149)
rituals, 197-277 (II, 155-300)
see also Roseae Rubae et Aureae Crucis
insects, 109 (I, 222)
Institute for the Study of American Religion, 697
instruments—*see* weapons, magical
Intelligences from (17th-century commentary on) *Sepher Yetzirah:*
Administrative, 159 (II, 78)
Collecting, 175 (II, 109-10)
Corporeal, 185 (II, 129)
Exacting, 191 (II, 142)
Imaginative, 212 (II, 181)
Natural, 187-8 (II, 134)
Perpetual, 172 (II, 103)
of Probation, 218 (II, 193)
Pure and Clear, 163 (II, 86)
Recondite, 194 (II, 147-8)
Renovating, 213 (II, 184)
Resplendent, 438, 615, 617 (III, 253; IV, 248, 251)
Wonderful or Hidden, 615 (IV, 248)
intelligences of the planets, 65 (I, 127)
sigils, 483, 485, 497-502 (IV, 58, 60, 80-6)
talismans, 503 (IV, 87-8)
intestines, 360, 361 (III, 126, 127, 128, 129)
Intra Nobis Regnum Dei, 241 (II, 234)
"Introduction to the Enochian System," 624-30 (IV, 260-73)
inverted pentagram—*see* pentagram, inverted
invisibility, 48 (I, 96)
Aleph (Air), 387 (III, 171)
Neophyte formula, 377, 378, 379, 387-9, 423-8 (III, 154, 156, 171-5, 229-38)
invisibility (continued):
Shin of Yeheshuah, 376, 387, 388 (III, 152, 171, 172)
Sign of Silence, 372 (III, 146)
invisible stations, 114-5, 346, 663 (III, 107-8; IV, 315)
"Invisible Stations, The," 342-4 (III, 101-4)
invocation, 44, 45, 377, 378, 379 (I, 87, 89; III, 154, 156)
alchemical operation, 395-9 *passim* (III, 184-91 *passim*)
Bornless Ritual, 443 (III, 260)
consecration of talismans, 384, 385, 413, 420, 422 (III, 166, 167, 171, 213, 224, 228)
divination, 393 (III, 182)
Enochian system, 624 (IV, 260)
skrying, 669, 671, 672, 673 (IV, 326, 329, 332)
evocation, 380, 382 (III, 159, 165)
invisibility ritual, 388 (III, 172)
purification and consecration of Body of Light, 464 (IV, 25)
requiem ceremony, 448 (III, 267)
spiritual development ritual, 391 (III, 178)
transformation ritual, 390, 391, 429, 432 (III, 175, 177, 239, 244)
Ioel, 443 (III, 262)
Iomd, 670 (IV, 326)
Ioou, 444 (III, 263)
Iophiel (Jophiel, Yophiel), 65, 97 (I, 127, 194)
consecration of Jupiter talisman, 414-9 *passim*, 421 (III, 214-6 *passim*, 218, 221, 223, 225)
sigil, 498 (IV, 81)
Iou, 444 (III, 263)
Ipsissmus, 21 (I, 30)
iron:
alchemy, 60 (I, 119)
Image of the Vision of Nebuchadnezzar, 206 (II, 171)
Isa, 444 (III, 262)
Isaiah, 207 (II, 172)
Isak, 444 (III, 262)
Ischure, 443 (III, 261)
Isha, 666 (IV, 319)
Isis, 12, 13, 56, 57, 187, 272, 425 (I, 112, 114; II, 132, 290; III, 232)
Ameshet, 361 (III, 129)
Bornless Ritual, 443 (III, 261)
description, 356 (III, 119-20)
Enochian:
chess queen, 686, 687, 691 (IV, 351, 352, 360)
pyramids, 663 (IV, 315)
Fire, 372 (III, 147)
Hathor, 343 (III, 101)
illustration, 664 (IV, 316)

Isis (continued):
Lotus Wand, 224, 262 (II, 203, 272)
called upon in consecration, 304 (III, 43)
of Nature, 163, 508 (II, 86; IV, 92)
Neophyte ritual, 369 (III, 140, 141)
see also Isis, station, invisible
Osiris, 56, 691 (I, 112; IV, 359)
Pillar, 344, 346 (III, 103-4, 108)
Praemonstrator, 342, 344, 352, 354, 356, 663 (III, 101, 103-4, 114, 116, 119-20; IV, 315)
station, invisible, 343, 344 (III, 101, 103-4)
step, 371 (III, 144)
Tarot:
The Empress, 589, 590 (IV, 210, 213)
Judgment, 172 (II, 104)
The Star, 188 (II, 135)
The Universe, 159, 592 (II, 79; IV, 216)
Toumathph, 692 (IV, 361)
transformation, 429-34 (III, 239-47)
Vault, 38 (I, 71)
veil, 342 (III, 100)
Venus symbol, 79, 195 (I, 158; II, 149)
Water, 184, 692 (II, 127; IV, 361)
see also keyword analysis
Isis-Sothis, 188 (II, 135)
Isis-Urania, 272, 276 (II, 290, 298)
Isis-Urania Temple, ix, 16, 17, 202n, 272 (I, 17, 21; II, 290)
Israel, 83, 190, 418 (I, 165; II, 138-9; III, 220)
Tribes, 149, 305 (II, 60-1; III, 44)
Issachar, 305 (III, 44)
Izaz (Eezodahzod), 669 (IV, 325)

- J -

J Document, 43 (I, 84, 85)
Jachin, 81 (I, 161-2)
jackal:
Anubis, 355 (III, 118)
Tou-mathaph, 343, 357, 361 (III, 103, 122, 128)
Jackson, Howard M., *The Lion Becomes Man,* 375n
Jaho, 375n
Jeheshua—*see* Yeheshua
Jehovah, 73, 333 (I, 144; III, 86)
human, 101 (I, 205-6)
see also Tetragrammaton, YHVH
Jehovah Elohim, 97 (I, 194)
see also YHVH Elohim
Jehovah Tzabaoth, 97 (I, 196)
see also YHVH Tzabaoth
Jehovashah—*see* Yehovashah
Jesuits and I.N.R.I., 11
Jesus, 11, 14, 94, 214, 240 (I, 188; II, 186, 234)
see also Christ
Jesus Nazarenus Rex Judecorum, 240 (II, 234)
Jewish Gnosticism, Merkabah Mysticism and Talmudic Tradition (Gershom G. Scholem), 375n
Jim (Jimel), 650 (IV, 297)
Job 19:25—239, 264, 440, 444-5, 449 (II, 231, 277; III, 257, 263, 269)
St. John, Gosepl According to, 12
3:8—102 (I, 207)
1:25-26—237 & 239, 264, 444, 449 (II, 229, 277; III, 257, 263, 269) 14:6—239, 264, 276, 440, 445, 449 (II, 231, 277, 299; III, 257, 263-4, 269)
Johnson, Charles, 628, 629 (IV, 267)
Johnson, Wendell, *People in Quandaries,* 6
Johoel, 375n
Jonas, Hans, *The Gnostic Religion,* 13, 202n
Jophiel—*see* Iophiel
journal, magical, x, xix-xx, xxiii
Judah, 305 (III, 44)
Jude, 280 (III, 10)
Judge, 530, 531, 538, 539 (IV, 120, 123, 133, 134, 135)
see also geomancy
Judgement—*see* Judgment
Judges 5:4, 5:23, 5:21—190 (II, 139-40)
Judges of the Dead—*see* Forty-two Judges of the Dead
Judgment (Tarot), 166, 172, 592 (II, 92, 104-5; IV, 216)
divination:
example, 577, 579, 580, 581 (IV, 194, 196, 199)
meaning, 585 (IV, 206)
Juggler, The—*see* Magician, The
Jung, Carl Gustav, xix, xxi, xxiv, 34, 46, 47 (I, 62-3, 91-2, 93)
Man and His Symbols, 5
Psychology of Transference, The, xxv
Secret of the Golden Flower, The, commentary to, 26-7, 33, 365 (I, 43, 58; III, 135)
see also analytical psychology
Jupiter (god), 75, 628 (I, 149; IV, 266)
sphere or orb, 221n
Jupiter (planet), 63, 65 (I, 125, 127)
alchemical operation, 398 (III, 189)
angel, intelligence, and spirit, 65 (I, 127)
aspiration, ruler of, 209, 210n, 214, 215 (II, 177, 185, 187)
Chesed, 19, 97, 218 (I, 26, 194; II, 195)
construction, 474 (IV, 41)
ear, left, 103 (I, 210)
Enochian letters and geomantic figures, 495 (IV, 77)
Fire, 215, 648 (II, 187; IV, 294)
hexagram, 218, 288, 289, 414 (II, 195; III, 21-22, 213, 214)

Jupiter (continued):
- Kaph, 215, 493 (II, 187; IV, 72)
- Kether, 643 (IV, 287, 288)
- lineal figures, 493 (IV, 72)
- magic square, 498 (IV, 81)
- Maltese cross, 204 (II, 168)
- Mars, balanced by, 215 (II, 187)
- Pisces, 495 (IV, 77)
- Sagittarius, 215, 495 (II, 187; IV, 77)
- seal, 498 (IV, 81)
- Spirit, 210n
- square, 70, 506 (I, 136; IV, 90)
- talisman, consecration, 413-22 (III, 212-28)
- Tarot:
  - Nine of Cups, 541, 560 (IV, 140, 169)
  - Six of Wands, 541, 553 (IV, 139, 158)
  - Swords:
    - Four, 541, 555 (IV, 139, 162)
    - Eight, 541, 563 (IV, 140, 173)
  - Two of Pentacles, 541, 558 (IV, 140, 165, 166)
  - The Wheel of Fortune, 71, 72, 542 (I, 139, 142; IV, 141)
- 25th Path, 214 (II, 185)
- Vault symbolism, 268 (II, 283)
- Water, 215 (II, 187)
- Zodiac, position in, 414 (III, 213)
- *see also* planets

Justice, 590 (IV, 213)
- divination:
  - example, 577, 578, 579 (IV, 194, 195, 196)
  - meaning, 584 (IV, 205)
- Nephthys, 589, 590 (IV, 210, 213)
- *see also* Tarot, trumps

- K -

K Document, 43 (I, 84)
- *see* "The Consecration Ceremony of the Vault of the Adepti," 258-69 (II, 264-86)

kabalah, kabballah—*see* Qabalah

Kaballah Unveiled, The (trans. MacGregor Mathers), 8, 16 (I, 18-9)

Kabexnuv (Kabexnuf), 344, 352, 358, 359 (III, 103, 114, 124, 125)
- description, 358 (III, 122)
- Enochian:
  - chess pawn, 687, 692 (IV, 353, 361)
  - pyramids, 663 (IV, 315)
- Fire, 692 (IV, 361)
- Horus, 692 (IV, 361)
- illustration, 665 (IV, 317)
- liver and gall bladder, 360, 361 (III, 127, 128)
- North, 361 (III, 128)
- Northwest, 344, 352, 358, 663 (III, 103, 114, 122; IV, 315)
- Sakhet, 361 (III, 129)

Kabexnuv (continued):
- West, 361 (III, 128)
- *see also* Qebhsenef

Kabiri, 31, 87, 169-71 (I, 53, 176; II, 97-101)
- Judgment, 172 (II, 104-5)

Kadesh, 191, 418 (II, 140; III, 220)

Kalah or Kallah, 72, 77 (I, 141, 155)

Kamael, 62, 64, 97, 318, 419 (I, 123, 126, 195; III, 64, 222)

kamea—*see* magic squares

Kaph:
- Air, 221n
- astral projection, 471 (IV, 36)
- construction, 474 (IV, 41)
- Jupiter and 25th Path, 214, 215 (II, 185-188 passim)
- lineal figures, 493 (IV, 72)
- skrying, 470 (IV, 34)
- 21st Path (Jupiter, The Wheel of Fortune):
  - Air, 210n
  - Hegemon's sceptre, 339 (III, 95)
  - Philosophus ritual, 192-3 (II, 144-5)
  - Portal ritual, 198, 209, 210 (II, 155, 177, 178)
- *see also* Hebrew alphabet; Jupiter; Paths; Wheel of Fortune

Kaph Cheth, 194 (II, 147)

Karma, 479-80 (IV, 52-3)

Karmaim, 191 (II, 141)

Kasmillos, 169-74 *passim* (II, 97-100 *passim*, 105-8 *passim*)

Kedemel, 65 (I, 127)
- Enochian:
  - chess, 690 (IV, 357)
  - letters, geomantic figures, Zodiac, 495 (IV, 77)
- geomancy, 524, 526 (IV, 113, 114)
- sigil, 500, 526 (IV, 84, 114)

Kehethel, 86, 554 (I, 172; IV, 160)

Kelial, 86, 555 (I, 173; IV, 162)

Kelly, Edward, 625-6, 628, 629, 658 (IV, 262-3, 267, 268, 309)

Kena Upanishad, 628 (IV, 267)

Kephra—*see* Khephera

Kerub, 80, 324, 405, 408, 471, 656 (II, 158; III, 72, 199, 206; IV, 36, 306)

Kerubic squares—*see* Enochian tablets, Kerubic squares

Kerubic Stations, Rite of the, 156-60, 464 (II, 72-81; IV, 24)
- formula, 420-2 (III, 223-8)

Kerubim, 27, 30, 46, 61 (I, 45, 52, 90, 120)
- angelic choir, 62, 64, 98 (I, 123, 126, 197)
  - transformation ritual, 430, 431, 433, 434 (III, 241, 243, 246, 247)
- angelic choir of Chokmah, 96 (I, 194)
- Apocalypse, 207 (II, 173)
- Ark of the Covenant, 146, 162 (II, 54, 85)

Kerubim (continued):
  Ark of the Covenant (continued):
    Shekinah between, 276, 375 (II, 298; III, 151)
  Circular Altar, 235, 243 (II, 224, 240)
  Eden, guardians of, 147, 233 (II, 54-5, 222)
  Egyptian gods, 663 (IV, 315)
  elements, lords of, 361 (III, 128)
  Enochian:
    chess, 688 (IV, 355)
    tablets:
      Kerubic squares, 644 (IV, 288)
      pyramids, 661 (IV, 313-4)
  Equinox ceremony, 374 (III, 149)
  Ezekiel, Vision of, 207, 233, 618 (II, 172-3, 222-3; IV, 253)
  Flaming Sword of the, altar diagram, 141, 145, 147, 154, 161 (II, 44, 52, 55, 56, 69, 82)
  Malkuth, 405 (III, 200)
  pentagram, 507 (IV, 90)
  signs or sigils, 280, 281, 282 (III, 10, 11, 12)
    consecration of elemental weapons, 325, 326-7 (III, 74, 75, 76, 77)
    Enochian pyramids, 649 (IV, 295)
    hexagram rituals, 296 (III, 31)
  sphinxes, 659, 660, 661 (IV, 310, 311, 314)
  stations, invisible, 342-3, 353, 356, 357 (III, 101-2, 115, 120, 121-2)
    Children of Horus between, 358 (III, 124)
  32nd Path, 155, 159, 209 (II, 71, 79, 176)
  Tomb of Christian Rosenkreutz guarded by emblems of, 224, 233, 242 (II, 203, 222, 273)
  The Universe, 160, 592 (II, 80; IV, 216)
  Vault symbolism, 246, 268 (II, 240, 284, 285)
  Veil of the Tabernacle, 159 (II, 79)
  voices, 653 (IV, 300)
  see also bull; eagle; lion; man
Kerux, 27, 339-40, 341-2 (I, 44; III, 96-7, 98-9, 100)
  angelic, 438 (III, 254)
  see also angel torch-bearer
  Anubis, 341, 346, 347, 352, 355, 356, 369, 663 (III, 98, 108, 109, 114, 118, 119, 142; IV, 315)
  astral/cosmic Neophyte temple in Sphere of Sensation, 452, 453 (III, 273, 274)
  elemental grade rituals, 139
  Equinox ceremony, 248, 249, 250, 255, 256, 257, 374 (II, 245-50 *passim*, 261, 262, 263; III, 149)
    installed, 256 (II, 262)
    lays down lamp and wand, 249 (II, 247)
  lamen, 139, 340 (III, 97)
    illustration, 351 (III, 113)
    see also caduceus
Kerux (continued):
  lamp—*see* lamp, Kerux
  Neophyte formula, speeches:
    evocation, 381 (III, 161, 162)
  Neophyte ritual, 116-22 *passim*, 124-7 *passim*, 129-33 *passim*, 344, 347, 364, 366-70 *passim*, 379-80 (II, 11-20 *passim*, 22, 25-9 *passim*, 32, 36, 38, 39, 40, 42, 43; III, 105, 109, 133, 137, 139, 141, 142, 143, 157-8)
    explains station, duties, lamp, wand, 119 (II, 15)
  station, 119, 160, 341 (II, 15, 81; III, 99)
  Theoricus grade required for, 137, 342 (III, 100)
  Theoricus ritual, 154-62 *passim*, 164 (II, 69, 70, 71, 73-8 *passim*, 81, 82, 83, 88, 89)
    station represents Gehenna, 160 (II, 81)
  wand (or staff)—*see* Wand, Kerux
  woman, office more natural for, 342 (III, 100)
  Zelator ritual, 141, 142, 144, 145, 146, 148, 149, 151, 152 (II, 44, 45, 46, 49-54 *passim*, 57-60 *passim*, 65, 66, 67)
Kether, 11, 19, 20, 21, 96, 97, 98, 615, 616, 617 (I, 24, 25, 28, 30, 193, 195, 198; IV, 248-51 *passim*)
  Aima Elohim, crown of, 177 (II, 114)
  Air, 345 (III, 106)
  alchemical operation, 399 (III, 190, 191)
  archangel, 374 (III, 150)
    see also archangels; Metatron
  of Assiah, 358, 362, 476, 614, 615, 617, 618, 619, 621 (III, 124, 130; IV, 46, 247, 248, 249, 252, 253, 254, 256, 257)
    Rashith ha Gilgalim, 614 (IV, 247)
  Atziluth, 617 (IV, 251)
  of Atziluth, 375, 614 (III, 151; IV, 246)
  Bornless Ritual, 442, 443, 444 (III, 259, 261, 263)
  of Briah, 614 (IV, 246)
  caduceus, 162, 340 (II, 83; III, 97)
  consecration of talisman, 413 (III, 212)
  crook, 242 (II, 237)
  Cup of Stolistes, 70, 177, 340 (I, 138; II, 113; III, 97)
  de Bry, Franciscus, 275 (II, 296)
  divine name, archangel, and angelic choir, 62, 64, 96 (I, 123, 126, 193)
  Draco, 451, 596, 603, 607 (III, 271; IV, 221, 231, 236)
  Eheieh, 188 (II, 135)
  Enochian:
    chess king, 693 (IV, 363)
    tablets, 656 (IV, 305)
  Hegemon's lamen, 339 (III, 95)
  Heh, 617, 641 (IV, 251, 282)
  hexagram, 293 (III, 27)
  Hierophant's lamen (collar), 336 (III, 91)
  Hierophant's sceptre, 335 (III, 90)

Kether (continued):
Hua, 276 (II, 299)
Jupiter, 643 (IV, 287, 288)
knowledge of through Chokmah and Binah, 331 (III, 82)
lineal figure, 493 (IV, 72)
Macroprosopus, 656 (IV, 305)
Malkuth, 613 (IV, 246)
Mercury, not included on symbol of, 71 (I, 138)
microcosm, 100, 101, 103, 105, 106 (I, 203, 205, 206, 209, 213, 214, 216)
above crown of head, 100, 405, 442, 448 (I, 203; III, 200, 259, 268)
individual, 373 (III, 148)
Neophyte ritual, 367 (III, 138)
Neophyte symbol (0=0), 347 (III, 119)
no planetary attribution, 268 (II, 286)
North Pole of heavens, 547, 549, 596, 602, 603, 655 (IV, 150, 152, 221, 231, 304)
Pan drawing, 213 (II, 184)
point, 204-5, 505 (II, 168; IV, 89)
Primum Mobile, 63, 96, 506 (I, 125, 193; IV, 89)
of Qlippoth, 614 (IV, 247)
requiem ceremomy, 448 (III, 268)
Rising on the Planes, 464 (IV, 24)
robe, white, 470 (IV, 40)
Rose-Cross lamen, 310, 311 (III, 51, 53, 54)
Serpent of Widsom, 275 (II, 297)
Sign of the Enterer, 371 (III, 144)
spiritual development ritual (as Crown), 437, 440 (III, 251, 256)
-st suffix (Coptic), 337, 663 (III, 92; IV, 315)
Tarot:
Aces, 542, 596 (IV, 142, 221, 222)
The High Priestess, 589 (IV, 210)
The Magician, 588 (IV, 210)
Temperance, 217 (II, 192)
Thaumiel, 359 (III, 125)
Thma-Ae-St, 339 (III, 96)
Thoth, 330n
Tiphareth, 609 (IV, 241)
titles, 77 (I, 153)
transformation ritual (as Crown), 431, 433 (III, 243, 245)
Vau, 641 (IV, 282)
vibration of divine names, 487, 491, 492 (IV, 62, 63, 70, 71)
Wonderful or Hidden Intelligence, 615 (IV, 248)
Yechidah, 67 (I, 129)
of Yetzirah, 614 (IV, 246)
see also Sephiroth
Keveqiah, 86, 559 (I, 174; IV, 167)
Keys of Tarot—*see* Tarot, trumps
keyword analysis, xviii, 11-4, 225, 240-1, 258, 262-3, 299, 311 (II, 204, 234, 265, 273-4; III, 35, 53)
keyword analysis (continued):
consecration of Sword, 318 (III, 64)
consecration of talisman, 414 (III, 213)
invisibility ritual, 423, 425, 428 (III, 229, 230, 233, 237)
Ritual of the Rose-Cross, 307-8 (III, 48-9)
transformation ritual, 430, 433 (III, 240, 246)
Khabs Am Pekht, Konx om Pax, Light in Extension, 13, 59, 120-1, 126, 132-3 (I, 117; II, 19, 29, 43)
consecration of talismans, 386, 417 (III, 169, 219)
evocation, 410 (III, 208)
explained, 128, 347 (II, 34; III, 109-10)
invisibility ritual, 427 (III, 236)
spiritual development ritual, 439 (III, 256)
transformation ritual, 433 (III, 246)
Khem:
The Devil (Tarot), 213 (II, 182)
see also Egypt
Khephera (Khephra), 158, 425 (II, 77; III, 232)
The Moon (Tarot), 185 (II, 130)
kilt: Knave (Princess) of Wands, 546 (IV, 147)
King:
alchemy, 60 (I, 120)
Great Hermetic Arcanum, 206 (II, 170)
King, Francis, ed., *Astral Projection, Magic and Alchemy,* 199n
The King Must Die (Mary Renault), xxii
King of the Hosts of the Sea, The; King of Undines and of Nymphs—*see* Knights (Kings), Cups
King of the Spirits of the Air, The; King of Sylphs and Sylphides—*see* Knights (Kings), Swords
King of the Spirits of Fire, The; King of the Salamanders—*see* Knights (Kings), Wands
King of the Spirits of the Earth, The; King of the Gnomes—*see* Knights (Kings), Pentacles
King scale of color, 95-6, 99 (I, 192-3, 199-202)
Enochian tablets, 630 (IV, 274)
planets, 287 (III, 20)
Rose-Cross lamen, 310, 312 (III, 51, 55)
Kingdom—*see* Malkuth
Kings, II, 13:14—418, 425 (III, 220, 232)
Kings (Princes), 544 (IV, 144-5)
celestial sphere, 596 (IV, 221)
Cups, 547 (IV, 149)
divination example, 571, 572, 574-8 *passim*, 580, 581, 586 (IV, 185, 186, 187, 190, 191, 192, 194, 195, 196, 199)
divinatoy meaning, 578, 582 (IV, 195, 201)
Enochian chess bishops, 686, 691, 696 (IV, 351, 360, 367)
Pentacles, 550 (IV, 153)
divination example, 568, 569, 577, 579, 586 (IV, 181, 281, 194, 197, 207)

Kings (Princes) (continued):
Swords, 548-9 (IV, 151)
divination example, 571, 572, 577, 578, 579 (IV, 185, 187, 194, 195, 197)
Enochian chess, 687 (IV, 353)
Tiphareth, 615 (IV, 249)
Vau, 615 (IV, 249)
Wands, 545-6 (IV, 147)
divination example, 571, 572, 577, 578, 579 (IV, 185, 186, 187, 194, 196)
see also Knights (Kings); Tarot, court cards
Kings of Edom, 190, 193 (II, 138-9, 146)
see also Edom
Kings, Elemental—*see* Enochian tablets, Kings, Elemental Kings
Kings of elements, 80 (I, 158-9)
Kings, Enochian—*see* Enochian tablets, Kings
Kings, Enochian chess—*see* Enochian, chess, pieces
Kirkala, 515 (IV, 97)
Kishon, 189, 190 (II, 138, 139)
Knaves (Princesses), 544 (IV, 145)
celestial sphere, 596, 597, 601, 607, 611, 615, 617, 618 (IV, 221, 222-3, 229, 236, 237, 241, 249, 250, 251)
Cups, 547 (IV, 149-50)
divination example, 570, 571, 572, 577, 578 (IV, 184, 185, 187, 194, 195, 196)
divination, 567, 568, 569, 573 (IV, 178, 180, 183, 189)
divinatory meaning, 582 (IV, 201)
elements, 607 (IV, 237)
Enochian chess castles, 686, 691, 696 (IV, 351, 360, 367-8)
Heh, 615, 616 (IV, 249)
Malkuth, 615, 616 (IV, 249)
Pentacles, 550 (IV, 153-4)
divination example, 571, 572, 574, 575 (IV, 185, 187, 190, 191)
Seven Palaces of Malkuth, 568 (IV, 180)
Swords, 549 (IV, 152)
Tetragrammaton, 607 (IV, 237)
Wands, 546 (IV, 147-8)
divination example, 568, 569, 587 (IV, 181, 182, 208)
Zodiac, 607 (IV, 237)
see also Tarot, court cards
Kneph, 685 (IV, 350)
Knights (Kings), 544 (IV, 144)
celestial sphere, 596 (IV, 221)
Chokmah, 615 (IV, 249)
Cups, 546 (IV, 149)
divination example, 568, 569, 570, 571, 572 (IV, 181, 182, 184, 185, 187)
divinatory meaning, 582 (IV, 201)
Enochian chess knights, 686, 691 (IV, 351, 360)
Pentacles, 549 (IV, 152)
divination example, 580, 581 (IV, 199)
Knights (Kings) (continued):
Swords, 548 (IV, 150)
Wands, 545 (IV, 146)
divination example, 571, 572 (IV, 185, 186, 187)
Yod, 615 (IV, 249)
see also Tarot, court cards
Knights, Enochian chess—*see* Enochian, chess, pieces
knocks:
how signified, 117 (II, 13)
invisibility ritual, 427 (III, 235)
Neophyte ritual, 364, 366, 367, 368 (III, 133, 136, 137, 138, 139)
see also Neophyte ritual
Knousou Pekht, 686 (IV, 350)
Knowledge and Conversation of the Holy Guardian Angel, 11, 12, 45 (I, 89)
Knowledge Lectures, xxii-xxiii, 5-6, 39, 50-111, 115, 624, 643 (I, 74, 99-227; IV, 260, 287)
Kokab, 63, 65, 98 (I, 125, 127, 196)
see also Mercury (planet)
Konx om Pax—*see* Khabs Am Pekht
Kor, 275 (II, 297)
Korzybski, Alfred, 6
Kotha, 443 (III, 262)
Krishna, 588 (IV, 210)
Kumara, 274 (II, 294)
Kumaric condition, 273 (II, 292)
Kundalini, 276 (II, 298)
Kurmana, 515 (IV, 97)

- L -

L Document (History Lecture), 43, 44 (I, 84, 85)
L.V.X., xviii, xxi, 13-4, 207, 233, 263, 276 (II, 172, 223, 274, 299)
signs:
Adeptus Minor ritual, 224, 225, 247 (II, 202, 205, 244)
astral projection, 471, 472 (IV, 37, 39)
Bornless Ritual, 444, 445 (III, 263, 264)
consecrations:
Lotus Wand, 304 (III, 42)
Sword, 318 (III, 64)
Vault, 263, 264, 265 (II, 274, 277, 279)
Equinox ceremony, 252, 255 (II, 253, 259)
evocation, 402, 412 (III, 195, 210)
hexagram rituals, 293, 299 (III, 27, 35)
illustrated, 134 (II, illus. f. 43)
pentagram rituals, 285, 286 (III, 18, 19)
Portal ritual, 220 (II, 197)
skrying, 662, 666, 667 (IV, 318, 319, 321)
spiritual development ritual, 435, 436, 441 (III, 248, 250, 258)

L.V.X. (continued):
  signs (continued):
    transformation ritual, 433 (III, 245)
    Vault, 270, 271 (II, 288, 289)
    vibration of divine names, 491 (IV, 70)
  see also keyword analysis
Labo-Ae (Leo), 343, 353 (III, 102, 115)
Lacerta, 596, 597, 598 (IV, 222, 223, 225)
  Chokmah, 603 (IV, 231)
Laetitia, 494, 495, 527, 533 (IV, 75, 77, 115, 126)
  see also geomancy, figures
La Fargue, J. Michael, *Language and Gnosis,* 375n
Laidrom, 325, 407, 409 (III, 73, 203, 206)
Laird, Charlton, *The Miracle of Language,* 6
Lalaphenourphen, 207n
Lam, 520 (IV, 105)
Lamb, 274, 275 (II, 295, 297)
Lamed:
  Libra, 305, 311 (III, 44, 53)
  telesmatic image, 486, 489, 491 (IV, 61, 66, 67, 69)
  see also Hebrew alphabet
lamen, 39, 45, 139 (I, 74, 89)
  Dadouches, 240 (III, 98)
    see also Fylfot cross
  Cancellarius, 332 (III, 84)
  Hegemon, 79, 139, 193, 338, 339 (I, 157; II, 145; III, 95, 96)
    burnt in brazier, 216 (II, 189)
    Equinox ceremony, 250 (II, 250)
  Hiereus, 139, 209, 213-4, 221, 226, 337-8 (II, 176, 184-5, 198, 205; III, 92, 93)
    burnt in brazier, 216 (II, 189)
    Equinox ceremony, 250 (II, 250)
  Hierophant, 218-9, 250, 252, 254, 334, 336 (II, 194-5, 250, 253, 257; III, 88, 90-1)
    evocation, 380, 402 (III, 159, 195)
    versions worn by other officers, 331, 332 (III, 83, 84, 85)
  illustrations, 351 (III, 113)
  Imperator, 331 (III, 83)
  Kerux, 139, 340 (III, 97)
    see also caduceus
  officers in Portal ritual, 198-9, 198n (I, 156)
  Past Hierophant, 332 (III, 85)
  Praemonstrator, 332 (III, 84)
  Stolistes, 340 (III, 97-8)
    see also Cup of Stolistes
  surrendered in Equinox ceremony, 250 (II, 250)
  see also Rose-Cross
lamp:
  consecration of elemental weapons, 323 (III, 70)
  consecration of Sword, 317 (III, 63)
  Kerux, 341 (III, 98)
    Equinox ceremony, 249, 250, 374 (II, 247, 249, 250; III, 150)
lamp (continued):
  Kerux (continued):
    Lamp of Hidden Knowledge, 124, 126 (II, 25, 29)
    Neophyte ritual, 124, 126, 380 (II, 25, 29; III, 158)
      explains, 119 (II, 15)
      explained by Hierophant, 129 (II, 35)
  skrying, 468, 473 (IV, 31, 40)
  spiritual development ritual, 392 (III, 180)
  Theoricus ritual, 154-60 *passim* (II, 69-80 *passim*)
lamps:
  Neophyte ritual, 128-9 (II, 34-35)
  Portal ritual, 198-204 *passim*, 216, 218 (II, 156-63 *passim*, 167, 170, 188, 193, 194)
Lamps Before the Throne, Seven, 150 (II, 62)
lamp(s), red:
  Equinox ceremony, 249, 250 (II, 247, 248, 250)
  Fire (on altar), 333 (III, 87)
  Philosophus ritual, 188, 190, 192, 194 (II, 137, 138, 140, 148)
  Practicus ritual, 166, 169, 170, 173, 174 (II, 92, 97, 99, 100, 106, 107, 108)
Langs, Robert, *Psychotherapy: A Basic Text,* xxv
Language and Gnosis (J. Michael La Fargue), 375n
Language in Action (S. I. Hayakawa), 6
Lanoo, 274 (II, 294)
lantern: The Hermit, 590 (IV, 212)
Laoaxrp, 325 (III, 73)
Larz, 638 (IV, 279)
Last Judgment, The, (Tarot)—*see* Judgment
Latent Heat, 70, 172 (I, 137; II, 103)
  Aral, 172 (II, 105)
Latin:
  Christian Rosenkreutz, 231 (II, 216, 217)
  Equinox ceremony, 251, 252, 255 (II, 251, 253, 254, 259)
Laver of Brass, 149 (II, 59)
Laver of Water of Purification, 61 (I, 121)
Laviah, 86, 554, 555 (I, 172; IV, 161, 162)
"The Law of the Convoluted Revolution of the Forces Symbolised by the Four Aces Round the Northern Pole," 603, 607-21 (IV, 236-57)
Lazarus, 592 (IV, 216)
lead, 60 (I, 119)
Leader of the Lion—*see* Strength
Leaping or Darting Formula, 619-20 (IV, 254-5)
Lebanon, Cedars of, 191, 418 (II, 140; III, 220)
"Lecture on Shemhamphoresch," 85 (I, 170)
Left Witness—*see* Witnesses
Legis Jugum, 235 (II, 224)
Lehachiah, 86, 558 (I, 174; IV, 167)

Lekabel, 86, 558 (I, 174; IV, 166)
Lelahel, 86, 553 (I, 172; IV, 159)
Leo, 10, 158 (II, 76)
  Cancer and Virgo, 601 (IV, 229)
  Cor Leonis—*see* Regulus
  crook, 242 (II, 237)
  divine and angelic names, 86 (I, 172)
  divine name, Hebrew letter, Tribe of Israel, angel, and color, 305 (III, 44)
  Enochian chess, 690, 694 (IV, 357, 365)
  Fortuna Major, 650 (IV, 300)
  Great Hermetic Arcanum, 206 (II, 170)
  Kerub of Fire, 343, 357 (III, 192, 121)
    see also Kerubim; lion
  Labo-Ae, 343, 353 (III, 102, 115)
  Lotus Wand, 302, 305, 315 (III, 40, 44, 60)
  Oip, 669 (IV, 325)
  Regulus—*see* Regulus
  star map, 595 (IV, 219)
  symbol, 50, 61, 182, 286, 402 (I, 99, 120; II, 124; III, 19, 195)
    consecration of talisman, 420 (III, 225)
    hexagram rituals, 296 (III, 31)
    see also lion, Kerub, symbol
  Tarot:
    The Chariot, 600 (IV, 227)
    Knight (King) of Pentacles, 549, 597 (IV, 152, 223)
    Queen of Cups, 599 (IV, 225)
    Strength, 71, 72, 542, 589, 599 (I, 139, 142; IV, 141, 210, 225)
    Wands:
      Ace, 607, 610 (IV, 237, 240)
      Five, 541, 550, 552, 553 (IV, 139, 156, 158)
      Six and Seven, 541, 553 (IV, 139, 158-9)
      King (Prince), 546, 597 (IV, 147, 223)
  Vault symbolism, 266 (II, 280)
  see also Zodiac
Leo, Alan, *1001 Notable Nativities,* 91 (I, 183)
Leo Minor, 546, 597 (IV, 147, 223)
leopard:
  body of Evil One, 344 (III, 103)
  Queen of Wands, 545, 551 (IV, 146, 155)
Lepus, 600, 601 (IV, 227, 228)
Lesser Arcana—*see* Tarot, court cards; Tarot, numbered cards
Lesser Banishing Ritual of the Hexagram—*see* Hexagram Ritual
Lesser Banishing Ritual of the Pentagram, x, xxi, xxiii, 3, 4, 8, 39-40, 42, 43, 48, 90, 281-2, 284, 293-4, 296 (I, 74-6, 81, 84, 95, 181; III, 11, 15, 28, 31)
  astral performance, 54-5 (I, 108-9)
  astral projection, 466 (IV, 27)
  Bornless Ritual, 446 (III, 265)
  ceremonial magic, 377 (III, 154)
Lesser Banishing Ritual of the Pentagram (continued):
  Consecration rituals:
    elemental weapons, 323, 328 (III, 70, 78)
    Lotus Wand, 303, 304 (III, 42, 45)
    Rose-Cross, 314, 316 (III, 57, 61)
    Sword, 319 (III, 65)
    talismans, 413, 480 (III, 212; IV, 53)
    Vault (with Lotus Wand), 258 (II, 264)
  Crowley, Aleister, 698
  described, 53-5 (I, 106-9)
  dreams, remembering, 94 (I, 188-9)
  evocation, 384, 402, 412 (III, 166, 195, 211)
  invisibility ritual, 423, 428 (III, 229, 238)
  Portal ritual, 199 (I, 158)
  skrying, 469, 669 (IV, 32, 325)
  spiritual development ritual, 435 (III, 248)
  transformation ritual, 434 (III, 247)
  uses, 54-5 (I, 108-9)
  vibration of divine names, 491 (IV, 70)
Lesser Countenance, 77-8 (I, 153-5)
Lesser Invoking Ritual of the Hexagram, 299 (III, 35-6)
  Mars, 318, 319 (III, 64, 65)
  see also Hexagram Rituals
Lesser Ritual of the Hexagram, 296-9 (III, 32-5)
  see also Hexagram Rituals
Levanah, 63, 65, 98 (I, 125, 127, 197)
  see also Moon
Levi, Eliphas, xxiii, 15, 43 (I, 16, 85)
Leviathan, 76, 194 (I, 150-1; II, 146)
Lexarph—*see* Elexarpeh
Liber Æmeth sive Sigillum Dei, 657 (IV, 308)
Liber AL (The Book of the Law), 698, 699
Liber V. vel Reguli, 698
Libertas Evangelii, 235 (II, 224)
libido, xxi, 33 (I, 59)
Libra:
  alchemical operation, 397 (III, 187)
  divine and angelic names, 86 (I, 173)
  divine name, Hebrew letter, Tribe of Israel, angel, and color, 305 (III, 44)
  Enochian:
    chess, 690, 694 (IV, 357, 365)
    letter and geomantic figure, 495 (IV, 77)
    skrying, 667 (IV, 321)
  equinox, 609 (IV, 241)
  Pdoce, 669 (IV, 325)
  Rose-Cross lamen, 311 (III, 53)
  star map, 595 (IV, 219)
  symbol used in spelling divine names, 83 (I, 166)
  Tarot:
    Justice, 71, 72, 542, 599 (I, 139, 142; IV, 141, 226)

Libra (continued):
  Tarot (continued):
    King (Prince) of Cups, 547, 598 (IV, 149, 224)
    Knave (Princess) of Cups, 597 (IV, 223)
    Swords:
      Queen, 548, 598 (IV, 151, 224)
      Two, Three, and Four, 541, 555 (IV, 139, 161-2)
    Temperance, 591 (IV, 214)
  telesmatic image, 486 (IV, 61)
  Venus, 495 (IV, 77)
  see also Zodiac
library, occult, 1-6
license to depart, 384 (III, 165)
Ligdisa, 325 (III, 73)
Light in Extension—*see* Khabs Am Pekht
Light On The Path (Mabel Collins), xx-xxi
lightning, 611 (IV, 242)
  The Tower, 591 (IV, 214)
Lightning Flash, 61-2, 162 (I, 122-3; II, 85)
Liiansa, 325, 407, 409 (III, 73, 203, 206)
Lilacza, 672 (IV, 330)
lilies, water, on Tarot cards:
  Ace of Cups, 543 (IV, 143)
  numbered cards, Cups, 556, 560, 564 (IV, 162, 163, 169, 170, 175)
Lilith, 82 (I, 163)
Lily of the Valley, 143, 403, 424 (II, 46; III, 197, 231)
Limitless Light—*see* Ain Soph Aour
Linea Dei Patris Filiique—*see* Enochian tablets
Linea Spiritus Sancti—*see* Enochian tablets
lineal figures:
  planets, 70 (I, 136)
  Sephiroth, 43, 44, 492-3 (I, 84, 85; IV, 72-3)
    talismans, 503, 505, 506 (IV, 88, 89)
lion, 419 (III, 223)
  alchemy, 84 (I, 167)
  Blood of the, 217 (II, 192)
  Chaldean Oracles, 171, 214 (II, 102, 186)
  Evil One, 344 (III, 103)
  Great Hermetic Arcanum, 206 (II, 170)
  Green, 60, 206 (I, 120; II, 170)
  head (crest), 545, 551 (IV, 146, 155)
  jackal, 361 (III, 128)
  Kerub, 46, 61, 158, 182, 343, 357 (I, 90, 120; II, 76, 124; III, 101, 102, 121)
    Circular Altar, 235, 243, 259 (II, 224, 240, 266)
    consecration of Fire Wand, 325 (III, 74)
      see also altar, Circular Altar
    Oip, 653 (IV, 300)
    symbol, 280, 283 (III, 10, 14)
    see also Kerubim; Leo
  tail, worn by Egyptian deities, 356, 357 (III, 119, 120, 121)
  Temperance, 217 (II, 192)
  Venus, 481 (IV, 55)
Lion Becomes Man, The, (Howard M. Jackson), 375n
lion-serpent (Leo), 283 (III, 14)
Little, Robert Wentworth, 17 (I, 20)
liver, 360, 361 (III, 126, 127, 128)
Livoyah, 86, 556 (I, 173; IV, 163)
Llewellyn Publications, xxv, 2
London, xxiv
  Warburg Institute, xxi
"Long hast thou dwelt in darkness," xvii, 7, 23, 126, 379 (I, 35-6; II, 28; III, 158)
  alchemical operation, 397 (III, 187)
  consecration of talismans, 386, 417 (III, 169, 219)
  evocation, 382, 409 (III, 162-3, 208)
  requiem ceremony, 449 (III, 269)
  transformation ritual, 433 (III, 245)
longitude—*see* celestial longitude
Looped or Flying Formula, 618-9 (IV, 253-4)
Lord of:
  Abandoned Success—*see* Eights (Tarot), Cups
  Abundance—*see* Threes (Tarot), Cups
  Blended Pleasure—*see* Fours (Tarot), Cups
  Defeat—*see* Fives (Tarot), Swords
  Despair and Cruelty—*see* Nines (Tarot), Swords
  Dominion—*see* Twos (Tarot), Wands
  Earned Success—*see* Sixes (Tarot), Swords
  Earthy (or Earthly) Power—*see* Fours (Tarot), Pentacles
  Established Strength—*see* Threes (Tarot), Wands
  the Fire of the World—*see* Sun, The (Tarot)
  Flame and Lightning—*see* Knights (i.e., Kings), Wands
  the Forces of Life—*see* Wheel of Fortune, The
  the Gates of Death—*see* Death (Tarot)
  the Gates of Matter—*see* Devil, The
  Great Strength—*see* Nines (Tarot), Wands
  Harmonious Change—*see* Twos (Tarot), Pentacles
  the Hosts of the Mighty—*see* Tower, The
  Illusionary Success—*see* Sevens (Tarot), Cups
  Loss in Pleasure—*see* Fives (Tarot), Cups
  Love—*see* Twos (Tarot), Cups
  Material Gain—*see* Nines (Tarot), Pentacles
  Material Happiness—*see* Nines (Tarot), Cups
  Material Success—*see* Sixes (Tarot), Pentacles
  Material Trouble—*see* Fives (Tarot), Pentacles
  Material Works—*see* Threes (Tarot), Pentacles
  Oppression—*see* Tens (Tarot), Wands

Lord of (continued):
the Paths of the Portal of the Vault of the Adepti, 35, 218, 225, 226, 426 (I, 65; II, 194, 205, 205; III, 233)
see also Portal grade
Peace Restored—*see* Twos (Tarot), Swords
Perfected Success—*see* Tens (Tarot), Cups
Perfected Work—*see* Fours (Tarot), Wands
Perpetual Success—*see* Tens (Tarot), Cups
Pleasure—*see* Sixes (Tarot), Cups
Prudence—*see* Eights (Tarot), Pentacles
Rest from Strife—*see* Fours (Tarot), Swords
Ruin—*see* Tens (Tarot), Swords
Shortened Force—*see* Eights (Tarot), Swords
Sorrow—*see* Threes (Tarot), Swords
Strife—*see* Fives (Tarot), Wands
Success Unfulfilled—*see* Sevens (Tarot), Pentacles
Swiftness—*see* Eights (Tarot), Wands
the Triumph of Light—*see* Chariot, The
Unstable Effort—*see* Sevens (Tarot), Swords
Valour—*see* Sevens (Tarot), Wands
Victory—*see* Sixes (Tarot), Wands
the Waves and the Waters—*see* Knights (Kings), Cups
Wealth—*see* Tens (Tarot), Pentacles
the Wide and Fertile Land—*see* Knights (Kings), Pentacles
the Wind and the Breezes—*see* Knights (Kings), Swords
Los Angeles, xix, xxi, xxv
Loss in Pleasure, Lord of—*see* Fives (Tarot), Cups
lotus, 55, 224, 262 (I, 110; II, 203, 272)
Harparkrat, 357, 424, 428, 465 (III, 121, 231, 232, 237; IV, 26)
Lotus Wand, 301, 302, 303, 432 (III, 38, 39, 41, 245)
Sign of Silence, 372 (III, 146)
Tarot, Cups:
Ace, 543 (IV, 143)
court cards, 547, 551 (IV, 149, 150, 155)
numbered cards, 556, 560, 561, 563, 546 (IV, 162, 163, 164, 169, 170, 175, 176)
Lotus of the Palace of Air, The—*see* Knaves (i.e., Princesses), Swords
Lotus Wand, 8, 43, 46-7, 221, 224, 262, 300-5 (I, 84, 92-3; II, 198, 202-3, 272; III, 37-45)
alchemical operation, 395-8 *passim* (III, 185-8 *passim*, 190)
astral projection, 466, 471 (IV, 28, 36)
Bornless Ritual, 442-5 *passim* (III, 259, 263, 264)
Chesed, 473 (IV, 40)
consecration, 303-5 (III, 41-5)
astrological chart for time of working, 303, 304 (III, 41, 43)
elemental weapons, 323, 324, 325 (III, 70, 71, 73)
Lotus Wand (continued):
consecration rituals:
Rose-Cross, 314-6 (III, 57-61)
Sword, 317-8 (III, 63-5)
talismans, 385, 413 (III, 168, 213)
Earth, 300 (III, 37)
evocation, 382, 402, 403, 404 (III, 162, 195, 197, 198)
Egyptian deities, carried by, 355, 356, 357 (III, 118, 119, 120)
elements, invoking and banishing, 303 (III, 40)
hexagram rituals, 296 (III, 32)
illustrated, 300-1 (III, 37-8)
invisibility ritual, 388, 426 (III, 172, 234)
Lesser Banishing Ritual of the Pentagram, 258 (II, 264)
pagan use, 698
Phoenix Wand, combined with, 355 (III, 118)
planets, invoking and banishing, 302-3 (III, 40)
requiem ceremony, 447 (III, 266)
skrying, 468, 470 (IV, 31, 34)
Spirit, 300 (III, 37)
spiritual development ritual, 391, 435-8 *passim* (III, 178, 248, 249, 250, 252, 253)
Tiphareth, 224n
transformation ritual, 390, 429, 431, 432 (III, 176, 240, 242, 243, 245)
use, 302-3 (III, 39-41)
Zodiac, 46-7, 224, 262, 300, 392 (I, 93; II, 202-3, 272; III, 37, 39-40)
Love, Lord of—*see* Twos (Tarot), Cups
Lovers, The, 589 (IV, 211-2)
divination:
example, 575 (IV, 191)
meaning, 584 (IV, 204)
Enochian pyramids, 649, 650 (IV, 296)
Lsrahpm, 325 (III, 73)
Lucifer, 11, 34 (I, 61)
Venus, 276 (II, 298)
Luna—*see* Moon
Luna Philosophorum, 60 (I, 119)
lunar month, 516 (IV, 98)
lungs, 360, 361 (III, 126, 127, 128)
Air, 101 (I, 205)
Lupus, 599 (IV, 226)
Lux, 478 (IV, 49)
see also L.V.X.
Lynx (constellation), 598 (IV, 225)
Lyra, 597 (IV, 223)
Binah, 603 (IV, 232)
Lzinopo, 325, 407, 409 (III, 73, 203, 206)

- M -

M, Book, 231 (II, 217, 218)
M Document:
lineal figures of Sephiroth, 43, 44, 492-3 (I, 84, 85; IV, 72-3)

"The Vision of the Universal Mercury," 43, 44, 476-8 (I, 84, 85; IV, 47-50)
M.E.V. = Magna Est Veritas (William Robert Woodman), 15 (I, 17, 18)
M.W.T. = Ma Wahanu Thesi (Marcus Worsley Blackden), 56 (I, 111-2)
Ma, 57, 443 (I, 113; III, 262)
Maarab (West), 80 (I, 159)
see also Mearab
Maat:
Hall of, 114-5
see also Thmaah
Mabahiah, 86, 562 (I, 171; IV, 172)
Machen, Arthur, ix, 16 (I, 18)
Machinery of the Mind, The (Violet Firth, aka Dion Fortune), 88 (I, 178)
Mackenzie, Kenneth M., 15, 17 (I, 16, 19)
MacNiece, Louis, *Astrology,* 10
macrocosm:
Banner of the East, 336 (III, 91)
breath, 347 (III, 109)
divination, 393 (III, 192)
hexagram, 277, 287, 293, 507 (II, 299; III, 20, 27; IV, 91)
man, 593 (IV, 217)
microcosm:
link with in Neophyte ritual, 369 (III, 141, 142)
reflected in, 100-10, 217, 451-4 (I, 203-25; II, 191; III, 271-6)
skrying, 469, 666 (IV, 32, 312)
Tiphareth, 205 (II, 169)
union with perfected microcosm, 475 (IV, 40)
Macrocosmos, 107-8, 467 (I, 219-20; IV, 29)
Macroprosopus, 77-8, 655, 656 (I, 153-5; IV, 304, 305)
Aima and Abba, 375 (III, 150)
Madathanus, Henricus, 478 (IV, 49)
Madim, 63, 65, 97, 318 (I, 125, 127, 195; III, 64)
see also Mars
madness, 104 (I, 211-2)
magic squares, 9, 70, 140, 493, 496, 498-502 (I, 136; IV, 74, 78-9, 81-6)
Jupiter, 498 (IV, 81)
Mars, 499 (IV, 82)
Mercury, 179, 501 (II, 117; IV, 85)
Moon, 164, 502 (II, 87; IV, 86)
Saturn, 70, 220, 498 (I, 136; II, 196; IV, 81)
sigils, 483, 496-502 (IV, 58, 78-86)
Sun, 499 (IV, 83)
Venus, 500 (IV, 84)
magical diary, x, xix-xx, xxiii
magical motto—*see* motto
"Magic of Light, The Formulae of the," 376-400 (III, 152-92)
see also Neophyte, formula
Magical Mirror of the Universe, 100 (I, 203-4)
see also microcosm; Sphere of Sensation
Magician, The, 558 (IV, 210)
Chokmah, 643 (IV, 287-8)
divination:
example, 575, 576 (IV, 192)
meaning, 584 (IV, 204)
Magick in Theory and Practice (Aleister Crowley), 464, 699 (IV, 25)
Magister Templi, 21 (I, 30)
Magus, 21 (I, 30)
of Power—*see* Magician, The
of the Eternal Gods—*see* Hierophant, The (Tarot)
of the Voice of Light—*see* Hermit, The
Magus, The (Francis Barrett), 9
Mahashiah, 86, 553 (I, 172; IV, 159)
Maim, 80, 179, 183 (I, 159; II, 118, 125)
Pyramid of the Elements, 187 (II, 134)
see also Water
Maladi, 672 (IV, 330)
Malakim, 97 (I, 196)
see also Melekim
Malkah, 60, 72, 77-8, 150 (I, 120, 141, 153-5; II, 61)
Malkah be Tarshisim ve-ad Ruachoth Schechalim (Malcah Betarshisim ve-ad Ruachoth Ha-Schechalim), 65 (I, 127)
sigil, 502 (IV, 86)
Malkuth, 11, 20, 21, 29, 34, 98, 615-8 *passim* (I, 27, 28, 30, 48, 62, 197, 198; IV, 248-51 *passim*, 253)
Air, 345 (III, 106)
altar, 151 (II, 63)
altar diagrams:
The Fall, 76, 193-4 (I, 150-1; II, 146-7)
The Flaming Sword of the Kerubim, 146 (II, 53)
altar in Eastern part of, 333 (III, 86)
of Assiah:
Cholem Yesodoth, 614 (IV, 247)
Neophyte temple, 331 (III, 82)
Outer Order rituals, 115, 205 (II, 168-9)
of Atziluth, 614 (IV, 246)
Binah, 615, 617 (IV, 248, 251)
of Briah, 614 (IV, 246)
Calvary cross of six squares, 193 (II, 145)
censer (transmits Fires of Netzach to Malkuth), 341 (III, 99)
cosmic Sphere of Sensation, 451 (III, 271, 272)
Cup of Stolistes, 71, 177, 340 (I, 138; II, 113; III, 97)
Cup (transmits Waters of Hod to Malkuth), 341 (III, 99)
dekagram, 510 (IV, 93)
diagram or symbol, 209 (II, 176)
divine name, archangel, and angelic choir, 62, 64 (I, 123, 126)
dodekangle, 506 (IV, 89)
Dragon, rescued from by Justified One, 239 (II, 229)

Malkuth (continued):
elements, 98, 506 (I, 198; IV, 89)
Eve, 74, 178 (I, 145; II, 115)
evocation, 406, 408-11 *passim* (III, 202, 206, 207, 209, 210, 211)
geomancy, 527, 539 (IV, 115, 136)
Hegemon's lamen, 79, 339 (I, 157; III, 96)
Hegemon's sceptre, 339 (III, 95)
Heh, 615, 616 (IV, 249)
hexagram, 293 (III, 27)
Hiereus:
Portal ritual, 199n
station, 337 (III, 92)
sword, 337 (III, 93)
Hierophant's sceptre, 335 (III, 90)
Kerubim, 405 (III, 200)
Kether, 613 (IV, 246)
Knave of Tarot, 79 (I, 156)
Malkah, kingdom of, 150 (II, 61)
Maltese cross, 204, 205 (II, 168)
Metatron and Sandalphon, 375 (III, 151)
microcosm, 102, 103, 106 (I, 207, 208-9, 216)
invisibility ritual, 424 (III, 231)
Neophyte ritual, 114, 364, 365 (III, 133, 134)
Nephesch, 67 (I, 129)
no planetary attributions, 268 (II, 286)
occult symbol, 205 (II, 168-9)
Paths:
from/to, 73, 76, 95, 147, 160 (I, 144, 150, 191; II, 55, 80)
Banner of the West, 338 (III, 93)
29th Path, 185 (II, 129)
31st Path, 172 (II, 103)
32nd Path, 159, 209, 215 (II, 78, 176, 187)
see also Paths; Tarot
pentacle (Earth), 224n
Phrath, 73 (I, 145)
Pillars, bases, 333 (III, 85-6)
qabalistic cross, 53, 403, 444 (I, 106; III, 197, 262)
Resplendent Intelligence, 438, 615, 617 (III, 253; IV, 248, 251)
Rising on the Planes, 464 (IV, 24)
Rose-Cross lamen, 310, 311 (III, 52, 54)
Salt, 84 (I, 168)
Sephiroth:
receives wisdom and power of, 411 (III, 210)
throne of, 405, 409 (III, 199, 207)
Serpent of Wisdom, 275 (II, 297)
Seven Palaces of—*see* Palaces, Seven
South Pole of heavens, 596, 600, 602, 603, 655 (IV, 221-2, 227, 231, 304)
spiritual development ritual, 438 (III, 253)

Malkuth (continued):
Tarot:
colors, 588, 590 (IV, 209, 213)
Knaves (Princesses), 615, 616 (IV, 249)
Tens, 552, 588 (IV, 157-8, 209)
Cups, 561 (IV, 170)
Pentacles, 554 (IV, 161)
Swords, 563 (IV, 174)
Wands, 558 (IV, 165)
Thm-a-Oe, 375 (III, 151)
telesmatic images, 492 (IV, 71)
transformation ritual, 430 (III, 241)
Tree of the Knowledge of Good and Evil, 177 (II, 114)
Vault symbolism, 269 (II, 286)
of Yetzirah, 358, 362, 614, 615, 617, 618, 619, 621 (III, 124, 130; IV, 247, 248, 249, 252, 254, 256, 257)
Aschim, 614 (IV, 246)
Zelator grade, 152, 163 (II, 65-6, 85)
see also Sephiroth
Mals, 495 (IV, 77)
see also Enochian, letters
Maltese cross, 204-5 (II, 168-9)
Ace of Pentacles, 543, 553 (IV, 144, 159)
Hierophant's cloak, 335 (III, 89)
Rose-Cross lamen, 311 (III, 53)
sceptre of Praemonstrator, 332 (III, 84)
man (Kerub), 46, 61, 157, 235, 343 (I, 90, 120; II, 75, 224; III, 101)
Oro, 653 (IV, 300)
symbol, 280, 281 (III, 10, 11)
see also Aquarius; Kerubim
Man and His Symbols (C. G. Jung), 5
Manas, 32 (I, 57)
Manasseh, 305 (III, 44)
man's head, held by Queen of Swords, 548, 551 (IV, 151, 155)
mantle:
court cards of Tarot, 545, 546, 547, 549, 550, 551 (IV, 146, 147, 150, 152, 154, 155)
see also cloaks
Manvantara, 274 (II, 294)
Mariodam, 443 (III, 261)
Mars, 63 (I, 125)
alchemical operation, 397 (III, 188)
angel, intelligence, and spirit, 65 (I, 127)
anger and impatience, 474 (IV, 41)
Aries, 495, 642 (IV, 77, 286)
consecration of Sword, 317, 318, 319 (III, 62-5 *passim*)
Enochian letters and geomantic figures, 495 (IV, 77)
Fire, 215 (II, 187)
Geburah, 19, 97, 215, 218, 644 (I, 26, 195, II, 187, 195; IV, 288)

Mars (continued):
hexagram, 218, 290, 318, 319 (II, 195; III, 23, 64, 65)
Jupiter, balanced by, 215 (II, 187)
Lesser Invoking Ritual of the Hexagram, 318, 319 (III, 64, 65)
magic square, 499 (IV, 82)
microcosm, 424 (III, 231)
nostril, right, 103 (I, 210)
pentagram, 70, 507 (I, 136; IV, 90)
Pisces, 642 (IV, 286)
see also Mars, Tarot, Cups, Ten
planetary hour, 317 (III, 62)
Scorpio, 495 (IV, 77)
seal, 499 (IV, 82)
Tarot:
Cups:
Five, 541, 556 (IV, 139, 162, 163)
Ten, 541, 550, 560, 561 (IV, 140, 156, 170)
The Emperor, 589 (IV, 211)
Nine of Swords, 541, 563 (IV, 140, 174)
Temperance, 591 (IV, 214)
Three of Pentacles, 541, 558 (IV, 140, 166)
The Tower, 71, 73, 191-2, 542, 644 (I, 139, 143; II, 142; IV, 141, 288)
Wands:
Two, 541, 550, 561 (IV, 140, 156, 170)
Seven, 541, 553 (IV, 139, 159)
27th Path, 31, 182, 181, 215 (I, 55; II, 123, 142, 187)
Vault symbolism, 268 (II, 283)
Water, 215, 648 (II, 187; IV, 294)
see also planets
Maruts, 273 (II, 292)
mask, astral assumption of, 381, 382, 408 (III, 160, 162, 205)
Masloth—*see* Mazloth
Masons—*see* Freemasons
Masonic Encyclopedia, 15 (I, 16)
Massachusetts, Salem, xviii
material basis in production of natural phenomena, 384-7 *passim* (III, 166, 167, 169, 170, 171)
Material Gain, Lord of—*see* Nines (Tarot), Pentacles
Material Happiness, The Lord of—*see* Nines (Tarot), Cups
Material Success, Lord of—*see* Sixes (Tarot), Pentacles
Material Trouble, Lord of—*see* Fives (Tarot), Pentacles
Material Works, The Lord of—*see* Threes (Tarot), Pentacles
Mathers, Mina, 453 (IV, 23)
"Of Skrying and Traveling in the Spirit-Vision," 467-74 (IV, 29-42)
Mathers, Mina (continued):
Tattwa visions, 474-8 (IV, 43-50)
Mathers, S. L. MacGregor, ix, 2, 8, 10, 11, 16, 17, 375n, 514. 624n, 625, 699, 700 (I, 17-21 *passim*; IV, 95, 262)
astral projection, 463, 464 (IV, 23, 24)
"Book of the Concourse of the Forces," 625, 630-96 (IV, 261, 274-368)
"Book 'T'—The Tarot," 540-65 (IV, 137-76)
Chaldean oracles, 31 (I, 54)
D.D.C.F. = Deo Duce Comite Ferro, 16-7, 45, 624, 625 (I, 19, 89; IV, 260, 261)
Enochian, 653-5 (IV, 300-3)
chess, "Official Ritual," 690-6 (IV, 359-68)
Flying Roll X, 199n
"Formulae of the Magic of Light, The," (Document Z.2), 376-400 (III, 152-92)
The Greater Key of King Solomon, 8, 16, 493 (I, 18; IV, 76)
The Kabbalah Unveiled, 8, 16 (I, 18-9)
"The Law of the Convoluted Revolution of the Forces Symbolised by the Four Aces Round the Northern Pole," 603, 607-21 (IV, 236-57)
"The Microcosm-Man," 2, 100-6, 199n (I, 203-16)
"Notes on the Tarot," 72-3 (I, 141-3)
"The Path of the Chameleon," 2, 95-9 (I, 191-202)
S.R.M.D. = S'Rhiogail Ma Dhream—*see* S.R.M.D.
The Sacred Magic of Abramelin, 8, 11, 16 (I, 18)
The Sorcerer and His Apprentice, 202n
Tattwa visions, 459, 462, 478 (IV, 16, 21, 49-50)
Tattwas, 517 (IV, 100-1)
"The Tree of Life as Projected in a Solid Sphere," 594-621 (IV, 218-57)
Matter—*see* First Matter
Matthew, The Gospel According to:
3:11—341 (III, 99-100)
16:24—235 (II, 224)
Mau, 158 (II, 76)
Maut, 375 (III, 151)
Mayim, 187 (II, 134)
see also Maim
Mazloth (Masloth), 63, 96 (I, 125, 194)
see also Zodiac
McDougall, William, *Psychology,* 88 (I, 177)
Mdio, 670 (IV, 326)
Mead, G. R. S., *Thrice-Greatest Hermes,* 201n
Mearab (West), 324 (III, 71)
see also Maarab
Mebahel, 86, 555 (I, 173; IV, 161)
Med, 495, 648 (IV, 77, 294)
see also Enochian, letters

medicina metallorum, 82 (I, 163)
meditation, xxiii, 4, 23, 52-3, 63, 68, 72, 87, 94-5, 136, 270, 308, 519-20 (I, 34, 105, 124, 133, 140, 175, 189-90; II, 288; III, 49-50; IV, 103-4)
  Enochian pyramids, 653-5 (IV, 300-3)
  god-forms, 372, 465 (III, 147; IV, 26)
  requiem ceremony, 450 (III, 270)
  Sandha, 517 (IV, 100)
  spiritual development ritual, 392, 393 (III, 180, 181)
  Tattwa vision, 459 (IV, 15)
Medusa, 549, 551, 598 (IV, 152, 155, 224, 225)
Melchel, 86, 557 (I, 173; IV, 164)
Melchidael, 86, 304, 305 (I, 171; III, 43, 44)
  Enochian letter, geomantic figure, Zodiac, 495 (IV, 77)
Melechim—*see* Melekim
Melekim, 62, 64 (I, 123, 126)
Mem, 8, 151 (II, 64)
  cup on cross and triangle, 178-9 (II, 117)
  caduceus, 162, 340 (II, 84; III, 97)
  scourge, 242 (II, 237)
  23rd Path (Water, The Hanged Man):
    Philosophus ritual, 188 (II, 137)
    Portal ritual, 198, 209, 210n, 212 (II, 155, 177, 181)
    Practicus ritual, 176, 179 (II, 112, 117)
  Vault symbolism, 269 (II, 286)
  Water, 158, 159 (II, 77)
    transformation ritual, 389 (III, 175)
  see also Hanged Man; Hebrew alphabet; Paths; Water
Mem He, 163, 168 (II, 86, 96)
memorization, 45, 48, 130, 135 (I, 89, 95; II, 37)
Mendes, Goat of, 212, 213, 217 (II, 182, 191)
Mendial, 86, 559 (I, 174; IV, 167)
Menelaus, 360 (III, 127)
Menqal, 86, 563 (I, 171; IV, 174)
Me-Ouroth, 152 (II, 66)
Mercabah, 145 (II, 52)
  see also Merkabah mysticism
Merciful Exempt Adept—*see* Chief Adept
Mercury (alchemical principle)
  alchemical operation, 397 (III, 189)
  de Bry, Franciscus, 275 (II, 296)
  elements, 310-11 (III, 52)
  imagination, 474 (IV, 41)
  Rose-Cross lamen, 310-11 (III, 52)
see also alchemy, principles
Mercury (god), 374-5 (III, 150)
  "The Vision of the Universal Mercury," 43, 44, 476-8 (I, 84, 85; IV, 47-50)
Mercury (metal), 60, 72, 206, 666 (I, 119, 141; II, 172; IV, 320)
Mercury (planet), 63 (I, 125)
Mercury (planet) (continued):
  Air, 648 (IV, 294)
  alchemical operation, 397 (III, 189)
  angel, intelligence, and spirit, 65 (I, 127)
  Chokmah, 643 (IV, 287)
  Enochian:
    letters and geomantic figures, 495 (IV, 77)
    pyramids, 648 (IV, 294)
  Gemini, 495 (IV, 77)
  hexagram, 218, 289 (II, 195; III, 22)
  Hod, 20, 98, 218, 497 (I, 27, 196; II, 195; IV, 80)
  magic square, 179, 497, 501 (II, 117; IV, 80, 85)
  mouth, 103 (I, 210)
  octagon, 508 (IV, 92)
  octagram, 70 (I, 136)
  planets, synthesis of, 588 (IV, 210)
  Practicus grade, 30, 167, 179 (I, 53; II, 93, 117)
  seal, 501 (IV, 85)
  symbol, 50, 71, 71, 179 (I, 99, 138, 140; II, 117)
    circle smaller than that of Venus, 79, 195 (I, 158; II, 149)
  Tarot:
    Eight of Wands, 541, 557 (IV, 140, 164)
    The Magician, 71, 72, 542, 588 (I, 139, 141; IV, 140, 210)
    Pentacles:
      Five, 541, 562 (IV, 140, 172)
      Ten, 541, 554 (IV, 139, 160)
      Six of Swords, 541, 559 (IV, 140, 168)
  Three of Cups, 541, 564 (IV, 140, 175)
  Third Adept in Portal ritual, 221n
  Virgo, 495 (IV, 77)
  see also planets
Mercy—*see* Chesed
Mercy Seat—*see* Kerubim, on Ark of the Covenant
Merkabah mysticism, 375n
  see also Mercabah
mermaids and mermen—*see* undines
Meroz, 190 (II, 139)
Messiah, 276, 375 (II, 298; III, 151)
Mesti, 358 (III, 123)
  see also Ameshet
metals, 61, 109 (I, 119, 120, 223)
  Enochian angels, 670 (IV, 327)
  prayer of Earth Spirits, 152-3, 406-7 (II, 67; III, 202-3)
  Tree of Life, 82 (I, 163)
  see also brass; copper; gold; iron; lead; Mercury; silver; tin
Metatron (Mettatron), 61, 62, 64, 96, 98, 145, 146, 152, 375n (I, 122, 123, 126, 193, 198; II, 52, 53, 66)
  evocation, 405, 406, 407 (III, 200, 201, 204)

Metatron (Mettatron) (continued):
Kerub on Ark of the Covenant, 146, 152 (II, 54, 85)
Kether of Briah, 614 (IV, 246)
Malkuth, 625 (IV, 248)
of Briah, 614 (IV, 246)
guardian over, 375 (III, 151)
sigil, 483 (IV, 57-8)
spiritual development ritual, 437-8, 439 (III, 252, 253, 254)
Thoth (Tho-oth), 365, 374 (III, 135, 150)
metempsychosis, 55 (I, 110)
Metraton, 96 (I, 193)
see also Metatron
Mettatron—*see* Metatron
Mevamayah, 86, 564 (I, 172; IV, 176)
Meynsicht, Adrian a, 478 (IV, 49)
Mezla, 621 (IV, 257)
Michael, 280, 656 (III, 10; IV, 306)
angel by night of Seven of Swords, 86, 560 (I, 174; IV, 169)
angel of the Sun, 65, 207n (I, 127)
consecration of Rose-Cross, 314 (III, 58, 59)
archangel of Fire, 80, 182, 207n, 673 (I, 159; II, 124; IV, 332)
consecration of Fire Wand, 324 (III, 72)
consecration of talisman, 421 (III, 225)
Lesser Banishing Ritual of the Pentagram, 54, 444 (I, 107; III, 262)
archangel of Hod, 62, 64, 98 (I, 123, 126, 196)
Judgment, 172 (II, 104)
Metatron, 375n
microcosm, 217 (II, 191)
astral projection, 464 (IV, 25)
macrocosm:
reflection of, 100-10, 217, 451-4 (I, 203-25; II, 191; III, 271-6)
union with, 475 (IV, 40)
man, 593 (IV, 217)
pentagram, 217, 219-20, 277, 287, 507 (II, 190-1, 196, 299; III, 20; IV, 90)
skrying, 661 (IV, 313)
"Microcosm—Man, The", 2, 100-6, 467 (I, 203-16; IV, 29)
Microcosmos, 201 (I, 160)
Microprosopus, 60, 72, 77-8, 101, 103, 655, 656 (I, 120, 141, 153-5, 206, 210; IV, 304, 305)
altar diagram, The Fall, 193 (II, 146)
Calvary cross of six squares, 79, 193 (I, 157; II, 145)
Hegemon's lamen, 339 (III, 96)
hexagram, 287 (III, 21)
Microscopium (Microscope), 599 (IV, 226)
Middle Pillar, 11, 276 (II, 298)
Air, 345 (III, 106)
Middle Pillar (continued):
Bornless Ritual, 444 (III, 263)
celestial sphere, 603, 655 (IV, 231, 304)
Hegemon's station, 338 (III, 94)
Hierophant's sceptre, 335 (III, 89)
Neophyte ritual, 364, 365, 367 (III, 134, 138)
ritual, x, xviii, xxi, 3, 5, 41, 45, 89-90, 378, 699 (I, 79-80, 90, 179-81; III, 155)
stations in, invisible, 356 (III, 120)
Thma-Ae-St, 339 (III, 96)
Thmaah, 375 (III, 151)
Vibratory Formula—*see* Vibratory Formula of the Middle Pillar
Middle Pillar, The (Israel Regardie), xxv, 4, 55, 92, 378 (I, 109, 185; III, 155)
Midian, 191 (II, 141)
Might—*see* Geburah
Mighty Adeptus Major—*see* Adept, Second
Mihal, 86, 561 (I, 174; IV, 170)
minerals, 109 (I, 223)
Minerva, 548 (IV, 152)
Minutum Mundum, 42, 43, plate f. 118, 237, 241-2, 246, 614, 615 (I, 81, 84, plate f. 190; II, 229, 234-7, 242; IV, 247, 249)
see also Path of the Chameleon
Miracle of Language, The (Charlton Laird), 6
mistakes in ceremonies—*see* errors in ceremonies
Mithra, 36 (I, 68)
mitre, 686, 693 (IV, 351, 363)
see also sceptre, Hegemon
Mitzrael, 86, 562 (I, 171; IV, 173)
Mizrach (East), 80, 324 (I, 158; III, 71)
Mnizourin, the Stone, 171 (II, 102)
Moab, 190 (II, 139)
Mochayel, 86, 563 (I, 171; IV, 174)
Modorio, 443 (III, 261)
monkeys, 110 (I, 223-4)
Monnastre, Cris, ix, x, xii
Introduction to the Fifth Edition, xvii-xxv
Monoceros, 600 (IV, 227)
Monocris de Astris, 179, 183, 186, 189 (II, 118, 125, 126, 132, 138)
monomania, 104 (I, 212)
Moon, 63 (I, 125)
alchemical operation, 396, 397 (III, 186-7, 188)
angel, intelligence, and spirit, 65 (I, 127)
Binah, 643 (IV, 288)
Cancer, 495 (IV, 77)
crescent and silver, 83 (I, 165)
Earth, 648 (IV, 294)
enneagram, 70, 510 (I, 136; IV, 93)
Enochian:
letters and geomantic figures, 495 (IV, 77)
pyramids, 648 (IV, 294)

Moon (continued):
eye, left, 103 (I, 210)
Garden of Eden diagram, 73 (I, 144)
hexagram, 218, 288, 430 (II, 195; III, 21, 241)
Supreme Invoking Ritual of the Hexagram, 430 (III, 240)
symbol, 288, 289 (III, 21, 22)
lunar month, 516 (IV, 98)
magic square, 164, 502 (II, 87; IV, 86)
Malkah, 60 (I, 120)
nodes (Caput Draconis and Cauda Draconis), 50-1, 524 (I, 100; IV, 112)
enneagon, 508 (IV, 92)
enneagram, 508 (IV, 93)
hexagrams, 288, 293 (III, 26, 28)
phases:
goddesses, 589, 590 (IV, 210, 211, 213)
Tree of Life, 68, 81, 164 (I, 131, 161; II, 87)
Portal grade, 219, 220 (II, 196)
seal, 502 (IV, 86)
Tarot:
Four of Cups, 541, 564 (IV, 140, 176)
The High Priestess, 71, 72, 542 (I, 139, 141; IV, 140)
Nine of Wands, 541, 557 (IV, 140, 164, 165)
Six of Pentacles, 541, 562 (IV, 140, 172)
Swords:
Two, 541, 555 (IV, 139, 161)
Seven, 541, 559 (IV, 140, 168)
see also Moon, The (Tarot)
Theoricus grade, 30, 155, 164 (I, 52; II, 71, 87)
Thoth, 330n
Tiphareth, reflection of Sun of, 68, 217 (I, 133; II, 191)
Vault symbolism, 267 (II, 282)
wandering thoughts, 474 (IV, 41)
Yesod, 20, 98, 217, 218, 603 (I, 27, 197; II, 191, 195; IV, 232)
see also planets
Moon, The, (Tarot), 181, 185, 591-2 (II, 121-2, 129-30; IV, 215)
divination:
example, 568, 569, 577, 578, 579 (IV, 181, 182, 194, 196, 197)
meaning, 585 (IV, 206)
see also Tarot, trumps
Moon breath, 68, 516, 522 (I, 133; IV, 98, 99, 108-9)
Moon nerve, 516 (IV, 98)
see also Chandra Nadi; Ida
moonstone, 669 (IV, 323)
Mo-ooth, 375 (III, 151)
Mor, 653 (IV, 300)
Mor Dial Hctga—*see* Emor Dial Hectega
mortar, 395 (III, 184)
Moses, 16, 165, 177, 340, 359 (I, 16, 83; II, 113; III, 197, 125)
Law of, 370 (III, 143)
Mother, 38, 150 (I, 71; II, 61)
see also Supernal Mother
Mother letters—*see* Hebrew alphabet, Mother letters
Mothers, Four—*see* Four Mothers
motto, 16-7, 310, 311, 317, 320, 322, 364 (III, 51, 54, 62, 68, 69, 133)
Mount Abiegnus—*see* Abiegnus, Mount
Mount Ebal, 202, 510 (II, 164; IV, 94)
Mount Paran, 191 (II, 140)
Mourning, Robe of—*see* Robe of Mourning
Mph:
eagle, 653 (IV, 300)
Enochian pyramids, 654 (IV, 302)
Mph Arsl Gaiol—*see* Empeh Arsel Gaiol
Müller, Max, 627 (IV, 265)
mummification, 358-9 (III, 124-5)
Munn, Norman, *Psychology,* 5
Muriel, 86, 305 (I, 172; III, 44)
Enochian letters, geomantic figures, Zodiac, 495 (IV, 77)
Musca ("Musea"), 600 (IV, 227)
mushrooms, 667 (IV, 321)
mutable signs—*see* Zodiac
My Rosicrucian Adventure (Israel Regardie), 1, 18 (I, 22)
Mysteria Magica (Melita Denning and Osborne Phillips), 682n
mystery cults, ancient, 22, 38, 370 (I, 32-3, 71; III, 142)
Egyptian mysteries, 374 (III, 150)
Eleusinian mysteries, 128 (II, 34)
Samothracian mysteries, 172 (II, 105)
Mystical Repast, 132, 370 (II, 41; III, 143)

- N -

N Document, 43, 540 (I, 84; IV, 137)
N.N., Frater, 232, 233, 237 (II, 220, 223, 227, 228)
N.O.M. = Non Omnis Moriar (William Wynn Westcott), 266, 658, 687 (II, 280; IV, 309, 347-8)
Naaom, 327 (III, 76-77)
Nachash, 276 (II, 298)
Nadis, 516 (IV, 98)
Nag, 515 (IV, 97)
Nag Hammadi, 207n
Naher, 73-4, 177, 315 (I, 144-5; II, 114; III, 59)
Nakhiel, 65 (I, 127)
sigil, 499 (IV, 83)
Nanael, 86, 561 (I, 171; IV, 171)

Nanta:
Enochian call (fifth), 672, 673, 676 (IV, 329, 330, 331, 336)
evocation, 407 (III, 204)
pronunciation, 650 (IV, 300)
see also Exarp, Hcoma, Nanta, Bitom; key-word analysis; Opening by Watchtower
Naochi (?), 601 (IV, 228)
Naphthali, 305 (III, 44)
Natural Intelligence, 187-8 (II, 134)
natural phenomena, production of, 384-7 (III, 166-71)
Heh of Yeheshua, 376, 384 (III, 152, 166)
Nature's Finer Forces, or the Science of Breath
(Rama Prasad), 514 (IV, 95)
Nboza, 327 (III, 77)
Nebuchadnezzar, 206 (II, 170-1)
negative confession, 58, 115 (I, 116)
Nehushtan, 83 (I, 165-6)
Neith, 361, 489 (III, 129; IV, 66)
Nelapr, 672 (IV, 330)
Nelokhiel, 86, 556 (I, 173; IV, 163)
Nemamiah, 86, 562 (I, 171; IV, 172)
nemyss, 333, 350 (III, 85, 112)
astral projection, 466 (IV, 27)
Egyptian deities, worn by, 354-8 *passim*, 662, 665 (III, 117-22 *passim*; IV, 317, 318)
Third Adept, 473 (IV, 40)
Neo-Pagan movement, 697, 698
see also New Paganism
Neoph-tho-osest, 352 (III, 114)
see also Nephthys
Neophyte, 31, 40, 44, 519, 521 (I, 55, 77, 87; IV, 104, 107)
drawing of Mount Abiegnus, 242 (II, 238)
consecration of talisman, 414 (III, 215)
evocation, 405 (III, 200)
grip, word, password, 144 (II, 49)
knowledge lecture, 50-9, 130 (I, 99-117; II, 37)
Lesser Banishing Ritual of the Pentagram, 281-2 (III, 11)
meditation, 52-3 (I, 105)
obligation or oath, 122-3, 365, 366, 379 (II, 21-4; III, 135, 136, 157)
Neophyte formula, place of Hierophant in, 381 (III, 160)
ritual—*see* Neophyte ritual (below)
Sentinel, qualified for office, 137, 342 (III, 100)
signs—*see* signs, Neophyte
step and sign, 144 (II, 49)
invisibility ritual, 389, 427 (III, 174, 236)
"The Symbolism of the Four Genii of the Hall of the Neophytes," 358-62 (III, 124-30)
Neophyte (continued):
temple, 11, 116-7, 213-4, 331, 379 (II, 11-2, 184; III, 82, 157)
consecration of talisman, 413 (III, 212)
divination, 451-4 (III, 271-6)
Enochian system, 624 (IV, 260)
evocation, 380, 402 (III, 159, 195)
invisibility ritual, 423 (III, 229)
requiem ceremony, 447 (III, 266)
"Symbolism of the Temple, The," 333-4 (III, 85-8)
transformation ritual, 429 (III, 239)
transformation ritual, 430 (III, 241)
Zelator ritual, 144-50 *passim* (48-62 *passim*)
see also candidate
Neophyte formula (formulae of the Magic of Light), 376-400 (III, 152-92)
alchemy, 395-9 (III, 184-92)
consecration of talismans, 384-7 (III, 166-71)
divination, 393-5 (III, 182-4)
evocation, 380-4 (III, 159-66)
invisibility, 387-9 (III, 171-5)
spiritual development, 391-3 (III, 178-81)
transformations, 389-91 (III, 175-7)
Neophyte ritual, xvii-xxv *passim*, 4, 8-9, 11, 12-3, 23-4, 27-9, 39, 42, 43, 58, 114-33, 201n, 336, 698 (I, 35-6, 44-50, 75, 82, 84, 116; II, 11-43; III, 91)
admission of candidate, 121-2, 379 (II, 20-1; III, 157)
"The Symbolism of the Admission of the Candidate," (Document Z.3), 363-75 (III, 131-51)
cardinal points and other directions:
East, 117, 120, 124, 125, 126, 127, 131, 132, 331, 332, 366, 367, 368, 379 (II, 12, 17, 18, 25, 26, 27, 29, 31, 40, 41; III, 82, 85, 136, 139, 140, 143, 157, 158)
see also Throne of the East
North, 119, 124, 126, 127, 346, 379 (II, 15, 24, 25, 26, 29, 32, 107, 157)
see also Stolistes, station
Northeast, 118, 120, 124, 127, 129, 131 (II, 13, 17, 18, 25, 32, 36)
Northwest, 127 (II, 32)
South, 118, 124, 131, 346, 379 (II, 14, 25, 40, 107, 157)
see also Dadouches, station
Southeast, 131 (II, 40)
West, 118, 119, 124, 125, 126, 129, 131, 334, 367, 379 (II, 14, 16, 25, 26, 27, 29, 36, 39, 41, 42, 87, 137, 158)
see also Throne of the West
see also invisible stations; Horus, Children of; Kerubim
chief officers, 118 (II, 14)
see also Three Chiefs, Neophyte ritual

Neophyte ritual (continued):
circumambulations:
candidate:
darkness (or knowledge), 124-5, 366-7, 379 (II, 25-7; III, 137-8, 157)
light, 127, 346, 369, 380 (II, 32; III, 107-8, 141, 158)
closing (reverse), 131, 346, 370 (II, 40; III, 107, 108; III, 143)
opening, 120 (II, 17)
closing, 131-3, 370, 380 (II, 39-43; III, 143, 158)
used in Equinox ceremony, 257 (II, 263)
consecration:
of candidate, 121, 124-5, 126, 127, 364, 367, 368, 369, 379, 380 (II, 20-1, 25-7, 29-30, 31; III, 133, 138, 140, 141, 157, 158)
of hall, 119-20, 131, 346 (II, 17, 40; III, 107)
Enochian system, 624 (IV, 260)
exhortation, 129-30, 380 (II, 36-7; III, 158)
god-forms, 114-5, 337-44, 346-7, 352-3, 364 (III, 92-104, 108-9, 114-5, 132-3)
"The Egyptian God-Forms of the Neophyte Grade," 354-62 (III, 116-30)
"Index for general reference to the Enterer [Neophyte] Ceremony," 379-80 (III, 157-8)
instruction, 128-31, 380 (II, 32-9; III, 158)
lesser officers, 118 (II, 14)
Mystical Repast, 132, 370 (II, 41; III, 143)
oath or obligation, 122-3, 379 (II, 21-4; III, 157)
opening, 117-21, 379 (II, 12-20; III, 157)
divination, 451 (III, 271)
"The Symbolism of the Opening of the 0=0 Grade of Neophyte," 344-7, 465 (III, 105-10; IV, 26)
used in Equinox ceremony, 248 (II, 245)
performance, 363-4 (III, 132-3)
sign, grip, step, word, password, 126-7, 370-3 (II, 30-1; III, 143-8)
signs register, 130 (II, 39)
stations, 114-6, 122, 129 (II, 11, 22, 35)
temple arrangement, 11, 116-7 (II, 11-2)
see also "Z" documents
Neoplatonism: Psellus, 25-6 (I, 40-1)
Nephesch, 33, 67, 102, 103, 104, 106 (I, 58, 129, 208-12 *passim*, 216)
invisibility ritual, 424 (III, 231)
Sephiroth in (Seven Palaces), 103 (I, 209)
Nephesch ha-Messiah (ha-Messiach), 98, 276, 375 (I, 198; II, 298; III, 151)
evocation, 402, 405, 407 (III, 195, 200, 204)
Malkuth of Briah, 614 (IV, 246)
Nephews, Four—*see* Four Nephews
Nephthys, 56, 57, 181 (I, 112, 114, 132)
Ahephi, 361 (III, 129)
Nephthys (continued):
Ameshet, 692 (IV, 361)
Bornless Ritual, 443 (III, 262)
description, 356 (III, 119)
Earth, 692 (IV, 361)
Enochian:
chess castle, 686, 687, 691 (IV, 351-2, 361)
pyramids, 663 (IV, 315)
Hathor, 343 (III, 101)
illustration, 664 (IV, 316)
Imperator, 342, 344, 352, 354, 356, 663 (III, 101, 103-4, 114, 116, 119; IV, 315)
Osiris, 56, 691 (I, 112; IV, 359)
Pillar, 344, 346 (III, 103-4, 108)
station, invisible, 343, 344 (III, 101, 103-4)
step, 371 (III, 144)
Tarot:
Judgment, 172 (I, 104)
Justice, 589, 590 (IV, 210, 213)
The Star, 188 (II, 135)
veil, 342 (III, 100)
Water, 372 (III, 147)
Neptune:
god, 600 (IV, 227)
planet, 51, 537n, 592 (I, 100; IV, 216)
Nequaquam Vacuum, 235 (II, 224)
nerves, nervous system, 515-6 (IV, 97, 98)
Neschamah, 32, 37, 38, 67, 100, 101, 103, 105, 417 (I, 58, 69, 71, 129, 203, 205, 206, 210, 213, 214; III, 219)
animals, lacking in, 110 (I, 224)
Briah of microcosm, 105 (I, 214)
invisibility ritual, 424 (III, 231)
Neophyte, 365, 366 (III, 134-5, 136)
Netzach, 20, 21, 97, 98 (I, 26-7, 30, 196, 197, 198)
angle of triangle on altar, 162 (II, 85)
Calvary cross of six squares, 193 (II, 145)
censer (transmits Fires of Netzach to Malkuth), 341 (III, 99)
divine name, archangel, and angelic choir, 62, 64 (I, 123, 126)
Fire from Geburah reflected in, 331 (III, 83)
Hegemon:
lamen, 79, 339 (I, 157; III, 96)
sceptre, 339 (III, 95)
heptangle, 506, 508 (IV, 89, 91)
hexagram, 218 (II, 195)
Hiereus's lamen, 213, 337 (II, 184; III, 93)
Isis, station of, 344 (III, 103)
Maltese cross, 204 (II, 168)
microcosm, 102, 103 (I, 207, 209)
invisibility ritual, 424 (III, 231)
left leg, 102 (I, 207)
Neophyte temple, 331 (III, 82)
Nephesch, 103 (I, 209)

Netzach (continued):
Paths:
to/from, 76 (I, 150)
21st Path, 215 (II, 187)
27th Path, 31, 191, 215 (I, 55; II, 142, 187)
28th Path, 186, 210 (II, 131, 177)
29th Path, 185 (II, 129)
see also Paths; Tarot
Philosophus, 31, 76, 194, 195, 331 (I, 54, 150; II, 147, 149; III, 83)
Entry into Netzach, 192-5 (II, 144-50)
temple arrangement, 192 (II, 144)
Pillar, White, base of, 333, 338 (III, 85, 94)
station of Dadouches, 341 (III, 99)
Portal ritual, 200 (158)
scourge, 242 (II, 237)
Second Adept in Portal ritual, 199n, 221n
Tarot:
Sevens, 552 (IV, 157)
Cups, 557 (IV, 164)
Pentacles, 562 (IV, 173)
Swords, 560 (IV, 169)
Wands, 553 (IV, 159)
Temperance, 217, 218 (II, 192)
Wheel of Fortune, 590 (IV, 212)
Venus, 218 (II, 195)
wand (Fire), 224n
see also Sephiroth
New Age, ix
New Magus, The (Donald Tyson), 505n
New Mexico, xxv, 700
New Paganism, ix, 700
see also Neo-Pagan movement
New Testament, 83 (I, 165-6)
New Zealand, xxii
Newton, Isaac, xviii
Nfrm, 650 (IV, 297)
Nhdd, 552 (IV, 318)
Nichsa, 80 (I, 159)
Nile, 57, 361 (I, 114; III, 129)
nine months waiting period at Portal, 92-4, 219 (I, 185-9; II, 196)
Nines (Tarot), 552 (IV, 157)
Cups, 560 (IV, 169-70)
divinatory meaning, 582 (IV, 202)
Pentacles, 554 (IV, 160)
divination example, 577, 579, 586 (IV, 194, 197, 207)
Swords, 563 (IV, 174)
divination example, 574, 575, 585, 586 (IV, 190, 191, 207)
Wands, 557 (IV, 164-5)
divination example, 571, 572, 577, 579, 586 (IV, 185, 186, 187, 194, 196, 207)
see also Tarot, numbered cards
Nirmanakayas, 273 (II, 282)
Nirvana, 273, 274 (II, 292, 294)
Nithahiah, 86, 557 (I, 173; IV, 164)
Nithal, 86, 561 (I, 171; IV, 171)
Noalmr, 672 (IV, 330)
nodes of Moon—*see* Moon, nodes
Nogah, 63, 65, 97 (I, 125, 127, 196)
serpent, 83 (I, 166)
see also Venus
Non Omnis Moriar (William Wynn Westcott), 266, 658, 687 (II, 280; IV, 309, 347-8)
Norma, 599 (IV, 226)
North, xxiii, 80 (I, 158)
Ahephi, 361 (III, 129)
alchemical operation, 396 (III, 186)
alimentary system, 360, 361 (III, 127, 128)
altar, russet side, 333 (III, 86)
Ammehitt, 353 (III, 115)
Black Pillar, 81 (I, 161)
Bornless Ritual, 443 (III, 260, 261)
bread and salt on altar (Earth), 334 (III, 87)
consecration of talismans, 385, 416, 422 (III, 167, 168, 216, 217, 227)
Crown of the, 355 (III, 118)
evocation, 381, 382, 402, 403, 404, 408, 409, 410 (III, 161, 162, 195, 196, 198, 205, 206, 209)
hexagram rituals, 298 (III, 34)
invisibility ritual, 388, 426 (III, 173, 235)
Kerub of Earth, 357 (III, 122)
North Pole of heavens, 92, 542, 594, 602, 603, 607, 615, 655 (I, 184; IV, 142, 218, 231, 236, 249, 304)
Knaves (Princesses) of Tarot, 544, 546, 547, 549, 550, 597 (IV, 145, 148, 150, 152, 154, 223)
see also Kether, North Pole of Universe
pentagram rituals, 53, 286 (I, 106; III, 19)
spiritual development ritual, 392, 435, 438, 439 (III, 179, 249, 253, 254)
transformation ritual, 390, 432 (III, 176, 243, 244)
see also cardinal points; Neophyte ritual, cardinal points and other directions
Northeast:
evocation, 382, 405 (III, 162, 201)
see also Ameshet; Neophyte ritual, cardinal points and other directions
Northwest:
Neophyte ritual, 127 (II, 32)
see also Kabexnuv
"Note on the Opening Exordium of 'Z,'" 374-5 (III, 150-1)
Nphra, 327 (III, 77)
Nroam, 327, 407, 410 (III, 77, 204, 208)
Nu, 56, 157, 185, 417, 424, 602 (I, 112; II, 75, 129; III, 220, 232; IV, 230)
Number, Mystic:
Adeptus Minor, 223, 261 (II, 201, 270)
Philosophus, 194 (II, 147)

Number, mystic (continued):
Practicus, 178, 183 (II, 115, 125)
Theoricus, 163, 168 (II, 86, 96)
Zelator, 147, 157 (II, 55, 73)
numbers:
Enochian calls, 671 (IV, 329)
6—371 (III, 144)
see also hexagram; Tiphareth
7—*see* seven, significance of number
10—*see* Sephiroth; Tree of Life
12—*see* Zodiac
21—223, 240, 261 (II, 201, 233, 270)
22—275 (II, 297)
see also Hebrew alphabet; Paths; Tarot
28—194 (II, 147)
32—*see* Thirty-two Paths of Wisdom
36—178, 183 (II, 115, 125)
40—*see* forty squares, Vault symbolism
42—*see* Forty-two Judges of the Dead; Forty-two letter name of God
45—163, 168, 220 (II, 86, 96, 196)
55—147, 157 (II, 55, 73)
72—*see* Shemhamphorash; Zodiac, quinances
84—275 (II, 296)
106—273 (II, 292)
120—224-5, 228, 233, 247, 262, 265, 275, 276 (II, 203-4, 211, 223, 244, 273, 279, 297, 299)
220—275 (II, 297)
463—237, 273, 275 (II, 228, 292, 297)
495—237, 273, 275 (II, 228, 292, 297)
496—205 (II, 169)
541—275 (II, 296)
576—237, 273, 275 (II, 228, 292, 297)
671—152 (II, 65)
776—275 (II, 296)
see also gematria
Nun:
Enochian pronunciation, 650 (IV, 297)
Scorpio, 305 (III, 44)
telesmatic image, 488, 489, 491, 492 (IV, 66, 67, 69, 71)
24th Path (Scorpio, Death):
Hiereus's lamen, 214, 337 (II, 185; III, 93)
Philosophus ritual, 192-3 (II, 144-5)
Portal ritual, 198, 200, 209, 210 (II, 155, 158, 177, 178)
Spirit, 210n
Temperance, 217-8 (II, 192)
see also Death; Hebrew alphabet; keyword analysis; Paths; Scorpio
Nun He, 147, 157 (II, 55, 73)
Nuremberg, 17 (I, 19, 21)
Nymphs and Undines:
Prince and Emperor of—*see* Kings (Princes), Cups
Nymphs and Undines (continued):
Princess and Empress of—*see* Knaves (Princesses), Cups
Queen of—*see* Queens, Cups
see also undines

- O -

O Document, 43, 540 (I, 84; IV, 137)
O.T.O, 697
oath or obligation:
Adeptus Minor—*see* Adeptus Minor, obligation
Hierophant, 253 (II, 256)
Neophyte—*see* Neophyte, obligation
Philosophus, 182 (II, 126)
Portal, 203-4 (II, 165-6)
Practicus, 168 (II, 96)
Theoricus, 156-7 (II, 73-4)
Zelator, 144-5 (II, 50)
Oblgotca, 672 (IV, 330)
Obligation, Cross of—*see* Cross of Obligation
obsession, 111, 389 (I, 226; III, 174)
occult, the, xviii
occultism, ix
octagon, 508, 509 (IV, 92)
octagram, 70, 508, 509 (I, 136; IV, 91)
octangle, 508 (IV, 92)
Octans, 600, 601 (IV, 228, 229)
Odyssey, 478 (IV, 49)
"Of the Four Elements and Their Natural Qualities," 611-3 (IV, 242-6)
"Of Obsession, Trance, Death," 111 (I, 226-7)
"Of Skrying and Traveling in the Spirit Vision," 467-74 (IV, 29-42)
"Of the Three Chiefs," 342 (III, 100-1)
"Of Traveling in the Spirit Vision," 108-9 (I, 220-21)
"Officers, The Stations of the," 334-44 (III, 88-104)
Ogdoad, 508 (IV, 92)
ogres, 110 (I, 224)
Ohooohaatan, 658 (IV, 309)
oil, in evocation, 409 (III, 207)
Oip, 653 (IV, 300)
Leo, 669 (IV, 325)
Oip Teaa Pedoce (Oip Teaa Pdoce), 182, 194, 281, 285, 315, 635, 653 (II, 124, 148; III, 10, 18, 60; IV, 276, 300)
consecration of Fire Wand, 325 (III, 73)
consecration of talisman, 421 (III, 226)
Enochian calls, 669 (IV, 325)
Opening by Watchtower:
evocation, 402 (III, 196)
spiritual development ritual, 435 (III, 248)
Vault consecration, 258 (II, 265)
Okmiah, 86, 553 (I, 172; IV, 159)
Ol sonuf vaorsagi..., 201, 422, 425, 444, 448, 627, 673 (II, 161; III, 228, 233, 262, 267; IV, 265, 333)

Ol sonuf vaaorsagi (continued):
see also Enochian, calls (keys), numbered calls, First
Olam (Olahm):
qabalistic cross, 53, 444 (I, 106; III, 262)
Pyramid of the Elements, 79, 187, 659 (I, 156; II, 134; IV, 310)
Olam Yesodoth, 63, 98 (I, 125, 198)
olive (color), 98, 241, 310 (I, 197; II, 235; III, 52)
altar (South side), 333 (III, 86)
Malkuth, 614, 616, 617 (IV, 247, 250, 251)
termination of 29th Path, 337 (III, 92)
Pentacle, 322 (III, 69)
olive branch, on Ace of Swords, 543 (IV, 143)
olive oil, 150 (II, 62)
olive tree, 58 (I, 116)
Olympic planetary spirits, 109 (I, 223)
sigils, 497, 503 (IV, 80, 87)
skrying, 497 (IV, 80)
telesmatic images, 490 (IV, 68)
Om, Oma, 628 (IV, 267)
Omdi, 669, 670 (IV, 325, 326)
Omebb, 654 (IV, 302)
Omega, 658 (IV, 309)
Ommoo-Szathan (Omoo-Sathan), 344, 353, 357, 365 (III, 103, 115, 121, 135)
On, 55 (I, 111)
1001 Notable Nativities (Alan Leo), 91 (I, 183)
Oomdi, 669 (IV, 325, 326)
Opening by Watchtower, xviii, 258-9, 377, 402-3, 413, 423, 429, 435-6, 447 (II, 264-7; III, 154, 195-7, 212, 229, 239, 248-50, 266)
"Opening of the Key, The," 567-81 (IV, 178-99)
Ophir, 80, 406, 409 (I, 158; III, 202, 207)
Ophiuchus, 598, 599 (IV, 224, 226)
opposition, 538 (IV, 134)
see also astrology, aspects
Oppression, The Lord of—*see* Tens (Tarot), Wands
Oracles of the Mighty Gods, The—*see* Lovers, The
Oracles of Zoroaster—*see* Chaldean Oracles
Orat, 592 (IV, 216)
orders:
A.A. (Argentum Astrum), ix, 10, 699
B.O.T.A. (Builders of the Adytum), xix
Hermetic Order of the Golden Dawn—*see* Golden Dawn
O.T.O. (Ordo Templi Orientis), 697
Societas Rosicruciana in Anglia, 17-8 (I, 19-21)
Society of the Inner Light, ix
Spiritus Sanctus, 14 (I, 13)
see also Collegium ad Spiritum Sanctum
see also Roseae Rubae et Aureae Crucis; Stella Matutina
organs of body, 359-61 (III, 125-9)
orgone energy, xxi
Orion, 595, 600 (IV, 220, 227)
Oro:
Enochian pyramids, 648 (IV, 294)
man kerub, 653 (IV, 300)
Oro Ibah Aozpi, 156, 164, 205, 281, 285, 315, 635 (II, 72, 87, 170; III, 10, 18, 60; IV, 276)
consecration of Dagger, 325 (III, 73)
consecration of talisman, 420 (III, 225)
Opening by Watchtower:
evocation, 403 (III, 196)
spiritual development ritual, 435 (III, 249)
Vault consecration, 259 (II, 266)
skrying, 667 (IV, 321)
transformation ritual, 439 (III, 240)
Oroiael, 207n
Orpheus (a misprint)—*see* Cepheus
Orth, 495 (IV, 77)
see also Enochian, letters
Osiris, 12-3, 27, 35, 36, 37, 56-9, 76, 157, 276 (I, 45, 63, 68, 70, 111-7, 149; II, 75, 299)
body broken up, 359, 362 (III, 125, 130)
description, 354 (III, 116-7)
elements, 334 (III, 87)
Enochian:
chess king, 686, 687, 688, 691, 693 (IV, 351, 352, 354, 359, 363)
pyramids, 663 (IV, 315)
Equinox ceremony, 374 (III, 149)
Evil One, slain by, 344 (III, 103)
evocation, 410 (III, 209)
Hierophant, 114, 337, 344, 352, 354, 358, 364, 366, 663 (III, 92, 104, 114, 116-7, 124, 132-3, 136-7; IV, 315)
Hori (Coptic letter), 345 (III, 105)
Horus, father of, 347 (III, 108)
illustration, 664 (IV, 316)
Isis and Nephthys, 56, 691 (I, 112; IV, 359)
Neophyte ritual, 114, 367, 369, 370 (III, 138, 140, 141)
Judgment Hall, 358 (III, 123)
Phoenix Wand, 224, 262, 354 (II, 203, 272; III, 117)
Portal ritual, 201, 208 (I, 160, 174)
requiem ceremony, 448 (III, 268)
Spirit, 372, 693 (III, 147; IV, 363)
spiritual development ritual, 438, 440, 441 (III, 254, 256, 258)
step, 371 (III, 144)
Tarot:
Death, 211 (II, 179)
Judgment, 172 (II, 104)
transformation ritual, 432 (III, 245)
Water, 184 (II, 127)
see also keyword analysis
Osiris Onnophris (Osiris on-Nophris), 223, 239, 261, 265, 334 (II, 201, 231, 270, 278; III, 87)

Osiris Onnophris (continued):
Adeptus Minor ritual, 223, 239 (II, 201, 231)
Bornless Ritual, 445 (III, 264)
consecration of talisman, 418 (III, 220)
requiem ceremony, 448, 449 (III, 267, 268, 269)
spiritual development ritual, 439, 440, 441 (III, 255, 257, 258)
Vault consecration, 261, 265 (II, 270, 278)
Osiris Risen, Sign of, 270 (II, 288)
see also keyword analysis; L.V.X., signs
Osiris Slain, Sign of, 239 (II, 202)
see also keyword analysis; L.V.X., signs
Osoronnophris (Osorronophris), 406, 442 (III, 201, 259, 260)
Ospmnir, 672 (IV, 330)
Outer Order:
grades referred to symbolically by 120 years, 224, 242 (II, 203, 273)
rituals, 113-96 (II, 11-152)
robes, sashes, 333 (III, 85)
see also elemental grades; Neophyte; Stella Matutina
ox, 143, 158, 159, 235 (II, 47, 77, 78, 224)
symbol, 280, 281 (III, 10, 11)
Ursa Major, 597 (IV, 221-2)
see also bull; Kerubim; Taurus

- P -

P Document, 43, 540 (I, 84; IV, 137)
P.A.L., Frater, 231 (II, 216)
P.D., Frater, 232 (II, 218)
Pachad, 97 (I, 195)
see also Geburah
Padmasambhava, 376n
Paganism, New, ix, 697, 698, 700
Pages (Tarot)—*see* Knaves (i.e., Princesses)
pagination of this edition, x, xii
Palaces, Seven, 82, 103, 159, 223, 261 (I, 164, 209; II, 79, 201, 271)
hexagram, 508 (IV, 91)
Knaves (Princesses) of Tarot, 568 (IV, 180)
microcosm, 424 (III, 231)
Seven-Branched Candlestick, 150 (II, 62)
Palaces, Seven Infernal, 177 (II, 114)
palm branch on Ace of Swords, 543 (IV, 143)
palm trees on Veil of the Tabernacle, 159, 161 (II, 79, 83)
Pam, 520 (IV, 105)
Pan, 212-3 (II, 182-4)
Pantacle—*see* Pentacle
Paphro Osoronnophris (Paphro Osorronophris), 406, 442 (III, 201, 260)
Papyri Graecae Magicae, 207n
Paralda, 80 (I, 158)
Paran, Mount, 191 (II, 140)
Paroketh, 200, 215, 223, 260, 331, 334-5, 342 (II, 159, 188, 200-1, 268, 269; III, 82, 85, 88, 100)
see also veil
Part of Fortune, 530, 538 (IV, 121, 134)
participation mystique, 43 (I, 61-2)
Paricular Exordium, The, 330, 375 (III, 81-2, 151)
Paschal, 419 (III, 222)
Pasht, 343 (III, 102)
Enochian pyramids, 663 (IV, 315)
illustration, 665 (IV, 317)
Kerub of South, 663 (IV, 315)
passive elements, 281 (III, 10)
see also elements, active and passive
passwords:
Adeptus Minor, 223, 240, 261 (II, 201, 233-4, 270)
Equinox ceremony, 248, 250, 373-4 (II, 245, 247, 250; III, 149, 150)
Neophyte, 127, 144, 373 (II, 31, 49-50; III, 148)
invisibility ritual, 389 (III, 174)
Philosophus, 194 (II, 147)
Portal, 217 (II, 190)
Practicus, 178, 183 (II, 115, 125)
Theoricus, 163, 168 (II, 86, 96)
Zelator, 147, 157 (II, 55, 73)
Past Hierophant—*see* Hierophant, Past
Pastos, 33, 37-8, 222, 225, 236-9 *passim*, 244, 245, 246, 268, 277 (I, 63, 70, 71; II, 199, 204, 226-31 *passim*, 238, 239, 240, 244, 283, 288)
foot of, 245, 246 (II, 241, 242)
lid of, illustration, 112 (II, 4)
see also Sword and Serpent
Osiris, 359 (III, 125)
Vault consecration ceremony, 258, 264, 265 (II, 264, 275-8 *passim*)
paten of bread and salt—*see* bread and salt
"Path of the Chameleon, The," 2, 95-9 (I, 191-202)
Path of the Chameleon, 267, 476 (II, 282; IV, 47)
see also Hodos Chamelionis; Minutum Mundum
Paths, 36, 39, 61, 275, 276 (I, 66, 74, 121; II, 297, 298)
altar diagram, The Serpent on the Tree of Life, 62, 162 (I, 123; II, 84)
animals, 109 (I, 222)
celestial sphere, 603, 605 (IV, 231, 234)
colors and color scales, 95-6, 99 (I, 191-2, 199-202)
elemental grade rituals, 137, 139, 140
First (Kether), 615 (IV, 248)
Hebrew alphabet, 162 (II, 84)
Hierophant's sceptre, 325 (III, 90)

Paths (continued):
  Rose-Cross lamen, 310 (III, 51)
  skrying, 464 (IV, 24, 25)
  starry sphere, 451 (III, 271)
  Tarot, 72-3 (I, 141-3)
    Ace of Wands, 343 (IV, 142)
  Tenth (Malkuth), 615, 617 (IV, 248, 251)
  see also Ayin; Kaph; Mem; Nun; Peh; Qoph; Resh; Samekh; Shin; Tau; Teth; Tzaddi
Pathway of Evil, 146 (II, 52-53)
Pathway of Good, 146 (II, 53)
Pathworking, 463-4 (IV, 23-4)
Paul, St., 588 (IV, 209)
Pavo, 599, 600 (IV, 226, 227)
pawns, Enochian chess—*see* Enochian, chess, pawns
Pdoce, 669 (IV, 325)
  see also Oip Teaa Pedoce
Pe, 405 (IV, 77)
  see also Enochian, letters
Peace Restored, Lord of—*see* Twos (Tarot), Swords
peacock, 546, 551 (IV, 148, 155)
  constellation—*see* Pavo
Pegasus (constellation), 546, 595, 598 (IV, 148, 219, 224, 225)
  Chesed, 603 (IV, 231)
Peh:
  anger and impatience, 474 (IV 41)
  Mars, 215 (II, 187)
  telesmatic image, 489, 491 (IV, 66, 67, 70)
  27th Path (Mars, The Tower), 31, 76 (I, 55, 150)
    admission badge—*see* admission badges, Paths, 27th Path
    Hegemon's station, 338 (III, 94)
    Hiereus's lamen, 214, 337 (II, 185; III, 93)
    Philosophus ritual, 182, 188-92, 193, 194 (II, 123, 137-43, 144-5, 147, 149)
      temple arrangement, 189 (II, 137)
    Portal ritual, 215 (I, 187)
    Practicus ritual, 176, 179 (II, 112, 117)
  see also Hebrew alphabet; Paths
Pehilyah, 86, 556 (I, 173; IV, 163)
Pelial, 97 (I, 196)
Peniel, 97 (I, 196)
Pentacle:
  elemental weapon (Earth), 47, 322 (I, 94; III, 69)
    astral projection, 471 (IV, 36)
    consecration, 323-5, 327 (III, 70-4, 76-8)
    illustration, 321 (III, 67)
    Knight (King) of Pentacles, 548 (IV, 152)
    Malkuth, 224n
    Opening by Watchtower:
      evocation, 403 (III, 196, 197)
Pentacle (continued):
  elemental weapon (Earth) (continued):
    Opening by Watchtower (continued):
      spiritual development ritual, 435, 436 (III, 249)
    Portal ritual, 200, 201 (II, 159, 160, 161)
    skrying, 469, 474 (IV, 32, 33, 41)
    Tattwa vision, 475 (IV, 43)
    see also weapons, magical, elemental
  evocation, 380, 402 (III, 159, 195)
  invisibility ritual, 388 (III, 172)
  production of natural phenomena, 384 (III, 166)
  Theoricus ritual, 154, 155, 156 (II, 69-72 *passim*)
Pentacles, 322, 553-4, 558-9, 562 (III, 69; IV, 159-61, 165-7, 172-3)
  court cards, 549-50 (IV, 152-4)
  divinatory meaning, 582, 584 (IV, 201, 203-4)
  see also individual cards [e.g., Tens (Tarot), Pentacles]
  see also Tarot
Pentad, 507 (IV, 90)
pentagon, 506, 507 (IV, 90)
Pentagonal Examination, 226 (II, 206)
pentagram, 4, 7, 29, 35, 40, 68, 506, 507, 508 (I, 50, 65, 76, 133; IV, 90-1)
  Aima, 150, 507 (II, 61; IV, 91)
  Air—*see* Air, pentagram
  astral projection, 472 (IV, 39)
  dekagram, 510, 512 (IV, 93)
  discharging talismans, 481 (IV, 54)
  Earth—*see* Earth, pentagram
  elemental grade rituals, 138, 140
  elements, 507 (IV, 90)
    attributed to points, 36, 281, 284, 310 (I, 66; III, 10, 16, 51)
    Enochian tablets, 210n, 630 (IV, 274)
      Tablet of Union (Spirit), 635 (IV, 275)
  Enochian:
    chess, 685 (IV, 350)
    Linea Spiritus Sancti, 653 (IV, 300)
    names from Sephirotic Calvary Cross, 637 (IV, 279)
  Fire—*see* Fire, pentagram
  geomancy, 524, 525, 539 (IV, 113, 116, 136)
  Great Mother, 150 (II, 61)
    see also pentagram, Aima
  Heh, 276-7, 507 (II, 299; IV, 91)
  120 years, 224, 242 (II, 203, 273)
  inverted, 213, 217, 280, 507 (II, 183, 191; III, 9; IV, 90)
  Mars, 70 (I, 136)
  microcosm, 217, 219-20, 277, 287, 507 (II, 190-1, 196, 299; III, 20; IV, 90)
  Portal ritual, five paths in, 209-10 (II, 177)
  Rite of the Pentagram and the Five Paths, 208-220 (II, 175-196)

pentagram (continued):
rituals, 280-6, 463 (III, 9-19; IV, 22)
Enochian system, 624 (IV, 260)
skrying, 668 (IV, 323)
Supreme Banishing Ritual of the Pentagram:
consecration of elemental weapons, 328 II, 88)
see also Lesser Banishing Ritual of the Pentagram; Supreme Invoking Ritual of the Pentagram; Supreme Ritual of the Pentagram
skrying, 470 (IV, 34)
Spirit, 507 (IV, 90)
coverts cross into pentagram, 217 (II, 190)
pentagrams—*see* Spirit, pentagrams
Sword, 317 (III, 62)
Tarot:
Death, 211 (II, 179)
The Devil, 213 (II, 183)
divination, 566 (IV, 177-8)
Water—*see* Water, pentagram
Wizard's Foot, 213 (II, 183)
Pentagrammaton, 8, 376, 466 (III, 153; IV, 27)
see also Yeheshuah
pentagrams, 699
astral projection, 464, 465, 466 (IV, 24, 26, 27)
banishing, 280-4 (III, 9-17)
consecration of elemental weapons, 323-7 *passim* (III, 71-7 *passim*)
invoking, 258, 259, 280-6, 315 (II, 265, 266, 267; III, 9-19, 59)
King (Prince) of Swords, 548 (IV, 151)
Rose-Cross lamen, 310, 312 (III, 51, 55)
Tattwa vision, 460 (IV, 18)
tracing, 328 (III, 88)
Zodiac, signs of, 283-4, 299 (III, 15, 35)
consecration of Lotus Wand, 304 (III, 43)
consecration of Sword, 318 (III, 64)
pentangle, 506 (IV, 90)
People in Quandaries (Wendell Johnson), 6
Per-em-Hru—*see* Book of the Dead, Egyptian
Pereclinus de Faustis, 151-2, 157, 161 (II, 64-5, 73, 83)
Perfected Success, The Lord of—*see* Tens (Tarot), Cups
Perfected Work, Lord of—*see* Fours (Tarot), Wands
permutations of YHVH, 149 (II, 60)
Perpetual Intelligence, 172 (II, 103)
Perpetual Success, The Lord of—*see* Tens (Tarot), Cups
Persephone, 172 (II, 104)
see also Proserpine
Perseus, 589 (IV, 211)
constellation, 595, 598 (IV, 219, 225)
Persia, 231 (II, 216)
Phaeton, 600 (IV, 227)
Phalarthao, 443 (III, 261)
phallic religions, 490 (IV, 68)
Pharos Illuminans, 195, 202, 203 (II, 149, 164)
Phi, 443 (III, 260)
Phillips, Osborne, and Melita Denning, *Mysteria Magica,* 682n
philology, 627, 628, 629 (IV, 265, 266, 269)
Philosopher's Stone, xxii, 25 (I, 38, 40)
evocation, 406, 407, 409, 411 (III, 202, 203, 207, 210, 211)
see also Stone of the Wise
Philosopher's Stone, The (Israel Regardie), 365, 377 (III, 135, 153-4)
philosophic egg, 84, 395, 398 (I, 167; III, 184, 185, 189)
Philosophus, 21, 35, 41, 95, 646, 659 (I, 30, 64, 79, 191; IV, 291, 310)
Adeptus Minor ritual, 226 (II, 206)
admission badge—*see* admission badges, Philosophus; cross, Calvary, Six squares
Enochian tablets, 656 (IV, 305)
Hiereus, grade required for, 195, 226, 342 (II, 150, 206; III, 100)
knowledge lecture, 77-86 (I, 153-74)
meditation, 80-1 (I, 160)
Netzach, 31, 76, 192-5, 331 (I, 54, 150; II, 144-50; III, 83)
Paths from, 195 (II, 149)
Paths to, 141, 147, 148, 154, 157, 161, 163, 169, 174, 181, 182, 195 (II, 44, 55, 58, 69, 74, 82, 87, 87, 107, 121, 123, 149)
Portal ritual, 202-20 *passim* (II, 163-97 *passim*)
Regimen of the Elements, 228 (II, 211)
Regimen of the Planets, 228 (II, 211)
ritual, 31, 181-96 (I, 54-5; II, 121-52)
adoration, 182-3 (II, 123-4)
closing, 195-6 (II, 150-2)
elemental prayer, 196 (II, 151-2)
The Entry into Netzach, 192-5 (II, 144-50)
oath, 182 (II, 126)
opening, 181-3 (II, 122-4)
The Path of Tzaddi, 186-8 (II, 131-6)
temple arrangement, 181 (II, 121-2)
The Entry into Netzach, 192-3 (II, 144-5)
The Path of Tzaddi, 186 (II, 131)
The 27th Path of Peh, 188-9 (II, 137)
The 29th Path of Qoph, 183-185 (II, 124-30)
The 27th Path of Peh, 188-192 (II, 137-43)
sign, 194, 200, 208, 215 (II, 147, 158, 159, 173, 174, 188)
consecration of Rose-Cross, 315 (III, 60)
pentagram rituals, 285 (III, 18)
Tattwa vision, 475 (IV, 43)

Philosophus (continued):
sign, grip, word, number, password, 194, 202 (II, 147, 163)
see also Fall, The, altar diagram
"Philosophus, The Grade of: Additional Lecture on the Tattwas of the Eastern School," 514-22 (IV, 95-109)
Phoenix (constellation), 599, 600 (IV, 226, 228)
Phoenix Collar, 233 (II, 220)
Phoenix Wand, 221, 224, 262 (II, 198, 203, 272)
Egyptian deities, held by, 354, 355, 356 (III, 117, 118, 119)
Oriris, 686 (IV, 351)
Lesser Banishing Ritual of the Hexagram, 258 (II, 265)
Lotus Wand, combined with, 355 (III, 118)
Vault consecration ceremony, 258 (II, 265)
Phorlakh (Phorlach), 80, 324 (I, 158; III, 72)
evocation, 404, 405, 408 (III, 199, 201, 206)
Tattwa vision, 459 (IV, 17)
Phraestt (South), 353 (III, 115)
Phrath, 73, 177, 195, 200, 202, 260 (I, 145; II, 114, 149, 158, 163, 268)
Phrithithi (Aquarius), 343, 353 (III, 102, 115)
physics, new, xviii
physiology, 5
Pictor—*see* Equuleus Pictoris
A Pictorial Key to the Tarot (A. E. Waite), 6, 39, 91 (I, 75, 183)
Pillars, 28, 38, 46, 55-9, 61-3, 81, 114, 162, 333 (I, 47, 71, 90, 110-7, 122, 161-2; II, 85; III, 85-6)
Adeptus Minor ritual, 222, 234, 238 (II, 199, 221, 230)
alchemical operation, 397 (III, 188)
bases, 333, 341 (III, 85-6, 99)
Black:
sash, 212, 333 (II, 181; III, 85)
Third Adept in Portal ritual, 203 (II, 165)
black and white, 81, 209, 333 (I, 161-2; II, 176; III, 85-6)
Bornless Ritual, 444 (III, 263)
capitals, 333 (III, 86)
celestial sphere, 603 (IV, 231)
of cloud and fire, 61, 62, 162, 348, 390, 391, 392, 427 (I, 122; II, 85; III, 173, 176-9 *passim*, 235)
consecration of talismans, 386, 387, 413, 418, 419, 420, 422 (III, 169, 170, 212, 221, 223, 224, 228)
drawing of Mount Abiegnus, 242 (II, 237)
Eve, supported by, 74, 76, 178, 193 (I, 145, 150; II, 115, 146)
evocation, 382, 383, 403, 410, 411 (III, 163, 197, 208, 209, 210)
five Pillars, 655, 656 (IV, 303, 304)
Hegemon, station between, 338 (III, 94)
Pillars (continued):
invisibility ritual, 388, 389, 427 (III, 173, 174, 235, 236)
Isis and Nephthys, 344, 346 (III, 104, 108)
Jachin and Boaz, 81 (I, 161-2)
Mercy:
Hegemon's sceptre, 339 (III, 95)
Thmaa-ett, 339 (III, 96)
Wheel of Fortune, 590 (IV, 212)
Metatron and Sandalphon, 375 (III, 151)
microcosm, 100, 102 (I, 204, 207)
Middle—*see* Middle Pillar
Mildness—*see* Middle Pillar
Neophyte ritual, 116, 119, 121, 126-9 *passim*, 131, 364-9 *passim*, 380 (II, 11, 15, 19, 29-35 *passim*, 40; III, 134-41 *passim*, 158)
explained, 128 (II, 34)
Philosophus ritual, 181, 183-4, 186, 188, 189, 190, 192 (II, 121-2, 126, 131, 132, 137, 138, 144)
Portal ritual, 198, 201, 208 (II, 155, 161, 175)
Practicus ritual, 166, 169 (II, 92, 97)
requiem ceremony, 449 (III, 269)
Samson, 212 (II, 181)
sash of the Black Pillar, 212, 333 (II, 181; III, 85)
Severity, 30 (I, 53)
Hiereus's sword, 337 (III, 93)
Thma-Aesh, 339 (III, 96)
see also Pillars, Black
spiritual development ritual, 391, 392, 393, 438, 439, 440 (III, 178-81 *passim*, 254-7 *passim*)
Temple, 81 (I, 161-2)
Theoricus ritual, 154, 156, 161, 162 (II, 69, 73, 82, 85)
transformation ritual, 390, 391, 429, 432, 433 (III, 176, 177, 239, 244, 246)
27th Path, 315 (II, 187)
Yesod, supported by, 163 (II, 86)
Zelator ritual, 141-9 *passim* (II, 44, 46, 50-54 *passim*, 58, 59, 60)
see also Tree of Life
Pingala, 515, 516, 517, 522 (IV, 97, 98, 100, 108)
Pisces:
crescent, 185 (II, 130)
divine and angelic names, 86 (I, 174)
divine name, Hebrew letter, Tribe of Israel, angel, and color, 305 (III, 44)
Enochian letter and geomantic figure, 495 (IV, 77)
Jupiter, 495 (IV, 77)
Mars, 642 (IV, 286)
see also Pisces, Tarot, Cups, Ten
pentagram, 283 (III, 15)
Pillar of Mercy, 603 (IV, 232)

Pisces (continued):
Tarot:
Cups:
Eight and Nine, 541, 560 (IV, 140, 169)
Ten, 541, 550, 560-1 (IV, 140, 156, 170)
Knight (King), 546, 598 (IV, 148, 225)
The Moon, 71, 73, 542, 592, 599 (I, 139, 143; IV, 141, 215, 226)
Queen of Wands, 545, 598 (IV, 147, 225)
Swords:
King (Prince), 598 (IV, 224)
Knave (Princess), 597 (IV, 223)
29th Path, 182, 185 (II, 123, 129)
Vault symbolism, 269 (II, 286)
see also Paths; Zodiac
Pisces Nautica—*see* Pyxis Nautica
Piscis Australis (Piscis Austrinus), 599 (IV, 226)
Piscis Volans ("Pisces Volcun"), 600 (IV, 227)
Pison, 73, 177, 315 (I, 144; II, 114; III, 60)
planetary hours: Mars, 317 (III, 62)
planetary spheres—*see* spheres, heavenly or planetary; planets
planetary spirits:
Enochian Kings, 659 (IV, 309)
see also Olympic planetary spirits; spirits, planetary
planets, 50-1, 65 (I, 100-1, 127)
alchemic powers (seven letters in vitriol, sulphur, and mercury), 206 (II, 172)
angels, 65 (I, 127)
sigils, 483, 485 (IV, 58, 60)
apertures of head, 103, 371 (I, 210; III, 145)
colors, 241, 267, 268, 287, 481 (II, 236, 282, 283, 285, 286; III, 20; IV, 55)
enneagram, 508 (IV, 93)
enneangle, 508 (IV, 92)
Enochian:
letters, 495 (IV, 77)
seniors, 637, 670 (IV, 278, 326)
tablets, 656 (IV, 305)
Great Cross, 648 (IV, 293, 294)
Lesser Angles, 645 (IV, 290)
pyramids, 651 (IV, 298)
Sephirotic Calvary Crosses, 643-4 (IV, 287-8)
geomancy, 524, 526, 537 (IV, 112, 113, 114, 132)
geomantic figures, 495 (IV, 77)
Great Hermetic Arcanum, 206 (II, 170)
Hebrew letters, 179, 311 (I, 78; III, 53)
heptagon, 508 (IV, 91-2)
hexagram, 508 (IV, 91)
hexagrams, 287-99 (III, 20-36)
attribution to points, 287, 312 (III, 20-1, 55)
planets (continued):
hexagrams (continued):
consecration of Rose-Cross, 315 (III, 59)
for one planet, 299 (III, 35-36)
for several planets, 299 (III, 36)
Zodiac, location in, 293 (III, 28)
hexangle, 507 (IV, 91)
inferior and superior, 293 (III, 27)
intelligences–*see* intelligences of the planets
lineal figures, 70 (I, 136)
Lotus Wand to invoke or banish, 302-3 (III, 40)
Mercury synthesis of, 588 (IV, 210)
named in elemental grade rituals, 137
Olympic spirits—*see* Olympic planetary spirits
order, 267 (II, 282)
Pan (seven-reeded pipe), 213 (II, 183)
Phoenix Wand, 224, 262 (II, 223, 272)
Regimen of the Planets, 228 (II, 211)
Rose-Cross lamen, 310, 311, 482 (III, 51, 53; IV, 57)
seals or sigils, 497, 498-502 (IV, 80, 81-6)
Seven-Branched Candlestick, 150 (II, 62)
spirits—*see* spirits, planetary
symbols, 51, 83 (I, 101, 165)
doors, 463 (IV, 22)
tracing, 288, 293 (III, 21-2] 26, 28)
talismans, 481, 494-5 (IV, 55, 76)
Tarot:
divination, 568 (IV, 181)
Judgment, 172 (II, 105)
numbered cards, 541, 550 (IV, 139-40, 156)
The Star, 188 (II, 135)
trumps, 71, 72-3, 542, 600 (I, 139, 141-3; IV, 140-41, 227)
Tree of Life, 642 (IV, 286)
see also spheres, heavenly or planetary
Vault symbolism, 246, 267, 268 (II, 240, 282-5 *passim*)
Zodiac, decanates, 642, 648 (IV, 286, 293, 294)
see also planets, Tarot, numbered cards
see also individual planets
plants, 109 (222-3)
Plato, 611 (IV, 244)
Pleasure:
Lord of—*see* Sixes (Tarot), Cups
The Lord of Blended—*see* Fours (Tarot), Cups
Lord of Loss in—*see* Fives (Tarot), Cups
Pluto, 172, 537n (II, 104)
Poemandres, Corpus Hermeticum, 201n
point, Kether, 204-5, 505 (II, 168; IV, 89)
polar bears, 666 (IV, 320)
Polaris, 451 (III, 271)
Binah, 603 (IV, 232)
Tarot, 597 (IV, 222, 223)

Polarity Therapy, 699
Pollux—*see* Castor and Pollux
"Polygons and Polygrams," 504-13 (IV, 88-94)
Pooyal, 86, 562 (I, 171; IV, 172)
Populus, 494, 495, 527, 536-7, 538 (IV, 75, 77, 115, 131, 134)
  Eight of Pentacles, 553-4 (IV, 159)
  Enochian pyramids, 649, 650 (IV, 296, 297)
  see also geomancy, figures
Poraios de Rejectis, 164, 168, 174 (II, 88, 96, 107)
Portal document, 3, 4, 5, 6, 87-95 (I, 175-90)
Portal grade, 35-6, 41, 422, 425 (I, 64-6, 79; III, 228, 233)
  meditation, 87, 88, 94-5 (I, 175, 189-90)
  nine months waiting period, 92-4, 219 (I, 185-9; II, 196)
  Paths to, 161, 163, 174 (II, 82, 87, 107)
  Regimen of the Planets, 228 (II, 211)
  ritual, 35-6, 95, 198-220 (I, 64-6, 191; II, 155-97)
    closing, 220 (II, 196-7)
    Enochian call, 201, 627 (II, 161; IV, 264)
    oath, 203-4 (II, 165-6)
    opening, 199-201 (II, 156-161)
    Rite of the Pentagram and the Five Paths, 208-220 (II, 175-196
    The Ritual of the Cross and the Four Elements, 201-208 (II, 163-174)
    temple arrangement, 198, 208 (II, 155, 175)
  sash, 203, 212, 216 (II, 165, 181, 189)
    Adeptus Minor ritual, 225 (II, 205)
    First Order Temple, that of no higher grade worn in, 332 (III, 85)
    white, 216 (II, 190)
  signs, 199, 200, 215-6, 216-7 (II, 157, 159, 188, 190, 200)
    see also Closing of the Veil; Rending of the Veil
  sign, grip, word, number, password, 216 (II, 190)
  thesis, 87 (I, 175-6)
  25th Path, 163 (II, 87)
Post annos CXX patebo, 15 (I, 14)
Post Annos Lux Crucis Patebo, 233 (II, 222)
Post Centum Viginti Annos Patebo, 225, 247, 262, 265 (II, 203, 244, 273, 279)
Post CXX Annos Patebo, 232, 233 (II, 220, 222)
power, xxiv, 4
Power—*see* Geburah
Powers (angelic choir), 97 (I, 195)
"Practical Z. Preparation for Divination" (J. W. Brodie-Innes), 451-4 (III, 271-6)
Practicus, 21, 30-1 (I, 30, 53-4)
  admission badge, 70-1 (I, 137-8)
  Hegemon, grade required for, 342 (III, 100)
Practicus (continued):
  Hod, 30, 73, 176-9, 331 (I, 53, 144; II, 112-8; III, 83)
  knowledge lecture, 69-76 (I, 135-51)
  meditation, 72 (I, 140)
  Paths from, 176, 179, 189-90 (II, 112, 117, 138)
  Paths to, 141, 147, 148, 154, 157, 161, 163, 166, 169, 173, 174, 177 (II, 44, 55, 58, 69, 74, 82, 87, 92, 97, 106, 107, 115)
  Philosophus ritual, 183-96 *passim* (II, 124-34 *passim*, 138-45 *passim*, 149, 151)
  Regimen of the Elements, 228 (II, 211)
  ritual, 30-1, 166-80 (I, 53-4; II, 92-120)
    adoration, 167-8 (II, 94-5)
    closing, 179-80 (II, 118-20)
    Cup of Stolistes explained, 177, 340 (II, 113; III, 97)
    oath, 168 (II, 96)
    opening, 167-8 (II, 93-5)
    temple arrangement, 166-7 (II, 92-3)
      The Thirtieth Path of Resh, 173 (II, 106)
      Temple in Hod, 176 (II, 112)
    Temple in Hod, 176-9 (II, 112-8)
    Thirtieth Path of Resh, 173-6 (II, 106-11)
    Thirty-First Path, 168-73, 214, 363 (II, 95-105, 185; III, 131)
  sign, 178, 183, 199, 200, 207, 208, 215 (II, 115, 125, 158, 160, 173, 174, 188)
    astral projection, 471, 472 (IV, 37, 39)
    consecration of Rose-Cross, 315 (III, 60)
    consecration of talisman, 413 (III, 212)
    pentagram rituals, 286 (III, 19)
  sign, grip, word, number, password, 178, 183 (II, 116, 125)
  see also Garden of Eden, altar diagram
Praemonstrator:
  Chesed, 204, 331, 332, 342 (II, 168; III, 82, 83, 101)
  Equinox ceremony, 250, 255 (II, 250, 259, 261)
    function, 252 (II, 254)
  functions and duties, 332 (III, 83)
  Isis, 342, 344, 352, 354, 356, 663 (III, 101, 103-4, 114, 116, 119-20; IV, 315)
  lamen, 332 (III, 84)
  mantle, 332 (III, 83)
  Neophyte ritual, 116-7, 132, 331-2 (II, 11-2, 42; III, 82-4)
  sceptre, 204, 332 (II, 168; III, 84)
    illustration, 348 (III, 110)
  wand—*see* Praemonstrator, sceptre
  Water, 332 (III, 82, 84)
Prana, 20, 360, 515 (I, 27; III, 127; IV, 97, 98)
pranas, 457 (IV, 12)
pranayama, xxi, 53, 515-6, 519-22 *passim* (I, 105; IV, 98-9, 103-8 *passim*)
Prasad, Rama, *Nature's Finer Forces, or the Science of Breath,* 514 (IV, 95)

prayers, elemental—*see* elemental prayers
precession of the equinoxes, 10, 594 (IV, 218)
Priestess of the Silver Star, The—*see* High Priestess, The
primates, 110 (I, 223-4)
  descended rather than ascended from human beings, 110 (I, 224)
Primum Mobile, 63, 96, 346, 506 (I, 125, 193; III, 108; IV, 89)
  see also Rashith ha-Gilgalim
Prince of:
  the Chariot of Earth; Prince and Emperor of the Gnomes—*see* Kings (Princes), Pentacles
  the Chariot of Fire; Prince and Emperor of Salamanders—*see* Kings (Princes), Wands
  the Chariot of the Waters; Prince and Emperor of Nymphs and Undines—*see* Kings (Princes), Cups
  the Chariots of the Wind; Prince and Emperor of Sylphs and Sylphides—*see* Kings (Princes), Swords
Prince scale of color, 95, 99 (I, 192, 199-202)
Princes (Tarot)—*see* Kings (Princes)
Princess of:
  the Echoing Hills; Princess and Empress of the Gnomes—*see* Knaves (Princesses), Pentacles
  the Rushing Winds; Princess and Empress of the Sylphs and Sylphides—*see* Knaves (Princesses), Swords
  the Shining Flame; Princess and Empress of Salamanders—*see* Knaves (Princesses), Wands
  the Waters and the Lotus; Princess and Empress of Nymphs and Undines—*see* Knaves (Princesses), Cups
Princess scale of color, 95, 99 (I, 192, 199-202)
Princesses (Tarot)—*see* Knaves (Princesses)
Principalities (angelic choir), 97 (I, 196)
Prithivi, 457, 458-60, 514, 516-22 *passim* (IV, 12-3, 14-6, 96, 99, 100, 101, 103, 105-8 *passim*)
  of Akasa, 458, 516 (IV, 14, 99)
  of Apas:
    astral projection, 470-4 (IV, 35-42)
    skrying, 469-70 (IV, 32-35)
  Lam, 520 (IV, 105)
Probation, Intelligence of, 218 (II, 193)
Probationer (A.A.), 10
Problem of Good and Evil, The or *The Christos* (Vitvan), 6
Prometheus, 32, 34 (I, 57, 62-3)
Prophet, The, (Tarot)—*see* Hermit, The
Prophet of the Gods, The—*see* Hermit, The
Proserpine, 550 (IV, 153)
  see also Persephone
protections, 465-6 (IV, 27)
  see also circle; Lesser Banishing Ritual of the Pentagram
Prudence—*see* Hermit, The
  Lord of—*see* Eights (Tarot), Pentacles
Psalms:
  24:7—419, 425 (III, 223, 232) 18th, 77th, and 29th, 190-1 (II, 139-40)
  139th, 107, (I, 217)
Psellus, 25-6 (I, 40-1)
psychic protection, 309 (III, 50)
Psychoanalysis for Normal People (Geraldine Coster), 88 (I, 178)
Psychology (William McDougall), 88 (I, 177)
Psychology (Norman Munn), 5
Psychology of Transference, The (C. G. Jung), xxv
Psycho-Synthesis (the Dean of Chester Cathedral), 88 (I, 178)
psychotherapy, xix, xx-xxi, xxiv-xxv, 5
  see also individual types
  see also Freudian psychoanalysis; Jung, Carl Gustav; Reich, Wilhelm
Psychotherapy: A Basic Text (Robert Langs), xxv
Ptah, 686, 692, 693-4, 695 (IV, 350, 362, 364-7 *passim*)
Ptolemy, Claudius, 594 (IV, 219)
Puella, 494, 495, 527, 533-4 (IV, 75, 77, 115, 127)
  Enochian chess, 690 (IV, 357)
  see also geomancy, figures
Puer, 494, 495, 527, 534 (IV, 75, 77, 115, 127)
  see also geomancy, figures
Pur, 444 (III, 263)
Pure and Clear Intelligence, 163 (II, 86)
purification—*see* consecration and purification
putrefaction, 395 (III, 185-6)
pyramid:
  admission badges, 39 (I, 74)
  cross, 335 (III, 88)
  elements, 659 (IV, 310, 311)
  see also Enochian tablets, pyramids
Pyramid of the Elements, 79, 186, 187, 217, 646, 659 (I, 156; II, 131, 132, 134, 190; IV, 291, 311)
  see also Enochian tablets, pyramids
Pyramid of Fire, 70, 168-72 *passim* (I, 137; II, 95, 96-104 *passim*)
  sides explained, 171-2 (II, 103)
Pyramids, the, 55 (I, 111)
pyramids, Enochian—*see* Enochian tablets, pyramids
Pyxis Nautica ("Pisces Nautica"), 599, 500 (IV, 226, 227)

- Q -

Q Document, 43, 540 (I, 84; IV, 137)
Q.L. = Quaero Lucem (Harriet Miller Davidson, aka Mrs. R. W. Felkin), 588 (IV, 209)
Qabalah—*see Holy Kabbalah, The* (A. E. Waite); *Sepher Yetzirah; Zohar*
Qabalah of Nine Chambers—*see* Aiq Beker
qabalistic cross, 39, 55, 81, 90 (I, 75, 109, 162, 181)
  Bornless Ritual, 442, 444 (III, 259, 262)
  consecration of elemental weapons, 328 (III, 77)
  consecration of talisman, 414 (III, 213)
  described, 53 (I, 106)
  evocation, 403, 404 (III, 197, 198)
  hexagram rituals, 296 (III, 32)
  invisibility ritual, 423, 425, 428 (III, 229, 233, 237)
  pentagram rituals, 284, 285, 286 (III, 16, 18, 19)
  Portal ritual, 199, 200, 201, 209, 215, 220 (II, 158, 159, 160, 176, 188, 197)
  requiem ceremony, 448, 449 (III, 267, 270)
  spiritual development ritual, 435 (III, 248)
  transformation ritual, 430 (III, 240)
  Vault consecration ceremony, 258, 260 (II, 271, 278)
  vibration of divine names, 491 (IV, 70)
Qebhsenef, 358 (III, 123)
  see also Kabexnuv
Qesheth, 95, 147, 214 (I, 191-2; II, 55-6, 185, 186)
Qlippoth, 61, 82, 98, 202 (I, 121, 163, 197; II, 164)
  altar diagrams:
    The Fall, 193 (II, 146)
    The Flaming Sword of the Kerubim, 146 (II, 52)
  animal sacrifice, 149 (II, 59)
  astral projection, 464 (IV, 25)
  bodily functions and organs of elimination, 359, 360 (III, 126, 128)
  cosmic Sphere of Sensation, 451 (III, 271)
  endekagram, 510 (IV, 94)
  endekangle, 506 (IV, 89)
  Hiereus guardian against, 337, 359 (III, 92, 125)
  Kether of, 614 (IV, 147)
  microcosm, 101, 102, 106, 107 (I, 206, 208, 215-6, 217)
  Neophyte ritual, 114
  Omoo-Sathan, 357 (III, 121)
  "The Qlippoth of the Qabalah," 202n
  telesmatic images, 488, 490 (IV, 65, 68)
  The Tower, 192 (II, 143)
  32nd Path, 155, 159 (II, 71, 79)
  Vault symbolism, 243 (II, 238)
Qoph, 147 (II, 55)
  circumambulation, reverse, 346 (III, 107)
  The Moon, 591 (IV, 214)
  Pisces, 305 (III, 44)
  29th Path (Pisces, The Moon), 76 (I, 150)
    admission badge, 79 (I, 156)
    Hegemon's sceptre, 339 (III, 95)
    Malkuth, terminates in olive quarter of, 337 (III, 92)
    Philosophus ritual, 182, 183-5, 192-3, 194 (II, 122, 123, 124-30, 144-5, 147, 150)
      temple arrangement, 181 (II, 121-2)
    Practicus ritual, 169 (II, 97)
    Theoricus ritual, 154, 157 (II, 69, 74)
    Zelator ritual, 141, 147, 148, 154, 157 (II, 44, 55, 58)
  see also Hebrew alphabet; Moon, The; Paths; Pisces
quantum mechanics, xviii
Quaternary, 506 (IV, 90)
Queen:
  alchemy, 60 (I, 120)
  Great Hermetic Arcanum, 206 (II, 170)
Queen of:
  Gnomes—*see* Queens, Pentacles
  Nymphs and Undines—*see* Queens, Cups
  the Canticles, 159 (II, 79)
  the Salamanders or Salamandrines—*see* Queens, Wands
  the Sylphs and Sylphides—*see* Queens, Swords
  the Thrones of:
    Earth—*see* Queens, Pentacles
    Flames—*see* Queens, Wands
    the Air—*see* Queens, Swords
    the Waters—*see* Queens, Cups
Queen scale of color, 95-9 (I, 191-202)
  planets, 287 (III, 20)
Queens (Tarot), 544 (IV, 144)
  Binah, 615 (IV, 249)
  celestial sphere, 596 (IV, 221)
  Cups, 547 (IV, 148-9)
    divination example, 568, 569, 571, 572, 573, 582 (IV, 181, 185, 187, 188, 201)
  divinatory meaning, 582 (IV, 201)
  Enochian chess queens, 686, 691, 695 (IV, 351, 360, 367)
  Heh, 615 (IV, 249)
  Pentacles, 549 (IV, 153)
  Swords, 548 (IV, 150-1)
    Enochian pyramids, 654 (IV, 301, 302)
  Wands, 545 (IV, 146-7)
    divination example, 575, 576, 586 (IV, 192, 207)
    Enochian:
      chess, 687 (IV, 353)
      pyramids, 654-5 (IV, 303)
see also Tarot, court cards

Queens, Enochian chess—*see* Enochian, chess, pieces
Quesheth—*see* Qesheth
quicksilver—*see* mercury (metal)
quinances of Zodiac:
angels, 85-86 (I, 170-74)
The Sun, 175 (II, 110)
quintile aspect, 510, 538 (IV, 93, 133)
see also astrology, aspects

- R -

R Document, 43, 540 (I, 84; IV, 137)
R.C., Frater, 232 (II, 218)
R.R. et A.C.—*see* Roseae Rubae et Aureae Crucis
Ra, 56-7, 158, 424, 425 (I, 112-3; II, 76; III, 232)
Enochian chess Fire knight, 685 (IV, 350)
Raagios, 207n
Ra-Agiosel (i.e., Raagiosl), 168, 325, 413, 421 (II, 95; III, 73, 213, 227)
Ragon, 15 (I, 16)
Raguel, 207n
Rahael, 86, 564 (I, 172; IV, 175)
Ra-hoor-Khuit, 698
Ram, 520 (IV, 105)
ram's head (crest), 546, 550, 551 (IV, 148, 153, 155)
Raphael:
angel of Mercury, 65, 207n (I, 127)
archangel of Air, 80, 156, 205, 207n, 673 (I, 158; II, 72, 170; IV, 332)
consecration of Dagger, 324 (III, 72)
consecration of talisman, 420 (III, 225)
Lesser Banishing Ritual of the Pentagram, 54, 444 (I, 107, 262)
transformation ritual, 429 (III, 240)
archangel of Tiphareth, 62, 64, 97 (I, 123, 126, 195-6)
consecration of Rose-Cross, 314 (III, 58, 59)
Rashith ha-Gilgalim, 63, 96, 346, 375 (I, 125, 193; III, 108, 150)
Kether of Assiah, 614 (IV, 247)
Ratziel, 96, 419, 438 (I, 194; III, 222, 254)
see also Raziel
raven, alchemy, 84 (I, 167)
Raziel, 62, 64, 96 (I, 123, 126, 194)
see also Ratziel
Re—*see* Ra
Real History of the Rosicrucians, The (A. E. Waite), 37 (I, 69-70)
Reconciler, 530, 538, 539 (IV, 120-1, 134, 135)
see also geomancy
Recondite Intelligence, 194 (II, 147-8)
Red Dragon, 12, 37, 76, 177, 239 (I, 70, 150; II, 114, 229)
Red Dragon (continued):
Vault symbolism, 243 (II, 238)
red lamp—*see* lamp(s), red
Red Rose and Gold Cross, 223n
see also Roseae Rubae et Aureae Crucis
red shoes—*see* shoes, red
Regardie, Israel, ix, xii, xvii-xxv, 683n, 699, 700
A.M.A.G. = Ad Majorem Adonai Gloriam, 272, 277, 405 (II, 290, 300; III, 200)
The Art of True Healing, 3, 41, 92 (I, 80, 185)
Ceremonial Magic, xviii
The Eye in the Triangle, xx, 1
The Formulae of the Magic of Light (Document Z.2), Foreword, 376-9 (III, 153-6)
The Garden of Pomegranates, 2
"Introduction to the Enochian System," 624-30 (IV, 260-73)
The Middle Pillar, xxv, 4, 55, 92, 378 (I, 109, 185; III, 155)
The Philosopher's Stone, 365, 377 (III, 135, 153-4)
My Rosicrucian Adventure, 1, 18 (I, 22)
"The Three Chiefs," 272-7 (II, 290-300)
The Tree of Life, 2, 18, 23, 39, 41, 52n, 377 (I, 23, 34, 75, 79, 104n, 153)
Twelve Steps to Spiritual Enlightenment, 4
Regimen of the Elements, 228 (II, 211)
Regimen of the Planets, 228 (II, 211)
Regulus, 10, 550, 594, 596, 599, 600, 606, 609 (IV, 156, 218, 222, 225, 227, 235, 241)
Tiphareth, 596 (IV, 221)
Rehaayal, 86, 559 (I, 174; IV, 168)
Reticulum (Reticulum Rhomboidalis; "Reticulus"), 600, 601 (IV, 228, 229)
Reyayel, 86, 558 (I, 173; IV, 165)
Reich, Wilhelm, xx-xxi, xxiv-xv
The Function of the Orgasm, 5
reincarnation—*see* metempsychosis
relaxation, xxi, 88, 90 (I, 178-9)
religious tolerance, xviii, 129 (II, 36)
Remiel, 207n
Renault, Mary, *The King Must Die,* xxii
Rending of the Veil, 200, 215-6, 223, 260, 403, 419, 422, 444 (II, 159, 188, 200, 268; III, 197, 223, 228, 262)
illustrated, 134 (f. 43)
Renovating Intelligence, 213 (II, 184)
Repast, Mystical—*see* Mystical Repast
Requiem ceremony, 377, 447-50 (III, 154, 266-70)
Resh:
with hexagrams, as a letter of the name Ararita:
Jupiter, 289 (III, 22)
Sun, 291-2 (III, 24-5)

Resh (continued):
lineal figures, 493 (IV, 72)
Sun, 215 (II, 187)
30th Path (Sun, The Sun), 30-1, 73, 161, 163 (I, 53, 144; II, 82, 87)
admission badge, 70 (I, 137)
circumambulation, 346 (III, 107)
Philosophus ritual, 186, 188 (II, 131, 137)
Portal ritual, 212, 215 (II, 181, 187)
Practicus ritual, 167, 173-6, 178, 179 (II, 93, 106-112, 115, 117)
temple arrangement, 172 (II, 106)
Theoricus ritual, 161, 163 (II, 82, 87)
vanity, 474 (IV, 41)
see also Hebrew alphabet; keyword analysis; Paths; Sun
residuum, 395-9 *passim* (III, 184, 186, 189, 191)
see also Caput Mortuum; Dead Head
Resplendent Intelligence, 438, 615, 617 (III, 253; IV, 248, 251)
Rest from Strife, The Lord of—*see* Fours (Tarot), Swords
Resultants, Four—*see* Four Resultants
Reuben, 305 (III, 44)
Revelation, The:
1:11—540 (IV, 137)
1:12-16—35 (I, 63-4)
1:12-18—239, 264, 440, 444, 449 (II, 229, 231, 277; III, 257, 263, 269)
2:7—239 (II, 231)
5:1—540 (IV, 137)
10:1-3—205-6 (II, 170-1)
see also Apocalypse
Revolving or Flowing Formula, 621 (IV, 256-7)
Reyayel, 86, 558 (I, 173; IV, 165)
Rheibet, 443 (III, 260)
rhomboid, 72 (I, 140)
Rhombus—*see* Reticulum
right ascension, 594 (IV, 218)
Right Witness—*see* Witnesses
Rishis, Seven, 597 (IV, 222)
see also Ursa Major
Rising on the Planes, 464-5 (IV, 24-5)
Rite of the Kerubic Stations, 156-60, 464 (II, 72-81; IV, 24)
formula, 420-2 (III, 223-8)
rituals, 27-39, 697 (I, 43-74)
Adeptus Minor—*see* Adeptus Minor, ritual
banishing rituals never used in Vault, 270 (II, 287)
Bornless, 377, 442-6 (III, 153, 259-65)
Ceremony of the Equinox, 26, 248-57, 373-4 (I, 41-2; II, 245-63; III, 148-50)
consecration, 303-5, 312-9, 323-8 (III, 41-5, 57-61, 63-5, 70-8)
Consecration Ceremony of the Vault of the Adepti, 258-65 (II, 264-78)
rituals (continued):
elemental, xxiii-xxiv, 135-96 (II, 44-152)
Equinox, 26 (I, 41-2)
grade, ii-xxiv, 44, 45, 135-96 (I, 86-7, 88; II, 44-152)
see also individual grades
Hexagram, 287-99 (III, 20-36)
see also Hexagram Rituals
Pentagram, 280-6 (III, 9-19)
see also Lesser Banishing Ritual of the Pentagram; Supreme Invoking Ritual of the Pentagram
Middle Pillar—*see* Middle Pillar, ritual
Neophyte—*see* Neophyte ritual
Philosophus—*see* Philosophus, ritual
Portal—*see* Portal, ritual
Portal thesis, 87 (I, 175-6)
Practicus—*see* Practicus, ritual
Requiem, 377 (III, 154)
Rose-Cross, 4, 8, 306-9 (III, 46-50)
skrying, 463-4, 465 (IV, 23-4, 25-6)
Theoricus—*see* Theoricus, ritual
Zelator—*see* Zelator, ritual
see also Neophyte formula
Rivers of Daath, Infernal, 239 (II, 229)
Rivers of Eden—*see* Garden of Eden, Rivers of
Roam, 410 (III, 208)
Robe of Darkness—*see* cloak, Hiereus
Robe of Mourning, 226, 228, 231, 263 (II, 207, 210, 216, 275)
robes:
black and white, 332-3 (III, 85)
Hierophant's, 252, 254 (II, 253, 257)
Queen of Wands, 545 (IV, 146)
white, 468, 471 (IV, 31, 35)
Kether, 473 (IV, 40)
see also cloaks
rock music, xviii
Rome, 628 (IV, 266)
rooks (castles), Enochian chess—*see* Enochian, chess, pieces
Roots of the Powers of the elements—*see* Aces (Tarot)
rope—*see* cord
rose, xx, xxv
altar (Air), 333, 334 (III, 86-7)
consecration rituals:
elemental weapons, 323 (III, 70)
Lotus Wand, 303 (III, 41)
Rose-Cross, 312, 314 (III, 57)
Sword, 317 (III, 63)
Equinox ceremony, 249, 50 (II, 247, 248, 250)
evocation, 409 (III, 207)
Neophyte ritual, 116-7, 132 (II, 11-2, 41)
requiem ceremony, 448 (III, 267)
Rose of Creation, 149-50 (II, 60-61)

rose (continued):
Rose of Sharon, 143, 403, 424 (II, 46; III, 197, 231)
Rose-Cross lamen, 310, 311, 312 (III, 51, 53, 55)
consecration, 315 (III, 61)
spiritual development ritual, 439, 441 (III, 255, 258)
transformation ritual, 429 (III, 240)
Vault symbolism, 242 (II, 238)
Rose-Cross, xxv, 42, 43, 47, 218, 219, 224, 233, 235, 236, 240, 243, 246, 270 (I, 81, 84, 94; II, 195, 202, 220, 222, 224, 226, 234, 240, 287)
consecration of elemental weapons, 323 (III, 70)
Equinox ceremony, 251, 252, 253, 255 (II, 250, 254, 256, 259)
Hierophant's lamen, 335 (III, 90)
lamen, 310-6 (III, 51-61)
astral projection, 466 (IV, 28)
Bornless Ritual, 442 (III, 259)
colors, 312 (III, 54-5)
consecration, 312-6 (III, 57-61)
consecration of Sword, 317 (III, 63)
consecration of talisman, 414 (III, 213)
sigils, 311, 317, 320, 322, 402, 482-5, 486, 487, 491, 493, 496 (III, 53, 62, 68, 69, 195; IV, 57-60, 61, 63, 70, 73, 74, 78)
colors, 483 (IV, 57)
skrying, 468, 473 (IV, 31, 40)
symbol (traced), 306, 422, 442, 448 (II, 46; III, 228, 260, 267)
astral projection, 466 (IV, 27)
consecration of talismans, 482 (IV, 56)
vibration of divine names, 492 (IV, 70)
Tiphareth, 473, 487, 491 (IV, 40, 63, 70)
Vault:
consecration, 252 (II, 272)
symbolism, 243 (II, 240)
Rose-Cross, Ritual of the, 4, 8, 306-9 (III, 46-50)
astral performance, 308-9 (III, 50)
Bornless Ritual, 445 (III, 264)
uses, 308-9 (III, 49-50)
rose leaves, in Portal ritual, 200, 205, 208, 216 (II, 159, 169, 170, 175, 189)
Rose of Ruby and the Cross of Gold, the, 226, 227, 228, 270 (II, 206, 209, 211, 287)
see also Roseae Rubae et Aureae Crucis
Rose of the:
Palace of Earth, The—*see* Knaves (Princesses), Pentacles
Palace of Fire, The—*see* Knaves (Princesses), Wands
rose branch, on Tarot cards, 554, 558, 562 (IV, 160, 166, 167, 172, 173)
rose tree:
Ace of Pentacles, 543 (IV, 143)
Eight of Pentacles, 553 (IV, 159)
The Fool, 588 (IV, 209-10)
Roseae Rubae et Aureae Crucis, 42, 223, 247, 251, 252, 254, 260, 265, 272, 405, 415, 426, 430, 442, 466, 624, 697, 699 (I, 80; II, 221, 243, 251-4 *passim*, 258, 269, 279, 291; III, 200, 215, 233, 241, 260; IV, 27, 260)
rituals, 197-277 (II, 155-300)
Rosenkreutz, Christian, 14-5, 37, 223, 229, 231-2, 223, 261, 266, 267, 270, 271-7 *passim*, 625 (I, 13-4, 69-70; II, 201, 212, 217-20, 221, 270, 280, 283, 287, 289, 292-300 *passim*, 262)
see also Pastos; Vault
roses, on Tarot cards:
Ace of Pentacles, 543 (IV, 144)
numbered cards, 553, 554, 555, 558, 559, 562, 563 (IV, 159-62 *passim*, 166, 167, 168, 172, 173, 174)
Rosicrucian chess—*see* Enochian, chess
Rosicrucians, xxii, xxv, 14-6, 18, 37, 231-2 (I, 13-7, 21-2, 69-70; II, 216-20)
Dee, John, and Edward Kelly, 626 (IV, 262)
Fama Fraternitatis, viii, 14-5, 37 (I, 13-5, 69-70)
The Brotherhood of the Rosy Cross (A. E. Waite), 18 (I, 22)
identification, 230, 246 (II, 215, 243)
Real History of the Rosicrucians, The (A. E. Waite), 37 (I, 69-70)
Rota, 232, 592 (II, 220; IV, 216))
Roubriao, 443 (III, 261)
Ruach, 34, 417 (I, 60-1; III, 219)
consciousness, 101 (I, 205)
ego, 33 (I, 58)
Neophyte, 365, 366 (III, 134, 135, 137)
Pyramid of the Elements, 187 (II, 134)
reasoning faculties, 27 (I, 44)
soul, part of, 67, 100-5 *passim* (I, 129, 203-14 *passim*)
Theoricus grade, 164, 168 (II, 88, 96)
see also Air
Ruach Elohim, 31, 55, 167, 183, 218, 413 (I, 54, 110; II, 94, 125, 126, 195; III, 212)
Banner of the East, 336 (III, 91)
Shin, 240, 280 (II, 234; III, 9)
Rubeus, 495, 525, 527, 528, 529, 534, 537, 539 (IV, 77, 115, 116-9 *passim*, 128, 133, 135)
Enochian pyramids, 650 (IV, 300)
see also geomancy, figures
Rudhyar, Dane, *Astrology of Personality,* 5
Ruin, Lord of—*see* Tens (Tarot), Swords
Ruler of Flux and Reflex—*see* Moon, The (Tarot)

Rulers of Elements, 80 (I, 158-9)
Rururet, 57 (I, 114)
russet, 98, 241, 310 (I, 197; II, 235; III, 52)
altar (North side), 333 (III, 86)
Malkuth, termination of 31st Path, 337 (III, 92)
Pentacle, 322 (II, 69)
Rzionr, 672 (IV, 330)
Rzla, 637-8 (IV, 279)

- S -

S Document, 43 (I, 84)
see "Introduction to the Enochian System," 624-59 (IV, 260-309)
S.A. = Sapere Aude (William Wynn Westcott), 16, 17, 576, 650, 658, 668 (I, 17-8, 19-20; IV, 193, 300, 308, 309, 323)
S.D.A. = Sapiens Dominabitur Astris (Anna Sprengel), 17 (I, 19)
S.R.M.D. = S'Rhiogail Ma Dhream (MacGregor Mathers), 16, 574, 585, 594, 601, 603, 644, 650, 653, 661 (I, 17, 18; IV, 190, 207, 218, 229, 236, 289, 300, 300, 313)
S.S.D.D = Sapienta Sapienti Dono Data (Florence Farr), 56 (I, 111-2)
Sa, 520 (IV, 105)
Sabao, 445 (III, 265)
Sabaoth, 444 (III, 262)
see also Elohim Tzabaoth; YHVH Tzabaoth
Sabriam (Sabrium), 444 (III, 263)
Sachiel, 65 (I, 127)
consecration of Jupiter talisman, 414, 415, 417, 418 (III, 214, 216, 218, 221)
Sacred Magic of Abramelin, The (trans. MacGregor Mathers), 8, 11, 16 (I, 18)
Sagitta, 598 (IV, 224)
Sagittarius, 214 (II, 185, 186)
divine and angelic names, 86 (I, 173)
divine name, Hebrew letter, Tribe of Israel, angel, and color, 305 (III, 44)
Enochian:
chess, 694 (IV, 365)
letter and geomantic figure, 495 (IV, 77)
Jupiter, 215, 495 (II, 187; IV, 77)
Pillar of Severity, 603 (IV, 232)
Tarot:
Death, 599 (IV, 226)
Knave (Princess) of Cups, 597 (IV, 223)
Queen of Pentacles, 549, 598 (IV, 153, 224)
Temperance, 71, 73, 542, 591, 599 (I, 139, 143; IV, 141, 214, 226)
Wands:
Eight, Nine, and Ten, 541, 557 (IV, 140, 164-5)
Knight (King), 545, 598 (IV, 146, 224)
telesmatic image, 487 (IV, 66)
Sagittarius (continued):
Vault symbolism, 269 (II, 286)
see also Zodiac; Paths
Sahiah, 86, 557 (I, 173; IV, 165)
Saiinor, 325 (III, 73)
Saitel, 86, 553 (I, 172; IV, 159)
Sakarah, 55 (I, 111)
Sakhet, 362 (III, 129)
see also Pasht; Sekhet
salamanders, 30, 80, 160 (I, 52, 159; II, 80)
King of the—*see* Knights (Kings), Wands
prayer, 196 (II, 151-2)
Prince and Emperor of—*see* Kings (Princes), Wands
Princess and Empress of—*see* Knaves (Princesses), Wands
Queen of the Salamanders or Salamandrines—*see* Queens, Wands
see also elementals
Salem, Massachusetts, xviii
Saliah, 86, 560 (I, 174; IV, 170)
Salt, 63, 478 (I, 124; IV, 49)
Hugo Alverda, 275 (II, 296)
consecration rituals
elemental weapons, 323 (III, 70)
Lotus Wand, 303 (III, 41)
Rose-Cross, 312 (III, 57)
Sword, 317 (III, 63)
elements, 310-11 (III, 51-2)
Rose-Cross lamen, 310-11 (III, 51-2)
Subtilis Aqua Lux Terra, 206 (II, 172)
Tree of Life on symbol, 84 (I, 168)
Portal ritual, 198, 200-1, 204, 208, 216 (II, 155, 160, 167, 175, 189)
Theoricus ritual, 154-60 *passim* (II, 69-73 *passim*, 67-80 *passim*)
Zelator ritual, 145 (II, 50-1)
see also alchemy, principles; bread and salt
Samael, 82, 145, 146, 406 (I, 163; II, 52, 53; III, 201)
Judgment, 172 (II, 104)
Samana, 515 (IV, 97)
Samekh:
Egyptian language, 650 (IV, 297)
Sagittarius, 304 (III, 44)
telesmatic image, 488, 489, 491 (IV, 66, 67, 69)
25th Path (Sagittarius, Temperance), 95-6, 161 (I, 191-2; II, 82)
Fire, 210n
Harpocrates, station of, 344, 356 (III, 103, 120)
Hegemon's station at intersection with 27th Path, 338 (III, 94)
Hiereus's lamen, 214, 337 (II, 185; III, 93)
Hierophant's sceptre, 335 (III, 90)
Neophyte ritual, 379 (III, 158)

Samekh (continued):
25th Path (continued):
Philosophus ritual, 186 (II, 131)
Portal ritual, 198, 209, 214, 216, 217, 218 (II, 155, 177, 185-6, 190, 191, 193)
Practicus ritual, 174 (II, 107)
Rising on the Planes, 464 (IV, 24)
stations, invisible, 356 (III, 120)
Temperance, 217 (II, 192)
Theoricus ritual, 161, 163 (II, 82, 87)
Throne of the East, 334-5 (III, 88, 89)
see also Hebrew alphabet; Paths; Sagittarius; Temperance
Samothrace, 31, 231 (I, 53; II, 216)
mysteries, 172 (II, 105)
Samson, 212 (II, 181)
San Francisco, xix
Sanctum Sanctorum, 161 (II, 83)
Sanctus Spiritus (order), 14 (I, 13)
see also Collegium ad Spiritum Sanctum
Sandalphon, 62, 63, 64, 98, 146 (I, 122, 123, 126, 198; II, 52)
evocation, 405, 406, 407 (III, 200, 201, 202, 204)
Kerub on Ark of the Covenant, 146, 159, 162 (II, 54, 79, 85)
Malkuth:
of Briah, 614 (IV, 246)
guardian over, 375 (III, 151)
telesmatic image, 488-9 (IV, 65-6)
The Universe, 159 (II, 79)
Sandha, 517 (IV, 100)
Sangha, 21 (I, 29)
Sanskrit, 628, 629 (IV, 266, 267)
sash, 350 (III, 112)
Adeptus Minor, 221 (II, 198)
astral projection, 466, 471 (IV, 27, 35)
skrying, 468 (IV, 31)
Equinox ceremony, 250 (II, 250)
illustration, 350 (III, 112)
Neophyte, 127, 369, 380 (II, 31-2; III, 141, 158)
temple, 332, 333 (III, 85)
Philosophus, 194 (II, 148)
Portal:
Adeptus Minor ritual, 225 (II, 205)
First Order Temple, highest grade sash worn in, 332 (III, 85)
ritual, 203, 212, 216 (II, 165, 181, 189)
white, 216 (II, 190)
Practicus, 178 (II, 116)
Theoricus, 163 (II, 86-7)
Zelator, 147 (II, 55)
Satan, 34, 214, 280 (I, 61; II, 186; III, 10)
Satanism, xvii
Satem, 158 (II, 77)
Sati-Ashtoreth, 685 (IV, 350)
Saturn, xxi, 63 (I, 125)
Air, 648 (IV, 294)
alchemical operation, 396 (III, 186)
angel, intelligence, and spirit, 65 (I, 127)
Aquarius, 495 (IV, 77)
Binah, 19, 96-7 (I, 25, 194)
Capricorn, 495 (IV, 77)
Daath, 218 (II, 195)
ear, right, 103 (I, 210)
Earth, 644 (IV, 289-90)
Enochian:
chess, 690 (IV, 357)
letters, 495 (IV, 77)
tablets:
Sephirotic Calvary Crosses, 643 (IV, 287)
geomantic figures, 495 (IV, 77)
hexagram, 218, 288, 289 (II, 195; III, 21, 22)
consecration of elemental weapons, 325 (III, 73)
evocation, 407, 409 (III, 203, 206)
general purpose hexagram, 296 (III, 31)
invisibility ritual, 423 (III, 230)
requiem ceremony, 447 (III, 267)
lineal figures, 493 (IV, 72)
magic square, 70, 220, 498 (I, 136; II, 196; IV, 81)
memory, 474 (IV, 41)
seal, 498 (IV, 81)
Tarot:
Eight of Cups, 541, 560 (IV, 140, 169)
Seven of Pentacles, 541, 562 (IV, 140, 172, 173)
The Star, 591 (IV, 215)
Temperance, 591 (IV, 214)
Three of Swords, 541, 555 (IV, 139, 161, 162)
Wands:
Five, 541, 550, 552, 553 (IV, 139, 156, 158)
Ten, 541, 557 (IV, 140, 165)
The Universe, 71, 73, 542, 592 (I, 139, 143; IV, 141, 216, 217)
Tau, 215 (II, 187)
Theta (Coptic letter), 345 (III, 105)
32nd Path, xxi, 159, 209, 213, 215 (II, 71, 176, 184, 187)
triangle, 70, 506 (I, 136; IV, 89-90)
Vault symbolism, 267 (II, 282)
see also planets
scales: Justice, 590 (IV, 213)
scarabeus: The Moon, 185, 591 (II, 130; IV, 215)
sceptre, 379 (III, 158)
Cancellarius, 332 (III, 84)
illustration, 348 (III, 110)
Chief Adept, 198, 200, 201, 216, 217 (II, 155, 159, 160, 161, 188-91 *passim*)

sceptre (continued):
Hegemon, 119, 127, 249, 338, 339, 365, 368 (II, 16, 32, 247; III, 95-6, 134, 139)
illustration, 349 (III, 111)
Hierophant, 11, 249, 254, 334, 335, 347, 368 (II, 247, 257; III, 88, 89-90, 109, 139)
Bornless Ritual, 442 (III, 259)
illustration, 349 (III, 111)
Neophyte ritual, 119, 120, 125, 131, 132 (II, 16, 17, 27, 28, 40, 41)
Past Hierophant, 332 (III, 85)
Praemonstrator, 332 (III, 84)
illustration, 348 (III, 110)
Sceptre of Power—*see* sceptre, Hierophant
Sceptre of Wisdom—*see* sceptre, Hegemon
sceptres in Neophyte ritual, 117, 120, 125, 131, 132 (II, 13, 18, 28, 29)
Schad Barschemoth ha-Shartathan—*see* Shad Barschemoth ha-Schartathan
Schemhamporesch (Schemhamephoresch, Schem-ha-Mephoresch, Shemhamphoresch), 85, 160, 172, 553, 565 (I, 170; II, 80, 105; IV, 158, 159, 176)
The Sun (Tarot), 175 (II, 110)
Scholem, Gershom G, *Jewish Gnosticism, Merkabah Mysticism and Talmudic Tradition,* 375n
Schrödinger's Cat, 700
Schueler, Gerald J., 682n
Scorpio:
alchemical operation, 397 (III, 187)
divine and angelic names, 86 (I, 173)
divine name, Hebrew letter, Tribe of Israel, angel, and color, 305 (III, 44)
Enochian:
chess, 694 (IV, 365)
letter and geomantic figure, 495 (IV, 77)
pyramids, 6543 (IV, 302)
Fire, 209, 210n (II, 177)
Kerub of Water, 343 (III, 102)
see also eagloe; Kerubim
Lotus Wand, 302, 305, 315 (III, 43, 44, 60)
Mars, 495 (IV, 77)
Rubeus, 650 (IV, 300)
scorpion, eagle, or snake, 269 (II, 284)
scourge, 242 (II, 237)
Szlae-Ee, 343, 353 (III, 102, 115)
Tarot:
Cups:
Ace, 607, 610 (IV, 237, 240)
Five, Six, and Seven, 541, 556 (IV, 139-40, 162-4)
King (Prince), 547, 598, (IV, 149, 224)
Death, 71, 73, 211, 214, 542, 599 (I, 139, 142; II, 179, 186; IV, 141, 226)
Justice, 599 (IV, 226)
Knight (King) of Wands, 545, 598, (IV, 146, 224)
Scorpio (continued):
Vault symbolism, 268 (II, 284)
see also keyword analysis; Zodiac
scorpion, 268 (II, 284)
Sakhet, 362 (III, 129)
Tarot:
Death, 211 (II, 180)
King (Prince) of Cups, 547, 551 (IV, 149, 155)
Temperance, 217 (II, 192)
Scotland, 18 (I, 22)
Scotts Hermetica, 201n
Scriptures—*see* Apocalypse; Bible; Chronicles; Daniel, Deuteronomy; Ezekiel; Exodus; Genesis; Habakkuk; Job; John; Judges; Kings; Matthew; Psalms; Revelation
Sculptor—*see*Apparatus Sculptoris
seagulls, 666 (IV, 320)
seals, 666, (IV, 320)
Seb, 686 (IV, 350)
Sebek, 686 (IV, 350)
Second Adept—*see* Adept, Second
Second Order—*see* Inner Order; Roseae Rubae et Aureae Crucis
secrecy, 16, 22, 126 (I, 18, 33; II, 36)
Neophyte obligation, 123 (II, 22-23)
Secret Chiefs, 1
Secret Doctrine, The (H.P. Blavatsky), 32, 272, 273, 274, 596 (I, 57; II, 290-1, 292-3; IV, 220)
Secret of the Golden Flower, The (trans. Richard Wilhelm), 26-7, 33, 365 (I, 43, 58; III, 135)
Sedona, Arizona, xxii
Seir, 190, 419 (II, 139; III, 222)
Sekhet, 663 (IV, 315)
see also Pasht; Sakhet
Self, xvii, xviii, xxi, 26, 27 (I, 41, 45)
self-initiation, 45 (I, 88)
semi-sextile aspect, 510 (IV, 94)
see also astrology, aspects
seniors (Enochian)—*see*Enochian tablets, seniors
Sentinel, 341 (III, 98)
Anubis, 334, 352, 356 (III, 88, 114, 119)
lamen, 139
illustration, 351 (III, 113)
Equinox ceremomy, 249, 258 (II, 248, 263)
Neophyte ritual, 116, 117, 120, 121, 131, 346, 363 (II, 11, 12, 17, 19, 39, 40; III, 108, 131, 132)
station and duties explained by Hiereus, 118 (II, 14)
Neophyte, office open to, 137, 341 (III, 100)
Zelator ritual, 152 (II, 66)
Sephardic, 52n, (I, 104n)
Sepher Yetzirah, 12, 44, 55, 61, 128, 152, 162, 178, 194, 493 (I, 87, 110, 122, 129; II, 33, 65, 66, 84, 103, 109, 116, 147; IV, 72)

Sepher Yetzirah (continued):
Intelligences, 159, 163, 172, 175, 185, 187-8, 191, 194, 211, 213, 218, 615, 617 (II, 78, 86, 103, 109-10, 129, 134, 142, 147-8, 181, 193; IV, 248, 251)
see also Intelligences of *Sepher Yetzirah*
Sephiroth, 11, 18021, 41, 43, 45, 47, 61-5, 275 (I, 23-9, 80, 84, 92, 121-7; II, 297)
AETERNITAS (Ab Kether Ex Chokmah Tu Binah Ex Chesed Regina Geburah. Nunc tiphareth In Netzach Totius Hod Ad Yesod Saeculorum Malkuth), 477, 478 (IV, 48, 49)
altar, 151 (II, 63)
angelic hosts, 62, 64 (I, 123, 126)
archangels, 62, 64 (I, 123, 126)
Averse, 177, 194 (II, 114, 148)
drawing of Typhon, 211 (II, 180)
celestial sphere, 657 (IV, 306)
*see also*Tree of Life, celestial sphere
colors, 95-9, (I, 191-202)
dekagon, 510, 511 (IV, 93)
dekagram, 510 (IV, 93)
divine names, 62, 64 (I, 123, 126)
elemental attributions, 84 (I, 168-9)
elemental grade rituals, 137, 139
elemental weapons, 224n
Enochian tablets, 643-4, 648 (IV, 287-8, 295)
Linea Spiritus Sancti, 650, 653 (IV, 300)
see also Tree of Life, Enochian system
Equinox ceremony, 374 (III, 149(
grades, tabulated with, 21 (I, 30)
Hebrew spellings and list, 51-2 (I, 102)
hexagrams, 287, 293 (III, 20, 21, 27)
Hierophant's sceptre, 335 (III, 90) 120 years, 225, 242 (II, 203-4, 273)
lineal figures—*see* lineal figures, Sephiroth
Outer Order temple, only four shown, 115, 331 (III, 82)
Palaces, Seven, 82 (I, 164)
Rose-Cross lamen, 310 (III, 51)
sigils, 483, 484 (IV, 58, 59)
skrying, 464 (IV, 24, 25)
starry sphere, 451 (III, 271)
Tarot, 67, 550, 552 (I, 130; IV, 156-7)
Ace of Wands, 543 (IV, 142)
divination, 567, 568, 579, 580 (IV, 178, 180, 197, 198)
see also Tree of Life, Tarot
Three Chiefs, 274 (II, 295)
Vault symbolism, 223, 266, 268 (II, 201, 280, 284)
Venus symbol, 79, 195, 268, 272, 275-6 (I, 157-8; II, 149, 284, 291, 297)
Yesod, purified and made clear by, 163 (II, 86)
see also Binah; Chesed; Chokmah; Daath; Geburah; Hod; Kether; Malkuth; Netzach; Supernal Sephiroth; Tiphareth; Tree of Life; Yesod
Sephirotic Calvary Crosses—*see* Enochian tablets, Sephirotic Calvary Crosses
Septemtriones, 597 (IV, 222)
see also Ursa Major
Seraph, 80, 324 (I, 159; III, 72)
Seraphim, 62, 64, 97, 207 (I, 123, 126, 195; II, 172)
angelic choir of Kether, 96 (I, 193)
consecration of Sword, 318 (III, 64)
Fiery Serpents, 83 (I, 165)
Judgment, 172 (II, 104)
telesmatic image, 486 (IV, 62)
Serpens:
star map, 595 (IV, 219)
serpent, 93 (I, 165-6)
altar diagram, The Fall, 193 (II, 146)
Kundalini, 276 (II, 298)
Tarot:
Death, 211 (II, 179-80)
King (Prince) of Cups, 546, 551 (IV, 149, 155)
Two of Pentacles, 558 (IV, 166)
see also dragon
Serpent Formula, 617-21 (IV, 251-7)
Serpent on the Tree of Life, The (altar diagram), 61-2, 161, 162-3 (I, 121-3; II, 82, 84-5)
Serpent of Wisdom, 162, 226, 275, 276 (II, 84, 206, 297, 298)
Mount Abiegnus drawing, 242 (II, 238)
Vault symbolism, 242-3 (II, 238)
serpents:
caduceus, 162, 340 (II, 84; III, 97)
Winged-Sphere Wand, 224, 262, 340 (II, 203, 272; III, 97)
servient squares—*see* Enochian tablets, servient squares
Set, 13, 58, 114 (I, 115)
see also Apophis; Typhon
Seth, Pillars of—*see* Pillars
Seven, The, 207n
Seven:
Churches—*see* Churches, Seven
Days of Creation, 223, 261 (II, 201, 271)
Infernal Palaces—*see* Palaces, Seven Infernal
Lamps Before the Throne—*see* Lamps Before the Throne, Seven months between Philosophus and Portal (Regimen of the Planets), 228 (II, 211)
number of officers, 341 (III, 100)
Palaces—*see* Palaces, Seven
Rishis, 597 (IV, 222)
see also Ursa Major
Seven-Branched Candlestick—*see* Candlestick, Seven-Branched
significance of number, 150-51, 207 (II, 63, 172)
Thrones, 207n
Tomb of Christian Rosenkreutz, 223, 261, 266-9, 271 (II, 201, 271, 280-6, 288-9)

Sevens (Tarot), 552 (IV, 157)
Cups, 556-7 (IV, 163-4)
divination example, 577, 578, 586 (IV, 194, 195, 196, 207)
divinatory meaning, 582 (IV, 202)
Enochian pyramids, 654 (IV, 302)
Pentacles, 562 (IV, 172-3)
divination example, 580, 581 (IV, 199)
Swords, 559-60 (IV, 158-9)
Enochian pyramids, 648 (IV, 294)
Wands, 553 (IV, 159)
divination example, 577, 579 (IV, 194, 196)
see also Tarot, numbered cards
Severity—*see* Geburah
sex of telesmatic images, 488, 489, 490, 660 (IV, 65, 67, 68-9, 312)
Sextans, 599, 600 (IV, 225, 227)
sextile aspect, 507, 538, 539 (IV, 91, 133, 134, 135)
see also astrology, aspects
Shaar, 152 (II, 65)
Shabbathai, 63, 65, 96 (I, 125, 127, 194)
invisibility ritual, 424, 428 (III, 230, 238)
requiem ceremony, 447 (III, 266)
sigil, 483, 485 (IV, 58, 60)
spiritual development ritual, 436 (III, 250, 251)
see also Saturn
Shad Barschemoth ha-Schartathan (Schad Barschemoth ha-Shartathan), 65 (I, 127)
sigil, 502 (IV, 86)
Shaddai, 98 (I, 197)
Shaddai El Chai, 62, 64, 80, 205 (I, 123, 126; II, 169-70)
consecration of talisman, 420 (III, 225)
elemental grade rituals, 155, 156, 163, 164, 165, 168 (II, 71, 72, 86, 88, 90, 96)
with hexagram of Moon, 289 (III, 22)
transformation ritual, 429, 430, 431, 433, 434 (III, 240, 241, 243, 246, 247)
shadow, xvii, xviii
Shatranju, 687 (IV, 348)
sheepskin mantle: Knave (Princess) of Pentacles, 550 (IV, 154)
Shekinah, 251, 272, 276, 375, 423, 428, 431, 436, 447 (II, 252, 290, 298; III, 151, 230, 237, 242, 250, 266)
shells, 34, 73, 76, 83, 177 (I, 62, 144, 150, 166; II, 114)
altar diagram, The Fall, 193 (II, 146)
Gehenna, 161 (II, 81)
32nd Path, 159 (II, 79)
see also Qlippoth
Shemesh, 63, 65, 97, 314, 315 (I, 125, 127, 195; II, 58, 59)
see also Sun
Shemhamphoresch—*see* Schemhamporesch
Shew Bread, Table of, 67 (I, 130)
Zelator ritual, 148, 149-50 (II, 58, 60-1)
Shewstone (Dee and Kelly), 626 (IV, 263)
Shiatsu, 699
Shin (Hebrew letter), xxv, 8, 147, 151, 159 (II, 55, 64, 77)
caduceus, 340, 162 (II, 84; III, 97)
Circular Altar, 235, 243, 258, 259 (II, 224, 240, 264, 267)
crown of Microprosopus, 101 (I, 206)
Fire, 172, 419 (II, 105; III, 222)
invisibility, 376, 387, 388 (III, 152, 171, 172)
Judgment, 591 (IV, 214)
Spirit—*see* Yeheshuah
spiritual development, 376, 388, 391 (III, 152, 172, 178)
31st Path (Fire, Judgment), 30, 73 (I, 53, 144)
admission badge, 70 (I, 137)
Hiereus's sword, 337 (III, 93)
Malkuth, terminates in russet quarter of, 337 (III, 92)
Practicus ritual, 166-7, 168-173, 176, 178, 179, 363 (II, 92-93, 95-105, 112, 115, 117; III, 131)
temple arrangement, 166-7 (II, 92-3)
Philosophus ritual, 184, 188 (II, 126, 137)
temple arrangement, 181 (II, 121)
Theoricus ritual, 154, 157 (II, 69, 74)
Zelator ritual, 141, 147, 148, 154, 157 (II, 44, 55, 58)
transformation ritual, 376, 388 (III, 152, 172)
see also Fire; Hebrew alphabet; Judgment; Paths
shoes:
blue, 198 (II, 156)
red, 117, 198, 199, 350, 466 (II, 12, 156; III, 112; IV, 27)
yellow, 198, 221, 442, 466 (II, 156, 199; III, 259; IV, 27)
Shooeu-tha-ist, 686 (IV, 350)
Shortened Force, Lord of—*see* Eights (Tarot), Swords
Shroud of Concealment or Darkness, 387-9, 423-8 *passim* (III, 171-5, 230-8 *passim*)
Shu, 55, 57, 158 (I, 110, 113-4; II, 77)
Shu Zoan, 686 (IV, 350)
sickle, 548 (IV, 151)
Sigillum Dei Æmeth, 657, 658 (IV, 308, 309)
sigils, 9, 42, 43, 44, 47, 482-5, 486, 493-503, 699 (I, 81, 84, 87, 94; IV, 57-60, 61, 74-88)
Ace of Wands, 542 (IV, 142)
angels of Tarot and Zodiac, 85 (I, 170)
consecration of talisman, 417 (III, 218)
doors, 463 (IV, 22)
Enochian system, 625 (IV, 261)
letters, 627 (IV, 264)
tablets, 657-9 (IV, 307-9)

sigils (continued):
evocation, 380-4 *passim*, 402, 405-10 *passim* (III, 159-65 *passim*, 195, 200-6 *passim*, 208, 209)
geomantic figures, 493, 494 (IV, 74, 75)
doors, 493 (IV, 74)
magic squares, 496-502 (IV, 79-86)
Olympic planetary spirits, 497, 503 (IV, 80, 87)
skrying, 497 (IV, 80)
planetary spirits, 524, 525, 526, 539 (IV, 113, 114, 116, 136)
planets, 497, 498-502 (IV, 80, 81-6)
Rose-Cross lamen—*see* Rose-Cross, lamen, sigils
telesmatic images, 486 (IV, 62)
tracing, 283, 284, 318, 324 (III, 15, 16, 64, 71)
alchemical operation, 395 (III, 185)
consecration of talisman, 414, 415, 416 (III, 212, 214, 215, 218)
evocation, 404, 405, 406, 408, 410, 411 (III, 199, 200, 202, 206, 208, 210)
requiem ceremony, 447 (III, 266, 267)
spiritual development ritual, 436 (III, 250)
transformation ritual, 430, 431 (III, 241, 242)
Zodiac, 698
see also Zodiac, signs and symbols
Signet Star, 287, 293 (III, 20, 27)
Significator (Tarot divination), 567, 581-2 (IV, 179, 200)
divination examples, 568-71 *passim*, 573-80 *passim* (IV, 181-5 *passim*, 189-5 *passim*, 198, 199)
signs:
Adeptus Minor—*see* L.V.X., signs
benediction, 372 (III, 147)
grade:
consecration of Rose-Cross, 315 (III, 60)
elemental grade rituals, 137
illustrated, 133-4 (II, illus. following 33)
pentagram rituals, 283 (III, 15)
Portal ritual, 220 (II, 196-7)
Tattwa vision, 460, 461 (IV, 17, 18)
see also individual grades
L.V.X.—*see* keyword analysis; L.V.X., signs
Neophyte, 126, 144, 149, 168, 199, 201, 202, 208, 368 (II, 30, 49, 60, 96, 157, 160, 164, 174; III, 140)
astral projection, 473, 474 (IV, 39, 41-2)
consecration of Lotus Wand, 304 (III, 42)
consecration of Rose-Cross, 314 (III, 58)
Enterer, 117-8, 126, 136-7, 345-6, 347, 365, 371-2 (II, 12-14, 30; III, 106, 109, 135, 144-5, 146)
consecration of talismans, 386, 418 (III, 169, 170, 221)
signs (continued):
Neophyte (continued):
Enterer (continued):
evocation, 382, 383, 410 (III, 163, 209)
Forty-two Judges, 358, 367 (III, 123, 137)
invisibility ritual, 389 (III, 174)
requiem ceremony, 449 (III, 270)
spiritual development ritual, 392, 393 (III, 180, 181)
Tattwa vision, 459, 461, 475 (IV, 15, 20, 43)
Thoth, 330, 366 (III, 81, 136)
transformation ritual, 390 (III, 175, 177)
invisibility ritual, 389, 427 (III, 174, 237)
Silence, 126, 136-7, 346, 371, 372 (II, 30; III, 106, 108, 145-6)
consecration of talismans, 386, 418 (III, 169-70, 221)
evocation, 383, 410 (III, 163, 209)
invisibility ritual, 428 (III, 237)
Tattwa vision, 459, 460 (IV, 15, 20)
Thoth, 366 (III, 136)
transformation ritual, 433 (III, 246)
Osiris Risen, 270 (II, 288)
see also keyword analysis; signs, L.V.X.
Osiris Slain, 239 (II, 202)
see also keyword analysis; signs, L.V.X.
Outer Order, all used in Vault consecration ceremony, 260 (II, 268)
Philosophus—*see* Philosophus, sign
Portal—*see* Portal grade, signs
Practicus—*see* Practicus, sign
R.R. et A.C., 252 (II, 253)
Theoricus—*see* Theoricus, sign
Typhon, 357 (III, 121)
see also keyword analysis; L.V.X., signs
Zelator—*see* Zelator, sign
signs of the Zodiac—*see* Zodiac
silence, 93-4, 127, 129 (I, 187; II, 30, 36)
silver:
alchemy, 60 (I, 119, 120)
crescent and Moon, 83 (I, 165)
Image of the Vision of Nebuchadnezzar, 206 (II, 171)
skrying, 666 (IV, 320)
Simeon, 305 (III, 44)
Sioda, 669 (IV, 325)
Sirius, 188 (II, 135)
six days of Creation, 507 (IV, 91)
Sixes (Tarot), 552 (IV, 156)
Cups, 556 (IV, 163)
divination example, 568, 569, 577, 578, 586 (IV, 181, 182, 194, 195, 196, 207)
divinatory meaning, 582 (IV, 202)
Pentacles, 562 (IV, 172)
divination example, 586 (IV, 207)
Swords, 559 (IV, 168)

Sixes (Tarot) (continued):
  Swords (continued):
    divination example, 570, 571, 572, 585 (IV, 184-7 *passim*, 207)
    Enochian pyramids, 648 (IV, 294)
  Wands, 553 (IV, 158-9)
    divination example, 571, 572, 577, 579 (IV, 185, 187, 194, 197)
  see also Tarot, numbered cards
skeleton, 590 (IV, 213)
Skinner, B. F., xviii
skrying, 463, 467-70, 473-4 (IV, 22-3, 29-35, 39-41)
  Enochian (Dee and Kelly), 625, 629 (IV, 262, 268)
  geomantic sigils, 493 (IV, 74)
  sigils of Olympic planetary spirits, 497 (IV, 80)
  Tattwas, 514 (IV, 95)
    see also Tattwa vision
Skrying in the Spirit Vision, 9-11 *passim*, 107-9, 283, 463 (I, 218-21; III, 14; IV, 23)
  Enochian:
    chess, 684 (IV, 347)
    tablets, 624, 653 (IV, 260, 300)
      servient squares, 660-70 (IV, 312-27)
        testing, 662, 667 (IV, 318, 321)
  god-forms, 372 (III, 147)
  "Of Skrying and Traveling in the Spirit Vision," 467-74 (IV, 29-42)
Slavonic languages, 628 (IV, 267)
Slgaiol, 325 (III, 73)
Sloane manuscripts, 44, 625, 629 (I, 85; IV, 262, 268)
snake, 268 (II, 284)
  see also serpent
Sobha, 650 (IV, 297)
Socharis, 686 (IV, 350)
Societas Rosicruciana in Anglia, 17-8 (I, 19-21)
Society of the Inner Light, ix
Sol—*see* keyword analysis; Sun
Sol Philosophorum, 60 (I, 119)
Solar Fire, 70, 171, 346 (I, 137; II, 103; III, 107)
  Axieros, 169 (II, 99)
  Michael, 172 (II, 104)
solitary work, ix, xviii-xix, xxii-xxiv, 2, 3, 44, 45-6 (I, 87, 90)
Solomon, 177, 340 (II, 113; III, 97)
  pillars of—*see* Pillars
Solomon, The Greater Key of (trans. MacGregor Mathers), 8, 16, 493 (I, 18; IV, 76)
solve et coagula, 32, 666 (I, 56-7; IV, 320)
Son of God, 657 (IV, 307)
Son of Man, 413, 429, 445, 449 (III, 212, 239, 264, 270)
Son of the Morning—*see* Emperor, The
Soniznt, 325 (III, 73)
Sons of Light, 207n
Sorath, 65 (I, 127)
  Enochian:
    chess, 690 (IV, 357)
    letters, geomantic figures, Zodiac, 495 (IV, 77)
  geomancy, 524, 526 (IV, 113, 114)
  sigil, 499, 256 (IV, 83, 114)
Sorcerer and His Apprentice, The, (ed. R. A. Gilbert), 202n
Sorrow, Lord of—*see* Threes (Tarot), Swords
Sothis, 663 (IV, 315)
  illustration, 614 (IV, 316)
  Kerub of West, 663 (IV, 315)
Sothou, 443 (III, 261)
soul, 697
  guidance and purification of, 74-6 (I, 146-9)
  parts of, 67, 105-6 (I, 129, 213-4)
South, xxiii, 80 (I, 159)
  altar, olive side, 333 (III, 86)
  Bornless Ritual, 443 (III, 261)
  circulatory system, 360, 361 (III, 127-8)
  consecration of talismans, 385, 416, 421 (III, 167, 217, 225)
  Crown of, 354, 355 (III, 116, 119)
  evocation, 381, 402, 404, 408 (III, 161, 195, 198, 205)
  hexagram rituals, 294-5, 297 (III, 29, 33)
  invisibility ritual, 388, 427 (III, 173, 235)
  Kerub of Fire, 357 (III, 121)
  lamp, red, on altar (Fire), 334 (III, 87)
  pentagram rituals, 53, 285 (I, 106; III, 18)
  Phraestt, 353 (III, 115)
  South Pole of heavens, 596, 600, 602, 603, 655 (IV, 221-2, 227, 231, 304)
  spiritual development ritual, 392, 435, 438 (III, 179, 180, 248, 254)
  Toumathaph, 361 (III, 128)
  transformation ritual, 390, 432 (III, 176, 244)
  White Pillar, 81 (I, 161)
  see also cardinal points; Neophyte ritual, cardinal points and other directions
Southeast:
  consecration of talismans, 385 (III, 168)
  evocation, 406 (III, 201)
  Neophyte ritual, 131 (II, 40)
  spiritual development ritual, 391 (III, 178)
  transformation ritual, 390 (III, 176)
  see also Toumathph
Southwest:
  evocation, 381 (III, 161)
  see also Ahephi
Spain, 14, 231 (I, 13; II, 217)
Sphere of the Elements—*see* Malkuth
Sphere of Sensation, xix, xxiii, 36, 39, 40, 41, 46, 92, 100-11, 345, 378 (I, 66, 75, 76, 79, 90, 184, 200-26; III, 106, 155)
  astral/cosmic Neophyte temple, 451-4 (III, 271-6)

Sphere of Sensation (continued):
- consecration of talisman, 413, 422 (III, 212, 228)
- earth, vitalized by Tattwas, 457 (IV, 12)
- evocation, 405 (III, 200)
- invisibility ritual, 387 (III, 172)
- Neophyte, 363, 364, 367, 369 (III, 131, 134, 138, 141, 142)
- skrying, 467, 469 (IV, 29, 33)
- spiritual development ritual, 391 (III, 178)
- transformation ritual, 389-90 (III, 175)
- *see also* aura

Sphere of the Zodiac—*see* Mazloth; Zodiac

spheres, heavenly or planetary, 45, 63 (I, 89, 125)
- Seven-Branched Candlestick, 150 (II, 62)
- sigils, 483, 485 (IV, 58, 60)
- *see also* planets

sphinx (sphynx), 157, 590 (II, 75; IV, 213)
- Enochian pyramids, 659-62, 666 (IV, 311-4, 318, 319)
- forms, 660 (IV, 311)
- Kerubim, 659, 660, 661 (IV, 310, 311, 314)
- making figures, 661-2 (IV, 313-4)
- telesmatic images, 660, 661 (IV, 311-12, 313)

Spirit:
- of Air, 687 (IV, 352-3)
- Akasa, 457, 458 (IV, 12, 13, 14)
- alchemical operation, 398 (III, 190)
- Aroueris, 691 (IV, 360)
- blood, 101 (I, 205)
- Chief Adept in Portal ritual, 199n
- cross of four elements, center of, 214 (II, 186)
- cross into pentagram, 217 (II, 190)
  - Enochian tablets, 233 (II, 222)
- dekagram, 510 (IV, 93)
- Enochian:
  - chess, 684, 685, 686, 687, 690, 691, 692, 693 (IV, 348, 350, 351, 352, 359, 360, 361, 363)
  - tablets:
    - Elemental Kings, 659 (IV, 309)
    - pyramids, 646, 648 (IV, 291, 293-4)
    - Sephirotic Calvary crosses, 656 (IV, 305)
    - Tablet of Union, 635, 645 (IV, 275, 290)
      - pyramids, 649, 654 (IV, 296, 301, 302)
  - Hegemon, 375 (III, 151)
- Kether, 19, 21 (I, 25, 30)
- Lotus Wand, 300 (III, 37)
- Osiris, 372, 693 (III, 147; IV, 363)
- pentagram, 507, 635 (IV, 90, 91, 275)
  - ritual, 668 (IV, 323)
- pentagrams, 201, 216, 220, 281, 284 (II, 160, 189, 197; III, 11, 16)
  - active, 280-1, 284, 285 (III, 10, 11, 16, 17, 18)

Spirit (continued):
- pentagrams (continued):
  - active (continued):
    - Bornless Ritual, 443, 444 (III, 260, 261, 262)
    - skrying (Enochian), 669 (IV, 325)
  - closing, 281 (III, 11)
  - equilibrating, 281, 285, 315 (III, 11, 18, 59)
    - consecration of elemental weapons, 327 (III, 77)
    - consecration of talisman, 413, 420, 421, 422 (III, 212, 224-8 *passim*)
    - evocation, 403 (III, 197, 198)
    - invisibility ritual, 423, 425 (III, 229, 233)
    - Opening by Watchtower:
      - evocation, 403 (III, 197)
      - spiritual development ritual, 436 (III, 249)
      - Vault consecration, 259 (II, 267)
    - skrying (Enochian), 669 (IV, 325)
  - passive, 280-1, 284 (III, 10, 11, 16, 17)
    - Bornless Ritual, 443, 444 (III, 261, 262, 263)
  - point of pentagram, 220, 280, 281, 282 (II, 192; III, 9-13 *passim*)
  - transformation ritual, 429 (III, 239)
- Portal grade, 35 (I, 65)
- Rose-Cross lamen, 350 (III, 51)
- Ruach, 102 (I, 207)
  - Yetzirah of microcosm, 105 (I, 214)
- Shin—*see* Yeheshuah
- Supreme Invoking Ritual of the Pentagram, 436 (III, 250)
- symbol, 283 (III, 14)
- *see also* wheel
- Tarot:
  - Aces, 542 (IV, 142)
  - divination, 568 (IV, 180)
  - The Star, 591 (IV, 215)
- Tau, 209 (II, 176)
- thumb, 100 (I, 204)
- Vault symbolism, 246, 267, 268 (II, 240, 282, 284)
- white cross and circle, 233 (II, 222)
- Winged-Sphere Wand, 224, 262 (II, 203, 272)

spirit:
- consecration of talismans, 385, 386, 387 (III, 167, 169, 171)
- evocation, 380-4 (III, 159-66)

spirit and body, 616-7 (IV, 249-51)

Spirit Tablet—*see* Tablet of Union

Spirit of:
- Ether—*see* Fool, The
- the Ether, 489 (IV, 67)
- the Mighty Waters—*see* Hanged Man, The
- the Primal Fire—*see* Judgment

Spirit Vision—*see* Skrying in the Spirit Vision
spirits:
  evil, 280, 381, 613 (III, 9, 160; IV, 245)
  good, 613 (IV, 245)
  Olympic—*see* Olympic planetary spirits
  planetary, 65, 109 (I, 127, 223)
    Enochian:
      chess, 689 (IV, 355)
      letters, geomantic figures, Zodiac, 495 (IV, 77)
    geomancy, 524, 525, 526, 537, 689 (IV, 113, 114, 132, 355)
    sigils, 483, 485, 498-502, 526 (IV, 58, 60, 81-6, 114)
    talismans, 503 (IV, 87-8)
    telesmatic images, 490 (IV, 68)
    see also planets, spirits
  true order of the Rose Cross, 231 (II, 218)
Spirits and Apparations (John Dee), 630n
spiritual consciousness, 103-7 *passim*, 110, 111, 451 (I, 210-4 *passim*, 218, 219, 224, 225, 226; III, 272)
  see also Daath, in microcosm
spiritual development:
  Neophyte formula, 377, 391-3, 435-41 (III, 153, 178-81, 248-58)
  Shin of Yeheshuah, 376, 388, 391 (III, 152, 172, 178)
Splendour—*see* Hod
Sprengel, Anna, 17 (I, 19, 21)
  S.D.A. = Sapiens Dominabitur Astris, 17 (I, 19)
square, 70, 506 (I, 136; IV, 90)
  aspect, 538, 539 (IV, 133, 135)
    see also astrology, aspects
  Chesed, 505, 506 (IV, 89, 90)
  elements, 506 (IV, 90)
  lineal figures of Sephiroth, 493 (IV, 72)
  Prithivi, 457-61 *passim*, 469, 489 (IV, 12-6 *passim*, 18, 19, 33, 67)
  Temperance, 218 (II, 192-3)
squares, magic—*see* magic squares
S'Rhiogail Ma Dhream (MacGregor Mathers), 16, 565 (I, 17, 18; IV, 176)
-*st* suffix (Coptic), 337, 663 (III, 92; IV, 315)
staff:
  Hermes, 476-7, 478 (IV, 47, 49)
  see also Wand
stag, 549, 551 (IV, 152, 155)
Stanzas of Dzyan, 272 (II, 192)
Star, The, 186, 188, 591 (II, 131, 134-6; IV, 214-5)
  divination:
    example, 577, 579, 580, 581 (IV, 194, 197, 199)
    meaning, 585 (IV, 205)
  Isis, 188 (II, 135)
  see also Tarot, trumps
star maps, 43, 595 (I, 84, 219, 220)
Star of Great Light, 280 (III, 9)
Star Ruby ritual, 698
Star Wave (Fred Alan Wolf), xviii
"Stations of the Officers, The," 334-44 (III, 88-104)
Stella Matutina, ix, 18, 116, 118, 131, 142, 155, 167, 226, 248, 252, 254, 255, 272, 414-5, 466, 624n, 683n (I, 21; II, 11, 13, 39, 45, 70, 93, 206, 245, 253, 256, 258, 259, 290; III, 215; IV, 27)
  rituals, 113-96 (II, 11-152)
step:
  Neophyte, 126, 370-1 (II, 30; III, 144)
    invisibility ritual, 389 (III, 174)
  Zelator, 147, 156 (II, 45, 73)
stigmata, 236 (II, 226)
Stimcul, 207n
Stolistes, 81, 340, 341, 342 (I, 161; III, 97-8, 99, 100)
  astral/cosmic Neophyte temple in Sphere of Sensation, 453 (III, 274)
  Aura-Mo-Ooth, 341, 352, 355 (III, 99, 114, 118)
  Cup—*see* Cup of Stolistes
  elemental grade rituals, 137
  Equinox ceremony, 248, 249, 250, 256, 374 (II, 246, 247, 249, 250, 262; III, 149)
  lamen—*see* Cup of Stolistes
  Neophyte ritual, 116, 117, 119-22 passim, 124, 125, 127, 131, 132, 364, 367, 369 (II, 11, 12, 15, 17, 20, 22, 25, 26, 27, 31, 32, 39, 40, 42; III, 133, 137, 139, 140-1)
    explains station and duties, 119 (II, 15)
    station explained by Hierophant, 129 (II, 35)
  station:
    circumambulation begins at, 346 (III, 107)
    and duties, 119, 341 (II, 15; III, 99)
    Kerub of Earth behind, 343, 357 (III, 101, 102, 122)
  woman, office more natural for, 342 (III, 100)
  Zelator grade required for, 137, 342 (III, 100)
  Zelator ritual, 141, 142, 143, 145, 148, 149, 151, 152 (II, 44-48 *passim*, 51, 58, 59, 67)
stomach, 360, 361 (III, 127, 128)
Stone of the Wise, xxii, xxv, 236, 448 (II, 227; III, 268)
  see also Philosopher's Stone
stones, 670 (IV, 326)
Stooping Dragon, 330, 344, 353 (III, 81, 103, 115)
Strength (Fortitude), 590 (IV, 212)
  divination:
    example, 577, 578, 579 (IV, 194, 195, 197)

Strength (Fortitude) (continued):
divination (continued):
meaning, 584-5 (IV, 205)
see also Tarot, trumps
Strength, The Lord of Established—*see* Threes (Tarot), Wands
Strength, The Lord of Great—*see* Nines (Tarot), Wands
Strife, The Lord of—*see* Fives (Tarot), Wands
Strophalos, 171 (II, 102)
Studio City, California, xx
Sub Spe—*see* Brodie-Innes, J. W.
Subtilis Aqua Lux Terra, 206 (II, 172)
Success, Lord of:
Abandoned—*see* Eights (Tarot), Cups
Earned—*see* Sixes (Tarot), Swords
Illusionary—*see* Sevens (Tarot), Cups
Material—*see* Sixes (Tarot), Pentacles
Perfected—*see* Tens (Tarot), Cups
Perpetual—*see* Tens (Tarot), Cups
Unfulfilled—*see* Sevens (Tarot), Pentacles
Sukshma Sharira, 515 (IV, 96)
Sulphur (alchemical principle), 206 (II, 172)
elements, 310-11 (III, 51-3)
Philosophus ritual, 192, 194 (II, 144, 148)
Rose-Cross lamen, 310-11 (III, 51-3)
Tree of Life, 84 (I, 167-8)
Zata, Elman, 275 (II, 296)
see also alchemy, principles
Sun, 12, 63 (I, 125)
Air, 215 (II, 187)
alchemical operation, 396-9 passim (II, 187, 188, 189, 191)
angel, intelligence, and spirit, 65 (I, 127)
Aries (exaltation), 589 (IV, 211)
circle and gold, 83 (I, 165)
Enochian:
kings, 637 (IV, 278)
letters, 495 (IV, 77)
Linea Spiritus Sancti, 655 (IV, 304)
Equinox ritual, 373-4 (III, 148-50)
eye, right, 103 (I, 210)
Fire, 175, 648 (II, 109; IV, 294)
Fylfot cross, 68, 148, 340 (I, 131; II, 57; III, 98)
Garden of Eden diagram, 73 (I, 144)
geomantic figures, 495 (IV, 77)
Greek cross, 70 (I, 137)
Hathor, Sun Disc on headpiece, 356 (III, 120)
hexagram, 70, 218, 508 (I, 136; II, 195; IV, 91)
hexagrams, 288 (III, 21] 26)
banishing, 292 (III, 25)
invoking, 291 (III, 24)
Hierophant's lamen, 336 (III, 90)
Kabiri, 174-5 (II, 107-9)
lineal figures, 493 (IV, 72)
magic square, 499 (IV, 83)
Sun (continued):
Moon, full, reflected by, 68, 217 (I, 133; II, 191)
Resh, 215 (II, 187)
seal, 499 (IV, 83)
Tarot:
Aces, 609 (IV, 241)
The Devil, 212 (II, 182)
Pentacles:
Eight, 541, 553, 554 (IV, 139, 159)
Four, 541, 558 (IV, 140, 167)
Six of Cups, 541, 556 (IV, 140, 163)
The Sun, 71, 73, 542, 592, 644 (I, 139, 143; IV, 141, 215, 288)
Temperance, 217 (II, 192)
Ten of Swords, 541, 563 (IV, 140, 174)
Three of Wands, 541, 561 (IV, 140, 171)
see also Sun, The (Tarot)
Tattwas, 457 (IV, 12)
30th Path, 167, 215 (II, 93-4, 187)
Tiphareth, 20, 60, 97, 215, 218, 603, 644 (I, 26, 120, 195; II, 187, 195; IV, 232, 288)
vanity, 474 (IV, 41)
see also planets
Sun, The (Tarot), 173, 175-6, 592, 644 (II, 106, 110-11; IV, 215, 288)
divination:
example, 574, 575 (IV, 190, 191)
meaning, 585 (IV, 206)
see also Tarot, trumps
Sun breath, 516, 522 (IV, 98, 99, 108-9)
Sun nerve, 516 (IV, 98)
see also Pingala; Surya Nadi
Sundt, Hal, x, xxv
footnotes, 198, 199, 201, 202, 205, 207, 210, 216, 221, 223, 224, 330, 331, 338, 375, 376, 624, 625, 630, 683
Sunyata, 21 (I, 29)
superconscious, 20 (I, 26)
Supernal Eden, 188, 194 (II, 135, 146)
Supernal Father, 77 (I, 153)
see also Abba; Chokmah
Supernal Mother, 72, 77 (I, 141, 153)
Tarot:
Ace of Cups, 543 (IV, 143)
The Star, 188 (II, 135)
see also Aima; Binah
Supernal Sephiroth, 19, 26, 28, 31, 33, 38, 96, 187, 251, 276, 345 (I, 24-5, 42, 46, 55, 59, 71, 194; II, 133, 252, 298, 299; III, 105)
altar diagrams:
The Flaming Sword of the Kerubim, 145 (II, 52)
The Garden of Eden, 177 (II, 113-4)
Banner of the West, 338 (III, 94)
caduceus, 68, 162, 340 (I, 131; II, 84; III, 97)
cord, 363 (III, 132)
Enochian tablets, 643 (IV, 288)

Supernal Sephiroth (continued):
Enochian tablets (continued):
Linea Spiritus Sancti, 653 (IV, 300)
geomantic figures, 526 (IV, 114)
hexagrams, 293, 413 (III, 27, 212)
Hiereus's lamen, 213 (II, 184)
Judgment, 592 (IV, 216)
Kerux's wand, 344-5 (III, 105)
Lesser Invoking Ritual of the Hexagram, 413, 447 (III, 212, 266)
microcosm, 100 (I, 203)
Neophyte ritual, 367-70 *passim* (III, 137-41 *passim*, 143)
Nephesch, 103 (I, 209)
Neschamah, 67 (I, 129)
Oracles of Zoroaster, 169 (II, 98)
requiem ceremony, 447 (III, 266)
Rose-Cross lamen, 311 (III, 53-4)
Supreme Invoking Ritual of the Hexagram, 436 (III, 250)
Three Chiefs, 274, 275 (II, 295, 296)
transformation ritual, 430, 431, 432 (III, 241, 243, 247)
triangle, 439, 465, 506 (III, 254; IV, 27, 89)
altar, 333, 335, 347, 366, 370 (III, 86, 88, 109, 136, 143)
Vault symbolism, 242 (II, 238)
Supreme Banishing Ritual of the Pentagram:
consecration of elemental weapons, 328 (III, 78)
Supreme Invoking Ritual of the Pentagram, 43, 48, 138, 284, 285-6 (I, 84, 95; III, 16-17, 18-19)
Adeptus Minor Obligation, 230 (II, 214)
alchemical operation, 398 (III, 189)
astral projection, 473 (IV, 39)
consecrations:
elemental weapons, 323, 437 (III, 71, 77)
Lotus Wand, 304 (III, 42)
Rose-Cross, 314 (III, 58)
talismans, 482 (IV, 56)
evocation, 404 (III, 198)
invisibility ritual, 423 (III, 229)
skrying, 469 (IV, 33)
spiritual development ritual, 436 (III, 250)
Supreme Ritual of the Pentagram, 280, 293, 310, 698-9 (III, 10, 27, 51)
consecration of elemental weapons, 323, 327 (III, 71, 77)
Supreme Ritual of the Hexagram, 287, 293, 299, 310 (III, 21, 27, 35, 51)
Surya, 522 (IV, 108)
Surya Nadi, 516 (IV, 98)
see also Pingala; Sun nerve
Surya Swara, 516, 517 (IV, 98, 100, 101)
Sushumna, 276, 515, 516, 517 (II, 299; IV, 97-100 *passim*)
swan, 33 (I, 60)
Knave (Princess) of Cups, 547, 551 (IV, 150, 155)
Swara, 515, 516, 517, 521, 522 (IV, 96-7, 98, 100, 106, 108)
swastika, 39, 489 (I, 74; IV, 67)
see also Fylfot cross
Sword, 43, 47, 317-9, 321, 322 (I, 84, 94; III, 62-5, 67, 69)
consecration, 317-9 (III, 63-5)
astrological chart for time of working, 317 (III, 63)
consecration of elemental weapons, 323, 325-8 *passim* (III, 70, 73-8 *passim*)
consecration of talismans, 385, 386, 387, 414-8 *passim* (III, 167-70 *passim*, 214-9 *passim*, 221)
evocation, 381, 382, 383, 402, 405-8 *passim*, 410, 411 (III, 160-4 *passim*, 195, 201-6 *passim*, 208, 209, 210)
Geburah, 470 (IV, 40)
see also Geburah, Sword
hexagram rituals, 296, 669 (III, 32; IV, 325)
Hiereus, 119, 249, 337, 368, 379 (II, 16, 247; III, 92, 93, 139, 158)
illustration, 349 (III, 111)
Imperator, similar one used by, 331 (III, 83)
Neophyte ritual, 118, 120, 123, 124, 125, 126 (II, 13, 17, 24, 26, 28, 29)
illustration, 321 (III, 67)
Imperator, 331, 332 (III, 83, 84)
illustration, 348 (III, 110)
Justice, 590 (IV, 213)
pentagram rituals, 280, 669 (III, 9; IV, 325)
skrying, 468 (IV, 31)
spiritual development ritual, 392, 438 (III, 179, 253)
see also Flaming Sword
Sword and Serpent, in Adeptus Minor ritual, 221, 226, 242 (II, 198, 207-8, 237)
see also Pastos, lid of
Sword of Strength and Severity—*see* Sword, Hiereus
Sword of Vengeance—*see* Sword, Hiereus
Swords (Tarot), 555, 559-60, 563 (IV, 161-2, 167-9, 173-4)
court cards, 548-9 (IV, 150-2)
Dagger, 322 (III, 68)
divinatory meaning, 582, 583-4 (IV, 201, 203)
Enochian chess, 685 (IV, 349)
see also individual cards [e.g., Nines (Tarot), Swords]
see also Tarot
sylphs, 30, 80, 160 (I, 52, 158; II, 80)
prayer, 164-5 (II, 89-90)
see also elementals

Sylphs and Sylphides:
  King of—*see* Knights (Kings), Swords
  Prince and Emperor of—*see* Kings (Princes), Swords
  Princess and Empress of the—*see* Knaves (Princesses), Swords
  Queen of the—*see* Queens, Swords
"Symbolism of the Admission of the Candidate, The," (Document Z.3), 363-75 (III, 131-51)
"Symbolism of the Four Genii of the Hall of the Neophytes, The," 358-62 (III, 124-30)
"Symbolism of the Opening of the 0=0 Grade of Neophyte, The," 344-7 (III, 105-10)
"Symbolism of the Seven Sides, The," 266-9 (II, 280-6)
"Symbolism of the Temple, The," 333-4 (III, 85-8)
symbols, 479 (IV, 51)
Synergetic Geometries, 700
Synesius, 28 (I, 47)
Synoches, 169 (II, 98)
Szathan Toophon, 344, 353 (III, 103, 115)
Szlae-Ee (Scorpio), 343, 353 (III, 102, 115)

- T -

T, Book—*see* Book T
T Document, 43 (I, 84)
  see "The Concourse of Forces: The Forty-Eight Angelical Keys or Calls," 671-82 (IV, 328-45)
Taad, 638 (IV, 279)
Taasd, 650 (IV, 297)
Ta-Aur (Taurus), 343, 353 (III, 102, 115)
Tabitom—*see* Elexarpeh, Comananu, Tabitom
Table of Shew Bread—*see* Shew Bread, Table of
Tablet of Union, 624n, 627, 628, 630, 638 (IV, 265, 267, 274, 279-81)
  Bornless Ritual, 442 (III, 259)
  celestial sphere, 655, 669 (IV, 306, 324)
  colors, 635 (IV, 275)
  consecration of talisman, 422 (III, 228)
  elements, 645 (IV, 290)
  Enochian:
    calls, 671-4 *passim* (IV, 318-31 *passim*, 333, 334)
    chess, 684 (IV, 347)
  illustration, 674 (IV, 333)
  invisibility ritual, 423, 425, 426 (III, 229, 233, 234)
  names, first letter, 660, 661 (IV, 311, 312)
  Opening by Watchtower:
    evocation, 403 (III, 197)
    spiritual development ritual, 436 (III, 249)
    Vault consecration, 259 (II, 267)
  pentagram rituals, 281 (III, 19)
  Portal ritual, 217, 218, 220 (II, 190, 194, 197)
Tablet of Union (continued):
  pyramids, 649, 654 (IV, 296, 301-2)
  skrying, 668, 669 (IV, 323, 324)
  Spirit, 635, 645 (IV, 275, 290)
  Tarot, 645 (IV, 290)
  Tattwa vision, 463 (IV, 22)
  transformation ritual, 430 (III, 240)
Tablets, Enochian—*see* Enochian, tablets
Tablets, Flashing—*see* Flashing Tablets
Tahaoelog, 658 (IV, 308)
Tahuti—*see* Thoth
Tai Chi, 699
Tal, 495 (IV, 77)
  see also Enochian, letters
Taliahad, 80, 324 (I, 159; III, 72)
talismanic emblems (from geomantic figures), 493, 494, 495 (IV, 74, 75, 77, 78)
talismans, 3, 9, 43, 44, 282, 479-81, 493-503 (I, 83, 87; III, 12; IV, 51-4, 74-88)
  Adeptus Minor Obligation, 229, 230 (II, 213, 214)
  consecration, 43, 465, 480, 481-2 (I, 83; IV, 27, 53, 55-6)
    Heh of Yeheshuah, 376, 384 (III, 152, 166)
    Neophyte formula, 378, 384-7 (III, 156, 166-71)
      Jupiter, 413-22 (III, 212-28)
  designing, 503 (IV, 88)
  discharging, 481, 482 (IV, 54, 56)
  elementals, 481 (IV, 54)
  Enochian system, 624, 627 (IV, 260, 264)
    chess boards, 687 (IV, 348)
  lineal figures of Sephiroth, 503, 505, 506 (IV, 88, 89)
  love, 480 (IV, 53)
  planetary intelligences and spirits, 503 (IV, 87-8)
  Sign of the Enterer, 371 (III, 145)
Taphthartharath, 65 (I, 127)
  Enochian:
    chess, 690 (IV, 357)
    letters, geomantic figures, Zodiac, 495 (IV, 77)
  geomancy, 524, 526 (IV, 113, 114)
  sigil, 497, 501, 526 (IV, 80, 85, 114)
Taro, 592 (IV, 216)
Tarot, xix, xx, 6, 9, 10, 12, 30, 43, 66, 540-93, 697 (I, 52-3, 84, 127-8; IV, 137-217)
  Aces—*see* Aces (Tarot)
  Adeptus Minor Obligation, 229 (II, 214)
  angels of numbered cards, 85, 553-64 *passim* (I, 170: IV, 158-76 *passim*)
  celestial sphere, 92, 100, 364, 594-611, 655 (I, 184-5, 203; III, 134; IV, 218-42, 304)
  color scales, 95, 99 (I, 192, 199-202)

Tarot (continued):
court cards (honours), 66, 68, 72, 79, 540, 544-50, 588 (I, 128, 130, 141, 156; IV, 138-9, 144-54, 209)
celestial sphere, 596, 597-9, 601, 602 (IV, 221, 222-5, 229, 230)
divination, 567, 573 (IV, 178, 188-9)
divinatory meaning, 567, 582 (IV, 179, 200-1)
Enochian:
chess, 685, 690 (IV, 350, 357)
Tablet of Union, 645 (IV, 290)
titles, 540 (IV, 138-9)
see also individual cards
divination, 39, 40, 42, 91, 566-87 (I, 75, 76-7, 82-3, 183; IV, 177-208)
"The Opening of the Key," 567-81 (IV, 178-99)
counting, 568, 571, 574, 575-6, 578, 579, 581, 587 (IV, 180-1, 185-6, 190, 192, 193, 195, 197-8, 199, 208)
Operations:
First, 569-73 (IV, 182-8)
Second, 573-5 (IV, 188-91)
Third, 575-6 (IV, 191-2)
Fourth, 576-9 (IV, 193-7)
Fifth, 579-81 (IV, 197-9)
pairing, 572, 575, 576, 578-9, 581, 586 (IV, 186-7, 191, 192, 193, 196-7, 198, 199, 207-8)
doors, 463 (IV, 22)
elemental grade rituals, 139
Enochian, 624 (IV, 260)
chess, 685, 686, 687, 689, 690, 692 (IV, 349-53 *passim*, 355, 356, 357, 362)
pyramids, 648, 649, 651 (IV, 295, 296, 298)
tablets, 642-5 *passim* (IV, 285-8 *passim*, 290)
Lesser Arcana, colors, 588 (IV, 209)
numbered cards, 78-9, 541, 550-65 (I, 156; IV, 139-40, 156-76)
celestial sphere, 596, 600-1 (IV, 221, 227-9)
divination, 567, 576 (IV, 178, 193)
divinatory meanings, 553-64 *passim*, 583-4 (IV, 158-76 *passim*, 202-4)
Enochian tablets, 642 (IV, 285, 286)
Great Cross, 642, 648 (IV, 286, 293-4)
Sephirothic Calvary Crosses, 644 (IV, 288)
titles, 541 (IV, 139-40)
Zodiac, decanates, 541, 642 (IV, 139-40, 285, 286)
Enochian chess pieces, 685 (IV, 350)
see also individual cards
Paths, 72-3, 78-9 (I, 141-3, 156)

Tarot (continued):
A Pictorial Key to the Tarot (A. E. Waite), 6, 39, 91 (I, 75, 183)
Sephiroth and/or Tree of Life, 67, 72-3 (I, 130, 141-3)
suits:
divinatory meaning, 570 (IV, 183)
elemental weapons, 320, 322 (III, 66, 68, 69)
elements, 607, 639 (IV, 237, 281)
Enochian tablets:
Kerubic squares, 644 (IV, 288-9)
Lesser Angles, 644 (IV, 288)
Four Worlds, 77 (I, 155)
Tetragrammaton, 67, 77, 639 (I, 130, 155; IV, 281)
see also Cups; Pentacles; Swords; Wands
telesmatic images, 486 (IV, 61)
trumps:
attribution of Hebrew letters and Zodiac, 71, 542 (I, 139; IV, 140-1)
celestial sphere, 596, 599-600, 601, 602, 689 (IV, 221, 225-7, 229, 230, 356)
colors, 588-93 (IV, 210-7)
divination, 567,573, 575 (IV, 178, 188, 191)
divinatory meanings, 582, 584 (IV, 201, 204-6)
Enochian chess, 689, 690 (IV, 355, 356, 357)
Hebrew mother letters, 568 (IV, 180)
"The Tarot Trumps" (Harriet Miller Davidson), 588-93 (IV, 209-17)
titles, 542 (IV, 140-1)
see also individual cards
Worlds, Four, 31 (I, 130)
see also Book T
"Task Undertaken by the Adeptus Minor," 106-8 (I, 217-20)
Tattwa vision, 39, 41, 91, 458-63, 467-78, 662 (I, 75, 78-9, 182; IV, 14-22, 29-50, 314)
delusion, 462 (IV, 20)
return, 461 (IV, 19-20)
testing, 460, 461, 462 (IV, 17-20 *passim*)
Tattwas, 42, 87, 456-8, 603 (I, 82, 175; IV, 12-15, 236)
colors, 517, 518-9 (IV, 101, 102-3, 104)
consecration of elemental weapons, 323 (III, 70, 71)
"The Grade of Philosophus: Additional Lecture on the Tattwas of the Eastern School," 514-22 (IV, 95-109)
symbols, 457 (IV, 12, 13)
cards:
ESP cards, 468 (IV, 30-31)
making, 458 (IV, 14)
telesmatic images, 489 (IV, 66-7)

Tattwas (continued):
  tests, 519 (IV, 102)
  time of day, 473 (IV, 40)
  see also Akasa; Apas; Prithivi; Tejas; Vayu
Tau (Hebrew letter), xxi, 77, 147 (I, 155; II, 55)
  astral projection, 471 (IV, 36)
  with hexagram of Mercury, as a letter of the name Ararita, 289 (III, 22)
  lineal figures, 493 (IV, 72)
  memory, 470, 471, 474 (IV, 34, 36, 41)
  Saturn, 215 (II, 187)
  skrying, 470 (IV, 34)
  32nd Path (Saturn, The Universe), xxi
    admission badge, 70 (I, 136-7)
    Hierophant's sceptre, 335 (III, 90)
    Philosophus ritual, 184 (II, 126)
      temple arrangement, 181 (II, 121)
    Portal ritual, 205-9, 215 (II, 169-77, 187)
    Practicus ritual, 169 (II, 97)
    Saturn, 213 (II, 184)
    skrying, 464, 667 (IV, 23, 24, 321)
    Theoricus ritual, 154, 155, 156-62 (II, 69, 71-81, 83)
      "Ceremony of Advancement in the Path of TAU," 156-160 (II, 72-81)
    Thoth, 330n
    transformation ritual, 431 (III, 243)
    Zelator ritual, 141, 147, 148 (II, 44, 55, 58)
  see also Hebrew alphabet; Paths; Saturn; Universe
Tau cross, 209, 215, 218 (II, 176, 188, 193)
  ankh, 224, 262 (II, 202, 272)
  Banner of the East, 218, 336 (II, 195; III, 91)
  Death (Tarot), 211 (II, 179)
  Enochian sigils, 658 (IV, 308)
  Phoenix Wand, 224, 262 (II, 203, 272)
Tau Portal, 209 (II, 176-7)
Taurus, 63 (I, 124)
  Amissio, 650 (IV, 300)
  Circular Altar, 259 (II, 266)
    see also altar, Circular Altar; ox, kerub
  crook, 242 (II, 237)
  divine and angelic names, 86 (I, 171)
  divine name, Hebrew letter, Tribe of Israel, angel, and color, 305 (III, 44)
  Enochian:
    chess, 694 (IV, 365)
    letter and geomantic figure, 495 (IV, 77)
  Kerub of Earth, 343 (III, 102)
    see also bull; Kerubim; ox
  Lotus Wand, 302, 305, 315 (III, 40, 44, 60)
  star map, 595 (IV, 220)
  symbol, 50, 61, 159, 283, 286 (I, 99, 120; II, 77; III, 14, 19)
    consecration of Pentacle, 327 (III, 77)
    consecration of talisman, 422 (III, 227)
Taurus (continued):
  symbol (continued):
    evocation, 403, 404, 405, 407 (III, 196, 198, 199, 203)
    hexagram rituals, 296 (III, 31)
    see also ox
  symbol used in spelling divine names, 83 (I, 166)
  Ta-Aur, 343, 353 (III, 102, 115)
  Tarot:
    The Emperor, 599 (IV, 226)
    The Hierophant, 71, 72, 542, 575, 589, 599 (I, 139, 142; IV, 140, 191, 211, 226-7)
    Knight (King) of Swords, 548, 598 (IV, 150, 225)
    Pentacles:
      Ace, 607, 610 (IV, 237, 240)
      Five, Six, and Seven, 541, 562 (IV, 140, 172-3)
      King (Prince), 550, 598 (IV, 153, 225)
    The Sun, 175 (II, 110)
  Venus, 495 (IV, 77)
  see also Zodiac
Taxir, 407, 410 (III, 204, 208, 209)
Teaa, 669 (IV, 325)
  see also Oip Teaa Pedoce
teacher, xxiv, 1
Tebunah, 188 (II, 135)
Tehuti—*see* Thoth
Tejas, 317, 457, 514, 516-22 *passim* (III, 62; IV, 12, 13, 96, 99, 100, 101, 103, 105, 106, 108)
  of Akasa, 458, 516 (IV, 14, 99)
  of Prithivi, 458, 475-6 (IV, 14, 43-5)
  Ram, 520 (IV, 105)
Telescopium (Telescope), 599 (IV, 226)
telesma, telesmata, 384, 385, 386, 388 (III, 166, 167, 168, 169, 172)
telesmatic images, 3, 11, 44, 378, 486, 487-93 (I, 85; III, 156; IV, 61-2, 64-73)
  angels of Tarot and Zodiac, 85 (I, 170)
  Enochian system, 624 (IV, 260)
    angels, 660 (IV, 311)
    skrying, 661 (IV, 313)
    sphinxes, 660, 661 (IV, 311-2, 313)
  gender, 488, 489, 490, 660 (IV, 65, 67, 68-9, 312)
Tem, 343 (III, 102)
  see also Thoomoo; Tmu; Toum; Tum
Teman, 191 (II, 140)
temenos, xxv
Temperance, 217-8, 591 (II, 191-193; IV, 214)
  divination:
    example, 574, 575, 577, 578 (IV, 190, 191, 194, 196)
    meaning, 585 (IV, 205)
  25th Path, 464 (IV, 24)
  see also Tarot, trumps

temple, 11, 23, 27, 28, 45, 45-6 (I, 34, 45, 46, 88, 90)
  Adeptus Minor ritual, 37 (I, 69)
  arrangement:
    Neophyte ritual, 116-7 (II, 11-2)
    Philosophus ritual:
      Entry into Netzach, 192 (II, 144)
      The Path of Peh, 189 (II, 137)
      The Path of Qoph, 181 (II, 121-2)
      The Path of Tzaddi, 186 (II, 131)
    Practicus ritual:
      The Path of Resh, 172 (II, 106)
      The Path of Shin, 166-7 (II, 92-3)
      Temple in Hod, 176 (II, 112)
    Theoricus ritual, 154-5, 161 (II, 69-70, 82)
    Zelator ritual, 141-2, 148 (II, 44-5, 58)
  door, 334 (III, 87-8)
  Neophyte—*see* Neophyte, temple
  "Symbolism of the Temple, The," 333-4 (III, 85-8)
  Tree of Life, 115, 331 (III, 82)
Tens (Tarot), 552 (IV, 157-8)
  Cups, 560-1 (IV, 170)
    divination example, 571, 572, 586 (IV, 185, 186, 187, 207)
  divinatory meaning, 582 (IV, 201-2)
  Pentacles, 554, 588 (IV, 160-1, 209)
    divination example, 571, 572 (IV, 185, 186, 187)
  Swords, 563 (IV 174)
    divination example, 577, 579, 585, 586 (IV, 194, 197, 207)
  Wands, 557-8, 588 (IV, 165, 209)
    divination example, 570, 571, 577, 579, 585, 586 (IV, 184, 185, 194, 196, 207)
  see also Tarot, numbered cards
testing, 474 (IV, 41)
  astral projection, 465, 470, 471 (IV, 26, 35, 36, 37)
  skrying, 460-3 *passim*, 469, 470 (IV, 17-20 *passim*, 23, 33, 34)
    Enochian tablets, 662, 667 (IV, 318, 321)
Teth:
  Great Hermetic Arcanum, 206 (II, 170)
  Leo, 305 (III, 44)
  19th Path (Leo, Strength), 214 (II, 188)
  see also Hebrew alphabet; Leo; Strength
Tetrad, 224, 262, 506 (II, 202, 272; IV, 90)
  Enochian tablets, 653 (IV, 300)
Tetragrammaton, 8, 29, 30, 47, 61, 147 (I, 51, 52, 94, 120-1; II, 54)
  color scales, 95 (I, 192)
  elements—*see* YHVH, elements
  Four Worlds, 77, 641 (I, 155; IV, 283)
  human, 103 (I, 210)
  Tarot, 67, 77 (I, 130, 155)
    Aces, 607 (IV, 237)
Tetragrammaton (continued):
  Tarot (continued):
    divination, 568 (IV, 180)
    suits, 67, 77 (I, 130, 155)
  see also Yeheshuah; YHVH
Tetragrammaton Elohim, 145, 177 (II, 52, 114)
  see also YHVH Elohim
tetrahedron, 70 (I, 137)
  bases of Pillars, 333 (III, 86)
  see also pyramid; triangle
Thahaaothe, 409, 410, 658 (III, 206, 208; IV, 308)
Thahebyobeaatanun, 658 (IV, 308)
Tharpesh (Tharpeshest), 343, 353, 357 (III, 102, 115, 121)
  Enochian chess Air castle, 686 (IV, 350)
Tharpheshest, 343 (III, 102)
Tharsis, 80, 324, 471 (I, 159; III, 72; IV, 36)
Thaum-Aesch-Nia-eth (Thaum-aesch-niaeth, Thaum-aesh-Neith), 341, 352, 424, 425 (III, 99, 114, 230, 233)
  description, 355 (III, 119)
Thaumiel, 82, 359 (I, 163; III, 125)
  Kether of Qlippoth, 614 (IV, 247)
Theban alphabet, 652, 660 (IV, 299, 311)
Thebes, Egypt, 55-6 (I, 111)
Thelema, 698, 699
Theoricus, 21, 30 (I, 30, 52-3)
  admission badge, 161 (II, 82-3)
  Kerux, grade required for, 137, 342 (III, 100)
  knowledge lecture, 67-8 (I, 129-33)
  meditation, 68 (I, 133)
  Paths from, 161, 163, 173, 174 (II, 82, 87, 106, 107)
  Path to, from Zelator (32nd), 141, 147, 148, 154, 157, 169 (II, 44, 55, 58, 69, 74, 97)
  ritual, 30, 154-65, 420, 464 (I, 52-3; II, 69-91; III, 224; IV, 24)
    adoration, 155-6 (II, 71-2)
    caduceus explained, 162, 340 (II, 83-4; III, 97)
    closing, 164-5 (II, 87-91)
    "Ceremony of Advancement in the Path of TAU" (Rite of the Kerubic Stations), 156-60, 659 (II, 72-81; IV, 310)
      skrying, 464 (IV, 24)
    opening, 155-6 (II, 70-72)
    temple arrangement, 154-5, 161 (II, 69-70, 82)
  Practicus ritual, 166-79 *passim* (II, 92-118 *passim*)
  sign, 163, 168, 199, 200, 205, 208, 215 (II, 86, 96, 158, 159, 169, 174, 188)
    consecration of Rose-Cross, 315 (III, 60)
    pentagram rituals, 285 (III, 18)
    skrying, 666 (IV, 320)
    transformation ritual, 429 (III, 239)

Theoricus (continued):
sign, grip, token, word, mystic number, password, 163, 168 (II, 86, 96)
Yesod, 163, 331 (II, 85, 86; III, 83)
Theoricus Adeptus Minor, 44, 603 (I, 87; IV, 236)
Theosophical Reduction, 275, 276 (II, 296, 297, 299)
Theosophy, 514 (IV 95)
see also Blavatsky, H. P.
Theta (Coptic letter), 345 (III, 105)
Thiao, 443 (III, 260)
Thirty-Two Paths of Wisdom, 162 (II, 84)
The Moon, 185 (II, 130)
see also Tree of Life
Thitasoe, 443 (III, 260)
Thmaah (Thmaest, Thma-Est, Thmaa-est, Thma-Ae-St), 331, 339, 346, 347, 352, 366, 453 (III, 82, 96, 108, 109, 114, 136, 275)
description, 355 (III, 118)
forms of:
Thma-Ae-St, Thma-Aesh, and Thmaa-ett, 339 (III, 96)
Thmae-st, Thmae-sh, and Thmaae-tt, 352 (III, 115)
Thma-oe-Sh, Thma-oe-Tt, Thma-a-oe-St, and Thm-a-Oe, 375 (III, 151)
invisibility ritual, 424 (III, 230)
Theta (Coptic letter), 345 (III, 105)
see also Maat
Thoomoo (Tho-oom Moo-oo), 343, 353 (III, 102, 115)
see also Tem; Tmu; Toum; Tum
Tho-oth (Tho-ooth), 202, 300, 342, 352, 356, 366 (II, 164; III, 81, 101, 114, 120, 136)
Metatron, 365, 374 (III, 135, 150)
see also Thoth
Thor, 148, 340 (II, 57; III, 98)
Thoteth, 443 (III, 261)
Thoth, 59, 330 (I, 116-7; III, 81)
Bornless Ritual, 444 (III, 262)
Cancellarius, 342, 352, 354, 356 (III, 101, 114, 116, 120)
description, 356 (III, 120)
evocation, 410 (III, 209)
invisibility ritual, 423 (III, 229)
The Magician, 588 (IV, 210)
Thouerist, 686 (IV, 350)
Thraa, 152 (II, 65)
Three Chiefs:
Adeptus Minor ritual, 272-7 (III, 290-300)
Neophyte ritual, 331-3, 342, 346 (III, 82-5, 100-1, 107)
"Three Chiefs, Of the," 342 (III, 100-1)
"Three Chiefs, The," 272-7 (II, 290-300)
Three Great Secret Holy Names of God—*see* Enochian tablets
Threes (Tarot), 552 (IV, 156)
Cups, 564 (IV, 175)
divination example, 572, 572 (IV, 185, 187)
divinatory meaning, 583 (IV, 202)
Pentacles, 558 (IV, 165-6)
divination example, 577, 578 (IV, 194, 196)
Swords, 555 (IV, 161-2)
divination example, 586 (IV, 207)
Wands, 561 (IV, 171)
divination example, 577, 579 (IV, 194, 197)
see also Tarot, numbered cards
Thrice-Greatest Hermes (G. R. S. Mead), 201n
Throne:
of the East, 114, 334-5, 344, 367, 368 (III, 88, 104, 139, 140)
consecration of talismans, 386, 418, 420 (III, 170, 221, 224)
evocation, 381, 383, 408 (III, 161, 163, 164, 205)
Neophyte ritual, 117, 118, 119, 120, 123, 126, 127, 129, 131 (II, 12, 13, 16, 18, 24, 29, 32, 35, 40, 42)
spiritual development ritual, 392, 393 (III, 179, 180)
transformation ritual, 390 (III, 176)
Isis, head-dress. 686 (IV, 351)
of the West, 119, 123, 129, 337 (II, 16, 24, 35; III, 92)
Thrones (choir of angels), 97 (I, 194)
Thrones:
of the Aces of the Tarot—*see* Knaves (Princesses)
of the Elders, 225, 242 (II, 203, 273)
Queens of Tarot, 544, 545, 547, 548, 549 (IV, 144, 145, 146, 149, 150-1, 153)
Thummim, 341 (III, 99)
Tibetan Book of the Dead (W. Y. Evans-Wentz), 21 (I, 29)
Tibetan Buddhism, 21 (I, 29), 376n
tiger, 546, 551 (IV, 147, 155)
tin, 60 (I, 119)
Tiphareth, xxi, 11, 19-20, 21, 97, 98 (I, 26, 30, 195-6, 197)
Adam, 74, 178 (I, 145; II, 115)
Adeptus Minor grade, 35 (I, 65)
Air, 215, 345 (II, 187; III, 106)
alchemical operation, 399 (III, 191)
Banner of the West, 338 (III, 94)
Bornless Ritual, 444, 445 (III, 263, 264)
Calvary cross of six squares, 193, 335, 336, 374 (II, 145; III, 88-9, 90, 91, 150)
Cancellarius, 331 (III, 82, 83)
celestial sphere, 603, 604, 655, 656 (IV, 231, 233, 304, 305)

Tiphareth (continued):
- Chief Adept in Portal ritual, 199, 199n, 221n (II, 156)
- colors in the four color scales, 96, 99 (I, 193, 199)
- consecration of Rose-Cross, 314 (III, 58-9)
- crook, 242 (II, 237)
- cross and triangle, 333, 602 (III, 86; IV, 230)
- divine name, archangel, and angelic choir, 62, 64 (I, 123, 126)
- Equinox ceremony, 374 (III, 149)
- Great Hermetic Arcanum, 206 (II, 170)
- Hegemon's lamen, 79, 339 (I, 157; III, 96)
- hexagram, 84, 205, 217, 218, 293, 333, 465 (I, 168; II, 169, 191, 195; III, 27, 86; IV, 27)
- hexangle, 507 (IV, 91)
- Hiddikel, 73 (I, 145)
- Hiereus's lamen, 214, 337 (II, 184; III, 93)
- Hierophant's lamen, 218, 336 (II, 194; III, 90)
- Hierophant's sceptre, 335 (III, 89)
- Kether, 609 (IV, 241)
- Knight of Tarot, 79 (I, 156)
- Lotus Wand, 224n
- Microprosopus, 60 (I, 120)
- microcosm, 101-6 *passim* (I, 208-15 *passim*)
  - human consciousness, 106 (I, 214)
  - trunk of body, 101 (I, 204-5)
- Nephesch, 103 (I, 209)
- Pillars, bases of, 333 (III, 86)
- Portal grade, 35 (I, 65)
  - ritual, 200, 212 (II, 158, 181)
- Regulus, 596 (IV, 221)
- Rising on the Planes, 464 (IV, 24)
- Rose-Cross lamen, 310, 311, 473, 487, 491 (III, 51, 52, 53-4; IV, 40, 63, 70)
- Sephiroth, center of, 609 (IV, 241)
- sceptres (gold band), 332 (III, 84)
- scourge, 242 (II, 237)
- step, 371 (III, 144)
- Sulphur symbol, 84 (I, 168)
- Sun—*see* Sun, Tiphareth
- Sun reflected by full Moon, 68, 217 (I, 133; II, 191)
  - Hathor, 589 (IV, 210)
- Tarot, 552 (IV, 156)
  - High Priestess, 589 (IV, 210)
  - Kings (Princes), 615 (IV, 249)
  - Sixes:
    - Cups, 556 (IV, 163)
    - Pentacles, 562 (IV, 172)
    - Swords, 559 (IV 168)
    - Wands, 553 (IV, 159)
  - The Sun, 644 (IV, 288)
  - Temperance, 217, 218 (II, 192, 193)
- Third Adept in Adeptus Minor ritual, 221n

Tiphareth (continued):
- Thm-a-oe-St, 375 (III, 151)
- 25th Path, 214, 335 (II, 185, 186; III, 88)
- Vau, 615 (IV, 249)
- Venus, 481 (IV, 55)
- vibration of divine names, 487, 491 (IV, 63, 70)
- Zauir Anpin, 77-8 (I, 163-5)
- *see also* Sephiroth

Tiriel, 65 (I, 127)
- sigil, 501 (IV, 85)

Tmo-oumathv, 352 (III, 114)
- *see also* Toumathph

Tmoumathaph (Tmoumathph)—*see* Toumathph

Tmoumathv, 344 (III, 103)
- *see also* Toumathph

Tmu, 343, 357 (III, 102, 121)
- *see also* Tem; Thoomoo; Toum; Tum

tomb—*see* Pastos; Vault

torch, Tarot:
- The Devil, 213 (II, 183)
- Temperance, 217 (II, 192)

Toucan (constellation), 600 (IV, 228)

Toum, 158, 357 (II, 77; III, 121)
- Enochian chess Fire bishop, 685 (IV, 350)
- *see also* Tem; Thoomoo; Tmu; Tum

Toumathph (Tmo-oumathv, Tmoumathv, Tmoomathaph, Tmoumathaph, Tmoumathph, Tou-mathaph, Tto-oumathph), 343-4, 352, 358, 359 (III, 103, 114, 123, 124, 125)
- description, 357-8 (III, 122)
- Enochian:
  - chess pawn, 687, 692 (IV, 353, 361)
  - pyramids, 663 (IV, 315)
- heart and lungs, 360, 361 (III, 127, 128)
- illustration, 665 (IV, 317)
- Isis, 692 (IV, 361)
- Neith, 361 (III, 129)
- South, 361 (III, 128)
- Southeast, 343-4, 352, 357, 663 (III, 103, 114, 122; IV, 315)
- Water, 692 (IV, 361)
- *see also* Duamutef

Tower, The, 31, 189, 191-2, 210, 591 (I, 55; II, 137, 142-3, 178; IV, 214)
- divination:
  - example, 568, 569, 575, 576 (IV, 181, 182, 192)
  - meaning, 585 (IV, 205)
- Enochian chess castles, 693 (IV, 364)
- Geburah, 644, 693 (IV, 288, 364)
- *see also* Tarot, trumps

Tower Struck by Lightning—*see* Tower, The

Traherne, Thomas, *Centuries of Meditation*, 25 (I, 39-40)

trance, 111 (I, 226-7)

transference (in psychotherapy), xxv

transformation, 48 (I, 96)
Mem (Water), 389 (III, 175)
Neophyte formula, 378-9, 389-91 (III, 156, 175-7)
Isis, 429-34 (III, 239-47)
Shin of Yeheshuah, 376, 388 (III, 152, 172)
transmutation, 670 (IV, 327)
traveling in the spirit vision—*see* Skrying in the Spirit Vision
Tree of the Knowledge of Good and Evil, 33, 73, 76, 83, 98, 177 (I, 59, 144, 150, 166, 197-8; II, 114)
altar diagrams:
The Fall, 193 (II, 146)
The Flaming Sword of the Kerubim, 145 (II, 52)
The Star, 188, 592 (II, 135; IV, 215)
Tree of Life, xxi, 2, 3, 18-21, 27, 29, 30, 33-5, 39, 41, 45, 51, 61-2, 617, 618, 697 (I, 23-9, 44, 48, 53, 59-63, 74, 79, 89, 101-2, 121-3; IV, 251, 253)
Adeptus Minor Obligation, correlated with, 229-30 (II, 212-5)
Adeptus Minor ritual, 226 (II, 206)
alchemical attributions, 82 (I, 163)
altar diagrams:
The Fall, 193-4 (II, 146-7)
The Flaming Sword of the Kerubim, 145 (II, 52)
The Garden of Eden, 177 (II, 115)
Serpent on the Tree of Life, 62, 162 (I, 123; II, 84)
ankh, 224, 245, 262, 274 (II, 202, 241, 272, 295)
aura, 90 (I, 180)
see also Middle Pillar ritual
Banner of the East, 218 (II, 195)
caduceus, 68, 162, 340 (I, 131; II, 83; III, 97)
Calvary cross of ten squares, 79, 191, 656 (I, 157; II, 141; IV, 305)
celestial sphere, 594, 595, 596, 600, 602-5, 655 (IV, 219, 220, 221, 227, 231-4, 303)
colors and color scales, 95-9 (I, 191-202)
Cup of Stolistes, 70-1, 177, 340 (I, 138; II, 113; III, 97)
elemental grade rituals, 139
Enochian system, 624 (IV, 260)
Sephirotic Calvary Crosses, 641, 642, 643 (IV, 283, 286, 287)
every created material thing, 602 (IV, 231)
Four Worlds, 77 (I, 155)
geomantic figures, 526-7 (IV, 114-5)
Hermetic Order of the Golden Dawn, 272-3 (II, 291)
Mercury, symbol, 71 (I, 138)
microcosm, 100-6 *passim* (I, 203-16 *passim*)
Tree of Life (continued):
Moon, phases, 68, 164 (I, 133; II, 87)
Pan drawing, 213 (II, 184)
planets, 642 (IV, 286)
see also spheres, celestial or planetary
Portal drawing, 87, 88 (I, 175, 177)
Qlippoth, 82 (I, 163)
Rising on the Planes, 464 (IV, 24)
Salt symbol, 84 (I, 168)
Sephiroth, within each, 77, 602, 614 (I, 155; IV, 231, 246)
Serpent of Wisdom, 276 (II, 298)
Sulphur symbol, 84 (I, 167-8)
Tarot, 72-3, 78-9 (I, 141-3, 155-6)
divination, 567, 579, 580 (IV, 178, 197, 198)
The Star, 188, 591 (II, 135; IV, 215)
The Tower, 192 (II, 142)
temple, 115, 331 (III, 82)
Thoth, 330n
"The Tree of Life as Projected in a Solid Sphere," 92 (I, 184-5)
Vault symbolism, 246, 266 (II, 240, 280)
Venus symbol, 79, 195, 268, 272, 274, 275-6 (I, 157-8; II, 149, 284, 291, 295, 297-8)
see also altar diagrams; Sephiroth
Tree of Life, The (Israel Regardie), 2, 18, 23, 39, 41, 52n, 377 (I, 23, 34, 75, 79, 104n; III, 153)
Triad, 187, 192, 220, 240, 506 (II, 133, 142, 196, 233; IV, 89)
Banner of the East, 336 (III, 91)
dekagram, 510, 512 (IV, 93)
Enochian tablets, 643 (IV, 288)
heptagram, 508 (IV, 92)
Neophyte ritual, 366, 367, 368, 370 (III, 136, 139, 140, 143)
octagram, 508, 509 (IV, 92)
The Star, 188 (II, 135)
see also Supernal Sephiroth
triangle, 505-6 (IV, 89-90)
alchemical principles, 506 (IV, 90)
altar, 333, 335, 345, 347 (III, 86, 88, 105, 109)
alchemical operation, 395-9 *passim* (III, 185, 187, 188, 190, 191)
consecration of talismans, 385, 415, 416, 417 (III, 167, 215, 218, 219)
evocation, 381, 406, 408 (III, 160, 202, 206)
invisibility ritual, 388, 426 (III, 172, 234)
see also cross, Calvary, with triangle
Banner of the West, 338 (III, 93, 94)
Binah, 505, 506 (IV, 89)
decanates of Zodiac, 149, 601-2 (II, 60; IV, 229-30)
Enochian chess pawns, 692 (IV, 361)

triangle (continued):
evocation, 377, 384, 402, 406, 407, 409, 410, 411 (III, 154, 166, 195, 202, 204, 206, 207, 208, 210)
Fire, 70, 506 (I, 137; IV, 90)
Cup of Stolistes, 71, 177 (I, 138; II, 113)
Kabiri, 169-71 (II, 97-101)
hexagram:
forms of, using paired triangles, 294-6 (III, 28-31)
made up of triangles of Fire and Water, 287 (III, 21)
Hiereus's lamen, 213, 214, 337 (II, 184, 185; III, 93)
lineal figures of Sephiroth, 493 (IV, 72)
Neophyte ritual, formed by officers, 379 (III, 158)
over head, 368 (III, 139)
Saturn, 70, 506 (I, 136, 89-90)
Seven-Branched Candlestick, 150 (II, 62)
Supernal Sephiroth—*see* Supernal Sephiroth, triangle
Tejas, 457, 469, 489 (IV, 12, 13, 18, 67)
Vault symbolism, 242, 243 (II, 238, 240)
Water, 185 (II, 128)
see also cross, Calvary, with triangle
Triangulum, 598 (IV, 225)
Triangulum Australe, 600 (IV, 228)
Tribes of Israel, 149, 305 (II, 60-1; III, 44)
trident, 476 (IV, 45)
trine aspect, 538, 539 (IV, 133, 134, 135)
see also astrology, aspects
Trinity, 213, 230 (II, 184, 215)
triplicities—*see* Air, signs; Earth, signs; Fire, signs; Water, signs; Zodiac, triplicities
Tristitia, 494, 495, 527, 533 (IV, 75, 77, 115, 126)
Enochian:
chess, 690 (IV, 357)
pyramids, 650 (IV, 300)
see also geomancy, figures
Triumphal Chariot of Antimony (Basil Valentine), 1
True and Invisible Rosicrucian Order, The (Paul Foster Case), xxv
Trumps—*see* Tarot
Tto-oumathph, 352 (III, 114)
see also Toumathph
Tucana—*see* Toucan
Tum, 56, 57 (I, 112, 114)
see also Tem; Thoomoo; Tmu; Toum
turtle, Knave (Princess) of Cups, 547, 551 (IV, 149, 155)
Twelve Steps to Spiritual Enlightenment (Israel Regardie), 4
Twos (Tarot), 550 (IV, 156)
Cups, 563-4 (IV, 175)
divination example, 577, 579 (IV, 194, 196)
Twos (continued):
divinatory meaning, 583 (IV, 202)
Pentacles, 558 (IV, 165-6)
divination example, 568, 569, 571, 572, 575, 576 (IV, 181, 182, 185, 187, 192)
Swords, 555 (IV, 161)
divination example, 575, 576, 577, 579 (IV, 192, 194, 196)
Wands, 561 (IV, 170-1)
divination example, 585, 586 (IV, 207)
see also Tarot, numbered cards
Typhon, 114, 357 (III, 121)
Portal ritual, 210, 211-2 (I, 178, 180)
sign of, 357 (III, 121)
see also keyword analysis; L.V.X., signs
Tarot:
Death, 211 (II, 179)
Judgment, 172 (II, 104)
see also Apophis; keyword analysis; Set
Tyson, Donald, *The New Magus,* 505n
Tzaddi:
Aquarius, 305 (III, 44)
Egyptian language, 650 (IV, 297)
28th Path (Aquarius, The Star), 76, 161 (I, 150; II, 82)
admission badge—*see* admission badges, Paths, 28th Path; Pyramid of the Elements
circumambulation, 236 (III, 107)
Philosophus ritual, 182, 185, 186-8, 192-3, 194 (II, 123, 130, 131-6, 144-5, 147, 150)
temple arrangement, 186 (II, 131)
Practicus ritual, 174 (II, 107)
Theoricus ritual, 161, 163 (II, 82, 87)
see also Aquarius; Hebrew alphabet; Paths; Star
Tzadqiel, 62, 64, 97 (I, 123, 126, 195)
consecration of Jupiter talisman, 414, 415, 417, 418 (III, 214, 216, 218, 221)
Tzaphon (North), 80, 324 (I, 158; III, 71)
Tzaphqiel, 62, 64, 97 (I, 123, 126, 194)
invisibility ritual, 423, 424, 428 (III, 230, 237)
requiem ceremony, 447 (III, 266)
sigil, 483, 484 (IV, 58, 59)
spiritual development ritual, 436, 438 (III, 250, 254)
Tzedek, 63, 65, 97 (I, 125, 127, 194)
consecration of Jupiter talisman, 414-9 *passim*, 421, 422 (III, 213-6 *passim*, 218, 221, 223, 225, 227)
see also Jupiter

- U -

U Document, 43 (I, 84)
see "The Microcosm—Man," 100-11 (I, 203-27)

ultraviolet, 267 (II, 283)
Um, 628 (IV, 267)
Uma Haimavati, 628 (IV, 267)
Un, 495 (IV, 77)
see also Enochian, letters
unbalanced power/mercy/severity, 4-5, 75, 125, 129-30, 439 (I, 148; II, 27, 36-7; III, 255)
unconscious, xvii, xix, xxii, xxiii, 20, 21, 24, 28, 34, 46 (I, 25, 29, 37, 46, 61, 62, 63, 91-2)
Nephesch, 33 (I, 58)
Undana, 515 (IV 97)
Understanding—*see* Binah
undines, 30, 80, 160 (I, 52, 159; II, 80)
astral projection, 472 (IV, 37)
King of Undines and of Nymphs—*see* Knights (Kings), Cups
prayer, 179-80 (II, 119-20)
skrying, 470 (IV, 34)
Tattwa vision, 476 (IV, 45)
see also elementals; Nymphs and Undines
unicorn, 179 (II, 118)
Universe, The, 154, 155, 159-60, 592 (II, 69, 70, 79-80; IV, 216)
divination:
example, 575, 576 (IV, 192)
meaning, 585 (IV, 206)
Isis, 159, 592 (II, 79; IV, 216)
The Star, 188 (II, 135)
32nd Path, 209 (II, 176)
see also Tarot, trumps
unpardonable sin, 75 (I, 148)
Unstable Effort, The Lord of—*see* Sevens (Tarot), Swords
"Unto Thee, Sole Wise, Sole Eternal, and Sole Merciful One...," 413, 429, 449 (III, 212, 239, 270)
"Unto Thee, Sole Wise, Sole Mighty and Sole Eternal One...," 235, 445 (II, 225; III, 264)
Upanishads, 628 (IV, 267)
Ur, 495 (IV, 77)
see also geomancy, figures
uraeus (pl. uraei), 58, 59 (I, 115, 117)
Uranus, 51, 537n, 592 (I, 100; IV, 216)
Uriel, 207n
see also Auriel
Urim, 341 (III, 99)
Ursa Major, 595, 596, 597, 599 (IV, 219, 222, 223, 225)
Ursa Minor, 597 (IV, 222, 223)
Uu, 444 (III, 263)
Uvolbxdo, 672 (IV, 330)

- V -

V. vel Reguli, Liber, (Aleister Crowley), 698
V.N.R. = Vestigia Nulla Retrorsum (Mina Mathers), 463, 467-78 (IV, 23, 29-49)
Vadali, 672, 673 (IV, 330, 331)
Vahaviah, 86, 553 (I, 172; IV, 158)
Valentine, Basil, *Triumphal Chariot of Antimony,* 1
Valentinus, 375 (III, 150)
Valour, Lord of—*see* Sevens (Tarot), Wands
Vam, 520 (IV, 105)
Vast Countenance, 77 (I, 153)
Vau (Enochian letter), 495 (IV, 77)
see also Enochian, letters
Vau (Hebrew letter):
Air, 644 (IV, 289)
see also YHVH, elements
Circular Altar, 235 (II, 224)
Dagger, 322 (III, 68, 69)
divination, 376, 393 (III, 152, 182)
Enochian:
chess bishop, 695 (IV, 366)
pyramids, 650 (IV, 296)
hexagram, 277 (II, 299)
Kether, 641 (IV, 282)
Kings (Princes) of Tarot, 544, 615 (IV, 144, 249)
16th Path (Taurus, The Hierophant):
Hegemon's sceptre, 339 (III, 95)
telesmatic image, 489, 491 (IV, 66, 69)
Thm-a-oe-St, 375 (III, 151)
Zodiac:
mutable signs, 644 (IV, 289)
Taurus, 305 (III, 44)
see also Hebrew alphabet
Vaughan, Thomas, 33, 39 (I, 60, 73)
Coelum Terrae, 19 (I, 25)
Vault (tomb of Christian Rosenkreuz), 14-5, 20, 311 (I, 14, 27; III, 53)
Adeptus Minor ritual, 23, 35, 37-8, 43, 222-8 *passim*, 232-47 *passim* (I, 36, 63, 69-71, 84; II, 199-211 *passim*, 219-31 *passim*, 238, 239, 240, 244)
symbolism of seven sides, 223 (II, 201)
banishing rituals never used in, 270 (II, 287)
"Concerning the Use of the Vault," 270-1 (II, 287-9)
Consecration ceremony, 258-65 (II, 264-78)
garments to be worn in, 270 (II, 287)
"The Symbolism of the Seven Sides," 266-9 (II, 280-6)
talismans, 481 (IV, 55)
Venus, 270, 276 (II, 287, 297)
Vaus, on Ace of Swords, 543 (IV, 143)
Vavaliah, 86, 560 (I, 174; IV, 169)
Vayu, 457, 514-22 *passim* (IV, 12, 13, 96-103 *passim*, 105, 106, 108)
Pam, 520 (IV, 105)
Vayu of Akasa, 458, 516 (IV, 14, 99)
Vayus, 515 (IV, 97)
vegetotherapy, 5
Vehooel, 86, 561 (I, 171; IV, 171)

veil, 36, 332 (I, 66; III, 84-5)
  light from behind attracted by Hierophant's sceptre, 347 (III, 109)
  see also Paroketh
Veil of the Tabernacle, 159, 217, 260, 370 (II, 79, 190, 268; III, 143)
Veils of Negative Existence, 77, 358, 362 (I, 153; III, 124, 130)
Vemibael, 86, 563 (I, 171; IV, 174)
Venus, 63, 272 (I, 125; II, 290, 291)
  alchemical operation, 399 (III, 191)
  angel, intelligence, and spirit, 65 (I, 127)
  Chesed, 643 (IV, 288)
  Earth, 648 (IV, 294)
  Enochian:
    chess, 690 (IV, 357)
    letters and geomantic figures, 495 (IV, 77)
    pyramids, 648, 654 (IV, 294, 302)
  heptagram, 70, 508 (I, 136; IV, 92)
  hexagram, 218, 290 (II, 195; III, 23)
  Isis, 589 (IV, 219)
  Libra, 495 (IV, 77)
  lion, 481 (IV, 55)
  Lucifer, 276 (II, 298)
  magic square, 500 (IV, 84)
  Netzach, 20, 97, 218 (I, 26, 196; II, 195)
  nostril, left, 103 (I, 210)
  Philosophus grade, 31, 182, 195 (I, 54; II, 123, 149)
  pleasure, 474 (IV, 41)
  seal, 500 (IV, 84)
  serpent, 83 (I, 166)
  symbol, 79, 80, 193, 195, 243, 274, 275-6 (I, 157-8, 160; II, 145, 149, 240, 295, 297-8)
    circle larger than that of Mercury, 79, 195 (I, 158; II, 149)
  Tarot:
    Cups:
      Two, 541, 563-4 (IV, 140, 175)
      Seven, 541, 556 (IV, 140, 163-4)
    The Empress, 71, 72, 542, 589 (I, 139, 141; IV, 140, 210, 211)
    Five of Swords, 541, 559 (IV, 140, 167)
    Four of Wands, 541, 561 (IV, 140, 171)
    Nine of Pentacles, 541, 554 (IV, 139, 160)
    The Star, 188, 591 (II, 135; IV, 214)
  Taurus, 495 (IV, 77)
  Tiphareth, 481 (IV, 55)
  Vault symbolism, 243, 266, 268, 270, 276, 589 (II, 240, 280, 283, 284, 287, 297; IV, 211)
  Water, 481 (IV, 55)
  see also planets
Verchiel, 86, 305 (I, 172; III, 44)
  Enochian letters, geomantic figures, Zodiac, 495 (IV, 77)
Veshiriah, 86, 558 (I, 174; IV, 166)
vesica, 72 (I, 140)
Vestigia—*see* Mathers, Mina; V.N.R.
Via, 495, 527, 536 (IV, 77, 115, 131)
  see also geomancy, figures
vibration of names, 3, 4, 35, 40, 45, 54, 138, 378, 487, 491-2 (I, 65, 76, 90, 108; III, 156; IV, 62-3, 70-1)
  Adeptus Minor Obligation, 230 (II, 214)
  astral projection, 465, 466 (IV, 26, 27)
    Rising on the Planes, 464 (IV, 24)
  Bornless Ritual, 442 (III, 260)
  description of method, 284, 345-6 (III, 16, 106-7)
  consecration of talismans, 413, 414, 417, 418, 422, 482 (III, 212, 214, 218, 219, 220, 228; IV, 56)
  evocation, 404, 406, 407 (III, 199, 202, 203, 204)
  with hexagrams, 299 (III, 35)
  invisibility ritual, 424, 428 (III, 231, 237)
  requiem ceremony, 449 (III, 269)
  skrying, 464, 469, 470, 661, 666, 667, 669 (IV, 24, 33, 34, 313, 319, 321, 325)
  spiritual development ritual, 436, 437, 440 (III, 250, 252, 257)
  Tattwa vision, 459-62 *passim* (IV, 16, 17, 18, 20, 21)
  transformation ritual, 429-33 *passim* (III, 239, 241, 243-6 *passim*)
Vibratory Formula of the Middle Pillar, xviii, 346, 378, 453 (III, 239, 241, 274)
  see also vibration of names
Victory:
  Cross of—*see* Cross of Victory
  Lord of—*see* Sixes (Tarot), Wands
  see also Netzach
virgin, 63 (I, 124)
Virgo, 12, 63 (I, 124)
  Chesed, 603 (IV, 231)
  divine and angelic names, 86 (I, 172)
  divine name, Hebrew letter, Tribe of Israel, angel, and color, 305 (III, 44)
  Enochian:
    chess, 694 (IV, 365)
    letter and geomantic figure, 495 (IV, 77)
    pyramids, 655 (IV, 303)
  Leo, influence on, 601 (IV, 229)
  Mercury, 495 (IV, 77)
  Pillar of Mercy, 603 (IV, 232)
  star map, 595 (IV, 219)
  symbol used in spelling divine names, 83 (I, 166)
  Tarot:
    The Hermit, 71, 72, 542, 599 (I, 139, 142; IV, 141, 226)
    Knave (Princess) of Wands, 597 (IV, 222)

Virgo (continued):
Tarot (continued):
Pentacles:
Eight, Nine, and Ten, 541, 553-4 (IV, 139, 159-60)
Knight (King), 549, 597 (IV, 152, 223, 224)
Queen of Swords, 548, 598 (IV, 151, 224)
Teaa, 669 (IV, 325)
telesmatic image, 486 (IV, 61)
Vault symbolism, 269 (II, 286)
see also keyword analysis; Zodiac
Virtues (angelic choir), 97 (I, 196)
"Vision of the Universal Mercury, The," 43, 44, 476-8 (I, 84, 85; IV, 47-50)
Vitriol, 206 (II, 172)
Vitriolum, 206 (II, 172)
Vitvan, *The Problem of Good and Evil* or *The Christos,* 6
Volans—*see* Piscis Volans
Volcanic Fire, 70, 171 (I, 137; II, 103)
Axiokersos, 170 (II, 99)
Samael, 172 (II, 104)
volcano, 218, 591 (II, 192; IV, 214)
Volexdo, 669 (IV, 325)
Vulpecula, 597, 598 (IV, 223, 224)
vulture head-dress, worn by Egyptian deities, 355, 356 (III, 118, 119)
Isis, 686 (IV, 351)
Vyana, 515 (IV, 97)

- W -

W Document, 43 (IV, 84)
see "Concerning the Tree of Life," 95-9 (I, 191-202)
Waite, Arthur Edward, ix, 43 (I, 85)
The Brotherhood of the Rosy Cross, 18 (I, 22)
The Holy Kabbalah, 44 (I, 87)
A Pictorial Key to the Tarot, 6, 39, 91 (I, 75, 183)
The Real History of the Rosicrucians, 37 (I, 69-70)
Tarot cards, 30, 589 (I, 53; IV, 211)
Wand:
Cancellarius—*see* sceptre, Cancellarius
Earth Fire Wand, 475 (IV, 43, 44)
Egyptian deities, 354-7 *passim* (III, 117-20 *passim*)
elemental weapon (Fire), 47, 320 (I, 94; III, 66-8)
consecration, 323-6, 327-8 (III, 70-5, 77-8)
illustration, 321 (III, 67)
Netzach, 224n
Wand (continued):
elemental weapon (Fire) (continued):
Opening by Watchtower:
evocation, 402 (III, 195, 196)
spiritual development ritual, 435 (III, 248)
Tarot:
Five of Wands, 552 (IV, 158)
King (Prince) of Wands, 545-6, 551 (IV, 147, 155)
skrying (Enochian), 669 (IV, 325)
Tattwa vision, 475 (IV, 43)
see also weapons, magical, elemental
geomancy, 539 (IV, 136)
Hegemon—*see* sceptre, Hegemon
Hierophant—*see* sceptre, Hierophant
Kerux, 249, 341, 344 (II, 247; III, 98, 105)
Neophyte ritual, 118, 120, 124 (II, 13, 18, 25, 26)
explains, 119 (II, 15)
explained by Hierophant, 129 (II, 35)
Lotus—*see* Lotus Wand
Phoenix—*see* Phoenix Wand
Praemonstrator, 204 (II, 168)
Winged-Sphere, 221, 224, 233, 236, 262, 340 (II, 198, 203, 222, 225, 226, 227, 272; III, 97)
wands, officers in Portal ritual, 198-9 (II, 156)
Wands (Tarot), 552-3, 557-8, 561 (IV, 158-9, 164-5, 170-1)
astral/cosmic Neophyte temple in Sphere of Sensation, 453 (III, 274)
court cards, 545-6 (IV, 146-8)
divinatory meaning, 582, 583 (IV, 201, 202)
Enochian chess, 685 (IV, 349)
see also individual cards [e.g., Sevens (Tarot), Wands]
see also Tarot
Warburg Institute, xxi
Ward, J. S. M., *Freemasonry and the Ancient Gods,* 11-2
Watcher for/of the Gods, 341, 355, 366, 370, 374 (III, 99, 118, 137, 143, 149, 150)
Watchtower, Opening by—*see* Opening by Watchtower
Watchtowers—*see* Enochian, tablets
Water, xxiii, 8
of Air:
Queen of Swords, 548 (IV, 151)
Rose-Cross lamen, 310 (III, 52)
alchemical operation, 398 (III, 189-90)
Alverda, Hugo, 275 (II, 296)
Apas, 457, 459, 469, 489 (IV, 12, 13, 15, 32, 33, 67)
Banner of the East, 336 (III, 91)
bread and fish, 593 (IV, 217)
caduceus, 162, 340 (II, 84; III, 97)
Chesed, 84, 215 (I, 169; II, 187)

Water (continued):
Chesed (continued):
Water from reflected in Hod, 331 (III, 83)
consecration by, 28 (I, 47)
consecration of talisman, 413, 414, 421-2 (III, 212, 213, 226-7)
Cup:
altar, 334 (III, 87)
transmits Waters of Hod to Malkuth, 341 (III, 99)
see also Cup, elemental weapon (Water); Cup of Stolistes
divine name, archangel, angel, ruler, king, etc., 80 (I, 159)
of Earth:
Malkuth, 614 (IV, 247)
of Yetzirah, 621 (IV, 256)
Queen of Pentacles, 549 (IV, 152)
Rose-Cross lamen, 310 (III, 52)
Tattwa, 489 (IV, 67)
Enochian chess:
boards, 694 (IV, 365)
queens, 691, 695 (IV, 360, 367)
Enochian tablets or Watchtowers:
pyramids, 649, 654-5 (IV, 296, 302, 303)
Water angle:
Air tablet, 667 (IV, 321)
call (seventh), 672, 677 (IV, 330, 337)
Enochian chess, 690 (IV, 357)
angels, 670 (IV, 327)
Earth tablet, call (fourteenth), 672, 679 (IV, 330, 341)
Enochian chess queen, 686 (IV, 351)
Fire tablet, 655 (IV, 303)
call (seventeenth), 672, 680 (IV, 330, 342)
Kether of Heh, 641 (IV, 283)
Water tablet, 167, 168, 178 (II, 94, 96, 97, 116)
Air angle, 326, 638, 649, 650, 670 (III, 75; IV, 280, 296-7, 327)
call (tenth), 672, 678 (IV, 330, 339)
skrying, 662, 666 (IV, 318-9)
archangels of angles, 326 (III, 75)
calls, 671, 672, 675 (IV, 329, 330, 336)
consecration of talisman, 413, 421, 428 (III, 212, 213, 226)
Earth angle, 645 (IV, 290)
call (eleventh), 672, 678 (IV, 330, 340)
Fire angle, 638 (IV, 280)
call (twelfth), 672, 678 (IV, 330, 340)
illustration, 632 (IV, 271)
Opening by Watchtower:
evocation, 402 (III, 196)
spiritual development ritual, 435 (III, 248)

Water (continued):
Enochian tablets or Watchtowers: (continued):
Water tablet (continued):
Opening by Watchtower (continued):
Vault consecration, 258 (II, 265)
Practicus ritual, 167, 168, 178 (II, 94, 96, 97, 116)
pyramids, 654 (IV, 302)
Water angle, 649, 654 (IV, 295, 302)
call (fourth), 671, 672 (IV, 329, 330)
see also Enochian tablets
finger, index, 100 (I, 204)
Fire, produced by, 151 (II, 64)
of Fire: Queen of Wands, 545, 655 (IV, 147, 303)
fish, 109 (I, 222)
Gihon, 73, 177 (I, 145; II, 114)
Heh, 639, 644 (IV, 281, 289)
see also YHVH, elements
hexagram, 298, 336 (III, 34, 91)
Hierophant's lamen, 218, 336 (II, 194; III, 90)
Hod, 20, 21, 31 (I, 27, 30, 55)
Water reflected from Chesed, 331 (III, 83)
Isis, 692 (IV, 361)
Kabexnuf, 361 (III, 128)
Kerub, 343, 357 (III, 102, 121)
see also eagle; Kerubim; Scorpio
Malkuth, olive quarter, 337 (III, 92)
Mars, 215, 648 (II, 187; IV, 294)
material basis, 384, 387 (III, 166, 171)
Osiris, Horus, Isis, 184 (II, 127)
pentagram, 282, 283, 284, 286 (III, 12, 13, 15, 16, 19)
astral projection, 471 (IV, 36)
Bornless Ritual, 443 (III, 261)
consecration:
Cup, 324 (III, 75)
Rose-Cross, 315 (III, 60)
talisman, 413, 421 (III, 212, 226)
Opening by Watchtower:
evocation, 402 (II, 196)
spiritual development ritual, 435 (III, 248)
Vault consecration, 258 (II, 265)
Portal ritual, 307 (II, 173)
Practicus ritual, 167, 179 (II, 94, 118)
skrying, 470 (IV, 34)
pentagram, point of, 280, 281, 282 (III, 10-13 *passim*)
Practicus grade, 29, 30, 32, 72, 167, 178 (I, 50, 53, 58, 140; II, 93, 115, 116)
Praemonstrator, 332 (III, 83, 84)
prayer, 179-80 (II, 119-20)
Root of the Powers of—*see* Aces (Tarot), Cups

Water (continued):
Rose-Cross lamen, 310-13 (III, 52-3, 55, 56)
alchemical principles and other elements in Water, 311 (III, 52-3)
location of petal (Mem), 311 (III, 53)
Water arm of cross and colors, 311, 312 (III, 52-3, 55)
consecration, 315 (III, 60)
Supreme Invoking Ritual of the Pentagram, 469 (IV, 33)
symbol:
eagle, in pentagram rituals, 283 (II, 14)
triangle:
part of hexagram, 287 (III, 21)
used in spelling divine names, 83 (I, 166)
see also eagle; Scorpio; Water, triangle
Tarot:
The Devil, 213 (II, 183)
The Hanged Man, 71, 73, 542, 592 (I, 139, 142; IV, 141, 216)
Temperance, 217, 218, 591 (II, 192; IV, 214)
Tattwa vision, 476 (IV, 45)
Theoricus ritual, 158 (II, 77)
Third Adept in Portal ritual, 199n
Thma-oe-Tt, 375 (III, 151)
Toumathph, 687, 692 (IV, 353, 361)
triangle, 185 (II, 128)
Venus, 481 (IV, 55)
of Water: Queen of Cups, 547 (IV, 149)
Zodiac:
fixed signs, 644 (IV, 289)
water signs, 50, 72 (I, 100, 140)
Enochian pyramids, 650 (IV, 297)
see also elements; Stolistes
Water-horse, 344 (III, 103)
water lilies, on Ace of Cups, 543 (IV, 143)
Waters Above the Firmament, 185 (II, 129)
Cup of Stolistes, 71, 177, 340 (I, 138; II, 113; III, 97)
Waters of:
Babylon, 251 (II, 252)
Creation, 61, 149, 162, 194, 220, 340, 413 (I, 121; II, 59, 84, 147, 195; III, 97, 212)
Banner of the East, 336 (III, 91)
Canopus, 360 (III, 127)
The Star, 188 (II, 135)
Stolistes, 346 (III, 107)
Edom, 194 (II, 148)
Life, 74, 177 (I, 145; II, 115)
Nu—*see* Nu
weapons, magical, 46-7 (I, 91-5)
consecration, 7, 42, 47 (I, 82, 95)
elemental, 43, 47, 320-2 (I, 84, 94; III, 66-9)
Adeptus Minor Obligation, 229 (II, 213)
Adeptus Minor ritual, 37 (I, 70)
weapons, magical (continued):
elemental (continued):
alchemical operation, 395, 398 (III, 185, 189, 190)
astral projection, 466 (IV, 78)
consecration, 8, 42, 43, 47, 320, 322, 323-8, 638 (I, 82, 84, 95; III, 66, 68, 69, 70-8; IV, 281)
illustration, 321 (III, 67)
skrying, 468, 469, 668, 669 (IV, 31, 32, 323, 325)
Tarot divination, 566 (IV, 178)
see also Cup; Dagger; Pentacle; Wand, Fire
Lotus Wand, 8, 46-7 (I, 92-3)
Sephiroth, 224n
sword, 43, 47 (I, 84, 94)
Wealth, Lord of—*see* Tens (Tarot), Pentacles
Webster, Sam, ix, x
Epilogue, 697-700
Weschcke, Carl Llewellyn, xi, xxv
footnotes, 343, 405, 570, 681, 692, 697
Foreword and Appreciation, ix-x
West, xxiii, 80 (I, 159)
alchemical operation, 396 (III, 186)
alimentary system, 360, 361 (III, 128)
altar, black side, 333 (III, 86)
Banner of the—*see* Banner of the West
Bornless Ritual, 442-5 *passim* (III, 259, 261, 262, 265)
consecration of talismans, 384, 385, 386, 413-6 *passim*, 418 (III, 166-9 *passim*, 212-5 *passim*, 217, 218, 221, 226)
Cup on altar (Water), 334 (III, 87)
Emantt, 353 (III, 115)
evocation, 380, 381, 382, 402, 403, 405, 406, 408, 410 (III, 159, 160, 161, 163, 196, 197, 200, 201, 202, 205, 206, 208)
hexagram rituals, 295, 297-8 (III, 30, 33-4)
Hiereus's station, 337 (III, 92)
invisibility ritual, 388, 426, 427 (III, 173, 234, 235, 236)
Kabexnuf, 361 (III, 128)
pentagram rituals, 53, 286 (I, 106; III, 19)
Pillar, Black, base, 333 (III, 86)
requiem ceremony, 448 (III, 267, 268)
spiritual development ritual, 391, 392, 435-9 *passim*, 441 (III, 178, 179, 180, 248, 249, 252, 254, 255, 258)
transformation ritual, 390, 431, 432, 433 (III, 176, 242, 244, 246)
see also cardinal points; Neophyte ritual, cardinal points and other directions
Westcott, William Wynn, ix, 8, 10, 17, 625 (I, 19-21; IV, 262)
The Chaldean Oracles of Zoroaster, 31 (I, 53-4)
Data of the History of the Rosicrucians, 16 (I, 16-7)

Westcott, William Wynn (continued):
"Further Rules for Practice," 668-70 (IV, 323-7)
N.O.M. = Non Omnis Moriar, 266, 658, 687 (II, 280; IV, 309, 347-8)
S.A. = Sapere Aude, 16 (I, 17-8)
see also S.A.
"The Symbolism of the Seven Sides," 266-9 (II, 280-6)
Tarot divination, 576 (IV, 193)
Weston-super-Mare, U.K., 18 (I, 22)
wheel:
circumambulation, 346 (III, 108)
symbol of Spirit, 280, 281, 285, 286, 507 (III, 10, 11, 18, 19; IV, 90)
consecration of talisman, 420, 421, 422 (III, 212, 224, 226, 227)
Wheel of the Aces, 621 (IV, 257)
Wheel of Fortune, The, (Tarot), 210, 590 (II, 178; IV, 212-3)
divination:
example, 571, 572 (IV, 185, 186, 187)
meaning, 584 (IV, 205)
Kether, 643 (IV, 287)
see also Tarot, trumps
Wheels:
angelic choir, 96 (I, 194)
see also Auphanim
Ezekiel's vision, 233 (II, 222)
whirl, in aura, expanding and invoking, 492 (IV, 71)
Wicca, ix, 698
Wilhelm, Richard, *The Secret of the Golden Flower,* 26-7, 33 (I, 43, 58)
Wilmshurst, W. L., *The Ceremony of Initiation,* 9
Wilson, George, x, xxv
footnotes, 117, 342
winds and attribution of elements to cardinal points, 283 (III, 14)
wine:
altar (Water), 334 (III, 87)
Adeptus Minor ritual, 221, 229, 230, 233 (II, 200, 212, 215, 222)
Equinox ceremony, 249, 250 (II, 247-50 *passim*)
evocation, 409 (III, 207)
requiem ceremony, 448 (III, 267)
spiritual development ritual, 439, 441 (III, 255, 258)
Winged-Sphere Wand—*see* Wand, Winged-Sphere
Wisdom—*see* Chokmah
Witchcraft, 698
witches, Salem, xviii
Witnesses, 529-30, 531, 538, 539 (IV, 120, 123, 133, 135)
see also geomancy
Wizard's Foot, 213 (II, 183)
wolf, The Fool, 588 (IV, 210)
Wolf, Fred Alan, *Star Wave,* xviii
Wonderful or Hidden Intelligence, 615 (IV, 248)
Woodman, William Robert, 15, 17 (I, 17, 18, 20, 21)
M.E.V. = Magna Est Veritas, 15 (I, 17, 18)
words of grades:
Neophyte (Har-Par-Krat), 127, 144, 344, 373 (II, 30, 49; III, 103, 147-8)
invisibility ritual, 389 (III, 174)
Philosophus (Yod He Vau He Tzabaoth), 194 (II, 147)
Practicus (Elohim Tzabaoth), 178, 183 (II, 115, 125)
Theoricus (Shaddai El Chai), 163, 168 (II, 86, 96)
Zelator (Adonai ha-Aretz), 147, 156 (II, 55, 73)
see also passwords
World, The—see Universe, The
Worlds, Four, 63, 613-5 (I, 125; IV, 246-9)
color scales, 95, 99 (I, 192, 199-202)
sigils, 483, 484, 485 (IV, 58, 59, 60)
Tarot, 67, 77 (I, 130, 155)
telesmatic images, 488, 489 (IV, 64, 65, 67)
Tetragrammaton, 77, 641 (I, 155; IV, 283)

- X -

X Document, 43 (I, 84)
see "Part Two: The Concourse of Forces," 659-68 (IV, 310-22)
xi (Coptic letter), 337, 663 (IV, 92, 315)

- Y -

Y Document, 43 (I, 84)
see "Part Four: The Concourse of Forces; Enochian or Rosicrucian Chess," 683-96 (IV, 346-68)
Yah, 62, 64, 96, 375n (I, 123, 126, 194)
suffix, 486, 487 (IV, 62, 64)
see also Yod He
Yeats, William Butler, ix, 16, 624n (I, 18)
Yebomayah, 86, 564 (I, 172; IV, 175)
Yechavah, 86, 558 (I, 174; IV, 167)
Yechidah, 67, 105-6, 345 (I, 129, 213-5; III, 106)
Yeheshua Mihi Omnia, 235 (II, 224)
Yeheshua Yehovasha (Yeheshuah Yehovashah), 264, 438, 439, 450 (II, 276; III, 253, 255, 256, 270)
Yeheshuah (Yeheshua), 8, 76, 101, 359 (I, 149, 206; III, 125)
Adeptus Minor ritual, 224, 225, 235, 240 (II, 202, 205, 224, 234)
consecration of talisman, 414, 420 (III, 222, 223)

Yeheshuah (continued):
dismissal of spirits, 304, 316, 319, 328, 387, 412, 420, 434, 441, 446 (III, 43, 61, 65, 78, 171, 211, 223, 247, 258, 265)
individual, 376n
invisibility ritual, 423-7 *passim* (III, 229, 231, 232, 234, 236)
Outer Order, not expressed in, 333 (III, 86)
Portal ritual, 201, 220 (II, 160, 197)
requiem ceremony, 449 (III, 269)
Ritual of the Rose-Cross, 306, 307 (III, 46, 47, 48)
rituals classified according to letters of, 376 (III, 152)
skrying (Enochian), 668 (IV, 323)
spelled with symbols of Yetziratic attributions of letters, 83 (I, 166)
Tattwa vision, 463 (IV, 22)
Tetragrammaton (YHVH), formed from by addition of Shin (Spirit), 235, 240, 274, 280, 376n (II, 224, 234, 295; III, 9)
Vault consecration ceremony, 261, 263, 265 (II, 271, 274, 279)
Yehohel, 86, 563 (I, 171; IV, 174)
Yehovashah (Yehovasha), 307, 387, 420, 423, 426 (III, 48, 171, 223, 229, 234)
skrying (Enochian), 668 (IV, 323)
Yelahiah, 86, 560 (I, 174; IV, 169)
Yelavel, 86, 553 (I, 172; IV, 158)
yellow shoes—*see* shoes, yellow
Yesod, 20, 21, 98 (I, 27, 30, 196-7)
Air from Tiphareth reflected in, 331, 345 (III, 83, 106)
automatic consciousness, 102, 105, 106 (I, 208, 214, 217)
Calvary cross of six squares, 193 (II, 145)
celestial sphere, 603, 604 (IV, 231, 232, 233)
Cup of Stolistes, 340 (III, 97)
dagger (Air), 224n
enneangle, 508 (IV, 92)
Evil One, station of, 344 (III, 103)
divine name, archangel, and angelic choir, 62, 64, 98 (I, 123, 126, 197)
Hathor, 589 (IV, 210)
Hegemon in Portal ritual, 199n
Hegemon's lamen, 79, 339 (I, 157; III, 96)
hexagram, 218, 287, 293 (II, 195; III, 21, 27)
Hiereus's lamen, 214, 337 (II, 185; III, 93)
Maltese cross, 204 (II, 168)
microcosm, 102, 103, 106 (III, 207-8, 209, 214)
generative and excretory organs, 102 (I, 207-8)
invisibility ritual, 424 (III, 231)
Moon, 218 (II, 195)
Neophyte ritual, station in, 114
Neophyte temple, 331 (III, 82)
Yesod (continued):
Nephesch, 103 (I, 209)
Paths:
from/to, 73, 76 (I, 144, 150)
30th Path, 175, 215 (II, 110, 187)
32nd Path, 209, 215 (II, 176, 177, 187)
see also Paths; Tarot
Philosophus ritual, temple in, 186 (II, 131)
Portal grade, 217, 219, 220 (II, 191, 196)
ritual, 199n, 212, 213, 214 (II, 181, 184, 185)
Rising on the Planes, 464 (IV, 24)
Tarot, Nines, 552 (IV, 157)
Cups, 560 (IV, 170)
Pentacles, 554 (IV, 160)
Swords, 563 (IV, 174)
Wands, 557 (IV, 165)
Theoricus grade, 30, 163, 331 (I, 52; II, 85, 86; III, 83)
Thoth, 330n
Tiphareth, Air from reflected in, 331 (III, 83)
transformation ritual, 430-4 *passim* (III, 241, 242, 243, 245, 246, 247)
triangle on altar, 162 (II, 85)
see also Sephiroth
Yetzer, 488 (IV, 65)
Yetzirah (Yetsirah), 63 (I, 125)
Kether of, 614 (IV, 246)
Enochian chess bishops, 696 (IV, 367)
Malkuth of, 358, 362, 614, 615, 617, 618, 619, 621 (III, 124, 130; IV, 246, 247, 248, 249, 252, 253, 254, 256, 257)
Palaces of, 42-lettered name in, 365 (III, 134)
Ruach in microcosm, 105 (I, 214)
sigils, 483, 484 (IV, 58, 59)
Tarot:
Aces, 542 (IV, 142)
Kings (Princes), 696 (IV, 367)
The Moon, 185 (II, 130)
Tattwa vision, 476 (IV, 45-6)
telesmatic images, 488, 489 (IV, 64, 65, 67)
32nd Path, 159 (II, 79)
Yeyayel, 86, 556 (I, 173; IV, 163)
Yeyelal, 86, 562 (I, 171; IV, 172)
Yeyeziel, 86, 559 (I, 174; IV, 168)
Yezalel, 86, 555 (I, 173; IV, 161)
YHShVH, 441, 443, 446, 466 (III, 258, 260, 265; IV, 27)
Enochian chess pieces, 685 (IV, 350)
pentagram, 507 (IV, 90)
see also Yeheshuah
YHVH, 8, 11, 76, 156, 165, 177, 220, 359 (I, 149; II, 71, 90, 114, 197; III, 125)
Adonai, 508 (IV, 92)
altar, symbolized on, 333 (III, 86)
animals, 109 (I, 222)

YHVH (continued):
consecrations:
Dagger, 324 (III, 71, 72)
Lotus Wand, 304, 305 (III, 43, 44)
Rose-Cross, 314, 315 (III, 59, 60, 61)
talismans, 386, 416, 419, 420 (III, 168, 217, 221, 225)
elemental weapons, 320, 322 (III, 66, 69)
elements, 160, 199n, 220, 506, 607, 638-9 (II, 80, 197; IV, 90, 237, 281)
cross, 225 (III, 89)
Enochian chess, 695 (IV, 366)
Enochian tablets, 638-9, 642, 646-7, 688 (IV, 281-2, 285, 291-2, 354)
Great Cross, 639, 640, 642 (IV, 282, 283, 285)
Kerubic squares, 641, 644, 688 (IV, 283-4, 288, 357)
pyramids, 649 (IV, 295)
Lesser Angles, 640 (IV, 282-3)
pyramids, 651 (IV, 298)
Sephirotic Calvary Crosses:
pyramids, 648 (IV, 295)
servient squares, 641-2, 644, 688 (IV, 284-5, 289, 357)
skrying, 668 (IV, 323)
evocation, 382, 408 (III, 162, 205)
Four Worlds—*see* Tetragrammaton, Four Worlds
invisibility ritual, 426, 427 (III, 234, 236)
microcosm, 105 (I, 214)
Neophyte temple, 331 (III, 82)
pentagram rituals, 53, 281, 285 (I, 106; III, 10, 18)
permutations, 86, 149, 305 (II, 60, 171-4; III, 44)
Portal ritual, 200 (II, 160)
spelled with symbols of Yetziratic attributions of letters, 83 (I, 166)
spiritual development ritual, 438 (III, 253)
square, 506 (IV, 90)
Tarot:
divination, 569, 570, 571 (IV, 182-3, 184, 185)
Judgment, 172 (II, 104)
see also Tarot, suits, Tetragrammaton
transformation ritual, 429, 430, 432, 434 (III, 240, 244, 247)
Vault symbolism, 268, 268, 269 (II, 283, 284-5, 286)
Zodiac, triplicities, 642 (IV, 285)
see also Tetragrammaton; Yeheshuah
YHVH Adonai, 508 (IV, 92)
YHVH Eloah Ve-Daath, 62, 64 (I, 123, 126)
consecration of Rose-Cross, 314 (III, 58, 59)
hexagrams of Sun, 291-2 (III, 24-5)
YHVH Eloha va-Daath, 97 (I, 195)
see also YHVH Eloah Vedaath
YHVH Elohim, 62, 64, 76, 194 (I, 123, 126, 150; II, 146-7)
hexagram of Saturn, 288 (III, 21)
invisibility ritual, 423-8 *passim* (III, 230, 233, 234, 235, 237)
requiem ceremony, 447 (III, 266)
sigil, 483, 484 (IV, 58, 59)
spiritual development ritual, 436 (III, 250)
YHVH of Hosts, 195 (II, 150)
YHVH Tzabaoth, 62, 64, 80, 97, 182, 183, 194, 195, 196 (I, 123, 126, 159, 196; II, 123, 124, 147, 149, 152)
consecration of talisman, 420 (III, 225)
hexagram of Venus, 290 (III, 23)
Yirthiel, 86, 557 (I, 173; IV, 165)
Yod:
ceremonial magic, 376 (II, 152)
Chokmah, 331 (III, 82)
Circular Altar, 235 (II, 224)
Earth, 694 (IV, 364-5)
Enochian:
chess knight, 695 (IV, 366)
pyramids, 650 (IV, 296)
evocation, 376, 380 (III, 152, 159)
Fire, 644 (IV, 289)
see also YHVH, elements
Fire Wand, 320 (III, 68)
with hexagram of Venus, as a letter of the name Ararita, 290 (III, 23)
Knights (Kings) of Tarot, 544 (IV, 144)
telesmatic image, 486, 491, 492 (IV, 61, 69, 71-2)
Thma-oe-Sh, 375 (III, 151)
Zodiac:
Cardinal signs, 644 (IV, 289)
Virgo, 305 (III, 44)
see also Hebrew alphabet; keyword analysis
Yod He, 438 (III, 254)
see also Yah
Yod He Vau He:
sigil, 485 (IV, 60)
see also YHVH
Yod He Vau He Elohim—*see* YHVH Elohim
Yod He Vau He Tzabaoth—*see* YHVH Tzabaoth
Yods:
Enochian Air sigil, 657, 658 (IV, 707, 708)
Fire Wand, 320 (66, 68)
Tarot:
Ace of Wands, 543 (IV, 142)
Judgment, 172 (II, 105)
The Moon, 185 (II, 130)
The Sun, 175 (II, 110)
yoga, xxi, 21, 47, 519, 699 (I, 29, 93; IV, 103)
Yogi, 515, 516, 517, 519-22 *passim* (IV, 96, 98, 99, 100, 103-8 *passim*)
Yophiel—*see* Iophiel
Yyphtho, 207n

- Z -

Z documents, xxiv, 8-9, 11, 27, 42, 43, 48, 114, 133, 202n, 276, 329-400, 697 (I, 44, 82, 83, 84, 95; II, 43, 298; III, 81-192)
  Enochian system, 624 (IV, 260)
  Z.1—The Enterer of the Threshold, 330-62, 465 (III, 81-130; IV, 26)
  Z.2—The Formulae of the Magic of Light, 376-400 (III, 152-92)
  Z.3—The Symbolism of the Admission of the Candidate, 363-75 (III, 131-51)
  see also Neophyte ritual
ZAA, 673, 680 (IV, 332, 343)
Zamael, 65 (I, 127)
Zanoni (Bulwer-Lytton), 517 (IV, 100)
Zata, Elman, 237, 273 (II, 228, 292)
  Sulphur, Chokmah, Fire, 275 (II, 296)
Zazel, 65 (I, 127)
  Enochian:
    chess, 690, 694 (IV, 357, 364)
    letters, geomantic figures, Zodiac, 495 (IV, 77)
  geomancy, 524, 526 (IV, 113, 114)
  sigil, 485, 497, 498, 526 (IV, 60, 79-80, 81, 114)
Zazi (Zodazodee), 669 (IV, 325)
Zayin:
  Enochian pyramids, 649, 650 (IV, 296)
  Gemini, 305 (III, 44)
  see also Hebrew alphabet
Zebulun, 305 (III, 44)
Zelator, 21, 28-30, 30 (I, 30, 48-51, 52)
  Dadouches, grade required for, 137, 342 (III, 100)
  Enochian side lecture, 627 (IV, 265)
  knowledge lecture, 60-6, 152 (I, 119-28; II, 66)
  meditation, 63 (I, 124)
  origin of name, 151 (II, 64)
  Paths from, 141, 147, 148, 154, 157, 166, 169 (II, 44, 55, 58, 69, 74, 92, 97)
  ritual, 28-30, 141-53 (I, 48-51; II, 44-68)
    adoration, 142-3 (II, 46-8)
    advancement:
      first part, 144-8 (II, 48-57)
      second part, 148-52 (II, 58-66)
    Banner of the West explained, 147, 338 (II, 56; III, 93-4)
    closing, 152-3 (II, 66-8)
    consecration and purification, 145 (II, 51)
    elemental prayer, 152-3 (II, 67-8)
    Fylfot cross explained, 148, 340 (II, 57; III, 98)
    oath, 144-5 (II, 50)
    opening, 142-3 (II, 45-7)
    temple arrangement, 141-2, 148 (II, 44-5, 58)
Zelator (continued):
  sign, 147, 156, 157, 199, 200, 204, 208, 215 (II, 55, 73, 74, 158, 160, 167, 174, 188)
    astral projection, 471, 472 (IV, 37, 39)
    consecration of Rose-Cross, 315 (III, 60)
    evocation, 403 (III, 197)
    pentagram rituals, 286 (III, 19)
    Tattwa vision, 460 (IV, 17)
  sign, step, grip, word, password, 147, 156 (II, 55, 73)
  Stolistes, grade required for, 137, 342 (III, 100)
  Theoricus ritual, 156-64 *passim*, (II, 72-88 *passim*)
Zelator Adeptus Minor—*see* Adeptus Minor, Zelator
Zend-Avesta, 109 (I, 223)
Zerachiel, 207n
Zeus, 172, 667 (II, 104; IV, 321)
Zion, 251 (II, 251, 252)
Ziza (Zodeezodah), 659, 669 (IV, 297, 325)
Zlar, 638 (IV, 279)
Zodazodee—*see* Zazi
Zodeezodah—*see* Ziza
Zodiac, 10, 609, 698 (IV, 241)
  alchemical operation, 397 (III, 187)
  animals ruled by signs, 109 (I, 223)
  Calvary cross, 79, 185 (I, 158; II, 129)
  cardinal signs, 269, 618-9 (II, 286; IV, 253, 254)
    Fire, 644, 650 (IV, 289, 297)
  cardinal, fixed, and mutable signs, 269, 611 (II, 285-6; IV, 241-2)
    Enochian:
      chess, 690 (IV, 356, 357)
      tablets, 642, 644 (IV, 285-6, 289)
    YHVH, 644 (IV, 289)
  charts for time of working:
    consecration:
      Jupiter talisman, 414 (III, 213)
      Lotus Wand, 303, 304 (III, 41, 43)
      Sword, 317 (III, 63)
    hexagrams, 293 (III, 28)
    pentagrams, 283-4 (III, 15)
  Chokmah, 19, 63, 506 (I, 25, 125; IV, 89)
    see also Mazloth
  colors, 241 (II, 236)
  decanates, 149 (II, 60)
    angels, 85-86 (I, 170-74)
    Enochian:
      chess pieces, 685 (IV, 350)
      tablets, Great Cross, 642 (IV, 285-6)
    Tarot, 550, 564-5, 600, 642 (IV, 156, 176, 227, 286)
      The Sun, 175 (II, 110)
  of Denderah, 597 (IV, 222)

Zodiac (continued);
divine and angelic names, 85-86 (I, 169-74)
divine names, Hebrew letters, Tribes of Israel, angels, and colors, 305 (III, 44)
dodekangle, 506, 510, 513 (IV, 89, 94)
Dragon or Serpent Formula, 618-21 (IV, 253-7)
elemental attribution of signs, 50 (I, 100)
elements, 611 (IV, 242)
cardinal points, 283 (III, 14)
Enochian:
chess, 689 (IV, 355)
tablets, 642-3 (IV, 285-7)
divine names, 669 (IV, 325)
Great Cross, 642, 648 (IV, 285, 293, 294)
Linea Spiritus Sancti, 655 (IV, 304)
Lesser Angles, 645 (IV, 290)
pyramids, 651 (IV, 298)
Sephirotic Calvary Crosses, 644 (IV, 288)
servient squares, 644 (IV, 289)
pyramids, 649 (IV, 295)
fixed (kerubic) signs, 61, 269 (I, 120; II, 286)
elements, 607 (IV, 237)
Enochian tablets, 669 (IV, 325)
geomantic figures and gematria, 650 (IV, 300)
Kerubim not to be confused with, 343 (III, 102)
Knaves (Princesses) of Tarot, 544, 607 (IV, 145, 237)
Tetragrammaton, 607 (IV, 237)
Fylfot cross, 68, 148, 340 (I, 131; II, 57; III, 98)
Greek cross, 70, 175 (I, 137; II, 109)
geomantic figures, 69, 524, 526, 537 (I, 135; IV, 112, 114, 132)
Hebrew letters, 150, 159, 305, 311 (II, 61, 77; III, 44, 53)
hexangle, 507, 508 (IV, 91)
kerubic signs—*see* Zodiac, fixed (kerubic) signs
Lotus Wand, 46-7, 224, 262, 300, 302 (I, 93; II, 202-3, 272; III, 37, 39-40)
mutable signs, 269 (II, 286)

Zodiac (continued):
mutable signs (continued):
Air, 644, 650 (IV, 289, 296)
North Pole, 607 (IV, 236)
pentagrams, 283-4, 299 (III, 15, 35)
precession, 594 (IV, 219)
quinances:
angels, 85-86 (I, 170-74)
The Sun, 175 (II, 110)
Rose-Cross lamen, 311, 482 (III, 53; IV, 57)
signs and symbols, 50 (I, 99)
doors, 463 (IV, 22)
Enochian letters, 627 (IV, 264)
with hexagrams, 299 (III, 35)
Sphere of the—*see* Mazloth; Zodiac, Chokmah
Sphere of Sensation, 451 (III, 451)
Table of Shew Bread, 149 (II, 60)
Tarot:
Aces, 610, 611, 613 (IV, 240, 241, 246)
attributions, 71, 72-3, 541-2 (I, 139, 141-3; IV, 139-41)
court cards, 544-5 (IV, 145)
divination, 568, 573, 575 (IV, 181, 188, 191)
The Magician, 588 (IV, 210)
The Sun, 175 (II, 110)
The Universe, 160, 592 (II, 80; IV, 216)
The Wheel of Fortune, 590 (IV, 212-3)
see also Zodiac, decanates, Tarot
triplicities, 185, 268, 269, 618, 619 (II, 129, 285-6; IV, 253, 254)
Enochian tablets, 642, 648 (IV, 285, 294)
geomancy, 537 (IV, 132)
talismans, 482 (IV, 55, 56)
Tarot, 607, 610 (IV, 237, 240)
YHVH, 642 (IV, 285)
twelve signs of Zodiac times ten Sephiroth = 120 years, 225, 242 (II, 203-4, 273)
Vault symbolism, 246, 268, 269 (II, 240, 284, 285, 286)
see also astrology; Mazloth
see also individual signs and triplicities
Zohar, 16, 44, 83, 152, 276 (I, 18-9, 87, 166; II, 66, 299)
Zoroaster, Oracles of—*see* Chaldean Oracles
Zuriel, 86, 305 (I, 173; III, 44)

STAY IN TOUCH

On the following pages you will find listed, with their current prices, some of the books and tapes now available on related subjects. Your book dealer stocks most of these, and will stock new titles in the Llewellyn series as they become available. We urge your patronage.

However, to obtain our full catalog, to keep informed of new titles as they are released and to benefit from informative articles and helpful news, you are invited to write for our bi-monthly news magazine/catalog. A sample copy is free, and it will continue coming to you at no cost as long as you are an active mail customer. Or you may keep it coming for a full year with a donation of just $2.00 in U.S.A. ($7.00 for Canada & Mexico, $20.00 overseas, first class mail). Many bookstores also have *The Llewellyn New Times* available to their customers. Ask for it.

Stay in touch! In *The Llewellyn New Times'* pages you will find news and reviews of new books, tapes and services, announcements of meetings and seminars, articles helpful to our readers, news of authors, advertising of products and services, special money-making opportunities, and much more.

The Llewellyn New Times
P.O. Box 64383-Dept. 663, St. Paul, MN 55164-0383, U.S.A.

• • •

TO ORDER BOOKS AND TAPES

If your book dealer does not have the books and tapes described on the following pages readily available, you may order them direct from the publisher by sending full price in U.S. funds, plus $2.00 for postage and handling for orders of $10 and under. Orders over $10 will require $3.50 postage and handling. There are no postage and handling charges for orders over $100. UPS Delivery: We ship UPS whenever possible. Delivery guaranteed. Provide your street address as UPS does not deliver to P.O. Boxes. UPS to Canada requires a $50 minimum order. Allow 4-6 weeks for delivery. Orders outside the U.S.A and Canada: Airmail—add $5 per book; add $3 for each non-book item (tapes, etc.); add $1 per item for surface mail.

FOR GROUP STUDY AND PURCHASE

Because there is a great deal of interest in group discussion and study of the subject matter of this book, we feel that we should encourage the adoption and use of this particular book by such groups by offering a special "quantity" price to group leaders or "agents."

Our Special Quantity Price for a minimum order of five copies of *THE GOLDEN DAWN* is $59.85 Cash-With-Order. This price includes postage and handling within the United States. Minnesota residents must add 6% sales tax. For additional quantities, please order in multiples of five. For Canadian and foreign orders, add postage and handling charges as above. Credit Card (VISA, Master Card, American Express) Orders are accepted. Charge Card Orders only may be phoned free ($15.00 minimum order) within the U.S.A. by dialing 1-800-THE MOON (in Canada call: 1-800-FOR-SELF). Customer Service calls dial 1-612-291-1970. Mail Orders to:

LLEWELLYN PUBLICATIONS
P.O. Box 64383-Dept. 663 / St. Paul, MN 55164-0383, U.S.A.

THE NEW MAGUS
by Donald Tyson
The New Magus is a practical framework on which a student can base his or her personal system of magic.

This book is filled with practical, usable magical techniques and rituals which anyone from any magical tradition can use. It includes instructions on how to design and perform rituals, create and use sigils, do invocations and evocations, do spiritual healings, learn rune magic, use god-forms, create telesmatic images, discover your personal guardian, create and use magical tools and much more. You will learn how *YOU* can be a *New Magus!*

The New Age is based on ancient concepts that have been put into terms, or *metaphors*, that are appropriate to life in our world today. That makes *The New Magus* the book on magic for today.

If you have found that magic seems illogical, overcomplicated and not appropriate to your lifestyle, *The New Magus* is the book for you. It will change your ideas of magic forever!
0-87542-825-8, 368 pgs., 6 x 9, illus., softcover **$12.95**

MODERN MAGICK
by Donald Michael Kraig
Modern Magick is the most comprehensive step-by-step introduction to the art of ceremonial magic ever offered. The eleven lessons in this book will guide you from the easiest of rituals and the construction of your magickal tools through the highest forms of magick: designing your own rituals and doing pathworking. Along the way you will learn the secrets of the Kabalah in a clear and easy-to-understand manner. You will also discover the true secrets of invocation (channeling) and evocation, and the missing information that will finally make the ancient *grimoires*, such as the **Keys of Solomon**, not only comprehensible, but usable. *Modern Magick* contains a comprehensive bibliography, glossary, and thorough index. It is not intended to supplant any other book; its purpose is to fully train and prepare anyone to use other books as he or she wills, with a full understanding of what the other writers are trying to present, along with what the other authors omit. *Modern Magick* is designed so anyone can use it, and is the perfect guidebook for students and classes. It will also help to round out the knowledge of long-time practitioners of the magickal arts.
0-87542-324-8, 608 pgs., 6 x 9, illus., softcover **$14.95**

GODWIN'S CABALISTIC ENCYCLOPEDIA
by David Godwin
This is the most complete correlation of Hebrew and English ideas ever offered. It is a dictionary of Cabalism arranged, with definitions, alphabetically, alphabetically in Hebrew, and numerically. With this book the practicing Cabalist or student no longer needs access to a large number of books on mysticism, magic and the occult in order to trace down the basic meanings, Hebrew spellings, and enumerations of the hundreds of terms, words, and names that are included in this book.

This book includes: all of the two-letter root words found in Biblical Hebrew, the many names of God, the Planets, the Astrological Signs, Numerous Angels, the Shem Hamphorash, the Spirits of the Goetia, the Correspondences of the 32 Paths, a comparison of the Tarot and the Cabala, a guide to Hebrew Pronunciation, and a complete edition of Aleister Crowley's valuable book *Sepher Sephiroth.*

0-87542-292-6, 500 pgs., 6 × 9, softcover **$15.00**

A GARDEN OF POMEGRANATES
by Israel Regardie
What is the Tree of Life? It's the ground plan of the Qabalistic system—a set of symbols used since ancient times to study the Universe. The Tree of Life is a geometrical arrangement of ten sephiroth, or spheres, each of which is associated with a different archetypal idea, and 22 paths which connect the spheres.

This system of primal correspondences has been found the most efficient plan ever devised to classify and organize the characteristics of the self. Israel Regardie has written one of the best and most lucid introductions to the Qabalah.

A Garden of Pomegranates combines Regardie's own studies with his notes on the works of Aleister Crowley, A.E. Waite, Eliphas Levi and D.H. Lawrence. No longer is the wisdom of the Qabalah to be held *secret!* The needs of today place the burden of growth upon each and every person—each has to undertake the Path as his or her own responsibility, but every help is given in the most ancient and yet most modern teaching here known to humankind.
0-87542-690-5, 176 pgs., softcover **$6.95**

THE MIDDLE PILLAR
by Israel Regardie
Between the two outer pillars of the Qabalistic Tree of Life, the extremes of Mercy and Severity, stands THE MIDDLE PILLAR, signifying one who has achieved equilibrium in his or her own self.

Integration of the human personality is vital to the continuance of creative life. Without it, man lives as an outsider to his own true self. By combining Magic and Psychology in the Middle Pillar Ritual/Exercise (a magical meditation technique), we bring into balance the opposing elements of the psyche while yet holding within their essence and allowing full expression of man's entire being.

In this book, and with this practice, you will learn to: understand the psyche through its correspondences on the Tree of Life; expand self-awareness, thereby intensifying the inner growth process; activate creative and intuitive potentials; understand the individual thought patterns which control every facet of personal behavior; regain the sense of balance and peace of mind—the equilibrium that everyone needs for physical and psychic health.
0-87542-658-1, 176 pgs., softcover **$6.95**

MYSTERIA MAGICA
by Denning and Phillips
For years, Denning and Phillips headed the international occult Order Aurum Solis. In this book they present the magickal system of the order so that you can use it. Here you will find rituals for banishing and invoking plus instructions for proper posture and breathing. You will learn astral projection, rising on the planes, and the magickal works that should be undertaken through astral projection. You will learn the basic principle of ceremonies and how to make sigils and talismans. You will learn practical Enochian magick plus how to create, consecrate and use your magickal tools such as the magickal sword, wand and cup. You will also learn the advanced arts of sphere-working and evocation to visible appearance.

Filled with illustrations, this book is an expanded version of the previous edition. It is now complete in itself and can be the basis of an entire magickal system. You can use the information alone or as the sourcebook for a group. It is volume 3 of **The Magical Philosophy**, the other two books being *The Sword and The Serpent* and *The Foundations of High Magick.* If you want to learn how to do real magick, this is the place you should start.
0-87542-196-2, 480 pgs., 6 x 9, illus., softcover **$15.00**